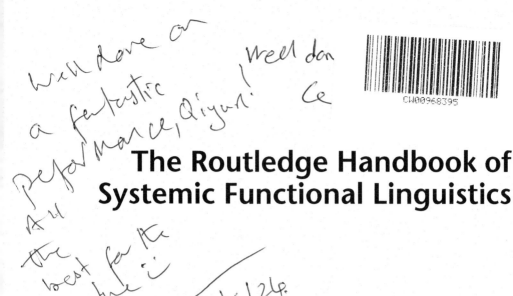

well done on a fantastic performance, Qiyun! Well done Ce All the best for the future ☺ 26/6/24.

The Routledge Handbook of Systemic Functional Linguistics

The Routledge Handbook of Systemic Functional Linguistics brings together internationally renowned scholars of systemic functional linguistics (SFL) to provide a space for critical examination of the key tenets underpinning SFL theory. Uniquely, it includes description of the three main strands within contemporary SFL scholarship: Halliday's *Introduction to Functional Grammar*, Martin's discourse semantics and Fawcett's Cardiff Grammar.

In five sections and thirty-eight interdisciplinary chapters, this is the first handbook to cover the whole architecture of SFL theory, comprising:

- the ontology and epistemology of SFL;
- SFL as a clause grammar;
- lexicogrammar below the clause and SFL's approach to constituency;
- SFL's vibrant theory of language above the clause; and
- SFL as a theory of praxis with real-world applications.

With a wide range of language examples, a comprehensive editors' introduction and a section on further reading, *The Routledge Handbook of Systemic Functional Linguistics* is an essential resource for all those studying and researching SFL or functional grammar.

Tom Bartlett is Reader in Language and Communication Research at Cardiff University, UK. He is the author of *Hybrid Voices and Collaborative Change* (Routledge, 2012) and *Analysing Power in Language* (Routledge, 2014).

Gerard O'Grady is Senior Lecturer in the Centre for Language and Communication Research at Cardiff University, UK. He is the author of *A Grammar of Spoken English Discourse* (2010).

Routledge Handbooks in Linguistics

Routledge Handbooks in Linguistics provide overviews of a whole subject area or subdiscipline in linguistics and survey the state of the discipline, including emerging and cutting-edge areas. Edited by leading scholars, these volumes include contributions from key academics from around the world, and are essential reading for both advanced undergraduate and postgraduate students.

The Routledge Handbook of Linguistic Anthropology
Edited by Nancy Bonvillain

The Routledge Handbook of the English Writing System
Edited by Vivian Cook and Des Ryan

The Routledge Handbook of Metaphor and Language
Edited by Elena Semino and Zsófia Demjén

The Routledge Handbook of Systemic Functional Linguistics
Edited by Tom Bartlett and Gerard O'Grady

The Routledge Handbook of Migration and Language
Edited by Suresh Canagarajah

The Routledge Handbook of Phonological Theory
Edited by S. J. Hannahs and Anna Bosch

The Routledge Handbook of Language and Media
Edited by Daniel Perrin and Colleen Cotter

The Routledge Handbook of Theoretical and Experimental Sign Language Research
Edited by Annika Hermann, Roland Pfau and Josep Quer

The Routledge Handbook of Systemic Functional Linguistics

Edited by
Tom Bartlett and Gerard O'Grady

Routledge
Taylor & Francis Group

LONDON AND NEW YORK

First published 2017
by Routledge
2 Park Square, Milton Park, Abingdon, Oxon OX14 4RN

and by Routledge
605 Third Avenue, New York, NY 10017

First issued in paperback 2020

Routledge is an imprint of the Taylor and Francis Group, an informa business

British Library Cataloguing-in-Publication Data
A catalogue record for this book is available from the British Library

Library of Congress Cataloging-in-Publication Data
Names: Bartlett, Tom, 1962- editor. | O'Grady, Gerard, editor.
Title: The Routledge handbook of systemic functional linguistics / edited by
    Tom Bartlett and Gerard O'Grady.
Description: Milton Park, Abingdon, Oxon ; New York, NY : Routledge,
    [2017] |
Series: Routledge Handbooks in linguistics | Includes bibliographical
    references and index.
Identifiers: LCCN 2016028576| ISBN 9780415748407 (hardback) |
    ISBN 9781315413891 (ebook)
Subjects: LCSH: Functionalism (Linguistics)—Handbooks, manuals, etc. |
    Systemic grammar—Handbooks, manuals, etc.
Classification: LCC P147 .R69 2017 | DDC 410.1/833—dc23
LC record available at https://lccn.loc.gov/2016028576

ISBN 13: 978-0-367-73649-1 (pbk)
ISBN 13: 978-0-415-74840-7 (hbk)

Typeset in Times New Roman
by Swales & Willis Ltd, Exeter, Devon, UK

Contents

Contents

Contents

Figures

Tables

Contributors

Tom Bartlett is Reader in Language and Communication Research at the University of Cardiff. His research interests are participatory democracy, the sociolinguistics of voice and the relation between text and context. He is the author of two books, *Analysing Power in Language: A Practical Guide* (Routledge 2014) and *Hybrid Voices and Collaborative Change: Contextualising Positive Discourse Analysis* (Routledge 2012), and co-editor of *Systemic Functional Linguistics: Exploring Choice* (Cambridge University Press 2013, with Lise Fontaine and Gerard O'Grady) and *Choice in Language: Applications in Text Analysis* (Equinox 2013, with Lise Fontaine and Gerard O'Grady). His most recent journal publication is 'Phasal dynamism and the unfolding of meaning as text', *English Text Construction* (2016) 9(1): 143–64.

Gerard O'Grady is Senior Lecturer at the Centre for Language and Communication Research at Cardiff University. He researches spoken discourse, with a particular focus on how textual and interpersonal meanings are co-constructed by speakers and hearers. His work is grounded in linear grammar, discourse and systemic intonation, systemic functional linguistics (SFL), functional sentence perspective (FSP) and relevance theory. He is the author of *A Grammar of Spoken English Discourse: The Intonation of Increments* (Bloomsbury 2010) and *Key Concepts in Phonetics and Phonology* (Palgrave 2012), and co-editor of *Systemic Functional Linguistics: Exploring Choice* (Cambridge University Press 2013, with Lise Fontaine and Tom Bartlett) and *Choice in Language: Applications in Text Analysis* (Equinox 2013, with Lise Fontaine and Tom Bartlett). His most recent journal publication is 'Given/New: What do the terms refer to? A first (small) step', *English Text Construction* (2016) 9(1): 9–32.

Thomas Hestbæk Andersen, PhD, is Associate Professor in International Business Communication and director of the Centre for Multimodal Communication, University of Southern Denmark. He is founding chairman of the Nordic Association for Systemic Functional Linguistics. His scholarly focus areas are social semiotic text analysis and text production, mainly focusing on Danish business communication. This focus includes research on multimodal copywriting, communication planning, organisational self-presentation and (as pure research) a systemic functional description of Danish.

Elizabeth Armstrong is Foundation Chair in Speech Pathology at Edith Cowan University, Western Australia. Her research focuses on the application of SFL theory to the everyday discourse of people with aphasia, to assist in both diagnosis and treatment issues.

Jorge Arús Hita, PhD, has been teaching English language and linguistics at Universidad Complutense de Madrid (UCM) since 1997. His publications, using systemic functional grammar (SFG) as a theoretical framework, include articles on corpus-based typological description, contrastive linguistics and teaching English as a foreign language (TEFL), published in various national and international journals and edited volumes. He has been copy-editor of the English studies journal *Atlantis* and is currently Associate Dean for Innovation and Technologies at the School of Philology, UCM, where he was previously e-learning coordinator. Jorge has participated in several nationally and internationally funded research and innovation projects. Among his publications, he is co-author of *Systemic-Functional Grammar of Spanish: A Contrastive Study with English* (Bloomsbury 2010), as well as co-editor of *English Modality: Core, Periphery and Evidentiality* (De Gruyter 2013), *Languages for Specific Purposes in the Digital Era* (Springer 2014) and *The Dynamicity of Communication below, around and above the Clause* (Benjamins 2016).

Elissa Asp is Professor of English and Linguistics, and Coordinator of Linguistics, at Saint Mary's University, Halifax, NS. She was educated at Glendon College and York University in Toronto, where she specialised in linguistic description of discourse and linguistic theory. She is interested in functional and formal theories of language, and developing models that elucidate language processing in context. Ongoing research addresses three main areas: (a) discourse correlates of dementias – especially neurodegenerative diseases associated with ageing, such as Alzheimer's disease; (b) magnetoencephalography (MEG) studies of neurocognitive networks supporting language production; and (c) the theoretical implications of (a) and (b) for models of language. She collaborates with colleagues at the Geriatric Medicine Research Unit and the Neurocognitive Imaging Lab at Dalhousie University on these projects.

John A. Bateman is Professor of Applied Linguistics in the Linguistics and English Departments of the Faculty of Linguistics and Literary Sciences at the University of Bremen. His research areas revolve around multimodal and multilingual semiotic descriptions, functional and computational linguistics (focusing particularly on accounts of register, genre, functional variation, functional natural language semantics, lexicogrammatical description and theory) and computational instantiations of linguistic theory. He has published widely in all of these areas, as well as authoring several introductory and survey articles on social semiotics, natural language generation and film and static document analysis. He is currently the coordinator of the Bremen Transmedial Textuality Research Group (http://www.fb10.uni-bremen.de/bitt).

Margaret Berry, now retired, was Reader in English Language at the University of Nottingham. She has published introductory books on systemic linguistics and articles on SFL theory, context of situation, exchange structure, Theme and Rheme, register variation and the application of SFL to the teaching of English. She has lectured in China, Australia and Canada, as well as in European countries.

Wendy L. Bowcher is Professor of Linguistics at Sun Yat-sen University, China. Her research interests include multimodal discourse analysis, context in SFL theory and English intonation. She is editor of *Multimodal Texts from Around the World: Cultural and Linguistic Insights* (Palgrave 2012), and co-editor of *New Directions in the Analysis of Multimodal*

Discourse (Erlbaum/Routledge 2007, with Terry D. Royce), *Systemic Phonology: Recent Studies in English* (Equinox 2014, with Bradley A. Smith) and *Language in Society, Society in Language: Essays in Honour of Ruqaiya Hasan* (Palgrave 2016, with Jennifer Yameng Liang). Wendy was instrumental in the formation of the Japan Association of Systemic Functional Linguistics (JASFL) in 1993 and served for several years as vice president of the Association. She also served as the vice-chair of the International Systemic Functional Linguistics Association (ISFLA) from 2011 to 2014.

David G. Butt is Associate Professor of Linguistics at Macquarie University in Sydney and was the Director of the University Research Centre for Language in Social Life. Over the last decade and more, this centre has conducted projects across communities and institutions for which SFL provided significant evidence about the management of change. Through the Centre, David has been actively engaged with professionals in medicine (surgery and psychiatry), counselling, care for people with disabilities, intelligent systems design and brain sciences, cultural analysis (literature, theatre, world Englishes), complexity theory and 'smart spaces', Vygotskyan approaches to education and training, financial reporting, courtroom explanations and forensic evidence, media and journalism, and language development in schools. The Centre has also investigated the interrelations between linguistics, verbal art (especially poetry), philosophy and the arguments of natural sciences (especially biology, genetics and physics). The Centre has participated in educational projects in various cultures beyond Australia – including Singapore, India, Japan, China and close neighbours in Timor and in Indonesia.

Alice Caffarel-Cayron is Senior Lecturer in French and Linguistics in the Department of French Studies at the University of Sydney. Her main research interests are the grammar and semantics of French, discourse analysis, stylistics and language typology. She has developed a systemic functional description of the grammar of French that she has applied to the teaching of French, linguistics, discourse analysis and stylistics in the Department of French Studies. Her *Systemic Functional Interpretation of French Grammar* was first published by Continuum in 2006 and republished as paperback in 2008. She is currently conducting research on the language of Simone de Beauvoir and the impact that her writings had on readers.

Ben Clarke is a Lecturer in English Language and Linguistics at the University of Portsmouth. His research interests include corpus-informed inquiries into the semantic and contextual motives for lexical and grammatical features and trends, the intersection of the media and the political, ideological discourses used to reinforce the political, economic and cultural status quo, and the proliferation, and increasing centrality to social life, of manifold discourses of public participation.

Kristin Davidse is Professor of English Linguistics at the University of Leuven. Her main research interest is the description of English grammar from a functional perspective. In the area of clause grammar, she has published on such topics as transitive–intransitive versus lexically ergative clauses, as well as middle, existential, copular and ditransitive constructions. In addition, she has dealt with it- and there-clefts, and clauses containing fact projection. She has also published on various processes of change such as grammaticalisation, deictification and intersubjectification in the English nominal group, as well as on structure and functions of the nominal group per se. She was one of the founding editors of the journal *Functions of Language*.

Y. J. Doran is a Researcher in the Department of Linguistics at the University of Sydney. His research centres on SFL and legitimation code theory, particularly in relation to semiotic description and typology, and knowledge building in education. His recent focus has been on the interaction of mathematical symbolism, images and English in the discourse of physics.

Robin P. Fawcett is Emeritus Professor of Linguistics at Cardiff University and former Director of the Computational Linguistics Unit in the Centre for Language and Communication Research. His main research interest is the development of a comprehensive systemic functional model of language in use. A key method of research has been implementing computer models of many components of this architecture, in both generating and understanding texts (spoken and written), in the twelve-year COMMUNAL Project. His *Invitation to Systemic Functional Linguistics* was published in 2008 in English, Chinese and Spanish, and his 2000 book *A Theory of Syntax for Systemic Functional Linguistics* was reissued in 2010 as a paperback. He has so far published ten books, more than eighty papers in journals or as book chapters and around seventy research reports, reviews and interviews. He is currently working on three major books: *An Integrative Architecture for Systemic Functional Linguistics and Other Theories of Language*, and two handbooks for analysing discourse, one in terms of its functional syntax and the other its functional semantics. He was the founding chair of what has grown to be the International Systemic Functional Linguistics Association; he is on the editorial board of the journals *Functions of Language*, *Annual Review of Functional Linguistics* and *Functional Linguistics*, and he is a series editor for Equinox Publishing.

Alison Ferguson is Conjoint Professor of Speech Pathology at University of Newcastle, Australia. She is well known for her research in applications of the methodology of conversation analysis to aphasia and as a contributor to the research applying SFL to aphasia.

Lise Fontaine is Senior Lecturer in the Centre for Language and Communication Research at Cardiff University, Wales. She lectures mainly on functional grammar, word meaning, corpus linguistics and psycholinguistics. Her research interests include functional grammar and, more specifically, the study of referring expressions as realised in the nominal group. In addition to grammatical analysis, she is also interested in related fields of linguistics study, including corpus linguistics and psycholinguistics. She is the author of *Analysing English Grammar: A Systemic-Functional Introduction* (Cambridge University Press 2012) and co-author of *Referring in Language: An Integrated Approach* (Cambridge University Press forthcoming, with Katy Jones). She is also co-editor of *Systemic Functional Linguistics: Exploring Choice* (Cambridge University Press 2013, with Tom Bartlett and Gerard O'Grady), *Choice in Language: Applications in Text Analysis* (Equinox 2013, with Tom Bartlett and Gerard O'Grady) and *The Cambridge Handbook of Systemic Functional Linguistics* (Cambridge University Press forthcoming, with G. Thompson, W. Bowcher, J. Liang and D. Schönthal).

Gail Forey is Associate Professor at the Hong Kong Polytechnic University, where she is programme lead for the Doctorate in Applied Language Sciences. Gail has carried out research and published in the areas of written and spoken workplace discourse, language issues related to offshore outsourcing, SFL, discourse analysis, language education and teacher development. Gail was awarded the PolyU President's Award for Excellent Performance in Teaching 2013/14 and the prestigious Hong Kong University Grants Council Teaching Award in 2014/15.

Sheena Gardner is Professor of Applied Linguistics in the School of Humanities at Coventry University. Her research in educational linguistics centres on academic genres and registers in the British Academic Written English Corpus (BAWE) of university student writing and on young learner classroom discourse. Her publications include *Genres across the Disciplines* with H. Nesi (2012), *Multilingualism, Discourse and Ethnography* with M. Martin-Jones (2012) and *Systemic Functional Linguistics in the Digital Age* with Siân Alsop (2016).

Bob Hodge is Emeritus Professor of Humanities at the Institute for Culture and Society, Western Sydney University, Australia. He has researched and published extensively in social semiotics and critical discourse analysis within a broad SFL framework. His best-known books are *Social Semiotics* (Polity 1988) and *Language as Ideology* (Routledge 1993), both co-authored with Gunther Kress.

Guowen Huang is Chair Professor of the Changjiang Programme, selected by the Ministry of Education of the People's Republic of China (PRC), and is Professor of Functional Linguistics at South China Agricultural University. Between 1996 and 2016, he was Professor of Functional Linguistics at Sun Yat-sen University, China. He is editor-in-chief of the journal *Foreign Languages in China*, and is co-editor of the journals *Functional Linguistics* and *World Languages*. During 2011–14, he chaired the Executive Committee of the International Systemic Functional Linguistics Association; during 2003–15, he chaired the China Association of Functional Linguistics. He publishes extensively both in China and internationally, and serves or has served as an editorial board or advisory committee member for several journals, including *Linguistics and the Human Sciences*, *Researching and Teaching Chinese as a Foreign Language*, *Journal of Applied Linguistics* and *Social Semiotics*. He is also a member of the editorial board of the monograph series Discussions in Functional Approaches to Language (Equinox). He was educated in the UK and holds two PhD degrees: one in applied linguistics (University of Edinburgh, 1992); the other in functional linguistics (Cardiff University, 1996). His research interests include SFL, discourse analysis, ecolinguistics, applied linguistics and translation studies.

Kerstin Kunz is Head of the Department of Translation and Interpretation at Heidelberg University, with expertise in linguistic typology, semantics and discourse analysis. She has published widely on language learning and translation, including her monograph *Cohesion in English and German: A Corpus-Based Approach to Language Contrast, Register Variation and Translation* (Universität des Saarlandes 2015).

Eden Sum-hung Li is Assistant Professor and programme lead in the School of Arts and Social Sciences at the Open University of Hong Kong. He has taught at Macquarie University and the University of Hong Kong. He is the author of *A Systemic Functional Grammar of Chinese* (Bloomsbury 2007) and *Language, Society and Culture in Hong Kong* (Open University Press 2015), and the co-author of *Analysing and Applying English Grammar* (Open University Press 2009, with C. Green and Y. Han) and *English Today: Forms, Functions and Uses* (Pearson 2012, with A. Mahboob).

Anne McCabe is a faculty member of the English Department at Saint Louis University – Madrid Campus, where she teaches linguistics, English as a second language (ESL) and writing pedagogy to undergraduate and graduate students. She holds a PhD in language studies from Aston University, and has published numerous book chapters and articles using a functional linguistics perspective to analyse educational and media texts. She has co-edited two volumes published by Bloomsbury (Continuum), both with Rachel Whittaker and Mick O'Donnell: *Language and Literacy: Functional Approaches* (2007) and *Advances in Language and Education* (2009). She recently co-edited a special issue of the TESOL international journal *Systemic Functional Linguistics and English Language Teaching*.

Edward McDonald is Professor in Functional Linguistics in the School of Foreign Languages at Sun Yat-sen University, China. He gained his bachelor's degree from the University of Sydney in 1988, his MA from Peking University in 1992 and his PhD from Macquarie University in 1999, with theses on the clause and verbal group grammar of modern Chinese. Between 1999 and 2012, he taught linguistics, Chinese language, translation, semiotics and music at the National University of Singapore, Tsinghua University Beijing, the University of Auckland and the University of New South Wales. Between 2003 and 2005, he worked as a language consultant at China Central Television International (CCTV 9). Edward has drawn on his cross-cultural study and work experience to inform his teaching and research work: crossing linguistic boundaries in his work on applying systemic functional theory to a range of languages, including modern Chinese and Scottish Gaelic (*Meaningful Arrangement: Exploring the Syntactic Description of Texts*, Equinox 2008); spanning national cultures in his work on Chinese language teaching and the hybrid concept of 'sinophone' (*Learning Chinese, Turning Chinese: Challenges to Becoming Sinophone in a Globalised World*, Routledge 2011) and bridging academic cultures in his work on European and Chinese traditions of language scholarship and the interactions between them (*Grammar West to East: European and Chinese Traditions in the Making of Modern Linguistics*, Springer forthcoming).

Karl Maton is Director of the LCT Centre for Knowledge-Building at the University of Sydney and Honorary Professor at Rhodes University. Karl is the creator of legitimation code theory (LCT). He is the author of *Knowledge and Knowers* (Routledge 2014) and *Knowledge-Building: Educational Studies in Legitimation Code Theory* (Routledge 2016), and co-editor of *Disciplinarity* (Continuum 2011, with F. Christie).

Donna R. Miller is Chair of English Linguistics at the Department of Modern Languages, Literatures and Cultures of the University of Bologna, where she heads the Research Centre for Linguistic-Cultural Studies (CeSLiC). Her research has focused on register analysis in institutional text types, her corpus-assisted investigations exploring the grammar of evaluation in terms of appraisal systems. She is co-editor of *Language and Verbal Art Revisited* (Equinox 2007, with Monica Turci) and in recent years has taken up the defence of Ruqaiya Hasan's framework for the study of the literature text, at the same time reflecting on Jakobson's potential place within it, for example 'The Hasanian framework for the study of "verbal art" revisited . . . and reproposed', *Textus* (2010) 23(1): 29–52, 'Another look at social semiotic stylistics: Coupling Hasan's "verbal art" framework with "the Mukařovský-Jakobson theory"', in C. Gouveia and M. Alexandre (eds) *Languages, Metalanguages, Modalities, Cultures: Functional and Socio-Discursive Perspectives* (Bond 2013) and 'Jakobson's place in Hasan's social semiotic stylistics: "Pervasive Parallelism" as Symbolic Articulation of Theme', in W.L. Bowcher and J.Y. Liang (eds) *Society in Language, Language in Society: Essays in Honour of Ruqaiya Hasan* (Palgrave Macmillan 2015).

Alison Rotha Moore is Senior Lecturer in English Language and Linguistics at the University of Wollongong and an Honorary Research Associate with the Language in Social Life Research Network at Macquarie University, led by David Butt. She has conducted several nationally funded research projects on interaction in health care, and currently publishes on medical discourse, animal studies and functional linguistics – in particular, register theory. Recent work includes a chapter on message semantics in W. L. Bowcher and J. Y. Liang (eds) *Society in Language, Language in Society: Essays in Honour of Ruqaiya Hasan* (Palgrave Macmillan 2015), and two chapters in *Communication in Surgical Practice*, edited by (Equinox 2016, edited by Sarah White and John Cartmill).

Amy Neale carried out her research at Cardiff University, completing her PhD under the supervision of Professor Robin Fawcett in 2002. Her professional career has focused on the commercialisation of new technologies, having supported researchers and entrepreneurs to get their innovations to market at University of Brighton, Queen Mary University of London, and the National Digital Research Centre. She has continued to find opportunities to publish, with a variety of publications appearing focused on her research into transitivity and the Cardiff Grammar.

Mick O'Donnell is a Lecturer at Universidad Autónoma de Madrid. He is best known for his application of SFL in the areas of computational linguistics and corpus linguistics. He has been developing corpus annotation software for the last twenty-five years, including Systemic Coder, RSTTool and UAM Corpustool, all of which have been widely used. He has worked in areas related to automatic text generation, syntactic parsing and dialogue systems, and his most recent area of interest relates to exploring the EFL learning process via corpus analysis of learner writing.

Teresa Oteíza is Associate Professor and Director of the Doctorate Programme in Linguistics at the Pontifical Catholic University of Chile. Her interests include the areas of critical discourse analysis, educational linguistics and SFL. Her articles have appeared in journals such as *Discourse and Society*, *Discourse Studies*, *Text and Talk*, *ALED* and *Signos*, among others.

Clare Painter is Honorary Associate of the Department of Linguistics at the University of Sydney, where she was first trained in SFL by M.A.K. Halliday. Her principal research interests are in the fields of children's language and literacy development, educational linguistics and multimodal discourse analysis. Her publications include *Into the Mother Tongue* (Bloomsbury 1984), *Learning through Language in Early Childhood* (Continuum 2000) and *Reading Visual Narratives: Image Analysis of Children's Picturebooks* (Equinox 2014, with J R Martin and Len Unsworth).

Beatriz Quiroz is Assistant Professor at the Department of Language Sciences in the Faculty of Letters of the Pontificia Universidad Católica de Chile (PUC-Chile), where she teaches and supervises undergraduate and postgraduate students in linguistics. She completed her PhD at the University of Sydney, Australia, in 2013. Her current research, informed by SFL, focuses on a metafunctionally integrated description of clause systems in Chilean Spanish, with special emphasis on the system-structure principle embodied by the theoretical dimension of axis. Other research interests include systemic functional language typology, as well as the interaction between lexicogrammar and discourse semantics. Relevant publications include 'Towards a systemic profile of the Spanish MOOD', recently reprinted in the multi-volume *Systemic Functional Linguistics* (Routledge 2015, edited by J. Martin and Y. Doran).

Nicholas Sampson is Research Assistant Professor at the Department of English, The Hong Kong Polytechnic University, Hong Kong. He has been involved in education for the past thirty years, during which time he has taught English to students at all levels of learning in countries such as Hong Kong, Singapore and the UK. He is also an established English language teaching (ELT) author with Macmillan and Pearson Education, having written more than eighty ELT textbooks for the Asian market, including Hong Kong, China, Japan, Vietnam, Taiwan and South Korea. Dr Sampson moved to the Department of English at the Hong Kong Polytechnic University, where he is currently the MA in English Language Studies (MAELS) programme lead. His current research interests include SFL, multimodality and teacher autonomy.

Serge Sharoff is Senior Lecturer in Translation Studies, University of Leeds. His research focuses on natural language processing and computer-assisted language learning, including automated methods for collecting corpora from the web, their analysis in terms of domains and genres and extraction of lexicons and terminology from corpora. He has been active in SFL since his work on multilingual generation in the 1990s.

Elizabeth Spencer is a Lecturer and speech pathologist, with specialist expertise in the areas of clinical discourse analysis, and a long-standing interest in clinical applications of SFL to adult speech and language disorders. She currently teaches in the area of child language disorders and research processes. Her current research focus explores the relationship between language and ageing in the general population, through the development of clinical research applications for computerised linguistic analyses for large, naturally occurring language samples.

Ken Tann is Lecturer in Communication Management at the University of Queensland Business School. He was personally trained by Jim Martin in SFL for ten years at the University of Sydney. Ken has applied SFL to organisational and institutional studies in interdisciplinary collaborations, and has pioneered a systemic framework for analysing identity discourse. He currently teaches business literacy, organizational communication and business semiotics at the UQ Business School.

Miriam Taverniers is Associate Professor of Functional Approaches to English Linguistics at Ghent University. Her research into the nature of grammatical metaphor in SFL (PhD 2002) led to a deep interest in fundamentally theoretical concepts – especially the design and conception of differentiating dimensions and theoretical categories in structural-functional and semiotically oriented linguistic frameworks, such as: the relation between lexis and grammar; stratification, especially the syntax–semantics interface; the relation between instance, norm/register and system; syntagmatic layering and functional diversity; and the concept of 'construction' and its relation to paradigmatic modelling in functional theories. She also works on more descriptive topics, but always with a special dedication to what a scrutiny of those topics can contribute to our understanding of the aforementioned theoretical issues. Current descriptive topics include (secondary) predication and labile verbs in relation to ergativity/unaccusativity in English and in a contrastive perspective.

Chris Taylor is Professor of English Language and Translation in the Department of Law and Languages at the University of Trieste and Director of the University Language Centre in Trieste. Film translation, in its many aspects, has been his major pursuit in recent years, with significant publications relating to such issues as dubbing, subtitling and localisation, and (more recently) audiovisual translation for the deaf and audio description for the blind. His numerous publications in this field include 'Multimodal transcriptions in the analysis, translation and subtitling of Italian films', *The Translator* (2003) 9(2): 191–205, in a special issue on screen translation; ' "I knew you'd say that!": A consideration of the predictability of language use in film',. in L. Zybatow (ed.), *Translation: Neue Entwicklungen in Theorie und Praxis* (Peter Lang 2009); and 'Multimodal text analysis and subtitling', in E. Ventola, C. Charles and M. Kaltenbacher (eds) *Perspectives on Multimodality* (John Benjamins 2004). In 2012, Christopher co-authored with Elisa Perego *Tradurre l'audiovisivo* (Carocci). He has recently coordinated a European Union project entitled Audio Description: Lifelong Access for the Blind (ADLAB), which achieved 'Success Story' status.

Elke Teich is Professor of English Linguistics and Translation Studies at Universität des Saarlandes, Saarbrücken, and principal investigator in the German Cluster of Excellence in Informatics Multimodal Computing and Interaction (MMCI – http://www.mmci.uni-saarland.de/) and the German Common Language Resources and Technology Infrastructure (CLARIN) project (http://de.clarin.eu/de/). Since 2014, she has been head of the Saarbrücken Collaborative Research Center Information Density and Linguistic Encoding, which is funded by the German Research Foundation (DFG) and covers fourteen projects with around fifty members (http://www.sfb1102.uni-saarland.de). Elke's expertise ranges from descriptive grammar of English and German over (multilingual) register analysis (with a special focus on scientific registers) to translatology. She is currently a member of the editorial/ advisory boards of journals *Languages in Contrast, Fachsprache – International Journal of LSP, Linguistics and the Human Sciences* and *Corpus Linguistics and Interdisciplinary Perspectives on Language*.

Paul Tench was formerly Senior Lecturer in the Centre for Language and Communication Research at Cardiff University, but retired in 2007 after forty years' service. His main teaching responsibilities were in phonetics, the phonology of English, applied linguistics and introductory SFL. His research focused mainly on the description of British English intonation, which resulted in *The Roles of Intonation in English Discourse* (Peter Lang 1990), *The Intonation Systems of English* (Cassell 1996) and *Transcribing the Sound of English* (Cambridge University Press 2011). Since retirement, Paul has devoted time to exploring system networks at the level of word phonology, and to working with minority language groups in devising orthographies for hitherto unwritten languages in Nigeria and Zambia.

Kazuhiro Teruya is Associate Professor in the Department of Chinese and Bilingual Studies at Hong Kong Polytechnic University, where he is also a founding member of the PolySystemic Research Group and the International Research Centre for Healthcare Communication (IRCCH). He is author of *A Systemic Functional Grammar of Japanese* (Continuum 2007, two volumes) and co-author of *Key Terms in Systemic Functional Linguistics* (Continuum 2010, with Christian Matthiessen and Marvin Lam).

Gordon Tucker was formerly Senior Lecturer at Cardiff University and has, since his retirement, retained an affiliation with the University as an Honorary Research Fellow. He is the co-developer, along with Robin Fawcett, of the systemic functional model of language known as the Cardiff Grammar.

Jonathan J. Webster is Professor in the Department of Linguistics and Translation and Director of The Halliday Centre for Intelligent Applications of Language Studies at City University of Hong Kong. Before joining City University in 1987, Jonathan taught at the National University of Singapore. He is the managing editor for the journal *WORD*, co-editor for the *Journal of World Languages* and founding editor of the journal *Linguistics and the Human Sciences*. He is editor of the multi-volume collected works of M.A.K. Halliday, Ruqaiya Hasan and Braj Kachru, co-author of *Text Linguistics: The How and Why of Meaning* (Equinox 2005, with M.A.K. Halliday) and author of *Understanding Verbal Art: A Functional Linguistic Approach* (Springer 2014).

Acknowledgements

Over the course of producing this book, there are numerous people who have helped us, and whom we would like to acknowledge and thank. First of all, we thank our colleagues and friends at the Centre for Language and Communication Research at Cardiff University, and the School of English, Communication and Philosophy (ENCAP) that houses it, for providing us with an academic home. Second, we would like to acknowledge the kind support of Louisa Semlyen at Routledge for encouraging us to edit this book. Thanks are also due to Laura Sandford at Routledge for helping us to bring the book to completion. We could not have worked with better publishers.

We are especially grateful to Chris Butler, Lise Fontaine, Paul Tench, Ed McDonald, Michael Willett, Gordon Tucker, Brad Smith, Martin Davies, David Banks, Rebekah Wegener, Sabine Bartsch and Wendy Bowcher for taking the time to review and comment on various chapters in the book.

Finally, Tom would like to thank Mary, Sadie and Jamie for providing such entertaining linguistic data over the years, while Gerard would like to thank Georgia and Myrto for putting up with his extended absences, and for keeping him sane during the production of this book.

Introduction

Reading systemic functional linguistics

Tom Bartlett and Gerard O'Grady

We are very pleased to present the current volume of work bringing together forty chapters that, between them, present a critical overview of the 'extravagant architecture' of systemic functional linguistics (SFL). SFL is unique amongst linguistic theories in attempting to account for the structural, social and developmental features of language within a single coherent – though far from simple – framework, and in the current volume our overriding concern was to provide an overview of this theoretical architecture in as much breadth and critical depth as possible, allowing full chapters for areas that are often treated as subsections in other collections. But there are many ways into the theory and many interconnections between the concepts to be explained. This makes the editors' job of imposing a schematic structure on the book a daunting task and one that is based, ultimately, on a somewhat arbitrary decision. The particular direction we have chosen largely follows the hierarchical arrangement of Halliday's *Introduction to Functional Grammar* (1994) in considering language from within, below and above the cause, with sections on general theoretical issues and applications framing these descriptions within the wider contexts of linguistics and social life. The approach we have taken is, we believe, a distinctive and productive one, and in this brief introduction we first describe the ways in which we think the book is an original contribution to the literature, then suggest alternative ways of navigating the highways and by-ways of the theory.

Distinctive features of this Handbook

The last decade or so has seen the appearance of a great many handbooks bringing together chapters by respected authors on various aspects of specific linguistic theories, issues and topics, and SFL has been the focus of several excellent recent volumes. So why another Handbook of SFL? That is certainly the question that we, the editors, asked ourselves before committing ourselves to such an extensive task; in response, we decided that we would encourage the following features that we feel make the Handbook distinctive and hence complementary to, rather than competing with, the existing works.

1   We decided to include the volume within the theoretical handbook series rather than its applied counterpart. For SFL, given Halliday's (1978) conception of language as a social semiotic, there is no sharp distinction between theory and application: they are just different ends of a cline of instantiation from the system as a meaning potential to the selection of resources in specific contexts of use. However, we felt that there had been an emphasis on SFL as an *appliable linguistics* in most compendium volumes and that it would therefore be timely to produce a complementary volume with a distinctly theoretical edge. In this way, we also hope to reach out to linguists from a wider range of theoretical persuasions than has perhaps been the case to date with SFL publications. Part I of the book is particularly aimed at such an audience, locating the SFL approach with respect to other linguistic theories (Bateman), outlining the principle theoretical concepts that drive SFL (Asp; Berry), and discussing alternative formulations and elaborations of central concepts (Fawcett). The three parts following then develop individual elements of the theory in terms that should make sense to specialists from other areas of linguistics, with applications and their connection to these theoretical chapters addressed in Part V.

2   The chapters in the book provide more than just an overview of the current state of the art in SFL, as is the remit of many handbooks, and authors were encouraged to take a critical stance to their topics, and to suggest what areas of research are needed to strengthen and expand the theory and, in so doing, potentially to connect aspects of SFL to seemingly incompatible elements of other theories. One of the perceived failings of SFL has been that the emphasis on application has meant that, while some aspects of the overall model have been continuously developed and refined, some theoretical concepts and description dating back half a century have become reified and beyond critique. Generally, those areas that have shown least development are the nuts and bolts of the grammar, so it is hoped that the distinctive emphasis on these areas in the current volume might inspire new work in the field.

3   The three different models of SFL – which we refer to as the 'IFG model' (after Halliday's *Introduction to Functional Grammar*), the 'Sydney Model' (after Martin's home university) and the 'Cardiff Model' (after Fawcett and Tucker's institution) – are all treated in some depth. While the IFG approach is privileged in this volume, the chapters specifically on the Cardiff Model (Fawcett; Huang; Neale) and the Sydney Model (Tann; Oteíza; Gardner) allow various aspects of these approaches to be developed on their own terms rather than as a simple bolt-on chapter in which the main differences from IFG are set out. Other chapters (McDonald; Tucker; Quiroz; Caffarel-Cayron; Taverniers) refer to more than one model in their linguistic descriptions, and debate the merits and pitfalls of each.

4   There are several chapters that deal with the specifics of languages other than English (LOTE) rather than only a single chapter discussing the phenomenon of cross-linguistic difference.[1] These chapters (Arús Hita; Teruya; Caffarel-Cayron; Li) not only apply SFL methods to new languages (although Chinese was, of course, the grammar on which Halliday sharpened his theoretical and descriptive teeth), but also test the theory in doing so, forcing us to consider what are theoretical and universal categories, and what are descriptive and language-specific categories – a distinction that fifty years of emphasis on descriptions of English has, at times, blurred. As well as these language-specific profiles, the contributions from Quiroz and Oteíza include discussions of LOTE and the implications of these for different aspects of the theory, while Kunz and Teich demonstrate how computational approaches can be used for language typology and comparison.

The 'extravagant architecture of SFL', or 'different ways to read this book'

As the French linguist Meillet (1937: ix) said, 'une langue est un système où tout se tient' (a language is a system where everything hangs together)– an aphorism that applies in spades to the complexity of SFL, as the extravagance of its architecture is a function not only of the scope of the theory, covering the phenomenon of language from morphemic contrasts to the analysis of text as discourse, but also of the several different functional relationships that are theorised to hold between the different elements within the model. Unlike other linguistic theories, SFL does not focus exclusively on relations of constituency or on meaning-to-form algorithms, but posits a number of theoretical relations between different elements. In the remainder of this chapter, we will give a brief outline of the 'extravagant architecture' of SFL so as to provide what David Butt (2007: 103) refers to as the 'semiotic addresses' of the different elements covered in the various chapters and, in so doing, outline the essential connections between these concepts.[2] To cover this multidimensional diversity in the linear format of a book entails imposing a structure of categorisation and sequencing, and so privileging one relational category over the others. In this Handbook, we have opted for a largely hierarchical approach, but to see this as a defining principle of SFL rather than as a simple editorial artefact would be to misunderstand the theory. One purpose of this chapter (and the many cross-references throughout the book) is thus to signal what other readings of the architecture are possible.

Stratum and rank

Starting from the notion of hierarchy, then, SFL relies on two key notions: stratum and rank (see Berry's chapter in this volume for full account). Of these, stratum is most distinctive to SFL, providing the theoretical means for modelling the relationship between linguistic form, utterance meaning and social interaction. To account for the relations between these phenomena, the IFG architecture comprises five strata: phonetics, phonology, lexicogrammar, semantics and context. There is a non-arbitrary relationship between strata with, for any pair of adjacent strata, the lower stratum construing the higher, while the higher stratum activates the lower (with the bidirectional concept of realisation conflating both processes). So, for example, lexicogrammatical elements, with their own meaning, combine to construe the semantics of the text, with the various semantic features construing the context as a form of social action. Conversely, the context activates semantics, which then activate lexicogrammatical form. Thus one way of following the architecture of the theory is via the realisation of one category by another. From this perspective, the chapters in Part IV, above the clause, include social phenomena (Bartlett; Bowcher; Gardner) realised through the semantics (Clarke; Moore; Oteíza), with the semantics in turn realised by the lexicogrammatical (Davidse; Butt and Webster; Andersen; Forey and Sampson) and intonational (O'Grady) features of the clause (Part II), which are in turn realised by phonemic and phonological features (Tench) below the clause (Part III).

In general, however, the hierarchical relationship between the phenomena in Parts II (at clause rank) and III (below the clause) is rather different from interstratal realisation, and is closer to the notion of constituency in more formal theories of linguistics. Rank refers to levels of structure within a single stratum; thus, for the lexicogrammar, SFL posits a number of functional-structural units intermediate between the word and the clause, and refers to these as *groups*. (McDonald offers an etic overview of group theory in SFL, while Fontaine, Tucker and Quiroz outline applications to the grammar of English.) The elements that constitute a group, and the meanings they bring with them, is an area of significant cross-linguistic difference; for this reason, the chapters by Caffarel-Cayron and Li provide examinations of French and Mandarin, while Quiroz includes a contrastive discussion of Spanish and English in her general overview of the verbal group. Rank is also an area of intra-theoretical difference, with the IFG and Cardiff Models differing significantly on this question (Fawcett; Quiroz; Caffarel-Cayron). Within Part III (below the clause), we also include the concept of metaphor (Taverniers), the phenomenon by which, for example, processes in the semantic stratum are realised as nominal groups in the lexicogrammar, thus combining the meanings associated with both strata in a complex blend.

While the clause is generally considered the largest structure on the rank scale in terms of the lexicogrammar, the concept of constituency has also been applied within the semantics. From the IFG perspective, a text is the largest semantic unit, with cohesion (Clarke; Moore) the defining feature of a text comprising multiple clauses, and various intermediate ranks have been suggested (Cloran 1995: 399). Within the Sydney architecture, however, semantic realisations are modelled in terms not of textual relations between clauses, but of ideational, interpersonal and textual relations (see 'Metafunctions' below) across the text as a whole, in what is referred to as the 'discourse semantic stratum' (Tann). Berry and Bartlett suggest different ways in which the stratum of context might be layered.

Metafunctions

As well as the vertical relations of stratum and rank, SFL theorises a three-way horizontal relationship across the strata, collectively known as the 'metafunctions'. In describing the lexicogrammar, Halliday found that the features clumped into three tightly intraconnected, but loosely interconnected, groupings corresponding to ideational (Davidse; Butt and Webster), interpersonal (Andersen) and textual (Forey and Sampson) functions of different sorts (hence metafunctions), with these responsible in a *relatively* autonomous way (although see Taverniers on metaphor) for the construal of ideational, interpersonal and textual meanings at the semantic stratum (Moore). Following from Halliday's (1978: 4) famous dictum that 'language is as it is because of the functions it has evolved to serve in people's lives', this suggests that the three metafunctions correspond in a significant, but non-absolute, way to distinct aspects of social activity, labelled field, tenor and mode (Bowcher). This relationship is known as the 'context–metafunction hook-up hypothesis' or, more recently, 'context–metafunction resonance' (Hasan 2014), and is a central pillar in SFL's concept of social life as a semantic construct.

Axis and delicacy

Two further closely interconnected dimensions that are crucial to SFL theory and description are axis and delicacy. Axis relates to the fundamental distinction in SFL between system and structure (Asp), which derives from Halliday's reformulation of his Scale and Category Grammar into SFL. In this earlier model, Halliday drew on his teacher Firth's concept that meaning is function in context to develop a structural model of language in which the inclusion of an element of structure at one level (rank) opened up a limited set of structural options (a system) at the rank below, the meaning of which was their function within that unit as determined in opposition to the functions of the other choices available (following the Saussurean concept of *valeur*). In this model, therefore, meaning derived from the structures chosen. In Halliday's later approach, which became SFL and which was based on the idea of language as a *meaning potential*, choices in meaning were given primacy and structure theorised as the output of the meaning choices made in a particular context (Fontaine, Bartlett and O'Grady 2013; O'Grady, Bartlett and Fontaine 2013). Such an approach was not designed to dismiss the importance of structure, however, because – following from Halliday's basic tenet that meaning and the lexicogrammar are coevolutionary – no options in meaning can be postulated without a reactance in the grammar and, conversely, every distinction in the grammar must represent a reactance to a change in meaning. Thus, for example, three moods (functional categories) can be recognised in English on the basis of structural variation, while structural variations such as passive and active clauses have to be accounted for not merely as structural alternatives, but as reflective of differences in meaning of some kind. The lexicogrammar, therefore, is modelled as a series of functional choices, each of which is realised through a structural reactance in what is known as the 'system–structure cycle'. Importantly, once a functional choice is made, the related structure is *inherited* (there are no transformations) as further systems of options are selected from, each with their own structural realisations.[3]

To illustrate: the choice of major clause in English is realised by the inclusion of a finite verb (F); once this choice has been made, further choices exist as to the mood of the clause, with the choice of indicative leading to the insertion of a subject (S) alongside the inherited F. Both S and F are then inherited as the choice of indicative opens up a further choice between declarative and interrogative, which lead to the structural sequences S^F and F^S respectively (where ^ signals compulsory ordering). This increasingly detailed description of the grammar as more choices are made is referred to as the 'cline of delicacy', with more delicate options related to less delicate ones through the concept of inheritance. Within this model, less delicate options are realised by grammatical variants, while the most delicate options are realised as lexis. Thus the relationship between lexis and grammar is seen not as categorical, but as a cline – a conception that accounts for the grouping of individual processes (lexis) into process types according to similar grammatical patterns in transitivity (Davidse). Similarly, group structures are the result of a simultaneous cluster of choices that become available midway along the cline of delicacy from clause to lexeme as, for example, when a subject or complement is more delicately classified as a participant with all the attendant possibilities that choice opens up. In this way, the structural hierarchy of rank can be related to the semantically oriented concept of delicacy – a demonstration of the interconnectedness of the various SFL categories.

It should be noted here that the meaningful options at the lexicogrammatical (LG) stratum are seen as the meanings of the lexicogrammatical categories themselves, which are not the same as the meanings realised at the semantic stratum. Thus, at the LG stratum, the declarative has a meaning that derives from its systemic contrasts with the indicative and the imperative, while, at the semantic stratum, the contrast between, say, a probe and a check is the sum of the contrasts between the LG features that construe them. In other words, delicacy operates at all strata (and see Bowcher for the contextual stratum and Moore for the semantic stratum). The system–structure cycle as described above, however, is not quite the approach as developed for the Cardiff Model. In the latter model, the features of the LG stratum resemble those of the IFG semantic stratum, yet choices are realised directly through structural variation without an intermediary stratum of abstract grammatical relations (Fawcett this volume; Zhang 2014).

Instantiation

The last relationship modelled in the SFL architecture is that of instantiation, the movement from the system as potential to the production of texts as specific instances of the system, the result of choices made in real time. Given the SF concept of language as social semiotic, instantiation is best thought of across the different strata simultaneously, so that at the potential end of the cline we have the context of culture being realised by the language system (again, the idea that social life is semiotic), while at the instance end we have individual contexts of situation being realised by individual concrete texts (Bartlett). Between these poles we have subpotentials of the language system, *code* (Maton and Doran) and *register* (Moore), relating to variation by user-group and situation type as subpotentials of the cultural system. SFL's work on code theory dates back to the 1960s, and Halliday and Hasan's collaboration with British sociologist Basil Bernstein on the socialisation of children into distinct language practices (Painter) according to their social background, and in linking educational achievement to the resulting uneven distribution of linguistic resources across the social system and the privileging of middle-class coding orientation in key institutional and educational settings. This critical educational research has left a rich legacy in applied SFL work and has been a driving force in the extensive application of the theory in pedagogical practice (McCabe), particularly in Australia.

The other angle on instantiation is variation by use. Given that instantiation is a cline, the level of specification is theoretically along a sliding scale, but for the purposes of analysis two principle subcategories are considered: institutional sites and the registers associated with them, towards the system end; and situation types and text types, towards the instance end. There is a difference in terminology here between the IFG and Sydney Models, which relates to differences in the overall architectures. The term 'register' was originally used within the IFG approach to refer to the semantic subpotential *corresponding to* a particular contextual subpotential, defined in terms of field, tenor and mode variables; within the Sydney Model, however, the term refers to the configuration of field, tenor and mode, and hence to the context directly, because this is seen as an entirely linguistic construct, realised by the discourse semantic stratum below and realising the stratum of genre, seen as a social process, above (Gardner). In these terms, culture is seen as the set of potential genres as determined by ideology, which constitutes a still higher stratum in the Sydney Model. From the IFG perspective, in contrast, genre is not seen as a separate stratum, but would be considered as an intermediary point along the cline of instantiation, as an activity type (Matthiessen 2015: 154).

Moving to the instance pole of the cline of instantiation brings SFL into contact with individual texts, which are analysed as the output of specific choices from the meaning potential of the system as a whole as constrained by the situational features of the context of situation. It is this combination of viewing texts in systemic terms – that is, in discussing what the choices made mean in contrast to the options not taken and in considering the options available within context – that defines the distinctive contribution of SFL to textual analysis, whether it be in the field of forensic linguistics (Ferguson, Spencer and Armstrong), verbal art (Miller) or in the critical analysis of language as embedded in social practice (Hodge). The functional and social-semiotic basis of SFL, throughout its whole interconnected architecture, means that the labelling of grammatical features provides an interface to analysis at higher levels of abstraction that formal mark-up cannot, and does not aspire to, achieve.

Given SFL's conception of language as a semiotic system and the focus on variable emic structure at the service of more generalisable social functions, the analysis of texts as instances can be extended to non-verbal modes – in particular, image, but also music and even architecture – being accounted for in terms of the ideational, interpersonal and textual meanings and relations they construe (Taylor). The detailed and multiple functional labelling of individual features that an SFL analysis entails further lends itself to fine-grained qualitative analysis for the close reading of individual texts, as well as to more representative quantitative approaches (Sharoff) in which the complex labelling allows for multiple angles of comparison, often bringing together functional similarities between categories that form-based analysis fails to capture. Reversing the angle of analysis, the creation of functional corpora allows for the possibility of both computerised production of language and the rapid and extensive analysis of texts, as well as the analysis of instances against the background of usage, normativity and markedness at different scales (O'Donnell).

Conclusion

In this chapter, we have offered a brief overview of the chapters in the book in an attempt to show the different ways in which the individual contributions relate to each other, and to hint at the rich and interrelated architecture of the theory – not extravagance for extravagance's sake, but because language as a social-semiotic phenomenon is itself extravagant. It is often claimed that Occam's Razor is the tool of science, but we are of the contrary opinion: that the simplest 'solution' to a problem may often be guilty of redefining that problem to suit the solution and that complexity reduced is merely complexity bypassed, complexity that will have to be accounted for somewhere down the line. Such an approach necessitates the continual development and interrelation of theoretical orientations towards the multiple aspects of language and their testing and refining in applied work. As it is customary to say at this point, we hope the chapters in this book – not as isolates, but as multiply connected nodes – go some way towards forwarding this endeavour.

Notes

1 For a detailed SFL profile of a variety of languages, see Caffarel et al. (2004).
2 See Matthiessen (2007) for a much fuller overview.
3 See Asp, this volume, for illustrations and note this slightly different use of the term 'realisation' from its use earlier in the chapter.

References

Butt, D.G. 2007. Method and imagination in Halliday's science of linguistics: From theory to practice. In R. Hasan, C.M.I.M. Matthiessen and J.J. Webster (eds) *Continuing Discourse on Language: A Functional Perspective, Vol. 1*. London: Equinox, pp. 81–116.

Caffarel, A., J.R. Martin and C.M.I.M. Matthiessen (eds). 2004. *Language Typology: A Functional Perspective*. Amsterdam: John Benjamins.

Cloran, C. 1995. Defining and relating text segments: Subject and theme in discourse. In R. Hasan and P. Fries (eds) *On Subject and Theme: A Discourse Functional Perspective*. Amsterdam: John Benjamins, pp. 361–402.

Fontaine, L., T. Bartlett and G. O'Grady (eds). 2013. *Systemic Functional Linguistics: Exploring Choice*. Cambridge: Cambridge University Press.

Halliday, M.A.K. 1978. *Language as Social Semiotic: The Social Interpretation of Language and Meaning*. London: Arnold.

Halliday, M.A.K. 1994. *Introduction to Functional Grammar*. 2nd edn. London: Arnold.

Hasan, R. 2014. Towards a paradigmatic description of context: Systems, metafunctions, and semantics. *Functional Linguistics* 1(9): 9–54.

Matthiessen, C.M.I.M. 2007. The 'architecture' of language according to systemic functional theory: Developments since the 1970s. In R. Hasan, C.M.I.M. Matthiessen and J.J. Webster (eds) *Continuing Discourse on Language: A Functional Perspective, Vol. 2.* London: Equinox, pp. 505–61.

Matthiessen, C.M.I.M. 2015. Christian M.I.M. Matthiessen. In T. Andersen, M. Boeriis, E. Maagerø and E.S. Tønnessen (eds). *Social Semiotics: Key Figures, New Directions.* London and New York: Routledge, pp. 16–41.

Meillet, A. 1937. *Introduction a l'étude comparative des langues indo-européennes.* Paris: Hachette.

O'Grady, G., T. Bartlett and L. Fontaine (eds). 2013. *Choice in Language: Applications in Text Analysis.* London and Oakville: Equinox.

Zhang, D. 2014. The meaning of function: Syntax in systemic functional linguistics. In Fang Yan and J. J. Webster (eds) *Developing Systemic Functional Linguistics: Theory and Application.* Sheffield: Equinox, pp. 48–67.

Part I
A theoretical overview

2

The place of systemic functional linguistics as a linguistic theory in the twenty-first century

John A. Bateman

Introduction

In this chapter, I attempt to briefly position systemic functional linguistics (SFL) in relation to the major streams of current linguistic theorising. It will become clear that many of the differences to be observed can be traced back to differences in basic philosophical orientations adopted in the early phases of SFL's development. This makes any straightforward characterisation or comparison across accounts a considerable challenge and, without some common basis for discussion, meaningful points of contact will be difficult to find. The chapter therefore begins by presenting an abstract scaffold for viewing linguistic accounts of all kinds, then proceeds to address some selected points on which an alignment between SFL and other current theories has been seen as problematic. Particular areas of discussion will include *pragmatics*, the relationship to *cognition*, the place of *syntax*, and general questions of *data, validation, verification* and *explanation*.

Classifying linguistic theories and linguistic theorising

The scaffold for comparison that I will employ will be defined by treating the various domains within which 'language' manifests itself as 'starting points' for systematic investigation. Such manifestations of language are to be understood in a very broad sense, taking 'language' as an observable phenomenon already somewhat for granted. In any situation of assumed language use, the systematic study of that phenomenon can adopt one of four points of departure. Language can be studied in terms of the properties of performances and products ('in texts'); in terms of the coordination and interaction of collections of speakers, from small groups to entire societies ('in groups'); in terms of the operations and mechanisms that might be responsible for the capabilities and actions of the individual speakers observed ('in heads'); and in terms of properties of those situations, generally social, in which language is occurring ('in contexts'). These starting points are characterised graphically by the four vertices of the pyramid shown in Figure 2.1. The labels selected for these vertices deliberately avoid established theoretical constructs proposed in the linguistics literature so as also to avoid the accompanying theoretical 'baggage' that often makes more foundational comparisons across approaches difficult. There are also naturally differences in how precisely such starting points are handled – that is, the *methods* drawn upon by particular approaches when drilling deeper into their selected vertices may differ. For example, within an 'in texts' perspective, accounts may, on the one hand, employ increasingly formal techniques for building models that 'generate' the patterns found in the adopted data, as pursued in (but not only in) *generative* models; on the other hand, they may rely more on statistical methods for producing distributional descriptions of that data. In contrast, *cognitive* approaches, most readily aligned with the 'in heads' perspective, commonly distinguish themselves from generative or 'formalist' approaches on the basis of very different foundational assumptions. Whereas for cognitive approaches observational data with respect to actual language behaviour plays a central role, for generative approaches introspection and judgement data generally play the primary role. This marks a long-running debate summarised well by Butler and Gonzálvez-García (2014: 6–17), drawing on positions articulated in Newmeyer (1998), Croft (1999), Haspelmath (2000) and others, and to which we will return later in the chapter. The labels in the scaffold thus mark out common 'fault lines' drawn between accounts that we can use to characterise those accounts more abstractly.

It is also relevant to consider the philosophical foundations assumed when exploring language. Individual linguistic accounts or schools may themselves engage in philosophical considerations of language and linguistics to a greater or lesser extent. The broader philosophical positions thus developed by individual accounts demarcate important sources of motivations for adopting (or not adopting) particular points of departure. Discussions that address philosophical foundations need to be differentiated from discussions playing out within particular paradigms: the former set the horizons of interpretation and evaluation for the latter. Consequently, the 'forms of discourse' employed in discussions of language constitute a further complex dimension for characterising differences between approaches. These forms of discourse vary according to their levels of abstraction – that is, how far they lie from observable linguistic data; a corresponding organisation of the interrelationships among these levels is suggested graphically in Figure 2.2.

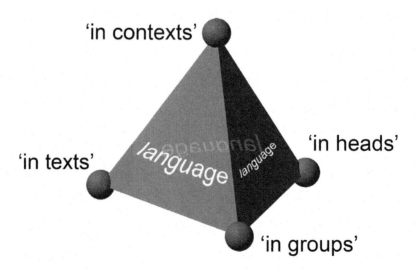

Figure 2.1   Points of departure for the systematic study of language, languages, texts and their users

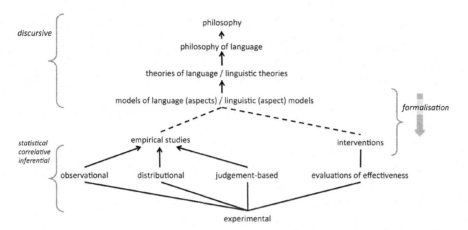

Figure 2.2   *Types of discourse available for couching reflective consideration of language and language phenomena*

Note: The vertical dimension correlates with degree of abstraction and distance from linguistic data, and covers several quite distinct kinds of relationships. The form of the diagram overall is *not* to be taken to indicate that all of these forms of discourse necessarily rest on, or 'bottom out' in, empiricism.

At the top of Figure 2.2 – seen as the farthest removed from actual instances of language use – we have those types of discourse best situated alongside other endeavours within *philosophy*, but focusing specifically on how language may impinge on the broad questions addressed. The purpose of these forms of discourse is then primarily to raise issues such as what it means to be human or to be conscious, or to build and partake in societies and culture, or to have or to be language at all. Within such broad orientations in the *philosophy of language*, particular *theories of language* may emerge. This level of abstraction marks the beginning of linguistics proper, whereby certain broader philosophical assumptions are worked through with respect to their consequences for thinking and systematising our thoughts about language. This may in turn lead on to particular, but still abstract, *models of language* situated among models proposed for other aspects of human behaviour or being. Taken further, such models offer paradigms within which varying degrees and kinds of 'formalisation' may be pursued. Any of these forms of discourse may tell us useful things about language and, moreover, any particular 'school' of linguistics may find itself employing differing forms of discourse with respect to different areas within its general focus of attention.

Finally, differences between approaches may arise due to the *direction* of the investigative movements they employ – that is, particular approaches can often be seen most beneficially in terms of the 'path' that they take along the edges of the pyramid between multiple selected points of departure. Beginning 'in heads', for example, means that cognitive principles and methods appropriate for such research – primarily experimental – will be adopted, but test cases may be defined in terms of linguistic behaviour ('in texts'). Alternatively, proceeding in the other direction, particular structural regularities may be observed and described (again employing appropriate methods, such as corpus studies or traditional linguistic structural description), and then motivations for these organisations are sought in cognitive principles – thus distributional features or syntactic generalisations over such features ('in texts') may be used to motivate discussion of cognitive capabilities ('in heads') as argued in terms of *construction grammar* (Gries 2012) or of *functional discourse grammar* (Hengeveld and Mackenzie 2008).

13

All positions and paths within the pyramid of points of departure are commonplace in the contemporary field of linguistics, and it is easy to find a multitude of exemplars. Moreover, some directions of development are seen as particularly important at this time, with significant research energy being expended on them across the field, and this chapter will draw these out more specifically in relation to SFL as it proceeds.

The nature of SFL

The point of departure for SFL and the motivation for this choice relates directly to its philosophical position on the role and nature of language. This in turn shapes the kind of *linguistics* that SFL takes itself to be. It will be useful to consider SFL's view of itself by addressing the basic components making up its name – that is, 'systemic', 'functional' and 'linguistics'. I will begin with 'linguistics' to anchor the account explicitly against the relevant philosophical forms of discourse set out in Figure 2.2.

Why systemic functional linguistics?

SFL is, first and foremost, an 'in contexts' form of linguistic activity. The motivation for this is a strong one, running through all facets of the theory and its discourses. It is therefore important to understand how SFL construes 'context' to see the role it takes within the theory. The emergence of SFL is traditionally traced back to the anti-dualist approach to language developed in Britain in the 1930s–50s by J.R. Firth (1890–1960). Firth's position on language drew, on the one hand, on philosophical critiques of the mind–body distinction that were becoming prominent through the work of Ludwig Wittgenstein, Gilbert Ryle and others, and, on the other, on earlier anthropological proposals that language be treated essentially as contextualised action for social and individual purposes (cf. Malinowski 1923). This led to Firth placing concrete 'contexts' of language use at the centre of his approach as the basic objects of inquiry for linguistics, *but without making any prior assumptions about what might be occurring in society or in the minds apparently participating in such contexts*.

For Firth, contexts involved signifying practices that could be captured in terms of 'statements of meaning' pitched at various levels of abstraction (Firth 1957 [1950]). Such statements of meaning were descriptions of language patterning that are (a) selected on the basis of their role in characterising how the linguistic events being described could be seen as 'meaningful' for their participants, and (b) formulated to help researchers to understand the processes observed without assuming that the categories introduced were themselves causally involved. The purpose of making these statements of meaning was to bring systematicity to any textual phenomena observed, thereby revealing 'patterns of life', the processual flux of meaningful activities. Linguistic statements of meaning could then be judged by virtue of how well they made such patterns visible to reflection.

Three important points should be made about these 'statements of meaning', because they remain relevant for understanding the positions taken within SFL today.

1   Firth took the philosophical positions of his time seriously and saw any statements that were made as linguistic entities in their own right – that is, linguistics in Firth's sense was 'just language turned back on itself' (Firth 1957 [1950]: 181). We shall see shortly that this is used to both negative and positive effect in current argumentation within SFL.

2   Given the complexity of linguistic behaviour, it was taken as axiomatic that such statements would span very diverse kinds of patterns and bring out differing kinds of generalisations. Firth expressed this usefully in terms of his well-known 'prism' metaphor, whereby linguistic behaviour is seen as analogous to white light and linguistic statements of meaning act as a methodological prism for splitting that light according to its components (cf. Firth 1968 [1956]: 108). Firth proclaimed all of these component descriptions to be 'meaningful' in that they contribute positively to (our understanding of) the meaning of any situation so described.

3   Since these statements of meaning were just language turned back on itself, they are also seen to have the properties of language themselves: they are not distinguished as some other kind of entity independent of the principles of linguistic discourse in general and so raise no ontological claims. In other words, linguistic terms used in statements of meaning remain manners of speaking and cannot (and should not) be 'hypostatised' as actually existent; statements of meaning are simply a scaffold that is used as a tool to get the job of linguistic description done and which should be removed when no longer needed. This orientation has also had both positive and negative consequences for subsequent linguistic theorising within SFL.

The starting point formed by combining these organising principles led to many questions and preconceptions concerning language being construed anew, but also faced various critiques.

It was in the work of M.A.K. Halliday, Firth's student, that a more systematic 'map' of an approach to language consistent with Firth's basic assumptions first appeared (Butt 2001: 1818). This framework, beginning with 'pre-SFL' models in the early 1960s, gradually moved in the 1970s towards Halliday's (1978) view of language as a *social semiotic* and SFL proper. The resulting framework continues many of the basic Firthian philosophical concerns, complemented with details of linguistic theory and models of language calling for the application of empirical methods at all levels of analysis. Linguistic descriptions were still seen as language turned back on itself – that is, a scaffold for making statements of meaning – but throughout the 1970s and 1980s the properties of those descriptions, and the metalanguage for their expression, became substantially more codified and capable of supporting more precise analyses.

Why systemic *functional linguistics?*

The philosophical commitment of SFL to characterising language from an 'in contexts' position led to a focus on the notion of 'possible actions' – that is, what speakers and hearers *can do*. A very significant component of this potential was then naturally taken to concern language. Thus, within the overall 'behaviour' potential, we find what is commonly termed in SFL the 'meaning potential' – that is, what speakers and hearers 'can mean'. SFL consequently sees its principal theoretical and descriptive task as characterising this meaning potential, and its uses and consequences as *resources* for meaningful action.

The notion of 'potential' and its use as a resource is a central design feature of the theory, and leads on directly to the most distinctive feature of SFL *descriptions*: the **system network**. All levels of the linguistic system are characterised as resources by describing them as interlinked collections of alternations accompanied by specifiable distinctions in their associated linguistic forms; many examples of such descriptions appear in the other contributions to this Handbook. The alternations constitute speaker's options – that is, their resources for action, meaning, etc. – at the level of abstraction considered. 'System' in SFL

15

is then used in a double sense: both individual groups of alternatives standing in contrast and the entire set of networks formed from these collections – as in 'the language system' – are commonly termed 'systems'. One theoretical goal of SFL as a whole is then to describe language as a collection of such systems – that is, 'systemically'.

Why systemic functional linguistics?

One of the most common ways in which SFL has been compared and contrasted with other kinds of linguistic theorising draws on the final component of its name: its characterisation as a 'functional' school of linguistics. Since there are many linguistic schools that are 'functionalist' in orientation, it has been natural to consider correspondences between these theories and SFL. The most detailed comparisons of this kind have been pursued by Butler and colleagues (for example Butler 1988; Butler and Taverniers 2008; Butler 2013; Butler and Gonzálvez-García 2014) precisely with the aim of improving dialogue across distinct, but arguably related, approaches wherein notions of language function play a role.

The broad family of approaches labelling themselves as 'functional' do share certain principles. In particular, properties of the linguistic system, such as grammatical organisation, are taken to be motivated more or less directly from features 'external' to that organisation itself. Butler and Taverniers (2008: 690) usefully characterise functional approaches as follows, annotated here in addition with respect to the vertices of Figure 2.1:

> [T]he central claim of functionalism is that language should be seen first and foremost as a system of communication between human beings ['in groups'], and that the shapes which languages take ['in texts'] are strongly conditioned by both the nature of human cognitive capacities ['in heads'] and the sociocultural contexts ['in contexts'] in which, and purposes for which, language is used.

This shows both the points of contact with our labelling system and the particular relationships presumed to hold among those contributing features. What is then definitional for the functional programme is that 'in texts' properties depend on cognitive and/or social facets. This illustrates that the dimensions employed not only refer to points of departure (such as cognitive, 'in heads'; structural, 'in texts'), but also pick out specific movements between vertices as suggested earlier.

The family of approaches classified as 'structural-functional' (Van Valin 1992: 2) picks out approaches that take communicative function to be a crucial motivating force for grammatical structure – a position common to all European approaches to linguistics since Hjelmslev and the Prague School – and so adopts a selection of 'in texts' as one pole combined with the assumption that regularities in texts (the 'structural' component) will be motivated from other poles. Those sources of motivation are most typically sought 'in heads' or 'in groups'. Approaches classified as 'functional-cognitive' consequently form a subfamily that attempts to motivate properties of linguistic behaviour specifically by virtue of cognitive principles or mechanisms. These approaches are situated along the edge of the pyramid between 'in heads' orientations and 'in texts' orientations, and correlate with cognitive approaches in the general tradition often attributed to Piaget (1985) and eventually taken up in 'cognitive science'. Positions that move between 'in texts' and 'in groups' correlate more with approaches that assume that language is primarily a social phenomenon. This can be traced back to work such as that of Vološinov (1986 [1929]) in social psychology or even to positions in social anthropology such as that of Malinowski (1923), to which SFL remains strongly aligned (cf., for example, Halliday 1978; Hasan 1985). This is picked up again in so-called *usage-based* approaches, of which there are now several variants, some also taking in the 'in heads' pole on their journey (Bybee 2010; Evans 2014; Tomasello 2005).

As shown by Butler and Gonzálvez-García (2014), however, the broad functionalist orientation is anything but homogeneous: simply to characterise a linguistic account as 'functionalist' or 'formalist' or 'cognitive' and so on will generally be insufficient (cf. Nuyts 2005), and one has to look closer at philosophical and methodological orientations as well. Approaches within the *cognitive linguistics* family, for example, contrast with many other approaches by positing a far closer relationship between the grammatical descriptions that they offer and assumed cognitive or neural mechanisms. This binding of the 'in texts' and 'in heads' perspectives draws primarily on philosophical argument and informal psychological models, such as theories of prototypes and metaphors (Evans and Green 2006; Langacker 1987), rather than psychological or psycholinguistic experimentation directly. In terms of their forms of discourse, therefore, they remain in the upper half of Figure 2.2. The gap that this opens up between the assumed 'cognitive' of cognitive linguistics and actual cognition, as revealed in psycholinguistics and neurolinguistics, is increasingly recognised as potentially problematic (cf. discussions in Butler and Gonzálvez-García 2014; Evans 2014). It is, moreover, also possible to consider cognitive linguistics and SFL as duals in certain respects: both claim to be usage-based and see language as a phenomenon that is learned without universals. Cognitive linguistics places its mechanisms 'in heads', while 'mainstream' SFL relies on 'semiotic' principles emerging out of the need for 'in groups' coordinated social activity.

Some common questions raised with respect to SFL

In this section, I turn to some of the frequently reoccurring questions that are raised by those coming to SFL for the first time or those attempting to make sense of SFL research in terms of other theories. Answering these questions relies on the definitional components of SFL that we have just seen, while also opening up some of the directions that might be beneficial for SFL to explore more deeply in the future.

What happened to syntax?

As with all linguistic accounts, one of the levels of description pursued in SFL is naturally that concerned with grammatical phenomena – or 'syntax' using the three-way distinction of syntax–semantics–pragmatics introduced by Morris (1938) and now assumed in many other schools of linguistics. Here, however, SFL exhibits a rather different orientation, which is a common source of non-alignments in treatments and a lack of communication across approaches. Although the syntax–semantics–pragmatics distinction is in many respects natural for accounts adopting an 'in texts' starting point, it is considerably less compelling when an 'in contexts' point of departure is pursued.

With the 'in texts' starting point, it is assumed that regularities will be observable in the linguistic forms and their combinations (syntax). These regularities may then be coordinated with distinctions in decontextualised meanings (semantics), which are subsequently contextualised by language users. This latter is the concern of pragmatics, to which I will return shortly. Such an orientation is found, for example, throughout approaches in Chomsky's generative linguistics tradition, in which patterns 'in texts' are to be accounted for first and foremost in terms of elegant systems of formal description (as in early transformational

grammars). These might then be taken as making predictions concerning cognitive principles and architectures. Along this path, contexts are met only at the end of the road, leaving
pragmatics as an area to be added (Hasan 2009).

A more fundamental background assumption of this orientation is that the nature of the
enterprise is not substantially changed by working towards, rather than out of, context – that
is, pursuing descriptions of syntactic regularities 'in texts' can proceed in its own right.
Whether this is actually the case is not yet entirely clear. For several phenomena addressed
in pragmatics, the differing starting points certainly lead to very different placements of
phenomena in SFL and non-SFL accounts; indeed, as we shall see in the next subsection,
for some phenomena central to pragmatics it is not straightforward to find SFL equivalents
at all. This can be seen in terms of Thibault and van Leeuwen's (1996) characterisation of
different demarcations and positioning of phenomena as involving a distinction between an
'importing' view and an 'exporting' view. Whereas SFL brings many alternations directly
motivated by contextual distinctions into its grammars (importing), many other accounts
move such distinctions into other components external to grammar itself (exporting).

The consequences of adopting the importing view when developing grammars can be
seen as follows. Grammatical representation within SFL relies throughout on paradigms
of alternations, or systems, that construe grammar as a resource as explained above. SFL's
primary source of evidence when constructing a grammar is the existence of regular patterns
of alternations that can be captured informally as proportionalities. Martin (1992: 8) offers
the following example of an *experiential* proportionality – that is, an alternation that makes
a difference within the area of meaning traditionally considered the realm of propositional
content:

Trillian is cooking dinner: Dinner is cooking::
Zaphod is marching the troops: The troops are marching::
Ford is boiling the kettle: The kettle is boiling

In terms of the meanings expressed, we have a (systematically) different combination of a
semantic process or predicate and participants or arguments in that process. Proportionalities
of this kind then correspond to alternations, which correspond in turn to individual systems of choice as defined within SFL. In this case, then, we have grammatical motivation
for a system distinguishing two grammatical features standing in opposition: 'effective' vs.
'middle' (Halliday and Matthiessen 2013: 334–6). The former labels clauses that can stand
in the first half of each proportion; the latter labels all clauses that can stand in the second
half of each proportion. Grammar development then continues by specifying structural properties sufficient for distinguishing the two groups from each another.

There are, however, *other* kinds of proportionalities to which SFL demands we pay equal
attention. For example, the following utterances *also* exhibit proportionalities that may well
need to find a place in the overall grammatical resource being constructed:

Trillian is cooking dinner: It is dinner that Trillian is cooking::
Zaphod is marching the troops: It is the troops that Zaphod is marching::
Ford is boiling the kettle: It is the kettle that Ford is boiling

Whereas an *exporting* account of grammar might consider such proportionalities to be
more pragmatic in nature – to do with language use, perhaps – and so remove them from the
tasks of grammar, SFL makes no such division and *imports* potential alternations into its

grammatical descriptions. This means that grammar in SFL is not limited a priori to some notion of 'core' grammatical phenomena that restrict the task.

This aligns with SFL's notion of grammar as a resource. The grammatical description provides precisely those options for making distinctions in meaning (considered broadly in terms of what would make a difference for the *communicative context*) that are available for a language user. In formulating an SFL grammar, we are therefore guided more by what speakers *can* say rather than what they cannot. This is a concrete consequence of only moving to an 'in text' description from the starting point of the 'in context' pole rather than vice versa: the context establishes distinctions in meaning with which distinct proportionalities in the grammar may both correlate and also co-construct.

These contrasting orientations have further consequences requiring attention when comparing SFL and many other approaches. Within the 'in texts' orientation, for example, the starting point entails that a grammatical description should first attempt to capture just what forms are 'in' any texts characterised and which not. This leads to a reliance on grammaticality whereby grammatical descriptions are evaluated by procedures that test whether those descriptions cover the range of data considered to be grammatical. Relating descriptions to data reliably in this fashion constitutes a central component of the argumentation employed in this orientation. SFL, in contrast, favours grammatical descriptions that provide compelling explanations in contextual terms of why some forms have occurred rather than others. Such explanations typically include statements concerning the other possibilities that a speaker might have followed, but did not, again expressing this in terms related to the differential contextual effects that would have been brought about. Grammaticality judgements per se are not, then, a principal driving force.

It is not straightforward to evaluate these differing orientations by direct comparison, because they each bring benefits for different kinds of tasks and also occupy different positions with respect to their adopted forms of discourse from that illustrated in Figure 2.2. Some quite substantial results concerning the nature of grammar have now been achieved on the basis of the more narrowly circumscribed grammatical descriptions from the 'in texts' starting point. Current evidence suggests, for example, that a certain family of grammatical descriptions may be adequate for characterising all structural regularities observed in descriptions of grammar – the so-called *mildly context-sensitive* grammar formalisms, which combine the kind of flexibility that appears necessary for natural occurrences of language with restricted computational complexity so that they are readily used in processing. The two most well-known formalisms of this kind are *tree adjoining grammar* (Joshi 1987) and *combinatory categorical grammar* (Steedman 2000); further detailed comparison of these frameworks with SFL is offered in Bateman (2008). Restricting computational complexity is considered a necessary goal within this tradition because otherwise there is little expectation that human performance on natural data will be accounted for. Similarly, Culicover and Jackendoff (2006) argue that syntax should be only as complex as it need be to 'establish interpretation'; such a syntax then acts as an integrator of information specified elsewhere for the purposes of that information's expression in language.

Many current accounts of syntax consequently move in this direction, paring down their syntactic components to provide a backbone sufficiently strong to carry other components of meaning, but not stronger. This supports, and is supported by, pushing the form of discourse employed 'downwards' in the direction illustrated by Figure 2.2, over the formalisation gap towards empirical studies. In contrast, one of the main goals of SFL has always been that it can be applied in specific areas in which knowledge of language must be taught or communicated, for example in both first and foreign language teaching as explicit cases of 'intervention' (again, see Figure 2.2). Here, the ability to explain convincingly *why* one grammatical form rather than another might be preferable and what consequences accrue from other choices is clearly of considerable value. This is not a capability that need follow directly from questions of grammaticality; instead, it is precisely an awareness of the *possibilities* of expression that is required, which is SFL's focus.

And where has pragmatics gone?

Following on from these issues raised with respect to grammar and syntax, there is the dual question concerning pragmatics – that is, language *use*. For a theory supposedly concerned centrally with the use of language and with the relation of language use to context, those coming to SFL theory are often perplexed by the lack of explicit treatments – and, for the most part, even *mention* – of pragmatics. Fairclough (1995), for example, adopts many SFL categories in his critical discourse analysis, but considers the lack of central pragmatic (and, in some respects, also semantic) notions such as 'presupposition', 'implicature' (cf. van Dijk 2008: 184–5), 'metaphor' and 'blending' (cf. Hart 2008) deeply problematic.

Practitioners of SFL are, however, often equally perplexed when confronted with these questions – in much the same way as a car owner might not be sure how to respond when asked why his or her car does not appear to have a fifth wheel. As we saw in the previous subsection, substantial differences in the placement of 'pragmatic' phenomena arise from SFL's 'importing' perspective. Since the starting point of Firthian, and then SFL, statements of meaning is always language use in contexts, descriptions are always confronted with issues of interpretation. What is taken to make patterns of linguistic phenomena 'in texts' into relevant patterns at all is precisely their functioning meaningfully 'in contexts'; thus *all* description in SFL sees itself as involved with language use and so a separate designation of an area of 'pragmatics' within this theoretical orientation is considered redundant.

Particularly for pragmatics, the assumption set out that whether we start 'in texts' or 'in contexts' makes little difference is of questionable validity. This can be seen well in the case of 'speech acts', a central area of study usually placed within pragmatics. Thibault and van Leeuwen (1996) argue, for example, that it is just those linguistic distinctions that would be most useful for characterising the speech functions of utterances that speech act theorists regularly *export* from grammatical description. This makes the grammar simpler, but at the same time complicates formulations of the relation between grammar and social action, since information relevant for interpretation is no longer available. The formalist tradition limits syntactic descriptions essentially to that motivated by a transparent encoding of a referential view of logical representation, and so the task within an exporting orientation becomes one of accounting for how language manages to achieve actions (such as 'threatening', 'promising', 'blackmailing' and so on) even though it lacks grammatical forms dedicated to such actions. Within SFL approaches, grammatical and semantic markers of such contextual distinctions are more naturally included in descriptions as characterisations of differences in what speakers can say (and thereby what they can mean), and so there is more information available to bridge the distinct levels of linguistic abstraction.

Nevertheless, there are also further areas commonly addressed within pragmatics towards which SFL approaches have so far directed less attention. There is a continuing deficit in SFL, for example, in accounts of dynamics and process – despite SFL researchers always having placed this particular aspect of theorising about language high on their list of priorities. Whereas it is justifiable that SFL considers all of its modelling decisions to be 'pragmatically' motivated in some sense, the modelling decisions taken towards describing 'potential' for action have not so far been accompanied by equal attention to areas of action that require *inference*. Here, the relation drawn in traditional pragmatics to logical formalisations has been more beneficial and so considering how this may be developed further within SFL constitutes an important open issue. Interactions to date have been limited largely due to the fact that work on dynamics within other areas of linguistics is strongly formal in orientation, for example (cf. Kamp 1981; Asher and Lascarides 2013). This will require more SFL linguists to engage with formal approaches, to which end a lingering suspicion within SFL that formal descriptions are automatically 'generative' in nature, and therefore aligned with the Chomskyan 'in texts'– 'in heads' perspective, needs to be overcome.

The relation of SFL to cognition and the brain

Within SFL, largely due to its early rejections of brain–body duality, explicitly 'cognitive' models have long been suspected of reversing explanatory accounts – that is, much psycholinguistic discourse is seen as a simple refinement of folk psychology driven by resonances in the linguistic system rather than as revealing genuine 'cognitive' processes (Butler 2013; Halliday and Matthiessen 1999). Consequently, there has traditionally been a gap in discussions of SFL concerning just how the individual language user processes or produces language – a gap bolstered by the lack of treatments of dynamics and inference just mentioned.

Positions vary within SFL on this issue. Fawcett, for example, has always proposed models that he explicitly sets up as cognitive (for example Fawcett 2000) – although, these, like most models within cognitive linguistics, have not been subjected to experimental investigation. Similarly, Davidse, a prominent SFL theorist and grammarian, has moved in recent years to position herself more explicitly within cognitive linguistics following a lack of broader take-up of cognitive or processing issues within much of SFL itself (Davidse 2000). As Butler (2013) sets out, this apparent rejection of results from psycholinguistics has led to a number of criticisms of other core components of the SFL framework as well. In a review exhibiting signs of frustration, for example, van Dijk (2008: 46) takes considerable exception to the account of context that SFL provides, characterising it as unmotivated and unempirical largely because of SFL's unwillingness to engage with cognitive modelling.

There can now be little doubt, however, that many facets of context are indeed being 'modelled' by the human cognitive system and fine-grained empirical predictions at many levels of abstraction have been verified (cf. Jones et al. 2011). In one long series of studies ranging over Zwaan, Langson and Graesser (1995), Zwaan and Radvansky (1998), Zacks (2010) and others, for example, increasingly robust cognitive models of the information that is constructed and maintained during discourse comprehension have been developed and supported experimentally. Important results, such as the centrality of events and the use of time and space to index changes as discourse unfolds, are now well established. This means that there needs to be far more attention and cross-fertilisation of the results of such experimental studies with the accounts of SFL. And, indeed, in many areas this need not necessarily be that difficult. It is striking, for example, how many of the constructs argued for in psycholinguistic studies correspond to the kinds of configurations posited to be at work during *logogenesis* within SFL – that is, the temporal dimension of a text's unfolding (Halliday and Matthiessen 1999: 18; Halliday and Matthiessen 2013: 601). There is much here to explore and more openness to the 'in heads' pole of our pyramid will be of considerable benefit. Although some earlier 'cognitive' discussions may well have been folk psychology recast in the genre of scientific discourse, as SFL often suggests, this can no longer be generalised to 'in heads' discussions as such. Indeed, critiques of this nature sound increasingly hollow when fine-grained predictions concerning measurable brain activity are supported by experiment. This empirical basis therefore needs to be incorporated more firmly within SFL methodology as well.

A further, relatively recent, development among 'in heads' positions that is very much in line with some of the philosophical orientations of SFL is the move to include *embodiment* as a crucial feature in both linguistic treatments and philosophical accounts (Johnson 1987). Many frameworks now consider it essential to include the role of the body, and its systems of perception and action, as integrally involved in characterisations of language, of language processing and of situated action, and this position is also increasingly supported by empirical research (Fischer and Zwaan 2008). Much of language and language use is consequently seen as inherently embodied action.

One way of characterising embodied action currently receiving considerable attention draws on the notion of *image schemas* (Lakoff and Johnson 1999; Talmy 2006). Image schemas offer a bridge between, on the one hand, routinised, embodied action and, on the other, conceptual representations. This position therefore constitutes a very broad sense of 'in heads' that may actually be more appropriately characterised in terms of a synthesis of 'in bodies' – since it is not assumed that language is a purely cognitive affair – and a particular reading of 'in contexts' – since perception, action and language are all seen to rely on an embodied entity that is 'in' its environment rather than a disembodied 'brain-mind'. Important frameworks being developed here include Roy's (2005) 'semiotic schemas' and Bergen and Chang's (2005) *embodied construction grammar*. These variants of 'in heads' theorising are well aligned with SFL preoccupations, even though those preoccupations have remained seriously underdeveloped within SFL itself (cf. the critical discussions in Thibault 2006; Butler 2013).

The reasons for this lack of development are also largely historical. It is sometimes suggested within SFL, for example, that the theory in fact already has a natural relationship with neural approaches to language because of an early alliance during SFL's formative period in the 1960s and 1970s with Lamb's *stratificational grammar* (for example Lamb 1999). Lamb proposed his account to be explicitly related to models of the brain as 'networks' of neurons and consequently adopted a network representation for linguistic phenomena. Drawing an analogy between SFL and neural accounts on the basis of a network representation confuses several of the levels of discourse given in Figure 2.2, however. Expressing linguistic descriptions as networks is as little an easy ticket for neurobiological plausibility as it is a replacement for detailed linguistic argumentation (*contra* Butt 2001: 1825). Considerably more empirical investigation of how best to relate the levels of abstraction involved will be necessary, again drawing on the state of the art in all of the relevant contributing fields.

Conclusions and outlook

This chapter should have made it clear that the field of linguistics has never been so diverse and vibrant, with approaches clustering around all of the distinct perspectives from which language can be approached. Further variations arise due to accounts choosing to *value* the contributions of their starting points differently, as well as by selecting rather different methods of *securing access* to details of the language phenomena at issue at those poles (such as by collecting natural data, by generating examples from introspection, by experimentation). Even within SFL there is considerable variation: whereas some areas focus on fine-grained linguistic description, other areas are more appropriately classified as contributions to the philosophy of language, while still others may offer educational guidelines – which diverse directions operate with rather different parameters and so do not necessarily combine as single theoretical constructs. Some theorists within SFL, as elsewhere, attempt highly integrative work of this kind, but the path is long and does not follow as an automatic consequence of the distinct endeavours themselves.

SFL commonly describes itself as an 'extravagant' theory with respect to the constructs and mechanisms it employs. This notion goes back to Firth's characterisation of linguistics as 'language turned back on itself'. A philosophical position of this kind is quite the reverse of approaches that are engaged in theory building within deliberately (and often usefully, as suggested at various points in this chapter) restricted formalisations. SFL can, in this sense, be used to actively explore properties of language and language use that, in many other accounts, have been difficult to gain access to. While this is very positive during exploration phases, it is also beneficial to be able to focus that extravagance so as to support more fine-grained articulations of linguistic descriptions. And here, again, there are many possibilities for interaction and exchange with other frameworks.

To support this, I have set out some of the ways in which SFL can be positioned against this broader background of linguistic research. The points of departure in Figure 2.1 and the distinct types of discourse set out in Figure 2.2 have suggested ways of picking out those aspects that (a) define SFL as a distinct approach and (b) may need to be considered more carefully to lower boundaries for communication across frameworks. For the former, the distinctive 'in contexts' orientation has led to a treatment of language as a resource for meaning making, whereby each level of description is considered a way of articulating differences in communicative context. The view of 'meaning' that results from this is considerably broader than that found in approaches more influenced by the development of formal or logic-based accounts of meaning. Within SFL, meaning is a matter of characterising how differences in social context can be created, maintained and manipulated by linguistic means; the referential notion of meaning as propositional semantics is included as only one facet. This has had considerable consequences for just which phenomena are treated where within the overall account, and has made SFL particularly strong in its attention to areas of the linguistic system and language use that have not so far received sufficient attention in other frameworks. The philosophical position adopted concerning language and its relation to social contexts is still therefore best described as a *social semiotic*, as suggested in Halliday (1978).

Some traditional boundaries or fractures between approaches need nevertheless to be considered critically. Any approach, for example, that concerns itself with making a grammatical account sufficiently explicit to 'cover' the structural configurations provided by a language or language variety will necessarily have components strongly focused at the 'in texts' pole, be those approaches structural, generative, formalist, cognitive or whatever. Any of these approaches may have points of significance for linguistic work more generally. For example, we saw that purely formal 'in texts' considerations have led to the discovery of the 'mildly context-sensitive' family of grammatical formalisms – a family with very specific properties beneficial for real-time, dynamic language processing. It is then natural to move towards the 'in heads' pole and ask whether there is also some relation to the kinds of behaviours of which our neural machinery is capable (cf. Steedman 2002). Moreover, as we have seen, the current explosion in brain-related linguistic theorising and description, ranging from more traditional psycholinguistic explorations to accounts of embodied semantics, all have much to add and will no doubt be of considerable relevance, even for SFL, in the future. In all cases, we will need movements 'downwards' in the levels of abstraction shown in Figure 2.2.

Linguistics as a whole can now benefit only when contributions across a broad range of linguistic schools are drawn upon, since no one orientation to the phenomenon of human language can claim to cover all the angles. This is also, in essence, to reaffirm an early position advocated by Halliday (1964: 13): 'I would defend the view that different coexisting models in linguistics may best be regarded as appropriate to different aims, rather than as competing contenders for the same goal.'

Although we have also seen points in this chapter that are not simply a matter of different accounts for differing aims – there are points of overlaps between goals that allow, and indeed insist upon, critical comparison and evaluation – it certainly needs to be recalled that there are more goals in linguistics as a field than those currently defined within any single programme of research. There is therefore now not only a considerable utility in engaging in productive dialogue, but also a need. Moreover – and this is perhaps the major message of this chapter – such dialogue requires both an openness and a readiness to hear what others are saying and why they are saying it.

References

Asher, N., and A. Lascarides. 2013. Strategic conversation. *Semantics & Pragmatics* 6(2): 1–62.

Bateman, J.A. 2008. Systemic functional linguistics and the notion of linguistic structure: Unanswered questions, new possibilities. In J.J. Webster (ed.) *Meaning in Context: Strategies for Implementing Intelligent Applications of Language Studies*. London: Equinox, pp. 24–58.

Bergen, B.K., and N. Chang. 2005. Embodied construction grammar in simulation-based language understanding. In J.-O. Östman and M. Fried (eds) *Construction Grammar(s): Cognitive and Cross-Language Dimensions*. Amsterdam: Johns Benjamins, pp. 147–90.

Butler, C.S. 1988. Pragmatics and systemic linguistics. *Journal of Pragmatics* 12: 83–102.

Butler, C.S. 2013. Systemic functional linguistics, cognitive linguistics and psycholinguistics: Opportunities for dialogue. *Functions of Language* 20(2): 185–218.

Butler, C.S., and F. Gonzálvez-García. 2014. *Exploring Functional-Cognitive Space* (Studies in Language Companion Series 157). Amsterdam: John Benjamins.

Butler, C.S., and M. Taverniers. 2008. Layering in structural-functional grammars. *Linguistics* 46(4): 689–756.

Butt, D.G. 2001. Firth, Halliday and the development of systemic functional theory. In S. Auroux, E.F.K. Koerner, H.-J. Niederehe and K. Versteegh (eds) *History of the Language Sciences: An International Handbook on the Evolution of the Study of Language from the Beginnings to the Present, vol. 2, 1806–1838*. Berlin and New York: de Gruyter, pp. 1806–38.

Bybee, J. 2010. *Language, Usage and Cognition*. Cambridge: Cambridge University Press.

Croft, W. 1999. What (some) functionalists can learn from (some) formalists. In M. Darnell, E. Moravcsik, F. Newmeyer, M. Noonan and K. Wheatley (eds) *Functionalism and Formalism in Linguistics. Volume I: General Papers*. Amsterdam and Philadelphia, PA: John Benjamins, pp. 87–100.

Culicover, P.W., and R. Jackendoff. 2006. The simpler syntax hypothesis. *Trends in Cognitive Sciences* 10(9): 413–18.

Davidse, K. 2000. The semantics of cardinal versus enumerative existential constructions. *Cognitive Linguistics* 10(3): 203–50.

Evans, V. 2014. *The Language Myth: Why Language is Not an Instinct*. Cambridge: Cambridge University Press.

Evans, V., and M. Green. 2006. *Cognitive Linguistics: An Introduction*. Edinburgh: Edinburgh University Press.

Fairclough, N. 1995. *Critical Discourse Analysis: The Critical Study of Language*. London: Taylor & Francis.

Fawcett, R.P. 2000. *A Theory of Syntax for Systemic Functional Linguistics* (Current Issues in Linguistics 206). Amsterdam: John Benjamins.

Firth, J.R. 1957 [1950]. Personality and language in society. In *Papers in Linguistics 1934–1951*. London: Oxford University Press, pp. 177–89. Reprinted from *The Sociological Review: Journal of the Institute of Sociology* 42(2): 37–52.

Firth, J.R. 1968 [1956]. Descriptive linguistics and the study of English. In F.R. Palmer (ed.) *Selected Papers of J.R. Firth 1952–1959*. London: Longmans, pp. 96–113.

Fischer, M.H., and R.A. Zwaan. 2008. Embodied language: A review of the role of the motor system in language comprehension. *The Quarterly Journal of Experimental Psychology* 61(6): 825–50.

Gries, S.T. 2012. Frequencies, probabilities, and association measures in usage-/exemplar-based linguistics: Some necessary clarifications. *Studies in Language* 36(3): 477–510.

Halliday, M.A.K. 1964. Syntax and the consumer. In C.I.J.M. Stuart (ed.) *Report of the Fifteenth Annual (First International) Round Table Meeting on Linguistics and Language Study* (Monograph Series in Languages and Linguistics 17). Washington, D.C.: Georgetown University Press, pp. 11–24. Reprinted in M.A.K. Halliday. 2003. *On Language and Linguistics: The Collected Works of M.A.K. Halliday, Vol. 3*. London: Equinox, pp. 36–49.

Halliday, M.A.K. 1978. *Language as Social Semiotic*. London: Arnold.

Halliday, M.A. K. and C.M.I.M. Matthiessen. 1999. *Construing Experience through Meaning: A Language-Based Approach to Cognition*. London: Cassell.

Halliday, M.A.K., and C.M.I.M. Matthiessen. 2013. *Halliday's Introduction to Functional Grammar*. 4th edn. London and New York: Routledge.

Hart, C. 2008. Critical discourse analysis and metaphor: Toward a theoretical framework. *Critical Discourse Studies* 5(2): 91–106.

Hasan, R. 1985. Meaning, context and text: Fifty years after Malinowski. In J.D. Benson and W.S. Greaves (eds) *Systemic Perspectives on Discourse, Vol. 1*. Norwood, NJ: Ablex, pp. 16–49.

Hasan, R. 2009. A view of pragmatics in a social semiotic perspective. *Linguistics and the Human Sciences* 5(3): 251–79.

Haspelmath, M. 2000. Why can't we talk to each other? Review of Newmeyer 1998. *Lingua* 110(4): 235–55.

Hengeveld, K., and J.L. Mackenzie. 2008. *Functional Discourse Grammar: A Typologically Based Theory of Language Structure*. Oxford: Oxford University Press.

Johnson, M. 1987. *The Body in the Mind*. Chicago, IL: University of Chicago Press.

Jones, N.A., H. Ross, T. Lynam, P. Perez and A. Leitch. 2011. Mental models: An interdisciplinary synthesis of theory and methods. *Ecology and Society* 16(1): 46.

Joshi, A.K. 1987. An introduction to tree adjoining grammar. In A. Manaster-Ramer (ed.) *Mathematics of Language*. Amsterdam: John Benjamins, pp. 87–114.

Kamp, H. 1981. A theory of truth and semantic representation. In J.A.G. Groenendijk, T.M.V. Janssen and M.B.J. Stokhof (eds) *Formal Methods in the Study of Language. Part 1* (Mathematical Centre Tracts 136). Amsterdam: Mathematisch Centrum Amsterdam, pp. 277–322.

Lakoff, G., and M. Johnson. 1999. *Philosophy in the Flesh: The Embodied Mind and its Challenge to Western Thought*. New York: Basic Books.

Lamb, S.M. 1999. *Pathways of the Brain: The Neurocognitive Basis of Language* (Current Issues in Linguistic Theory 170). Amsterdam and Philadelphia, PA: John Benjamins.

Langacker, R.W. 1987. *Foundations in Cognitive Grammar, Vol. 1: Theoretical Prerequisites*. Stanford, CA: Stanford University Press.

Malinowski, B. 1923. *The Problem of Meaning in Primitive Languages*. New York: Harcourt, Brace, and Co.

Martin, J.R. 1992. *English Text: Systems and Structure*. Amsterdam: John Benjamins.

Morris, C.W. 1938. *Foundations of the Theory of Signs*. Chicago, IL: University of Chicago Press.

Newmeyer, F.J. 1998. *Language Form and Language Function*. Cambridge, MA: MIT Press.

Nuyts, J. 2005. Brothers in arms? On the relations between cognitive and functional linguistics. In F.J. Ruiz de Mendoza Ibáñez and N.S. Peña Cervel (eds) *Cognitive Linguistics: Internal Dynamics and Interdisciplinary Interaction* (Cognitive Linguistics Research 32). Berlin: Mouton de Gruyter, pp. 69–100.

Piaget, J. 1985. *The Equilibration of Cognitive Structures: The Central Problem of Intellectual Development*. Chicago, IL: University of Chicago Press.

Roy, D. 2005. Semiotic schemas: A framework for grounding language in action and perception. *Artificial Intelligence* 167(1–2): 170–205.

Steedman, M.J. 2000. *The Syntactic Process*. Cambridge, MA: MIT Press.

Steedman, M.J. 2002. Plans, affordances, and combinatory grammar. *Linguistics and Philosophy* 25(5–6): 723–53.

Talmy, L. 2006. The fundamental system of spatial schemas in language. In B. Hampe (ed.) *From Perception to Meaning: Image Schemas in Cognitive Linguistics*. Berlin: Mouton de Gruyter, pp. 37–47.

Thibault, P.J. 2006. *Brain, Mind and the Signifying Body: An Ecosocial Semiotic Theory*. London: Continuum.

Thibault, P.J, and T. van Leeuwen. 1996. Grammar, society, and the speech act: Renewing the connections. *Journal of Pragmatics* 25: 561–85.

Tomasello, M. 2005. *Constructing a Language: A Usage-Based Theory of Language Acquisition*. Cambridge, MA: Harvard University Press.

van Dijk, T.A. 2008. *Discourse and Context: A Sociocognitive Account*. Cambridge: Cambridge University Press.

Van Valin, R.D. 1992. A synopsis of role and reference grammar. In R.D. Van Valin (ed.) *Advances in Role and Reference Grammar* (Current Issues in Linguistic Theory 82). Amsterdam: John Benjamins, pp. 1–166.

Vološinov, V.N. 1986 [1929]. *Marxism and the Philosophy of Language*. Cambridge: Harvard University Press.

Zacks, J.M. 2010. How we organize our experience into events. *Psychological Science Agenda* 24(4).

Zwaan, R.A., and G.A. Radvansky. 1998. Situation models in language comprehension and memory. *Psychological Bulletin* 123(2): 162–85.

Zwaan, R.A., M.C. Langson and A.C. Graesser. 1995. The construction of situation models in narrative comprehension: An event-indexing model. *Psychological Science* 6(5): 292–7.

3

What is a system?
What is a function?

A study in contrasts and convergences

Elissa Asp

Everything having to do with languages as systems needs to be approached, we are convinced, with a view to examining the limitations of arbitrariness.[1]

(de Saussure 1986: 131)

Introduction

Ferdinand de Saussure (1857–1913) articulated some of the key concepts that framed linguistics in the twentieth century. Among his contributions was the distinction between **syntagmatic** and **paradigmatic** (or 'associative') relations (de Saussure 1986). Syntagmatic relations have to do with combinatorial possibilities – with constituency (one unit composed of one or more others) – but also (and perhaps more significantly in de Saussure's formulations) with aspects of serial order and dependencies between items that allow, signify or constrain constituency. Serial order involves both permissible and impossible sequences that are language particular. For example, in English, except in a few loan words, the phoneme /s/ can precede, but not follow, a voiceless stop /t/ in a syllable onset (/st/ but not */ts/); articles precede, rather than follow, nouns with which they are in construction (*a miracle* not *miracle a*); verbs precede their complements in unmarked orders (*Sam eats squid* not *Sam squid eats*), and so on.

Viewed synchronically, such serial ordering for canonical syntagms is largely **arbitrary**, although historical and comparative linguistics may provide accounts of when – and sometimes even why – a language has acquired a feature and what the allowable range of orderings is. Dependency relations, on the other hand, may be **motivated** by semantic features. For example, differences between prototypical intransitives (*laugh, collapse, sneeze*) and transitives (*tickle, exclude, slice*) are grounded in the participant roles associated with the meaning of the verbs. Similarly, features such as number and grammatical gender may be construed as motivated insofar as they index structural relations, although grammatical gender is referentially arbitrary, while number is motivated. And, again, languages vary in terms of whether and how such relations are expressed. These different types of syntagmatic relation may appear between items that are **present** in a construction.

27

In contrast, de Saussure (1986: 122) describes paradigmatic relations in terms of **absence**. What is present in a syntagm gets part of its **value** from its associates or 'mnemonic group', which may include not only morphosyntactic associates such as the inflectional paradigms for verbs or declensions of nouns, but also items related via semantic, lexical, phonological or phonetic features. Consider the following example.

(1) Sam slept through an afternoon

In example (1), the value of any particular item is partially determined by the absent items with which it is in contrast: the referent *Sam* versus relevant other participants; past not present tense; contrasts for semantic features of *sleep* versus, for instance, *doze*; and so on for the other selections. This value is partial since selection and interpretation may also be affected by items copresent in a syntagm. For example, simple past tense verbs may be ambiguous between habitual and single-instance interpretations. Features of an accompanying time adjunct can push interpretation towards one of these. So a partial paraphrase of example (1) with singular indefinite *an* is *on some occasion Sam did this*, but *the* in the same environment leaves the interpretation ambiguous. Thus the selection of items present in a syntagm can be seen as functionally motivated not only by contrast with their absent associates, but also by the syntagmatic environments in which they appear. For de Saussure, these axes – the syntagmatic and the paradigmatic; the arbitrary and motivated – were the central linguistic relations to be accounted for.

Curiously, although all linguistic models recognise paradigmatic contrasts to some extent, most frame grammars in terms of syntagmatic structures. This focus may follow from the cognitive salience of structural units. It may also follow from twentieth-century developments that foregrounded the importance of structure over meaning and, in work deriving from Chomsky's research, the associated characterisation of syntax as the autonomous generative component of language, which had the effect of limiting paradigmatic relations to only those contrastive features necessary to define grammatical classes and structural potentials – although these are turning out to be rather many. In contrast, systemic functional linguistic (SFL) models treat paradigmatic relations as defining for language, and so focus extensively on formalising paradigmatic options in particular languages as **systems** and **system networks**. This reflects the largely European and British intellectual traditions in which SFL developed, which give prominence to the **functions of language**.

Interest in the uses or functions of language has a history in the Western tradition that dates back to antiquity insofar as classical and later scholars were concerned with language use in logic, rhetoric and poetry, as well as with ontological questions bearing, broadly, on relationships between language, thought and reality. Distinctions between language function and language form, and debates about the relative importance of each, appear equally ancient and persist in modern linguistics, marking differences that shape theoretical discussion insofar as linguists identify models as either primarily formal or functional.

This chapter outlines, first, what systems and functions are, and sketches their development in SFL. It then briefly explores approaches to systems and functions in recent work in the minimalist program (MP). Arguably, SFL occupies the functional and paradigmatic extremity of functional-formal and paradigmatic-syntagmatic axes, while MP occupies the other. Despite the contrastive positioning of models, there are points of convergence that suggest that systems and functions are among the ways in which the arbitrariness of language is limited.

Definitions and contexts

What is a system, broadly speaking?

In its broadest sense, the term 'system' refers to the relationships between any collection of elements (concrete or abstract; living or not; designed or natural) that are interconnected with each other such that changing some part of the system, for instance by removal or addition of items, affects the system as a whole or some part of it. Systems are **open** insofar as they may gain or lose elements through interaction with their environments. Such gains or losses change the internal structure, function and/or output of the system. If change results in continued existence and/or improved performance of the system, it is adaptive; otherwise, we see system failures of one sort and another. Systems are **closed** if they have finite elements (they neither lose nor gain elements – matter in physical systems), but interact with environments in other ways, such as the addition or loss of heat in closed physical systems. Closed systems are **isolated** if they do not interact with their environment at all, although genuine isolation appears to be hypothetical or approximate, rather than a real state in the physical world (Kolesnikov et al. 2001: 136). Systems in these broad senses include not only natural physical and biological systems, but also natural and designed social and semiotic systems, and are studied in specific disciplines ranging from thermodynamics and biology to sociology, psychology and cybernetics, and, following von Bertalanffy (1968), in general systems theory.

What is a system in SFL?

The notion that language may be characterised by systems takes both forms in SFL. On the one hand, language is defined as a large, open, dynamic system network, evolving and adapting in response to environmental demands (the uses speakers make of it) and also shaping the environments with which it interacts. In SFL, the primary environments of interest have been social (language as a social semiotic), instantial (discourse in interaction) and ontogenetic (language as both instrument and result of primary and secondary socialisation processes in development). There has also been a resurgence of interest in the origin of language and its relationships to human evolution. Halliday (1995), for example, proposes that the emergence of language provides the basis for evolving human consciousness and cognition.

On the other hand, the characterisation of systems in particular languages in SFL conventionally begins with closed systems as representations of grammatical phenomena and, although the closed systems of the grammar have often been contrasted with open set relations of the lexicon, early on Halliday (1961) described 'the grammarian's dream' as the extension of system networks to encompass the lexicon as 'most delicate' grammar. Investigation into the possibility of realising the grammarian's dream has periodically been taken up, for example by Hasan (1987), Tucker (1998), Neale (2002), Fawcett (2014) and Matthiessen (2014).

Grammatical systems are **closed** insofar as the number of options is finite and relatively small, though not necessarily binary. All systems are specified for environments. In early scale and category models (such as Halliday 1961; Gregory 2009 [1966]), these environments were grammatical construction types such as nominal/verbal group, major/minor clause and so on in a constituent hierarchy or **rank scale**. For instance, in English, the nominal group is the environment for a system (NUMBER) contrasting count and non-count nouns; major clause is the environment for the system (MOOD) that specifies clause types as indicative or imperative and so on. One or more features of such syntagmatic environments constitute **entry condition(s)** for systems: clauses must have the feature +major (that is, +verb) for MOOD options to be available, while the feature +nominal is the entry condition for a system of NUMBER. The choices in a system are referred to as its 'terms': singular/plural are terms in the count system. Since some choices are dependent on others, a term in one system (such as count) can function as an entry condition for another. Movement from left to right through a system leads to finer classification and is referred to as 'increasing the **delicacy** of descriptions'. The choice between terms in a system is **mutually exclusive** and **obligatory** insofar as one cannot, for example, choose a count noun and not select either singular or plural in a system that includes these options and no others. In systems in which selection of some feature is **optional** (such as +/– modality), the system-network will include negative (–modal) and positive (+modal) options.

Thus a simple system for the number feature in modern English might look like Figure 3.1a, in which the environment is specified for nominal groups and the (square) brackets (that is, [and]) indicate a mutually exclusive 'or' relation. In more elaborated system networks, some systems may be **conjunct**, while others are **hierarchically ordered**. Figure 3.1b represents both situations. Modern English personal pronouns may be represented as involving conjunctive systems of case and person. Selections from both systems must be made. If first or third person are selected, there is a further option of number, while selection of third-person singular opens up options for gender. Braces (curly brackets – that is, { and }) are conventionally used for conjunct systems. The right brace in Figure 3.1b indicates that selection of gender is available as a choice for personal pronouns only with the features singular and third person. These thus form a

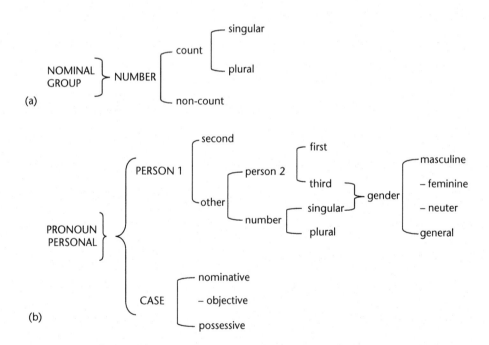

Figure 3.1 (a) A simple number system; (b) A consolidated personal pronoun system

conjunct entry condition for gender. A disjunct entry condition – 'if a or b, then c or d' – would simply substitute a bracket ('or') for the brace ('and').

In early scale and category models, systems were used for conventional morphosyntactic features of classes of units and their output was a feature (such as singular) or a bundle of features such as those for personal pronouns. The features (or feature bundles) were conceptualised as abstract 'formal items/exponents' related to other categories by the **scale of exponence**, or later **realisation rules** (for example Halliday 1961, 1968). In a system like that for personal pronouns, the ultimate exponents define single item subclasses whose realisations are words. In other cases, such as the NUMBER system or the MOOD system, exponents may have more distributed realisations. A feature such as plural in the nominal group might be overtly realised on a head noun or a determiner (or both) or not at all.[2] From 1966 onward, Halliday argued that linguistic systems are 'deeper' semantic characterisations of meaning potential. One interpretation of this is that the systems are exclusively semantic and related to syntax and phonology by realisation rules. The Cardiff Grammar (CG) has explicitly developed this approach, as we shall see later in the chapter.[3] However, Halliday himself has actually continued to work with distributed systems, primarily, although not exclusively, in lexicogrammar and phonology. The change, in the late 1960s, was that the syntactic systems became extensively semanticised and ultimately Halliday relabelled this stratum (between phonology and semantics) as 'lexicogrammar'.

Three further features are necessary to complete this sketch of systems in SFL. First, the options in systems characterising the grammar of a language will ideally be **weighted for probability of occurrence**. For instance, Halliday and James (2005 [1993]) estimated the probability of selecting positive versus negative in a polarity system as approximately 0.9:0.1, whereas in the tense system simple past versus simple present are equiprobable at 0.5:0.5. Halliday (2013) observes that such probabilities are inherent features of semiotic systems, links them to entropy in information theory (Shannon and Weaver 1949), and further points out that probability distributions have implications for language learning and theories of markedness. For example, with the caveat that probability distributions will vary somewhat with text types, the selection of a 0.1 option in a low-entropy system will be more marked than its 0.9 alternative and none of the terms in an equiprobable system will appear marked. With respect to language learning, Halliday (2013) points to the association of probabilities with frequency of occurrence and its importance for acquisition, with more probable (hence more frequently encountered) constructions being acquired first. He also suggests that a bimodal system, in which terms are either equiprobable (0.5:0.5) or maximally skewed (0.1:0.9), might be easier to learn than one in which skewness is more variably distributed. He does not pursue this particular line, but the implications for English systems of polarity and tense are, obviously, that positive will be acquired before either tense or negation, but also that the markedness of negation – and perhaps also its affective salience – relative to the unmarked status of past/present may provide it with an 'acquisitional advantage'. If other grammatical systems turn out to be either equiprobable or maximally skewed, one might hypothesise, and indeed empirically test, feature-systems acquisition stages based on probability distributions in children's input.

Second, systems and system networks are conceptualised as representations of choices available to speakers. Halliday (1966, 1970, 2013) states that system networks are abstract formal representations of semiotic potential relevant at the level of a population, emphasising the idea that speakers make choices from them not as predictive of the behaviour of individuals on any specific occasion nor to suggest conscious choice on the part of speakers, but to foreground language function as the primary object of interest. Halliday (1966, 1995, 2013) normally qualifies statements about unconscious choice to the effect that choices may be brought to conscious awareness and consciously made, should circumstances demand it. Thus choice and choosing characterise speakers as agents of their discourse, consciously choosing this or that from an explicitly known array of options, only exceptionally. However, the choices themselves are often referred to as processes for which systems are procedural algorithms guiding production, perhaps especially in computationally implemented models for text production (for example Fawcett 2013; O'Donnell 2013), but also generally as reflected in the habit of describing hierarchic systemic structure as temporal, sequential selection: one chooses this and then that. That there is some ambivalence around the status of systems as abstract representations of potential or as procedural algorithms, and around the notion of choice as involving conscious agents or not, is evidenced in the papers directly addressing aspects of these questions in Fontaine, Bartlett and O'Grady (2013).

Third, and relatedly, SFL models posit **intrinsic functionality**: that linguistic systems naturally cluster into networks whose boundaries are specified by broad **metafunctions** common to all natural languages. Specifically, the expectation is for significant interdependence amongst systems serving the same function such that choices within a function are more likely to be mutually or hierarchically constraining, whereas choices from different functions are relatively independent of each other. Similarly, change in a system, through addition or deletion of terms for instance, may affect the value of terms in systems localised to the same function, but not the value of terms in systems localised to other functions (Halliday 1968). From the point of view of systems theory, this is exactly what one should expect, so it may not seem particularly novel or insightful. However, it means that the systems in SFL are functionally localised – the metafunctions constituting another dimension of the environment for system networks – and motivated by use in context. This in turn opens the way to using systems not only as an interpretative linguistic base for discourse analyses ranging from instance to genre – work in which SFL linguists have extensively engaged – but also invites predictions about language acquisition, historical change, language typology and potential neural instantiations of language that deserve investigation. Exploration of these points and the metafunctional hypothesis necessarily refers to the conceptualisation of language functions, so we turn now to these.

What is a language function, broadly speaking?

If one asks 'what is language?', a common sort of response is that it is a system for communication – that is, a definition that refers to a global function or purpose (and to system). If one presses for more specific characterisations, one may get, among other possibilities, lists of functions or uses. We use language to express thoughts and emotions, to tell stories and jokes, to index identity, to get others to do things, to engage in social interactions ('we were just talking'), to make poems, to think, and so on. These examples foreground two of three senses in which language is broadly understood as 'functional': it is construed as an instrument (variously of thought, emotion, communication and contact) and as action (storytelling, lying, joking, gossiping and so on). The third sense is related to the notion of language as systems – the contrasts internal to languages that are the bases for value. Collectively, these three perspectives on language function as instrument, action and system inform both common sense and theoretical models of language in some measure.

In addition to the pervasive influence of de Saussure, early-to-mid-twentieth-century European and British thinking about language reflected different dimensions of these broad functions. Among these, Carl Bühler's (1934) *organon* model was explicitly instrumental.

Modelled on Plato's discussion in *Cratylus* of the function of language as an *organum* (tool) for communication, Bühler (1990 [1934]: 35) proposed **expressive**, **representative** and **conative** functions, which he described as 'largely independent variable semantic relations' that configured in complex language signs. The representative function had to do with 'objects and states of affairs' (a modification of Plato's 'things') and as symbolic, in the sense that the associations of phonological form and representation are arbitrary (Bühler 1990 [1934]: 37). The expressive function indexically marked states in the speaker and the conative function as the appeal (or signal) to the addressee. The three functions are presented as simultaneously configured in speech events, and although Bühler says that the representational function takes precedence, he argues that the expressive and conative functions are equally important insofar as they warrant language in the first instance. The organon model was influential in part because it projected the roles of addresser and addressee into the signifying process, not merely as senders and receivers of messages nor as automata reacting to external stimuli, but as the source of conative and expressive functions that shape and motivate discourse.

Among many contributions, Prague school linguists developed functional characterisations of information structure. Of particular importance was Mathesius' work beginning in the 1920s on prosodic and syntactic variations that signal speakers' presentation of information as given or new, and as marked or unmarked for thematic prominence (for example Firbas 1964; Vachek 1966; Mathesius 1975). Bühler's organon model complemented Prague school theories of information structure insofar as the former's notion of the complex sign as simultaneously symbolic (representational and arbitrary), indexical (of the speaker's state) and signalling (shaped with the addressee in mind) is consonant with the distinctions made between the unmarked form of a sentence and its coherent organisation in discourse, from the speaker's perspective, into Theme (a message starting point, typically given information) and Rheme (the message highlight, new information), and the various syntactic and prosodic options for markedness. Thus Prague school linguists developed Bühler's functional insights through characterisations of language-internal resources for message organisation and its discourse consequences.

Focus on language as action was a primary preoccupation of early-to-mid-twentieth-century British scholars. For instance, anthropologist Malinowski (1923) coined the terms 'context of situation' and 'phatic communion' to name factors relevant to conceptualisation of language function as a mode of action. He made two main points about context of situation.

1   Speech situations affect language use and function to such an extent that achieving coherent equivalence for translations requires not only access to a language, but also ethnographic description relating the context of situation to its 'context of culture' and to the pragmatic and interactional features of the situation in which speech is embedded.
2   Observation of language use in many contexts of situation suggests that it is not primarily an instrument for the expression of complex thought, but a mode of action for coordinating joint activities.

Malinowski (1923) argues that phatic communion – that is, talking about nothing in particular to establish and maintain social contact – is a special case of this second, more general, actional character of language. Phatic communion differs only because it is not an adjunct to other activities; rather, it *is* the social activity. In the philosophy of language, Wittgenstein (1953) developed related arguments that word meaning is defined by use(s) in context(s).

And Austin (1962) presented his theory of speech acts in the late 1950s – arguing that every utterance performs an action the interpretation of which requires inferential work on the part of addressees.

British linguist J.R. Firth was a major figure in this milieu, as professor of phonetics at University College London (1928–44) and later holding the chair in general linguistics at the School of Oriental and African Studies (1944–56). The approach to language that he initiated, the 'London school', informed many aspects of Halliday and colleagues' work in developing SFL, and shared much with European and British functionalism. Firth (1957a: 137–67) adopted and adapted Malinowski's insights on the importance of context of situation in accounting for text meaning and textual variation, and on the nature of language as primarily a mode of action rather than reflection. Wittgenstein's insights on the contextual determination of word meanings influenced Firth's elaboration of the idea of **collocation** – that is, the **mutual expectancy** of words co-occurring in texts – as a way of investigating the meaning of individual words, stylistic patterns and **restricted languages** (Firth 1957b: 181). Collocation anticipates probabilistic and concordance studies in corpus linguistics, while the idea of restricted languages evolved in later work into functional varieties or **registers** associated with specialised fields and contexts of situation (for example Gregory 1967; Halliday and Hasan 1980). Continental influences, especially of de Saussure and Hjelmslev, were evident in Firth's insistence on the importance of systemic contrast and syntagmatic colligation (Firth 1955), and the relational and stratified character of language (Firth 1957b). He argued for a polysystemic approach to the analysis of language (or preferably varieties within a language), with systems dispersed through the different levels (from context to phonetics) (Firth 1957b). In common with other functionalists of his time, he believed that the proper object of linguistic inquiry is text and the goal is to elucidate meaning (for example Firth 1955). Where he differed from Bühler and Prague school linguists was in his anti-mentalist stance, for example thinking it inappropriate to 'regard language as "expressive" or "communicative"' because that would 'imply that it is an instrument of inner mental states' which (to paraphrase him) we do not understand and cannot observe (Firth 1957b: 169). Instead, he argues that we should approach meaning with a 'thoroughgoing contextual technique' that 'does not emphasise the relation between the terms of a historical process or of a mental process, but the interrelations of the terms – set up as constituents of the situation itself' (Firth 1957b: 170). What he seems to have envisioned, given the dispersion of meaning into systems of contrasts in different levels, is an account of meaning in text that referred to systemic values (contrastive features), which, correlated with each other and with features of the context of situation, would cumulatively characterise meaning. If one were to transport Firth – unchanged in his views, but willing to engage with the neurosciences – into the present, he might be advocating for parallel distributed, bottom-up competition models in which 'meaning' is an emergent property.

The functional aspect that transformed 'systemic linguistics' to systemic-**functional** linguistics emerged out of the confluence of these European and British traditions, and understandably inherits much from them. The 'scale and category' models of the 1960s elaborated and synthesised many of Firth's proposals, and (saliently) were polysystemic and functional insofar as they formalised features such as transitivity, mood, voice and so on as syntactic systems with structural outputs (for example Halliday 1961, 2002 [1964]; Gregory 2009 [1966]). The first shift away from this 'distributed systems' approach was Halliday's (1966) paper 'Some notes on "Deep Grammar"' in which he proposed that system networks represent 'underlying' paradigmatic specifications of feature contrasts for surface syntagmatic structures. Theoretically, structural representations could then be relatively simple, since they would not be required to do all of the work of relating (deep/semantic) paradigmatic feature selections to surface structures. The paper and the project can be read as an explicit alternative to Chomsky's approach to characterising relations between different, but related, syntagms as structural transformations.

What is a language function in SFL?

Sydney Grammar

Halliday seems to have first used the term 'metafunction' in 1973 – but the ideas appeared somewhat earlier. Influenced by Prague school work on theme and information and semantic structure (for example Firbas 1964, 1966; Vachek 1966), Halliday (1967a, 1967b, 1968, 1969a, 1969b, 1970) made explicit arguments for the metafunctional hypothesis. As noted earlier, the hypothesis is that the systems of a language naturally cluster into system networks that correspond to four broad language functions common to all languages. Languages have an **experiential function**: they allow the representation of experience in terms of events, states and relations, the participants in them and the circumstances in which they are embedded, as well as the **logical** relations between events and states in that experience. Halliday (1968: 209) associates this with the representational function in Bühler and semantic structure in Prague school work. Experiential and logical functions were later labelled as two components of an **ideational function** (Halliday 2002 [1979]). Drawing on Bühler's and Malinowski's insights, Halliday also posited an **interpersonal function**: languages are used as social action, to get or offer information or goods, to direct the behaviour of others, and to enact attitudes, evaluations and so on. And, influenced by the Prague school, natural languages have a **discourse** (later, **textual**) **function**: they allow information to be organised in terms of speakers' assessments of focus and newsworthiness, and as related or not to prior discourse, to extra-textual context(s) or as anticipatory of upcoming news. The metafunctional hypothesis thus claims intrinsic functionality reflected not only in systemic contrasts, but also in the clustering of systems into functionally bounded networks that answer to demands of language use. These broad functions reflect components of contexts of situation conceptualised in terms of **fields** of experience that the language must represent and in which talk is embedded, the **tenor** that speakers take in relation to addressees and the **mode** of communication (as spoken, written, signed, spontaneous or not, and so on) (Gregory 1967; Halliday and Hasan 1980; Martin 1992).

Illustrated from the perspective of the clause in English, the experiential function is represented in the TRANSITIVITY network in systems of process type and agency, the interpersonal function in the MOOD system and the textual function in the Theme system. These systems are posited as conjointly, rather than hierarchically, organised, with feature selections from systems in different functions contributing to different aspects of clause structure. The logical function accounts for structural recursion in terms of hypotactic and paratactic relations. These different functional selections contribute layers of different structural types to the clause that are conflated with each other such that any clause simultaneously configures selections from all functions.[4]

The different layers of structural representation are said to be functional in the sense that they represent feature selections from systems localised to different metafunctions that are relatively independent of each other, show dependencies between systems within metafunctions, are simultaneous and are contextually motivated. Metafunctional independence is evidenced in the relative freedom with which selections from systems such as MOOD and

TRANSITIVITY may be made, interdependence in the interaction of interpersonal systems such as MOOD and MODALITY, and the 'relative' quality of independence of systems located in different metafunctions in the interaction of systems such as TRANSITIVITY and VOICE or Theme and MOOD. The structures also exhibit some unusual properties from formalist perspectives. These include that clauses are not 'headed' (but groups are) and there is no movement nor are there any empty constituents. Each of these points reflects a position that contrasts with (some) other functional models and/or formal models, and is relevant in comparisons of other approaches to systems and functions. Not all of them can be addressed in this brief chapter, but they are worth keeping in mind.

Cardiff Grammar

The Cardiff Grammar (CG) developed by Fawcett and colleagues shares SFL assumptions about the systemic and intrinsically functional character of language.[5] However, it is useful to highlight some of the key differences here in considering systems and functions. Fawcett (2013) has pursued a research agenda that respects Halliday's (1966) arguments for treating systems as the generative semantic base, weighting them for probability and relating strata via realisation rules. The work has also been informed by Fawcett's explicit rejection of the 'anti-mentalist' stance that Halliday seems to have inherited from Firth and by the research task of developing a computationally implemented text generation system. The result is a model that locates all systems in the semantics as algorithms (not choices) guiding production, with realisation rules relating features to syntax and phonology. The semantic systems are organised not into metafunctions, but into eight 'strands of meaning'. In addition to experiential, interpersonal, logical and thematic networks, there are strands for negativity, validity, affect and information. This organisation sidesteps some of the complexity involved in including, for instance, affect, validity and mood in a single interpersonal network, while also avoiding 'forced choice' assignment of metafunctionally ambiguous (polarity) or heterogeneous (validity) strands to one or another metafunction. The Cardiff Grammar also differs in not positing systems as simultaneous (for example experiential and interpersonal selections precede textual selections). This is partly driven by the pragmatics of computer implementation, but Fawcett (forthcoming) also argues that it is functionally motivated insofar as message organisation presupposes something to organise. The semantic systems are in turn related to higher order conceptual and discourse planning components wherein 'choices' are actually made (Fawcett 2013). Conceptually, this organisation means that the syntax and phonology are outputs of the semantics in CG. The syntax itself is represented in flat, relationally labelled, constituent-like structures. Like the Sydney Grammar, clauses are not headed (but groups are), and since the grammar is organised realisationally, the syntax involves no movement; nor are any empty positions associated with movement, although null subjects are recognised in imperatives and non-finite clauses. The move away from simultaneous systems for the clause and the metafunctional hypothesis makes CG computationally tractable and demonstrates that it is possible to write a generative grammar along SFL lines.

What roles do systems and functions play in the minimalist program?

The MP is robustly 'formalist' and arguably 'anti-functional' in many senses, so it may seem odd to ask what role(s) systems and functions play within it. However, recent work in MP suggests that, in fact, systemic contrasts and intrinsic functions are an inescapable part of language – to which one is inexorably led regardless of where or with what assumptions one starts. In the following, I briefly make the case for this observation. The research goals of MP are directed towards discovery of universal grammar (UG), assumed to be a generative procedure that makes language possible. Its focus is formal syntax, which in MP is generated by a bottom-up process (**Merge**) that selects pairs of lexical items defined by their formal contrastive features, combines them into sets and labels them with one of the terms in the set or a shared feature (Chomsky 1995). The features are checked by a matching process. Merge can apply to its own output, so is said to be recursive.

In MP, clause representations comprise a lexical layer consisting of a 'bare phrase structure' (the VP, a verb and its arguments) and a functional layer of phrases headed by features such as tense, agreement, aspects, voice and also, since the work of Rizzi (1997) and Cinque (1999), overtly textual (Topic and Focus) and interpersonal features associated with speech function, mood and modalities. Cinque and Rizzi (2008) hypothesise a version of UG in which every morphosyntactic feature will correspond to a functional head that is ordered in a universal structural hierarchy. They call this the 'cartographic' approach to syntax. They estimate that there may be some 400 features in the world's languages, although not all languages will express all features and differences in orders will arise through movement (or adjustment of the hierarchy). They observe that the features and their orders arise at least in part from semantics and say in closing:

> Syntax is organized to express meaning, but does not dissolve into the mere organization of meaningful units: UG expresses the possible items of the functional lexicon and the way in which they are organized into hierarchies, tailored on the needs of the expression of meanings, but not reducing to them.
>
> *Cinque and Rizzi 2008: 53*

Note that the cartographic approach proposes that UG has a rich functional structure built on contrastive features that correspond to metafunctional components.

Two recent studies challenge the cartographic approach to UG. In a study comparing Holkomelem, Blackfoot and English, Ritter and Wiltschko (2009) make an argument in favour of hierarchically ordered universal functions, but against fixed content for functional categories. Specifically, they argue for a universal function (inflection phrase) that serves to deictically ground reported events to the utterance event. In English, TENSE serves this function. However, in Holkomelem and Blackfoot (respectively), LOCATION and PERSON do. Here, notice that UG is being set up as defining functional structures with cross-linguistically variable instantiations. Cowper and Hall (2014) take things a bound further in asking, 'Where do features come from?' Their delightfully de Saussurean response is that 'the ability to search for systematic contrast in the linguistic input, by correlating differences at various levels, is the only mechanism required to account for the abstract building blocks that make up . . . the formal features of grammatical systems' (Cowper and Hall 2014: 17). Universal functions (which they do assume) arise from interpersonal and experiential functions (the conceptual–intentional interface) – such as the need to express speech functions, to deictically ground propositions, to express relations between processes and participants and the aspectual character of events – and from the articulatory–perceptual interface as both a resource for the development of phonological contrasts, for instance, and a source of constraints imposed by the requirements of serial or spatial ordering. Notice where we have arrived: this is a version of UG grounded in universal (experiential, interpersonal, textual and logical) functions that languages must serve one way or another, plus Merge and 'the ability to posit formal features from correlated categorical differences' (Cowper and Hall 2014: 17) – a surprisingly systemic, or at least paradigmatic, and functional view.

To be sure, the representation and conception of language, and the goals, of MP differ from SFL in many fundamental ways. In MP, functions are conceptualised as 'atomic' morphosyntactic particles, akin to phonological features (such as +/–voice, +/–coronal), which head binary constituent structures, over which movement is ubiquitous; SFL avoids movement by grounding the grammar in paradigmatic contrasts and allowing realisation rules to specify structure. The 'bottom-up' conception of functions in MP contrasts with the global perspective provided by the metafunctional hypotheisis. The lexicogrammatical divide is still assumed in MP and there is no evidence of any interest in using functionally informed descriptions of natural language texts as resources for the wide range of applications at which SFL linguists have excelled. Moreover, Chomsky (2005, 2013) regularly states that language is not for communication, is likely not evolved and is ill adapted for expression, and suggests instead that it is better conceptualised as 'an instrument of thought'. The latter claim – by which he means that Merge made thought possible (for example Chomsky 2005) – curiously positions him in parallel with Halliday and Matthiessen (1999) insofar as they also see language as central for thought. However, they see interaction in social contexts as the ground for phylogenetic and ontogenetic development of language, whereas for Chomsky these too appear as incidental by-products of Merge. Chomsky (2005, 2013) further speculates that language (UG) may be a 'perfect' system – closed, with no redundancy, and isolated. The 'isolated' status is an inference from his arguments against gradual evolution from older domain general neurocognitive systems and associated attempts to detach UG from cultural and neurobiological environments. These positions are, of course, antithetical to SFL (and many other functionalist) conceptions of language and languages.

Prospects for systems and functions

Looking at the treatments of function and system in SFL and MP not only provides some scaffolding for seeing the theoretical contrasts listed above, but also highlights some convergence amongst models with very different theoretical objects and goals, suggesting that system, and the contrasts that systems formalise, and function, both global metafunctions and the atomic features realising them, are not ways of seeing language, but central to it, whatever one's interests and preoccupations. The evidence of convergence also suggests areas in which theoretically motivated research, debate and fruitful interaction may be warranted. An obvious target is more typological and historical work exploiting the metafunctional hypothesis as a means of investigating differences that make a difference, particularly insofar as it suggests where to expect (or not) interactions amongst functional features. Another obvious target is experimental corpus work in language acquisition to empirically test feature-systems acquisition stages based on probability distributions in children's input.

There should also be empirical investigations into neural bases for intrinsic functionality, including experimental testing of the trifunctional hypothesis, and into how selection processes are neurally supported, using functional imaging and neuropsychological testing. Additionally, the fact that system networks with simultaneous entry conditions are computationally intractable because of the complexities of the interactions (Fawcett, forthcoming) does not necessarily mean that they are cognitively intractable. Indeed, the metafunctional hypothesis suggests that, where there are significant interactions (and hence computational complexity), we should expect that the systems belong to the same functional domain.

Identifying the neural networks that support metafunctions (or not) and selection processes would be significant first steps in addressing these questions. This kind of research promises different lines of evidence for thinking about our models. Such evidence would arguably have a bearing on what we take as central linguistic functions, whether we see choice as only extrinsic (in action systems) and systems as only semantic, as saturating linguistic processing or as limited to binary choices in local syntactic domains. Evidence that helps us to think about these kinds of questions should contribute to our understanding not only of the roles of systems and functions in a particular class of descriptions and models, but also of language, its relationships to contexts and the limits of the arbitrary.

Notes

1 Permission to reproduce the quote granted by Cricket Media.
2 See Berry, this volume, for more detail on realisation rules.
3 See also Fawcett, this volume.
4 See the chapters in Part II for detailed structural representations, and Halliday (1985, 1994) and Halliday and Matthiessen (2004, 2014).
5 See Fawcett, this volume.

References

Austin, J.L. 1962. *How to Do Things with Words*. Cambridge, MA: Harvard University Press.
Bühler, C. 1990 [1934]. *Theory of Language: The Representational Function of Language*. Trans. D.F. Goodwin. Amsterdam: John Benjamins.
Chomsky, N. 1995. *The Minimalist Program*. Cambridge, MA: MIT Press.
Chomsky, N. 2005. Three factors in language design. *Linguistic Inquiry* 36(1): 1–22.
Chomsky, N. 2013. Problems of projection. *Lingua* 130: 33–49.
Cinque, G. 1999. *Adverbs and Functional Heads: A Cross-Linguistic Perspective*. New York: Oxford University Press.
Cinque, G., and L. Rizzi. 2008. The cartography of syntactic structures. *Studies in Linguistics, CISCL Working Papers* 2: 42–58.
Cowper, E., and D.C. Hall. 2014. *Reductiō ad discrimen:* Where features come from. *Nordlyd* 41(2): 145–64.
de Saussure, F. 1986. *Course in General Linguistics*. Trans. R. Harris. Peru, IL: Open Court.
Fawcett, R.P. 2013. Choice and choosing in systemic-functional grammar. In L. Fontain, T. Bartlett and G. O'Grady (eds) *Systemic Functional Linguistics: Exploring Choice*. Cambridge: Cambridge University Press, pp. 115–34.
Fawcett, R.P. 2014. The cultural classification of 'things': Towards a comprehensive system network for English noun senses. In M. de los Ángeles Gómez González, F. Ruiz de Mendoza Ibáñez and F. Gonzálves García (eds) *Theory and Practice in Functional-Cognitive Space*. Amsterdam: John Benjamins, pp. 53–84.
Fawcett, R.P. Forthcoming. *The Many Types of Theme in English: Their Syntax, Semantics, and Discourse Functions*. Sheffield: Equinox.
Firbas, J. 1964. On defining the theme in functional sentence analysis. *Travaux linguistiques de Prague* 1: 267–80.
Firbas, J. 1966. Non-thematic subjects in contemporary English. *Travaux linguistiques de Prague* 2: 239–56.
Firth, J.R. 1955. Structural linguistics. In F. Palmer (ed.) 1968. *Selected Papers of J.R. Firth 1952–59*. Bloomington, IN, and London: Indiana University Press, pp. 35–52.
Firth, J.R. 1957a. A Synopsis of Linguistic Theory, 1930–55. In F. Palmer (ed.) 1968. *Selected Papers of J.R. Firth 1952–59*. Bloomington, IN, and London: Indiana University Press, pp. 168–205.

Firth, J.R. 1957b. Ethnographic analysis and language with reference to Malinowski's views. In F. Palmer (ed.) 1968. *Selected Papers of J.R. Firth 1952–59*. Bloomington, IN, and London: Indiana University Press, pp. 137–67.

Fontain, L., T. Bartlett and G. O'Grady (eds). 2013. *Systemic Functional Linguistics: Exploring Choice*. Cambridge: Cambridge University Press.

Gregory, M. 1967. Aspects of varieties differentiation. *Journal of Linguistics* 3(2): 177–98.

Gregory, M. 2009 [1966]. English patterns. In J. de Villiers and R. Stainton (eds) *Michael Gregory's Proposals for a Communication Linguistics: Volume 2 of Communication in Linguistics*. Toronto: Editions du Gref, pp. 3–142.

Halliday, M.A.K. 1961. Categories of the theory of grammar. *Word* 17(3): 241–92.

Halliday, M.A.K. 1966. Some notes on 'deep' grammar. *Journal of Linguistics* 2(1): 57–67.

Halliday, M.A.K. 1967a. Notes on transitivity and theme in English, part I. *Journal of Linguistics* 3(1): 37–82.

Halliday, M.A.K. 1967b. Notes on transitivity and theme in English, part II. *Journal of Linguistics* 3(2): 199–244.

Halliday, M.A.K. 1968. Notes on transitivity and theme in English, part III. *Journal of Linguistics* 4(2): 179–215.

Halliday, M.A.K. 1969a. Options and functions in the English clause. *Brno Studies in English* 8: 82–8.

Halliday, M.A.K. 1969b. A brief sketch of systemic grammar. *La Grammatica; La Lessicologia*. Rome: Bulzoni Editore.

Halliday, M.A.K. 1970. Language structure and language function. In J. Lyons (ed.) *New Horizons in Linguistics*. Harmondsworth: Penguin, pp. 145–65.

Halliday, M.A.K. 1985. *Introduction to Functional Grammar*. London: Arnold.

Halliday, M.A.K. 1994. *Introduction to Functional Grammar*. 2nd edn. London: Arnold.

Halliday, M.A.K. 1995. On language in relation to the evolution of human consciousness. In A. Sture (ed.) *Of Thoughts and Words (Proceedings of Nobel Symposium 92: The Relation between Language and Mind)*. London: Imperial College Press, pp. 45–84.

Halliday, M.A.K. 2002 [1964]. English system networks. In J.J. Webster (ed.) *Collected Works of M.A.K. Halliday, Vol. 1: On Grammar*. London: Continuum, pp. 127–51.

Halliday, M.A.K. 2002 [1979]. Modes of meaning and modes of expression: Types of grammatical structure, and their determination by different semantic functions. In D.J. Allerton, E. Carney and D. Holdcroft (eds) *Function and Context in Linguistic Analysis: Essays Offered to William Haas*. London: Cambridge University Press, pp. 57–79.

Halliday, M.A.K. 2013. Meaning as choice. In L. Fontaine, T. Bartlett and G. O'Grady (eds) *Systemic Functional Linguistics: Exploring Choice*. Cambridge: Cambridge University Press, pp. 15–36.

Halliday, M.A.K., and R. Hasan. 1980. *Text and Context: Aspects of Language in a Social Semiotic Perspective*. Tokyo: Sophia Linguistica.

Halliday, M.A.K., and Z.L. James. 2005 [1993]. A quantitative study of polarity and primary tense in the English finite clause. In J.M. Sinclair, M. Hoey and G. Fox (eds) *Techniques of Description: Spoken and Written Discourse*. London: Routledge, pp. 32–66.

Halliday, M.A.K., and C.M.I.M. Matthiessen. 1999. *Construing Experience through Meaning: A Language-Based Approach to Cognition*. London and New York: Cassell.

Halliday, M.A.K., and C.M.I.M. Matthiessen. 2004. *Introduction to Functional Grammar*. 3rd edn. London: Arnold.

Halliday, M.A.K., and C.M.I.M. Matthiessen. 2014. *Halliday's Introduction to Functional Grammar*. 4th edn. London: Routledge.

Hasan, R. 1987. The grammarian's dream: Lexis as most delicate grammar. In M.A.K. Halliday and R. Fawcett (eds) *Theory and Description: New Developments in Systemic Linguistics*. London: Pinter, pp. 184–211.

Kolesnikov, I.M., S.I. Kolesnikov, V.A. Vinokurov and G.E. Zaikov. 2001. *Thermodynamics of Spontaneous and Non-spontaneous Processes*. Huntington, NY: Nova Science.

Malinowski, B. 1923. The problem of meaning in primitive languages. In C.K. Ogden and I.A. Richards (eds) *The Meaning of Meaning: A Study of the Influence of Language upon Thought and of the Science of Symbolism*. New York: Harcourt, Brace, & World, pp. 296–336.

Martin, J.R. 1992. *English Text: System and Structure*. Philadelphia, PA, and Amsterdam: John Benjamins.

Mathesius, V. 1975. *A Functional Analysis of Present Day English on a General Linguistic Basis*. Ed. J. Vachek and trans. L. Dušková. The Hague and Paris: Mouton.

Matthiessen, C.M.I.M. 2014. Extending the description of process type within the system of transitivity in delicacy based on Levinian verb classes. *Functions of Language* 21(2): 139–75

Neale, A. 2002. More delicate TRANSITIVITY: Extending the PROCESS TYPE system networks for English to include full semantic classifications. Unpublished PhD thesis. Cardiff University.

O'Donnell, M. 2013. A dynamic view of choice in writing: Composition as text evolution. In L. Fontain, T. Bartlett and G. O'Grady (eds) *Systemic Functional Linguistics: Exploring Choice*. Cambridge: Cambridge University Press, pp. 247–66.

Ritter, E., and M. Wiltschko. 2009. Varieties of INFL: TENSE, LOCATION, and PERSON. In H. Broekhuis, J. Craenenbroeck and H. van Riemsdijk (eds) *Alternatives to Cartography*. Berlin and New York: Mouton de Gruyter, pp. 153–201.

Rizzi, L. 1997. The fine structure of the left periphery. In L. Haegeman (ed.) *Elements of Grammar*. Amsterdam: Kluwer, pp. 281–337.

Shannon, C., and W. Weaver. 1949. *The Mathematical Theory of Communication*. Urbana, IL: University of Illinois Press.

Tucker, G. 1998. *The Lexicogrammar of Adjectives: A Systemic Functional Approach to Lexis*. London: Cassell Academic.

Vachek, J. 1966. *The Linguistic School of Prague*. Bloomington, IN: Indiana University Press.

von Bertalanffy, L. 1968. *General Systems Theory: Foundations, Developments, Applications*. New York: Brazziler.

Wittgenstein, L. 1953. *Philosophical Investigations*. Oxford: Blackwell.

Stratum, delicacy, realisation and rank

Margaret Berry[1]

Introduction

This chapter is responsible for discussing some of the main pillars of the architecture of systemic functional linguistics (SFL). In 1961, when he first put forward a coherent and comprehensive architecture for the theory of grammar, Halliday included layers (levels), categories (system, structure, unit and class) and scales (rank, delicacy and exponence). These are all still relevant to SFL today, although levels are now called 'strata', under the influence of Lamb's stratificational linguistics (for example Lamb 1964) and they have been joined by a second kind of layering, that of the metafunctions. Exponence has been further distinguished as realisation and instantiation.

System and metafunction are discussed elsewhere in this volume (Asp), these being the two concepts that most characterise SFL and distinguish it from other approaches to linguistics. The present chapter will focus on stratum, delicacy, realisation and rank, but will also consider the interrelations of these with system and metafunction.

The chapter will adopt the perspective of 'mainstream' SFL, the aim being to provide an outline framework that will be filled out by subsequent chapters in this volume. Relevant matters from the perspective of other forms of SFL will also be discussed in later chapters in this volume, including from the perspective of Cardiff Grammar (Fawcett) and from the perspective of discourse semantics (Tann).

Stratum and metafunction

Most approaches to linguistics recognise some kind of layering in language, to represent different kinds and levels of abstraction. SFL now recognises two kinds of layering: stratal and metafunctional. The following are regarded as strata: context, semantics, lexicogrammar, phonology, phonetics and, for written language, graphology (sometimes called orthography). The metafunctions are: ideational (subdivided into experiential and logical), interpersonal and textual (Asp, this volume). The strata are assumed to be hierarchically ordered, context being the highest stratum and phonetics the lowest; the metafunctions are assumed to be in parallel with each other.[2]

This section will discuss these two kinds of layering, paying particular attention to the main ways in which SFL differs from other approaches to linguistics. Many of the differences can be explained by the fact that SFL is a theory of language as choice: language is seen as a set of resources from which choices are made. As such, while the main focus of most approaches to linguistics is on syntagmatic relations, the main focus of SFL is on choice relations – that is, on paradigmatic relations – although it is also concerned to relate the paradigmatic relations to the syntagmatic relations. The distinction between paradigmatic and syntagmatic relations is further discussed by Asp (this volume).

Just how unusual SFL is in this respect can be seen from the fact that Butler and Gonzálvez-García (2014: 488–9) report that, of the sixteen functional/cognitive/constructionist models they discuss, only one other besides SFL, the Columbia school, could be said to give particular attention to paradigmatic relations – and Butler and Gonzálvez-García have reservations about even this one.

SFL is also unusual among approaches to linguistics in including context – that is, context of situation – in its hierarchy of strata.[3] As has been said, SFL is a theory of language as choice; the view is that it is impossible to make sense of linguistic choices without reference to context and also that it is impossible to make sense of context without reference to linguistic choices. Linguistic choices are strongly influenced by the contexts of the situation in which they occur, but in certain circumstances linguistic choices may bring about a change in the context, for instance leading it to become more formal or more informal. More generally, context is regarded as explaining the form of the language system as a whole. The clusterings of choices in the language system are hypothesised to derive from clusterings of contextual features. It is assumed that language is the way it is because of the uses to which it is put in the real world. Hasan (2001) goes as far as saying 'there can be no language without context'. Although itself extralinguistic, context is regarded as integral to accounting not only for individual linguistic choices, but also for the nature of the whole language system. Butler (2004: 164) notes that SFL is 'the only functional theory to have built in a specific model of social context, through the parameters of field, tenor and mode'.[4]

It is not really possible to offer insightful examples when the concepts under discussion are as general as those in this chapter. However, for light relief, if nothing else, I will be referring at intervals to examples (1) and (2). These, like the other examples in this chapter (except occasionally where otherwise stated), are taken from Robert Browning's *The Pied Piper of Hamelin* (1842).

(1) "If I can rid your town of rats
   "Will you give me a thousand guilders?"
   "One? fifty thousand!" – was the exclamation
   Of the astonished Mayor and Corporation.

(2) . . . – when suddenly, up the face
   Of the Piper perked in the market-place,
   With a, "First, if you please, my thousand guilders!"

   A thousand guilders! The Mayor looked blue;
   So did the Corporation too.

The contexts of situation of the two passages are in some ways similar, in some ways different. Both are set in the centre of Hamelin; in both, the participants are the Pied Piper and the

Mayor and Corporation. However, in between the two passages, the Pied Piper actually gets rid of the rats and this changes the context. In the first passage, both the Pied Piper and the Mayor and Corporation need something and are negotiating to their mutual advantage. By the second passage, both sides feel themselves to be in a position of strength: the Pied Piper because he has got rid of the rats, the Mayor and Corporation because they no longer need the rats got rid of. As I shall suggest below, this leads to different linguistic choices.

Semantics, the next stratum down in the hierarchy after context, is interpreted more broadly in SFL than in most approaches to linguistics. Traditionally in linguistics, 'semantics' has been concerned with what SFL regards as ideational meaning, the term 'pragmatics' being used for what is left over. SFL includes in semantics all types of meaning – interpersonal and textual, as well as ideational – not wishing to privilege any one of these types of meaning. Meaning is central to SFL. The three main types are regarded as equal and parallel; choices under the heading of ideational are assumed to be simultaneous with interpersonal choices and with textual choices (Butler and Gonzálvez-García 2014: 382; Asp, this volume).

If we now focus on the Pied Piper's *Will you give me a thousand guilders?* in example (1) and his *First, if you please, my thousand guilders!* in example (2), semantically these are again in some ways alike, but in some ways different. The semantic similarities and differences can be drawn out by reference to the metafunctions. Ideationally, the two utterances are alike in that both are about the Mayor and Corporation giving a thousand guilders to the Pied Piper. Interpersonally, they are alike to the extent that the Pied Piper is trying to get the Mayor and Corporation to give him the thousand guilders. However, more delicately, from an interpersonal point of view, the Pied Piper's utterance in example (1) could be characterised as a polite request, while his utterance in example (2) looks more like a peremptory demand. It would seem reasonable to suggest that his semantic choice in (2) reflects his contextual greater position of strength (see above). Textually, it is relevant to note that (1) includes the first mention of the giving of the thousand guilders, while in (2) the Pied Piper can expect the Mayor and Corporation to remember the earlier mention. This too is reflected in his linguistic choices, as will be discussed further shortly.

Where most approaches to linguistics include a level/stratum called syntax, SFL has lexicogrammar. Halliday avoids using the term 'syntax':

> This word suggests proceeding in a particular direction, such that a language is interpreted as a system of forms, to which meanings are then attached. . . . In a functional grammar, on the other hand, the direction is reversed. A language is interpreted as a system of meanings, accompanied by forms through which the meanings can be realized. The question is rather: 'how are these meanings expressed?'. This puts the forms of a language in a different perspective: as means to an end, rather than as an end in themselves.
>
> *Halliday 1994: xiv*

A further point that needs explaining is that in SFL, as the name 'lexicogrammar' suggests, lexis/vocabulary and grammar/syntax are considered to form one stratum, rather than two, as in some other approaches. Lexis is regarded simply as more delicate grammar. Lexical choices can be shown to be related to grammatical choices, but in a system network lexical choices are usually at the right-hand, more delicate, end of the network, while grammatical choices are usually at the left-hand, less delicate, end.[5] In regarding lexis and grammar as forming a continuum, SFL is not unusual: Butler and Gonzálvez-García (2014: 493) indicate that, of their sixteen approaches, only five do not see it that way.

The semantic choices in the Pied Piper's utterances from examples (1) and (2) are reflected in the lexicogrammatical choices. The ideational similarity is reflected by, among other things, the repetition of the lexical items *thousand* and *guilders* (see Davidse, this volume). The interpersonal difference is reflected in the choices from the MOOD system (see Andersen, this volume): the choice in example (1) is 'interrogative'; the choice in example (2) is of a 'minor' clause. The textual distinction between first mention of the giving of a thousand guilders and subsequent mention is reflected in example (2) by the ellipsis of *give* and the use of *my* (see O'Grady, this volume).

A problem with SFL is that the boundary between semantics and lexicogrammar is not always clear. Halliday (1994: xix) regards this as a strength of the approach: '[T]here is no clear line between semantics and grammar, and a functional grammar is one that has been pushed in the direction of the semantics.' However, more recently in SFL, approaches to semantics have been developing that recognise a semantic stratum which is independent of, although relatable to, the lexicogrammar.[6]

Phonetics in SFL owes a certain amount to the prosodic approach of Firth, but despite this remains rather traditional. Phonology, however, again recognises systems of choices – choices between different intonational patterns, for instance – and these can be related to the meanings they express (Halliday and Greaves 2008; O'Grady 2010; O'Grady, this volume; Tench, this volume). And similar things can be said about graphology/orthography as about phonology.[7]

It is relevant to note here that the Pied Piper's utterance in example (1) is marked with a question mark; his utterance in example (2), with an exclamation mark. This reflects the contextual, semantic and lexicogrammatical differences, and has implications for the intonation.

It should also be said that SFL is unusual among approaches to linguistics in the very fact that it regards the stratal and metafunctional layering as two distinct kinds of layering. Other approaches recognise distinctions that roughly approximate to SFL's distinction between the experiential and interpersonal metafunctions, but they include the resulting layers with their other levels or strata. Functional discourse grammar (FDG), for instance, recognises an interpersonal level and a representational level (Hengeveld and Mackenzie 2008: 13), roughly corresponding to SFL's interpersonal and experiential metafunctions,[8] but FDG includes these in the general hierarchy of levels, along with a morphosyntactic level and a phonological level. For SFL, metafunctional layering is a distinct form of layering. In fact, the metafunctions cut across the strata, in the sense that they have implications for each of the main strata. The metafunctions are primarily semantic, representing different types of meaning, but give rise to the layering of the lexicogrammar and are themselves hypothesised to relate to the main parameters of context. The intonational systems of phonology can be shown to relate to different metafunctions.[9]

Delicacy

Halliday (1961) distinguished three scales of abstraction that were necessary to relate linguistic categories to each other: rank, exponence and delicacy – exponence later being further distinguished as realisation and instantiation. Delicacy will be discussed in this section of this chapter; realisation and rank, in subsequent sections. Instantiation will be discussed in Part IV of the volume.[10]

As has been said elsewhere in this volume (Asp), paradigmatic relations are modelled in SFL via systems in system networks. Each system is assumed to represent a choice, a choice between options, the options being represented by the terms in the system. The individual systems are combined in system networks in such a way as to show the various types of dependency that hold between them. This results in a left-to-right arrangement, which is known as the 'scale of delicacy', systems on the left being the least delicate systems, systems on the right, the most delicate. Originally the concern of lexicogrammar, system networks are now being drawn for other strata, including semantics and context of situation, to model the choices relevant to those strata. Within each stratum, it is at least theoretically possible to distinguish ideationally relevant system networks, interpersonally relevant system networks and textually relevant system networks.

Halliday devised a notation to represent the different kinds of dependency relation that hold between systems in a system network.[11] Martin (2013) provides a step-by-step guide on how to draw system networks and also discusses the motivation for the distinctions proposed.[12]

It is important to recognise that a system network is hypothetical.[13] For instance, the dependency relations between the systems may turn out not to be as originally expected. In this case, the ordering in delicacy will change.

SFL linguists differ as to precisely what is meant by 'choice' and so about precisely what is being modelled by a system network. For some linguists, a network is an attempt to model real choices available to, and made by, human individuals; for others, the use of the word 'choice' is metaphorical and intended merely to represent certain aspects of the inner workings of language.[14] In some cases, the different views lead to different arrangements on the scale of delicacy.

Earlier in the chapter, I discussed linguistic choices in an informal and ad hoc manner; as subsequent chapters of the volume will show, however, it is the formalism of the system network that makes possible more organised discussion and enables the setting up of precise hypotheses.

Realisation

Halliday proposed realisation as a relation both between and within strata.

Realisation between strata

The relationship between strata is a relationship of realisation. Viewed from the top, context is realised by semantics; semantics by lexicogrammar; lexicogrammar by phonology/graphology; phonology by phonetics. Viewed from the bottom, phonetics realises phonology; phonology/graphology realise lexicogrammar; lexicogrammar realises semantics; semantics realises context. There are some exceptions to these general statements – for instance, in some cases, semantics can be realised directly by phonology or graphology. The simplest glosses for 'realise' are 'encode' or 'make manifest'; for example semantics can be said to encode or make manifest the context and lexicogrammar can be said to encode or make manifest the semantics.

Hasan (1995: 209) argues that realisation should be seen as a two-way relationship – as a dialectic – in which the choices of a higher stratum activate the choices of a lower stratum and the choices of a lower stratum construe the choices of a higher stratum. So, for instance, contextual choices activate semantic choices and are construed by semantic choices; semantic choices activate lexicogrammatical choices and are construed by lexicogrammatical choices. Hasan (1995: 206) points out that a further argument for regarding context as a stratum, in spite of the fact that it is extralinguistic, is that the same relationships hold between context and semantics as between semantics and lexicogrammar.

The notion that choices of a higher stratum activate choices of a lower stratum seems to be quite straightforward. However, there may be problems with the notion of construal. The word 'construe' is used in SFL in a rather unusual way. In ordinary English, it would be expected to have an animate – indeed, a human – subject: it is people who do construing. But in SFL an aspect of language is frequently said to construe another aspect of language, as when the semantics is said to construe the context or lexicogrammar is said to construe the semantics.[15] There seem to be different views in SFL as to exactly what is meant by 'construe' in this connection, although this is not usually explicitly discussed. When a lower stratum is said to construe a higher stratum, does it mean (a) simply that the lower stratum represents/encodes the higher stratum? Or (b) that the lower stratum provides clues that enable human language users to construe the higher stratum? Sometimes, it seems to mean (c) that the lower stratum actually creates the higher stratum. There are two variants of (c) – that (c1) in actual instances of language, a lower stratum creates a higher stratum to the extent that one cannot analyse one without the other (for example that the only way of analysing the context is via the semantics) and (c2) that, more generally in language, the possibilities at a lower stratum shape the possibilities at a higher level (for example that the possibilities in lexicogrammar shape the possibilities in the semantics, so that we can mean semantically only in ways that the resources of the lexicogrammar permit).

There would seem to be problems with both (c1) and (c2): (c1) can lead to circular reasoning and make it impossible to test hypotheses about relations between the strata (see below); (c2) would seem to allow the lower stratum to control innovation and change at the higher stratum.[16]

Halliday put forward some precise hypotheses about the realisation relationships between the strata. For instance, of the realisation relationships between context and semantics, he says:

> Let us postulate that the relevant features of a situation in which language has some place are the **field** of social process, the **tenor** of social relationships and the **mode** of discourse itself: that is, (i) what is going on, (ii) who are involved, and (iii) what part the text is playing – whether written or spoken, in what rhetorical mode and so on. We shall then find a systematic relationship between these components of the situation and the functional components of the semantic system. It appears that, by and large, the field – the nature of the social activity – determines the ideational meanings; the tenor – the social statuses and roles of the participants in the situation – determines the interpersonal meanings; while the mode – the part assigned to the linguistic interaction in the total situation – determines the textual meaning.
>
> *Halliday 2002 [1979]: 201, emphasis original*

The set of realisation relationships outlined here has become known as the 'context–metafunction hook-up hypothesis (CMHH)' (Hasan 1995: 222)[17], of which Butler (2003a: 204) says: 'The problem, in my view, is that once formulated, such hypotheses seem to be reinterpreted by practitioners of [SFL] as accepted fact, rather than submitted to rigorous testing and modification or even outright rejection.' And it certainly is the case that many SFL linguists seem to regard the CMHH as accepted fact.

Problematically, if contextual features are established via semantic features and semantic features are established via contextual features, the reasoning is circular and the hypothesis becomes untestable. The way to break out of the circle would seem to be to ensure that contextual features are established independently of the semantic features and that semantic features are established independently of the contextual features. It should then be possible to see whether (a) the contextual choices form mutually dependent clusters, (b) the semantic choices form mutually dependent clusters and (c) there really is a relationship of probable co-occurrence between certain of the contextual clusters and certain of the semantic clusters.

Studies testing aspects of the CMHH are beginning to appear, although in a small way (for example Thompson 1999; Clarke 2012, 2013; Berry 2016). In the meantime, it should be said that Halliday's hypotheses have led to insightful research even before they have been properly tested – this will be discussed further by Bowcher elsewhere in this volume.

Halliday (2002 [1979]) has also put forward hypotheses about the realisation relationships between the semantics and the lexicogrammar. Experiential meanings will tend to be realised particularly; a structure that represents experiential meanings 'will tend to have this form: it will be a configuration, or constellation, of discrete elements' (Halliday 2002 [1979]: 203). Interpersonal meanings will tend to be realised prosodically; the interpersonal meaning is 'strung throughout the clause as a continuous motif or colouring' (Halliday 2002 [1979]: 205). Textual meanings will tend to be realised culminatively: 'What the textual component does is to express the particular semantic status of elements in the discourse by assigning them to the boundaries; this gives special significance to "coming first" and "coming last"' (Halliday 2002 [1979]: 208). Logical meanings will tend to be realised recursively, but Halliday (2002 [1979]: 211–15) regards this statement as more problematic than the statements concerning the other three metafunctions.

Realisation within strata

As well as proposing realisation relations between strata, Halliday also proposed realisation relations within strata. He suggested that syntactic paradigmatic relations (systems) were in some way closer to the semantics than syntagmatic relations (structures) and that the structures could be regarded as realising the choices from systems (Halliday 1966a). It is now assumed – in theory, at least – that within each stratum it is possible to identify paradigmatic relations and that these will be realised by the syntagmatic structures of that stratum.

Halliday (1969, 2009: 84) gives details of **realisation statements** – procedures that show how one gets from the choices to the structures. The 2009 list of these is as follows:

insertion	+x	[insert function X]
conflation	X/Y	[conflate function X with function Y]
expansion	X(P+Q)	[expand X to P plus Q, unordered]
ordering	X^Z	[order Z after X]
(note also #^X 'put X first')		
preselection	:w	[preselect feature w]
classification	::z	[classify lexically as z]
(where grammatical features have not yet been assigned)		
lexification	= t	[lexify as t] (specify lexical item)

To generate, say, a clause, the realisation statements have to be applied in the order in which they are needed for the generation; for example functions have to be inserted before they can be conflated. And if conflation has taken place, ordering realisation statements will be applied to the conflated functional bundles.

To give a very brief example, if the option 'indicative' is chosen from one of the MOOD systems (see Andersen, this volume), this is realised in English by the presence of a Subject and a Finite Verb. So we have two insertion realisation statements, +Subject and +Finite Verb. If a choice from the TRANSITIVITY systems (Davidse, this volume) has produced the function Actor, we have another insertion statement, +Actor. If a choice from a VOICE system were to lead to Actor and Subject being realised by the same element of structure, we would then need a conflation realisation statement: conflate Actor with Subject. If a choice from a THEME system (Forey and Sampson, this volume) were to mean that the combined Actor and Subject is to be thematised, we would need an ordering realisation statement: #^Actor+Subject, meaning put Actor+Subject first. If a further option from a MOOD system, 'declarative', were selected, we would need another ordering realisation statement: order Finite Verb after Actor+Subject. Assuming appropriate lexification, we would so far have generated something like example (3).

(3) The rat bit . . .

If a similar set of choices and realisation statements, involving the conflation of Goal and Complement, were also to be applied, we could generate example (4).

(4) The rat bit the dog.

A different set of choices and realisation statements would be needed to generate examples (5)–(7).

(5) The dog was bitten by the rat
    or

(6) The dog the rat bit, (but not the cat)
    or

(7) Did the rat bite the dog?

The insertion realisation statements would be the same, but the conflation and/or the ordering statements would differ.[18]

A question that is sometimes asked is whether 'realisation' within a stratum means the same as 'realisation' between strata. I think the answer is probably 'Yes': one can use the same glosses for both. A lower stratum 'realises'/'encodes'/'makes manifest'/'construes' a higher stratum and structures 'realise'/'encode'/'make manifest'/'construe' choices from systems. From the other direction, choices from a higher stratum 'activate' choices from a lower stratum and choices from systems 'activate' structures.[19]

Rank

A rank scale of units is set up to account for the stretches of language of different sizes that carry patterns (structures) and choices (systems). The original and best-known rank scale in SFL is the rank scale for lexicogrammar, but rank scales have also been set up for other strata. The concept of rank has been much criticised over the years, beginning with Matthews (1966). However, much of the criticism has been from an exclusively syntagmatic point of view, and has missed the importance of unit and rank in relation to paradigmatic options. These points will be discussed further later in the chapter.

The rank scale for lexicogrammar

The lexicogrammatical rank scale is assumed to consist, in hierarchical order, of the following units: clause, group, word and morpheme. Halliday and Matthiessen (2014: 9) present this as the rank scale for the lexicogrammar of English, but regard it as 'typical of many' languages.

Each rank of unit is associated with particular sets of patterns and choices. For instance, the clause is associated with patterns and choices of TRANSITIVITY, of MOOD and of THEME, while the group is associated with such patterns and choices as those of NUMBER and PERSON.[20]

A simple example of a clause analysed into groups, words and morphemes would be as in example (8a).

(8a)	clause							
	group			group		group		
	word	word		word		word	word	
	morpheme	morpheme	morpheme	morpheme	morpheme	morpheme	morpheme	morpheme
	The	rat	s	kill	ed	the	cat	s

A linear analysis would be presented as in example (8b).

(8b) || The rat+s | kill+ed | the cat+s ||[21]

The default position for a rank scale is that each unit consists of one or more of the unit next below: a clause consists of one or more groups; a group consists of one or more words; a word consists of one or more morphemes. However, there is provision for 'rank shift' or 'embedding', whereby a unit of one rank may function in the structure of a unit of its own rank or of a unit of rank below. Consider the clause in example (9).

(9) ||They | bit | the babies | in [the cradles] ||

Here, *the cradles* is a nominal group, a particular class of group, in that it shares the patterns and choices associated with nominal groups. But here it is functioning as part of the group/phrase *in the cradles* – that is, it is functioning in the structure of a unit of its own rank.[22]

Consider the clause in example (10).

(10) ||I | chiefly | charm | creatures [[that do people harm]] ||

Here, *that do people harm* is a clause in that it largely shares with other clauses the patterns and choices associated with clauses. But here it is qualifying *creatures*, which means that it is functioning as part of a group – that is, it is functioning in the structure of a unit of a rank below itself.

SFL linguists differ over when it is appropriate to invoke the notion of rank shift/embedding and this has recently led to some lively debates on Sysfling and Sysfunc, the email channels for SFL.[23]

Unit complexes

So far, the units discussed have been what might be thought of as the basic units for lexico-grammar. Each of the basic units can combine with other units of its own rank to form a unit complex. Example (11) is an example of a clause complex.

(11) ||*They fought the dogs* || *and killed the cats* || *And bit the babies in the cradles*||

An example of a group complex appears in **bold italics** in example (12).

(12) ||*And* | *nobody* | *could < enough > admire* | ***The tall man and his quaint attire***||

An example of a word complex, again in **bold italics**, appears in example (13).

(13) ||*And* | *here*| *they*| *noticed* | *round his neck*| *A scarf of **red and yellow** stripe*||

It is not so easy to find examples of morpheme complexes, though they do occur. A radio programme in the UK (Radio 5 Live, 12 April 2014) included the following phrase (example (14)).

(14)   ***pro-and-anti-***Russian demonstrations in Ukraine

Of course, not all unit complexes involve a simple linking through 'and'. Examples (15) and (16) are further examples of clause complexes.

(15) ||*Into the street the Piper stept,*|| *Smiling first a little smile*||

(16) ||*If we've promised them aught,*|| *let us keep our promise!*||[24]

Rank scales for other strata

Rank scales of units have also been proposed for other strata, again to account for the stretches that carry the patterns and choices of those strata.

For phonology, the units that have been proposed are tone group, foot, syllable and phoneme (Berry 1977: 82–3; Halliday and Matthiessen 2014: 5–6;); for graphology, sentence, sub-sentence, word and letter (Halliday and Matthiessen 2014: 6–7). I also included paragraph and phrase in my graphological rank scale (Berry 1977: 97–102). Hasan and Cloran have proposed a rank scale for semantics, comprising text, rhetorical unit, message, message component (for example Hasan 1996: 117–18).

Sinclair and Coulthard (1975), drawing on early work by Halliday, adopted a rank-based framework for their analysis of the structure of discourse, the units being lesson, transaction, exchange, move and act. While their initial work was on classroom discourse – hence the name of their highest unit – they later adapted the framework for work on other registers such as doctor–patient interviews. They commented:

> We decided to use a rank scale for our descriptive model because of its flexibility. The major advantage of describing new data with a rank scale is that no rank has any more importance than any other and thus if, as we did, one discovers new patterning it is a fairly simple process to create a new rank to handle it.
>
> *Sinclair and Coulthard 1975: 20*

A rank scale then can be heuristically useful. If one discovers a new set of patterns or choices, one of the first questions to ask is: over how big a stretch do these patterns/choices operate? This, I would suggest, is relevant to current experiments in the description of contexts of situation. In a study of the choices that speakers and writers make when construing the contexts of situation in which they find themselves (Berry 2016), it seems that some of the choices relate to whole language events, but that others relate only to particular stages of language events. An embryonic rank scale for context would then include the units language event and stage. Others are likely to emerge.[25]

Criticism of the notion of rank

The notion of rank has been much criticised over the years, beginning with Matthews (1966), to which Halliday (1966b) replied, and followed by, for example, Huddleston (1988: 140–55) and Fawcett (2000: 309–38). There is no room in this chapter for full discussion. The criticism has, however, been well discussed by Butler (1985: 29–33; 2003a: 187–8; 2003b: 279–90).[26]

As noted earlier in the chapter, much of the criticism seems to be from an exclusively syntagmatic perspective and has missed the importance of rank in relation to paradigmatic options. Units are characterised as much by the choices that they carry as by their structures. Indeed, for me, the most important work that units/classes of units do is to provide points of origin for system networks – that is, to show where/how often the choices in the networks become relevant. If a network has the clause as its point of origin,[27] its choices become relevant every time there is a new clause. If the nominal group is the point of origin, the choices become relevant every time there is a new nominal group.

Butler (1985), while acknowledging the justice of many of the criticisms, nevertheless finds arguments in favour of a rank-based grammar. One of these has to do with the applicability to texts:

> Given that one of Halliday's aims is to develop a model which will be applicable to text analysis, the rank concept is extremely useful as a search aid in such a study. Breaking a text up into units of a particular rank, with no (or little?) residue, and then further division of these units into units of a lower rank (while mindful of the possibility of rank shift) is a way of making sure that every bit of the text is accounted for, and that both its larger-scale and smaller-scale patterns can be recorded.
>
> *Butler 1985: 32*

Summary

The framework outlined in this chapter can be summarised as follows. SFL recognises the following strata: context, semantics, lexicogrammar, phonology, graphology and phonetics. At each stratum, it recognises a rank scale of units. Within each unit of each stratum, SFL distinguishes choices associated with the experiential, interpersonal and textual metafunctions. Within each metafunction of each unit of each stratum, the systems of choices are related on a scale of delicacy. The strata are related on a scale of realisation. Realisation also relates the choices of each stratum to the structures of each stratum via realisation statements.

However, this is only an outline of the theory and not all of the details have yet been fully worked out. Some parts of the jigsaw are nearer completion than others. Moreover, the main motivation for distinguishing the strata, the ranks of unit and the metafunctions is the way in which choices cluster in networks of mutually dependent systems. If future research casts doubt on what are presently thought to be the clusterings, the details of the theory – and maybe even the basic architecture – may need to change. The outline theory and details developed in this chapter should therefore be regarded as hypothetical.

Notes

1 I am grateful for comments on the first draft of this chapter from the editors of the volume and also from Chris Butler. Of course, I alone am responsible for any errors or misrepresentations.
2 Except that textual meaning is regarded as second-order meaning. For discussion, see Matthiessen (1992).
3 Functional discourse grammar includes a contextual component, but this largely relates to the co-text rather than to the context of situation (Hengeveld and Mackenzie 2008: 9–12).
4 For more on the relevance of context to a comparison of SFL with other approaches, see Bateman, this volume. For more detailed discussion of context itself, see Part IV. See also Hasan (2001).
5 For further discussion, see Hasan (1987) and Tucker (1998).
6 See Halliday and Matthiessen (2006 [1999]); Moore, this volume, for message semantics; Tann, this volume, for discourse semantics; Fawcett, this volume, for the Cardiff Grammar view of semantics. For general discussion, see Butler (2003a: 178–84; 2003b: 290–1).
7 For discussion, see Halliday and Matthiessen (2014: 6–7); Berry (1977: ch. 5). A distinction should probably be drawn between graphology and graphetics, to parallel that between phonology and phonetics, but as far as I am aware no SFL linguist has drawn this distinction. However, see Butler and Gonzálvez-García (2014: 45, 381).
8 FDG's interpersonal seems to include both SFL's interpersonal and SFL's textual.
9 A detailed comparison of the layering of SFL with that of FDG and role and reference grammar can be found in Butler and Taverniers (2008).
10 It is assumed here that while delicacy, realisation and rank relate layers and categories of the theory, instantiation is a relationship between the theory and the data.
11 For examples, see Asp, this volume.
12 Martin (2013) is a bilingual volume, part English, part Chinese. The English sections include examples from English and Tagalog. The Chinese sections, by Wang Pin and Zhu Yongsheng, include examples from Chinese, Japanese, Korean and Tibetan.
13 See Berry (2013: 379–80) for discussion.
14 See Fontaine (2013) and Berry (2014) for discussion.
15 Butler and Gonzálvez-García (2014: 486) report that twelve of their sixteen approaches, in addition to SFL, are concerned with construal, but these other approaches see construal as a cognitive operation, so for them, as for ordinary language, it is people who do the construing.
16 For further discussion of these matters, see Bartlett, this volume.
17 Hasan later came to prefer the term 'context–metafunction resonance (CMR) hypothesis' (e.g. Hasan 2015: 128).
18 These realisation statements will be exemplified more fully in Parts II and III of this volume. See also Berry (1977: ch. 2).
19 However, Taverniers (2016: 20) argues that the two types of realisation are *not* the same.
20 Martin (2013: 61–6) discusses the motivation for recognising clause and group as different units.
21 For a discussion of minimal versus maximal bracketing in relation to rank and unit, see Butler (2003a: 164–6).
22 Halliday and Matthiessen (2014: 362–3) use both the terms 'group' and 'phrase', and distinguish between their meanings. However, they seem to ignore the distinction when exemplifying group/phrase in group/phrase rankshift (Halliday and Matthiessen 2014: 10). The example here is, in fact, grammatically ambiguous: *in the cradles* could be regarded as qualifying *babies*, rather than as an Adjunct indicating where the biting took place, which is how I have analysed it.

23 For discussion of the issues involved, see Fawcett (2000: 26–30) and Butler (2003b: 279–91).

24 For discussion of the range of ways in which unit complexes can be formed, see Butt and Webster, this volume. For more on lexicogrammatical units, rank and rank shift, see Berry (1975: chs 6 and 7).

25 For Martin, genre is a staged, goal-oriented social process (e.g. Martin 1992: 505).

26 Cardiff Grammar rejects the concept of a rank scale: see Fawcett (2000: 309–38) and in this volume.

27 For 'point of origin', see Halliday (2009: 66–7).

References

Berry, M. 1975. *An Introduction to Systemic Linguistics, vol. 1: Structures and Systems*. London: Batsford.

Berry, M. 1977. *An Introduction to Systemic Linguistics, vol. 2: Levels and Links*. London: Batsford.

Berry, M. 2013. Towards a study of the differences between formal written English and informal spoken English. In L. Fontaine, T. Bartlett and G. O'Grady (eds) *Systemic Functional Linguistics: Exploring Choice*. Cambridge: Cambridge University Press, pp. 365–83.

Berry, M. 2014. Changes in systemic functional linguistics: Past developments, ongoing developments (and future developments?). Paper presented to the European Systemic Functional Linguistics Conference, Paris, July.

Berry, M. 2016. On describing contexts of situation. In W.L. Bowcher and J.Y. Liang (eds) *Society in Language, Language in Society: Essays in Honour of Ruqaiya Hasan*. Basingstoke: Palgrave Macmillan, pp. 184–205

Butler, C.S. 1985. *Systemic Linguistics: Theory and Applications*. London: Batsford.

Butler, C.S. 2003a. *Structure and Function: A Guide to Three Major Structural-Functional Theories, Part I – Approaches to the Simplex Clause* (Studies in Language Companion Series 63). Philadelphia, PA, and Amsterdam: John Benjamins.

Butler, C.S. 2003b. *Structure and Function: A Guide to Three Major Structural-Functional Theories, Part II – From Clause to Discourse and Beyond* (Studies in Language Companion Series 64). Philadelphia, PA, and Amsterdam: John Benjamins.

Butler, C.S. 2004. Corpus studies and functional linguistic theories. *Functions of Language* 11(2): 147–86.

Butler, C.S., and F. Gonzálvez-García. 2014. *Exploring Functional-Cognitive Space*. Amsterdam: John Benjamins.

Butler, C.S., and M. Taverniers. 2008. Layering in structural-functional grammars. *Linguistics* 46(4): 689–756.

Clarke, B.P. 2012. Do patterns of ellipsis in text support systemic functional linguistics' 'context-metafunction hook-up' hypothesis? A corpus-based approach. Unpublished PhD thesis, Cardiff University.

Clarke, B.P. 2013. The differential patterned occurrence of ellipsis in texts varied for contextual mode: Some support for the 'mode of discourse-textual metafunction' hook-up? In G. O'Grady, T. Bartlett and L. Fontaine (eds) *Choice in Language: Applications in Text Analysis*. Sheffield: Equinox, pp. 269–97.

Fawcett, R.P. 2000. *A Theory of Syntax for Systemic Functional Linguistics*. Philadelphia, PA, and Amsterdam: John Benjamins.

Fontaine, L. 2013. Introduction. In L. Fontaine, T. Bartlett and G. O'Grady (eds) *Systemic Functional Linguistics: Exploring Choice*. Cambridge: Cambridge University Press, pp. 1–12.

Halliday, M.A.K. 1961. Categories of the theory of grammar. *Word* 17(3): 241–92. Reprinted in M.A.K. Halliday. 2002. *Collected Works, Vol. 1*. Ed. J.J. Webster. London: Continuum, pp. 37–94.

Halliday, M.A.K. 1966a. Some notes on 'deep' grammar. *Journal of Linguistics* 2(1): 56–67. Reprinted in M.A.K. Halliday. 2002. *Collected Works, Vol. 1*. Ed. J.J. Webster. London: Continuum, pp. 106–17.

Halliday, M.A.K. 1966b. The concept of rank: a reply. *Journal of Linguistics* 2(1): 110–18. Reprinted in M.A.K. Halliday. 2002. *Collected Works, Vol. 1*. Ed. J.J. Webster. London: Continuum, pp. 118–26.

Halliday, M.A.K. 1969. Options and functions in the English clause. *Brno Studies in English* 8: 81–8. Reprinted in F.W. Householder (ed.). 1972. *Syntactic Theory I: Structuralist*. Harmondsworth: Penguin, pp. 248–57. Also reprinted in M.A.K. Halliday. 2005. *Collected Works, Vol. 7: Studies in English Language*. Ed. J.J. Webster. London: Continuum, pp. 154–63.

Halliday, M.A.K. 1994. *An Introduction to Functional Grammar*. 2nd edn. London: Edward Arnold.

Halliday, M.A.K. 1979. Modes of meaning and modes of expression: Types of grammatical structure and their determination by different semantic functions. In D. Allerton, E. Carney and D. Holdcroft (eds) *Function and Context in Linguistic Analysis: A Festschrift for William Haas*. Cambridge: Cambridge University Press, pp. 57–79. Also reprinted in M.A.K. Halliday. 2002. Collected Works, Vol. 1: On Grammar. Ed. J.J. Webster. London: Continuum, pp 196–218.

Halliday, M.A.K. 2009. Methods – techniques – problems. In M.A.K. Halliday and J.J. Webster (eds) *Continuum Companion to Systemic Functional Linguistics*. London: Continuum, pp. 59–86.

Halliday, M.A.K., and W.S. Greaves. 2008. *Intonation in the Grammar of English*. London: Equinox.

Halliday, M.A.K., and C.M.I.M. Matthiessen. 2006 [1999]. *Construing Experience through Meaning: A Language-Based Approach to Cognition*. London: Continuum.

Halliday, M.A.K., and C.M.I.M. Matthiessen. 2014. *An Introduction to Functional Grammar*. 4th edn. London: Routledge.

Hasan, R. 1987. The grammarian's dream: Lexis as most delicate grammar. In M.A.K. Halliday and R.P. Fawcett (eds) *New Developments in Systemic Linguistics. Vol. 1: Theory and Description*. London: Pinter, pp. 184–211.

Hasan, R. 1995. The conception of context in text. In P.H. Fries and M. Gregory (eds) *Discourse in Society: Systemic Functional Perspectives – Meaning and Choice in Language: Studies for Michael Halliday*. Norwood, NJ: Ablex, pp. 183–283.

Hasan, R. 1996. *Ways of Saying: Ways of Meaning*. London: Cassell.

Hasan, R. 2001. Wherefore context? The place of context in the system and process of language. In Ren Shaozeng, W. Guthrie and I.W. Ronald Fong (eds) *Grammar and Discourse: Proceedings of the International Conference on Discourse Analysis*. Macau: Universidad de Macau, pp. 1–21.

Hasan, R. 2015. Systemic functional linguistics: Halliday and the evolution of a social semiotic. In J.J. Webster (ed.) *The Bloomsbury Companion to M.A.K. Halliday*. London: Bloomsbury, pp. 101–34.

Hengeveld, K., and J.L. Mackenzie. 2008. *Functional Discourse Grammar: A Typologically Based Theory of Language Structure*. Oxford: Oxford University Press.

Huddleston, R.D. 1988. Constituency, multi-functionality and grammaticalization in Halliday's Functional Grammar. *Journal of Linguistics* 24: 137–74.

Lamb, S.M. 1964. On alternation, transformation, realization and stratification. *15th Georgetown Round Table*, pp. 105–22.

Martin, J.R. 1992. *English Text: System and Structure*. Philadelphia, PA, and Amsterdam: John Benjamins.

Martin, J.R. 2013. *Systemic Functional Grammar: A Next Step into the Theory – Axial Relations*. Beijing: Higher Education Press.

Matthews, P.H. 1966. The concept of rank in 'neo-Firthian' grammar. *Journal of Linguistics* 2(1): 101–9.

Matthiessen, C.M.I.M. 1992. Interpreting the textual metafunction. In M. Davies and L. Ravelli (eds) *Advances in Systemic Linguistics: Recent Theory and Practice*. London: Pinter, pp. 37–81.

O'Grady, G. 2010. *A Grammar of Spoken English Discourse: The Intonation of Increments*. London: Continuum.

Sinclair, J.M., and R.M. Coulthard. 1975. *Towards an Analysis of Discourse: The English Used by Teachers and Pupils*. London: Oxford University Press.

Taverniers, M. 2016. Verb patterns in a typological perspective. Paper presented to the LinC Summer School, Cardiff University, 31 August–2 September.

Thompson, G. 1999. Acting the part: Lexico-grammatical choices and contextual factors. In M. Ghadessy (ed.) *Text and Context in Functional Linguistics*. Philadelphia, PA, and Amsterdam: John Benjamins, pp. 101–24.

Tucker, G.H. 1998. *The Lexicogrammar of Adjectives: A Systemic Functional Approach to Lexis*. London: Cassell.

5

From meaning to form in the Cardiff Model of language and its use

Robin P. Fawcett

CARDIFF UNIVERSITY

Language is not simple; its complexity is the complexity of the human brain, and it is of no help to anyone to pretend that it is simpler than it really is.

Halliday 2008: 9

Introduction[1]

Goals

The main goals of this chapter are:

1   To introduce you to the major characteristics of the version of Systemic Functional Linguistics (SFL) known as 'the Cardiff Model' (CM) and
2   to show how it relates 'meaning' to 'form' – in two meanings of 'meaning' (roughly 'sense' and 'reference'), so in two major stages.

We begin by (a) establishing the principles of the Linguistics that underpins the Cardiff Model, and (b) identifying a crucial distinction between two types of 'description of a language'.

Six variables on which linguistic theories differ

The CM's positions on these variables are as follows:

1   The main goal of Linguistics is to understand human language **and its use**.
2   The primary function of language is to enable **communication between human minds**; it is only secondarily for thinking, expletives etc.
3   Linguistics is – or should be – a science, so linguists and applied linguists should study both languages and language-texts **scientifically** – even when their primary motivation is an application.

4   **Theorising** about language and **describing** specific languages are mutually dependent activities. Valuable research methods include:

- **building models** of **languages**, especially **languages in use** (realized in written and diagrammatic descriptions, and/or computer modelling), then recursively **testing, evaluating, revising** and **re-testing** them;
- the **analysis of texts** following **scientific procedures** (so a demanding type of testing); and
- **systemic thought experiments** (so thinking paradigmatically).

5   It is a bonus of great value if a theory of language is 'appliable' (Halliday's term, 2008) to solving real-world problems.
6   As scientists, linguists should be open to the innovative ideas of other scholars, but we should evaluate them scientifically before incorporating them in our models of language and its use.

Describing language and describing language-texts

It is essential to distinguish between two types of linguistic description. The distinction is rarely made explicit, and this has led to serious misunderstandings about what constitutes a 'grammatical description' of a language.

- The first type is a **scientific description** (or **model**) of a language. The goals are to make the description: (a) **comprehensive** (as far as is possible); (b) **explicit** (so 'generative', in one sense of the term, so **testable**); (c) **valid** (so describing what it claims to describe); (d) **reliable** (so replicable by other scholars using the same evidence); and (e) **clear** (so understandable).
- The second type of grammatical description is a **text-descriptive framework**. This describes the categories and relationships needed for analysing **text-sentences**. Since these are the observable **outputs** from using a language, whether spoken or written, the categories and relationships used in text analysis should be derived from those of the scientific model.

Interestingly, almost all published SFL 'grammars', including Halliday's IFG and Fawcett's *Invitation to SFL* (2008), are essentially text-descriptive frameworks, as Halliday has pointed out (e.g. 1994:ix). Yet both works are derived from scientific descriptions of English, both having been implemented in large computer models for generating language texts.

The basic principles and concepts of the Cardiff Model

All but one of the basic principles of the CM are derived from Halliday. We shall start with those that define language itself.

Six CM principles derived from Halliday's revolutionary 1970s proposals

Between 1966 and 1973 Halliday introduced six innovatory principles that transformed his earlier **Scale and Category** theory of grammar (Halliday 2002 [1961]) into **Systemic Functional Grammar**. This constituted a revolution in Linguistics that challenged all users of the theory (and arguably all linguists) to develop more comprehensive and more insightful descriptions of languages than his predecessors had envisaged.

The following six principles are derived directly from Halliday's writings, sometimes with considerable adaptation, as indicated below.

1   **System** (choice) has priority over **structure**. Systems combine into **system networks**.
2   The system networks for TRANSITIVITY, LOGICAL RELATIONS, MOOD, THEME, etc are choices between **meanings**, i.e. they represent the **meaning potential** of a language. In the 1970s Halliday frequently referred to them as **semantic** choices, but we shall see shortly that he later adopted a different theoretical position. However, all systemic functional linguists would agree that the core of a SFL model is a vast network of systems, covering many types of meaning, and that **choice between meanings** is the key SFL concept - whatever label they use for the level at which these system networks occur in their theoretical statements.
3   Meanings are **realized** in **forms**: i.e. in **items** (words and morphemes), **syntax**, and **intonation** or **punctuation**. So a full grammar must include **realization rules**. These state how the **meanings** of features in system networks are expressed as **forms**. Such a grammar is a **generative** grammar.
4   A clause is a single syntactic structure that **integrates**, via the realization rules, **several major areas of meaning**. The CM separates Halliday's four 'strands of meaning' (aka 'metafunctions') into eight: experiential, logical relations, interpersonal, validity, negativity, affective, thematic and informational, plus two 'minor' strands: inferential and discoursal (see Fawcett 1980: 26–34 and 2008: 168–71).
5   The meanings and forms of **lexical items** (vocabulary) should also be modelled by system networks and realization rules, and integrated with those for grammatical items and structures. The CM implements this concept it on a large scale: see Tucker (1998) for adjectives, Neale (2002a and 2002b) for lexical verbs, and Fawcett (2014a) for nouns.
6   **Intonation** should similarly be included in the model (as should **punctuation**), with system networks displaying their meanings and realization rules generating their forms. The CM implements intonation and punctuation as alternative **sub-components** within form, in parallel with **syntax** and **items** (Fawcett 2014b: 331–4).

Taken together, these six principles gave Linguistics both a new theory of language and a vastly increased specification of the phenomena that a comprehensive description of a language should cover.

Now let's see what a model of language that implements these principles is like.

The 'core' model of language

Figure 5.1 shows the SFL model of language that was implemented in both of the large SFL computer models of language in the 1980s: (a) Penman, containing Halliday's 'Nigel' grammar (and reflected in *IFG*) and (b) COMMUNAL, containing the GENESYS grammar and embodying further developments by Fawcett and his colleagues. This equivalence is demonstrated by the similarity between the figure in Matthiessen and Bateman (1991: 102) and that in Fawcett, Tucker and Lin (1993: 121) - and so essentially as in Figure 5.1. (But we shall see shortly that Halliday later changed his position on the theoretical status of the levels of language identified in Figure 5.1.)

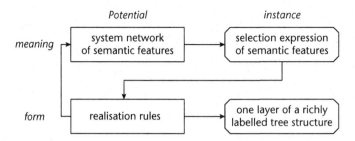

Figure 5.1 The components and their outputs in a generative SFL lexicogrammar

The grammar's main **components** are on the left and their **outputs** are on the right. Each component specifies a 'potential'. The **system network** of semantic features at the level (or stratum) of **meaning** specifies the language's 'meaning potential', and the **realization rules** state how these are expressed at the level of **form**, so specifying the language's **form potential**. The **meaning potential** constitutes the model's generative base.

A lexicogrammar is not a 'thing' but a procedure. Here is how it works. The first traversal of the **system network** produces a **selection expression** of semantic features that will typically be realized as a **clause**. These features are the input to the **realization rules**, which state how they will be realized at the level of form. The first traversal generates both the **elements** of the clause and the **items** that directly **expound** some (or occasionally all) of them, plus the associated **intonation** or **punctuation**.

In most text-sentences some clause elements are **filled** by a **unit**. So some realization rules specify a **re-entry** to the network to generate these 'lower' units (represented by the arrow on the left of Figure 5.1). These subsequent traversals of the network generate **nominal** or other **groups** and **embedded clauses** to fill the first clause's unexpounded elements – and later still lower units to fill some of those units' elements.

Thus a grammar is the sentence-generating component of a full model of language and its use. (In SFL, the term 'grammar' is short for **lexicogrammar** – a term introduced as a reminder that a model of language must include lexis/vocabulary.) We shall shortly come to a major section headed 'How to get meaning to form in the Cardiff lexicogrammar', and this will give you a detailed description of one part of the lexicogrammar. But see Fawcett, Tucker and Lin (1993) for the fullest published description of the generation of a text-sentence in SFL.

The CM incorporates a seventh and equally important principle from Halliday's theory. This is that language must be studied in its social and cultural contexts. See the later sections of this chapter and Bartlett, Chapter 23; Bowcher, Chapter 24; Moore, Chapter 26; and Gardner, Chapter 29.

The CM's additional major principle

But the CM is also shaped by an eighth major principle: one that is largely ignored in Halliday's writings. This is the idea that a comprehensive model of language and its use needs to locate the lexicogrammar within an adequately complex model of a 'communicating mind' (Fawcett 1980). Specifically, the CM provides a **cognitive-interactive** model of an interacting mind that also incorporates knowledge of (i.e. beliefs about) the **socio-cultural** factors relevant to **generating** and **understanding** language-texts. It is this type of comprehensive model that is needed if we are to model the way in which each **Performer** tailors their contribution to the text/discourse to reflect their **beliefs** (real or pretended) about the informational requirements of a specific **Addressee** (or class of Addressees) at a particular point in an unfolding discourse.

Two problematical later developments in Halliday's theoretical model

However, in the period in the 1970s when the model described here was emerging, Halliday was also exploring another innovatory principle: that a full model of language needs a higher 'sociosemanic' system network. Such additional networks initially represented options in 'behaviour' in Bernstein's specific 'critical contexts of socialization', but they were later generalized to become 'the semantics'. (See Tann, Chapter 27.)

For many years, therefore, Halliday was exploring simultaneously two concepts of 'semantics' – and so, in effect, two models of language. In the first, the networks for TRANSITIVITY, LOGICAL RELATIONS, MOOD, THEME etc. constitute the level of meaning, and Halliday often describes them as **semantic** options. But in the second model he treats them as part of the level of 'wording' (i.e. **form**) – and so as **realizing** a higher 'semantics'. In the end he opted for the second. So some adherents of the SM may consider that the model described here is less insightful, on the grounds that it doesn't have a level of language that corresponds to the sketch for the 'ideational' component of a higher 'semantics' in Halliday and Matthiessen (1999) or the exploratory networks in Martin (1992) for a higher 'discourse semantics'.

However, by working for two decades on the twin tasks of (a) semanticizing all of the system networks at the level of TRANSITIVITY, LOGICAL RELATIONS, MOOD, THEME etc. (a task begun by Halliday in the late 1960s but never completed) and (b) providing their complementary realization rules, the CM has already developed very many near-comprehensive **semantic system networks**. For example, the expressions generated from Hasan's semantic network for 'speech function' (Hasan 1992) are essentially the same as those that are generated from the CM's semantic network for MOOD, as illustrated in the next major section and more fully in Fawcett (2011). The main difference is that the CM's outputs are generated directly from the semantics whereas Hasan's are derived via an additional lexicogrammatical stratum.

A second potential SM criticism of the model of language described here might be that, because it doesn't have a 'higher' semantics, it cannot provide for the phenomena that Halliday originally described as exhibiting **incongruence** and now terms **grammatical metaphor**. But the CM architecture for language and its use does in fact provide for these types of incongruence (and indeed others), as a later section will illustrate.

We shall come shortly to the description of how the CM gets from meaning to form. But first we should establish the key concepts that underpin the CM's functional syntax, since it is through this that the meanings are realized.

Six key concepts in functional syntax

The CM's descriptive syntactic categories (so occasionally its theoretical syntactic categories) have been subject to continual development since the 1970s. Thus the process of semanticizing the CM's **system networks** has been complemented by further 'functionalizing' the CM's **syntax** – with both types of advance incorporating the new evidence from Corpus Linguistics available from the 1980s onwards. As Halliday himself has pointed out (2003 [1993]: 433–41), later work in the SM has mainly been on extensions to new areas rather than revisions of the existing SM grammar. And the result is that there are now two sister 'dialects' of SFL: the SM and the CM, these being described and evaluated in Butler (2003a and 2003b: passim).

Here are the key concepts that underpin the CM's functional syntax:

1   Each **unit** in **syntax** realizes a feature in the system network that denotes a **semantic unit**. For English the initial choice in the semantic system for ENTITY TYPE is (simplifying slightly) between [situation], [thing], [minor_relationship_with_thing], [quality] and [quantity]. Typically, these are realized respectively as **clause, nominal group, prepositional group, quality group** and **quantity group**.

2   A **unit** and its **elements** are mutually defining. Each element represents a different aspect of a typical **referent** in the **input** for that unit, e.g. an **event** for a **clause** and an **object** for a **nominal group**. (See the penultimate section of this chapter for the concept of the 'input'.) The elements of each unit are different from those of every other unit – except for two that are relevant to virtually all units: the **linker** (e.g. *and*) and the **inferer** (e.g. *even*). Thus:

   - A **clause** typically represents an **event** in the input, and its elements represent the participants, circumstances, validity, polarity, time etc. of the event. (See Fawcett 2008 and 2010 [2000].)
   - A **nominal group** typically represents an **object** in the input, so also its 'cultural classification', 'number' (singular/plural/mass), particularization, quantification, qualities etc. (See Fawcett 2007 and Fontaine, Chapter 17.)
   - A **prepositional group** represents a **minor relationship with an object**.
   - A **quality group** represents a **quality** of an object or event and various associated meanings (see Tucker (1998) and Tucker, Chapter 18).
   - A **quantity group** represents a **quantity** and its associated meanings.
   - Three classes of **cluster (genitive, human proper name,** and **address)** may fill nominal group elements to express complex meanings within some types of object.

   For fuller descriptions of these units, see the above references and Fawcett (2010 [2000]: 193–213), and compare McDonald, Chapter 16.

3   The grammar typically generates **several layers** of **units** in a text-sentence, frequently **embedding** one unit within another. (Contrast Halliday's position, summarized in Berry, Chapter 4.)

4   The **categories** used in the realization rules – so in representations of the outputs (usually omitting place) – are: **(class of) unit, place** (in unit), **element** (of structure of a unit) and **item** (word or morpheme).

5   The four main **relationships** used in the realization rules – and in analyzing functional syntax – are **componence, conflation, filling** and **exponence**. Thus:

   - Potentially, a unit is **composed** of two or more **elements**, and any **instance** of a unit has one or more elements;
   - A unit's **elements** are located at sequenced **places** in the unit;
   - One **element** is often **conflated** with another, e.g. an Auxiliary Verb with the Operator as O/X, and a Participant Role with a Subject, e.g. S/Ag;
   - Some clause elements are directly **expounded** by **items**, e.g. the Operator, Auxiliaries and Main Verb (see Quiroz, Chapter 19, for a discussion of the 'verbal group' in the CM and SM);
   - Almost all other elements are **filled** by a **unit** (or two or more **co-ordinated units**);

- Any such unit is itself **composed** of one or more elements (so repeating the relations so far); and
- The lowest element is **expounded** by an **item** (or items, e.g. *eat* + *ing*).

Figure 5.2 illustrates the most important syntactic categories and relationships (while omitting Participant and Circumstantial Roles).

6   In principle, the grammar should state, for every feature in every system, the **general probability** (expressed as a percentage) that the feature will be selected. However, **probabilities** are often **reset** in mid-generation of a text-sentence, then reinstated. See the next section for examples of the two types of resetting. Knowledge of these **filling probabilities** is very helpful in analyzing text-sentences, and should be included in grammars designed for use as **text-descriptive frameworks**. (See the first section of this chapter for this key concept, and Fawcett (2010 [2000]: 305–7) for summarizing diagrams.)

From meaning to form within the Cardiff lexicogrammar

This section illustrates the concept of getting 'from meaning to form' in the lexicogrammar for MOOD in English. Thus it illustrates CM **theory** through a CM **description** of how this part of English works.

First, however, we should consider how best to **represent** (a) a **system network** and (b) its accompanying **realization rules.**

Note: In SFL, the names of subnetworks are usually written in capitals and the features in lowercase. But when features are referred to in running text they are typically shown in square brackets, e.g. [information], with informal representations sometimes being written in single quotation marks (e.g. 'information giver'). In a system network, three dots (...) means 'This leads to further systems not shown here.' Finally, an item to be inserted in the text-sentence being generated is indicated by double quotation marks, e.g. "can".

The problem of how best to represent a SFL grammar

Consider the simplified representation in Figure 5.3 of part of the CM's semantic system network for MOOD. Here we are considering it as a representation of certain concepts, and in the next section we shall discuss concepts themselves.

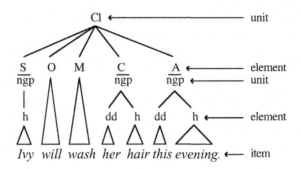

Figure 5.2   The basic categories of functional syntax

Source: Fawcett (2008: 74)

Figure 5.3 represents the system network in the **graph** format that is typically used in introductory texts. However, the representation that follows expresses the same concepts as a set of rules, and this more compact **linear** format actually provides more information. It includes several **realization rule** numbers and, in the first line, a **same pass rule** number (sp1.3, which will be explained shortly). And it is not limited by page-width, as the graph format is.

> MOOD → 98% information (1.2) / 2% proposal_for_action (sp1.3) ...
> information → 98% giver / 1.4% seeker / 0.2% confirmation_seeker (1.3) /
>   0.1% exclamation ... / 0.3% (others).
> giver → 99% simple_giver / 1% plus_confirmation_seeker (1.213) ...
> seeker → 38% polarity_seeker / 60% new_content_seeker /
>   2% choice_of_alternative_contents_seeker.

Both representations model the system network as a 'resource' (Halliday's preferred description), but the linear version demonstrates that a system network is equivalent to 'a set of rules'.

What sort of rule is sp1.3 on [proposal_for_action], in line 1? It is a **same pass preference re-setting rule**. This is a CM innovation that enables a relatively simple system network to model the great variation in the **probabilities** that a given feature in a system will be chosen. A same pass (sp) rule on a feature states that, if this feature is selected, the probabilities will be reset in a system (or systems) that will be entered later in the same traversal of (i.e. pass through) the network. Consider sp1.3:

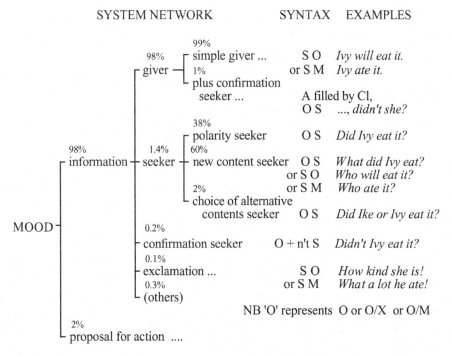

Figure 5.3 Part of a simplified semantic system network for MOOD

Source: Figure 11.1 in Fawcett (2008).

sp1.3 : for same_pass prefer [0.1% period_marked / 99.9% not_period_marked].

This says that, if [proposal_for_action] is chosen, the feature [not_period_marked] (e.g. realized as *Read it!*) will almost certainly be preferred over [period_marked] (e.g. realized as *Be reading it!*).

Now consider the subnetwork below. It is a linear representation that provides some of the visual advantages of the graph form, while also illustrating the meanings by examples. It represents some early features in the systems entered from [proposal_for_action] in Figure 5.3, and the section on realization rules (to which we shall come shortly) will refer to some of its realization rules.

proposal_for_action →	Examples of realizations
90% by_addressee /	*Read it! Could you read it, please?*
4% by_self_and_addressee.../	*Let's read it!*
5% by_self.../	*Shall I read it?*
1% by_outsider...	*(Let) Ivy read it!*
by addressee →	
50% directive (20).../	*Read it!*
40% request (1.33).../	*Can/Could/Will/Would you read it?*
10% suggestion...	*What about you reading it?*
request →	
60% appeal_to_ability (1.331) /	*Can / Could you read it?*
40% appeal_to_willingness (1.332)	*Will / Would you read it?*
&	
30% direct ap /	*Can / Will you read it?*
70% indirect ap.	*Could / Would you read it?*

For a near-comprehensive eight-page semantic system network for MOOD in English, see Appendices A and B in Fawcett (2011).

Finally, how should we represent **realization rules**? Again, there are two main ways: in a **tabular** or a **linear** format. Tables with columns suffice for simple grammars, but for the complexity of a comprehensive grammar we need the flexibility of a linear representation (as used in the next subsection but one).

Meanings in the system network for MOOD

There are three reasons for using the MOOD network to illustrate the way in which the CM models choice between meanings.

- It illustrates clearly the difference between a **semantic** system network for MOOD (as in the CM) and one that reflects contrasts at the level of **form** (as in the SM).
- It complements the two other chapters in this volume that describe the CM's approach to the English clause: Huang, Chapter 11 on THEME and Neale, Chapter 12 on TRANSITIVITY. But see Neale (2002a and 2002b) for a detailed description of **process types** and **participant roles** in English.
- It illustrates the complex nature of realization rules required in any adequately comprehensive systemic functional grammar.

MOOD meanings assign communication roles to the Performer and the Addressee, such as the 'giver' or 'seeker' of 'information'.

We start by noting the features that have been selected in the overall network before reaching MOOD (one being needed for a realization rule in the next section). They are: [entity, situation, congruent_situation, independent]. So the **entry condition** for MOOD is [independent].

Let me now comment briefly on the semantic features in the network in Figure 5.3.

Since [information] leads to a system that includes [giver] and [seeker], [giver] entails 'information-giver', so corresponding to the everyday term 'statement'. Similarly, [seeker] entails 'information-seeker', so corresponding to 'question'. The third option in the first system is [confirmation_seeker], a typical example being *Didn't Ivy eat it?* So, although it has the **form** of a 'negative' 'polarity-seeker' (see below), it has the **meaning** suggested by its name (and further inferences, necessarily omitted here). The fourth option is [exclamation], and its meaning is clear.

An 'information giver' can be either [simple] (e.g. *Ivy ate it*) or [plus_confirmation_seeker] (e.g. *Ivy ate it, didn't she?*).

Similarly, [seeker] leads to a dependent system: [polarity_seeker] (in traditional grammar: 'Yes-No question'), [new_content_seeker (traditionally: '*Wh*-question') and [choice_of_alternative_contents_seeker] (traditionally: 'alternative question').

The first stage in getting from meaning to form within the lexicogrammar is therefore to traverse the semantic system network (from left to right in Figure 5.3) and so to generate a **selection expression**, e.g. [information, giver, simple_giver], so generating as the output *Ivy will eat it*, etc.

Standard SM networks for MOOD reflect clause patterns at the level of form. They omit choices such as [confirmation_seeker] and most of the choices to which [proposal_for_action] leads, including many types of [request], [suggestion] and [offer]. They also typically omit [choice_of_alternative_contents_seeker] and other options not included here. The closest SM equivalent to the CM's system network for MOOD is Hasan's network for 'speech functions' (e.g. Hasan 1992). But her network is intended to be part of the SM's 'higher semantics', so that its realizations are not directly as **forms** (as here) but as 'pre-selections' in the standard SM MOOD network. So, from the CM viewpoint, the SM approach adds an unnecessary level of networks and realization rules. (See Andersen, Chapter 8.)

Some realization rules for MOOD and their outputs

In explaining how the grammar turns **meanings** into **forms,** the key component is the **realization rules**. This section is therefore central to the lexicogrammar and so to this chapter.

An introductory approach to the realization rules for MOOD in English typically focusses on the sequential relationship between the Subject (S) and the Operator (O), or, if there is no Operator, the Main Verb (M), as shown in the 'SYNTAX' column in Figure 5.3. But in a large-scale generative grammar the realization rules for MOOD need to be integrated with those that generate other clause elements, especially Auxiliary Verbs. This is because most Auxiliary Verbs and the Main Verb (if a form of *be*) frequently also function as the Operator (for example, in "Ivy is here", "is" expounds O/M (using the 'conflation' operation described below).

Many realization rules for MOOD features include **conditions**, and some involve **re-entry** to the system network to **preselect** the features required to generate a **lower unit** in the structure, e.g. a **clause** as in Rule 1.213 below, or a **nominal group** as in Rule 1.33 below.

Realization rules must be applied in their numerical order. Each consists of one or more **realization statements**, each specifying, under stated conditions, one of the following **operations**:

1   Insert a **unit** to fill an **element** (e.g. ngp).
2   Insert an **element** (e.g. h) at a numbered **place** in a **unit** (e.g. 84 in ngp).
3   **Conflate** (= insert one element by another) (e.g. 'Ag by S', creating 'S/Ag').
4   **Expound** an **element** by an **item**, e.g. h < "she".
5   **Fetch** from the relevant part of the **belief system** the version of the referent's **name** that realizes the meaning, e.g. "Ivy" or "Dr Idle".
6   **Reset preferences**, i.e. probabilities in systems, including resetting to 100% and 0%. This operation is used to limit options on re-entering the network to generate another unit.
7   **Re-enter** the network at [entity] (to ensure continuity of choices in register).
(To compare these with Halliday's set, see Berry, Chapter 4.)

Now for some examples.

Rule 1.1 is for a feature that we met when listing the entry conditions for MOOD. Whenever a new text-sentence is generated, a sigma ($\sum$, representing 'sentence') is automatically generated as the topmost category (omitted in Figure 5.2). In the CM the concept of 'sentence' is used as a variable that represents whatever **act** in **discourse structure** the text-sentence expresses.

> **1.1 : congruent_situation :**
>   Cl, S @ 33, if not being then M @ 100.

Note: throughout this section italicized text indicates either an explanatory comment or an example of a realization.

*Rule 1.1 means 'Insert a **clause** (Cl), then insert the element **Subject** (S) at **Place 33** in the clause, and, if the semantic feature [being] has not been selected, insert a **Main Verb** (M) at **Place 100**. Note the useful simplifying CM concept of a **negative condition**.*

*Why 'Place 100'? Since most clause elements can occur at two or more places, a comprehensive grammar needs around 250 **places** to provide for all possible sequences.*

*Rules from TRANSITIVITY generate (a) the realization of the **Process** as a **Main Verb** (M), e.g. "eat" or "ate" in the examples in Figure 5.3, and (b) its associated **Participant Roles** - that is, an **Agent** (typically conflated with the **Subject** as S/Ag), and an **Affected** (typically conflated with a **Complement** as C/Af). Sometimes a PR is left unfilled, e.g. an Agent in some types of [proposal_for_action], as in "Eat it!". For TRANSITIVITY in the CM, see Neale (2002a and 2002b) and Neale, Chapter 12.*

Now consider the complex yet elegant Rule, 1.2. Its sole purpose is to locate the **Operator**, if there is one, at its **place** in the **clause**.

*The rule has three sections. The first lists the semantic features that must have been chosen in other parts of the system network for the rest of this rule to be applied. The examples on the right illustrate some of the many words that may **realize** the corresponding semantic feature by expounding the Operator (O). Thus 'retrospective' is the CM's functional name for the traditional term 'perfect', and it is realized in an Auxiliary Verb (X) that can be conflated with O as O/X, as in "Ivy has nibbled it". (Note that two or more of these features can be* *co-selected, e.g. by adding [period-marked] (traditionally 'continuous' or 'progressive'), as in "Ivy has been nibbling it." So here 'or' means 'or or and'.*

1.2 : information:	***Examples of realizations***
if (being or	*is/was/will be*
unmarked_passive or	*is/was/will be + -en/ed*
retrospective_from_trp or	*has/had/will have + -en/ed*
period_marked or	*is/was/will be + -ing*
future_trp or	*will/shall*
validity_assessed or	*may/must* etc
modulated or	*can/should* etc
contrast_on_polarity or	*She DID eat it*
negative or	*She did + n't/not eat it*
(seeker and not subject_theme_sought) or	*Did she eat it? What did she eat?*
confirmation_seeker)	*Didn't she eat it?*
then. . . .	

*The next section specifies the **place** in the clause where the Operator will be located, under each of two slightly complex conditions. Later realization rules will generate the **item** that **expounds** it.*

then (if giver or (seeker and subject_theme_sought)	*Ivy will eat it* or *Who has eaten it?*
then O @ 35,	
if (seeker and not subject_theme_sought) or	*What did Ivy eat?*
confirmation_seeker)	*Didn't Ivy eat it?*
then O @ 31),	

The final section identifies four key features which, if one or more is chosen, require that there be an Operator. So, if no feature is chosen that results in O being expounded by an item (e.g. "may"), the 'do_insertion_subrule' (omitted here for reasons of space) inserts "do", "does" or "did", as appropriate.

if (seeker or confirmation_seeker or negative or contrast_on_polarity)
then do_insertion_subrule.

Undeniably, Rule 1.2 is pretty complex. However, by bringing together the many different semantic motivations for introducing an Operator, we greatly increase the elegance of the grammar as a whole.

The next rule illustrates a different type of complexity.

1.213 : plus_confirmation_seeker:	*Ivy ate it, <u>didn't she</u>?*

A/CSTag @ 237,
for A/CSTag prefer [situation, tag, confirmation_seeking_tag],
for A/CSTag re_enter_at entity.

*This rule places a **Confirmation-Seeking Tag Adjunct (A/CSTag)** near the end of the clause. Then it **resets** the **probabilities** for [situation] etc., **re-enters the network**, and fills A/CSTag with a 'truncated' **clause** (one with only O and S). Finally, it applies an* *if_on_mother_pass rule that re-uses features of the mother clause to generate automatically the items to expound O ("didn't") and the head of the ngp at S ("she") – so generating "didn't she?' – just as competent English-speakers do.*

The next rule illustrates two more characteristics of realization rules: (a) a rule may serve two or more features, and (b) it may use **register** *variables (which reflect variables in* **context of situation***) as conditions. Note that '<+' means 'is expounded by adding this suffix', and 'N' is the clause element Negator.*

> **1.3 : confirmation_seeker or negative:**
> if casual or (consultative and spoken) then O <+ "n't",
>
> > *Didn't Ivy eat it? or Ivy didn't eat it.*
> if formal or (consultative and written) then (N @ 38, N < "not").
>
> > *Did Ivy not eat it? or Ivy did not eat it.)*

Finally, here are some interesting rules for a few features entered from [proposal_for_action].

> **1.33 : request:** *Can/Could/Will/Would you read it?*
> O @ 31,
> for S prefer [thing, congruent_thing, interactant, addressee],
> for S re_enter_at entity.

The first line places the Operator but doesn't expound it. (For this see the next two rules.) The next two lines concern the Subject. As in Rule 1.213 above, realization is by **re-entering** *the network and generating a* **nominal group (ngp)** *to fill S, and then adding "you" to expound its head. So the grammar neatly preselects the entire lower unit from this one rule. The next two rules are both simple and self-explanatory.*

> **1.331 : appeal_to_ability :**
> if direct_ap then O < "can", if indirect_ap then O < "could".
> **1.332 : appeal_to_willingness :**
> if direct_ap then O < "will", if indirect_ap then O < "would".

Interestingly, SM linguists would treat these examples as either an 'interpersonal grammatical metaphor' (in Halliday's writings) or 'semantic choices' (in Hasan's 'speech function' networks).

This section has illustrated (a) how the CM works, as it gets 'from meaning to form', and (b) the inevitable complexities in some of the rules that are needed for any adequately comprehensive lexicogrammar. The area of English grammar described here presents a stern challenge to any theory of language. The key factor in CM's ability to model these complexities relatively economically is that it uses **semantic features** as **conditions** in the **realization rules**.

The need to go beyond the lexicogrammar

In recent decades Halliday and other SM linguists have firmed up on the general concept that an additional higher level of system networks is needed. It is termed 'discourse semantics' by Martin (e.g. 1992) and simply 'semantics' by Halliday and Matthiessen (e.g. 1999) and Hasan (e.g. 1992). (See also Moore, Chapter 26; Tann, Chapter 27.) However, detailed description has lagged behind theory (other than in Hasan's work), so that it is hard to evaluate these proposals scientifically.

The corollary of adopting the current SM position on 'semantics' is that the standard system networks for TRANSITIVITY, LOGICAL RELATIONS, MOOD etc. are no longer seen as 'semantic', and so as the level of 'meaning', but as being at the level of 'wording' (i.e. 'form'). So a SM linguist might object that the account of getting 'from meaning to form' given so far omits the level of meaning, i.e. semantics.

The CM position is that our work since the 1970s on expanding our networks as explicitly **semantic system networks** has made a higher semantic system network unnecessary – but that other types of 'higher' component are needed. For these, see the next two sections.

The first section of these assesses SM linguists' progress in providing descriptions of this new level, and then introduces the linguistic phenomena that are seen by SM scholars as a major motivation for adding the higher semantic network. Halliday originally characterized these phenomena as **incongruent**, but they are now usually referred to as types of **grammatical metaphor** (see Taverniers, Chapter 22). The following section then introduces the full CM architecture, illustrating it by providing a more comprehensive model of how to get 'from meaning to form' – including modelling both the grammatical metaphor phenomena and certain other incongruent phenomena.

Is there a level of 'meaning' above the networks for TRANSITIVITY etc?

The challenge of grammatical metaphor and other incongruent phenomena

We saw earlier that Halliday's original motivation for adding a higher semantic system network above those for TRANSITIVITY, etc. was to provide for certain 'sociosemantic' options. But Halliday (2003 [1984]) presents a sketch for the 'mood' part of a new model of language that is unrestricted by social context. It has three levels of networks: one for 'moves' (actually 'acts') in **discourse**, one for the **semantics** of 'mood' ('speech function') and one for the **forms** of 'mood'. Later, Hasan developed detailed networks for the semantics of 'mood' (e.g. Hasan 1992). These were only partially complemented by Halliday and Matthiessen's 1999 exploratory sketch of a generalized 'ideational semantics'.

That work also included a growing list of **grammatical metaphor (GM) phenomena**, these being presented as a major justification for the additional level of networks. In broad terms, these proposals were at a similar level to the outline system networks for 'discourse semantics' in Martin (1992). The GM phenomena are also a challenge to the CM, and the next section describes how we handle them – and other incongruent phenomena.

The need for a scientific approach to modelling incongruent phenomena

Since SM scholars have so far provided networks for only some parts of this higher network, most being exploratory sketches, many questions remain unanswered. In a scientific approach to modeling the GM and other incongruent phenomena, SFL scholars should ask at least these five questions:

1   Has any alternative way of modelling these phenomena been proposed?
2   If so, how should we test and evaluate the alternative proposals?

3   Where and how are decisions between semantic features made?
4   Are system networks the most appropriate formalism for representing choices/decisions at every 'level/stratum' of the overall model?
5   What other formalisms should be considered?

Let me now describe how the CM handles incongruent phenomena. It uses one or other of the following three ways.

- Our work since the 1970s on semanticizing and expanding the system networks provides for some types of GM phenomena, e.g. the requests in the MOOD network introduced earlier.
- We have expanded a higher component that was already required (**equivalences**; see Figure 5.4), so that it now handles not only many GM phenomena but also other challenging phenomena such as 'fresh' metaphors and idioms. (We shall see how this works in the next section.)
- Certain other phenomena that exhibit 'incongruence' are handled in one or other of the **microplanners** (see Figure 5.4). For example, the **theme microplanner** changes the input's logical form to enable the grammar to generate **experiential**, **evaluative**, and **existential enhanced theme** constructions - examples being respectively: *It was Ivy who read it*, *It was nice that she did that* and *There's a bee in your hair*). (For **enhanced theme** constructions, see Huang (2003) and Huang, Chapter 11. For the **thematization** microplanner see Fawcett (1997).

Our conclusion is therefore that no higher semantic system network is needed. For a full discussion of this major issue, see Fawcett (forthcoming).

We turn finally to the overall architecture of the CM, beginning with the reasons for the differences between the CM and the SM.

From 'input meaning' to form in the full Cardiff Model

Goals and architectures in the two SFL models

The major theoretical differences between the CM and the SM are reflected in their different overall architectures.

The CM architecture seeks to model the way that an **individual** human (the **Performer**, P) generates and understands texts in **specific** situations. It is the product of over two decades of work, involving over two dozen scholars, working to combine SFL (including its 'socio-cultural' aspects) with the 'cognitive-interactive' approach to modelling language and its use that is required in Computational Linguistics.

It is essentially a **consulting** architecture in which components in the generation procedure 'consult' aspects of P's **belief system** as P generates text-sentences, as described below and more fully in Fawcett (2013 and forthcoming).

In contrast, Halliday's watchword is 'I stop at the skin.' His goal, and so that of many of his colleagues, is to relate language-texts to their **generalized social** and **cultural** (including **ideological**) contexts – but without trying to model the complex cognitive unconscious planning that results in texts addressed to a specific Addressee, e.g. when generating **referring expressions**.

SM scholars make two simplifying assumptions about how we generate language-texts: (a) that the concept of **realization** between form and meaning can be extended 'upwards' to the 'higher' components, and (b) that each such level/stratum of language consists of a **system network** of choices (and structures, in some proposals), such that a selection expression of features at each higher stratum is realized in the stratum below, by realization rules that predetermine choices, eventually reaching the lexicogrammar.

However, from a scientific viewpoint current descriptions of this model are merely exploratory sketches, because there have been no large-scale illustrative descriptions or computer implementations of this simplifying **multi-stratal** model. And, interestingly, the computer implementation of Halliday's 1970s model in the Penman Project (Matthiessen and Bateman 1991) was in fact a 'consulting' architecture, as is the CM; see Fawcett (2013 and forthcoming).

Unlike the SM, the CM's cognitive-interactive architecture introduces several different types of component, each with a processor or structure appropriate to its function (e.g. **decision trees** for the **microplanners**, and **taxonomies** for the **belief system**). Together, these model the way in which the **Performer(s)** of a text produces it, making multiple instantaneous subconscious decisions by consulting relevant sub-components of the **belief system**. This has sub-components for all the socio-cultural factors foregrounded in the SM, plus many others omitted here. Several of these higher components have been tested by being implemented in the computer as parts of a working text-sentence generator. See below and Fawcett (forthcoming) for a fuller picture.

The CM's architecture, with its many different types of task-specific component, is more complex than the SM's relatively simple multi-stratal model. This is inevitable, because it seeks to model how an individual plans and produces a specific text, so that it must provide for **cognitive-interactive** as well as **socio-cultural** factors.

The full CM architecture

We have been assuming so far that 'meaning' is located in the semantic features of the system network. And so it is; this is 'meaning' as the 'sense' of the text's wording. But to demonstrate that the CM can handle 'meaning' in a sense that encompasses grammatical metaphor and other types of incongruence, we need a much fuller model of generation: one that can also handle 'meaning' as 'reference'. And this requires us to model the **input** to the process of generation. This 'input is the ultimate 'meaning' of a text-sentence, and so the starting point for the description that follows of how to handle a typical GM.

For a general overview of the CM's architecture, I invite you to 'read' the diagram in Figure 5.4, focussing here on the **generation** side. Fawcett (2013) gives a brief introduction to this architecture, with summaries and evaluations of six different SFL proposals for architectures for generating texts, but Fawcett (forthcoming) provides a far fuller account of both. For an overview of the model's **understanding** side, see Fawcett (1994 and forthcoming); for the CM's **corpus-consulting probabilistic parser**, see Day (2007); and for its **semantic interpreter** see O'Donoghue (1994).

Generating a sentence that contains a nominalization

Let us consider the generation of a text-sentence that includes a nominalization. The context of situation is that Ivy's mother is telling a friend about an event in Ivy's life, and she concludes with this coda: *So Ivy's loss of her keys was pretty disastrous.* Unusually, the **referent** of the Subject/Carrier is not an **object** but, incongruently, an **event**, expressed as *Ivy's loss of her keys.*

Ivy's mother (the Performer, P) could have expressed this 'lose' event in various other ways, each with a slightly different meaning, including: *Ivy's losing her keys*, *this loss* and *the fact that Ivy lost her keys*. Clearly, a comprehensive model of language and its use must be able to show where and how, in the overall model, such planning decisions are made, and how they are implemented.

Here is an outline of how the architecture described here models such cases, referring to Figure 5.4. We shall assume that the decisions have already been made about (a) **genre** structure, (b) **exchange structure** and **rhetorical structure** and (c) **register, social code** etc.

1 P's **planner** constructs an appropriate **input** to generation, this being represented in **systemic functional logical form** (SFLF): see Fawcett (forthcoming). Essentially, this is the **event** to which the sentence being generated **refers** plus its **purpose** (expressed as an **act** in the **discourse structure**). So the **input** is the 'meaning' of the text-sentence, in P's mind, in the 'reference' sense of *meaning*. Informally, the input is '(Ivy lose keys) be bad'. We focus here on the embedded event, i.e. '(Ivy lose keys)'.

2 P's Planner makes its decisions after consulting the relevant sub-components of P's large and complex **belief system**, aka its 'database' (the internal subcomponents being omitted in Figure 5.4). These subcomponents include P's beliefs about the **context of situation**, the **context of culture**, the **preceding discourse structure**, its **wording** (the latter two affecting the degree of **recoverability** by the **Addressee** (A) of each **referent**) etc – and beliefs about **A's beliefs** about these variables. These are all represented in SFLF.

3 The **planner** then consults the relevant sub-components of the belief system, as it decides between the available **equivalences.** One decision is whether to present the event **congruently** or **incongruently**. Here, it decides to present it **incongruently**, as a **nominalization** (the most compact option), and it 'enriches' the SFLF of the input appropriately.

4 Next, each of the dozen **microplanners** in turn consults the relevant sub-components of the **belief system** and enriches the current SFLF by adding to it appropriate **referring expressions, time specifications**, expressions of **affective attitudes** etc.

5 The result is an **enriched logical form**.

6 **Predetermination rules** then automatically translate the enriched SFLF into **preferences** in . . .

7 . . . the **semantic system network** within the **lexicogrammar**, . . .

8 so generating a **selection expression** of semantic features.

9 The **realization rules** then convert these features into . . .

10 . . . a functionally-labelled **tree structure**.

11 Finally, the **syntax stripper** removes everything except the string of words and the intonation or punctuation, so generating (after further re-entries to the system network). . . .

12 . . . the underlined portion of the **text-sentence** *So Ivy's loss of her keys was* pretty *disastrous.*

Thus many unconscious planning decisions, including the **reification** of the 'lose' event in the sub-component for EQUIVALENCES, converts a **referent event** into a simple string of **items**.

To summarize: the CM handles some 'GM-type phenomena' in its semanticized system networks, others in the **equivalences** sub-component, and others in microplanners such as the thematization microplanner. From the CM viewpoint, then, there are no grounds for introducing an additional 'semantic' system network, as many users of the SM appear to assume (some with qualms).

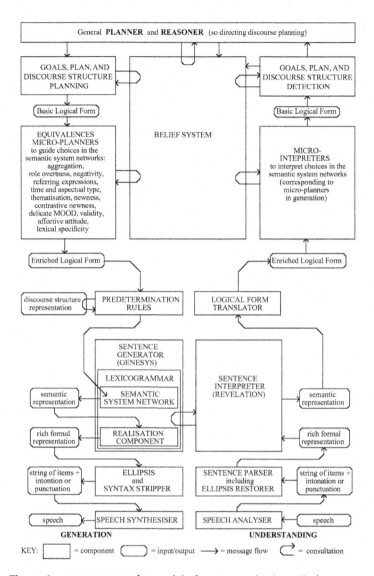

Figure 5.4   The major components of a model of a communicating mind

Source: Figure 8.1 in Fawcett (forthcoming).

We have also seen that the many socio-cultural factors that affect decisions in generating and understanding language-texts have a natural place within a cognitive-interactive architecture.

Locating the Cardiff Model in the language-related disciplines of the twenty-first century

As we saw in the first section of this chapter, the Cardiff Model of language and its use was originally conceived as a SFL model of the human mind in social interaction (Fawcett

1980, 1981 [1973]). It is this that explains its natural fit with the requirements of **Natural Language Generation** and, in a later development, **Natural Language Understanding**, so contributing to those fields as well as to **Linguistics**.

The CM's increasingly comprehensive descriptions of the lexicogrammar of English (always at the levels of both meaning and form) have been subject to a continual process of scientific development, drawing on advances in linguistic methodology in the period since the 1970s, especially **Computational Linguistics** and **Corpus Linguistics**. It therefore now offers a far more complete model of language and its use than it did in the 1980s, with further major publications that describe it scheduled to appear in 2017 and 2018.

The CM therefore belongs squarely within the broad family of functional and cognitive theories of language, as is demonstrated in two recent surveys of such approaches: Butler (2003a and 2003b) and Butler and Gonzales-Garcia (2014).

Despite the title of my 1980 book - *Cognitive Linguistics and Social Interaction* - there is little similarity, sadly, between the CM version of SFL and the more recently developed theory of language known as 'Cognitive Linguistics', e.g. Langacker (1987a and 1987b). (A more suitable name for that theory might have been 'Conceptual Linguistics', because it focuses overwhelmingly on the area of meaning termed 'experiential' in SFL, so its 'cognitive range' is quite limited.)

The early years of the twenty-first century have seen ever-increasing interest in modelling language in its natural mental and social setting i.e. spoken and written communication between humans. I therefore believe that there is a promising future for a model of language in use (in contrast with language abstracted from its context, as in various formalist theories) – and especially for one that combines the inherent strengths of both SFL models with a scientific approach to the many remaining challenges presented by the ever-fascinating phenomenon that is human language.

Note

1 The COMMUNAL Project, which was the computer implementation of what became the Cardiff Model of language and its use, was supported by grants from the Speech Research Unit at DRA Malvern (now QinetiQ) for over ten years, by ICL (now Fujitsu) and Longman in Phase 1, and throughout by Cardiff University. I thank these institutions for their support for this 'blue sky' research. I also thank the two friends and colleagues to whom I am particularly indebted: Michael Halliday, to whom I owe most of the basic concepts of my model of language, and Gordon Tucker, who has worked closely with me for many years in developing the version of Systemic Functional Grammar that has come to be known as the Cardiff Grammar and implementing it as the core component of the COMMUNAL computer model of language and its use. Finally, I thank Yuen Lin and the two dozen or so other fine scholars who have worked closely with us in developing the Cardiff Model. (Note that in this chapter 'CM' is used to refer to (a) the full Cardiff Model of language and its use and (b) the lexicogrammar that is its core component – aka 'the Cardiff Grammar'.)

References

Butler, C.S. 2003a. *Structure and Function: An Introduction to Three Major Structural-Functional Theories, Vol. 1 – Approaches to the Simplex Clause*. Amsterdam: John Benjamins.

Butler, C.S. 2003b. *Structure and Function: An Introduction to Three Major Structural-Functional Theories, Vol. 2 – From Clause to Discourse and Beyond*. Amsterdam: John Benjamins.

Butler, C.S., and F. Gonzálves-García. 2014. *Exploring Functional-Cognitive Space*. Amsterdam: John Benjamins.

Day, M. D., 2007. *A Corpus-Consulting Probabilistic Approach to Parsing: the CCPX Parser and its Complementary Components*. PhD Thesis. Cardiff: Dept. of Computer Science, Cardiff University, Cardiff.

Fawcett, R.P. 1980. *Cognitive Linguistics and Social Interaction: Towards an Integrated Model of a Systemic Functional Grammar and the Other Components of a Communicating Mind*. Heidelberg: Julius Groos and Exeter University.

Fawcett, R.P. 1981 [1973]. Generating a sentence in systemic functional grammar. University College London (mimeo). Reprinted in M.A.K. Halliday and J.R. Martin (eds) *Readings in Systemic Linguistics*. London: Batsford, pp. 146–83.

Fawcett, R.P., 1994. 'A generationist approach to grammar reversibility in natural language processing'. In T. Strzalkowski (ed.), *Reversible Grammar in Natural Language Generation*. Dordrecht: Kluwer, pp. 65–413.

Fawcett, R.P. 1997. *Equivalence Rules in an Algorithm for Generating Five Types of Theme*. COMMUNAL Working Papers No. 8. Cardiff: Computational Linguistics Unit, Cardiff University. Available from fawcett@cardiff.ac.uk.

Fawcett, R.P. 2007. Modelling 'selection' between referents in the English nominal group: An essay in scientific inquiry in linguistics. In C.S. Butler, R. Hidalgo Downing and J. Lavid (eds) *Functional Perspectives on Grammar and Discourse: In Honour of Angela Downing*. Amsterdam: John Benjamins, pp. 165–204.

Fawcett, R.P. 2008. *Invitation to Systemic Functional Linguistics through the Cardiff Grammar: An Extension and Simplification of Halliday's Systemic Functional Grammar*. 3rd edn. London: Equinox.

Fawcett, R.P. 2010 [2000]. *A Theory of Syntax for Systemic Functional Linguistics* (Current Issues in Linguistic Theory 206). Amsterdam: John Benjamins.

Fawcett, R.P. 2011. A semantic system network for MOOD in English. Available from fawcett@cardiff.ac.uk.

Fawcett, R.P. 2013. Choice and choosing in systemic functional grammar: What is it and how is it done? In L. Fontaine, T. Bartlett and G. O'Grady (eds) *Systemic Functional Linguistics: Exploring Choice*. Cambridge: Cambridge University Press, pp. 115–34.

Fawcett, R.P. 2014a. The cultural classification of 'things': Towards a comprehensive system network for English noun senses. In M. de los Ángeles Gómez González, F. Ruiz de Mendoza Ibáñez and F. Gonzálves García (eds) *Theory and Practice in Functional-Cognitive Space (Studies in Functional and Structural Linguistics)*. Amsterdam: John Benjamins, pp. 53–84.

Fawcett, R.P. 2014b. The meanings and forms of intonation and punctuation in English: The concepts required for an explicit model. In W.L. Bowcher and B.A. Smith (eds) *Systemic Phonology: Recent Studies in English*. London, Equinox, pp. 360–437.

Fawcett, R.P. Forthcoming. *An Integrative Architecture of Language and Its Use for Systemic Functional Linguistics and Other Theories of Language*. London: Equinox.

Fawcett, R.P., G.H. Tucker and Y.Q. Lin. 1993. How a systemic functional grammar works: The role of realization in realization. In H. Horacek and M. Zock (eds) *New Concepts in Natural Language Generation*. London: Pinter, pp. 114–86.

Halliday, M.A.K. 1984 [1975]. Language as code and language as behaviour: A systemic-functional interpretation of the nature and ontogenesis of dialogue. In R. P. Fawcett, M.A.K. Halliday, S.M. Lamb and A. Makkai (eds) *The Semiotics of Culture and Language, Vol. 1: Language as Social Semiotic*. London: Pinter, pp. 3–35.

Halliday, M.A.K. 1985. *An Introduction to Functional Grammar*. London: Arnold.

Halliday, M.A.K. 1994. *An Introduction to Functional Grammar*. 2nd edn. London: Arnold.

Halliday, M.A.K., 2002 [1961]. Categories of the theory of grammar. In *Word* 17, pp. 241–92. Reprinted in M.A.K. Halliday, 2002. *Collected Works of M.A.K. Halliday*, Vol. 1: *On Grammar*. Ed. J. Webster. London: Continuum, pp. 37-94.

Halliday, M.A.K. 2003 [1993]. Systemic theory. In R.E. Asher (ed.). 1993. *Encyclopaedia of Languages and Linguistics*, Oxford: Pergamon Press, pp. 4905–8. Reprinted in M.A.K. Halliday.

2003. *Collected Works of M.A.K. Halliday, Vol. 3: On Language and Linguistics*. Ed. J. Webster. London: Continuum, pp. 433–41.

Halliday, M.A.K. 2008. Opening address: Working with meaning – Towards an appliable linguistics. In J.J. Webster (ed.) *Meaning in Context: Implementing Intelligent Applications of Language Studies*. London: Continuum, pp. 7–23.

Halliday, M.A.K., and C.M.I.M. Matthiessen. 1999. *Construing Experience through Meaning: A Language-Based Approach to Cognition*. London: Cassell Academic.

Hasan, R. 1992. Meaning in sociolinguistic theory. In K. Bolton and H. Kwok (eds) *Sociolinguistics Today: International Perspectives*. London: Routledge, pp. 80–119.

Huang, G. 2003. *Enhanced Theme In English: Its Structures and Functions*. Shangxi: Shangxi Educational Press.

Langacker, R.W. 1987a. *Foundations of Cognitive Grammar, Vol. 1: Theoretical Prerequisites*. Stanford, CA: Stanford University Press.

Langacker, R.W. 1987b. *Foundations of Cognitive Grammar, Vol. 2: Descriptive Application*. Stanford, CA: Stanford University Press.

Martin, J.R. 1992. *English Text: System and Structure*. Amsterdam: John Benjamins.

Matthiessen, C.M.I.M., and J.A. Bateman. 1991. *Text Generation and Systemic Functional Linguistics*. London: Pinter.

Neale, A. 2002a. *More delicate TRANSITIVITY: Extending the PROCESS TYPE system networks for English to include full semantic classifications*. Unpublished PhD thesis. Cardiff University. Available from amy.neale@gmail.com.

Neale, A. 2002b. *The Process Type Data Base*. Available from amy.neale@gmail.com.

O'Donoghue, T.F. 1994. Semantic interpretation in a systemic grammar. In T. Strzalkowski, (ed.), *Reversible Grammar in Natural Language Generation*. Dordrecht: Kluwer, pp. 415–447.

Tucker, G.H. 1998. *The Lexicogrammar of Adjectives: A Systemic Functional Approach to Lexis*. London: Cassell Academic.

Part II
At clause rank

Systemic functional linguistics and the clause

The experiential metafunction

Kristin Davidse

Introduction

To broach the experiential analysis of the clause in systemic functional linguistics (SFL), it is essential to start from the principled distinction between theory and description made by Halliday (1961; 1994: xxxiv). Linguistic theories specify one's fundamental assumptions about language and the nature of the linguistic sign. It is within these assumptions that the facts of a language are described – that is, its categories identified and interpreted. The *theoretical* assumptions of SFL relevant to the experiential organisation of the clause are as follows.

1   Assuming Hjelmslev's (1961 [1943]) view of the linguistic sign, a distinction is made between semantic purport, that factor of the content which is inter-translatable between languages, and *coded* meaning, which is language-specific. The lexicogrammatical structures and systems of an individual language 'form' its specific semantics, 'just as an open net casts its shadow down an undivided surface' (Hjelmslev 1961 [1943]: 57).[1] This coding relation commits analysts to the requirement that 'all the categories employed must be clearly "there" in the grammar of the language' (Halliday 1994: xix).
2   The grammar is a purely abstract code, which can be looked at only through the meaning or through the expression. In Halliday's (1985: xxxv) view, 'our understanding of the meaning system itself is very deficient; so the face of the grammar that is turned towards the semantics is hardly illuminated at all'; hence the code has to be cracked basically through the form.
3   Besides the coding (or 'realisation') relation between semantics and lexicogrammar, the second basic semiotic relation is that of instantiation (Halliday 1992). It defines structures and systems at various levels of delicacy (Halliday 1961: 267), ultimately linking the abstract language system to its concrete instantiations, or usage tokens (Halliday and Matthiessen 2004: 21).
4   Grammar and lexicon are viewed as one unified resource, with lexis as the 'most delicate grammar' (Halliday 1961: 267).

5 The whole clause, rather than the verb, determines experiential semantics (Halliday 1961, 1967a), which are conceived of as process-participant configurations (that is, interactions between, or relations involving, things) to which circumstances may be related.

6 Whilst being schematisable into general intransitive and transitive structures, experiential semantics involve distinct types of configuration in three primary domains: (a) material, (b) mental and (c) relational – that is, (a) actions and events observed 'out there' in the material world, (b) conscious mental processing experienced 'in here', in the 'egoic' field (Whorf 1956: 163*ff*) and (c) relational processes such as attribution and identification.

These theoretical assumptions have informed different *descriptions* in the SFL tradition. Even though work on other languages has also been done (as we shall see throughout this chapter), descriptions of English (still) predominate. About his work on English, Halliday (1994: xxxiv) himself wrote: 'There are many aspects of English that need to be much more fundamentally re-examined than I have managed to achieve here; one obvious example is the circumstantial elements in the clause, which I have treated in very traditional fashion.' Cautioning against dramatic paradigm shifts per se, he continued:

> Twentieth-century linguistics has produced an abundance of new theories, but it has tended to wrap old descriptions up inside them . . . The old interpretations were good, but not good enough to last for all time. . . . What are needed now are new descriptions.
> *Halliday 1994: xxxiv*

As we have moved well into the twenty-first century, this adage is still the crucial one to heed. It is therefore proper to look in the next section at Halliday's early work on the general experiential categories of English (Halliday 1967a, 1967b, 1968), which inaugurated a distinctive dialectic between theory and descriptive heuristics.

Historical perspective

Halliday's (1967a, 1967b, 1968) 'Notes on transitivity and theme' and Fillmore's (1968) 'Case for case' appeared at about the same time. Both deal with the representational semantics of the clause and, because they both defined sets of roles that have been used extensively in their respective traditions, they have sometimes been perceived as comparable proposals. In fact, they could not be more different in a number of fundamental ways.

Halliday's primary types of process-participant relations are identified in terms of (a) the specific agnation paradigms of English, and (b) the different selection restrictions obtaining on participants and on the relation between participants and process types, such as [+conscious] for the Processer of mental verbs (Halliday 1968: 193). Gleason (1966: 199) defined *agnates* as regular *structural variants* that can accommodate identical lexical elements. In analytical languages like present-day English, the different readings of 'apparently identical structures' can be shown up by their different agnation paradigms. Gleason's agnates are akin to Whorf's (1956: 89) 'reactances' – that is, the distinct alternates triggered by 'submerged meanings', which constitute the formal side of 'cryptotypical' (Whorf 1956: 105) linguistic categories (categories without systematic overt marking).

Halliday (1967a, 1967b, 1968) identified different agnation paradigms that reveal distinct process-participant relations in, at first sight, identical one- and two-participant syntagms, such as examples (1) and (2), below. He captured their distinct semantics by means of the different role configurations of (a) Actor + Goal versus (b) Initiator + Actor.

Examples (1a)–(1c) constitute the 'goal-directed' paradigm, in which all clauses express action being directed onto a Goal by an Actor (including (1b) *John threw*, which has an inherent, rather than an overt, Goal). Examples (2a)–(2c) form the 'causative' paradigm, which does not express an Actor targeting action onto a Goal, but in which 'causation' can be expressed by adding an Initiator to the (non-goal-directed) action of an Actor.

(1a) *John threw*   *the ball.*
     Actor   Goal

(1b) *John threw.*
     Actor

(1c) *The ball was thrown*   *by John.*
     Goal   Actor

(2a) *Mary jumped*   *the horse.*
     Initiator   Actor

(2b) *The horse jumped.*
     Actor

(2c) *The horse was jumped* *by Mary.*
     Actor   Initiator

Semantic features such as [+goal-directed] and [+causative] capture the different ways in which the agentive participant relates to the verb and the second participant. Halliday (1968: 198) also points out the latter's different 'inherent voice' relation to the verb: *the ball* is an undergoer only in (1a)–(1c), but *the horse* is both doer and undergoer in (2a)–(2c). Specific selection restrictions attach to this second participant in (2a)–(2c) in that it requires the features [+animate], but [–control]. The distinct agnation paradigms are related to 'verb classes [, which] represent the potentiality on the part of each verb of entering into each of the sets of relations involved' (Halliday 1967a: 52).

Halliday (1967a, 1967b, 1968) set out the following participant roles within the primary domains:

- Initiator–Actor–Goal–Range for material processes;
- Processer–Phenomenon for mental processes;
- Attribuant–Attribute, and Value–Variable/Identified–Identifier for relational processes.

In *An Introduction to Functional Grammar* (Halliday 1985), some of these roles were renamed: Processer became Senser, Attribuant became Carrier and Variable was renamed Token. Besides the primary process types, three secondary process types were introduced, each combining formal and semantic characteristics of two primary types.

- Behavioural processes such as *watch* and *listen* construe an external ('material') perspective on processes of consciousness.
- Verbal processes are in between mental and relational processes, describing the sending of symbolic representations by typically conscious sources.
- Existential processes are in between relational and material processes, construing an external perspective on the instantiation of categories.

At the most schematic level of the grammar, which transcends the domain-specific configurations, Halliday (1968) formulated the following generalisation: English clauses always have a participant that is critically involved in the process, the Affected (which became the Medium in Halliday 1985). To this nucleus, an Agent may be added, making for a fully transitive configuration, like examples (1a) and (2a), the transitivity of which can be tested by the possibility of an unmarked passive in examples (1c) and (2c) (Halliday 1994: 165). Halliday characterised this as an 'ergative' generalisation because, just as in ergative case marked languages, there is always a participant embodying the change or relation described by the verb (like the participant in the absolutive case), while the cause of this change or relation (like the participant in the ergative case) may or may not be expressed. On the other hand, the Medium-process nucleus may be extended by a Range specifying the 'extent' of the action, as in examples (3a) and (4a), yielding a configuration of low transitivity, which does not have a reflexive agnate, as shown in examples (3b) and (4b), and a marked passive only (Halliday 1967a: 58–60), as in examples (3c) and (4c).

(3a) John threw a tantrum.

(3b) ⁺John threw himself.

(3c) A tantrum was thrown by John.

(4a) The horse jumped the fence.

(4b) *The horse jumped itself.

(4c) A fence was jumped by the horse.

The configurations specific to material, mental and relational processes can, in principle, also be taken further *down* in delicacy. An example of this is Hasan's (1987: 185) fine-grained lexicogrammar of verbs of 'gain/loss of access to things', which she presents as 'an enquiry into what Whorf 1956 called "reactance"', and which takes the description up to the specific features and agnates of individual verbs. Relating Halliday's (1968, 1985) most general part of the experiential network to Hasan's (1988) part at the most delicate end, we see that we move from maximally distinct functional configurations, such as intransitive vs. transitive, to increasingly similar, *sub*types of configurations. Intransitive, transitive and ditransitive clauses differ from each other in the sense of *not* sharing whole clusters of agnates or reactances. As we move down in delicacy, for example specifying different subtypes of ditransitive structures, as in Hasan (1987), we move into (partial) subcategorisation: '[E]ach progressive step in the network specifies identity and uniqueness between classes of structures' (Hasan 1987: 187).

In its use of agnates as a descriptive heuristic, Halliday's work is compatible with other approaches using 'diathesis alternates' – that is, the different possible expressions of the participant roles of lexical verbs – to 'probe for linguistically pertinent aspects' (Levin 1993: 1) of clausal representational semantics. Matthiessen (2014: 143–4) characterises Levin's (1993) description of verb classes and alternations as:

> located somewhere mid-way between the least delicate pole of the cline, grammar, and the most delicate, lexis. . . . Looked at from the grammar end of the cline, her description can be seen as dealing with micro-grammars of transitivity with specifications of 'syntactic alternations', like the transitivity of motion or the transitivity of perception;

and looked at from the lexis end, it can be seen as identifying grammatical generalizations about verb senses that form lexical fields, like the field of motion or the field of perception.

Fillmore (1968), by contrast, proposed one set of universal, purely semantic, roles, such as Agent, Objective, Instrument and Location, defined independently from syntax and assigned on the basis of their 'objectively' perceived involvement in a state-of-affairs. Thus *poison* and *a sword* are, irrespective of their codings in examples (5a), (5b) and (6a), viewed as Instrument. DeLancey (1984) contrasted the Fillmorean analysis with an alternation-based one, arguing that construing *poison* as Agent in example (5b) represents it as capable of *in*dependent action and *direct* causation, whereas *a sword* cannot be represented as an Agent in example (6b), but only as an Instrument manipulated by an animate Agent in example (6a).

(5a)   John killed Mary with poison.

(5b)   Poison killed Mary.

(6a)   Gareth beheaded the dragon with a sword.

(6b)   *A sword beheaded the dragon.

Fillmore's semantic approach was taken much further in delicacy in his 'Frame semantics' (Fillmore 1982), which relates the meaning of verbs to all of the encyclopaedic knowledge surrounding it, specifying verbs' characteristic interactions with things necessarily or typically associated with them. Whilst different in theoretical and methodological orientation, purely semantic theories such as these can suggest possible semantic features to linguists who want to interpret the different semantic fault lines drawn in specific languages by covert categories residing in alternations – and by overt categories such as case marking and verbal morphology (see 'Experiential analyses of languages different from English').

Critical issues

The following sections will look at some issues and different positions assumed with regard to them, as well as at methodologies that can contribute to description and theory formation in the area of experiential clause grammar. Different positions will be juxtaposed, which is not to suggest that some are wholly 'right' and others 'wrong', and different methodologies will be looked at, but not with the idea that there is one that is good for all purposes; rather, what matters is to keep linguistic thought, argumentation and analytical practice alive in ongoing debates. The three main challenges incumbent on linguists working on experiential clause grammar in the systemic functional tradition are, arguably:

1   to critically compare the different positions found in various descriptions by Halliday and by other SFL linguists with optimal form-meaning correlation as a standard;
2   to increase the granularity of descriptions of experiential grammar, as has always been stressed on the theoretical level and
3   to draw up experiential analyses of languages different from English and to engage in cross-linguistic analysis, given the theoretical commitment to linguistically construed process-participant relations.

Kristin Davidse

In what follows, we will discuss these three critical issues in SFL descriptive practice, in each case linking them to areas that are in need of further development.

Alternative descriptive proposals

The argued comparison of alternative proposals is an important aspect of any theoretical approach bent on progress. A typical set of phenomena for which different analyses are available within SFL is that of locative constructions, such as examples (7a) and (8a). Halliday (1976: 160) analysed the prepositional phrases *at the bridge* in (7a) and *with stones* in (8a) as participants 'inherent' in the verb, but he did not return to this idea in later work. Later, Halliday (1994: 159) stipulated that 'systematic alternation between a prepositional phrase and a nominal group' is required to interpret an element as a participant, as is the case with Agents, which can be coded by a nominal or a *by*-phrase. This criterion does not apply systematically to locative verbs, because some such as *pelt* alternate, as in example (8b), but others such as *throw* do not, as in example (7b).

(7a) He threw stones at the bridge.

(7b) *He threw the bridge with stones.

(8a) He pelted the dog with stones.

(8b) He pelted stones at the dog.

Fawcett (1987), on the other hand, has always viewed constructions such as examples (7a) and (8a)–(8b) as three-participant constructions. Concurring with Halliday's (1976) earlier position, Fawcett (1987: 134) views them as 'inherently associated with the process expressed by the Main verb'. In further support of the three-participant analysis of locative constructions, Laffut (2006: 113) argues that:

> The key difference between participants and circumstances is that participants *participate* in the process and have a specific (basically agentive or patientive) 'voice' relation to the verb, whereas circumstances are *attendant on* the process but do not interact with it.

Locative actions such as *throwing* and *pelting* 'affect' both the Locatum being relocated and the Location to which it is relocated. The resulting contiguity relation between the Locatum and the Location is the 'telos' of the process (Laffut 2006: 117). By contrast, in a case like example (9), below, the prepositional phrase *in this tiny room* is not affected by the process of *cooking*, but adds circumstantial modifications to the process and its participants (Laffut 2006: 121).

(9) She used to cook their meals in this tiny room.

Fawcett (1987: 131) not only proposes a three-participant analysis for locative constructions like examples (7a), (8a)–(8b) and (12a), below, but also for ditransitive and complextransitive constructions, as in examples (10a) and (11a) respectively. He argues that this provides a better semantic generalisation: it reveals the systematic relation that exists between the three-participant constructions that express the *causation* of possessive (10a), intensive (11a) and locational relations (12a) and the corresponding two-participant possessive (10b), intensive (11b) and locational (12b) configurations:

[A] systemic grammar provides a natural means of bringing out the remarkable similarities in the semantic features of clauses with (a) *have* . . . and *give* [example (10)], etc. (b) *be* . . . and *make* [example (11)], etc. and (c) *be* . . . *send* [example (12)], etc.

Fawcett 1987: 131

(10a) I've given Oliver a tie.

(10b) Oliver has a tie.

(11a) Ike made Ivy the boss.

(11b) Ivy is the boss.

(12a) He put all his jewels in the wash.

(12b) All his jewels are in the wash.[2]

Questions that have puzzled linguists for decades are addressed, but not fully solved, in either approach. For instance, why do some locative verbs alternate and others not? And why can the notion of participants 'inherent' in the meaning of the verb not be related to a foolproof test such as their non-omissibility? According to Pinker (1989: 108), 'it's not what possibly or typically goes in an event that matters; it's what the verb's semantic representation is choosy about in that event that matters'. Pinker's (1989: 124–30) narrow semantic characterization of alternating locative verbs such as smear, spray and dribble is summarized by Laffut (2006: 34) as containing 'only verb meanings that . . . allow one to predict both a particular type of motion and a particular type of end state'. However, it is not fully clear how this lexical-functional approach can cope with gradience and change affecting alternations. Later in this chapter, it will be suggested that the study of agnates/alternations might be expected to make progress with the quantitative and qualitative interrogation techniques of extensive corpus data that are currently being developed.

Delicacy

One area that, in the general debate, has tended to be taken one step further down in delicacy (Halliday 1961: 267) is the different types of intransitive. Halliday (1968: 188) identified the primary contrasts in English intransitives as instantiated by examples (13) and (14), and then considered the question how the different types of process-participant relation in the examples could be captured. On the one hand, the distinction 'can be represented in terms of actor and goal, the one being an actor–action relation and the other a goal–action relation', or, alternatively, *John* in example (13a) and *Mary* in example (14a) – 'where there is no external cause' – can be viewed as 'causer/affected' and *John* in example (13b) and *the clothes* in example (14b) as 'affected' only. On the other hand, Halliday (1968: 188) ventured that '[we] may postulate some feature distinction, perhaps that of action, or "doing", as opposed to supervention, or "happening" '.

(13a) John sat down.

(13b) John fell down.

(14a) Mary washed (*sc.* 'herself').

(14b) The clothes washed.

In both functionally and formally oriented work, a subset of Halliday's 'superventive' intransitive clauses was singled out for more delicate characterisation – namely, those allowing the causative-inchoative, or 'ergative', alternation, in which the two-participant construal expresses the causation of the one-participant variant, as in example (15), below. Davidse (1999 [1991]: 108) proposed to reserve the role Medium for the core participant of lexically ergative verbs such as *broke* in example (15):

> An intransitive Actor is the sole energy source of the action, whereas the Medium is not. Even when expressed by middle clauses such as *the branch moved, the glass broke, the door opened*, [they] are felt to have a second potential energy source.

Levin and Rappaport (1994: 50) argued that the subset of intransitive verbs allowing the ergative alternation are inherently dyadic: they 'inherently imply the existence of an external cause', even when no cause is explicitly specified in the intransitive. In both approaches, the causative alternation is, as it were, 'projected behind' the syntagm in determining its meaning (van den Eynde 1995: 118). From a comparative typological point of view, Haspelmath (1993), by contrast, elucidates the meaning of the intransitive alternates as 'spontaneously occurring events' and associates the meaning 'externally caused' only with the transitive variant of morphologically alternating verbs. Indirectly, this raises the question of the cognitive status of alternation-based generalisations, which will be looked at from the point of view of sorting experiments later in this chapter.

(15a) The glass broke.

(15b) Who/what broke the glass?

Levin and Rappaport (1994) also pointed out the importance of selection restrictions. It is typical of the external cause, *who/what* in example (15b), that it can be 'natural forces or causes, as well as agents or instruments' (Levin and Rappaport 1994: 50). On the other hand, specific lexical selection restrictions have to be present for the subject + intransitive verb alternate to be available (Levin and Rappaport 1994: 46). For instance, corresponding to example (16a), we can get (16b) (Levin and Rappaport 1994: 45), but there is no intransitive counterpart of example (17a), as shown by the impossibility of (17b) (Levin and Rappaport 1994: 46).

(16a) Antonia broke the glass/the radio.

(16b) The glass/the radio broke.

(17a) He broke his promise.

(17b) *The promise broke.

Interestingly, the fact that English verbs mostly do not allow the ergative alternation in all of their sub-senses had already been recognised in the corpus-based *Collins COBUILD English Language Dictionary* (Sinclair 1987). The authors systematically identify ergative sub-senses (marked 'V-erg') on the basis of their attesting the ergative alternation and they point out specific collocational restrictions, thus distinguishing the ergative sub-senses from purely intransitive and transitive ones. For *break*, for instance, besides many transitive and some intransitive uses, four ergative sub-senses are distinguished:

(i) an object . . . splits into pieces . . . for example because you have dropped it or hit it too hard; (ii) something long and narrow . . . snaps into two pieces . . . for example because you are pulling or pushing it at one end; (iii) a tool or piece of machinery . . . is damaged and no longer works; (iv) a piece of news . . . is told to people.

Sinclair 1987: 165

In this respect, *Collins COBUILD English Language Dictionary* is a treasure house of finely observed interactions between alternations and selection restrictions at the most delicate end of the lexicogrammar, waiting for insightful generalisations across the whole lexis-grammar continuum to be formulated.

Experiential analyses of languages different from English

Most of the work in SFL has been done on English, the experiential categories of which are strongly cryptotypical. In this section, we turn to languages that mark their experiential categories mainly overtly – namely, by morphological marking on nouns and verbs. We will focus on one question: how does the issue of generalised models of participant roles present itself from the perspective of languages typologically different from English?

From an explicitly typological position, McGregor (1997: 99) converges with Halliday's position: 'Halliday . . . has proposed that both . . . the ergative . . . and the transitive . . . [systems of participant roles] are relevant to the grammars of all languages. Evidence from a number of languages supports this generalization.' The studies in *Language Typology: A Functional Perspective* (Caffarel et al. 2004) by and large concur with this with regard to French (Caffarel), German (Steiner and Teich), Japanese (Teryua), Chinese (Halliday and McDonald), Vietnamese (Duc Thai), Telugu (Prakasam) and Pitjantjatjara (Rose).

However, Martin's (1996) in-depth study of Tagalog arrived at a somewhat different position. Martin (1996: 260*ff*) argued that Tagalog's distinctive agnation patterns cannot be generalised either as having 'Medium-process' as the basic nucleus, to which an Agent may be added (that is, the ergative model) or as having 'doer-process' as the primary nucleus, to which a done-to may be added (that is, the transitive generalisation). More specifically, neither model can capture the very systematic opposition between -*mag*- and -*um*- marked processes in Tagalog, which Ramos (1974) interpreted as marking 'centrifugal' versus 'centripetal' actions – that is, actions exporting or importing done-tos, as in examples (18) and (19) below, respectively, or actions occurring outside of the agent versus internally induced actions by an agent, as in examples (20) and (21).[3]

(18)	<u>nag</u>-bili	ang	babae ng	gulay[4]
	sold	TM	woman	vegetables
	'The woman <u>sold</u> some vegetables'			

(19)	b-<u>um</u>-ili	ang	babae ng	gulay
	bought	TM	woman	vegetables
	'The woman <u>bought</u> some vegetables'			

Kristin Davidse

(20) *ang*	*pari*	*'y*	*nag-bangon*	*ng*	*bago-ng*	*bahay*[5]
TM	priest	IM	erected	new	LK	house
'The priest built a new house'						

(21) *Ako*		*'y*	*b-um-angon*
I (Topic)		IM	got up
'I got up'			

Martin (1996: 292) ventures:

> One way to generalize these . . . oppositions is to argue that action clauses in Tagalog are based on two different types of clause nucleus, where the nucleus consists of a Process and a Medium through which that process is actualized. One of these, the *-um-* type, is basically implosive (or centripetal): It involves events in which the Medium either simply acts, or acts on done-tos in such a way as to draw them into the nucleus. The other, the *mag-* type, is basically explosive (or centrifugal . . .): It involves more volatile events in which the Medium acts in a way that has repercussions for other participants.

Martin (1996: 294) concludes that 'a functional grammar whose terms are carefully motivated with as many reactances as possible does in fact lead, as Whorf initially suggested, to an interpretation of languages as individuals'.

While McGregor (1997: 99) holds that the transitive and ergative systems suffice to characterise the experiential semantics of all languages, his approach differs from Halliday's in one important respect: McGregor (1997: 114) views only the roles associated with general agentive and patientive voice relations as 'emic' distinctions – that is, as 'linguistically significant experiential signs'. The 'micro-roles' associated with distinct semantic types of situation clause are, in his view, only etic – that is, contextually defined, semantic types.[6] The emic transitive roles are Actor and Undergoer, to which McGregor (1997: 96) adds the Affected – that is, the animate participant affected in some way by the situation, for example by receiving the Undergoer. The Actor is the participant who enacts some action, event, behaviour, state or cognitive process, irrespective of whether or not it is within its control. The Undergoer suffers the action (or other type of state-of-affairs), which is not within its control. The ergative roles are the Agent, who directs action either onto another entity or onto itself, and the Medium, who materialises or actualises the state-of-affairs (McGregor 1997: 98).

Conceived of as a typological parameter, the question is to which extent the two systems apply to individual languages. At one extreme are languages in which the two systems apply throughout all clauses, which McGregor (1997: 99) argues is the case in the Australian Aboriginal language Gooniyandi. Actor, Undergoer and Affected are 'cross-referenced in the verb by a pronominal prefix or enclitic' (McGregor 1997: 97), and the ergative 'Agent is realized by an NP which may be marked by the ergative postposition *-ngga*, while the Medium is realized by an unmarked NP' (McGregor 1997: 98). Example (22) below illustrates the nominal and verbal morphology realising the two sets of roles (McGregor 1997: 97) : the Actor is cross-referenced in the verb by the nominative pronominal prefix *l-* 1sg,

88

the Undergoer is cross-referenced by the accusative prefix –ø–3sg, and the Affected is cross-referenced by the oblique enclitic –*nhi* 3sg. The ergative Agent is marked by the postposition –*ngga*.

(22)	*ngaarri*	*nganyi*	*-ngga*	*doow*	*-l+ø+a*	*-nhi*	*yoowooloo*	*-yoo*
	money	I	-ERG	get	1sgNOM+3sgACC+A	-3sgOBL	man	-DAT
	'I got money from the man.'							

McGregor (1997: 99–100) further sets out his typological generalisation of experiential clause grammar as follows:

> At the other extreme would be languages in which the two systems are completely disjoint . . . I know of no such languages. In between these two extremes are two main possibilities. First, it may be that all clauses are organized according to one system, and only some according to the other. This is probably the case in English, where the transitive system appears to apply to all situation clauses . . . , while the ergative system appears to be restricted to a proper subset. . . . Second, it may be that some clause types are organized transitively, some ergatively, and that in some the two intersect.

Current contributions and research

Within recent and current contributions to experiential grammars, a difference can be made between 'core' SFL work and more eclectic studies, which enter into dialogue with frameworks such as cognitive grammar, lexical functional grammar and construction grammar to realise the aim of 'unearthing' a language's experiential semantics from its distinct, language-specific reactances and more overt coding.

From a core SFL perspective, there has been a stream of work on English from various SFL centres such as the Sydney school (for example Halliday 1985, 1994; Hasan 1987; Halliday and Matthiessen 2004; Matthiessen 2014) and the Cardiff school (Fawcett 1987; Tucker 1996). Core SFL work on languages other than English was brought together in Caffarel and colleagues (2004). Quiroz's (2013) study of Chilean Spanish, like Martin's (1996) study of Tagalog, picks up on Pike's (1971: 76) idea that participants and circumstances can be characterised in terms of a cline from nuclear to peripheral relations in the clause as a whole. Quiroz's (2013: 199–218) description of the participants in Chilean Spanish clause grammar is based on their different agnates. The most central element, Participant 1, is that which involves person selection in the verbal group and which may or may not be overtly realised as a nominal group. It is also the most central participant interpersonally, in which the speaker vests the responsibility for the truth of the proposition (Halliday 1985: 76). Participant 2, the traditional second participant of a transitive configuration, is the element that can be cliticised by an accusative pronominal element. Modal responsibility can be shifted to it in the passive. Participant 3 is the element involved in ditransitive constructions. It is associated with dative cliticisation and cannot be assigned modal responsibility. The participant status of both Participants 2 and 3 is additionally signalled by clitic doubling – that is, realisation by both a nominal group and a clitic – and adposition with pre-positional *a*, which Quiroz (2013: 201) shows to be different from prepositional phrases realising more peripheral elements such as circumstances and attributes on the basis of their different agnation patterns.

Participants 2 and 3 are nuclear experiential elements, which in their clitic realisation are also part of the basic 'negotiator' unit of interpersonal structure. Quiroz's analysis shows how systematic configurational relations can be perceived in structure and process-participant-circumstance relations interpreted in terms of nuclearity.

More eclectic studies of sub-areas of English are Lemmens (1998), engaging in dialogue with cognitive grammar, and Laffut (2006), who incorporates insights from the lexical-functional approach (for example Pinker 1989; Levin 1993). Further eclectic work includes contrastive work such as the studies by Guerrero Medina (2002) and Lavid, Arús & Zamorano Mansilla (2010) about English and Spanish, and Nordrum's (2015) study of Swedish, Norwegian and English. The added benefits of contrastive and historical work will be discussed next. To further realise SFL's project of describing individual languages' experiential grammars, which emerged in dialogue with linguists such as Whorf, Gleason and Pike, some form of reconnection with like-minded theoreticians and analysts on the current scene is a necessity.

Main research methods

The description of the process types in Halliday (Halliday 1985, 1994; Halliday and Matthiessen 2004) has been used widely in such applications as critical discourse analysis and educational linguistics. Methods that might take this description further have received less attention. This section will consider two research methods that can contribute greatly to progress in the analysis of language-specific experiential grammars and which tie in with the strongly empirical turn that linguistics has taken in the twenty-first century. First, it is essential to team up further with the neo-Firthian strain of corpus methodology, pioneered by Sinclair in such works as *Corpus, Concordance and Collocation* (1991). In addition, essential new perspectives can come from psycholinguistic studies, in which SFL traditionally has not invested.

In the realm of corpus-based study of experiential lexicogrammar, Tucker's (1996) analysis of the pattern *not have the faintest/foggiest/etc. idea* was pioneering in many ways. Not only did it propose a way of integrating Halliday's 'lexis as most delicate grammar' and Sinclair's 'lexis-driven grammar', but it also offered an SFL treatment of an issue that has since become a pet topic in construction grammar – namely the analysis of semi-productive idioms.

Stefanowitsch and Gries's (2003) collostructional analysis is an important addition to corpus-based heuristics for the semantic description of experiential constructions. Whereas collocational measures quantify the degree to which lexical items are attracted to a lexical node, collostructional analysis measures the degree to which lexical items are attracted to, or repelled by, particular slots of a construction. Interestingly, Gries and Stefanowitsch (2004) immediately applied their method to alternations such as the ditransitive versus the to-dative variant.[7] Their findings offer support for the construction grammar position that each member of an alternation is a form-meaning pairing in its own right, not only mapping onto different information structures, but also encoding different general semantics. The ditransitive construction in example (23), most strongly attracted the verb *give,* followed by *tell, offer, cost* and *teach,* and the *to*-dative construction *send* and *play,* with *take* and *pass* as runners-up. The sets of the most strongly attracted collexemes are compatible with the semantic distinctions assigned to the two constructions (for example Pinker 1989): the ditransitive construction is said to mean 'causing to receive' and the *to*-dative construction 'causing (accompanied) motion to', typically involving physical distance between the theme and the receiver. However, Gries and Stefanowitsch (2004: 107) point out that '[t]he suggested constructional meanings do not straightforwardly account for all differences between the two constructions'. Despite being attracted to the *to*-dative construction, *sell*, *supply* and *pay* involve 'causing to receive', and *read*, *hand* and *feed* typically do not entail physical distance. This shows the need for 'a more refined analysis of the two constructions' semantics' (Gries and Stefanowitsch 2004: 107), which tallies completely with the collostructional analysis.

In its more extreme forms, construction grammar's insistence that semantic generalisations are associated with syntagmatic 'surface patterns' very much challenges the assumption that alternations are semantically revealing. For instance, Goldberg (2002: 329) holds that 'relying on explicit or implicit reference to a possible alternative paraphrase' in the analysis of argument structure patterns 'puts blinders on, and limits a theory's ability to state the full extent of the relevant generalizations'. Goldberg's position entails that there is stronger semantic similarity between syntagms whose surface form is similar, like examples (23) and (24), which are said to express 'caused motion', than between alternates such as examples (23) and (25), which instantiate the locative alternation, and examples (24) and (26), which instantiate the dative alternation. [8]

(23) *to*-locative: spray the substance to all parts of the plan

(24) *to*-dative: give the money to the poor

(25) *with*- applicative: spray all parts of the plant with the substance

(26) ditransitive: give the poor the money

An interesting reply to this is Perek's (2012) study entitled 'Alternation-based generalizations are stored in the mental grammar: Evidence from a sorting task experiment'. Perek (2012: 604) explicitly recognises (as do the SFL and lexical functional traditions) that variants of an alternation differ semantically, for example the *to*-locative 'construes the event as an action by the agent on the theme, causing it to move, whereas the *with*-variant construes it as an action affecting the location'. However, it is the stronger claim that subjects sort semantic similarity between examples on the basis of surface similarity rather than alternation that he wants to test. Perek set up a sorting experiment, in which he offered stimuli sets of ditransitives, as in example (23), *to*-locatives, as in (24), *to*-datives, as in (25), *with*-applicative and ditransitives, as in (26), to his subjects in the form of cards. He instructed his subjects to sort them into the three groupings that best reflected the semantic similarities between the sentences as a whole. Under Goldberg's construction hypothesis, the *to*-dative and *to*-locative are expected to form one group (the 'caused motion' construction), and the *with*-applicatives and ditransitives, the other two groups. Under the alternation hypothesis, either a dative sorting (*to*-dative and ditransitive) or a locative sorting (*to*-locative and *with*-applicative) are expected to come out as one group. Of the twenty-six subjects, eleven produced a locative sorting, six produced a dative sorting and none produced a caused motion sorting. Statistical processing of the results – namely, deviations scores and hierarchical clustering – further confirmed that the subjects relied more strongly on alternation-based generalisations than on surface-structure generalisations to detect semantic similarity. Perek (2012: 628) concludes that it is reasonable to assume that alternation-based generalisations are mentally stored, and that they involve '(i) a constructional meaning abstracted from the meanings of the variants of the alternation, with (ii) an underspecified form which contains only the commonalities between variants'.

In the current polemic surrounding agnation/alternation, it is apt to extend the debate to *external* non-linguistic standards. Lucy (1992) made exactly this point in his reformulation of Whorf's linguistic relativity hypothesis: to avoid the danger of circularity, one has to verify the existence of correlations between linguistic structure and non-linguistic behaviour such as sorting experiments. With its tradition of agnation-based generalisations in experiential grammar, SFL is ideally placed to set up follow-up experiments and to contribute crucially to this debate.

Finally, in eclectic SFL work on experiential clause grammar, contrastive and historical methods can be seen to cast new light on questions of long standing, as can be illustrated with some studies of spontaneous event marking. Guerrero Medina (2006) compares the semantic effects of *sich* and *se* versus the use of intransitives to express 'spontaneous events' in German and Spanish. In both languages, the middle marker deprofiles the agent and presents the subject as affected. However, in Spanish, the use of *se* (rather than the intransitive) may additionally be associated with increased punctuality, perfectivity, unintentionality and increased affectedness. In German, no such semantic and aspectual values are coded by *sich*. Adhering to the general methodology of 'seeing language(s) through multilingual corpora' (Johansson 2007), Nordrum (2015) investigates Norwegian and Swedish translations of English ergative intransitives from parallel corpora. Her aim is to gain more insight into spontaneous-event marking in the two Scandinavian languages, which subsumes reflexive marking, *seg* (N) / *sig* (S), morphological –s marking, diachronically related to the reflexive, but synchronically homonymous with the morphological passive and (less commonly) the ergative intransitive. She finds that whereas, in Norwegian, the reflexive is the main marker of spontaneous events, in Swedish there is a division of labour between the –s marker and the reflexive: the former, with its natural kinship to the passive, is the prototypical marker of spontaneous events, whereas the latter requires 'potent' subjects, such as entities endowed with biological life, or organisations, which can be interpreted as capable of self-instigation. One explanatory factor why the Norwegian –s marker largely disappeared may be that its close neighbour, the s– passive, fossilised into a generic passive. By contrast, the s-passive and the –s spontaneous event marker retained a wider distribution in Swedish.

Lemmens (1998) reconstructs some historical changes in the verb-specific application of the ergative alternation in English. The directionality of change is assumed to be generally towards ergativisation (Halliday 1985: 146), but Lemmens (1998: 191–219) also documents cases of de-ergativisation, such as the verb *abort*. It came into English from Latin in the sixteenth century, depicting spontaneous miscarriage. In metaphorical uses of this meaning, it is clearly ergative, as shown by examples (27) and (28), which add a cause to the event of 'aborting' (Lemmens 1998: 202).

(27)   When peace came so near to the birth, how it abortived . . . (OED, 1692)

(28)   This is that which abortives the Perfection of the most glorious and useful Undertakings (OED, 1699)

In modern English, *abort* came to be construed as a transitive verb to express the meaning of 'deliberately terminating a pregnancy', as in *to abort a child* in example (29) below (Lemmens 1998: 210). Its one-participant alternate, the first clause of (29), is an 'absolute' transitive, whose overt participant, *pregnant teen-agers*, is construed as intentionally targeting the action of termination onto the implied 'their child'.

(29) Too many pregnant teen-agers are urged to take the 'easy way' and abort, convinced by twisted logic that it is kinder to abort than to bear a child and place it
for adoption. (WSJ)

Contrastive and historical studies reveal language-specific and diachronic differences in the
selection restrictions on participants, and differences in voice and nuclearity in the construal
of process-participant-relations. In this way, they alert us to the Hjelmslevian tenet that each
language's content-form constructs a different content-substance (as we saw at the start of
this chapter).

Recommendations for practice

The challenge for SFL is to integrate empirical methods such as those discussed in the last
section into its own 'grammatics' – that is, its theory of description for experiential clause
grammar. Some elements of its long tradition in this area dovetail with current trends, such
as the notion that the lexicogrammar in its representational function is a unified resource
and the emphasis on the meaning of the whole construction. Others are currently controversial, such as the status of agnation-based semantic generalisations. This suggests the need
for more *meta-descriptive* reflection on all of the formal 'reactances' to experiential clause
meaning, their relation to overt coding and the nature of the semantic distinctions that we
can draw from them. To promote innovative work on experiential clause grammar, it will be
essential to develop and teach analytical methods, and descriptive heuristics, from a specifically systemic functional perspective.

Future directions

From its specific theoretical perspective, SFL is very well placed to contribute to many current
trends in the description of the representational semantics of clauses: fine-grained language-
specific descriptions, comparative and diachronic studies, and typological work. From its broad
neo-Firthian perspective, SFL can develop distinctive positions on topical issues such as:

- how observations about lexical – that is, collocational – *syntagmatic* structure might be
  integrated with the description of grammatical structure (cf. Tucker 1996); and
- how study of the lexical *classes* that are defined by attraction to elements of structure,
  both the verbal element and its participants, might contribute to insight into the semantics of a construction (cf. Stefanowitsch and Gries 2003).

All of these areas constitute important challenges that might allow SFL to contribute crucially to a more precise understanding of the lexicogrammar in its representational function.

Notes

1 In the SFL tradition, the coded meaning and its lexicogrammar are equated with Hjelmslev's content-
substance and content-form, respectively. In parallel fashion, phonetic substance and phonological
structures and systems are equated with Hjelmslev's expression-substance and expression-form
(Taverniers 2008).
2 Example (10) is taken from Fawcett (1987: 146); example (11) appears in Fawcett (1987: 151);
example (12) is found at Fawcett (1987: 157).

3 TM = topic marker (Martin 1996: 230); IM = inner motion; LK = linker (Martin 1996: 259).
4 Martin (1996: 258).
5 Martin (1996: 259).
6 The distinction *emic – etic* was coined by Kenneth Pike (1971). *Emic*, as in 'phonemic', refers to fundamental, systemic distinctions, whereas *etic*, as in 'phonetic', refers to phenomena that depend on context.
7 The collostructional analyses reported on in Gries and Stefanowitsch (2004) are based on the British component of the *International Corpus of English*.
8 Examples (23)–(26) were extracted from *Wordbanks*Online (http://wordbanks.harpercollins.co.uk).

References

Caffarel, A., J. Martin and C.M.I.M Matthiessen. 2004. *Language Typology: A Functional Perspective*. Amsterdam: John Benjamins.

Davidse, K. 1999 [1991]. *Categories of Experiential Grammar* (Monographs in Systemic Linguistics 7). Nottingham: University of Nottingham.

DeLancey, S. 1984. Notes on agentivity and causation. *Studies in Language* 8(2): 181–213.

Fawcett, R. 1987. The semantics of clause and verb for relational processes in English. In M.A.K. Halliday and R. Fawcett (eds) *New Developments in Systemic Linguistics, Vol. 1: Theory and Description*. London: Pinter, pp. 130–83.

Fillmore, C. 1968. The case for case. In E. Bach and R.T. Harms (eds) *Universals in Linguistic Theory*. London: Holt, Rinehart & Winston, pp. 1–88.

Fillmore, C. 1982. Frame semantics. In Linguistic Society of Korea (ed.) *Linguistics in the Morning Calm: Selected Papers from SICOL-1981*. Seoul: Hanshin, pp. 111–37.

Gleason, H.A. 1966. *Linguistics and English Grammar*. New York: Holt, Reinhart & Winston.

Goldberg, A. 2002. Surface generalizations: An alternative to alternations. *Cognitive Linguistics* 13(4): 327–56.

Gries, S., and A. Stefanowitsch. 2004. Extending collostructional analysis: A corpus-based perspective on 'alternations'. *International Journal of Corpus Linguistics* 9(1): 97–129.

Guerrero Medina, P. 2006. The grammatical expression of the spontaneous middle type in German and Spanish. In C. Mourón Figueroa and T. Moralejo Gárate (eds) *Studies in Contrastive Linguistics: Proceedings of the 4th International Contrastive Linguistics Conference*. Santiago de Compostela: University of Santiago de Compostela, pp. 343–53.

Halliday, M.A.K. 1961. Categories of the theory of grammar. *WORD* 17(3): 241–92.

Halliday, M.A.K. 1967a. Notes on transitivity and theme in English 1. *Journal of Linguistics* 3(1): 37–81.

Halliday, M.A.K. 1967b. Notes on transitivity and theme in English 2. *Journal of Linguistics* 3(2): 199–244.

Halliday, M.A.K. 1968. Notes on transitivity and theme in English 3. *Journal of Linguistics* 4(2): 179–215.

Halliday, M.A.K. 1976. Types of process. In G. Kress (ed.) Halliday: *System and Function in Language*. London: Oxford University Press, pp. 159-173.

Halliday, M.A.K. 1985. *An Introduction to Functional Grammar*. London: Arnold.

Halliday, M.A.K. 1992. How do you mean? In M. Davies and L. Ravelli (eds) *Advances in Systemic Linguistics*. London: Pinter, pp. 20–35.

Halliday, M.A.K. 1994. *An Introduction to Functional Grammar*. 2nd edn. London: Arnold.

Halliday, M.A.K., and C.M.I.M. Matthiessen. 2004. *An Introduction to Functional Grammar*. 3rd edn. London: Arnold.

Hasan, R. 1988. The grammarian's dream: Lexis as delicate grammar. In M.A.K. Halliday and R. Fawcett (eds) *New Developments in Systemic Linguistics, Vol. 1: Theory and Description*. London: Frances Pinter, pp. 184–212.

Haspelmath, M. 1993. More on the typology of inchoative/causative verb alternations. In B. Comrie (ed.) *Causatives and Transitivity*. Amsterdam: John Benjamins, pp. 87–111.

Hjelmslev, L. 1961 [1943]. *Prolegomena to a Theory of Language*. Revised English edn. Madison, WI: University of Wisconsin Press.

Johansson, S. 2007. *Seeing through Multilingual Corpora: On the Use of Corpora in Contrastive Studies*. Amsterdam: John Benjamins.

Laffut, A. 2006. *Three-Participant Constructions in English: A Functional-Cognitive Approach to Caused Relations*. Amsterdam: John Benjamins.

Lemmens, M. 1998. *Lexical Perspectives on Transivity and Ergativity: Causative Constructions in English*. Amsterdam: John Benjamins.

Lavid, J., J. Arús & J.R. Zamorano Mansilla. 2010. Systemic Functional Grammar of Spanish. A Contrastive Study with English. London: Continuum.

Levin, B. 1993. *English Verb Classes and Alternations*. Chicago, IL: Chicago University Press.

Levin, B., and M. Rappaport. 1994. A preliminary analysis of causative verbs in English. *Lingua* 92: 35–77.

Lucy, J. 1992. *Language Diversity and Thought: A Reformulation of the Linguistic Relativity Hypothesis*. Cambridge: Cambridge University Press.

Martin, J. 1996. Transitivity in Tagalog: A functional interpretation of case. In M. Berry, C. Butler, R. Fawcett and G. Huang (eds) *Meaning and Form: Systemic Functional Interpretations – Meaning and Choice in Language: Studies for Michael Halliday*. Norwood, NJ: Ablex, pp. 229–96.

Matthiessen, C.M.I.M. 2014. Extending the description of process type within the system of transitivity based on Levinian verb classes. *Functions of Language* 21(2): 139–75.

McGregor, W. 1997. *Semiotic Grammar*. Oxford: Clarendon.

Nordrum, L. 2015. Exploring spontaneous-event marking though parallel corpora: Translating English ergative intransitive constructions into Norwegian and Swedish. *Languages in Contrast* 15(2): 230–50.

Perek, F. 2012. Alternation-based generalizations are stored in mental grammar: Evidence from a sorting task experiment. *Cognitive Linguistics* 23(3): 601–35.

Pike, K. 1971. *Linguistic Concepts: An Introduction to Tagmemics*. Lincoln, NE, and London: University of Nebraska Press.

Pinker, S. 1989. *Learnability and Cognition: The Acquisition of Argument Structure*. Cambridge, MA: MIT Press.

Quiroz, B. 2013. The interpersonal and experiential grammar of Chilean Spanish. Towards a principled systemic-functional description based on axial argumentation. Unpublished PhD thesis. University of Sydney.

Ramos, T. 1974. *The Case System of Tagalog Verbs* (Pacific Linguistics Series B 27). Canberra: The Linguistic Circle of Canberra.

Sinclair, J. 1987. *Collins COBUILD English Language Dictionary*. London: Harpercollins.

Sinclair, J. 1991. *Corpus, Concordance and Collocation*. Oxford: Oxford University Press.

Stefanowitsch, A., and S. Gries. 2003. Collostructions: Investigating the interaction of words and constructions. *International Journal of Corpus Linguistics* 8(2): 209–43.

Taverniers, M. 2008. Hjelmslev's semiotic model of language: An exegesis. *Semiotica* 171(1–2): 367–94.

Tucker, G. 1996. So grammarians haven't the faintest idea: Reconciling lexis-oriented and grammar-oriented approaches to language. In R. Hasan, C. Cloran and D. Butt (eds) *Functional Descriptions: Theory in Practice*. Amsterdam: John Benjamins, pp. 145–78.

van den Eynde, K. 1995. Methodological reflections on descriptive linguistics: Knud Togeby's principles and the pronominal approach. In L. Schøsler and M. Talbot (eds) *Studies in Valency*. Odense: Odense University Press, pp. 111–31.

Whorf, B.L. 1956. *Language, Thought and Reality: Selected Writings of Benjamin Lee Whorf*. Ed. J. Carroll. Cambridge, MA: MIT Press.

The logical metafunction in systemic functional linguistics

David G. Butt and Jonathan J. Webster

The logical metafunction: In brief

Each step in a message must proceed by one of three principles of extension: (a) the simple adding of a structural element (*parataxis*, a linking between 'equals'); (b) a link of dependency (*hypotaxis*, a subordination) between what emerges and what has gone before, or what may be coming next and (c) a sequence that is built by *reiteration* of the last structural selection (*iteration*, or recursion). The resources by which these three options are enacted throughout the structures of language, along with their systems of typical semantic motivation, can be thought of as the *logical metafunction*.

When we speak or write, we are fashioning our meanings through linguistic options, whether unconsciously or consciously. We rarely attend to the dance-like 'choreography' of our clause-to-clause structures; they appear to be the most unconscious, 'backgrounded' of our combinatorial systems. This unconsciousness of patterning is the case despite the remarkable complexity and rate of utterance of which humans are capable. Consider children haggling over the rules of a game or anyone in a flight of passion, or observe (when the opportunity arises) the impassioned speech of someone expressing the profound moral earnestness of his or her state of mind. Shakespeare is renowned for producing such states in his debates and soliloquys. Here is Macbeth, weighing up in his own mind how to proceed in the regicide he is about to commit:[1]

> If it were done,|| when 'tis done || then 'twere well
> [[It were done quickly.]]||| If th'assassination
> Could trammel up the consequence || and catch
> With his surcease, success;|| that but this blow
> Might be the be-all and the end-all – here,
> But here, upon this bank and shoal of time,||
> We'ld jump the life [[to come]]|||.

Macbeth 1. vii. 1–7

Such combinations of messages have both *structure* and *function*. These are ways of seeing the same evolved phenomenon from two different perspectives: all natural structures (including languages) have structures that incorporate action and the history of the conditions under which the action has had to be performed.

Function and structure are reciprocally dependent dimensions of any living form. And the combinatorial virtuosity in textual expansion and composition needs accurate depiction in any theory of human language. Theories of language with very different motivations – such as those of Halliday and of Chomsky – do allocate careful consideration to a 'logical' dimension, albeit with very different roles in each theory. Yet while we shall seek to explain what modern linguistics has to reveal about this domain of linguistic creativity, it is useful to set out from the traditional view of the phenomenon from Western grammars and rhetorical theory.

Those of us with a European-styled primary education will recall being trained in distinctions between clause and sentence, and between *compound sentences* and *complex sentences*. Clauses could be characterised as either *independent* (*main* or *principal*) or *dependent*. Among the dependent clauses, we could identify *adjectival* and a challenging spectrum of *adverbial* clauses. Furthermore, there were the clauses that themselves could hold a single-case role (usually objective/accusative case) within an overarching clause: these were the *noun* clauses of Latin, in which a clause was embedded inside a matrix clause. The combination of independent, main clauses produced a *compound sentence* (the use of 'sentence' here indicating that we were working on written clauses marked off by punctuation). Any combination of independent and dependent clauses produced a *complex sentence*.[2]

The insights of the rhetorical tradition in the West have been overlooked in many educational texts and contexts, although they are still somewhat in evidence in accounts of romance languages. What was important for oratory and meaning was how an argument or *trope* (a swerve or tendency in the meaning; a figure of speech) was mapped onto, or realised in, *schemes* (the grammar and words). It was the dynamic of this cross-stratal mapping (for us, how semantics is realised in the lexicogrammar) that produced the actual meaning. Meaning was, as for the Roman orator Cicero (107–44 BCE), a vigorous performance of action, not some ideal mental form awaiting an expression. Let us put this view of mapping to work.

The following conversation between an adult and a child aged 3 years and 9 months took place very early on a Sunday morning. The parent had already been out and had arrived home to find – very unusually for that time of the morning – that the child was dressed and ready to go out.

    Child: I am dressed already.
    Adult: [nods]
    Child: I was thinking . . . in my room,
              if I put my shoes on,
              we might go round to Auntie Jennie's.

If we look at the logical relations (the logical *order*), we have a simple structure with two depths below the main clause and something of a marked *sequence* (×ββ before 'βα) (see Figure 7.1):

    α   I was thinking . . . in my room
    ×ββ   if I put my shoes on
    'βα   we might go round to Auntie Jennie's

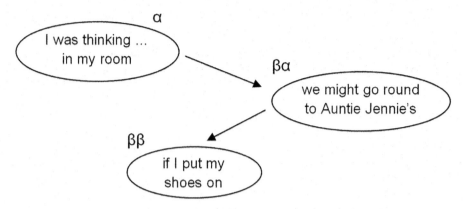

Figure 7.1 Logical relations

Grammatically, the projecting first clause (α) is the dominant. We know, however, that the issue between the parent and the 3-year-old is 'we might go round to Auntie Jennie's' ($\beta\alpha$), which is said *last* in the *sequence* of thematic organisation of the clause complex. The 'if I put my shoes on' ($\beta\beta$, or two depths of subordination) is a concession thrown in ahead of the main business, to enhance negotiations in the face of previous quarrels. The semantic picture, by comparison with the grammatical one, brings out a **non**-1:1 mapping between the level of semantics (with the semiotic weight being on the indirect petition). On the other hand, the lexicogrammar, in which an ambivalent projection (note the durative, present-in-present verbal group, 'was thinking'), together with the late addition of a circumstance ('in my room'), suggest that the child is trying to pass off the petition more as a reflective 'statement' than as a demand for 'goods and services'. The test for this is simply to imagine the parent replying to the reflection with 'That's nice', rather than to the petition with 'Perhaps we could'.

In fact, we can extract three levels of significance from this exchange. There is a situational or contextual level at which we need to narrow down the parameters of context: the social roles, with their assumptions about authority; the field of relatives, and their social

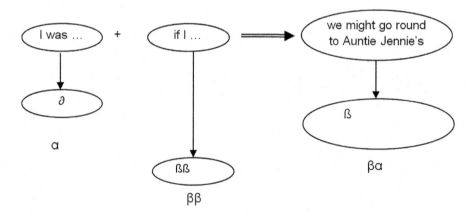

Figure 7.2 Logical relations: projection

and physical proximities; and the typical uses of spoken styles in phonic channel between parents and children (for instance the indirect strategy here is not every child's semantic style). The contextual configuration for the situation might include the syntagmatic moves.[3]

The semantic stratum (that is, level) might be characterised as a sequence, with the interactive 'nub' coming in late news, not thematically up front:

Prefacing (device) → Concession (condition) → Petition (modalised)

This brings out the way in which a speaker can use both alignment and counterpoint between context, semantics and lexicogrammar. We can also see from this why Halliday's supervisor, J.R. Firth, distinguished carefully between *semantics* as a level and *meaning*, the latter being the ensemble effect of choice across all levels. Hence we can follow how Halliday has improved upon the traditional terminology, how he offers a consistent coding system and how we need to keep in mind that the combinatorial principles that we are discussing are in evidence at other ranks of the lexicogrammar and at other strata (namely, across semantic and phonological units).

For clause complexes in English, Halliday and Matthiessen (2014) represent the simultaneous choices with the network in Figure 7.3.[4] Such resources are 'logical' because they imply a principle by means of which the world represented in the language 'hangs together'. They are elements of a metafunction because the principle behind this linguistic architecture is relatively abstract. (The Greek word *meta* suggests *beyond* something and, in this case, it is *beyond* the general level of abstraction in a principle; hence *meta*function suggests something that is over and above the more concrete instances of function.)

With the name 'metafunction', the *logical* becomes a fourth generalised principle in the meaning potential that languages typically offer – that is, alongside the *interpersonal*, *experiential* and *textual* metafunctions (all set out in detail elsewhere in this volume[5]). But where do we place the resources that we are seeking to display in the linguistics? In other words, are there meaning options tightly tied in with the logical arrangements? The two competing relationships appear to be to the world-building properties of language – that is, how we

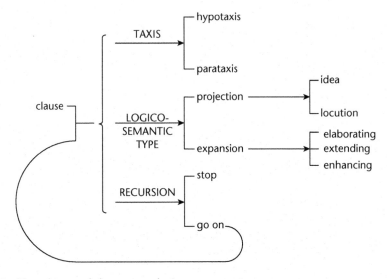

Figure 7.3 The systems of clause complexing

regard experience – or to the texture-weaving resources of the textual metafunction. Both are relevant. But it is the combination of experiential and logical resources that gives us a bloc of resources for modelling a world, whether natural or virtual. Halliday has seen the interrelationship of these two functions as an ideational bank of choices; hence we have in his work the three metafunctions – interpersonal, ideational and textual – as well as the four divisions – *interpersonal, experiential, logical* and *textual*, which last ties them all together and to the immediate context.

The significance for different languages and in different theories

Different tendencies towards paratactic, hypotactic and iterative structures are in evidence across different languages, and even across the different strata and ranks of a single language. This variation of tendency regarding how structure will be built may be also in evidence across the historical stages of what is putatively one language. The 'function' in meta*function* also reminds us that we are dealing with semantic choices: the architecture is a structure of meaning, not merely a 'structure' with no consequences for the purposes of communication. This becomes an important point to note, since, as we will later review, the linguistics of Chomsky, by contrast to systemic functional linguistics (SFL), has consistently held that the central and crucially human properties of the linguistic system 'cannot be' for communication and 'cannot be' due to pressures of functionality and semantic adaptation.[6]

The consideration of the theoretical term 'logical metafunction' is, then, a means of bringing to light the principles in a given language by which speakers build up:

1   complexity within a linguistic unit;
2   complexity between units of the same scale; and
3   complexity between units that vary in structure, but which may be contributing at the same semantic weight or value in a specific context.

So too there is the corollary of 3: the situation of *rank shift* – whereby, say, a clause may do service within the elements of a group and the group is but one element in the configuration of elements of a clause. This 'down-ranking' is also referred to as 'embedding' or, in previous decades of linguistics, as 'nesting'.

In this chapter, we wish to emphasise the semantic consequences of *taxis* in the formation of grammatical combinations, and in the relation between such combinations and semantic and rhetorical structure. While the rhetorical traditions of Europe maintained the resources of *taxis* as one of the routine topics of scholarly training, the continuing areas of discussion in text studies today include the relation with reported speech (hence between clauses), with tense (verbal group combinations in serial tense systems) and, in language typology, with serial choices in clause combinations representing events and causation. This last case of serial choice refers to the cross-linguistic differences between a greater experiential load on relations between groups in a single clause (a configurational realisation) or on the cumulative effect of a sequence of clauses that may seem, from the perspective of a different language, to 'break up' the experience into partial 'event-ings'. The most cited instance in the literature may be of a case in which the English clause could be glossed, such as *A man threw a stick over the fence into the garden*. According to research conducted by Pawley (1987: 353*ff*), the meaning in Kalam (a language of Papua New Guinea) would need to be handled by Kalam's small set of generalised verb choices, set out in a serial order:

Cl 1 *man stick hold* Cl 2 *he displaced-different* Cl 3 *fence above it-went* Cl 4 *garden-inside it-fell*.

As Pawley (1987: 136–7) emphasised and Matthiessen (2004: 575–8) elaborated, this difference is a contrastive allocation of distinctions across linguistic systems. As Matthiessen (2004) formulates the issue, there is a difference between allocating the descriptive task to a configuration within a clause and the potential for serial array to render process or 'quanta of change' (Halliday and Matthiessen 1999). Readers may have other cases to evaluate: Sapir (1884–1939) wrote of a specific verb for a group crossing a river from a westerly direction (and English has, at the same pole, an archaic form, 'westering', v: intrans./ adj., but usually applied specifically to the sun or other archetypal journeying). As an example of the opposite extreme for synthetic referential word building, Sapir also offered:

wiitokuchumpunkurüganiyugwivantümü,
meaning
'they-who-are-going-to-sit-and-cut-up-with-a-knife-a-black-female-or-male-buffalo'.

In SFL, in light of Halliday's practical and theoretical attention to discriminating between metafunctional organisation, stratification, rank scale and grammatical 'depth' across a language, there has been a considerable effort to describe how the choices of the logical metafunction 'play out' across texts and across languages. These have tended to be elaborations of the schema offered by Halliday, which will guide what follows. We would emphasise at this point that it is now difficult to summarise or extend the elaborate chapters that set out the logical metafunction in the different editions of *An Introduction to Functional Grammar* – that is, those of Halliday (1985, 1994) and Halliday and Matthiessen (2004, 2014). It broadens our view if we remind ourselves of the work on another rank and with a different orientation to meaning – namely, Poynton's (1984) work on the interpersonal semantics of vocatives – essentially the way in which the logical resources at the ranks of word display the combinatorial creativity of language from 'below'. By examining the patterns and constraints on name-building in English, Poynton shows how the motivation of the forms is interpersonal contact:

James → Jim → Jimbo → Jimmikins

The network representations of Poynton's version of these patterns of meaning making are complex, but clearly systemic.

Our aim here will have to be modest – namely, to demonstrate the significance and practicality of analysis of the logical patterns of text. In particular, we wish to show how the metafunctional 'division of labour' in SFL and the coding of logical choices as patterns help us to see consequences for meaning. We will illustrate logical relations mainly from the complexing between clauses, since these choices of grammatical construction are somewhat like the 'molecular' level in physics: it is at this level that we are dealing with the actual elements of the world, the way in which wording has been fashioned to enter human exchanges as texts.

Halliday's coding of clause combinations and their semantic consequences

Given the intricacy of the webs we can weave with clauses – balancing them one against another to grade the content and force of our communicative exchanges – the process of analysis demands a notation system that (a) serves to represent the complexity without 'running out' of notational potential and (b) maintains consistency without ambiguous coding. It helps with notation, in some cases at least, if the representation can be iconic. We mean by this that the shape and terms of analysis might be most effective if a quick survey can impart the overall character of the structure being represented.

In what follows, we offer a version of analysis that is guided by Halliday's system of coding, as well as by the distinctions that he and Matthiessen (and others) have utilised.[7]

Preceding the application of the notation, one needs to establish clause boundaries and the status of each clause: does it involve rank shift or embedding – namely, the service whereby the clause contributes a role *within* another clause, as a head in a nominal group or as a qualifier in a nominal group, or as an adverbial of comparison (for example *so fast* [[*that he fell over his own feet*]])? A suggestion that we add is that the clauses be rendered in iconic form using screen or page to represent the *order* (that is, depths down the page) and *sequence* (passage from left to right). So, if Caesar ever did utter that famous sequence (which we will take the licence to extend), then we could quite easily describe the logical relations as follows.

I came;   I saw;   I conquered,

                                 when it suited me

                                                to fight the barbarians.

1   +2   +3α

                                ×3$\beta\alpha$

                                          ×3$\beta\beta$

The explication of this coding and setting out is relatively straightforward: the three paratactic structures are simply numbered in the sequence of their appearance – 1+2+3. The semantic character of the parataxis can be appositional (marked by a diacritic =), or simply additive (+), or circumstantial relation (×). But the third clause has two dependent clauses for which it is the main clause. We have the address of the third clause (the '3'), but we must attach a signal to '3' to indicate that it is working as the origin for at least one dependent clause (here, two). So the α needs to be attached because it dominates over other structures. These structures need their code at their lower *depth* (*not* 'rank' or 'level', which have specific meanings in terms of constituency and stratal differences, respectively). The hypotactic clauses need their signature origin (the '3'), and then a β, to show the subordination or dependency. As we go another depth down, we retain the signature of the origin in the upper depth – now 3β – and add the parent label α, giving this depth as 3$\beta\alpha$. The second dependency also needs to be marked for its dependency: hence 3$\beta\beta$. Embedded clauses are indicated as [[. . .]]. Embedded groups, if to be indicated because of their relevance to the research question(s), are simply [. . .]. Embedded clause complexes are consistently marked by the same system within the embedding brackets, for example:

When it suited me || to fight those barbarians
[[who were brazen || and remained || to oppose us]] → [[1 + 2α × 2β]].

Example 7.1 illustrates the full complexity and the notation inherent in mapping out the logical relations between clauses.

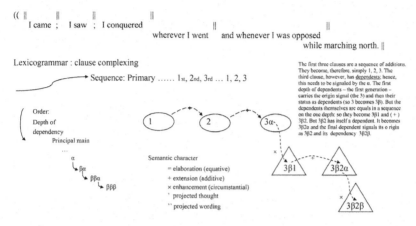

```
(( ||          ||          ||              ||
  I came  ;   I saw   ;   I conquered
                                      wherever I went     and whenever I was opposed
                                                                       while marching north. ||
```

Lexicogrammar : clause complexing

→ Sequence: Primary ...... 1st, 2nd, 3rd ... 1, 2, 3

Order:
Depth of
dependency
Principal main

α
βα
ββα
βββ

Semantic character

= elaboration (equative)
+ extension (additive)
× enhancement (circumstantial)
' projected thought
'' projected wording

The first three clauses are a sequence of additions. They become, therefore, simply 1, 2, 3. The third clause, however, has dependents; hence, this needs to be signalled by the α. The first depth of dependents – the first generation – carries the origin signal (the 3) and then their status as dependents (so 3 becomes 3β). But the dependents themselves are equals in a sequence on the one depth: so they become 3β1 and (+) 3β2. But 3β2 has itself a dependent. It becomes 3β2α and the final dependent signals its o rigin as 3β2 and its dependency 3β2β.

Example 7.1   The notation of logical relations

Introductory passage: David Malouf, *Fly Away Peter* (1982)

What follows is the first of a number of increasingly involved clause complexes from a novel, *Fly Away Peter*, by David Malouf (1982: ch.4), an award-winning author who maintains what the Romans would have appreciated as 'the plain style'. The purpose of these selections, and of this chapter, is to invite some of those who may not have used Halliday's scheme to engage with the rewarding accounts of Chapter 7 of his *Introduction to Functional Grammar*, across its four editions. The principles are straightforward. The evidence achieved by the analysis is relevant to linguistic issues from register analysis and stylistics to the biological debates.[8] By using Malouf's text, we can see how 'variations on the theme' of complexing provide deep, semantic effects and constructive opportunities in text.

The novel is set just before and during the First World War, initially on the coast in southeast Queensland. Ashley Crowther, who has returned from Cambridge to attend to his family property, plans to preserve the remarkable birds and natural lagoons of the region. He has hired Jim, a quiet bird enthusiast, to be the keeper of this natural sanctuary. The situation begins thus:

||Sometimes, << when Ashley Crowther
had a party of friends
down for the weekend,
or for the Beaudesert races >> Jim
would take them out
in a flat-bottomed boat,|| 1α << ×1β >>

|| and for an hour or two they would drift
between dead white trees and brackish water,
its depths the colour of brewed tea,
its surface a layer of drowned pollen
inches thick in places, a burnished gold.|| 2

|| Parting the scum, || $\times\beta$

they would break in among clouds.|| α

The clausal architecture is quite resolvable in relation to the combinatorial principle of dominance or dependency: Jim would do something – 1α main issue – but this would have a circumstantial issue appended to it – ×β (*when Ashley* . . .). Furthermore, another dominant action – 2 (*they would* . . .) – is simply added. It is an issue with no appended qualification in the architecture of the second sentence.[9] Hence:

Clause Complex 1: **1**α << ×**1**β >> **2** Clause Complex 2: ×β α

Logical metafunction: a multidisciplinary perspective

The *logical metafunction* is, then, a theoretical term representing the ensemble of resources by which we make sense through *order*, combination and the forms of complex *sequence* in our syntagmatic expectations. As these resources are dispersed systemically – that is, as they cross the strata and the rank scales of the architecture of a natural language – they need to be regarded from a number of perspectives. The multiple perspectives are required to capture the broad range of linguistic motivations that might be expressed by sequence.

Certainly, one might respond at this point by saying that all aspects of language are employing *order* – namely, that sequence, combination and *taxis* (the term from classical grammars) are ubiquitous. This degree of order and interconnectedness is what J.R. Firth, Halliday's teacher, emphasised by invoking the term 'prehension'. This word (originally used by A.N. Whitehead in 'process philosophy') referred to the expectancies between systems: how one choice *prehends* others. We could simply say that the choice of *x* will raise the probability of *y* and *z*. But much linguistic *prehension* remains latent, with the job of linguists being to bring the connectedness to light. Still, as Saussure (1959) emphasised, linearity is the second fundamental resource of language as a semiotic system. We can therefore reasonably ask: why do we need to discriminate a *logical* order or sequencing from the ubiquity of *order*?

One answer appears to be that the 'choose over' sequencing of the logical combinations is just one of the simultaneous patterns by which consistencies of meaning can be folded into the multifoliate potential of a clause complex, and of a clause, and of a group, and even of words (after Poynton 1984, 'little poopsy, woopsy').

A second reason, often underestimated in accounts of discourse, is that such principles carry with them significant semantic consequences, for example in the way that a complex of clauses gives us a strong sense of an experiential model of the world that is accumulating in a text. Previously, Butt (1988a/b) has referred to this as the 'existential fabric' of a text. Because of the generality of combinatorial principles in a language, much of the semantic pressure from the logical function is experienced as a tide of meaning that seems unmarked and unremarkable. The wide-scale combinatorial engineering between clauses may be among the deepest and consequently least conscious of our linguistic resources. For this reason, we refer to the *latent* character of options that many people regard as random (Butt 1988a/b). It is as if clause complexing, for example, provides only a proscenium or stage for the more overt 'actors' of intra-clausal and lexical choices – systems that declare their presence at centre stage. We propose that the logical patterns of our language take on a peculiar cultural force in a metaphysics of the world of our primary socialisation. They are the deepest form of how things are in our world. They become the loose architecture for our adult reasoning and thence the subtle rhetorical face of our linguistic persona.

As a third reason for focusing on the logical function, we would emphasise that, in a lexicogrammar for instance, clause complexing becomes the dramatic interface between the grammar as meaning and information units (tone groups) as sound. The tone groups realise certain grammatical choices *and* enjoin the affective grounding of meanings in bodily sound – that is, the rhythms and musicalities of communication (Malloch and Trevarthen 2009). Such alignments between the shaping of wording and the shaping of tones provide the speaker with systems of possible variations between the unmarked parallelisms – between clause and information unit – and forms of concord or counterpoint. Through this potential for concord and contrast between grammar and our speech melodies, the structures of combination in the logical metafunction bring us back to confront the deeply embodied character of human language. According to neurobiologists Panksepp and Trevarthen (2009), it is in the subcortical areas of the brain (those that we share with many members of the animal kingdom in their systems of emotional expression) that a communicative musicality supplies the interpersonal foundation to language and human intersubjectivity. Cortical-based learning came later in evolution and comes later in our lives (Porges 2011). It is through this layering of language structures that we can conceive of the architecture of language having a direct bearing on the 'surds' of emotion that were part of the traditional and classical views of musical modes, and which seem most insistent in the powers of poetry and all verbal arts.[10] It is a form of tonal accumulation, tension and release that we can feel in the drama of feeling throughout Shakespeare's sonnets, as in the opening eight lines of Sonnet 65:

(1)   Since brass, nor stone, nor earth, nor boundless sea,
        But sad mortality o'er-sways their power, ||

(2)   How with this rage shall beauty hold a plea, ||

(3)   Whose action is no stronger than a flower?||

(4)   O, how shall summer's honey breath hold out
        Against the wreckful siege of battering days,||

(5)   When rocks impregnable are not so stout,||

(6)(7) Nor gates of steel [E] so strong,|| but Time decays?||

(8)   O fearful meditation! || . . .

---

	(2)α		(4)α				(8)1	and then simple aggregation 1	1	2	1	2
(1)β1		(3)β2		(5)β1	(6)β2[E]	(7)β3						

The logical metafunction also brings us close to the nub of argument over broad general issues concerning the nature of grammar and the place of linguistics in a biology of human nature (as mentioned earlier). Towards the conclusion of this chapter, then, we need to return to the implications of this form of linguistic complexity for evolutionary thinking, and for social and brain sciences. Included here ought to be the ferment in linguistics as to what, if anything, is natural, innate and universal about human communication. We now have the Chomskyan position on innateness based *completely* on the role of 'recursion' in syntax (Chomsky 2012: e.g. 30, 176–81), as well as on something compositional about the concept 'merge' (Chomsky 2012: e.g. 15–17, 200–1, 263). This position differs from iteration and recursion ('choose over from the same system') in the lexicogrammatical networks of SFL, particularly because these latter terms in functional linguistics are only one of many ways of elaborating structure and of creating many simultaneous structures in the expression substance in a language.

Also controversial are the ways in which specific systems in grammar do or do not exemplify principles of combination, for example the degree to which the tense system of contemporary English should be characterised as a serial tense system (with a build-up from three tense choices being selected over and over from primary tense) or whether we are dealing with a two-tense system with a modal 'future' (that is, with a strong resemblance to the verbal group concatenations of earlier forms of English). This is an interesting debate because it shows how historical change in a grammatical system may closely parallel the adaptive 'descent with modification' (or natural selection) of the Darwinian conception of change in living systems. The point here is that the earliest system of 'English' was clearly oriented to two-tense systems – namely, the past tense and the non-past (along with various periphrastic strategies) in Anglo-Saxon of 1,000 years ago (Cummings 2010, 2015). In Chaucer's work (c. 1380), we see the potential of a realis/irrealis distinction with the subjunctive force of auxiliary verbs, which subjunctive meaning is still evident in Shakespeare's writing (c. 1600). But, in modern-day English, the subjunctive force and its expressions in the verbal group as a system have diminished, and the vestigial signs of what was once a system have been brought into a new relationship of consistent serial choice. We might reflect here on an analogy with the way in which the human systems of jaw control and communicative intonation and hearing (the bones of the middle ear) are derivations of the gill arches in fish (Porges 2011: 37–40, 160, 251), or how the frailties of the human knee reflect the aquatic origins of humans (Shubin 2009). Clearly, the origins of a system clarify the range of its possible functions – as is the case in the polyvagal theory of the mammalian nervous system (Porges 2011).

But with this diachronic, evolutionary reflection, we move to illustrate the basic workings of the logical function in the grammar of clause complexes. The rank of clause complex, in the lexicogrammatical stratum, has drawn the most attention in the SFL literature on the logical metafunction. Certainly, there is a strong semantic connection between the semiotic construction of a world and the architecture of clause-to-clause relations.

Clause complexing as meaning potential: variations of intensity by *taxis* in the prose of the Malouf passage

Our claim here may be summed up as 'structure enables function; and function directs structure': the clausal structures in the following two passages are examples of the 'reciprocal delimitation' between the signified and the signifier that Saussure (1959) pointed out as one of the paradoxical conditions of signs in a sign system. More concretely, we can say that the novelist David Malouf achieves certain effects by means of the choices he makes in the relations between clauses – choices that may be unconscious, but which certainly mark his style as an artist: plain diction (lexis) set against subtle, perhaps latent, grammatical accumulations.

Extended complexity: one sentence from Malouf, *Fly Away Peter (1982: ch. 4)*

[[What he could not know]] *WAS* to how great a degree
[[these trips into the swamp, in something very like a punt *were* for Ashley recreations of long still afternoons on the Cam ||
||but *translated* here not only to another hemisphere, but back, far back, into some pre-classical, prehistoric, primaeval and haunted world . . .
<< it *was* this [[that *accounted* for his mood of suspended wonder]] >>
[[in which the birds [[Jim *pointed* out || and *might* almost *have been calling up* || as he *named* them in a whisper out of mists before creation]] *WERE* extravagantly disguised spirits of another order of existence || and the trip itself – despite the picnic hamper and the champagne bottles [[*laid* in ice]] and the girls, one [[of whom *was* the girl [[he *was about to marry* – a water journey in another deeper sense]]]]];
||which IS [[why he occasionally *shivered* || and *might* << *looking back* >> *have seen* Jim, << where he *leaned* on the pole || *straining*, a slight crease in his brow and his teeth || *biting* his lower lip >> as the ordinary embodiment of a figure [[already *glimpsed* in childhood || and *given* a name in mythology, || and only now *made* real]]]]].||

This passage presents us with an interlacing of around twenty-five clausal elements (there are grounds for debate over the number). These create a sense of many forms of qualification all being added and held together – semantically suspended – awaiting a full unravelling as the sentence comes to its end. In fact, the complex resolves itself into only two main or matrix clauses. Both of these are identifying clauses: X (what he could not know) = Y (to how great a degree); and X (which) is Y (Why . . .) (see Figure 7.4). The narratorial thought is taking us into a complex convergence of autobiographical and cultural symbolism in which the experience represented takes on the numinous character of a different order of reality.

This 'suspension of interpretation' is set out in all its structural consistency, and authorial virtuosity, in Example 7.2. It is a liminal moment for the character Ashley and consequently

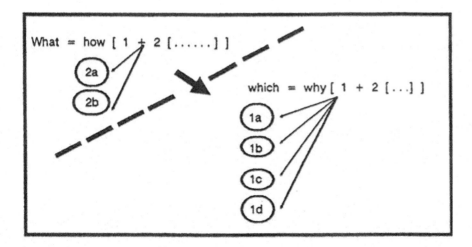

Figure 7.4 Logical relations in *Fly Away Peter*

it becomes a 'crossing' for the reader – over into a state in which atomistic summaries in an additive form will not serve to express how many elements depend on one another in the rendering of a human psyche.

In Example 7.3, you can view a different clausal strategy for this protracting and delaying in the aesthetic interpretation of crucial moments of understanding for the character Ashley. The text can be read off from chapter 15 of Malouf's novel and from the diagram Example 7.2, along with its image of a farmer as symbolic 'grim reaper'.

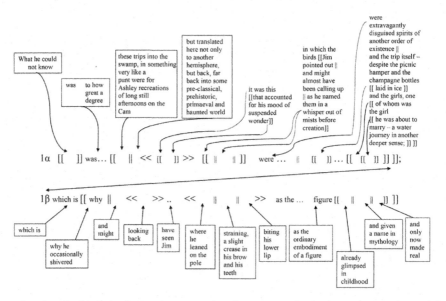

Example 7.2   The logical relations between the clauses in Malouf, *Fly Away Peter* (1982: ch. 4)

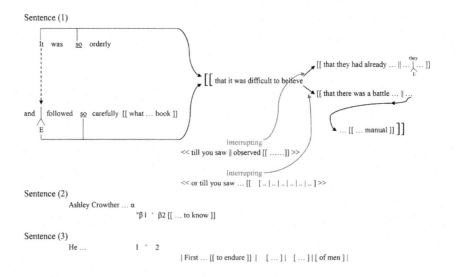

Example 7.3   The logical relations in representing Ashley's psyche

We have, then, a grammar of what philosopher of science Feyerabend (1975: ch. 16) called the opposition between a 'hypotactic system' and a 'paratactic aggregate'. Feyerabend had been reading Whorf's writings, and saw the relevance of the ideas to complexity in nature and art. The density, variety and depth of complexing serve in the novel as resource for the intimation of felt, but hard-to-specify, significance, excitement and anxiety. The unit of the clause is the interface with the information unit in language (the tone contour and prominence through pitch). This interface, whether through congruent or counterpoint in alignment, engages the older, subcortical systems of our organism.[11]

The sense of a background of emotional intensification is a recurring motif in Malouf's novel. The clausal 'music' (or a shifting tide in the grammar) provides the context at which the images and other lines of consistency in the work converge. Such points of convergence create what used to be referred to as 'cruces' in a literary text. A more inclusive concept of organisation, which looks for multiple alignments of semantic structure, is in Hasan's level of 'symbolic articulation' (for example Hasan 1979, 1985a/b).

In this novel, for example, there are a number of cases of this structural concentration. These are marked by at least three features – two overt 'literary' strategies, and the less overt (but here insistent) interrelation and accumulation of clauses. The literary choices are the introduction of a primary symbol of Western myth of iconography (the Stygian boatman or, later, the scythe of the grim reaper) and a confusion in a reference chain, producing a double value or 'dropped stitch' in the texture. For example, after a description of the brightly blazered and privileged young women at a boating party, who are also watching the exotic kingfishers across the mist heavy lagoon, there is the text:

He liked to show *them* off – his birds . . .

Multivariate vs. univariate constructions

Let us reconsider, at this point, the variety of perspectives from which we can interpret structure and how these might be usefully applied to language. One relevant distinction is between multivariate and univariate structures. A *multivariate* structure is a unit made up of parts that make individual, qualitatively different contributions to the whole. A *univariate* structure is built by repeated steps, or steps that make a similar contribution to an overall pattern. These two valuable notions of structure can also be applied to the *same* phenomenon when we change the generality, or *depth of field*, in our analysis. If we consider a spider's web, for example, most of the segments of structure appear to be repeats of the one pattern – albeit a pattern at different scales. We might refer to this as 'univariate building'. From another angle, however, the web has a distinctive centre and layers from core to periphery. If the spider is fed caffeine, the spider's web-making becomes inconsistent or irregular – that is, its regularity fails (Andrei 2013). By being distorted, it becomes more complex, less predictable, perhaps approaching uniqueness. Patterns of fingerprints and many biological consistencies have this same character: overwhelming similarity, but unique if seen in high degrees of discrimination or *delicacy* (the term used in SFL). What Darwin called 'the economy of nature' produces mechanisms with the paradoxical character of all life forms – 'descent with modification', or *variation*. Reflect again on the way in which the 154 sonnets of Shakespeare revolve about the same two preoccupations (namely, advice to a young man and an ambiguous 'dark lady'), yet each sonnet is remarkable also in its uniqueness.

This is an important point. Structure statements concerning language (and meaning more generally) are dismissed by some theorists because there may be some element of difference

David G. Butt and Jonathan J. Webster

between the linguistic statement and the actuality of speech, as if the uniqueness of human interactions 'defies' utterly the tools of rational description or sciences. Text patterns will always be unique, at some degree of analysis. This will be the case even when a text is utterly unremarkable, or clichéd. Structure statements assist us in revealing the ground of variation among phenomena and between instances of the systems we capture in our observations of experience – that is, in modelling our world through the ideational metafunction (the combination of experiential meanings with logical architectures).

The next section introduces other distinctions and concepts that extend our ideas about what constitutes structure.

Building a clause and building the units by which one can build a clause

It is useful, even with our focus on clause complexing, to survey briefly the logical structure of the nominal and verbal groups in English. What emerges is a better sense of how the concatenation of group structure in both cases can be represented according to multivariate *and* univariate interpretations. Nominal group structure invites a multivariate interpretation. There are a number of apparently distinct functional contributions, for example:

Deictic   Numerative   Epithet(s)   Classifier(s)   Thing   Qualifier

But this multivariate interpretation can be revised by changing the depth of field in our lens: we have a Thing/Head structure that has various options for modification, for choosing over. This iterative view echoes the iterative structure of the verbal group in English. It sets out from the deictic force of primary tense or modality and then enters a series of choices of sequent tenses, in this sense 'presetting' the conditions of the process:

$$\alpha \rightarrow \quad \beta \rightarrow \quad \gamma \rightarrow \quad \delta \rightarrow \quad \varepsilon \rightarrow \quad \ldots$$

This gives us further motivation to think of structural arrangements in languages as resources that are utilised by homology with structures repeated throughout the natural order. This assists us in seeing the adaptation or, as proposed by Darwin, the 'descent with modification' that is the rationale for using the classifier 'natural' with languages. We might reflect here on the iterative character of the structural resource in Fibonacci proportions – that is, 3:5:8:13:21:34:55 . . . (see Figure 7.5).

The contrast between this position and Chomsky's claims for his 'biolinguistics' becomes clearer. The uniqueness of language is now, according to his recent thinking, solely in the structural power of recursion. The position of those in SFL who have engaged with evolutionary issues and the wider views of biologists, geneticists and neuroscientists is that language has derived from a convergence of structural conditions, and that systemic resources of very many different origins have been integrated in its evolved multileveled organisation. The logical function is but one line of these robust patterns of order. In evolution, we see numerous cases of renewal of a previously 'successful' pattern or relationship – but this will always be under the conditions of an ecological opportunity or pressure. Consider the direct relation between the gill of a fish and the ultimate form of our ear, and the cranial nerves we share with sharks, for example (Shubin 2008: ch. 5).

We need to appreciate that the power of the lexicogrammatical units of clause complexing derive from the potential to mean by different alignments and by counterpoint with divisions

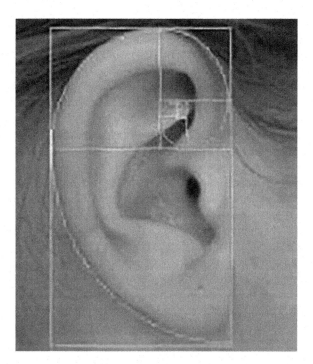

Figure 7.5 The ear structured in Fibonacci proportions

of structures on other strata. A speaker's choice in expression – and thence the cadence of an actor – derives from the relationship between the tone group and the clausal architecture (Halliday and Greaves 2008). Above the clause, semantic units and rhetorical choices have been represented in SFL, including Matthiessen's (2015) adaptation of rhetorical structure theory (RST), first developed by Mann and colleagues (1989), and the rhetorical units (RUs) as argued by Cloran (1994). The role of semantic units, between the generic elements and the lexicogrammatical realisations, is well illustrated in Hasan (1984).

Evolutionary implications: behavioural ensembles across species

The logical metafunction brings us directly to many of the most intense debates in linguistics: are there communicative behaviours among birds, ants, honey bees, bonobo chimps, whales or even between single-cell bacteria (such as E. coli), or viruses, which display combinatorial intricacies of logical patterning either analogical or homologically related to those in human communication? To answer this question, we need to turn to various disciplines, as well as to linguistics. This wide issue is raised here since the notion of recursion, and an allied notion of conceptual 'merge', have become the central ideas in Chomsky's theory of innatism in language acquisition.

The uncompromising argument of the Chomskyan school of thought since the 1960s has been that universal grammar (UG) is unique to humans. Emphasis was given to the peculiar, supposedly 'non'-functional and counter-intuitive character of some syntactic processes (since the motivation for such could not have come from broad evolutionary adaptation: Chomsky 1972, 2012: 50*ff*).[12]

In a series of discussions and explanatory notes (Chomsky 2012), Chomsky re-enlivens his views – on the limits of Darwinian natural selection when applied to the emergence of language (for example Chomsky 2012: 170); on the essential nature of merge (for example Chomsky 2012: 13–17, 50–4) and on what is universal without exception (for example Chomsky 2012: 245). The language characteristic emphasised is still the *computational* properties of what humans do, but free of systems for externalisation. Chomsky (2012: 30) also dismisses any current claims concerning the computational property *recursion* in animal and bird communications, as well as continuing the attack on the studies by Daniel Everett – that is, on Everett's data from twenty-five years of work with the Pirahã in the Amazon (Everett 2009, 2012). Those data suggest an absence of Chomsky's universal recursion in a natural language.[13]

The logical metafunction in Halliday's systemic functional model of language has been underestimated in its meaning-making potential. The significant loss to our approaches to language from this underestimation appears when we note how the resources of the logical metafunction are implicated in our most human of exchanges – especially in:

1 unconsciously managed affective reactions – through the embodied systems of emotion and reasoning in those moments of profound seriousness in human communication; or
2 consciously trialled and edited in peaks and flats of discoursal complexity – illustrated in the logical architecture of Shakespearean sonnets and in the cruces of the 'plain style' novel by David Malouf.

Systemic functional work on the logical metafunction is now extremely diverse and detailed. In this short chapter, we hope we have offered you an aperture into the wider vista of works by Halliday and also by Matthiessen. The essential sources from which to set out in order to develop this introduction are Halliday and Matthiessen (1999), Halliday and Matthiessen (2014: ch. 7) and the vast exemplification given in Halliday and Webster (2015: 272–366).

Other primary sources are listed in the references. These include some differences of theory, expository style and focus (including emphases on other ranks in the lexicogrammar or on other strata). Martin (1992) and Fawcett (2000) are examples of somewhat different managements of related textual architecture, with some differences of theoretical stance (for example Fawcett 2000: 263–72 and 315*ff*).

Coda

The combinatorial power of logical organisation applies to every level and rank of linguistic composition, from our modifications of morphology with children ('daddy baddy!') to the various elaborations of rhetorical choreography.

But the metafunction is only one of many resources from which human groups have fashioned their ways of interacting through speech. In this regard, we might suggest that the role of the logical metafunction has come to be overstated in debate around universal grammar. The uniqueness of humans does not depend on us being the only species with strategies of construction that we can combine and extend by repeating. The textual metafunction, for example, involves resources that bring humans into the special relationship of intervening in the form of the code – namely, it enables us to have choices about our choices. Any claims, therefore, about the unique character of human languages must include the logical function – but must not stop there.

Notes

1 In this extract, ‖ represents the clause boundary; [[. . .]] represents the embedded clause.
2 Note that the kudos and power of the written form have meant that 'sentence' has been carried over into some linguistic discussions as if it could do service for spoken clause complexes – an unhelpful conflation of terms.
3 See Hasan (1985a/b) for contextual configuration and Hasan (1984) for the sequencing of 'generic structure potential'.
4 Note the various explanations of network conventions in this volume.
5 See Anderson, Davidse, and Forey and Sampson, all this volume.
6 See Chomsky (1972, 1975, 1993, 2012) and the total focus on 'recursion' and 'merge', referred to later in this chapter.
7 See Halliday and Matthiessen (2004, 2014) and revisit Halliday (1985).
8 See the references to the role of language in human evolution, under 'Evolutionary implications: Behavioural ensembles across species'.
9 Note that we are taking a sentence boundary in written text to constitute a clause complex boundary in grammar. This is a convenience that serves for most situations, but not all.
10 Literary critic Blackmur (1932) used the metaphor of 'surds' of feeling in the depiction of the irreducible and seemingly irrational effects of poetry.
11 See again Porges (2011: 251); see also, on subcortical systems, Panksepp and Biven (2012: 222*ff*) and Panksepp and Trevarthen (2009: 132–3).
12 See also Anderson and Lightfoot (2002).
13 But note the academic 'storm' around this. It is addressed by a documentary, *The Grammar of Happiness* (2012), available through the Smithsonian Channel and elsewhere.

References

Anderson, D.W., and Lightfoot, S.R. 2002. *The Language Organ: Linguistics as Cognitive Physiology.* Cambridge: Cambridge University Press.
Andrei, M. 2013. Spiders on drugs: See how they web. *ZME Science*, 16 January. Available online at http://www.zmescience.com/medicine/mind-and-brain/spiders-drugs/
Blackmur, R.P. 1932. Examples of Wallace Stevens. *Hound and Horn* 5(2): 233–5.
Butt, D. 1988a. Ideational meaning and the existential fabric of a poem. In R. Fawcett and D. Young (eds) *New Developments in Systemic Linguistics, Vol. 2: Theory and Application.* London and New York: Pinter, pp. 174–218.
Butt, D. 1988b. Randomness, order and the latent patterning of text. In D. Birch and M. O'Toole (eds) *Functions of Style.* London and New York: Pinter, pp. 74–97.
Chomsky, N. 1972. *Problems of Knowledge and Freedom: Russell Lectures.* London: Fontana/Collins.
Chomsky, N. 1975. *Reflections on Language.* New York: Pantheon Books.
Chomsky, N. 1993. *Language and Thought.* Wakefield, Rhode Island and London: Moyer Bell.
Chomsky, N. 2002. *On Nature and Language.* Cambridge and New York: Cambridge University Press.
Chomsky, N. 2012. *The Science of Language: Interviews with James McGilvray.* Cambridge: Cambridge University Press.
Cloran, C. 1994. *Rhetorical Units and Decontextualisation: An Enquiry into Some Relations of Context, Meaning and Grammar.* Nottingham: University of Nottingham.
Cummings, M.J. 2010. *An Introduction to the Grammar of Old English: A Systemic Functional Approach.* Sheffield and Oakville, ON: Equinox.
Cummings, M.J. 2015. Systemic functional diachronic linguistics: Theory and application. Paper presented at the 42nd International Systemic Functional Congress, Aachen, July.
de Saussure, F. 1959. *A Course in General Linguistics.* Trans. W. Baskin. New York and London: McGraw Hill.

Everett, D.L. 2009. *Don't Sleep, There Are Snakes: Life and Language in the Amazonian Jungle*. New York: Vintage Books.

Everett, D.L. 2012. *Language: The Cultural Tool*. New York: Vintage Books.

Fawcett, R.P. 2000. *A Theory of Syntax for Systemic Functional Linguistics* (Amsterdam Studies in the Theory and History of Linguistic Science 206). Amsterdam and Philadelphia, PA: John Benjamins.

Ferroni, F. 2012. Occhi indiscreti sul neutrino. *Il Sole* 24.

Feyerabend, P. 1975. *Against Method: Outline of an Anarchistic Theory of Knowledge*. Atlantic Highlands, NJ, and London: Humanities Press.

Halliday, M.A.K. 1985. *An Introduction to Functional Grammar*. London: Arnold.

Halliday, M.A.K. 1994. *An Introduction to Functional Grammar*. 2nd edn. London: Arnold.

Halliday, M.A.K., and W. Greaves. 2008. *Intonation in the Grammar of English*. London and New York: Equinox.

Halliday, M.A.K., and C.M.I.M. Matthiessen. 1999. *Construing Experience through Meaning: A Language-Based Approach to Cognition*. London: Cassell.

Halliday, M.A.K., and C.M.I.M. Matthiessen. 2004. *An Introduction to Functional Grammar*. 3rd edn. London: Arnold.

Halliday, M.A.K., and C.M.I.M. Matthiessen. 2014. *An Introduction to Halliday's Functional Grammar*. 4th edn. London: Arnold.

Halliday, M.A.K., and J.J. Webster. 2015. *Text Linguistics. The How and Why of Meaning*. Sheffield and Bristol, CT: Equinox.

Hasan, R. 1979. Language in the study of literature (Workshop Report No. 6). In M.A.K. Halliday (ed.) *Working Conference on Language in Education: Report to Participants*. Sydney: University of Sydney.

Hasan, R. 1984. The nursery tale as a genre. *Nottingham Linguistic Circular* 13: 71–102.

Hasan, R. 1985a. *Linguistics, Language and Verbal Art*. Geelong, Vic: Deakin University Press.

Hasan, R. 1985b. Part B. In M.A.K. Halliday and R. Hasan (eds) *Language, Context and Text: Aspects of Language in a Social Semiotic Perspective*. Geelong, Vic: Deakin University Press. pp. 52–121.

Malloch, S., and C. Trevarthen (eds). 2009. *Communicative Musicality: Exploring the Basis of Human Companionship*. New York: Oxford University Press.

Malouf, D. 1982. *Fly Away Peter*. New York: Random House. Retrieved from http://www.oocities.org/grantandrewjeffery/Flyaway2.doc

Mann, W.C., C.M.I.M. Matthiessen and S.A. Thompson. 1989. *Rhetorical Structure Theory and Text Analysis*. Marina del Rey, CA: USC/Information Sciences Institute.

Martin, J.R. 1992. *English Text: Systems and Structure*. Amsterdam: John Benjamins.

Matthiessen, C.M.I.M. 2004. Descriptive motifs and generalizations. In A. Caffarel, J.R. Martin and C.M.I.M. Matthiessen (eds) *Language Typology: A Functional Perspective*. Amsterdam: John Benjamins, pp. 537–673.

Matthiessen, C.M.I.M. 2015.

Panksepp, J., and L. Biven. 2012. *The Archaeology of Mind: Neuroevolutionary Origins of Human Emotions* (Norton Series on Interpersonal Neurobiology). New York: W.W. Norton.

Panksepp, J., and C. Trevarthen. 2009. The neuroscience of emotion in music. In S. Malloch and C. Trevarthen (eds) *Communicative Musicality: Exploring the Basis of Human Companionship*. New York: Oxford University Press, pp. 105–46.

Pawley, A. 1987. Encoding events in Kalam and English: Different logics for reporting experience. In R.S. Tomlin (ed.) *Coherence and Grounding in Discourse*. Amsterdam: John Benjamins, pp. 329–60.

Porges, S. 2011. *The Polyvagal Theory: Neurophysiological Foundations of Emotions, Attachment, Communication, and Self-regulation* (Norton Series on Interpersonal Neurobiology). New York: W.W. Norton.

Poynton, C. 1984. Forms and functions: Names as vocatives. *Nottingham Linguistic Circular* 13: 1–34.

Shubin, N. 2008. *Your Inner Fish: A Journey into the 3.5-Billion-Year History of the Human Body*. New York: Pantheon.

Shubin, N. 2009. This old body. *Scientific American* 300(1): 64–7.

8

Interpersonal meaning and the clause

Thomas Hestbæk Andersen

The interpersonal metafunction represents 'the idea that language can be used as a means of communicating information' (Halliday 1975: 21). The fundamental nature of any communication process is that of dialogue (Halliday 1975: 31); hence the interpersonal resources of language designate 'the area of the language in which choices are made which assign communication roles to the performer (whether speaker or writer) and to the addressee (whether listener or reader)' (Fawcett 2011: 1). In this way, the interpersonal resources (both the lexicogrammatical and semantic resources) reflect and construe an intersubjective aspect of semiosis; as Halliday (2002 [1992]: 354, emphasis original) points out, '[m]eaning is **inter**subjective activity, not subjective'.

Central to the systemic functional description of dialogue is Halliday's notion of speech function and Fawcett's somewhat corresponding notion of MOOD meaning. The idea of speech functions (or MOOD meanings) is to some extent comparable to the idea of *Sprachspiel* in Wittgenstein's thinking (Wittgenstein 1958: §§ 7, 10, 23, 43) and to the idea of speech acts in speech act theory (Austin 1962; Searle 1969). The latter comparison is also made by Taverniers (2011: 1109), who states that the options in Halliday's system for speech functions 'define different types of speech acts'. It should be noted, however, that where speech act theory embraces a notion of intention, this is avoided by Halliday, who is concerned with intersubjectively negotiated purposivity in using language, not with individual intention.

This chapter will take as its point of departure Halliday's description in his *Introduction to Functional Grammar* (1985) – hence the 'IFG traditional' description – of the interpersonal realm of language and it will introduce Fawcett's description of – or the Cardiff grammar (CG) perspective on – interpersonal meaning.[1] From these initial presentations of the IFG tradition's and the CG's descriptions, the chapter will proceed to discuss of a number of problematic issues in both frameworks; the discussion will similarly focus on Halliday's description, but it will also be contrastive of the two.

In the final part of the chapter, necessary reflections and clarifications for future work on the interpersonal meaning of the clause will be sketched out.

Interpersonal meaning and the clause in the IFG tradition

According to Halliday and Matthiessen (2014: 134), the clause is 'organized as an interactive event'.

As an interactive event, the clause contributes to the development of an exchange (of meaning) between a speaker (or writer) and a listener (or reader). The notion of exchange is central in the IFG tradition's description of the interpersonal metafunction and, as a broad, non-technical term, it covers a description of how the semantic system of SPEECH FUNCTIONS is realised in the lexicogrammar by different clause types (and in phonology by different intonation contours). Different clause types in English[2] are structured by different orderings of Subject and Finite. Subject and Finite together constitute the Mood element of the clause; interpersonally speaking, this is the pivotal lexicogrammatical element.

The speech functions

The semantic taxonomy of speech functions contains four basic and primary speech functions – namely, statement, question, command and offer. Their fundamental properties are shown in Table 8.1 (Halliday and Matthiessen 2014: 136–7), which also gives an example of each of the speech functions.

Table 8.1 combines two variables: (a) the nature of the commodity that is being exchanged, and (b) the roles that are defined by the exchange process (Halliday 1984: 11).

In a linguistic exchange, we can position ourselves in one of two roles: either we can give something, or we can demand something – that is, (b) – and this 'something' that we are giving or demanding can be either a semiotic commodity or a non-semiotic commodity – that is, (a). A semiotic commodity is labelled *information* and non-semiotic commodities are labelled *goods-and-services*.

The notion of exchange is closely tied to the second variable – that is, the positioning of the performer and the addressee in the roles of 'giver' or 'demander'. Halliday and Matthiessen (2014: 135, emphasis original) describe the roles played in an exchange as follows:

> The speaker is not only doing something himself; he is also requiring something of the listener. Typically, therefore, an 'act' of speaking is something that might more appropriately be called an **interact**: it is an exchange, in which giving implies receiving and demanding implies giving in response.

Table 8.1 Basic speech functions and their properties

		COMMODITY EXCHANGED	
		goods-and-services	*information*
ROLE IN EXCHANGE	*giving*	'offer' *Shall I give you this teapot?*	'statement' *He's giving her the teapot.*
	demanding	'command' *Give me that teapot!*	'question' *What is he giving her?*
		Proposal	Proposition

Table 8.2 Basic speech functions and their responses

Speech function	Expected response	Discretionary response
Offer	Acceptance	Rejection
Shall I give you this teapot?	*Yes, please do!*	*No, thanks.*
Command	Undertaking	Refusal
Give me that teapot!	*Here you are.*	*I won't.*
Statement	Acknowledgement	Contradiction
He's giving her the teapot.	*Is he?*	*No, he isn't.*
Question	Answer	Disclaimer
What is he giving her?	*A teapot.*	*I don't know.*

It follows that statement, question, offer and command are to be regarded as dialogically initiating speech functions, to which there are a number of possible and typical responses.

The four basic speech functions and their respective sets of responses are shown in Table 8.2 (Halliday and Matthiessen 2014: 136–7).

The speech functions and mood types

The semantic taxonomy of speech functions (the system of SPEECH FUNCTION) is realised in the lexicogrammar by different mood types (that is, clause types) in the system of MOOD, and on the phonological level by their intonation contour (Halliday and Matthiessen 2014: 166–70), in the following typical (congruent) way:

1   a statement is realised by a declarative clause;
2   a question is realised by an interrogative clause (either a 'yes–no' interrogative or a WH-interrogative);
3   a command is realised by an imperative clause and
4   an offer is realised by an interrogative clause, where the Finite is formed by a modal verb (Halliday 1984: 15, 20; Halliday and Matthiessen 2014: 137, 146).

It is debatable whether the offer indeed has a typical realisation. On the one hand, the examples in IFG seem to suggest this and Hasan (1985) contributes significantly to an understanding of the lexicogrammar of offers in her *Offers in the Making*. On the other hand, in his *Lexicogrammatical Cartography*, Matthiessen (1995: 438) largely avoids talking about the offer, stating that '[t]here is no special grammatical category for offers'. And in the section on grammatical metaphors of MOOD in IFG, there is no description of any congruent (or any metaphorical) realisations of the offer – that is, there is no account of any typical (or atypical) realisations of the offer (Halliday and Matthiessen 2014: § 10.4).

The declarative and the interrogative are types of indicative clause, meaning that they are structured around the Mood element, which in English consists of Subject and Finite. They are structurally distinct from one another, since the declarative is characterised by the word order Subject before Finite, while the 'yes–no' interrogative is characterised by the word order Finite before Subject. The WH-interrogative has the order of Subject before Finite, when the WH element is the Subject, and Finite before Subject otherwise (Halliday and Matthiessen 2014: 143). The imperative is different from the indicative in that it does not necessarily involve a Mood element – that is, a Subject and a Finite (this goes for the unmarked positive imperative, such as *look*); however, there are forms of imperatives with a Mood element, such as *Don't you look* (Halliday and Matthiessen 2014: 165), and the imperative is considered a Mood type.

According to Halliday and Matthiessen (2014: 144, emphasis original), the Finite:

> brings the proposition down to earth, so that it is something that can be argued about. . . . This can be done in one or two ways. One is by reference to the time of speaking; the other is by reference to the judgement of the speaker . . . In grammatical terms, the first is **primary tense**, the second is **modality**. . . . What these have in common is **interpersonal deixis**: that is, they locate the exchange within the semantic space that is opened up between speaker and listener.

The Subject is 'responsible for the functioning of the clause as an interactive event' (Halliday and Matthiessen 2014: 146), since it is said to carry 'the **modal responsibility**: that is, responsibility for the validity of what is being predicated (stated, questioned, commanded or offered) in the clause' (Halliday and Matthiessen 2014: 148, emphasis original).[3]

In addition to the three clause types of MOOD, Halliday and Matthiessen operate with minor clauses and exclamatives. Minor clauses have no verbal element and do not realise propositions or proposals, but minor speech functions – namely, 'exclamations, calls, greetings and alarms' (Halliday and Matthiessen 2014: 195). The description of the exclamative is very brief and primarily consists of a number of examples, and the exclamative is nowhere to be seen in the system network of MOOD (Halliday and Matthiessen 2014: 162). In other words, its status is somewhat unclear in the IFG tradition.[4]

The speech functions and MODALITY (and POLARITY)

POLARITY and MODALITY are interconnected systems: the options in POLARITY (positive and negative) designate the extremes to which the options in MODALITY function as intermediate degrees. In other words, MODALITY construes 'the region of uncertainty that lies between "yes" and "no"' (Halliday and Matthiessen 2014: 176), as illustrated in Figure 8.1.

Any type of speech function can function with any of the two options in POLARITY. For MODALITY, the picture is different. The speech functions associated with the exchange of information (propositions) and the speech functions associated with the exchange of goods-and-services (proposals) connect with different types of modality – namely, modalisation (that is, probability and usuality) and modulation (that is, obligation and inclination), respectively (Halliday and Matthiessen 2014: 177–8). MODALITY is realised in the Mood element of the clause, either through the Finite or through Mood Adjuncts.

Figure 8.1   POLARITY and MODALITY

Interpersonal meaning and the clause in the CG: a perspective

In the CG, the linguistic domain of dialogue is called MOOD, which here designates the interpersonal strand of meaning. Polarity and validity (these cover roughly the same as polarity and modality in the IFG tradition) are two other, separate strands. MOOD 'covers the roles of the **interactants in the act of communication**' (Fawcett forthcoming: 53, emphasis original). These roles – played out by the notions of the Performer and the Addressee – are grouped in two main areas of meaning. The first is concerned with meanings that assign 'communication roles in giving, seeking, confirming, etc., **information** about events' (Fawcett 2011: 21, emphasis original); the second area covers meanings that assign communication roles 'in proposals for events that are actions. . . . Any such meaning is termed . . . a **proposal for action**' (Fawcett 2011: 21, emphasis original).

There are some 150 different MOOD meanings in the CG and it is not possible to give a complete description of all of these in this chapter.[5] A small part of the total system network is presented by Fawcett elsewhere in this volume.

In the CG, the different MOOD meanings (such as 'information giver' and 'information seeker') are associated with different syntactic[6] structures. In other words, the various MOOD meanings are expressed on the level of form, primarily through the ordering of Subject, Operator and Main Verb. Subject, Operator and Main Verb are elements of the clause, and they do not have any meaning on their own (level).[7] What is significant for these elements in relation to the MOOD meanings is that the structure of the elements expresses different meanings:

> [T]he major distinction at the level of form between an 'information giver' and an 'information seeker' is this: an 'information giver' has the structure of **Subject + Main Verb (S M)**, . . . or **Subject + Operator (S O)**, . . . whereas an 'information seeker' typically – but not always – has the structure **O S**.
>
> *Fawcett 2011: 22, emphasis original*

The options in the system of MOOD are associated with clauses that function as initiating moves in an exchange structure – that is, a sequencing and turn-changing structure (Fawcett 2010: ch. 8).

Problematic issues and uncertainties

In this section, we shall consider some of the ambiguities and problematic issues with the description of exchange in the IFG tradition, and then relate these to the description of MOOD in the CG tradition.

How many speech functions are there?

Halliday (1984) is key to understanding the IFG account of speech functions. Matthiessen (2007: 522) calls the article 'seminal' in his chronological overview of the developments in systemic functional linguistics (SFL), and Fawcett (2011: 18) describes it in the same way, while noting that the ideas presented in the article were first formulated in the mid-1970s. The article is seminal for a number of reasons. On a more abstract theoretical level, it provides a description of interstratal realisational relations between semantics and lexicogrammar, thereby emphasising the need (as perceived by the IFG tradition) for a dual stratification of the content plane of language. As Taverniers (2011) shows, the introduction of an explicit semantic network (functioning on a higher level than lexicogrammatical networks) was an addition to Halliday's earlier model of SFL and in fact marks a fundamental difference from the CG's description of language, in which we do not find a dual stratification of the content plane of language (Fawcett 2011: 19). On a more descriptive level, Halliday's article provides the first account of the system of SPEECH FUNCTION – with the set of the four basic speech functions: statement, question, offer and command – with which we still operate today in the IFG tradition.

Until Halliday's 1984 article, speech functions in SFL were different sets of speech functions that were more or less described in detail and more or less transparently substantiated. In 1963, Halliday (2005 [1963]: 255) talks of 'sentence functions', which are motivated by the MOOD system in combination with the TONE system, and he identifies the total set of sentence functions to be 'statement, question, command, answer and exclamation'. Nearly the same set is posited in 1970, in a high-profile article in Lyons' *New Horizons in Linguistics*, where Halliday mentions in passing the 'basic "speech functions" of statement, question, response, command and exclamation' (Halliday 2002 [1970]: 189). Also in 1970, he presents a set of speech functions that are primarily argued for by intonation patterns – that is, the set is tied to the meanings of different tones. This set contains seven distinct speech functions – namely, the four major speech functions statement, the WH question, the 'yes/no' question and command, and the three minor speech functions, response, exclamation and call (Halliday 1970: 26).

Apart from the fact that (a) the number and labelling of speech functions is inconsistent, and (b) Halliday seems to express a kind of tentativeness to the status of his description given that, at one point, he talks of sentence functions and at another puts the notion of speech function in quotation marks. Two things should be noted in these early accounts of speech functions. First, there is no mention of the speech function offer; secondly, the system for SPEECH FUNCTION is motivated by the system of MOOD – that is, by clause syntax (Halliday 2002 [1970]: 189; Halliday 2005 [1963]: 254). It is likely that these two aspects are interwoven: there is no immediate syntactical motivation for four basic (or major) speech functions, hence no place for the offer, when the speech functions are to be argued for with the MOOD system that has only three basic clause types – that is, declarative, interrogative and imperative – as its principal options.

The offer does not become part of the basic set of speech functions until Halliday's 1984 introduction of the two fundamental variables on which to build the taxonomy of speech functions – namely, commodity and role. When combined, these two variables make it necessary to operate with four basic speech functions and this makes way for the offer. This semantic approach, taking the variable of commodity and role as point of departure, causes the problem that four basic speech functions are to be realised by only three basic clause types in MOOD. It could be argued that this makes up for a fuzzy grammatical evidence for semantic categories, even though Hasan (1985) has contributed with a long and insightful defence for the offer, and even though Halliday himself has suggested the notion of grammatical metaphor,[8] and thereby loosened the ties between the system of SPEECH FUNCTION and the system of MOOD.

This possible problematic issue is not at stake in the CG. Here, the MOOD meanings (at the level of meaning) are explicitly mapped onto syntax (at the level of form) – that is, onto different structures of (primarily) Subject and Operator. There is therefore no room for a difference between the number of MOOD meanings and the number of realising syntactical structures. And there is no need for concepts such as congruence and grammatical metaphor to explain MOOD (Fawcett 2010). A challenge to the CG regarding the question of how many MOOD meanings there are is that it operates within the area of 150 MOOD meanings (Fawcett 2011: 49–54). This, of course, provides for an incredibly rich resource for computer-based analysis and generation, but it is a fairly immense network of which to derive an overview when engaging in manual text analysis. One could also argue that there is a limited degree of generalisation in the network.

Are the system of SPEECH FUNCTION and the system of MOOD really semantic systems?

In the IFG tradition, it is not lucidly clear whether SPEECH FUNCTION is a semantic or a contextual system; in the CG, it is not clear how the allegedly semantic system of MOOD is related to context. So, in different respects, the question of whether the two systems are really semantic systems is relevant when scrutinising both the IFG tradition and the CG.

In the figures and tables in their *Introduction to Functional Grammar*, Halliday and Matthiessen (2014: 136) describe the speech functions as options in a semantic network, which are realised in lexicogrammar, and the figures show how the semantic system of SPEECH FUNCTION is organised (in part) in two subsystems – namely, INITIATING ROLE (with the options give and demand) and COMMODITY (with the options information and goods-and-services). If we then look carefully at the prose accompanying the figure and table in question, the picture becomes blurred. In the body text, there are traces to suggest that one of the subsystems in SPEECH FUNCTION is more contextual than semantic: Halliday and Matthiessen (2014: 135) state that the exchange of goods-and-services concerns 'an object or an action' – that is, 'the exchange commodity is strictly nonverbal'. If indeed goods-and-services are defined by a material difference and not by a semiotic difference (Thibault 1995: 71, 83), then it is hard to see goods-and-services as a semantic entity.

If we now compare the network for SPEECH FUNCTION in the IFG with the system of dialogue on the level of social context in Halliday's 1984 article, the plot thickens even more.[9] The two networks are reproduced here as Figures 8.2 and 8.3.

Other than the fact that the subsystem ROLE ASSIGNMENT in the earlier network is split into the two subsystems of MOVE and INITIATING role in the later network, the networks are identical. In other words, what is regarded in 1984 as a contextual system is regarded in 2014 as a semantic system. This stratal relocation is nowhere argued for by Halliday (or Matthiessen).

Halliday (1984) does not only seem inconsistent when compared to the *Introduction to Functional Grammar* (Halliday and Matthiessen 2014). The article is also somewhat problematic per se: the commodity exchanged is treated both as a semantic and a contextual concept. This becomes apparent when we compare the figures reproduced here as Figures 8.4 and 8.5, which are said to describe the ontogenesis of 'Nigel' (on the late transition phase and on the threshold of adult language, respectively). In Figure 8.4, goods-and-services and information are elements of meaning, while they are part of the description of context in Figure 8.5. No explanation is provided in the article's body text for this apparent inconsistency.

In the CG, the network for MOOD is explicitly thought of as semantic, and for Fawcett (2011: 10) it is a cardinal point to 'push MOOD all the way to semantics'. As described earlier, this is done by positing a network with explicit semantic features (on the level of meaning) combined with syntactic realisations (on the level of form). From Fawcett's (2011: 4) point of view, Halliday's network for MOOD is not semantic, and Halliday's (stratal) differentiation between a semantic network for speech functions and a lexicogrammatical network for

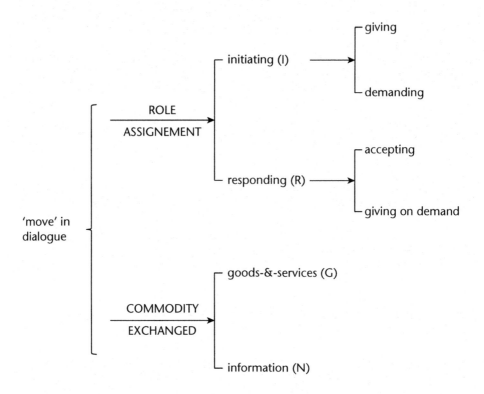

Figure 8.2 The system of dialogue (a): Level of social context – the 'move'
Source: Halliday (1984: 12)

MOOD is not necessary, since Fawcett maps syntax – that is, what he sees as equivalent to Halliday's MOOD – directly onto *his* MOOD meanings. Halliday's stratal differentiation is at odds with what Fawcett (2011: 19, emphasis original) calls '[t]he great beauty of the systemic functional approach to understanding . . . language' – namely, 'that the core component is A SINGLE, UNIFIED SYSTEM NETWORK OF MEANINGS'. From a Hallidayan point of view, however, Fawcett's approach is problematic since it loses sight of the relation between meaning and culture:

> [Fawcett's approach] removes the cultural base for meaning as postulated in Halliday's SFL; instead for Fawcett, this base is replaced by cognition, or an individual's belief system, which becomes the primary term in the game of human existence. Semantics in these two models is not the same thing; and mind in Fawcett's model is not made semiotically.
>
> *Hasan et al. 2007: 711*

Hasan's critique is tantamount to saying that Fawcett's system networks are not concerned with meaning in a (social-)semiotic sense (even though he explicitly regards them as system networks for meaning) and that his categories are more of a pragmatic (Levinson 1983) or cognitive kind, maybe even posited on an a priori basis.

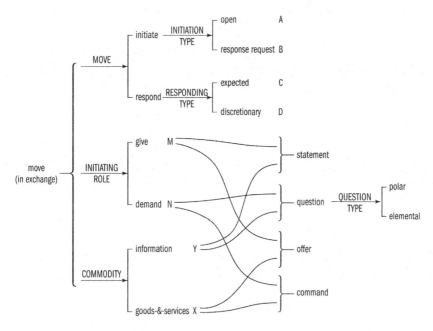

Figure 8.3 The semantic system of SPEECH FUNCTION

Source: Halliday and Matthiessen (2014: 136)

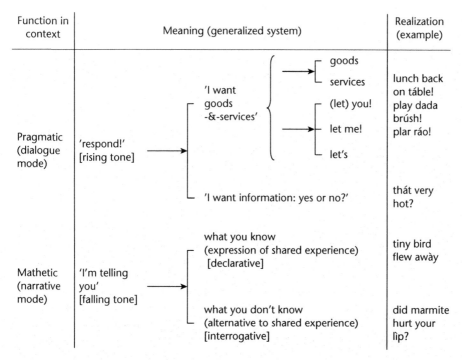

Figure 8.4 Transition, late (1;10)

Source: Halliday (1984: 28)

Thomas Hestbæk Andersen

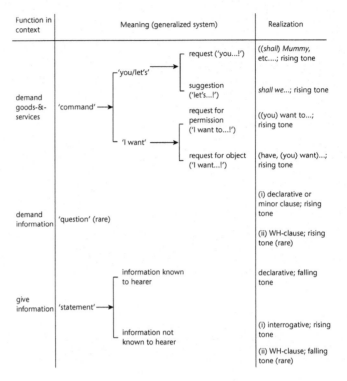

Figure 8.5   Incipient adult (2;0): Nigel on the threshold of the adult system of dialogue
Source: Halliday (1984: 30)

Why a distinction between information and goods-and-services?

Halliday's notion of speech function has been used by many systemic functional scholars to describe communicative purpose. It has been done with different emphasis on, for example, phonology (Halliday 2005 [1963], 1970; Halliday and Matthiessen 2014), clause structure (Halliday 1984; Halliday and Matthiessen 2014; Matthiessen 1995), discourse (Martin 1992) and message semantics (Hasan 1985, 1996; Moore, this volume), and it has been done for a large number of languages (Teruya et al. 2007). These accounts of speech function have been rich and have proven valuable in a large number of applied contexts. Strikingly, though, no description has ever debated Halliday's axiomatic distinction between role and commodity, comprising the distinction between information and goods-and-services; rather, this distinction has simply been reiterated and taken for granted. Since these (interrelated) distinctions are fundamental – and since their description holds a number of uncertainties (as we saw in the last section) – it is reasonable to discuss them in further detail.

The variable describing the roles of the interlocutors in an exchange as giver or demander seems fairly unproblematic. In an exchange, two parties are necessary and there is some directionality to the exchange, so it seems adequate to see the speaker as either giver or demander and to see the listener as taking up a complementary, responding role. The speaker's role as either giver or demander is also very clearly reflected in the way in which the declarative, interrogative and imperative clause types realise the speaker's role.

The other variable – that describing the commodity (that is, the variable with which Halliday distinguishes information from goods-and-services) – seems more problematic. When Halliday (1984: 11) introduces this variable, he simply states that '[t]he commodity may be either (a) goods-&-services or (b) information (cp. Ervin-Tripp 1964. . . . The distinction between information and goods-&-services is theoretically a very fundamental one.' In other words, when introduced, the only support for the distinction between information and goods-and-services is (i) a reference to work by Ervin-Tripp (1964) and (ii) an unsubstantiated claim that the distinction is indeed theoretically very fundamental. The latter is posited without any references or further argumentation, so we are left to look at Ervin-Tripp's work for support. Halliday refers to Ervin-Tripp's article 'An analysis of the interaction of language, topic, and listener', which scrutinises a number of key concepts in sociolinguistics. In the article's description of 'dyadic interactions' (Ervin-Tripp 1964: 88), we find wordings that create a link to Halliday's account of speech functions. Ervin-Tripp posits a number of interactions, including 'a. Requests for goods, services, or information' (Ervin-Tripp 1964: 88) and 'c. Offering information or interpretation' (Ervin-Tripp 1964: 89). These formulations are the only parts in Ervin-Tripp's article where we can find some sort of connection to Halliday's work on speech functions – but even this connection is only terminological, since Erwin-Tripp nowhere defines the terms, or groups 'goods' together with 'services', or posits these terms as an opposition to 'information'. Ervin-Tripp's article may have served as inspiration for Halliday, but it hardly suffices as a theoretical substantiation of his distinction between information and goods-and-services.

A possible substantiation for the distinction between information and goods-and-services is ontogenesis – or, to be more precise, Halliday's case study of the ontogenesis of 'Nigel'. This study is brought into the picture in some detail in Halliday (1984), and also Halliday and Matthiessen (2014: 138) indicate that his account of ontogenesis can substantiate the distinction.[10] It is therefore appropriate (briefly) to consider Halliday's description of ontogenesis in a search for the substantiation for which we are looking.

According to Halliday (1973, 1978), there are three phases in a child's learning of its mother tongue, as follows.

I   First, the child develops a proto-language, which helps it to express the 'instrumental, regulatory, interactional, personal, heuristic, imaginative' communicative functions (Halliday 1978: 71).

II   Next is a transition phase, in which the child starts to combine the six communicative functions from Phase I into two more general functions – namely, the 'pragmatic' and the 'mathetic'. In Phase II, '[t]he semiotic substance of the pragmatic/mathetic distinction, between language as doing and language as learning, has now been incorporated into the grammar, in the form of the functional distinction between interpersonal and ideational in the adult system' (Halliday 1978: 72). In addition to the interpersonal and the ideational metafunction, a third component appears in the language system in Phase II – namely, the textual metafunction – which helps to organise interpersonal and ideational meaning.

III When all three metafunctions are simultaneously in play, the child has learned its mother tongue and has entered Phase III, which 'consists in mastering the adult language. Phase III, of course, continues throughout life' (Halliday 1978: 72).

Halliday's description of the phases of ontogenesis provides for an argument for the metafunctional hypothesis in the IFG tradition – that is, for its three metafunctions – but it does not substantiate the distinction between information and goods-and-services. There is nothing in Halliday's writing to suggest that 'language as doing and language as learning' should be equal to a distinction between proposal and proposition, hence to the distinction between speech functions associated with goods-and-services and speech functions associated with information. If we add to this that Halliday uses information and goods-and-services as both semantic and contextual components in the sections of his 1984 article where he describes ontogenesis (as we saw earlier in the chapter), it becomes quite problematic to claim an ontogenetic support for the distinction between information and goods-and-services.

A further problematic issue with the distinction between information and goods-and-services is that the definition of goods-and-services seems incoherent with (maybe) the most fundamental of all definitions in SFL – namely, the definition of meaning. In SFL, 'social' equals 'cultural' (Halliday 1984: 9; Halliday and Hasan 1985: 4) and SFL can be thought of as a 'culture semiotics' (social semiotics) in the sense that meaning is theorised as a superindividual, social concept (Lemke 1995).[11]; 'Meaning is **inter**subjective activity, not subjective' (Halliday 2002 [1992]: 354, emphasis original; Halliday and Matthiessen 1999: 2), and culture is theorised as 'an edifice of meanings – a semiotic construct. . . . [T]he formulation "language as social semiotic" . . . means interpreting language within a sociocultural context, in which the culture itself is interpreted in semiotic terms' (Halliday 1996: 89; cf. Halliday 1984: 8).

Culture is meaning and 'all activities are cultural', ascertains van Leeuwen (2005: 74) in his reading of Malinowski. In line with this, Halliday (1978: 191) states that 'reality is a social construct, [and] it can be constructed only through an exchange of meanings'. With such axiomatic ideas of meaning, it is paradoxical to operate with entities that have no meaning. In other words, it is problematic to operate with the notion of goods-and-services, which are said to be 'non-symbolic [things and] acts.[12] As non-symbolic entities, goods-and-services are not brought into being 'through language (or perhaps other semiotic systems)' (Halliday 1984: 11) – that is, they are without meaning, since semiotic in the systemic functional theory means 'having to do with meaning' (Halliday 2005 [1995]: 198–9).

The idea of goods-and-services as entities without meaning is furthermore incoherent with the fact that this notion is part of the description of the clause as exchange; in an exchange '[the] non-linguistic physical acts are not . . . independent of the meaning potential of the lexicogrammatical form. They are a necessary and fully semiotic part of the total social act' (Thibault 1995: 71).

In the CG, there is no use of the dichotomy of information vs. goods-and-services; instead, there is a distinction between information and proposal for action. Butler (2003: 46) argues that this distinction corresponds to Halliday's distinction between information and goods-and-services, but the somewhat unsubstantiated notion of goods-and-services is (largely) avoided in the CG. How, then, does the CG substantiate its distinction between information and proposal for action, one could ask? This is not overtly addressed by Fawcett, so we are left to speculate. One possible inspiration for this distinction could be Austin's (1962) distinction between constatives and performatives. If one compares Fawcett's definitions and formulations with those of Austin, there are some similarities, not least the fact that Austin describes *How to do things with words* and MOOD with Fawcett's (2008: 52, emphasis original) words 'expresses the meaning of WHAT WE ARE DOING THROUGH LANGUAGE'. Fawcett operates with information and action, while Austin (1962: 132) talks about 'saying' and 'doing', where the latter means 'performing . . . an action' (Austin 1962: 6). Actually, Fawcett (2011: 17) himself notes speech act theory as an early influence (Butler 2003: 45).

Future directions

In this section, we shall very briefly consider some reflections and necessary clarifications for future work on the interpersonal meaning of the clause.

First and foremost, the distinction between information and goods-and-services should be either substantiated or avoided. In an ontological setting in which reality is a social construct, it is hard to see how the distinction could be substantiated in a way that is theoretically coherent with the systemic functional definition of meaning. If one were to attempt substantiation, albeit this theoretical issue, one would – for starters – have to clarify that goods-and-services is not an ecological, material commodity, but a semiotic construct, just as information is. If we uphold a contrast between 'material' and 'semiotic' as two orders of phenomena in our world, then this contrast is eventually semiotically made. This clarification leads to a number of questions: if both goods-and-services and information are semiotic constructs, what then differentiates them? Most often – but not always (for example Halliday 1978: 99) – Halliday defines information as linguistic semiosis (for exxample Halliday 1984, 2005 [1995]) and this could possibly differentiate information from goods-and-services, which meanings are (also) constructed by semiotic systems other than language. This stance, however, opens up a discussion of whether it is fruitful to uphold a distinction between linguistic semiosis and multisemiotic semiosis, when one brings multimodal theory (for example Kress 2010) and contemporary communication channels into the picture. All in all, there are severe problems in upholding a distinction between information and goods-and-services. If one were to avoid the distinction, an alternative way of mapping out speech functions could be found – and this leads to the following reflections.

In relation to stratification, it should be made clear to what extent any description of speech functions is approached primarily from below – as per the modelling of the ideational part of the semantic stratum in Halliday and Matthiessen (1999) – or from above – as per the current modelling in the IFG tradition, in the CG and in Martin's work on discourse semantics – or perhaps even from both perspectives. One might consider a bidirectional approach, which would involve two steps: first, approaching the speech functions from below and describing them as semantic interpretations of the various clause types, for example statement for declarative, question for interrogative and request for imperative; and secondly, through analysis of dialogue, relating these rather general semantic interpretations of clause types – that is, of grammatical structures – to actual contexts, whereby one could both determine their precise meaning (in the particular dialogue) and more generally map out subtypes. These would now be motivated from above, from contextual cues and semantic patterning. Such a bidirectional approach lends its rationale to Silverstein's (1985: 257) assertions that 'a bidirectional dialectic constitutes the minimalest [*sic*] total linguistic fact' and that a 'bidirectional dialectic' is necessary, since 'structure . . . "determines" presupposable use-value' (Silverstein 1985: 256) and since 'structure . . . "is determined by" entailing use-value' (Silverstein 1985: 256). In relation to metafunctional diversity, one could consider pursuing a multi-metafunctional perspective when describing speech functions. This means not only describing the interpersonal lexicogrammatical resources that realise each type of speech function (such as Subject and Finite), but also looking for resources from experiential lexicogrammar (such as volitional Process) and textual lexicogrammar (such as Subject Theme) (Hasan 1985; Thibault and van Leeuwen 1996: 574–5).[13]

Notes

1 See Fawcett, this volume.
2 It should be noted that the description of the interpersonal lexicogrammar covers English only. Descriptive categories such as Subject, Finite and clause types differ in function and form in different languages. See Teruya et al. (2007) for a presentation of MOOD in a number of languages other than English.
3 Halliday's interpersonal definition of the Subject has been one of the most heavily criticised definitions in his language description: see, e.g., Butler (2003); Fawcett (1999, 2008); Huddleston (1988, 1991); Hudson (1996); Matthiessen and Martin (1991). Since the Subject is central to the way in which a clause construes interpersonal meaning, it is worthwhile looking into the critique.
4 An illustration of the speech functions at work and the way in which different speech functions are realised by different Mood types with different (meanings of) Subject and Finite is provided by Halliday in his analysis and interpretation of 'The "silver" text' in his second edition of *An Introduction to Functional Grammar* (Halliday 1994: 368–91).
5 See, e.g., Fawcett (2011) for elaborate descriptions of MOOD.
6 In the CG, there is an explicit level of (and use of the word) syntax; the notion of syntax is largely avoided in the IFG tradition.
7 See Fawcett, this volume.
8 See Taverniers, this volume.
9 See Steffensen (2008) for a discussion of this issue.
10 See also Davidse (1997).
11 See also Halliday's (2002 [1992]) use of Vygotsky.
12 See also Halliday (1989: 3).
13 See also Martin's (2011) notion of 'coupling'.

References

Austin, J.L. 1962. *How to Do Things with Words*. Oxford: Oxford University Press.
Butler, C.S. 2003. *Structure and Function: A Guide to Three Major Structural-Functional Theories, Part 2 – From Clause to Discourse and beyond*. Amsterdam: John Benjamins.
Davidse, K. 1997. The subject–object versus the agent–patient asymmetry. *lb leuvense bijdragen* 86(4): 413–31.
Ervin-Tripp, S. 1964. An analysis of the interaction of language, topic, and listener. In *The Ethnography of Communication*, 66(2): 86–102.
Fawcett, R.P. 1999. On the subject of the Subject in English: Two positions on its meaning (and how to test for it). *Functions of Language* 6(2): 243–73.
Fawcett, R.P. 2008. *Invitation to Systemic Functional Linguistics through the Cardiff Grammar*. London: Equinox.
Fawcett, R.P. 2010. *Alternative Architectures for Systemic Functional Linguistics: How Do We Choose?* (Discussions in Functional Approaches to Language). London: Equinox.
Fawcett, R.P. 2011. A semantic system network for MOOD in English (and some complementary systems). Paper available from fawcett@cardiff.ac.uk.
Fawcett, R.P. Forthcoming. *Functional Syntax Handbook: Analysing English at the Level of Form*. London: Equinox.
Halliday, M.A.K. 1970. *A Course in Spoken English: Intonation*. Oxford: Oxford University Press.
Halliday, M.A.K. 1973. *Explorations in the Functions of Language*. London: Arnold.
Halliday, M.A.K. 1975. *Learning How to Mean: Explorations in the Development of Language*. London: Arnold.
Halliday, M.A.K. 1978. *Language as Social Semiotic*. London: Arnold.
Halliday, M.A.K. 1984. Language as code and language as behaviour: A systemic-functional interpretation of the nature and ontogenesis of dialogue. In R.P. Fawcett, M.A.K. Halliday, S.M. Lamb and A. Makkai (eds) *The Semiotics of Culture and Language, vol. 1*. London: Pinter, pp. 3–36.

Halliday, M.A.K. 1985. *An Introduction to Functional Grammar*. London: Arnold.

Halliday, M.A.K. 1989. *Spoken and Written Language*. 2nd edn. Oxford: Oxford University Press.

Halliday, M.A.K. 1994. *An Introduction to Functional Grammar*. 2nd edn. London: Arnold.

Halliday, M.A.K. 1996. Introduction: Language as social semiotic – The social interpretation of language and meaning. In P. Cobley (ed.) *The Communication Theory Reader*. London: Routledge, pp. 88–93.

Halliday, M.A.K. 2002 [1970]. Language structure and language function. In *Collected Works of M.A.K. Halliday, vol. 1: On Grammar*. London: Continuum, pp. 173–95.

Halliday, M.A.K. 2002 [1992]. How do you mean. In *Collected Works of M.A.K. Halliday, vol. 1: On Grammar*. London: Continuum, pp. 352–68.

Halliday, M.A.K. 2005 [1963]. The tones of English. In *Collected Works of M.A.K. Halliday, Vol. 7: Studies in English Language*. London: Continuum, pp. 237–63.

Halliday, M.A.K. 2005 [1995]. On language in relation to fuzzy logic and intelligent computing. In *Collected Works of M.A.K. Halliday, vol. 6: Computational and Quantitative Studies*. London: Continuum, pp. 196–212.

Halliday, M.A.K., and R. Hasan. 1985. *Language, Context, and Text: Aspects of Language in a Social-Semiotic Perspective*. Geelong, Vic: Deakin University Press.

Halliday, M.A.K., and C.M.I.M. Matthiessen. 1999. *Construing Experience through Meaning*. London: Cassell.

Halliday, M.A.K., and C.M.I.M. Matthiessen. 2014. *An Introduction to Functional Grammar*. 4th edn. London: Routledge.

Hasan, R. 1985. *Offers in the Making: A Systemic-Functional Approach*. Sydney: Macquarie University.

Hasan, R. 1996. *Ways of Saying, Ways of Meaning: Selected Papers of R. Hasan*. London: Cassell.

Hasan, R., C. Cloran, G. Williams and A. Lukin. 2007. Semantic networks: The description of linguistic meaning in SFL. In R. Hasan, C.M.I.M. Matthiessen and J.J. Webster (eds) *Continuing Discourse on Language, Vol. 2: A Functional Perspective*. London: Equinox, pp. 697–738.

Huddleston, R. 1988. Constituency, multi-functionality and grammaticalization in Halliday's functional grammar. *Journal of Linguistics* 24: 137–74.

Huddleston, R. 1991. Further remarks on Halliday's functional grammar: A reply to Matthiessen & Martin. *Occasional Papers in Systemic Linguistics* 5: 75–129.

Hudson, R. 1986. Systemic grammar. *Linguistics* 24: 791–815.

Kress, G. 2010. *Multimodality: A Social Semiotic Approach to Contemporary Communication*. London: Routledge.

Lemke, J. 1995. *Textual Politics*. London: Taylor & Francis.

Levinson, S.C. 1983. *Pragmatics*. Cambridge: Cambridge University Press.

Martin, J.R. 1992. *English Text: System and Structure*. Amsterdam: John Benjamins.

Martin, J.R. 2011. Multimodal semiotics: Theoretical challenges. In S. Dreyfus, S. Hood and M. Stenglin (eds) *Semiotic Margins: Meaning in Multimodalities*. London: Bloomsbury Academic, pp. 243–70.

Matthiessen, C.M.I.M. 1995. *Lexicogrammatical Cartography: English Systems*. Tokyo: International Language Science Publishers.

Matthiessen, C.M.I.M. 2007. The 'architecture' of language according to systemic functional theory: Developments since the 1970s. In R. Hasan, C.M.I.M. Matthiessen and J.J. Webster (eds) *Continuing Discourse on Language, Vol. 2: A Functional Perspective*. London: Equinox, pp. 505–62.

Matthiessen, C.M.I.M., and J.R. Martin. 1991. A response to Hoddleston's review of Halliday's *Introduction to Functional Grammar*. *Occasional Papers in Systemic Linguistics* 5: 5–74.

Searle, J.R. 1969. *Speech Acts: An Essay in the Philosophy of Language*. Cambridge: Cambridge University Press.

Silverstein, M. 1985. Language and the culture of gender: At the intersection of structure, usage, and ideology. In E. Mertz and R.J. Parmentier (eds) *Semiotic Mediation: Sociocultural and Psychological Perspectives*. Orlando, FL: Academic Press, pp. 219–59.

Steffensen, S.V. 2008. Reassessing the systemic functional subject: A hologrammatical interpretation. In N. Nørgaard (ed.) *Systemic Functional Linguistics in Use*. Odense: OWPLC 29, pp. 782–806.

Taverniers, M. 2011. The syntax–semantics interface in systemic functional grammar: Halliday's interpretation of the Hjelmslevian model of stratification. *Journal of Pragmatics* 43(4): 1100–26.

Teruya, K., E. Akerejola, T. Andersen, A. Caffarel-Cayron, J. Lavid, C. Matthiessen, U. Petersen: Patpong and F. Smedegaard. 2007. Typology of MOOD: A text-based and system-based functional view. In R. Hasan, C.M.I.M. Matthiessen and J.J. Webster (eds) *Continuing Discourse on Language, Vol. 2: A Functional Perspective*. London: Equinox, pp. 859–920.

Thibault, P.J. 1995. Mood and the ecosocial dynamics of semiotic exchange. In R. Hasan and P.H. Fries (eds) *On Subject and Theme: A Discourse Functional Perspective*. Amsterdam: John Benjamins, pp. 51–90.

Thibault, P.J., and T. van Leeuwen. 1996. Grammar, society, and the speech act: Renewing the connections. *Journal of Pragmatics* 25: 561–85.

van Leeuwen, T. 2005. *Introducing Social Semiotics*. London: Routledge.

Wittgenstein, L. 1958. *Philosophische Untersuchungen*. Frankfurt: Suhrkamp.

Textual metafunction and theme

What's 'it' about?

Gail Forey and Nicholas Sampson

The textual metafunction

As established by Halliday (Halliday and Matthiessen 2014),[1] systemic functional linguistics (SFL) models language in social context and recognises three general social functions for which language is used: (a) enacting our social relationships; (b) representing our experience to each other and (c) organising our enactments and representations as meaningful text. These are known as the 'metafunctions': the *interpersonal* metafunction enacts relationships; the *ideational* metafunction represents experience and the *textual* metafunction organises text. When discussing the three metafunctions, Halliday (1978: 113) points out that 'the textual function has an enabling function with respect to the other two; it is only in combination with textual meanings that ideational and interpersonal meanings are actualized'. The textual metafunction is realised by the choices a speaker or a writer makes in combining the ideas and reality that he or she wishes to express (ideational), along with the relationship that he or she hopes to project and develop (interpersonal). The organisation of the ideational and the interpersonal plays a key role in developing what it is we mean and how we relate to those with whom we want to interact through language. Halliday (1977: 181) states that the function of the textual metafunction is:

> specifically that of creating a text, of making the difference between language in the abstract and language in use in other words, it is through the semantic options of the textual component that language comes to be relevant to its environment.

Within the textual metafunction, the choice of Theme and Rheme creates the major system. Halliday (1977) attributes the development of Theme to Prague school linguists. However, his interpretation differs from that of the Prague school. He separates the two aspects of Prague school Theme, point of departure and basis/foundation into Theme/Rheme and Given/New, respectively. *Theme* refers to the elements that function as the point of departure, while *Given* refers to the elements that function as the basis or foundation of the clause (Davidse 1987). In many instances, but not all, Theme is conflated with Given information, while New information is contained within the Rheme. Halliday and Matthiessen (2014: 118) elaborate the distinction between Given and New as 'information that is presented by the speaker as recoverable (Given) or not recoverable (New) to the listener'. Thompson (2007: 672) points out that Theme/Given, followed by Rheme/New, 'constructs the clause as a movement from the speaker's point of departure . . . to the information presented as newsworthy for the hearer'. Theme realises what the writer wishes to highlight as the point of departure around which the story unfolds and the New elaborates the field, developing it in experiential terms (Martin 1992a: 452). Halliday argues while the two pairs of clause functions – that is, Theme/Given and Rheme/New – are similar, they are two distinct systems each construing different semantic choices for the text producer (speaker or writer) and being construed in different ways (Halliday and Matthiessen 2014). Martin (1992a) adds that Theme is generally restricted to grounding the genre of the text, while the New is not restricted in this way and is far more flexible.[2] The focus of this chapter is the textual metafunction and Theme, where Theme is the 'glue' that structures and binds together the ideational and interpersonal meanings.

Definition of Theme

Theme is seen as a universal element where the point of departure for the clause is indicated in some way; in every language, there is a way of identifying the message of the clause – that is, what the clause is about. Theme in English is used to refer to 'the first group or phrase that has some function in the experiential structure of the clause' (Halliday and Matthiessen 2014: 91) and everything else is the Rheme. However, in other languages, Theme may not be what comes first in the clause; other languages have different ways of marking the Theme. The Theme of a clause in Japanese, for example, is followed by the particle *wa* or *ga* (Teruya 2009; Thomson 2005); in Tagalog, the particle *ang* is used to identify the Theme of the message (Martin 1983). Gouveia and Barbara (2001) discuss the role of the elided subject in Portuguese. Arús Hita (this volume) provides detailed insights into Theme in Spanish, while Rose (2001) reports on the variation and the role of Theme in different languages such as Chinese, French, Gaelic, German, Japanese Pitjantjara, Tagalog and Vietnamese.

The point of departure is the semantic label and Theme is the lexicogrammatical element. Theme plays a crucial role in focusing and organising the message, and contributes to the coherence and success of the message. Theme can be identified as 'the element that serves as the point of departure; it is that which locates and orients the clause within its context' (Halliday and Matthiessen 2014: 89). Within the clause, everything that is not Theme is classified as Rheme. Rheme is the part of the clause where the Theme is developed (Halliday and Matthiessen 2014). For example, in the clause *I'm not athletic*, *I* is the Theme and *[a]m not athletic* is the Rheme. In English, the focus of the present chapter, special status is given to what comes first (Thompson 2007: 677). The choice of what comes first is 'a textual resource systematically exploited' to effect different patterns (Martin 1992b: 12).

The constituents of Theme: topical, interpersonal and textual Theme

Theme must include an ideational feature and, within the textual metafunction, this is referred to as *topical* or *experiential* Theme. Theme acts as a representation of the experiential elements of the message and is a participant, a process or a circumstance.[3] However, within the clause, that which is found in initial position may include other choices, such as an element that links one clause to a preceding clause, for example *and*, *but*, and such choices are referred to as a *textual* Theme.[4] In addition, another feature often found in initial position before an ideational element is the speaker or writer's viewpoint, such as *sadly, unfortunately*, and this is referred to as *interpersonal* Theme. Halliday and Matthiessen (2014) state that textual and interpersonal Themes do not exhaust the potential of Theme, because they cannot carry any ideational meaning. When a textual or interpersonal Theme is found before the topical Theme, we refer to this as a *multiple* Theme.

A textual Theme may include any combination of a (a) continuative, (b) structural and (c) conjunctive, in that order, which is found preceding the topical Theme. Their role is to relate the clause to the previous clause. A continuative is frequently found in texts to link two clauses together, for example *yes, no, oh, OK, well*. A structural element generally refers to a conjunction, such as *and, because, if*, etc., or a relative, such as *which, who, wherever*. Throughout the discussion, we will draw examples from one text: a moving speech given by Harry Smith, a veteran of the Second World War, at the Labour Party Conference in Brighton in September 2014 (Sky News 2014). Our analysis will uncover how the speaker links together interpersonal and ideational features into a coherent opening, as in example (1).

(1)	Well,	I	came in to this world in the rough and ready year of 1923.
		I	'm from Barnsley
	And	I	can tell you . . .
	textual Theme	topical Theme	Rheme
	Multiple Theme		

The speaker chooses a continuative *well* and an additive conjunction *and* to link a clause to the previous clause. The *well* introduces a discursive element into the monologue to indicate that the speaker wishes to retain the floor. A conjunctive establishes a relationship between two parts of a clause into a single structural unit. A conjunction is a distinct class in the grammar.[5] Textual elements, while typically thematic, may occur other than in initial position in a clause.

Interpersonal Themes function to explicitly construe writer/speaker viewpoint and are realised by Modal Adjuncts, for example *unfortunately, in my opinion, generally* (Halliday and Matthiessen 2014). In addition, vocatives (formal or informal forms of address) and the choice of Mood, such as whether utterances are questions (interrogatives), commands (imperatives) or statements (declaratives), also indicate an interpersonal element. Within an imperative clause such as *don't touch that*, the implicit subject is *you*. The clause therefore has an interpersonal element embedded within the structure. Similarly, an interrogative implicitly carries some form of interpersonal meaning, because an interrogative tacitly involves an interlocutor. The choice of Theme is directly related to the Mood of the clause.[6] Owing to space limitations, we will focus only on declarative mood choice in the present chapter, leaving a fuller discussion of the choice of Mood and Theme in imperatives and interrogatives for a follow-up paper.

Modal Adjuncts are intrinsically interpersonal in nature, adding information that reflects the writer or speaker's judgement. Modal Adjuncts may be found in the Theme and the Rheme of the clause. However, as Halliday and Matthiessen (2014) point out, they are commonly found in thematic position, because if the speaker includes some element that presents his or her own angle on the matter, it is natural to make this the point of departure:

I'll tell you what I think. Modal Adjuncts have two subtypes, Comment Adjuncts and Mood Adjuncts. Comment Adjuncts are realised by expressions, which comment on the clause as a whole, such as *sadly, unfortunately*. As shown in example (2), below, Harry Smith chooses to start a clause complex with the Comment Adjunct, *sadly*, to build up a vivid and persuasive picture of the poverty experienced in his youth, and to express his attitude towards that being the norm in Britain at the time.[7]

(2)	Sadly	rampant poverty and no health care	was the norm for the Britain of my youth
	interpersonal Theme	topical Theme	
			Rheme
	Multiple Theme		

The interpersonal Theme *sadly* sets up the prosodic development of the negative experiences. The term 'prosody' is used to refer to the patterning of meaning found in a text – the waves of meaning that give a text its texture, which Halliday and Hasan (1989) identified as one of two crucial attributes of a text (the other being structure). Texture refers to the way in which resources such as patterns of cohesion create texts that are both cohesive and coherent: 'Texture results where there are language items that tie meanings together in the text as well as tie meanings in the text to the social context in which the text occurs' (Paltridge 2012: 130).

Thematic organisation above the clause

Through the analysis of Theme, we can identify how the textual metafunction weaves a text together through a range of resources to give it a texture and to structure the text as a complete whole. For example, Martin and Rose (2007) suggest that the opening stage of a text can be considered to be the hyperTheme of the text.[8] In addition to hyperTheme, which functions at the level of units above the clause, such as the paragraph, there is also macro-Theme, which is realised as the heading, title or other overarching point of departure for a complete text.[9] While Theme refers to the patterning of discourse within the clause, hyper-Theme refers to the packaging of information within phases of a text. It predicts what will be in the message within each phase (Martin and Rose 2007). For example, the opening of Harry's speech, in example (3), below, is the springboard for the rest of the message, indicating that the text is a personal anecdote, retelling a *barbarous* time without *public health care*. Harry starts by establishing the period and contrasting the fictional upper-class characters of *Downton Abbey*, a British television drama set within this period, with people from Barnsley (a working-class town in the north of England).

(3)　As *you* can see// *I'm* not athletic//// well, *I* came in to this world in the rough and ready year of 1923////*I'm* from Barnsley// and *I* can tell you //*that my childhood* [[like so many others from that era]] was not like an episode from Downton Abbey//// Instead, instead *it* was a barbarous time//*it* was a bleak time// and *it* was an uncivilised time // because *public health care* didn't exist////

Within this hyperTheme, the speaker establishes a context for the text that follows. The most frequent topical Theme is *I* and there are a number of textual Themes, for example *and* and *instead.* The textual Theme *instead* contrasts the experience of the upper class with the *barbarous* experience of the working class. The coordinating conjunction *and* combines with the parallel clause structure, and the development of the new information heightens and provides the opportunity to increase the intensity of this *barbarous, bleak* and *uncivilised* time in history. The repetition of the referent *it* gives the text a rhythm and allows the speaker to highlight the negative New information.

Focusing more closely on the texture and the patterns of Theme within a text, a key feature is thematic progression, first introduced by Daneš (1974). Thematic progression clearly demonstrates the enabling factor of the textual metafunction: how the organisation of clauses within a complete text is linked and developed to form a cohesive whole. Theme 'is the most significant factor in the development of the text' (Halliday and Matthiessen 2014: 132) and provides an opportunity to understand the development of how the choice of what comes first in a clause is made, and how these choices function to link ideas together and develop the text.

Coherence, according to Daneš (1974: 114), as seen through thematic progression, can be seen as 'the choice and ordering of utterance themes, their mutual concatenation and hierarchy, as well as their relationship to hyperThemes of superior text units (such as paragraph, chapter, etc.).' Both Daneš (1974) and Fries (1995a) illustrate the role of Theme in the organisation of a text. Daneš (1974) viewed similar patterns in English and Czech, but was using a feature referred to as 'communicative dynamism' to identify thematicity. Communicative dynamism focuses on the distribution of dynamic elements within sentences (Daneš 1974; Firbas 1992). In looking at the distribution of elements across sentences, Daneš (1974) introduced the notion of thematic progression. Fries (2005, 2009), taking a Hallidayian perspective with a focus on Theme as predominantly the point of departure, analysed the thematic development of texts. Daneš (1974) and Fries (2005, 2009) demonstrated the patterns in thematic progression/development, and both agree on four basic patterns of thematic progression in a text, as shown in Figure 9.1. Throughout all of the examples in the chapter, we will be using **bold** to highlight the marked Theme of the clause and *italics* to identify the Subject.

To illustrate the organisation of a text, we can review thematic development in an extract from Harry's speech, as outlined in Figure 9.2.

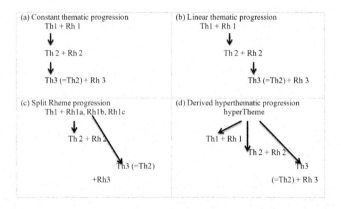

Figure 9.1   Four patterns of thematic progression

Note: Th = Theme; Rh = Rheme

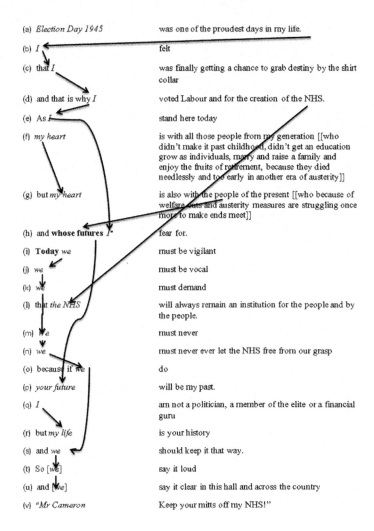

(a) *Election Day 1945*	was one of the proudest days in my life.
(b) *I*	felt
(c) that *I*	was finally getting a chance to grab destiny by the shirt collar
(d) and that is why *I*	voted Labour and for the creation of the NHS.
(e) As *I*	stand here today
(f) *my heart*	is with all those people from my generation [[who didn't make it past childhood, didn't get an education grow as individuals, marry and raise a family and enjoy the fruits of retirement, because they died needlessly and too early in another era of austerity]]
(g) but *my heart*	is also with the people of the present [[who because of welfare cuts and austerity measures are struggling once more to make ends meet]]
(h) and **whose futures** *I**	fear for.
(i) **Today** we	must be vigilant
(j) we	must be vocal
(k) we	must demand
(l) that *the NHS*	will always remain an institution for the people and by the people.
(m) We	must never
(n) we	must never ever let the NHS free from our grasp
(o) because if we	do
(p) *your future*	will be my past.
(q) *I*	am not a politician, a member of the elite or a financial guru
(r) but *my life*	is your history
(s) and we	should keep it that way.
(t) So [we]	say it loud
(u) and [We]	say it clear in this hall and across the country
(v) *"Mr Cameron*	Keep your mitts off my NHS!"

Figure 9.2 Thematic progression: Harry's speech

*The element *I* is included in the Theme because, as shown in example (8b), Theme can be extended to include both the first ideational element and the Subject, and different approaches to identifying the boundary of Theme are discussed in the next section.

As shown in Figure 9.2, the text is extremely cohesive, with all but one of the Themes being derived from Given information, constituting either constant Theme such as the repetition of *I* and *we*, or linear thematic progression as shown in (b), (h) and (l). In addition, we can see that the dominant Theme choice is an unmarked one, in which the Subject and topical Theme are conflated. The limited use of marked Themes, where something other than Subject such as *today* and *your futures* realises topical Theme, emphasises the importance of the 'now' and highlights that our immediate actions have a dramatic influence on the future. There are some textual Themes *and, but, so*, which hold the text together, but these are not the dominant forms that create cohesion and coherence. Only Theme (v) *Mr Cameron* is New information – a thematic choice primed to change the rhythm and afford a prominence to New information placed in initial position. The combination of New information in the Theme and Rheme of clause (v) construes a memorable, conclusive and forceful accumulation of meaning developed throughout the text – that is, a hyperNew for the text as a whole.[10]

Studies of thematic progression – or 'method of development', as Fries (1995a) calls it – have been carried out focusing on professional discourse (Forey 2004; Iedema 1999; Kong 2004; Thompson and Thompson 2009). Banks (2008) discusses thematic development in scientific texts. Most notable are studies that discuss thematic progression within education. Crossley and McNamara (2010), Christie and Derewianka (2008), and Crossley and McNamara (2010) all point out that organisation and coherent writing contribute to the overall success of assessed tasks in written school exams. Coffin (2006) and Coffin and Derewianka (2009) focus on history texts, and identify the key role of Circumstantial Adjuncts that are found in initial position and the role that these choices make in the organisation of history texts. Hood (2009), also focusing on academic writing, highlights the role of hyperTheme in linking ideas at a text level and explicates the paragraph as a key component in successful writing. Owing to space limitations, we are unable to discuss thematic progression in detail in this chapter, but we hope that our brief overview has provided insights into the appliable nature of Theme and the role of the textual metafunction in organising a text.

The studies mentioned above are only a few of the key works that illustrate the role of Theme and the variation of thematic choice across registers. All studies focusing on Theme make the 'invisible' organisation of a text 'visible'. However, such studies have often adopted different units of analysis when analysing Theme, which makes a comprehensive picture of the role of Theme in different registers difficult.

Subject, topic and Theme

A more detailed review of Theme raises a number of contentious issues related to Theme, such as: the difference between Subject, topic and Theme; the unit of analysis of what is classified as Theme and the role and function of marked Theme. All such issues need to be addressed if we are to conduct an analysis of the textual metafunction.

In non-SFL grammars, 'subject' refers to the part of the sentence or clause that usually indicates what the clause is about or who (or what) performs the action (that is, the agent). In SFL, Subject specifically refers to the grammatical Subject, which, in English, is the modally responsible nominal of that which is predicated. Halliday and Matthiessen (2014: 79) identify three different functions for Subject: *psychological, grammatical* and *logical* Subject, which three distinctions have been used to identify:

- the psychological Subject – 'psychological' referring to what the speaker/writer chooses as the point of departure for the message, 'that which is the concern of the message';
- the grammatical Subject, the structure – 'that on which something is predicated' and
- the logical Subject – referring to the doer of the process (the 'doer of the action' being the agent).

Halliday points out that, in some instances, all three – psychological, grammatical and logical Subject – can be conflated, as shown in example (4).

(4)	no one in our community	was safe from poor health, sickness and disease
	psychological Subject	
	grammatical Subject	
	logical Subject	

However, all three are 'quite different things' and therefore different labels are adopted: psychological Subject: Theme; grammatical Subject: Subject and logical Subject: Actor (Halliday and Matthiessen 2014: 80), providing a clear definition of what is meant by the grammatical Subject in English – that is, Subject is that on which something is predicated.[11] The distinction between grammatical Subject and what the message is about can be significantly different. In example (5), below, the Subject and Theme are both conflated, and *my parents* is the Subject and the first element with a 'function in transitivity' in the clause; hence it is not only Theme, but also considered the 'unmarked' Theme.[12]

(5)	*my parents*	did everything in their power to keep Marion alive and comfortable
	unmarked Theme	Rheme

In examples (6) and (7), below, the first element with a 'function in transitivity' is not the Subject, but a Circumstantial Adjunct of Location: Place, *in our home*, and a Circumstantial Adjunct of Manner: Quality, *in my heart*. Circumstantial Adjuncts carry ideational meaning; hence Halliday and Matthiessen (2014) identify this, and only this, element as Theme. When something other than Subject is in initial position, we refer to this as a 'marked' Theme.

(6)	**in our home**	*TB* came for my eldest sister, Marion
	marked Theme	Rheme

Harry deliberately foregrounds another ideational element, *in our home*, invoking an image of warmth and security – *our home* – before introducing the Subject (*TB* – that is, tuberculosis). We refer to this Theme as the marked Theme, where something other than the Subject is found in initial position. As shown in example (7), Harry chooses a Circumstantial Adjunct of Manner to express his anguish, establishing the context before he introduces the Subject of the clause, *I*.

(7)	**in my heart**	*I* can still feel my mum and dad's desperation
	marked Theme	Rheme

A marked Theme is a Theme where the text-producer consciously or unconsciously affects the organisation of the text by choosing something other than the Subject in a declarative clause as the starting point of his or her message. Marked Themes may be realised by a variety of grammatical elements, particularly Circumstantial Adjunct and (less often) Complement. Marked Themes do not merely realise Theme, but exhaust it.

Martin (1992a), Berry (1996) and Martin and Rose (2007) argue that when a marked Theme occurs in first position, it receives more prominence in the clause than if it occurs elsewhere. For example, Coffin's (2006) discussion of the role of Circumstantial Adjunct of time as marked Theme in history texts illustrates their role in organising a text chronologically. Davies (1997: 55) argues that the marked Theme is not recurrent, but rather signals 'changes/shifts or stages in the progression of the discourse'. She further contends that marked Theme choices act as framing elements. All agree that the choice of marked Theme is important and that it plays a crucial role in the interpretation of the message, as shown in Figure 9.2, in which marked Theme is used to emphasise time.

Drawing the boundary for Theme

Gómez-González (2001) points out that topic or Subject is often equated with Theme, and, as Thompson (1996: 121) cautions, 'it is easy to confuse Theme and Subject since we can say that, in some sense, the clause is about both'. Fries (1995a) and Thompson (1996) raise an important question concerning where we should draw the boundary of Theme.

The standard approach to identifying Theme in a clause is based on Halliday and Matthiessen's (2014: 89) definition: 'Theme extends from the beginning of the clause and up to (and including) the first element that has a function in transitivity.' There are a number of divergences from Halliday and Matthiessen (2014) in the identification of Theme, for example Berry (1995), North (2005), Martin and Rose (2007), Forey (2009), Montemayor-Borsinger (2009), Huang (this volume) and others include everything up to the Subject of the clause as Theme. These scholars argue that Theme need not necessarily be restricted to the first ideational element in a clause. They believe that, by including Subject within the Theme, the orientation of the text – the continuity to phases in the discourse – is more visible. The focus here is the text and the choice of Theme in the unfolding at a discourse level, which can help us to understand the organisation and 'periodicity' – a term used by Martin and Rose (2007) to refer to the waves of information flow found in a text. Berry (1996) argues that if only the first ideational element is analysed as Theme, then some co-referential elements will not be captured by an analysis of Theme in a text. She claims that 'the priority concerns, discoursal or causal, of a speaker or writer need not be ideational' (Berry 1996: 19) and that the writer may choose to select a feature as Theme because it relates to the surrounding text, or the concerns of the immediate clause, or something more closely related to the reader's concerns. She argues that the Theme can be seen to act as an interpersonal Theme at a discourse level and that such interpersonal Themes will influence the meaning of a number of clauses or a paragraph – similarly to Halliday and Matthiessen (2014) assigning the clause an interpersonal function through the four basic speech moves (dialogic interactions) of informs, questions, requests and undertakings.

The main argument in favour of analysing the Subject as part of Theme is that the thematic progression and the information flow of a text may thereby be more easily understood (Berry 1995, 1996; Matthiessen 1992, 1995; Ravelli 1995). Matthiessen (1992: 50) points out that 'experiential Adjuncts may pile up at the beginning of the clause and the effect is clearly one of successive Thematic contextualisation'. He refers to this as a 'clustering' of ideational elements. This clustering of ideational elements was found in texts written by civil servants in which there is a cluster of Circumstantial Adjuncts prior to the Subject establishing the context of the clause (Forey 2009).

In defence of counting only the first ideational element as Theme, Thompson and Thompson (2009) add that if the Subject is included, then the grammaticality of the category of Theme will be compromised. This will blur the distinction between the textual and ideational metafunctions. They point out that the mandatory inclusion of the Subject shifts Theme from its intended unit to a wider, and perhaps more vague, semantic meaning. Fries (2009) and Thompson and Thompson (2009: 47) suggest that 'thematic prominence does not end abruptly but fades in a diminuendo'. Thompson and Thompson (2009) coin the term 'minimal Theme' to refer to only the first ideational element and 'maximal theme' where the boundary of Theme extends to include the Subject where preceded by other ideational elements. Fries (1995a: 15), in reviewing the different approaches to what should be included in Theme, posits that the inclusion of the Subject 'finesses the issue of exactly how Theme and Subject interact'. Thompson and Thompson (2009) suggest that, where possible, two levels of analysis should be undertaken, with a focus on the clause and the discourse semantics;[13] 'the two threads of meaning, while both contributing to texture, operate independently' (Thompson and Thompson 2009: 58). A focus on the clause requires attention to minimal Theme (only the first ideational element), because this provides the difference between the metafunctions. At the same time, those looking to understand the logocentric growth of a text may wish to include the Subject within Theme.[14] However, conducting a double analysis of Theme is not always practicable owing to time constraints or necessary given that the most important issue is the analysts' aims, for example depending on whether they are investigating how the textual metafunction operates at the detailed level of the clause or the bigger prosody across a text.

Martin (1992a) advocates analysing Theme in relation to the clause, clause complex, paragraph and text. Whichever unit one chooses to analyse, this choice is motivated by the purpose. Pedagogically motivated work often uses the clause complex or orthographic sentence as the unit of Theme analysis, because sentences are easily recognisable by students with little or no knowledge of grammar (Whittaker 1995). As noted, the analyst's decision on the unit of analysis needs to be motivated by his or her analytical focus. A comparison of examples (8a) and (8b) is illustrative. In example (8a), only the first ideational element is analysed as minimal Theme; in example (8b), analysis of the maximal Theme reveals that the clause is front loaded with a 'cluster' of Circumstantial Adjuncts before the Subject of the clause, *I*, is introduced.

(8a) **in 1945**	after a long hard great depression and a savage and brutal war, at the age of 22 and still in the RAF, *I* voted for the first time.
marked Theme	Rheme

(8b) **in 1945 after a long hard great depression and a savage and brutal war, at the age of 22 and still in the RAF,**	*I*	voted for the first time.
marked Theme	Subject Theme	
		Rheme
Theme		

Both analyses of example (8) are acceptable; however, they highlight the different textual choices, with example (8a) identifying only the time, *in 1945*, and example (8b) including Harry's conscious decision to amplify the negative context of post-war England.

As shown in Table 9.1, through these Circumstantial Adjuncts, Harry emphasises important framing factors: the time, the extent, the conditions, his age (which was well past the age to exercise the right to vote) and where he was – *still in the RAF*. The choice to have a cluster of Circumstantial Adjuncts in initial position is clearly important and its significance would be lost if analysts were to count only the first ideational element as Theme.

If we look at example (9), below, we can see the difference between including Subject in Theme or only the first ideational element.

(9) *I* **still remember hearing** [[while I played as a child on my front step]] ///*the anguished cries* that floated from a nearby neighbour's window/// *they* were the screams from a woman dying from cancer [[who couldn't afford morphine to ease her passage from this life]]///*no one in our community* was safe from poor health, sickness and disease/// **in our home** *TB* came for my eldest sister, Marion/// *tuberculosis* tortured my sister //and *[tuberculosis]* left her an invalid [[who had to be restrained with ropes tied around her bed]]/// *my parents* did everything in their power to keep Marion alive and comfortable// but *they* just didn't have the dosh [[to get her the best clinics, [[find her the best doctors or the right medicines]]]]] instead *she* wasted away before our eyes// **until** *my mother* could no longer handle her care// and *she* was dispatched to the workhouse infirmary // where *she* died at the age of ten, 87 years ago. *Mum and dad* couldn't afford to bury their darling daughter/// **so, like the rest of our country's indigent,** _she_ was dumped nameless into a pauper's pit///

The text of example (9) conforms to Halliday and Matthiessen's (2014) reporting genre, chronicling in a linear and chronological order important and significant occasions in Harry's life. We distinguish unmarked from marked Theme in examples (10) and (11).

The hyperTheme of this extract is identified in example (9). Harry chooses a mental projecting clause *I still remember hearing [[. . .]]*, as a means of creating a powerful visual image of a small boy playing outside his home – an image that should ostensibly be a fondly recalled memory from childhood, but which here sets up the awfulness of what follows: *the anguished cries that floated from the nearby neighbour's window*. When analysing projecting clauses in initial position, there is some agreement that the projecting clause carries the interpersonal meaning – the stance of the speaker – and that the projected clause indicates the main ideational meaning of the clause complex (Forey 2009; Halliday and Matthiessen 2014; Thompson and Thompson 2009).

Table 9.1 Circumstantial Adjuncts

Circumstantial Adjuncts prior to I	Type
in 1945	Circumstantial Adjunct of time
after a long hard great depression and a savage and brutal war	Circumstantial Adjunct of extent and condition
at the age of 22	Circumstantial Adjunct of time
and still in the RAF	Circumstantial Adjunct of location

Generally, at text level, the entire projecting clause is classified as a marked Theme (see example (10)). However, within such clause complexes, the Theme of each clause can be analysed at a more delicate level. Where *I* is seen as the Theme of the projecting clause, *the anguished cries* are the Theme of the projected clause, and *while I* is the textual and topical Theme of the embedded clause.[15]

In reviewing unmarked Theme, in example (10), we see that when the Subject is conflated with the Theme, we have an extremely coherent text centred on family and illness.

(10) *they*	were the screams from a woman dying from cancer
my parents	did everything in their power to keep Marion alive and comfortable
tuberculosis	tortured my sister
she	was dispatched to the workhouse infirmary
unmarked Theme	Rheme

However, as we can see in example (11), Harry has foregrounded a number of marked Themes. In all instances except one, that choice is a circumstantial element: *in our home, until, like the rest of the country's indigent*.

(11) **I still remember hearing [[while I played as a child on my front step]]**	*the anguished cries*	that floated from a nearby neighbour's window
Until	*my mother*	could no longer handle her care
so, like the rest of the country's indigent,	*she*	was dumped into a nameless pauper's pit
marked Theme	Subject Theme* Rheme*	Rheme*

* Two possible interpretations for Theme and Rheme

As in example (9), instead of focusing on the Subject as the Theme, Harry has deliberately foregrounded another ideational element as the marked Theme to draw attention to various elements: Harry uses a marked ideational Theme *until* to highlight the gap in time during which his sister's pain was manageable by his mother and before his sister was sent to the workhouse infirmary, thus stressing the lack of medical care available to the poor at that time in England. In a similar way, Harry foregrounds the marked Theme *so, like the rest of the country's indigent*, instead of the Subject (*she*) to highlight and emphasise just how badly treated the poor were before the establishment of the National Health Service (NHS), thus building upon the main focus of his speech: how terrible life was for many people before universal health care afforded them access to the care, treatment and dignity available to others. As shown in example (11), which offers two possible interpretations for Theme and Rheme, the choice depends on the reason for undertaking the analysis: the analyst might include only the marked Theme choice as Theme, classifying everything else as Rheme, or (taking a maximal approach) might choose to include the Subject as Theme and review how this inclusion reveals patterns in the text. Unfortunately, we do not have the space to discuss in full the benefits of both maximal and minimal Theme; when in doubt, the analyst could use both and compare the different patterns revealed by these different choices.

While Halliday and Matthiessen's (2014) definition of Theme has achieved consensus, the unit of analysis that we classify as Theme remains contentious. When studying the textual metafunction, how a text has texture and hangs together, clear definitions of Theme and the unit of analysis are needed.

Conclusion

The textual metafunction is a theoretical framework that 'enables' the organisation of ideational and interpersonal meaning, construing language from abstract words into language as meaning within a social context (Halliday 1977). Theme identifies the choices made by the speaker or writer with respect to the point of departure for the message. The choice of Theme and thematic progression provides insights into the organisational features of the message, cohesion and development of meaning within and between clauses. Thematic cohesion can be modelled and made explicit, and the ability to make what was previously invisible explicit and visible affords opportunities for analysts, teachers, students and text users to appreciate the flow and the texture of a text, and the patterns that can be identified in language. When undertaking thematic analysis, the purpose of the investigation will determine the unit of analysis. In this sense, what is analysed as Theme is dependent on the aim and purpose of the analysis.

There is therefore some scope for what constitutes the unit of analysis – that is, whether Theme includes only the first ideational element in a clause, as per Halliday and Matthiessen (2014), or extends to the Subject of the clause, as suggested by Berry (1995) and Martin and Rose (2007). The decision of the unit of analysis of Theme needs to be justified and established prior to starting any analysis. A strong argument for including the Subject as part of Theme is that the thematic progression and information flow of a text can more readily be seen and understood if the Subject is included. In contrast, if the focus is at the clause level, analysing only the first ideational element can reveal interesting choices made within a text. Another contentious issue concerns the difference between Subject, topic and Theme, with Subject and topic often conflated into Theme. A further point is the role and function of marked Theme, whereby the way in which the writer or speaker consciously or unconsciously impacts on the organisation of a text by choosing something other than the Subject as the starting point of their message raises the issue of how marked Themes are realised.

More research on Theme needs to be carried out in terms of cross-linguistic differences, multimodal choices and registerial differences of different texts if analysts and text producers are to develop a greater understanding of how Theme choices structure text. Research focusing on Theme provides revealing information about texts not only for analysts, but for everyone involved in constructing texts. Ideally, a shared archive of digitally available analysis of Theme, to include a range of different registers and languages, would be extremely beneficial in helping us to understand how meaning is enabled through the textual metafunction.

Notes

1 See also Bateman and Asp, both this volume.
2 See also O'Grady, this volume, for a fuller discussion of Given and New.
3 See Davidse, this volume, for a discussion of transitivity.

4 Within the Cardiff Grammar, these features would not be classified as Theme: see Huang, this volume.

5 See Martin and Rose (2007) and Halliday and Matthiessen (2014) for a more detailed discussion.

6 For a detailed discussion of Mood, see Anderson, this volume.

7 See Halliday and Matthiessen (2014) for an overview of Mood and Comment Adjuncts.

8 See also Hood (2009).

9 See Martin and Rose (2007) for a detailed discussion.

10 See Martin and Rose (2007) for a full discussion of hyperNew.

11 See Arús Hita, this volume, for a discussion of Subject in Spanish.

12 For transitivity, see Davidse, this volume.

13 See Tann, this volume.

14 See Martin (1992a: ch. 6) for additional discussion.

15 See Berry, this volume, for an overview of embedded clauses.

References

Banks, D. 2008. The significance of thematic structure in the scientific journal article, 1700–1980. *Odense Working Papers in Language and Communications* 29: 481–502.

Berry, M. 1995. Thematic options and success in writing. In M. Ghadessy (ed.) *Thematic Development in English Texts*. London: Pinter, pp. 55–84.

Berry, M. 1996. What is Theme? A(nother) personal view. In M. Berry, R. Fawcett and G. Huang (eds) *Meaning and Form: Systemic Functional Interpretations*. Norwood, NJ: Ablex, pp. 1–64.

Christie, F., and B. Derewianka. 2008. *School Discourse*. London: Continuum.

Coffin, C. 2006. *Historical Discourse: The Language of Time, Cause and Evaluation*. London: Continuum.

Coffin, C., and B. Derewianka. 2009. Mulitmodality layout in school history books: The texturing of historical interpretation. In G. Forey and G. Thompson (eds) *Text Type and Texture: In Honour of Flo Davies*. London: Equinox, pp. 191–215.

Crossley, S.A., and D.S. McNamara. 2010. Cohesion, coherence, and expert evaluations of writing proficiency. In S. Ohlsson and R. Catrambone (eds) *Proceedings of the 32nd Annual Conference of the Cognitive Science Society*. Austin, TX: Cognitive Science Society, pp. 984–9.

Daneš, F. 1974. Functional sentence perspective and the organisation of the text. In F. Daneš (ed.) *Papers on Functional Sentence Perspective*. The Hague: Mouton, pp. 106–28.

Davidse, K. 1987. M.A.K. Halliday's functional grammar and the Prague school. In R. Dirven and V. Fried (eds) *Functionalism in Linguistics* (Linguistic and Literary Studies in Eastern Europe 20). Amsterdam and Philadelphia, PA: John Benjamins, pp. 39–79.

Davies, F. 1997. Marked Theme as a heuristic for analysing text-type, text and genre. In J. Pique and D. Viera (eds) *Applied Languages: Theory and Practice in ESP*. Valencia: Servei de Publications Universitat de Valencia, pp. 45–71.

Firbas, J. 1992. *Functional Sentence Perspective in Written and Spoken Communication*. Cambridge: Cambridge University Press.

Forey, G. 2004. Workplace texts: Do they mean the same for teachers and business people? *English for Specific Purposes* 23(4): 447–69.

Forey, G. 2009. Marked interpersonal themes: Projecting clauses in workplace texts. In G. Forey and G. Thompson (eds) *Text Type and Texture: In Honour of Flo Davies*. London: Equinox, pp. 151–74.

Fries, P.H. 1995a. Themes, methods of development, and texts. In R. Hasan and P.H. Fries (eds) *On Subject and Theme: A Discourse Functional Perspective*. Amsterdam: John Benjamins, pp. 317–59.

Fries, P.H. 1995b. Patterns of information in initial position in English. In P.H. Fries and M. Gregory (eds) *Discourse in Society: Systemic Functional Perspectives*. Norwood, NJ: Ablex, pp. 47–66.

Fries, P.H. 2009. The textual metafunction as a site for discussion of the goals of linguistics and techniques of linguistic analysis. In G. Forey and G. Thompson (eds) *Text Type and Texture: In Honour of Flo Davies*. London: Equinox, pp. 8–44.

Gómez-González, M.A. 2001. *The Theme–Topic Interface: Evidence from English*. Amsterdam and Philadelphia, PA: John Benjamins.

Gouveia, C.A.M., and L. Barbara. 2001. *Marked or Unmarked That Is Not the Question, The Question Is: Where's The Theme?* (Direct Working Papers 45). Liverpool: University of Liverpool.

Halliday, M.A.K. 1977. Text as semantic choice in social contexts. In T.A. van Dijk and J. Petofi (eds) *Grammars and Descriptions.* Berlin and New York: de Gruyter. pp, 176–225.

Halliday, M.A.K. 1978. *Language as a Social Semiotic: The Social Interpretation of Language and Meaning.* London: Arnold.

Halliday, M.A.K., and R. Hasan. 1989. *Language, Context, and Text: Aspects of Language in a Social-Semiotic Perspective.* Oxford: Oxford University Press.

Halliday, M.A.K., and C.M.I.M. Matthiessen. 2014. *Halliday's Introduction to Functional Grammar.* 4th edn. London and New York: Routledge.

Hood, S. 2009. Texturing interpersonal meanings in academic argument: Pulses and prosodies of value. In G. Forey and G. Thompson (eds) *Text Type and Texture: In Honour of Flo Davies.* London: Equinox, pp. 216–33.

Iedema, R. 1999. Formalising organizational meaning. *Discourse & Society* 10(1): 49–66.

Kong, K. 2004. Marked themes and thematic patterns in abstracts, advertisements and administrative documents. *Word* 55(3): 343–62.

Martin, J.R. 1983. Participant identification in English, Tagalog and Kate. *Australian Journal of Applied Linguistics* 3(1): 45–74.

Martin, J.R. 1992a. *English Text.* Amsterdam: John Benjamins.

Martin, J.R. 1992b. Theme, method of development in existentiality: The price of reply. *Occasional Papers in Systemic Linguistics* 6: 147–84.

Martin, J.R., and D. Rose. 2007. *Working with Discourse.* London: Continuum

Matthiessen, C.M.I.M. 1992. Interpreting the textual metafunction. In M. Davies and L. Ravelli (eds) *Advances in Systemic Linguistics: Recent Theory and Practice.* London: Pinter, pp. 37–81.

Matthiessen, C.M.I.M. 1995. Theme as an enabling resource in ideational 'knowledge' construction. In M. Ghadessy (ed.) *Thematic Development in English Texts.* London: Pinter, pp. 20–47.

Montemayor-Borsinger, A. 2009. Text-type and texture: The potential of Theme for the study of research writing development. In G. Forey and G. Thompson (eds) *Text Type and Texture: In Honour of Flo Davies.* London: Equinox, pp. 108–24.

North, S. 2005. Disciplinary variation in the use of theme in undergraduate essays. *Applied Linguistics* 26(3): 431–52.

Paltridge, B. 2012. *Discourse Analysis: An Introduction.* London: Bloomsbury.

Ravelli, L. 1995. Metafunctional interaction from a dynamic perspective: Implications for the description of Theme. In R. Hasan and P.H. Fries (eds) *On Subject and Theme: From the Perspective of Functions and Discourse.* Amsterdam: John Benjamins, pp. 187–234.

Rose, D. 2001. Some variations in Theme across language, *Functions of Language* 8(1): 109–46.

Sky News. 2014. 92-year-old war veteran Harry Smith at the Labour Party Conference. 24 September. Available online at https://www.youtube.com/watch?v=CsmIfDNeKLY

Teruya, K. 2009. Grammar as a gateway into discourse: A systemic functional approach to subject, theme, and logic, *Linguistics and Education* 20(1): 67–79.

Thompson, G., 1996. *Introducing Functional Grammar.* London: Arnold.

Thompson, G. 2007. Unfolding Theme: The development of clausal and textual perspectives on Theme. In R. Hasan, C.M.I.M. Matthiessen and J. Webster (eds) *Continuing Discourse on Language: A Functional Perspective.* London: Equinox, pp. 671–96.

Thompson, G., and S. Thompson. 2009. Theme, Subject and the unfolding of text. In G. Forey and G. Thompson (eds) *Text Type and Texture: In Honour of Flo Davies.* London: Equinox, pp. 45–69.

Thomson, E. 2005. Theme unit analysis: A systemic functional treatment of textual meanings in Japanese. *Functions of Language* 12(2): 151–79.

Whittaker, R. 1995. Theme, processes and the realisation of meaning in academic articles. In M. Ghadessy (ed.) *Thematic Development in English Texts.* London: Pinter, pp. 105–28.

Intonation and systemic functional linguistics

The way forward

Gerard O'Grady[1]

Introduction

The systemic functional linguistics (SFL) theory of intonation in English developed by Halliday, in a series of publications in the early 1960s, presented in a monograph in 1967 and subsequently in a textbook in 1970 with accompanying sound files, is paradoxically both radical and traditional. It is traditional in the sense that it adopted the forms of traditional intonation analysis – notably, the primary nuclear tones – and chunked speech into units containing a complete intonation curve. Yet it is simultaneously radical in the sense that intonation is described in terms of abstract phonological choices that are themselves the realisation of grammatical choices.

In SFL, the tone group is the highest ranked unit in the phonological rank scale. It is formed from one or more feet, which are themselves formed from one or more syllables, which are in turn formed from one or more phonemes. Each foot contains a mandatory ictus followed by an optional remiss. The ictus is realised by a salient syllable or a silent beat. Intonation is described in a rank scale analogous to that of clause grammar. Halliday inherited from scholars at Edinburgh – chiefly, David Abercrombie – the view that English is a stress-timed language. The consequences of these two theoretical presuppositions will be examined in this chapter to illustrate how they have obscured areas of commonalities with other approaches to intonation and to open up areas for future research in SFL.

Critical issues and topics

Before examining the SFL description of intonation in English, its function as a meaning-making resource will first be described. The intention is to foreground how different theoretical underpinnings create space to allow for different and richer interpretations of the meaning-making contribution of intonation. SFL's unique view of intonation as a dynamic meaning-making grammatical resource contrasts with one whereby intonation is considered to be an attitudinal overtone, for example Bolinger's (1972: 20) famous metaphorical description of intonation as the waves and swells superimposed on the tide of communication. Swells are, in SFL terms, tone groups and waves are tones.

SFL views language as a social-semiotic meaning-making resource that has evolved along complementary, but independent, strands of meaning: the SFL metafunctions. Unlike earlier editions of Halliday's *Introduction to Functional Grammar*, intonation is no longer presented in a separate section, as it was in the second edition (Halliday 1994), in which it was restricted to Chapter 8, but is now thoroughly integrated into the description of the grammar. In the fourth edition (Halliday and Matthiessen 2014: 114–21), the systems of Tonality and Tonicity are described as part of the Textual Metafunction; intonation functions as a resource for creating relevance to context by demarking the extent of the units of information and projecting which part(s) of the information unit is (are) irrecoverable information. Halliday now describes Tone as an Interpersonal resource, with the opposition between falling and rising tones signalling the opposition between certainty and uncertainty (Halliday and Matthiessen 2014: 166–70). Moreover, SFL's polysystemic picture of language enables Halliday to note that Tone also functions to signal logical relations between tone groups (Halliday and Matthiessen 2014: 553–4).

Tench (1996a), presenting the Cardiff variety of SFL, has proposed that intonation realises six functions. These functions are presented in Table 10.1. As implied above, the fact that the tone group is postulated to be the highest element of the phonological rank restricts discussion of how speakers group (at least in pre-scripted genres) tone groups into spoken paragraphs. SFL considers non-tonic prominences as primarily rhythmical saliences and has not focused on how pitch declination[2] is used by speakers to organise their text into spoken paragraphs.

At the end of this chapter, some suggestions for showing how Hallidayan SFL could usefully incorporate concepts such as declination into its description of intonation will be presented. Before that, however, "I will set out how SFL formalises intonation and, subsequently, SFL's formalism will be contrasted with that of the tones and breaks indices (ToBI) framework – that is, an alternate approach to the study of intonation. This is done with the aim of illustrating the overlaps and divergences between the two approaches.

Current contributions and research: a critical overview

SFL, along with traditional British analyses of intonation such as O'Connor and Arnold (1973), recognises that speakers segment their speech into chunks, known as 'tone groups', each of which contain one complete intonation contour. Halliday (1967: 33) argued that each tone group represented a unit of information, which he labelled an 'information unit'. Boomer and Laver (1968), in a series of studies investigating speech errors, found that slips

Table 10.1 The six functions of intonation

Function	Metafunction/System	Realisation
Organisation of Information	Textual	Declination
	Logical	Tone
Realisation of communicative functions	Interpersonal/Mood	Tone
Expression of attitude	Interpersonal/Attitude	Secondary tone
Syntactic meanings	Textual/Tonality	Tone group
Textual structure	Textual/Tonicity	Tonic syllable
Identification of spoken genres	All	All[3]

Source: Tench (1996a)

of the tongue tended to occur prior to tonic words and that pauses within, but not between, tone groups were perceived as markers of hesitation (cf. O'Grady 2010: 106–10). This led Boomer and Laver (1968: 9) to state that 'the tone unit is handled in the central nervous system as a unitary behavioural act'. The intonation unit (IU) storage hypothesis developed by linguists such as Chafe (1994: 55) and Croft (1995: 872) similarly claims that IUs are pre-compiled in short-term memory and that their restricted size reflects biological processing limits. Thus it seems that Halliday's equation of tone group and information unit rests on solid foundations.

In SFL, the chunking of speech is known as Tonality and the segmentation may be marked or unmarked. In the unmarked case, the tone group is coterminous with a single ranking clause. Halliday and Greaves (2008: 101) claim that unmarked tonality occurs around 60 per cent of the time in continuous dialogue. Corpus evidence from non-SFL scholars such as Crystal (1975) and Croft (1995) provides clear evidence for the correspondence between tone groups and clauses – although both scholars note that tone groups are frequently coterminous with structural units below the clause. Croft (1995) argues that a tone group will be coterminous with grammatical structures other than the clause if the clause is syntactically complex and exceeds the limits of short-term memory storage. Furthermore, speakers tend to place parallel structures into separate tone groups. Elements that are not central to clause structure, such as adjuncts, tend to be placed within their own tone group and produced with a rising tone. Croft's findings are very much in line with those expressed by SFL, which notes that long clauses are often realised in speech as two tone groups, with the division occurring either between Theme and Rheme or between nucleus and Adjunct. Similarly, SFL recognises that marked examples of tonality with circumstantial elements placed in separate tone groups are likely.

In the SFL phonological scale, tone groups consist of one or more feet, which themselves consist of one or more syllables, themselves consisting of one or more phonemes. Thus, as well as normally equating with clauses and realising information units, tone groups are units of rhythm. Halliday's view of rhythm was heavily influenced by Abercrombie (1967), who developed the insight that most languages patterned towards a stress-timed or a syllable-timed rhythm. Abercrombie argued that English was a stress-timed language containing isochronous descending feet. While such a view elegantly captures the perceptual difference between rhythmic patterns in languages with and without reduced vowels, it has been empirically falsified (for example Roach 1982; Dauer 1983; Grabe and Low 2002). While SFL no longer explicitly claims that feet in English are isochronous, as Halliday (1994: 293–4) earlier stated, neither has it ever explicitly distanced itself from the claim.

Halliday and Matthiessen (2014: 13) simply note that the perception of English rhythm 'derives from the marked contrast between strong and weak syllables'. This claim agrees with numerous studies of rhythm – notably, Bolinger (1981), a hugely influential paper that notes that English rhythm derives from the presence of three weak vowels, /ə/, /ɪ/ and /ʊ/ – and the unique properties of English syllable structure. It must be admitted, however, that the claim 'that strong syllables tend to occur at roughly even intervals', and the approving mention of Catford's now discredited claim that rhythm results from the modulation of the airstream mechanism by chest and stress pulses (Halliday and Matthiessen 2014: 13), illustrates an unhealthy and unhelpful lingering attraction to the notion of isochrony.

Thus, while not denying the importance of rhythm as a meaning-making device, for present analytical purposes we can focus on the contribution of pitch in isolation from rhythm, although we must be cognisant of the danger of not focusing solely on

(A)Non-salience^<u>Salience</u>^Non-salience^<u>Salience</u>^Non-salience^(B)**Tonic**^Non-salience^(C)**Tonic**(D)^<u>Salience</u>^Non-salience^**Tonic**(E)^Non-salience^(F)<u>Salience</u>^Non-salience^**Tonic**

Figure 10.1 Chunking speech into four tone groups

phonological structure and remember that the structure itself is the result of systemic – that is, meaningful choice. Yet separating pitch from rhythm has important consequences: first, it allows SFL analyses to be compared more easily with non-SFL work on intonation, such as ToBI; and secondly, it allows for a new view of the function of pre-tonic saliences in signalling information structure and of the role of pitch in organising tone groups into paragraph-like units.[4]

In speech, the exact boundaries between tone groups may be indistinct (Brown et al. 1980). Yet, as Greaves (2007) observes, indeterminacy in the actual location of tone group boundaries is not functionally significant; what matters is that the exact number of tone groups/information units can be determined. Each tone group consists of a mandatory tonic or nuclear syllable, with optional salient and non-salient syllables. A tone group may commence with a tonic syllable, a pre-head or a head. A pre-head contains one or more non-salient syllables; a head contains an initial salience followed by other optional saliences and non-saliences. The combination of pre-head and head form the pre-tonic. This, if present, is followed by a tonic, which may itself be followed by a tail consisting of one or more non-tonic syllables. Thus, perceptually, the speech signal consists of a succession of syllables, some salient, some non-salient and others tonic. These are chunked into a series of tone groups containing a single tonic syllable (see Figure 10.1).

The presence of the four tonics entails the presence of four tone groups. (There will be a discussion of compound tone groups shortly.) The first tone group, marked in Figure 10.1 by (A), commences with a pre-head, contains a head and culminates either with the tonic marked by (B) or the immediately following non-salient segment. However, the tonic marked by (C) is unquestionably part of the second tone group; the exact boundary lies between the two tonics.[5] The boundary between the third and fourth tone group, marked by (D), is unambiguous, falling between the tonic and the following head (onset). However, the boundary between the third and fourth tonic is again ambiguous, and falls somewhere after the tonic syllable marked by (E) and the start of the head marked by (F). In summary, the speech signal consists of significant events, the saliences and tonics, and the non-significant transitions between the points of significance. This is a view that we will see towards the end of the chapter is remarkably similar to that set out by ToBI theorists (Ladd 2008).

When studying the functional significance of intonation, we, as analysts, need concern ourselves only with the significant events. Halliday (1967) noted that lexical items could be presented as recoverable or non-recoverable through variations in the placement of the tonic syllable. Unmarked Tonicity occurs when the final lexical item contains the tonic syllable; any other tonic placement represents marked Tonicity. Examples (1)–(3), with salient and tonic syllables underlined, illustrate.[6]

(1) // <u>Geo</u>rgia   <u>bought</u> | a new <u>book</u> //   Unmarked

| NEW FOCUS |

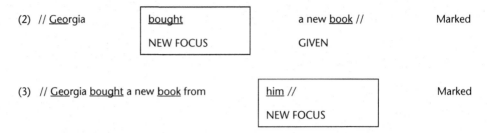

In all of the examples, the final lexical item in the tone group is *a new book*. However, it is the focus – that is, 'the portion that the speaker is drawing particular attention to' (Halliday and Greaves 2008: 103) – only in example (1). Example (2) focuses on the buying and appears be a response to a possible question, such as *What was done to a new book?* The presence of *a new book* is signalled to be recoverable. The focus on the object pronoun in example (3) contrasts *him*, a non-lexical item, with some other possible source of the new book. Thus, informationally, the tonic syllables represent the foci of the messages. The elements following the Tonic syllable are Given.

The informational status of the lexical items preceding the tonic is, Halliday claims, ambiguous. They may be Given or New depending on whether or not they are recoverable from the context. However, Halliday and Matthiessen (2014: 117) note that the presence of a rhythmic salience suggests that *needs* is the beginning of the New in example (4) and its absence in example (5) indicates that it is part of the Given.

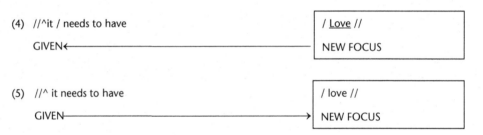

While *needs* in example (4) is rhythmically salient as the ictus element in the foot, it is also pitch-prominent. Dauer (1983) and Ladd (2008) state that, in English, rhythmically salient syllables serve as turning points in the intonation contour. The spectrographs of my own reading of examples (4) and (5), in Figures 10.2 and 10.3, illustrate the role of pitch in signalling the salience of *needs* in example (4) and in signalling its non-salience in example (5).[7]

The pitch turning on the vowel nucleus on *needs* signals the perceptual salience of the syllable and hence the lexical item. Conversely, in Figure 10.3, *needs* is deaccented (Ladd 2008) and backgrounded. Unlike in Figure 10.2, there is only a single point of intonational salience: in this case, the tonic.

There will be a further discussion of the significance of salient pre-tonic syllables in the following section, once SFL's view of intonation has been contrasted with that of ToBI. Tonic placement signals which lexical items are presented as not recoverable. In instances of marked tonality, tonic placement signals that post-tonic items are presented as recoverable.[8] If salient syllables are not a reflex of rhythm, it would seem likely that they also represent informationally meaningful choices. Speakers make pre-tonic syllables salient to signal their view that the syllables are contained within lexical items of informational significance.

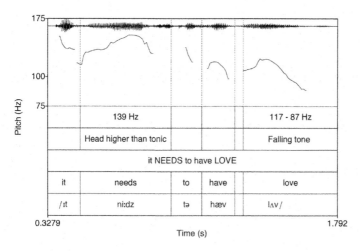

Figure 10.2 Spectrograph of example (4)

As with tonic syllables, analysts cannot simply assume that the informational status of a head depends on whether or not it has been previously mentioned or is in the air; they must factor in the speaker's intonational choices.

The final system of intonation is tone. Halliday (1967) and Halliday and Greaves (2008) propose a tonal inventory of seven primary tones. In declarative mood, falling tone (tone 1) signals certainty and rising tone (tone 2) signals uncertainty. A fall-rise (tone 4) signals that something seemed certain, but is not, while a rise-fall (tone 5) signals that something seemed uncertain, but is in fact certain. A level tone, phonologically commutable with a low-rise (tone 3), signals opt-out: the speaker is neither certain nor uncertain.

The remaining two tones 13 (pronounced 'one three') and 53 (pronounced 'five three') are compound. Halliday (1967: 16) labelled them as 'double tonics', with the second tonic projecting a minor focus. He treats them as a single tone because he claims that the tones

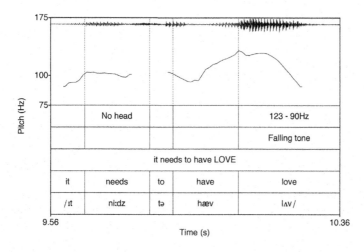

Figure 10.3 Spectrograph of example (5)

have fused into one single tone group with a single, optional, initial pre-tonic selection. There can be no possibility of introducing a pre-tonic element between the two (Halliday 1967: 13, fn 4). Tench (1990: 168–70) rejects the necessity of incorporating the description of sequences of tones 1 and 5, followed by tone 3, as compounds because there is, in fact, the possibility of inserting a pre-tonic segment between the tones in certain cases. He points out a number of examples from Halliday (1970) in which compound tones are notated despite the presence of an intervening pre-tonic segment. Indeed, there are further examples found in Halliday and Greaves (2008) – as illustrated in example (6) (Halliday and Greaves 2008: 12) – in which it is difficult to interpret *take* as anything other than a pre-tonic segment in the second tone group.

(6)   // 13 Roger 'll / take you / home //

Furthermore, the criterion of information structure posits that a tone group equates to an information unit. This is compromised by positing two foci, albeit of different status, within a compound tone group. There is overwhelming support for the view that tone 3 following tone 1 signals that the content of the second tone group represents a minor point of information that modifies what comes before (Cruttenden 1997). For these reasons, compound tone groups will be treated as sequences of independent tone groups in the remainder of this chapter.

Secondary tone realises more delicate meanings in the interpersonal systems of key. For instance, in a declarative mood utterance, a wide fall (tone 1+) signals strong commitment to a proposition, as in example (7).

(7a) // 1 it is going to be sunny today //

(7b) // 1+ it is going to be sunny today //

The initial height and depth of the fall in example (7b) conveys a stronger key and is a more forceful utterance. Like tone 5, it signals greater commitment to the expressed proposition. Table 10.2 lists the form and function of primary tones in declarative, interrogative and imperative mood. Readers interested in exploring all the available key choices are invited to pronounce the example utterances contained within the table with agnate tone choices.

Tone groups may have optional pre-tonic segments that represent what Halliday and Greaves (2008: 168) label 'indirect secondary tone choices'. A pre-tonic segment choice is constrained by the following tone choice and, like secondary tone choices, it represents a more delicate, but still systemic, tonal selection.

- There are three potential pre-tonics available with a tone 1 choice. The unmarked pre-tonic, notated as tone.1, tends to follow a steady course by either drifting downwards, remaining fairly level or (less usually) drifting upwards. Tone –1 is a bouncing pre-tonic, with each salient syllable starting from a low dipping tone and going rapidly up to about mid-high (Halliday and Greaves 2008: 171). This option conveys an argumentative or contrastive key. A further option is the listing pre-tonic notated as tone ...1, which functions to coordinate a list of items within a single tone group.
- There are two pre-tonic options associated with tone 2. The first is the neutral tone.2, which is high and tends to be fairly level. There is a significant jump down to the tonic syllable prior to the tone movement. The other option, tone –2, represents an involved variant and is realised by low-level pitch prior to the tonic.

Table 10.2 The primary tones of English: form and function

Tone	Primary/Secondary	Realisation	Function
DECLARATIVE MOOD e.g. // <u>john</u> / <u>stole</u> the rhi / <u>no</u>ceros //			
Tone 1	**Primary**	**Fall**	**Statement**
Tone 1*	Secondary	wide fall	Strong statement
Tone 1.	Secondary	mid fall	Neutral statement
Tone 1 -	Secondary	low fall	Mild statement
Tone 2	**Primary**	**Rise**	**Querying statement**
Tone 2.	Secondary	High rise	Neutral querying statement
Tone <u>2</u>	Secondary	Sharp fall-rise	Querying point specified
Tone 3	**Primary**	**Level**	**Uncommitted statement**
Tone 4	**Primary**	**Fall-Rise**	**Contingent statement**
Tone 4.	Secondary	High fall-rise	Contingent statement
Tone <u>4</u>	Secondary	Low fall-rise	Stronger contingent statement
Tone 5	**Primary**	**Rise-Fall**	**Committed statement**
Tone 5.	Secondary	Mid to high rise-fall	Committed statement
Tone <u>5</u>	Secondary	low to mid rise-fall	Highly committed
INTERROGATIVE MOOD Y/N e.g., // ^ did he / <u>steal</u> the rhi / **no**ceros //			
Tone 1			Strong demand, conducive
Tone 2			Neutral polar interrogative
Tone <u>4</u>			Assertion
Tone 3			Uncommitted
Tone 5			Committed or surprised
INTERROGATIVE MOOD WH e.g. // who / <u>stole</u> the rhi / **no**ceros //			
Tone 1			Neutral
Tone 2			Mild
INTERROGATIVE MOOD WH e.g. // **who** / stole the rhi / noceros // (Marked tonicity)			
Tone 2			Echo question
IMPERATIVE MOOD e.g. // shut the / **win**dow //			
Tone 1			neutral
Tone 3			mild
IMPERATIVE MOOD e.g. // don't / **go** //			
Tone 1			neutral
Tone 3			warning
IMPERATIVE MOOD e.g. // an<u>swer</u> the / **quest**ion //			
Tone 1			neutral
Tone 3			answer
Tone <u>4</u>			compromise
Tone 5			insistent

- There are also two pre-tonic options associated with tone 3. The first, the neutral one, is notated as tone.3 and, like tone.2, is realised with a significant jump down prior to the tonic. The marked variant tone –3, like tone –2, is realised by a low-level pitch and there is no significant jump down to the tonic. In declarative mood, tone –3 realises a jokey or casual key, but in imperative mood, it may draw attention to the seriousness of what is being requested (Halliday and Greaves 2008: 179).
- SFL does not recognise any systematic pre-tonic options that are associated with tones 4 and 5.

Figure 10.4 summarises the resulting nineteen options.

Tone functions not only to signal Interpersonal meaning, but also Logical meaning. Halliday and Greaves (2008: 130–5) propose the relationships set out in Table 10.3. It details the proposed Logical function of tone in sequences of tone groups.

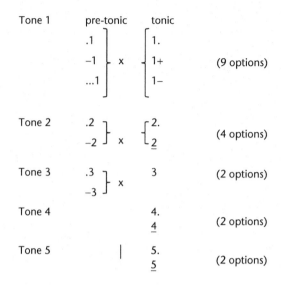

Figure 10.4 The primary, secondary and secondary indirect tones of English

Source: Adapted from Halliday and Greaves (2008: 181)

The details set out in Table 10.3 are not prescriptive. Halliday and Greaves (2008: 131) acknowledge that any tone can follow any tone regardless of the tactic relations created by the lexicogrammar. However, they also claim that sequences not set out in Table 10.3 are marked, and represent a tension between the intonation and the lexicogrammar. These marked meanings consequently create new meanings through the recombination of independent systems. Yet, other than El-Menoufy (1969) and O'Grady (2013), there has been

Table 10.3 The Logical function of tone[y]

Tone 1 followed by tone 1 = two unrelated tone groups, e.g.

// 1 I went to <u>town</u> // 1 I met <u>Jane</u> //

Tone 3 followed by tone 1 = one paratactic tone group complex, e.g.

// 3 I went to <u>town</u> // 1 and met <u>Jane</u> //

Tone 4 followed by tone 1 = one hypotactic tone group complex, e.g.

// 4 to meet <u>Jane</u> // 1 I went to <u>town</u> //

Tone 1 followed by tone 4 = one hypotactic tone group complex, e.g.

// 1 I went to <u>town</u> // 4 to meet <u>Jane</u> //

Tone concord expansion, elaborating parataxis = tone repetition,[10] e.g.

// 1 I met <u>Jane</u> // 1 she is an old <u>school</u> friend // 1 and she is Mike's <u>sister</u> //

Tone concord expansion, elaborating hypotaxis = tone repetition, e.g.

// 1 I met <u>Jane</u> // 1 who is an old <u>school</u> friend // 1 besides being Mike's <u>sister</u> //

---

scant investigation of tone sequencing in discourse, so these claims remain in need of empirical verification.

Where the relationship between the clauses is one of projection, the unmarked realisation is that the projecting clause does not constitute its own tone group. While example (8) is illustrated with tone 1, any tone choice is possible.

(8a) // 1 he said Jane is buying a new <u>car</u> //   Paratactic projection locution

(8b) // 1 he said that Jane was buying a new <u>car</u> //   Hypotactic projection locution

Because no extensive corpus investigation of this claim has been undertaken, this claim too remains empirically unverified.

Tench (1990, 1996a), building upon the work of Halliday (1967: 37), argues that tone choice signals the informational status of the propositions contained within tone groups and also the dependency relationship between adjoining tone groups. His claim is that, no matter the tactic relationship set up by the lexicogrammar, the relationships set out in Table 10.4 hold.

Tench's claims are very much in accord with those expressed by scholars working within the ToBI tradition. However, once again, there has not yet been an empirical investigation of a large corpus to validate his claims. For instance, while there seems to be a tendency for tone 4 to accompany tone groups containing only thematic material (Cruttenden 1997) and especially those coinciding with marked theme, we simply do not know, without examining large-scale corpora, how prevalent this tendency is. O'Grady (2010) has noted that separating the theme,

Table 10.4 The organisation of intonation

Tones 1 or 5 = Major information, e.g.

// 1 I went to <u>town</u> //

Tone 2 or 3 followed by tone 1 = Major incomplete information, e.g.

// 3 I went to <u>town</u>   // 1 to see <u>Jane</u> //

   Incomplete   Complete

Tones 2 or 3 preceded by tone 1 = Minor information

// 1 I went to <u>town</u>   // 3 to see <u>Jane</u> //

   Major   Minor

Tone 4 in final position

// 1 I went to <u>town</u>   // 4 to see <u>Jane</u> //

   Major   Major implication

Tone 4 in non-final position

// 4 Yesterday   // 3 I went to <u>town</u>   // 1 to see <u>Jane</u> //

   Theme highlighting   Incomplete   Major

Source: Tench (1990, 1996a)

marked or not, into its own tone group gives the theme extra prominence irrespective of tone choice. There will be a further discussion of the relationship between tone and the status of information in the final section.

ToBI and SFL compared and contrasted

ToBI is currently the dominant paradigm for the study of intonation. It represents a collective attempt at creating standardised conventions for the transcription of speech in individual languages. Like SFL, proponents of ToBI do not claim that their system is universal and recognise that their transcriptions apply only to individual languages. To date, there are numerous ToBi transcriptions of languages such as English, Japanese, French, Greek, German and Korean (Jun 2005).

In the remainder of this section, discussion of the ToBI description refers only to the description of English. Scholars working within the ToBI framework position intonation as a pragmatic resource that adds contextualised meaning to unfolding discourse. ToBI practitioners neither work with nor recognise grammatical systems such as Tonality and Tonicity. Nor, indeed, does the ToBI description even include any formal notation for identifying tonic syllables and tone movements.

On its face, the ToBI description seems very different to the SFL one, but, as the following paragraphs indicate, this is not the complete picture. Ladd (2008) notes that a ToBI transcription conceptualises the speech contour as a string of pitch accents, with intervening deaccented syllables.[11] ToBI claims that only pitch accents are meaningful and that the transitions between them are of no consequence. Such a conceptualisation naturally obscures the paradigmatic choices that underpin the syntagmatic realisation of the pitch accents and decouples the intonation system from the grammar. Yet the decision to accent a syllable and the resultant choice of pitch accent is itself a systemic and generative choice.

The original ToBI description (Pierrehumbert 1980) identified pitch accents as turning points in the F0 (pitch) contour. The pitch accents consist of either a single H or L, or a combination of H and L tones, representing movement towards or from the peak or trough. The peak or trough is indicated with a *. Thus ToBI allows H*, L*, L+H*, L*+H, H*+L, H+L* and H*+H. A tone may be followed by two types of edge tone: phrase accents (either H– or L–) and boundary tones (either H% or L%). Pierrehumbert's (1980) claim was that all combinations of pitch accents and edge tones were legal, and that the resulting pitch contour itself was of no functional significance. Yet she produced a series of annotated figures illustrating the correspondence between the final pitch accent and the following edge tones and the tone movements identified by SFL (Pierrehumbert 1980: 390*ff*).

In Figure 10.5, the pitch accents are all L+H*.[12] The sound file has been transcribed into SFL conventions with primary tone. Each accented syllable was salient with the combination of the final pitch accent, and the following phrase accent and boundary tone movement representing a tone 1 movement.

While ToBI systems do not overtly prioritise the psychological significance of information units, the break index tier annotates the degree of juncture between words and between the final word and the silence at the end of the utterance. The break index is scaled from 0 to 4, with 3 and 4 indicating junctures between intermediate and intonational phrases, respectively. A juncture of 1 represents the normal juncture between words, 0 represents no juncture and 2 represents any other type of juncture.

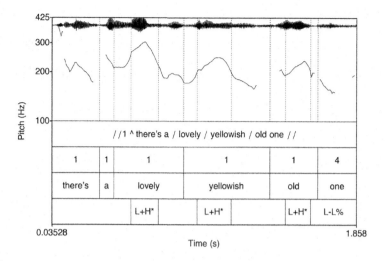

Figure 10.5 ToBI and SFL compared

Teich and colleagues (2000) present the results of a mapping experiment comparing how SFL and ToBI practitioners annotated sound files. They found that SFL tones are easily describable in terms of the ToBI system. Tonic syllables regularly corresponded with the final pitch accents, while earlier pitch accents always fell on the first syllable in a foot. Ladd (2008: 259*ff*) noted that pitch accents fall on syllables perceived as being relatively prominent in part because they are metrically stronger. Yet while SFL argues that that salient syllables are epiphenomenal choices caused by the timing of English, ToBI approaches recognise that they signal meaningful decisions. An H* accent signals that the items made salient in the discourse are new, while an L* accent signals that the lexical item is salient, but not new (Pierrehumbert and Hirschberg 1990).

Halliday's (2005: 288) examples hint that there may be a rhythmic signal of givenness in example (9) but not in example (10).[13]

    (9) //^it's supposed to be / very / **good** /

   (10) //^it's sup / posed to be / very /**good** //

This is intriguingly close to the ToBI view that, because *supposed* in example (11) contains a pitch accent, it is signalled as salient. Brazil (1997) claims that a pre-tonic prominence signals that the lexical item represents a selection from 'an existential paradigm' – that is, a set of possible lexical items that the speaker could have chosen in the context. In this case, the speaker contrasts *supposed* with other possible lexical items such as *may be, could be*, etc.

Hirschberg (2004) lists the functions of intonation as captured by a ToBI transcription system, but crucially does not link them to a wider view of the language system. Consequently, her proposal reads as a series of mappings between independent systems rather than a unified description illustrating how tensions caused by recombinations of two parts of the lexicogrammatical system function to create meaning. Yet the meanings she illustrates in her series of minimal pairs (Hirschberg 2003: 523) are identical to those that Halliday (1967) and Tench (1996a) ascribe to differing tonality placements.

Similarly, Hirschberg's (2003) description of 'nuclear stress' is compatible with SFL's notion of focus. Her discussion of how an utterance final pitch accent and following edge tones combine with syntactic ordering to produce illocutionary force (Hirschberg 2004: 532–6) is, to all intents and purposes, identical to SFL's description of the Interpersonal function of primary Tone (see Table 10.2). For instance, she notes that statements and WH questions (Why, How, etc.) are normally produced with a falling contour (H*L–L%), while 'yes/no' questions are normally produced with a rising contour (L*H–H%). A continuation rise is signalled by a low rising contour formed from the combination of pitch accent with L–H% contour. Pierrehumbert and Hirschberg (1990) discuss how Intonation phrase final contours signal dependency relations: rising contours signal that the interpretation of the proposition contained in the Intonation phrase is dependent on the following speech; falling contours signal that the Intonation phrase is independent.

Unlike SFL, ToBI treats intonation as a pragmatic marker and, as a result, does not treat it as integral to the language system. This, despite the obvious similarities, leads to two significant differences in the claims that ToBI makes in how intonation contributes to the production of meaning. The first concerns Given and New. ToBI argues that de-accenting typically signals the givenness of a particular lexical item.[14] Yet ToBI scholars such as Hirschberg note that lexical items that are clearly available from the context are, on occasion, accented. They attribute this to the syntactic form of the item, itself a reflex of identifiabilty, rather than the speaker's decision to present an item as if it were not recoverable (Hirschberg 2003: 530).

The second difference is what Hirschberg labels 'topic structure' – that is, how prosodic choices function above the tone group in the signalling of the opening and closure of macro units of speech. ToBI argues that a high initial onset, following an extended pause, signals the opening of a spoken paragraph, whereas a fall to the bottom of the speaker's pitch range, followed by an extended pause, closes the topic. While Halliday and Greaves (2008) are silent on phonological units above the tone group, others within the broad SFL tradition (Brazil 1997; O'Grady 2013; Tench 1990;) do incorporate at least a preliminary description of spoken paragraphs into their accounts of English intonation, as we shall see in the next section.

The next section will attempt to incorporate insights from ToBI into an SFL description. This is not meant to imply that, as a theory of intonation, SFL is in any way inferior to other approaches. Indeed, there is much that ToBI could learn from SFL's integration of intonation within the grammar, for example in relation to the Interpersonal systems of Key and the Textual systems of Information. It is not, however, the purpose of this chapter to suggest to other theories how insights from SFL can improve their descriptive apparatus; it is the purpose of the final section to suggest future directions for SFL's theory of intonation. Like any living theory, SFL's theory of intonation cannot remain static. If it is to develop, it must be open to dialogue with cognate approaches.

Future directions

In this section, four areas of potential development are suggested for SFL intonation. The first relates to the possibility of including a rigorous description of intonation above the tone group; the second, to the position of pre-tonic saliences within the theory; the third, to the use of corpora to validate descriptions; and the fourth, to descriptions of the intonation of languages other than English.

Phonological paragraphs

Iwamoto (2014) argues that most SFL descriptions of intonation have not included a description of spoken paragraphs or paratones because the criteria used to identify such units are phonetic and not systemic. This view, however, largely depends on what one considers to be the necessary criteria. Tench (1996a) and O'Grady (2013) recognise that the start of a paratone signals a transition in the discourse; it is, in other words, textually disjunctive. The closure of a paratone is textually exhaustive and, once again, disjunctive. As such, it is probable that two paratones will be separated by a pause. But pausing is not necessarily a defining criterion; rather, it seems useful to postulate that paratones can be identified by the presence of high initial onset and a final fall to the bottom of the speaker's range. Pitch height – albeit not necessarily the height of an initial onset[15] – is, contra Iwamoto (2014), treated as a semiological resource in SFL, for example the choice between tone 1. and tone 1+. O'Grady (2013) provides a more delicate description in his attempt to describe a short speech in terms of major and minor paratones. While he demonstrates that differing paragraph choices led to the foregrounding of different listening paths, he did not manage to establish the systemic options required to identify paratones. A fruitful extension of his work would be to look at the tension between paratone structure and theme choices – especially hyperthemes (Martin 1992: 437–9).

Pre-tonic saliences

Mainstream SFL theory regards pre-tonic saliences as primarily rhythmic choices that do not represent meaningful selections in a manner analogous to Tonicity selections. Yet, as illustrated in this chapter, it is not accurate to describe English as a foot-timed language and hence to treat the salient syllable as a reflex of timing. The work of ToBI scholars and others such as Brazil (1997) demonstrates that tonic syllables and pre-tonic salient syllables result from the same choices: the decision to accent the syllable or not. There is evidence from outside SFL that any accented syllable is presented as New, although, as noted elsewhere in this chapter, the description of Given and New across the literature is wholly inadequate. It is hoped that, once a more encompassing and robust definition of Given and New is adopted, progress will be made in describing the pre-tonic saliences as a systemic meaning-making resource.

Corpora

While there have been descriptions of intonation grounded in the close study of recorded texts, such as Halliday (1970), there has not yet been a serious SFL corpus investigation of a language or dialect. This needs to change, so that the SFL description of intonation can be empirically tested. Major obstacles to intonational corpus research are the plethora of transcription systems and the thorny issue of inter-transcriber reliability. A potential time-saving way forward would be to use the existing ToBI corpora, and to employ studies such as Teich and colleagues (2000) to develop a reliable means of translating ToBI notation into SFL. Ideally, this could be developed into an automatic program. With access to large and reliable corpora from a number of genres, SFL analysts could usefully probe the issues raised in the previous two subsections. Two other areas that could be fruitfully examined in large corpora are how tone choices combine with clause taxis to create logical meaning and the contribution of intonation to the creation of spoken genres.[16] In addition, the availability of large reliable corpora would allow analysts to extend the description of English to include features such as high rising tone, routine listing intonation (Tench 2003) and, potentially, even dialectal variation.

Intonation outside of English

Regrettably, there has been no mention of intonation in any language other than English. This is simply because there is, to date, limited literature to review. Within SFL, Tench (1996b) is an interesting attempt to explore differences in tonality choices between English and German, but it does not attempt to provide a robust description of German intonation. Rose (2001) incorporates intonation descriptions of the Western Desert Aboriginal language. His careful emic approach illustrates how intonation descriptions of non-English codes could be developed. Like Rose's work, ToBI has developed transcription systems that treat each language in their own terms. This is the approach that SFL scholars need to adopt to see how (or if) intonation functions as a meaning-making resource in languages outside of English. Were an automatic ToBI/SFL translation program to be developed, SFL scholars would have immediate access to useful corpora. A thorough description of intonation in numerous languages would not only enrich the grammatical descriptions, but also potentially provide evidence for the balance and interplay between biology – that is, Gussenhoven's (2004: 79–96) three codes of intonation, biological, frequency and effort – the cultural evolution of semiosis within an individual language and semiosis as the epiphenomenal result of language drift.

Notes

1 The author thanks the four anonymous referees, who looked at this chapter, for their thoughtful comments and insightful remarks. Any errors or omissions are entirely the author's own.
2 Declination or downdrift is the gradual decline in pitch level on the first salient syllable (onset) of a series of tone groups. Each onset in the sequence is produced at a slightly lower pitch. Wichmann (2000) notes that while speakers may arrest the drift in onset level, they signal the introduction of a new paragraph by resetting the onset height to a value high in their pitch range. They signal the closure of the topic by a fall to the bottom of their pitch range.
3 The examples and discussion in Tench (1990: 476–511) suggest that intonation is not the sole, or even the most significant, prosodic resource in the identification of spoken genres.
4 It also allows us to investigate the role that the patterning of speech as more or less rhythmic has in signaling information structure and in managing hearer expectations. For instance, Szczepek Reed (2010) observes that speakers produce relatively rhythmic or isochronous segments of English speech to foreground parts of their message and to signal their alignment with their interlocutor.
5 A phonetician would use clues such as syllable lengthening, decrescendo, accelerando, creaky voice, pitch reset and pausing to determine the boundary between the tone groups.
6 The tonic is by definition the final salience. Tone group boundaries are indicated by //.
7 The open-access speech analysis software Praat was used to record and make the spectrographs.
8 O'Grady (2014) critiques the nebulous nature of recoverability as defined in the SFL literature and elsewhere by illustrating that, as presently stated, the concept of recoverability is neither operationalisable nor broad enough to cover all instances of information structuring.
9 For convenience, only tonic syllables are notated within the tone groups.
10 The choice of tone depends on the informational status of the tone groups. In this example, the choice of tone 1 indicates that the speaker signals that each tone group contains major and complete information.

11 The pitch accents are – at least in English – rhythmically salient (Ladd 2008). There is no claim, however, of isochrony for English.
12 The sound file *yellow.wav* is available online at http://www.ling.ohio-state.edu/~tobi/ame_tobi/ annotation_conventions.html
13 See also the previous discussion of examples (4) and (5).
14 Like the present author, Hirschberg (2004) expresses her discontent at the vagueness of the term 'givenness'.
15 But it is possible to find tone groups consisting of a single lexical item in which the tonic syllable is necessarily also the first accented syllable (onset) in the tone group.
16 Among linguistic theories, SFL is without doubt uniquely qualified to conduct such an investigation: see the chapters in Part IV.

References

Abercrombie, D. 1967. *Elements of General Phonetics*. Edinburgh: Edinburgh University Press.
Bolinger, D. 1972. *Intonation*. Harmondsworth: Penguin.
Bolinger, D. 1981. *Two Kinds of Vowels, Two Kinds of Rhythm*. Bloomington, IN: Indiana University Linguistics Club.
Boomer, D., and J. Laver. 1968. Slips of the tongue. *British Journal of Discorders of Communication* 3(1): 2–12.
Brazil, D. 1997. *The Communicative Value of Intonation in English*. Cambridge: Cambridge University Press.
Brown, G., K.L. Currie and J. Kenworthy. 1980. *Questions of Intonation*. London: Croom Helm.
Chafe, W. 1994. *Discourse Consciousness and Time*. Chicago, IL: University of Chicago Press.
Croft, W.S. 1995. Intonation units and grammatical structure. *Linguistics* 71(3): 490–532.
Cruttenden, A. 1997. *Intonation*. Cambridge: Cambridge University Press.
Crystal, D. 1975. *The English Tone of Voice*. London: Arnold.
Dauer, R. 1983. Stress-timing and syllable-timing reanalysed. *Journal of Phonetics* 11(1): 51–62.
El-Menoufy, A. 1969. A study of the intonation in the grammar of English. Unpublished PhD thesis. London University.
Grabe, E., and E. Ling Low. 2002. *Durational Variability in Speech and Rhythm Class* (Hypothesis Papers in Laboratory Phonology 7), Berlin: Mouton.
Greaves, W.S. 2007. Intonation in systemic functional linguistics. In R. Hasan, C.M.I.M. Matthiessen and J.J. Webster (eds) *Continuing Discourse on Language: A Functional Perspective*. London: Equinox, pp. 979–1025.
Gussenhoven, C. 2004. *The Phonology and Tone of Intonation*. Cambridge: Cambridge University Press.
Halliday, M.A.K. 1967. *Intonation and Grammar in British English*. The Hague: Mouton.
Halliday, M.A.K. 1970. *A Course in Spoken English*. Oxford: Oxford University Press.
Halliday, M.A.K. 1994. *An Introduction to Functional Grammar*. 2nd edn. London: Arnold.
Halliday, M.A.K. 2005. Intonation in English grammar. In J.J. Webster (ed.) *The Collected Works of M.A.K. Halliday, Vol. 7: Studies in English Language*. London: Continuum, pp. 264–86.
Halliday, M.A.K., and W.S. Greaves. 2008. *Intonation in the Grammar of British English*. London: Equinox.
Halliday, M.A.K., and C.M.I.M. Matthiessen. 2014. *An Introduction to Functional Grammar*. 4th edn. London: Routledge.
Hirschberg, J. 2004. Pragmatics and intonation. In L. Horn and G. Ward (eds) *Handbook of Pragmatics*. Oxford: Blackwell, pp. 515–37.
Iwamoto, K. 2014. A multi-stratal approach to paragraph-like organization in lectures. In W.L. Bowcher and B.A. Smith (eds) *Systemic Phonology: Recent Studies in English*. Sheffield: Equinox, pp. 116–50.
Jun, S.A. 2005. *Prosodic Typology: The Phonology of Intonation and Phrasing*. Oxford: Oxford University Press.

Ladd, D.R. 2008. *Intonational Phonology*. 2nd edn. Cambridge: Cambridge University Press.

Martin, J.R. 1992. *English Text: System and Structure*. Amsterdam: John Benjamins.

O'Connor, J.D., and G.F. Arnold. 1973. *Intonation of Colloquial English*. 2nd edn. London: Longman.

O'Grady, G. 2010. *A Grammar of Spoken English Discourse: The Intonation of Increments*. London: Continuum.

O'Grady, G. 2013. Choices in Tony's talk: Phonological paragraphing information unit nexuses and the presentation of tone units. In G. O'Grady, T. Bartlett and L. Fontaine (eds) *Choice in Language: Applications in Text Analysis*. Sheffield: Equinox, pp. 125–57.

O'Grady, G. 2014. An investigation of how intonation helps to signal information structure. In W.L. Bowcher and B.A. Smith (eds) *Systemic Phonology: Recent Studies in English*. Sheffield: Equinox, pp. 27–52.

Pierrehumbert. J. 1980. The phonology and phonetics of English intonation. Unpublished PhD dissertation. Massachusetts Institute of Technology, Cambridge, MA.

Pierrehumbert, J., and J. Hirschberg. 1990. The meaning of intonation contours in the intrepretation of discourse. In P.R. Cohen, J. Morgan and M.E. Pollack (eds) *Intentions in Communication*. Cambridge, MA: MIT Press, pp. 271–312.

Roach, P.J. 1982. On the distinction between 'stress-timed' and 'syllable-timed' languages. In D. Crystal (ed.) *Linguistic Controversies*. London: Arnold, pp. 73–9.

Rose, D. 2001. *The Western Desert Code: An Australian Cryptogrammar*. Canberra: Pacific Linguistics.

Szczepek Reed, B. 2010. *Analysing Conversation: An Introduction to Prosody*. Basingstoke: Palgrave Macmillan

Teich, E., C. I. Watson and C. Pereira. 2000. Matching a tone-based and tune-based approach to English intonation for concept-to-speech generation. *Proceedings of the 18th Conference on Computational Linguistics* 2: 829–35.

Tench, P. 1990. *The Roles of Intonation in English Discourse*. Bern: Peter Lang,

Tench, P. 1996a. *The Intonation Systems of English*. London: Cassell.

Tench, P. 1996b. Intonation and the differentiation of syntactical patterns in English and German. *International Journal of Applied Linguistics* 6(2): 223–56.

Tench, P. 2003. Processes of semogenesis in English intonation. *Functions of Language* 10(2): 209–34.

Wichmann, A. 2000. *Intonation in Text and Discourse: Beginnings Middles and Ends*. London: Longman.

11

Theme in the Cardiff Grammar

Guowen Huang

Introduction

The concept of 'Theme' is closely linked with Halliday's (1967, 1968, 1973, 1985, 1994) metafunctional hypothesis (especially the Textual metafunction), which is in contrast with the proposal in the Cardiff Grammar that there are eight different 'strands of meaning' rather than only three metafunctions.

The aim of this chapter is to illustrate the various kinds of 'theme' in the Cardiff Grammar, which include Subject theme, multiple theme, enhanced theme, the 'referent as role in event' construction and the 'event-relating enhanced theme' construction. The chapter will also analyse elements that are generally treated as Theme in the Hallidayan writings, which are not regarded as thematic element in the Cardiff Grammar.

The description of theme in the Cardiff Grammar was initially inspired and influenced by Halliday's early writings (for example Halliday 1967, 1968, 1970a, 1973), but has been developed into a substantially different account of theme from that which Halliday proposed in the late 1960s and early 1970s. This is in line with the fact that Fawcett's systemic functional approach to language began with Halliday's ideas in his late 1960s and early 1970s writings, but has departed from there since the mid-1970s (for example Fawcett 1981 [1974–76], 1980, 2000, 2008, forthcoming*a*, forthcoming*b*).

The discussion below will focus on (a) Theme and (b) Fawcett's approach to theme. But there are three points that are worth mentioning at the outset.

1   We shall assume that the reader is familiar with Halliday's description of Theme, as presented in Halliday (1994).
2   Halliday uses the term Theme with an initial capital letter, whereas Fawcett usually uses it with a lower case – that is, theme – the reason probably being that, for Halliday, in an English clause there is an element that is to be identified as *the* Theme, while, for Fawcett, there may be more than one type of theme.
3   Fawcett uses modifiers to distinguish between various types of theme, for example 'Subject theme', 'experiential enhanced theme' and 'marked Participant Role theme'.

In this chapter, we shall use 'Theme' and 'theme' where appropriate. When we are talking of Halliday's concept, we use 'Theme', and 'theme' when addressing Fawcett's idea.

In the Cardiff Grammar, in the identification of theme, the focus is on the theme in the clause itself – that is, theme within the clause. Therefore the discussion is not concerned with either 'thematic progression' (Daneš 1974) or 'hyperTheme' and 'macroTheme' (Martin 1992).

Defining the term 'Theme/theme'

Fawcett (forthcoming*a*) strongly challenges the widely held assumption that there is 'a unified concept of Theme' and suggests that one possible way of characterising all of the types of theme is to say that they are all types of 'prominence in the message'. He argues that there are various other types of 'prominence' besides theme – including 'informational' prominence, as either New or Contrastively New information. For Fawcett, the term 'prominence' does not seem a natural cover term to use in the case of some of the types of theme (cf. Downing 1991; Berry 1995).

In the Cardiff Grammar, the term 'theme' is treated as an umbrella label for a broad range of semantic phenomena. As Fawcett suggests, this concept of theme may be (a) a generalising concept, such as the idea that each type of theme reflects some specified type of 'prominence', (b) a 'contextualising' of the clause or (c) something that reflects the viewpoint of the Performer.

Defining 'the Cardiff Grammar'

Fawcett's understanding of the concept of theme was first inspired by the writings of Halliday in the 1960s and the 1970s. But, because of the influence from studies such as discourse analysis, corpus linguistics, natural language generation and cognitive linguistics, his view on theme has changed into one that is significantly different from Halliday's. Fawcett (forthcoming*a*) firmly believes that his approach is equally systemic-functional, that 'this new account of theme in English is simply one part – one strand of meaning – of a very large and fully integrated description of all aspects of the lexicogrammar of English' and that 'this description is set within the framework of a model of a communicating mind', 'while the key principles upon which this new version of [systemic functional linguistics] SFL is based are essentially the same as those that underlie Halliday's model'.

Fawcett emphasises the importance of system networks because 'the concept of a system network that expresses choices between meanings is the most fundamental concept in SFL' (Fawcett forthcoming*a*) and, in his discussion on issues related to theme, he presents simple, yet adequate, system networks for the different types of choice in theme, other than providing structural analyses.

Fawcett (forthcoming*a*) argues that the most basic assumption of his SFL description is that 'thematic meanings are linguistic meanings between which a user of a language chooses, in order to serve the various purposes that may arise in a developing discourse'; this is similar to the fact that 'we choose between the available meanings of transitivity, mood and so on'. He then adds that 'the principle that thematic meanings, like other types of meaning, necessarily involve a choice is . . . one which Halliday sometimes ignores'.

As is pointed out in Fawcett in a number of publications (for example Fawcett 2000, 2008 and in this volume), in the Cardiff Grammar the system networks of choices in Transitivity, Mood, Theme and so on are interpreted as the semantics. The Cardiff Grammar is an approach in which a system network that models the 'meaning potential' of a language constitutes its semantics.

As a descriptive grammar, the Cardiff Grammar is designed to be capable of being used to describe both languages and texts; as a generative grammar, it is so well formalised that it can be run in a computer as part of a text-generation system (Fawcett et al. 1993).

The Cardiff approach to the identification of theme

In the Cardiff Grammar, a clause is not treated as having a 'Theme–Rheme structure', which is in clear contrast with Halliday's (1994) description of the thematic structure.

In the Cardiff Grammar, there is no such a thing as 'multiple Theme' having more than one metafunctional element. In the second edition of Halliday's *Introduction to Functional Grammar* (IFG; hence the 'IFG approach') (Halliday 1994), any element that occurs before the experiential element is treated as a type of theme. In the Cardiff Grammar, the clause *but surely he is on my side* is analysed as '(*but*) [not treated as theme] *surely* [Thematised Adjunct] *he* [Subject Theme]', as is illustrated in example (1).

(1) But	surely	he	is on my side
	Thematised Adjunct	Subject Theme	

In the Cardiff Grammar, a simple English clause may have one or more different types of Theme and these different types of Theme are treated as grammatical phenomena in their own right. For instance, example (1) contains the thematised Adjunct (*surely*) and the Subject theme (*he*). This means that a simple clause may have one or more elements that have one or other of several types of thematic status.

Illustration of theme in the Cardiff Grammar

In this section, we shall try to illustrate the different types of theme that are recognised in the Cardiff Grammar. The major types of theme to be dealt with are Subject theme, multiple theme, enhanced theme, the 'referent as role in event' construction and the 'event-relating enhanced theme' construction. Finally, we shall discuss cases that some scholars regard as 'theme', but which are not considered such in the Cardiff Grammar.

Subject theme

In SFL, the most fundamental concept is the concept of a system network that expresses choices between meanings. One of Fawcett's (forthcoming*a*) aims is to present simple, yet adequate, system networks for the various types of choice in theme, other than presenting structural analyses of the various types of 'thematic' structure.

Fawcett (forthcoming*a*) discusses what is called 'Subject theme' and 'marked Participant Role (PR) theme' by presenting the system network illustrated in Figure 11.1.

Although the system network in Figure 11.1 is a simplified one, it is good enough to illustrate the differences between the Subject theme and the marked PR theme, as well as the probabilities in the three systems. The examples given to illustrate the systems are 'Action' – that is, Material (Halliday 1994) Processes. In the two-role agentive process (clause) *Ivy ate*

Guowen Huang

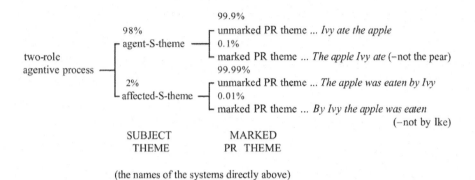

SUBJECT
THEME

MARKED
PR THEME

(the names of the systems directly above)

Figure 11.1 Typical systems for Subject theme and marked PR theme

Note: This pattern of choices occurs, with different PRs, for many other two- and three-role Process types, e.g. Agent + Created, Perceiver + Phenomenon, etc.

the apple, Ivy is the Agent – that is, Actor (Halliday 1994) - while *the apple* is the Affected – that is, Goal (Halliday 1994) – with regard to TRANSITIVITY and both are Participant Roles. In *Ivy ate the apple, Ivy* is the theme and it is an unmarked theme, which is in contrast with *The apple Ivy ate*, in which case *the apple* is a marked theme. These two themes are called 'agent Subject theme', with the Agent as the unmarked theme and the Affected as the marked theme. In *The apple was eaten by Ivy*, the theme is the affected Subject theme, which is an unmarked PR theme; in contrast, in *By Ivy the apple was eaten*, the theme is *by Ivy*, which is a marked PR theme.

Figure 11.1 also tells us that, in 98 per cent of cases, we have the agent-S-theme and, within this system, we usually have the unmarked PR theme (99.9 per cent of cases). Within the affected-S-theme system, we usually have unmarked PR theme (99.99 per cent of cases), in contrast with marked PR theme, which rarely occurs (0.01 per cent of cases).

If we analyse the four clauses in examples (2)–(5) below by using the method of analysis presented in Halliday (1994), we can see that there are slight differences between the Cardiff Grammar and the Sydney Grammar.

(2) Ivy ate the apple.   [Ivy: unmarked Theme; Subject as Theme]

(3) The apple Ivy ate.   [The apple: marked Theme; Complement as Theme]

(4) The apple was eaten by Ivy.   [The apple: unmarked Theme; Subject as Theme]

(5) By Ivy the apple was eaten   [By Ivy: marked Theme; Adjunct as Theme]
     (not by Ike).

According to Halliday (1994), if the element that serves as Theme is the Subject of the clause, it is an unmarked Theme. If it is not the Subject – for example a Complement (C) or an Adjunct – it is a marked Theme. Note also that, according to Halliday (1994), *by Ivy* in example (4) is an Adjunct, which is treated as a Participant Role (that is, Complement) in the Cardiff Grammar. Semantically, *by Ivy* functions as the Agent of the action of eating, but syntactically, it is a prepositional phrase. Therefore we may say that the motivation for Halliday's (1994) analysis is based on syntax, whereas that in the Cardiff Grammar is based on semantics.

Multiple themes

Both Halliday (1994) and Fawcett (forthcoming*a*) use the term 'multiple theme', but in doing so they are referring to different constructions.

Halliday (1994: 52–5) clearly states that the element that serves as Theme must be an experiential element: '[T]he Theme extends from the beginning of the clause up to (and including) the first element that has a function in transitivity' and 'this element is called the 'topical Theme' (Halliday 1994: 53). If there is a non-experiential element that occurs before the experiential element that functions as the topical Theme, it is also regarded as part of the Theme.

Halliday (1994: 55) gives a complicated example – example (6), below – to illustrate the complexity of a multiple Theme, with the first seven elements (three textual elements, three interpersonal elements and one experiential element) together forming the multiple Theme.

(6a)   <u>Well but then Ann surely wouldn't the best idea</u> be to join the group?

(6b)   well [textual: continuative] but [textual: structural] then [textual: conjunctive] Ann [interpersonal: vocative] surely [interpersonal: modal] wouldn't [interpersonal: finite] the best idea [experiential: topical] {Theme} be to join the group {Rheme}

Halliday's (1994) analysis suggests that there is one principle underlying the analysis of multiple Theme: '[E]very clause must contain one and only one topical Theme' (Eggins 2004: 302). According to the Cardiff Grammar, there are a number of problems with Halliday's analysis of multiple Theme, one of which is that some of the elements that are regarded as part of the multiple Theme are not the result of choice. This point will be picked up again later in the chapter.

In the Cardiff Grammar, the term 'multiple theme' is used to illustrate the phenomenon such as that in example (7).

(7)   Last night Ivy and half a million others watched the new Tom Hanks film.

The first element (*last night*) in example (7) is a Circumstantial Element in terms of Transitivity analysis and an Adjunct with respect to syntactic analysis. According to Halliday's (1994) analysis, *last night* is the marked Theme (Circumstance as Theme) and the rest of the clause is Rheme, while the Theme is a simple Theme (as opposed to multiple Theme). However, according to the analysis in the Cardiff Grammar, *last night* is a thematised Adjunct and *Ivy and half a million others* is the Subject theme. Thus, for the Cardiff scholars, example (7) contains a multiple theme realised by two independent elements.

Example (8) (cited in Fawcett forthcoming*a*) is another that can be used to illustrate the analysis in the Cardiff Grammar.

(8)   (I've seen King Lear several times –) but Coriolanus I haven't seen.

With the clause *but Coriolanus I haven't seen* in example (8), there are different analyses. For Halliday (1994), *but Coriolanus* is a multiple Theme, with *but* as a 'textual: structural Theme' and *Coriolanus* as a (marked) 'experiential: topical Theme'. For Fawcett, *but* is not counted as part of the theme (since there is no choice involved), and *Coriolanus* is a marked Participant Role (PR) theme and *I* a Subject theme. Although both Halliday and Fawcett assume that there is a multiple Theme/theme in example (8), they are talking about different things with very different analyses.

To summarise, for Halliday (1994), 'multiple Theme' refers to the construction that has one, and only one, experiential element and one or more non-experiential element(s); for Fawcett, 'multiple theme' refers to the co-occurrence of two or more types of simple theme.

Enhanced themes

The term 'enhanced theme' came to be used in the early 1990s by people working within the Cardiff SFL community (for example Fawcett and Huang 1995; Huang and Fawcett 1996) and it later was used by others (for example Thompson 2004: 164; Thompson 2014: 170). It is used to describe the kind of theme that is found in clauses such as examples (9)–(11a).

> (9)   There's a bee in Ivy's hair.

> (10)   It is obvious that he is right.

> (11a)   It was Henry that kissed Helen.

There is one thing in common in these three clauses, in that each has an empty Subject and an Operator/Main Verb (that is, *there is, it is, it was*), which form the 'thematic build-up'. In the Cardiff Grammar, *a bee* in example (9) is regarded as an existential enhanced theme because the clause is an existential one; *obvious* in example (10) is called an evaluative enhanced theme because the focus expresses a kind of evaluative meaning and *Henry* in example (11a) is treated as an experiential enhanced theme because the theme is realised by an experiential element.

Instead of following Halliday's metafunctional hypothesis, which assumes that there are three strands of meaning in the clause, Fawcett (1980, 2008) identifies different strands of meaning in his analysis of examples such as example (9). Figure 11.2 illustrates both the semantics and his syntactic analysis of example (9). With respect to functional syntax, *there* is the Subject, *is* is the Main Verb (M) conflated with the Operator, *a bee* is the Complement conflated with Carrier and *in Ivy's hair* is another Complement expressing Location (Lo), which, for Halliday (1994), would be treated as an Adjunct.

Note too that, in Figure 11.2, *there is* is marked as 'thematic build-up' and *a bee* is treated as an enhanced theme. If we follow Halliday's (1994) analysis, *there* is the (simple) Theme and the rest of the clause (*is a bee in Ivy's hair*) is the Rheme.[1]

The analysis of example (10) is similar to that of example (9). With regard to syntactic analysis and Transitivity analysis, *it* is the Subject, *is* is the Main Verb conflated with the Operator, *obvious* is the Complement conflated with Attribute and *that he is right* is another Complement conflated with Carrier. Since *that he is right* is a clause, it can be further analysed as follows: *that* is a Binder, *he* is the Subject conflated with Carrier, *is* is the Main Verb and *right* is a Complement conflated with Attribute. Like *there is* in example (9), *it is* in example (10) is the thematic build-up, with *obvious* being the enhanced theme. The embedded clause *he is right* can also be analysed by looking at the Transitivity and thematic

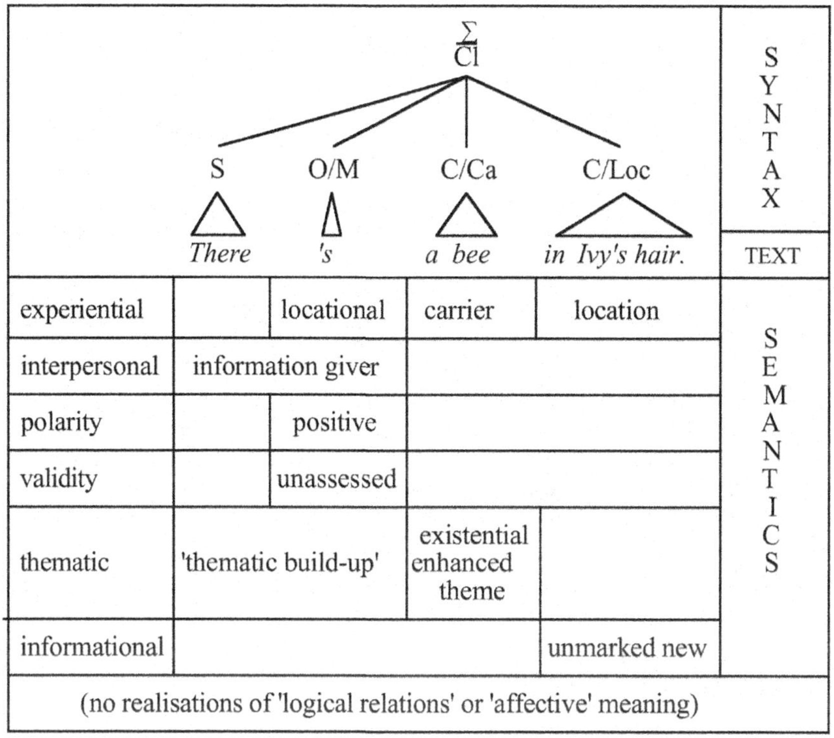

					SYNTAX
	S	O/M	C/Ca	C/Loc	
	There	*'s*	*a bee*	*in Ivy's hair.*	TEXT
experiential		locational	carrier	location	
interpersonal	information giver				
polarity		positive			SEMANTICS
validity		unassessed			
thematic	'thematic build-up'	existential enhanced theme			
informational				unmarked new	
(no realisations of 'logical relations' or 'affective' meaning)					

Figure 11.2 The syntactic and semantic analysis of an existential enhanced theme construction
Source: Fawcett (forthcoming*a*)

status: *he* is the Carrier and *right* is the Attribute, with *he* being the Subject theme with respect to thematic analysis.

As is illustrated in Thompson (2014: 156–7), *it is obvious that* in example (10) is treated as Theme, with *he is right* as Rheme (cf. Halliday 1994: 60). This analysis is against the basic principle of clause organisation in that *that* is the Binder, the function of which is to introduce the embedded clause and which cannot be taken away from the clause it introduces.[2]

Example (11a) is called the 'cleft construction' or 'it-cleft construction' in traditional grammar; Halliday (1994: 58–61) calls it a 'predicated Theme construction'. This construction is often compared with an 'uncleft' construction, as in example (12) below.

(12)   Henry kissed Helen.

The main difference between examples (11a) and (12) can be phrased as follows: with regard to information focus, in example (12) *Henry kissed Helen*, the potentially new information tonic falls on the last lexical element (that is, *Helen*), while in example (11a) *It was Henry that kissed Helen*, the information focus is on the element that is identified as the enhanced theme (that is, *Henry*). In example (11a), there is presupposed information involved, which is not to be found in example (12) in normal circumstances. The new information in example (12) is potentially new, which is in contrast with another kind of new information in example (11a), which is contrastively new with the tonic falling on the enhanced theme (that is, *Henry*). If we want to put the contrastively new information tonic on *Helen* in example (11a), we can reorganise the clause (sentence) by changing the order of the two elements involved (example (11b)).

>   (11b)   It was Helen that Henry kissed.

The syntactic analysis and semantic analysis of example (11) are similar to those of examples (9) and (10). There are two levels of experiential analysis and thematic analysis. In terms of experiential analysis, at the first level, *it* is the Subject, *was* is the Main Verb conflated with the Operator, *Henry* is a Complement conflated with Attribute and *that kissed Helen* is the other Complement conflated with Carrier. At the second level, the embedded clause *that kissed Helen* is an Action Process, with *that* serving as the Subject conflated with Agent, *kissed* as the Main Verb and *Helen* as the Affected. With respect to thematic analysis, *it was*, like *there is* in example (9) and *it is* in example (10), is the thematic build-up and *Henry*, like *a bee* in example (9) and *obvious* in example (10), is the enhanced theme. The element *that* in the embedded clause in example (11) is the Subject theme. With example (11b) above, the theme is expounded by *Henry*, which is a Subject theme.

Huang's (1996, 2003) study of the experiential enhanced theme construction suggests that there are two basic types, with the well-recognised type represented by example (13) and the less well-known type represented by example (14) (Huang 2003: 173).

>   (13)   'We can't ignore what's going on,' he said, getting straight to it. 'We're going to have to face it.'
>   'It's you who have to face it,' Deena said, trying to keep her fury under control.

>   (14)   I sat numbly behind the wheel as Big Ben chimed the single stroke of 1 a.m., the sound carrying clearly across the river. My dressing-gown was soaked in dark blood, my hands were sticky, and my feet felt slippery by the pedals.
>   *It was then that I heard the voice.* It came from both outside and within me, deep and gentle, with a calm, almost hypnotic quality that transfixed me in my seat.

In example (13), the constrastive meaning is obvious: *you* conveys information that is not only 'new', but also 'contrastively new', and the embedded clause *who have to face it* expresses presupposed information. In Halliday's (1970b) terms, this is typically realised by a tone 3, but it is also regularly presented as the 'tail' that follows the Tonic on the enhanced theme, when it is deemed to be recoverable (O'Grady, this volume).

In example (14), the item *then* signals 'recoverability'. In Halliday's terms, 'givenness' is realised intonationally and it would certainly be possible to read this sentence, in a natural manner, with a single Tonic on 'voice', so that only the embedded clause contains potentially new information. The analysis of information types indicates that the two constructions in examples (13) and (14) are of different types, with the former being more widely recognised.[3]

The 'referent as role in event' construction

Halliday (1994: 40–1) used example (15), below, to illustrate 'a special thematic resource whereby two or more separate elements are grouped together so that they form a single constituent of the Theme + Rheme structure'.

>   (15)   What the duke gave to my aunt was that teapot.

Halliday calls this kind of construction 'thematic equative', because 'it sets up the Theme + Rheme structure in the form of an equation, where "Theme = Rheme"' (Halliday 1994: 40). In example (15), the Theme is *what the duke gave to my aunt*, which is a simple Theme, although it is a clause in structure.

In the Cardiff Grammar, example (15) is called the 'referent as role in event' construction. The reason for having this functionally motivated term is that the existing terms 'wh-cleft' and 'pseudo-cleft' in traditional grammar are misleading as if there were some pre-existing syntactic unit that had been 'cleft', which is not true because there is no such syntactic transformation involved. To explain the meaning of the term 'referent as role in event', let us analyse example (15). In this example, the element of an event (*what the duke gave to my aunt*) that may otherwise have been realised in a nominal group (*the thing that the duke gave to my aunt*) is instead presented as a referent that is identified by its role in the event. And that is why examples such as example (15) above and examples (16) and (17) below are called the 'referent as role in event' construction in the Cardiff Grammar.

(16)   What she had was a Margarita.

(17)   What we saw was a badger.

The reason for giving up Halliday's (1994) term 'thematic equative' is that the Theme in this construction is not always equal to the Rheme. Although it is true that the majority of the 'referent as role in event' constructions are 'identifying' and the second role (as *that teapot* in example (15)) is often filled by a 'particularised' (or 'definite') nominal group, there are also cases in which this second role is filled by an 'unparticularised' (or 'indefinite') entity, as *a Margarita* and *a badger* in examples (16) and (17), respectively (cited in Fawcett forthcoming*a*). It is for this reason that, in the Cardiff Grammar, the clauses in examples (15)–(17) are regarded as attributive (rather than identifying) relational Processes consisting of 'Carrier + Process + Attribute'. Therefore the Participant Roles of *what the duke gave to my aunt* in example (15), *what she had* in example (16) and *what we saw* in example (17) are all 'Carrier'.

With respect to experiential analysis, according to the Cardiff Grammar, *what the duke gave to my aunt* in example (15) is the Carrier and *that teapot* is the Attribute; in thematic terms, *what the duke gave to my aunt* is the Subject theme.

As we can see, the identification of the theme in the 'referent as role in event' construction, as in example (15), does not depend on a choice in theme, but on a choice in how to identify a referent.[4]

The 'event-relating enhanced theme' construction

Apart from the existential, evaluative and experiential enhanced theme constructions, another type of enhanced theme construction is recognised in the Cardiff Grammar, which is called the 'event-relating enhanced theme' construction. It is so called because, with examples such as example (18) below, there are two events (that is, the underlined parts) to which event-relating Process relates (Fawcett forthcoming*a*). The Process type in this construction is concerned with a set of relationships that can occur between pairs of events – no matter whether those events are expressed in nominalisations (that is, as nominal groups) or clauses at the level of form.

(18)   <u>That he failed to put the issue to the voters</u> implies <u>a lack of genuine confidence</u>.

In terms of Transitivity analysis, *that he failed to put the issue to the voters* is the Carrier and *a lack of genuine confidence* is the Range. In contrast, we can express the meaning in example (18) in another way, in example (19), below, without changing the basic conceptual information.

> (19)   It implies a lack of genuine confidence that he failed to put the issue to the voters.

In example (19), the Range (*a lack of genuine confidence*) that comes second in example (18) is made the enhanced theme, with *it implies* performing the function that is similar to the thematic build-up, like *there is* in example (9), *it is* in example (10) and *it was* in example (11). In the Cardiff Grammar, the relationships between examples (18) and (19) are dealt with as a type of Transitivity in their own right.

The 'event-relating enhanced theme' construction should be distinguished from the existential, evaluative and experiential enhanced theme constructions in that, in the former, it is the Process that is thematised, whereas in the latter it is the Participant Role – including Halliday's (1994) Circumstantial Element – that is thematised. Compared with the latter, the 'event-relating enhanced theme' construction is rare and it is still debatable whether it is necessary to recognise it as a major type of enhanced theme construction.

Summary: enhanced themes

The existential, evaluative and experiential, and the 'event-relating' enhanced theme constructions recognised in the Cardiff Grammar have similarities and differences. One of the obvious similarities is that, in each of the constructions, there is an element that is highlighted so that enhancement is achieved. Through the thematic build-up, the Performer is able to signal to the Addressee that an enhanced element is about to be presented. As Fawcett (forthcoming*a*) explains, by not making the very first element of the clause theme, the Performer creates 'the delay between announcing that the theme is coming and its actual presentation builds up the Addressee's expectations, so enhancing the effect when finally – but in fact only milliseconds later – the Performer presents the Enhanced Theme itself'. It is for this reason that those four constructions are treated as enhanced theme constructions in the Cardiff Grammar.

The 'referent as role in event' construction is similar to the other four constructions in that it is closely related to them in expressing more or less the same meaning, which suggests that example (15) (repeated below) and example (20) are more or less equivalent in conveying the basic message of 'the duke gave my aunt that teapot'.

> (15)   What the duke gave to my aunt was that teapot.
>
> (20)   It was that teapot that the duke gave to my aunt.

Since both examples (15) and (20) express the basic meaning of 'the duke gave my aunt that teapot', these two constructions are respectively called 'pseudo-cleft' and 'cleft' sentences in traditional grammar.

Elements not treated as theme

In this section, we shall describe the elements that are treated as Theme or thematic by Halliday (1994), but are not regarded as theme in the Cardiff Grammar.

In deciding which types of element can be regarded as theme, we should remind our-selves of a basic principle in SFL: Meaning implies choice, or 'Theme is a meaningful choice' (Downing 1991: 122). This principle is in the root of the Cardiff Grammar in dealing with all language phenomena, including the identification of theme of all kinds.

According to this principle, a number of cases that Halliday (1994) treats as Theme are not regarded as theme in the Cardiff Grammar, as in examples (21) and (22).

(21) But he is right.

(22) Because she was ill, she was not able to come.

According to Halliday's (1994) analysis, *but he* in example (21) is a multiple theme, with *but* being a 'textual: structural Theme' and *he*, an 'experiential: topical Theme'. In example (22), the dependent clause *because he was ill* is treated as the Theme of the whole clause complex, and both the Sydney Grammar and the Cardiff Grammar have no disagreement on this respect. If both clauses are further analysed in terms of their own thematic structures, according to Halliday (1994), the Theme of the dependent clause in example (22) is a multiple one, with *because* as a 'textual: structural Theme' and *she*, an 'experiential: topical Theme'. In the Cardiff Grammar, Linkers (that is, 'coordinating conjunctions') such as *and, but, or* and *for*, and Binders (that is, 'subordinating conjunc-tions'), such as *because, when, before, if,* etc., are not regarded as thematic elements simply because they are in those positions in the clause not as a result of semantic choice; they have to be there because they introduce the clause that follows. They are not like ele-ments such as Subject, Complement and Adjunct, which can occur in other positions as a result of thematic choices.

Let us look at some other examples.

(23) Does he speak French?

(24) Who did you see?

(25) How beautiful it is!

(26) Let's do that.

Examples (23)–(26) are concerned with interpersonal issues rather than textual (thematic) ones. According to Halliday (1994), *does he* in example (23) is a multiple Theme, with *does* as an 'interpersonal: Mood Theme' and *he*, an 'experiential: topi-cal Theme'. In example (24), although the wh-element *who* occurs early (in the first position), it is not the result of a thematic choice to make it a theme. Similarly, *how beautiful* in example (25) occupies the first position of the clause not as a result of a choice in theme, but as a choice of Mood.

Example (26) deserves special attention in that it is a special construction. According to the analysis in Halliday (1994: 87), *let's* is interpreted 'as a wayward form of the Subject "you and I" ', and in Thompson (2014: 152) it is identified as the Theme of the clause. In the Cardiff Grammar (Fawcett 2008: 162), *let* is called the 'Let Element' and *us/'s* is the Subject. However, the theme in this construction – for example *'s* in example (26) – if it is regarded as the theme, is not a result of thematic choice.

As Fawcett (forthcoming*a*) argues:

[I]n a fully semantic systemic functional grammar, all of the 'mood-related' elements . . . are placed at their positions in the clause as a direct result of the realization rules for the relevant features in the MOOD network, so that once again . . . they are *not* where they are in the clause as the result of a thematic choice.

This argument leads to the question of whether we should strictly stick to thematic choices and disregard other metafunctional choices when we are talking about the identification of Theme/theme.[5]

A different case

The Cardiff Grammar approach to theme reflects the characteristics, the underlying assumptions and the principles of the model. Some of the differences between the Cardiff Grammar and the Sydney Grammar are the result of the different assumptions, interpretations and ways of analysis in both approaches. Let us illustrate the difference in analysing the thematic structure with four examples (slightly adapted from Fawcett forthcoming*a*).

(27a) 'I love you,' said Ike to Ivy.

(27b) 'I love you,' Ike said to Ivy.

(27c) Said Ike to Ivy, 'I love you.'

(27d) Ike said to Ivy, 'I love you.'

According to Halliday (1994), the two clauses in example (27) form a clause nexus of parataxis. Thus, with regard to thematic analysis, each example will have two thematic structures. Example (27e) is an analysis of example (27a).

(27e) *'I*	*love you,'*	*said*	*Ike to Ivy*
Unmarked Theme	Rheme	Marked Theme	Rheme

It shows that there are two thematic structures in example (27a), each of which has its own Theme and Rheme; in the second thematic structure, the Theme is a marked one, because it is the Process that is thematised.

The thematic analysis of example (27b) indicates that the two Themes are (simple) Subject Theme, expounded respectively by *I* and *Ike*. With example (27c), the Theme of the first clause is a marked one, because it is realised by the Process *said*, and the Theme in the second clause is a Subject theme. And the two thematic structures in example (27d) are the same, because they both have an unmarked Theme (Subject Theme).

The Cardiff Grammar does not follow Halliday's (1994) classification of clause complexes nor does it distinguish between hypotaxis and parataxis the way that he does; instead, it takes an approach that is the same as that of Quirk and colleagues (1985). For scholars following the Cardiff Grammar approach, example (27) is made up of four elements in each instance: *Ike* [Subject] *said* [Main Verb] *to Ivy* [Complement] *'I love you'* [Complement]. In terms of Transitivity analysis, the Subject is conflated with the Agent (Ag), the first Complement with the Affected-Cognisant (Af-Cog) and the second Complement with Phenomenon (Ph). Obviously, the terminology used to describe the different elements in these four examples is different from that in Halliday (1994), but the important difference is that *'I love you'* (Complement/Phenomenon) is treated as an embedded clause or a 'text' filling an element of the clause, which is a Complement of the clause. For Halliday (1994), example (27) is a clause complex in each instance, whereas for Fawcett, each is a simple clause (sentence).

Since the syntactic analysis of example (27) suggests that the structural elements of these four instances are basically the same, the difference between them lies in the different positions of the four elements in the clause.

(27a-i)   C/Ph + M + S/Ag + C/Af-Cog

(27b-i)   C/Ph + S/Ag + M + C/Af-Cog

(27c-i)   M + S/Ag + C/Af-Cog + C/Ph

(27d-i)   S/Ag + M + C/Af-Cog + C/Ph

Key: Af-Cog = Affected-Cognisant; Ag = Agent; C = Complement; M = Main Verb; Ph = Phenomenon; S = Subject; / = conflated with

Since the syntactic analysis in the Cardiff Grammar is different from that in the Sydney Grammar with regard to example (27), it is expected that we will have different thematic analyses of these four examples. With both examples (27a) and (27b), the C/Ph (*'I love you'*) is the theme; with example (27c), the theme is a marked one, because it is realised by the thematized Process (the Main Verb) and the theme in example (27d) is realised by *Ike*, which is the Subject of the clause, thus making the theme a Subject theme.

The discussion so far shows that, in talking about the differences in thematic analysis between the Sydney and Cardiff Grammars, the differences of their different assumptions, different interpretations and different ways of analysis should be taken into consideration. It is because of these differences that both approaches produce very different syntactic and semantic analyses of the same clause.

Concluding remarks

Although there have been many writings on 'Theme' in SFL, both in monograph forms (Deng 2012; Ghadessy 1995; Gómez-Gonzàles 2001; Hasan and Fries 1995; Huang 2003; Wang 2008) and journal papers, in the literature to date, the concept of Theme is not as clear as one may think. For Fawcett, theme/Theme is not a unified concept, but a general term for a constellation of phenomena. In the Cardiff Grammar, there is no place for the concept for Halliday's term of 'topical Theme', because this term is too broad to be useful, since it refers to both Participant Roles and Circumstantial Elements. And clearly, if the Theme/theme is realised by a Circumstantial Element, it does not go with Halliday's definition of Theme, which is 'that which the clause is about', as *last night* in example (7).

The analysis of theme (or Theme) in this chapter indicates that the Cardiff approach has its reasons for alternative analysis, but it is firmly based on both the belief that the principle that meaning implies choice should be applied to any analysis of thematic structures and the assumption that thematic meanings are linguistic meanings between which the Performer chooses for his or her purposes in communication in the given context of situation.

We might say something here, as a concluding remark, that is important, but which may arouse controversy in the SFL community: that the Cardiff Grammar, an alternative model of language that is designed with the aim of being 'an extension and simplification of Halliday's Systemic Functional Grammar' (Fawcett 2008), has its own characteristics and needs more attention from SFL scholars other than those associated with Cardiff.

Notes

1 There are a number of studies on this construction. For a book-length treatment of this construction involving English and Chinese, see Deng (2012).
2 For the study of other issues concerning the evaluative enhanced theme construction, see Wang (2008) and Fawcett (forthcoming*a*).
3 For further analysis, see Huang (2003) and Fawcett (forthcoming*a*).
4 For more discussion on this construction, see He (2004) and Fawcett (forthcoming*a*).
5 See Forey and Sampson, this volume.

References

Berry, M. 1995. Thematic options and success in writing. In M. Ghadessy (ed.) *Thematic Development in English Texts*. London: Pinter, pp. 55–84.
Daneš, F. 1974. Functional sentence perspective and the organization of text. In F. Daneš (ed.) *Papers in Functional Sentence Perspective*, The Hague: Mouton, pp. 106–28.
Deng, R. 2012. *Xitong Gongneng Yufa de Cunzaiju Yanjiu* [*Studies on the Existential Sentences from a Systemic Functional Perspective*]. Guangzhou: Sun Yat-sen University Press.
Downing, A. 1991. An alternative approach to theme: A systemic-functional perspective. *WORD* 42(2): 119–43.
Eggins, S. 2004. *An Introduction to Systemic Functional Linguistics*. 2nd edn. London: Pinter.
Fawcett, R.P. 1980. *Cognitive Linguistics and Social Interaction: Towards an Integrated Model of a Systemic Functional Grammar and the Other Components of an Interacting Mind*. Heidelberg: Julius Groos and Exeter University.
Fawcett, R.P. 1981 [1974–76]. *Some Proposals for Systemic Syntax*. Cardiff: Polytechnic of Wales.
Fawcett, R.P. 2000. *A Theory of Syntax for Systemic Functional Linguistics* (Current Issues in Linguistic Theory 206). Amsterdam: John Benjamins.
Fawcett, R.P. 2008. *Invitation to Systemic Functional Linguistics through the Cardiff Grammar: An Extension and Simplification of Halliday's Systemic Functional Grammar*. 3rd edn. London: Equinox.
Fawcett, R.P. Forthcoming*a*. *The Many Types of Theme in English: Their Syntax, Semantics and Discourse Functions*. London: Equinox.
Fawcett, R.P. Forthcoming*b*. *An Integrative Architecture of Language and its Use for Systemic Functional Linguistics and Other Theories of Language*. London: Equinox.
Fawcett, R.P., and G.W. Huang. 1995. A functional analysis of the enhanced theme construction in English. *Interface: Journal of Applied Linguistics* 10(1): 113–44.
Fawcett, R.P., G.H. Tucker and Y.Q. Lin. 1993. How a systemic functional grammar works: The role of realization in realization. In H. Horacek and M. Zock (eds) *New Concepts in Natural Language Generation*. London: Pinter, pp. 114–86.
Ghadessy, M. (ed.) 1995. *Thematic Development in English Texts*. London: Pinter.
Gómez-Gonzàles, M.A. 2001. *The Theme–Topic Interface: Evidence from English*. Amsterdam: John Benjamins.
Halliday, M.A.K. 1967. Notes on transitivity and theme in English, Part 2. *Journal of Linguistics* 3(2): 199–244.

Halliday, M.A.K. 1968. Notes on transitivity and theme in English, Part 3. *Journal of Linguistics* 4(2): 179–215.

Halliday, M.A.K. 1970a. Language structure and language function. In J. Lyons (ed.) *New Horizons in Linguistics*. Harmondsworth: Penguin, pp. 140–65.

Halliday, M.A.K. 1970b. *A Course in Spoken English: Intonation*. Oxford: Oxford University Press.

Halliday, M.A.K. 1973. *Explorations in the Functions of Language*. London: Arnold.

Halliday, M.A.K. 1985. *An Introduction to Functional Grammar*. London: Arnold.

Halliday, M.A.K. 1994. *An Introduction to Functional Grammar*. 2nd edn. London: Arnold.

Hasan, R., and P.H. Fries (eds). 1995. *On Subject and Theme: A Discourse Functional Perspective*. Amsterdam: John Benjamins.

He, H. 2004. An alternative perspective on pseudo-clefts: Sphere shifts in English. Unpublished PhD thesis. Sun Yat-sen University, Guangzhou.

Huang, G.W. 1996. Experiential enhanced theme in English. In M. Berry, C.S. Butler, R.P. Fawcett and G.W. Huang (eds) *Meaning and Form: Systemic Functional Interpretations – Meaning and Choice in Language: Studies for Michael Halliday*. Norwood, NJ: Ablex, pp. 65–112.

Huang, G.W. 2003. *Enhanced Theme in English: Its Structures and Functions*. Shanxi: Shanxi Education Press.

Huang, G.W., and R.P. Fawcett. 1996. A functional approach to two 'focussing' constructions in English and Chinese. *Language Sciences* 18(1–2): 179–94.

Martin, J.R. 1992. *English Text: System and Structure*. Amsterdam: John Benjamins.

Quirk, R., S. Greenbaum, G. Leech and J. Svartvik. 1985. *A Comprehensive Grammar of the English Language*. London: Longman.

Thompson, G. 2004. *Introducing Functional Grammar*. 2nd edn. London: Arnold.

Thompson, G. 2014. *Introducing Functional Grammar*. 3rd edn. London: Arnold.

Wang, Y. 2008. *A Functional Study of the Evaluative Enhanced Theme Construction in English*. London and Singapore: Pearson (Prentice Hall).

12

Transitivity in the Cardiff Grammar

Amy Neale

Introduction

TRANSITIVITY is the linguistic system that enables a speaker to refer to events, happenings and 'goings-on'. In the second half of the twentieth century, some key works on transitivity relations emerged that shifted the concept from concern with the number of direct objects and verb arguments that a predicate in a clause can take to a system that provides for the semantic functioning of verb senses and their arguments. This system facilitates the classification of verbal arguments in the form of semantic roles, and provides a model in which the presence and type of the semantic roles serve as a predictor of the clause's 'Process type'.

Halliday (1994: 106) states that the TRANSITIVITY system allows us to 'construe the world of experience into a manageable set of process types'. This type of 'experiential' meaning is manifested at the level of form in the Main Verb and its extensions. In the Cardiff Grammar (CG), these formal items realise the 'Process' in the clause and the associated 'Participant Roles' at the level of meaning.

Fawcett (1980: 134) describes the 'experiential component' of language – which includes TRANSITIVITY – as expressing 'the meanings through which a language reflects the objects, qualities and relationships that a person finds in the world around him'. He goes on to describe that:

> [T]he referent situation that has been formulated by the performer's problem solver for transmission to the addressee is viewed as 'process', and then the term 'process' is to be interpreted in a sense that includes 'relationships' and 'states' as well as 'actions' and 'changes of relationship and state'.
>
> *Fawcett 1980: 134*

Within Fawcett's early works, we find the roots for the CG approach to TRANSITIVITY. Here, Fawcett begins to describe language as a programme that entails system networks, which enable the expression of the language's 'meaning potential' at the same time as proposing a model compatible with cognitive approaches to human communication.

This chapter is concerned with the system through which the TRANSITIVITY elements of the clause are realised. The chapter provides some broad context for TRANSITIVITY, as well as a full description of the current CG system. As such, much of what appears here is a summary of works already published, with references provided within the chapter.

Other approaches to TRANSITIVITY

To appreciate the motivations behind CG and the present-day development of the model, it is useful to consider other approaches to this area of language. The CG is a model that is both influenced by, and developed in response to, such other approaches, and the following historical context points towards some of the ways in which the CG approach to TRANSITIVITY incorporates both a social and cognitive approach to linguistics.

Within transformational grammar, perhaps the most far-reaching work relating to TRANSITIVITY is Fillmore's (1968) theory of case grammar (later, frame semantics). This theory has been influential, not least because of the prominence it gives to semantics, and is used and developed through FrameNet, a human- and machine-readable lexical database of word senses and their associated frames. This tool has been used for computational linguistics and natural-language processing tasks, particularly as a data-training set for semantic role parsing.

Fillmore (1968) departs from what was increasingly becoming a mainstream approach to linguistics. His proposal for case grammar recognises two types of relation: 'pure' and 'labelled'. *Pure* relations are those that hold, for example, between the 'Subject' and the constituent Noun Phrase in the sentence, and the 'direct object' and the constituent Noun Phrase in the sentence. A *labelled* relation is that which holds between the Noun Phrase and Verb Phrase, 'which is mediated by a pseudocategory label such as Manner, Extent, Location, Agent' (Fillmore 1968: 16). In case grammar, it is this second category of labelled relations that assigns the 'case forms' and which involves a determination of the semantic function. Fillmore sees these cases as being innate and universal, and as determining the types of judgement that human beings are capable of making about the world. Moreover, he claims that these case forms serve the purpose of classifying the verbs in a language.

Fillmore (1968) provides semantic specifications and restrictions for his model: his Agent case role, for example, must be animate, plus each case category can occur only once in a sentence. These specifications reflect Fillmore's proposition that 'case assignments' take place in the deep structure of the sentence and not in the surface structure. In this way, Fillmore's work paved the way for Levin's work on alternations, at which we will look shortly.

Within the transformational grammar approach, Gruber (1965) also proposed that information about the semantic and pragmatic properties of the predicate should be included in the lexical entry. In so doing, he pioneered the way for what became Chomsky's 'theta theory'. Theta roles are ways of further describing the arguments associated with the predicate in a sentence. For Chomsky, like Fillmore, the theta roles are a restricted, finite, universal set. It is because of theta theory that Chomsky's 'subcategorisation' was abandoned and selection information became redundant, leading us to infer that semantic information has primacy over syntactic information about a word and its context in the clause.

While Fillmore and Chomsky were beginning to introduce semantics into TRANSITIVITY, they provided frameworks that are fundamentally syntagmatic in nature. In contrast, systemic functional linguistics (SFL) provides a system that is paradigmatic and thus enables us to think more broadly about possible applications.

Developing out of the Fillmore paradigm, Levin's (1993) *English Verb Classes and Alternations* provides a large classificatory analysis of verbs in English (3,262 in total), providing syntactic and semantic categories for each, and is configured paradigmatically. Levin's hypothesis is that a verb's 'alternations' and its internal structures are determined by its meaning. Levin's work goes further than Chomsky's theta theory by proposing that the semantic information in the lexicon determines the syntactic behaviour of the verb.

Levin's large and well-known classification of verbs in English has now been configured as a database in the VerbNet project, in which 'each verb class . . . is completely described by thematic roles, selectional restrictions on the arguments, and frames consisting of a syntactic description and semantic predicates with a temporal function'.[1] Like FrameNet, VerbNet is being widely deployed for natural language-processing tasks.

Fellbaum's (1998) *A Semantic Network of English Verbs* provides an account of how the verbal lexicon is classified for entry into the WordNet lexical database, through which its creators seek to cover all aspects of language. The classification that the WordNet creators have produced recognises syntactic frames for each verb, but does not link these frames to the semantic, or 'thematic', roles.

As with Fillmore and Levin, the goal for WordNet is to carve up the 'verb lexicon' into semantically related fields. These domains were then rebuilt into groups of synonyms, which are referred to as 'synsets'. These sets are constituted of verbs that can be substituted for each – that is, which are claimed to be synonyms of each other, such as *shut* and *close*.

Within a functional linguistic paradigm, Hopper and Thompson (1980) developed a model of transitivity based on cross-linguistic discourse. They proposed a number of transitivity variables, which, when combined, define whether a clause displays what they term 'high transitivity' or 'low transitivity'.

Hopper and Thompson's approach is related to the systemic functional approach, with a model for transitivity that is based on a semantic continuum, from low to high – but it does not account for levels of delicacy through a system that moves from grammar to lexical item. It is this systemic approach that marks out SFL, and thus CG, and an element that ensures that the model is as applicable to modelling the production of language as the description of language. While Hopper and Thompson's model supports discourse analysis, it does not enable language generation, whereas CG aims to provide for both.

More recently, Faber and Mairal Uson's (1999) *Constructing a Lexicon of English Verbs* is carried out in the framework of Dik's functional grammar (FG). Faber and Mairal Uson propose the value of organising predicates into coherent semantic classes, encoding both syntactic and semantic regularities. They have developed the 'functional-lexematic model' (FLM) and their intention is to expand the FG lexicon – particularly in the area of verbs, because they propose that a verb's semantic components can reflect their syntactic properties. While their starting point is similar to Levin's, Faber and Mairal Uson are working within a different framework, and seek to map both paradigmatic and syntagmatic information onto each verb entry in the lexicon, aiming to include information in their lexicon of how lexemes are related to other lexemes, as 'dynamic representations within a conceptual network' (Faber and Mairal Uson 1999: 3).

Faber and Mairal Uson move away from a flat taxonomy to something more akin to the system network model of SFL, with a hierarchical structure with classifications and further subclassifications. They also recognise that verbs in the lexicon should be accompanied by 'meaning components' or 'semantic features', such as Agent, Goal/Patient and Beneficiary, similar to Chomsky's theta roles, Fillmore's 'cases', and Halliday and Fawcett's Participant Roles. Their syntactic analysis of the verbs in the lexicon consists of observing the complementation patterns for each verb, and they suggest that semantic parameters constrain and filter the syntax of a verb. They provide a large-scale demonstration of the FLM approach, providing 'synsem' (syntactic-semantic) information for a large and impressive number of interrelated lexical domains and subdomains.

TRANSITIVITY in SFL

In his article, 'Categories of theory of grammar', Halliday (1961) had no concept of 'system network' for TRANSITIVITY and, at this stage, the system is referred to only in relation to structure – that is, the syntagmatic description of verbs and the arguments they might take. Halliday's (1976: 69) seminal publication is, however, the first description of 'lexis as most delicate grammar' and is therefore an important precursor.

Halliday's first published system network showing how TRANSITIVITY might be modelled is presented in Kress (1976). This network is accompanied by a set of 'realization statements' (Halliday 1976: 111) giving an indication of the possible surface forms that might result from a traversal of the network. His 'Notes on Transitivity and Theme, Part 2' (Halliday 1968) is both a review and a refinement of his earlier description of TRANSITIVITY (Halliday 1967), including the introduction of the 'ergative' pattern in English and thus the introduction of the semantic role 'Affected' for Processes involving causation.

Importantly, Halliday recognises the prevalence of ergative functions in all types of Process – not only action clauses (which are typically transitive), but also relational and mental Processes. The recognition of ergativity leads to the introduction of further semantic roles of Agent and Medium, and the development of his concept of TRANSITIVITY towards a more 'semantic' system network. It is not, however, until his paper 'Language structure and language function' that Halliday (1970) really begins to elevate the status of 'system' within his theory. In this publication, he begins to introduce the idea that the meaning potential of language is modelled by semantic choices in a system network. This work, which emphasises the semantics of the clause, is where Halliday explicitly disputes the need for a dichotomy between 'competence' and 'performance', and it is from this point on that Process types and Participant functions become the centre of the 'ideational' metafunction. It is also in this work that Halliday begins to propose semantically based labels for the Participants associated with the different Process types.

Fawcett's (1981 [1973]) publication 'Generating a sentence in systemic functional grammar' began to specify the detail for what was to become the CG system of TRANSITIVITY. In this publication, Fawcett took up the challenge of Halliday's (1961) earlier proposal to generate lexis through a system network. The means that Fawcett provided for doing this did not involve the merging of grammar and lexis into the continuum of a single network, but rather maintaining them as two networks equally dependent on each other, which are entered simultaneously. What Fawcett's simultaneity did not encompass, however, was how to account for the fact that choices made in the TRANSITIVITY network (that is, the type of Process or the type of Role to be generated) may influence or even direct the choices to be made in the lexicon.

In his book *Cognitive Linguistics and Social Interaction*, Fawcett (1980) provides his first full treatment of TRANSITIVITY and it is in this description that we see the centrality of Participant Roles within the system. In his system for TRANSITIVITY, the roles are clearly central to defining the Process type, with the detailed description of the system for 'action' Processes being defined by the roles chosen in the network. This description lays the foundation for Fawcett's later introduction of Re-expression tests – a set of defined semantic tests used for determining Process type and Participant Role.

In his book, Fawcett (1980) discusses what the network should be concerned with, concluding as follows:

1   The network will generate a 'selection expression', which specifies the Process type. Thus the Process type generated by the network will produce an Inherent Role configuration, 'including a specification of whether they will be realized "overtly" or "covertly", and so whether or not an Inherent Role will be realized in items at the level of form' (Fawcett 1980: 136).
2   The entry conditions to other system networks.
3   Associated lexical verbs that are produced as a result of the Process type classifications and the Inherent Role configurations.

Fawcett's approach is one whereby TRANSITIVITY belongs fundamentally at the level of semantics, which differs greatly from a view of it being concerned merely with complementation patterns.

To bring in another systemic functional perspective on TRANSITIVITY, it is useful to consider Davidse's approach to 'experiential meaning' (Davidse 1991, 1992; Davidse and Geyskens 1998). Davidse takes Halliday's framework as her basis, but pushes his system network approach for TRANSITIVITY further.

Davidse's uses Whorf's definition of 'reactances' as the covert markers that identify cryptotypes in language and, similarly to Fawcett, she sees the configuration of Participant Roles as the 'reactance' for reaching TRANSITIVITY categories in English. This use of Process and Participant Role configuration as reactance is similar to the manner in which Fawcett (1980) models different 'material' Process types as 'agent-centred' Processes and 'affected-centred' Processes.

Essentially, the distinction between these two types enables the modelling of causation and non-causation of the Process, and the central tenet of Davidse's (1991: 27) description is that the 'transitive' is 'Actor-centred' and the 'ergative' is 'Medium-centred'.

Davidse (1992) takes the distinction between transitive and ergative forms, and examines certain fine distinctions within each. In the 'transitive' type, the Goal is an 'inert affected' and the 'process is being done to it, but the Goal itself does not "do" the process' (Davidse 1992: 118). In the 'ergative' type, the Process *happens* to the Medium. Through the investigation of cryptotypes at work in the system of TRANSITIVITY, Davidse suggests a number of distinctions within each of the transitive and ergative types in order to produce a full picture of TRANSITIVITY. Importantly, she identifies certain TRANSITIVITY types that are not found in Halliday's network, thus extending the system of TRANSITIVITY by allowing for the transitive and ergative distinctions to be modelled through Participant Role configuration within the main TRANSITIVITY system.

The Cardiff Grammar model of TRANSITIVITY

The CG is a model of language that finds its basis in SFL and which has grown from the work of a number of scholars mainly at Cardiff University. The tenets of this branch of systemic functional theory come, in particular, from the ideas first presented by Fawcett (1981 [1973]), which he expanded upon in his book *Cognitive Linguistics and Social Interaction* (Fawcett 1980). The scholar who has written most on the area of Transitivity in CG is Fawcett (1980, 1981 [1973], 1987, 1996, 2010 [2001], 2008, 2009, 2011, 2012, forthcoming), but with contributions from others, including Fawcett and colleagues (1996), Tucker (1995, 1996, 1998)

Table 12.1 Comparing Cardiff Grammar and Sydney Grammar Process types

Cardiff Grammar Process type	Sydney Grammar Process type
Action	Material
	Behavioural
Relational	Relational
	Existential
Mental	Mental
	Verbal
Influential	Mental
	Material
Event-relating	Relational
Environmental	

and Neale (2002, 2006, 2011). As a description of the CG system of TRANSITIVITY, what follows is a summary of work that has already been presented in these various publications.

In the current CG TRANSITIVITY system network, there are three main Process type categories – 'action' processes, 'relational' processes and 'mental' processes – plus three further categories of 'influential' processes, 'event-relating' processes, and the minor and referentially limited 'environmental' processes.

For readers who may be more familiar with the Sydney SF dialect, Table 12.1 outlines the main differences between the Sydney and Cardiff descriptions of Process type.

As Halliday and Matthiessen (2004: 174) state: 'Systemic terms are not Aristotelian categories. Rather, they are fuzzy categories; they can be thought of as representing fuzzy sets rather than "crisp" ones.' This approach is embedded within the CG model of language. Rather than categories for Process types based on their meaning as defined at a point in time, each area of semantically related Processes is distinguishable according to its Participant Role configuration. It is exactly this approach that has led to the introduction of the new Process type categories of 'influential' and 'event-relating' in CG. Based on a corpus approach, these new categories have been incorporated into the TRANSITIVITY system to allow for the generation of verb senses whereby the Participant Roles associated do not pass the re-expression tests.

Fawcett (2011) provides an objective test for each possible Participant Role. The re-expression tests serve as reactances that allow us to identify the cryptotypical TRANSITIVITY categories that exist. Fawcett's grammatical tests are ways in which the clause can be re-expressed that will enable the analyst to understand the semantic function that is taking place.

The following sections address each of the CG Process types, describing the meanings that each construes, the Participant Role configurations that realise them and the requisite re-expression tests for the Participant Roles as footnotes.

'Action' Processes

In recent years, Fawcett has returned to the description of 'action' Processes, for the reason that a large number of 'non-material action' Processes exist that must be included in this category of Process type. In particular, there are many 'social action' Processes that pass the requisite tests for Processes of this type, but which do not involve material action. The 'action' Process network therefore incorporates 'material action' Processes and 'social action' Processes.

Amy Neale

The processes that are realised through the 'action' system network broadly realise clauses that Halliday and Matthiessen (2004: 179) would describe as 'processes of doing-&-happening'.

Examples of action Process clauses, covering all options in the action Process system network, along with the associated probes, are as illustrated in Table 12.2.

Table 12.2 Action Processes

Example clause, with Participant Roles identified	Probe / test for Participant Roles
(1) Action, one-role, Agent only: *We all* (Ag) *used to cheat* (Pro) *in exams*	If X is the possible Agent (Ag), the clause can be re-expressed as *What X did was to . . .* The Agent is typically animate and usually human OR has 'creature-like' qualities
(2) Action, one-role, Affected only: *His mother* (Af) *died* (Pro) *of pneumonia*	If X is the possible Affected (Af), the clause can be re-expressed as *What happened to X was that . . .* , plus failure in the Agent test
(3) Action, one-role, Created only: *The race* (Cre) *started* (Pro)	If X is the possible Created (Cre), the clause can be re-expressed as *What came into being was X* or, in the case of 'preventing', etc., *What didn't come into being was X* In Action process clauses, the Created occurs either in a two-role process with an Agent or in a one-role process. The Created role also occurs with influential Processes (see examples (40)–(52)).
(4) Action, one-role, Carrier only: *A ship* (Ca) *appeared* (Pro) *in the distance*	If X is the possible Carrier (Ca), the clause can be re-expressed as *The thing about X is that . . .* (adding *as a result* if it is an Agent-Carrier or Affected-Carrier)
(5) Action, two-role, plus Affected: *He* (Ag) *hit* (Pro) *the burglar* (Af) *on the head*	Tests as above
(6) Action, two-role, plus Created: *I* (Ag) *make* (Pro) *cakes* (Cre)	Tests as above
(7) Action, two-role, plus Range: *Have you* (Ag) *read* (Pro) *that article* (Ra)?	If X is the possible Range (Ra) and Y is the other possible PR, the clause can be re-expressed as *What Y (Main Verb) was X* (plus failure in the other relevant tests (Affected, Created, Matchee, etc)' OR, for a complex example, re-express as *What was it that Y (Main Verb)? It was X* Typically, a non-sentient object, either a distance (e.g. *two miles*) or a reified Process (e.g. *a shower*), or – in the case of 'influential' and 'event-relating' Processes – an embedded event filled by either clause or nominalisation; typically occurs as second PR
(8) Action, two-role, plus Manner: *A circuit* (Ag) *behaves* (Pro) *in exactly the same way* (Ma)	If X is the possible Manner (Ma) and Y is the possible Agent (Ag), the clause can be re-expressed as *X is how Y behaved*
(9) Action, three-role, plus Affected plus Manner: *Artie* (Ag) *treated* (Pro) *most women* (Af) *with indifference* (Ma)	Tests as above

The primary distinction in the system network is the number of Participant Roles that will accompany the Process in the clause. This is a change in CG from that described in Fawcett (1980), and reflects the abandonment of the system that offers a choice between 'agent-centred' and 'affected-centred' Processes, which allowed for the capture of transitive and ergative Process constructions. In the Sydney Grammar, provision is made for transitive and ergative clauses through the use of different Participant Roles (Actors and Goals occur in transitive clauses, and Agents and Mediums occur in ergative clauses).

In CG, there is no generalisation to capture the ergative and transitive uses of a verb form; rather, the two uses are now recognised as different verb senses, which are generated from different places within the system network. The abandonment of the 'agent-centred' or 'affected-centred' distinction is the result of refining the set of Participant Roles within the TRANSITIVITY system. The participant is no longer both 'Agent' and 'Actor', but simply an 'Agent'. By classifying all of the Participant Roles in the 'action' Process system network as either Agents or Affecteds, or both, the CG framework has enough labels to indicate the degree of causation.

'Relational' Processes

The CG 'relational' Process system includes an important generalisation: all five sub-classes of relational Process type ('attributive', 'locational', 'directional', 'possessive' and 'matching') take the same Participant Role configurations. Therefore, on a pass through the system network, both the system for choosing Participant Role *and* Process type must be entered simultaneously.

Examples of all the relational Process clauses that can be generated through the system network are laid out in Table 12.3.

In CG, the 'relational' Process system also allows for the generation of compound roles; thus an Agent and an Affected can each be conflated with a Carrier to specify the

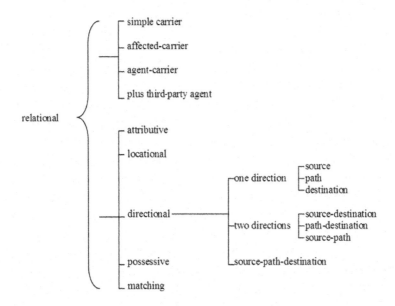

Figure 12.1 The current system network for relational Processes in the Cardiff Grammar

Table 12.3 Relational Processes

Example clause, with Participant Roles identified	Probe/test for Participant Roles
(10) Relational, Attributive, Simple Carrier: *He* (Ca) *doesn't resemble* (Pro) *the robber* (At)	If X is the possible Carrier (Ca), the clause can be re-expressed as *The thing about X is that . . .* (adding *as a result* if it is an Agent-Carrier or Affected-Carrier) If X is the possible Attribute (At) and Y is the possible Carrier (Ca), the clause can be re-expressed as *X is what (or how or who) Y was* (adding *as a result* if necessary)
(11) Relational, Attributive, Affected Carrier: *She* (Af-Ca) *broke out in* (Pro) *a rash* (At)	The test for Af-Ca is the same as the test for Carrier above, adding *as a result*
(12) Relational, Attributive, Agent Carrier: *I* (Ag-Ca) *maintained* (Pro) *my friendship with her* (At)	The test for Ag-Ca is the same as the test for Carrier above, adding *as a result*
(13) Relational, Attributive, plus third-party Agent: *Martin Luther* (Ag) *translated* (Pro) *the bible* (Af-Ca) *into German* (At)	Tests as above
(14) Relational, Locational, Simple Carrier: *She* (Ca) *is* (Pro) *in Australia* (Loc)	If X is the possible Location (Loc) and Y is the possible Carrier (Ca), the clause can be re-expressed as *X is where (or when) Y was*
(15) Relational, Locational, Affected Carrier: *Soviet Territory* (Af-Ca) *borders* (Pro) *on Poland* (Loc)	Tests as above
(16) Relational, Locational, Agent Carrier: *I* (Ag-Ca) *sank* (Pro) *into his biggest armchair* (Loc)	Tests as above
(17) Relational, Locational, plus third-party Agent: *He* (Ag) *tied* (Pro) *her hands* (Af-Ca) *behind her back* (Loc)	Tests as above
(18) Relational, Directional, Simple Carrier: *Icy wind* (Ca) *swept* (Pro) *through the streets* (Des)	If X is the possible Destination (Des) and Y is the possible Carrier (Ca), the clause can be re-expressed as *Y went to/towards X* The two other possible roles that can occur in a Directional process clause are Source (So) and Path (Pa). Respectively, the re-expression test for Source is *Y went away from X* (referred to by Fawcett as T10) and for Path is *Y went via X*
(19) Relational, Directional, Affected Carrier: *The bus* (Af-Ca) *ran* (Pro) *into the car* (Des)	Tests as above
(20) Relational, Directional, Agent Carrier: *She* (Ag-Ca) *pulled back* (Pro) *from the window* (So)	Tests as above
(21) Relational, Directional, plus third–party Agent: *Mrs Kaul* (Ag) *led* (Pro) *him* (Af-Ca) *to his seat* (Des)	Tests as above
(22) Relational, Possessive, Simple Carrier: *The land* (Ca) *belongs to* (Pro) *the big family* (Pos)	If X is the possible Possessed (Pos) and Y is the possible Carrier (Ca), the clause can be re-expressed as *X was what Y had/lacked* (adding *as a result* if necessary)

(23) Relational, Possessive, Affected Carrier: Tests as above
The train (Af-Ca) *gathered* (Pro) *speed*
(Pos)

(24) Relational, Possessive, Agent Carrier: *We*   Tests as above
(Ag-Ca) *hired* (Pro) *a car* (Pos)

(25) Relational, Possessive, plus third–party   Tests as above
Agent: *The taxman* (Ag) *gave* (Pro) *me*
(Af-Ca) *a £783 rebate* (Pos)

(26) Relational, Matching, Simple Carrier: *You*   If X is the possible Matchee (Mtch) and Y is the
(Ca) *don't take after* (Pro) *your sister*   possible Carrier (Ca) or Phenomenon (Ph), the
(Mtch)   clause can be re-expressed as *It was X that Y*
matched (or didn't match) OR *It was X that Y was*
matched with (or was not matched with) OR *It was*
X that Y became joined with (or unjoined from)

(27) Relational, Matching, Affected Carrier: Tests as above
Her disdain (Af-Ca) *changed* (Pro) *to*
respect (Mtch)

(28) Relational, Matching, Agent Carrier: *Len*   Tests as above
(Ag-Ca) *tied the knot* (Pro) *with Kate*
(Mtch)

(29) Relational, Matching, plus third-party   Tests as above
Agent: *We* (Ag) *will combine* (Pro)
liberty (Af-Ca) *with order* (Mtch)

---

precise semantic function of the role. Particularly important is the configuration within a clause of an Agent with the compound role of Affected-Carrier, which is central to the three role Processes that can be generated through the 'relational' system. In the network, they are termed 'plus third-party Agent' Processes, because a 'third party' is introduced to what would otherwise be a two-role Process. This configuration facilitates the generation of 'possessive' Processes such as example (25).

'Mental' Processes

In the mental Process system, different Participant Roles are associated with sub-Process type and four separate single Participant Roles are offered to fulfil these different Participant Role configurations: Emoter, Perceiver, Cognisant and Phenomenon. All of these can occur with the fourth Participant Role of Phenomenon. This set of Participant Role configurations allows for a delicate semantic specification, in turn allowing for revealing analyses of the Process in a clause.

In the Sydney Grammar, all 'mental' Processes occur with the Participant Role configurations of 'Sensor' and 'Phenomenon'. The CG proposes different Participant Roles associated with each 'mental' Process type – Emoter, Perceiver, Cognisant – each of which can occur with the fourth Participant Role of Phenomenon, thus allowing for a more delicate semantic specification.

Examples of all the mental Process clauses that can be generated through the TRANSITIVITY system network are given in Table 12.4.

'Influential' Processes

Fawcett (forthcoming: ch. 2, §3.7) describes the 'influential' Process type to model a set of Processes in the grammar that is not accounted for elsewhere in the TRANSITIVITY system.

Table 12.4 Mental Processes

Example clause, with Participant Roles identified	Probe/test for Participant Roles
(30) Mental, Emotion, Emotive, Emoter-oriented: *She* (Em) *is in love with* (Pro) *him* (Ph)	If X is the possible Emoter (Em) and Y is the possible Phenomenon (Ph), the clause can be re-expressed as *X had a good/bad feeling about/need for Y* (adding, if necessary, *the idea of* before Y) If X is the possible Phenomenon (Ph), the clause can be re-expressed as *Y had a good/bad feeling about X'* (where Y is the Emoter), OR *Y physically perceived* (where Y is the Perceiver), OR *Y knew/thought/didn't know X* (where Y is the Cognisant) (adding *as a result* in all cases if necessary) While most PRs are typically filled by a 'thing', the Phenomenon is typically filled by an 'event'
(31) Mental, Emotion, Emotive, Phenomenon-oriented: *Her performance* (Ph) *absolutely knocked* (Pro) *me* (Em) *out* (PrEx)	Tests as above In this example, 'out' is a Process Extension (labelled 'PrEx') and therefore part of the Process and not a PR
(32) Mental, Emotion, Desiderative: *Be careful what* (Ph) *you* (Em) *wish for* (Pro)	Tests as above
(33) Mental, Perception, Simple-Perceiver: *He* (Perc) *experienced* (Pro) *a pang of sadness* (Ph)	If X is the possible Perceiver (Perc) and Y is the possible Phenomenon (Ph), the clause can be re-expressed as *X physically perceived Y* (adding *as a result* if necessary) The term 'physically' is needed because many verbs are also used in 'cognition' Processes
(34) Mental, Perception, Agent-Perceiver: *He* (Ag-Perc) *tasted* (Pro) *the wine* (Ph)	The test for Ag-Perc is the same as the test for Perceiver above, adding *as a result*
(35) Mental, Perception, plus third-party Agent: *Francis* (Ag) *concealed* (Pro) *the machine* (Ph) *from us* (Af-Perc)	The test for Af-Perc is the same as the test for Perceiver above, adding *as a result*
(36) Mental, Cognition, Simple-Cognisant: *We* (Cog) *know* (Pro) *the Smiths* (Ph)	If X is the possible Cognisant (Cog) and Y is the possible Phenomenon (Ph), the clause can be re-expressed as *X knew/thought/didn't know Y* (adding *as a result* if necessary).
(37) Mental, Cognition, Affected-Cognisant: *I* (Af-Cog) *remember* (Pro) *cabling home for money* (Ph)	The test for Af-Cog is the same as the test for Perceiver above, adding *as a result*
(38) Mental, Cognition, Agent-Cognisant: *They* (Ag-Cog) *were choosing* (Pro) *sweets from the stall* (Ph)	Tests as above
(39) Mental, Cognition, plus third-party Agent: *We* (Ag) *persuaded* (Pro) *them* (Af-Cog) *we were genuinely interested* (Ph)	Tests as above

Processes of this type all include an embedded event in the matrix clause that is somehow 'influenced' in one way or another by the Process.

In his description of the 'influential' Processes, Fawcett states that some 'causation' Processes could be interpreted as 'three-role' 'cognition' Processes. However, the processes of 'making', 'forcing', 'allowing' and 'preventing' do not 'explicitly express the meaning of the Process of "communication" ' (Fawcett forthcoming: ch. 2, §3.7) and so do not involve verbal causation. Therefore this new category shares some of the characteristics of 'action' Processes. As such, they are defined by the Participant Role configuration that they can take.

Examples of all the influential Process clauses that can be generated through the TRANSITIVITY system network are as follows.

(40) Influential, with agent, control, causative: *The state* (Ag) *must ensure* (Pro) *law-abiding people are protected* (Cre)

(41) Influential, with agent, control, permissive: *He* (Ag) *let* (Pro) *Jack lead the way* (Cre)

(42) Influential, with agent, control, preventative: *The policy* (Ag) *hindered* (Pro) *reform* (Cre)

(43) Influential, with agent, control stage of process, starting: *They* (Ag) *kicked off* (Pro) *a two month tour* (Cre)

(44) Influential, with agent, control stage of process, continuing: *They* (Ag) *kept on* (Pro) *walking* (Ra)

(45) Influential, with agent, control stage of process, delaying: *The flight* (Ra) *had been postponed* (Pro)

(46) Influential, with agent, control stage of process, ceasing: *He* (Ag) *killed* (Pro) *the conversation* (Ra)

(47) Influential, with agent, tentative: *The crowd* (Ag) *attempted* (Pro) *to break through* (Ra)

(48) Influential, with affected, success, succeeding: *He* (Af) *managed to* (Pro) *find us* (Ra)

(49) Influential, with affected, success, failing: *She* (Af) *failed* (Pro) *in her attempt to swim the channel* (Ra)

(50) Influential, with affected, stage of process, starting: *I* (Af) *have come* (Pro) *to like him* (Cre)

(51) Influential, with affected, stage of process, continuing: *The girder* (Af) *kept on* (Pro) *bending* (Ra)

(52) Influential, with affected, stage of process, ceasing: *The clock* (Af) *stopped* (Pro) *ticking* (Ra)

In the case of 'influential' Process clauses, where an Agent brings an event into being, the Created Participant Role is realised as either a full clause or a nominalisation.

'Event-relating' Processes

'Event-relating' Processes are a new addition to the CG TRANSITIVITY system, described by Fawcett as a 'work in progress' that recognises a Process type that is a relatively new phenomenon in the language. This category allows for Processes whose meaning has been extended through metaphor to relate two events to each other.

While Halliday deals with these Processes as grammatical metaphor, meaning that both a 'congruent' and an 'incongruent' analysis must be provided for such occurrences, Fawcett proposes that these Processes should be analysed as a separate Process type, suggesting that 'there is no longer any semantic connection with (their) historical origin' (Fawcett forthcoming).

The full set of event-relating Process clauses that can be generated through the TRANSITIVITY system network are as in examples (53)–(67).

(53) Event-relating, cause-to-effect, causing effect: *A degree in English* (Ca) *could lead to* (Pro) *a career in journalism* (Ra)

(54) Event-relating, cause-to-effect, requiring effect: *Lack of money* (Ca) *necessitated* (Pro) *a change in plan* (Ra)

(55) Event-relating, cause-to-effect, allowing effect: *A 24 hour ceasefire* (Ca) *allowed* (Pro) *the two armies to reach an agreement* (Cre)

(56) Event-relating, cause-to-effect, affecting effect: *The downturn in consumer spending* (Ca) *has affected* (Pro) *trading* (Ra)

(57) Event-relating, cause-to-effect, preventing effect: *The rain* (Ca) *stopped* (Pro) *us from enjoying the trip* (Ra)

(58) Event-relating, cause-to-effect, ending effect: *Safety concerns* (Ca) *have halted* (Pro) *work on the dam* (Ra)

(59) Event-relating, effect-from-cause: *Inflation* (Ca) *results from* (Pro) *an excess of demand over supply* (Ra)

(60) Event-relating, inferential, premise-to-inference: *The merger* (Ca) *will mean* (Pro) *the closure of the company's Sydney office* (Ra)

(61) Event-relating, inferential, inference-to-premise: *The idea of heaven* (Ca) *presupposes* (Pro) *the existence of God* (Ra)

(62) Event-relating, temporal, earlier-to-later: *Political journalism shakeups* (Ca) *precede* (Pro) *midterms* (Ra)

(63) Event-relating, temporal, later-to-earlier: *Sunshine* (Ca) *followed* (Pro) *rain* (Ra)

(64) Event-relating, comparison, identity: *A remote control car race* (Ca) *symbolises* (Pro) *how easy it is to let their lives go off track* (Ra)

(65) Event-relating, comparison, similarity: *The situation on the ground* (Ca) *resembles* (Pro) *a conflict in the last stages* (Ra)

(66) Event-relating, comparison, difference: *These results* (Ca) *contrast* (Pro) *sharply with other medical tests* (Ra)

(67) Event-relating, simple co-occurrence: *Childhood diagnosis* (Ca) *was not associated with* (Pro) *changes in peak height velocity* (Ra)

Fawcett recognises that, when these verbs are used in their 'event relating' sense, the Participant Role configurations are different from what Halliday would recognise as their 'congruent' realisation.

Fawcett uses the example *lead to*, which is a 'three–role' 'directional' Process, as seen in example (21), repeated here for ease of reference.

(21)   *Mrs Kaul* (Ag) *led* (Pro) him (Af-Ca) *to his seat* (Des).

The sense of *lead to* as an 'event-relating' Process must be analysed differently from this. The 'event-relating' version has only two Participant Roles, which do not pass the test for the 'three-role' 'directional' type, as per example (53).

(53)   *A degree in English* (Ca) *could lead to* (Pro) *a career in journalism* (Ra)

This justifies recognising a new Process type category of 'event-relating' Processes, rather than these senses being metaphorised senses of a congruent 'directional' Process.

'Environmental' Processes

Finally, CG includes a system for recognising a referentially limited Process type, but one that is necessary in a full model of language. This is the system for 'environmental' Processes, for which there are two options, as follows.

(68)   Environmental, as process: *It rained* (Pro)

(69)   Environmental, as attribute: *It is* (Pro) *sunny* (At)

These Processes are not only frequent, especially in casual conversation, but also constructed in a unique manner.

The subject has no real-world referent, thus the item is referentially empty. This choice is the only option in the whole TRANSITIVITY system network that involves no Participant Roles, as per example (69) above.

This full set of Process types within the CG system of TRANSITIVITY describes an attempt to account satisfactorily for all relevant aspects of meaning. The full set has been tested against the analysis of 5,400 frequently occurring English verb senses (Neale 2002).

Future directions

As a theory that seeks to provide for language as both a cognitive and a social system, the CG approach has a great deal to tell us about TRANSITIVITY.

Considering the importance of 'language in use' as a cornerstone for developing and amending the systemic functional approach to linguistics, now, more than ever, we have a huge opportunity (a) to test the theory, using extremely large corpora to demonstrate instances of language in use, (b) to use the theory to explain what is going on when people are using language and (c) to expand the theory as language usage changes over time.

The centrality of choice within the theory is largely interdependent on the notion of 'probability'. Choice within the system is not a question of an individual user's choice, but of the likelihood of one element occurring over another based on previous language in use, plus a collective agreement on how the system works. It is this concept of language as social contract that, when combined with Fawcett's more programmatic approach, makes the Cardiff Grammar particularly powerful.

In conclusion, the advent of computing power combined with the volumes of user-generated content online presents us with an opportunity to really understand the probabilities of one feature occurring versus another based on choice. Perhaps more than anywhere else in the theory, it is the area of TRANSITIVITY for which this can be most readily applied.

Frequency of occurrence of individual verb senses – and, more importantly, co-occurrence and collocation – is what really leads us to understand what is happening within TRANSITIVITY. Back in 2001, when carrying out research for a doctoral degree, it was still extremely difficult to determine with scientific precision what verb senses are most frequently used in the language and how they are used; hence researchers relied not only on new studies based on corpora (such as Cobuild and Longman dictionaries), but also on old texts such as West's Service List (1953). Now, it is possible to access large bodies of data not only to learn at a point in time what is going on in a language, but also to enable machine learning approaches to create intelligent systems for natural-language processing.

For the system of TRANSITIVITY in the twenty-first century, we are now able to implement the full system network in a computational framework powered by real instances of language that can update probabilities of use to drive the generation of real instances of language, moving away from a pure theory to an application that tests the theory completely.

Note

1 http://verbs.colorado.edu/~mpalmer/projects/verbnet.html

References

Davidse, K. 1991. Categories of experiential grammar. Unpublished PhD thesis. Department of Linguistics, Katholieke Univeriteit, Leuven.

Davidse, K. 1992. Transitivity/ergativity: The Janus-headed grammar of actions and events. In M. Davies and L. Ravelli (eds) *Advances in Systemic Linguistics: Recent Theory and Practice*. London: Pinter, pp. 105–35.

Davidse, K., and S. Geyskens. 1998. 'Have you walked the dog yet?' The ergative causativization of intransitives. *WORD* 48(2): 155–80.

Faber, P., and R. Mairal Uson. 1999. *Constructing a Lexicon of English Verbs*. Berlin: Mouton.

Fawcett, R.P. 1980. *Cognitive Linguistics and Social Interaction: Towards an Integrated Model of a Systemic Functional Grammar and the Other Components of a Communicating Mind*. Heidelberg: Juliu Groos and Exeter University.

Fawcett, R.P. 1981 [1973]. Generating a sentence in a systemic functional grammar. In M.A.K. Halliday and J.R. Martin (eds) *Readings in Systemic Linguistics*. London: Batsford, pp. 146–83.

Fawcett, R.P. 1987. The semantics of clause and verb for relational processes in English. In M.A.K. Halliday and R.P. Fawcett (eds) *New Developments in Systemic Linguistics, Vol. 1: Theory and Description*. London: Pinter, pp. 130–83.

Fawcett, R.P. 1996. A systemic functional approach to complementation in English. In M. Berry, C. Butler, R.P. Fawcett and G.W. Huang. (eds) *Meaning and Form: Systemic Functional Interpretations*. Norwood, NJ: Ablex, pp. 297–366.

Fawcett, R.P. 2008. *Invitation to Systemic Functional Linguistics through the Cardiff Grammar: An Extension and Simplification of Halliday's Systemic Functional Grammar*. London: Equinox.

Fawcett, R.P. 2009. *Functional Syntax Handbook: Analysing English at the Level of Form*. London: Equinox.

Fawcett, R.P. 2010 [2001]. *A Theory of Syntax for Systemic Functional Linguistics* (Current Issues in Linguistic Theory 206). Amsterdam: John Benjamins.

Fawcett, R.P. 2011. Problems and solutions in identifying Processes and Participant Roles in discourse analysis, part 1: Introduction to a systematic procedure for identifying Processes and Participant Roles. *Annual Review of Functional Linguistics* 3: 34–87.

Fawcett, R.P. 2012. Problems and solutions in identifying Processes and Participant Roles in discourse analysis, part 2: How to handle metaphor, idiom and six other problems. *Annual Review of Functional Linguistics* 3: 27–76.

Fawcett, R.P. Forthcoming. *The Functional Semantics Handbook: Analysing English at the Level of Meaning*. London: Equinox.

Fawcett, R.P., G.H. Tucker and Y.Q. Lin. 1996. *The GENESYS Lexicogrammar Version 5.3*. Software. Computational Linguistics Unit, Cardiff University, Cardiff.

Fellbaum, C. (ed.). 1998. *WordNet: An Electronic Lexical Database*. Cambridge, MA: MIT Press.

Fillmore, C.J. 1968. The case for case. In E. Bach and R.T. Harms (eds) *Universals in Linguistic Theory*. New York: Holt, Rinehart & Winston, pp. 1–25.

Gruber, J. 1965. Lexical structures in syntax and semantics. Unpublished PhD dissertation. Massachusetts Institute of Technology, Cambridge, MA.

Halliday, M.A.K. 1961. Categories of the theory of grammar. *WORD* 17(3): 1–7.

Halliday, M.A.K. 1967. Notes on transitivity and theme, part 1. *Journal of Linguistics* 3(1): 37–81.

Halliday, M.A.K. 1968. Notes on transitivity and theme, part 2. *Journal of Linguistics* 4(2): 179–215.

Halliday, M.A.K. 1970. Language structure and language function. In J. Lyons (ed.) *New Horizons in Linguistics*. Harmondsworth: Penguin, pp. 141–65.

Halliday, M.A.K. 1976. English system networks. In G. Kress (ed.) *System and Function in Language: Selected Papers by M.A.K. Halliday*. Oxford: Oxford University Press, pp. 36–51.

Halliday, M.A.K. 1994. *An Introduction to Functional Grammar*. 2nd edn. London: Arnold.

Halliday, M.A.K., and C.M.I.M. Matthiessen. 2004. *An Introduction to Functional Grammar*. 3rd edn. London: Arnold.

Hopper, P., and S.A. Thompson. 1980. Transitivity in grammar and discourse. *Language* 56(2): 251–99.

Kress. 1976.

Levin, B. 1993. *English Verb Classes and Alternations: A Preliminary Investigation*. Chicago, IL: Chicago University Press.

Neale, A. 2002. More delicate TRANSITIVITY: Extending PROCESS-TYPE system networks for English to include full semantic classifications. Unpublished PhD thesis. Cardiff University, School of English Studies, Communication and Philosophy.

Neale, A. 2006. Matching corpus data and system networks: Using corpora to modify and extend the system networks for transitivity in English. In S. Hunston and G. Thompson (eds) *System and Corpus: Exploring Connections*. London: Equinox, pp. 143–63.

Neale, A. 2011. Alternation and participant role: A contribution from systemic functional grammar. In P. Guerrero Medina (ed.) *Morphosyntactic Relations in English: Functional and Cognitive Perspective*. London: Equinox, pp. 83–112.

Tucker, G.H. 1995. The treatment of lexis in a systemic functional model of English with special reference to adjectives and their structure. Unpublished PhD thesis. University of Wales, Cardiff, School of English Studies, Communication and Philosophy.

Tucker, G.H. 1996. 'So grammarians haven't the faintest idea': Reconciling lexis-oriented and grammar-oriented approaches to language. In R. Hasan, D. Butt and C. Cloran (eds) *Functional Descriptions: Language, Form and Linguistic Theory*. Amsterdam: John Benjamin, pp. 145–79.

Tucker, G.H. 1998. *The Lexicogrammar of Adjectives: A Systemic Functional Approach to Lexis*. London: Cassell Academic.

13

Theme in Spanish

Jorge Arús Hita

Introduction

In order to speak about Theme, we need at the same time to refer to functions such as Subject or Agent, in Spanish as well as in English. In Spanish, however, the combination –or conflation, in systemic terms– of Theme with Subject or Finite does not play a role in the expression of interpersonal meaning as it does in English (as we shall see later in the chapter). The way in which the different metafunctions interact has long been recognised as asymmetric –mostly concerning the relationship of the textual metafunction, the one within which the THEME system is found, with the others: '[I]t is only in combination with textual meanings that ideational and interpersonal meanings are actualized' (Halliday 1978: 113). In spite of the existence of systemic literature dealing with the internal workings of this interaction – for example Matthiessen (1992: 44), who speaks of '(i) the experiential and (ii) interpersonal modes of organizations as carriers of textual waves' – the second-order nature of textual meaning has arguably made of this metafunction the least transparent one and is perhaps the reason why it has been the most controversial.[1]

The textual metafunction is the hardest one to pin down, but at the same time it is that which arguably opens up more possibilities to look into the intricacies of the lexico-grammar of a particular language. Because 'the description of a particular language is the realization of the general theory' (Caffarel et al. 2004: 12), findings made in the description of the textual resources of a language other than English (LOTE) can be expected not only to shed light on that language's textual systems and their relationship with the ideational and interpersonal systems, but also to enrich systemic functional linguistics (SFL) theory by adding to the theoretical understanding of the textual metafunction and its interplay with the other metafunctions. While our focus in this chapter will remain on Spanish Theme, a number of issues will spring up that extend beyond the textual to implicate interpersonal factors, as well as the interrelation between textual and interpersonal meaning. The revision, in the second section of the chapter, of the existing research on Theme in Spanish will reveal some of those issues and how they have been addressed. Among them, the following stand out.

1 As will be seen, there tends to be an agreement that Theme in Spanish is manifested in clause-initial position. This brings about the following question: because the Subject is often left unexpressed in Spanish, for example *llegaron al mediodía* ('[they] arrived at midday'), is there an unexpressed Subject Theme – as in example (1a) – or is the clause-initial Process the Theme – as in example (1b)?

(1a) *ellos*	*llegaron*	*al mediodía*
they	arrived	at midday
Theme	Rheme	

(1b) *llegaron*		*al mediodía*
arrived		at midday
Theme		Rheme

2 Should elided Subjects be considered unrealised Themes – that is, if example (1b), above, were to be favoured, how should Process^Subject structures such as example (2), below, be analysed? Would the Process be the ideational Theme, as in example (2a), or should the Theme include also the post-verbal Subject, as in example (2b)?

(2a) *llegaron*	*más personas*	*al mediodía*
arrived	more people	at midday
Theme	Rheme	

(2b) *llegaron*	*más personas*	*al mediodía*
arrived	more people	at midday
Theme	Rheme	

The next question is not so much about Theme, but rather about how thematisation reveals an important interpersonal issue.

3 English statements typically thematise the Subject, whereas 'yes/no' questions have Finite^Subject as Theme (Halliday and Matthiessen 2013: 102). Since Spanish does not necessarily reflect this functional distinction on its interpersonal structure –as seen in example (3), below– is it worth speaking of a 'Mood structure' in Spanish?

(3a) *Han*	*llegado*
[They] have	arrived
Finite	Predicator
'They have arrived'	

(3b) ¿Han		llegado?
[They] have		arrived
Finite		Predicator
'Have they arrived?'		

These issues have been addressed in recent research, and will be revised and discussed here. Other problematic points will arise during our discussion of Spanish Theme that affect other areas of the lexicogrammar and which will not be thoroughly examined here, for reasons of space and focus. As will be seen in the concluding section, this chapter opens a number of avenues for future research.

The chapter is structured as follows: the next section looks at the existing views on Spanish Theme and the answers given to the issues mentioned above. The chapter then complements the views previously presented with a proposal that tries to account for the questions that the existing literature has so far left unresolved and which will help to carry out the thematic analysis of Spanish clauses, as is done in the more practical subsequent section. In conclusion, the final chapter recapitulates the main points made throughout and suggests future research directions.

Views on Spanish Theme

This section presents Theme in Spanish as treated by a number of authors. The interpersonal and the textual Theme are quite non-controversial in the literature. We will simply offer a description based on Lavid and colleagues (2010). Although this will also be the main source for the explanation of ideational Theme in Spanish, the discussion will here include a number of sources offering alternative views on more controversial issues, such as those presented in the introduction.

As the review of the literature will show, Theme in Spanish is characterised, according to the vast majority of sources, by its clause-initial position. Although this view is not so uniform when looking at ideational Theme (as we shall see), it can be safely applied to the identification of interpersonal, textual and absolute Themes (which different kinds of Theme are described in what follows). Following Halliday and Matthiessen (2013) for English, Lavid and colleagues (2010: 74) describe textual Theme as '[e]lements which are instrumental in the creation of the logical connections in the text, such as linkers, binders and other textual markers', and interpersonal Theme as '[e]lements which express the attitude and the evaluation of the speaker with respect to his/her message, including those expressing modality and polarity'. In this light, we can now analyse example (4) as shown below, with the linker *pero* as textual Theme[2] and the Comment Adjunct *en mi opinión* as interpersonal Theme.[3] As in English, textual Themes typically precede interpersonal Themes in Spanish – but note that the beginning of example (4) could be re-expressed as *en mi opinión, sin embargo, ...* ['in my opinion, however, ...], in which formulation the interpersonal precedes the textual Theme in a more marked realisation. We will come across the same example below with a specification of its ideational Theme.

(4) pero	en mi opinión	ha nacido para narrador de historias
but	in my opinion	has been born for storyteller
textual Theme	interpersonal Theme	
'But in my opinion he was born a storyteller'		

Lavid and colleagues (2010: 76–7) also speak about the other type of Theme that may precede the ideational Theme – that is, the absolute Theme, which is syntactically and prosodically independent, and therefore not controlled by polarity and/or modality features. Examples (5)–(7) include absolute Themes. As we can see in examples (5) and (6), the absolute Theme can be a syntactic constituent of the clause –*eso* in example (5) is Complement and *Modestia* in example (6) is Subject – and can be co-referential with a nuclear participant – with a Phenomenon in example (5) and an Actor in example (6). What makes them absolute Themes is the prosodic detachment with which they are expressed. Absolute Themes are often preceded by a textual Theme, as in example (7a). Absolute Themes have also been called 'Theme matter' (Lavid 2001; Taboada 1995) and they should not be confused with actual circumstances of matter, such as the one in example (8a). An easy way in which to differentiate an absolute Theme from a circumstance of matter is to try to place that element at the end of the sentence; if you can do so, then it is a circumstance, as in example (8b), otherwise it is an absolute Theme, as in example (7b). Absolute Themes are much more frequent in spoken, than in written, Spanish (Hidalgo-Downing 2003). As with example (4), the ideational Theme is, for the time being, left out of the analysis in these examples.

(5)	*Eso*	*no te lo crees ni tú*
	That	don't believe even you
	absolute Theme	
	'You don't believe that yourself'	

(6)	*Modestia, lo que se dice modestia,*	*tampoco parece acompañar a las explicaciones de la doctora Langer*
	Modesty, what one would call modesty	does not really seem to accompany Dr Langer's explanations
	absolute Theme	

(7a)	*Pero*	*en cuanto a la producción de crudos,*	*ésta se mantiene sobre los 25 millones de barriles diarios*
	But	as for crude production	this remains at about 25 million barrels per day
		textual Theme	absolute Theme

(7b) **ésta se mantiene sobre los 25 millones de barriles diarios en cuanto a la producción de crudos*

(8a)	*En cuanto a calidad,*	*las principales cervezas peruanas pueden competir con las mejores del mundo*
	Concerning quality	the main Peruvian brewers can compete with the best in the world
	Circumstance: matter	

(8b)	*las principales cervezas peruanas pueden competir con las mejores del mundo*	*en cuanto a calidad*
	The main Peruvian brewers can compete with the best in the world	concerning/in quality
		Circumstance: matter

We now turn to ideational Theme, where, as stated above, the main issue in Spanish is what to do when the Subject is not present. When it is present, the analysis is quite unproblematic: the clause-initial Subject is the ideational Theme, whether alone, as in examples (9) or (10), or in a multiple Theme – that is, preceded by other kinds of Theme, as in example (7), analysed for ideational Theme below.

(9)	*Yo*	*me fui sola*
	I	left alone
	ideational Theme	Rheme

(10)	*Tus palabras*	*me afectan hasta no sé donde*
	Your words	affect me more than I can imagine
	ideational Theme	

(7)	*Pero*	*en cuanto a la producción de crudos,*	*ésta*	*se mantiene sobre los 25 millones de barriles diarios*
	But	as for crude production	this	remains at about 25 million barrels per day
	textual Theme	absolute Theme	ideational Theme	Rheme

If the clause starts with a nuclear participant other than the Subject, then the analysis is also quite uncontroversial. For instance, in examples (11) and (12), the ideational Themes are the initial Complement and Adjunct, respectively. Incidentally, notice that if the Complement in example (11) or the Adjunct in example (12) were to be prosodically isolated from the rest of the clause, they would be absolute Themes. In writing, that would usually – although not necessarily (see example (5)) – be indicated by means of a comma after the absolute Theme. Complement and Adjunct Themes are not as frequent as Subject Themes, and their presence often reflects specific informational motivations, which makes them *marked* themes.[4]

(11)	*Esta*	*me la compré hace más de 20 años*
	This	I bought it over 20 years ago
	Complement	
	ideational Theme	Rheme

(12) *a mí*		*me apetece menos ir al teatro*
To me		I fancy less going to the theatre
Adjunct		
ideational Theme		Rheme
'I don't really feel like going to the theatre'		

We now turn to those structures that cause disagreement among researchers on Theme in Spanish – that is, verb-initial clauses, such as examples (13) and (14). The literature shows two main standpoints here, which can be summarized as follows: either the verb – that is, the Process – is the Theme, as in examples (13a) and (14a), or the unrealised Subject is the Theme, as in examples (13b) and (14b).

(13a) *Tengo*		*mucho que hacer*
(I) Have		a lot to do
Process		
ideational Theme		Rheme

(13b) *(Yo)*	*tengo*	*mucho que hacer*
(I)	Have	a lot to do
Subject/Carrier	Process	
ideational Theme	Rheme	

(14a) *¿fuiste*		*alguna vez creyente?*
Were (you)		ever a believer?
Process		
ideational Theme		Rheme

(14b) *(tú)*	*¿fuiste*	*alguna vez creyente?*
(you)	Were	ever a believer?
Subject/Carrier	Process	
ideational Theme	Rheme	

Process as Theme is the option most widely held (for example Taboada 1995; McCabe and Alonso 2001; McCabe 2002; Arús 2010; Lavid et al. 2010; Martín García and Gil 2011). The main argument in favour of the thematic status of clause-initial verbs in Spanish is the fact that the verbal suffix provides the person and number information necessary for

---

the tracking of participants in pretty much the same way as the personal pronoun does in English. In order to account for this, Lavid and colleagues (2010) put forward a more delicate type of thematic analysis in which the first element allowing the tracking of participants is called Thematic Head. This Thematic Head can be a whole word or a clitic, when the clause begins with a participant (Actor, Goal, Senser, Phenomenon, etc.), or a verbal suffix, when the clause begins with a verb. In that light, example (10) would be analysed as shown in example (10b), below, whereas verb-initial examples (13) and (14) above would be analysed as shown in examples (13c) and (14c) below. Notice that what this analysis does is identify what, in mainstream literature, is called 'ideational (or topical) Theme', now under the label of *thematic field*, and then pinpoint the Thematic Head, which, in the case of Processes, is just the verbal affix.

(10b) *Tus palabras*		*me afectan hasta no sé donde*
Your words		affect me more than I can imagine
Phenomenon		
Thematic Head		
Thematic field		Rhematic field

(13c) *Teng-*	*-o*	*mucho que hacer*
have	1st sing.	a lot to do
Process		
Pre-Head	Thematic Head	
Thematic field		Rhematic field

(14c) *¿fu-*	*- iste*	*alguna vez creyente?*
was/were	2nd sing.	ever a believer?
Process		
Pre-Head	Thematic Head	
Thematic field		Rhematic field

Arús (2010) gives a number of reasons supporting the Process-as-Theme approach. These reasons can be summarised as follows.

1   If the Theme is realised in initial position, it is problematic to think of an unrealised participant as Theme (but see, however, Moyano's view, which we consider shortly).
2   Relatedly, the order in Spanish clauses – notably, middle processes such as example (15) – is often Process^Subject. If the elided Subject were expressed, it would not necessarily have to be in initial position.

(15) *Entraron*	*los fotógrafos*	*para hacer las fotos*
Entered	the photographers	to take the photos
Process	Subject	
ideational Theme		
'The photographers entered to take the photos'		

3   The information necessary for the tracking of participants as the text unfolds is conveyed in Spanish by the verbal inflection. As noted, this fulfils a similar textual role to that of the personal pronoun in English. There is no reason, then, not to assign thematic status to the element bearing this inflection – that is, the Process.

4   The reason for eliding the Subject in Spanish is very often the same as the reason for using the personal pronoun in English: the element elided/pronominalised is Given from the point of view of the information structure. Because the verbal inflection, as stated above, allows the tracking of participants, there is no need to express such a participant in Spanish. Subjects are therefore elided precisely because they are Given. Just as in English, in Spanish Given and Theme often coincide, but not in elided-Subject structures, which actually allow us to capture the nature of the Given/Theme interaction. An elided Subject is an elided Given, not an elided Theme, which is the first expressed ideational constituent. This is captured by the analysis of example (16), which contrasts with an English structure such as example (17), from the BNC (Davies 2004). Participant tracking, and therefore thematic progression, in example (16) is thus enabled by the Process *Subieron*, by dint of the information provided by the verbal inflection, in very much the same way as the Subject *They* does in example (17).

(16)		*Subieron*	*al automóvil*
	(they)	got into	their vehicle
		ideational Theme	Rheme
	Given	→ New	

(17)	They	left	for Beirut by sea on 25 April
	Theme	Rheme	
	Given	→ New	

Moyano (2010, forthcoming) provides the strongest opposition to Process as Theme and support for elided Subject as Theme. In her view, there is an elided Theme when this conflates with an elided agreeing Participant – that is, the nominal group agreeing with the verb affix in the Spanish clause. The reasons adduced by Moyano are very much in line with what has already been explained in relation to the treatment by Lavid and colleagues (2010) of the verbal inflection as Thematic Head: '[O]nce the agreeing Participant/Theme is introduced in a clause initiating a series in a text, it is elided in the subsequent clauses until the participant identity is changed to start another phase' (Moyano forthcoming). This is made possible, as seen above, by the verbal inflection. Moyano's explanation mostly applies to written texts – notably essays. However, her analysis could be safely extended to spoken discourse. For instance, examples (13) and (14) would be analysed as shown in examples (13b) and (14b), which we now repeat with agreeing Participant instead of Subject to reflect Moyano's terminology.

(13b) *(Yo)*	*tengo*	*mucho que hacer*
(I)	have	a lot to do
Agreeing Participant/Carrier	Process	
ideational Theme	Rheme	

(14b) *(tú)*	*¿fuiste*	*alguna vez creyente?*
(you)	were	ever a believer?
Agreeing Participant /Carrier	Process	
ideational Theme	Rheme	

The most radical difference between Moyano's model and the rest of the literature on Theme in Spanish is found in those structures in which the agreeing Participant is realised in New position – that is, after the Process, at least in clauses starting with a Process or a Circumstance (although nothing is said about Complement or Adjunct-first clauses). In such cases, according to Moyano, there is a conflation between New and Theme. This is illustrated by the analysis in example (18), where we see that *se*-clitic constructions – that is, *no se utilizó*– often favour a post-verbal agreeing Participant – that is, Subject – realisation. Further research should also look at whether this kind of approach does not risk equating Theme with Subject –see example (15) – thus making syntactic criteria prevail over textual ones for Theme identification, something rather non-functional.

(18) *Sin embargo,*	*no se utilizó*	*un lenguaje hostil contra Gómez*
However,	wasn't used	a hostile language against Gómez
	Process	Agreeing Participant
textual Theme		ideational Theme/New
'However, no hostile language was used against Gómez'		

The discussion about the thematic status of clause-initial verbs has led us to one more conflictive point – that is, whether Theme is to be identified in Spanish, as it is in English, as the first sequential element in the clause. Concerning the former issue, given that Process as Theme wins over elided Subject as Theme in terms of the number of scholars advocating one or the other analysis, we will, for the rest of this chapter, adhere to the Process-as-Theme position. As for the sequential realisation of Theme, pending further research on the conflation of Theme and New, we will here adopt the widely held position that the Theme is realised in Spanish, as in English, by the first experiential element of the clause.

The last thematic option we will be discussing is Circumstance as Theme, as in example (19), below. While it is generally agreed that the Circumstance is part of ideational Theme and that circumstantial Themes are marked, the issue here – not only in Spanish, but across languages – is whether the Circumstance exhausts the clause's thematic potential – that is, whether, as illustrated by example (19a), the ideational Theme coincides exclusively with the Circumstance, which is the stance taken by Halliday and Matthiessen (2013) for English, or, as in example (19b), where it extends beyond the Circumstance to also include the first non-circumstantial participant or Process, as sustained by the Cardiff Grammar.[5] Although there is research in which circumstantial Theme is treated as one more kind of Theme (for example McCabe and Alonso 2001; Sheldon 2013), descriptions of Spanish textual resources tend to favour the option illustrated in example (19b), thus extending ideational Theme to include the first nuclear participant.[6]

Although there still is a great deal of work to be done concerning this issue, there are arguments that compel us to adhere to the second interpretation. Notably, it seems clear that the Circumstance in example (19) basically sets up a temporal framework, as defended by Downing (1991) for this kind of Circumstance in English, and the clause has not been properly started until the Process *noto* has been introduced. Teruya (2004) identifies as a typical feature of Japanese the sequence circumstantial Theme^participant Theme, the former serving to stage the process; the latter, to add one more link to the identity chain – something which, as pointed out by Rose (2001: 126–7), also happens in other languages, including English. On the other hand, it also seems quite clear that the staging role of the Circumstance in example (19) is different from that of the Circumstance in example (20), which could arguably be said to be more involved in the chaining of identities. Should both kinds of Circumstance be granted the same thematic status, or should the one in example (20) be considered to exhaust the thematic potential? As stated, there is a potential research niche here.

(19a)	*Desde hace algún tiempo*		*noto cambiada a mi hija*
	For some time		I feel my daughter changed
	Circumstance: time		
	ideational theme		Rheme
	'For some time now I have been observing changes in my daughter'		

(19b)	*Desde hace algún tiempo*	*noto*	*cambiada a mi hija*
	Circumstance: time	Process	
	ideational theme		Rheme

(20)	*y*	*con el martillo y las tenazas*	*hizo a Aquiles un escudo invencible*
	and	with the hammer and the pincers	Achilles made an invincible shield
		Circumstance: matter	
	textual Theme	ideational Theme?	Rheme?

Before ending the review of what the existing literature says on Theme in Spanish, a last word should be said on Theme markedness, which has simply been mentioned in passing so far. As is well known, Theme markedness depends on MOOD type – that is, declarative clauses have Theme markedness systems that differ from those of interrogatives or imperatives. Views on this issue vary greatly in the literature. There are those like Taboada (1995) for whom all Themes are unmarked in Spanish, which view tries to reflect the flexibility of Spanish syntax. Conversely, other sources such as Arús (2010) and Lavid and colleagues (2010) recognise the existence of marked and unmarked Themes in Spanish. Arús (2010) offers a system network of Theme markedness in Spanish declarative clauses. This system includes varying degrees of markedness based on how frequent each type of Theme is, as illustrated in Table 13.1 and the corresponding examples (21)–(28).[7] The classification in Table 13.1 is not exhaustive, but it provides a fair view of thematic realisations in Spanish. As we can see, Theme markedness in Spanish is one more research area about which there still is a lot to be said.

Table 13.1 Markedness cline in Spanish Theme

Theme markedness	Realisation		Example
Unmarked	Subject/Theme; Subject = non-pronominal	(21)	***Tus palabras*** *me afectan hasta no sé dónde* ('**Your words** affect me more than I can imagine')
	Process/Theme	(22)	***Entraron*** *los fotógrafos para hacer las fotos* ('The photographers **entered** to take the photos'; lit. '**Entered** the photographers . . . ')
	Complement/Theme; Complement = pronominal	(23)	*Pero* ***la*** *vieron 42 millones de personas en un solo año* ('But **it** was seen by 42 million people in one year'; note that the Spanish clause is active)
	Impersonal *se*/Theme	(24)	***Se*** *está muy bien* ('**One** feels very good')
Marked	Circumstance/Theme^Subject; Subject = non-pronominal	(25)	*Y en* ***estos tiempos el socialismo*** *debe jugar un papel central* ('And **nowadays socialism** must play a key role')
	Circumstance/Theme^Process	(26)	***Desde hace algún tiempo noto*** *cambiada a mi hija* ('**For some time now [I] have been observing** changes in my daughter')
	Non-circumstantial Adjunct/Theme	(27)	***A mí*** *me apetece menos ir al teatro* ('I don't really feel like going to the theatre'; lit. '**To me** me pleases less . . . ')
	Complement/Theme; Complement = non-pronominal	(28)	***Esta*** *me la compré hace más de 20 años* ('I bought this one over 20 years ago'; lit. '**This** myself it bought . . . ')
Marked +	Subject/Theme ; Subject = pronominal	(29)	***Yo*** *me fui sola* ('**I** left alone')

Note: / = 'conflates with';^= 'followed by'

Source: Adapted from Arús (2010: 42)

Theme in Spanish and systemic functional theory

The review of the literature in the last section has set the stage for our analysis of Theme in Spanish. It is also important to remember what we said at the beginning of this chapter: the study of thematic structure in Spanish has important consequences for the analysis of Mood and, ultimately, for systemic-functional theory, because the combination of Theme with Subject or Finite does not play a role in the expression of interpersonal meaning in Spanish. In the last section, we answered questions 1 and 2 from the introduction by deciding to analyse clause-initial Processes as Theme. In this section, we will try to find an answer to the third issue raised in the introduction about the role of the Mood structure in Spanish. Let us remember that English – mostly in writing, where intonation cannot play its role – thematises the Subject or the Finite^Subject string to indicate whether the utterance is a statement or a 'yes/no' question, respectively, as illustrated by example (30), from the BNC Corpus (Davies 2004).

(30a) They	have	arrived!
Subject	Finite	
Theme	Rheme	

(30b) Have	they	arrived yet?
Finite	Subject	
Theme		Rheme

We saw in the discussion in the last section that Spanish does not use this resource to differentiate between statements and questions, precisely because the Subject is often left unexpressed and because, when expressed, it may be placed before or after the verb. The reasons for the relative position of Subject and verb have been discussed elsewhere (Arús 2004a, 2004b) and we will not go into them here; what matters to us is that the motivations for the order in which they appear have nothing to do with whether the clause is a statement or a question. This has led authors such as Quiroz (2013; see also in this volume) to question the existence of a Subject in Spanish, or at least the functional need to identify one. This author proposes the category Negotiator – after Caffarel (2006) for French – to explain interpersonal meanings in Spanish – notably, concerning the enactment of dialogic exchange. The Negotiator comprises the Predicator, which for Quiroz (2013) is the Process (no need for a Finite), together with any clitics that may go with it and any Modal Adjuncts that may precede the Predicator. Her analysis of a clause such as example (31) is shown below. Notice the concentration of clitics, which makes it quite hard to provide a complete translation into English.

(31) o	tal vez	se lo estaba diciendo	a sí mismo
or	maybe	him it (he) was saying	to himself
	Modal Adjunct	Predicator	
	Negotiator		Remainder
'or maybe he was saying that to himself'			

Although the kind of analysis illustrated by example (31) is very suitable for describing the structure of discourse exchange in Spanish (Quiroz 2013: 299–305), the interrelation of the Negotiator with thematic systems has not yet been studied. For instance, if the Subject is left out of the picture, how does it affect thematic analysis? Or, do the clitics preceding the Predicator in example (31) have thematic status? In a similar line to Quiroz's proposal – that is, disposing of a Mood structure for Spanish, but more compatible with thematic analysis – is the stance taken by Lavid and colleagues (2010). In this model, the Finite is also considered redundant in Spanish and therefore not recognised. The only necessary interpersonal element is the Predicator –which, unlike Quiroz's model, does not include clitics– and if the Subject is explicit, it is identified as such – that is, Subject. Example (32) shows the interpersonal and thematic analysis of a Spanish clause according to this model.

(32)	*Ya*	*han llegado*	*las rebajas*
	Already	have arrived	the sales
	Adjunct	Predicator	Subject
	ideational Theme		Rheme
	'The sales have finally arrived'		

Both proposals – that is, those of Quiroz (2013) and Lavid and colleagues (2010) – seem to clearly support the view that there is no need to recognise a Mood structure in Spanish, at least not in terms of Subject + Finite. This answers the third question set out earlier – yet only partially. If the Mood structure in terms of Subject and Finite plays no role in Spanish, these categories are not really interpersonal. Disposing of the Finite for the functional analysis of Spanish seems to be no problem at all, as shown by example (32) – but what about the Subject? If it is not interpersonal, what is it?

The textual–interpersonal interplay therefore seems to call for a metafunctional relocation of the Subject, which in mainstream systemic functional grammar (SFG) belongs to the interpersonal structure. We actually do not need to look outside SFG to find a solution. The Cardiff Grammar (Fawcett, in this volume) treats the Subject – as well as other elements that, in the Sydney Grammar, are included within the interpersonal metafunction – as syntactic elements that interact with the other systems of the grammar. Fawcett (2000: 115) makes an interesting point when he says, talking about Predicators, Complements and Adjuncts, that 'in *IFG* [Halliday's *Introduction to Functional Grammar*] their role seems to be little more than a way of labelling another row of boxes that would otherwise remain empty'. Additionally, placing the Subject, Complement, etc. outside the interpersonal metafunction and having them interact with the different systems in the way it is done in the Cardiff Grammar seems to make the theory more easily amenable to the description of Spanish – and perhaps other languages. In an analysis such as that in example (32), therefore, the sequence Adjunct^Predicator^Subject refers to the clause's syntactic structure, which interacts with the other metafunctions. As far as the textual metafunction is concerned, the interaction with syntax allows us to speak of example (32) as one with Adjunct^Predicator as Theme, in pretty much the same way as the textual–experiential interaction highlights the fact that, experientially speaking, the Theme is Circumstance^Process. The complete analysis showing this three-way interaction is provided in example (33) below.

(33) *Ya*	*han llegado*	*las rebajas*
Circumstance	Process: existential	Existent
Adjunct	Predicator	Subject
ideational Theme		Rheme

Analysing Spanish for theme: contrasts with English

In this section, we adopt the stance of Subject as a syntactic element to fully exploit the analysis of Theme in Spanish. This is done contrastively with English, because this comparison clearly illustrates the different ways in which syntax interacts with the textual metafunction – notably, the system of THEME. For instance, example (34) shows that, in English, Mood regulates syntactic order, thus requiring Subject^Finite, whereas Theme regulates experiential order, thus requiring Actor/Theme in the active example (34a) and Goal/Theme in the passive example (34b), which creates a tension between experiential (speaker-subjective) and syntactic (language-specific) requirements.[8]

(34a) The Prime Minister	is	meeting	industry representatives
Actor	Process		Goal
Theme	Rheme		
Subject	Finite	Predicator	Complement
Mood		Residue	

(34b) These	had	previously	been met	by the Industry Secretary
Goal	Pro-	Circumstance	-cess	Actor
Theme	Rheme			
Subject	Finite	Adjunct	Predicator	Adjunct
Mood		Residue		

Conversely, example (35), below, shows that whereas Theme in Spanish regulates experiential order, as it does in English, thus requiring Actor/Theme in example (35a) and Goal/Theme in example (35b), there is no tension between experiential (speaker-subjective) and syntactic (language-specific) requirements, because other resources, such as verb/Subject agreement or the preposition *a* before a human Complement, guarantee the identification of the Subject. No specific order of the Subject and the Finite is expected or required; that is why there is no Mood in the analysis of example (35) and also why Spanish does not need to resort to a passive in example (35b). Incidentally, example (35b) also shows a typical feature of Spanish – that is, the clitic reduplication of a thematised Complement or Adjunct, the latter in this case by means of *los*. We will not delve into this phenomenon here, yet it is worth pointing out that research on this point could shed new light, among other things, on issues having to do with the cline from absolute Theme to ideational Theme, because the clitic in these cases could be taken to bring about a prosodic detachment of sorts.

(35a)	El Primer Ministro		va a reunirse		con representantes industriales
	The Prime Minister		is meeting		industry representatives
	Actor		Process		Circumstance
	Subject		Predicator		Adjunct
	Theme		Rheme		

(35b)	A estos	los	había recibido	previamente	el ministro de industria
	To these	them	had received	Previously	the Industry Secretary
	Go-	-al	Process	Circumstance	Actor
	Adjunct	Complement	Predicator	Adjunct	Subject
	Theme	Rheme			

Examples (34) and (35) show not only cross-linguistic differences, but also resemblances. For instance, they allow us to see that the textual systems of THEME and INFORMATION interplay in similar ways in both languages. In Spanish, as in English, there tends to be a newsworthiness cline on which less newsworthy elements are placed earlier in the clause and more newsworthy ones are placed towards the end. In examples (34) and (35), we see that whereas the syntactic order of examples (34b) and (35b) is very different, the experiential order is very similar, with the Goal as Theme and the Actor in end-focus position in both cases. Thematic choices are therefore as highly motivated by newsworthiness constraints in Spanish as they are in English.

In spoken language, as illustrated by example (36) for English and example (37) for Spanish, intonation renders (textually motivated) experiential ordering less important, thus letting syntax dictate the order, if necessary. Thus, whereas examples (36a) and (36b) resemble the structure of written discourse, example (36c) is a typical realisation of spoken English, without relevant thematic or modal structures: intonation is enough, the same as example (37c) in colloquial spoken Spanish. Spanish examples (37a) and (37b), and English examples (36a) and (36b), are also comparable in that whereas, as said above, intonation may take over Mood arrangement in English, in Spanish it is punctuation – the initial question mark – that is replaced by intonation.

(36a)	Would	you	like	something to drink?
	Pro-	Senser	-cess	Phenomenon
	Theme		Rheme	
	Finite	Subject	Predicator	Complement
	Mood		Residue	

(36b)	I'	ll	have	a coke
	Actor	Process		Goal
	Theme	Rheme		
	Subject	Finite	Predicator	Complement
	Mood		Residue	

(36c) A: (Want) a drink?

B: Sure; a coke for me, please

(37a)	¿Quieres	una bebida?
	(Do you) want	a drink?
	Process	Phenomenon
	Predicator	Complement
	Theme	Rheme

(37b)	Voy a tomar	una cerveza
	(I)'m going to have	a beer
	Process	Goal
	Predicator	Complement
	Theme	Rheme

(37c) A: ¿Una bebida? ('A drink?')

B: Una cerveza, por favor ('A beer, please')

The discussion in examples (34)–(37) has been circumscribed to declarative and interrogative clauses, because it is there that the Spanish/English contrast is clearest concerning the different ways in which syntactic structure and Theme interact. Commands, for instance, are analysed similarly in both languages, because they have no explicitly realised Finite in English either. The only difference in the analyses of examples (38) and (39) is that the Mood element is specified in English. The main issue in the analysis of the Spanish command in example (39) is to decide how far the Theme extends, because the clause starts with two experiential constituents merged in a single word – that is, the Process *da* ('give') and the cliticised Recipient *me* ('me'). In our analysis, the ideational Theme has been taken to include both the Process and the clitic, because it arguably makes more sense to think of at least a whole word as the beginning of the clause.

(38) Give	me	that paper
Process	Recipient	Goal
Theme	Rheme	
Predicator	Complement	Complement
Mood	Residue	

(39) Dame		ese vaso de leche
Give me		that glass of milk
Process	Recipient	Goal
Predicator	Complement	Complement
Theme		Rheme

Before moving on to the concluding section, the analysis of example (40), below, serves as a synopsis of much of what this chapter has covered concerning Theme in Spanish. This multiple-Theme clause starts with the Linker *pero* as a textual Theme, followed by the comment Adjunct *personalmente* as interpersonal Theme. Comment Adjuncts, just like Mood Adjuncts such as *tal vez* ('maybe'), are modal Adjuncts, which belong to the interpersonal metafunction; that is why they are interpersonal Adjuncts. They contrast with the other Adjuncts, which are sometimes called 'residue Adjuncts', such as *en arte*, *al ingenio* and *más que al diablo* in example (40). The first of these – that is, *en arte* – starts the experiential part of the clause in example (40) and, together with the first element from nuclear transitivity – that is, the Phenomenon *al ingenio* – makes up the clause's ideational Theme.

(40) *pero*	*personalmente,*	*en arte,*	*al ingenio*	*le*	*temo*	*más que al diablo*
but	personally	in art	to inventiveness	it	(I) fear	more than to the devil
		Circumst: matter	Phenom-	-enon	Process	Circumstance: quantity
		Adjunct	Adjunct	Compl.	Predicator	Adjunct
Textual Theme	Interpersonal Theme	Ideational Theme		Rheme		

'but personally, in art, I fear inventiveness more than the devil'

Conclusions and pointers to the future

This chapter has answered some questions related to Theme in Spanish and, more interestingly, has brought up a number of issues that remain open for future research. Among the former, clause-initial Processes (verbs) have been analysed as Themes to the detriment of the alternative interpretation defending the existence of implied Subject Themes. The other big question for which an answer has been provided concerns the interplay between the textual and the interpersonal metafunctions, which suggests that there is no Mood structure in Spanish – as opposed to English – and, closely related to this and as postulated by the Cardiff Grammar, that elements which in the Sydney Grammar have traditionally been considered to belong to the interpersonal metafunction (notably, the Subject) are best treated as components of syntactic structure.

Among the questions left unanswered, the following areas have been identified as in need of further research:

1   Circumstance as Theme, so as to distinguish between those Circumstances that do not exhaust the thematic potential and those that may present a higher degree of involvement in textual unfolding;
2   theme markedness in Spanish – notably, across speech functions and across genres;
3   the interrelation of the interpersonal Negotiator, as described by Quiroz (2013), with thematic systems – notably, what to do about clause-initial clitics in terms of thematic analysis (see example (31));

4   the cline from absolute Theme to ideational Theme, because there are cases – for example those with clitic reduplication of a thematised Complement or Adjunct – that seem to have an intermediate status (such as example (35b)); and

5   clitics, again, on this occasion when they are suffixed to an imperative, in that we have suggested analysing them as part of the Theme (see example (39)), but might there be grounds not to include them in the Theme?

To these questions raised throughout the chapter, one more issue could be added with important implications for the theory – namely, the possibility of exploring whether syntactic structure is better left outside the metafunctions, as has been done here following the Cardiff Grammar, or whether, on the contrary, there are grounds to consider it a metafunctional resource. In other words, if categories such as the Subject and the Adjunct are not interpersonal, does it necessarily mean that they are not metafunctional at all? At any rate, the study of Theme in Spanish not only sheds more light on the nature of this textual category, but also shows the need for a streamlining of some aspects of the theory so as to make it more readily adaptable to the description of LOTE.

Notes

1 See, e.g., the critical views of the Hallidayan approach to Theme in Hudson (1986) and Huddleston (1988, 1991, 1992).
2 See Halliday and Matthiessen (2013: 454) for the distinction between Linkers and Binders, which same distinction applies to Spanish.
3 This and all subsequent Spanish examples have been taken from the *Corpus de Referencia del Español Actual* (CREA).
4 See Arús (2010: 42) for a system network of Theme markedness in Spanish.
5 See Forey and Sampson, and Huang, both in this volume.
6 See Matthiessen (1995) for the distinction between nuclear and circumstantial transitivity.
7 Some of these examples appeared above and are now renumbered; the ideational Theme is highlighted in **bold**.
8 For the sake of convenience, and following common SFL practice, in this section we analyse all ideational Themes as simply *Theme*.

References

Arús, J. 2004a. English and Spanish structures: The textual metafunction as a contrastive tool for the analysis of language. In D. Banks (ed.) *Text and Texture*. Paris: L'Harmattan, pp. 173–90.
Arús, J. 2004b. Understanding 'how' we mean through discourse analysis: A contrastive example using systemic-functional grammar. In M. Carretero, H. Herrera, G. Kristiansen and J. Lavid (eds) *Estudios de lingüística aplicada a la comunicación*. Madrid: Departamento de Filología Inglesa de la Universidad Complutense de Madrid, pp. 29–64.
Arús, J. 2010. On Theme in English and Spanish: A comparative study. In E. Swain (ed.) *Thresholds and Potentialities of Systemic Functional Linguistics: Multilingual, Multimodal and Other Specialised Discourses*. Trieste: EUT, pp. 23–48.
Caffarel, A. 2006. *A Systemic Functional Approach to the Grammar of French: From Grammar to Discourse*. London and New York: Continuum.
Caffarel, A., J.R. Martin and C.M.I.M. Matthiessen (eds). 2004. *Language Typology: A Functional Perspective*. Amsterdam: John Benjamins.
Davies, M. 2004. *BYU-BNC*. Based on the British National Corpus from Oxford University Press. Available online at http://corpus.byu.edu/bnc/

Downing, A. 1991. An alternative approach to Theme: A systemic-functional perspective. *WORD* 42(2): 119–43.

Fawcett, R. 2000. *A Theory of Syntax for Systemic Functional Linguistics*. Amsterdam: John Benjamins.

Halliday, M.A.K. 1978. *Language as Social Semiotic: The Social Interpretation of Language and Meaning*. London: Arnold.

Halliday, M.A.K., and C.M.I.M. Matthiessen. 2013. *Halliday's Introduction to Functional Grammar*. 4th edn. London: Routledge.

Hidalgo-Downing, R. 2003. *La tematización en el español hablado*. Madrid: Gredos.

Huddleston, R. 1988. Constituency, multi-functionality and grammaticalization in Halliday's functional grammar. *Journal of Linguistics* 24: 137–74.

Huddleston, R. 1991. Further remarks on Halliday's functional grammar: A reply to Matthiessen and Martin. *Occasional Papers in Systemic Linguistics* 5: 75–130.

Huddleston, R. 1992. On Halliday's functional grammar: A reply to Martin and Martin and Matthiessen. *Occasional Papers in Systemic Linguistics* 6: 197–212.

Hudson, R. 1986. Systemic grammar. *Linguistics* 24(1): 791–815.

Lavid, J. 2001. Using bilingual corpora for the construction of contrastive generation grammars: Issues and problems. *Technical Papers–University Centre for Computer Corpus Research on Language* 13: 356–66.

Lavid, J., J. Arús and J.R. Zamorano. 2010. *Systemic Functional Grammar of Spanish: A Contrastive Study with English*. London: Continuum.

Martín García, A., and J.M. Gil. 2011. Una perspectiva sistémico-funcional del español: Acerca de la multifuncionalidad en la cláusula castellana simple. *Revista de Investigación Lingüística* 14(1): 191–214.

Matthiessen, C.M.I.M. 1992. Interpreting the textual metafunction. In M. Davies and L. Ravelli (eds) *Advances in Systemic Linguistics: Recent Theory and Practice*. London and New York: Pinter, pp. 37–81.

Matthiessen, C.M.I.M. 1995. *Lexicogrammatical Cartography: English Systems*. Tokyo: International Language Science.

McCabe, A. 2002. Everything's a Theme: Where's the value? Plenary presentation at the 14th Euro-International Systemic-Functional Workshop, University of Lisbon, July.

McCabe, A., and I. Alonso. 2001. Theme, transitivity and cognitive representation in Spanish and English written texts. CLAC 7. Available online at http://pendientedemigracion.ucm.es/info/circulo/no7/mccabe.htm

Moyano, E. 2010. El sistema de Tema en español: Una mirada discursiva sobre una cuestión controvertida. In E. Ghio and M.D. Fernández (eds) *El discurso en español y portugués: Estudios desde una perspectiva sistémico-funcional*. Santa Fe: Universidad Nacional del Litoral, pp. 39–87.

Moyano, E. Forthcoming. *Theme in the Spanish Clause: Outline for a Systemic Description*. Santa Fe: Universidad Nacional del Litoral.

Quiroz, B. 2013. The interpersonal and experiential grammar of Chilean Spanish: Towards a principled systemic-functional description based on axial argumentation. Unpublished PhD thesis. Sydney University.

Rose, D. 2001. Some variation in Theme across languages. *Functions of Language* 8(1): 109–45.

Sheldon, E. 2013. The research article: A rhetorical and functional comparison of texts created by native and non-native English writers and native Spanish writers. Unpublished PhD thesis. University of New South Wales, Kensington, NSW.

Taboada, M. 1995. Theme markedness in English and Spanish: A systemic-functional approach. Unpublished manuscript. Universidad Complutense de Madrid.

Teruya, K. 2004. Metafunctional profile of the grammar of Japanese. In A. Caffarel, J.R. Martin and C.M.I.M. Matthiessen (eds) *Language Typology: A Functional Perspective*. Amsterdam: John Benjamins, pp. 185–254.

14

Mood in Japanese

Kazuhiro Teruya

Introduction

Humans create meanings in action in shared contexts of situation (Halliday 2007 [1984]: 303) by enacting their social roles and relationships in exchanges of information or goods-&-services. Here, the core interpersonal resource with which humans enact the exchanges in their dialogic interaction is the interpersonal system of MOOD (Halliday and Matthiessen 2014; Matthiessen et al. 2008; Teruya 2007). It is a grammatical system working at clause rank: if a clause is 'free', it selects for mood as a realisation of the semantic system of speech function in negotiating the assignment of speech roles and as a realisation of the tenor relationship by calibrating and defining social power and status in speech situations. This chapter is concerned with this negotiation strategy and illustrates how the system of MOOD in Japanese operates in discourse.

Japanese is a Eurasian language spoken primarily on five main islands and more than 400 adjacent inhabited islands by more than 130 million speakers on these islands and in other countries. The genealogical classification to language families is much debated, for example whether to affiliate it with the Altaic or Austronesian language families, or to interpret it as a mixture of these language families, or else treat it as a language isolate, all of which are currently untestable hypotheses (Miller 1971; Shibatani 1990). A common view is to link Japanese to the Ryukyuan languages spoken in the Ryukyu Islands, although they are mutually unintelligible.

Historical perspectives

The linguistic study of modern Japanese has a long tradition going back to the late nineteenth century. It started out by defining the word as a linguistic unit and identifying paradigms of classes of words based on the morphological notion of 'mood', introduced from European linguistics (Otsuki 1897, cited in Suzuki 1996 [1972]: 230). This influence of European linguistics of that time brought about the morphology-based approach to the study of Japanese (at which we look later in the chapter). A functional school has, however, emerged since the mid-1950s, led by Okuda and his colleagues. Their approach to language is, in some respects, comparable to systemic functional linguistics (SFL), for it sees and describes, for example, the unity of lexis and grammar as lexicogrammar – nuclear configurations of experiential meaning – and foregrounds the paradigmatic organisation of the language. While the theoretical underpinnings and dimensions of Okuda's (1985) functional linguistics are different from Halliday's SFL (for example Halliday 2005 [1996]), the SFL account, in particular, on the system of MOOD in Japanese has gained insight from the Okudayan school's descriptive accounts (for example Miyajima 1972; Suzuki 1996 [1972]; Uemura 1989; Takahashi 1994; Okuda 1996). What follows is an overview of the historical development of SFL accounts of interpersonal grammar in Japanese since the late 1980s. It is not intended to be comprehensive.

Systemic functional accounts of Japanese started in the context of natural-language processing in the 1980s (Matthiessen and Bateman 1991) by adopting the framework of NIGEL, one of the largest machine grammars.[1] For example, as part of modelling interaction base, Matthiessen and Bateman (1991) specified the organisation of politeness distinctions in reference to social distance and roles between interactants in a communicative situation. Their explicit specification of linguistic choices helped to make succeeding accounts of Japanese as specific as necessary in describing the core systems of TRANSITIVITY, MOOD and THEME in Japanese (for example Teruya 1998).

From the mid-1990s, a number of SFL accounts of the interpersonal grammar started to emerge, first among which was the 'pre-systemic' stage at which interpersonal functions were studied with a specific focus on instantial features of interpersonal functions in discourse. Hori (1995) argued for the interpretation of the 'subjectlessness' of Japanese by showing that Subject is typically implicit when the Noun Phrase (NP) is marked in honorific expressions. Her argument was presented without having to identify the functional role that the NP plays in the interpersonal organisation of the clause. Teruya (1998), however, presented an overview of the interpersonal grammar and identified core mood types in Japanese. His study identified interpersonal functions of Subject, Predicator, Complement and Negotiator, and their relationships with reference to relevant interpersonal systems such as POLARITY, POLITENESS and MODALITY.

Following this account, in the 2000s, came the 'systemic' stage. Based on the functional account of the grammar in the pre-systemic stage, the relevant interpersonal systems came to be represented systemically in the form of system networks. It was the early 2000s that saw the development of the system network of the interpersonal grammar as part of the endeavour to profile the metafunctional organisation of Japanese based on corpus evidence (Teruya 2004). A more detailed, large, corpus-based account follows in the second half of the 2000s (Teruya 2007). Around this time, descriptive accounts of interpersonal grammar that are registerially specific started to appear, 'exploring' texts in a range of persuasive texts (Sano 2006 on ATTITUDE) and the 'doing' texts of written business directives (Mizusawa 2008). In another development, a new 'dialect' of SFL appeared in Japan: the 'Kyoto Grammar' (Tatsuki 2009), drawing partly on the Cardiff Grammar (Fawcett, this volume). Here, the account of the system of MOOD is still in the early pre-systemic stage.

In the second decade of the twenty-first century, more register-based accounts, the 'reporting' texts of news reports (Ochi 2012) and an account based on texts from three registers (Fukui 2013) have emerged around the same time, with the issues addressed in what follows.

Critical issues and topics in linguistic study of MOOD in Japanese

Japanese has a complex verbal morphology that involves various bound affixes. As for nominals, they are followed by 'postpositions' *ga, o, wa, ni*, etc., which are traditionally referred to as 'case particles'.[2] These postpositions are grammatically very general, but help to distinguish experiential roles of participants (*ga, o, ni*) and circumstances (*kara, made, e*, etc.). Verbs, adjectives and verbal suffixes or endings including the copula inflect and realise various interpersonal meanings such as tense, politeness and modality. In examples (1)–(9),[3] these morphemes are linked to the element that they follow by a hyphen (-) (Teruya 2004).

In Japanese, the clause final position is interpersonally significant because this is where the Predicator is realised by a nominal, adjectival or verbal group enacting various interpersonal meanings not only based on the variations in form of the element by which the Predicator is realised, such as *kak-u* ('write') in 'decisive' form, *kak-oo* ('will write') in 'volitional', *kak-e* ('write!') in 'imperative' etc., but also in concert with other interpersonal functions such as Subject and Negotiator. The Negotiator follows the Predicator and is realised by various clause final particles. Some of these interpersonal particles are specific to the realisation of MOOD types such as *ka* for the interrogative mood, while others realise the speaker's attitude towards the meaning being negotiated, such as *ne* (confirmation) and *yo* (assertion), or gender differences such as *ze* (strong insistence: masculine) and *wa* (mild insistence: feminine). The Subject is modally responsible for the various interpersonal meanings realised through the Predicator. It appears somewhere in the clause initial position, but is often implicit when the identity of the Subject can be inferred in the environment of discourse. These interpersonal functions will be discussed in reference to the grammaticalisation of different MOOD types.

In the traditional account of Japanese, the verbal morphological make-up has been taken as motivation for mood categories. For example, interpersonal morphological contrasts such as conclusive/imperative/hortative (cf. Shibatani 1990) have been taken as indicative of different 'moods' and the derived MOOD types are included under the larger category of 'modality'. Under this large umbrella category, not only verbal mood, but also modality, evidentiality, politeness and interpersonal particles, are studied (Nihongo Kijutsu Bunpo Kenkyukai 2003).

In systemic functional accounts of the system of MOOD, these verbal contrasts are dealt with as different 'modes' at group rank and taken as items realising interpersonal operators. The traditional morphology-based approach is a consequence of the way in which language is theorised; it is the result of the way in which the phenomena have been studied, not of the phenomena themselves. In other words, the primary syntagmatic orientation in language theorising fails to show the realisation of relationships between variables that are organised paradigmatically as a network of interrelated options for meaning-making.

The socio-semiotic context in which language is embedded for meaning-making according to SFL (Bateman, this volume) is not often part of linguistic theory. In SFL, semantics is seen as a distinctive level of coding that interfaces with both the socio-semiotic context and the grammatical system (Halliday 1984: 229), but in many other theories this 'interlevel' nature of semantics has not been recognised. The lack of semantics in modelling language limits the range of perspectives in which language can be observed. Consequently, traditional grammar comes to be described based primarily on formal evidence such as the inflectional categories of verbs. SFL operates with not only such overtly marked categories, but also cryptotypic ones that appear only in the form of reactances.

Let us consider the interrogative particle *ka* as an example (as abbreviated as 'Q' in example (1)). This clause final particle *ka* functions as Negotiator – that is, the interpersonal clause function that enacts the clause as one of 'yes/no' interrogative mood. In terms of politeness, it is marked by a politeness ending (formal) *desu* ('be'), which contrasts with examples (2)–(9), which are unmarked in politeness (informal).

(1) *Shokuji-wa*	*oishikatta desu*	*ka* [a rising tone]
meal	tasty-past be-formal	Q
Subject	Predicator	Negotiator
'Was the meal tasty?'		

In example (1) above, the clause is concerned with the exchange of information – more specifically, demanding information (that is, the speech function of 'question'). Intonationally, the clause carries a rising tone and thus realises the question. Example (2) is another for comparison: the clause has the same interrogative particle *ka*, which carries a falling tone, with a different type of Predicator marked morphologically in the volitional form *-(y)oo* ('let's').

(2) X: *Shokuji-o*	*shi-yoo*	*ka* [a falling tone]
meal	do-informal-volitional	Q
Complement	Predicator	Negotiator
'Shall we have a meal?'		

Y: *Un,*	*soo*	*shi-yoo*
yes	so	do-informal-volitional
Adjunct	Complement	Predicator
'Let's do so'		

If the perspective is limited to, or biased towards, the formal make-up of the clause, it would then seem to be natural to analyse the clause as a type of interrogative mood owing to the presence of this interrogative particle. Contrary to example (1), however, the clause in example (2) is identified as:

1 being concerned with the exchange of goods-&-services, since the expected reply is an acceptance, not an answer, thus concerned with the here-&-now of the speech event;
2 involving the Negotiator at the clause ending that is mapped onto the intonational contour of a falling tone, as with imperative and declarative mood, and, unlike the declarative mood, with no tense distinction between 'present' and 'past' because the imperative mood is always concerned with the present speech event and
3 realising the verbal group by the verb in the volitional form, which is followed by an interrogative particle.

These three properties derive from the 'trinocular' perspective in SFL (Halliday 1978, 2005 [1996]). All descriptive categories are identified from them: (a) the higher level, 'from above'; (b) the same level, 'from around' and (c) the lower level, 'from below'. In systemic grammar, (a) has priority (Halliday 2003 [1992]: 203). Since property (c) is derived from (a), the clause in question is an exchange of goods-&-services that enacts a subtype of imperative – namely, 'oblative' mood. Here, the interrogative particle *ka* indicates that the speaker is seeking reconfirmation from the addressee of the proposal being put forward, which is why it is marked by a falling tone (Halliday and Greaves 2008; O'Grady, this volume; Uemura 1989;). As mentioned, in SFL, the approach 'from above' has the priority. This means that it is possible to keep in check the realisational relationship between grammatical and semantic systems in terms of how relevant systems co-define their relationship by means of which a network of options in the systems – systems that we may call 'co-systems' – can be ordered in delicacy. This is another issue that is pertinent in particular to the 'systemic' stage in the ongoing development of accounts of Japanese.

The system of MOOD in Japanese has a number of co-systems such as POLARITY, MODALITY and HONORIFICATION. Let us consider the system of POLARITY as an example. This interpersonal system has two options – namely, 'positive' and 'negative' – and it intersects with the different mood types. However, how they co-select negative polarity depends on a given mood type. In other words, not all mood types can select negative and the interpersonal meaning that it expresses is correspondingly different.

In Japanese, negative polarity is expressed by the suffix [non-past:] -*(a)na-i* ('not (non-past)'), [past:] -*(a)na-katta* ('was/did not') in the verbal or adjectival group realising the Predicator. In a declarative clause, negative polarity negates the proposition put forward, as in example (3).

(3) *Hon-o*	*yom-ana-katta*
book	read-negative-past-informal
Complement	Predicator
'(I) didn't read the book'	

The fact about the past experience – that is, whether or not the speaker read the book – can be interrogated by adding to it the negotiatory particle *ka*, as we have observed already.

(4) *Hon-o*	*yom-ana-katta*	*ka*
book	read-negative-past-informal	Q
Complement	Predicator	Negotiator
'Didn't (you) read the book?'		

However, if the declarative clause is about the here-&-now of a speech event – that is, if the Predicator is not marked in the past tense – the interrogative marker in the negative question enacts not 'question', but 'suggestion', as in example (5).

(5)	*Biichi-ni*	*ik-ana-i*	*ka*
	beach-to	go-negative-informal	Q
	Adjunct	Predicator	Negotiator
	'Shall we go to the beach?'		

While morphologically different, the imperative mood can also be marked in negative polarity by the negative particle *na*. This, however, enacts different speech functions. For example, the clause in example (6) below may mean either 'prohibition' (it prohibits the addressee from going to the beach at the time of speaking) or 'restraint' (it restrains him or her from going to the beach no matter when), depending on whether it is initiated before or at the point of the actualisation of the addressee's going to the beach. Grammatically, it forms a subtype of the imperative mood – that of 'prohibitive'.

(6)	*Biichi-ni*	*ik-u*	*na*
	beach-to	go-informal	negative-prohibitive
	Adjunct	Predicator	Negotiator
	'Don't go to the beach'		

As far as the relationship between the formal marking of negative polarity and mood types are concerned, the oblative mood, which enacts 'offer' in the structure of Predicator^Negotiator, is the odd one out, because the verbal operator of the volitional form with ending *-(y)oo* takes neither the negative suffix nor negative particle, as in example (7).

(7)	*Biichi-ni*	*isshoni*	*ik-oo*	*ka*
	beach-to	together	go-volitional-informal	Q
	Adjunct	Adjunct	Predicator	Negotiator
	'Shall we go to the beach together?'			

Incidentally, the volitional form may also express 'intention' when the Subject is the speaker, as in example (8) below. This contrasts with the volitional form used to enact 'offer', whose Subject is both the speaker and addressee.

(8)	*Ashita kara*	*oyog-oo*
	tomorrow-from	swim-volitional-informal
	Adjunct	Predicator
	'I will swim from tomorrow'	

Having said that, negative oblative equivalent may be realised by an alternative wording, as in example (9) below, in which an auxiliary marked in the volitional form *-ok-oo* ('let's put in advance') is preceded by the participle marked in negative *-nai* ('not') as in *ika-nai-de* ('not to go').

(9) *Beechi-ni*	*ika-nai-de okoo*	*ka*
beach-to	go-negative-aspect-volitional	Q
Adjunct	Predicator	Negotiator
'Let's not go to the beach'		

Here, the issue is whether the view obtained from below is motivating enough to generalise the system of MOOD as having the most general mood opposition between 'oblative' and 'non-oblative' (Fukui 2013) – that is, one without negative form and the others with relevant negative forms, into which all of the subtypes of mood are to be systematised. The answer is that it is not: if there were to be this split in the system, it would mean that offers contrast with statements, questions and commands in Japanese, and so the oblative would stand in opposition to the declarative, interrogative and imperative, simply because the negative suffix and particle cannot be appended to its verbal operator [*ik-*]*oo* ('let/will [go]') to realise the 'negative' in the system of POLARITY. In the social context, the fact about not offering goods or services can be expressed simply by not undertaking it, which is the reason why grammatical resources for offers are not congruently realised unlike the other primary speech functions: 'commands' and 'statements' have specific forms of verbs that realise the Predicator, while 'questions' are typically realised by the presence of an interrogative particle that realise the Negotiator.

Seen in the light of the clause as exchange, it is thus useful to observe propositions first. Many languages have developed distinctive grammars for statements and questions (Halliday and Matthiessen 2014: 139; Teruya et al. 2007), which can serve as a descriptive way into the MOOD system. Once the orientation for observation for describing the system of MOOD is set to the exchange of propositions and the perspective 'from above', variations in wording can be sorted, so that an overall landscape can be systematically described.

Current contribution and research

Interpersonal functions and their realisation

In systemic functional accounts of the system of MOOD (Teruya 2004, 2007), the verbal contrasts described so far in this chapter are dealt as different 'modes' at group rank and taken as items realising the interpersonal function of Predicator in the clause. But these realisations need to be understood in terms of the nature of the interpersonal mode of expression, as first theorised by Halliday (1979). Interpersonal features such as those in the system of MOOD tend to be realised prosodically in languages – that is, in the case of a clause, they are realised in more than one place, the prototypical prosody being an intonation contour. In discussing the prosodic mode of expression in different languages around the world, Matthiessen (2004) shows that interpersonal prosodies may be manifested through different media of expression.

In general, the media of expression of the prosodic mode of realisation of interpersonal features has three general types: *sequential* (such as relative sequence of Subject and Finite in English), *intonational* (for example rise and fall of pitch movements), or *segmental* (such as 'tags' or interpersonal particles). In Japanese, interpersonal features are manifested intonationally and segmentally, as in many other languages (Caffarel et al. 2004). In terms of their grammatical realisation, relevant operators are the grammatical deployment of the intonation, such as a rising tone and falling tone, and the interpersonal functions of Subject, Predicator and Negotiator.

Given that the prosody of interpersonal meanings is realised differently through the generalised interpersonal functions such as the Subject and the Predicator, the functions that they play are accordingly different. The Predicator in Japanese, for example, is the locus of interpersonal meanings. It is a composite of both experiential and interpersonal meanings: experientially, it is conflated with the Process, representing a process unfolding in time of happening, doing, sensing, saying, being or having; interpersonally, it realises the meanings of polarity, modality and evidentiality, but also politeness and honorification. It is thus complex in its morphological make-up. The Negotiator, whose involvement is either obligatory or optional depending on the interpersonal meaning at risk, may be realised by (a) modal particles, such as *na*, *to*, etc., indicating different mood types and the source of information as hearsay or as a report, or (b) attitudinal particles, such as *ne*, *wa*, *ze*, etc., by means of which the speaker identity may be expressed in terms of gender (as noted earlier).

This structural realisation of the Predicator and the possible presence of the Negotiator is the basic clause pattern that is deployed as negotiation strategies in Japanese. The Subject, as the element that is held modally responsible for the proposition or the proposal put forward, may be introduced in the clause. Thus the interpersonal structure of the clause as exchange in Japanese is generally 'Subject (^ Complement)^Predicator (^ Negotiator)', wherein the Complement is what is not functioning as Subject, but has the potential to do so. Having said that, the Subject is often implicit when it can be inferred from the Predicator or the environment of discourse. In fact, in a dialogic interaction, what is tossed back and forth in an ongoing exchange is the Predicator together with or without the Negotiator, because these functions are those that carry the exchange forward.

The context in which the Subject is ellipsed varies, but, interpersonally, one reason for the ellipsis of the Subject is associated with the nature of commodity being exchanged and the involvement of interactants in it. Simply put, if the commodity being exchanged is goods-and-services, the Subject is most likely implicit, for it is restricted to the interactants. Table 14.1 is an illustration of major mood types.

Mood types

The most general mood distinction in Japanese is between 'indicative' and 'imperative' (see Figure 14.1). They differ with respect to speech function in terms of the commodity being exchanged – namely, information and goods-&-services, respectively. Within 'indicative' and 'imperative', there are more delicate speech functional distinctions grammaticalised as different mood types. In general, the systemic contrasts in mood are realised through the Predicator, which is realised by a verbal, adjectival or nominal group to which a copula may be attached to realise interpersonal meanings.

Indicative mood type

The indicative mood is differentiated into two indicative types based on the direction of information exchange: 'giving' information – that is, 'statement' – is realised as 'declarative'; 'demanding' information – that is, 'question' – is realised as 'interrogative'. Each type is further differentiated into subtypes based on the nature of information being exchanged.

Table 14.1 Subtypes of the system of MOOD and their structural realisation

ORIENTATION OF EXCHANGE	SUBTYPES OF MOOD	FUNCTION STRUCTURE (realisation statement*)	POLITENESS	
			Unmarked	Marked
Indicative mood types				
giving	declarative: conclusive	Predicator Pred.: 'decisive' form	*watashi-wa tegami-o kaku* 'I write a letter'	*watashi-wa tegami-o kakimasu* 'I write a letter'
	declarative: suppositive	Predicator Pred.: 'conjectural' form	*kare-wa tegamio-o kakudaroo* 'he will probably write a letter'	*kare-wa tegami-o kakudeshoo* 'he will probably write a letter'
demanding	interrogative: 'yes/no' interrogative	Predicator^Negotiator Pred.: 'decisive/ conjectural' form; Neg.: interrogative particle	*anata-wa tegami-o kaku ka* 'will you write a letter?'	*anata-wa tegami-o kakimasu ka* 'will you write a letter?'
	interrogative: D-interrogative	+ D-word; Predicator^Negotiator Pred.: 'decisive/ conjectural' form; Neg.: interrogative particle	*dare-ga tegami-o kaku ka* 'who will write a letter?'	*dare-ga tegami-o kakimasu ka* 'who will write a letter?'
giving/ demanding	explanative	[co-selective with indicative mood] Pred.: + *no da/no ka* ('[the explanation for that] is/ is it?') etc.	*dare-ga tegami-o kaku no ka* 'who [is it that] will write a letter?'	*dare-ga tegami-o kaku n desu ka* 'who [is it that] will write a letter?'
Imperative mood types				
demanding	jussive	Predicator Pred.: v.g: 'imperative' form	*kake* 'write!'	*kakinasai* '(please) write!'
	requestive	Predicator Pred.: v.g. in 'participle'^*kureru* ('give') in 'imperative' form	*kaite kure* 'write it (for me)'	*kaite kudasai* 'please write it (for me)'
	suggestive	Predicator Pred.: 'volitional' form	*kakoo* 'let's write'	*kakimashoo* 'let's write'
	prohibitive	Predicator^Negotiator Pred.: 'decisive' form; Neg.: 'prohibitive' particle *na*	*kaku na* 'don't write!'	-
	optative	Predicator Pred.: v.g.: + 'optative' suffix *–tai* ('want to')	*kakitai* 'want to write'	-
giving	oblative	Predicator^Negotiator Pred.: 'volitional' form; Neg.: 'interrogative' particle *ka*	*kakoo ka* 'shall write?'	*kakimashoo ka* 'shall write?'

* Pred. = Predicator; Neg. = Negotiator; v.g. = verbal group

Kazuhiro Teruya

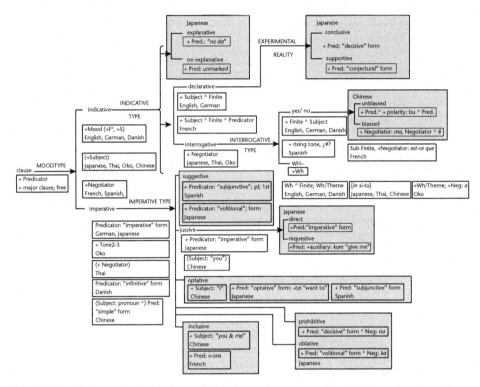

Figure 14.1   System of MOOD in Japanese in the environment of a multilingual system of MOOD

Note: Partitions indicate options/systems that are specific to one or more languages and thus not general to all the language represented by the system network.

Source: Based on Teruya et al. (2007); see also Teruya and Matthiessen (2015).

The declarative mood in Japanese has two subtypes: 'conclusive' and 'suppositive'. The distinction is based on how the experience represented as information in a proposition is derived from the perspective of the speaker: either from the world of speaking, or from the world of imagination or speculation.

The conclusive type is realised through the Predicator by a verbal or adjectival group, or a nominal group accompanying a copula in the decisive form *da* ('be'). It indicates a tense distinction between the non-past and the past as in *mi-ru* ('see') vs. *mi-ta* ('saw'), *da* ('is') vs *da-tta* ('was'). The suppositive type is always marked by the 'conjectural' equivalent of the copula *da-roo* ('will be'). This copula indicates only the suppositive nature of the proposition being put forward, thus the tense distinction is made in the experiential content of the proposition rather than in the copula itself, for example *i-ku da-roo* ('will go'; *lit.* go + copula-conjectural;) vs. *i-tta da-roo* ('would have gone'; *lit.* went + copula-conjectural).

The contrast between the two subtypes indicates that the event is either 'certain' (to be the case) or 'uncertain' (to be the case). Here, the un/certainty is derived from the way in which the event is experienced or understood subjectively in a given context (Okuda 1984). The speaker thus implies this speculative mode of knowing and thinking about the event through the suppositive mood. In this respect, this type differs from the modality of probability, for example *kamoshirenai* ('may'), which indicates the speaker's subjective judgement about the 'degree' of probability associated with the proposition put forward.

Unlike probability, the suppositive mood cannot be used if the proposition is concerned with the speaker's own goings-on, as in example (10).

(10)	*Watashi-wa	denki-o	keshi wasureta daroo
	I	light	switch-off forgot-conjectural-informal
	Subject	Complement	Predicator
	'I may have forgotten to switch off the light'		

The suppositive mood may also indicate probability: the speaker's subjective assessment of the certainty of the proposition may be specified objectively by a mood Adjunct, such as *osoraku* ('probably'), and/or through the Predicator involving a modal auxiliary, such as *ni chigainai* ('must'). The sequence is modality^suppositive mood, as in example (11).

(11)	Osoraku	keshiwasureta-ni chigainai daroo
	probably	swich-off forgot-must-conjectural-informal
	mood Adjunct	Predicator
	'must have probably forgotten'	

Contrasting with the 'declarative' mood is the 'interrogative' mood. It realises the speech function of 'question' and is further differentiated into two subtypes: the 'yes-no' interrogative, realising polar questions, and D-interrogative (or WH-interrogative),[4] realising content-question.

As discussed earlier, one of the major structural features of the interrogative mood is the presence of the Negotiator. Among the set of negotiatory markers, a small set of interpersonal particles – *ka, kai* or *no* – carrying a rising tone enacts interrogative mood.

The difference between these two types of the interrogative mood lies in the response that they demand from the addressee. While the 'yes/no' interrogative demands a 'yes' or 'no' answer, the D-interrogative demands missing or unknown information in the transitivity structure of the clause, either participant or circumstance, which is queried by the relevant interrogative D-word.

In principle, the insertion of an interrogative clause-final particle realising Negotiator into a declarative clause shifts its mood to that of interrogative. However, when the suppositive mood is interrogativised this way, it gives rise to the meaning of 'doubt' serving as a self-imposed rhetorical question – especially when politeness is unmarked. If marked in politeness, on the other hand, the speaker's indecisiveness about the validity of the proposition is communicated to the addressee. Intonationally, the clause is marked with a falling tone and thus similar to that of declarative mood.

(12)	Kare-wa	kuru deshoo	ka
	he	come-informal-conjectural	Q
	Subject	Predicator	Negotiator
	'will he probably be come?'		

The system of indicative mood type is simultaneous with another system, the 'explanative', which adds a meaning of 'explanation' to the statement or question. It is thus co-selective with the declarative and interrogative mood; together, these two systems express the interpersonal judgement about the causal relationship between what is to be explained and what explains it, from the perspective of the interactants. In the explanative mood, the Predicator is marked with an ending *no da* ('[the explanation for that] is') in writing or *n da, n desu, no*. Here, the explanation covers a broad range of causal relationships such as cause, reason, motivation, source and grounds, which are conceived to exist in the co-text or in the given context. Grammatically, when the causal relationship is established co-textually, it is typically realised prosodically – that is, the orientation of the explanation is sensitive to the indicative type: interrogative ('you explain to me') vs. declarative ('I explain to you').

Example (13) is a conversation between two old friends, a female (X) and a male (Y), in which X tries to find out what Y has said to a woman whom they both know (Higashino 2014: 34). X's question is marked in the explanative and it is followed by Y's reply, also marked in the explanative.

(13) X:

Anata,	*kanojo-ni*	*nani-o*	*itta no?*
you	her-to	what	say-past-explanative
Subject	Complement	Complement	Predicator

'What did you say to her?'

Y:

Nani-mo	*ittenai.* [. . .],	*nakayoku*	*shanpan-o*	*nonda n da*
nothing	say-negative-inf.	happily	champagne	drank-explanative-inf.
Complement	Predicator	Adjunct	Complement	Predicator

'(I) didn't say anything, [. . .], we just had champagne happily'

X:

Sona wake	*nai deshoo*
such reason	-modality be-negative-conjectural
Predicator	

'That can't be true.

Dattara,	*dooshite*	*kanojo-ga*	*totsuzen*	*son'na koto-o*	*iidasu no?*
if so	why	she	suddenly	such thing	begin to speak-explanative
		Subject	Adjunct	Complement	Predicator

If so, why does she suddenly start saying thing like that?'

Y:	*Wakan nai*	*yo*
	know-negative	emphasis
	Predicator	Negotiator
	'(I) don't know'	

Imperative mood type

The imperative mood is concerned with the exchange of goods-&-services and realises a proposal through which the speaker involves 'you' and/or 'me' – the interactants – in the here-&-now of an interactive event. In this sense, all of the imperative mood types indicate present time, distinguishing them from all of the indicative mood types.

The 'imperative' mood has two contrasting types: 'jussive' and 'optative'. The *jussive* mood directly prompts the exchange through various kinds of command, while the *optative* mood does so indirectly by the speaker expressing his or her desire or intention. In terms of the addressee's response, however, both evoke a response by complying or refusing in the case of demanding a proposal, or accepting or rejecting in the case of offering. Responses may be expressed paralinguistically by simply nodding or exchanging eye contact. However, the response is often linguistically codified in Japanese so as to reflect the difference in social roles and relationship between the speaker and the addressee. Example (14) is an exchange between a customer (C) and a travel consultant (T) in the context of a service encounter wherein the travel consultant's expression of acceptance of a command, *kashikomari mashita* (*lit.* a verb, *kashikomaru*, marked in politeness meaning 'accept in a humble manner'), codifies vertical tenor relationship between interactants based on their socially conceived superior–inferior relationship.

(14) C:	*Panfuretto-o,*	*chotto*	*onegaishitai n desu*	*keredomo*
	Pamphlet	a bit	favour-optative-explanative be-formal	but
	Complement	mood Adjunct	Predicator	Negotiator
	'(I) want to ask for a pamphlet'			

T:	*Kashikomarimashita*
	accept- formal-past
	Predicator
	'Certainly'

In terms of realisation, both jussive and optative moods are realised either by Predicator alone or by a combination of Predicator^Negotiator. All of the imperative moods, except the oblative and prohibitive moods, are realised by the Predicator only because of two features related to the imperative type: (a) verbals that realise the Predicator are morphologically specific to each given mood type (see Table 14.1); and (b) the Subject is generally implicit because it is restricted to interactants only – that is, the speaker ('I' or 'we') and/or the addressee ('you').

The imperative mood has five 'demanding' types – jussive, suggestive, prohibitive, requestive and optative mood – and one 'giving' type – oblative. Of all the imperative moods, the jussive mood is the most prototypical type because it expresses a direct 'command'. The Predicator is realised by verbs in the imperative form and only those with the semantic feature of 'volition' – that is, processes of doing brought about by an instigator with 'consciousness', like humans – can realise this mood type. For example, processes of happening such as *ochir-u* ('drop') cannot enact commands; if used in the imperative form, it instead enacts the speech function of 'desire', as in *ochir-o* ('[I wish it] drop!').

Similar to the jussive mood is the requestive mood. It is realised by a verbal group complex in which the verb of 'give', *kureru* ('give [me]'), marked in the imperative form augments the preceding main verb that represents the nature of 'service' or 'favour', as in *kai-te kure* ('write it [for me]') (*lit.* 'write' in the participle^'give [a favour to speaker]' in the imperative). The auxiliary *kure* (or its polite form, *kudasai*) is often elided and the main process alone is used in the spoken discourse as in *kaite* ('write it [for me]!').

This requestive mood type is less forceful in enacting commands because it experientially construes the service demanded as a favour to the speaker. It thus can be used in conjunction with the more forceful jussive type, as in *Suwa-tte. Suwa-tte. Suwa-re!* ('Please sit. Please sit. Sit!'), which is an extract from a television programme in which a female superintendent addressing her female subordinate to sit down at a bar shifts her interpersonal strategy from the requestive (the first two clauses) to the jussive (the last one) to receive the service demanded. This shift indicates the change of the experiential role of the speaker in relation to the addressee. In the requestive mood, the speaker is construed as a beneficiary, (experientially Client) – that is, the one who benefits from the exchange, as in *watashi (no tame) ni* ('for [the sake of] me'). In the jussive, on the other hand, the speaker is a commander (experientially Initiator) – that is, the one who causes the addressee to take an action demanded.

The suggestive and the oblative moods are distinguished by the presence or absence of a Negotiator realised by an interrogative particle *ka* because the Predicator is the same in both mood types, for example *kak-oo* ('shall we/let us write'). This means that the presence of the Negotiator changes the speech role of a clause from a demanding (command) to a giving (offer). In other words, the Negotiator marks the orientation of exchange being one of giving. This complementary relationship is similar to that between the declarative and the interrogative mood. However, the role of the Negotiator is different in the exchange of information because the Negotiator changes the role of a clause from the giving (statement) to the demanding (question).

As discussed, the optative mood is slightly different from those just described. It is an expression of the speaker's desire or intention or urge to do something, which prompts the addressee into the exchange of goods-&-services. There are two types of optative expression: (a) the adjectival morpheme *-ta-i* ('wish to . . .') suffixed to a verbal participle, as in *tabe-tai* ('wish to eat'); and (b) the adjective *hoshii* ('want'). The exchange of goods is expressed by (b), while that of service, either (a) or (b).

In either case, the Subject is restricted to the speaker and is implicit. In terms of tense selection, the optative mood always selects the present time, which is another distinctive property that is shared by all of the imperative moods. Contrary to these properties, the optative markers *-ta-i, hoshi-i* ('wish/want [to]') may indicate past tense and enact the speaker's 'present' wish or desire that is potentially or inherently unrealisable, as in example (15).

(15) *Neko-ni*	*umare-tak-atta*
cat	born-past-informal
Adjunct	Predicator
'(*lit.* I wanted to be born as a cat) I wish I was born as a cat'	

The optative mood may alternatively select the addressee or a non-interactant as Subject. This brings about a borderline case in which the optative mood comes to resemble the declarative mood. However, when a clause marked with the optative expression has a non-interactant Subject, it must be marked in the explanative mood, as in [Subject:] *kare wa* [Adjunct:] *neko ni* [Predicator:] *umare-tak-atta n da* ('[the explanation for that is] he wanted to be born as a cat'). As discussed already, this optional explanative marking is open only for indicative mood. In other words, when the Subject is realised by other than speaker, the optative clause must be declarativised to enact a statement about the Subject.

Future direction: system of MOOD in Japanese

This chapter has illustrated the most general mood options available in the interpersonal system of MOOD in Japanese. Japanese operates with a set of distinct mood types that are distinguished in both meaning and wording, being associated structurally with the functions of Subject, Predicator and Negotiator, and combinations thereof. Since the task of this chapter was to discuss the system of MOOD, it did not systematically contrast the MOOD system with its co-systems such as SUBJECT PERSON, MODALITY, HONORIFICATION, POLARITY, EVIDENTIALITY and TENSE. However, where relevant, a number of co-systems were brought in to clarify differences: the distinction between the speech functions of 'question' and 'suggestion', both of which are realised through interrogative mood, was clarified by referring to the interpersonal systems of TENSE, POLARITY and POLITENESS; the distinction between 'command' and 'desire', realised through imperative mood, was related to the experiential processes of doing and happening.

The different mood types described in this chapter are independent variables within the system of MOOD; however, they are at the same time partially dependent on other simultaneous systems that are at risk in enacting exchanges. As pointed out, the description of the mood system presented here could be developed further in delicacy to the point at which increased delicacy still yields further systems; the probabilistic profiling of systemic terms (Matthiessen 2015), such as 'declarative' and 'explanative', in the system of MOOD in Japanese could also be explored. It not only helps us to identify the relationships between grammar and lexis (cf. Hasan 1987) within different mood types and the morphological make-up of verbs realising the Predicator in a particular mood type, but also enables us to expand our understanding of the partial interdependence between the terms of mood system and simultaneous systems. Options that look similar in a subsystem of MOOD may well be probabilistically different in terms of their realisational weight or frequency of occurrences.

Notes

1 See O'Donnell, this volume.
2 See Suzuki (1996 [1972]) and Matthiessen and Bateman (1991) for discussion.

3   In the examples given here, each clause is numbered in Arabic numerals. The first line of each clause provides the original wording; the second gives an interlinear gloss and morphological information; the third includes a functional analysis and the fourth is a rough English translation.

4   The 'D-' represents the initial letter /d/ of interrogative words such as *dare* ('who'), *doko* ('where'), *dore* ('which'), *doo yatte* ('how') – except for *itsu* ('when'). Note in the English translations the root of the 'WH'.

References

Caffarel, A., J.R. Martin and C.M.I.M. Matthiessen (eds). 2004. *Language Typology: A Functional Perspective*. Amsterdam and Philadelphia, PA: John Benjamins.

Fukui, N. 2013. Description of mood in Japanese: Examining mood types in a selected set of text. In E.A. Thomson and W.S. Armour (eds) *Systemic Functional Perspectives of Japanese: Descriptions And Applications*. Oakville, TN: Equinox, pp. 65–100.

Halliday, M.A.K. 1978. *Language as Social Semiotic: The Social Interpretation of Language and Meaning*. London: Arnold.

Halliday, M.A.K. 1979. Modes of meaning and modes of expression: Types of grammatical structure and their determination by different semantic functions. In D.J. Allerton, E. Carney and D. Holdcroft (eds) *Function and Context in Linguistic Analysis: A Festschrift for William Haas*. Cambridge: Cambridge University Press, pp. 57–79.

Halliday, M.A.K. 2003 [1992]. Systemic grammar and the concept of a 'science of language'. In J.J. Webster (ed.) *The Collected Works of M.A.K. Halliday, Vol.3: On Language and Linguistics*. London and New York: Continuum, pp. 199–212.

Halliday, M.A.K. 2005 [1996]. On grammar and grammatics. In J.J. Webster (ed.) *The Collected Works of M.A.K. Halliday, Vol. 1: On Grammar*. London and New York: Continuum, pp. 384–417.

Halliday, M.A.K. 2007 [1984]. Language as code and language as behaviour: A systemic-functional interpretation of the nature and ontogenesis of dialogue. In J.J. Webster (ed.) *The Collected Works of M.A.K. Halliday, Vol. 4: Language of Early Childhood*. London: Bloomsbury, pp. 227–50.

Halliday, M.A.K., and W.S. Greaves. 2008. *Intonation in the Grammar of English*. London and Oakville, TN: Equinox.

Halliday, M.A.K., and C.M.I.M. Matthiessen. 2014. *Halliday's Introduction to Functional Grammar*. 4th edn. London and New York: Routledge.

Hasan, R. 1987. The grammarian's dream: Lexis as most delicate grammar. In M.A.K. Halliday and R.P. Fawcett (eds) *New Developments in Systemic Linguistics: Theory and Description*. London: Pinter, pp. 184–211.

Higashino, K. 2014. *Masukareedo Ibu* [*Masquerade Eve*]. Tokyo: Shueisha Bunko.

Hori, M. 1995. Subjectlessness and honorifics in Japanese: A case of textual construal. In R. Hasan and P.H. Fries (eds) *On Subject and Theme: A Discourse Functional Perspective*. Amsterdam: John Benjamins, pp. 151–85.

Matthiessen, C.M.I.M. 2004. Descriptive motifs and generalisations. In A. Caffarel, J.R. Martin and C.M.I.M. Matthiessen (eds) *Language Typology: A Functional Perspective*. Amsterdam and Philadelphia, PA: John Benjamins, pp. 537–674.

Matthiessen, C.M.I.M. 2015. Halliday's conception of language as a probabilistic system. In J.J. Webster (ed.) *The Bloomsbury Companion to M.A.K. Halliday*. London, New Delhi, New York and Sydney: Bloomsbury, pp. 137–202.

Matthiessen, C.M.I.M., and J.A. Bateman. 1991. *Text Generation and Systemic-Functional Linguistics: Experiences from English and Japanese*. London: Pinter.

Matthiessen, C.M.I.M., K. Teruya and C. Wu. 2008. Multilingual studies as a multi-dimensional space of interconnected language studies. In J.J. Webster (ed.) *Meaning in Context*. London and New York: Continuum, pp. 146–221.

Miller, R.A. 1971. *Japanese and the Other Altaic Languages*. Chicago, IL: University of Chicago Press.

Miyajima, T. 1972. *Dooshi no imi yoohoo no kijutsuteki kenkyuu* [*A Descriptive Study on the Meaning and Usage of Japanese Verbs*]. Tokyo: Shuei.

Mizusawa, Y. 2008. Investigating the directive genre in the Japanese and Australian workplace: A systemic functional approach. Unpublished PhD thesis. University of Wollongong.

Nihongo Kijutsu Bunpo Kenkyukai. 2003. *Gendai Nihongo Bunpo 4: Dai 9 bu Modariti* [*Modern Japanese Grammar, Vol. 4: Part 8 – Modality*]. Tokyo: Kuroshio.

Ochi, A. 2012. A text-based study of the interpersonal grammar of modern Japanese: Mood, odality and evidentiality. Unpublished PhD thesis. Macquarie University.

Okuda, Y. 1984. Osihakari 1 [Supposition 1]. *Nihongogaku* 12: 54–69.

Okuda, Y. 1985. *Kotobano kenkyu josetsu* [*An Introduction to the Study of Language*]. Tokyo: Mugi Shobo.

Okuda, Y. 1996. Bun no koto [On clause]. *Kyooiku Kokugo* [*Educational Linguistics*] 2(22): 2–14.

Otsuki, F. 1897. *Ko nihon bunten bekki* [*General Japanese Grammar Additional Note*]. Available online at http://kindai.ndl.go.jp/info:ndljp/pid/992498

Sano, M. 2006. A linguistic exploration of persuasion in written Japanese discourse: A systemic functional interpretation. Unpublished PhD thesis. University of Wollongong.

Shibatani, M. 1990. *The Languages of Japan*. Cambridge: Cambridge University Press.

Suzuki, S. 1996 [1972]. *Keitairon: Josetsu* [*Morphology: An Introduction*]. Tokyo: Mugi Shobo.

Takahashi, T. 1994. *Dooshi no kenkyuu: Dooshi no dooshi rashisa no hatten to shooshitsu* [*Studies of Verbs: The Development and Disappearance of Verbhood*]. Tokyo: Mugi.

Tatsuki, M. 2009. The Kyoto grammar to Nihongo bunseki [The Kyoto grammar and Japanese language analysis]. *Nihongogaku* 28(4): 60–72.

Teruya, K. 1998. Exploration into the world of experience: A systemic function interpretation of the grammar of Japanese. Unpublished PhD thesis. Macquarie University.

Teruya, K. 2004. Metafunctional profile of the grammar of Japanese. In A. Caffarel, J.R. Martin and C.M.I.M. Matthiessen (eds) *Language Typology: A Functional Perspective*. Amsterdam and Philadelphia, PA: John Benjamins, pp. 185–254.

Teruya, K. 2007. *A Systemic Functional Grammar of Japanese*. Two volumes. London: Continuum.

Teruya, K., and C.M.I.M. Matthiessen. 2015. Halliday in relation to language comparison and typology. In J.J. Webster (ed.) *The Bloomsbury Companion to M.A.K. Halliday*. London, New Delhi, New York and Sydney: Bloomsbury, pp. 427–52.

Teruya, K., E. Akerejola, T.H. Andersen, A. Caffarel, J. Lavid, C.M.I.M. Matthiessen, U.H. Petersen, P. Patpong and F. Smedegaard. 2007. Typology of MOOD: A text-based and system-based functional view. In R. Hasan, C.M.I.M. Matthiessen and J.J. Webster (eds) *Continuing Discourse on Language: A Functional Perspective, Vol. 2*. London: Equinox, pp. 859–920.

Uemura, Y. 1989. Nihongo no intoneeshon [Intonation in Japanese]. *Kotoba no Kagaku* [*Science of Language*] 3: 193–220.

Part III
Below the clause

The phoneme and word phonology in systemic functional linguistics

Paul Tench

Introduction

The principal function of phonology is to provide each discrete unit in the lexicogrammar of a language with distinctive acoustic forms. Each lexicogrammatical unit has to have its own form to distinguish it from all other units in a system. Phonology provides those forms. Phonology is not simply an inventory of phonemes that operates in a given language, but a set of systems that functions at all levels of the lexicogrammar. Systemic functional linguistics (SFL) has achieved a high degree of sophistication in specifying the phonological systems that operate with clauses and sentences (that is, intonation), but has largely neglected the description of systems that operate at other, lower, ranks in the lexicogrammatical hierarchy. This chapter seeks to contribute to redressing that imbalance by looking specifically at those systems that operate at the level of words.

Without phonology, there can be no lexicogrammar. Words are identified by their phonological form so that they can be distinguished from all of the others. As distinct forms, they are stored in the mental lexicon and thus are capable of being listed paradigmatically, as potential items in a system. Words thus have both meaning and form, *signifiés* and *signifiants* as de Saussure referred to this duality. Each distinctive form, or *signifiant*, is composed of phonetic material, which is the physical basis for the other main function of phonology, which is to provide the means for speaking a language.

It will be objected that not all of the *signifiants* of a language might in fact be uniquely distinctive, as in English *right*, *write*, *rite*, *wright*, but that is largely a matter of historical accident: [rɪçt], [ʋritə], [ritə], [ʋrɪçt] all eventually became [ɹaɪt] through various historical processes. Secondly, it will be objected that lexicogrammatical items can also be conveyed non-phonologically, by orthography; however, most writing systems in the world are based on replications of phonology, for example either directly as in alphabets and syllabaries, or indirectly as in Braille, Morse code, semaphore, etc. It is also true that some writing systems are not based on phonology at all, but on lexis, such as Chinese characters ('ideographs'), numbers and icons used in visual displays on computers, washing instructions on clothing, etc. – but in all such cases, the written forms were preceded culturally and psycholinguistically by oral forms. 'Rebus' writing is a hybrid system, mixing phonologically and non-phonologically based systems, for example in texting *before* as *b4*. Apart from ideographs and icons, it remains true to say that lexicogrammatical items in any language are directly or indirectly realisations of the phonology of that language.

Phonology is therefore an integral part of language. Phonology is the systemic organisation of phonetic material for all of the distinctive units of lexicogrammar. The phonology of a language is the systemic organisation of phonetic material peculiar to that language; thus each language has its own specific categories, inventories and patterns of sound. Phonology can consequently be examined in general terms that are valid for all languages and, indeed, particular phonological universals can be identified. All language theories should therefore accommodate phonology and, in doing so, each phonological theory reflects the dominant characteristics of an overarching theory of language. SFL has its own major principles and priorities that get reflected in its theory of phonology.

Historical perspectives

Systemic phonology is most closely associated with Halliday, although it grew out of an earlier approach to phonology developed by J.R. Firth and the so-called prosodic phonologists at the School of Oriental and African Studies at London between the 1930s and the 1960s. A succinct summary of the distinctives of their prosodic analysis is found in Tench (1992: 8):

> Prosodic Analysis is a non-universalist approach to the description of the phonology of a language that highlights the syntagmatic as well as the paradigmatic dimensions of the phonic material, in terms of structures and systems and is prepared to recognize different systems appropriate to different components of the language and to reflect grammatical categories wherever necessary, in such a way as to conform as fully, appropriately and elegantly as possible to a general linguistic theory.

Prosodic analysis eschewed a universalist goal, as systemic phonology does today. The phonology of each language is to be described in terms of its own set of units, features and categories. Although there are general universal features in all languages, for example all languages have vowels, consonants, syllables, etc., and languages that have three vowels all maintain the principle of maximum discrimination so that they 'choose' /i, a, u/, etc., each language displays categories, inventories and patterns that are unique to itself.

Prosodic analysis, furthermore, was not primarily concerned with written transcription conventions or a strictly linear presentation of the phonetic material; rather, it sought to draw as much attention to sequential features of the sound of utterances as to the paradigmatic. Sequential features stretched beyond single segments and were called 'prosodies'; examples include nasalisation through a whole or part of a syllable, vowel harmony, palatalisation through a whole or part of a word, lexical tone and intonational tone over a whole clause or utterance. These 'prosodies' were also known as 'plurisegmental' features.

Systems represent small sets of choices, for example all of the strong vowels that appear in stressed syllables or all of the weak vowels that appear only in unstressed syllables, as in the case of English. But systems may vary according to position in a structure. There is, for example, one system of consonants that operates at the onset of a syllable in English, but a different system that operates at its coda: there is a different set of choices in final position, since /ŋ/ becomes available in final position, but it is not available in initial position, while /h, j, w/ (and /ɹ/ in non-rhotic accents) are not available in final position, but are available in initial position. This 'polysystemic' principle extends in delicacy to other possibilities at the onset: if the syllable has two initial consonants, then the first consonant belongs to a much smaller system and the second consonant likewise. (Note that, in a triconsonantal onset in English, the obligatory /s/ does not form a system, because there is no choice at that point of structure.) Similar, delicate, systems operate at the coda.

There was also no 'compartmentalisation' of units in prosodic analysis. In other traditions, reference to units across phonology, grammar and lexis was strictly forbidden; the units of phonology, grammar and lexis were tightly 'compartmentalised'; in prosodic analysis, on the other hand, phonological description was directly related to grammatical units such as words, phrases and clauses. There might even be a separate phonology for nouns and pronouns in a language, for example, and separate phonologies for 'native' and 'loan' words.

Halliday (1961) developed the notion of a hierarchy of phonological units, such that, in English, 'tone groups' consisted of 'feet', which consisted of 'syllables', which consisted of 'phonemes' (Halliday et al. 1964: 25–7) and, conversely, phonemes had various functions in syllables, which had various functions in feet, which had various functions in tone groups (Halliday 1967: 12–15). This 'structure–function' relationship was not apparent in the earlier model; the units in prosodic analysis were simply domains in which prosodies operated. Each language would need to be described in terms of its own phonological hierarchy, which might not be parallel to that of English. The case is made in what follows for such a difference in the phonological hierarchy of a language called Etkwen.

Tench (1976) also suggested an extension of the structure of the hierarchy with double ranks to capture the structure and function of phonemes in clusters, of syllable sequences in rhythm groups and of intonation unit sequences in intonation groups; he also suggested an extension to the ranks of the hierarchy to embrace phonological paragraphs ('paratones'), exchanges and discourse. In this respect, he was indebted to Pike's (1967) larger perspective on phonological hierarchy.

Halliday (1967) also developed the notion of system networks in phonology. System networks are graphic displays of the choices available in the phonology of a language, the conditions under which the choices are made and the degrees of delicacy of those choices. He produced whole, comprehensive displays for all of the intonation systems of English and syllable finals of standard Chinese (Halliday 1992), as did Young (1992) for the consonant cluster systems of English.

It has to be conceded, however, that, within the sixty-year tradition of SFL, relatively little attention has been paid to the systemic phonology of words. The phonological hierarchy is presented in Berry (1977), but without much explication at the level of words; more appears in Butler (1985), but fuller descriptions appear in Tench (1992) in a range of languages including English, Chinese, Welsh, Arabic, Telegu and Australian language Gooniyandi. Tench (2014) is an attempt to produce a more comprehensive description of the phonological structure of monomorphemic words in English.

Most attention has been given to the level of intonation, principally because, in intonation, the semantic functional dimension is prominent, which has been the bedrock of SFL, and also because as much attention is paid to spoken discourse as to written. Intonation systems appear regularly in all SFL descriptions of English, and intonation description and theory have readily been advanced (Halliday and Greaves 2008; Tench 1990, 1996, 1997). The discourse intonation approach of Brazil and the Birmingham school of linguists is basically an adaptation of Halliday's systemic-functional approach (Brazil 1975, 1978, 1997; Brazil et al. 1980; O'Grady 2010). Halliday's influence may also be seen in Wells' (2006) description of English intonation.

Phonology is viewed as the formal aspect of the acoustic image (*signifiant*) of linguistic units (*signifiés*); thus words and morphemes constitute phonological units, as well as grammatical and semantic units. This is the case for other units as well: rhythm units are acoustic images of phrases/groups and clauses, and intonation provides systems at the level of clause, sentence and discourse. (Phonetics is the phonic substance that 'articulates' the phonological units and systems in actual instances of spoken language.) A phoneme is the minimal unit of phonology; it provides a distinctive unit in sequences for the identification of individual basic lexicogrammatical units – that is, words and morphemes. It has a contrastive function, distinguishing lexicogrammatical units that would otherwise be identical, such as *light* /laɪt/ and *right* /ɹaɪt/, and *light* /laɪt/ and *plight* /plaɪt/.

Current contribution: networks for word phonology

System in word phonology is not like system in lexicogrammar or intonation, a set of options from which a speaker chooses to create meaning; rather, system in phonology at the level of word (and also at the level of groups/phrases) is the specifications of what the speakers of a language recognise as having been established in, or 'selected' by, the language to represent its words.

One current contribution is the attempt to produce system networks for the phonological units of English words (Tench 2014). What follows here is an attempt to produce system networks for another, less well-known, language, to see if the same practical principles of network design can apply.

A full statement of the phonology of words of any language would ideally include statements about:

- the permissible number of syllables (syllabic count) in a (monomorphemic) word;
- the permissible features of suprasegmental marking;
- the permissible kinds of structure in a syllable;
- the inventory of phonemes at the nucleus of the syllable and at the margin (or margins, in the case of closed syllables);
- their allophonic distribution and
- their permissible phonotactic distribution.

Here, we will attempt to describe as fully as possible the phonology of monomorphemic words in Etkwen, a Jukunoid Benue-Congo language spoken in the south of Taraba State, Nigeria.[1] Reference will also be made to English as a language more familiar to the reader.

This description of Etkwen word phonology follows the model presented in Tench (2014) for Southern England Standard Pronunciation (SESP), traditionally known as 'received pronunciation' (RP).

1   The number of syllables allowed for a 'monomorphemic' word – that is, words that consist of a single morpheme (for example English *bed*, *hotel*, *hospital* are monomorphemic, but *bedding*, *hotels*, *hospitalised* are not)
2   The suprasegmental features of syllables (in the case of English, this means the degrees of word stress – that is, primary, secondary and no stress; in the case of Etkwen, it means the pitch of syllables – that is, a lexical tone system)

3   The structure of syllables (English has closed, as well as open, syllables and certain per-
     missibilities of consonant clusters; Etkwen has only open syllables and a very different
     set of permissible clusters at syllable onset)
4   The actual inventory of phonemes at the nucleus of the syllable and at margins (in the
     case of Etkwen, there is only the onset margin)
5   Some allophonic variation (only briefly for Etkwen, whereas for English there an
     abundance of information).

The hierarchy of systems can be displayed as in Figure 15.1.

Syllable count

As in English, there appears to a maximum of five syllables for a single word[2] in
Etkwen. Also, as in English, this maximum is a very rare occurrence: only one instance
in 1,000 Etkwen words in a first mini-dictionary (WeSay 2012), <a.ya.gwa.mo.kpwa>,
chimpanzee.[3] In English, there are words such as <a.bra.ca.da.bra> and <mul.li.ga.taw.ny> –
clearly, words borrowed from elsewhere, but, from an English language point of view,
without internal morphemic boundaries; similarly, place names of non-English origin
such as Ystalyfera /ʌ.stə.lə.vɛə.ɹə/ from Wales.

Words with four syllables are more common in Etkwen (1.3 per cent), but still relatively infrequent, just as in English: <a.de.de.re> (kind of tree); <a.dgyen.ta.hwi>, *fire finch*;
<a.la.kwa.bin> (kind of vegetable); <e.bwi.fə.zən>, *blind*; <e.tso.tso.ro>, *toad*. Words with
three syllables are more common again (approximately 13.1 per cent): <a.gwa.gwa>, *goose*;
<a.kpe.te>, *tray*; <bi.ya.zon>, *bear* (animal); <shin.ge.re>, *singlet*. Words with two syllables
form approximately 40.2 per cent of the total: <a.cha>, *net*; <bi.tin>, *trousers*; <cha.shən>,
back (of the body). Finally, monosyllabic words constitute 45.3 per cent: <a>, *in, on, at*;
<ban>, *to lean on*; <chin>, *waist, fly* (insect); <sə>, *mat*. A simple display of the syllable
count of Etkwen (and English) words might appear as illustrated in Figure 15.2.

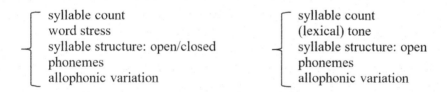

Figure 15.1   The system hierarchies of English and Etkwen

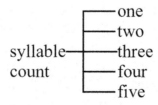

Figure 15.2   A simple system network syllable counts (Etkwen and English)

Suprasegmental marking

The suprasegmental feature of Etkwen syllables is tone. Rhythmical timing appears to be syllabic, unlike the (alleged) stress timing of English. However, each syllable is marked by tone – register tone, rather than contour tone: either high, mid or low. There are abundant illustrations of tone contrasts, particularly in monosyllabic words.[4]

<bá>	*to write, to follow, roof*
<ba>	*to thresh* (kind of tree)
<bà>	*to burn, to stick/gum*
<bgé>	*cooked, miserly*
<bge>	*dog, to slice* (something) *off*
<bgè>	*fresh* (leaves)

Similar contrasts occur with each vowel; this is also the case for Etkwen nasal vowels. In disyllabic words, there is a high tendency for both syllables to carry the same tone, 86 per cent of the total number in the mini-dictionary:

<átá>	*house*
<ata>	*under*
<àtà>	*father*
<ébá>	*dove*
<eba>	*pancreas*
<èbà>	*small hoe, scrounger*

However, there does also appear to be some freedom for each syllable to be accompanied by any of the three tones (14 per cent):

<éhwí>	*lower part of the back* [high + high]
<ehwi>	*assistance* [mid + mid]
<ehwí>	*thin string made from palm fronds* [mid + high]
<ehwì>	*bundle of grass* [mid + low]
<gúkpèn>	*leopard* [high + low]

In words of three syllables, there appears to be the same kind of preponderance of identical tones:

<ásúkú>	*storage sacks*
<atafan>	(kind of yam)
<èfíkà>	*hog*
<adedere>	(kind of tree)

But:

<ádgyéntahwi>	*fire finch* [high + high + mid + mid]

(Unfortunately, the tone pattern of the one five-syllabled word – <ayagwamokpwa>, *chimpanzee* – is not certain.)

The network for tones and tone patterns for mono- and polysyllabic words might be displayed as in Figure 15.3.

Contrast this network with the equivalent at the same level in the phonological hierarchy for English (Tench 2014), in which the stress patterns are more complicated and numerous (Figure 15.4).

Syllable structure

The Etkwen syllable structure system is much simpler than that of English for two reasons. First, it does not feature closed syllables; rather, every syllable ends in a vowel. (In the orthographic transcriptions shown in this chapter, the final *−n* represents a nasal vowel, as we shall see.) However, the onset system is just as 'full' as the English one, yet with a totally different inventory of permissible consonant clusters. Just as English permits up to

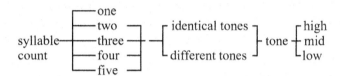

Figure 15.3   A system network of lexical tone patterns in Etkwen words

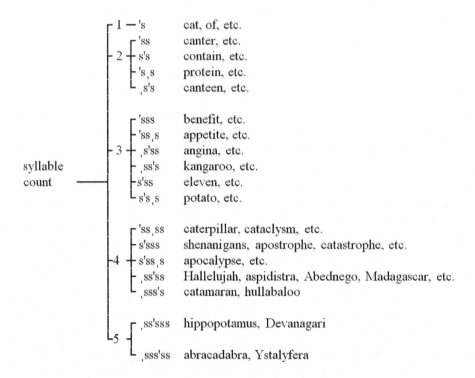

Figure 15.4   A system network of lexical stress patterns in English

Note: 's = primary stress; ˌs = secondary stress; s (without a mark) = unstressed

239

three consonants, so does Etkwen; both languages also admit zero onsets – that is, a syllable beginning with a vowel – although this means that, in Etkwen, the vowel will appear alone in the syllable, since no coda margins are allowed.

Secondly, Etkwen does not distinguish between strong and weak syllables. Their distinction between high, mid and low tones does not appear to have any effect on syllable structure in the way that the features of 'strong' and 'weak' have on English, as is evident in the network with twenty-five forms illustrated in Figure 15.5.

In Etkwen, the onset may be zero, as noted in example (1) for V.[5]

The onset may otherwise have a single consonant or a double consonant cluster: C, CC, as in examples (2) and (3). The initial consonant may be pre-nasalised: nC, nCC, as in examples (4) and (5). Pre-nasalisation in Etkwen is a brief nasal articulation before a voiced plosive that is non-syllabic – that is, it does not constitute a separate syllable, because it does not carry tone. In addition, the onset may be palatalised: Cy, CCy, as in examples (6) and (7). Alternatively, it may be labialised: Cw, CCw, as in examples (8) and (9). A single labialised consonant may also be pre-nasalised: nCw, as in example (10).

The full inventory of consonants is listed later in the chapter.[6] The plain double-consonant clusters maintain a consistent voice feature and are restricted to taking either /k/ or /g/ as the second item following /f/, /t/, /b/ and /d/: /fk/, /tk/, /bg/ and /dg/.

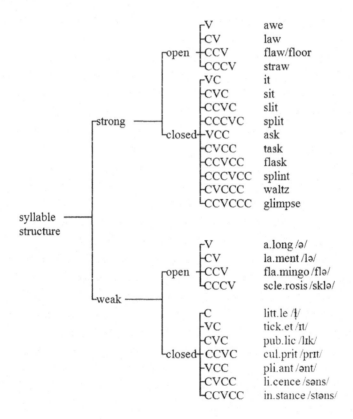

Figure 15.5 A system network of syllable structures in English

Source: Tench (2014)

Pre-nasalisation is widespread: as [ᵐ] before labials /p, b, bg, f/; as [ⁿ] before /t, d, ts, tʃ, tk, s, ʃ/; and as [ŋ] before /k, g/. It also occurs with a few cases of labialisation: [ᵐbw]; [ⁿdwe]; [ŋgwa]. Labialisation also affects the consonants /p, b, t, d, k, g, kp, ts, tʃ, dʒ, m, f, s, ʃ/ and consonant clusters /bg, dg, fk, tk/. Palatalisation, spelt <y>, affects far fewer consonants: mainly labials /p, b, ʍ, f, v, m/ and the consonant clusters / bg, dg/.

Examples (1)–(10) illustrate all of the permitted onsets, in their orthographic representations.

(1) V   a   *in, on, at*
                 a.bé   *they*
                 è.bí   *turtle*
                 o   *you* (sg)

(2) CV   bə   *black, to cross legs*
                 fè   *close, compact*
                 nó   *to mix*

(3) CC   bgo   *to ask, beg*
                 fken   *to shine, kind of tree*
                 e.tken   *to stand*

(4) nC   mba [ᵐba]   *to labour*
                 nda [ⁿda]   *to seek*
                 ngge [ŋge]   *with*

(5) nCC   mbga [ᵐbga]   *children*

(6) Cy   byo   *ugly*
                 vyi   *cold*
                 mya   *fast*

(7) CCy   bgya   *flute*
                 dgyen   *stomach*
                 é.dgyán   *to love*

(8) Cw   bwe   *to do*
                 jwèn   *rabbit, hare*
                 shwa   *neck*

(9) CCw   bgwá   *plenty*
                 fkwa   *to roast*
                 E.tkwen   *Etkwen* (language)

(10) nCw   mbwá [ᵐbwá]   *to give birth*
                 ndwe [ⁿdwe]   *four*
                 nggwa [ŋgwa]   *to be wide*

In contrast to the twenty-five forms in the English syllable structure system (see Figure 15.5), Etkwen has just these nine forms, which can be displayed in the network illustrated in

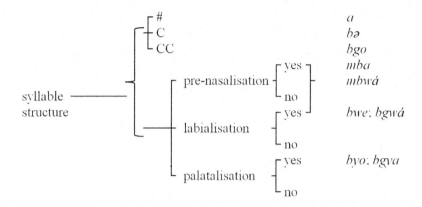

Figure 15.6 A system network of syllable structures in Etkwen

Figure 15.6. The Etkwen network specifies that there is a simultaneous 'choice' between onset consonants and systems of pre-nasalisation, labialisation and palatalisation, which themselves can be either positive or negative – and, in one case, double (pre-nasalisation and labialisation).

Syllable nucleus

Etkwen has an inventory of eleven vowels. Six are oral, /i, e, ə, a, u, o/; only five are nasal, /ĩ, ẽ, ɔ̃, ã, õ/, with /u/ having no nasal equivalent. All vowels take the full tone system.

There are three vowel systems: one set of vowels operates word-initially; another set operates only word-finally – namely, the nasal vowels and the third set operates word-medially and word-finally.

The word-initial system contains three items /a, e, o/, while /a/ alone, as we have seen, can constitute two words: <a> as a locative preposition (*at, in, on*) or as a grammatical marker of the future tense. It also occurs as the first syllable of many words. The item /e/ does not stand alone, but it does occur as the first syllable of many words. The item /o/ alone, as we have also seen, constitutes the pronoun *you* (sg), but otherwise it does not lead any other word. The other vowels can neither stand alone nor lead any word.

All of the oral vowels occur medially and finally. The nasal vowels occur only finally; their orthographic representation is with following <n>, as noted earlier, which is common to other Jukunoid Benue-Congo languages in Taraba State and other major languages in Nigeria, such as Yoruba (Dunstan 1969: 167). When <n> occurs word-medially it is interpreted either as consonant /n/ or as pre-nasalisation before a consonant. In the word *Etkwen*, <n> signals nasalisation of the preceding vowel (/ẽ/); in <ano>, *what?*, it is the consonant /n/; in <ando>, *spinach*, it is interpreted as pre-nasalisation of /d/: [a.ⁿdo].

The three Etkwen vowel systems can be displayed as in Figure 15.7.

Contrast this network of eleven vowels with that of English, with its separate systems of strong/weak syllables, closed/open syllables and long/short vowels, and a total inventory of twenty-three vowels and three syllabic consonants (Figure 15.8).

Syllable onsets

Etkwen has open syllables only. The onset may be zero, as with words with initial /a, e/ and the word <o>. The onset may be a single consonant or a double consonant cluster, with

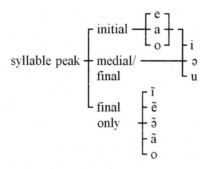

Figure 15.7 A system network of syllable peaks in Etkwen

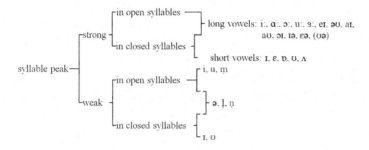

Figure 15.8 A system network of syllable peaks in English

Source: Tench (2014)

pre-nasalisation, labialisation, pre-nasalisation and labialisation, or palatalisation. The single consonant system is /p, t, k, kp, b, d, g, ts, tʃ, dʒ, f, s, ʃ, h, v, z, y, ʍ, w, m, n, ɲ, ŋ, l, r/, with examples as follows.

/p/	\<pe\>	*to close*
/t/	\<te\>	*medicine, guinea fowl*
/k/	\<kə\>	*to reproduce*
/kp/	\<kpé\>	*tomorrow*
/b/	\<be\>	*they*
/d/	\<dá\>	*dream*
/g/	\<ge\>	*he/she, him/her*
/ts/	\<tsen\>	*laughter*
/tʃ/	\<chá\>	*torn*
/dʒ/	\<jé\>	*across the river*
/f/	\<fè\>	*close, compact*
/s/	\<sé\>	*to press*
/ʃ/	\<shin\>	*to plant*
/h/	\<hi\>	(grammatical marker of past tense)
/v/	\<vən\>	*to throw*
/z/	\<zə\>	*place*
/j/	\<ye\>	*those*

/ʍ/ <hwe>   *fool*
/w/ <wá>   *to farm*
/m/ <me>   *breast*
/n/ <ne>   *big*
/ɲ/ <nyé/   *to cross a river*
/ŋ/ <ngá>   *to be dry*
/l/ <lá>   *to jump*
/r/ <ra>   *not*

Note that both /l/ and /r/ occur very infrequently, but they do contrast with each other.

The network of Etkwen onset systems is, of course, identical to the network of syllable structures.

Phoneme features

To illustrate a network of the features of the vowel system, the more familiar system of English strong vowels is presented here first (Tench 2014). (A separate system is necessary for the weak vowels of English, as we shall see shortly.) The incidental advantage of this display is that it separates not only the two systems, strong and weak, but also, within the strong vowel system, short vowels with their particular phonological constraint in distribution from long vowels. Also, the display integrates diphthongs with monophthongs into one single strong vowel system. The parentheses around /ʊə/ are intended to indicate that not all SESP (RP) speakers have this vowel in their speech, it being replaced either by /ɔː/, as in *poor* /pɔː/, or by /u:+ə/, as in *dour* /'du:ə/.

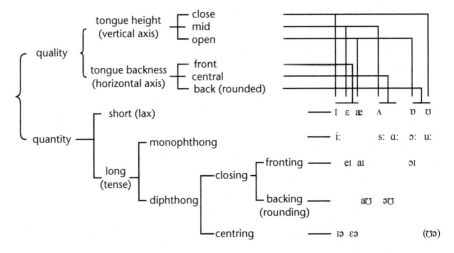

Figure 15.9   A system network of the strong vowels of SESP

Figure 15.10   A system network of the weak vowels of SESP

The design of the network is intended to show the three most relevant systems of tongue height, tongue backness and quantity, with their realisations (Figure 15.9).

The network for weak vowels is very much simpler, with no system for quantity and much-reduced systems for tongue height and backness. The system for closed syllables is shown on the left-hand side of Figure 15.10 and that for open syllables on the right.

On the other hand, Etkwen, as noted above, has only an inventory of eleven vowels: six oral and five nasal. The six oral vowels consist of three close vowels: /i, ə, u/, and three non-close /e, a, u/; /ə/ is actually a close central vowel [ɨ], but is spelt <ə> in common with many languages in the Middle Belt and North of Nigeria. The vowels /e, o/ have mid height; /a/ is open.

The five nasal vowels have the equivalent phonetic qualities as their oral counterparts, thus /ɔ̃/ is phonetically [ĩ]. They are all spelled with a following <n>: <in, en, ən, an, on>.

The Etkwen system is obviously much simpler than English, comprising only eleven items, and without the distinctions between long and short, monophthongs and diphthongs, closing and centring, and fronting and backing. The tongue height system is also simpler (Figure 15.11).

The inventory of English consonants is, likewise, presented first as being more familiar. The classification criteria are presented in a system network for syllable-initial consonants as in Figure 15.12; that for syllable-final consonants would require the addition of /ŋ/ (nasal

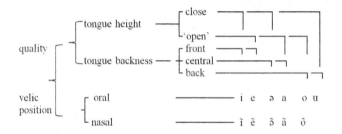

Figure 15.11   A system network of the vowels of Etkwen

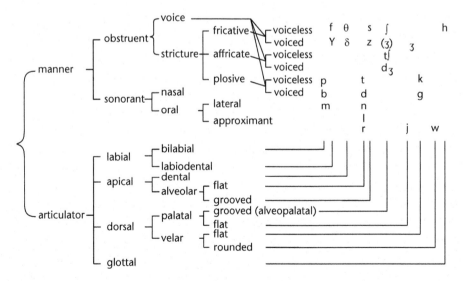

Figure 15.12   A system network of the syllable-initial consonants of SESP

Source: Tench (2014)

velar flat), and also the deletion of /h/, the 'articulator' row 'glottal' and also the 'manner' row 'approximant'.

The incidental advantages of this display over traditional consonant charts include the close link between affricates and both fricatives and plosives, the close link between nasals and both plosives (in points of articulation) and approximants (as 'fellow' sonorants), the labelling of grooved articulations and the close links between them, and the avoidance of redundant 'cells' for voicelessness for sonorants. (There is, however, a redundant voiced 'cell' accompanying /h/.) The parentheses around /ʒ/ indicate its marginal status in the syllable-initial system; parentheses would not be required in the network for the syllable-final system.

As in the English consonant network, the close link between both fricatives and plosives is shown in Figure 15.13, as is the close link between nasals and plosives/affricates (in points of articulation) and other sonorants. Again, there are no redundant voiceless cells with the sonorants. It may be surprising, and even counter-intuitive, to separate /w/ and /ʍ/ quite considerably, but, as it happens, /ʍ/ acts like the other fricatives in taking palatalisation, whereas /w/ does not. Their similarity in articulation is nevertheless shown explicitly.

A number of asymmetries show up here. First, there is no voiced counterpart to either /ʃ/ or /ts/, whereas there is for /tʃ/. There is also no voiced counterpart to the double articulation /kp/, while there is no voiceless counterpart to /j/, as there is for /w/. Finally, there is no nasal counterpart to /kp/, as there is for all of the other points of articulation for plosives and affricates.

Allophones

It is frequently maintained that *allophonic variation* does not belong to phonology as such, but rather to phonetics. It is maintained that, because allophones do not have the contrastive function of phonemes, they do not constitute a lower order in the phonological hierarchy. However, SFL follows Firthian prosodic analysis, noting that allophonic features of phonemes vary according to the specifications of a given language. For instance, English and French both have a phoneme that is symbolised as /p/, but although they have much in

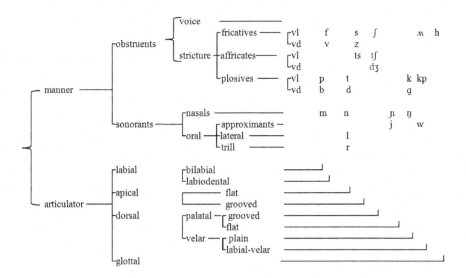

Figure 15.13   A system network of the consonants of Etkwen

common ('bilabial', 'voiceless', 'fortis', 'plosive' and a number of contrastive and distributional characteristics), they have nevertheless quite a different set of allophones: English /p/ is most often 'aspirated', whereas the French /p/ is not; English /p/ has glottal reinforcement in some environments, whereas the French does not. The word phonology of a language must therefore also specify what allophonic variation is permissible; it is as if a language has selected certain phonetic realisations for its phonemes and not others that another language might have selected. So, having specified that, within the permitted consonant inventory, English has /p/, we can then specify what allophonic variation is permitted; this amounts to specifying what forms the phonetic realisation of /p/ may take.[7]

Figure 15.14 is an example of how an allophonic network might look for Etkwen /j/. It is a 'normal' approximant with clear voicing in initial and intervocalic position, but when it acts as palatalisation of consonants, it takes on a noticeable degree of friction. Voiceless friction is rather like [ʃ] or [ç].[8]

Voiced friction is like fricative [ʝ]: byo (*ugly*) [bʝo]. The system network for /j/ might be presented as in Figure 15.14, with square brackets containing an allophonic transcription.

Conclusion and future directions

What has been presented in this chapter is an attempt at adapting the practical principles of system network design to phonological systems at the level of monomorphemic words in English and Etkwen. They have purposely been presented as 'surface' structures to be as readily comprehensible as possible.

The systemic phonology enterprise requires scrutiny by others of the networks produced in this chapter and in Tench (2014), the development of complete system networks for allophonic realisations and their distribution, and the incorporation of phonotactic information into the networks.

Phonotactics

'Phonotactics' refers to the specification of permissible distributions and combinations of vowels and consonants in a language. Phonotactics, as a term, is often employed to refer specifically to the permissible combinations of consonants in clusters in syllable initial and final margins. A brief discussion of the phonotactic possibilities in English appears in Tench (2014), but see also Young (1992).

Full phonotactic charts of English appear in Gimson (1989: 241–56), but it should be noted that they do include inflected forms of words and hence are not strictly monomorphemic. Gimson (1989: 256) points out that not all possible combinations that conform to general patterns are utilised; thus there happen to be no words like /faʊd/, /saɪdʒ/, /mɒmp/, /bɹuːtʃ/, /pliːk/, /splʌk/, /strɛdʒ/. This underutilisation of all possible combinations is not, it should be noted, subject to specifications in English word phonology, but rather to the specifications of the lexicon itself. More new words with permissible phonotactics may well

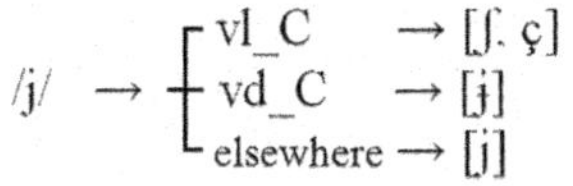

$$/j/ \rightarrow \begin{cases} vl\_C & \rightarrow [\int \cdot ç] \\ vd\_C & \rightarrow [ʝ] \\ elsewhere & \rightarrow [j] \end{cases}$$

Figure 15.14 A system network for the allophones of Etkwen /j/

yet enter the lexicon. Incorporating phonotactic information into systemic networks is a task for future researchers.

Phonology of bound morphemes

A parallel study needs to be made of the phonological characteristics of bound morphemes, both inflectional and derivational. Most bound morphemes in English consist either of non-syllabic consonants, such as /-s, -z/, /-t, -d/ or /θ/, or of one or two unstressed syllables, such as /bɪ-/, /ʌn-/, /-ə/, /-əst/, /-əd/, /-nəs/, etc. However, there are some that require a syllable with either primary or secondary stress: examples of those requiring primary stress are /-ˈɛsk/ as in *picturesque*, /-ˈɛt/ as in *kitchenette* and /ˈɛə/ as in *millionaire*; examples with secondary stress include /ˌɹiː-/ as in *rework*, /ˌpɹəʊ-/ as in *proactive*, /ˌkəʊ-/ as in *cooperate*, /ˌnɒn-/ as in *non-nuclear*, etc. System networks will be needed for prefixes and suffixes.

Parametric phonetics

A 'parametric' approach to phonetics highlights the continuous activity of organs of speech, as opposed to the more static 'segmental' approach that is adopted in most studies of the phonology of languages (Tench 1978). It was characteristic of the earlier prosodic analysis approach to the study of pronunciation in the form of 'prosodies'. Such 'plurisegmental' features are observed in English as in the rounding ('labialisation') of consonants adjacent to rounded vowels, the nasalisation of vowels adjacent to nasal consonants, the devoicing of voiced consonants adjacent to voiceless consonants and silence, the voicing of /h/ between voiced articulations and the quality of /h/ and aspiration depending on the ensuing vowel. System networks for allophonic variation could usefully include such a parametric dimension.

The parametric approach affects phonemes in English too. The distribution of bound morphemes for 'past forms' depends on the phonological form of the stem: if it ends in /t, d/, then a whole syllable is required /-əd/; if it ends in any other voiced articulation, then the (voiced) /d/ is required and if it ends with a voiceless consonant, then the form will be (voiceless) /t/. In other words, the non-syllabic form maintains vocal fold activity. Likewise the /-əz, -z, -s/ forms of the third-person singular of verbs, and the plural and possessive suffixes of nouns.

Another example is the place of the articulation of nasals adjacent to other consonants, especially plosives. A nasal adjacent to the bilabials /p, b, m/ will be (bilabial) /m/, as in *temper, number, impossible, imbalance*, etc. This is also observable in informal speech, in which <m> does not appear in standard orthography, as in *input* (sometimes 'mis-spelt' as *imput*), *unbalanced, unmixed*. Bilabial articulation is maintained as a plurisegmental feature. Velar articulation is also likewise maintained, as in *ink, language, incorrect, ingratitude, unkind, ungrateful, non-conformist*. This assimilation is either phonemic, as in these cases, or allophonic, whereby the adjustment of the nasal articulation does not conform with a phoneme in English, as [ɱ] in *triumph*, [n̪] in *tenth*, [ɲ] in *onion*.

This kind of assimilation affects /t, d/ likewise in informal speech, so that *utmost* is frequently mis-spelt as *upmost*, *good morning* is pronounced as [ˌɡʊbˈmɔːnɪŋ], etc. It also affects /t, d, s, z/ when /j/ follows: *statue* as [ˈstaˌtʃuː], *due, dew* as [dʒuː] making it homophonous with *Jew*, and *issue* and *usual* as [ˈɪʃuː], [ˈjuːʒʊəl]. In all of these cases, a point of articulation is maintained across segments.

A parametric dimension to system networks would therefore be appropriate for allophonic variation, for bound morphemes and, eventually, for phrases/groups, words in sequence.

Cultural associations

The vast majority of words in a language maintain an arbitrary association between *signifié* and *singifiant*, such that there is absolutely no symbolic association between the notion of 'cat' and the sequence of sounds transcribed as /kæt/. But there is obviously a linguistic attempt to replicate the sound of a cat with the sound sequence /mi'aʊ/, usually spelt as <meow>. Animal sounds and other natural sounds such as the blowing of the wind as *whoosh*, the 'creaking' of doors and the 'rattling' of windows, etc., are reproduced as closely as possible to the phonological units of English.

Beside such onomatopoeia, or 'primary sound symbolism', there is a 'secondary sound symbolism', or phonaesthetics, which associates certain phonemes not with physical sounds, but with qualities. The vowels /iː, ɪ/ often seem to refer to notions of smallness in size, movement, time, sound and sense: consider *pip, pinch, minute* /'mɪnɪt/, *ping, piffle.* But the relationship is by no means absolute – that is, it is not a purely phonological phenomenon: consider *small* with the vowel /ɔː/, *minute* /ˌmaɪ'njuːt/, and with the said vowel, *big*. Nevertheless, this cultural association is reflected in recent coinages such as *zip, blip, kitsch* and *niche*. There appears to be a readiness, at least in British culture, to render the notions of smallness with the vowels /iː, ɪ/. There also appears a readiness to associate other vowels with other notions. A separate 'lexicophonological' system network might be constructed, which could extend to the association of certain vowel preferences and syllable structures that distinguish femininity and masculinity in personal names: why *Chloe* sounds feminine and *Butch* does not.

Another dimension to cultural associations is what might be called permissible poetic forms. What constitutes rhyme/rime, alliteration, rhythm, etc., is peculiar to a culture and its language. Rhyming schemes in Welsh poetry, for instance, seem to be more complex than those in English.

Variation

System networks that identify historical processes might be envisaged. Certainly, networks for other accents of English need to be produced, in their own right and for contrastive purposes; likewise, in the great applied linguistics enterprise, networks in phonological 'interlanguage'. Tench (2003) published a study, highlighting the polysystemic principle of systemic phonology, which shows how Korean learners of English had consistently greater difficulty in producing intelligible renditions of final consonants than initial; this seems to be because Korean has a much simpler coda system than its onset system.

Other languages

Perhaps the biggest need in the immediate future is the presentation of system networks in the phonology of other languages besides English (and Etkwen), to produce a more rigorous set of procedures.

In the whole theoretical and applied linguistics enterprise, the primary role of the linguist is to present full and adequate accounts of the nature of language in general and of languages in particular (Halliday et al. 1964: x–xi) in all of their complexity. Descriptions of different languages allow comparison and contrast, which brings vital information to the attention of linguists, teachers, textbook writers and other language professionals, and also to others who are involved in related matters politically, administratively, academically, commercially, socially, therapeutically, forensically and technically.

Notes

1 It is also spelt 'Etkywan' in *Ethnologue* (ISO 639-3 ich) and known as 'Ichen' (hence the *Ethnologue* code) in Hausa, the regional language of wider communication (Ichen Language Team 2014).
2 Henceforth 'word' will refer to 'monomorphemic word', to save unnecessary repetition.
3 < and > indicate orthographical representation; . indicates a syllable break.
4 Acute accent (e.g. á) = high tone; unmarked (e.g. a) = mid tone; grave accent (e.g. à) = low tone.
5 Note that the orthographical representations above (and below) show nasalisation of a vowel by a following <n>, for example <atafan> = /atafã/; Etkwen = /etkwẽ/.
6 See 'Syllable onsets'.
7 See Tench (2014) for an initial attempt to draw up networks for the allophonic variations of English /p/ and /b/.
8 Note that the alternative spelling of Etkwen is 'Etkywan', with a purported palatalisation of /k/: /ky/; this would yield phonetically [kʃ] or [kç] and is probably responsible for the Hausa rendering of the language name as *Ichen* [itʃen].

References

Berry, M. 1977. *An Introduction to Systemic Linguistics, Vol. 2: Levels and Links*. London: Batsford.
Brazil, D.C. 1975. *Discourse Intonation*. Birmingham: English Language Research.
Brazil, D.C. 1978. *Discourse Intonation II*. Birmingham: English Language Research.
Brazil, D.C. 1997. *The Communicative Value of Intonation in English*. Cambridge: Cambridge University Press.
Brazil, D.C., M. Coulthard and C. Johns. 1980. *Discourse Intonation and Language Teaching*. London: Longman.
Butler, C. S. 1985. *Systemic Linguistics: Theory and Applications*. London: Batsford.
Dunstan, E. (ed.). 1969. *Twelve Nigerian Languages*. London: Longmans.
Gimson, A.C. 1989. *An Introduction to the Pronunciation of English*. 4th edn. London: Arnold.
Halliday, M.A.K. 1961. Categories of the theory of grammar. *WORD* 17(3): 241–92.
Halliday, M.A.K. 1967. *Intonation and Grammar in British English*. The Hague, NL: Mouton.
Halliday, M.A.K. 1992. A systemic interpretation of Peking syllable finals. In P. Tench (ed.) *Studies in Systemic Phonology*. London: Pinter, pp. 98–121.
Halliday, M.A.K., and W.S. Greaves. 2008. *Intonation in the Grammar of English*. London: Equinox.
Halliday, M.A.K., A. McIntosh and P. Strevens. 1964. *The Linguistic Sciences and Language Teaching*. London: Longmans.
Ichen Language Team. 2014. *Ba we Ka Hwi Ichen* [*Writing and Reading Ichen Language*]. Taraba: Zing.
O'Grady, G. 2010. *A Grammar of Spoken English Discourse*. London: Continuum.
Pike, K.L. 1967. *Language in Relation to a Unified Theory of the Structure of Human Behavior*. 2nd rev'd edn. The Hague: Mouton.
Tench, P. 1976. Double ranks in a phonological hierarchy. *Journal of Linguistics* 12(1): 1–20.
Tench, P. 1978. On introducing parametric phonetics. *Journal of the International Phonetics Association* 8: 34–46.
Tench, P. 1990. *The Role of Intonation in English Discourse*. Frankfurt aM: Peter Lang.
Tench, P. (ed.). 1992. *Studies in Systemic Phonology*. London: Pinter.
Tench, P. 1996. *The Intonation Systems of English*. London: Cassell.
Tench, P. 1997. The fall and rise of the level tone in English. *Functions of Language* 4(1): 1–22.
Tench, P. 2003. Non-native speakers' misperceptions of English vowels and consonants: Evidence from Korean adults in UK. *International Review of Applied Linguistics* 41: 145–73.
Tench, P. 2014. Towards a systemic presentation of the word phonology of English. In W.L. Bowcher and B.A. Smith (eds) *Systemic Phonology*. London: Equinox, pp. 267–94.
Wells, J.C. 2006. *English Intonation: An Introduction*. Cambridge: Cambridge University Press.
WeSay. 2012. WeSay Etkwen dictionary. Unpublished.
Young, D. 1992. English consonant clusters: A systemic approach. In P. Tench (ed.) *Studies in Systemic Phonology*. London: Pinter, pp. 44–69.

Form and function in groups

Edward McDonald

Introduction: defining 'group'

The concept of group in systemic functional linguistics (SFL) is more complex than its equivalents in other theories of grammar or syntax for a number of reasons.

1   It is not an autonomous structural notion, but rather is understood as the **realisation** of systemic features – that is, the **syntagmatic** combinations recognised in the group, as in other grammatical units, are the realisation of **paradigmatic** options.
2   In standard ranked constituency versions of SFL (for example Halliday 1994 [1985]), the group takes its place on the **rank scale** whereby units of different ranks play different kinds of functional role and exhibit different kinds of structural patterning.
3   By means of this notion of rank scale, the group takes an intermediate position: linked by one trajectory to the structure of the **clause**, in that each group realises a particular function in the clause structure, and by another trajectory to classes of **word**, in that words are classified according as they play functions in the structure of the group.
4   The group incorporates two principles of structure: **univariate**, in which a single kind of functional relationship is seen as multiplied recursively, for example modification involving a Head and one or more Modifiers; and **multivariate**, in which a number of different functional roles can be recognised, for example Deictic^Numerator^Thing, with all groups able to be analysed in both ways.
5   In many languages, group rank accommodates two distinct kinds of structure: the **group** proper, which is the expansion of a central word and contains a Head plus Modifiers and/or Qualifiers; and the **phrase**, which is the contraction of a clause and mimics the Process–Participant structure.

The structure of groups combining to form a clause, alongside the internal structure of groups made up of words, provides the basic constituency framework on which functional analysis depends. It is the need to clarify the function structure of the clause that prompted the positing of a 'rank scale' (Halliday 1961) whereby constituency structure is separated into different 'sizes' of unit – for example, for English, clause, group/phrase, word, morpheme – on the grounds that each rank is characterised by different kinds of structural patterns. By this structural principle, the **functions** (functional elements) of the rank above are realised by **classes** of the rank below. The basic functional principle here is an **experiential** one, with the basic experiential clause functions of Participant, Process and Circumstance, in English at least, corresponding to the group classes of nominal, verbal and adverbial, respectively, and with the prepositional phrase realising Circumstances and certain types of Participant. This link-up between clause function and group class is, however, complicated by the multifunctional analysis of the clause, whereby different kinds of structures, not necessarily constituency-based like the experiential clause structure, are superimposed on this basic constituency structure.

Problems with the requirement of 'total accountability' (Halliday 1966) – that is, that each clause function must be realised by a group structure and that each word must be a realisation of a group function – have led some scholars to suggest that rank scale be done away with altogether, on the basis that it is neither descriptively useful nor theoretically coherent that each word must be part of a group in order to be part of a clause (Fawcett 2000a: ch. 10; Matthews 1966;). Moreover, because the conceptualisation of classes of word is dependent on their function in classes of group, which are in turn dependent on their function in the clause, only those word classes that commonly function as the Heads of groups are 'assigned' to a discrete group class. So, for example, the adjective in English is assimilated to the group class of the noun, the most common Head of groups in which the adjective appears (an analysis with deep roots in European linguistics, as we shall see later in this chapter), leading some scholars to claim that its own individual patterning is neglected (for example Tucker 1998, and in this volume). Furthermore, the experiential bias of the constituency-based rank scale has led some scholars to suggest that it be restricted to experiential structure only (for example McDonald 2004; McGregor 1991, 1996).

Although in the description of English, group and phrase are regarded as functionally equivalent, in that each realises clause-rank functions, other languages do not necessarily show the same equivalence. For example, in Japanese, the group–phrase difference is elided, with the equivalents of English nominal groups and prepositional phrases both constructed like phrases, with a mini-Process-like marker of their Participant or Circumstance role. More problematically, in a language such as Chinese, it is possible to interpret the 'preposition' of a prepositional phrase and the 'verb' of a clause as forming a 'serial verb construction', rendering the boundary between phrase and clause unclear – something that may cause problems for the 'separation of powers' assumed by the rank scale

The concept of group is a relatively recent one in the history of linguistics. In Europe, ancient and medieval grammatical frameworks recognised only 'word' (Gr. λέξις *léxis*; L. *dictiō*) and 'sentence' (Gr. λόγος *lógos*; L. *orātiō*), and the in-between concept of 'group' has gone through a process of evolution within linguistics since it was first introduced in the eighteenth century. The concept of 'group' derives from that of *groupe des mots* ('group of words') used by French and German scholars from the eighteenth century onwards to capture relationships in the European vernacular languages between words not marked by inflections for government or agreement as in the classical languages (see 'Historical perspectives' below). The notion of group can also be understood as an elaboration of the traditional notion of 'parts of speech' (a long-standing mistranslation for 'parts of the sentence'), which, over a long period of evolution, had come to be interpreted as, in effect, 'classes of word', with a word appearing either by itself or in company with other like elements, hence forming a 'group'.

It may thus seem as if the concept of group bears a heavy weight of both history and analytical necessity. This chapter will attempt to lay out the evolution of this concept through history and across SFL theory, not so much to argue for any one model of groups as to reveal the implications of certain theoretical and descriptive choices. To throw light on these issues, examples will be cited from a number of the typologically different languages examined in McDonald (2008), as well as from English and other languages treated in Part III of the current volume.

The descriptive base

There has been a tendency for lexicogrammatical descriptions using SFL to largely neglect the morphological aspect of languages in favour of a focus on the grammatical links between words and groups, and thus largely, apart from considerations of word order, to take their formal realisation for granted. Whatever the historical reasons for this, which arguably may be traced to the roots of SFL descriptive work in Chinese (Halliday 1956, 1959) and English (Halliday 1967a, 1967b, 1968, 1994 [1985]; Halliday and Hasan 1976; Martin 1992), both of which languages have minimal explicit marking of clause and group relations, it is perhaps a temptation for SFL practitioners to identify clause functions more or less 'intuitively' from above and to be less careful in 'reading the signals' from below. For this reason, there is a need to be aware of a greater range of structural types and realisational modes across languages than the Chinese/English type, and not to assume that one model will work for all.

This section represents a quick and unrepresentative survey, drawing on McDonald (2008). The possibilities cover a range of languages, from those in which almost every clause and group relation is marked by an inflectional ending, such as Old English (example (1)), through those in which almost no structural relation is marked, such as Old Chinese (example (2)), to in-between languages, such as Scottish Gaelic (example (3)), in which there is minimal marking, but of a slightly different sort. A short example from each language is discussed, given in Latin orthography, with word-for-word glossing and contextual translation in English provided beneath. In the case of the inflected Old English, another inflected form is provided in italics underneath each inflected word - to give some idea of the range of morphological variation, for example waes ~ *wesan*, while uninflected words are enclosed in square brackets, for example [in].

(1) *Old English*

Wæs	hē	sē	mon	in	weoruldhāde	geseted
Was	he	that	man	in	worldhood (secular life)	set
	▸	▸	◂	↳	↵	
→	↵					←
wesan	*his*	*þæs*	*mannes*	*[in]*	*weoruldhād*	*setan*
'That man was settled in secular life'

oð	þā	tīde	þe	hē	wæs	gelȳfdre	ylde
till	the	time	that	he	was	of-lived (advanced)	of-age
	▸	◂		↳	↵	▸	◂
↳		↵		↳			↵
[oð]	sēo	tīd	[þe]	hine	wære	gelȳfode	yldo

'Until he was of advanced age'

ond	hē	næfre	nænig	lēoð	geleornode.
and	he	never	not-any	song	learned
	↳		▸	◂	↵
				↳	↵
		↳			↵
[ond]	him	[næfre]	nænige	lēoðe	leornan

'And he had never learned any song'

Old English is a language of the familiar Indo-European type with two kinds of relations marked by nominal and certain verbal inflections:

1   **government** relations, which mark clause relations of a kind roughly equivalent to transitivity in modern terms, but understood in terms of verbs or prepositions 'governing' nouns or pronouns in particular inflectional cases – indicated above by bent arrows, ↳   ↵ – for example the relations between *geleornode* ('learned') and *lēoð* ('song'), or between *in* ('in') and *weoruldhāde* ('secular life'); and

2   **agreement** relations, which mostly mark group relations, specifically between nominal elements, whereby particular words match or 'agree' in terms of case, number and gender, for example the participle + noun combination *gelȳfdre ylde* ('of lived age') in which each is marked by a syncretic ending that indicates simultaneously genitive [case], singular [number] and feminine [gender] – indicated above by arrow heads ▸   ◂ .

Traditionally, the subject and the finite verb – Participant and Process in transitivity terms – are also understood as falling under the latter relation, since they agree in number and person. They are indicated above as linked by *both* government and agreement, for example *wæs hē . . . geseted* ('he was set'), in which the subject *hē* ('he') comes in between the two parts of the verb *wæs . . . geseted* ('was set').

The Indo-European inflectional type of language is that which forms the basis of the Western grammatical tradition and the study of grammar arose in this tradition out of the need to explain the patterns of inflections. It will be discussed in more detail under 'Historical perspectives'.

(2)   *Old Chinese*

Sòng	rén	yǒu	géng	tián	**zhě**
Song	people	exist	plough	field	NOM

'(Among the) people of Song there was a man who ploughed the fields'

tián zhōng	yǒu	zhū
field in	exist	trunk

'in his field there was a tree stump'

tù	zǒu
hare	run

'a hare ran (out)'

chù	zhū
strike	trunk

'hit the stump'

zhé	jǐng
break	neck

'broke its neck'

ér	sǐ
CONJ	die

'and died'

Old Chinese is an example of a maximally isolating language in which there is a clear distinction between lexical and grammatical words, dubbed *shí* ('full, real') and *xū* ('empty, virtual'), respectively, by traditional Chinese philologists, which operate together in order to realise clause and group functions. The bulk of both clause and group relations are marked by word order and collocational relations, with extensive use of ellipsis for reference and a single structural marker *zhī*, which could be glossed as 'subordinator' and marks a Modifier^Head relationship. For example, an alternative form of the opening group could be given as *Sòng guó zhī rén* ('Song state SUB person', roughly equivalent to the English 'Song State's people'). Word order conventions are quite similar to English: the main grammatical marker needing explanation here is *zhě* (in bold in example (2)) glossed as 'nominaliser', which turns a preceding verb, adjective or clause into the equivalent of a noun and can be translated as 'the one who [does something]', so *géng tián zhě* ('plough field NOM') is equivalent to 'farmer'. The only other grammatical morpheme here is the generalised conjunction *ér* (also in bold), which links verbs or clauses in a temporal or causal relation and can be translated as 'then, afterwards, therefore' according to context. This kind of language has very little 'visible' grammatical form and therefore, in traditional Chinese linguistics, there was little or no recognition of grammar as such, but more of a focus on the semantic interpretation of words in their textual contexts. In Whorfian terms, this means that much of the grammar is 'cryptotypic' and a particular grammatical category may have a number of 'reactances', which may pose a challenge for analysts to identify.

(3) *Gaelic*

Fear	a bhitheas	fada	gun phòsadh
man	REL be+FUT	long	without marrying
'A man who goes long without getting married'			

fàsaidh	feur is fraoch is fireach		air;
grow+FUT	grass and heather and moor		on-him
'grass and heather and moor (= ill humour) grow on him;'			

fear	a bhitheas	fada	gun phòsadh
man	REL be+FUT	long	without marrying
'A man who goes long without getting married'			

fàsaidh	feusag mhòr		air.
grow+FUT	beard big+FEM		on-him
'a great beard grows on him.'			

Modern Scottish Gaelic is an example of an Indo-European language that has lost most of its original inflections, but, like the other Celtic languages, has developed a range of new morphological processes that mostly serve to indicate links within groups or phrases. In the extreme case, this leads to what would have originally been a two-word phrase becoming a single word, for example *air* ('on him'), and these so-called prepositional pronouns, which 'inflect' for three persons and two numbers, play a very prominent role in the language. In other cases, what were originally phonetic assimilation phenomena have been reinterpreted as markers of grammatical relations. For example, the ancestors of feminine nouns such as *feusag* ('beard') would have ended in a vowel in the nominative or subject case: when pronounced together with a following adjective such as *mòr* ('big'), the now intervocalic /m/ would be softened or 'lenited' to a voiced nasal fricative /ṽ/; when the final vowels dropped, it was this softening or 'lenition' that came to mark feminine gender. So, in the modern language, unlenited *fear mòr* /fɛr mōr/ ('man big ~ big man') (masculine) contrasts with lenited *feusag mhòr* /fiəsaġ v̄ōr/ ('beard big ~ big beard') (feminine). Such lenition, indicated orthographically by a following <h>, also operates after certain prepositions, thus marking the link between them and the following noun – for example *gun phòsadh* ('without marrying'), in which the unlenited verbal noun is *pòsadh* – or is used to mark, often with a preceding particle, certain verb forms, such as the special modifying or 'relative' form of the future tense of the verb 'to be', *bhitheas*, as opposed to *bidh* for the ordinary future. The overall effect, syntagmatically, is to 'bind' certain particular group or phrase elements closely to each other and, paradigmatically, to single out certain forms as 'marked' formally and semantically. So, based on the evidence of languages such as Gaelic, morphological marking is not necessarily directed towards the marking of major clause functions, as we might expect from the 'classic' Indo-European type from which it is descended, but may operate mainly at group rank.

Structurally, languages may operate with a range of types. For example, in Japanese, Processes are realised by verbal or adjectival groups in the form of inflected words, in contrast to Participants and Circumstances, which are alike realised by a postpositional phrase – that is, a nominal group followed by a postposition (the rough equivalent of a preposition in languages such as English or French). Although traditional classifications tend to identify a whole language as 'inflectional' or 'isolating', a language such as French, as pointed out by Caffarel (2004, and in this volume), while inflectional in some aspects of the verbal group, for example in how it realises tense, in expressing given participants instead 'incorporates' them pronominally into the verbal group in the manner of 'polysynthetic' languages.

As noted at the beginning of this section, it is perhaps the minimally formally marked nature of Chinese and English grammar that has left systemic functional linguists relatively uninterested in the morphological aspect of lexicogrammar. However, it is not simply the descriptive need to be able to accommodate a wide range of languages that calls for a focus on morphology, important though this is, but also a recognition of the fundamental nature of language as a network of linkages between meaning and form – between signified and signifer in Saussurean terms – that requires linguists of any school to constantly be aware of the interplay between the two. From a historical point of view, theories of grammar, and hence conceptualisations of group/phrase structure, have always started from the explanation of formal features. It is to this historical perspective that we now turn.

Historical perspectives

It is perhaps necessary to stress the need for an understanding of the historical background of the notion of group, both within the development of SFL itself and in the broader linguistic tradition. Not only is the SFL framework one solution to a suite of analytical problems with which European linguists have been struggling over several centuries, but it also represents a semanticisation of a number of grammatical categories, commonly regarded as merely 'grammatical' or 'formal', in a way that will make them useful for text analysis. Thus it is necessary to understand the antecedents of the SFL formulation of group–phrase relations to appreciate how it solves these common problems and how effectively it does so. In the following discussion, we will examine the historical development of the analysis of word and group classes. Since, typologically, as noted in the previous section, there is still excessive reliance within SFL on English as the yardstick for descriptive categories, with concomitant blurring of the crucial distinction between descriptive and theoretical

Edward McDonald

Table 16.1 Clause function and word type in Indo-European languages

Clause function	Default word class	Morpho-syntactic features
Process	Verb	inflected for tense, mood, person, number
Participant	Noun	inflected for gender, number, case – with cases indicating participant functions (agent, patient, beneficiary) and circumstantial relations (location, goal, source)
circumstance	adverb	a small set of uninflected elements indicating position, direction, etc.
clause-linker	conjunction	a set of uninflected elements indicating addition, contrast, etc.

categories (Halliday 1992), there is a relative lack of understanding of the range of ways in which clause and group relations may be marked across languages.

The classical languages that form the basis of the European grammatical tradition, Greek and Latin, are both very similar in how they preserved the common Indo-European inheritance. Their lexical word classes were highly inflected, while their grammatical word classes were mostly uninflected; hence word inflections became the explanandum of the European analytical tradition, which, until quite recently, was very much a word-based one (cf. Hockett 1954; Robins 1959).

From a 'bottom-up' perspective, we can recognize two large sets of inflected word classes, **nominal** and **verbal**, and two sets of uninflected, **adverbial** and **conjunctional**. Verbal inflections, involving suffixes and some prefixes, as well as changes in the internal vowel and/or consonant structure of the lexical root, realised meanings of tense, aspect and mood. Nominal inflections, involving suffixes with occasional changes in the lexical root, realised meanings of number, gender and case (this last realising both participant and circumstance roles, as we shall see). Table 16.1 sets out the relationship between clause function and word class in these languages.

From a 'top-down' perspective, the main experiential clause functions – Process, Participant, Circumstance – were largely realised by the distinct classes of verb, noun and adverb. The circumstantial use of noun cases inherited from proto-Indo-European became increasingly restricted in Greek and Latin to particular lexical items, or 'frozen' in particular lexemes (often then reinterpreted as adverbs). 'Adverbs' became increasingly linked structurally either to a verb within a compound or to a following nominal group, thus forming a prepositional phrase. The Old English example (4) shows the same lexeme *þurh* (modern English 'through') in both roles in sequential clauses.

(4) *Old English*

and hrædlīce	þæt	hūs	**þurh**flēo
and quick+DAT	that+ACC+SG+NEUT	house+ACC+SG	through-fly+SUBJ+3+SG
'and quickly flies through the house'			

cume	**þurh** ōðre	duru	in
come+SUBJ+3+SG	through one-of-two+ACC+SG	door+ACC+SG	in
'(He) comes in through one door'			

258

and	**þurh** ōðre	ūt	gewite.
and	through one-of-two+ACC+SG	out	depart+SUBJ+3+SG
'and departs out through the other'			

From a 'round-about' perspective, relations between Process and Participants were marked by explicit inflectional endings indicating transitivity (case) and voice (active/middle/passive); some Circumstances were marked by nominal case inflections, while others were realised by uninflected adverbs. Modification relations, mainly confined to nominal word classes, were marked in the substantive subtype by the genitive (possessive) case or, in the adjective subtype, by inflectional endings indicating agreement in number, gender and case. Given this broad coverage of relations marked by inflectional endings, it made descriptive sense to work with only two grammatical units, word and sentence. Clause elements belonging to inflected word classes were all linked to each other through inflections, while uninflected word classes were understood either as related to the verb (hence 'adverbs') or functioning as clause linkers ('conjunctions').

It was only when European scholars began to analyse their own less inflected vernaculars that this model began to break down. In attempting to devise grammars for the European vernaculars, scholars began to move away from the word-focused morphologically based Latin model ('this verb governs the accusative case') to a clause-focused, syntactically based model ('this clause consists of subject, verb and object'). The earliest typologies of group classes classified them by their function in the clause; hence what, in his grammar of French *Les vrais principes de la langue française*, Girard (1982 [1747]) called *membres de phrase* ('sentence elements') or *parties constructives* ('constituent parts') included the following (Graffi 2001: 27):

- *subjectif* (subject);
- *attributif* (verb and its nearest concomitants, such as negation);
- *objectif* (direct object);
- *terminatif* (indirect object);
- *circonstanciel* (circumstance/adjunct);
- *conjonctif* (conjunction) and
- *adjonctif* (vocative and interjection).

This can be understood as part of the increasing move away from morphologically based to syntactically based grammars: rather than words 'governing' or 'agreeing with' each other, different (groups of) words are understood as playing particular roles in the sentence.

Later scholars took this in the direction of greater abstractness. For example, in his *Organism der Sprache*, German scholar Becker (1970 [1827]) based his theory of *Satzglieder* ('sentence members') on the notion of three main *Satzverhältnisse* ('sentential relationships'), under which the clause functions were grouped as follows:

- predicative – Subject and Predicate;
- attributive – Attribute and
- objective – Object and Adverbial.

This model became the basis for pedagogical grammars in German-speaking countries for the subsequent century (Graffi 2001: 136–8).

Later typologically oriented accounts, such as Humboldt (1988 [1836]), Weil (1978 [1844]), von der Gabelentz (1869, 1874, 1875), characterised groups in terms of the internal ordering of their elements, using such logical (in the SFL sense) notions as 'determined' and 'determining'. Jespersen (1924) was the first to distinguish groups from clauses as realising different kinds of structural relations, characterising group elements as joined by 'junction' relations, while clause elements were joined by 'nexus' (not in the SFL sense) relations, both of which were further subdivided according to different 'ranks' (not in the SFL sense): 'primary', 'secondary' and 'tertiary'. From the 1930s, Tesnière began working on a dependency model, published posthumously as Tesnière (1959), which brought clause and group structures back into a single structural *stemma* of different levels of *régissant* ('controller') and *subordonné* ('dependant'), but which interpreted the highest level of these in terms of a semantic framework of *procès* ('process'), *actants* ('participants') and *circonstants* ('circumstances').

Most of these models, which can be generally classed as dependency ones – that is, as recognising varying levels of functions between sentence elements – were developed in Europe. In the United States, from the 1930s another model, that of constituency, began to be imported from phonology, based on the principle of distribution – that is, the possibility of co-occurrence in structure (Bloomfield 1933; Harris 1951). Although constituency and dependency models could easily be regarded as complementary or even roughly equivalent (Matthews 1981: ch. 4), with the rise of formalist syntax, dependency, which had clear semantic implications, came to be downgraded in favour of constituency, while dependency part–part relations were largely superseded in favour of constituent part–whole relations.

Critical issues and topics

The concept of group is, in effect, an elaboration of traditional word-class notions, in which a notion of group was implicit in the dependency-based theories of government (Process vs. Participant(s)) and agreement (Head and Modifier(s)). In Latin, for example, the inflectional endings made clear the dependency relations between most of the elements of the clause. For languages like many of the European vernaculars, which lack the inflectional endings of Latin or of Old English, the only way in which the analyst could show the relatedness of such elements was to 'group' them together – at first using dependency relations such as 'modification'; then using constituency notions such as 'distribution' (Bloomfield 1933) – and then to characterise each element in terms of function and/or class.

Within the history of the systemic functional tradition itself – from system structure theory, scale and category grammar, systemic functional grammar, to SFL (Fawcett 2000a: 16–17) – the category of group has been hugely complexified, without, however, its fundamental conceptualisation as part of the ranked constituency model being changed. The basic principle of system structure theory is that structures at each rank are made up of functions and that these functions are realised by classes of element from the rank below. This model was carried basically unchanged into scale and category grammar (Halliday 1961), within which classes of group were defined in constituency terms as realisations of the clause functions of Subject, Predicator (and Finite), Complement and Adjunct (SPCA). In the first major descriptive statement of systemic functional grammar (Halliday 1967a, 1967b, 1968), this neat model was disturbed when this basic SPCA structure was reinterpreted in functional, specifically interpersonal terms and two extra function structures were 'added': the experiential one of Process, Participant(s), Circumstance(s); and the textual one of Theme, Rheme.

The clause was now regarded as the conflation of three distinct structures, picking out different elements of the clause as significant, but still realised by the same classes of group, thus giving rise to a potential clash between the different function structures and their group realisation. At the same time, another kind of structure was introduced, realised entirely differently from the others, in the form of intonationally marked INFORMATION structure. Even at this point, it was clear that the more 'traditional' TRANSITIVITY structure was entirely constituency-based, while the MOOD structure showed strongly constituency-like features only in the interaction between Subject and Finite. Interpersonally speaking, the rest of the clause could be seen as a variably 'coloured' transitivity structure, with numbers of functions having different degrees of interpersonal relevance, such as Complement as potential Subject, and different interpersonal Adjuncts. At the same time, there were 'redundant' elements in this structure, in which a whole section of the clause was specifically identified as 'Residue' – that is, not significant in expressing features of MOOD or MODALITY – and in which functions such as Predicator and (non-interpersonal) Adjunct(s) seemed merely to be 'reflections' of the experiential functions of Process and Circumstance(s). Between them, the experiential and interpersonal structures achieved more or less 'full coverage' of clause elements, while the two textual structures of THEME and INFORMATION simply 'picked' out a most prominent element as Theme or New, leaving the rest of the clause as 'remainder'.

A decade later, in another seminal paper, Halliday (1979) posited the existence of distinct kinds of structure corresponding to each of the metafunctions: constituent for experiential; prosodic for interpersonal; periodic for textual and culminative for an extra kind of structure, the logical, which was mostly relevant for relations between clauses. However, in textbook presentations of SFL (Berry 1975, 1977; most influentially Halliday 1994 [1985]), in which these realisational complexities were presented as accessible for analytical use, all of the structures were 'fitted into' an overarching constituent framework in the form of 'rows of boxes'. Although such a presentational convention is useful, the visual logic of 'boxes on top of other boxes' has given rise to pseudo-arguments such as 'where the Theme ends' – before the Subject or after the Subject – as if a textual function necessarily needs to be matched up with a differently defined experiential or interpersonal function, rather than, by the nature of periodic structures, being characterised as a gradual lessening of thematic potential from, in English, the thematically prominent beginning of the clause.

As already noted, within the group itself, early on Halliday had identified two distinct structures: the group proper and the phrase. The group and the phrase were seen as structurally different, but functionally equivalent, in that both realised functions in the clause structure. This notion of phrase could be seen as implicit in traditional theories of government, whereby both verb and preposition were seen as 'governing' an 'object'. In Halliday's functional reinterpretation of such relations, the prepositional phrase was seen as a contraction of the Process Participant core of the clause, with the basic structure of (minor) Process and (minor) Range. By the same token, Halliday's notion of group could be seen as 'calqued' on the traditional notion of agreement, for instance an adjective 'agreeing' with its head noun, whose functional interpretation sees the group as an expansion of a head word, with the basic structure Head Modifier.

The first (and so far only) major attempt to delink this increasingly complex clause 'multi-structure' from the constituent structure realised by classes of group has been made by Fawcett (2000a, 2000b). Fawcett, one of the few systemic linguists to incorporate linguistic-historical reasoning in his arguments for theoretical-descriptive system-building, has gone back to the point at which the basic SPCA clause structure was decisively transformed into four simultaneous function structures as defined by the three metafunctions of experiential (TRANSITIVITY), interpersonal (MOOD) and textual (THEME and INFORMATION) (Halliday 1967a, 1967b, 1968), with the later-introduced logical metafunction dealing with relations between clauses (Halliday 1979, 1985). Specifically, Fawcett identifies a particularly historical moment when the four metafunctional structures were still seen as being realised by a 'combined' structure identical to the fundamental SPCA structure. Although this is not stressed by Fawcett, who is more concerned to identify this model as a 'Cardiff Grammar' in embryo, such a move would obviate the potential mismatch between the multifunctional clause structure – that is, simultaneous function structures – and the group classes, since the group classes would presumably relate only to the fundamental SPCA structure. Thus the SPCA structure would be understood as purely experiential in terms of its composition by groups, but with ordering determining the conflation of Mood and Theme functions with an experiential element.

With regard to group/phrase types, the greatest difference from many other syntactic theories, such as those in the generative grammar tradition, is the restriction of the notion of a 'verb phrase' mixing verbal and nominal elements – historically speaking, the syntactic equivalent of the 'predicate' of logic – to a verbal group composed entirely of verbal elements, in accord with other kinds of groups. This move, however, has been criticised by Fawcett, who denies that verbal group exhibits the same Modifier Head relations as other kinds of groups and sees all verbal elements as slotting into positions in one large single 'starting structure' that realises all of the metafunctionally distinct semantic options in the clause. In a comparable move, McDonald (2004), in the context of a descriptive challenge in Mandarin Chinese whereby the different metafunctions define structures that do not seem to coincide with a common clause structure, restricts the scope of the verbal group to experiential elements only, with the pre-verbal interpersonal elements expressing meanings of mood and modality understood as operating directly in the clause structure. Similarly McGregor (1996a), for a largely equivalent notion of 'verb phrase', recognises a rank scale for experiential elements only and, in further work revisiting the whole issue of types of structure and their hook-up with different metafunctional meanings (cf. Halliday 1979), makes this claim for the rank scale and constituency relations more generally (McGregor 1991, 1997).

From the multifunctional viewpoint of, in Fawcett's terms, both systemic functional grammar (Halliday 1967a, 1967b, 1968) and SFL (Halliday 1985), groups are analysed in both constituency (experiential/interpersonal) and dependency (logical) terms; less formally, the overall group structure is also interpreted textually (Halliday 1994 [1985]). It may thus seem as though the whole notion of group structure has become, as it were, 'overloaded' and that its application in lexicogrammatical analysis is well overdue for an overhaul, as we shall see shortly (and see Tucker, this volume).

One of the most controversial issues with regard to the conceptualisation of the group/ phrase in SFL has been that broached in the so-called rank-scale debate, which, in Fawcett's (2000a) account, has spanned the mid-1960s to the present and whose theoretical resolution should be regarded an urgent task for the theory. Since the historical facts have already been laid out by Fawcett with admirable clarity, it might be more useful here to reflect on the nature of such public controversies, which seem often to have just as much to do with the politics of the discipline as with substantive theoretical and descriptive issues. This particular 'debate' seems largely to have missed the chance to realise, or at least acknowledge, that 'rank' and 'constituency' are not in fact equivalent: although the former is based on the latter, rank is ultimately determined by the function structure of the clause, which then determines function structures at lower ranks. Rank, in other words, is a more abstract notion than constituency and the structures that come in under its scope exist in a symbiotic relationship with the relevant systems: structure that is realising system is not the same thing as structure *tout court*. Thus if it is the paradigmatic options that are 'driving' the description, with syntagmatic structures seen as realising those options, certain analytical and descriptive decisions might need to be taken that would seem unnecessary from a strictly structural viewpoint.

It is perhaps significant in light of the oft-cited 'evolutionary' nature of SFL theory – which, in the area of grammatical structure, could perhaps more accurately be characterised as 'accretionary' – that a solution to the problem of rank was in fact put forward in Halliday (1979), whose textual implications were then followed up by Martin (1992): the recognition of different types of structure for each metafunction, with constituency reserved for the experiential metafunction. This means that there would be no need for the prosodic interpersonal structure or periodic textual structure to fit into a constituency straitjacket. However, the next step of modifying the lexicogrammatical analysis has never been taken – except, of course, in the work of Fawcett and his colleagues operating within a very different conceptualisation of the relationship between system and structure. In work on Chinese (McDonald 1998, 2004), a language with even more sparse structural marking than English, this author has been led to define the constituency structure in solely experiential terms, with various parts of this structure given an interpersonal 'colouring' or identified as part of a textual 'wave'. So, without going into more detail here, it could be argued that problems with the rank scale are but one symptom of the much broader problems of a lexicogrammar that is somewhat straining at the seams.

Current contributions and research

As noted a number of times throughout this chapter, in SFL this area of the lexicogrammar has been relatively neglected in favour of descriptions of clause grammar. There are number of common themes raised by the contributors to the other chapters in this part of the volume that provide pointers towards how the theoretical conceptualisations and lexicogrammatical descriptions of the group/phrase in SFL might or should develop. These can be summed up under a number of headings, as follows.

- The need to elaborate the description of groups beyond what is required for clause analysis, in the direction of greater lexical delicacy and semantic specificity (Fontaine, Tucker, both this volume)
- The need to revisit the metafunction–structure relation at this rank to rethink the descriptive decision whereby metafunctional contributions to each group/phrase 'are not represented in the form of separate whole structures, but as partial contributions to a single structural line' (Halliday 1994 [1985]: 279) (Fontaine, Tucker, both this volume)
- The need to account for a structural marker that is not itself part of a structure, such as *of* in English, *de* in French, *zhi* in classical Chinese or *de* in modern Chinese, or *no* in Japanese, and whether such elements, functioning more like conjunctions 'between' rather than 'inside' clauses, cause problems for the conceptualisation of the rank scale (Fontaine, this volume)
- The need to maintain a clear distinction between descriptive and theoretical categories, for example the danger of privileging constituency as a key notion to explain the ways in which (classes of) units relate to one another, to the extent of regarding it as 'metafunctionally neutral' (Quiroz, this volume)

- The need for what Davidse (this volume) describes as 'meta-descriptive reflection', whereby, for example, an account of the systems realised through the verbal group in French is calibrated against other descriptions of French within and outside SFL (Caffarel, this volume).

Also meriting mention here is the comparative-theoretical work of Butler (2003a, 2003b) who brackets SFL with functional grammar (FG) and role and reference grammar (RRG) as examples of 'structural-functional theories', and carries out a detailed comparison of all three theories across a number of parameters, as well as the recent recommendation by Davies (2014: 6–7) that 'one respect in which SFL could be broadened now would be to explore links with other approaches'.

Recommendations for practice and future directions

Tucker (this volume) quotes Halliday (1961) as identifying 'constant territorial expansion' as a key aim of the theory that was to become SFL, but, as Tucker notes, 'the thrust of territorial expansion in SFL has tended to be "outwards and upwards" into broader areas of linguistic organisation, such as discourse and discourse semantics, genre and register, appraisal, etc.', while the coverage of the lexicogrammar has 'remained essentially stable'. Since the topic of group function and structure is arguably one of the oldest and least modified areas of the theory, now is perhaps a good time for a rethink. Davidse (this volume) makes a similar recommendation specifically in relation to the experiential lexicogrammar:

> This suggests the need for more *meta-descriptive* reflection on all of the formal 'reactances' to experiential clause meaning, their relation to overt coding and the nature of the semantic distinctions we can draw from them. To promote innovative work on experiential clause grammar, it will be essential to develop and teach analytical methods and descriptive heuristics from a specifically systemic functional perspective.

As already noted earlier, it is crucial to clearly distinguish theoretical categories from descriptive categories so as to escape the straitjacket of English. Many so-called theoretical debates within SFL, such as that around the verbal group, are in fact almost exclusively framed in terms of the descriptive categories of English. We need to articulate explicit principles for identifying group structures, which are likely to be more distinct across languages than clause structure, for dealing with issues such as:

- the range of structural types within groups/phrases;
- whether there *is* a distinction between group and phrase;
- the internal 'allegiance' of words in group classes, such as whether 'adjectives' go together with nouns or verbs and
- the realisation of group structures.

It is not possible to specify 'future directions' in terms of specific areas in which the theory should develop. This will quite rightly depend on the needs of particular research applications, the interests of individual researchers and the particular features of the languages under study. Rather, on the basis of the developmental history of group/phrase notions within grammatical constituency in general within SFL, we might put forward certain 'useful trajectories' to guide future work, such as:

- the need to formulate explicit guiding principles in the move from theoretical to descriptive categories;
- the need to justify descriptive decisions in relation to overall theoretical goals, with no need for all versions of SFL to 'dance to the same tune';
- the need for a range of multilingual descriptions to serve as models in the descriptive base of SFL, so that descriptions are not always 'coming from English' and
- a more proactive use of the concept of delicacy (Halliday 1961: 267) in developing a range of descriptions from the more general grammatical types, for example for pedagogical uses, to the more specific lexical types, for example for analytical uses or for machine translation, text generation, etc.

If the grammar is the 'powerhouse' of SFL theory, it is arguably the group/phrase rank that provides much of its fuel. For both theoretical and practical needs, then, it is time for the group/phrase to attract some more attention.

References

Becker, K.F. 1970 [1827]. *Organism der Sprache*. 2nd edn. Hildesheim: Georg Olms.
Berry, M. 1975. *Introduction to Systemic Linguistics, Vol. 1: Structures and Systems*. London: Batsford.
Berry, M. 1977. *Introduction to Systemic Linguistics, Vol. 2: Levels and Links*. London: Batsford.
Bloomfield, L. 1933. *Language*. New York: Holt & Reinhart.
Butler, C. 2003a. *Structure and Function: A Guide to Three Major Structural-Functional Theories, Part 1 – Approaches to the Simplex Clause*. Amsterdam: John Benjamins.
Butler, C. 2003b. *Structure and Function: A Guide to Three Major Structural-Functional Theories, Part 2 – From Clause to Discourse and beyond*. Amsterdam: John Benjamins.
Caffarel, A. 2004. Metafunctional profile of the grammar of French. In A. Caffarel, J.R. Martin and C.M.I.M. Matthiessen (eds) *Language Typology: A Functional Perspective*. Amsterdam: John Benjamins, pp. 77–137.
Davies, E. 2014. A retrospective view of systemic functional linguistics, with notes from a parallel perspective. *Functional Linguistics* 1(4): 1–11.
Fawcett, R.H. 2000a. *A Theory of Syntax for Systemic Functional Linguistics* (Current Issues in Linguistic Theory 206). Amsterdam: John Benjamins.
Fawcett, R.H. 2000b. In place of Halliday's 'verbal group', Part 1: Evidence from the problems of Halliday's representation and the relative simplicity of the proposed alternative. *WORD* 51(2): 157–203.
Girard, G. 1982 [1747]. *Les vrais principes de la langue française*. Geneva and Paris: Droz.
Graffi, G. 2001. *200 Years of Syntax: A Critical Survey* (Studies in the History of the Language Sciences 98). Amsterdam: John Benjamins.
Halliday, M.A.K. 1956. Grammatical categories in modern Chinese. *Transactions of the Philological Society* 55(1): 177–224.
Halliday, M.A.K. 1959. *The Language of the Chinese: Secret History of the Mongols* (Philological Society Publications 17). Oxford: Blackwell.
Halliday, M.A.K. 1961. Categories of the theory of grammar. *WORD* 17(3): 241–92.
Halliday, M.A.K. 1966. The concept of rank: A reply. *Journal of Linguistics* 2(1): 110–18.
Halliday, M.A.K. 1967a. Transitivity and Theme in English, part 1. *Journal of Linguistics* 3(1): 37–81.
Halliday, M.A.K. 1967b. Transitivity and Theme in English, part 2. *Journal of Linguistics* 3(2): 199–244.
Halliday, M.A.K. 1968. Transitivity and Theme in English, part 3. *Journal of Linguistics* 4(2): 179–215.
Halliday, M.A.K. 1979. Modes of meaning and modes of expression: Types of grammatical structure and their determination by different semantic functions. In D. Allerton, E. Carney and D. Holdcroft (eds) *Function and Context in Linguistic Analysis: Essays Offered to William Haas*. Cambridge: Cambridge University Press, pp. 57–79.

Halliday, M.A.K. 1985. *An Introduction to Functional Grammar*. Oxford: Arnold.

Halliday, M.A.K. 1992. Systemic grammar and the concept of a 'science of language'. *Waiguoyu [Journal of Foreign Languages]* 2(78): 1–9.

Halliday, M.A.K. 1994. *An Introduction to Functional Grammar*. 2nd edn. Oxford: Arnold.

Halliday, M.A.K., and R. Hasan. 1976. *Cohesion in English*. London: Longman.

Harris, Z.S. 1951. *Methods in Structural Linguistics*. Chicago, IL: University of Chicago Press.

Hockett, C. 1954. Two models of grammatical description. *WORD* 10: 210–34.

Humboldt, W. 1988 [1836]. *Über die Verschiedenheit des menschlichen Sprachbaues und ihren Einfluss auf die geistige Entwicklung des Menschengeschlechts [On Language]*. tr. P. Heath. Cambridge: Cambridge University Press.

Jespersen, O. 1924. *The Philosophy of Grammar*. London: George Allen & Unwin.

Martin, J.R. 1992. *English Text: System and Structure*. Amsterdam: John Benjamins.

Matthews, P.H. 1966. The concept of 'rank' in neo-Firthian linguistics. *Journal of Linguistics* 2(1): 101–9.

Matthews, P.H. 1981. *Syntax*. Cambridge: Cambridge University Press.

McDonald, E. 1998. Clause and verbal group systems in Chinese: A text-based functional approach. Unpublished PhD thesis. Macquarie University, Sydney.

McDonald, E. 2004. Verb and clause in Chinese: Issues of constituency and functionality. *Journal of Chinese Linguistics* 32(2): 200–48.

McDonald, E. 2008. *Meaningful Arrangement: Exploring the Syntactic Description of Texts*. London: Equinox.

McGregor, W. 1991. The concept of rank in systemic linguistics. In E. Ventola (ed.) *Functional and Systemic Linguistics: Approaches and Uses*. Berlin: Mouton, pp. 121–38.

McGregor, W. 1996. Arguments for the category of verb phrase. *Functions of Language* 3(1): 1–30.

McGregor, W. 1997. *Semiotic Grammar*. Oxford: Clarendon.

Robins, R.H. 1959. In defense of WP. *Transactions of the Philological Society* 58(1): 116–44.

Tesnière, L. 1959. *Éléments de syntaxe structurale [Elements of Structural Syntax]*. Paris: C. Klincksieck.

Tucker, G. 1998. *The Lexicogrammar of Adjectives: A Systemic Functional Approach to Lexis*. London: Cassell Academic.

von der Gabelentz, G. 1869. Ideen zu einer vergleichenden Syntax. *Zeitschrift für Völkerpsychologie und Sprachwissenschaft* 6: 376–84.

von der Gabelentz, G. 1874. Weiteres zur vergleichenden Syntax. *Zeitschrift für Völkerpsychologie und Sprachwissenschaft* 8: 29–165.

von der Gabelentz, G. 1875. Wort- und Satzstellung. *Zeitschrift für Völkerpsychologie und Sprachwissenschaft* 8: 300–38.

Weil, H. 1978 [1844]. *De l'ordre des mots dans les langues anciennes comparées aux langues modernes. [The Order of Words in the Ancient Languages Compared with that of the Modern Languages]*. tr. C.W. Super. Amsterdam: John Benjamins.

17

The English nominal group
The centrality of the Thing element

Lise Fontaine[1]

Introduction

The nominal group[2] is a relatively understudied area of the grammar within systemic functional linguistics (SFL). There has been very little dedicated attention[3] given to grammatical units below the clause within SFL, with the exception of Tucker (1998) on the lexicogrammar of adjectives, Bache (2008) on the verbal group (focusing on tense and aspect), and Fontaine and Jones (forthcoming), who examine referring expressions. The relative lack of a concentrated body of work on this grammatical unit is surprising since it plays such an important role, serving to express the participating entities, in the clause and in discourse. It carries the majority of the lexical content in any text and, as has been established in several studies, it is a sensitive index of register (Biber et al. 1998; Fontaine 2007).

Like the clause, the nominal group is a meaning-driven unit. As Halliday (1994: 193–4) explains, it is the 'grammatical resource for representing things'. From a discourse perspective, the nominal group is the principal resource for expressing the participating entities, for introducing them to the discourse and for maintaining them once they are there (Martin 1992: 95). It is well established that participants play a significant role in transitivity (Davidse and Neale, both in this volume; Halliday 2005 [1966]: 61). The nominal group also most frequently expresses the Subject of the clause (Andersen, this volume) and the Theme element of the clause (Forey and Sampson, this volume), making it the only unit that can simultaneously express the main functional elements for all three main metafunctions of the clause. However, perhaps most importantly, understanding the nominal group is central to understanding of how reference is handled in the grammar (Fawcett 1980: 89), giving access to meaning across strata (Berry, this volume). When we consider the nominal group, we are considering the lexicogrammar of referring expressions.

By means of examining the current status of the nominal group and how it is handled in SFL, this chapter will surface some important issues that need attention and will offer a solution to one of them – namely, a reversal of the relative importance of the Head and Thing elements. In particular, it will explore the cases in which different theories separate out Thing and Head, and consider the semantic and grammatical implications of the different positions. In the next section, the nominal group will be introduced, along with a historical perspective of how its description has developed within SFL. The subsequent section describes the elements of the nominal group individually, focusing on the distinction made between the Thing and Head elements. Finally, the argument for the centrality of the Thing element is put forward by considering the function of Thing in comparison with the purely structural role of Head. The proposals offered here intend to drive forward the development of this area of the grammar.

Developments in the description of the nominal group

Fries (1970), although not writing within an SFL framework, was the first scholar to publish a detailed functional account of the noun phrase. His description has much in common with nominal group developments within SFL, as will be shown shortly. Almost all accounts assume a head-plus-modifier relationship in which, in most cases, the 'head' element is a noun[4] and any modifying elements can either be determiners (including deictics and numeratives), pre-head modifiers, such as Epithet (typically adjectives) or Classifier (typically nouns), and post-head modifiers, often called Qualifiers, as in example (1).

(1) a little **house** with a yard

There is a considerable amount of consistency in nominal group descriptions, as shown in Table 17.1, which offers a comparison of this example as analysed following different, but related, grammars.

The term 'head' is normally related to structure rather than function in descriptions of the noun phrase. However Fawcett (1980) adopted 'head' as a semantically motivated term, later defining it as 'the "cultural classification" of the referent'[5] (Fawcett 2000: 217). Halliday (1985: 167) uses both Head[6] and Thing in the description of the nominal group, where the more semantic term, Thing, functions as the 'semantic core' of the nominal group. What Fawcett calls 'head' is roughly equivalent to what Halliday calls 'Thing'. The Head, for Halliday, is an element of logical structure, which suggests a more structuralist account based on a 'head' element that can be expanded into a group through modification (McDonald, this volume). Having retained the term 'Modifier' as an element of logical meaning, other terms are used for the experiential meanings of the nominal group: 'Deictic', 'Numerative', 'Epithet', 'Classifier' and 'Qualifier'. The various elements of the nominal group will be discussed later in the chapter, but first we will continue with a brief view of how it developed within SFL.

The first significant SFL discussion of the nominal group appeared in Fawcett (1980), offering a more cognitively oriented systemic account including system networks.

Table 17.1 Basic analysis of example (1) by various grammars

	a	*little*	**house**	*with a yard*
Fries (1970)	determiner 2	loose-knit modifier	**head**	restrictive modifier
Halliday (1985 onwards)	Deictic	Epithet	**Thing**	qualifier
		Premodifier	**Head**	Post-modifier
Fawcett (1980, 2000)	quantifiying determiner	modifier	**head**	qualifier
Martin (1992)	Deictic	Epithet	**thing**	Qualifier
Fontaine (2012)	deictic determiner	modifier	**thing**	qualifier

His approach introduced a focus on referring expressions with respect to the nominal group, using the term 'referent thing' for the input to the system network, in which referent thing is 'a more or less well-defined mental construct to which the performer wishes to refer' (Fawcett 1980: 90).[7] Following this, Halliday (1985) provided a detailed account of the nominal group as an element below the clause and then Martin (1992) published his discourse-oriented treatment of participants. However, before this, we can glean something from the early system networks. As suggested earlier, nominal group descriptions generally place Thing or Head as the central element – but the distinction is not as simple as it may at first seem. While the Thing element is the semantic core, it is not essential; it is the Head element that is prioritised as the central obligatory element, as will be explained later in the chapter. This section aims to cover the key conceptual positions in the nominal group as concerns Thing and Head.

Two key features of SFL that must be kept in mind throughout this discussion are the system networks (Asp, this volume) and the concept of choice (Fontaine et al. 2013). Some early English system networks for the nominal group were published in 1964 (Halliday 1976 [1964]: 131–5), but because they were not annotated, it is difficult to be certain about what information we can draw from them. The 1964 system network had the concept of 'head' as central to the nominal group. For Halliday, all nominal groups must have a Head element and this was reflected in the options in the network in terms of what could be selected as Head – that is, a nominal or non-nominal item in head position. This distinction is shown in examples (2) and (3), in which the Head element is underlined. The Head element in example (2) is *apples*, whereas in example (3) it is a non-nominal (not a noun) item.[8]

(2) those two <u>apples</u>

(3) those <u>two</u>

These examples show the importance given to the Head element in the early accounts, since the distinction between nominal and non-nominal as Head indicates that it is the Head element that is prioritised in terms of working out the nature of this unit. As we will see, this remains strong even in later versions.

Halliday and Hasan (1976: 44) provide the first discussion of the experiential structure of the nominal group and, although there is very little detail, the basic elements of experiential structure are introduced as Deictic, Numerative, Epithet, Classifier, Thing and Qualifier. However, since they deal primarily with reference in terms of cohesion, the discussion relates to pronominal, rather than lexical nominal groups. To get a more complete view of the nominal group, we need to turn to Halliday (1977).

The system networks for the nominal group in Halliday (1977) offer more detail, but they remain unannotated. To illustrate Halliday's first complete theoretical account of the nominal group, let us consider example (4), taken from Halliday (1977: 208). This is a complex example, but the only one discussed.

(4) a pair of unoiled garden shears

As stated earlier, Halliday considers that the nominal group expresses three metafunctions (Halliday and Matthiessen 2004: 328–9): *ideational*, which is further divided between the logical and the experiential component, *interpersonal* and *textual*, each of which is covered in detail in this volume (Anderson; Butt and Webster; Davidse; Forey and Sampson).

As Halliday (1977: 178) states, 'the logical component is distinct from the other three [components] in that all logical meanings, and only logical meanings, are expressed through the structure of "unit complexes": clause complex, group complex and so on'.[9] Therefore, for the nominal group, we are currently considering, *a pair of unoiled garden shears*, there is no logical structure at group rank, since this nominal group is a simplex and logical structure applies only to complexes. However, at the level of word, Halliday (1977: 210) states that there is a complex – that is, 'groups consisting of more than one element are simultaneously structured both as word constructions (multivariate) and as word complexes (univariate)' – and therefore there is a logical analysis to be made at the level of word for the word complex formed by *unoiled garden shears*, as shown in Table 17.2.

Nominal groups such as these are straightforward and there is general consensus about their description. However, problems arise with the full nominal group *a pair of unoiled garden shears* owing to the presence of multiple nouns.

The experiential system network for Halliday's (1977) nominal group is shown in Figure 17.1. The entry point to the system network (Asp, this volume) for the nominal group is (+Thing). Consequently, 'thing' is also at least one of the entry conditions for the system network for Participant Type. This is an important functional development since the entry condition for the system is the more semantic feature of Thing, rather than the structural element of Head, as it was in 1964. There is distinction as between Thing:common and Thing:proper, which accounts for whether *John* or *the man* is expressed, for example. There is also a distinction made between self or speaker reference (*I*, *me*) and non-self.

The absence of determiners in this system network is because they were considered as only expressing textual meaning (see below). Each metafunction has its own system network. Figure 17.2 illustrates the interpersonal system network for the nominal group, with the same entry point (that is, 'nominal group' (+Thing)). We find two main systems here: 'person' and 'connotation'. The distinction for person ('role') system replicates the person system in Halliday and Hasan (1976). The interpersonal system networks maintain the speech role of the referring expression and any connotation assigned to it. Although 'connotation' is unlikely to apply to 'speech roles' (that is, *I*, *you*, *we*), it is certainly relevant to 'other person role' in the selection of nouns (Thing:object).

Finally, Figure 17.3 provides a sample of the system network for 'deixis' and determiners – that is, textual meaning. As Halliday (1977: 224) points out, the order of the elements within the nominal group is fixed, 'but it is the thematic principle that determines this fixed sequence and explains why in the verbal and nominal group, the element that has deictic value comes first: this is the element that relates to the "here and now"'. Basic distinctions modelled here include the difference between *his garden shears* (specific: selective: personal: possessive), *whose garden shears* (specific: selective: interrogative) and *any garden shears* (non-specific: unrestricted).

While the logical system for the nominal group was not presented in Halliday (1977), we do find a description in the form of an analysis, which is shown, along with the other

Table 17.2 Logical and experiential components for unoiled garden shears

	unoiled	garden	shears
Logical	γ	β	A
	←	Modifier	Head
Experiential	Epithet	Classifier	Thing

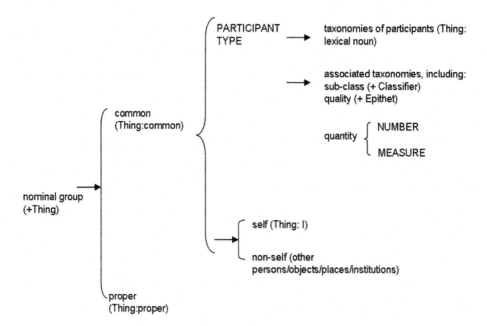

Figure 17.1 Simplified system network for nominal group with respect to the experiential component

Source: Halliday (1977: 213)

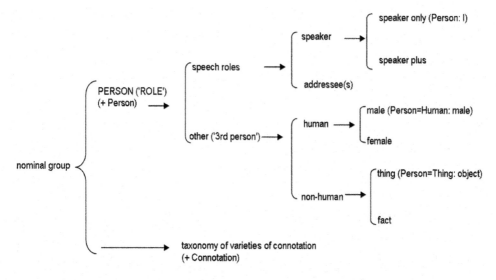

Figure 17.2 Simplified system network for the nominal group with respect to the interpersonal component

Source: Halliday (1977: 217)

Lise Fontaine

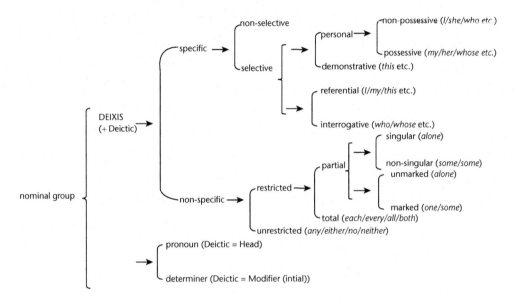

Figure 17.3 Simplified system network for the nominal group with respect to the textual component

Source: Halliday (1977: 219)

three components, in Table 17.3. This description can be related to the system networks as follows: in the Participant Type system (see Figure 17.1), features would be selected (for example common object, artefact, agriculture tool) to get *shears* as Thing in the nominal group; the selection of *unoiled* would be made in the quality system, which functions as Epithet; and selections in the measure system result in *pair of* expressing the Numerative function of the nominal group. The example shows how the functional elements of the nominal group correspond to the options in the system networks.

The analysis in Table 17.3 is difficult to understand and Halliday (1977) does not discuss it in detail. The reason it merits some commentary here is that it highlights one of the challenging areas in the lexicogrammar of the nominal group. At this point in the development of the nominal group, the four main metafunctions were maintained separately, for example the Deictic expresses textual meaning, Head expresses logical meaning, Thing expresses experiential meaning and Connotation expresses interpersonal meaning. As we

Table 17.3 Full analysis for a pair of unoiled garden shears

	a	pair	of	unoiled	garden	shears
Logical	β: Modifier	α: Head				
		α: Head	β: Modifier			
				γ: Modifier	β: Modifier	α: Head
Experiential		Numerative:		Epithet	Classifier	Thing:Common
		Measure				
Interpersonal				Connotation		Person:other
Textual	Deictic					

Source: Halliday (1977: 219)

272

will see later, experiential, interpersonal and textual meanings are conflated in the current description of the nominal group, and only logical meaning is retained as a separate strand of meaning. Because this chapter argues that the logical strand of meaning should also be conflated within the nominal group, we will now briefly consider how logical structure is applied to this example.

In SFL, head–modifier relations are captured in terms of logical meaning. Halliday (1977: 209) classifies the nominal group *unoiled garden shears* as a simplex (therefore as having no logical structure); with regard to *a pair of unoiled garden shears*, he states that it 'contains no logical structures' – that is, it is neither a group complex nor a word complex. However, his analysis does provide for a logical structure for the nominal group in addition to the logical structure of the word complex (*unoiled garden shears*). One possible interpretation is that the logical structure is in fact meant to account for the entire nominal group, *a pair of unoiled garden shears*, as a word complex. In this case, we would expect an analysis such as that given in Table 17.4, which would match the structure of a nominal group such as *the five unoiled door hinges*.

At one point in Halliday's (1977) discussion, *pair-of* is hyphenated, showing some recognition of its status.[10] In the experiential analysis of this nominal group, *pair-of* is expressing the Numerative element, in which *of* is not seen as a preposition introducing a prepositional phrase.

Halliday's (1977) view of the nominal group with associated system network has remained relatively unchanged with no further major developments in the functional elements themselves, except for the development of different types of Numerative in Halliday and Matthiessen (2004). However, maintaining a logical structure in the nominal group even with these developments remains problematic, as will be shown in the next section.

Current descriptions and related issues

In this section, each element of the nominal group is presented in turn, drawing attention to relevant specific issues where appropriate. As was shown briefly above, the nominal group is considered to be multifunctional, with ideational, interpersonal and textual meanings; however, the experiential functions of the nominal group have greater prominence, since the interpersonal and textual elements have been integrated into one strand of experiential meaning. For example, whereas in 1977 Deictic was an element of the textual structure of the nominal group, it is now also part of the experiential description (Halliday 1985: 160). In the most recent account of the nominal group, Halliday and Matthiessen (2014) maintain the same functional elements of the nominal group as defined in Halliday and Hasan (1976) – that is, Deictic, Numerative, Epithet, Classifier, Thing and Qualifier, although the current model includes an extended account of Numeratives. An example of the full functional account of the nominal group is given in Table 17.5. The only condition on the nominal group

Table 17.4 Possible logical structure of the word complex

	a	pair	of	unoiled	garden	shears
Logical	← Modifier	← Modifier		← Modifier	← Modifier	Head
	the	five		unoiled	door	hinges

Table 17.5 Sample nominal group analysis (invented example)

The	two	lovely	wooden	rockers	that my father made for us
Deictic	Numerative	Epithet	Classifier	Thing	Qualifier
Pre-modifier	Pre-modifier	Pre-modifier	Pre-modifier	Head	Post-modifier

is that one element must serve as the Head element. Halliday and Matthiessen (2004: 332) explain that the dissociation of Head from Thing means that 'it can be conflated with any of the premodifying functions', including Classifier and Numerative. For example, 'This' in *This will never work* is considered a Deictic conflated with Head, and here the Thing element is not expressed. This separation of Head and Thing may have this advantage, but it is not clear that it outweighs the disadvantages, as we will see.

While the nominal group itself is a structure, its elements are considered to be functional. We noted in Table 17.1 that different descriptions generally agree on what to call the different elements. However, the distinction that Halliday makes between experiential structure and logical structure causes his description to diverge from others. The most significant distinction is the dissociation of Head and Thing. For this reason, we will begin the discussion of the elements of the nominal group with the distinction between Head and Thing, before moving on to consider the remaining elements in turn.

Head and Thing

While the interpersonal and textual meanings of the nominal group have conflated in the experiential strand of meaning, as discussed above, the logical strand remains separate. In English, there is a strong relation between what expresses the Thing element and what expresses the Head element. In the most usual instance, the Head (logical) element and the Thing (experiential) element are conflated (Bloor and Bloor 2004: 150; Halliday and Matthiessen 2004: 331). Since the Thing element is defined as the semantic core of the expression, it would be reasonable to assume that it will also form the structural core in the role of Head. While there is a denotational relationship between the 'thing' selected (cf. 'class at head' in the early description) and the classification of the entity being referred to, the Head itself does not refer to a particular thing. It is the expression in its entirety that is used by the speaker to refer to a particular object, as in *John, he, the man from upstairs*. An important point must be made at this point: the referent of any nominal group is in the mind of the speaker, rather than in the external world.[11] As Rijkhoff (2002: 27) explains, 'referents of NPs [noun phrases] are rather mental representations of entities as they are created, stored, and retrieved in the minds of the speech participants'. The Thing element is a representation of the class of the entity.[12] In Fontaine (2008), it is argued that it is this experiential element that is semantically a representative of the referent (the cognitive construct); the Head has only a structural role to play in the expression. This relationship is shown in Table 17.6, adapted from Halliday and Matthiessen (2004: 332).

In Table 17.6, the class of object (that is, the semantic core) being referred to is a *cup* and specifically, the speaker is referring to a particular *white cup*. The main distinction between Thing and Head for Halliday and Matthiessen (2004: 325) is that Thing is an element of experiential structure and Head is an element of logical structure. As stated earlier, while every nominal group must have a Head, the Thing element is not always expressed and Head could conflate with any other pre-modifying element such as Deictic,

Table 17.6 Relation between Thing and Head

the	white	*cup*
Deictic	Epithet	**Thing**
Modifier	Modifier	**Head**

Numerative, Epithet or Classifier (for example ***those*** *are not mine, those five are not mine, the **poor** cannot be left out, the **city** of Lausanne is beautiful*), although never Qualifier (Halliday and Matthiessen 2004: 332).

There is one construction in which, for Halliday, the nominal group contains only an Epithet. This concerns relational processes whereby the Attribute at clause level is expressed as an adjective, as for example (5), taken from Halliday and Matthiessen (2004: 331). The analysis for this example is shown in Table 17.7. There are alternative approaches to this,[13] which include the unit of quality group or adjective group as the unit expressing the Attribute.

(5) you're very lucky

In example (5), the Epithet is considered to be the Head element (Halliday and Matthiessen 2014: 391). Tucker (this volume) provides a detailed discussion of what is given here as Epithet, so we will not explore the arguments other than to comment on what it has to say about the nominal group and referring. In Halliday's framework, the Head, as an element of logical structure, must conflate with at least one element of experiential structure in the nominal group, but this is not necessarily with the Thing element; indeed, the Thing element is not obligatory. This gives priority to the Head element (logical structure) over the Thing element (experiential meaning), which is arguably undesirable in a functional approach to language. We could say that the Thing element is always included and is left implicit if it is not expressed, but the priority given to the logical structure means that the description of the nominal group both in systemic terms and in the functional description is structurally oriented.

Fawcett's (2000) approach shows how the experiential and logical strands of meaning can conflate in the nominal group resulting in there being only one element that expresses both types of meaning. For Fawcett, this element is the Head element.[14] Halliday maintains a logical strand of meaning and an experiential strand of meaning for the nominal group, giving priority to the Head (logical structure) and forcing structure, rather than meaning, to lead the way. There is no clear definition of Head other than by means of its role of constraining the Thing element by determining its value in the Mood system and its potential as Subject (Halliday and Matthiessen 2004: 333). In other words, Head, as an element, is kept and prioritised essentially in order to account for subject–verb agreement (for example

Table 17.7 Epithet as Head in the nominal group

You	're	very	lucky
Carrier	Relational Process	Attribute	
Nominal Group	Verbal Group	Nominal Group	
		Epithet	
		pre-modifier	**Head**

*This woman **is** voting, These women **are** voting*). However, Fawcett (forthcoming) argues that this is unnecessary: '[I]t is NOT the case that there is "agreement" between the head of the nominal group that is the Subject and the Operator or Main Verb.' Fawcett uses coordinated nominal groups (for example *my best friend and his sister*) to make the point that the Subject, rather than any head noun, is either plural or singular, since each nominal group is singular, but, as a Subject, the grammar treats the coordinated group as plural (for example *my best friend and his sister **are** coming for dinner*).

Furthermore, Halliday (1985: 169) states that, 'in analysing group structure, it is not necessary to set up three distinct "lines" corresponding to the experiential, interpersonal and textual metafunctions'. This is because, for groups, while we can still recognise the different metafunctions, 'they are not represented in the form of separate whole structures' (Halliday 1985: 158). However, as already mentioned, this type of conflation of the different strands of meaning has not included the logical structure and, as a result, it is handled separately from experiential meaning. This raises an important question about the need for this extra layer of structure. As we will see, identifying Head first forces the analysis to be resolved based on this determination – that is, knowing what expresses the Head element must happen first before consideration of the Thing element.

We will turn now to the remaining elements of the nominal group, and consider how the distinction between Thing and Head is affected by having Head as the central element.

Deictic

While most descriptions of the nominal group have two categories of element before the central element, Halliday has four: Deictic, Numerative, Epithet and Classifier (and this includes post-Deictic, as will be discussed shortly). Other descriptions, such as Fawcett (2000), tend to treat deictic items and numerative items as determiners, and this would then mean that there are various types of determiner.[15] Similarly, they combine qualities and sub-classifiers under the more general label of modifiers, although the modifier–head relationship is handled in logical terms – that is, the experiential elements of Deictic, Numerative, Epithet, Classifier and Qualifier are all modifiers in logical terms. We will return to this later in a comparison of how this is handled by different grammars.

As discussed earlier, Halliday and Matthiessen (2004: 312) state that 'the Deictic element indicates whether or not some specific subset of the Thing is intended; and if so, which'. In this sense, it is a kind of specificity marker in the process of referring – that is, is the speaker referring to a specific entity or not. This is significant and reflects the collaborative nature of referring (Clark and Wilkes-Gibbs 1986). As Martin (1992: 98) states, 'every time a participant is mentioned, English codes the identity of that participant as explicitly recoverable from the context or not'. For every nominal group, then, the speaker will mark the expression for specificity (on the part of the speaker) and recoverability (on the part of the addressee) by anticipating what his or her addressee knows. In every description of the nominal group, the Deictic has this function, but of course it is worth noting that pronouns also do this, as do proper names, which is why they are inherently deictic or indexical. This can be a surprisingly complex area of the grammar, especially when considered along with Numeratives.

Numerative

For Halliday and Matthiessen (2004: 317–18) Numeratives 'indicat[e] some numerical feature of the particular subset of the Thing: either quantity or order, either exact or inexact'.

This means that if the Thing element is expressed by *dog*, for example, in an expression such as *one dog* or *some dogs*, the referent being referred to is, respectively, an exact quantified subset of all dogs and an inexact quantified subset of all dogs. In example (4) (*a pair of unoiled garden shears*), we saw how *pair of* was an example of a type of Numerative. Halliday and Matthiessen (2004: 333) extend Numeratives to include nominal expressions linked with *of*, as in example (6), in which *pack of* expresses Numerative and *cards* expresses the Thing element. This is also an example of an instance in which Thing and Head do not conflate: the Head element here is *pack*.

(6) pack of cards

Epithet and Classifier

As explained, 'modifier' is the term used by Halliday for an element of logical structure. Halliday has two main categories of modifier: Epithets, which express the qualities of the Thing, and Classifiers, which sub-categorise the Thing. As Bloor and Bloor (2004: 141) explain, '*bus* in *a bus station* pinpoints something that is distinctive and classificatory'. The function of Classifiers is to identify a particular subtype of Thing.

In contrast, Epithets 'indicate features or characteristics' (Bloor and Bloor 2004: 141) of the Thing rather than identify a particular subset of it. This is not a classification function, but rather a description by qualities assigned to the Thing.

There is also a distinction made between two main types of Epithet: interpersonal and experiential. The difference relates to the function of the Epithet in terms of whether it sub-classifies, functioning like a Classifier (typically not gradable or modifiable, for example *a wooden spoon*) or whether it expresses interpersonal meaning relating to the opinion or stance of the speaker (for example *a really lovely dress*). While interpersonal Epithets are clearly indicating a quality, there are times when, in the process of referring, it is a quality that is used to sub-classify the Thing. Halliday and Matthiessen (2004: 318–19) explain that interpersonal Epithets express the speaker's attitude and 'represent an interpersonal element in the meaning of the nominal group'. Experiential Epithets are types of modifier that function between interpersonal Epithets and Classifiers.

Before completing the picture with the Qualifier element, it is worth noting at this point that the foregoing elements (Deictic to Classifier) are not necessarily pre-modifiers in logical structure. Where any of these conflate with Head (as in example (6)), they express the central element of the nominal group and are therefore not pre-modifying the Head; rather, they are the Head.

Qualifier

Qualifiers have been defined as the element that occurs after the Thing element (Halliday and Matthiessen 2004: 323). They differ from other elements of the nominal group because they are generally expressed by prepositional phrases and clauses, which means that they are not operating at the same level or rank as the rest of the nominal group.[16] In traditional terms, the units expressing the Qualifier are embedded or rank-shifted in that they operate at a rank that is either equivalent to or higher than the nominal group. Like the other elements of the nominal group, Qualifiers also function as modifiers, but as Halliday and Matthiessen (2004: 324) explain, 'the characterization is in terms of some process within which the Thing is, directly or indirectly, a participant'. This description has not been thoroughly examined in the literature except perhaps by Fontaine (2007, 2008), but to better understand what is meant by this, let us consider example (7), taken from Halliday and Matthiessen (2004: 324).

(7) the children who are wearing blue hats

If we imagine that this nominal group were expressed as the Subject of a clause as in example (8), then it is easy to see that the Thing element is involved in a relational process of *being* at the same time as being involved in a material process of *wearing*.

(8) The children who are wearing blue hats will be on your team

On the surface, there is little difference between Epithets and Qualifiers, if we accept that the invented examples (9) and (10) are roughly similar in terms of the descriptions.

(9) The children <u>who are tall</u> will be on your team

(10) The <u>tall</u> children will be on your team

The nature of referring in each case is quite different. In example (9), the referent is represented as participating in two situations (*being on your team* and *being tall*); in example (10), the referent is represented as participating in only one situation (*being on your team*). The grammar expresses this need for an additional situation quite nicely through the Qualifier element.

This account of the nominal group seems relatively straightforward, but in practice there are some complex issues that require some consideration. For example, in the nominal group expressing the Subject in example (11) taken from Fontaine (2008), there are six nouns that could be Thing and, depending on which it is, there may be one or more Deictics or Numeratives, or indeed Qualifiers. This author's preferred analysis for this is to consider angle as Thing,[17] but what this example is intended to show is that, as soon as a nominal group has more than one noun, the relationship between them must be established – and this is the main area of challenge in this area of the grammar, as we will see in the next section.

(11) The angle of elevation of the top of a tree from a point P on the ground is 30°.

The centrality of Thing

Without discussing example (11) in detail, it illustrates the two main areas that, in this author's view, require attention from scholars: the account of determiners (Deictics–Numeratives) and qualifiers. These two issues are related because, from the analyst's perspective, the identification of Thing is what determines what is Qualifier, or indeed whether there is a one, since the Qualifier is defined as 'that which follows Thing' (Halliday 1985: 166) and anything before Thing will be a Deictic, Numerative, Epithet or Classifier. A post-modifier is a modifier that occurs in the position following the Head element. When Head conflates with Thing, any post-modifier will conflate with Qualifer. So while it is possible to have a post-modifier without a Qualifier (as in example (6), in which Thing is said to be embedded in the Post-modifier), it is not possible to have a Qualifier without a Post-modifier since it is the identification of the Head element that determines whether there is a Post-modifier because, by definition, a Post-modifier is a modifier that occurs after the Head. This suggests that the Head must be identified prior to any determination of Thing and this is entirely problematic from a referring perspective (Fontaine 2013), whereby the semantic core is prioritised as part of the referring process.

It is typically the case that where Head does not conflate with Thing, the nominal group includes the structural item *of*. It is not always clear whether the function of *of* is as a reduced process in a prepositional phrase (Halliday 1985: 189) or as a grammatical item, marking 'a structural relationship between nominals' (Halliday and Matthiessen 2014: 394). This distinction is significant because, in nominal groups with more than one noun, the researcher or analyst must determine which one is Thing and which is Head, and then reconcile the functions of the remaining elements. The important point here is that if Head is the central element, then this drives the analysis.

One of the great challenges for grammarians with regard to the determiners (Deictics and Numeratives) is that they both have the potential to be expressed by nouns and the group structure that follows them. This kind of embedding adds to the complexity of the nominal group. Rather than attempt to illustrate this complexity with example (11), we will consider example (12), taken from Martin (1992: 133). Here, the nominal group includes a 'partitive' (meronymic) relation signalled by *of*. Halliday and Matthiessen (2004) call this type of extended Numerative a 'Facet' (Table 17.8); for Fawcett (2000), it is a 'partitive determiner' (Table 17.9); Martin (1992) calls it a 'Pre-Deictic' (Table 17.10).

(12)   the top of the mountain

This *of*-item is problematic for all scholars. As noted earlier, Halliday and Matthiessen (2014: 394) consider it a structural marker linking two nominals. It is not given any status of its own and is included with the Post-modifier in logical meaning and with the Numerative in experiential meaning. Martin (1992: 133) treats it as a 'structure marker' and it is not

Table 17.8 Facet expression following Halliday and Matthiessen (2014)

	the	*top*	*of*	*the*	*mountain*
Logical	Pre-modifier	**Head**	Post-modifier		
Experiential	Facet	Facet	Facet	Deictic	**Thing**

Table 17.9 Partitive expression following Fawcett (2000)

nominal group				
	partitive determiner	selector	deictic determiner	**head**
nominal group				
deictic determiner	head			
the	*top*	*of*	*the*	*mountain*

Table 17.10 Pre-Deictic expression following Martin (1992)

nominal group				
	Pre-Deictic		Deictic	**Thing**
nominal group				
Deictic	Thing			
the	*top*	*of*	*the*	*mountain*

considered as an element of the nominal group. Fawcett (2000) considers it as an element of the nominal group, called the 'selector element'. It can occur in various places and must always be preceded by a certain type of determiner.[18]

The separation of logical meaning in the nominal group causes a problem for nominal groups with one or more *of*-items. If we compare examples (13) and (14), we find that the Head and Thing elements conflate in example (13), but not in example (14), and while both express Numerative + Thing experientially, they differ in logical meaning. Most importantly, the central or core element in example (13) is *coffee* and in example (14) it is *cup*.

(13)   some coffee

(14)   a cup of coffee

While the referent may cognitively be represented as <coffee> in whatever non-linguistic form, the speaker's intentions and plans would be clear: the entity being referred to is coffee. If, by definition, Thing is the semantic core of the nominal group and representative of the class of the referent, then it is reasonable to assume this must be activated for the speaker. Consequently, it is difficult to see how Thing is best placed in an embedded structure in a post-modifier.

It would be simple to say that the problem can be identified as one relating to expressions with *of*. It is well-known that *of*-expressions are problematic and while we have briefly surveyed some of the proposals here, some others are in development (for example Schönthal, 2016). The real problem is that accounts of these functional elements must be developed within a referring perspective and consideration for the choices available to speakers. There are implications related to these expressions that are not being taken into account and these are related to the system networks. If the networks are meant to model the options available to the speaker in creating meaning, then it is critical to ask what the nature of these options is in terms of leading to one description rather than another. One real difficulty in discussing these issues concerns the fact that the literature that has been published to date is scarce on detail. Except in Fries (1970), Fontaine (2008) and Fawcett (forthcoming), we do not ever see much detail in terms of the realisation of these functional components. What is needed is a view of this unit that prioritises its role in expressing a referring expression – that is, in the way in which it achieves the purposes intended by the speaker. This involves prioritising the Thing element since it is this element that represents the class of the referent (Fontaine 2008, 2013). In other words, as the semantic core, the Thing element must lead the way, in the same way in which this is true in the transitivity system for the clause. Halliday and Matthiessen (2014: 397) identify a 'striking parallelism' between the verbal group (Quiroz, this volume) and the nominal group in terms of their structure, but whereas they see the logical structure as that which 'embodies the single most important semantic feature of the English verb' (Halliday and Matthiessen 2014: 398), the same cannot be said for the English noun and the nominal group. It is the experiential functional element, Thing, that should be central to a full description of the nominal group.

Future work in this area should approach issues related to the nominal group by considering their production as referring expressions. This means recognising the role of the Thing element as representing the conceptual entity to which the speaker is referring. What we know about referring is that it is context-dependent and addressee-oriented (Clark and Wilkes-Gibbs 1986; Jones 2014). The idea of taking a more cognitive approach to the nominal group has support from other scholars. Both Fries (1999) and Keizer (2004), after extensive consideration of the problem of qualifiers, have concluded that a more cognitive approach is needed to explain why these elements are present. Basing the account on head–modifier relations carries structuralist baggage from an earlier era of traditional approaches to grammar.

In a functionally oriented approach such as SFL, adhering to a notion of headedness complicates things more than is necessary. In fact, as is hopefully clear at this point, the logical functions are encoded in the experiential elements (for example Qualifier is defined as that which follows Thing and Classifiers precede Thing). As Halliday and Matthiessen (2014: 397, emphasis original) state, 'the structure of groups recapitulates, in the *fixed* ordering of their elements, the meaning that is incorporated as *choice* in the message structure of the clause'. While there is no question about order or relationship within the nominal group, we ought not to suggest that there is no relevance of the logical function in the nominal group at all, but rather that it should not be interfering with the semantics of their nature as referring expressions. The Thing element, with its function of expressing an entity, must be central.

Notes

1 The author would like to thank the anonymous reviewer, as well as Tom Bartlett, James Martin, Peter Fries, Katy Jones and David Schönthal, for valuable comments on drafts of this chapter.
2 'Nominal' is the term used within SFL (Halliday and Hasan 1976: 39). Halliday does make a distinction between group and phrase (see McDonald, this volume).
3 It is worth noting that the following key publications include detailed sections related to units below the clause: Fawcett (1980, 2000); Halliday (1985, 1994); Matthiessen (1995); Halliday and Matthiessen (2004, 2014).
4 Some argue for a determiner headedness, see, e.g., Hudson (2004) or Carnie (2007).
5 Space does not permit a full comparison with the Cardiff Grammar approach to the nominal group, but see Fawcett (2007) and Fontaine (2008, 2013).
6 Halliday uses initial capital letters to indicate functional labels, but the term 'head' also has a general sense as the pivotal constituent of any group.
7 See also Fontaine (2008) for a detailed discussion of this.
8 See 'Numeratives' below.
9 See Butt and Webster, this volume, for more detail on logical structure.
10 See Fawcett's (1980, 2000) and Martin's (1992) approaches under the heading 'The centrality of Thing'.
11 Cf. Fawcett's (1980) 'referent thing'.
12 Cf. Fawcett's (2000) cultural classification.
13 See Tucker (1998) and in this volume; also Fawcett (2000) and Fontaine (2012).
14 But see Fontaine (2012) for arguments in favour of having the Thing element as the conflated element, as is proposed here.
15 See, e.g., Fawcett (2007).
16 See Berry, this volume, for a discussion of rank in SFL.
17 See Fontaine (2008) for full discussion.
18 See Fawcett (2006, 2007) for detail on these determiners and on his principle of selection.

References

Bache, C. 2008. *English Tense and Aspect in Halliday's Systemic Functional Grammar: A Critical Appraisal and an Alternative*. London: Equinox.
Biber, D., S. Conrad and R. Reppen. 1998. *Corpus Linguistics: Investigating Language Structure and Use*. Cambridge: Cambridge University Press.

Bloor, T., and M. Bloor. 2004. *The Functional Analysis of English: A Hallidayan Approach*. 2nd edn. London: Arnold.

Carnie, A. 2007. *Syntax: A Generative Introduction*. 2nd edn. Malden, MA: Blackwell.

Clark, H., and D. Wilkes-Gibbs. 1986. Referring as a collaborative process. *Cognition* 22(1): 1–39.

Fawcett, R. 1980. *Cognitive Linguistics and Social Interaction: Towards an Integrated Model of a Systemic Functional Grammar and the Other Components of an Interacting Mind*. Heidelberg: Julius Groos and Exeter University.

Fawcett, R. 2000. *A Theory of Syntax for Systemic Functional Linguistics*. Amsterdam: John Benjamins.

Fawcett, R. 2006. Establishing the grammar of 'typicity' in English: An exercise in scientific inquiry. In G. Huang, C. Chang and F. Dai (eds) *Functional Linguistics as Appliable Linguistics*. Guangzhou: Sun Yat-sen University Press, pp. 159–262.

Fawcett, R. 2007. Modelling 'selection' between referents in the English nominal group. In C.S. Butler, R. Hidalgo Downing and J. Lavid (eds) *Functional Perspectives on Grammar and Discourse: In Honour of Angela Downing* (Studies in Language Comparison Series 85). Amsterdam: John Benjamins, pp. 165–204.

Fawcett, R. Forthcoming. *Functional Syntax Handbook: Analysing English at the Level of Form*. London: Equinox.

Fontaine, L. 2007. The variability of referring expressions: An alternative perspective on the noun phrase in English. In D. Coleman, W. Sullivan and A. Lommel (eds) *LACUS Forum XXXIII: Variation*. Houston TX: LACUS, pp. 159–70.

Fontaine, L. 2008. A systemic functional approach to referring expressions: Reconsidering post-modification in the nominal group. Unpublished PhD thesis. Cardiff University.

Fontaine, L. 2012. *Analysing English Grammar: A Systemic Functional Introduction*. Cambridge: Cambridge University Press.

Fontaine, L. 2013. Semantic options and complex functions: A recursive view of choice. In L. Fontaine, T. Bartlett and G. O'Grady (eds) *Systemic Functional Linguistics: Exploring Choice*. Cambridge: Cambridge University Press, pp. 95–114.

Fontaine, L., and Jones, K. Forthcoming. *Reference: Atypical Referring in Language, Discourse and Cognition*. Cambridge: Cambridge University Press.

Fontaine, L., T. Bartlett and G. O'Grady (eds). 2013. *Systemic Functional Linguistics: Exploring Choice*. Cambridge: Cambridge University Press.

Fries, P. 1970. *Tagmeme Sequences in the English Noun Phrase*. Santa Ana: Summer Institute of Linguistics.

Fries, P. 1999. Post-nominal modifiers in the English noun phrase. In P. Collins and D. Lee (eds) *The Clause in English: In Honour of Rodney Huddleston*. Amsterdam: John Benjamins, pp. 93–111.

Halliday, M.A.K. 1976 [1964]. English system networks. In G. Kress (ed.) *Halliday: System and Function in Language*. Oxford: Oxford University Press, pp. 101–35.

Halliday, M.A.K. 1977. Text as semantic choice in social context. In T.A. van Dyck and J. Petofi (eds) *Grammars and Descriptions*. Berlin: Mouton, pp. 176–225.

Halliday, M.A.K. 1985. *An Introduction to Functional Grammar*. London: Arnold.

Halliday, M.A.K. 1994. *An Introduction to Functional Grammar*. 2nd edn. London: Arnold.

Halliday, M.A.K. 2005 [1966]. Grammar, society and the noun. In J.J. Webster (ed.) *On Language and Linguistics*. New York: Continuum, pp. 50–76.

Halliday, M.A.K. and R. Hasan. 1976. *Cohesion in English*. London: Longman.

Halliday, M.A.K., and C.M.I.M Matthiessen. 2004. *An Introduction to Functional Grammar*. 3rd edn. London: Arnold.

Halliday, M.A.K., and C.M.I.M Matthiessen. 2014. *An Introduction to Functional Grammar*. 4th edn. London: Arnold.

Hudson, R. 2004. Are determiners heads? *Functions of Language* 11(1): 7–42.

Jones, K. 2014. Towards an understanding of the use of indefinite expressions for definite reference in English discourse. Unpublished PhD thesis. Cardiff University.

Keizer, E. 2004. Postnominal PP complements and modifiers: A cognitive distinction. *English Language and Linguistics* 8(2): 323–50.

Martin, J.R. 1992. *English Text: System and Structure*. Philadelphia, PA, and Amsterdam: John Benjamins.

Matthiessen C. 1995. *Lexicogrammatical Cartography: English Systems*. Tokyo: International Language Sciences.

Rijkhoff, J. 2002. *The Noun Phrase*. Oxford: Oxford University Press.

Schönthal, D. 2016. The constructions of English of-NPs: A corpus, contextual and cognitive approach. Unpublished PhD thesis. Cardiff University.

Tucker, G. 1998. *The Lexicogrammar of Adjectives: A Systemic Functional Approach to Lexis*. London and New York: Cassell.

18

The adjectival group

Gordon Tucker

Introduction and aims

The notion of 'adjectival phrase/group' is widely recognised in grammatical descriptions across constituency- and construction-based linguistic theories, whether formal, functional or cognitive (for example Biber et al. 1999: 101; Ouhalla 1994: 31), and generally refers to a phrase (AP/AdjP) whose head word is an adjective. The unit 'group', as recognised in systemic functional grammar (SFG), is discussed in detail by McDonald (this volume), with detailed discussions of two other classes of group, the 'nominal group' and the 'verbal group', discussed by Fontaine and Quiroz (both in this volume), respectively.

Among grammatical units in SFG theory and description, the adjectival group still has the least clear status. Yet its status, or lack of it, in such descriptions has never aroused strong debate or controversy, unlike, for example, the status or otherwise of the verbal group (for example Fawcett 2000b). Furthermore, its recognition or otherwise does not appear to depend upon strongly competing models within the general framework of systemic functional linguistics (SFL). Nevertheless, some of the positions on both sides of the argument derive from substantial differences in theory- or model-specific criteria or in the principles established by competing SFL models.

In a certain sense, those that do not recognise an adjectival group in their description nonetheless usually recognise some kind of functional structure associated with the adjective as a major lexical class. And, of course, the adjective, as a class of the unit 'word', is fully recognised within all SFG descriptions of English. However, given that, in some descriptions, adjectives are exponents of modifiers within the nominal group or sometimes of the head of the nominal group (as in attributive relational clauses such as example (1)), little attention is given to any related structure, beyond the notion of 'sub-modification'.

(1) Writing your own pieces can be very exciting[1]

In this survey, we shall attempt to answer the following two central questions.

1   What, if any, are the theory-specific reasons given for excluding or including an adjectival group as a class of the unit group?
2   Where the adjectival group is recognised, how are the elements concerned described and labelled, and what functions are attributed to them?

Several other grammatical aspects of adjectives and their potential structures, for example the external environments in which they are found, will also be briefly discussed, as will the close relationship between adjectival and adverbial structures.

Finally, we shall explore the possibility of reconciling approaches for and against the adjectival group, in an attempt at least to illuminate the descriptive benefits that have been gained from in-depth studies on adjectival structures.

Units, classes of unit and recognition or otherwise of an adjectival group class

Michael Halliday's early and subsequent position

Befittingly, we need to return to the earliest work of the founder of SFL, Michael Halliday, to throw light on the theoretical underpinning of grammatical units and classes of units as used in many SFL descriptions. It is important to understand that, here, we are concerned specifically with SFL approaches and no attempt will be made to discuss the establishment of grammatical categories in other linguistic theories.

Halliday sets out the theoretical and descriptive principles for what came to be known as 'scale and category grammar' and, later, 'systemic functional grammar' in his early published work on Chinese (Halliday 1956). It is indeed here that we first find the statement of the theoretical principle/criterion that has influenced positions on the status of an 'adjectival group'. Halliday (1956: 36–7, emphasis added) states that 'classes [of unit] are systemic and are stated as paradigms in interrelation with the elements [of structure], that is, as exhaustive inventories of forms *classified as operating at a given place in the structure of the unit next above*'. On this basis, for Chinese, Halliday recognises three primary group classes – namely, the verbal group, the nominal group and the adverbial group.

In an influential paper, Halliday (1961) sets out – this time, in general terms – his definition of central theoretical categories such as 'unit', 'structure' and 'class'. Again, he makes a crucial point in respect of the category of 'class' – namely, that '[t]he class is that grouping of members of a given unit which is defined by operation in the structure of the unit next above' (Halliday 1961: 64). The category of 'structure', on the other hand, is determined 'with reference to classes of the unit next below' (Halliday 1961: 65).

These theoretical clarifications militate against the recognition of an adjectival class of group, essentially on the basis that one of the primary environments for adjectives is the Complement in attributive relational clauses, as illustrated in example (1), and if it functions as Complement in the structure of the unit, it is therefore classified as a nominal group. This raises two issues for the grammar of English, as pointed out in detail by Fawcett (2000: 198–9). First, adjectival structures such as *very exciting* in example (1) are not found as the Subject of clauses, unlike structures with a noun as head. Secondly, there seems little alternative to simple 'sub-modification' within the nominal group for the analysis of *very exciting*, as in example (2), without recognising the class of 'adjectival group'.

(2) He made a very exciting companion for the evening!²

One concession that Halliday does make to the notion of an adjectival group proper is found precisely in respect of attributive relational clauses. He notes that, in the case of an adjective (Epithet) as head of the nominal group at Attribute/Complement, this type of nominal group is 'sometimes referred to distinctively as "adjectival group"' (Halliday and Matthiessen 2014: 391) – by other systemicists, he means, not by himself.

Those adopting a similar position to that of Halliday

Given the importance of Halliday's early seminal writings in setting out the theoretical criteria and principles on which, first, scale and category grammar, and, later, SFG were based, it is unsurprising and reasonable that his position in respect of classes of unit is adopted by a number of writers. Halliday's central descriptive account of the functional grammar of English, *Introduction to Functional Grammar* (IFG, hence 'the IFG approach'), did not appear until 1985, by which time there had appeared a number of textbooks adopting a systemic functional account of language. Since the appearance of IFG, further complementary texts have appeared, many accepting Halliday's theoretical principles, although clearly with different emphases and with different readerships in mind, and focusing on different aspects of the description of English.

Muir (1972) adopts Halliday's position and treats adjectives functioning as Complement/ Attribute, as in example (1), as head of a nominal group. The structure he sets up for the nominal group is m(odifier), h(head), q(ualifier). With regard to adjectives at head, he states that they have a restrictive range of modifiers, such as *very, rather, quite*, etc., and qualifiers, such as *enough, indeed*, or 'complete clauses or groups or restricted types, such as *as* (m) *fit* (h) [*as possible*] (q)' (Muir 1972: 29).

Sinclair (1972) introduces three 'kinds' of group, which are, like Halliday's, the nominal, verbal and adverbial groups. Sinclair (1972: 133) does use the term 'adjectival group' for adjectival Complements, such as *he went away, A HAPPY MAN*, although in other places – for example with his description of the adverbial group – he uses the term 'adjective-headed' for instances such as *that's quite fast enough* (Sinclair 1972: 207). The structure given to such examples is, again, m, h and q.

Berry (1975: 74), in stating that '[a]ny formal item is more likely to represent certain elements of structure than to represent others, and on this basis it can be assigned to a class', espouses Halliday's position on the definition of 'class', as set out earlier in the chapter, and consequently (although not explicitly expressed) adjectival structures, for her, are part of the nominal group. Berry also introduces the term 'type', which applies to the type of internal structure of units. So m(odifier), h(headword), q(ualifier) versus b(efore preposition) p(reposition), c(ompletive) are two different 'types' of group, differentiated on the basis of their own structure. Again, one assumes that structures such as *very easy indeed*, for Berry, would belong to the type m, h, q and to the class 'nominal group', because she accepts Halliday's definition of class as determined by its function in the unit above, rather than by the type of internal structure.

Gregory (2009 [1969]: 96), in his early writings in the scale and category tradition, likewise defines 'class', in respect of groups, in terms of potentiality of operation in the structure of the unit above on the rank scale, the clause'. Gregory's (2009 [1969]: 98) nominal group class includes a type with an adjectival nominal head expounded by the adjectival nominal word class, for example *nice, large, shiny, young*, etc.

In his impressive and substantial account of the systemic functional grammar of English, Matthiessen (1995) again adopts Halliday's position in respect of classes of group. In cases such as *very nice* in *he was very nice*, Matthiessen (1995: 686) points out that, where 'the participant is construed as a property . . . [the] Head of the nominal group is . . . realised by an adjective rather than a noun'.

Those adopting a position different from that of Halliday

Of all alternative approaches to the question of adjectival structures and, indeed, to the overall architecture of an SFG, that of Fawcett (1974–76) is arguably the most significant. The significance is the result of at least two aspects of Fawcett's early work: first, that it remained – and still remains – fully within the theory of SFG; and second, that Fawcett provides substantial arguments for his theoretical differences from Halliday's scale and category model.

Without attempting to summarise the bulk of the differences between Halliday's and Fawcett's early models, we can focus on the specific and important distinction that Fawcett makes in terms of establishing classes of unit. Fawcett (1974–76: 10) completely rejects Halliday's criterion for establishing a class of unit on the basis of its role in the unit next above. In fact, for Fawcett (1974–76: 10, emphasis original):

> Potentiality of operation in a higher unit is not relevant at all . . . [and it] obscures one of the most elegant characteristics of a grammar, namely that a relatively small number of units can carry a very large number of complex meanings precisely because there is *not* a one-to-one relationship between unit and element of structure.

For Fawcett (1974–76: 10), units are defined by their 'componence', in terms of their elements of structure, and the elements that are recognised for a given class of unit (here, the group) are those needed to realise 'the relevant semantic options'. The semantic options are those that are available and realised at that particular level in the grammar. On the basis of this criterion, Fawcett sets up a number of classes of group: nominal group, adverbial group, adjectival group and prepend group.

A further consequence of establishing classes of unit on the basis of the semantic role of their respective elements of structure is the rejection of generalised element labels, such as m, h and q. Whilst Fawcett retains their use for his nominal group, elements in the other classes of group have distinctive labels and he adds that 'such labels may be nmemonics for the type of meaning that they realise' (Fawcett 1974–76: 11).

Again of significance, in respect of the elements of structure that Fawcett recognises for his 'adjectival group', is that they are the same as those recognised in his 'adverbial group'. This later leads Fawcett (1980: 92) to posit a single class of group, labelled the 'quantity–quality' group, whose core element of structure, the apex (a), will be filled respectively by an adverb or adjective. With the publication of Fawcett (2000), as in Tucker (1998), this class of group is renamed the 'quality group'.[3] In the discussion here, for the sake of clarity, this chapter will predominantly use the label 'adjectival group'.

In Fawcett's earliest description, then, the adjectival–adverbial group/quantity–quality group has a componence of four separate elements – the **temperer** (t); the core element, or **apex** (a); the **scope** (s); and the **limiter** (l) – as illustrated in example (3).

(3) although large animals are generally **more** (t) **efficient** (a) **at walking** (s) **than small ones** (l)[4]

Fawcett borrows the terms 'temperer' from Turner (1970) and Muir (1972), 'apex' from Muir, rather than Turner's 'vortex', and 'limiter' again from Muir, although later he adopts Turner's term 'finisher'. Despite these borrowings from Turner and Muir, neither of these scholars recognises a separate adjectival group, their use being confined to adverbial structures.

Fawcett's unique contribution to the structure of this class of group is the introduction of the scope element, illustrated by *at walking* in example (3). This would appear to be the only place where post-apex/post-'head' material is separated out into two distinct elements on the basis of their semantic difference.

Over the course of the development of the Cardiff Grammar, a number of functional labelling changes have taken place; none, however, radically modifies the description as set out briefly above. The 'lexicogrammar of adjectives' is taken up in detail by Tucker, in the framework of the COMMUNAL project, leading to a number of publications – notably, Tucker (1998).[5] Tucker further develops Fawcett's original description, adding a number of elements and importantly providing system network descriptions for the meaning potential realised by adjectives and their structures.[6]

The only other substantial SFG descriptive account of the grammar of adjectives, as realised by an adjectival group, is provided by Downing and Locke (2006). Their twenty-five-page description explores this resource and its realisations in terms of 'describing persons and things'. Downing and Locke (1992) originally adopted a modifier, head, qualifier analysis of the elements of structure in the adjectival group, but introduced slightly different post-head elements – namely, modifier and complement – in their revised account (Downing and Locke 2006).

Importantly, Downing and Locke provide abundant examples of the kinds of modification and complementation of adjectival heads.[7] In their description of the various kinds of complementation, they provide instances of various kinds of complement, including those that correspond to the Cardiff Grammar 'scope' element; unlike the Cardiff Grammar, Downing and Locke posit no separate element of structure for the 'scope' type nor do they give an example of both types co-occurring post-head.

It should be noted that the adjectival group/phrase is also recognised within SFG writing by Young (1980), Thompson (1996), Morley (2000) and Fontaine (2013). With the exception of Fontaine (2013), whose experiential analysis of this group reflects the Cardiff Grammar, the analysis offered is essentially in terms of Pre-modifier/Modifier, Head, Qualifier/Post-modifier elements.

Adjectival structures and their meanings

Experiential description and analysis

We have seen that SFG accounts of lexicogrammatical structure involving adjectives range from basic sub-modification within the nominal group, through the generic m, h and q elements applied to an 'adjectival group', to the more explicitly functionally labelled elements, such as t, a, f and s in the Cardiff Grammar approach. Irrespective of the description adopted in any given account, the grammar ultimately has to account for the linguistic potential (meaning potential/lexicogrammatical potential) that adjectival structures realise.

In their treatment of groups, Halliday and Matthiessen (2014: 361) point out a general difference between the metafunctional nature of the clause and that of structures at the rank of group. While it is possible to view the clause in terms of three distinct structures combined into one, the picture is different at the level of group, where although, as Halliday and

Matthiessen (2014: 361) say, the same three metafunctional components are recognisable, 'they are not represented in the form of separate whole structures, but as partial contributions to a single whole line'. In their detailed account of the nominal group, however, Halliday and Matthiessen (2014) do discuss its separate experiential and logical structure. It is in the discussion of the logical structure of the nominal group that we find reference to the Modifier, Head and Post-modifier (instead of Qualifier, which is considered experiential). In their experiential analysis, they recognise a number of functional elements: Deictic – Numerative – Epithet – Classifer – Thing – Qualifier, the first four experiential elements corresponding to the single element Modifer in the logical metafunction. Each of these elements has a distinct function, or semantic contribution, in the expression of Things. And the contribution of each to the overall potential needs to be set out in the form of the system network. While Halliday and Matthiessen (2014) have a limited account of the part of the system network relating to the experiential potential of the nominal group, much more is available in Matthiessen's (1995: 645–711) comprehensive account.

What is lacking, however, both in Matthiessen (1995) and Halliday and Matthiessen (2014), is any experiential account that corresponds to the sub-modification element in the logical structure of the nominal group, where structures such as *rather more impressive* are handled. Arguably, this lack of attention to that area of experiential description might, albeit unintentionally, reinforce the impression that there is nothing significant to say about 'adjectival group' elements of structure and the functions they realise. Indeed, in discussing the adverbial group, Matthiessen (1995: 640) argues that 'the modification is essentially (but not exclusively) concerned with intensification'. With the very close similarity between adverbial and adjectival structures, it is arguably this view of modification as essentially 'intensifying' in nature that has limited a more detailed experiential description in respect of adjectives.

The introduction to this chapter made reference to the possibility of reconciling approaches that differed in respect of recognition of an adjectival group. If we accept the observation that, in Matthiessen (1995) and Halliday and Matthiessen (2014), the experiential metafunctional perspective on adjective-based structures is simply not dealt with in their descriptions, we come very close to being able to reconcile the two opposing positions. And by considering the descriptions of Downing and Locke (2006) and those of the Cardiff Grammar (for example Tucker 1998), we are importantly adding to the coverage of SFGs. It is clearly beyond the possibility of any single work to cover the whole of the grammar of a language – even in the case of Matthiessen's (1995) impressive 978 pages of description.

Ultimately, 'constant territorial expansion', to use Michael Halliday's own expression, is, or should be, a key aim. Halliday (1961: 69) uses the expression in respect of the territorial expansion of grammar into lexis. In recent decades, the thrust of territorial expansion in SFL has tended to be 'outwards and upwards' into broader areas of linguistic organisation, such as discourse and discourse semantics, genre and register, appraisal, etc., all of which are represented in this Handbook. With fewer systemic linguists focusing on lexicogrammar, however, descriptions have not expanded: the coverage of IFG, for example, has remained essentially stable now over four decades and four editions.

Naturally, drawing on resources from different SFG models involves a willingness and ability to translate between them. This is not always easy and arguably, at times, theoretical differences may seem insurmountable. In the case of adjectival grammar, it may be suggested that there is no inherent problem.[8]

It is therefore worth looking at the descriptions of those who have provided fuller accounts, especially in experiential terms, of adjective-based grammar – in particular, the descriptions of the Cardiff Grammar (for example Tucker 1998) and Downing and Locke (1992, 2006).

What most SFG descriptions agree on is that the 'head' element realised by an adjective can be pre-modified and post-modified. This is illustrated in examples (4) and (5).

(4) very (pre-m) difficult (h) to understand (post-m)[9]

(5) more (pre-m) difficult (h) than it seems (post-m)[10]

Such a basic description, however, hides the considerable potential that English has for the various kinds of pre- and post-modification available. Clearly, there is a substantial difference between the experiential potential associated with 'Things' expressed in the structure of nominal group and the experiential potential associated with 'Qualities' through adjectival group structure.[11] As Halliday and Matthiessen (1999: 186) point out, 'Qualities tend to be experientially simple, specifying values along a single dimension', whereas 'Things . . . tend to be ideationally more complex'.

The resource for 'specifying values along a single dimension', however, is much richer than would at first appear and it is this richness that is captured in those fuller descriptions of adjectival grammar.

The central element

The principal, obligatory element in the adjectival group is that realised uniquely by adjectives. It is typically labelled 'head', by Downing and Locke (2006) among others, whereas the Cardiff Grammar prefers 'apex' (a) on the grounds of avoiding 'inappropriate parallels with the structure of the nominal group' (Tucker 1998: 66). Moreover, because 'head' is often used in the logical structural description of the nominal group (for example by Halliday and Matthiessen 2014), the Cardiff Grammar's preference for apex parallels the use of Deictic, Numerative, Epithet, etc., in Halliday and Matthiessen's experiential account of nominal group structure.

The semantic potential of adjectives is clearly substantial, given that they constitute a major, open-class lexical category. Various classifications of adjective meaning are available, including Halliday and Matthiessen's (1999: 211) 'tentative classification'. Naturally, although one can arguably dispense with the notion of 'adjectival group', the potential in respect of adjectives and 'Qualities' remains. Tucker's (1998) classification makes some attempt to correlate 'QUALITY TYPE' with lexicogrammatical consequences. He posits features such as [situation-oriented] versus [thing-oriented] Qualities and, within the latter, [epithetic] versus [classifying], which picks up on Halliday's original distinction between 'Epithet' and 'Classifier' in terms of modification within the nominal group. Phenomena such as gradability, subjectivity/objectivity, modifier sequence in the nominal group are associated with Tucker's classification. To the extent to which he is able to accomplish this correlation, Tucker is exploring and implementing wherever possible Halliday's (1961: 69) fundamental concept of **lexis as most delicate grammar**. Downing and Locke (2006: 480) provide a similar classification, including categories such as 'descriptors' and 'classifiers'.

Pre-head/apex elements

Pre-head/apex elements are essentially linked to Qualities that are gradable in the first place. Gradable Qualities can be expressed in 'more/less' terms, whereas Non-gradable Qualities are 'either/or'. To give a brief example, research, practice, science, etc., are either *medical* or not; they cannot be **very medical*, **quite medical*, **so medical*, etc. Note that there is a correlation here between Epithets (epithetic Qualities) and Classifiers (classifying Qualities) in the sense that Classifiers are associated primarily with non-gradable Qualities. It is the 'quantification' of gradable Qualities that is expressed (almost exclusively in English) by pre-head/pre-apex elements of structure.

Both the Cardiff Grammar and Downing and Locke (2006) give detailed accounts of pre-head/apex elements. Downing and Locke (2006) adopt the modification and pre-modification approach, given their use of modifier, head, qualifier elements to describe adjectival group structure. The Cardiff Grammar, on the other hand, adopts the general notion of **tempering**, introducing a number of types of **temperer** element, **degree temperer** (t^d or d^t), **emphasising temperer** (t^e or et) and **adjunctival temperer** (t^a or at).[12]

However rich the resource, the central contribution of the various pre-head/apex elements is to allow the expression of different degrees of the Quality in question. As a general principle, elements that are placed before others are further specifying the degree expressed by an element to the right. Logically, then, as Halliday and Matthiessen (2014: 390) show in the βγ – ββ – βα analysis in their Figure 6–8, reproduced here as Figure 18.1, it is a case of sub-modification.

In such sequences, some elements may themselves be realised by units in which modification/tempering is also found. This is often the case when an adverb is the head/apex of an adverbial group modifying an adjectival apex and is itself modified/tempered, as shown in example (6), using parentheses, and in Figure 18.2, using the Cardiff Grammar notation. Incidentally, here, we see an example of the similarity between the structure and meanings of the adjectival and adverbial groups – a matter which will be discussed later in the chapter.

(6) (so ((very largely) (tactical)))[13]

Downing and Locke (2006: 484) originally describe five systems of modification: **comparative and superlative** (for example *more difficult*), **intensification** (for example *very difficult*), **attenuation** (for example *slightly salty*), **quantification** (for example *a mile long*)

a	rather	more	impressive	figure
			Modifier	Head
γ		β		α
	Sub-Modifier		Subhead	
	βγ	ββ	βα	

Figure 18.1 Submodification in the nominal group

Source: Halliday and Matthiessen (2014: 390)

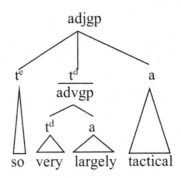

Figure 18.2   Cardiff Grammar structural representation of example (6)

and **description** (for example *socially acceptable*). In their 1992 version, they also posited three levels of submodification, **sssm**, **ssm** and **sm**, with examples such as that shown in Figure 18.3. Some doubt might be expressed, however, over the status of *at that time* and *still*, which would need to be analysed as clausal Adjuncts, with the adjectival group as an Attribute in a relational attributive clause, as in example (7).

(7)   He was at that time still very sadly impecunious

Furthermore, *very* in this example is not a direct sub-modifier of *impecunious*, but of the adverbial head/apex *sadly*, along the lines of the analysis shown in Figure 18.2. In their Downing and Locke's (2006) version, sub-modification is reduced to one level, essentially excluding material such as *at that time* and *still* in Figure 18.3.

   While allowing for the range of options available as described in Downing and Locke's account, the Cardiff Grammar conflates the first four of their categories under the label of 'tempered by degree', and treats their fifth as 'tempered by quality' (Tucker 1998: 183). Similar distinctions to Downing and Locke's first four categories are subsequently covered in the more delicate systems of the network for [tempered quality] (Tucker 1998: 185). These systems lead to realisation through the degree temperer (t^d/dt) or the adjunctival temperer (t^a/at) for 'tempering by quality' such as **economically** *significant*.

   The range of sub-modification described by Downing and Locke is covered in the Cardiff Grammar by a further temperer, the emphasising temperer (t^e/et), for examples such as *so* in *so very quickly*.

   Tucker (1998: 71) tentatively introduces a further 'pre-modifying' element, which he labels **extent (ex)**, to handle items such as *far* as in *far too quick* or *rather/somewhat* in *rather/somewhat more interesting*.

	sssm	**ssm**	**sm**	**m**	**h**
She divorced her	at that time	still	very sadly		impecunious husband

Figure 18.3   Downing and Locke's (1992) analysis of an adjectival group showing levels of submodification

Finally, the Cardiff Grammar recognises a determiner element (d^{qld}/qldd) within the adjectival group, necessary for superlative expressions such as that in example (8), and a quantifying determiner (d^{qlq}/qlqd), as in example (9).

(8) they were **the most** successful[14]

(9) This question, and the next, were perhaps **the two most** crucial with regard to . . . [15]

Post-head/apex elements

There is general agreement that there is a potential for post-head/apex meanings. Most adjectival group descriptions, including Downing and Locke (1992, 2006), recognise a post-head element, the **qualifier (q)**, typically realised by expressions such as those italicised in examples (10) and (11).

(10) very clever *at coping with unpleasantness*[16]

(11) more beautiful *than the flowers in the field*[17]

Again, Downing and Locke (1992: 531–9) dedicate a whole module to the range of expressions used in 'Qualification of the Attribute'. Clearly, the expression *than the flowers . . .* in example (11) introduces the explicit comparator in the overall comparative initiated by *more*. The post-head expression in example (10) has a very different function – one of narrowing down the domain or 'scope' of the Quality in question (here, *clever*). This distinction, however, is made only in the Cardiff Grammar, which recognises two post-apex elements, the **finisher (f)**, finishing off the comparison introduced by temperers such as *more*, and the **scope (sc)**, which expresses the domain to which the Quality applies. Importantly, both scope and finisher can be present, as shown in example (12), which suggests that the m, h, q approach would need to recognise two instances of the qualifier element.

(12) more (td) successful (a) at school (sc) than Afro-Caribbean boys (f)[18]

It should also be noted that the presence of a finisher will bring about adjectival group discontinuity wherever the group is found at modifier in a nominal group, as shown in Figure 18.4.

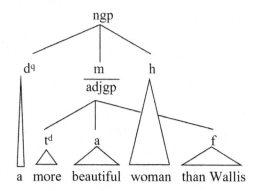

Figure 18.4 Adjectival group discontinuity
Source: BNC GV9

Of the two most detailed accounts of the adjectival group and the range of meanings that it realises, there is roughly parallel coverage, with some differences in description, such as the scope/finisher distinction discussed above. However, the two descriptions differ substantially in their purpose. Downing and Locke (1992: xi) was 'written primarily for students of English as a foreign or second language'; Tucker's (1998) account was written in the context of a 'generative SFG', providing (semantic) system networks, realisation rules and a functional structure. What both accounts do, however, is set out the range of meanings available through the adjectival group, albeit for a different readerships.

The syntactic environments of adjectival groups

Because we are concerned primarily with the internal structure and function of the adjectival group, the discussion of the external function of the group will be brief. The central syntactic environments of the adjectival group, where recognised, are:

1   modifier in nominal group (*a big parcel*); and
2   Complement in attributive relational clauses (*it was very big*).[19]

There are a number of less common environments that also need to be taken into consideration, including:

3   attributive Complement in material clauses with a resultative Attribute (*he washed the plates **clean***);
4   various types of clause Adjunct (*I'm receiving you loud and clear*; *strange, I never suspected him*; ***soaking wet**, he walked into the bathroom*);
5   temperer in an adjectival group (***pale** green, **bright** red*);
6   post-positive modifier in a nominal group (*something **very important***) and
7   completive in a prepositional group (*in **short**, for **good***).[20]

Arguably, many of these less frequent contexts, such as 3–7, militate against treating the adjectival group as a subtype of nominal group. As was discussed earlier in the chapter, the key argument for treating adjectives as heads of the nominal group is the unit's function in the structure of the unit at the rank above (here, the clause). Yet a number of the environments above – namely, 1, 5 and 6 – are not the clause, so the adjective in *pale green*, for example, or even *very pale green* is not nominal in any real sense.

Adjectival and adverbial groups

General similarities

The adverbial group is fully recognised in SFG descriptions that do not recognise the adjectival group. If we consider Halliday and Matthiessen's (2014: 419–23) account of the adverbial group, we find that the description bears considerable resemblance to descriptions of the adjectival group. Halliday and Matthiessen recognise a modifier–head–post-modifier functional structure of the adverbial group, and include the kind of examples of pre-modification that are described and discussed by Downing and Locke (1992: 520*ff*; 2006: 492) and in the Cardiff Grammar (Tucker 1998). Again, Halliday and Matthiessen's (2014) description focuses exclusively on the logical structure of the adverbial group as Figure 18.5 shows.

not	so	very	much	more	easily
				Modifer	Head
ζ	ε	δ	γ	β	α

Figure 18.5   The logical structure of the adverbial group
Source: Halliday and Matthiessen (2014: 420)

In their discussion of post-modifiers, such as *than I could count – for me to count*, they consider such examples to be embedded rank-shifted units.

The similarity of adjectival and adverbial group structures is unsurprising. Among the various types of adjective (Quality), it is predominantly the gradable type that have corresponding adverbs, for example *happy – happily, deft – deftly, certain – certainly*, etc. There are, of course, many adverbs in this often considered 'ragbag' lexical category that are not de-adjectival, such as *tomorrow, nevertheless, sometimes, furthermore*, etc. Some such adverbs present a dilemma for overall inclusion in the adverbial group because there is no potential for any kind of modification.

The Cardiff Grammar approach to adjectival and adverbial groups

In one of his earliest works, Fawcett (1974–76) recognises separate adjectival and adverbial groups, albeit with the same elements of structure (temperer, apex, scope and limiter). In a handwritten addendum in the mimeograph, he points towards his amalgamation, in his later work, of the two into a single group the **quantity–quality** group, on the basis that the only difference between the two is semantic (Fawcett 1980: 92*ff*), in the sense that the adjectival kind refer to Qualities of **Things** and the adverbial kind refer to Qualities of **Situation** – that is, the semantic unit realised through the clause. The 'quantity' in the label refers to the 'quantities' of the qualities, expressed through tempering, for example *very important*. With Fawcett (2000: 204), this group is relabelled **quality group**, with the use of **quantity group** – a novel addition to SFG – to cover what is essentially quantification, as in *very much, well over sixty*, etc. Fawcett (2000: 207*ff*) also defends his choice of such semantically oriented labels, rather than 'adjective–adverb group', for example, as reflecting the 'framework of an explicitly functional grammar'. This view seems reasonable, although it is not reflected elsewhere in the model, with the traditional word-class labelled **nominal group** and **prepositional group**.

Inter-model reconciliation

Towards an integrated description

Earlier in the chapter, it was suggested that perhaps the main difference between the alternative positions in the adjectival group debate is the lack of coverage of the experiential aspect of the structure associated with adjectives, as in Halliday and Matthiessen (2014). If the experientially oriented insights in the detailed descriptions of Downing and Locke and the Cardiff Grammar might enhance Halliday and Matthiessen's description, then it is worth attempting to model those insights and consequently make them available to those who draw substantially on the IFG model. This is not to disparage model-theoretic differences and certainly not self-interestedly to promote any one approach above the others, but it would arguably be of use to those who, for one reason or another, are unable or unwilling to work at times with two or more apparently conflicting descriptions.

Figure 18.6 is a tentative description within the IFG framework, using Halliday and Matthiessen's (2014: 390) example in their Figure 6–8 and showing the experiential elements within the nominal group. The Cardiff Grammar labels have been used for the string *rather more impressive*, although alternative experientially oriented labels could be used, such as 'Intensifier1', 'Intensifier2', as already adopted in the IFG framework. The Epithet element would also need to extend beyond the Thing element, to capture the Scope and Finisher elements.

It is crucially important that the added elements, Extent, Temperer, Apex, etc., are not considered elements proper of the nominal group – for if there is no Epithet/adjective, these added elements and their functions are also absent.

Whilst there is no inherent problem with the experiential analysis in Figure 18.6, the attributive relational use of adjective structures, as in example (13), is more problematic.

(13)   it was rather more impressive

First, the 'Epithet as Head' specification needs to be reconsidered. Figure 6–8 in Halliday and Matthiessen (2014: 391) makes it clear, as does Figure 18.6 here, that the Epithet is not exclusively the adjective, but also includes any modifying material, such as *rather more* in example (13). It is therefore the Quality as the central element in the experiential analysis of the Epithet that corresponds to the Head of the nominal group, rather than the whole of the Epithet. Moreover, some adjectives realising the Classifier can equally function as Head, as in examples (14)–(17) below, and some Classifiers as well may include modification of the Quality, as three of these examples show. Again, this observation suggests that 'Epithet as Head' is the wrong characterisation.

(14)   This is **purely medicinal**[21]

(15)   All the buildings were **wooden**[22]

(16)   Cooker was **all electric**[23]

(17)   Oh, I think I'm **wholly French**[24]

It would therefore seem more appropriate to characterise this kind of nominal group as having Quality as Head. Furthermore, no other function of the nominal group proper, such

a	rather	more	impressive	figure
Deictic	Epithet			Thing
	Extent	Temperer	Apex	

Figure 18.6   A tentative experiential analysis of a nominal group containing an Epithet

as Deictic, Numerative, etc., is possible in Quality-headed attributive relational clauses. However, modification of the Quality in terms of functions such as Temperer, Finisher, Scope, etc., does need to be available. This would give rise to the kind of analysis shown in Figure 18.7.

The difference in modification of a Thing-headed and a Quality-headed nominal group in an attributive relational clause would be characterised in the system network. In Matthiessen's (1995: 308–9) description, this involves the system of 'ascription' as either 'class ascription' (nominal head) or 'quality ascription' (adjectival head) in respect of the participant of Attribute in such clauses.

What Figure 18.8 shows is the consequences of each type of ascription. Class ascription leads to a default nominal group structure with its associated experiential functions, whereas quality ascription leads to the systems that specify Qualities and their modification, for example the system of EPITHESIS.

Such a system for EPITHESIS in respect of Matthiessen's account is suggested in Figure 18.9. This system is an adaptation of Tucker's Cardiff Grammar account (Tucker 1998: 119).

rather	*more*	*impressive*	*than the earlier one*
Epithet			
Extent	Temperer	Quality	Standard[i]
Modifier		Head	Qualifier

Figure 18.7   Proposed analysis for a nominal group with Quality as Head

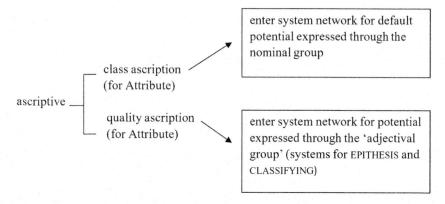

Figure 18.8   A proposed system for the system of ASCRIPTION

Source: Based on Matthiessen (1995)

297

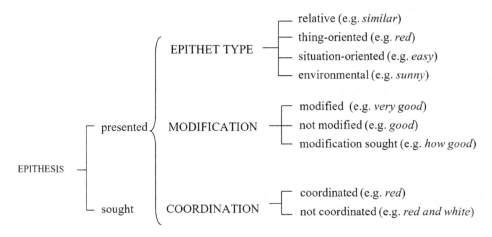

Figure 18.9 A proposed system for EPITHESIS

Reconciliation and SFL practice

It might well be considered disrespectful to make such suggestions for modifications in someone else's model of these phenomena. The above suggestions, however, should be read as tentative and in the spirit of model reconciliation. There is little doubt that Michael Halliday and Christian Matthiessen would have no real objection to other systemic grammarians modifying, and particularly expanding, their own model – provided, of course, that the theoretical and descriptive principles underpinning their model were respected. The intended purpose here is to provide an even fuller account of the area of the lexicogrammar that involves adjectival structures.

In a sense, there is also here a suggestion in respect of good practice on the part of those who use SFG analysis to inform their own research on language use. For example, those investigating language from the perspective of appraisal theory (Oteíza, this volume) should find fuller descriptions of adjectival structures and their meanings extremely useful. If such structures do not have any substantial coverage in one model, it surely makes sense to at least investigate models in which there is and in which the coverage is expressed in systemic functional terms. In this way, analysts might avoid resorting to non-systemic functional descriptions and so maintain a consistent theoretical underpinning to their analyses.

Future work

As this author has often maintained, the essential future work on SFG – and, here, specifically on adjective-related phenomena – is precisely that: 'future work'. Extant descriptions are never comprehensive, and can always be modified and expanded. It is unreasonable to criticise grammarians such as Michael Halliday and Christian Matthiessen for some 'lack of coverage' in works such as IFG and Matthiessen (1995). A handful of systemic functional grammarians alone cannot hope to provide increasingly detailed and more comprehensive descriptions. Yet if the SFG baton is not taken up by others, our descriptions will always fall short of the mark in many places. There is still much work to be done on the whole area of adjective-centred meaning and structure; it is a baton waiting for others to seize.

Notes

1 BNC A06. Wherever possible, examples are drawn from the British National Corpus (BNC).
2 BNC JYD.
3 See 'Adjectival and adverbial groups' below.
4 BNC AAG.
5 COMMUNAL stands for 'Convivial Man-Machine Understanding through Natural Language'.
6 Tucker's modifications are set out in the next section, 'Adjectival structures and their meanings'.
7 These are discussed under the heading 'Pre-head/apex elements'.
8 Suggestions for reconciling the two positions are discussed in some detail under the heading 'Inter-model reconciliation'.
9 BNC JAE.
10 BNC HUM.
11 The differences between 'Things' and 'Qualities' are discussed in detail by Halliday and Matthiessen (1999: 184*ff*).
12 The labelling used by Fawcett (e.g. Fawcett 2000) and by Tucker (e.g. Tucker 1998) sometimes exhibits slight differences, such as here, where there is a difference in the order of the symbols constituting the element's label, e.g. *et* against *t*^e.
13 BNC EF4.
14 BNC HYO.
15 BNC ALC.
16 BNC HHB.
17 BNC J1K.
18 BNC FAY.
19 In the Cardiff Grammar, elements of the structure of the clause are indicated with a capital letter, e.g. 'Complement', whereas elements in groups are indicated with a lower case letter, e.g. 'head'.
20 Although *short* and *good* in these expressions are adjectives, it is arguably better to treat the expressions as single items and not to analyse the adjectives as apexes of a putative adjectival group.
21 BNC C8T.
22 BNC FB4.
23 BNC FY5.
24 BNC GUK.

References

Berry, M. 1975. *Introduction to Systemic Linguistics, Vol 1: Structures and Systems*. London: Batsford.
Biber, D., S. Johansson, G. Leech, S. Conrad and E. Finegan. 1999. *Longman Grammar of Spoken and Written English*. Harlow: Pearson Education.
Downing, A., and Locke, P. 1992. *A University Course in English Grammar*. New York: Prentice Hall.
Downing, A., and Locke, P. 2006. *English Grammar: A University Course*. 2nd edn. London and New York: Routledge.
Fawcett, R.P. 1980. *Cognitive Linguistics and Social Interaction: Towards an Integrated Model of a Systemic Functional Grammar and the Other Components of an Interacting Mind*. Heidelberg: Julius Groos and Exeter University.
Fawcett, R.P. 1974–76. *Some Proposals for Systemic Syntax*. Cardiff: Polytechnic of Wales.
Fawcett, R.P. 2000a. *A Theory of Syntax for Systemic Functional Linguistics*. Amsterdam and Philadelphia, PA: John Benjamins.
Fawcett, R.P. 2000b. In place of Halliday's 'verbal group', part 1: Evidence from the problems of Halliday's representations and the relative simplicity of the proposed alternative. *WORD* 51(2): 157–203.
Fontaine, L. 2013. *Analysing English Grammar: A Systemic Functional Introduction*. Cambridge: Cambridge University Press.

Gregory, M. 2009 [1969]. *English Patterns*. In J. de Villiers and R.J. Stainton (eds) *Michael Gregory's Proposals for a Communication Linguistics* (Communication in Linguistics Series 2). Toronto: Éditions du Gref, pp. 3–142.

Halliday, M.A.K. 1956. Grammatical categories in modern Chinese. *Transactions of the Philological Society* 55(1): 177–224.

Halliday, M.A.K. 1961. Categories of the theory of grammar. *WORD* 17(3): 241–92.

Halliday, M.A.K., and C.M.I.M. Matthiessen. 1999. *Construing Experience through Meaning: A Language-Based Approach to Cognition*. London: Cassell Academic.

Halliday, M.A.K., and C.M.I.M. Matthiessen. 2014. *Halliday's Introduction to Functional Grammar*. 4th edn. London: Arnold.

Matthiessen, C.M.I.M. 1995. *Lexicogrammatical Cartography: English Systems*. Tokyo: International Language Sciences.

Morley, G.D. 2000. *Syntax in Functional Grammar: An Introduction to Lexicogrammar in Systemic Linguistics*. London and New York: Continuum.

Muir, J. 1972. *A Modern Approach to English Grammar: An Introduction to Systemic Grammar*. London: Batsford.

Ouhalla, J. 1994. *Transformational Grammar: From Rules to Principles and Parameters*. London: Arnold.

Sinclair, J. 1972. *A Course in Spoken English: Grammar*. Oxford: Oxford University Press.

Thompson, G. 1996. *Introducing Functional Grammar*. London: Arnold.

Tucker, G.H. 1998. *The Lexicogrammar of Adjectives: A Systemic Functional Approach to Lexis*. London: Cassell Academic.

Turner, G. 1970. A linguistic approach to children's speech. In G. Turner and B. Mohan (eds) *A Linguistic Description and Computer Program of Children's Speech*. London: R.K.P, pp. 1–154.

Young, D.J. 1980. *The Structure of English Clauses*. London: Hutchinson.

19

The verbal group

Beatriz Quiroz

In the Hallidayian tradition, the verbal group is a class of unit at group/phrase rank generally co-extensive with the Process in the experiential structure of the English clause, with Finite + Predicator in the interpersonal structure, and with part of the Rheme in the textual (thematic) structure. As is well known, each of these functional components in structure is assumed to contribute in turn to the realisation of features in key metafunctionally diversified **clause systems** – PROCESS TYPE, MOOD and THEME, respectively. In addition, the verbal group in English is described as the entry condition for a number of systems located below the clause, such as TENSE, VOICE, POLARITY and MODALITY (Halliday and Matthiessen 2014).

The aim of this chapter is to explore the status of the verbal group in light of a number of key theoretical, descriptive and methodological issues surrounding this class in the systemic functional linguistics (SFL) literature. To do this, the discussion is organised into three sections. First, the chapter begins with an historical overview of the place assigned to the verbal group since it was first introduced in the origins of SFL, including its description in the context of the general account of English lexicogrammar. Following this, a brief review of descriptive work specifically focusing on the verbal group in other languages is provided. The chapter then addresses critical issues arising from the description of the English verbal group, as presented in all four editions of *An Introduction to Functional Grammar* (Halliday 1985, 1994; Halliday and Matthiessen 2004, 2014) and through the discussion put forward by Fawcett (2000a, 2000b) within the framework of the Cardiff Model, and some cross-linguistic issues illustrated by the systemic functional description of the verbal group in Chilean Spanish (Quiroz 2013).

Historical perspective

The verbal group was first introduced as a descriptive category in the context of the 'scale and category' model, which Halliday (1961) put forward as his own development of the Firthian system–structure principle (for example Firth 1957). According to this principle, linguistic **structure**, across units and levels, is to be accounted for in close relation to underlying **systems** of oppositions, which ultimately explain the 'contextual meaning' of all linguistic categories. Following this principle, Halliday (1961) sets out to show that the system–structure principle can be applied to comprehensive grammatical descriptions, using English as an illustrative language.

Thus, in an early sentence–clause–group–word–morpheme model of the English rank scale, Halliday (1961: 274) uses the verbal group to illustrate the specific contribution of group/phrase rank units to sentence structure – specifically, its status as a specific 'primary' **class** of unit 'expounding' what was then described as the Predicator.

Figure 19.1 shows that the Predicator in English clause structure was 'expounded' (that is, realised) by the verbal group at the next rank below, the group/phrase rank. As a class of unit below the clause, the verbal group enters its own set of oppositions (which are 'expounded' by the possibilities of its own internal elements of structure). In other words, the 'consist of' relation between units and classes of units along the English rank scale is already, at this early stage, mediated by system–structure relations. Figure 19.2 diagrammatically represents this basic assumption in Halliday (1961).

Following Firth, Halliday also keeps two interrelated orders distinct already in his 'scale and category' model: the order of theoretical categories and the order of descriptive categories. General categories such as 'unit', 'class', 'system' and 'structure' refer to mutually defining interrelations within the theory. As a descriptive category, however, the verbal group presupposes specific ways in which those general categories relate to English lexico-gramatical patterns – that is, its status as grammatical category results from system–structure interrelations found across ranks in English, and not merely from the recognition and labelling of syntagmatically arranged constituents in the English sentence nor from straightforward compositional relations between 'larger' and 'smaller' units – as in the traditional approach to the description of units and classes of units.

With the later consolidation of the 'systemic' model (for example Halliday 1966a, 1981 [1964]), the description of the verbal group and other (classes of) units contributed to further

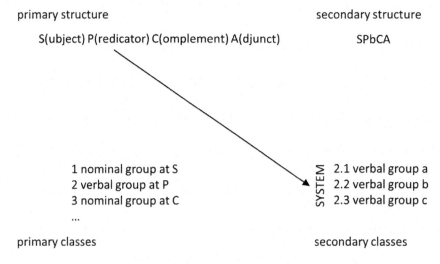

Figure 19.1 Systems of classes and their relation to clause structure

Source: Adapted from Halliday (1961: 254)

general theoretical categories ...

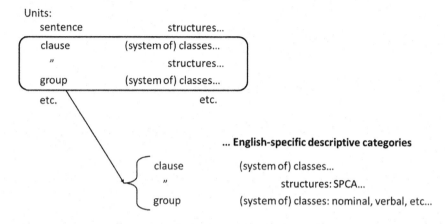

Figure 19.2   Relations among units, classes, system and structure in the 'scale and category' model

Source: Adapted from Halliday (1961: 266)

modelling of the metafunctional and rank-based diversification of grammatical systems in English. Three simultaneous systems of choice with the English clause as the entry condition were proposed: TRANSITIVITY, MOOD and THEME (for example Halliday 1969). Each of these systems was realised in structure by specific configurations of functions and each function was in turn realised by a given class at group/phrase rank, below the clause. Thus TRANSITIVITY (that is, PROCESS TYPE) choices within the domain of the English clause were realised by configurations of mutually defined elements of structure, including the Process; MOOD choices, on the other hand, were realised by a separate configuration of functions, including the Predicator. At that stage of the description of the English clause, both the Process and the Predicator, motivated by different systems, were realised by the same unit at the rank immediately below: the verbal group.

Still entirely in the context of the description of English lexicogrammar (McDonald, this volume), developments within the systemic model also paved the way for a complementary view on structure. According to Halliday (1981 [1965]), linguistic structure shows basically two kinds of pattern: multivariate and univariate. *Multivariate* structure involves more than one variable, with each variable making a distinct contribution to the whole, for example Deictic · Epithet · Thing in the internal structure of the English nominal group. *Univariate* structure, in turn, is understood as the recurrence of one single variable (potentially) forming open-ended series, in a way similar to traditional 'coordination' and 'subordination' relations in complex units. Univariate structures could, in fact, be of two types: *paratactic*, when elements involved have the same status, as in *cats, dogs and horses*; or *hypotactic*, when elements hold dependency relations among one another, as in Head · Modifier(s) within the nominal group. Elements in paratactic structures were represented by Arabic numbers, while elements in hypotactic structures were represented by Greek letters, as shown by examples (1) and (2) below, taken from Halliday (1981 [1965]).

(1)	*cats,*	*dogs*	*and horses*	**univariate structure: paratactic**
	1	2	3	

(2)	*staff*	*salary*	*increase*	**univariate structure: hypotactic**
	γ	β	α	

Univariate structure, in particular, came to be more fully explained in terms of **recursive systems** and the description of the English verbal group was crucial for this development. Halliday (1976 [1966]: 141) sees that the way in which the English verbal group is built up 'does not directly reflect the choices that have been made in various systems' – that is, its morphological make-up does not reveal, in a straightforward manner, neither its systemic organisation nor the configuration of elements in its internal structure. Halliday goes on to propose that the English verbal group can be seen as the result of selections in a three-term system that is **recursive** in nature – that is, each of its terms can be chosen more than once. This recursive systemic pattern allows Halliday to account for the English TENSE system, which includes a very small set of possibilities: 'past' (−), 'present' (0) and 'future' (+). Each term in this tripartite system can be repeatedly selected in English according to specific restrictions, or 'stop rules'. Possible iterations and restrictions to these are those generating univariate, chain-like patterns in the English verbal group.

This account of TENSE as a recursive system thus provided a fresh view on the specific organisation of the verbal group (as opposed to other classes of units at the same rank), but also a thought-provoking explanation that challenged traditional descriptions of English tense. The account of TENSE (systems) with the verbal group as an entry condition came to be later specifically associated with the logical component of the ideational metafunction (Halliday 2002 [1979]), and this interpretation was further enriched with the analysis of patterns described across English texts and registers (for example Matthiessen 1984). Figure 19.3 illustrates a 'standard model' account of the univariate structure of the English verbal group that foregrounds the realisation of tense selections in structure.

In Figure 19.3, hypotactically related functions represented by Greek letters do not show a strict one-to-one correspondence to verbal group constituents. In fact, such a univariate

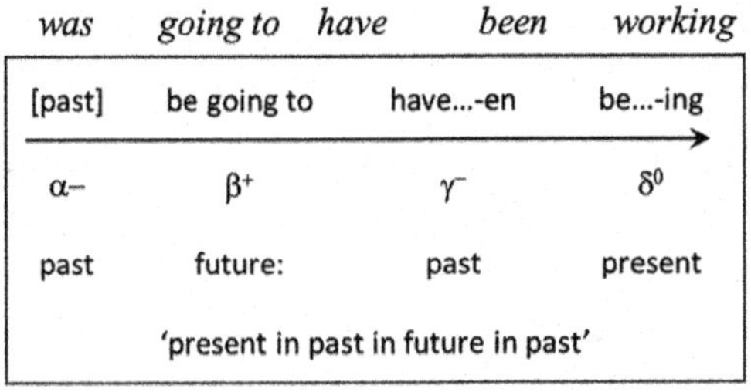

was	*going to*	*have*	*been*	*working*
[past]	be going to	have...-en		be...-ing
α−	β+	γ⁻		δ⁰
past	future:	past		present
	'present in past in future in past'			

Figure 19.3 Univariate structure of the English verbal group: realisation of recursive TENSE selections

Note: cf. Halliday and Matthiessen (2004: 400)

Source: Adapted from Halliday (1985: 178)

structural interpretation does not map onto the multivariate organisation of the verbal group in any self-evident way either – unless the fact that they are motivated by different systems (that is, non-recursive and recursive systems, in each case) is taken into account.[1] A critique of the standard interpretation of the structure of the English verbal group is provided by Fawcett (2000a: 162*ff*). Bache (2008) also challenges the standard account and offers an alternative explanation of serial (univariate) patterns within the domain of the 'verbal expression' (a term that he coins to avoid reference to rank-scale assumptions).

In Halliday (1985: 255*ff*), the logico-semantic expansion of simple verbal groups into complexes leads to three kinds of distinctions in meaning:

- elaborating verbal group complexes give way to PHASE distinctions, for example *seems to be* (reality-phase) and *starts doing/to do* (time-phase);
- extending complexes relates to CONATION distinctions, for example *try to do* (conative) and *manage to do* (reussive) and
- enhancing complexes lead to MODULATION distinctions, for example *tend to do* (time), *insist on doing* (manner) and *happen to do* (cause).

A basic system network for verbal group complexing is later provided by Matthiessen (1995: 718). An up-to-date account, including subtypes and system networks, can be found in Halliday and Matthiessen (2014: 567*ff*).[2]

Specific systemic representations of the English verbal group through **system networks** were first published in Halliday (1976 [1964]: 124–6), and further reworked in other, more simplified, versions provided by Matthiessen (1995) and Halliday (2002 [1996]). Matthiessen's (1995: 729) network includes a recursive TENSE system in the context of a comprehensive systemic account of English lexicogrammar. Halliday's (2002 [1996]: 394) network is introduced to illustrate the relative simplicity of systems when compared to the number of possible selection expressions that they can generate. An up-to-date English verbal group system network can be found in Halliday and Matthiessen (2004: 349; 2014: 410).

Over the years, the English verbal group has found itself contributing to simultaneous clause systems and the ensuing structures in various ways (for example Halliday 1970: 327). However, at least in early accounts, this class was not always necessarily and/or explicitly linked to rank-scale assumptions. An example of this is Halliday's (2002 [1970]) functional account of English clause structure, in which the terms 'verb' and 'verbal group' are used interchangeably in relation to the class realising relevant functions at clause rank: in structure associated with 'transitivity', the Process is said to be 'usually represented by a verb' (Halliday 2002 [1970]: 178); in interpersonal 'mood' clause types – that is, declarative, interrogative, etc. – the 'finite element of the verb' plus the 'grammatical subject' are at stake (Halliday 2002 [1970]: 190; no function labels are provided). It is only in the first fully fledged metafunctionally diversified model of English lexicogrammar (Halliday 1985) that the English verbal group is clearly analysed as realising the Process in the experiential clause structure, and as roughly co-extensive with Finite and Predicator in the interpersonal analysis.

Beyond these considerations, structural representations locating the English verbal group with respect to the full extent of inter-rank relations (for example by means of 'flat' trees or multi-tiered 'boxed' diagrams with 'minimal bracketing') are rather rare in SFL literature. A fairly comprehensive representation of such inter-rank relations can be found in Halliday and Matthiessen (2014: 77), as illustrated in Figure 19.4.

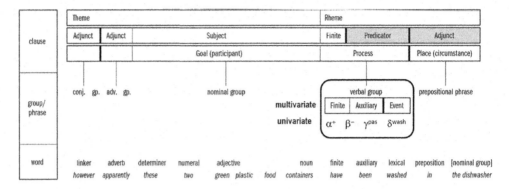

Figure 19.4 An account of constituency relations along the English rank scale

Note: Univariate layer added for the verbal group

Source: Adapted from Halliday and Matthiessen (2014: 77)

Specific accounts of the verbal group in languages other than English are relatively sparse. McDonald (2004), for example, provides an instantial system network for the Mandarin verbal group, describing choices in ASPECT and TENSE based on patterns found in texts across registers. Work conducted on French by Caffarel-Cayron (this volume) has productively inspired research on other Romance languages, by suggesting for the first time the centrality of the verbal group in SFL interpretations of this language family. Her account has led to important insights for the description of MOOD in both Portuguese (Figueredo 2011, on Brazilian Portuguese; Gouveia 2010, on European Portuguese) and Chilean Spanish (Quiroz 2013). However, apart from Caffarel's (1992) description of French TENSE and an account provided for Chilean Spanish by Quiroz (2013), no specific systemic accounts with associated networks seem to be available in languages other than English. As a general rule, the verbal group tends to be taken for granted as a class below the clause and/or to be described mainly in relation to compositional (whole–part) relations (for example Teruya 2007, in Japanese; Lavid et al. 2010, in Peninsular Spanish).

Critical issues

The verbal group in English: a critical view from the Cardiff Grammar

Fawcett (2000a, 2000b) provides an in-depth critique of the verbal group as a relevant grammatical category in SFL. His argument nonetheless needs to be considered against the background of the Cardiff Model, as laid out in Fawcett (2000c). This caveat is an important one, since Fawcett's dismissal of the English verbal group is based on discrepancies with the Sydney Model that are both theoretical and descriptive in nature.

It is beyond the scope of the present chapter to review the general discussion framed by Fawcett in terms of the rank-scale 'controversy' (McDonald, this volume). However, it is worthwhile noticing that the Cardiff Model does not assume the rank scale as a theoretical organising principle. In fact, Fawcett (2000c) makes a case against the rank scale, mostly as modelled by Halliday (1961), directing his critique towards the compositional 'consist of' principle that, in his view, is at the core of any rank-scale assumptions. Fawcett dismisses the 'total accountability' principle underlying whole–part relations among units at different ranks – that is, the idea that all clauses must consist of groups (of different classes), which in turn must consist of words (of different classes), which in turn must consist of morphemes (Halliday 1961: 253). Fawcett's (2000a: 177) claim is that this kind of 'whole–part' relation between units and classes of units is not critical or even desirable for grammatical description.

In the discussion specifically addressing the verbal group (mostly as described in Halliday 1994), Fawcett (2000a, 2000b) then offers a number of reasons why the verbal group, as a class of unit, is not necessary for the description of the English clause (also suggesting that this is the case for other languages). The main reasons can be summarised as:

1   the 'unnecessary' twofold treatment of the internal structure of the English verbal group (that is, multivariate and univariate);
2   the simultaneous analysis of a Finite function both at clause rank (in clause interpersonal structure) and at group rank (in the structure of the verbal group);
3   the 'inconsistent' treatment of the so-called phrasal verbs in standard SFL descriptions (for example particles such as *off* in *they called the meeting off* analysed as a separate element in the interpersonal structure of the clause – an Adjunct – but as an integral part of the Process in its experiential structure);
4   the treatment of the Finite as a clause constituent, despite the fact that it is not co-extensive with the corresponding unit at the rank immediately below the clause (that is, a whole group, not only a word);
5   the 'inconsistent' treatment of Finite as being directly realised by a (finite) verb in present and past tenses in clauses including copulative verbs, but as conflated with the Predicator in other clause types and
6   the lack of 'unity' of the English verbal group, which admits a number of discontinuities (for example the interpolation of the Subject in polar interrogatives, such as *you* in *Do you like chocolate*, or the interpolation of adverbial Modal Adjuncts between the Finite and the Predicator, such as *already* in *You will already have guessed the answer*).[3]

What the related objections 2–6 clearly show is the assumption that structural elements at one rank *must* correspond to a single, discrete constituent immediately below if a rank scale is to be taken seriously. In this respect, Fawcett's objections are thought-provoking: analyses provided by standard descriptions do not seem to be always explicitly and coherently related to the rank-scale assumptions that he is indeed foregrounding in his critique.

However, it is worthwhile noticing that, already in early versions of the standard model (for example Halliday 1966a: 57; 1981 [1965]: 29), functional elements of structure were *not* assumed to hold a one-to-one correspondence with discrete constituents at the rank immediately below. Conflation ('fusion') and discontinuity were already part of the picture in the early systemic model. The traditional example is portmanteau morphology, which involves the simultaneous realisation of a number of terms from different systems at higher ranks (word, group, clause, etc.) (Hudson 1981 [1972]). As for discontinuity, another traditional example is the structural realisation of (morphological) categories such as 'person', 'number' and 'gender' across languages: as noted by Firth (1957: 21), the realisation of these categories is 'distributed all over the sentence' and not by only one single constituent, whatever the rank. This idea can be related to the problem of accounting for the morphological make-up of the English verbal group, which Halliday (1976 [1966]) indeed addresses in terms of recursive systems.

With respect to discontinuity, it is also important to mention that the standard Sydney Model assumes that metafunctionally diversified systems (for example PROCESS TYPE, MOOD, THEME) tend to generate distinct structural configurations at clause rank (particulate, prosodic and periodic, respectively), which do not map onto one another neatly. Halliday (2002 [1979]) suggests that interpersonal structure, in fact, is prone to show prosodic, discontinuous patterns and only experiential structure within the ideational component seems to be more clearly 'constituent-like' – that is, it shows the kind of 'discreteness' that allows mapping functional components onto whole units at the rank immediately below.

As for the 'simultaneous' analysis of a Finite function at clause and group rank, Fawcett does not refer to the fact that clause rank functions and group rank functions are, in the Sydney 'standard' model, necessarily derived from systems located at different ranks. It could be fairly claimed that labelling a Finite function at both group and clause rank is indeed misleading, but if both theoretical and descriptive principles of the standard Sydney Model are taken into account, it is clear that there are two, not one, structural functions at stake, each of which is generated by a different system. Ultimately, then, the Finite function at clause rank in English needs to be seen in relation to MOOD distinctions within inter-personal systems in lexicogrammar, while the Finite function at group rank relates to the realisation of temporal and modal deixis, as shown by Figure 19.5.

The main inconsistency for which standard versions could be criticised has to do with the ways in which the rank scale is modelled as a theoretical category, which admittedly has important descriptive implications. Despite the fact that the theory had already established

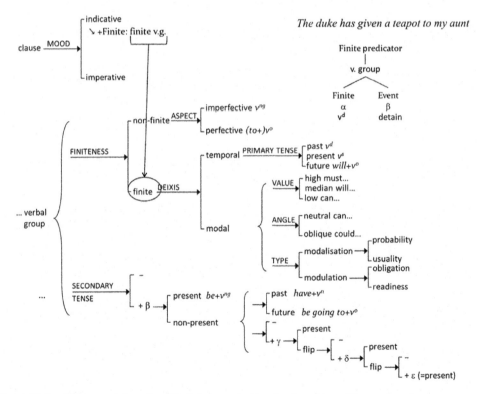

Figure 19.5 Clause-rank function (Finite) pre-selecting features down the rank scale

Source: Based on verbal group system in Halliday (2002 [1996]: 394)

from the beginning that units, classes of units and their organisation along the rank scale are integrated and motivated via system–structure interrelations, most mainstream SFL accounts do seem to privilege constituency in terms of straightforward compositional 'whole–part' relations along the local hierarchy of units in lexicogrammar.

In any case, in light of the 'problems' found in the Sydney Model, Fawcett (2000a: 182*ff*) offers a number of arguments for 'promoting' the internal elements of the verbal group, which he relocates as elements of clause **syntax** (as framed in the Cardiff Model). In Figure 19.6, English clause elements, as modelled by Fawcett, are highlighted to show their correspondence to the verbal group in the standard Sydney version. As seen in Figure 19.6, Halliday's Finite is replaced by the Operator (O), and appears at the same level as Auxiliaries (X) and the Main Verb (M) (roughly, Halliday's Event).

In the standard Sydney Model, these elements would be accounted for within the domain of the verbal group. A full representation of the Cardiff Model analysis, including its semantic motivation, can be found in Fawcett (2000b: 369).

Fawcett's critique, interestingly, leads to the key question of the motivation of grammatical categories in two different models. As already noted, when Fawcett points towards the various 'inconsistencies' in the Sydney framework, he is focusing on the constituency principle, which he primarily associates with compositional relations and the required 'total accountability' of such relations across ranks. Accordingly, constituency relations appear in this view as metafunctionally neutral, since Fawcett assumes neither metafunctionally diversified bundles of interconnected systems nor a multi-tiered view of structure deriving from such systems (although he posits eight alternative 'strands of meaning' underlying his own description of the 'form' of the English clause) (Fawcett 2000b: 369). Since no system–structure relations are assumed among units below the clause, elements of clause structure are not seen as 'pre-selecting' a class (of units) in systems at lower ranks (see Figure 19.5). Crucially, then, Fawcett does not model the same kind of system–structure interrelations motivating units and classes at different ranks; rather, he opts instead for a different interpretation of linguistic relations, the most fundamental being the relation between 'meanings' (system potential) and 'form' (syntax) (Fawcett 2000b: 362, and in this volume). Such an interpretation relies in turn on a complex set of assumptions, organised within a different theoretical framework, with different descriptive consequences for his account of the English clause.

Beyond these considerations, Fawcett (2000c) makes a fair point that the application of the 'consists of' principle is reductive in grammatical description. This has also been pointed out by McGregor (1996) and Morley (2001), who critique Fawcett's arguments against the

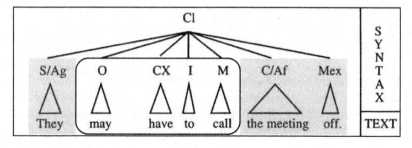

Figure 19.6   Analysis of the simple clause at the level of syntax
Source: Adapted from Fawcett (2000b: 369)

verbal group, but agree with him on that point. Indeed, a coherent integration of a rank-scale model based on system–structure diversification and one based on constituency (direct whole–part relations) is not self-evident in neither SFL theory nor 'standard' descriptions of English assuming a verbal group. This becomes even more problematic when the verbal group is assumed in the description of other languages, as is discussed in the next section.

The status of the verbal group in other languages: an illustration from Chilean Spanish

To complement the discussion of the verbal group in English, we can also consider its status in the description of Chilean Spanish. In this variety of Spanish, the verbal group is involved in the realisation of two fundamental clausal systems, MOOD and PROCESS TYPE (Quiroz 2013). Beginning with the interpersonal organisation of the clause, the finite verbal group as a whole realises the Predicator, the only function required to make the Spanish clause arguable. This is because the verb's inflectional morphology fully grounds the clause to the speech event in terms of modal responsibility, temporality and modality – in contrast to French and English, in which discrete Subject and Finite functions are required for the same purpose. In fact, the primary MOOD contrast between [indicative] and [imperative] is motivated in Spanish by both selections in portmanteau morphology and the relative positioning of clitic elements (pronominal, reflexive and/or recessive in nature). As for the more delicate distinction between [declarative] and [interrogative], only intonation or the presence of a Q-interrogative element is at stake. As shown in Table 19.1, a fully arguable clause serving as entry condition for MOOD in Spanish requires a Predicator 'pre-selecting' a finite verbal group at the rank below (underlined in the examples).

Depending on more delicate choices in MOOD, the Predicator may preselect a 'restricted' verbal group (as in imperative clauses, which allow selections in modal responsibility only through PERSON at group rank) or an 'open' verbal group (as in indicative clauses, which do admit potentially simultaneous choices in TENSE and MODALITY at group rank). Figure 19.7 shows a system network for the verbal group in (Chilean) Spanish.

From the point of view of the experiential organisation of the Spanish clause, the verbal group may realise a nuclear configuration of the Process and associated Participant(s) entirely on its own. Person selections in the verb inflection, along with the presence of pronominal clitics (accusative and/or dative), are enough for the realisation of a basic nuclear configuration in Spanish, again in contrast to English, in which Participants are necessarily realised at clause rank, primarily by nominal groups. Table 19.2 shows the main possibilities

Table 19.1 MOOD in Spanish: feature paradigm, realisation statements and examples

MOOD choice	realisation	example
[imperative]	↘ +Predicator: restricted v.g.	_Prende el cable_ 'Switch on the cable (TV)'
[indicative: informative: declarative]	↘ +Predicator: open v.g.	_Prendiste el cable_ 'You switched on the cable (TV)'
[indicative: interrogative: polar]	↘ rising tone	_¿Prendiste el cable?_ '(Did) you switch on the cable (TV)'
[indicative: interrogative: elemental]	↘ +Q-int; #^Q-int; Q-int^p	_¿Quién prendió el cable?_ 'Who switched on the cable (TV)?'

Note: Data from Quiroz (2013)

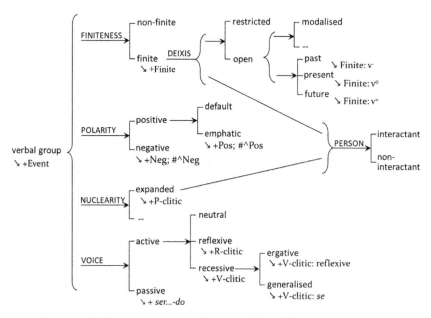

Figure 19.7 Verbal group system in (Chilean) Spanish

Source: Adapted from Quiroz (2013)

for experiential structure in Spanish (verbal group underlined; participants in bold; verbal inflection hyphenated).

The range of possibilities between a 'minimal' group-only realisation and a clause-rank realisation of nuclear configurations in experiential structure can be accounted for by selections in NUCLEARITY at group rank (see Figure 19.7). These realisational possibilities seem to be motivated by a number of higher-order factors, among which discourse-semantic considerations involving the recoverability or non-recoverability of participants (IDENTIFICATION) and/or the need to lexicalise participants in texts (IDEATION) are at stake.[4]

In addition, selections in VOICE within the domain of the Spanish verbal group contribute to a number of delicate clause-rank distinctions in PROCESS TYPE. For example, the potential choice between [ergative] and [generalised] (see Figure 19.7) motivating the presence of Voice-clitic in verbal group structure is relevant in the choice between process subtypes at clause rank (Quiroz 2013). The distinction between [ergative] and [generalised] indeed offers an alternative view on what is traditionally accounted for in terms of 'pseudo-reflexive' marking, as the *se* in *La puerta se cerró* ('The door closed') and 'impersonal/passive' marking, such as *se* in *Se vende esta propiedad* ('This property (is) sold'). Such an explanation contrasts with problematic and controversial bottom-up descriptions usually offered in descriptive work on Spanish, which tend to be centred on word-rank marking in isolation.[5]

Table 19.2 Nuclear experiential structure in Spanish: clause-rank and clitic-only realisation

Usted <u>no h-a dado</u> **un buen argumento**	**clause rank realisation of participants**
'You haven't given a good argument'	
<u>No **lo** h-**a** dado</u>	**group rank realisation of participants**
'You haven't given it'	

From the point of view of the internal organisation of the Spanish verbal group, this class can be productively seen from two complementary perspectives on structure, as in English. First, the structure of the Spanish verbal group can be analysed as an iterative patterning of elements, in a way that is similar to patterns described for verbal groups in English (for example Halliday 1985, 1994) and French (Caffarel-Cayron, this volume) – that is, its internal organisation can also be interpreted in terms of (hypotactically) univariate structure generated by comparable TENSE recursive systems, although the extent to which systemic features can be repeatedly selected in such systems is certainly limited in comparison to English and French. A good example is 'future', which in Spanish can be selected only once (cf. Quiroz 2013). Also, as in French (Caffarel-Cayron, this volume), selections in TENSE and MODALITY within the domain of the verbal group can be made simultaneously, for example through modal operators realised by finite verbs co-selecting for primary 'past', 'present' or 'future'. Example (3) below illustrates the univariate structure of the Spanish verbal group.

(3)

Pud-o	haber	sido	condenado	por homicidio
may-3s/ pst/ind	have-inf	be-prtcp	condemn-prtcp	for homicide

verbal group			
$\alpha^{-/mod}$	β^{-}	γ^{pass}	δ^{event}

'(He) could have been condemned   for homicide'

However, such a chain-like perspective on the internal organisation of the Spanish verbal group fails to account, on its own, for important structural patterns that cannot be described in terms of selections in recursive systems or in terms of iterative dependencies. This is the case, in particular, with the structural realisation of NUCLEARITY and VOICE systems at group rank (shown in Figure 19.7). Examples (4)–(6) show Participant-clitic (P-cl) and Voice-clitic (V-cl) as elements of verbal group structure generated by each of those systems, respectively (Quiroz 2013).

(4)

Usted	no	me	h-a	dado	un buen argumento
	neg	dat/1s	have-3s/ prs/ind	give- prctp	a good argument

	Predicator				STRUCTURE: INTERPERSONAL	rank: clause
Part1	Part3/Process			Part2	STRUCTURE: EXPERIENTIAL	
n. gr.	verbal group			nominal group	CLASS	rank: group
	Neg	P-cl	Finite	Event		STRUCTURE: MULTIVARIATE	
		$\alpha^{0/neg}$	β^{-}	γ^{event}		STRUCTURE: UNIVARIATE	
	neg	clitic	verb	verb		CLASS	rank: word

you   no me you-have given   a good argument

'You haven't given me a good argument'

(5)

No	se	me	h-a	dado	un buen argumento
neg	se	dat/1s	have-3s/ prs/ind	give- prctp	a good argument

				STRUCTURE: INTERPERSONAL	rank: clause
Predicator					
Part3/Part1/Process			**Part2**	STRUCTURE: EXPERIENTIAL	
verbal group			nominal group	CLASS	rank: group
Neg	V-cl	P-cl	Finite	Event		STRUCTURE: MULTIVARIATE
	$\alpha^{0/neg}$ β^- γ^{event}			STRUCTURE: UNIVARIATE	
neg	clitic	clitic	verb	verb	CLASS	rank: word

no 'se' me (someone)-have given   a good argument

'A good argument <u>hasn't been given to me</u>'

(6)

No	me	lo	h-a	dado
neg	dat/1s	acc/3s	have-3s/ prs/ind	give- prtcp

				STRUCTURE: INTERPERSONAL	rank: clause
Predicator					
Part3/Part2/Part1/Process				STRUCTURE: EXPERIENTIAL	
verbal group				CLASS	rank: group
Neg	P-cl	P-cl	Finite	Event	STRUCTURE: MULTIVARIATE
	$\alpha^{0/neg}$ β^- γ^{event}			STRUCTURE: UNIVARIATE	
neg	clitic	clitic	verb	verb	CLASS	rank: word

no me it you-have given

'<u>(You) Haven't given it to me</u>'

Examples (4)–(6) show that the verb and/or series of verbs within the Spanish verbal group act as a kind of 'nucleus' to which clitic elements can be closely associated as 'satellites'. The examples also show that such satellites cannot be adequately represented in univariate terms. A nucleus–satellite interpretation of structure has been associated in SFL literature with a 'molecular' view of experiential structure that goes beyond a strictly 'constituency-based' multivariate interpretation (Halliday 2002 [1979]).

Indeed, Martin (2010 [1996]) suggests that the general multivariate/univariate comple-mentarity can be reinterpreted, within the ideational perspective, as distinct 'nuclearity' patterns entirely dissociated from constituency considerations. For him, ideational clause structure, but also structure at lower ranks, can be generally seen as (both) 'mononuclear' and 'multinuclear'. A *mononuclear* perspective foregrounds one element as the 'centre of gravity' other elements revolve around (Martin 2010 [1996]: 379), while a *multinuclear* perspective foregrounds serial interdependency among elements. Martin (2010 [1996]: 351) interprets such structural patterns as **orbital** and **serial**, respectively. Further, he illustrates how both patterns are useful to interpret the structure of the English nominal group in ways the multivariate/univariate complementarity cannot fully reveal. In an interpretation of the structure of the Spanish verbal group, the orbital/serial complementary perspective also seems to be useful to understand the internal specificities of this class (even if a clear relation with experiential/logical meanings at this rank remains to be further explored): while TENSE selections appear to favour serial interdependencies that are similar to those suggested for the English verbal group, the relation between clitic elements and the verb(s) more clearly suggests an orbital pattern.

Spanish clitics are generally considered in descriptive work as closer to affixal particles than to words proper. Among the main reasons supporting this view, it can be mentioned that clitics are phonologically weak particles requiring the presence of at least one verb; there-fore they can never appear on their own in elliptical structures, unlike clause constituents such as nominal groups. As already seen in the examples (4)–(6), Spanish clitics include not only pronominal clitics (accusative and dative) realising Participants at clause rank, but also other morpheme-like elements involved in VOICE systems at group rank. In addition, clit-ics may form 'clusters' or fixed combinations of (generally up to) two particles, and these clusters are highly restricted in terms of both their internal sequence and their positioning with respect to the 'verbal part' of the verbal group. Finally, these particles in Spanish are also associated with a phenomenon known as 'clitic doubling' that allows the simultaneous realisation of Participants by nominal groups (at clause rank) and co-referential pronominal clitics (at group rank).[6]

The very brief exploration presented here suggests that the internal organisation of the Spanish verbal group cannot be accounted for only in terms of serial or univariate patterns; a complementary orbital perspective on structure, taking into account the specific pattern-ing of clitic elements, is needed to supplement it. The emphasis on any single perspective would fail to capture all of the relevant generalisations concerning the internal organisa-tion of this class in Spanish, as well as important contrasts with other languages, such as English and French.[7] This resonates with the descriptive generalisation that the twofold view on structure – associated with the complementarity between logical and experiential patterns – reveals different tensions across languages (Matthiessen 2004: 575*ff*). In rela-tion to the Spanish verbal group, it raises the question of the extent to which this class at group/phrase rank could be better analysed as a **verbal phrase** – that is, as a 'mini clause' – rather than the simple expansion of a 'verb word'.[8] It also shows that the contribution of clitic elements to clause structure (in different metafunctions) is far from straightforward. Importantly, this exploration shows that even if the same 'verbal group' label is used, the specific organisation of this group/phrase class can be – and needs to be – explicitly moti-vated. In the account proposed here, this motivation is ultimately based on the interaction of system–structure relations across ranks, not on the simple application of the 'consist of' principle associated with a narrow conceptualisation of the rank scale (Quiroz 2013).

Main research methods

The discussion in this chapter points towards the need for a meta-descriptive reflection (Davidse, this volume) that makes explicit theoretical and descriptive assumptions in relation to the status of the verbal group as a descriptive grammatical category both in English and in other languages. The more abstract theoretical constructs underlying descriptive principles seem rarely to be at stake in discussion leading to the establishment (or rejection) of this class; therefore the challenge is to frame comparison, assessment and criticism not only in terms of the descriptive approach adopted, but also, critically, in terms of the theoretical framework to which such an approach can be explicitly related. This also has, of course, an impact on the methods being assumed, whether these are conceptualised as part of a series of ordered 'stages', as in the Cardiff Model (for example Fawcett 2000c: 147), or else in terms of different sets of methodological assumptions revolving around (clause) systems, as in the Sydney Model (for example Halliday 2003 [1992]). In this regard, the key distinction between the theoretical and the descriptive plane is again highly relevant. This distinction can be even more critical when, within the same model, the status of classes (of units) that might be considered analogous (or not) to the English verbal group is at stake in the description of other languages.

The review of what has been proposed by the Cardiff Model reveals that a discussion around the English verbal group that does not take into account the system–structure interrelations underlying the standard Sydney Model can be difficult to relate to a number of issues in linguistic description. Likewise, addressing broader questions on the nature of abstract theoretical categories, such as the rank scale, may be also problematic when key assumptions are left out of the discussion. There remains the question of what is being privileged in the assessment of the rank scale as a theoretical dimension: constituency framed in terms of compositional relations, or mutually defining system–structure relations across ranks?[9]

On the other hand, the exploration of relevant patterns in Chilean Spanish indicates that the establishment of the verbal group as a general descriptive category capturing useful cross-linguistic generalisations can be problematic when seen solely from the point of view of whole–part relations and/or syntagmatic patterns. An attempt has been made to show that, within the Sydney Model, system–structure relations are crucial for an explicit account of what can be (or not) considered as analogous to the English verbal group, thus allowing for a principled cross-linguistic comparison (and assessment).

Consequently, rather than adopting a clear-cut position in relation to the methodological implications of the exploration presented here, a number of exploratory questions can be proposed around the descriptive status of the verbal group (or any other grammatical category), as follows.

- Generally speaking, are mutually defining system–structure relations being assumed, including interconnections *across ranks, strata and metafunctions*, when setting up units and classes of units (for example Martin 2013)? Or are we starting from a whole set of different (theoretical, descriptive and methodological) assumptions (for example Fawcett 2000c)?
- What is the point of departure in the description: interconnected systems of relations involving higher-rank units such as the clause, or a compositional, constituency approach to structure?
- How are elements in a metafunctionally diversified interpretation of clause structure mapped onto units at the rank immediately below in English and *across* languages?

- Are different types of structure associated with different metafunctions taken into account (for example Halliday 2002 [1979]; Martin 2010 [1996])? Or is the functionally neutral principle of 'total accountability' being favoured?
- Finally, is systemic recursion and/or serial structure the only possibility when accounting for the internal organisation of the verbal group in English (cf. Bache 2008) and other languages (cf. Quiroz 2013)?

Further, from the point of view of SFL language typology framed in the Sydney Model (for example Caffarel et al. 2004), one key question is to what extent different phenomena, from different languages, can be productively called by the same descriptive name (Halliday 2003 [1992]: 205) – that is, what the basis is for using the 'verbal group' as a label to capture relevant generalisations. If the same label is indeed productive, is this explicitly shown and argued for? Or is the 'transfer comparison' method being loosely applied without a critical and/or systematic argumentation and assessment (cf. Halliday 2003 [1992]: 204*ff*)? What happens in the SFL description of non-Indo-European languages in which the specific status (and motivation) of the verbal group may be even more obscure? Should a verbal group be assumed at all in SFL cross-linguistic work? Is such an assumption productive when looking at the specific organisation of different languages? Is it possible that we are simply forcing categories that have evolved from the description of English patterns onto other languages and, in so doing, making other languages look 'exotic' as a result (Halliday 1966b [1959–60]: 179)?

Notes

1 For an account of the English verbal group multivariate structure, including Finite, Polarity and Event functions, see, e.g. Halliday (1994: 198); Halliday and Matthiessen (2014: 398).
2 For a critical review of this description in relation to the treatment of 'aspectuality' in different functional frameworks, see Butler (2003: 490*ff*).
3 For alternative accounts of the main arguments provided by Fawcett, see McGregor (1996) and Morley (2001).
4 Cf. Martin (1992); for a different interpretation of the function of Spanish clitics in clause structure, particularly in relation to theme, see Arús, this volume.
5 For an alternative SFL account of these distinctions, see Arús (2006).
6 Cf. Quiroz (2013) for an in-depth discussion.
7 For a detailed argumentation, see Quiroz (2013).
8 For the conceptualisation of groups and phrases in SFL, see McDonald, this volume.
9 For the latter, see Halliday (2013) and Martin (2013).

References

Arús, J. 2006. Perspectiva sistémico-funcional de los usos de 'se' en español. *Revista signos* 39(61): 131–59.
Bache, C. 2008. *English Tense and Aspect in Halliday's Systemic Functional Grammar: A Critical Appraisal and an Alternative*. London: Equinox.
Butler, C. 2003. *Structure and Function: A Guide to Three Major Structural-Functional Theories, Part 1 – Approaches to the Simplex Clause*. Amsterdam: John Benjamins.
Caffarel, A. 1992. Interacting between a generalized tense semantics and register-specific semantic tense systems: A bistratal exploration of the semantics of French tense. *Language Sciences* 14(4): 385–418.

Caffarel, A., J.R. Martin and C.M.I.M. Matthiessen (eds). 2004. *Language Typology: A Functional Perspective*. Amsterdam: John Benjamins.

Fawcett, R. 2000a. In place of Halliday's 'verbal group', part 1: Evidence from the problems of Halliday's representations and the relative simplicity of the proposed alternative. *WORD* 51(2): 157–203.

Fawcett, R. 2000b. In place of Halliday's 'verbal group', part 2: Evidence from generation, semantics and interruptability. *WORD* 51(3): 327–75.

Fawcett, R. 2000c. *A Theory of Syntax for Systemic Functional Linguistics*. Amsterdam: John Benjamins.

Figueredo, G. 2011. Introdução ao perfil metafuncional do português brasileiro: Contribuições para os estudos multilíngues. Unpublished PhD dissertation. Universidade Federal de Minas Gerais, Belo Horizonte.

Firth, J.R. 1957. A synopsis of linguistic theory, 1930–55. In J.R. Firth, W. Haas and M.A.K. Halliday (eds) *Studies in Linguistic Analysis*. Oxford: Basil Blackwell, pp. 1–32.

Gouveia, C. 2010. Towards a profile of the interpersonal organization of the Portuguese clause. *Documentação de Estudos em Lingüística Teórica e Aplicada* 26(1): 1–24.

Halliday, M.A.K. 1961. Categories of the theory of grammar. *WORD* 17(3): 241–92.

Halliday, M.A.K. 1966a. Some notes on 'deep' grammar. *Journal of Linguistics* 2(1): 57–67.

Halliday, M.A.K. 1966b [1959–60]. Typology and the exotic. In M.A.K. Halliday and A. McIntosh (eds) *Patterns of Language: Papers in General Descriptive and Applied Linguistics*. London: Longmans, pp. 165–82.

Halliday, M.A.K. 1969. Options and functions in the English clause. *Brno Studies in English* 8: 81–8.

Halliday, M.A.K. 1970. Functional diversity in language as seen from a consideration of modality and mood in English. *Foundations of Language* 6(3): 322–61.

Halliday, M.A.K. 1976 [1964]. English system networks. In G.R. Kress (ed.) *Halliday: System and Function in Language*. London: Oxford University Press, pp. 101–35.

Halliday, M.A.K. 1976 [1966]. The English verbal group. In G.R. Kress (ed.) *Halliday: System and Function in Language*. London: Oxford University Press, pp. 136–58.

Halliday, M.A.K. 1981 [1964]. Syntax and the consumer. In M.A.K. Halliday and J.R. Martin (eds) *Readings in Systemic Linguistics*. London: Batsford, pp. 21–8.

Halliday, M.A.K. 1981 [1965]. Types of structure. In M.A.K. Halliday and J.R. Martin (eds) *Readings in Systemic Linguistics*. London: Batsford, pp. 29–41.

Halliday, M.A.K. 1985. *An Introduction to Functional Grammar*. London: Arnold.

Halliday, M.A.K. 1994. *An Introduction to Functional Grammar*. 2nd edn. London: Arnold.

Halliday, M.A.K. 2002 [1970]. Language structure and language function. In J.J. Webster (ed.) *Collected Works of M.A.K. Halliday, Vol. 1: On Grammar*. London: Continuum, pp. 173–95.

Halliday, M.A.K. 2002 [1979]. Modes of meaning and modes of expression: Types of grammatical structure and their determination by different semantic functions. In J.J. Webster (ed.) *Collected Works of M.A.K. Halliday, Vol. 1: On Grammar*. London: Continuum, pp. 196–218.

Halliday, M.A.K. 2002 [1996]. On grammar and grammatics. In J.J. Webster (ed.) *Collected Works of M.A.K. Halliday, Vol. 1: On Grammar*. London: Continuum, pp. 384–417.

Halliday, M.A.K. 2003 [1992]. Systemic grammar and the concept of a 'science of language'. In J.J. Webster (ed.) *Collected Works of M.A.K. Halliday, Vol. 3: On Language and Linguistics*. London: Continuum, pp. 199–212.

Halliday, M.A.K. 2013. Meaning as choice. In L. Fontaine, T. Bartlett and G. O'Grady (eds) *Systemic Functional Linguistics: Exploring Choice*. Cambridge: Cambridge University Press, pp. 15–36.

Halliday, M.A.K., and C.M.I.M. Matthiessen. 2004. *An Introduction to Functional Grammar*. 3rd edn. London: Hodder Arnold.

Halliday, M.A.K., and C.M.I.M. Matthiessen. 2014. *Halliday's Introduction to Functional Grammar*. 4th edn. London: Routledge.

Hudson, R.A. 1981 [1972]. An 'item-and-paradigm' approach to Beja syntax and morphology. In M.A.K. Halliday and J.R. Martin (eds) *Readings in Systemic Linguistics*. London: Batsford, pp. 371–409.

Lavid, J., J. Arús and J.R. Zamorano Mansilla. 2010. *Systemic Functional Description of Spanish: A Contrastive Study with English*. London: Continuum.

Martin, J.R. 1992. *English Text: System and Structure*. Amsterdam: John Benjamins.

Martin, J.R. 2010 [1996]. Types of structure: deconstructing notions of constituency in clause and text. In Z. Wang (ed.) *SFL Theory*. Shanghai: Shanghai Jiao Tong University Press, pp. 343–85.

Martin, J.R. 2013. *Systemic Functional Grammar: A Next Step into the Theory–Axial Relations*. Beijing: Higher Education Press.

Matthiessen, C.M.I.M. 1984. *Choosing Tense in English*. ISI Research Report. Information Sciences Institute, University of Southern California.

Matthiessen, C.M.I.M. 1995. *Lexicogrammatical Cartography: English Systems*. Tokyo: International Language Sciences.

Matthiessen, C.M.I.M. 2004. Descriptive motifs and generalizations. In A. Caffarel J.R. Martin and C.M.I.M. Matthiessen (eds) *Language Typology: A Functional Perspective*. Amsterdam: John Benjamins, pp. 537–664.

McDonald, E. 2004. Verb and clause in Chinese discourse: Issues of constituency and functionality. *Journal of Chinese Linguistics* 32(2): 200–47.

McGregor, W. 1996. Arguments for the category of verb phrase. *Functions of Language* 3(1): 1–30.

Morley, G.D. 2001. Reaffirming the Predicator and verbal group in systemic grammar: A reply to Fawcett's 'In place of Halliday's verbal group'. *WORD* 52(3): 339–55.

Quiroz, B. 2013. The interpersonal and experiential grammar of Chilean Spanish: Towards a principled systemic-functional description based on axial argumentation. Unpublished PhD dissertation, University of Sydney.

Teruya, K. 2007. *A Systemic Functional Grammar of Japanese*. London: Continuum.

20

The verbal group in French

Alice Caffarel-Cayron

This chapter explores the French verbal group from the perspective of systemic functional linguistics (SFL) theory and, more specifically, Hallidayan linguistics (Halliday 1976, 1994; Halliday and Matthiessen 2004). What, among other things, distinguishes SFL from other functional theories of language is its systemic orientation and its stratification of content into semantics and lexicogrammar (Berry, this volume), thus allowing for an interpretation of grammar as a meaning-making system, for example the interpretation of the semantics of time as realised by the grammatical system of TENSE, one of the verbal group systems that will be discussed in this chapter. Another aspect of SFL is that it prioritises functional categories over grammatical classes. As pointed out by Caffarel and colleagues (2004: 13):

> [A]ny particular descriptive categories such as the system of . . . TENSE, the structural functions of . . . Predicator and the grammatical classes of [verbal] group, verb . . . are realizations of categories defined by the theory – system, structural function, and class.

This chapter's account of the verbal group in French will explore both the systems that are realised at verbal group rank and the functions played by the verbal group within the clause, as well as how those functional components are then realised in the verbal group structure. Systemic functional typological work has shown that:

> Variation across languages seems to be more prominent in the structural or realizational output of the systems and in the more delicate subsystems than in the general systems. This is because the more delicate systems tend to reflect realizational differences whilst the more general systems tend to reflect functional differences.
>
> *Caffarel et al. 2004: 55–8*

First, we discuss some of the dimensions and categories of the theory as pathways for exploring the verbal group of any language, and explore the different contributions of the verbal group to the clause in terms of the three metafunctional components (see Berry, this volume). In addition to contributing to the realisation of meanings at clause rank, the verbal group is the rank location for a number of systems, such as tense, modality, polarity and aspect in French. We will then review some of the work done on French tense, with some reference to aspect.

Systemic functional grammar: metalanguage for exploring the French verbal group

The fundamental organisational principles of SFL – stratum metafunction and rank – provide a framework for exploring the verbal group. In French, the verbal group is a realisational unit that forms a constituent structure at the rank below the clause in the lexicogrammar (see McDonald, this volume). It realises interpersonal and experiential functions in the clause, but also serves as entry condition to the systems of TENSE and ASPECT (ideational grammatical construal of time), MODALITY (interpersonal: modulation and modalisation) and VOICE (textual: active versus passive).

Thus the verbal group in French is significant in realising meanings in the clause across the different metafunctions – ideational (clause as representation), interpersonal (clause as exchange) – and textual (clause as message), as illustrated in Tables 20.1 and 20.2 showing the metafunctional analysis of example (1), an active clause, and example (2), a passive clause, respectively, based on Caffarel's (2006) account of French grammar.

(1) *Le chat a attrapé une souris dans la cuisine*
('The cat caught a mouse in the kitchen')

(2) *Une souris a été attrapée par le chat dans la cuisine*
('A mouse was caught by the cat in the kitchen')

Tables 20.1 and 20.2 indicate that the verbal group is interpreted as the unit within which the Process and the Finite/Predicator are realised. Within the experiential metafunction, the function of Process encodes a particular domain of experience, such as material, mental or relational. It is the nucleus of the clause as representation and it can, at times, be interpreted as its sole realisational component, as we will see shortly. We will then go on to illustrate that, within the interpersonal metafunction, both the Finite and the Predicator are essential to the realisation of the exchange: the Finite expresses tense (and modality), whilst the Predicator specifies the content of the process, but also secondary tense, aspect and voice. Next, we will see that, textually, the verbal group of French does not realise a particular function, but is typically unmarked thematically and, in examples (1) and (2), it forms part

Table 20.1 Metafunctional analysis of example (1)

	Le chat	a	attrapé	une souris	dans la cuisine
systemic features of clause	{indicative: declarative: . . . ; material & effective: . . . ; unmarked theme & active . . . }				
interpersonal: modal structure	Subject	Finite	Predicator	Complement	Adjunct
experiential: transitivity structure	Actor/Agent		Process	Goal/Medium	Circumstance: Place
textual: thematic structure	Theme		Rheme		
features of realising unit	{nominal group}	{verbal group: active}		{nom. group}	{prepositional phrase}

Table 20.2 Metafunctional analysis of example (2)

	Une souris	*a été*	*attrapée*	*par le chat*	*dans la cuisine*
systemic features of clause	{indicative: declarative: . . . ; material & effective: . . . ; unmarked theme & passive: agentive . . . }				
interpersonal: modal structure	Subject	Finite	Predicator	Complement	circumstantial Adjunct
experiential: transitivity structure	Goal/Medium	Process		Actor/Agent	Circ: Place
textual: thematic structure	Theme	Rheme			
features of realising unit	{nom. gp.}	[verbal group: passive}		{prep. phrase}	{prep.phrase}

of the Rheme.[1] In addition, as shown in Caffarel (2006), participants that are pronominal-ised and prefixed to the verbal group function as Given in the informational structure of the clause. We will come back to this later in the chapter, when we highlight the textual motiva-tion between pronominalising participant or not.

As a preliminary insight into some of the features of the French verbal group, let us explore example (3), a clause complex taken from de Beauvoir's (1946) *Tous les hommes sont mortels*. The verbal groups in each clause are in bold italic. Example (3a) is a project-ing clause, with a mental process realised by a complex verbal group in which the main event is *savoir* hypotactically expanded from the modal verb *vouloir*; example (3b) is a pro-jected clause, with a material process realised by a verbal group with a complex tense, *avait enfermé*, which is a Past in relation to a Past (past-in-past).[2]

(3a) *Je **voudrais bien savoir***
    Lit. 'I would like well to know'
    ('I would really like to know')

(3b) *pourquoi on **l'avait enfermé***
    ('why they locked him up')

In example (3a), the verbal group consists of a modal verb, *vouloir*, followed by a 'modal Adjunct', *bien*, followed by the main Event, *savoir*. Unlike in English, modal verbs in French can select for primary tense and, in this particular instance, we have a future in rela-tion to the past. Note that, in English, we interpret *want* as a mental process rather than as a modal verb, because it can select for primary tense unlike modal verbs in English such as *must* and *can*. Typically, when *vouloir* is a modal verb in French rather than a mental process, it is translated as *like* in English, as in *je voudrais un café* ('I would like a coffee'). In example (3a), the verbal group *voudrais savoir* functions as a modulated mental process in the experiential structure and as Finite^Predicator in the interpersonal structure, which, with the Subject *je* and the Modal Adjunct *bien*, function as the Negotiator of the clause. The function of the Negotiator in the French clause as exchange will be explained later in the chapter.[3] In example (3b), the verbal group includes also the direct complement pronoun *le*. We will see below that once a function that pertains to what we call the 'Remainder' (analogous to the Residue in English) is pronominalised and placed before the verbal group, such as the Complement, it becomes part of the Negotiator.[4] The Negotiator will be shown to be the most salient element in the interpersonal structure of the clause, which maps onto what is experientially the clause nucleus. In the following sections, we will explore how the French verbal group contributes to the realisation of experiential, interpersonal and textual meanings in some more detail.

The role of the verbal group in the experiential structure

In this section, we further explore the function of the verbal group in the transitivity structure of the French clause. We argue that it forms the nucleus of the French clause as representation. The nuclear nature of the Process is foregrounded by the fact that nuclear participants and nuclear circumstances can agglutinate to the Process to construe experiential meaning. At times, when all participants are pronominalised, including the Subject, the verbal group can be interpreted as the only element through which the functional structures of the clause are realised even though French transitivity systems are clearly clausal systems. However, they may be realised at clause rank, as in example (4), or verbal group rank with pre-selection at clause rank, as in example (5). The choice between pronominalising or not pronominalising participants or circumstances is a textual one, which will be illustrated later in the chapter.

(4) *Marie **parle** à son fils*
   ('Marie speaks to her son')

(5) ***Elle lui parle***
   Lit. 'She to him speaks'
   ('She speaks to him')

Let us examine further the placement of complement pronouns in French in relation to the verbal group. Complement pronouns typically precede the verbal group, whether simple or complex. Thus, in a clause in which the verbal group realises a complex series of temporal relations, complement pronouns precede the finite, as we saw in example (3b) and is also illustrated in example (6) below.

(6) *Je le lui **avait réparé***
   Lit. 'I it to him had fixed'
   ('I had fixed it for him')

Similarly, in an analytically causative clause in which the verbal group is complex, complement pronouns precede the causative, *faire*, as in example (7).[5]

(7) *Je te le **ferai réparer***
   Lit. 'I to you it will make to fix'
   ('I will make you fix it')

On the other hand, in clauses in which there is a modal verb followed by a non-finite verb, the complement pronouns precede the non-finite verb, as in examples (8) and (9). This would suggest that the modal verbs are not expansions of the main verb, as is the causative *faire*, but are independent from it. We can argue that there are, in fact, two different types of verbal group complex in French: those in which the two verbs are closely related, as in example (7); and those that are serial verb constructions in which each verb has its own domain of participation, as in examples (8) and (9).

(8) *Je **veux** le lui **demander***
     Lit. 'I want it to him to ask'
     ('I want to ask him about it')

(9) *Il ne **pouvait** pas lui **répondre***
     Lit. 'He not could not to him to answer'
     ('He could not answer him')

In French, only the verb *vouloir*, when projecting an idea, can truly be considered as a mental process functioning at clause rank. In contrast, both *pouvoir* and *devoir* cannot project; rather, they modify the main Process and, as a consequence, can be used in clauses with non-conscious participants, as in *cet appartement doit être cher* ('this apartment must be expensive'). As shown in example (9), verbal group systems in French – TENSE, MODALITY and POLARITY – are all simultaneous choices: we can choose past tense + imperfective aspect + modality: ability, as in example (9), or past tense + perfective aspect + modality: obligation + negative polarity, for instance, as in example (10).

(10) *Il n'a pas **dû** écouter*
      Subj-3rd-pers-sg + negclitic + modal: primary past + perfective + negative Adj + Pred
      Lit. 'He not has not must to listen'
      ('He must not have listened')

In contrast, in English, it is not possible to choose modality and primary tense. There are not future and past options of *must*, for instance. In French, it can select simultaneously for a primary tense: *je dois* (present); *je devais* (imperfect past); *je devrai* (future), etc.[6]

In addition, one can add the feature of Voice, which distinguishes between an active and a passive verbal group. Example (10) has an active verbal group, but we could also have the feature passive added to it, as in example (11).

(11) *Il n'a pas **dû** être écouté*
      ('He must not have been listened to')

The verbal group can be expanded through hypotaxis not only to express modality, as in examples (8)–(11), but also to express phase/time (example (12)), causality (example (13)), time (example (14)), and more complex relations between ability, phase and time (example (15)).

(12) *Elle **a commencé** à écrire un livre*
      ('She has started to write a book')

(13) *Elle **a fait** mourir son poisson*
      Lit. She has made to die her fish
      ('She made her fish die')

(14) *Elle **va écrire** demain*
      ('She is going to write tomorrow')

(15) *Elle n'**arrive** toujours pas **à finir d'écrire** son livre*
      Lit. She not arrives always not to finish of to write her book
      ('She still has not succeeded in finishing writing her book')

This last example can be analysed in terms of the logical metafunction as a hypotactic expansion directed toward the main event *écrire*: (α *n'arrive toujours pas* β *à finir* γ *d'écrire*).[7]

This section has shown that the French verbal group can be simplex or complex and that it functions as Process in the transitivity structure of the clause. We also saw that, when participants are pronominalised, all transitivity functions can be interpreted as realised within the verbal group. Not only participants, but also some circumstances have the potential of being prefixed to the verbal group, as seen in examples (16)–(18). The constituents in bold italic/bold represent the circumstances that are nuclear in the sense that they can be pronominalised and positioned before the verbal group.

(16) *Elle va **à la plage***
      ('She goes **to the beach**')
      *Elle **y** (Circ: destination) va*
      ('She **there** goes')

(17) *Elle vient **de Bordeaux***
      ('She comes **from Bordeaux**')
      *Elle **en** (Circ: Source) vient*
      '(She **from there** comes')

(18) *Elle parle **de son travail***
      ('She is talking **of her work**')
      *Elle **en** (Circ: Matter) parle*
      ('She **of it** speaks')

The flexible nature of the order of constituents in the French clause respective to the realisational location of transitivity functions (*Elle regarde la lune* [Subject^Verb^Object]/ *Elle la regarde* [Subject^Object^Verb]) show that a word rank approach to typology, whereby French is typically seen as an SVO language, is limiting and that we need to have a top-to-bottom approach to bring out similarities across languages that may have been considered very different from a formal perspective (Caffarel et al. 2004).

The role of the verbal group in the interpersonal structure

In this section, we explore further the role of the verbal group in the interpersonal structure of the clause. We saw in the last section that, in the indicative clause, the main functional components of the verbal group are the Finite and Predicator, and that, together with the Subject and at times Complement and/or Adjunct (when pronominalised), they form the Negotiator of the clause, which are essential to the negotiation process, as shown in example (19), a text sample. The Negotiator in French is functionally analogous to the Mood element in English, but whereas in English the negotiation is carried forward by the Subject + Finite, in French it is carried forward by the Subject + Finite + Predicator, with the possibility of including pronominalised participants, as in the exchange in example (19). What does not enter in the Negotiator will be referred to as the 'Remainder' of the clause. The terms 'Negotiator' and 'Remainder' have also been used for the description of Vietnamese (Thai 2004) and Chilean Spanish (Quiroz 2013) – languages in which the Predicator is also crucial to the negotiation process and cannot be omitted as in English.

(19) A. [Negotiator] **Tu as vu** [Remainder] *le dernier film de Ken Loach?*
   Lit. 'You have seen the last film of Ken Loach?'
   ('Have you seen Ken Loach's new film?')

B. *Non,* [Negotiator] *je ne l'ai pas encore vu.*
   Lit. 'No, I not it have not yet seen.'
   ('No, not yet.')

A. [Negotiator] **Tu devrais aller le voir,** [Negotiator] *c'est* [Remainder] *super.*
   Lit. 'You should go it to see, it is great.'
   ('You should: it's great.')

In this exchange, the Complement introduced in the Rheme in the first move becomes part of the locus of the exchange, and so part of the Negotiator in the second and third moves, by being pronominalised and prefixed to the verbal group.

Caffarel's (1995, 2006) interpretation of the interpersonal structure of the French clause in terms of a Negotiator and Remainder has been criticised by Banks (2010: 406), who suggests that the two labels are interchangeable in that 'the Negotiator–Remainder works for English, and the Mood–Residue structure works for French'. However, his argument is essentially formal, and does not take into account the differences in the negotiation process in French and English, simply seeing those descriptive categories as labels that can be applied to any structure irrespective of their function. By applying the English interpersonal structure to French, the central nature of the verbal group in French, with Finite and Predicator functioning together with the Subject – and, at times, pronominalised Complement and Circumstances as previously shown – for the negotiation to move forward, is lost.

One of the examples that Banks (2010: 403) analyses is that in example (20a).

(20a) *Vous avez compris le message?*
   Lit. 'You have understood the message?'
   ('Have you understood the message?')

This might be analysed as in example (20b), based on Caffarel (2006).

(20b)	*Vous*	*avez*	*compris*	*le message?*
	Subject	Finite	Predicator	Complement
	Negotiator			Remainder

Banks (2010: 403), however, suggests that it could be analysed as in example (20c).

(20c) *Vous*	*avez*	*compris*	*le message?*
Subject	Finite	Predicator	Complement
Mood		Residue	

Banks (2010: 403) adds that '[t]he first example has a Mood made up of Subject + Finite, *Vous avez*, with *compris le message* constituting the Residue. This seems straightforward and poses no problems.'

The application of labels to constituents irrespective of their function in discourse can be considered to be a significant problem. Here, we have an analysis that applies the structure of English onto French, with the result of separating the Finite and Predicator in French, which is not the case for negotiation in French, as has been shown by the examples of exchanges in the previous discussion. A potential reply to the question *Vous avez compris le message?* could simply be *Oui* ('Yes') or *Non* ('No'), where both Negotiator and Remainder are elliptical, or *Oui, je l'ai compris* ('Yes, I've understood it') or *Non, je ne l'ai pas compris* ('No, I haven't understood it'), where the complement is pronominalised to the verbal group and enter the negotiation process. It is impossible in French to omit the Predicator in the reply as in English. So one cannot say **Oui, je l'ai* ('Yes, I have') or **J'ai* ('I have'). The central role of the Predicator in the negotiation is one of the main motivating factors for having labels different from those of English.

If we were to decide to keep the Mood–Residue labelling of English and apply it to the French interpersonal structure, then it would still have to reflect the discourse-semantic differences that exist between French and English in the way that they negotiate meaning and in the way they realise speech functions. Thus if we were to apply the labels Mood and Residue to example (20a), the analysis would have to reflect the semantics of exchange of French. The analysis proposed in example (20d), based on Banks (2010), would work, but new labels have been adopted because the notion of Mood is so closely associated with Subject and Finite alone. Since the terms 'Negotiator' and 'Remainder' were proposed for the analysis of the French interpersonal structure, they have also been used for the description of Vietnamese (Thai 2004) and Chilean Spanish (Quiroz 2013, 2015), and are also discussed in Gouveia (2010) in the context of the interpersonal structure of Portuguese.

(20d) *Vous*	*avez*	*compris*	*le message?*
Subject	Finite	Predicator	Complement
Mood			Residue

Similarly, if we were to apply the Negotiator–Remainder labels to English, the analysis should still reflect the specificities of English with regard to the negotiation of an exchange and the realisation of Mood options, as in example (21a), based on Banks (2010: 405).

(21a) *Have*	*I*	*misled*	*her?*
Subject	Finite	Predicator	Complement
Negotiator (Mood)		Remainder (Residue)	

Banks suggests that example (21) could easily be analysed with the categories of French as laid out in example (21b).

(21b) *Have*	*I*	*misled*	*her?*
Subject	Finite	Predicator	Complement
Negotiator			Remainder

Banks (2010: 405) concludes:

> Here we have an inversion with explicit Finite and Predicator, so that the Finite precedes, and the Predicator follows the Subject. The Finite + Subject + Predicator, *Have I misled*, is thus analysed as Negotiator, with *her* as Remainder. This seems to work perfectly well.

However, such an analysis does not bring out the crucial role of the Subject + Finite in realising Mood options in English and in carrying the negotiation, and implies that the Predicator is part of it.

The choice of new labels for French was motivated by the differences that exist between French and English modal structures, the realisation of Mood options and the process of exchange. In exploring the role of the verbal group in dialogue in French, it made sense to apply different labels from those of English to capture the different functions in discourse.

The role of the verbal group in the textual structure

From the point of view of the textual metafunction, the verbal group in French is non-prominent textually in the declarative clause. Also known as the 'enabling' function, the textual metafunction provides the resources for assigning different textual statuses to clausal elements. The system of THEME and the INFORMATION FOCUS system are two of the systems that are concerned with the assignment of textual statuses: thematic prominence and newsworthiness, respectively. From a discourse perspective, thematic information relates to the method of development – that is, the mode of expansion of the text – while the information that is new typically foregrounds the 'main point' (Fries 1981). In French, as in English, the Theme of the clause – that is, its point of departure – is located in initial position and functions similarly from a discourse perspective. For this reason, we find no need to change the labelling of the Theme–Rheme structure.

With regard to the INFORMATION FOCUS system, Halliday (1978: 133) writes:

> Since it is realized through intonation, which is not shown in the writing system, the information structure is a feature of the spoken language only; and any interpretation of the information structure of a written text depends on the 'implication of utterance' which is a feature of written language. There are two aspects to this: (i) the interpretation of the paragraphological signals that the written language employs, such as punctuation, underlining and other form of emphasis; (ii) the assumption of the 'good reason' principle, namely that the mapping of the information structure onto other structures will take the unmarked form except where there is good reason for it to do otherwise.

In French, as in English, new information typically falls at the end of the information unit, of which the grammatical correlate is, in the unmarked case, the clause. Thus the New often maps onto the Rheme of the thematic structure and this can be used as the default case for analysing new information in written texts. However, when the New and Rheme are separated, the grammar of French gives us other means of identifying the New. For example, in French, absolute Themes – that is, Themes that are outside the experiential/interpersonal structure, such as prominent pronominals (pronouns that cannot be positioned before the verbal group) – are typically New (see Figure 20.1). These grammatical clues provide a means for interpreting New elements in texts expressed graphically.

Although there appears to be a correlation between types of Theme and the mapping of Theme onto Given or New, it is important to stress here that, in SFL, 'the choice of whether to treat some item as Theme is basically independent of the choice of whether to treat that item as given or new information' (Fries 1981: 136). This separating approach to thematic and information structures contrasts with the combining approach of French functionalists such as that of Combettes (1975) and Hagège (1985).

As Figure 20.1 shows and as stated by Matthiessen (1995: 716), '[t]he verbal group is in fact often a textual transition between Theme and New'.

This is further illustrated by example (22), in which transitivity roles are prefixed to the verbal group, realised as non-prominent pronouns, and prominent pronouns (*Moi, à elle*), in addition to the nominal group, *l'article*, function as Absolute Themes outside the clause nucleus and are marked as New. Each absolute Theme is co-referential with a transitivity role within the experiential structure of the clause.

> (22)   *Moi, l'article, **je le lui ai donné**, à elle*
>   Lit. 'Me, the article, **I it to her have given**, to her'
>   ('I gave **her** the article')

Here, the first two elements *Moi* and *l'article* function as Absolute Theme and Contrastive New, and *à elle* is late News. As already mentioned, an absolute Theme is a Theme that does not have an experiential or interpersonal role. Its sole function is textual and it serves to indicate what the clause is about. The non-prominent pronouns – that is, those that can be prefixed to the verbal group and enter the negotiation – indicate the experiential and interpersonal roles of the participants introduced at the beginning and end of the clause as absolute Theme and late News.

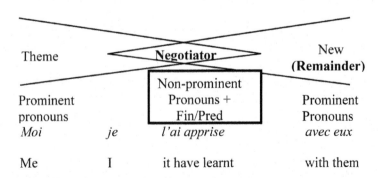

Figure 20.1   The verbal group: at the transition of the textual waves

Textually, the verbal group is also the locus for the realisation of the VOICE system: operative [active verbal group] versus receptive [passive verbal group]. In French, the system has fewer options than that of English: the bene-receptive option in French cannot be used with the *être* passive verbal group. In other words, the conflation of the Beneficiary and Subject functions is not possible with the basic types of receptive clause. However, as Judges and Healey (1985: 205–6) note:

> [A]n English passive sentence such as 'her father was offered a book' cannot be passivized in French in normal ways; but it can be translated into French by a passive substitute such as *son père s'est vu offrir un livre*.

To render the English receptive clause, the French uses a middle clause – that is, a clause without an Agent. The fact that middle clauses in French are very productive (Caffarel 2006) and can be used as an alternative to agentless receptive clauses partly explains why receptive clauses (with passive verbal group) in French are not as widely used as in English. An effective clause – that is, a clause with an Agent – may be operative (active) or receptive (passive) in voice. In an operative clause, the Subject, conflated with unmarked Theme, is the Agent; in a receptive clause, which has a passive verbal group, the Subject is the Medium. A receptive clause may be agentive or non-agentive. If agentive, then the Agent is realised by a prepositional phrase of which the preposition is *par*. The examples below are of material effective clauses. Example (23) is an operative clause; example (24) is a receptive: agentive clause; example (25) is a receptive: non-agentive clause.

(23a) *Jean a fermé la porte*
       ('Jean has closed/closed the door')

(23b)	Jean	a fermé	la porte
	Subject	Finite^Predicator	Complement
	Agent	Process: material: effective	Medium
	Theme	Rheme	

(24a) *La porte a été fermée par Jean*
       ('The door has been closed by Jean')

(24b)	La porte	a été fermée	par Jean
	Subject	Fin. pass. Pred	Adjunct
	Medium	Process: material: effective	Agent
	Theme	Rheme	

(25a) *La porte a été fermée*
       ('The door has been closed')

(25b)	La porte	a été fermée
	Subject	Fin. pass Predicator
	Medium	Process: material: effective
	Theme	Rheme

The event encoded in examples (24) and (25) could be construed without expressing what caused the Medium–Process nucleus (*fermer la porte*) and instead be construed by means of a middle clause with a reflexive verbal group, as in example (26).

(26)   [Medium] *La porte* [Process: material: middle] *s'est fermée* (the door shut)

Having discussed the main contributions of the French verbal group to the three metafunctions, we will now turn to the verbal group system of TENSE, which will lead us to discuss aspect as it is conflated with time in the primary past tenses.

The verbal group system of Tense

Formal and traditional approaches to French tense have tended not to recognise the differentiation between the logical and the experiential modes of construing time, because they have focused on word rank, producing morphologically based interpretations of tense resources. Most French grammars interpret tense as a subcategory of the 'tense–aspect' category. Within this macro-grammatical category, tense and aspect counterbalance each other; 'when one increases in strength, the other must necessarily lose strength' (Imbs 1960: 16). Complex tenses are interpreted as a combination of tense plus the perfect aspect (Guillaume 1929; Imbs 1960; Judges and Healey 1985; Wagner and Pinchon 1962), whilst simple tenses are considered to be unmarked for aspect (perfect). The perfect is potentially recursive (Guillaume 1929), which gives rises to the so-called double compound tenses. The main drawback with such an approach, which represents 'tenses' as experiential structures, is its inability to convey the serial meaning of tense, based on repeated tense choices (Halliday 1994).

Tense: a composition of time and aspect

The interpretation of French tense as a composition of time and aspect rather than as the realisation of serial time reflects a word-rank approach to tense complexes rather than exploring how time is realised in the grammar through series of tense selections. A word-rank approach focuses on form rather than on the complex temporal meanings of French complex tenses. For example, Wagner and Pinchon's (1962: 226, author's own translation) chapter on tense in their *Grammaire du Français classique et moderne* starts: 'The indicative comprises five tenses. Each of these tenses has three forms: a simple form, a compound form and a double compound form.' The compound forms are interpreted in terms of aspect rather than time.

Table 20.3 tabulates the five French tenses identified by Wagner and Pinchon (1962). In the first row, the tenses are unmarked for aspect, which Wagner and Pinchon characterise in terms of completion – which is problematic because the imperfect clearly embodies some aspectual meaning. In both the second and third rows, the tenses are marked for aspect. The double-compound forms, in the third row, mark anteriority with respect to the compound forms and thus do encode a temporal relation – but this fact is overlooked by Wagner and Pinchon.

There are a number of inconsistencies in Wagner and Pinchon's (1962) interpretation of French tense. If the *passé antérieur* is a past plus the perfect, why not call it a *passé défini parfait*? If both the *imparfait* and *conditionel* are tenses, why not term them accordingly? The terms *défini* and *indéfini* are also misleading, and contradict Wagner and Pinchon's

Table 20.3 The three forms of the five tenses

présent	*imparfait*	*passé defini*	*future*	*conditionel*
je chante	je chantais	je chantai	je chanterai	je chanterais
('I sing')	('I sang')	('I sang')	(' will sing')	('I would sing')
passé indéfini	***plus-que-parfait***	***passé antérieur***	***futur antérieur***	***conditionel passé***
j'ai chanté	j'avais chanté	j'eus chanté	j'aurai chanté	j'aurais chanté
('I have sung')	('I had sung')	('I have sung')	('I will have sung')	('I would have sung')
passé indéfini surcomposé	***plus-que-parfait surcomposé***	***passé antérieur surcomposé***	***futur antérieur surcomposé***	***conditionel passé surcomposé***
j'ai eu chanté	j'avais eu chanté	j'eus eu chanté	j'aurai eu chanté	j'aurais eu chanté
('I have had sung')	('I had had sung')	('I had had sung')	('I will have had sung')	('I would have had sung')

Source: Wagner and Pinchon (1962)

semantic interpretation of the *passé indéfini* form, *j'ai chanté*, as a present plus the perfect aspect. The label 'indefinite past' implies that the tense to which it refers expresses an unspecified past. The difficulty with this particular tense is that, depending on context, it may construe a simple past or a past in relation to a present (Caffarel 1992). Example (27), taken from *Le Monde*, 13 July 1989 (author's own translation), shows that, as a past, it is not always unspecified.

(27) *Comme je **l'ai indiqué** dans mon précédent article (*Le Monde *du 12 juillet) l'anglais, d'une manièreirrésistible, est en passe de devenir la langue mondiale par excellence comme **l'a été** autrefois le latin pendant des siècles.*

('As I mentioned it in my preceding article (*Le Monde*, 12 July) English, in an unstoppable manner, is about to become the world language *par excellence* as, in the old days, Latin was for centuries.')

In example (27), both past tenses (in bold italic) realise a 'simple' past with reference to a specific time, *12 juillet* and *autrefois*, respectively.

Table 20.3 highlighted an interesting feature of the French tense system – that is, the wide range of past tenses and past complex tenses – and we explore this in more detail in the next section.

Tense: a series of times

The other main approach to the description of French tense consists in exploring how TIME (semantics) is realised by the TENSE system (lexicogrammar) in the context of texts. This is the approach proposed by Halliday (1976) and Caffarel (1992). In systemic terms, 'tense serves to bridge the temporal gap between the interpersonal situation, the interaction between the speaker and listener and the ideational situation, the experience represented in the text by the process and its participants' (Bateman and Matthiessen 1991: 119). Such an approach reveals that the difference between the simple and compound tenses is a matter of 'time' rather than 'aspect'. It follows that the auxiliaries, *avoir* and *être*, are analysed as tense markers expressing a relation of anteriority rather than as aspect markers expressing 'completion'. This does not mean that aspect is not a feature of French, but that complex tenses express series of time (logical perspective) relations rather than time + aspect (experiential perspective). On the other hand, aspect is a feature that allows us to distinguish the primary past tense in French: past imperfect versus simple past/*passé compose*, for example. In *Le bon usage*, Grévisse (1986) insists that *avoir* and *être* are always time auxiliaries. He recognises three groups of tenses (see Table 20.4), in a temporal relationship, corresponding to the three forms, simple (*temps simples*), compound (*temps composés*) and double compound (*temps surcomposés*).

Table 20.4 foregrounds a temporal interpretation of all tenses. For example, *conditionel* has been replaced by *futur du passé* ('future from the past'), which reflects the temporal meaning of the tense to which it refers: that of 'future in relation to a past'. The misleading terms *défini* and *indéfini* are replaced by *simple* and *composé* ('compound') respectively. This has the advantage of highlighting that the two past tenses are formally distinct, but functionally similar, in that they both express a past in relation to the speech time. The *imparfait* does, of course, also construe an aspectual meaning in addition to time, at which we will look shortly. What is highlighted here is that tense complexity construes secondary tense rather than aspect. Aspect, on the other hand, is a distinction that we find in the primary tenses.

In Grévisse's view, a tense may comprise more than one time component, such as the *future antérieur*, which expresses a future time following a past time. Such an approach reflects a linear-time approach to tense (Jespersen 1933) whereby tense is analysed as grammaticalising time segments oriented towards each other on a timeline. On the other hand, the account of French tense that is presented in the next section reflects a serial interpretation of tense, whereby complex tenses are analysed as grammaticalising series of temporal relations rather than a composition of times or time and aspect, thus bringing to the fore the full temporal potential of the French tense system.

A systemic-functional account of the French tense potential

In Halliday's (1994: 198) model, it is 'the logical structure of the verbal group that realizes the system of tense in English and tense in English is a recursive system'; thus TENSE is interpreted in terms of the logical metafunction rather than the experiential metafunction. In French, it is also the logical structure of the verbal group that realises tense, but the system of tense is, contrary to that of English, only partially recursive, and primary past tenses realise both time and aspect.

Table 20.4 Grévisse's (1975) tabulation of French tenses

temps simples	temps composés	temps surcomposés
present	**passé composé**	**passé surcomposé**
je chante	j'ai chanté	j'ai eu chanté
imparfait	**plus-que-parfait**	**plus-que-parfait surcomposé**
je chantais	j'avais chanté	j'avais eu chanté
passé simple	**passé antérieur**	
je chantai	j'eus chanté	
futur simple	**futur antérieur**	**futur antérieur surcomposé**
je chanterai	j'aurai chanté	j'aurai eu chanté
futur du passé	**futur antérieur du passé**	**futur antérieur du passé**
je chanterais	j'aurais chanté	**surcomposé**
		j'aurais eu chanté

French has five primary tense options: three pasts, one present and one future. The three primary pasts – the simple past, the compound past and the imperfect past – are interpreted as identical in terms of their temporal meaning (that is, their semantic *valeur* in the general system), but as different in terms of their uses and aspectual *valeurs* (Caffarel 1992). The imperfect past, in addition to expressing precedence in relation to a reference time that is the speech time, also encodes an aspectual meaning embodied in the term 'imperfect'. This past tense presents the events from an internal perspective – that is, as seen from within the situation. The difference between the simple past and compound past is registerial: they are used in different textual environments, with the simple past being the tense of narration in literary text, whilst the compound past is the tense of narration in spoken language. Both present events from an external perspective as completed at a particular point in time.

The five primary tense options and their realisations can be mapped as in Table 20.5. The table represents the options available in the primary tense system with their realisations and an instantiation of their use. The realisations represent third-person endings.

The serial character of tense complexes implies a linearly recursive tense system. This means that the system may be re-entered. Whilst the tense system of English is fully recursive in that past, present or future may be reselected (Matthiessen 1996), the recursivity behind French tense is partial.[8] Only past and future options can be reselected. In other words, the French tense system does not allow for the selection of a second-order present. Moreover, the future may be reselected only once and under specific conditions. Thus the systemic recursivity of the French tense system is particularly elaborated for the past.

As we move from secondary to tertiary tense selection, the number of options is reduced. This shows that the recursivity of the French tense system is restricted, as shown in Table 20.6.

The notion of linear recursivity, highlighted by a group-rank approach to tense, is essential to the description of both English and French tense systems, and is the key to the dynamic process that leads to the realisation of serial time. This principle of recursivity makes possible the interpretation of the tense complexes of French in terms of repeated time selections. Whereas the tense simplexes presented in Table 20.6 relate the event time directly to the speech time, tense complexes do so through a chain or series of (maximally four) temporal relations. Accordingly, tense complexes are said to represent serial time.

Table 20.5 Primary tenses and their realisations

primary tense		realisation (based on third-person singular ending)	instantiation
present		–ø	George mange une pomme ('George is eating an apple')
	imperfect past	–ait	George mangeait une pomme et Pierre faisait la vaisselle ('George was eating an apple and Pierre was washing the dishes')
past	simple past	–a	Quand Pierre arriva, George chanta ('When Pierre arrived, George sang')
	compound past	a/est verb–é(e)	Quand Pierre est arrivé, George a chanté ('When Pierre arrived, George sang')
future		–ra	Quand Pierre arrivera, il sera trop tard ('When Pierre arrives, it will be too late')

Alice Caffarel-Cayron

Table 20.6 Reduction in systemic recursivity

	primary	secondary	tertiary	quaternary
past	Yes	Yes	Yes	Yes
present	Yes	No	No	No
future	Yes	Yes	No	No

Source: Caffarel (1992: 392)

Tense combinations are labelled 'backwards' – that is, 'beginning with the deepest and using the preposition *in* to express the serial modification' (Halliday 1994: 198). In other words, one names tenses moving from the last selection to the primary selection. Thus, the tense in *elle aura eu mangé* ('she will have eaten') is a 'past in past in future'. The interpretation of French tense in terms of a realisation of systemic recursivity allow us to account for the tenses as tabulated in Table 20.7.

The 'past in past in future in past' is the most complex tense within the French tense system. The temporal chain that it embodies is represented in Figure 20.2, which shows that the maximal temporal chain in French can realise no more than a series of four temporal relations between the speech time (Ts) and the event time (Te).

In this section, we have briefly reviewed the French tense system. A verbal group rank interpretation of French tense in terms of its logical structure allows us to accommodate all potential series of time and tense combinations. The French tense system consists of two simultaneous systems, one deictic and the other recursive. The *deictic* system (primary tenses) offers a range of five alternatives, three of which are past, for expressing a time in relation to the speech time. The *recursive* system allows the repeated selection of the future or the past for the expression of serial time. Unlike in the traditional models, French tense complexes are thus interpreted as time relations (logical viewpoint) rather than tense plus

Table 20.7 French tenses: realising serial time

primary tenses	secondary past	tertiary past	quaternary past
present je chante	**past in present** j'ai chanté		
imperfect past je chantais	**past in imperfect past** j'avais chanté	**past in past in past imperfect** j'avais eu chanté	
compound past j'ai chanté	**past in compound past** j'ai eu chanté		
simple past je chantai	**past in simple past** j'eus chanté **future in past** je chanterais secondary future	tertiary future	
future je chanterai	**past in future** j'aurai chanté	**past in past in future** j'aurai eu chanté	
	past in future in past j'aurais chanté		**past in past in future in past** j'aurais eu chanté

334

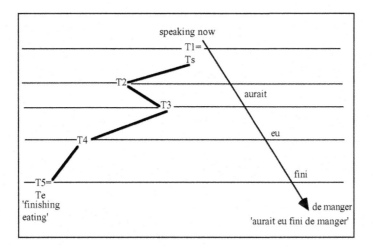

Figure 20.2   Structure of the past-in-past-in-future-in-past

Note: Ts = speech time; Te = event time

Source: Caffarel (1992: 397)

aspect (experiential viewpoint). Aspect is instead a feature that allows us to distinguish the primary past options, such as imperfect past versus simple past/compound past rather than something to be added to the primary tenses to form complex tenses.

Conclusion

This chapter aimed to offer an overview of some crucial features of the French verbal group from the point of view of SFL and to provide some insights into how to undertake the description of a language other than English. It highlighted the importance of the systemic and functional dimensions when establishing language-specific grammatical categories, and of keeping in mind that those categories are much more than formal labels; they reflect the functioning and semantics of the language in the context of texts.

This chapter also argued in favour of describing a language from the standpoint of the language in question by exploring the functioning of grammatical resources within texts rather than imposing categories from English, for instance. This was illustrated when we looked at the functioning of the verbal group within the interpersonal structure of the clause. The analysis of the verbal group within the experiential metafunction showed its centrality within the French clause, and drew attention to the potential agglutination of participants and nuclear circumstances to the verbal group.

The overview of French tense also highlighted some of the differences between French and English tense, with French tense having more delicate systems within the past tense options and reduced recursivity in the secondary options. The approach focused on the natural relationship that exists between the semantics of time and the lexicogrammatical system of TENSE, foregrounding secondary tense as a series of time relations. Systemic functional linguistics gives us the resources with which to interpret grammar as a meaning-making resource and thus, when exploring a grammatical class such as the verbal group, the main objective must be to explore how it makes meaning across the different dimensions of the theoretical spectrum.

Notes

1 See also Quiroz, this volume.
2 See 'The verbal group system of Tense' later in the chapter.
3 See also Caffarel (2006).
4 See also Quiroz, this volume.
5 See Baillard (1982) for a description of French complement pronouns in causative sentences.
6 See 'The verbal group system of Tense' on French tense.
7 For a detailed account of verbal group complexing in English, see Matthiessen (1995) and Quiroz, this volume.
8 See Caffarel (1992) for a more detailed account of French tense across different text types.

References

Baillard, J. 1982. The interaction of semantic and syntactic functions and French clitic case marking in causative sentences. In P.J. Hopper and S.A. Thompson (eds) *Syntax and Semantics, Vol. 15: Studies in Transitivity*. New York and London: Academic Press, pp. 49–69.

Banks, D. 2010. The interpersonal metafunction in French from a systemic functional perspective. *Language Sciences* 32(4): 395–407.

Bateman, J., and C.M.I.M. Matthiessen. 1991. *Systemic Linguistic and Text Generation: Experiences from Japanese and English*. London: Pinter.

Caffarel, A. 1992. Interacting between a generalized tense semantics and register-specific semantic tense systems. *Language Sciences* 14(4): 385–418.

Caffarel, A. 1995. The interpersonal structure of the French clause. In R. Hasan and P. Fries (eds) *On Subject and Theme: A Discourse Functional Perspective* (Current Issues in Linguistic Theory 118). Amsterdam and Philadelphia, PA: John Benjamins, pp. 1–49.

Caffarel, A. 2006. *A Systemic Functional Grammar of French*. London: Continuum.

Caffarel, A., J.R. Martin and C.M.I.M. Matthiessen. 2004. *Language Typology: A Functional Perspective*. Amsterdam: John Benjamins.

Combettes, N. 1975. *Pour une linguistique textuelle*. Nancy: Academie de Nancy-Metz.

de Beauvoir, S. 1946. *Tous les hommes sont mortels*. Paris: Gallimard.

Fries, P.H. 1981. On the status of theme in English: Arguments from discourse. *Forum Linguisticum* 6(1): 1–38.

Gouveia, C.A.M. 2010. Towards a profile of the interpersonal organization of the Portuguese clause. *DELTA* 26(1): 1–24.

Grévisse, M. 1886. *Le bon usage*. Paris: Editions DCULOT.

Guillaume, G. 1929. *Temps et verbe: Théorie des aspects, des modes et des temps* (Collection linguistique publiée par la société de linguistique de Paris 27). Paris: Champion.

Hagège, C. 1982. *La structure des langues: Que sais-je*. Paris: Presses Universitaires de France.

Halliday, M.A.K. 1976. The English verbal group. In G. Kress (ed.) *Halliday: System and Function in Language*. Oxford: Oxford University Press, pp. 136–58.

Halliday, M.A.K. 1978. *Language as Social Semiotic: The Social Interpretation of Language And Meaning*. London: Arnold.

Halliday, M.A.K. 1994. *An Introduction to Functional Grammar*. 2nd edn. London: Arnold.

Halliday, M.A.K., and C.M.I.M. Matthiessen. 2004. *An Introduction to Functional Grammar*. 3rd edn. London: Arnold.

Imbs, P. 1960. *L'emploi des temps verbaux en français moderne*. Paris: Klincksieck.

Jespersen, O. 1933. *Essentials of English Grammar*. London: Allen & Unwin.

Judges, A., and F.G. Healey. 1983. *A Reference Grammar of Modern French*. London: Arnold.

Martinet, A. 1978. *Grammaire fonctionnelle du français*. Paris: Didier.

Matthiessen, C.M.I.M. 1995. *Lexicogrammatical Cartography: English Systems*. Tokyo: International Language Sciences.

Matthiessen, C.M.I.M. 1996. Tense in English seen through systemic functional theory. In M. Berry, C. Butler, R. Fawcett and G. Huang (eds) *Meaning and Form: Systemic Functional Interpretations*. Norwood, NJ: Ablex, pp. 431–98.

Quiroz, B. 2013. The interpersonal and experiential grammar of Chilean Spanish: Towards a principled systemic-functional description based on axial argumentation. Unpublished PhD dissertation, University of Sydney.

Quiroz, B. 2015. La cláusula como movimiento interactivo: Una perspectiva semántico-discursiva de la gramática interpersonal del español. *DELTA* 31(1): 261–301.

Thai, M.D. 2004. Metafunctional profile of Vietnamese. In A. Caffarel J.R. Martin and C.M.I.M. Matthiessen. 2004. *Language Typology: A Functional Perspective*. Amsterdam: John Benjamins, pp. 397–431.

Wagner, R., and J. Pinchon. 1962. *Grammaire du français classique et modern*. Paris: Hachette.

21

The nominal group in Chinese

Eden Sum-hung Li

Introduction

The variety of Chinese described in this chapter is known in different parts of the Chinese-speaking world as *Putonghua* ('common speech'), *Guoyu* ('national language'), or *Huayu* ('Chinese language'), and in the English-speaking world as Mandarin. Sociolinguistically, it may be characterised as 'Modern Standard Chinese' (Chen 1999; Kratochvíl 1968), officially based on Beijing dialect for its pronunciation and style, as well as the classic works of modern vernacular prose for its grammatical norms (Chen 1999).

From the systemic functional perspective, Chinese, as any other language, is a higher-order semiotic system, which is tri-stratal (Berry, this volume). At the lexicogrammatical stratum, a rank scale for Chinese may be recognised as clause (including clause complex and clause simplex) – group/phrase – word – morpheme, whereby a clause is composed of one or more groups/phrases, a group/phrase is composed of one or more words and a word is composed of one or more morphemes (McDonald, this volume). However, the conception of morpheme and word in Chinese is somewhat different from that in English. Chinese is commonly characterised as a 'monosyllabic' language – that is, one in which a morpheme is usually phonologically mapped onto a single syllable and graphically onto a character. Owing to this regular mapping between morpheme, syllable and character, speakers of Chinese have a strong sense of this complex as an integrated unit in the language – referred to by the single term 字 *zi* ('character/morpheme/syllable') – and a correspondingly weak sense of units above or below, whether in grammar or in phonology (Halliday and McDonald 2004; Li 2007). As a result, the topic of word structure, especially in relation to word compounds, has been an important – even dominant – one among Chinese grammarians, from both traditional and structuralist approaches (for example Tiee 1990). A lot of confusion has resulted because of the tendency of some scholars to regard any word written with more than one character as a 'compound' even though many of these examples are compounds only in a historical sense, having become 'frozen' into a single morpheme centuries ago.

From the systemic functional perspective, the lowest rank in Chinese that bears implications for clause grammar in terms of the three metafunctions is at the rank of group rather than at the rank of word/morpheme (Li 2007: 16), since there is no inflectional morphology

Table 21.1 The abbreviations used for clause analysis

verbal	nominal	adverb	marker
aspect [ASP] coverb [CV] postverb [PV] modal auxiliary [MOD]	determiner [DET] measurer [MEAS] postnoun [POSTN]	degree adverb [DADV]	adjectival marker [ADJ] adverbial clause marker [ADM] negative marker [NEG] nominal clause marker [NOM] passive marker [BEI] plural marker [PL] possessive marker [POSS] relative clause marker [REL]

in Chinese realising clause functions. Hence this chapter will not discuss word structure, but will focus on a single group type, the nominal group, and how it relates to the structure of the clause in Chinese. Table 21.1 sets out the abbreviations used for clause analysis in this chapter.

The Thing in the nominal group

Apart from the case of nominalisation, which we will discuss later in this chapter, the essential element in the nominal group in Chinese is the Head, which performs the experiential function of Thing. The Head can be modified, but, unlike English, in Chinese all modifiers precede the Head. These pre-modifiers and the Head form a multivariate structure – that is, each component in the nominal group represents a distinctive variable that enters into a configuration of relations with the other components. Logically, these pre-modifiers are dependent on the Head in terms of taxis, forming a hypotactic nexus (Fang 2012: 101). We can illustrate this with the underlined nominal group in example (1).

(1)	有	個	表哥	是	耿	家	的	窮	親戚
	Yǒu	*gè*	*biǎogē*	*shì*	*gěng*	*jiā*	*de*	*qióng*	*qīnqi*
	have	MEAS	cousin	be	Geng	family	POSS	poor	relative

'(We) have a cousin who is a poor relative of the Geng family'

The nominal group 耿家的窮親戚 *Gěng jiā de qióng qīnqi* in example (1) forms a Premodifier + Head construction. There are two Premodifiers realised by a possessive 耿家的 *Gěng jiā de* ('Geng family + possessive marker *de*') and an adjective 窮 *qióng* ('poor'). Both of these modifiers are grammatically dependent on the Head 親戚 *qīnqi* ('relative') and serve different semantic functions in the nominal group. In the following section, we will examine the Head and the various semantic functions realised by different pre-modifiers, as well as their potential order.

According to the model set out in Halliday and Matthiessen (1999), in the experiential metafunction, a figure, or quantum of change, is realised by a clause; the Participant of a figure is typically realised by a nominal group or an adjectival group; a Process, by a verbal group; and a Circumstance, by an adverbial group or prepositional phrase. The Participant in a figure can be either a 'thing' or a 'quality' (Halliday and Matthiessen 1999: 61). In Chinese, while the Head functioning as the Thing is typically realised by a nominal group, the Quality is construed as verbal, realised by an adjectival verb (also known in the literature as an 'adjective' or a 'stative verb') (Li 2007: 52). The adjectival verb in Chinese, when used predicatively, is considered a type of verb because it possesses many properties of the verb.

First, an adjective may be directly pre-modified by a modal verb, as shown in example (2).

(2)	考試	答	題目	時,	你	應該	謹慎	些
	Kǎoshì	*dá*	*tímù*	*shí*	*nǐ*	*yīnggāi*	*jǐnshèn*	*xiē*
	exam	answer	question	ADM	you	MOD	careful	PL
	'[When you] answer the questions in an examination, you should be more careful'							

In example (2), the modal auxiliary verb 應該 *yīnggāi* ('should') is placed in front of the adjectival verb 謹慎 *jǐnshèn* ('careful') and directly modifies it.

In addition, an adjectival verb may be post-modified by a postverb, indicating a range of meanings to do with phase, as shown in example (3).

(3)	她	的	臉	立即	紅	起來
	tā	*de*	*liǎn*	*lìjí*	*hóng*	*qǐlái*
	She	POSS	face	immediately	red	PV
	'Her face immediately grew red'					

In this example, the adjective 紅 *hóng* ('red') is followed by a postverb 起來 *qǐlái*, indicating a type of phase (Halliday and McDonald 2004: 382–7).

The semantic features of the Thing can be formulated systemically as a typology, as shown in Figure 21.1.

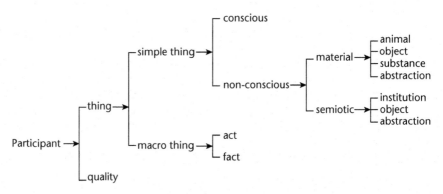

Figure 21.1 A typology of the semantic features of Participant in Chinese

Source: Adapted from Li (2003: 76)

The Thing can be either *simple* or *macro*. Simple things can be differentiated into *conscious*, such as 人 *rén* ('person'), 女孩 *nǔhái* ('girl') or *non-conscious*. Non-conscious things, in turn, are either *material* or *semiotic*. Material things can be further categorised into *animal*, such as 狗 *gǒu* ('dog'), *object (material)*, such as 桌子 *zhuōzi* ('desk'), *substance*, such as 木材 *mùcái* ('timber'), or *abstraction (material)*, such as 歷史 *lìshǐ* ('history'), whereas semiotic things can be *institution*, such as 政府 *zhèngfǔ* ('government'), *object (semiotic)*, such as 文件 *wénjiàn* ('document'), or *abstraction (semiotic)*, such as 理論 *lǐlùn* ('theory'). In contrast to simple things, macro things refer to macro-phenomena realised by a rank-shifted clause (Halliday and Matthiessen 1999: 10). In general, a macro thing is either an *act* or a *fact*. An act refers to a macro-phenomenon, which is known as extended reference as shown in example (4), while a fact refers to meta-phenomenon, which is known as reference to facts as shown in example (5) (Halliday and Hasan 1976; Halliday and Matthiessen 1999; Li 2003).

(4)	他們	被	發現!	這	也	太	不	小心	了!
	tā men	*bèi*	*fāxiàn!*	*zhè*	*yě*	*tài*	*bù*	*xiǎoxīn*	*Le!*
	he PL	BEI	discover	this	also	DADV	NEG	careful	ASP

'They were discovered! Their act was too careless!'

(5)	兒子	死	於	車禍,	這	事	對	她	的	打擊	很	大.
	érzǐ	*sǐ*	*yú*	*chēhuò*	*zhè*	*shì*	*duì*	*tā*	*de*	*dǎjī*	*hěn*	*dà*
	son	die	CV	car accident	this	matter	CV	she	POSS	blow	DADV	big

'Her son was killed in a car accident. This is a big blow to her.'

Premodifiers of the Thing

Concerning the Thing in Chinese, there is always the question of definiteness. The Thing can be realised by a proper noun, a pronoun or a common noun. Both proper nouns and pronouns are interpreted as definite even when they do not take any modifier. Thus they normally occur alone unless for the purpose of emphasis, for example 可憐的她 *kělián de tā* ('pitiable + ADJ + she – pitiful her'), 好一個武松 *hǎo yī ge Wǔ Sōng*[1] ('good + one + MEAS: individual + *Wǔ-Sōng* – what a good *Wǔ Sōng!*'). The case of the common noun is more complicated. A nominal group with a common noun as Head can contain many pre-modifiers. In such cases, the pre-modifiers, including Deictic, Numerative, Measurer, Epithet, Classifier and Qualifier, together with a Head, form a multivariate structure. These functions are realised by different word classes: the Deictic is realised by a determiner, including a demonstrative and possessive, or a quantifier; the Numerative, by a numeral; the Measurer, by a measure word; the Epithet, by an adjectival verb; the Classifier, by a noun or adjectival verb; and the Qualifier, by a coverbal phrase or relative clause. It should be noted that, unlike the case in English, the Qualifier is a pre-modifier.

Deictic

The notion of 'Deictic' refers to an element that indicates 'whether or not some specific subset of the Thing is intended; and if so, which' (Halliday 1994: 181). In short, a Deictic specifies the potential referent of the Thing by 'pointing' towards a subset of the type of Thing. In Chinese, this subset can be *specific* or *non-specific*, realised by a specific Deictic and non-specific Deictic, respectively.

A specific Deictic is realised by central determiners, which include article, demonstrative and possessive in English. Determiners of a nominal group can be classified in terms of their order into pre-determiners, central determiners and post-determiners. However, unlike in English, there is no article in Chinese. Central determiners in Chinese therefore include demonstratives and possessives only. Let us illustrate with the Chinese translation of the first paragraph of Agatha Christie's famous novel *Murder on the Orient Express* (examples (6) and (7)). The definiteness expressed by the definite article 'the' in the English original text in example (7) – that is 'the platform', 'the train' and 'the Taurus Express', has not been translated in the Chinese translation:

(6)	敘利亞	嚴冬	清晨	五時
	Xùlìyà	*yándōng*	*qīngchén*	*wǔshí*
	Syria	cold winter	early morning	five o'clock

'It was five o'clock on a winter's morning in Syria'

(7) 在 鐵路 指南 稱為 托魯斯特快車 的 一 列車 停靠 在 鈣勒頗 車站 月臺

[[*zài tiělù zǐnán chēng- tuōlǔsī tèkuài de*]] *yī lièchē tīngkào zài gàilèpō chēzhàn yuètái*
          wéi   chē

'At railway directory called Taurus Express REL one train stop at Aleppo station platform'

'Alongside the platform at Aleppo stood <u>the train</u> grandly designated in railway guides as <u>the Taurus Express</u>'

There are two demonstratives in Chinese: 這 *zhè* ('this') – near or associated with the speaker; and 那 *nà* ('that') – further away from the speaker or associated with the listener or third party. Both demonstratives point to or specify a particular potential referent, the Thing. For countable common nouns, when there is no other element indicating (specific) number such as a Numerative, the plural morpheme 些 *xiē* can be added to the demonstrative to indicate plurality, as shown in Table 21.2.

Table 21.2 Demonstrative in Chinese

Demonstratives	Singular	Plural
這 *zhè*	這個人 *zhè gè rén* ('this + MEAS: individual + person – this person')	這些人 *zhè xiē rén* ('this + PL + person – these people')
那 *nà*	那件事 *nà jiàn shì* ('that + MEAS: piece + matter – that matter')	那些事 *nà xiē shì* ('that + PL + matter – those matters')

It should be noted that the Measurers 個 *gè* and 件 *jiàn* are mostly obligatory, but they can be omitted when the meaning is clear and when the nominal group is functioning as Theme, as shown in example (8).

(8)

這	人	全身	禦寒	裝束,
Zhè	*rén*	*quánshēn*	*yùhán*	*zhuāngshù,*
this	person	whole body	against cold	clothing

'As for the man, his whole body was covered with heavy clothing,'

連	耳朵	也	戴上	了	耳帽,
lián	*ěrduǒ*	*yě*	*dài-shàng*	*le*	*ěrmào,*
even	ear	also	wear-on	ASP	ear muffs

'even his ears were covered with ear muffs,'

除了	一	顆	紅	鼻頭	和	兩	撇	上翹	的	仁丹鬍子	之外,
Chúle	*yī*	*kē*	*hóng*	*bítóu*	*hé*	*liǎng*	*piě*	*shàngqiào*	*de*	*réndān húzi*	*zhīwài,*
besides	one	MEAS	red	nose	and	two	MEAS	pointing-upward	ADJ	curled moustache	beside

'besides a red nose and two upward-curled moustaches,'

什麼	也	看不見.
shénme	*yě*	*kàn-bù-jiàn.*
whatever	also	look-NEG-see

'nothing could be seen.'

Possessive in Chinese can be either *marked* with 的 *de*, as in 我的父親 *wǒ de fùqin* ('my father: I + POSS + father') or *unmarked*, as in 我 *wǒ* ('my') in 我父親 *wǒ fùqin* ('my father: I + father'), with the former being the default. Like demonstratives, the use of a possessive also indicates a specific referent. For countable common nouns indicating persons, the plural morpheme 們 *men* can be added to indicate plurality.

Non-specific Deictics, on the other hand, are realised by pre-determiners – that is quantifiers, such as 每 *měi* ('each/every'), 所有 *suǒyǒu* ('all'), 一切 *yīqiè* ('all'), 一些 *yīxiē* ('some'), 別的 *biéde* ('others'). Each additional modifier, in general, increases the degree of specification and further limits the subset of potential referents of the Thing. It should be noted that this generalisation is applied not only to quantifiers such as 一些 *yīxiē* ('some'), 每 *měi* ('each/every') and 別的 *biéde* ('others'), but also to those such as 所有 *suǒyǒu* ('all'), 一切 *yīqiè* ('all') – and even to non-nominal quantifiers such as the adverbs 全 *quán* ('completely'), 都 *dōu* ('all') – because by pointing to a full set, or in the negative to an empty set, the quantifier also serves to further restrict the interpretation of potential referents.

As in English, a Deictic element is optional and a nominal group without a Deictic element does not mean that it has no value in the Chinese Deictic system. Cheng and Sybesma (1999, 2005) point out that, without any modifier, a common noun in the postverbal position in a clause can be interpreted as definite, indefinite, or generic, depending on the context and co-text; however, when it occurs alone in the preverbal position, it can only be interpreted as definite or generic, but not indefinite.

Let us illustrate with examples. In example (9), the common noun 槍 *qiāng* ('gun'), in a postverbal position, is not modified and is interpreted as indefinite. In contrast, in example (10), the two common nouns in a preverbal position – that is, 哨聲 *shàoshēng* ('whistle') and 火車 *huǒchē* ('train') – are not modified and are interpreted as definite, as shown in the translation. The common noun in the preverbal position in example (11), 熊貓 *xióngmāo* ('panda'), is interpreted as generic.

(9)	他	拿	了	槍,	便	働	了	出	去
	Tā	*ná*	*le*	*qiāng*	*biàn*	*dòng*	*le*	*chū*	*qù*
	He	take	ASP	gun	then	rush	ASP	exit	PV
	'He took a gun and rushed out'								

(10)	哨聲	響	起,	火車	要	動	了
	Shàoshēng	*xiǎng*	*qǐ*	*huǒchē*	*yào*	*dòng*	*le*
	whistle	blow	PV	train MOD	AUX	move	VERB
	'The whistle blew; the train was about to leave'						

(11)	熊貓	是	一	種	温馴	的	動物
	Xióngmāo	*shì*	*yī*	*zhǒng*	*wēnxún*	*de*	*dòngwù*
	Panda	be	one	MEAS	gentle	ADJ	animal
	'The panda is a gentle animal'						

Numerative

The Numerative function indicates numerical features of the Thing. In English, it is classified as a post-determiner. According to Li (2007: 26), numerals in Chinese can be classified into *simplex* or *complex*. Simplex numerals refer to the cardinal numbers from 零 *líng* ('zero') to 九 *jiǔ* ('nine') and basic units such as 十 *shí* ('ten'), 百 *bǎi* ('a hundred'), 千 *qiān* ('a thousand'), 萬 *wàn* ('ten thousand') and so on. Complex numerals, on the other hand, include any combination of the simplex numerals such as 一百二十五 *yībǎi èrshíwǔ* ('two hundred and fifteen'). Both the simplex and complex encode cardinal numbers.

For ordinal numbers, the prefix 第 *dì* is added in front of the numeral, for example 第一 *dìyī* ('first'), 第二 *dìèr* ('second'). Fractional numbers are encoded by inserting the morphemes 份之 *fēnzhī* between the denominator and numerator: denominator^份之 *fēnzhī*^numerator.

For example, 十份之一 *shífēnzhīyī* means 'one tenth'. Multiples are encoded by the Thing 倍 *bèi* ('time'), for example 三倍 *sānbèi* ('triple').

Measurer

The function Measurer is realised by measure words that classify the Thing into different categories according to a number of criteria. It should be noted that this notion of Measurer corresponds to the notion of 'classifier' in the wider literature in traditional grammar of Chinese. However, following the systemic functional convention, the notion of 'Classifier' is reserved for another pre-modifying function that will be discussed later in this chapter. In a Chinese nominal group, when the Thing is identified, for example introduced by a deter-miner, or quantified, for example introduced by a numeral, it is likely to be modified by a measure word. The measure word must agree with the Thing that it modifies. For example, it is acceptable to say 這本書 *zhè běn shū* ('this + MEAS: printed material + book – this book') or 這頁書 *zhè yè shū* ('this + MEAS: page + book – this page of the book'), but not 這條書 *zhè tiáo shū* ('this + MEAS: long flexible + book'). The system network of measure words in Chinese can be represented as in Figure 21.2. However, it should be noted that some measure words can be categorised into more than one subtype, depending on the nominal group that they modify. For example, the word 口 *kǒu* (lit. 'mouth') is categorised as a meta-phorical collective measure word in the nominal group 一口湯 *yī kǒu tāng* ('one mouthful of soup: one + MEAS: mouth + soup'); however, it is categorised as an individuative measure word in another nominal group 一口釘 *yī kǒu dīng* ('one nail: one + MEAS: piece + nail'), because the measure word here has no semantic relation with mouth. It can also be used as an individuative measure for things with a prominent opening, for example 一口井 *yī kǒu jǐng* ('one + MEAS: mouth + well – one well').

The system network in Figure 21.2 shows that measure words divide into four subtypes: *individuative*, *collective*, *quantitative* and *partitive*. The choice of individuative measure words can further lead to *intensive* and *macro*. While intensive individuative measure words are mainly associated with Things that can be counted as individual entities, for example 名 *míng* ('person'), as in 一名教師 *yī míng jiàoshī* ('one + MEAS: person + teacher – one teacher'), macro individuative measure words are associated with the Things that con-strue both macro-things such as events and occurrences, and macro-qualities, for example

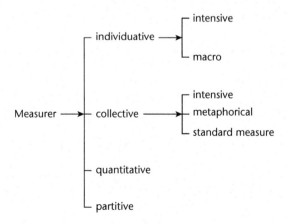

Figure 21.2 Types of Measurer in Chinese

場 *chǎng* ('field'), as in 一場演出 *yī chǎng yǎnchū* ('one + MEAS: field + performance – one performance'). Among various intensive individuative measure words, 個 *gè* is the general individuative that can map onto most Things and which therefore occurs most frequently. Apart from 個 *gè*, there are some comparatively specific ones for particular classes of the Things, such as 所 *suǒ* for certain types of institution.

The choice of collective measure words can further lead to three options: *intensive*, *metaphorical* and *standard*. The intensive collective measure words include container words used as measure pre-modifiers, for example 碗 *wǎn* ('bowl'), as in 一碗飯 *yī wǎn fàn* ('one + MEAS: bowl + rice – one bowl of rice'), 杯 *bēi* ('cup, glass'), as in 一杯水 *yī bēi shuǐ* ('one + MEAS: glass + water – one glass of water'). The metaphorical collective measure words include words that can stand alone as entities, but which are used temporarily to indicate quantities, for example 口 *kǒu* ('mouth'), as in 一口井 *yī kǒu jǐng* ('one + MEAS: mouth + well – one well'), 身 *shēn* ('body'), as in 一身債務 *yī shēn zhàowù* ('one + MEAS: body + loan – owing a lot of money to someone'). The standard collective measure words are used for measurements as such, and indicate the standards for length, weight, volume and area, for example 里 *lǐ* ('Chinese mile'), as in 一里路 *yī lǐ lù* ('one + MEAS: mile + road – one mile of road'), 尺 *chǐ* ('Chinese foot'), as in 一尺布 *yī chǐ bù* ('one + MEAS: foot + cloth – a foot of cloth').

While collective measure words are associated with a number of individual Things, quantitative measure words are associated with a group or kind of Thing. Among the quantitative measure words, 種 *zhǒng* ('a kind of') is the most common. In contrast, the partitive measure words are associated with part(s) of the Thing, for example 層 *céng* ('layer'), as in 一層泥土 *yī céng nítǔ* ('one + MEAS: layer + soil – one layer of soil'), 段 *duàn* ('section'), as in 一段路 *yī duàn lù* ('one + MEAS: section + road – one section of road'). Table 21.3 shows some common measure words in Chinese.

The choice of measure words is closely related to the field of the text, which relates to the experiential metafunction. There are more than 200 measure words in Chinese. The choice of measure words affects the delicacy of the description of the Head in a nominal group and partly contributes to the style of a creative work. It is noted that some nominal Heads can be pre-modified by more than one type of measure word, such as 一片藍天 *yī piàn lán tiān* ('one + MEAS: slice + blue sky – a stretch of blue sky'), or 一線天 *yī xiàn tiān* ('one + MEAS: thread + sky – one thread of sky') and 半邊天 *bàn biān tiān* ('half + MEAS: side + sky – half of the sky'). Some measure words can extend to pre-modify abstract nominal Heads, such as 一身銅臭 *yī shēn tóngchòu* ('one + MEAS: body + copper + stink – full of the stink of money').

Epithet

In Chinese, an Epithet can be realised by an adjectival verb. As the Epithet in a Chinese nominal group, an adjectival verb used attributively is usually followed by 的 *de*, a grammatical marker of an attributive pre-modifier, as shown in example (12).

(12)	眼	前	是	一	片	綠油油	的	草地
	Yǎn	*qián*	*shì*	*yī*	*piàn*	*lùyóuyóu*	*de*	*cǎodì*
	Eye	POSTN	be	one	MEAS	green	ADJ	grassland

'There is a field of green grassland before my eyes'

Table 21.3 Common measure words in Chinese

Measure-type	Measure words	Examples of potential Head
individuative intensive	本 *běn* ('printed material')	書 *shū* ('book'); 簿 *bù* ('notebook'); 日記 *rìjì* ('diary')
	名 *míng* ('person')	警察 *jǐngchá* ('police'); 消防員 *xiāofángyuán* ('firefighter'); 記者 *jìzhě* ('news reporter')
	幅 *fú* ('piece')	畫 *huà* ('printing'); 相片 *xiàngpiàn* ('photo'); 字畫 *zìhuà* ('orthography')
	間 *jiān* ('compartment')	房間 *fángjiān* ('room'); 屋 *wū* ('house'); 公寓 *gōngyù* ('apartment')
individuative macro	場 *chǎng* ('field')	演出 *yǎnchū* ('performance'); 歌劇 *gējù* ('opera'); 話劇 *huàjù* ('drama')
	次 *cì* ('time')	比賽 *bǐsài* ('competition'); 會議 *huìyì* ('meeting'); 演講 *yǎnjiǎng* ('talk')
	番 *fān* ('period')	準備 *zhǔnbèi* ('preparation'); 角逐 *juézhú* ('competition'); 理論 *lǐlùn* ('argument')
	單 *dān* ('case')	買賣 *mǎimài* ('trade'); 案件 *ànjiàn* ('crime'); 車禍 *chēhuò* ('car accident')
collective intensive	杯 *bēi* ('glass/cup')	開水 *kāishuǐ* ('boiled water'); 咖啡 *kāfēi* ('coffee'); 茶 *chá* ('tea')
	瓶 *píng* ('bottle')	牛奶 *niúnǎi* ('milk'); 酒 *jiǔ* ('wine'); 油 *yóu* ('oil')
	盆 *pén* ('plate')	生菓 *shēngguǒ* ('fruit'); 蔬菜 *shūcài* ('vegetable'); 水 *huǐ* ('water')
	箱 *xiāng* ('box')	蘋果 *píngguǒ* ('apple'); 香蕉 *xiāngjiāo* ('banana'); 芒果 *mángguǒ* ('mango')
collective metaphorical	笔 *bǐ* ('pen')	交易 *jiāoyì* ('exchange'); 錢 *qián* ('money'); 貸款 *dàikuǎn* ('loan')
	口 *kǒu* ('mouth')	英文 *yīngwén* ('English'); 謊言 *huǎngyán* ('lie'); 食物 *shíwù* ('food')
	線 *xiàn* ('thread')	希望 *xīwàng* ('hope'); 生機 *shēngjī* ('chance to be alive'); 天 *tiān* ('sky')
	身 *shēn* ('body')	華服 *huáfú* ('beautiful clothes'); 債務 *zhàowù* ('loan'); 銅臭 *tóngchòu* ('derogatory: rich')
collective standard measure	尺 *chǐ* ('feet')	布 *bù* ('cloth'); 床 *chuáng* ('bed'); 露台 *lùtái* ('balcony')
	度 *dù* ('unit')	電 *diàn* ('electricity'); 煤氣 *méiqì* ('gas'); 彩虹 *cǎohóng* ('rainbow')
	加崙 *jiālún* ('gallon')	奶 *nǎi* ('milk'); 水 *shuǐ* ('water'); 飲品 *yǐnpǐn* ('soft drink')
	噸 *dūn* ('ton')	垃圾 *lājī* ('rubbish'); 泥土 *nítǔ* ('soil'); 沙 *shā* ('sand')
quantitative	班 *bān* ('group: people')	人 *rén* ('people'); 匪徒 *fěitú* ('gang'); 警察 *jǐngchá* ('police')
	幫 *bāng* ('group: bad guy')	黑社會 *hēishèhuì* ('triad society'); 匪徒 *fěitú* ('bad guy'); 劫匪 *jiéfěi* ('robber')
	群 *qún* ('group: animal')	羊 *yáng* ('sheep'); 狼 *láng* ('wolf'); 狗 *gǒu* ('dog')
	雙 *shuāng* ('pair: thing')	皮鞋 *píxié* ('shoe'); 手套 *shǒutào* ('glove'); 襪子 *wàzi* ('sock')
partitive	邊 *biān* ('side')	天 *tiān* ('sky'); 土地 *tǔdì* ('field'); 面孔 *miànkǒng* ('face')
	層 *céng* ('layer')	洋房 *yángfáng* ('mansion'); 蛋糕 *dāngāo* ('cake'); 岩石 *yánshí* ('rock')
	點 *diǎn* ('spot')	希望 *xīwàng* ('hope'); 燭光 *zhúguāng* ('candle light')
	段 *duàn* ('section')	路 *lù* ('street'); 時間 *shíjiān* ('time'); 日子 *rìzǐ* ('period')

In the existential clause in example (12), the existent is 一片綠油油的草地 *yī piàn lǜyóuyóu de cǎodì* ('a field of green grassland'), in which the Thing is 草地 *cǎodì* ('grassland') and the pre-modifier is 一片綠油油的 *yī piàn lǜyóuyóu de*, in which 一 *yī* ('one') is the Numerative and 片 *piàn* is the Measurer, and 綠油油 *lǜyóuyóu* ('green') is the Epithet, an adjectival verb followed by the marker 的 *de*.

Classifier

As mentioned earlier, the notion of Classifier in systemic functional grammar does not correspond to the usual notion of classifier in the grammar of Chinese. From the systemic functional perspective, Classifier indicates 'a particular subclass of the Thing in question' (Halliday 1994: 184). In other words, while both Deictics and Classifiers restrict the potential referent of the Thing, Deictics indicate the subset of the Thing or the subset of the subclass of the Thing, while Classifiers indicate the subclass of the Thing. Classifiers are typically realised by a noun, for example 石 *shí* ('stone') in 石牆 *shí qiáng* ('stone wall'). Classifiers, to a certain extent, like Epithets, specify the quality of the Thing, such as the quality of being made of stone in 石牆 *shí qiáng* ('stone wall'). Halliday (1994) points out two criteria to differentiate Classifiers from Epithets in English: first, Classifiers do not accept degrees of comparison; and second, Classifiers tend to be organised in mutually exclusive sets. Generally speaking, these two criteria can also be applied in the nominal group in Chinese. For instance, we cannot say 一道更石牆 *yī dào gèng shí qiáng* ('a more stone wall') or 一道木石牆 *yī dào mù shí qiáng* ('a wooden stone wall'), but we can say 一道更美麗的牆 *yī dào gèng měi lì de qiáng* ('a more beautiful wall') and 一道小巧美麗的牆 *yī dào xiǎo qiǎo měi lì de qiáng* ('a tiny beautiful wall').

There are various functions of Classifiers in Chinese. The following list has been modified from Li and Thompson (1981), but is not exhaustive. The Classifier of a nominal group may serve as a spatial indicator, or as an indicator of the nature, or a metaphorical description, of the Thing.

1 A spatial indicator may further specify:

   a the location:

      i of the Thing, for example 田鼠 *tiánshǔ* ('field + mouse > field-mouse');

      ii where the Thing is applied, for example 唇膏 *chúngāo* ('lip + ointment > lipstick');

      iii where the Thing is sold, for example 快餐店 *kuàicān diàn* ('fast food + store > fast food store');

   b the period of time during which the Thing operates, for example 夜校 *yèxiào* ('night + school > night school');

2 the nature of the Thing, which may be further subcategorised as:

   a the source of the Thing, for example 煤礦 *méikuàng* ('coal + mine > coal mine');

   b the materials out of which the Thing is made, for example 銅像 *tóngxiàng* ('bronze + statute > bronze statue');

   c the cause of which the Thing is a result, for example 水漬 *shuǐzì* ('water + stain > water stain');

   d the sources of energy based on which the Head operates, for example 核能 *hénéng* ('nuclear + energy > nuclear energy');

   e the animal or instrument that uses the Thing, for example 馬房 *mǎfáng* ('horse + house > manger');

f an institution in which the Thing works, for example 機倉服務員 *jīcāng fúwùyuán* ('cabin + server > flight attendant')

g the merchandise that the Thing sells or delivers, for example 保險經紀 *bǎoxiǎn jīngjì* ('insurance + salesperson > insurance salesperson');

h a sport for which the Thing is a piece of equipment, for example 網球拍 *wǎngqiú pāi* ('tennis + racket > tennis racket');

i the part of the body of which the Thing is an ailment, for example 頭痛 *tóutòng* ('head + ache > headache');

j something against which the Thing functions as a protective device, for example 雨傘 *yǔsǎn* ('rain + umbrella > umbrella');

k the animal of which the Thing is a product, for example 蜂蜜 *fēngmì* ('bee + honey > honey');

l the body of which the Thing is a part, for example 車輪 *chēlún* ('car + wheel > the wheel of a car');

m the substance of which the Thing is an instrument or for which it is a container, for example 垃圾箱 *lājī xiāng* ('rubbish + bin > rubbish bin'); or

3 a metaphorical description of the Thing, for example 龍船 *lóngchuán* ('dragon + boat > dragon boat').

Qualifier in a nominal group

In the previous section, we discussed the multivariate structure of the Chinese nominal group: Deictic (realised by determiner or possessive)^Numerative (realised by numeral)^Measurer (realised by measure word)^Epithet (realised by adjectival verb)^Classifier (realised by noun or adjectival verb)^Thing (realised by noun). In addition, in Chinese, a nominal group may include a Qualifier. Like Circumstances, a Qualifier can also be realised by a coverbal phrase (Li 2007: 32–6) – that is, the Chinese equivalent of a prepositional phrase; alternatively, it can realised by a 'defining relative clause' – that is, an embedded clause preceding the Head. In English, a Qualifier always follows the Thing – that is, the Qualifier of a nominal group is a post-modifier. In other words, pre-modifiers of an English nominal head are words or word complexes, while post-modifiers are rank-shifted – that is, a phrase or a clause. In Chinese, a Qualifier, like other elements of the nominal group, always precedes the Thing. While a clause realises a figure consisting of a major process, a coverbal phrase consists of a minor process; as Halliday (2004: 324) argues, 'the characterisation here is in terms of some process within which the Thing is, directly or indirectly, a participant'. The Qualifier serves the function of characterising the Thing.

Coverbal phrase

Coverbal phrase is the only class of phrase in Chinese (Halliday and McDonald 2004; Li 2007). While a clause congruently realises a figure that consists of a major process 'within which the Thing is, directly or indirectly, a participant', a phrase consists of a minor process (Halliday and McDonald 2004: 324). A coverb in Chinese represents a minor process. The typical structure of a coverbal phrase in Chinese is coverb + nominal group, for example 在香港 *zài Xiānggǎng* ('in Hong Kong'), 當時 *dāngshí* ('at that time'). However, for coverbal phrases denoting spatial location or direction, the nominal group may be modified by a postnoun, which is the only element that follows the nominal Head. Letus illustrate with an example – example (13).

(13)	他	凝望	著	在	港灣	裏	那	艘	巨大	的	遠洋	郵輪
	tā	níngwàng	zhe	zài	gǎngwān	lǐ	nà	sōu	jùdà	de	yuǎnyáng	yóulún
	he	stare at	PV	CV	harbour	POSTN	DET	MEAS	giant	ADJ	ocean	cruise liner

'He stared at that giant ocean cruise liner in the harbour'

In the nominal group 在港灣裏那艘巨大的遠洋郵輪 *zài gǎngwān lǐ nà sōu jùdà de yuǎnyáng yóulún* ('the giant ocean cruise liner in the harbour'), the coverbal phrase 在港灣裏 *zài gǎngwān lǐ* ('in the harbour') is a Qualifier, which is realised by the nominal group 港灣 *gǎngwān* ('harbour') followed by a postnoun 裏 *lǐ* ('inside'), while 那 *nà* ('that') is the Deictic, 艘 *sōu* is the Measurer, 巨大 *jùdà* ('giant') is the Epithet, 遠洋 *yuǎnyáng* ('ocean') is the Classifier and 郵輪 *yóulún* ('cruise liner') is the Thing.

The Qualifier in example (13) is part of the nominal group, not the Circumstance in the clause as a whole. Functionally, a Qualifier is neither the Circumstance of a figure nor a Participant functioning as the Beneficiary in a ditransitive clause, nor the Goal or the Actor in a clause with dispositive voice (Li 2007: 189–206). A Qualifier indicates the spatial restriction of the Thing in a nominal group. Unlike a Circumstance, a Qualifier can be fronted to the beginning of a nominal group, but not be thematised to become a marked Theme.

There are two possible positions of the coverbal phrase in a nominal group: either preceding the Deictic or following the Measurer of the nominal group. In example (13), 在港灣裏那艘巨大的遠洋郵輪 *zài gǎngwān lǐ nà sōu jùdà de yuǎnyáng yóulún* ('the giant ocean cruise liner in the harbour'), the Qualifier precedes the Deictic and the Measurer. However, it is also possible for it to follow the Deictic and the Measurer, as in 那艘在港灣裏巨大的遠洋郵輪 *nà sōu zài gǎngwān lǐ jùdà de yuǎnyáng yóulún* ('the giant ocean cruise liner in the harbour').

Relative clause

As mentioned, a defining relative clause precedes the nominal Head, as shown in example (14).

(14)	我	最	喜歡	的	作家	是	魯迅
	Wǒ	zuì	xǐhuān	de	zuòjiā	shì	Lǔ Xùn
	My	most	like	REL	writer	be	Lǔ Xùn

'The writer (who) I like most is Lǔ Xùn'

In example (14), the Thing is 作家 *zuòjiā* ('author') and the pre-modifier is 我最喜歡的 *wǒ zuì xǐhuān de* ('my favourite'), which is a rank-shifted relative clause as Qualifier. 我 *wǒ* ('I') is the Subject, 喜歡 *xǐhuān* ('like') is the verb, 最 *zuì* ('most') is an adverb of degree and 的 *de* is a subordinating particle being placed in front of the Thing to indicate the modifying function of the embedded clause (Fang et al. 1987). However, Fang and Wu (2010) point out that the particle *de* may not always succeed in turning all embedded clauses into Qualifiers in the sense that, although grammatically acceptable, the embedded clause functioning as Epithet may sound unnatural. As with coverbal phrases, there are two possible positions for a defining relative clause embedded in the nominal group: preceding the determiner or following the measure word, as in examples (15) and (16).

(15)	他	買	回來	的	那	一	張	皮	沙發
	[(tā)	mǎi	huílái	de]	nà	yī	zhāng	pí	shāfā
	he	buy	PV	REL	that	one	MEAS	leather	sofa
	'the leather sofa that he bought'								

(16)	那	一	張	他	買	回來	的	皮	沙發
	nà	yī	zhāng	[(tā)	mǎi	huílái	de]	pí	shāfā
	that	one	MEAS	he	buy	PV	REL	leather	sofa
	'the leather sofa that he bought'								

Nominal clause rank shift as nominal group

According to Li and Thompson (1981: 575), the notion of 'nominalisation' refers to the grammatical process by which 'a verb, a verb phrase, a sentence or a portion of a sentence including the verb' functions as a nominal group. In systemic functional linguistics (SFL), however, it is known as one type of grammatical metaphor, of which 'nominalisation' is presented as the 'prototypical example' functioning as a nominal group (Halliday 2004). In this section, we focus on the nominal clause functioning as a nominal group.

In Chinese, a nominal clause is also marked with the marker 的 *de*, as shown in example (17).

(17)	在	香港,	爬	格子	的	很	難	生活
	Zài	Xiānggǎng,	pá	gézǐ	de	hěn	nán	shēnghuó
	CV	Hong Kong	climb	block	NOM	DADV	difficult	living
	'In Hong Kong, being a writer is very difficult to make a living'							

In example (17), [[爬格子]] 的 [[*pá gézǐ*]] *de* ('being a writer') is a nominal clause that consists of a verb 爬 *pá* ('climb') + 格子 *gézǐ* ('blocks') + 的 *de*. It is a clause rank-shifted to be a nominal group – that is, a component of a lower rank – realising a Participant role. The nominal clause here refers to the job of an author because, before the age of computers, authors used to write their manuscripts on a specific type of paper with vertical blocks on it. Each Chinese character fits within a block and each column of block is separated from the adjacent column by a space. Hence an analogy is drawn between writing on this kind of paper and climbing on ladders. The nominal clause here functions as the Thing, which can be pre-modified by a specific Deictic and a plural marker as in example (18).

(18)	在	香港,	那	些	爬	格子	的	很	難	生活
	zài	Xiānggǎng,	nà	xiē	pá	gézǐ	de	hěn	nán	shēnghuó
	CV	Hong Kong	DET	PL	climb	block	NOM	DADV	difficult	living
	'In Hong Kong, those working as a writer (find it) very difficult to make a living'									

A nominal clause should be differentiated from a defining relative clause, although both of them have a similar structure. While a nominal clause functions as the Thing, a defining relative clause functions as the Qualifier of the Thing. A defining relative clause is thus followed by the Head, while the nominal clause stands for the Head. Let us examine example (19).

(19)	在	香港,	那	些	爬	格子	的	人	很	難	生活
	zài	Xiānggang,	nà	xiē	pá	gézǐ	de	rén	hěn	nán	shēnghuó
	CV	Hong Kong	DET	PL	climb	block	REL	person	DADV	difficult	living

'In Hong Kong, those who work as writers (find it) very difficult to make a living'

Structurally, the defining relative clause [那些爬格子的] *nà xiē pá gézǐ de* ('who work as a writer') in example (19) seems to be identical with the nominal clause in example (18). However, the Head here is 人 'people' and the defining relative clause [[那些爬格子]]的 [[*nà xiē pá gézǐ*]] *de* is a pre-modifier of the Head. In other words, the relative clause is the Qualifier of the Thing.

Logical resources within a nominal group

In terms of logical structure, Fang (2012) analyses the nominal group in Chinese as either a simplex – that is, only one nominal Head can be identified – or a complex – that is, more than one Head can be identified. Fang points out that while the hypotactic relation is the only relation found between the pre-modifier and the Thing in a Chinese nominal group simplex, both hypotactic and paratactic relations are found among the components inside a Chinese nominal group complex. As for the logico-semantic types, while there is no projecting type in a Chinese nominal complex, all three expansion types – elaboration, extension and enhancement – are found among the components inside a Chinese nominal complex. This is a new research avenue for the nominal group in Chinese.

Owing to limitations of scope, this chapter has focused more on the structures and functions of the various pre-modifiers in Chinese nominal groups; however, further research on the nominal group in use would be worthwhile, such as possible combinations of pre-modifier in a nominal group and the preferential patterns in different kinds of discourse – that is, the employment of nominalisation in scientific writing and in creative writing – and the complexity of pre-modifiers in the nominal group in written Chinese and in spoken Chinese. Research in this direction will tell us the extent of the influence of personal preference – an essential element in building the probability of each option in the system network.

Note

1 *Wǔ Sōng* is a famous character in classical novel *The Water Margin*.

References

Chen, P. 1999. *Modern Chinese: History and Sociolinguistics*. Cambridge: Cambridge University Press.
Cheng, L.L.S., and R. Sybesma. 1999. Bare and not-so-bare nouns and the structure of NP. *Linguistic Inquiry* 30(4): 509–42.

Fang, J. 2012. Exploring the logical resources of Chinese nominal groups: A systemic functional approach. Paper presented at the 39th ISFC, University of Technology, Sydney, 16–20 July.

Fang, J., and C.Z. Wu. 2010. Exploring shifts in translating English nominal groups modified by embedded clauses: A corpus-based approach. Paper presented at the ASFLA Conference, *Practising Theory: Expanding Understandings of Language, Literature and Literacy*, Queensland University of Technology, Brisbane, 30 September–2 October.

Fang, Y., E. McDonald and M.S. Cheng. 1987. On Theme in Chinese: From clause to discourse. In R. Hasan and P.H. Fries (eds) *On Subject and Theme: A Discourse Functional Perspective*. Amsterdam and Philadelphia, PA: John Benjamins, pp. 235–74.

Halliday, M.A.K. 1994. *An Introduction to Functional Grammar*. 2nd edn. London: Arnold.

Halliday, M.A.K. 2004. *The Language of Science*. London: Continuum.

Halliday, M.A.K., and R. Hasan. 1976. *Cohesion in English*. London and New York: Longman.

Halliday, M.A.K., and C.M.I.M. Matthiessen. 1999. *Construing Experience through Meaning: A Language-Based Approach to Cognition*. London and New York: Cassell.

Halliday, M.A.K., and E. McDonald. 2004. Metafunctional profile of the grammar of Chinese. In A. Caffarel, J.R. Martin and C.M.I.M. Matthiessen (eds) *Language Typology: A Functional Perspective*. Amsterdam: John Benjamins, pp. 305–96.

Kratochvíl, P. 1968. *The Chinese Language Today: Features of an Emerging Standard*. London: Hutchinson University Library.

Li, C.N., and S.A. Thompson. 1981. *Mandarin Chinese: A Functional Reference Grammar*. Berkeley, CA: University of California Press.

Li, E.S.H. 2003. A text-based study of the grammar of Chinese from a systemic functional approach. Unpublished PhD thesis. Macquarie University, Sydney.

Li, E.S.H. 2007. *A Systemic Functional Grammar of Chinese*. London: Continuum.

Tiee, H.H.Y. 1990. *A Reference Grammar of Chinese Sentences*. Tucson, AZ: University of Arizona Press.

22

Grammatical metaphor

Miriam Taverniers

Introduction

One possible way of defining grammatical metaphor that can usefully be taken as a starting point is the notion of 'congruence'. In this perspective, expressions that are regarded as examples of grammatical metaphor are 'incongruent' in that they depart in one way or another (to be specified shortly) from the 'default' or 'congruent' way in which 'the same meaning' can be expressed. For instance, ideational meanings are typically realised in the clause by means of process configurations – that is, constellations of a process, participants and circumstances: in example (1a), *you examine* [a] *model, you . . . conclude that* [something is the case]. Clauses are congruently linked by means of conjunctions or other types of connective, for example *if* in example (1a). Example (1b) departs from this mode of expression: here, two configurations are realised as nominal groups – namely, *an examination of any typical model* and *the conclusion that this is not possible* – and the link between the two is realised as a modalised relational process, *will lead to*. Nominalisations and the realisation of a configuration link by means of a relational process are regarded as **ideational grammatical metaphors** in systemic functional linguistics (SFL) (Halliday 1985a).

    (1a)   If you examine any typical model, you will conclude that this (type of damage) is not possible.

    (1b)   ONE OF the most common types of damage which the novice pilot is likely to inflict on his model is that caused by one of the main rotor blades coming into contact with the tailboom. <u>An examination of any typical model will lead to the conclusion that this is not possible.</u>[1]

Interpersonal meanings of modal assessment are typically realised in the clause by means of modal auxiliaries, as in example (2a), or mood adjuncts, as in example (2b). When a modal assessment is coded by a projecting clause (see Butt, this volume), as in example (2c), the expression is regarded as an **interpersonal grammatical metaphor** (of modality) (Halliday 1985a).

(2a)　You <u>must</u> be the boldest man I ever met with.

(2b)　You are <u>probably</u> the boldest man I ever met with.

(2c)　<u>I think</u> you are the boldest man I ever met with.[2]

'Grammatical metaphor' is conceived of as the grammatical variant of the traditionally known type of (lexical) metaphor: in the same sense as a figurative expression is metaphorical because it differs from a (more) literal rendering of a meaning, grammatical metaphor is **metaphorical** in that it deviates from a more typical, or more congruent, means of expression.

Historical perspective

The notion of 'grammatical metaphor' as it is characterised in Halliday's SFL is intrinsically intertwined with the conception of two crucial dimensions of the SFL architecture (see Berry, this volume):

1　the flexible interface between lexicogrammar and semantics (**stratification**); and
2　the nature of the different metafunctional components (**metafunctions**).

This section will trace the initial development of the concept of grammatical metaphor in SFL, starting with the introduction of the notion in Halliday (1985a). It will briefly consider 'precursory' conceptions of congruence before 1985, to arrive at a better understanding of Halliday's thinking on grammatical metaphor. On the basis of this, some key themes in the initial conception of 'grammatical metaphor' will be identified; in this exploration, special attention will be paid to the way in which grammatical metaphor is hooked up with the theoretical dimensions of stratification and metafunctional complementarity.

Halliday's introduction of 'grammatical metaphor'

The concept of 'grammatical metaphor' as it is known today in SFL was originally introduced in the first edition of Halliday's (1985a) *Introduction to Functional Grammar*. According to Halliday, the traditional view of lexical metaphor, which takes a perspective 'from below' (that is, one word/lexeme may have different meanings, literal and metaphorical), needs to be complemented with a view 'from above' (that is, one meaning may be realised in various formal/lexicogrammatical expressions) (cf. Taverniers 2006). 'From below' and 'from above' refer to the model of stratification, with the higher strata (for example context, semantics) at the top and the lower strata (for example lexicogrammar, phonology/graphology) at the bottom.

Halliday (1985a) recognises two major types of grammatical metaphor – namely, *ideational* and *interpersonal*. The ideational type are introduced as **metaphors of transitivity** because they involve changes in the transitivity configurations (as in example (1b)). Within the interpersonal type, Halliday makes a distinction between **metaphors of modality** (as in example (2c)) and **metaphors of mood**. A typical example of this last is where a speech functional meaning of a 'command' is not realised by an imperative (which is its simplest and most congruent realization, according to Halliday), as in example (3a), but rather by means of a modalized interrogative, as in example (3b).

(3a)　Tell me the way to Leicester Square.

(3b)　Could you please tell me the way to Leicester Square?[3]

'Congruence' in pre-1985 work in SFL

Before the introduction of grammatical metaphor in Halliday (1985a), the notion of congruence appeared in some earlier work. Three different contexts can be distinguished, as follows.

1   In Halliday (1956, 1976, 1978), **congruence** is introduced in relation to 'markedness', 'norm' and 'probability value' in the study of (social) varieties of language: incongruent expressions are 'marked' in relation to what is normative in a variety of language and have lower probability values. Congruent and incongruent expressions are seen as **variants** – a term inspired by Labov's (1969) variation theory, in which variants are 'alternative ways of "saying the same thing"' (Labov, quoted in Halliday 1976: 577). Halliday (1976) calls these variants **metaphorical**, because it is impossible to decide whether or not they have exactly the same 'meaning' as Labov implies. These types of variant exist on all levels of language; hence Halliday (1976) proposes the terms 'phonological metaphors', 'grammatical metaphors' (which can be morphological, lexical or syntactic) and 'semantic metaphors'.

2   Fawcett (1980) takes up Halliday's concept of congruence and proposes a 'CONGRUENCE network' in which *nominalised* structures are represented, systemically, as less typical options and variants of other structures. In SFL terms, this thus provides a precursory network of how **ideational** metaphor could be dealt with. Within Fawcett's model – which later came to be known as the 'Cardiff' variant of SFL (see later in the chapter and Fawcett, this volume) – this network is regarded as the primary one – that is, as the first network before any other functionally specific network is entered. For instance, the selection in the congruence network of 'referent regarded as situation' and realised 'straightforwardly' (that is, as a full clause) forms the input (entry condition) for the more specific network of ILLOCUTIONARY FORCE.

3   Halliday (1984) focuses on the lack of a one-to-one relation, within the **interpersonal** metafunction, between speech functional meanings and lexicogrammatical structures that realise those meanings, and hence the need to model the 'content' side of language as containing (at least) two levels: lexicogrammar and semantics. Halliday (1984) thus introduces the system of SPEECH FUNCTION to model interpersonal semantics. Options from the system of SPEECH FUNCTION are said to have congruent realisations in the MOOD system, characterised as 'typical' or 'unmarked' realisations. For the interpersonal metafunction, Halliday (1984: 14) specifies a link between incongruence and increased delicacy: '[M]any of the more delicate distinctions within any system depend for their expression on what in the first instance appear as non-congruent forms.'

Reassessment of Halliday's introduction of grammatical metaphor

Grammatical metaphor was introduced into Hallidayan SFL at a time when **stratification** was a highly discussed topic (see Berry, this volume), with a focus on the question of how many strata are useful or needed (cf. Halliday 1985b). We saw how the notion of congruence was fleshed out in Halliday's (1984) treatment of SPEECH FUNCTION in relation to categories of MOOD, in the first publication in which a general semantic network is proposed,[4] in addition to a network of structures at the stratum of lexicogrammar. The stratification of the content side of language into a lexicogrammar and a semantics is thus intrinsically related to the role of grammatical metaphor in language: it is because the content is 'internally stratified' (Halliday et al. 1992) that language has metaphoric power. Indeed, Halliday (2008: 16) proposed the distinction between lexicogrammar and semantics to account for grammatical metaphor. This shows the great theoretical importance of the notion of grammatical metaphor to the development of the model as a whole.

In addition to its general hook-up with stratification, it is useful to specify some other themes that can be discerned in the initial view of grammatical metaphor, some of which form running threads in subsequent research.

- In relation to earlier SFL work on 'congruence', it should be noted that the concept of 'grammatical metaphor' is more **dynamic and creative**: it is no longer purely defined negatively, as 'what is *not* the norm', as '*in*congruent' is, and it is linked to the concept of a flexible relation between semantics and lexicogrammar, which makes the overall meaning potential as powerful as it is.
- There is a shift to a **perspective 'from above'**, which characterises much post-1985 work in SFL, because the stratum of semantics comes to play a crucial role in theorising 'grammatical metaphor'.
- Grammatical metaphor is relevant for the **ideational and interpersonal** metafunctions.
- Instead of a specification of 'incongruent' as different from 'congruent' (parallel to 'figurative' as different from 'literal' in the traditional perspective on metaphor, as we have seen), the focus is on **variation** in expression and in meaning, and this opens up the way towards recognise a **scale** of congruence (as we will see later in the chapter).
- In contrast to the traditional view on metaphor, the focus is on grammatical **configurations** rather than (lexical) items (in isolation) – a view that has far-ranging potential implications, which have especially been explored in relation to ideational metaphor, as we will see.

These themes set the scene for the further development of grammatical metaphor, to which we will turn in the next section.

Major theoretical and descriptive topics

After its introduction in Halliday (1985a), grammatical metaphor was explored intensively, from both theoretical and descriptive angles. From a theoretical perspective, the nature of grammatical metaphor in relation to stratification and the dynamics of language were especially highlighted. From a descriptive view, the definition, identification and analysis of ideational and interpersonal metaphors in different contexts became an important topic of research. In this respect, ideational metaphor has received much more attention than interpersonal metaphor, as we will see in what follows.

Grammatical metaphor in relation to stratification

In connection with the theme of stratification, grammatical metaphor is characterised as involving a **tension** between different interpretations and, in this sense, is reconnected with the traditional concept of metaphor, with its tension between literal and figurative meanings. Within the stratified model, this tension is defined as a 'stratal tension' (Martin 1997: 33) – that is, a tension between the wording and the meaning of an expression. This is often illustrated with examples of verbal play, as in example (4), taken from Martin (1995: 39).

(4)   Conversation between Dr. Watson and Sherlock Holmes
      'I'm inclined to think – ' said I.
      'I should do so,' Sherlock Holmes remarked impatiently.

Here, Watson uses an interpersonal metaphor of modality to assess the probability of a proposition, with *I'm inclined to think* meaning something like 'It might be the case that . . . ' or 'It may probably be that . . . '. Holmes interrupts him and takes up the literal meaning, in which *think* is a mental process of cognition. Similar tensions can be seen in interpersonal metaphors of mood – in which, for instance, an interrogative such as *Could you open the window?* can have 'literal' interpretation as a question (request for information) or a metaphorical one as a command (request for a service to be done) – and in ideational metaphors – in which, for instance, a nominalisation can be interpreted as a 'thing' or as a 'process'.

Halliday (1998: 192) characterises grammatical metaphor as a 'realignment between a pair of strata'; alternatively, as 'a cross-coupling (decoupling, and recoupling in a different alignment) between the semantics and the lexicogrammar)' (Halliday 2008: 16).

The semogenic power of grammatical metaphor

In the 1990s, language as a dynamic open system became an important theme in SFL. In this view, language is defined as **metastable** – that is, it persists by constantly adapting to new environments (Halliday 1990: 86). The internal stratification of the content plane of language plays a central role in this perspective. It is only when a system evolves different content strata that it has the power to adapt: it becomes flexible because different strata can be decoupled and recoupled in interaction with ever-changing environments. Language adapts by changing and, in this view, grammatical metaphor becomes a means to innovate in language at the level of structure (grammar), just like traditional metaphor can be the basis of innovations at the level of words (lexis). Metaphor (in general) is a means to expand the overall meaning potential of a language – that is, it is a 'powerful meaning-making resource' (Halliday 2003: 20).

Grammatical metaphor is an example of a higher-order semiotic resource, because it builds on existing resources (that is, existing form–meaning couplings) and further expands those. Thus Halliday (1992) hypothesises that, in each of the three timescales of **semogenesis** that he distinguishes, *congruent forms precede metaphorical ones*: in **ontogenesis**, the development of the language of an individual; in **phylogenesis**, the evolution of a language system and in **logogenesis**, the unfolding of language in a text (cf. Halliday and Matthiessen 1999: 235).

Ideational metaphor: fully packed

In the description and analysis of grammatical metaphor in texts, ideational metaphor has received extensive attention, and this chapter can offer only a cursory overview of the major themes that have emerged from this research.

It is well known that a highly nominalised 'style' is characteristic of scientific and bureaucratic discourse, and it is especially in those registers that ideational metaphor has been studied. What the SFL approach has brought to this domain of research can be summarised as follows.

1   As we saw earlier in the chapter, grammatical metaphor has to do with **variation** in form. For instance, a typical case of an ideational metaphor is that in which a meaning that could be encoded as a process configuration – that is, as a clause – is packaged in a more condensed form – that is, in a nominal group. In most cases, there is a range of variants that are possible, and Halliday (1998, for example) presents 'congruent' and 'metaphorical' as two poles of a **continuum**. In keeping with the view of ideational metaphor as a condensed, highly packaged form of expression, one can 'deconstruct' an ideational metaphor by **unpacking** it and this can be done in steps, as shown in example (5). Each step, from example (5a) to example (5e), produces a more congruent rewording compared to the previous one.

(a) Increasing failure to grow enough food on the part of farmers leads to a decline in productivity (5) through a lack of energy and malnutrition.
(b) If there is an increasing failure to grow enough food, then there will be a decline in productivity through a lack of energy and malnutrition.
(c) If the farmers are not able to grow enough food and this gets worse and worse, productivity will decline through a lack of energy and malnutrition.
(d) If the farmers are not able to grow enough food and this gets worse and worse, they will become less productive through a lack of energy and malnutrition.
(e) If the farmers are not able to grow enough food and this gets worse and worse, then they will become less productive because they will have less energy and will be malnourished.[5]

2   Nominalisation does not occur on its own, but is part of a larger **set of shifts** that occur simultaneously. For instance, if *less* in *people will become less productive because they will have less energy* (example (5e)) is nominalised (into the noun *decline*), at the same time *productive* will be nominalised (*a decline in productivity*) and the hypotactic *because*-clause will be reworded as a prepositional phrase (. . . *through* . . .) in which the preposition will then also necessarily be followed by a nominal expression (*lack of energy*) instead of a clausal process configuration. Ideational grammatical metaphors are thus described as occurring in **syndromes**. A more fine-grained analysis of such syndromes and the various steps that can be taken in unpacking highly condensed metaphors has led to a typology of ideational metaphor,[6] and has revealed an ordering in the types of metaphoric shifts that can occur – namely, 'relator → circumstance → process → quality → entity' (Halliday 1998: 211). This is an implicational hierarchy: all shifts to the right can occur, but no shift to the left. Halliday (1998: 211) refers to this ordering as a general 'drift' 'towards thinginess'.

The various steps are illustrated in example (6). The most straightforward (congruent) encoding of a causal link between two configurations is through a relator (in example (6a), *because*) and the most condensed, highly packaged encoding of this causal meaning is as an entity (in example (6e), *cause*).

(6a)	Heating costs are minimal <u>because</u> the weather is mild.	relator	↓
(6b)	Heating costs are minimal <u>because of the weather</u>.[7]	circumstance	↓
(6c)	The mild weather <u>results</u> in minimal heating costs.	process	↓
(6d)	The minimal heating costs are <u>ascribable</u> to the weather.	quality	↓
(6e)	<u>The cause of the minimal heating costs</u> is the weather.	entity	

3   The question of **why** grammatical metaphor is so common in certain types of register (and hence why a language user might choose a metaphorical, rather than a congruent, expression) has aroused considerable interest, as has (and to an even greater extent) the follow-up question of how the value of grammatical metaphor in specific registers can be assessed: is it a good or a bad thing, and for whom? Two distinct, but interrelated, motifs have been recognised for the use of ideational metaphor in scientific discourse (cf. Halliday and Martin 1993):

a   a **technicalising** (or categorising, or taxonomic) motif – that is, where nominalisations are the primary source of technical terminology;[8] and

b   a **rationalising** motif – that is, where nominalised 'packages' (as Halliday calls them) of information tend to occur in the Theme/Given position of a clause and hence form the point of departure for the further argumentation or reasoning.

The first is more *systemic*, in that new categories are formed that become part and parcel of a theory, whereas the second is *instantial*: it pertains to carrying forward the argument in specific discursive instances (Halliday 1998).

The question of the function of grammatical metaphor has been a recurrent topic of discussion. In Halliday's and Martin's work on scientific discourse, motifs for using grammatical metaphor are presented as positive: grammatical metaphor helps in construing knowledge and in organising the complex scientific reasoning that takes place. In this respect, this approach to grammatical metaphor stands in contrast to much work in critical discourse analysis, where nominalisation is primarily depicted as a mechanism to mystify agency (in the same vein as passivisation and one-participant ergative processes[9]). Thus the popular research on the use of grammatical metaphor in specific text genres (which forms a substantial strand of research for ideational metaphor) starts from the premise that 'ideational metaphor equals power' (Halliday 1990: 71) and oscillates between two ideological perspectives: one highlighting grammatical metaphor as a mechanism that has enabled (and that has even been essential in) the advancement of modern science (for example Goatly 1996); the other focusing on the nominalised discourse of the expert as 'a language of power and technocratic control' (Halliday 1998: 228) that creates a distance between scientific knowledge and the everyday experience of life – that is, between the expert and the layman/learner.

Interpersonal metaphor: more hedging please

Further explorations of Halliday's concept of interpersonal grammatical metaphor, both in terms of further theoretical refinement and in terms of applying the concept in the analysis of text instances, are much less numerous compared to the study of ideational metaphor. This probably has to do with a kind of 'indeterminacy' that is inherent in interpersonal metaphors. This is first true of interpersonal metaphors of mood, since 'languages do not display clearcut categories in the grammar corresponding to offers and commands' (Halliday 1984: 19), which makes it more difficult to determine what counts as 'congruent' in the realisation of speech functions and thus to motivate why other types of construction would be regarded as metaphorical (cf. Butler 1988a). For instance, the imperative, which Halliday views as the most congruent realisation of a command, is much limited in use, more 'polite' forms of command, containing different types of hedging, being more common. This is also the case in the context of ontogenesis, since the child often hears these 'alternative' expressions of command. This probably explains why Halliday's hypothesis that the congruent comes first in ontogenesis has not been demonstrated in the interpersonal domain (if one takes the imperative as congruent) (cf. Painter 2003), in contrast to the ideational one.

For interpersonal grammatical metaphor in general, there is no clear continuum from more to less congruent, as is found with ideational metaphor,[10] nor have recurrent patterns of shifts been identified that occur in interpersonal metaphor; hence there is no overview of interpersonal metaphor in terms of types of lexicogrammatical shift and possible relations between them.[11]

Butler (1988b: 94, for example) suggests that to formulate the principles behind **why** a speaker might choose a metaphorical, rather than a congruent, expression of mood or modality and also the principles by which interpersonal metaphors can be interpreted, one should approach 'interpersonal metaphor' from the perspective of pragmatics and take into account insights proposed by Grice, such as the cooperative principle and the relevance principle. However, this suggestion has never been taken up in SFL and the question of what are the functions (or even the *raison d'être*) of interpersonal metaphor is still relatively ignored, compared to ideational metaphor.[12]

One area of the Sydney Model onto which the concept of interpersonal grammatical metaphor has shed new light is that of the logico-semantic relation of projection. Halliday and Matthiessen (2004: 626) introduce the category of 'interpersonal projection', which includes constructions with projecting mental processes in the (traditional) strict sense (type: *I think . . . , I believe . . .*) and also relational modal assessment constructions containing a quality, which are projecting in a broader sense (such as *It's unbelievable that . . .*).

Grammatical metaphor phenomena in other frameworks

Table 22.1 offers a cursory overview of treatments, in other linguistic frameworks, of phenomena that are regarded as grammatical metaphors in (Sydney) SFL[13] and of some broader, related phenomena.

Evidently, the most crucial aspect in which the Sydney SFL approach differs from others is the very conception of these phenomena as 'metaphorical' and thus also the link that is made with 'metaphor' in the traditional sense. However, this itself is (only) a metaphorical extension of the use of the term 'metaphor'. More fundamentally, what sets the Hallidayan approach apart from all others is the fact these different phenomena are conceived of as pertaining to something similar, to a similar kind of mechanism that is at work – that is, the fact that they are subsumed under *one* theoretical category. The difference of this overarching approach is most visible in the link that is made between ideational and interpersonal phenomena – they are both instances of 'grammatical metaphor' – but it can also be seen within the metafunctions. The embedding of nominalisation – a phenomenon that is relatively well studied in various linguistic frameworks – within a larger set of shifts (called 'syndromes of metaphors') and the organisation of these shifts in terms of a hierarchy is unique to SFL. Similarly, within the interpersonal realm, the link that is made between two relatively well-established categories of phenomena – illocutionary speech acts (interpersonal metaphors of mood) and propositional attitude phenomena (interpersonal metaphors of modality) – is unseen elsewhere.

Table 22.1 'Grammatical metaphor phenomena' and related phenomena in other linguistic frameworks (and other disciplines)

	'Grammatical metaphor phenomena' in other linguistic frameworks	*Broader related phenomena in linguistics (and other disciplines)*	*Perspective*
Ideational grammatical metaphor		• nouniness vs. clausehood of different types of complement/ degrees of finiteness :: higher perspective in terms of rank scale: complexing & embedding • word formation :: lower perspective in terms of rank scale: word rank	← *synoptic perspective: lexicogrammar: rank scale*
	• research tradition on 'abstract nouns' (Halliday and Hasan 1976) or 'anaphoric nouns'/'A-nouns' (Francis 1986) as Themes; later also called 'shell nouns' (Schmid 2000)		← *dynamic perspective: logogenesis*
		• LEXICALISATION	← *dynamic perspective: phylogenesis*
		• (developmental) psychology and philosophy: theories of encapsulation/ reification; concept development (e.g. Piaget)	← *dynamic perspective: ontogenesis*
Interpersonal grammatical metaphor	Metaphors of mood	• illocutionary and perlocutionary speech acts	← *synoptic perspective: semantics/'pragmatics'*
		• adjacency pairs; preferred and dis-preferred seconds	← *dynamic perspective: logogenesis*

Metaphors of modality	• propositional attitudes	• non-factivity vs. factivity with mental process complementation	← synoptic perspective: semantics and lexicogrammar
	• work in pragmatics on hedging and politeness phenomena (also relevant for metaphors of mood)		← synoptic perspective: 'pragmatics'
		• GRAMMATICALISATION (of metaphors into discourse markers, e.g. *I think*)	← dynamic perspective: phylogenesis

Critical issues

The focus of this section is on a number of critical issues that have characterised the study of grammatical metaphor in SFL since its inception and which are primary challenges for the further refinement of the concept. These can be summarised in terms of three dimensions, as follows.

1   A first issue concerns the **theoretical representation** of grammatical metaphor in systemic functional terms – more specifically, the place of grammatical metaphor in a *stratified* model in which meaningful options are represented by *system networks*: how can the multiple-to-multiple relation between lexicogrammar and semantics be modelled? Does the recognition of this relation entail that we need separate system networks for both strata? How can grammatical metaphor be networked?

2   A second area of concern pertains to **metafunctional diversity** – more specifically, **metafunctional types of grammatical metaphor**: what is the specific nature of ideational and interpersonal metaphor? What do they share in addition to being 'incongruent' – that is, apart from the 'stratal tension' that they display?

3   A third major domain of development concerns the study of the **function of metaphor** in specific textual instances and text types (registers/genres), and also the role of metaphor (in addition to incongruence and markedness) in **semogenesis**: what is the role of specific types of grammatical metaphor in different registers/genres, and how does this role change along different timescales (across texts, in an individual or in a language)?

The first two dimensions are related to the two theoretical themes, pointed out earlier in the chapter, which are essential in understanding 'grammatical metaphor' from a theoretical perspective within the architecture of SFL – namely, *stratification* and *metafunctional diversity*. The third dimension looks more applied, because it thematises the use of metaphor in text (types), but it hinges on an additional theoretical theme that has to be taken into consideration: the link between system and text (*instantiation*), and, in relation to this, the nature of register as an intermediate category (between system and text). The three domains of development pointed out here can be used as running threads in exploring recent contributions to the study of grammatical metaphor, which is the topic of the next section.

Recent and current contributions

This section briefly reviews recent contributions in SFL that explicitly address the question of how grammatical metaphor can be incorporated into the architecture of the model. Three types of modelling can be distinguished, which thus represent three strands in current metaphor research in SFL (of which Table 22.2 offers an overview).

1   Recent proposals in **Sydney** SFL focus on the semantic stratum and its relation to lexicogrammar. Three different types of *new* semantic model (with *system networks*) have been proposed, each of which incorporates grammatical metaphor in its own way and each of which thematises a different metafunctional component: Martin's discourse semantics (which starts from textual considerations, but comprises all metafunctions); appraisal theory (which pertains to the interpersonal metafunction) and Halliday and Matthiessen's model of the ideation base (that is, ideational semantics).
2   **Cardiff** SFL incorporates phenomena that Halliday subsumes under 'grammatical metaphor' into *existing networks* of MOOD, VALIDITY ASSESSMENT, etc.
3   A third, **functional-constructional**, strand of SFL research can be recognised that incorporates insights from Langacker's cognitive grammar. The focus here is on *constructional* properties of grammatical metaphors.

Incorporating grammatical metaphor in semantic models: The Sydney approach

1   Martin's (1992: 19) **discourse semantics** starts from the view that grammatical metaphor and cohesion are semantic motifs that form the 'impetus for stratification'. Ideational grammatical metaphor is incorporated as a resource that contributes to the cohesion of a text in multiple ways. Grammatical metaphor creates participants (which

Table 22.2 Recent strands in grammatical metaphor studies in SFL

Strand of SFL	Model		Primary axis focused on to incorporate grammatical metaphor
Sydney	*textual* starting point (cohesion)	> **discourse semantics** (Martin 1992)	**paradigmatic and vertical integration** of grammatical metaphor
	interpersonal starting point (evaluative meaning)	> **appraisal theory** (Martin and White 2005)	
	ideational starting point (the ideation base)	> model of the **ideation base** (Halliday and Matthiessen 1999)	
Cardiff	'grammatical metaphor phenomena' incorporated in **existing networks** (regarded as 'semantic')		**paradigmatic and horizontal absorption** of grammatical metaphor phenomena
Functional-constructional	grammatical metaphor as a **doubling of semiosis** (Taverniers 2002, forthcoming)		**syntagmatic integration** of grammatical metaphor

may then play a role in reference chains) (Martin 1992: 138*ff*), and builds taxonomies and thus reconstrues lexical relations in a text (Martin 1992: 328). Ideational metaphor packages information as Theme or New, which is then linked to other information in the Rheme – that is, not through the system of CLAUSE COMPLEXING as in congruent expressions. Grammatical metaphor is seen as a 'gatekeeper' or a 'processing interface' between semantics and lexicogrammar: just as interpersonal grammatical metaphor mediates between the semantics of SPEECH FUNCTION and the lexicogrammar of MOOD, so ideational grammatical metaphor is an interface between the semantic system of CONJUNCTION and the lexicogrammatical systems of clause complexing – namely, TAXIS and LOGICO-SEMANTIC RELATION (Martin 1992: 389). The idea is then further expanded in that the 'processing interface' is regarded as sensitive to register variation (interpersonal metaphor is sensitive to tenor and ideational metaphor is sensitive to field) and the link with register provides the *raison d'être* of the processing interfaces (Martin 1992: 417).

2   **Appraisal theory** was set up in SFL to account for evaluative language in a systemic way. In this framework, numerous shades of evaluative meanings and the ways in which they can be expressed in language are classified and organised in a system network. The phenomenon of interpersonal grammatical metaphor formed an explicit source of inspiration for this work: it has been through the notion of interpersonal metaphor that systemic functional linguists recognised how the diversity of lexicogrammatical structures that are available to express interpersonal meanings pertain to a common semantic area (cf. White 1999). The model of appraisal is presented as an interpersonal component within the stratum of discourse semantics (Martin and White 2005). Its network contains various options that are realised by projecting clause complexes (in the broader sense of 'projection' pointed out earlier in the chapter).

3   Halliday and Matthiessen (1999) present a system network of the **ideation base**, or ideational semantics, of English. The introduction of a separate semantic stratum with its own network is again motivated in relation to the modelling of grammatical metaphor.[14] What they propose is, in essence, a semantic version of the systems of ideational lexicogrammar of TRANSITIVITY and CLAUSE COMPLEXING (LOGICO-SEMANTIC RELATIONS and TAXIS). A major innovation (other than a range of refinements of those earlier systems) lies in the primary options in the network. The network's starting point (entry condition) is called 'phenomenon', which then has three primary options: 'sequence', 'figure' and 'element'. Each of those can be realised by congruent or incongruent realisations in the lexicogrammar; hence the model assigns an important role to grammatical metaphor.

Incorporating 'grammatical metaphor phenomena' in existing networks: the Cardiff approach

In the Cardiff grammar (see Fawcett, this volume), 'grammatical metaphor' is not regarded as a (special) phenomenon in its own right. Relations between expressions as in examples (1)–(3), (5) and (6) are dealt with as **equivalences** – that is, alternatives in logical form that are pragmatically equivalent. In the Cardiff grammar, 'logical form' refers to the level above the (semantic) system networks, which is the input for the networks and which models the alternatives that are available in a language for expressing a particular meaning (cf. Fawcett forthcoming). Through a type of decision tree (called a 'microplanner') that consults relevant aspects of the 'belief system', a language user is able to decide which logical form to select from a number of possible alternatives. The higher level of logical form and the notion of equivalence (and microplanners) are thus the Cardiff grammar's tools to model the concept of choice in the (semantic) system networks in general, such as between an active or a passive voice, or between different types of thematisation. In this sense, what Halliday regards as grammatically metaphorical expressions are equivalent to other expressions (regarded as congruent in the Sydney Model) at the level of the belief system and thus the phenomena that Halliday regards as metaphorical are accommodated in the existing Cardiff Model without additional architecture.

Incorporating grammatical metaphor as a construction type: a functional-constructional approach

In Taverniers (2002, forthcoming), the focus is on grammatical metaphor as a possible construction type, starting from the question: what is it exactly, in the *structure* of ideational and interpersonal grammatical metaphors, that makes them metaphorical? The aim of this work is to provide a definition of grammatical metaphor that takes into account three prerequisites.

1   *Identify grammatical 'metaphoricity'*. The definition must characterise grammatical metaphor as a resource in its own right, while also recognising it as a second-order phenomenon of language, as metaphor in general is.
2   *Account for ideational and interpersonal metaphors*   The definition must be general enough to comprise ideational and interpersonal grammatical metaphor, yet at the same time flesh out the specific 'guise' of grammatical metaphor in the ideational and interpersonal metafunctions.
3   *Specify the content and expression sides of grammatical metaphor as a linguistic sign*   The definition must identify the semantic import and the lexicogrammatical expression form of grammatical metaphors.

As a first step towards this type of definition, one needs a clear view of the expression form and semantics that characterise the ideational and interpersonal metafunctions in general, regardless of grammatical metaphor. In defining this ideational and interpersonal 'default semiosis', Taverniers (2002, forthcoming) takes as a basis Halliday's (1979) characterisation of the metafunctional 'modes of meaning' and 'modes of expression' (which became known as his 'wave–particle–field' motif), and further specify those by including insights from Langacker's cognitive grammar and McGregor's semiotic grammar.

At the *content* side, the interpersonal component can be defined as having a **grounding** function, adapting a concept introduced by Langacker (1991): the enactment of social relations is fulfilled, linguistically, by grounding the message to the speaker–now context. Ideational semantics are **configurational** (Halliday 1979): experience is construed, linguistically, by configuring an event (or figure), a thing or a quality.

At the *expression* side, interpersonal meanings are realised in a field-like manner, through prosodies (Halliday 1979). Following McGregor (1997: 236), we can call this mode of expression 'scope'. An interpersonal element has **scope** over the unit through which it runs as 'a continuous motif or colouring' (Halliday 1979: 66). Ideational meanings are realised in a particulate way (Halliday 1979), by different building blocks of experience bundled together. We can call this mode of expression 'bundling' (a term intended to cover both constituency and dependency structure).

Grammatical metaphor is then defined as a **doubling of semiosis** – that is, a doubling of the default semiosis that characterises the ideational and interpersonal metafunctions. At the structural level, grammatical metaphors make a double use of the typical types of patterning. In ideational metaphor, there are two levels of configuration of figures, because one (nominalised) figure becomes a participant in another figure. In interpersonal metaphor, there are likewise two layers of grounding: one provided by a projecting clause, the other provided by the default grounding devices (that is, Finite, Adjuncts).

Through the concept of 'doubling of semiosis', we can attempt to identify structurally or syntagmatically the stratal tension that is typical of grammatical metaphor and the view that grammatical metaphor is a way of 'using existing resources more than once' (Martin and Matthiessen 1991: 350). In ideational metaphor, the tension is between a 'thing' and a 'figure' meaning, because a nominalisation occurs in a 'thing' slot in an event configuration, but internally has the structure of an event configuration of its own. In interpersonal metaphor, there is a tension between the 'literal' ideational meaning of the projecting clause that interpersonally assesses a projected clause that already has its default grounding (in its Finite and Modal Adjuncts, if there are any) and a (re)interpretation of this projecting clause as a grounding device itself. The projecting clause has this possibility because it construes the speaker–now context ideationally. This doubling effect, in ideational and interpersonal metaphor, is what the definition is intended to capture in structural terms.

Different ways of incorporating 'grammatical metaphor': a meta-theoretical comparison

The three models of grammatical metaphor described in this section approach the phenomenon and attempt to integrate it within an SFL architecture in different ways (cf. the last column in Table 22.2). A distinction can be made in terms of the **critical issues** identified earlier: the Sydney and Cardiff Models' focus on grammatical metaphor in relation to *stratification* and *system networks*, and the functional-constructional proposal's highlighting of the theme of *metafunctional complementarity* in focusing on what ideational and interpersonal metaphors have in common. From a meta-theoretical perspective, this distinction in approach can be further specified in terms of the **axis** that is taken as a primary 'entry point' to theorising the concept of grammatical metaphor: the Sydney and Cardiff Models take a *paradigmatic* look, while the functional-constructional model starts from the *syntagmatic* axis. Within the paradigmatic approach, there is a further contrast. The Sydney Model, on the one hand, incorporates grammatical metaphor by 'upgrading' the semantics – that is, by introducing new system networks for this stratum – and, in this way, grammatical metaphor is *integrated 'vertically'*. In the Cardiff Model, on the other hand, the view of levels of encoding (in this case, the semantics, where the networks are and the higher level of the belief system) is not changed to deal with grammatical metaphor and 'grammatical metaphor phenomena' are incorporated in existing (semantic) networks (which are seen as on a par with the Sydney lexicogrammatical networks); hence grammatical metaphor is *'horizontally' absorbed* into the existing networks. The vertical vs. horizontal approaches to incorporating grammatical metaphor are thus in keeping with the overall difference in architecture – more specifically, with regard to the number of strata. As noted earlier, the presence of (at least) two strata in the Sydney architecture is intrinsically intertwined with the conception of grammatical metaphor.

Future directions

It is consequently clear that there is no consensus on how to model 'grammatical metaphor' – how to incorporate it – within the overall architecture of a systemic functional theory of language. The challenge is all the more daunting and fascinating because 'grammatical metaphor' *par excellence* is intertwined with the major differentiating dimensions[15] of the architecture, not only *stratification* and *metafunctional diversity*, which appear first from a theoretical perspective and which we took as a starting point in this chapter, but also *systemic representation*, the *system–instance* interaction and *synoptic–dynamic* distinction, and the *lexis–grammar* continuum (which we have not considered in this chapter, but will briefly touch upon in this final section). A **theoretical study** of 'grammatical metaphor' in relation to these dimensions is evidently (still) on the research agenda; a **meta-theoretical comparison** of proposals that have been developed so far, focusing on how (in)compatible they are, would also be very welcome.

In addition to this evident path for the further study of grammatical metaphor within SFL, there are at least two further specific challenges. One is to **engage with work** on 'grammatical metaphor phenomena' in other frameworks, both within linguistics and between disciplines. Another challenge is to further develop the **dynamic perspective**, with a special focus on the role of grammatical metaphor in phylogenesis.

Table 22.1 highlights that grammatical metaphor can be connected with myriad linguistic phenomena that have received attention in other frameworks. Engaging with this work would be valuable in further developing our understanding of grammatical metaphor from different perspectives, as indicated in the last column in Table 22.1. Some steps have been taken in that direction: in various places, Butler (1988a, 1988b, 1996) identifies aspects of pragmatics that are relevant in relation to interpersonal metaphor and, in Butler (2003: 59), he points out other relevant frameworks, which Heyvaert (2003a, 2003b) and Taverniers (2008) incorporate insights from Langacker's cognitive grammar in looking at the internal variation within ideational and interpersonal metaphor, respectively.

The role of grammatical metaphor in a dynamic perspective is a topic that deserves more attention, especially in a phylogenetic view, which has been relatively little studied in SFL, compared to grammatical metaphor in ontogenesis and logogenesis. SFL should connect with the concept and process of 'grammaticalisation' (and its relation to lexicalisation), which has received much attention in other (functionalist) frameworks in the last few decades, and which is an important area for cross-fertilisation between theories.[16] From a meta-theoretical viewpoint, in this connection, the relation between synoptic and dynamic views should also be further looked into: what is 'metaphorical' from a synoptic, systemic view is not always 'metaphorical' in specific instances and clarifying this may provide a step forward into solving the problem of the 'indeterminate' nature of interpersonal grammatical metaphor.

Notes

1 BNC CAY. Examples labelled 'BNC' in the notes have been taken from the British National Corpus (BNC), distributed by Oxford University Computing Services on behalf of the BNC Consortium. All rights in the texts cited are reserved.
2 BNC FU4.
3 BNC A0U.
4 The attribute 'general' has to be added here, because Halliday explored situation-specific models with two levels of networks, semantic and lexicogrammatical, to account for meanings and expressions that are available in highly specific settings, e.g. threats and warnings in the context of parental control. Cf. Taverniers (2002) for an overview.
5 BNC APN.

6 For overviews, see Halliday (1998: 209–10) or Halliday and Matthiessen (1999: ch. 6).

7 BNC CH1.

8 In this respect, ideational grammatical metaphor contributes to the lexical density of a text, and, in this sense, Halliday's concept of (ideational) grammatical metaphor sheds new light on the register variables of 'lexical density' and 'grammatical intricacy' that had been proposed in earlier research on register (cf. Ure 1971). (High lexical density and low grammatical intricacy are typical of written texts, whereas spoken texts show a greater degree of grammatical intricacy and a lower lexical density: see, e.g., Halliday 1994b.)

9 Cf. Martin (2008) on the distinction between these two types of approach.

10 Cf. 'Ideational metaphor: Fully packed', point 1.

11 Cf. 'Ideational metaphor: Fully packed', point 2.

12 Cf. 'Ideational metaphor: Fully packed', point 3. In her theory of 'message semantics' (see Moore, this volume), Hasan focuses on the relation between semantic choices and their realisations in the lexicogrammatical system of mood, and also analyses the function of those choices in discourse (e.g. Hasan 2009). However, the concept of interpersonal metaphor does not feature in this model (or is at least regarded as problematic – cf. Hasan 2010: 287).

13 Fawcett's (forthcoming) expression of 'grammatical metaphor phenomena' is exapted to refer to phenomena that are regarded as grammatical metaphors in (Sydney) SFL, with the understanding that the phenomena covered are *not* necessarily regarded as grammatically metaphorical, or metaphorical, in other frameworks (including Cardiff SFL, as we will see later in the chapter).

14 See also Halliday in Thibault (1987).

15 Cf. Taverniers (2002, forthcoming) for a further exploration of these.

16 For some proposals stretching SFL in that direction, see Kissine (2010) and Taverniers (2014).

References

Butler, C.S. 1988a. Politeness and the semantics of modalised directives in English. In J.D. Benson, M.J. Cummings and W.S. Greaves (eds) *Linguistics in a Systemic Perspective*. Amsterdam: John Benjamins, pp. 119–53.

Butler, C.S. 1988b. Pragmatics and systemic linguistics. *Journal of Pragmatics* 12: 83–102.

Butler, C.S. 1996. On the concept of an interpersonal metafunction in English. In M. Berry, R. Fawcett, C.S. Butler and G. Huang (eds) *Meaning and Form: Systemic Functional Interpretations*. (Meaning and Choice in Language: Studies for Michael Halliday – Advances in Discourse Processes 57). Norwood, NJ: Ablex, pp. 151–181.

Butler, C.S. 2003. *Structure and Function: A Guide to Three Major Structural-Functional Theories, Part 2 – From Clause to Discourse and beyond* (Studies in Language Companion 64). Amsterdam: John Benjamins.

Fawcett, R.P. 1980. *Cognitive Linguistics and Social Interaction: Towards an Integrated Model of a Systemic Functional Grammar and the Other Components of a Communicating Mind*. Heidelberg: Groos.

Fawcett, R.P. Forthcoming. *Alternative Architectures for Systemic Functional Linguistics: How Do We Choose?* London: Equinox.

Francis, G. 1986. *Anaphoric Nouns* (Discourse Analysis Monographs 11). Birmingham: University of Birmingham.

Goatly, A. 1996. Green grammar and grammatical metaphor, or language and the myth of power, or metaphors we die by. *Journal of Pragmatics* 25(4): 537–60.

Halliday, M.A.K. 1956. Grammatical categories in modern Chinese: An early sketch of the theory. *Transactions of the Philological Society*, pp. 180–202.

Halliday, M.A.K. 1976. Antilanguages. *American Anthropologist* 78(3): 570–84.

Halliday, M.A.K. 1978. Language in urban society. In *Language as Social Semiotic: The Social Interpretation of Language and Meaning*. London: Arnold, pp. 154–63.

Halliday, M.A.K. 1979. Modes of meaning and modes of expression: Types of grammatical structure, and their determination by different semantic functions. In D.J. Allerton, E. Carney and D. Holdcroft (eds) *Function and Context in Linguistic Analysis: A Festschrift for William Haas*. Cambridge: Cambridge University Press, pp. 57–79.

Halliday, M.A.K. 1984. Language as code and language as behaviour: A systemic-functional interpretation of the nature and ontogenesis of dialogue. In R.P. Fawcett, M.A.K. Halliday, S. Lamb and A. Makkai (eds) *The Semiotics of Culture and Language, Vol. 1: Language as Social Semiotic*. London: Pinter, pp. 3–35.

Halliday, M.A.K. 1985a. *Introduction to Functional Grammar*. London: Arnold.

Halliday, M.A.K. 1985b. Systemic background. In J.D. Benson and W.S. Greaves (eds) *Systemic Perspectives on Discourse. Vol. 1: Selected Theoretical Papers from the 9th International Systemic Workshop* (Advances in Discourse Processes 15). Norwood, NJ: Ablex, pp. 1–15.

Halliday, M.A.K. 1990. New ways of meaning: The challenge to applied linguistics. In M. Pütz (ed.) *Thirty Years of Linguistic Evolution*. Amsterdam: John Benjamins, pp. 59–95.

Halliday, M.A.K. 1992. How do you mean? In M. Davies and L. Ravelli (eds) *Advances in Systemic Linguistics: Recent Theory and Practice*. London: Pinter, pp. 20–35.

Halliday, M.A.K. 1994a. *Introduction to Functional Grammar*. 2nd edn. London: Arnold.

Halliday, M.A.K. 1994b. Spoken and written modes of meaning. In D. Graddol and O. Boyd-Barrett (eds) *Media Texts: Authors and Readers*. Avon: Multilingual Matters, pp. 51–73.

Halliday, M.A.K. 1998. Things and relations: Regrammaticising experience as technical knowledge. In J.R. Martin and R. Veel (eds) *Reading Science: Critical and Functional Perspectives on Discourses of Science*. London: Routledge, pp. 185–235.

Halliday, M.A.K. 2003. Introduction: On the 'architecture' of human language. In J.J. Webster (ed.) *Collected Works of M.A.K. Halliday, Vol. 3: On Language and Linguistics*. London: Continuum, pp. 1–29.

Halliday, M.A.K. 2008. Opening address: Working with meaning – Towards an appliable linguistics. In J.J. Webster (ed.) *Meaning in Context: Implementing Intelligent Applications of Language Studies*. London: Continuum, pp. 7–23.

Halliday, M.A.K., and R. Hasan. 1976. *Cohesion in English*. London: Longman.

Halliday, M.A.K., and J.R. Martin. 1993. *Writing Science: Literacy and Discursive Power* (Critical Perspectives on Literacy and Education). London: Falmer.

Halliday, M.A.K., and C.M.I.M. Matthiessen. 1999. *Construing Experience through Meaning: A Language-Based Approach to Cognition* (Open Linguistics Series). London: Cassell/Continuum.

Halliday, M.A.K., and C.M.I.M. Matthiessen. 2004. *Introduction to Functional Grammar*. 3rd edn. London: Arnold.

Halliday, M.A.K., G. Kress, R. Hasan and J.R. Martin. 1992. Interview with M.A.K. Halliday, May 1986: Part II. *Social Semiotics* 2: 58–69.

Hasan, R. 2009. *Semantic Variation: Meaning in Society and in Sociolinguistics – The Collected Works of Ruqaiya Hasan. Vol. 2*. London: Equinox.

Hasan, R. 2010. The meaning of 'not' is not in 'not'. In A. Mahboob and N. Knight (eds) *Appliable Linguistics*. London: Continuum, pp. 267–306.

Heyvaert, L. 2003a. *A Cognitive-Functional Approach to Nominalization in English*. Berlin: Mouton.

Heyvaert, L. 2003b. Nominalization as grammatical metaphor: On the need for a radically systemic and metafunctional approach. In A.-M. Simon-Vandenbergen, M. Taverniers and L. Ravelli (eds) *Grammatical Metaphor: Views from Systemic Functional Linguistics* (Current Issues in Linguistic Theory 236). Amsterdam: John Benjamins, pp. 65–99.

Kissine, M. 2010. Metaphorical projection, subjectification and English speech act verbs. *Folia Linguistica* 44(2): 339–70.

Labov, W. 1969. Contraction, deletion, and inherent variation of the English copula. *Language* 45(4): 715–62.

Langacker, R.W. 1991. *Foundations of Cognitive Grammar, Vol. II: Descriptive Application*. Stanford, CA: Stanford University Press.

Martin, J.R. 1992. *English Text: System and Structure*. Amsterdam: John Benjamins.

Martin, J.R. 1995. Interpersonal meaning, persuasion and public discourse: Packing semiotic punch. *Australian Journal of Linguistics* 15(1): 33–67.

Martin, J.R. 1997. Analysing genre: Functional parameters. In F. Christie and J.R. Martin (eds) *Genres and Institutions*. London: Cassell, pp. 3–39.

Martin, J.R. 2008. Incongruent and proud: De-vilifying 'nominalization'. *Discourse & Society* 19(6): 801–10.

Martin, J.R., and C.M.I.M. Matthiessen. 1991. Systemic typology and topology. In F. Christie (ed.) *Literacy in Social Processes*. Darwin, NT: Northern Territory University, Centre for Studies in Language and Education, pp. 345–83.

Martin, J.R., and P. White. 2005. *The Language of Evaluation*. New York: Palgrave.

McGregor, W.B. 1997. *Semiotic Grammar*. Oxford: Clarendon.

Painter, C. 2003. The use of a metaphorical mode of meaning in early language development. In A.M. Simon-Vandenbergen, M. Taverniers and L. Ravelli (eds) *Grammatical Metaphor: Views from Systemic Functional Linguistics* (Current Issues in Linguistic Theory 236). Amsterdam: John Benjamins, pp. 151–67.

Schmid, H.-J. 2000. *English Abstract Nouns as Conceptual Shells: From Corpus to Cognition* (Topics in English Linguistics 34). Berlin: Mouton de Gruyter.

Taverniers, M. 2002. Systemic-functional linguistics and the notion of grammatical metaphor: A theoretical study and the proposal for a semiotic-functional integrative model. Unpublished PhD dissertation. Ghent University.

Taverniers, M. 2006. Grammatical metaphor and lexical metaphor: Different perspectives on semantic variation. *Neophilologus* 90(2): 321–32.

Taverniers, M. 2008. Interpersonal grammatical metaphor as double scoping and double grounding. *WORD* 59(1–2): 83–109.

Taverniers, M. 2014. Grammatical metaphor and grammaticalization: Fractal patterns in linguistic change. Paper presented at the 25th European Systemic Functional Congress, Paris, 9–12 July.

Taverniers, M. Forthcoming. *Grammatical Metaphor as a Construction Type*. London: Equinox.

Thibault, P.J. 1987. An interview with Michael Halliday. In R. Steele and T. Threadgold (eds) *Essays in Honour of Michael Halliday, Vol. 2: Language Topics*. Amsterdam: John Benjamins, pp. 601–27.

Ure, J.N. 1971. Lexical density and register differentiation. In G.E. Perren and J.L.M. Trim (eds) *Applications of Linguistics: Selected Papers of the Second World Congress of Applied Linguistics, Cambridge, 1969*. Cambridge: Cambridge University Press, pp. 443–52.

White, P. 1999. Beyond interpersonal metaphors of Mood: Modelling the discourse semantics of evaluation and subjectivity. Paper presented at the 11th Euro-International Systemic Functional Workshop, Ghent University, 14–17 July.

Part IV
Above the clause

Context in systemic functional linguistics

Towards scalar supervenience?

Tom Bartlett

Introduction: context in SFL as an appliable and exotropic theory of language

Systemic functional linguistics (SFL) has been described as an extravagant model of language with a bewildering array of technical terms, many of which seem, at first sight, to refer to the same concept (see Bateman, this volume). While, for proponents of other theories, this is seen as an unnecessary encumbrance, the reason for this extravagance lies in SFL's unique-ness as an *exotropic* theory of language that locates 'language in the social environment' (Hasan 2005, 2009: 37). By this definition, Hasan is simultaneously differentiating SFL from formalist theories of language, which do not locate language in the social environment, and from general sociolinguistics, which does not claim to be an integrated theory of language.[1] In line with this broad perspective, SFL aims to account *in an integrated way* for: meaning-to-form relations within language (linguistics); the relationship between language as a social construct and its contexts of use (sociology); and the acquisition and development of the language system by individuals as members of social groups (social psychology). The key points uniting these themes are that language is learnt in context, is used in context by social-ised speakers, and is altered as a system by its use in various contexts. Context is therefore a unifying element within the overall architecture of SFL, linking language as system and instance (*langue* and *parole*) to the material conditions of those who use it, in accordance with Halliday's Marxist orientation towards language and linguistics.[2]

This chapter will undertake a *critical genealogy* of the conceptualisation of context within SFL, outlining the orientations within psychology, sociology and linguistics that provided the intellectual conditions of possibility for the emergence of the concept, and identifying what can be seen as unresolved tensions arising from this theoretical trajectory. In doing so, it will focus on the interconnected critiques that:[3]

- Halliday's classical Marxist orientation entailed an intellectual programme to correlate variations in linguistic behaviour with variations in social structure (specifically, class and situation type), which has resulted in an overly deterministic/congruent modelling of the relationship between contextual and linguistic features, and which underplays divergence, diversity and the unique socialisation of the individual; and

- some of the core elements of the SFL theory of context have not developed in pace with the thinking that has surrounded them, with the result that such terms no longer have the same meaning, or *valeur*, as in their original context and cannot interact as previously theorised.

The concluding discussion will draw on recent developments in sociolinguistics to suggest ways in which these tensions may be resolved through a *scalar supervenience* conception of context, arguing that such an approach clarifies the contribution of SFL to socially oriented linguistics while establishing an expanded agenda for SFL.

Vygotsky, language and the mind in society

Tracing SFL's genealogy reveals what may, to many, be a surprising forebear: psychology.[4] Critics such as van Dijk (2008) take SFL to task for failing to take on board the cognitive aspects of context, while for some within SFL 'the mind' and 'cognition' are treated as taboo topics. However, while Halliday's approach to language is clearly socioculturally oriented, this does not mean that he discounts either the mind or the individual; rather, he follows an inter-individual over an intra-individual approach and, while he is quick to 'recognize the importance of the other kind' (Halliday et al. 1988: 2), he sees any approach that is not ultimately rooted in social interaction as untenable, maintaining that the development of individual linguistic potential is essentially a product of social interaction from infancy onwards:

> This sharing of [an infant's] language by at least one other person – typically in this very early stage his [*sic*] mother – is a prerequisite for his successful language development and therefore for his development as a whole; without it he cannot learn. Creating language, and creating through language, are essentially interactive processes; they can never take place inside one individual's skin.
>
> *Halliday 2007 [1977]: 56*

This conception of the cyclical relationship between the individual's development of language as *systemic potential* ('creating language') and the use of language acts as *instances* of the system in context ('creating through language') derives in large part from the writings of the Soviet psychologist Lev Vygotsky (1978) and his conception of 'the mind in society'. Whereas, for Piaget, the emergence and development of speech in the infant were explained as the externalisation of consciousness and thought, which develop in *autogenetic* fashion as the child matures, in Vygotsky's view a child first learns to interact with those around them, developing the reflexes and customs of situated behaviour, and only then *internalises* these routines. For both Piaget and Vygotsky, the child's private speech – that is, the self-directed talk that is used in undertaking tasks – is seen as a pivotal point of development, the difference being that for Piaget this represents the first emergence of thought as language, while for Vygotsky it is the reproduction of past interactions as a means of scaffolding present behaviour – 'the sociogenesis of human consciousness by means of semiotic mediation' (Hasan 2005: 150). Taking the complementary perspective on the same idea, Halliday (1978: 4) states that 'language is as it is because of the functions it has evolved to serve in people's lives'. Developing both perspectives simultaneously, we can add the corollary that, once the semiotic tool has developed to suit an existing functional need, then new functions can develop to suit the tool, which in turn leads to new contextual possibilities. In this way, we see the cogenetic relationships between language and thought, between system and parole, and between context and behaviour (linguistic or otherwise). SFL accounts for this development at three interconnected and simultaneously operating scales: *logogenesis*, the development of meaning in specific instances of use; *ontogenesis*, the development of language in the socialised individual; and *phylogenesis*, perturbations to the system as a result of variation in use. However, while Halliday (1975) himself has produced a theoretical study of the ontogenesis of language in an individual child, the emphasis in SFL has tended toward phylogenesis in relating stable variations in linguistic potential to differences in interactive practices *across social groups*, as in Cloran and Hasan's classic study (for example Cloran 1994). This emphasis on variation by social class can be traced to Halliday's Marxist approach to language – an approach that he shared with Basil Bernstein (Wegener 2011: 84), whose theory of coding orientations extends the Vygotskian account of linguistic socialisation, and has provided one of the most significant and enduring theoretical influences within the SFL model.[5]

Bernstein

Three principal limitations within Vygotsky's approach have been discussed in the development of SFL as a social-semiotic theory (Hasan 2005: 145–9).

1   There is no descriptive account given of language in use as a mediating tool between experience and thought, or (in more conventional SFL terms) between context and behaviour – an enterprise that has taken up a considerable amount of effort in SFL work on context.[6]
2   Vygotsky's consideration of language as the mediational means between experience and thought was intended to account only for higher-order cognitive functions and not for everyday practice.
3   Vygotsky limited his attention to the construction of experiential meaning – that is, to our representation of entities, activities and relations – without consideration of either the interpersonal aspects of language-in-use or the intratextual principles of organisation.

It was through the work of Halliday and Hasan, and their collaboration with British sociologist Basil Bernstein, that these concepts were to be developed. This section will focus on the second and third of these developments as they relate specifically to Bernstein's sociology; the following section will turn to Malinowski's anthropology and Firth's linguistics as they contribute to SFL's descriptive account of language in use.

Bernstein is best known for his work on 'class, codes and control', as it is summarised in the title of the five-volume collection of his own and others' works on the subject. While clearly within the Vygotskian tradition, or what is now called 'sociocultural theory' (SCT) within the field of language acquisition and socialisation, Bernstein was not so much concerned with language internalisation and the development of the higher cognitive functions in the individual as in broad differences across sectors of society as a function of the class system and the differential access to resources, both capital and linguistic, between the classes. In particular, Bernstein was keen to understand why working-class children were less successful in school than their middle-class peers – a situation he explained in terms of a devaluing within the school system of the ways of speaking, or 'coding orientations' (Bernstein 1971: 135), that the working class children had developed within their home context. The notion of coding comprises two connected factors, both of which are the result of individual socialisation into a particular social group: (a) the *recognition rules* that allow a participant in a situation to know exactly what it is that is 'going on' and what would be considered appropriate behaviour in the situation thus understood; and (b) the *realisation rules* that enable socialised speakers to encode their participation in the manner appropriate to that context. The relevance of Bernstein's work, therefore, is that he extends Vygotsky's concept of language socialisation and internalisation to include not only experiential meaning and higher-order concepts, but also the whole range of behaviours carried out through language, while relating these differences to variations in socialisation and the unequal distribution of linguistic resources across subcultures within a single society. However, in emphasising heterogeneity *between* social groups, it can be argued that the Bernsteinian approach within SFL assumes an excessive degree of homogeneity *within* social groups and downplays the fact that, building on Vygotsky, each individual is, to a greater or lesser degree *multicodal* (Bartlett 2013: 356, 358) in that they are socialised into a range of social contexts, each with their own linguistic practices and not determined purely on the basis of class membership.

Malinowski and Firth

Along with variation according to group (dialectal or codal variation), Halliday and Hasan have also focused on variation according to situation type (diatypic or register variation), the intellectual roots of which can be traced to the anthropology of Malinowski as elaborated in the linguistic theory of Firth.

If, for Bernstein, recognising the meaning of social situations as communicative events is the result of prior socialisation into similar contexts, for Malinowski, language itself is meaningless if divorced from such recognisable situations, as explained in comments on his attempts to understand and describe the Kiriwinian language of the Western Pacific:

> [I]t should be clear . . . that conception of meaning as *contained* in an utterance is false and futile . . . utterance and situation are bound up inextricably with each other and the context of situation is indispensable for the understanding of the words. Exactly as in the reality of spoken or written languages, a word without *linguistic context* is mere figment and stands for nothing by itself, so in the reality of a spoken, living tongue, the utterance has no meaning except in the context of situation.
>
> *Malinowski 1966 [1923]: 307, emphasis original*

While Malinowski (1966 [1923]: 307) originally made these comments with regard to 'primitive tongues' only, he later retracted this claim as 'an error, and a serious error', asserting now that 'between the savage use of words and the most abstract and theoretical one there is only a difference of degree' (Malinowski 1935: 58). The point that Malinowski is making here – and one that follows from Vygotsky and Bernstein's positions – is that language use is so embedded in culture that not only do all speech acts combine with material action in making meanings, but also behind both these verbal and non-verbal actions (the context of situation) is a cultural history (the context of culture), a knowledge of which is necessary to make sense of the interaction.

Malinowski's ideas were taken up by a colleague at the University of London, J.R. Firth, who later held the first Chair in General Linguistics in the United Kingdom. Within his specialist area of phonology, Firth proposed that what were traditionally classified as allophones were better analysed not as accidental variation of a single abstract variable, but as *prosodies*, the combined output of a whole configuration of contextual features (Firth 1957 [1935]: 48) – an idea that he expanded to suggest that the meaning of linguistic items at all levels is dependent on the context of situation in which they are produced and that each context commands its own repertoire of linguistic features:

> The multiplicity of social roles we have to play ... involves also a certain degree of linguistic specialisation. Unity is the last concept that should be applied to language ... There is no such thing as *une langue une* and there never has been.
>
> *Firth 1957 [1935]: 29*

This formulation is the basis for the categorisation and description of *registers* in SFL – that is, the distinct ways of speaking that at once respond to and characterise specific *contexts of situation* as categories of meaningful behaviour. An idea that will be developed in what follows is that diversity in language is, in fact, *under*played in current SFL theory, which ultimately posits not only *une langue une*, but also *une culture une* in characterising variation in terms of differences in frequency of selection with a single overarching context of culture – an approach that is hard to reconcile with the diverse and overlapping linguistic practices identified within and between often super-diverse speech communities.

Context of situation is described by Firth (1957 [1935]: 18), in words that parallel Vygotsky and foreshadow Bernstein, as a place in which 'whole stretches of personal biography, and cultural history are involved, and in which past, present and future all meet', and in various papers he attempts to systematise the relationship between context and language features at an abstract level, in contrast with Malinowski's context-specific and ad hoc approach. The basic categories that Firth (1957 [1950]: 182) developed as a 'context of situation for linguistic work' were as follows, with Halliday and Hasan's (1989: 8) words added in square brackets as a gloss and a point of comparison:

A The relevant features of participants: persons, personalities [corresponding, more or less, to what sociologists would regard as the statuses and roles of the participants]

    i   The verbal action of the participants
    ii The non-verbal action of the participants.

B The relevant objects [other relevant features of the situation: the surrounding objects and events in so far as they have some bearing on what is going on]

C The effect of the verbal action [what changes were brought about by what the participants in the situation had to say].

It is easy to criticise Firth's catalogue for its lack of specificity, but such an initial approach is in keeping with his ideas on context and meaning, with the generalisable categories presented at a high level of abstraction and the details to be added later for each specific context. A potentially more serious limitation is that this schema does not provide any specific suggestions as to what individual mappings of context and language might contribute to linguistic theory beyond a descriptive account; Firth (1957 [1935]: 182) does, however, drop a tantalising hint when he says that '[c]ontexts of situation and types of language function can then be grouped and classified', suggesting a motivated relationship between them. As described in Bowcher's contribution to this volume, identifying which features of the context correlate with which linguistic features has been one of the central concerns of SFL for the last half-century and is its most distinctive characteristic.

An important point to note before moving on from Firth to the genesis of SFL itself is that within Firth's context of situation – his 'past, present and future' – we have not only a mixture of first-order and second-order contexts (those features such as 'status' that pre-exist the interaction and those created through the real-time 'verbal [and] non-verbal action of the participants' respectively), but also what might be termed 'third-order' context: 'the effect of the verbal action' on the pre-existing situation. This, of course, makes sense for Firth's exploratory 'linguistic work' insofar as it describes what is there, what is said and done, and what happens as a result; however, I will argue in this chapter that developments in the theoretical architecture of SFL mean that these different orders of context can no longer be indiscriminately grouped together and related to the linguistic features of interaction by means of a single mechanism.

Halliday and Hasan

As Butt and Wegener (2007: 610) point out, while Firth's conception of the relationship between context and language related in theory to linguistic features at all levels, in practice his focus on context and phonology dealt with the two material ends of what was to become the stratal model of language in SFL (as we shall see and see Berry, this volume), while the abstract systems in between – the semantics and the grammar – remained to be explored. This was a task that fell to Firth's student Michael Halliday, whose early grammatical model, Scale and Category Grammar, represented linguistic structure in terms of the options (categories) that become available within the context of previously selected structures at a particular level (scale), with different meanings attached to the structures available at any point. A major shift in the development of SFL occurred, however, when Halliday turned the model on its side to represent grammar as a *meaning potential*, systems of contrasting meanings made available at any point as the result of previous selections and realised through distinct lexicogrammatical structures (see Asp, this volume). These structural features are then inherited and built upon to realise more delicate choices in meaning. What Halliday found as a result of this process was that the overall network of meanings divided into three relatively discrete sets, the choices within each being strongly interconnected, while largely independent of choices in the other sets. Given the semantic organisation of the grammar and Halliday's underlying conviction that language has evolved to suit the social functions that it needs to fulfil, he concluded that, within language, there are three distinct areas (or strands) of meaning corresponding to three requirements of social interaction: (a) to represent our experiences of the events, entities and states of affairs that comprise our lived experience (real or imaginary); (b) to negotiate our relationships with other speakers and (c) to shape our talk to make it more coherent and comprehensible. These areas of meaning are known as the 'ideational', 'interpersonal' and 'textual' metafunctions respectively, capturing the notion that, in each area, a range of semantic features combine to create a single higher-order meaning type.

Through its orientation to the demands of social interaction, it is the semantic stratum of language that mediates between the lexicogrammar and the context of situation, both as a response to the existing situation and as the dynamic means of its continuation and development. Context is thus seen as the outermost and most abstract of the linguistic strata, the overlap between language and non-language, prompting Hasan's (1995: 219) glossing of the context of situation as the 'relevant context' – that is, those aspects of the non-linguistic environment that are made relevant through language (which concept we shall discuss later in the chapter). Given the core SFL concept of the coevolution of language and society,

Halliday therefore hypothesises that each of the three language-internal metafunctions, the ideational, interpersonal and textual, will be particularly, although not exclusively,[7] associated with different aspects of the situation, labelled 'field', 'tenor' and 'mode' respectively. This claim is generally known as the 'context–metafunction hook-up hypothesis' (CMHH), although Hasan (2014) now prefers the term 'metafunctional resonance', and it is the source of much debate both within and outside of SFL.[8]

In perhaps the most accessible overview of the relationship between text and context – and in terms that have hardly altered in the half-century since their first formulation in Halliday (1964) – field, tenor and mode are described as follows:

> The FIELD OF DISCOURSE refers to what is happening, to the nature of the social action that is taking place: what is it that the participants are engaged in, in which language figures as some essential component?
>
> The TENOR OF DISCOURSE refers to who is taking part, to the nature of the participants, their statuses and roles: what kinds of role relationship obtain among the participants, including permanent and temporary relationships of one kind or another, both the types of speech role that they are taking on in the dialogue and the cluster of socially significant relationships in which they are involved?
>
> The MODE OF DISCOURSE refers to what part language is playing, what it is that the participants are expecting language to do for them in the situation: the symbolic organisation of the text, the status that it has, and its function in the context, including the channel (is it spoken or written or some combination of the two?) and also the rhetorical mode, what is being achieved by the text in terms of such categories as persuasive, expository, didactic, and the like.
>
> *Halliday and Hasan 1989: 12*

A central claim within SFL is that the concepts of field, tenor and mode combine Halliday's insight into the metafunctional organisation of the language system and the SFL view on the coevolution of language and society while refining Firth's atheoretical categorisation of the variables of context. In the following sections I will expand on various aspects of SFL's conceptualisation of context and its place in the overall theoretical architecture, before suggesting that there are unresolved tensions between these theoretical advances in the architecture and the different timescales incorporated within the definitions of field, tenor and mode, as inherited from Firth.

Context and the overall architecture of SFL: a supervenient model

In SFL theory, drawing on Malinowski, any context of situation can be regarded as a specific instance of a larger system, the context of culture, which comprises the set of systemically contrastive behaviours possible within that culture, as captured in Figure 23.1. In this schematisation, each situation type comprises a *contextual configuration* (Hasan 1995: 231) of selections in field, tenor and mode.

Corresponding to the context of culture, as the means of its semiotic realisation, is the linguistic system (cf. *la langue*), which, having coevolved with the culture, is coterminous with it. On the right-hand side of Figure 23.1, we have instances of the culture as contexts of situation, which are realised in real time through actual texts (*parole*). Instantiation is a cline, however, and in between the cultural and language systems and their specific instantiation as situations and texts we have, first, *cultural domains* with their corresponding *registers*

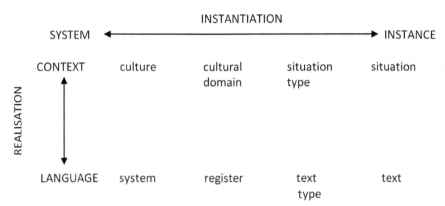

Figure 23.1 Relations between context and language: system and instance

(see Moore, this volume), then the *situation types* that make up these domains and the *text types* that typically realise them. It should be stressed again here, following from the earlier discussion of Vygotsky and Bernstein, that the relationship between the two systems and their instantiations is bidirectional: speakers come into contact with the system through language in use, while the system is an accumulation of such instances of language in use. To capture this idea, the literature (for example Hasan 2013: 279) refers to realisation as simultaneously the *activation* of language by the context and the *construal* of the context by the language. This relationship holds not only between context and text, but also within the language system itself, where each level (*stratum*) of language both activates and is construed by choices in the stratum below (see Figure 23.2).

In Figure 23.2, the outermost circle represents the context of situation as an instance of the context of culture. The next circle represents the semantics – that is, the meanings that realise the context in that they make certain features relevant in situ. The next circle is the lexicogrammar of the language – the linguistic nuts and bolts that work together to realise the semantic import of individual messages. The idea that the lexicogrammar realises the semantics, which realise the context, is known as 'metaredundancy' (Lemke 1984). Finally, but not included in Figure 23.2, we have the graphology or phonology by which the language is realised as substance. Reading the model horizontally, as well as vertically, we see the privileged relationship between each of the three metafunctions and specific aspects of the context: the ideational metafunction realising the field of context, the interpersonal realising the tenor and the textual realising the mode.

As a schematic representation of Hasan's concept of relevant context and Lemke's notion of metaredundancy, Figure 23.2 captures a central tenet within SFL theory, with its emphasis on language as behaviour, and the coevolution of language and culture: that context is itself semiotic – that is, a cultural artefact, rather than a set of external material features to which linguistic behaviour is merely a response. Martin (2014) refers to this as the *supervenient* perspective on context:

> [I]t may be useful to distinguish between two perspectives on the relation between language and social context, which we can refer to as supervenient and circumvenient. The supervenient perspective [which is the perspective represented in Figure 23.2], whereby context is treated as a higher stratum of meaning; the circumvenient one would alternatively see language as embedded in social context, where social context is interpreted as extra-linguistic.

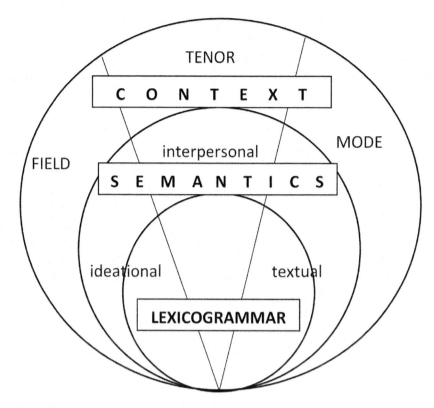

Figure 23.2 Context, language and metafunction

Between them, then, these two figures capture in brief the architecture of SFL, the place of context in that architecture, the relationship between language and parole, and the context-metafunction hook-up, with context as the glue that binds the whole model together. However, as with all models, this elegance hides tensions that become apparent only in application. In the remainder of this chapter I will elaborate on these tensions as they were outlined in the introduction and elaborate on the concept of supervenience.

Discussion

SFL's early development came about in a particular time and place, for a particular purpose and with specific resources available i.e. a Marxist orientation towards dialectal materialism, including an intellectual programme to relate behaviour to social structures; in reaction to Chomsky's asocial and mentalist approach to language; and with textual data more or less limited to written texts and the occasional transcription of oral texts, both within specific and highly institutionalised genres.[9] While these purposes and methods remain valid, society, sociolinguistic theory and methods of data collection have all altered, as have key aspects of SFL theory itself; hence this section develops the critiques referred to in the introduction that (a) the context/text relationship within SFL is overly congruent/deterministic, and (b) some of the core elements of the theory have not developed in tandem with later refinements, so that they no longer have the same meaning, or *valeur*, as in their original context and cannot interact as previously theorised. In light of the overview of the genealogy of context within

SFL theory and its current place within the overall architecture, these general critiques can now be explored in the following, more specific terms:

- the concept of relevant context and the relation between situation and text or first- and second-order contexts;
- the exact nature of realisation between strata and
- the possibility of a unitary context of culture.

Relevant context, activation and construal

Drawing on Firth and Malinowski, the SFL definitions of field, tenor and mode mix elements of both first- and second-order context: the activities, roles and relationships embedded in the culture, on the one hand, and those that are played out in the immediate interaction, on the other. As stated above, this makes sense in Malinowskian and Firthian terms, which are concerned with the *regular performance of ritual interactions* and the *regular correlations between the contextual and linguistic features*. But while these are both essential aspects of the relationship between texts and their conditions of production, it can be suggested that the continued schematisation of first-and second-order elements within a single undifferentiated stratum of context breaks down in light of developments within SFL – in particular, Hasan's (2013: 279, emphasis added) notion of relevant context and the conception of realisation as the *symmetrical and simultaneous* relationship of activation and construal:

> [C]ontext, semantics and lexicogrammar are related by a REALISATIONAL DIALECTIC whereby the higher stratum ACTIVATES the lower and the lower CONSTRUES the higher. Speakers do not happen to mean serendipitously in a meaning exchange: the meanings they mean are those called for by the CONTEXTUAL CONFIGURATIONS (henceforth CC), i.e. by the *interactants' sense of what is relevant to the social activity at that given point*. CC is that abstraction from the context of situation which activates linguistic meanings, activating lexicogrammar.

While the notion of relevant context (italicised in the quote) is an essential refinement of the theory, it cannot *on its own* account for the different degrees of involvement in the situation of those first-order features included in the still-extant definitions of field, tenor and mode. To put the problem in a nutshell: if two speakers choose to ignore in conversation the structural power differentials between them, then these differentials are not made relevant through language, yet this very act of not-making-relevant is in itself an extremely relevant feature of the situation taken as a whole and alters the significance of those features that are verbalised.

Between such a situation, in which first-order features are overridden or ignored by participants, and entirely *congruent* situations, in which first- and second-order features tally, there are situations in which there is only an indirect relationship between some first-order features and what the participants construe as relevant. As an example of this, Bartlett (2013) refers to the case a red-haired man 'first-footing' in Scotland, where tradition has it that it is bad luck for a redhead to be the first to cross your threshold in the New Year. Such an event might provoke an atmosphere of hostility, which becomes apparent in the language used – in which case, the first-footer's red hair is relevant and has an effect on the language used, so it can certainly be said to activate the linguistic reaction, but it would surely be an overextension of the term to claim it is *construed* by it. There is therefore a need to look in more detail at the relationship between realisation, activation and construal.

What do 'realise', 'activate' and 'construe' mean?

There are many different glosses in the SFL literature for the way in which contextual features activate linguistic meanings: as tendencies or preferences; as leaving a trace on, illuminating or being readable from the text.[10] All are superficially elegant, but with woolliness and metaphor masking real differences and tensions between them. The reason for such a proliferation is that activation is a very broad concept that subsumes a number of potential reactances besides that of construal, so jeopardising the concept of realisation as the bidirectional relationship between the activation/construal pairing. This has serious knock-on effects for descriptions of context in SFL in that either (a) those features of context that are directly construed as relevant within an interaction are mistakenly identified as the activating context in its entirety or, conversely, (b) realisation is rendered an underspecified concept that can be used to signal any relationship between two strata without accounting for the mechanisms by which they are related.

This suggests a need to combine a theory of context as what is construed as relevant through language with a theory of context that asks why that particular construal took place in that way and at that particular time, developing additional terminology to account for those features of the situation that are relevant to language-in-use but which are not (directly) construed as such so as to reintegrate these expanded categories into a single coherent model. In the following rough sketch, I first distinguish between the *environment* (everything that surrounds the situation, including social and individual histories, as well as material features of the setting) and what I shall refer to as the *sctx*[11] – that is, the second-order reality that is construed by, and which can be read off, the text itself – and describe in preliminary fashion four distinct, but interrelated, concepts that account for the relationship between text and context: *activation, construal, correlation* and *indexicality*.

The interplay of second-order field, tenor and mode at any point represents a specific *sctx* (by definition) that is *construed* by the linguistic features of the stratum below, the semantics, which are in turn construed by the lexicogrammar.[12] *Activation* is a wider concept, covering any of the ways in which environmental features leave a trace upon the text in a particular situation, whether this is through direct construal (social power correlating with linguistic power) or more oblique relationships (such as a first-footer's red hair). *Correlation* refers to the tendencies for particular language features and environmental features to co-occur (with the reasons for the correlation to be explored), and if the degree of correlation is strong enough, then the linguistic construal of a second-order context can be said to *index* a particular first-order category (Silverstein 2003), such as when a particular way of speaking is associated in the popular imagination with gender or writtenness.[13] Unlike construal, which (in relative terms) is a synchronically fixed and co-determining relation between signifier and signified across strata, indexicality is a relationship that can be broken in either direction: pre-empting a discussion to follow, bishops do not always speak like bishops and speaking like a bishop does not make you one.

There are several points in the above sketch that need considerable elaboration – in particular, the distinction between construal and indexicality as a function of synchronic stability, a distinction not made in the sociolinguistic literature but touched on in my conclusion. Figure 23.3 is a working model of context based on this snapshot (and see also Ochs 1992), which separates *sctx* from environment so as to capture some of the more delicate relations developed in this section. I shall return briefly to this model in the conclusion.

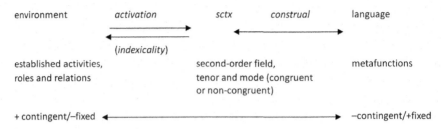

Figure 23.3 A sketch model of context

Congruence, reification and homogeneity

It has been claimed in this chapter so far that the SFL motivation in describing the relationship between the features of contexts and the language features through which they
are played out was the sociological goal of capturing robust generalisations of variety
according to use, or *register* variation, describable in terms of tendencies across the population as a whole. This is a natural starting point, given the materialist conception of
society underlying the theory, coupled with the limitations on the data available, but it
could be argued that the approach has led to a focus on *reified* situations, performed by
relatively *homogeneous* sectors of society, who both knew how to act out these situations
and conformed in doing so in a manner *congruent* with their longer-term social roles as
members of well-defined groups and the established role-relationship between groups. In
such situations, as when the Bishop of Woolwich 'does being' the Bishop of Woolwich
(Halliday and Hasan 1989: 12–14), any tensions between first- and second-order context
are neutralised and the 'relevant context' is the entire situation, because the pre-linguistic
features out there match those realised through the language, *so that to describe one is to
describe the other.*

In *steady-state situations* such as this, there appears to be no need for theoretical distinctions between indexicality and construal, and between direct and oblique construal, but
this masks a serious theoretical limitation. With reference to the Bishop of Woolwich's
sermon, for example, defining the context solely in terms of the activity, the interpersonal
relations and the rhetorical style construed through language (that is, field, tenor and mode
in Halliday and Hasan's terms) is not enough to demonstrate a construal of 'bishopness'
without an understanding of the link between the context so construed and what it is to be a
bishop in that particular time and place. In the congruent and reified situations that are the
focus of much analysis, this connection is imposed by a knowing analyst, who reads it off
the text as an instance of a familiar context of culture. While this may have been an effective mode of analysis in critiques of modernist post-war social relations in which semantics
construes context and context indexes position for those in the know, it is insufficient as a
means of analysis in situations in which social roles are being renegotiated and recalibrated
(see for example Bartlett 2012). These fall into at least the following three types, which are
unlikely to be discrete categories.

- *Non-congruent situations*, where interactants construe activities, relationships and/or
  styles other than those generally expected in the specific context. Providing a more
  complex account of context in such situations is essential in applying SFL within
  critical discourse analysis.

- *Non-homogeneous situations*, where interactants come from communities with distinct coding orientations and so are operating by a different set of rules. Providing a more complex account of context in such situations is essential in applying SFL within intercultural communication.
- *Non-reified situations*, where the activity being undertaken has not achieved generic status; in such cases there is no set formula for interaction, which may range from being entirely ad hoc to demonstrating the signs of an *immanent* genre (Bartlett 2012). Such situations are likely to be increasingly common in an age of super-diversity within single geographical areas.

Taking this argument a step further, the recent trend in sociolinguistics towards the study of super-diversity (for example Blommaert 2013) highlights the need for revision in the SFL concept of context of culture as a single overarching and metastable (Lemke 1984) system in which variation between groups and between contexts of situation is accounted for through a resetting of the probabilities for what language features are likely to be used in each case. Even assuming that every conceivable combination of contextual features could be catalogued and correlated with specific language features, such an approach would satisfy the conditions for descriptive adequacy but would fall a long way short of explanatory adequacy. As Hasan (2009: 36) herself acknowledges, the relationship between context and text as presently theorised is in danger of lapsing into descriptivism rather than addressing the paramount functionalist question, 'Why thus here and now?':

> [F]or a theory that introduces itself as a social semiotic one, it [SFL] is woefully neglectful of specifically sociolinguistic issues; its only substantial contribution is in the field of discourse analysis where it offers a framework for the analysis of social context as well as for that of discourse. However, in both cases the emphasis is classificatory and concerned with the description of linguistic phenomena rather than sociolinguistic ones; the social enters only somewhat superficially, especially in the description of the vectors of context, making no reference to any sociological framework, and often confusing the description of a phenomenon with its production.

Describing the relationship between context and language simply in terms of codependent variables within a unitary context of culture is not so far from the Labovian quantitative sociolinguistics dismissed within SFL, only with entire registers, rather than individual features such as phonemes, correlated with features of the environment. To bring up a well-worn analogy in SFL, where the system (*langue*) is compared to the climate and language-in-use (*parole*) to the weather, it is worth bearing in mind that meteorology does not simply catalogue the instances that continually perturb the system but attempts to *account for* the causes of that variation in terms of wider geographical features. Likewise, an appliable theory needs to be able to account for correlations, not only to identify them. Moreover, there comes a breaking point at which difference – even mutually intelligible difference – is no longer variation but a separate system and there is work to be done in this area in tandem with wider sociolinguistics.

Conclusion

Both Halliday (1978: 69) and Hasan (2001: 15) have drawn attention to the complexity and multiple layering of the conditions behind the context of situation, but this complexity is often overlooked in discussions or has been integrated into field, tenor and mode as if all of the interacting features were at the same scale and therefore in the same realisation relationship with language. In this chapter, I have argued that it is a theoretical necessity for SFL to model this complexity and multiple layering – in particular, separating out *sctx* from environment and recognising the range of different relationships that hold between these two elements, as discussed above. In this way, the model in Figure 23.3 will need to be elaborated to accommodate these different types of activation and their interaction with each other and the *sctx*.

Such a move might appear to be a betrayal of a core SFL principle that context is a semiotic construct, as captured in Martin's distinction between the supervenient and circumvenient perspectives. Within the proposed model, however, the environment remains a semiotic construct, though distinct from the *sctx*, which is the immediate semiotic response to the longer-term semiotics of the environment, and with both elements acting together to create additional meanings.[14] Or rather, different elements of the environment will be meaningful to different participants in different ways as a result of their semiotic histories (in the Vygotskian sense), while only a selection of these meaningful elements will be directly realised (or 'made relevant' in Hasan's terms) in response to the context of situation.

There is therefore, between environment and *sctx*, an enigmatic region that comprises those elements of the environment that are meaningful to different individuals and which may or may not be realised as text.[15] While this fits with the Firthian notion that the context of situation is a region in which 'whole stretches of personal biography, and cultural history are involved, and in which past, present and future all meet' (Firth 1957 [1935]: 18), the current conception of realisation between strata cannot account for these different features of context and their relationship to the text. What it can adequately describe is homogeneous, congruent and reified situations – but such cases must ultimately be accounted for in just the same way as heterogeneous, incongruent and non-reified behaviour. There is therefore a need for an approach to context that is neither simply supervenient or circumvenient, in Martin's sense, but which, following Blommaert's (2005) concepts of *scales* and *layered simultaneity*, recognises that multiple timescales and multiple contexts coalesce around each instance of interaction. In other words, the different social histories and relations that different individuals bring to bear within a single context of situation are all long-term semiotic constructs that affect each individual's reading of both the immediate linguistic interaction and the material environment in which it takes place. *Scalar supervenience* might be an appropriate name for such a conception of context.[16]

Notes

1 As pointed out by my colleague, Gerard O'Grady, West Coast functionalism and usage-based theories could also be considered exotropic, although their theoretical scope is more limited in that, unlike SFL, they remain theories of language and not theories of society.
2 See Wegener (2011) for a detailed discussion and Halliday (2015) for a personal reflection. For a more detailed account of the specifics of SFL modelling of the context–language interface, see Bowcher, this volume.
3 These relate primarily to the writings of Halliday and Hasan. Martin proposes an alternative architecture (see Tann, this volume), although much of the current discussion relates to this model also.
4 It could be argued that Vygotsky is a social psychologist rather than a psychologist per se, but this would be to miss the point that, from a Marxian position, social psychology *is* psychology.
5 See Maton and Doran, this volume, for recent developments in this field.
6 See Bowcher (2014) and in this volume, and Lukin (2015).
7 Not exclusively, because, under socio-evolutionary pressure, language features are put to use in novel and 'metaphorical' ways – see Taverniers, this volume.

8 There is not room in this chapter to discuss the CMHH, but see Berry and Bowcher, both this volume, as well as Clarke's (2012) discussion from within SFL and van Dijk's (2008) critique from outside.

9 My thanks to my colleagues Gerard O'Grady and Tereza Spilioti, each of whom suggested aspects of these constraints.

10 See Bartlett (2013) for a fuller discussion.

11 This is an awkward name I have used elsewhere as a placeholder to avoid confusion with the proliferation of similar terms for related concepts in this field. To avoid further confusion, I will continue to use it despite its inelegance. While it conforms more or less with Hasan's 'relevant context', I have not used that term because of the problems discussed with the concept of 'relevance'.

12 The term 'realisation' then being reserved for intrastratal signified/signifier relations, e.g. the lexicogrammatical feature interrogative being realised by F^S word order.

13 See Bartlett (2015) for a discussion focusing on mode as a problematic category.

14 Cf. Berry (2013) on second-order context.

15 My thanks to Jamie Williams for bringing to my attention this additional category, which would also qualify for the label 'semiotic context'.

16 See also Bartlett (forthcoming).

References

Bartlett, T. 2012. *Hybrid Voice and Institutional Change: Contextualising Positive Discourse Analysis*. London and New York: Routledge.

Bartlett, T. 2013. 'I'll manage the context': Context, environment and the potential for institutional change. In L. Fontaine, T. Bartlett and G. O'Grady (eds) *Systemic Functional Linguistics: Exploring Choice*. Cambridge: Cambridge University Press, pp. 342–64.

Bartlett, T. 2015. Mode as a troublesome category: Social expectations and/or the construal of textuality? In W.L. Bowcher and J.Y. Liang (eds) *Essays in Honour of Ruqaiya Hasan: Society in Language, Language in Society*. London and New York: Palgrave, pp. 166–83.

Bartlett, T. Forthcoming. Approaches to discourse. In W.L. Bowcher, J.Y. Liang, G. Thompson and L. Fontaine (eds) *The Cambridge Handbook of Systemic Functional Linguistics*. Cambridge: Cambridge University Press.

Bernstein, B. 1971. *Class, Codes and Control, Vol. 1: Theoretical Studies towards a Sociology of Language*. London: Routledge & Kegan Paul.

Berry, M. 2013. Towards a study of the differences between formal written English and informal spoken English. In L. Fontaine, T. Bartlett and G. O'Grady (eds) *Systemic Functional Linguistics: Exploring Choice*. Cambridge: Cambridge University Press, pp. 365–83.

Blommaert, J. 2005. *Discourse: A Critical Introduction*. Cambridge: Cambridge University Press.

Blommaert, J. 2013. *Ethnography, Superdiversity and Linguistic Landscapes: Chronicles of Complexity*. Bristol: Multilingual Matters.

Bowcher, W.L. 2014. Issues in developing unified systems for contextual field and mode. *Functions of Language* 21(2): 176–209.

Butt, D., and R. Wegener. 2007. The work of concepts: Context and metafunction in the systemic functional model. In R. Hasan, C.M.I.M. Matthiessen and J.J. Webster (eds) *Continuing Discourse on Language: A Functional Perspective, Vol. 2*. London and Oakville, CT: Equinox, pp. 589–618

Clarke, B. 2012. Do patterns of ellipsis in text support systemic functional linguistics' 'context-metafunction hook-up' hypothesis? A corpus-based approach. Unpublished PhD thesis. Cardiff University.

Cloran, C. 1994. *Rhetorical Units and Decontextualisation: An Enquiry into Some Relations of Context, Meaning and Grammar* (Monographs in Systemic Functional Linguistics 6). Nottingham: Nottingham University School of English Studies,

Firth, J.R. 1957. *Papers in Linguistics, 1934–1951*. Oxford: Oxford University Press.

Fontaine, L., T. Bartlett and G. O'Grady (eds). 2013. *Systemic Functional Linguistics: Exploring Choice*. Cambridge: Cambridge University Press.

Halliday, M.A.K. 1964. Comparison and translation. In M.A.K. Halliday, M. McIntosh and P. Strevens (eds) *The Linguistic Sciences and Language Teaching*. London: Longman, pp. 111–34.

Halliday, M.A.K. 1975. *Learning How to Mean: Explorations in the Development of Language*. London: Arnold.

Halliday, M.A.K. 1978. *Language as Social Semiotic: The Social Interpretation of Language and Meaning*. Baltimore, MD. University Park Press.

Halliday, M.A.K. 2007 [1977]. Some thoughts on language in the middle school years. In J.J. Webster (ed.) *The Collected Works of Michael Halliday, Vol. 6: Language and Education*. London and New York: Continuum, pp. 49–62.

Halliday, M.A.K. 2015. The influence of Marxism. In J.J. Webster (ed.) *The Bloomsbury Companion to M.A.K. Halliday*. London and New York: Bloomsbury, pp. 94–100.

Halliday, M.A.K., and R. Hasan. 1989. *Language, Context and Text*. 2nd edn. Oxford: Oxford University Press.

Halliday, M.A.K., S. Lamb and J. Regan. 1988. *In Retrospect: Using Language and Knowing How* (Twelfth in a Series of Seminars: Issues in Communication). Claremont, CA: The Claremont Graduate School.

Hasan, R. 1995. The conception of context in text. In P. Fries and M. Gregory (eds) *Discourse in Society: Systemic Functional Perspectives* (Meaning and Choice in Language: Studies for Michael Halliday). Westport, CT, and London: Ablex, pp. 183–283.

Hasan, R. 2001. Wherefore context? The place of context in the system and process of language. In R. Shaozeng, W. Guthrie and I.W.R. Fong (eds) *Grammar and Discourse: Proceedings of the International Conference on Discourse Analysis*. Macau: Universidad de Macau, pp. 1–21.

Hasan, R. 2005. Semiotic mediation and three exotropic theories: Vygotsky, Halliday and Bernstein. In J.J. Webster (ed.) *The Collected Works of Ruqaiya Hasan, Vol. 1: Language, Society and Consciousness*. London and Oakville, CT: Equinox, pp. 130–59.

Hasan, R. 2009. Wanted: A theory for integrated sociolinguistics. In J.J. Webster (ed.) *The Collected Works of Ruqaiya Hasan, Vol. 2: Semantic Variation – Meaning in Society and in Sociolinguistics*. London and Oakville, CT: Equinox, pp. 5–40.

Hasan, R. 2013. Choice, system, realisation: Describing language as meaning potential. In L. Fontaine, T. Bartlett and G. O'Grady (eds) *Systemic Functional Linguistics: Exploring Choice*. Cambridge: Cambridge University Press, pp. 269–99.

Hasan, R. 2014. Towards a paradigmatic description of context: Systems, metafunctions, and semantics. *Functional Linguistics* 1:9.

Lemke, J. 1984. *Semiotics and Education* (Toronto Semiotic Circle Monographs, Working Papers and Prepublications). Toronto: Victoria University.

Lukin, A. 2015. Language and society, context and text: The contributions of Ruqaiya Hasan. In W.L. Bowcher and J.Y. Liang (eds) *Essays in Honour of Ruqaiya Hasan: Society in Language, Language in Society*. London and New York: Palgrave, pp. 143–65.

Malinowski, B. 1935. *Coral Gardens and their Magic, Vol. 2*. New York: American Book Company.

Malinowski, B. 1966 [1923]. *The Problem of Meaning in Primitive Languages. Supplement to C.K. Ogden and I.A. Richards'* The Meaning of Meaning. 10th edn. New York: Harcourt.

Martin, J.R. 2014. Evolving systemic functional linguistics: Beyond the clause. *Functional Linguistics* 1:3.

Ochs, E. 1992. Indexing gender. In A. Duranti and C. Goodwin (eds) *Rethinking Context: Language as an Interactive Phenomenon*. Cambridge: Cambridge University Press, pp. 335–58.

Silverstein, M. 2003. Indexical order and the dialectics of sociolinguistic life. *Language and Communication* 23: 193–229.

van Dijk, T.A. 2008. *Discourse and Context: A Sociocognitive Approach*. Cambridge: Cambridge University Press.

Vygotsky, L.S. 1978. *The Mind in Society: The Development of Higher Psychological Processes*. Ed. M. Cole, V. John-Steiner, S. Scribner and E. Souberman. Cambridge, MA: Harvard University Press.

Wegener, R. 2011. Parameters of context: From theory to model and application. Unpublished PhD thesis. Macquarie University, Sydney.

24

Field, tenor and mode

Wendy L. Bowcher

Introduction

Field, Tenor and Mode together form a conceptual framework for describing the *context of situation* – that is, they represent the parameters across which the *relevant* features of a situation in which language is involved may be grouped. In systemic functional linguistics (SFL), Field, Tenor and Mode are important for describing the way in which context and language are interrelated. This chapter briefly traces the development of the concepts of Field, Tenor and Mode, their importance within SFL, and their relationship with other key concepts such as *register*, *context* and *metafunction* (see Moore, Bartlett and Asp, respectively, all in this volume). The chapter ends by introducing some current developments in the description of Field, Tenor and Mode.

Historical perspectives

Field, Tenor and Mode derive from the pioneering work in linguistics of J.R. Firth, who was the first Chair of General Linguistics in the United Kingdom. In investigating and describing the nature of language, Firth's central focus was on 'meaning' – that is, Firth (1968a: 97, emphasis original) was concerned with 'mak[ing] statements of *meaning* in purely linguistic terms . . . at a number of *levels of analysis*: for example, in phonology, grammar, stylistics, situation, attested and established texts'. We can see from this quotation that Firth considered 'situation' to be a level of analysis in describing language. Firth (1968b: 14) argues that '"meaning" is a property of the mutually relevant people, things, [and] events in the situation'. Firth (1968c: 177) presented these 'people, things, and events' as a framework for investigating language in context and formalised them in the following way:

1   The participants: persons, personalities, and relevant features of these.

    a   The verbal action of the participants.
    b   The non-verbal action of the participants.

2   The relevant objects and non-verbal and non-personal events.
3   The effect of the verbal action.

Perhaps the best-known application of Firth's framework is that of a study of buying and selling in Cyrenaica by Mitchell (1975). In this study, originally published in 1957, Mitchell analytically demonstrates the relationship between contextual features and language choices. He also shows how transactions in a marketplace follow specific and recognisable stages. This latter observation was an important forerunner to later work in analysing linguistic *genres* (see Gardner, this volume). McCarthy (2000: 85) contends that 'the enduring value of Mitchell's proposals is that they enable us to explain why utterance-types in different classes of service encounter might vary when other things appear to be equal'.

The recognition that language varies according to its contexts of use was important in developing the parameters of Field, Tenor and Mode. In fact, Hasan (2014) points out that the origin of the contextual concepts of Field, Tenor and Mode lies in Halliday's attempt to account for patterns in language variation, or in the description of *registers*. In his very early work, Halliday presents the concepts of Field, Style and Mode as 'aspects of the situation in which language operates' and as being useful for identifying different situation types 'to which formally distinct registers correspond' (Halliday et al. 1964: 90). Around the time that Halliday was formulating his views on the relationship between the parameters of context of situation and features of language, a number of scholars were involved in discussing the theoretical significance of 'context' and the features of context pertinent to language in use (for example Catford 1965; Ellis 1966). One of these scholars, Michael Gregory, attempted to delineate and standardise the various terms in use. Gregory (1967: 195) introduced the term 'Tenor', rather than 'style', to refer to the 'social role' dimension of situated language, because he felt 'tenor' was a less ambiguous term: 'TENOR (in the Oxford English Dictionary sense of "way of proceeding") is so little used nowadays except unambiguously in the discussion of music that it has some of the advantages of neutrality.' The term 'Tenor' was taken up by Halliday in his theory of language in place of the word 'style'.

Critical issues and topics

Field, tenor and mode within SFL theory

That the parameters of context in SFL are directly influenced by the work of Firth is not surprising, because Halliday, the founder of SFL, was a student of Firth. However, Halliday developed Firth's contextual features in a very important way – one on which the whole theory of SFL hinges.

Through observation of everyday language in use, Halliday's preferred approach to describing language has been to find linguistic consistencies, or patterns, rather than oddities. Language-in-use unfolds in situations and it does so not only in its materiality as sound or marks on a page, but also in its semantic characteristics, which are very much tied to the situation:

> [T]he context in which the text unfolds, is encapsulated in the text, not in a kind of piecemeal fashion . . . but through a systematic relationship between the social environment on the one hand, and the functional organization of language on the other.
>
> *Halliday 1985: 11*

In SFL, linguistic consistencies are shown to probabilistically correlate with situational features, such that language variation, or register, may be 'defined as systematic variation in probabilities' (Halliday 2005: 66). Halliday (2005: 66) explains that:

[A] register is a tendency to select certain combinations of meanings with certain frequencies, and this can be formulated as the probabilities attached to grammatical systems, provided such systems are integrated into an overall system network in a paradigmatic interpretation of the grammar.[1]

In theorising the correlation between language and context, Halliday (1985: 12) asks the questions 'How can we characterize a text in its relation to its context of situation?' and 'How do we get from the situation to the text?' The theoretical relation between context and text is described through organising the features of the context of situation under three main headings: Field, Tenor and Mode. These headings and their configuration of features not only 'serve to interpret the social context of a text, the environment in which meanings are exchanged' (Halliday 1985: 12), but also are 'encapsulated' in a systematic way in features of a text.

What is meant by 'encapsulated'? For Halliday, a key way of 'characteriz[ing] a text in relation to its context of situation' is to understand that 'although when we write [a text] down it looks as though it is made of words and sentences, [a text] is really made of meanings' (Halliday 1985: 10, 12). Thus 'text', in SFL, is defined as 'a semantic unit' (Halliday 1985: 10). Further, a text is both a product and a process: as a product, a text can be 'recorded and studied'; as a process, it represents 'a continuous process of semantic choice' intimately tied to a particular context of situation (Halliday 1985: 10–11). A text – and, indeed, any piece of real language – simultaneously expresses three strands of meaning, and meaning is understood in a specific way in SFL theory. To explain this, we need to understand how language is modelled in SFL (see Berry, Bateman and Asp, all in this volume).

Language is modelled as comprising three levels, or *strata*, along with the extralinguistic level of *context*. The three linguistic levels are: *semantic*, *lexicogrammatical* and *phonological/graphological*. The semantic stratum has four 'functions', or 'strands of meaning' (Halliday 1985: 23): *experiential*, *interpersonal*, *logical* and *textual*. These strands of meaning are organised under three headings, known as 'metafunctions': *ideational* (experiential + logical), *interpersonal* and *textual*. According to Halliday (1985: 23), these metafunctions are a characteristic of all natural languages, because they represent the 'inner organization of language whereby its form construes meanings relevant to the [contextual] parameters' (Hasan 2001: 9). *Experiential* meaning refers to the function of language to express 'some kind of a process, some event, action, state, or other phenomenal aspect of the real world to which it bears some kind of symbolic relation' (Halliday 1985: 18). *Interpersonal* meaning refers to the interactive function of language – the role of language in conveying speech roles, attitudes and social identity. *Logical* meaning has to do with the expression of relations between events and phenomena conveyed in the language. *Textual* meaning has to do with the way in which a text both unfolds and is organised into a coherent whole.[2]

The lexicogrammatical level comprises three main systems: TRANSITIVITY (participants, processes, circumstances), MOOD (Subject, Predicate, Modality), and THEME (Theme and Rheme, Given and New). The stratum of *phonology/graphology* is the level of linguistic 'expression'. An important point with regard to strata is that 'all strata are interdependent with consequences from above being articulated all down the spectrum' (Butt 2001: 1826).

The semantic stratum is the interface between the lexicogrammatical stratum and the stratum of context in the sense that 'the elements of context activate the elements of the semantic level, and meta-redundantly those of the lexicogrammatical level' (Hasan 2001: 10). Context is thus in a 'realisational' relation with language. Simply put, a *realisational* relation occurs

393

when features of one stratum, such as the stratum of context, are re-presented 'in a different guise' across the other strata (Hasan 2013: 278) – that is, there is no 'direct line' from specific contextual features to specific linguistic features. In other words, these contextual features do not 'cause' these linguistic features; rather, language and context are in a dialectical relation. Further, there is a non-random simultaneous patterning of choices at one stratum in relation to those of a different order at another – a simultaneous 'assemblage' of semiotic detail at each stratum (Halliday 1992; Butt and Wegener 2007; Butt 2008; Bowcher 2010; Hasan 2013). One final crucial point regarding realisation is the connection between realisation and 'metaredundancy'. *Metaredundancy* refers to the theoretical position that 'linguistic meaning is part of each level [and that] . . . statements about linguistic meaning are not the task of semantics alone' (Butt 2001: 1826). Thus linguistic meaning resides at all levels, but is realised differently at each level (see Berry, this volume).

This model of language in terms of strata and realisation has an important bearing on the relationship between the contextual parameters of Field, Tenor and Mode, and the language choices made in a situation. The contextual parameters can be described basically as follows (adapted from Halliday 1985: 12):

- *Field* – what is happening; the nature of the social action in which language is an essential component.
- *Tenor* – who is taking part; the nature of the participants, their social statuses and roles vis-à-vis one another and the types of speech role that they are taking on in the dialogue.
- *Mode* – what part the language is playing; the symbolic organisation of the text, and its status and function in the situation, including the channel (for example spoken or written mode) and the rhetorical mode.

As noted earlier, the contextual parameters Field, Tenor and Mode are theoretically motivated with respect to the language system – that is, the specific characteristics of Field, Tenor and Mode in a given situation are the *relevant features* of that situation (see Bartlett, this volume).

Relevancy means that the features of the specific situation are realised in the language used in that situation. Conversely, the language itself indicates the relevant features of the context in terms of the subject matter and type of activity, the role of language and the social relations between the interactants in the situation. Features not realised in the language, such as (perhaps) the material surroundings of the interaction, are not considered 'relevant'. Halliday provides a principle upon which we can investigate relevancy. He proposes that certain features of the context are realised in a non-random and systematic way through certain features in the system of LANGUAGE. He demonstrates that Field tends to be construed at the semantic level through ideational meaning and through choices in the grammatical system of TRANSITIVITY. Tenor, on the other hand, tends to be enacted through interpersonal meaning and through choices in the systems of MOOD and MODALITY, while Mode tends to be construed through textual meaning and through the grammatical systems of THEME and INFORMATION, as well as through choices in cohesion (Halliday 1977). This set-up has been referred to as the 'context–metafunction hook-up hypothesis' (Hasan 1995) and, more recently, the 'context–metafunction resonance (CMR) hypothesis' (Hasan 2014). This hypothesis of the relationship between context and language makes it possible to investigate 'the formal linguistic features capable of acting as the *typical* correlates of the features pertaining to each situational parameter; . . . identify[ing] them as patterns of transitivity, mood, aspects of modality, modulation, or the categories of cohesion' (Hasan 2014: 9).

Non-relevant features of the material surrounds of the situation fall within the category of *material situational setting* (MSS). In spoken situations, the features of the MSS may enter into the description of the context of situation and thus become 'relevant' only if they are 'mentioned'. For instance, consider a situation in which two speakers are talking about their plans for the summer holidays. They may be sitting in a coffee shop. Indeed, they could be located anywhere to be discussing these plans; hence the material situational setting is irrelevant to their talk. But let us say that one speaker mentions that the table is wobbly and bends down to place something underneath the table leg. After this brief interruption, the talk may then continue with the summer plans. In this case, the table and its wobbliness have entered the conversation; hence what was once in the material situational setting has become a part of the context of situation, albeit only momentarily, because these features were realised in certain choices in the language used. This short interruption, itself, takes on a different configuration of contextual features from the discussion of holiday plans. A description of this kind of phenomenon, in which different types of activity may be co-located or integrated with another activity, is found in Hasan (1999) and updated in Hasan (2014). These different types of activity may be 'integrated', 'aligned' or 'independent', and are accounted for in the system of ITERATION.

Although Field, Tenor and Mode are described as separate components of the context of situation, they actually work interdependently. This is because 'what we do', 'with whom' and 'how' are contingent on each other. Thus Field, Tenor and Mode work as a 'configuration', rather than a 'combination'. Hasan (1995: 231) has described this as analogous to a 'chemical solution', and she uses the term 'contextual configuration' (CC) to capture the way in which features of the context combine in specific ways in different situations of language use (Hasan 1985, 1995). This 'interdependency' of the contextual features is characteristic at all levels of description. In this regard, Halliday (1985: 23) makes the following comment:

> Every sentence in a text is multifunctional; but not in such a way that you can point to one particular constituent or segment and say this segment has just this function. The meanings are woven together in a very dense fabric in such a way that, to understand them, we do not look separately at its different parts; rather, we look at the whole thing simultaneously from a number of different angles, each perspective contributing towards the total interpretation. That is the essential nature of a functional approach.

The characteristic of interdependency is an important reason why realisation is a probabilistic, rather than a causal or one-to-one, phenomenon.

Representing the contextual parameters

One of the current critical issues with regard to the contextual parameters concerns how to represent their features in a way that enables more rigorous empirical investigations of the relationship between context and language.

One major suggestion that is in keeping with the SFL *paradigmatic* interpretation of language is the representation of the features of Field, Tenor and Mode in the form of *system networks* (see Asp, this volume). System networks can represent choice 'right across the strata' (Butt 2001: 1819) and those for context are typically called 'contextualisation system networks' (Hasan 2009).

System networks were first used by Halliday in the description of lexicogrammatical choices (Hasan 2014) and have been employed in various SFL descriptions of language.

A system network for context has Field, Tenor and Mode as its primary choices, with a fourth choice being 'iteration'. The choice of iteration allows for re-entry into the whole context system as a situation unfolds.[3] For instance, if we take our sample situation of two friends talking at a coffee shop, the brief talk about the wobbly table would be incorporated into the description of the situation through the choice of 'iteration' in the contextualisation system network. The analyst would show how there was a re-entry into the context of situation at the moment the talk about the table's wobbliness occurred, after which the re-entry to the previous features relevant to the main conversation would be made (Hasan 1999).

Within the system of CONTEXT, Field, Tenor and Mode are primary entry points to three different, but interrelated, semiotic domains in which an array of semiotic features are set out. The features relevant to a specific situation of language use can be mapped onto these networks and represented in *selection expressions*. Mapping the selections relevant to a corpus of texts would show clusters of choices correlating with text-types or registers.

System networks are arranged so that choices on the left are the most primary, and hence the most general, choices.[4] These selections at the more primary end of the networks are said to point towards the generalised structural features of texts/contexts (Hasan 1985, 2014; Bowcher and Liang 2015).[5] Those to the right represent more delicate choices, which may constitute choices reflecting optional features of context-types, and hence correlate with variations within specific registers (Hasan 1985; Urbach 2013; Bowcher 2014). Thus mapping the features within each semiotic domain provides analysts with the resources for making comparisons across various situations and for grouping situations into situation types. (A brief overview of current developments in representing Field, Tenor and Mode as networks of choices is provided later in this chapter.)

Variations in interpreting Field, Tenor and Mode in SFL

One main departure from Halliday's description of Field, Tenor and Mode is that proposed by Martin (1992) (see Tann, this volume). Within Martin's model, Field, Tenor and Mode are interpreted as register categories, while register, rather than being a linguistic entity, is equated with context of situation, in the sense that it 'describes the immediate situational context in which the text [is] produced' (Eggins 1994: 26). Register is thus 'realised' in language, rather than being interpreted as 'text type', and hence a linguistic category correlating with a configuration of choices within Field, Tenor and Mode. At a level above register is *genre*, or 'social purpose' (see Gardner, this volume). Genre is equated with context of culture in the sense that social purposes tend to be culturally defined and culturally structured (Eggins 1994). The genre, or the 'generic structure', steers the configuration of register choices (features of Field, Tenor and Mode) relevant to each stage of a text as it unfolds. Martin (1984: 25) defines genre as 'a staged, goal-oriented, purposeful activity in which speakers engage as members of our culture'. This view helps the analyst to see how the variables of field, tenor and mode may change across a specific situation, as realised in a text. However, other researchers, such as Hasan (1995, 1999 especially), have demonstrated that the changing variables of Field, Tenor and Mode can be accounted for without departing from the conceptions of register and context of situation as espoused by Halliday.

Another variation in the description of Field, Tenor and Mode is that proposed by Hasan (1999) – in particular, her descriptions of Field and Mode. Hasan argues that certain features of Mode, such as choices to do with the 'role of language', the expectations of the participants of the language in the situation, and the relation between the language and the rhetorical mode of the text – that is, 'what is being achieved by the text in terms of such categories as persuasive, expository, didactic, and the like' (Halliday 1985: 12) – are better placed within the parameter of Field. A common way of referring to the 'role of language' in SFL descriptions is through the use of the terms 'ancillary' or 'constitutive', which have been linked to 'rhetorical mode'. Situations in which language is said to be *ancillary* are characterised as those in which the language 'integrates' with other forms of activity and facilitates that activity. These include situations such as a cooking demonstration, a game or a service encounter. On the other hand, in other situations, 'the language activity tends to be self-sufficient, in the sense that it accounts for most or all of the activity relevant to the situation' (Halliday et al. 1964: 92). In these situations, the language is *constitutive* of the situation. An example of such a situation might be a university lecture on linguistics. Hasan's (1999: 282) point is that, 'just like material actions, verbal actions . . . specify what the interactants are doing: in the verbal action of explaining, one of the interactants explains just as in the material action of buying, one of the interactants buys'. She therefore proposes that the choices of ancillary and constitutive are better placed within Field and not in Mode. This then leaves Mode as largely concerned with the 'channel' (phonic or graphic) and the 'contact' between interactants in the situation, such as whether the situation involves two-way interaction or face-to-face interaction, or whether interaction between participants is mediated through technology (such as a telephone).

Bowcher (2013, 2014) discusses the validity of these modifications. While stating that 'Hasan presents a compelling case for bringing the choices of constitutive and ancillary within the Field network' (Bowcher 2014: 196), she argues against this change. She maintains that although both 'role of language' and 'rhetorical mode' have been placed within mode, they should be seen as different. Rhetorical mode has more to do with 'the experience around which the nature of the activity centres: its conceptual or practical focus' (Bowcher 2014: 197) and is thus more 'field-like'. Role of language, on the other hand, is a useful gloss for the 'degree to which language is involved in the event' – that is, its ancillary or constitutive role (Bowcher 2014: 198). Thus, for Bowcher, 'role of language' and the subcategories of 'ancillary' and 'constitutive' are better left within the contextual parameter of Mode, and 'practical' and 'conceptual' (features linked to rhetorical mode) within Field.[6]

Current contributions and research

Recent work in formalising the description of Field, Tenor and Mode has concentrated on developing system networks that set out possible choices representative of the situational features and subfeatures appropriate to these general domains. Although 'emerging' through 'Halliday's work on the grammar of English' (Butt 2001: 1822), system networks are available at varying degrees of development and delicacy for such systems as INTONATION, LEXICOGRAMMAR, SEMANTICS and CONTEXT. The main proponents of contextualisation system networks are Hasan (1999, 2009, 2014), Butt (2004, 2012), Bowcher (2007, 2013, 2014) and Berry (2015).

Hasan (1999, 2009) has proposed system networks for Field, arguing their features through specific text/context illustrations, and Hasan (1999, 2014) demonstrates through careful analysis and discussion of various texts how system networks may be developed and made use of, and how extended and complex situations may be accounted for in her networks. She also discusses the concept of 'default dependencies' and 'selection expressions' in relation to contextualisation system networks. *Default dependencies* are sets of choices that 'limit the conjunction' of other choices within a network (Hasan 1999: 279) – that is, if choice X is chosen in system H, then choice Y MUST be chosen in system K. Selection expressions set out in a systematic way the choices from the contextualisation system networks.[7] Hasan (2014) presents a detailed 'walk-through' of the meaning, value and utility of system networks for Field, Tenor and Mode, with ample illustrations of various options in each network.

Butt (2004) has developed systems for Field, Tenor and Mode in his (as yet unpublished) manuscript entitled *Parameters of Context*. He explains that his networks 'elaborate a wide range of contextual distinctions with semantic consequences' and are 'concerned with the semantic varieties of work and institutions in a technologically developed community' (Butt 2004: 7). While this may make it appear that Butt's networks are rather specific in nature, they are general enough in their scope to be utilised in analysing a range of contexts and for researchers to build into them contextual features identified in different contexts of language use. This is echoed in a comment by Urbach (2013: 316), that:

> Continuing clarification of the systemic values of context would greatly benefit linguistic research and increase the confidence and ability of linguists to control for contextual variables to evaluate the values of linguistic choices, particularly in register studies, where the analysis is focused on a mid-point of the cline of instantiation.

Bowcher's work has mainly focused on Field and less substantially on Mode. Bowcher (2007) considers Hasan's (1999) field network from the point of view of multimodal instructional texts, arguing that the concepts of 'material action', 'ancillary' and 'constitutive' need to be reinterpreted, especially for some written multimodal instructional texts in which the 'action' is construed both visually and verbally. Bowcher (2013) focuses on the variable of 'Material Action' in Butt's and Hasan's Field networks, and in relation to multimodal texts. Bowcher (2014) revisits the feature 'Material Action', but as part of a broader discussion of Field and Mode, and with a view to discussing issues related to the standardising or unifying of features from the current available networks, so that they can be used as the primary and defining features of Field and of Mode.

Berry (2015) has also developed system networks for the contextual parameters, but from a somewhat different perspective, considering contextual features from the point of view of the participants in the situation itself. This is reminiscent of some of her early work on the 'written genres of business and industry', in which she conducted interviews with writers themselves to ascertain what they judged as being successful or unsuccessful writing in their field (Berry 1995). Berry (2015: 187) aims to 'discover what contextual features adult native speakers and writers respond to . . . how the speakers and writers construe contexts and how they respond in the semantic choices they make to the contexts they have construed'. She is thus interested in what she calls 'pre-text relevant contextual features and via-text relevant contextual features', and the way in which these two categories of features affect a speaker's semantic choices in a situation.

Another approach to the description of the contextual parameters is that proposed by Matthiessen (2006, 2013, 2015).[8] Rather than utilising system networks, Matthiessen suggests that the parameters of context can be represented on a 'registerial map' in which Field, Tenor and Mode intersect. The map itself represents the registerial range of the language. With regard to the individual contextual parameters, Field, for instance, is interpreted in terms of 'field of activity' (socio-semiotic process) and 'field of experience' (subject matter). The field of experience is considered to be a more 'specific' feature of field than socio-semiotic process. Matthiessen (2006, 2013, 2015, for example) represents 'field of activity' as a pie chart divided into 'slices' of socio-semiotic processes: expounding, reporting, recreating, sharing, doing, recommending, enabling and exploring. Across these slices are 'mode values', which are arranged as concentric circles from the inner to the outer circumference of the pie. These values include spoken and monologic, spoken and dialogic, written and dialogic, and written and monologic (Matthiessen 2006). According to Matthiessen (2006: 45), tenor would need to be represented as a sphere, but he explains that the 'different regions' on the pie diagram 'tend to have different associations with tenor, and these can be mapped systematically'. The map represents a typological and topological interpretation of context by representing different types of context, and showing how their features intersect, blend or 'shade into one another' (Matthiessen 2006: 44).

Bartlett (2013, 2015) problematises the way in which non-contextual and non-material features of the general environment, be they cultural, personal, or socio-political, may leave a 'trace' on the choices made in a text, yet not be construed as 'relevant' context, in the sense that SFL defines 'relevancy' (as we saw earlier). This argument has obvious implications for decisions as to what features should be included in generalised system networks for Field, Tenor and Mode. Bartlett (2015, and this volume) suggests a 'scalar' model of the contextual features. This model would take into account first-order features, or those that have an influence over the overall nature of the context, as well as second-order features, or those features directly construed in the language of the text. He calls for a more rigorous means of accounting for these different 'orders' of contextual features within the architecture of the SFL model of language.

Main research methods and practices

Prior to the recent developments of contextualisation system networks, one of the clearest analyses of the relationship between language and the contextual parameters of Field, Tenor and Mode is found in Halliday (1985). Here, Halliday outlines several facets of how an analysis may be conducted, and also includes two detailed analyses showing the relationship between lexicogrammatical choices, meanings and contextual features: one involves the analysis and interpretation of two lines from a poem by Ben Jonson called 'To Celia'; the other involves an analysis and interpretation of a short dialogue between a father and a child. The first analysis begins at the lexicogrammatical level, moving from there to the level of meaning and then to context. The second begins with a description of the context of situation, then moves through the semantic choices to the lexicogrammatical realisations.

Aside from these analyses by Halliday, there are various analyses of the relationship between context and text throughout the SFL literature, too numerous to mention here. The following are some points to consider when developing a description of a specific configuration of Field, Tenor and Mode.

- The main purpose for the investigation should be clearly articulated.
- Naturally occurring discourse is preferred – that is, language that is used in real situations, whether those be spoken, written or some combination of these.
- The analysis of a corpus of texts or of texts that are comparable in some way is the most useful for highlighting and exploring specific contextual configurations, and for building hypotheses based on observations of how linguistic and contextual choices pattern.

This, in turn, aids in developing empirically based descriptions of registers or text-types that correlate with context-types, thus giving insights into the many ways in which language and society are connected.

- The analysis may begin at the level of context, at which the analyst makes a generalised description of the Field, Tenor and Mode based on his or her understanding of the text. However, the description of Field, Tenor and Mode must be confirmed through an analysis of the linguistic choices made. A formal description of the context may utilise features from the current system networks for Field, Tenor and Mode (Hasan 1999, 2009, 2014; Butt 2004, 2012; Bowcher 2007, 2010, 2013, 2014; Berry 2015), or may derive from the generalised descriptions provided by Halliday (1985), or may utilise Matthiessen's (2006, 2013, 2015, for example) registerial map. As already noted, the contextualisation system networks, are still in their early developmental stages and further empirical study is needed to increase their accountability and usability (Bartlett 2013, 2015, and this volume).
- Alternatively, an analysis may begin at the level of lexicogrammar at which the analyst first divides the text into clauses, then analyses each clause in terms of the choices made in systems such as TRANSITIVITY, MOOD, THEME and others (Halliday and Matthiessen 2014). The lexicogrammatical choices are then interpreted in terms of the meanings that are realised, which in turn aid in developing a description of the relevant features of the context of situation.

Future directions

The main task at hand is to further develop the descriptions of Field, Tenor and Mode in such a way that more rigorous analyses of various contexts of situations may be conducted (Hasan 2009, 2014). As mentioned in this chapter, one way of doing this is through the development of system networks of options for Field, Tenor and Mode. This work is likely to be enhanced by the development of more sophisticated digital visualisation techniques and software that can construct interdependent, detailed and complex system networks. Complementary to this is the exploration of more 'implicit' ways in which situations of language use come about and are characterised, and what this may mean for the descriptions of Field, Tenor and Mode (Bartlett 2013, 2015, and this volume; Berry 2015, and this volume). The development of the descriptions of Field, Tenor and Mode is thus an ongoing project in SFL, but one that provides a key means of describing and accounting for register variation and for the relationship between language, context and society.

Notes

1 See also Nesbitt and Plum (1988), Freddi (2013) and Teich (2013) for discussions and/or analyses of registers in terms of probabilities in grammatical choices.
2 See the chapters in Part II of this volume.
3 See, e.g., Hasan (2009, 2014).
4 See, e.g., Halliday (2009: 64–70, 84 especially).
5 See Gardner (this volume) on the generic structure potential (GSP).
6 See also Butt (2004).
7 See also Butt (2004) and Bowcher (2014).
8 See also Matthiessen and Teruya (2016).

References

Bartlett, T. 2013. 'I'll manage the context': Context, environment, and the potential for institutional change. In L. Fontaine, T. Bartlett and G. O'Grady (eds) *Systemic Functional Linguistics: Exploring Choice*. Cambridge: Cambridge University Press, pp. 342–64.

Bartlett, T. 2015. Multiscalar modelling of context: Some questions raised by the category of mode. In W.L. Bowcher and J.Y. Liang (eds) *Society in Language, Language in Society: Essays in Honour of Ruqaiya Hasan*. Basingstoke: Palgrave, pp. 166–83.

Berry, M. 1995. Thematic options and success in writing. In M. Ghadessy (ed.) *Thematic Development in English Texts*. London: Cassell, pp. 55–84.

Berry, M. 2015. On describing contexts of situation. In W.L. Bowcher and J.Y. Liang (eds) *Society in Language, Language in Society: Essays in Honour of Ruqaiya Hasan*. Basingstoke: Palgrave, pp. 184–205.

Bowcher, W.L. 2007. Field and multimodal texts. In R. Hasan, C.M.I.M. Matthiessen and J.J. Webster (eds) *Continuing Discourse on Language*. London: Equinox, pp. 619–46.

Bowcher, W.L. 2010. The history and theoretical development of 'context of situation' in systemic functional linguistics. *Annual Review of Functional Linguistics* 2: 64–93.

Bowcher, W.L. 2013. Material action as choice in field. In L. Fontaine, T. Bartlett and G. O'Grady (eds) *Systemic Functional Linguistics: Exploring Choice*. Cambridge: Cambridge University Press, pp. 318–41.

Bowcher, W.L. 2014. Issues in developing unified systems for contextual field and mode. *Functions of Language* 21(2): 176–209.

Bowcher, W.L., and J.Y. Liang. 2015. GSP and multimodal texts. In W.L. Bowcher and J.Y. Liang (eds) *Society in Language, Language in Society: Essays in Honour of Ruqaiya Hasan*. Basingstoke: Palgrave, pp. 251–74.

Butt, D. 2001. Firth, Halliday and the development of systemic functional theory. In S. Auroux, E.F.K. Koerner, H.-J. Niederehe and K. Versteegh (eds) *History of the Language Sciences: An International Handbook on the Evolution of the Study of Language from the Beginnings to the Present*. Berlin and New York: Walter de Gruyter pp. 1806–38.

Butt, D. 2004. Parameters of context: On establishing the similarities and differences between social processes. Unpublished mimeograph. Macquarie University, Sydney.

Butt, D. 2008. The robustness of realisational systems. In J.J. Webster (ed.) *Meaning in Context: Strategies for Implementing Intelligent Applications of Language Studies*. London: Continuum, pp. 59–83.

Butt, D. 2012. Practical sciences, interpersonal meaning, and networks for tenor. Paper presented at Register and Context Symposium, Macquarie University, Sydney, 6–8 February.

Butt, D., and R. Wegener. 2007. The work of concepts: Context and metafunction in the systemic functional model. In R. Hasan, C.M.I.M. Matthiessen and J.J. Webster (eds) *Continuing Discourse on Language*. London: Equinox, pp. 619–46.

Catford, J.C. 1965. *A Linguistic Theory of Translation: An Essay in Applied Linguistics*. Oxford: Oxford University Press.

Eggins, S. 1994. *An Introduction to Systemic Functional Linguistics*. London: Pinter.

Ellis, J. 1966. On contextual meaning. In C.E. Bazell, J.C. Catford, M.A.K. Halliday and R.H. Robins (eds) *In Memory of J.R. Firth*. London: Longman, pp. 79–95.

Firth, J.R. 1968a. Descriptive linguistics and the study of English. In F.R. Palmer (ed.) *Selected Papers of J.R. Firth 1952–59*. London: Longman, pp. 96–113.

Firth, J.R. 1968b. Linguistic analysis as a study of meaning. In F.R. Palmer (ed.) *Selected Papers of J.R. Firth 1952–59*. London: Longman, pp. 12–26.

Firth, J.R. 1968c. A synopsis of linguistic theory, 1930–55. In F.R. Palmer (ed.) *Selected Papers of J.R. Firth 1952–59*. London: Longman, pp. 168–205.

Freddi, M. 2013. Choice and language variation: Some theoretical reflections. In L. Fontaine, T. Bartlett and G. O'Grady (eds) *Systemic Functional Linguistics: Exploring Choice*. Cambridge: Cambridge University Press, pp. 56–71.

Wendy L. Bowcher

Gregory, M. 1967. Aspects of varieties differentiation. *Journal of Linguistics* 3(2): 177–274.

Halliday, M.A.K. 1977. Text as semantic choice in social contexts. In T. van Dijk and J. Petöfi (eds) *Grammars and descriptions*. Berlin: Walter de Gruyter, pp. 176–225.

Halliday, M.A.K. 1985. Part A. In M.A.K. Halliday and R. Hasan (eds) *Language, Context, and Text: Aspects of Language in a Social-Semiotic Perspective*. Geelong: Deakin University Press, pp. 1–49.

Halliday, M.A.K. 1992. How do you mean? In M. Davies and L. Ravelli (eds) *Advances in Systemic Linguistics: Recent Theory and Practice*. London: Pinter, pp. 20–35.

Halliday, M.A.K. 2005. Quantitative studies and probabilistic grammar. In J.J. Webster (ed.) *Collected Works of M.A.K. Halliday, Vol. 6: Computational and Quantitative Studies*. London: Continuum, pp. 63–75.

Halliday, M.A.K. 2009. Methods – techniques – problems. In M.A.K. Halliday and J.J. Webster (eds) *Continuum Companion to Systemic Functional Linguistics*. London: Continuum, pp. 59–86.

Halliday, M.A.K., and C.M.I.M. Matthiessen. 2014. *Halliday's Introduction to Functional Grammar*. 4th edn. London and New York: Routledge.

Halliday, M.A.K., A. McIntosh and P. Strevens. 1964. *The Linguistic Sciences and Language Teaching*. London: Longman.

Hasan, R. 1985. Part B. In M.A.K. Halliday and R. Hasan (eds) *Language, Context, and Text: Aspects of Language in a Social-Semiotic Perspective*. Geelong: Deakin University Press, pp. 52–118.

Hasan, R. 1995. The conception of context in text. In P. Fries and M. Gregory (eds) *Discourse in Society: Systemic Functional Perspectives* (Meaning and choice in language: Studies for Michael Halliday). Norwood, NJ: Ablex, pp. 183–283.

Hasan, R. 1999. Speaking with reference to context. In M. Ghadessy (ed.) *Text and Context in Functional Linguistics*. Amsterdam: John Benjamins, pp. 219–32.

Hasan, R. 2001. Wherefore context? The place of context in the system and process of language. In R. Shaozeng, W. Guthrie and I.W.R. Fong (eds) *Grammar and Discourse: Proceedings of the International Conference on Discourse Analysis*. Macau: University of Macau, pp. 1–21.

Hasan, R. 2009. The place of context in a systemic functional model. In M.A.K. Halliday and J.J. Webster (eds) *Continuum Companion to Systemic Functional Linguistics*. London: Continuum, pp. 166–89.

Hasan, R. 2013. Choice, system, realization: Describing language as meaning potential. In L. Fontaine, T. Bartlett and G. O'Grady (eds) *Systemic Functional Linguistics: Exploring Choice*. Cambridge: Cambridge University Press, pp. 269–99.

Hasan, R. 2014. Towards a paradigmatic description of context: Systems, metafunctions, and semantics. *Functional Linguistics* 1: 9.

Martin, J.R. 1984. Language, register and genre. In F. Christie (ed.) *Children Writing: Reader*. Geelong: Deakin University Press, pp. 21–30.

Martin, J.R. 1992. *English Text: System and Structure*. Amsterdam: John Benjamins.

Matthiessen, C.M.I.M. 2006. Educating for advanced foreign language capacities: Exploring the meaning-making resources of languages systemic-functionally. In H. Byrnes (ed.) *Advanced Language Learning: The Contribution of Halliday and Vygotsky*. London: Continuum, pp. 31–57.

Matthiessen, C.M.I.M. 2013. Registerial cartography: Context and semantics. Plenary address at the International Systemic Functional Congress (ISFC40), Sun Yat-sen University, Guagnzhou, China, 15–19 July.

Matthiessen, C.M.I.M. 2015. Register in the round: Registerial cartography. *Functional Linguistics* 2(9): 1–48.

Matthiessen, C.M.I.M., and K. Teruya. 2016. Registerial hybridity: Indeterminacy among field of activity. In D.R. Miller and P. Bayley (eds) *Hybridity in Systemic Functional Linguistics: Grammar, Text and Discursive Context*. Sheffield: Equinox, pp. 205–39.

McCarthy, M. 2000. Mutually captive audiences: Small talk and the genre of close contact service encounters. In J. Coupland (ed.) *Small Talk*. Harlow: Pearson Education, pp. 84–109.

Mitchell, T.F. 1975. The language of buying and selling in Cyrenaica: A situational statement. In T.F. Mitchell (ed.) *Principles of Firthian Linguistics*. London: Longman, pp. 167–200.

Nesbitt, C., and G. Plum. 1988. Probabilities in a systemic grammar: The clause complex in English. In R.P. Fawcett and D.J. Young (eds) *New Developments in Systemic Linguistics: Theory and Application*. London and New York: Pinter, pp. 6–38.

Teich, E. 2013. Choices in analysing choice: Methods and techniques for register analysis. In L. Fontaine, T. Bartlett and G. O'Grady (eds) *Systemic Functional Linguistics: Exploring Choice*. Cambridge: Cambridge University Press, pp. 417–31.

Urbach, C. 2013. 'Choice' in relation to context: A diachronic perspective on cultural *valeur*. In L. Fontaine, T. Bartlett and G. O'Grady (eds) *Systemic Functional Linguistics: Exploring Choice*. Cambridge: Cambridge University Press, pp. 300–17.

Cohesion in systemic functional linguistics

A theoretical reflection

Ben Clarke

This chapter is concerned with cohesion in systemic functional linguistics (SFL) specifically, but will have relevance for functional linguistics more generally. If a text is defined as a single semantic unit, cohesion is one of two properties of textuality; the other, coherence, can be defined simply as a text's being consistent in logical terms. Comparably, cohesion may be defined as links of a linguistic sort between two or more items in a text, be the items in question words, phrases or bigger units still. One can talk of a number of different types of cohesion, or 'cohesive device'; generally, these types are considered to consist of 'reference', 'substitution', 'ellipsis', 'conjunction', 'repetition', 'collocation' and a range of sense relations, such as 'synonymy', 'antonymy', etc. These are usually grouped into two main types: (a) grammatical cohesive devices ('reference', 'substitution', 'ellipsis' and 'conjunction'), in which the two parts of the link embody a one-way, dependency relation; and (b) lexical cohesive devices ('repetition', 'collocation' and the sense relations), in which the two parts of the link embody a two-way, mutually defining relation. In the main, this chapter limits consideration of cohesion to the grammatical cohesive devices for a number of reasons, many of which will become clear at relevant points in the ensuing discussion; that said, the overriding argument of the chapter[1] is as relevant to those cohesive devices not discussed in its main body.

The chapter has three purposes. The first two sections present the two descriptions of cohesive devices that have, at least until now, been the most prominent in the theory. This comparative task is necessarily informed by mapping the respective descriptive accounts in the wider theoretical architecture of SFL (see Bateman, Asp and Berry, all in this volume). A second goal of the chapter is to briefly chart some of the more applied work on cohesion in SFL since Halliday and Hasan's (1976) seminal work *Cohesion in English*. Third, and finally, the chapter proposes where future work on cohesion in SFL may usefully be invested to advance our understanding of these different cohesive devices, given the theory's orientation and goals.

Cohesion in SFL following Halliday and Hasan (1976)

The two systemic functional descriptions of cohesion referred to so far are those of Halliday and Hasan's (1976) *Cohesion in English* and Martin's (1992) *English Text*. Rather than offering a general comparison of these descriptions, this and the next section focus on the ability of each descriptive account to enable a contextualised and (particularly) a semanticised understanding of cohesive devices, which is an area in which future work on cohesion in SFL might concentrate efforts (as we will discuss later in the chapter). The comparative task of this and the next section therefore necessarily entails brief prior discussions of the wider theoretical architecture of the standard SFL model (although see Fawcett, this volume) – particularly, the theoretical relations of stratification and realisation (Berry, this volume) and the theoretical abstraction of metafunction (Asp, this volume).

Stratification is often informally glossed as the property that language has in being composed of 'a number of levels'. These 'levels' are different orders of abstraction. They can be defined more strictly by, and are mostly knowable as such because of, recurring realisational patterns, but also because the reality of stratification – the different levels, or 'strata', themselves – require different units of analysis and different methods of analysis to enable their description (Crystal 1997: 82–3). These recurring patternings are highly probabilistic relationships between pairs or groups of phenomena at these different orders of abstraction; when one choice is made at one level, it has, as a consequence, a highly likely effect on choices relative to the phenomenon to which it is related at the next level. Consider, as an illustrative example, the systems of MOOD, made up of the features 'imperative', 'indicative: declarative' and 'indicative: interrogative', and SPEECH FUNCTION, made up of the features 'command', 'question', 'statement' and 'offer'. These systems – the former, a lexicogrammatical one, and the latter, a semantic one – have a highly regular interaction. For example, the semantic feature of 'question', the demand for linguistic information, is usually formulated grammatically as an 'indicative: interrogative'. But the demand for linguistic information can be expressed by other grammatical means, such as 'indicative: declarative' (*It would be nice to know what you are planning for dinner*) or 'imperative' (*Tell me what you are planning for dinner*). As Berry (this volume) outlines in detail, standard accounts of SFL postulate four language strata – (from biggest to smallest) semantics, lexicogrammar, phonology and phonetics – as well as an extralinguistic stratum of context.

Based primarily on language-intrinsic[2] criteria (for example clusters of dependency between available resources, viewed systemically as a network), SFL's theory of language functions – its metafunctional hypothesis – states that language serves the following three functions:

1   to represent experience in discrete configurations, as well as to express the serial relations between such configurations of experience (the 'ideational metafunction');
2   to interact and exchange; to negotiate and enact inter-subjectivity (the 'interpersonal metafunction'); and
3   to present these ideational and interpersonal meanings as coherent and cohesive text in and given its context (the 'textual metafunction').

As implied by the last of these definitions, textual metafunctional language phenomena have a different status in the theory to their ideational and interpersonal counterparts: they are inherently second-order in kind, playing an enabling role to ideational and interpersonal language phenomena (Halliday 1978: 130–2; Matthiessen 1992). Put another way, it is the textual metafunction that makes possible the expression of the substantive functions carried forward in the ideational and interpersonal metafunctions.

For Halliday and Hasan (1976), all cohesive devices are operative at the textual metafunction (for example Halliday and Hasan 1976: 29) – that is, in different ways, the different cohesive devices play a role in organising the flow of linguistic information into meaningful discourse, coherent in its context. Cohesive devices thus assist in semiosis and the consequent creation of text. With the exception of 'reference' – a 'relation between meanings . . . a relation on the semantic level' (Halliday and Hasan 1976: 89) – Halliday and Hasan (1976: 29) argue that cohesive devices are operative at the lexicogrammatical stratum. Although they are lexicogrammatical resources, cohesive devices are viewed by Halliday and Hasan (1976) as non-structural because the two items related by a cohesive link usually exist across textual environments that are greater than the highest unit of lexicogrammatical rank, such as ellipsis (*When **are we meeting**? [**We are meeting**] At two o'clock*), substitution (*I wanted **the new version of the textbook**. Never mind. The old **one** will do*) and reference (*I saw **Gerard and Tom** disputing the game. **They** never agree when it comes to football!*),[3] and do not themselves bring about grammatical structure (Halliday and Hasan 1976: 6–7; Matthiessen et al. 2010: 74).

Given this approach, semantic and contextual motives for the cohesive device therefore largely lie outside Halliday and Hasan's (1976) account, although their approach does not deny the relevance of such work. They themselves go only so far in this direction as to posit general semantic motives for reference, conjunction, substitution and ellipsis, as well as lexical cohesion (Halliday and Hasan 1976: 298–323). These are all, in slightly different ways, a matter of semantic continuity. Conjunction, they argue, is motivated by *indication of semantic connection between two continuous passages of text*, such that the interpretation of one message depends on the relation in which it stands with respect to the other, either in ideational or interpersonal terms (Halliday and Hasan 1976: 308, 320–2). In marginally different ways, substitution and ellipsis are said to construe the meaning of *continuity where there is a broader environment of contrast* (Halliday and Hasan 1976: 306–8, 314–18). Both the continuity (for example of referent, of process, etc.) and the environment of contrast (for example in terms of class membership, polarity or modality, etc.) may take one of a range of forms (Halliday and Hasan 1976: 307, 315). Furthermore, in some instances, 'contrast' equates simply to 'new information', with the case of substitution/ellipsis construing continuative meanings via given information (for example *I fancy **an ale**. I'll try **this one***). Lexical cohesion construes meanings of *identity of reference* (repetition) or *similarity of the lexical environment* (collocation and sense relations) (Halliday and Hasan 1976: 318–20). Finally, the meaning of reference can be glossed as *continuity and potential identity of referent(s)* (Halliday and Hasan 1976: 304–6, 308–14). However, as the authors consider 'reference' to be a semantic phenomenon, this is little more than a restatement of its general treatment in their account.

While such semantic motives provide a useful starting point, such descriptive generalisations get us only so far in our understanding of some phenomena. Full semantic explanations for the occurrence of a lexicogrammatical cohesive device require detailed semantic descriptions, including both generalised meanings typically carried forward by the cohesive device in question, and nuanced meanings construed by more particular instances of the cohesive device and in register-specific usage. This point shall be returned to in different ways in both the next and subsequent sections.

Cohesion in SFL following Martin (1992)

Martin's (1992; Martin and Rose 2007) proposals are a significant reworking of Halliday and Hasan's (1976) account, involving consequences for the stratal and metafunctional location of cohesion and consequently wider theoretical implications for the architecture of SFL.[4] Rather than attempt to account for the generalised or more nuanced semantic and contextual motives for cohesive devices, Martin (1992: 1, 2009: 156, 2014: 9) models cohesive devices systemically *as* semantic phenomena per se. Martin (1992: 390, 2009: 156–7, 2014: 10) argues that the cohesive devices conceived in semantic terms are then metafunctionally diversified, thus putting his proposed description at odds with that of Halliday and Hasan (1976), who see all of the cohesive devices as textual metafunctional resources. 'Reference', considered as the phoric relations between participants (broadly conceived) presented in a text, is modelled by Martin (1992: 93–158) as a textual metafunctional discourse semantic system of IDENTIFICATION; 'conjunction' is re-presented in the logical metafunctional discourse semantic system CONJUNCTION as a matter of the relevance of one message to others in a text (Martin 1992: 159–270); and the resources of 'lexical cohesion', the range of meaning relations pertaining between lexical items, is presented as the metafunctionally experiential discourse semantic system IDEATION. (Martin 1992: 271–380). Substitution and ellipsis, Martin (1992: 388–9) concludes, cannot be treated as semantic phenomena, however, because they do not have variable lexicogrammatical realisations. Still, as phenomena modelled in a principally stratified theory of language (as seen in the last section), they are anticipated to be motivated by semantic and contextual factors; for Martin (1992: 389–90, 2014: 31–92), as a concern with the negotiation of meanings between interlocutors in communicative exchange, interpersonal metafunctional considerations.[5] Martin (1992: 14–27, 2014: 7–8) justifies this conceptual reworking of cohesion phenomena on structural grounds – namely, that cohesive devices introduce structure of a kind different to lexicogrammatical structure, defined in the unit of text, a semantically defined unit (Halliday and Hasan 1976: 2; Halliday 1985: 10; cf. Crystal 1997: 82–3).

Although not concerned to align herself with one rather than the other of these descriptive approaches to cohesion, Xueyan's (2013) contribution is relevant here. In contrast to the majority of work post-Halliday and Hasan (1976) on cohesion in SFL, which is of an applied sort (as we will see in the next section), Xueyan (2013) discusses semantic motives for, and construals of, particular types of ellipsis pattern in English as a foreign language (EFL) classroom discourse, finding that instances of clausal ellipsis are used in a range of speech functions – both as initiating and responding moves – to tie moves coherently across the sequencing of moves in dialogue. As important as her findings is her procedure. As Xueyan (2013: 239) says, 'in order to step further towards the general semantics of ellipsis, more text types need be studied'. This position aligns with the overriding argument of the present chapter: future SFL work on cohesion should offer detailed descriptions of the semantic and contextual motives for specific cohesive devices. The final section of this chapter describes the semantic potential of certain ellipsis patterns in a different text-type to that of Xueyan (2013).

Applied work on cohesion in SFL

Contra the descriptive and theoretical discussions of the last two sections, this section reviews more applied work on cohesion in SFL since Halliday and Hasan's (1976) *Cohesion in English*. Given the scope of this chapter, this review is necessarily limited as such, doing little more than to list some of the work undertaken on cohesion within a SFL paradigm since Halliday and Hasan (1976). This is done primarily to give a sense of with which kinds of enquiries work on cohesion in SFL has most been concerned since that time.

A common enquiry in systemic functional work on cohesion since 1976 has been to conduct work within language typology on cohesion generally and on specific cohesive devices particularly, comparing the behaviour of the phenomena involved in different languages.[6] Recent work by Steiner, Kunz and colleagues (for example Kunz and Steiner 2010, 2013; Degaetano-Ortlieb et al. forthcoming) is particularly notable. They compare types, functions and patterns of a range of cohesive devices in English and in German, using large amounts of corpus data and statistical methods for computing significance in their data. As with much language typological work on cohesion, Steiner, Kunz and colleagues are concerned with applications relating to translation (see Kunz and Teich, this volume). Another angle of applied enquiry is work on cohesion in clinical settings: Armstrong (1987, 1991), for example, has used cohesive devices to explore language impairment; Fine (1995), to explore the language of psychiatric patients; and Butt and colleagues (2007) to explore psychotherapeutic data. Other applied work includes Gardner (2012) and Paziraie (2013), who have both explored the enactment of cohesive relations in students' academic writing in their second language with a view to improving academic performance in such practices.

A number of scholars have looked at cohesion and coherence in the analysis of a range of different text types, for example Parsons (1990) on science texts and Cloran (1999) on mother–child interactions. With the increased interest in multimodality, work on cohesion between items instantiated in different semiotic systems has received attention: Martinec (1998) explores cohesion between different embodied modalities; Martinec (2004) considers instances of cohesion between language and gesture; Liu and O'Halloran (2009) explore the enactment and nature of cohesive relations between language and still image.

A proposal for future systemic functional work on cohesion

The chapter so far has highlighted that, although conducted on a range of text types and concerned with a variety of applications, much of the post-1976 work on cohesion in SFL has explored questions of a lexicogrammatical sort. If one accepts Halliday and Hasan's (1976) approach to describing cohesion – that is, that ('reference' aside) cohesive devices are operative at the lexicogrammatical stratum – this trend seems logical enough. Yet regardless of approach, in a functional and stratal view of language such as that of SFL, the descriptive task is not complete until a detailed account is offered of the semantic motives for, and the meanings construed by, lexicogrammatical phenomena such as cohesive devices and, in turn, the equivalent motives and construals for these at the level of context.[7] The chapter so far has, however, demonstrated both that (a) such works are rare and (b), for those accounts that do exist – that is, Halliday and Hasan (1976) and Martin (1992) – there is disparity in terms of how the task should be conducted.

This final section constitutes the main argument of the chapter, calling for future SFL work on cohesion to concentrate efforts on teasing out such full descriptions of the semantic and contextual motives for specific cohesive devices. It does so by demonstrating what might be entailed by such descriptive work. Here, we offer a more delicate description of the contextual, and particularly semantic, motives for certain types of ellipsis. The basis of this demonstration is empirical: specifically, the occurrence of particular patterns of ellipsis in Clarke (2012), for which there appears to be no existing explanation, are here reasoned along semantic and contextual grounds.[8]

Consider examples (1)–(3), drawn from a dataset of eighty-nine UK tabloid and broadsheet newspaper reports on football games, assembled during the second half of 2009.

(1) Rooney went straight for the ball, (*Rooney* [S])[9] put it on the spot and (*Rooney* [S]) promptly sent Almunia the wrong way.

(2) Gathering possession near the centre circle, he cantered forward, (*he* [S]) exchanged passes with Eboué, and (*he* [S]) crafted a curler into the top corner.

(3) Mancienne looked uncertain and (*Mancienne* [S]) failed to deal with a bouncing ball on the edge of the box and (*Mancienne* [S]) allowed Rodallega to send in his low shot which Hahnemann turned around the post.

Two characteristics that these examples have in common are that:

• in terms of functional structure, there is ellipsis of always and only the grammatical Subject, which is here termed 'Subject-only ellipsis'; and
• the cohesive relation extends from the antecedent clause, via ellipsis, to stand in as the Subject for the next two consecutive clauses

The frequency of such instances in the dataset in question – 30 of all 244 instances of any functional-structural type of ellipsis in this corpus are of this type – is not only particularly notable, but also statistically significant. As Clarke (2013: 277–8) notes, the potential for ellipsis is a matter of the clause, not some arbitrary number of words; given the number of instances of any type of ellipsis in this corpus, the likelihood of a clause chosen at random containing any case of ellipsis is slightly greater than 5 per cent (244 instances of ellipsis ÷ 4,732 clauses in the corpus = 0.0516). The consequent likelihood of *any* two random consecutive clauses in this corpus *both* containing ellipsis of any type is marginally greater than a quarter of 1 per cent ($0.0516 \times (0.0516 \div 4,642) \times 4,643 = 0.00264651$[10]). Yet this corpus actually engenders 16 instances of consecutive clauses containing ellipsis, all of which are Subject-only ellipsis[11] –a ratio that is in excess of 6,000 times more frequent than chance. Despite the fact that semiotic modalities such as language embody a range of relationships that are not random (Oakes 1998), such marked frequency of this patterned type of ellipsis certainly does not appear to be a chance occurrence; rather, on the basis of statistical computation of the empirical evidence, it appears that there is some factor motivating the occurrence of this very particular type of ellipsis pattern.

While Halliday and Hasan's (1976: 306–8, 314–18) 'continuity in the context of contrast' semantic motive for ellipsis is not irrelevant here, the evidence from conjunction-type patterns suggests that continuity meanings are not so prominent in the instances of ellipsis presently under discussion. Of all expressed conjunctive relations, continuative ones – or 'additive' ones, in Halliday and Hasan's (1976) terms – are proportionally less frequent in instances of consecutive Subject-only ellipsis than they are in all other (that is, non-consecutive) instances of Subject-only ellipsis (see Tables 25.1 and 25.2).

Moreover, 'continuity in the context of contrast', as a *generalised* semantic motivation (Halliday and Hasan 1976: 306–8, 314–18) – that is, one common to all cases of ellipsis – offers no explanation as to why there is such a statistically significant occurrence of ellipsis

Table 25.1 Conjunction types for consecutive Subject-only ellipsis

None (Ø)	Additive ('and')	Adversative ('but')
9 (30%)	15 (50%)	6 (20%)

Table 25.2 Conjunction types for non-consecutive Subject-only ellipsis

None (Ø)	Additive ('and')	Adversative ('but')	Temporal ('(and) then')
0 (0%)	102 (79.07%)	18 (13.95%)	9 (6.98%)

in consecutive clauses, and why so only and always with one particular functional structural type of ellipsis: Subject-only ellipsis. A full explanation can be offered only once one considers further empirical characteristics typifying the instances at hand.

> (4) Craig Bellamy, whose contribution across the pitch was colossal, collected a Lescott interception, (*Craig Bellamy* [S]) ran 40 yards, (*Craig Bellamy* [S]) exchanged passes with Richards and (*Craig Bellamy* [S]) gratefully lashed in on 74 minutes.

The average length in words of clauses involved in the particular type of ellipsis under discussion here[12] is notably shorter than the equivalent for all other clauses in the dataset. Whereas all other clauses in the dataset have an average word length that is greater than 10.5 words (49,843 wds ÷ 4,688 clauses = 10.6320392 wds), the average length of clauses involved in consecutive Subject-only ellipsis is a little greater than 8.5 words (377 words ÷ 44 clauses = 8.56818).[13] This means that the latter are nearly 20 per cent shorter in terms of word length than the former (8.56818 ÷ 10.6320392 = 0.80588303).

Examples (5)–(7), from the same newspaper football reports dataset, suitably illustrate the brevity typical of clauses involved in consecutive Subject-only ellipsis.

> (5a) He tamed a lofted pass, [5 words]
> (5b) (*he* [S]) left a bewildered Lorik Cana on his backside [8 words]
> (5c) and (*he* [S]) poked in a fabulous goal [6 words]

> (6a) . . . Zat Knight met Matt Taylor's free-kick in the 38th minute [11 words]
> (6b) but (*Zat Knight* [S]) was off balance [4 words]
> (6c) and (*Zat Knight* [S]) headed wide. [3 words]

> (7a) Lee walked the offside tightrope superbly [6 words]
> (7b) and (*Lee* [S]) rounded Hart, [3 words]
> (7c) but (*Lee* [S]) dragged his shot across goal and wide. [8 words]

One concern of work on literary narrative in the Barthesian structuralist tradition was with how text can function iconically to construe time in variable and meaningful ways (for example Barthes 1966; Chatman 1969, 1978; Genette 1980). In terms of the text as a vehicle to communicate temporal meanings of duration, for example, Chatman (1978: 72) claims that, where the reported actions or events happen in a short real-world time frame (the 'story-time'), yet are discussed at length in the text (the 'text-time'), events are slowed as if to submit them to necessary detailed examination. This Chatman (1978: 72) labels textual 'stretch'. In the reverse scenario, which Genette (1980: 95–9) terms textual 'summary', reported actions or events have a significant 'story-time', yet are granted only a very limited portion of the text. Such cases, says Genette (1980; 95–9), can be used to give the effect of an acceleration of the pace. Similar calculation methods to those employed above were adopted by these scholars as a means of determining 'text-time'. Genette (1980: 88–95), for example, analyses literary novels by taking a 'number of pages' measure; an alternative measure for 'text-time' of reading time has also been proposed (Toolan 1988: 55).

One does not have to think too long or hard to identify potential pitfalls in the approaches described, some of which concern the indelicate and unspecific nature of the units of measure in question. Conducting an analysis of a full text, it is possible to postulate an alternative approach that considers how textual patterns can construe meanings relating to time. The Appendix provides the full text from which the first illustrative example of this chapter (Figure 25.1) is drawn. This text is a report produced by British tabloid newspaper the *Daily Star* on the English football Premier League game between Manchester United and Arsenal on 29 August 2009. As with thirty-two of the eighty-nine texts in the entire corpus of Clarke (2012), all of the actions denoted by the processes of the report's main clauses fall within the time frame of the ninety-odd minutes of the football game itself. As such, time references for actions are relatively narrow and often stated in the relatively specific temporal currency of minutes. Consequently, a fine-grained analysis of the 'story-time' of the text is more feasible (see Figure 25.1).

Headline, sub-headline and other similar metadata-type information aside, the main text has twenty main clauses with the following main verb processes: *capped, won, won, scored, thought, ruled out, led to, turned, let fly, came (close), continued, seemed to be, were, was, went . . . for, put, sent, booked, was offered* and *got*. Of these main verb processes, fifteen are verbs of the dynamic type (Quirk et al. 1985: 177–8) and therefore, in the usual instance, have a deducible time reference that is consequently relatively precise: *capped, won, won, scored, ruled out, led to, turned, let fly, continued, went . . . for, put, sent, booked, was offered* and *got*. In contrast, *thought, came (close), seemed to be, were* and *was* are stative verbs, with, therefore, varying and often ambiguous, unspecific time references (Quirk et al. 1985: 179). In the text, three individual human referents are given multiple mentions as direct elements of main clauses: WAYNE ROONEY (five times: *Wayne Rooney, Ø,*[14] *Rooney, Ø* and *Ø*), ANDREY ARSHAVIN (three times: *Andrey Arshavin, Arshavin* and *Ø*) and ROBIN VAN PERSIE (three times: *Van Persie, Van Persie* and *his effort*). As is typical of newspaper report texts (Bell 1991), the presented order of events in the text-time is not congruent with their order in the story-time.

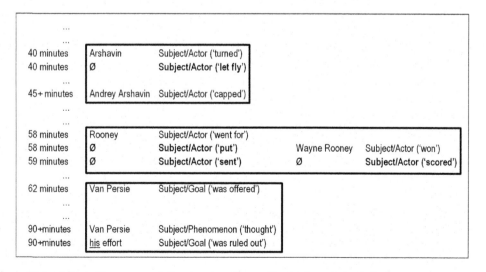

Figure 25.1 Schematic representation by story-time of text referents in *Daily Star* report

For the purposes of the present analysis, however, the chronology of events by story-time is more insightful; this is given diagrammatically in Figure 25.1 in respect of all mentions of the three referents just identified.

Earlier in this section, it was identified that adjacency of events in 'text-time', usually marked in form by coordination (see Tables 25.1 and 25.2), was a necessary condition for the kind of Subject-only ellipsis observed in this dataset.[15] The analysis contained in Figure 25.1 suggests that a further condition creates at least a preferential environment for instances of Subject-only ellipsis – namely, the proximity of the events in the 'story-time' references such that they are construed as all but simultaneous. The effect is only accentuated when the instances of Subject-only ellipsis are combined across successive clauses, yielding a pseudo-pace to the consequent events being reported on. With respect to the single instance of consecutive Subject-only ellipsis in this text, it is worth noting that a number of events that go unreported in the text occur in the 'story-time' in between Wayne Rooney's collecting the football (as referred to in the *went . . . for* clause) and his scoring the penalty (as referred to in the *sent* clause): the Arsenal goalkeeper is booked for the infringement that brings about the penalty; Wayne Rooney spends some 7 or 8 seconds placing the ball on the penalty spot; an Arsenal player is reprimanded by the referee for encroachment into the penalty area, etc.

A principle of Hallidayan description is to consider the *valeur* of certain choices against a backdrop of choices that might feasibly have been made, but were not (Berry 1975; Halliday and Matthiessen 2004; Caple 2008: 131). In that spirit, further support for the hypothesis *adjacent 'story-time' references render a favourable environment for consecutive cases of Subject-only ellipsis* is to be found in the fact that example (8a), as actually instantiated in the text, was not instead instantiated, as it might well have been, as example (8b).

(8a) Van Persie thought he had equalised deep into stoppage time but his effort was ruled out for an offside against William Gallas [. . . *12 intervening clauses . . .*] and Van Persie was offered the chance to curl a free-kick at Foster's goal which thudded against the crossbar.

(8b) Van Persie was offered the chance to curl a free-kick at Foster's goal and (*Van Persie* [S]) thought he had equalised deep into stoppage time but (*Van Persie* [S]) had his effort ruled out for an offside against William Gallas.

Not only do the 'story-time' time references in the case of ROBIN VAN PERSIE mentions in this text ([i]62 minutes, [ii]90+ minutes and [iii]90+ minutes) fail to satisfy the aforementioned condition, but also neither are all of the events in coordination in example (8b) realised as verbs of a dynamic sort (cf. *thought*) nor does ROBIN VAN PERSIE as referent bear/construe the necessary pace/pseudo-pace consequent from taking on the initiating participant role (*Van Persie was offered*; (*Van Persie* [S]) *had his effort ruled out*) in the events in question. Subsequent questions concerning causality may reasonably be raised at this point: what degree of bearing, for example, does the order of events in the 'story-time' have on their presented order in the text? How much of text-order, instead, is determined by events' satisfaction of news values? This chapter, however, avoids these, because such causal considerations are, again, typically outside the remit of Hallidayan linguistics (cf. Stubbs 1993); rather, it will consider only the statistical trends in evidence in the text.

The trends discussed in this section with respect to consecutive Subject-only ellipsis have been illustrated in the detailed analysis of only one full text, because of evident space constraints. Yet the same trends operate on larger scale in the wider dataset of Clarke

(2012), and they do so with respect to both the positive evidence – as is observable to a fair degree in the partially acontextual instances provided throughout this section[16] – and the negative evidence as akin to example (8b). One final extended example offers something of both the positive and negative evidence, illustrating many of the other points made so far. In example (9), succession between events adjacent in the 'story-time' is accentuated by the consecutive instances of Subject-only ellipsis, giving Keane's on-field actions consequent pseudo-pace. Features of the surrounding clauses, for example the presence of stative verbs (*are*, *have*, etc.) and the increased length of clauses in number of words, etc., provide a background against which the textual features of the ellipsis clauses can gain their semantic significance.

(9) Jermain Defoe exposed Andre Bikey's lack of manoeuvrability by rolling him with ease, only to be brought down by the central defender's despairing challenge. **Keane skipped up, (*Keane* [S]) shimmied, (*Keane* [S]) fooled keeper Brian Jensen into diving right and (*Keane* [S]) coolly slotted the ball into the other corner.** Burnley are not a team to park the bus on their away travels, despite their obvious weakness at the back. And they do have a bit of flair going forward, which is why they have won all three of their Premier League home games so far.

Returning to a discussion that reasons these patterns along semantic grounds as a way of concluding this section, then, we can modify the previous speculation by referring to the work of Genette and colleagues. While instances of consecutive Subject-only ellipsis contribute in construing an increase in speed – a quickening of the pace – 'speed' and 'pace' are not to be understood as the physical speed of singular actions. This is often the case in the present data (for example *ran, lashed in, promptly sent, went . . . for*, etc.), and when it is so, it probably owes to the second-order social action of the text per se (for example certain fast-paced recreational sports, and similarly fast-paced physical activities and domains). Yet exceptions – cases in which the speed referred to is not of a physically fast sort – are in evidence (for example *crafted, tamed*, etc., from the same text). 'Pace', then, is instead intended here in an iconic way as a matter of the rhythm and flow of the text (Matthiessen 1992); as referred to here, 'pace' is to be understood in textual terms, as the swift procession between neighbouring actions – cf. Genette's (1980) 'textual summary' – rather than in experiential terms, or at least rather than purely in experiential terms.

Conclusion

This chapter has served to review work conducted on cohesion in SFL since Halliday and Hasan's (1976) *Cohesion in English*, determining that theoretical and descriptive contributions have been limited. The two most detailed descriptive proposals for modelling cohesive devices in the theoretical architecture of SFL have been compared, particularly with a focus on the extent to which these allow semantic and contextual explanations for the patterned use of cohesive devices in text generally, and in particular text-types. This led to the mainstay of the chapter, in which a relatively small empirical investigation of a particular patterned usage of ellipsis – one that thus far is without a semantic explanation – was presented. Substantiated by the empirical evidence, more nuanced semantic and contextual reasons were offered as motives for the trends of ellipsis originally identified.

We can conclude that SFL work on cohesive devices might benefit significantly from taking a similar empirically based approach – that is, to explain the observed range and patterns of uses of any cohesive device by recourse to observed lexicogrammatical trends in text, working stratally upwards to reason semantically and contextually. The example of consecutive Subject-only ellipsis examined in this chapter is evidently but a drop in the ocean. Furthermore, the lack of a general – or in Hasan's (1996) terms, 'contextually open' – description of the semantic stratum (cf. Matthiessen 1995: 40), as well as the equivalent at the stratum of context, does not help in this venture (Matthiessen 1992: 76; Hasan 1996; Martin 2009: 164). Yet it is precisely by working upwards from lexicogrammatical trends that we are most likely to achieve that goal of attaining a better holistic understanding of phenomena at the semantic and contextual strata themselves.

As Firth (1950) argued, a full description of any linguistic phenomenon requires consideration from a number of perspectives. Through Halliday's (1996) formulation of 'trinocular principles' for descriptive practice, SFL finds itself in a position to be principally adept in offering the exhaustive descriptions of the type that Firth envisaged. In this way, the theory can offer valuable insights, worthy of due consideration by other functional approaches and linguistics at large, for cohesion and other linguistic phenomena.

Appendix *Daily Star*, 'United hit back to sink Gunners', 29 August 2009

Manchester United roared back from a half-time deficit to record a controversial 2–1 victory over Arsenal at Old Trafford.

Andrey Arshavin capped a brilliant first half by putting Arsenal ahead and if Ben Foster had not denied Robin van Persie with a brilliant feet-first save, Arsenal would probably have won.

Instead, Wayne Rooney won a debatable penalty when he went down under Manuel Almunia's challenge, and scored it himself before Abou Diaby turned Ryan Giggs' free-kick into his own net to give the hosts their victory.

Van Persie thought he had equalised deep into stoppage time but his effort was ruled out for an offside against William Gallas, and Arsene Wenger's protest against the disallowed goal led to him being sent from the dug-out.

Arshavin turned and let fly with a rasper of a drive in the first half to put the Gunners ahead.

Nemanja Vidic came close to levelling straight away for the hosts but Arsenal continued on top.

At that point, there seemed to be only one winner. How wrong those doubters were as Ferguson's team surged back, Giggs the architect behind the comeback just as Arshavin had sparked Arsenal earlier.

The difference was referee Mike Dean said yes when United claimed their penalty as Rooney went crashing to the ground after Giggs had supplied the pass that sent him through one-on-one with Almunia. Rooney went straight for the ball, put it on the spot and promptly sent Almunia the wrong way.

When Diaby was hacked at by Rooney and Wes Brown, both men were booked and Van Persie was offered the chance to curl a free-kick at Foster's goal which thudded against the crossbar. A minute later, from a very similar position, United got their second when Diaby inexplicably headed into his own net.

Notes

1 See 'A proposal for future systemic functional work on cohesion'.
2 Cf. Bühler (1934) and Jakobson (1960), among others.
3 Bold in each of these examples indicates the two parts, dependent and independent, of the grammatical cohesive tie.
4 See 'Cohesion in SFL following Halliday and Hasan (1976)'; cf. Tann, this volume.
5 For corresponding contextual considerations relevant to substitution and ellipsis, see Poynton (1985: 81) and Martin's (1992: 528–32) elaboration.
6 See, e.g., Martin (1983b) and Thomson (2005); also work in the edited collections by Steiner and Yallop (2001) and Caffarel et al. (2004).
7 Cf. Halliday (1979, 1996); see Clarke (2013) for an example of contextual variables in relation to ellipsis.
8 This work is more fully sketched out in Clarke (2016).
9 In examples (1)–(9), ellipted items are reconstituted in italics and surrounded by parentheses, with the functional structural role (e.g. Subject, Finite, Main Verb, etc.) of this ellipted item indicated in square brackets.
10 The figure 4,643 denotes the number of consecutive clauses in the corpus. Any single text has one fewer instances of consecutive clauses than it does individual clauses. With a corpus containing 4,732 clauses and 89 texts, there are therefore 4,643 consecutive clauses in the corpus.
11 The '16' refers to the number of pairs of consecutive clauses that both have Subject-only ellipsis. There are 30 instances of Subject-only ellipsis involved in these 16 pairs of consecutive clauses. Thus example (4) has three instances of Subject-only ellipsis, but only two pairs of consecutive clauses both attesting Subject-only ellipsis.
12 '[I]nvolved in' is intended to indicate that this calculation includes the clause containing the antecedent Subject.
13 The ellipsis of Subjects alone not accounting for this difference, because 20 of the 30 elliptied Subjects in question have one-word antecedents.
14 This indicates non-realisation of the referent – non-realisation of an ellipsis kind.
15 Cf. examples of situationally recoverable Subject-only ellipsis (e.g. (*I* [Subject]) *went to the game last night* in a text message between friends) – so-called Subject-dropping (Biber et al. 1999: 1104–5).
16 A full appreciation would require the same kind of analysis as that carried out on the Appendix text to be carried out on the full texts of all other examples presented in this section, i.e. an analysis that considers all process types in the text against its 'story-time' timeline and looks at the succession between these events, including seeing which other referents might have coordinated and had consecutive Subject-only ellipsis connecting them, but did not.

References

Armstrong, E.M. 1987. Cohesive harmony in aphasic discourse and its significance in listener perception of coherence. In R.H. Brookshire (ed.) *Clinical Aphasiology: Conference Proceedings*. Minneapolis, MN: BRK, pp. 210–215.

Armstrong, E.M. 1991. The potential of cohesion analysis in the analysis and treatment of aphasic discourse. *Clinical Linguistics and Phonetics* 5(1): 39–51.

Barthes, R. 1966. Introduction à l'analyse structurale des récits. *Communications* 8(1): 1–27.

Bell, A. 1991. *The Language of News Media*. Oxford: Wiley-Blackwell.

Berry, M. 1975. *An Introduction to Systemic Linguistics, Vol 1: Structures and Systems*. London: Batsford.

Biber, D., Johansson, S., Leech, G., Conrad, S. and E. Finegan. 1999. *Longman Grammar of Spoken and Written English*. London: Longman.

Bühler, K. 1934. *Sprachtheorie: Die Darstellungsfunktion der Sprache*. New York: Fischer.

Butt, D., A. Moore, C. Henderson-Brooks, R. Meares and J. Haliburn. 2007. Dissociation, relatedness and 'cohesive harmony': A linguistic measure of degree of 'fragmentation'? *Linguistics and the Human Sciences* 3(3): 263–93.

Caffarel, A., J.R. Martin and C.M.I.M. Matthiessen. 2004. *Language Typology: A Functional Perspective*. Amsterdam: John Benjamins.

Caple, H. 2008. *Intermodal Relations in Image Nuclear News Stories*. In L. Unsworth (ed.) *Multimodal Semiotics: Functional Analysis in Contexts of Education*. London: Continuum, pp. 125-138.

Chatman, S. 1969. New ways of analysing narrative structure. *Language and Style* 2: 3–36.

Chatman, S. 1978. *Story and Discourse: Narrative Structure in Fiction and Film*. Ithaca, NY: Cornell University Press.

Clarke, B.P. 2012. Do patterns of ellipsis in text support systemic functional linguistics' 'context-metafunction hook-up' hypothesis? A corpus-based approach. Unpublished PhD thesis. Cardiff University.

Clarke, B.P. 2013. The differential patterned occurrence of ellipsis in texts varied for contextual mode: Some support for the 'mode of discourse – textual metafunction' hook-up. In G. O'Grady, T. Bartlett and L. Fontaine (eds) *Choice in Language: Applications in Text Analysis*. Sheffield: Equinox, pp. 269–97.

Clarke, B.P. 2016. 'Textual dynamism as a heuristic for a delicate semantic description of ellipsis patterns'. *English Text Construction*, 9: 1, 99–114.

Cloran, C. 1999. Contexts for learning. In F. Christie (ed.) *Pedagogy and the Shaping of Consciousness: Linguistic and Social Processes*. London: Cassell, pp. 31–65.

Crystal, D. 1997. *The Cambridge Encyclopaedia of Language*. 2nd edn. Cambridge: Cambridge University Press.

Degaetano-Ortlieb, S., K. Kunz, E. Lapshinova-Koltunski, K. Menzel and E. Steiner. Forthcoming. GECCo: An empirically based comparison of English–German cohesion. In G. de Sutter, I. Delaere and M.A. Lefer (eds) *New Ways of Analysing Translational Behaviour in Corpus-Based Translation Studies*. Berlin: Mouton.

Fine, J. 1995. Towards understanding and studying cohesion in schizophrenic speech. *Applied Psycholinguistics* 16(1): 25–41.

Firth, J.R. 1950. Personality and language in society. *Sociological Review* 42(1): 37–52.

Gardner, S. 2012. Genres and registers of student report writing: An SFL perspective on texts and practices. *Journal of English for Academic Purposes* 11(1): 52–63.

Genette, G. 1980. *Narrative Discourse*. Oxford: Blackwell.

Halliday, M.A.K. 1978. *Language as Social Semiotic: The Social Interpretation of Language and Meaning*. London: Arnold.

Halliday, M.A.K. 1979. Modes of meaning and modes of expression: Types of grammatical structure, and their determination by different semantic functions. In D.J. Allerton, E. Carney and D. Holdcroft (eds) *Function and Context in Linguistic Analysis: Essays Offered to William Haas*. Cambridge: Cambridge University Press, pp. 57–79.

Halliday, M.A.K. 1985. Context of situation. In M.A.K. Halliday and R. Hasan (eds) *Language, Context and Text: Aspects of Language in a Social Semiotic Perspective*. Oxford: Oxford University Press, pp. 3–14.

Halliday, M.A.K. 1996. On grammar and grammatics. In R. Hasan, C. Cloran and D.G. Butt (eds) *Functional Descriptions: Theory in Practice*. Amsterdam: John Benjamins, pp. 1–38.

Halliday, M.A.K., and R. Hasan. 1976. *Cohesion in English*. London: Longman.

Halliday, M.A.K., and C.M.I.M. Matthiessen. 2004. *Introduction to Functional Grammar*. 3rd edition. London: Edward Arnold.

Hasan, R. 1996. Semantic networks: A tool for the analysis of meaning. In C. Cloran, D. Butt and G. Williams (eds) *Ways of Saying: Ways of Meaning*. London: Cassell, pp. 104–31.

Jakobson, R. 1960. Linguistics and poetics. In T. Sebeok (ed.) *Style in Language*. Cambridge, MA: MIT Press, pp. 350–77.

Kunz, K., and E. Steiner. 2010. Towards a comparison of cohesive reference in English and German: System and text. *Linguistics & the Human Sciences* 6(1–3): 219–51.

Kunz, K., and E. Steiner. 2013. Cohesive substitution in English and German: A contrastive and corpus-based perspective. In K. Aijmer and B. Altenberg (eds) *Advances in Corpus-Based Contrastive Linguistics: Studies in Honour of Stig Johansson*. Amsterdam: John Benjamins, pp. 201–31.

Liu, Y., and K.L. O'Halloran. 2009. Intersemiotic texture: Analysing cohesive devices between language and images. *Social Semiotics* 19(4): 367–88.

Martin, J.R. 1983a. Conjunction and continuity in Tagalog. In M.A.K. Halliday and J.R. Martin (eds) *Readings in Systemic Linguistics*. London: Batsford, pp. 310–36.

Martin, J.R. 1983b. Participant identification in English, Tagalog and Kâte. *Australian Journal of Linguistics* 3(1): 45–74.

Martin, J.R. 1992. *English Text: System and Structure*. Amsterdam: John Benjamins.

Martin, J.R. 2009. Discourse studies. In M.A.K. Halliday and J.J. Webster (eds) *Continuum Companion to Systemic Functional Linguistics*. London: Continuum, pp. 154–65.

Martin, J.R. 2014. Evolving systemic functional linguistics: Beyond the clause. *Functional Linguistics* 1(3): 1–24.

Martin, J.R., and D. Rose. 2007. *Working with Discourse: Meaning Beyond the Clause*. 2nd edn. London: Continuum.

Martinec, R. 1998. Cohesion in action. *Semiotica* 120(1): 161–80.

Martinec, R. 2004. Gestures that co-coccur with speech as a systematic resource: The realization of experiential meanings in indexes. *Social Semiotics* 14(2): 193–213.

Matthiessen, C.M.I.M. 1992. Interpreting the textual metafunction. In M. Davies and L. Ravelli (eds) *Advances in Systemic Linguistics: Recent Theory and Practice*. London: Pinter, pp. 37–82.

Matthiessen, C.M.I.M. 1995. *Lexicogrammatical Cartography: English Systems*. Tokyo: International Language Sciences.

Matthiessen, C.M.I.M., K. Teruya and M. Lam. 2010. *Key Terms in Systemic Functional Linguistics*. London: Continuum.

Oakes, M. 1998. *Statistics for Corpus Linguistics*. Edinburgh: Edinburgh University Press.

Parsons, G. 1990. *A Comparative Study of the Writing of Scientific Texts Focusing on Cohesion and Coherence*. Nottingham: Department of English Studies, University of Nottingham.

Paziraie, M.E. 2013. The effect of the textual metafunction on the Iranian EFL Learners' writing Performance. *English Language Teaching* 6(2): 71–83.

Poynton, C. 1985. *Language and Gender: Making the Difference*. Oxford: Oxford University Press.

Quirk, R., Greenbaum, S., Leech, G. and J. Svartvik. 1985. *A Comprehensive Grammar of the English Language*. Harlow: Longman.

Steiner, E., and C. Yallop. 2001. *Exploring Translation and Multilingual Text Production: Beyond Content*. Berlin: Mouton.

Stubbs, M. 1993. British traditions in text analysis: From Firth to Sinclair. In M. Baker, G. Francis and E. Tognini-Bonelli (eds.) *Text and Technology: In Honour of John Sinclair*. Amsterdam: John Benjamins, pp. 1-33.

Thomson, E. 2005. Theme unit analysis: A systemic functional treatment of textual meanings in Japanese. *Functions of Language* 12(2): 151–79.

Toolan, M.J. 1988. *Narrative: A Critical Linguistic Introduction*. London: Routledge.

Yang, X. 2013. Modelling ellipsis in EFL classroom discourse. In F. Yan and J.J. Webster (eds) *Developing Systemic Functional Linguistics: Theory and Application*. Sheffield: Equinox, pp. 227–40.

Register analysis in systemic functional linguistics

Alison Rotha Moore

Introduction

The term *register* has had considerable currency within and beyond systemic functional linguistics (SFL) for more than fifty years. But this currency masks a persistent conflation of disparate views, including views about the location and centrality of register in a functional theory of language, and views about the kinds of analytic methods that can best characterise register and 'capture' registerial variation. As a result of its position within the overall 'architecture' of SFL as a theory of language, the concept of register has been topicalised or implicated in most of the theory's development since the 1960s. Yet although the term register is still in frequent use, it has recently been argued that register classification itself is now 'in limbo' within SFL (Hasan 2014).

A particular concern is that Halliday's own view of register as a 'semantic configuration' (for example Halliday 2002 [1977]) and 'a setting of probabilities in the semantics' (Thibault 1987: 610) has not had sufficient critical explication (Lukin et al. 2011), nor has his claim that register is the product of settings in the three dimensions of field, tenor and mode (Bowcher, this volume).

The main thrust of this chapter, therefore, is to provide a picture of Halliday's concept of register, and to illustrate the empirical use of this concept and its centrality in the overall architecture of SFL. It is suggested that one line of continuity in SFL's development can be traced between Halliday's work on register, the work of his close associate Hasan on context and semantics, and work currently drawing on these approaches. To critically situate this particular line of continuity, brief comparisons are made with other approaches to register – both within and outside SFL – and some challenges for register analysis are canvassed.

What is Halliday's concept of register?

As pointed out some twenty years ago (Matthiessen 1993) and more recently (for example Lukin et al. 2011; Hasan 2014), there has been surprisingly little explication and testing of Halliday's specific view of register. This section surveys Halliday's articulation of the concept. It also touches on ideas about variation in language according to 'use' more generally, against which Halliday's specific conception of register emerged.

In one of his most accessible volumes, Halliday (1985: 29) describes register as 'a variety of language, corresponding to a variety of situation'. In the same book, he writes:

> A register is a semantic concept. It can be defined as a configuration of meanings that are typically associated with a particular situational configuration of field, mode and tenor. But since it is a configuration of meanings, a register must also, of course, include the expressions, the lexico-grammatical and phonological features, that typically accompany or realize these meanings.
>
> *Halliday 1985: 39*

Elsewhere, Halliday (2003) suggests that the semantic stratum is where language interfaces with the eco-social environment (see Figure 26.1). At this interface, register functions as 'the necessary mediating concept that enables us to establish the continuity between a text and its socio-semiotic environment' (Halliday 2002 [1977]: 58).

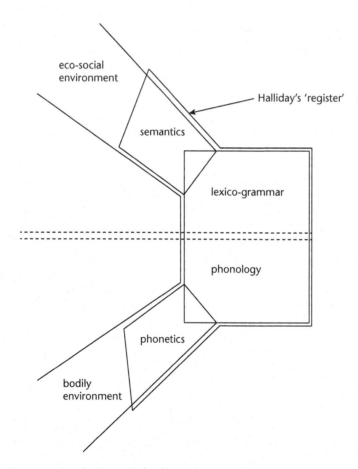

Figure 26.1 Language in relation to its bodily and eco-social environment
Source: Halliday (2003: 13)

Although the idea of characterising language variation by use can be found much earlier, such as in the work of Philipp Wegener (1848–1916) (Butt and Wegener 2007), the concept of 'register' was introduced into linguistics by T.R.W. Reid (1956, cited in Halliday 2009: 187) and gained currency largely through the work of Michael Halliday (for example Halliday 1973; Halliday and Hasan 1985; Halliday et al. 2007 [1964]).

Despite some changes over time, Halliday's view of register has consistently been that of:

1   a construct belonging within the semantic stratum;
2   a multifunctional, multidimensional construct that cannot be reduced to a single feature or cline such as 'degree of formality' or 'degree of spoken/writtenness';
3   a construct that is responsive to settings in field, tenor and mode;
4   a primary category that is centrally involved in motivating systems of grammatical distinction and handling indeterminacy – not an 'add on' to the architecture of the theory; and
5   a concept that is capable of detailed (and contested, disparate) application, not only a flag to fly over the notion of variation.

Register compared with dialect

Halliday's first extended articulation of register (Halliday et al. 2007 [1964][1]) describes register and dialect variation as together constituting 'institutional linguistics', which is presented as an essential complement to descriptive linguistics. Although by no means the final word on register theory, the paper contains an array of important theoretical statements about the nature of register and its place in a linguistic theory of language.

Dialects differ 'primarily, and always to some extent, in substance' (Halliday et al. 2007 [1964]: 17). In other words, dialects of a single language differ in the lexical, grammatical and phonological features that realise choices in meaning, but the choices of meaning in each dialect of the language are essentially the same. Registers 'differ primarily in form' (Halliday et al. 2007 [1964]: 17), which can be taken to mean difference in their internal semantic organisation or 'meaning potential' (as we will see later in the chapter). This is why we can translate a particular register from one language to another, such as science in Spanish to science in English, but cannot preserve dialect in translation (Halliday 2002 [1990]: 169).

Crucially, Halliday et al. (2007 [1964]: 18) is already saying that registers are not marginal varieties of language, but between them 'cover the total range of our language activity'. Registers are defined by formal, not situational, properties, such that:

> [I]f two samples of language activity from what, on non-linguistic grounds, could be considered different situation-types show no differences in grammar or lexis, they are assigned to one and the same register: for the purpose of the description of the language there is only one situation type here, not two.
>
> *Halliday et al. 2007 [1964]: 18[2]*

This last claim is an interesting one, which has had insufficient development in register studies.

An integrated sociolinguistics

A key driver of the development of register theory was Halliday's (1975) goal of moving towards a general sociolinguistic theory. Sociolinguistic and ethnomethodological thinkers were discussing how people manage the myriad possible meanings in social situations. For Halliday, the questions were: what are the components of social situations, how can they be mapped to the linguistic system itself and how are they related to actual texts?

Scholars such as Firth (1950) and Hymes (1972) had provided some guidance, but Halliday (1975) wanted a model that could predict what a speaker was going to say in the same way as the hearer does. He felt that existing models were hampered by confusions between distinct levels of abstraction. A particular target was sociolinguistics' macro–micro distinction, by which items of different orders – such as text and sentence – are related in terms of size, when the more salient relation is *realisation* (Halliday 1975).

Register: The necessary mediating concept

Halliday's (2002 [1977]: 58) alternative to a macro–micro view of language and context is his concept of register, which he called 'the necessary mediating concept that allows us to establish the continuity between a text and its socio-semiotic environment'.

Across Halliday's accounts of context–language relations, features of the context – namely, field, tenor and mode – tend to be given an agentive property in that they are often said to *determine* (Halliday et al. 2007 [1964]: 20) or *activate* (Halliday 2002 [1977]: 54) corresponding features in the semantics.

By the same token, reciprocal relations have also been posited between these two levels, whereby language has some agency: semantic features *realise* (Halliday 1975: 187), *reflect* (Halliday 1985: 34) or *construe* (Halliday 2002 [1994]: 232) the context of situation.

A good explanation of this reciprocal relation is Hasan's (1985: 55) account of shopping:

> The commonsense view is that we say 'Can I have . . . ', 'That'll be six dollars seventy', and so on, because we happen to be in a shopping situation. The un-commonsense view is that shopping as a culturally recognisable type of situation has been constructed over the years by the use of precisely this kind of language.[3]

Like the relation between situation and language, the relation between culture and language more generally is one of realisation, and in Halliday's model this means that 'situations' are not pre-existing categories outside linguistic and cultural systems. As Figure 26.2 shows, register takes a central theoretical place, acting as a pivot between the concepts of realisation and instantiation (Matthiessen 1993). An instance of language (a text), with its particular cluster of semantic features, brings into being an instance of some situation, because register variation allows different situational types to occur within cultures and to co-evolve with them.

It should be noted that there are several implications of Halliday's model of register that are still generating critical evaluation. For example, Figure 26.2 may be read as suggesting that a single culture houses a single language, reifying and homogenising each in an unhelpful way. Although this is probably an unintended implication of the diagram, further reflection on SFL's theoretical architecture could help to support the nuanced empirical work on linguistic and cultural co-variation undertaken within SFL (such as by Bartlett, this volume).

By the 1980s and 1990s, Halliday's concept of register had been further elaborated, and the link with the variables field, tenor and mode explicated via the metafunctional hypothesis – that is, the claim that language itself has three primary metafunctions, the ideational, interpersonal and textual (see Bowcher, this volume). Halliday (2002 [1990]:168) stresses that, when we talk of 'a register', this is really just a term of convenience: register is more

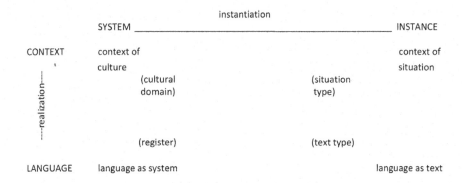

Figure 26.2   Instantial and realisational relations between culture, situation, language system and text, and the role of register

Source: Adapted from Halliday (1999: 8)

properly theorised as continuous variation along many linguistic dimensions, although in practice 'only a small fraction of the theoretically possible combinations of linguistic features will actually be found to occur'.

Throughout Halliday's writing, the concept of register retains this tension between register(s) as a count noun and register as a mass noun – between the mappable space, as it were, and the places known at specific locations on the map.

This articulation of register as continuous multidimensional variation is given extensive development by Matthiessen (1993) in his seminal paper 'Register in the round'. Drawing on Halliday's characterisation of register as a skewing of probabilities in the types of linguistic choice that can appear, Matthiessen shows how 'a register' can be thought of as one 'state' of the overall language system, activated by field, tenor and mode settings. Alternatively, register can be modelled as a partitioned system, in which access to options in the generalised language system can be seen as 'blocked' for certain registers. Empirical descriptions of register variation that exemplify this approach include Nesbitt and Plum's (1988) large-scale quantitative study of clause complexing in different narrative registers, and Caffarel's (1992) work on French tense in different registers.

As these empirical studies attest, and as Matthiessen (1993: 231) points out, if register is interpreted as an independent dimension of functional variation, 'a register' is just an idealised location along this dimension. We can then treat 'language' – and indeed 'a language' – as the assemblage of locations along the dimension of register variation. This last point, contra Bartlett (this volume), indicates that the Hallidayan approach does not inherently prioritise a unitary notion of language, or of culture, especially when one observes how other dimensions of variation are taken into account – for example diachronic (phylogenetic and ontogenetic) variation – and how multilingual systems can be similarly modelled as assemblages of systems from different languages that may have common parts and language-specific parts (Matthiessen 1993).

Register and texture

Within SFL generally, *texture* is a property of the theoretical construct *text*. For Halliday and Hasan (1976), in their book *Cohesion in English*, texture means something like 'texthood' and it arises out of semantic configurations of two kinds – namely, register and cohesion. A text is 'a passage of discourse which is coherent . . . with respect to the context of situation, and therefore consistent in register; and it is coherent with respect to itself, and therefore cohesive' (Halliday and Hasan 1976: 23). In this account, settings in register are describable by observing settings in grammatical systems across Halliday's function–rank matrix – namely, the systems TRANSITIVITY, MOOD and so on. Cohesion comprises the so-called non-structural resources, including reference (pronominal, etc.), substitution and ellipsis, general sense relations (synonymy, metonymy, etc.) and instantial relations (naming, equivalence, etc.), along with continuatives, conjunctives and adjacency pairs (Q and A, etc.).

Later, Hasan contrasts *texture* with *register*, narrowing the former term to cover only the non-structural, cohesive resources and relabelling the combination of textural configurations plus register configurations 'text unity' (Hasan 1985: 52), although register, structure and texture are consistently viewed as being activated by configurations of field, tenor and mode. Importantly, the least delicate options in field, tenor and mode correlate with structure (activity type) and the more delicate ones with texture – so, for example, the same shopping activity may have different content.

It should be noted that there are differences between Halliday's and Martin's models of relations between register, texture and genre. For Martin and colleagues, register is a setting in field, tenor and mode (context), not 'a variety of language' (Matthiessen 1993; Hasan 2014; Martin 2014; Tann, this volume).

Comparing SFL and other approaches more broadly

Halliday's concept of register has been compared with other approaches to characterising functional varieties of language (for example Lee 2001). To summarise grossly its distinctive features, Halliday's model:

- aims to explain variation in language generally, not only to identify and classify recognised professional or institutional varieties;
- is therefore realisational, rather than indexical, in that it brings out the co-constitutive relation between linguistic meaning and contextual variation;
- is multifunctional, rather than ideationally or interpersonally oriented alone; and
- offers a theoretical framework for large-scale comparative applications, but is not easy to automate, meaning that proxy or index measures of functional categories are generally used in automated register analysis.

As Ghadessy (1999) points out, most other approaches are either more formal, for example focusing on specific lexis and/or morphemes such as –*ed*, –*ing* (Crystal 1991; Biber 1995), or more structural, focusing on sequential 'moves' in discourse (Sinclair and Coulthard 1975; Swales 1990). An important caveat regarding comparability is that SFL approaches usually treat the clause as the unit at which options configure, whereas non-SFL approaches typically use the word or text as the basic unit, so that frequency statistics for relevant features can be quite different measures in SFL and non-SFL approaches.

With this outline of Halliday's concept of register in mind and after glimpsing alternative developments, we can now examine how register analysis is conducted within Halliday's framework.

Alison Rotha Moore

How is register analysis performed in SFL?

This section discusses how those following the Hallidayan tradition operationalise register in analysis – that is, how they use the idea of register as a 'semantic configuration' and a 'setting of probabilities in the semantics'. What makes the following studies examples of this approach is that they each treat register as *activated* by configurations of field, tenor and mode, while register itself is located on a lower stratum. Correspondingly, the analyses use contextual configurations to explain semantic patterns, or use the semantic patterns observed to problematise expected field, tenor and mode settings – an approach that helps to counter criticisms of circularity in the Halliday/Hasan view (see Bartlett, this volume).

In other words, if register is *not* context, one can explore the extent to which semantic configurations change within and between contexts by holding one term in the equation constant and varying the other – or at least observing what happens when we find variation and consistency on these different levels (to the extent possible, given the current development of the apparatus). It is not that other models of register cannot elucidate how language varies within and between contexts; certainly, they can and are used productively in this way.

Halliday's empirical work on register

Halliday's (2002 [1964]) earliest detailed analyses of specific domains focused on literature – in particular, poetry. Further studies of literature appeared over several decades, including of the novel *The Inheritors*, the play *An Inspector Calls* and a Thurber short story/modern fable (Halliday 2002a). Halliday has analysed political discourse (Halliday 2002 [1992]), professional discourse (Halliday 2002 [1994]), children's language (Halliday 2002b) and science (Halliday 2004). But, for Halliday, questions about linguistic systems in general – not only about specific domains – must also be addressed through the lens of register, for example the probabilistic nature of linguistic systems (Halliday 2005 [1993]).

Important theoretical positions invariably emerge in Halliday's empirical work. For instance, while describing how field, tenor and mode predict register in children's dialogue, Halliday (2002 [1985]: 284–5) notes that what makes such prediction possible is exactly what makes it possible for children to learn language at all: 'the systematic relationship between these categories of situation and the metafunctions'. Metafunctions and situations resonate in a probabilistic fashion, however; only 'by and large' does field rely on ideational grammatical choices.

Register and science

Halliday's most sustained and illuminating examination of any one register is his work on science. He shows how modern science – unlike quotidian registers – depicts relations, actions and events as if they were things, and relations *between* events as if they were events themselves (Halliday and Martin 1993: 52). The following is an outline of Halliday's account of how science deploys such semantic configurations, examining the contextual pressures and payoffs for doing so – phylogenetically, ontogenetically and logogenetically – and summarising his observations about the semantic and lexicogrammatical resources activated.

Most of Halliday's work on science is on 'scientific English', which he treats as 'a generalized functional variety, or register of the modern English language' that can be profiled with varying degrees of delicacy (Halliday 2004: 140). From the point of view of context, scientific English and its internal variation:

can be summarized in terms of field, tenor and mode: in field, extending, transmitting or exploring knowledge in the physical, biological or social sciences; in tenor, addressed to specialists, to learners or to laymen, from within the same group (e.g. specialist to specialist) or across groups (e.g. lecturer to students); and in mode, phonic or graphic channel, most congruent (e.g. formal 'written language' with graphic channel) or less so (e.g. formal with phonic channel), and with variation in rhetorical function – expository, hortatory, polemic, imaginative and so on.

Halliday 2004: 140

Scientific register(s) and their development can be explained only 'provided, first, that we consider the features together rather than each in isolation; and secondly, that we are prepared to interpret them at every level, in lexicogrammatical, semantic, and socio-semiotic (situational and cultural) terms' (Halliday 2004: 141).

Summarising the results of several studies on scientific discourse, we can say that Halliday's analyses have identified a number of semantic features as important characteristics of the register(s) of science, including *generalisation, abstraction* and *grammatical metaphor*. These semantic features are represented as 'three successive waves of theoretical energy' that reshape experience, each wave taking it further away from the common-sense view.

What this means is that individuating, concrete and congruent ways of speaking – for instance the common-sense *Sam smoked all his life, so now he's dying of lung cancer* – are not typical of the register of science; rather, we see construals such as *Lung cancer death rates are clearly associated with increased smoking*. In scientific discourse, the grammatical participants are:

- general – that is, rates across the population, not some individual's chance;
- abstract – not a concrete touchable person or the viewable event of dying, but abstract things (*rates of death*); and
- expressed via a kind of metaphor whereby 'entities', such as people, take the grammatical form of adjectives instead of nouns, whereas events, such as dying, are represented grammatically as nouns, as if they were things.

This does not mean that the features typical of science are not found in other registers. Halliday's (2004: 18) account of the rise of science shows that its mode of representing experience has colonised other areas of life, particularly 'those concerned with establishing and maintaining prestige or power' such as administration. Examples (1a) and (2a) are taken from science and administration/commerce, with examples (1b) and (2b) being their common-sense glosses (Halliday 2004: 28).

(1a) The goal of evolution is to optimise the mutual adaption of species.
(1b) Species evolve in order to adapt to each other as well as possible.

(2a) Failure to reconfirm will result in the cancellation of your reservations.
(2b) If you fail to reconfirm, your reservations will be cancelled.

Example (1a) exemplifies what Halliday calls the 'favourite clause type' of English scientific writing.

What makes this construction typical of science is the realisational relation between the grammar, semantics and context that it instantiates. At the semantic level, it is 'a sequence

425

of two figures, linked by a logical-semantic relation', but it is expressed, at the lexicogram-matical level, as a single clause, of the type 'identifying/intensive, circumstantial or possessive' (Halliday 2004: 74). The contextual 'payoffs' of such patterns include (a) the capacity to organ-ise experience taxonomically and (b) the capacity to enter into sequences of logical progression within reasoned argument, without which scientific practice could not have emerged.

In other words, the semantic and grammatical patterns of scientific English have function-ality with respect to the field, tenor and mode that they construe, and the way in which such parameters come together to both expand knowledge and restrict access to it. This functionality is further highlighted in studies of the emergence of scientific language/thought (Halliday 2004; Kappagoda 2005; Banks 2008). Note that, although they are functional, the linguistic patterns of science are part of what make science difficult for learners (Halliday and Martin 1993: 52).

From other scholars, we have manual, synchronic profiles domains such as news, advertising, sports commentary, religious discourse, business letters, tourism and medi-cal consultations (Ghadessy 1988, 1993). Diachronic accounts also appear (for example Bowcher 1999; Urbach 2013). There is a substantial body of computational work, often concerning translation (for example Steiner 2004; Neumann 2014), and including diachronic studies (for example Teich 2013). A challenge for register studies is to integrate quantitative research that is statistically sophisticated, but which relies on proxy measures of functional categories on the lexicogrammatical stratum, with 'thicker', direct analyses of functionally motivated categories on all strata.

Semantic networks in the service of register analysis

Situating register at the level of semantics opens up the possibility that an adequate specifica-tion of semantic variation in terms of semantic units could be the key to effective description of register variation. If so, the question becomes: what exactly is this semantic system and what are its options?

Halliday (2005 [1995]: 254–6) argues that while we cannot yet model the whole seman-tic system, we can 'specify its internal organization'. This, he suggests, is analogous to the lexicogrammatical function–rank matrix, but:

> with its own distinct categories – a 'rank scale' of structural units such as text, subtext, semantic paragraph, sequence, figure, element; and metafunctional regions defined in topological fashion, construing the activity patterns and ideological motifs of the culture (clusters relating to technology, to social hierarchy, to the sphere of activities of daily life, and so on). As with lexicogrammar, these are represented paradigmatically as net-works of meaning potential.
>
> *Halliday 2005 [1995]: 256*

Nevertheless, an ongoing question in SFL has been whether it is necessary, or even possi-ble, to draw up formalised accounts of meaning potential at the semantic stratum, and if so, whether such accounts should be built separately for different registers or unified to encom-pass registerial and codal variation within a language.

Context-specific networks

In Halliday's empirical work, the semantic categories through which register is to be inter-preted are, typically, contextually open but ad hoc (in Firth's non-pejorative sense). At times, however, Halliday developed formalised semantic models on a separate stratum from the lexicogrammar. These are often context-specific, the most famous being Halliday's (1973) network for threats and warnings as semantic options in a social context known to be critical for socialisation – namely, parents' verbal control of children (Hasan 2009b).

Halliday (1973) shows how a semantic network might be drawn up and describes its essential attributes for validity. These can be summarised as follows:

> [The semantic network is a] hypothesis about meanings accessible to speakers in some specific context type, and the form of the network represents how those meanings are related to one another; the semantic network is *the 'input' to the lexicogrammar*: in other words, its options are realized lexicogrammatically; the *input to the semantic network* is some sociologically significant and specific context.
>
> *Hasan et al. 2007: 307*

The threat–warning network is reproduced as Figure 26.3.[4] Selected realisation rules are given in Table 26.1.

The efficiency of the threat–warning network is that all possible threats and warnings in this context can be netted in, organised via clusters of semantic features that distinguish threats (such as *I'll smack you*) from warnings (such as *You'll get dirty*), and linked to

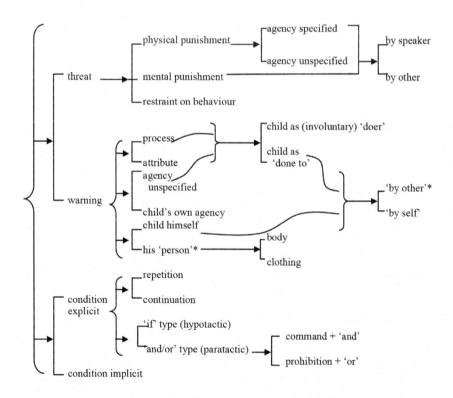

Figure 26.3   A context-specific network for threats and warning

Source: Adapted from Halliday (1973: 89)

Table 26.1 Selected realisation rules for the threat–warning network

Semantic feature	Lexicogrammatical realisation
threat	clause: declarative
physical punishment	clause: action: voluntary (*do* type); effective (two-participants): Goal = you; future tense; positive; verb from Roget ' 972 (or 972, 276)
agency specified	voice: active
by speaker	Actor/Attribuand = *I*
by other	Actor/Attribuand = *Daddy*, etc.
mental punishment	clause: relational: attributive: Attribute = adjective from Roget ' 900
warning	clause: declarative
attribute	clause: relational: attributive: mutative; Attribute = adjective from Roget ' 653, 655, 688, etc.
agency unspecified	clause: non-resultative: Affected (Actor, Goal or Attribuand) = *you/yourself* or some form of '*your person*'

Note: Although both [threat] and [warning] are shown as having the realisation 'clause: declarative', the selection of each of these options requires further delicacy.

lexicogrammatical features for recognising or realising each semantic feature. This network informed research on class and gender in children's socialisation, although contextually open networks were later preferred (as we will see later in the chapter). Other context-specific networks have been designed by Halliday and Matthiessen (1999) for network-based text generation, and by Butt and colleagues for clinical trial recruitment (Brown et al. 2004), and workers' compensation resolutions (Moore and Tuckwell 2006), although example-based recognition criteria often replace formal realisation rules.

Contextually open networks, message semantics, and inter- and intra-register variation

According to Hasan (1996; Hasan et al. 2007), the semantic systems of a language are contextually open: a robust semantic model must incorporate registerial variation, and must systematise it paradigmatically and exhaustively.[5] Put another way, it is not theoretically sound to draw up one 'semantics' at a time, context by context, or to leave variation out of the general model (Hasan 2014).[6] Like models of other strata, a paradigmatic semantics must be statable in terms of system networks, with realisation statements for each term in the system (Hasan 1989a, 2014; cf. Halliday 1973).

In Hasan's model, the primary unit is 'message', which stands in a constituency relationship with the semantic unit 'text' (potentially with intervening ranks). The unit 'message' is 'the smallest semantic unit capable of entering into the structure of a text' (as the realisation of an element of generic structure) and it is usually realised by a ranking clause, with some exceptions (Hasan 2009b: 243). Hasan's four networks trace the semantic contrasts of English and their dependencies within and between the four metafunctions (experiential, logical, interpersonal, textual[7]). Figure 26.4 exemplifies this with the network fragment 'Demand Information'.

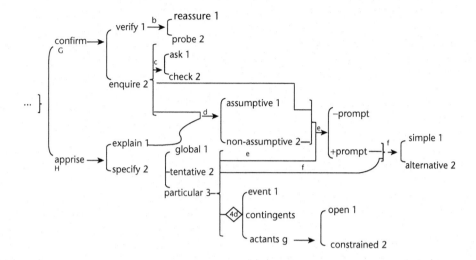

Figure 26.4 Options for demanding information, from Hasan's RELATION ENACTMENT network

Note: Entry condition is 'demand information'.

Source: Hasan (2013: 289)

Message semantic networks have been used to investigate 'fashions of meaning' within specific contexts – most famously, maternal control – in relation to social class (for example Hasan 1989a, 2009b) and gender (Cloran 1989). Other contexts include news reporting (Lukin 2013) and ordering pizza by telephone (Matthiessen et al. 2005).

Much less has been done on inter-registerial variation – that is, variation in register that corresponds to variation in context – although this is emerging. In fact, we may need a clearer map of such variation, using paradigmatic modelling for context (Butt 2004; Bowcher 2014; Hasan 2014) *and* semantics, before we can say what is and is not 'the same' versus a 'different' register (cf. Hasan 2014).

Table 26.2 Selected realisation rules for Hasan's DEMAND INFORMATION network

Semantic feature	Lexicogrammatical realisation
confirm	indicative
verify	declarative: tagged
enquire	declarative: (mood tag not possible)
reassure	declarative:tagged:reversed moodtag
probe	declarative:tagged:constant moodtag
ask	interrogative:polar
check	declarative:untagged/Tone2
assumptive	polarity negative
non-assumptive	polarity positive
simple	clause simplex
alternative	clause complex: paratactic extension: alternation or (includes ellipsis)

Register analysis with semantic networks: examples from health care

Hasan's network for RELATION ENACTMENT has been used in several healthcare contexts. In surgery, a key concern is how the parties direct and coordinate each other's action, especially when trainees are present, so an analysis was made of the sequence and distribution of options within DEMAND GOODS-AND-SERVICES in routine surgical practice, along with proxemic, graphic and intonational analyses not reported here.

Senior surgeons were found to use subtle variations in command type to control the phasing of surgery and to accomplish critical moments such as 'swapping sides' with their trainees (Moore et al. 2010; Lukin et al. 2011; Moore 2016). Such interpersonal registerial competence was shown to be a vital, but institutionally invisible, aspect of professional expertise. For instance, when safety and 'failure' are at stake, and agentive roles are being renegotiated, it is highly significant that a mentor uses more commands with Hasan's features [suggestive] and [consultative], for example *Can we swap sides?*, treating the mentored participant 'as if she has the right to demur' (Hasan 2009b: 293).

In the domain of palliative care, message semantic analyses of doctors' questions helped to identify prominent higher-order semantic features – *incipience*, *implicitness* and *individuation* – which play a crucial role in opening up space for patients to discuss end-of-life issues without forcing such discussion (Moore 2015). Hasan's (2009b) DEMAND INFORMATION network fragment was the primary tool (Figure 26.4).

One common pattern was to direct topic development with an [ask]^[verify] sequence, followed by a [specify]^[verify] sequence. Often, topic-initiating questions also had the feature [prefaced], as in *Are you finding any problems . . . ?* This feature here explicitly frames 'problemness' as the patient's point of view, as in Extract 26.1, which shows Doctor, Patient and Kin's turns.

In these two medical domains, message semantic analysis makes it easier than grammatical analysis alone to recognise relevant patterning and to net in all relevant contrasts, although see Moore (2015) for challenges and potential revisions to the networks. Although not a formal contrastive study, these patterns begin to distinguish, among other things, surgery and palliative care on repeatable, semantic measures. At a more delicate level, they distinguish between groups and between instances, within each healthcare domain. The semantic configurations can be related to the contextual configurations that motivate such registerial patterning – or such resonances can at least be tested.

Extract 26.1 Palliative care consultation

135	D	Are you finding any problems with nighttime? [DI: confirm: enquire: **ask**; preface]
136	P	No I just lay there and wait for daytime to come.
137	D	Do you? [DI: confirm: **verify**: elliptical probe]
138	P	Yes I can go to bed at 10 o'clock and wake up at 2 am and just lay awake there.
139	D	What are you thinking about? [DI: apprise: **specify**]
140	K	Listen to the radio most of the time.
141	D	Really? [DI: confirm: **verify**: elliptical probe]
142	P	Just listen to talkback radio, what's happening and think how much longer . . .

Source: Moore (2015)

Some remaining issues

Although the approach discussed here can be considered 'formally complete' (Lemke 2011), challenges remain, including questions about stratal isomorphism, differentiating realisation and delicacy, and differentiating code and register. It has not yet been possible to automate message semantic analysis (although this does not distinguish it from other semantic-level models). Disagreement about the (re)wiring of context-level networks – in particular, with respect to field–mode relations (Bowcher 2014) – limits study comparability. As Hasan (2014) points out, though, we must expect such problems given the recency of networks for semantics and context. One limitation of other approaches, expressed by Martin (2002) as the urgent need for a unit at the semantic level, has at least been addressed in message semantics.

A recurrent criticism of message semantics is that its options do nothing more than restate options available at the grammatical level, with a one-to-one relation between each semantic feature and a unique type of clause structure that realises it. This is not the case (Lukin et al. 2011; Hasan 2014; Moore 2015) although *some* semantic distinctions may remain too closely tied to reifications in the grammar, for certain analytic purposes.

Arguably, one gap in tool power concerns the construal of agency. Moore (2004, 2005) attributes this problem to a lack of integration between social-theoretical accounts of agency – which model agency as something more dialectical than unfettered action – and the interpretation of linguistic patterning by analysts. Although the grammar of agency has been articulated from several perspectives, including systemic functional grammar's complementarities (for example transitive/ergative), language users draw on various levels of discourse organisation in construing agency. Attempts to address this problem, such as Hasan's (1989b) cline of dynamism and van Leeuwen's (1995) representation of action, are important advances, but have underexploited the power of making statements at different orders of abstraction.

A brief example from HIV medicine will illustrate. In Extract 26.2, Michael, the patient (P), and Trevor, the doctor (D),[8] are discussing viral load test results and considering a change of medicine.

Together, they decide that the poor test results might be the result of the patient skipping doses. The patient depicts himself as, and enacts the role of, decider: . . . *we'll leave it for*

Extract 26.2 HIV medicine consultation

191	D	The viral load shows without question, that . . . the antivirals . . . aren't working, yeah.
192	P	Well maybe because . . . like that was a week before, would it show in that week?
193	D	Yeah.
194	P	When –
195	D	Yeah. If – if you'd stopped, for example. Yeah.
196	P	It probably would have shown in that? <u>Okay well, we'll leave it for another two weeks</u>. [DEMAND GS: **suggestive**; non-exhortative: **assertive; plea**]
198	D	Okay. [[43 turns omitted]]
242	D	Um, I'll put 'he'll probably need a change of antivirals, <u>but Michael has asked to postpone this for a two week period</u>', ah, what'll I write? 'while he improves his compliance'.

Source: Moore (2004, 2005)

another two weeks (Turn 196). In the doctor's subsequent reformulation of this decision (Turn 242), the patient is depicted quite differently, with little authority: *Michael has asked to postpone . . .*

From my reading, no networked, contextually open, (discourse) semantic account exists that adequately integrates the dynamic, cross-speaker and cross-metafunctional patterning that construes the contested agency here.[9] Of particular concern is the modelling of semiotic agency (effects on, or caused by, speaking and sensing).

As argued elsewhere, situating register at the *semantic* stratum opens up the possibility of 'describing language variation and consistency without making such language varia-tion isomorphic with social variation' (Lukin et al. 2011: 189). In other words, in a given context of situation, there may be some variation in the specific set of wordings that appears from one instance to the next. This is made possible in the Hallidayan model because register is one stratal remove from genre, and stratal separation allows recombination, non-congruent realisation and contextual metaphor.

However, one question that remains is: under what conditions, if not contextual dif-ference, might register variation occur? The question addresses the possibility of circular reasoning: if contextual configurations (social variation) determine semantic configurations (linguistic variation), then how can it also be true that linguistic variation happens *without* contextual variation?

Similar questions concern the relationship between 'delicacy' and stratal boundaries. One possible description of the differences in the healthcare examples discussed is to say that the patterns constitute *different contexts of situation*, for the very reason that changes in the configuration of field, tenor and mode have been observed to correlate with changes in semantic configurations, and in turn with lexicogrammatical ones. An alternative view is that such patterns constitute variations in the 'same' contextual configuration, seen paradig-matically from the point of view of a high degree of delicacy. Hasan's discussion of texture is relevant here.

While there is much to clarify about paradigmatic accounts (for example Butt and Wegener 2007; Hasan 2014; Martin 2014), it can be said that a robust realisational system that is continually perturbed by each instantiation and which accommodates an indefinite amount of variation (by use, by user and over time) cannot function on the basis that each term in one stratum has completely fixed relations with each term on the other strata – yet this is what isomorphic relations between linguistic and social variation would imply. As Hasan (2010: 277) puts it, '[t]he fact that realization between strata does *not* display a 1:1 relationship is a critical feature ensuring the semogenic power of language' – for example, the category 'imperative' overwhelmingly functions as a recognition criterion for the seman-tic category DEMAND GOODS-AND-SERVICES, unless there is good reason for doing otherwise.

An important part of the answer to such questions therefore comes from the notion of congruence as *typical* alignment. Halliday stresses that stratal alignments are probabil-istic, not fixed. Yet questions arise concerning the status of Hasan's 'good reason' for atypical realisations: if we can specify the 'good reason', does this not count as an addi-tional source of prediction, albeit conditioned? Halliday, Hasan, Matthiessen and their associates are ambiguous on this point: the probabilistic nature of register is sometimes treated as inherent fuzziness, with instantiations impossible to fully predict; elsewhere, register is treated as a system of dispersed realisations and dispersed activating features, which *could* be specified if only we could see the complexity involved (cf. Butt and Wegener 2007). This is, of course, an unresolved debate in philosophy of probability itself (Grossman 2006).

Often, quandaries around such issues indicate sites of crucial significance in the institutional domain. For example, the language that doctors and patients use to decide about novel, toxic treatments looks different lexicogrammatically from recurrent decisions about common infections, but arguably both realise the contextual configuration of 'shared decision-making' within that domain (Moore 2004). In palliative care, some doctors use an individuating style, which appears to be highly valued in the current institutional order. Should such varying linguistic patterns be called distinct registers? And what are the implications for our understanding of the relation between code and register, if institutionally preferred styles in medicine represent gender-typical or class-typical patterns more broadly as they appear to do (cf. Hasan 2009b)?

Concluding remarks

In 1993, Mohsen Ghadessy described register analysis as a fast-expanding 'sub-discipline of linguistics', equating 'register analysis' with 'working with examples of genuine texts in the hope of establishing the linguistic features that characterise each'. Now, more than twenty years later, fewer publications bear 'register' in their title, but the use of real texts, kept in contact with their contexts, has never been more prevalent in linguistic research and language teaching materials. This makes it important to keep reflecting on how 'register' is interpreted and positioned with respect to linguistic theory and practice. A recent survey of sixteen functional, cognitive and constructionist linguistic models (Butler and Gonzálvez-Garcia 2014) identified SFL as the model most concerned with factoring register into its architecture; thus register is something on which SFL must draw, but also something that it must explain.

The present chapter has foregrounded the concept of register as 'semantic configuration'. This Hallidayan tradition of register has continued to develop productive analyses and partnerships. From the theoretical point of view, Hasan in particular continued to test and refine her semantic networks until her untimely recent death, and Hasan, Butt and Bowcher have developed networks for analysing context of situation as part of a paradigmatic account of register. Current challenges include: building research partnerships in domains with the potential for new feedback into SFL theory (perhaps health care is one such domain); the 'computational enhancement' of register studies; teasing out theoretical coherence between variant models and interpretations of register; and testing the contextually open network approach across a large and sufficiently varied set of domains to better gauge its real capacity.

Notes

1 Written mostly by Halliday.
2 See Gardner, this volume.
3 For detailed discussion of this bidirectional relation, see Hasan (1999, 2009a, 2009b); for the related, but distinct, notion of meta-redundancy see Lemke (1984) and Martin (1992); for proposing 'reflection' and 'construal' as distinct relations, see Bartlett, this volume.
4 See Halliday (1973) and Hasan et al. (2007) for the iterative, dialogical process involved in its development.
5 Hasan acknowledges that the networks need extending in delicacy to account for all meanings within a message, i.e. to reach the goal of being language-exhaustive.
6 Hasan accepts context-specific modelling when contextually open modelling is not available (Hasan et al. 2007).

7 Unlike systemic functional grammar, message semantics has no internal bracketing of logical and experiential functions.
8 'Michael' and 'Trevor' are both pseudonyms.
9 Cf. Martin's (1992: 391) call for such integration.

References

Banks, D. 2008. *The Development of Scientific Writing: Linguistic Features and Historical Context*. London: Equinox.

Biber, D. 1995. *Dimensions of Register Variation*. Cambridge: Cambridge University Press.

Bowcher, W. 1999. Investigating institutionalization in context. In M. Ghadessy (ed.) *Text and Context in Functional Linguistics*. Amsterdam: John Benjamins, pp. 141–76.

Bowcher, W. 2014. Issues in developing unified systems for contextual Field and Mode. *Functions of Language* 21(2): 176–209.

Brown, R., P. Butow, D.G. Butt, A.R. Moore and M.H. Tattersall. 2004. Developing ethical strategies to assist oncologists in seeking informed consent to cancer clinical trials. *Social Science & Medicine* 58: 379–90.

Butler, C., and F. Gonzálvez-Garcia. 2014. *Exploring Functional–Cognitive Space*. Amsterdam: John Benjamins.

Butt, D.G. 2004. Parameters of context. Unpublished monograph. Department of Linguistics, Macquarie University, Sydney.

Butt, D.G., and R. Wegener. 2007. The work of concepts: Context and metafunction in the systemic functional model. In R. Hasan, C.M.I.M. Matthiessen and J. Webster (eds) *Continuing Discourse on Language*. London: Equinox, pp. 589–618.

Caffarel, A. 1992. Interacting between a generalized tense semantics and register–specific semantic tense systems: A bistratal exploration of the semantics of French tense. *Language Sciences* 14: 385–418.

Cloran, C. 1989. Learning through language: The social construction of gender. In R. Hasan and J.R. Martin (eds) *Language Learning Culture*. Norwood, NJ: Ablex, pp. 111–51.

Crystal, D. 1991. Stylistic profiling. In K. Aijmer and B. Altenberg (eds) *English Corpus Linguistics*. London: Longman, pp. 221–38.

Firth, J.R. 1950. Personality and language in society. *The Sociological Review* 42(1): 37–52.

Ghadessy, M. (ed.). 1988. *Registers of Written English*. London and New York: Pinter.

Ghadessy, M. (ed.). 1993. *Register Analysis: Theory and Practice*. London and New York: Pinter.

Ghadessy, M. 1999. Textual and contextual features in register identification. In M. Ghadessy (ed.) *Text and Context in Functional Linguistics*. Amsterdam: Benjamin, pp. 125–40.

Grossman, J. 2006. Inferences from observations to simple statistical hypotheses. Unpublished PhD thesis, University of Sydney.

Halliday, M.A.K. 1973. *Explorations in the Functions of Language*. London: Arnold.

Halliday, M.A.K. 1975. *Language as Social Semiotic: Towards a General Sociolinguistic Theory*. London: Arnold.

Halliday, M.A.K. 1985. Part A. In M.A.K. Halliday and R. Hasan (eds) *Language, Context, and Text: Aspects of Language in a Social-Semiotic Perspective*. Geelong: Deakin University Press, pp. 3–49.

Halliday, M.A.K. 1999. The notion of 'context' in language education. In M. Ghadessy (ed.) *Text and Context in Functional Linguistics*. Amsterdam: Benjamin, pp. 1–24.

Halliday, M.A.K. 2002a. *Collected Works of M.A.K. Halliday, Vol. 2: Linguistic Studies of Text and Discourse*. Ed. J.J. Webster. London: Continuum.

Halliday, M.A.K. 2002b. *Collected Works of M.A.K. Halliday, Vol. 4: The Language of Early Childhood*. Ed. J.J. Webster. London: Continuum.

Halliday, M.A.K. 2002 [1964]. The linguistic study of literary texts. In J.J. Webster (ed.) *Collected Works of M.A.K. Halliday, Vol. 2: Linguistic Studies of Text and Discourse*. London: Continuum, pp. 5–22.

Halliday, M.A.K. 2002 [1977]. Text as semantic choice in social context. In J.J. Webster (ed.) *Collected Works of M.A.K. Halliday, Vol. 2: Linguistic Studies of Text and Discourse*. London: Continuum, pp. 23–81.

Halliday, M.A.K. 2002 [1985]. Dimensions of discourse: Grammar. In J.J. Webster (ed.) *Collected Works of M.A.K. Halliday, Vol. 1: On Grammar*. London: Continuum, pp. 261–88.

Halliday, M.A.K. 2002 [1990]. The construction of knowledge and value in the grammar of scientific discourse: With reference to Charles Darwin's *The Origin of Species*. In J.J. Webster (ed.) *Collected Works of M.A.K. Halliday, Vol. 2: Linguistic Studies of Text and Discourse*. London: Continuum, pp. 168–94.

Halliday, M.A.K. 2002 [1992]. Some lexicogrammatical features of the zero population growth text. In J.J. Webster (ed.) *Collected Works of M.A.K. Halliday, Vol. 2: Linguistic Studies of Text and Discourse*. London: Continuum, pp. 197–227.

Halliday, M.A.K. 2002 [1994]. So you say 'pass' . . . thank you three muchly. In J.J. Webster (ed.) *Collected Works of M.A.K. Halliday, Vol. 2: Linguistic Studies of Text and Discourse*. London: Continuum, pp. 228–54.

Halliday, M.A.K. 2003. Introduction: On the 'architecture' of human language. In J.J. Webster (ed.) *Collected Works of M.A.K. Halliday, Vol. 3: On Linguistics and Language*. London: Continuum, pp. 1–29.

Halliday, M.A.K. 2004. *Collected Works of M.A.K. Halliday, Vol. 5: The Language of Science*. Ed. J.J. Webster. London: Continuum.

Halliday, M.A.K. 2005 [1993]. Quantitative studies and probabilities in grammar. In J.J. Webster (ed.) *Collected Works of M.A.K. Halliday, Vol. 6: Computational and Quantitative Studies*. London: Continuum, pp. 130–56.

Halliday, M.A.K. 2005 [1995]. Computing meanings: Some reflections on past experience and present prospects. In J.J. Webster (ed.) *Collected Works of M.A.K. Halliday, Vol. 6: Computational and Quantitative Studies*. London: Continuum, pp. 239–67.

Halliday, M.A.K. 2009. Methods–techniques–problems. In M.A.K. Halliday and J.J. Webster (eds) *Continuum Companion to Systemic Functional Linguistics*. London and New York: Continuum, pp. 59–86.

Halliday, M.A.K., and R. Hasan. 1976. *Cohesion in English*. London: Longman.

Halliday, M.A.K., and R. Hasan. 1985. *Language, Context, and Text: Aspects of Language in a Social-Semiotic Perspective*. Geelong: Deakin University Press.

Halliday, M.A.K., and J.R. Martin. 1993. *Writing Science: Literacy and Discursive Power*. London: Routledge Falmer.

Halliday, M.A.K., and C.M.I.M. Matthiessen. 1999. *Construing Experience through Meaning: A Language-Based Approach to Cognition*. London and New York: Cassell.

Halliday, M.A.K., A. McIntosh and P. Stevens. 2007 [1964]. The users and uses of language. In J.J. Webster (ed.) *Collected Works of M.A.K. Halliday, Vol. 10: Language and Society*. London and New York: Continuum, pp. 5–37.

Hasan, R. 1985. Part B. In M.A.K. Halliday and R. Hasan (eds) *Language, Context, and Text: Aspects of Language in a Social-Semiotic Perspective*. Geelong: Deakin University Press, pp. 52–118.

Hasan, R. 1989a. Semantic variation and sociolinguistics. *Australian Journal of Linguistics* 9: 221–75.

Hasan, R. 1989b. *Linguistics, Language and Verbal Art*. Oxford: Oxford University Press.

Hasan, R. 1996. Semantic networks: A tool for the analysis of meaning. In C. Cloran, D.G. Butt and G. Williams (eds) *Ways of Saying, Ways of Meaning: Selected Papers of Ruqaiya Hasan*. London: Cassell, pp. 104–31.

Hasan, R. 1999. Speaking with reference to context. In M. Ghadessy (ed.) *Text and Context in Functional Linguistics: Systemic Perspectives*. Amsterdam: Benjamin, pp. 219–28.

Hasan, R. 2009a. The place of context in a systemic functional model. In M.A.K. Halliday and J.J. Webster (eds) *Continuum Companion to Systemic Functional Linguistics*. London: Continuum, pp. 166–89.

435

Hasan, R. 2009b. *The Collected Works of Ruqaiya Hasan, Vol. 2: Semantic Variation – Meaning in Society and in Sociolinguistics*. Ed. J.J. Webster. London: Equinox.

Hasan, R. 2010. The meaning of 'not' is not in 'not'. In A. Mahboob and N. Knight (eds) *Appliable Linguistics*. London: Continuum, pp. 267–306.

Hasan, R. 2013. Choice taken in the context of realization. In L. Fontaine, T. Bartlett and G. O'Grady (eds) *Systemic Functional Linguistics: Exploring Choice*. Cambridge: Cambridge University Press, pp. 269–99.

Hasan, R. 2014. Towards a paradigmatic description of context: Systems, metafunctions, and semantics. *Functional Linguistics* 1: 9.

Hasan, R., C. Cloran, G. Williams and A. Lukin. 2007. Semantic networks: The description of linguistic meaning in SFL. In R. Hasan, C.M.I.M. Matthiessen and J.J. Webster (eds) *Continuing Discourse on Language: A Functional Perspective, Vol. 2*. London: Equinox, pp. 297–738.

Hymes, D. 1972. Models of the interaction of language and social life. In J. Gumperz and D. Hymes (eds) *Directions in Sociolinguistics: The Ethnography of Communication*. New York: Holt, Rinehart & Winston, pp. 35–71.

Kappagoda, A. 2005. What people do to know: The construction of knowledge as a social-semiotic activity. In R. Hasan, C.M.I.M. Matthiessen and J.J. Webster (eds) *Continuing Discourse on Language: A Functional Perspective, Vol 1*. London: Equinox, pp. 185–216.

Lee, D.Y.W. 2001. Genres, registers, text types, domains and styles: Clarifying the concepts and navigating a path through the BNC jungle. *Language Learning and Technology* 5(3): 37–72.

Lemke, J. 1984. *Semiotics and Education* (Toronto Semiotic Circle Monographs, Working Papers and Prepublications 1984.2). Toronto, ON: Victoria University.

Lemke, J. 2011. Review of Hasan (2009), *Semantic Variation*. *Linguistics and the Human Sciences* 4(3): 314–20.

Lukin, A. 2013. What do texts do? The context-construing work of news. *Text and Talk* 33(4–5): 523–52.

Lukin, A., A. Moore, M. Herke, R. Wegener and C. Wu. 2011. Halliday's model of register revisited and explored. *Linguistics and the Human Sciences* 4(2): 187–243.

Martin, J.R. 1992. *English Text: Systems and Structure*. Amsterdam: Benjamin.

Martin, J.R. 2002. Meaning beyond the clause: SFL perspectives. *Annual Review of Applied Linguistics* 22: 52–74.

Martin, J.R. 2014. Evolving systemic functional linguistics: Beyond the clause. *Functional Linguistics* 1: 3.

Matthiessen, C.M.I.M. 1993. Register in the round: Diversity in a unified theory of register analysis. In M. Ghadessy (ed.) *Register Analysis: Theory and Practice*. London: Pinter, pp. 221–92.

Matthiessen, C.M.I.M., A. Lukin, D.G. Butt, C. Clereigh and C. Nesbitt. 2005. A case study of multi-stratal analysis. *Australian Review of Applied Linguistics* 19: 123–50.

Moore, A. 2004. The discursive construction of treatment decisions in HIV medicine. Unpublished PhD thesis. Macquarie University, Sydney.

Moore, A. 2005. Modelling agency in HIV decision-making. *Australian Review of Applied Linguistics* 19: 103–22.

Moore, A. 2015. Can semantic networks capture intra- and inter-registerial variation? Palliative care discourse interrogates Hasan's message semantics. In W.L. Bowcher and J.Y. Liang (eds) *Society in Language, Language in Society: Essays in Honour of Ruqaiya Hasan*. London: Palgrave, pp. 83–114.

Moore, A. 2016. Lovers, wrestlers, surgeons: A contextually sensitive approach to modelling body alignment and interpersonal engagement in surgical teams. In S. White and J. Cartmill (eds.) *Communication in Surgical Practice*. London: Equinox, pp. 257–87.

Moore, A., and K. Tuckwell. 2006. A tenorless genre? Forensic generic profiling of workers' compensation dispute resolution discourse. *Linguistics and the Human Sciences* 2(2): 205–32.

Moore, A., D.G. Butt, J. Cartmill and J. Ellis-Clarke. 2010. Linguistic analysis of verbal and nonverbal communication in the operating room. *ANZ Journal of Surgery* 80(12): 925–9.

Nesbitt, C., and G. Plum. 1988. Probabilities in a systemic grammar: The clause complex in English. In R.P. Fawcett and D.L. Young (eds) *New Developments in Systemic Linguistics, Vol. 2: Theory and Application*. London: Pinter, pp. 6–38.

Neumann, S. 2014. *Contrastive Register Variation: A Quantitative Approach to the Comparison of English and German*. Berlin: de Gruyter.

Sinclair, J., and M. Coulthard. 1975. *Towards an Analysis of Discourse*. Oxford: Oxford University Press.

Steiner, E. 2004. *Translated Texts: Properties, Variants, Evaluations*. Frankfurt: Peter Lang.

Swales, J. 1990. *Genre Analysis*. Cambridge: Cambridge University Press.

Teich, E. 2013. Choices in analysing choice: Methods and techniques for register analysis. In L. Fontaine, T. Bartlett and G. O'Grady (eds) *Systemic Functional Linguistics: Exploring Choice*. Cambridge: Cambridge University Press, pp. 417–31.

Thibault, P. 1987. An interview with Michael Halliday. In R. Steele and T. Threadgold (eds) *Language Topics: Essays in Honour of Michael Halliday, Vol. 1*. Amsterdam: Benjamin, pp. 601–27.

Urbach, C. 2013. 'Choice' in relation to context: A diachronic perspective on cultural *valeur*. In L. Fontaine, T. Bartlett and G. O'Grady (eds) *Systemic Functional Linguistics: Exploring Choice*. Cambridge: Cambridge University Press, pp. 300–17.

van Leeuwen, T. 1995. Representing social action. *Discourse & Society* 6(1): 81–107.

27

Context and meaning in the Sydney architecture of systemic functional linguistics

Ken Tann

An introduction to the Sydney architecture

The Sydney architecture of systemic functional linguistics (SFL) is known for its wide applications in educational linguistics and social research, with a focus on power relations, the social distribution of semiotic resources and the building of communities. The model is strongly influenced by J.R. Martin's reading of Hjelmslev (1943, 1961) and Hartford stratificational linguistics (Gleason 1968; Gutwinski 1976), alongside Halliday's systemic functional grammar. It is commonly characterised by its text-orientation, discourse semantics (for example Martin 1992; Martin and White 2005; Martin and Rose 2003, 2007) and the modelling of genre (Martin and Rose 2008) as a contextual stratum. Building on Halliday and Hasan's (1980) initial work on cohesion and texture (see Clarke, this volume), the model takes an innovative approach to text as a unit of meaning with its own systems and structures (*discourse semantics*) that transcend the boundaries of the clause, and mediate between lexicogrammar and its context.[1] As such, descriptions of discourse semantics relate systematically to both of its adjacent strata, and it is therefore necessary to consider the way in which context is modelled in this approach to understand the motivation underlying the particular treatment of discourse semantics in this model and to locate it within its overall architecture. Most distinctly, the stratified model of context in the Sydney architecture theorises two levels of context – *register* and *genre* – as semiotic systems in themselves that are expressed by linguistic resources, including discourse semantics.[2] Beyond a mere redefinition of some SFL terminology, this difference in the formulation of context has significant implications for the understanding of the role and boundaries of linguistics. This chapter will outline the key concepts of context and discourse semantics by drawing attention to the differences between the model and other systemic models, before reviewing their practical implications for current directions in research (for example Bednarek and Martin 2010).

A stratified model of context: register and genre

The stratified model of context in the Sydney architecture distinguishes itself from other systemic functional models in three important ways: (a) its theorisation of the nature and status of context as connotative semiotic; (b) its modelling of a stratified context; and (c) the relationship of context to lower levels of abstraction – that is, to discourse semantics and, via discourse semantics, to lexicogrammar. Each of these aspects will be considered in this section to examine how they constitute an actual alternative to Halliday and Hasan's model of context (Matthiessen 1993), and to explore the theoretical motivations that underlie their innovation.

Context as a connotative semiotic

The model of context in the Sydney architecture draws on Hjelmslev's (1943, 1961) concept of *connotative semiotic*, which he defines as a semiotic that takes another semiotic as its expression plane. Context, in the Sydney Model, is similarly regarded as a connotative semiotic that is expressed by language, which is itself a denotative semiotic (Martin 1985). In this way, the relationship between the context plane (genre and register) and language (discourse semantics, lexicogrammar and phonology/graphology) is theorised as a symbolic one, in which language use symbolises its social context, as shown in Figure 27.1. This move takes Halliday's (1978) argument of 'language as social semiotics' further by extending it to its context in reconceptualising 'context' as itself a meaning-making resource – a notion that will be explored in this section, while the stratification of context and language will be discussed later.[3]

In contrast to other models of context that situate social context (as theoretical parameters) outside language (for example Hasan 1985, 2009), context in the Sydney Model is theorised as a higher stratum of meaning. Context is regarded as a semiotic plane (cf. Hjelmslev's connotators) expressed by language resources such as discourse semantics and lexicogrammar, which are in turn expressed by phonology/graphology in the form of *metaredundancy* (Lemke 1984) – that is, patterns of patterns. The shift allows the concept of the language

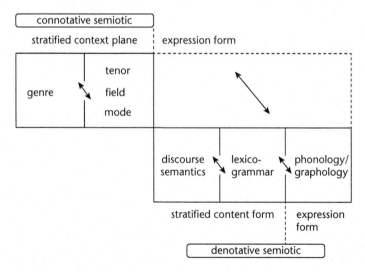

Figure 27.1 Stratified model of context and language

Source: Martin (1997)

strata as a meaning-making resource to be generalised to semiotics in general, including resources in modalities other than spoken and written texts, thus paving the way for multi-modality as a dominant research agenda in this approach (to which we will return later in the chapter). For instance, other semiotic resources can be theorised as part of the content form alongside language, which allows the consolidation of various semiotic systems, such as images, sound and language, as part of the same expression form for the context in which they operate. The distinction between connotative and denotative semiotic also serves to highlight the difference between the various kinds of realisational relationships at differ-ent levels. The notion of a connotative semiotic develops Halliday's notion of register as a characterisation of probabilities in language in terms of the weighting of selections within systems and the logogenetic unfolding of probabilities in a text, distinguishing it from the relationship between lexicogrammar and phonology as one of denotative semiotic.

This way of modelling context stands in contrast to Hasan's (1985, 2009) model of context in a number of significant ways. First, while Hasan considers context as theoreti-cal parameters for relating social conditions to language, thus requiring a separate level of sociological analysis for such aspects as institutions, material settings, personal histories and mental functions, among others (see Bartlett, this volume), context in Martin's model is understood as a pattern of its expression form (that is, the language plane), and there is con-sequently no strict distinction between linguistic and sociological levels of analysis. This is because, in this model, social institutions and identities are ultimately expressed by language or other forms of semiotics. However, the practical implication of this interpretation is that language use and the control of linguistic resources provide social access, which makes the model highly appealing to educators (see Gardner, this volume). This approach has been taken up in various educational projects to empower students from aboriginal, migrant and economically disadvantaged backgrounds (Martin 2000).

Second, the distinction between Martin and Hasan's approaches to context also leads to the vastly different ways in which it is modelled. Because Hasan regards context as the parameters that affect how the text is composed, she understandably finds it difficult to isolate a single aspect of context as responsible for a specific language feature observed in text and the entire configuration has to be taken as a set of interlocking features during analysis. Hence her concept of 'contextual configuration' (Hasan 1985) describes the values of field, tenor and mode as interpenetrating interdependently to affect the availability of options across metafunctions. Martin's model, on the other hand, assumes that language use is closely aligned metafunctionally to context. Because language is the primary means of access to context in his model, he rejects what he sees as an inconsistency when different contextual variables are held responsible for the same language features. He argues in favour of a description that aligns each metafunction in language to a specific aspect of context and asserts that such alignments are necessary for speakers' understanding of the context, because the three aspects of field, tenor and mode are meanings 'projected onto context' by the three metafunctions in language (Martin 1992: 494). This principle of *metafunctional solidarity* (Martin 1991) provides an important motivation for theorising discourse seman-tics as a distinct stratum (at which we look later).

Finally, it is important to note that the definitions of 'register' and 'field' in this model represent a considerable departure from Halliday and Hasan's (1985) original use of the terms. In both cases, the difference in terminology is a result of the difference in their con-ception of context, as mentioned earlier. On the one hand, *register* in the Sydney Model refers to a stratum of context that includes field, tenor and mode (Martin 1992), as shown in Figure 27.1, whereas Halliday and Hasan use the term to refer only to varieties of language in terms of probabilistic tendencies at the level of semantics. Because the Sydney Model defines context as an abstraction from language, such probabilistic tendencies in the language plane are regarded as expressions of register; conversely, register is an abstraction of these tendencies. On the other hand, *field* in the Sydney Model refers to the specialised taxonomies and activity sequences that are specific to particular kinds of discourse (Martin 1992: 289), whereas Halliday's (1985) field of discourse includes 'social actions' that 'participants are engaged in', which is, in fact, an aspect of genre in the Sydney Model. This distinction and the relationship between the two contextual strata will be explored further in the following section.

Stratification of context

Drawing on Gregory's (1967) concept of functional tenor, the Sydney architecture models *genre* as a distinct stratum of context from register. It also explicitly rejects a cognitive account of context such as participants' thoughts (cf. Fawcett 1980; van Djik 2006), regarding context as meaning-making practices available in a culture for achieving social goals.

Originally formulated as 'staged, goal-oriented purposeful activity' (Martin 1984: 25), Martin's concept of genre covers the notion of participants' 'social actions' in Halliday's (1985) description of field, as well as the notion of 'rhetorical mode' in Halliday's description of mode. For Halliday, the field of discourse refers to 'participants' purposive activity', in which language 'figures as some essential component', with the subject matter as 'one element in it' (Halliday and Hasan 1976: 22). While the component of subject matter has been developed as taxonomies and activity sequences in Martin's model, the 'purposive activity' is reinterpreted as genre in terms of 'purposeful activity'. One of the motivations behind differentiating between the two aspects is to separate activity sequences that are structured in field-time from generic structures that are structured in text-time (Martin 1999: 229). Halliday's mode, on the other hand, includes a component of 'rhetorical mode', or 'what is achieved by the text in terms of such categories as persuasive, expository, didactic, and the like' (Halliday and Hasan 1976: 12). This aspect of mode and its categories are adopted as the teleological dimension of 'goal-orientation' in the Sydney modelling of genre agnation. The consequent overlap between field and mode in the description of genre that can be seen here has to do with the way in which genre is characterised by all three metafunctions at a level of abstraction above register: in the same way as field, tenor and mode constrain patterns in language, genre constrains the combination of all three register variables. The stratified contextual model is therefore designed to account for the agnation of recurring combinations while allowing field, tenor and mode, at a separate stratum, to account for language patterns within each metafunction.

While the characterisation of genres by their schematic stages may bear some resemblance to Hasan's (1985) analysis of text structures, the two approaches are grounded in significantly different theoretical modellings that stem from Martin's stratification of context. Indeed, the use of schematic structures in Martin and Rose (2007) is attributed to Hasan's (1977) work, among others. However, in contrast to the Sydney Model that treats genre as a stratum with its own system (that is, genre agnates) and structure (that is, schematic structures) cycle, Hasan's model of context is not stratified and, because context is outside of language, text structure is a property of the text generated by particular contextual configurations. Hence the relationship between register/contextual configuration and these structures in the two models is, in fact, theoretically inverse: in Martin's (2010 [1985]: 49, for example) model, schematic structures of genres generate the register variables of field, mode and tenor, and constrain their recurring combinations; in Hasan's (1985, for example), contextual configurations activate the text structures in a given instance.

The practical implication of this opposite theoretical orientation is that Martin treats genre as a constant and the starting point in text analysis, with changes in register variables as the text unfolds, while Hasan treats the configuration of field, tenor and mode values as constants in a given text, with deviations in structures according to subtle differences in those values. Consequently, the two models deal with the analysis of complex situations very differently. For instance, where more than one social purpose is present in a long text or interaction, Martin (1994) analyses them as serial extensions and expansions in the form of 'macro-genres', while Hasan (1999) analyses them as forms of deviation in text design in the presence of modifying elements, or 'field integration'. Furthermore, Martin identifies common generic stages with more specific phases and optional phases within them (after Gregory and Malcolm 1981), such that the difference in staging is regarded as agnation, whereas Hasan's model distinguishes between obligatory and optional stages for comparing similar text types, and the two models have developed in rather different directions.

Stratification in the Sydney architecture

As the preceding sections show, the way in which stratification is theorised has significant impact on the development of analytical models in SFL. Even though the relationships across strata are all commonly glossed as 'realisation' and they share the quality of 'symbolic abstraction' (Halliday and Matthiessen 1999: 385), the relationship between context and language is not identical to that between levels of language (Martin and Rothery 1980). Moreover, the word 'realise' has itself been used in varied ways in the literature, synonymously with 'manifest', 'constitute', 'renovate' and 'symbolise' (Martin 1992: 378), and at times confused with instantiation and individuation (Martin 2008; also Bartlett, this volume). The notion of connotative semiotics, as introduced earlier, therefore serves to flag different forms of relationships that hold between levels of stratification in the model: the difference between a connotative and denotative semiotic marks and explains the characterisation of the relationship of register to language as probabilistic, as opposed to other levels.

While allowing for potentially different kinds of organisational relationships across strata, the Sydney Model holds to the central principle of stratification that each level constitutes a system–structure cycle, such that 'meaning is made at all levels' (Martin 1999: 30), with 'each level . . . contributing a layer of meaning to text' (Martin 1986: 226). In contrast to models that treat lexicogrammar as the structural output of meaning at the semantic level (for example Fawcett 1980, and in this volume), all levels in the Sydney Model are regarded as meaning-making resources in the sense that there are systemic selections made at every level of abstraction accompanied by their structural consequences; each selection is hence meaningful against the background of other potential choices within the same stratum (*valeur*) and functionally motivated by selections in the adjacent stratum (*metaredundancy*). The alignment of selections at every level can then be compared for congruence. It is in this line of reasoning that discourse semantics is introduced as a level of analysis that mediates between register and lexicogrammar.

Meaning at the level of the text: discourse semantics

Discourse semantics builds primarily on Halliday and Hasan's (1976) work on cohesion (see Clarke, this volume). Heavily inspired by Gleason's (1968) stratificational approach to discourse structures, it regards text as a semantic unit, in contrast to other approaches to semantics that focus on the level of message (such as Hasan 1983, 1996; Halliday 1984; Moore, this volume). It thereby provides a way in which to analyse cohesive ties as a network of relationships (cf. Gleason's reticulum) that run through the whole text, to preserve the text as an integral unit of analysis, rather than as a series of related clauses.

These cohesive ties are reinterpreted as a distinct stratum with its own *system–structure cycle* that mediates between register and lexicogrammar, by aligning itself metafunctionally with both.

Systems and structures

Halliday and Hasan's (1976) modelling of clause structures takes the boundary of the clause as its unit and treats those that transcend clausal boundaries as non-structural (Martin 1992: 23). Discourse semantics provides an alternative and integrated approach by modelling them as open-ended covariate chains that run through the text as a whole, to capture the continuity between them. Originally inspired by Hasan's (1984, 1985) cohesive harmony analysis, discourse semantics extends the analysis beyond coherence to texture in general (Martin 2001a,b), to capture the continuity within and between clauses.

Discourse semantics also differs from Halliday's and Hasan's concept of semantics in two fundamental ways. First, in contrast to Halliday's (1984) speech function based on the message as a unit and Hasan's (1983, 1996) semantic networks that relates the text to the message in terms of constituency, Martin's model treats the text as an irreducible unit of analysis. Secondly, while Halliday's and Hasan's models regard semantics as the analysis of meaning, the Sydney Model analyses meaning as the mapping of selections at all strata.

Using this method, Martin (1992) reinterprets Halliday and Hasan's (1980) work on reference, conjunction, substitution, ellipsis and lexical cohesion by consolidating them as discourse semantic systems: *ideation*, which construes experience as activity sequences, taxonomic relations and nuclear relations; *conjunction*, which connects messages; *negotiation*, in the exchange of information and goods and services in dialogues; and *identification*, which tracks participants in discourse. Martin and Rose (2003/2007) subsequently expand on the set with *periodicity*, which deals with information structure, and Martin and White (2005), with more recent work on *appraisal*, which deals with the intersubjective positioning of speakers (see Oteíza, this volume).

The model assumes three kinds of structuring principles (after Pike 1982), from a syntagmatic perspective, that are found in lexicogrammar – particulate, prosodic and periodic –corresponding to the three metafunctions (Martin 1996). *Particulate* structures are segmental and are associated with ideational meaning – that is, experiential meaning, with orbital structures such as the nuclear relations of process and participants in part–whole constituent relationships, and logical meaning, with part–part serial structures generating dependency chains such as those in clause complexing. *Prosodic* structures, such as intonation, are supra-segmental because they map over different segments and are associated with interpersonal meaning. *Periodic* structures are bound by waves of peaks and troughs, such as those of Theme and Rheme, and are associated with textual meaning. These three types of structure are reorganised by interdependency structures at the discourse semantic stratum known as 'covariate structures', which transcend clause boundaries. In doing so, covariate structures relate elements in different clauses to one another and provide coherence to the text.

Metafunctional solidarity across strata

The stratification of cohesive resources as discourse semantic systems and their structural basis in lexicogrammar allow them to be metafunctionally aligned to both lexicogrammar and register (see Table 27.1), to establish 'metafunctional solidarity' and the 'intrinsic functionality' (Martin 1991) of register, as described earlier.

For example, the nuclear relations in transitivity are organised by the orbital-structuring principle at the level of lexicogrammar, while the nuclear relations in each clause are in turn related to those in other clauses by covariate structures to form taxonomies and activity sequences at the level of discourse semantics and construe a particular field. The particulate-organising principle therefore informs the basis for the organisation of ideational meaning.

To understand the dynamics of a text or its texture, it would be necessary to consider the collective effect of all three kinds of structure in the text, or their *co-articulation* (Martin 1992: 548; Tann 2010), at every stratum. For instance, a line of enquiry in discourse analysis may be how the taxonomic relations and appraisal resources of a text map onto its periodicity to realise a particular context or ideology.[4]

A complementary and equally important concept to co-articulation between structures is that of co-selection between systems, which has been developed in the Sydney Model recently. Instances of co-selections from different systems in the text, including those across metafunctions, are described as *couplings* (Martin 2008, 2010), and couplings with higher probabilistic tendencies are described as *syndromes* (Zappavigna et al. 2008).

Meaning as interstratal relations: grammatical metaphors

The stratification of the content plane into lexicogrammar and discourse semantics provides a useful way in which to understand grammatical metaphors (see Taverniers, this volume), which are defined in the Sydney Model as the stratal tension between the two language strata (Martin 1992, 2008). Because meaning in the Sydney Model does not reside at a semantic level to be realised as grammatical forms, but at all levels, a tension can result between meanings at risk at different levels of organisation for metaphorical expressions. In this account, two layers of meaning are simultaneously present in a metaphorical expression – that is, two sets of *valeur* are present at different strata: one with respect to lexicogrammar; the other with respect to discourse semantics. The inclusion of discourse semantics as a stratum in the model makes it possible to distinguish between solidary (or congruent) and non-solidary realisations across all metafunctions as a mechanism that offers two competing interpretations for negotiation as the text unfolds.[5] For example, the ideational metaphor 'the high-speed chase' construes the discourse semantic process of chasing as a grammatical

Table 27.1 Metafunctional alignment of discourse semantic resources to context

Metafunction	Structure	Lexicogrammar	Discourse semantics	Register
Experiential	Orbital	Transitivity, etc.	Ideation	Field
Logical	Serial	Clause complex	Conjunction	
Interpersonal	Prosodic	Mood	Negotiation	Tenor
		Modality	Appraisal	
Textual	Periodic	Theme	Periodicity	Mode
		Ellipsis, etc.	Identification	

participant and the interpersonal metaphor 'I wonder if I may . . . ?' realises the question grammatically as a declarative clause, while the textual metaphor 'the following point . . . ' treats a part of the text as a grammatical participant.

The Sydney Model theorises grammatical metaphors as the intertextual relations that are opened up by the metaphorical expression, whereby one set of relations is agnate to its directly immanent texts through the paradigmatic relations in lexicogrammar and another is agnate to its indirectly immanent texts through those in discourse semantics. An important implication is that grammatical metaphor has consequences in a text's lexical relations at other levels. The use of nominalisation has the potential to change activity sequences (realised by processes, such as walking, running, jumping, etc.) into taxonomic relations (realised by participants, for example kinds of movement) to build up specialised fields (such as biomechanics). Interpersonal metaphors have the potential to repackage modulation in negotiation (for example 'you must do X') as the appraisal resource of attitudes ('it is prudent to do X') and shift the focus from power to solidarity, while entire reference chains can be constructed in written texts with the semiotic entities produced through textual metaphors (for example 'the first point is . . . ; the second point is . . . ') in terms of identification. These shifts in lexical relations in the text also consequently produce a change in register, such as a shift away from an everyday field towards a specialised one, from a highly asymmetric tenor towards a more egalitarian or perhaps patronising one, or from a more spoken mode towards a written one, as shown in these examples.

Recent research and applications of the Sydney Model: commitment, iconisation and affiliation

A model of language that treats discourse semantics as a distinct stratum has enabled a number of new directions in this research, including multimodality in children's picture books, newspapers, music, body language and physical space, and, more recently, identity research (for example Bednarek and Martin 2010; Martin et al. 2013; Painter et al. 2014). Recent research in Sydney has taken on a focus on semogenesis, or the unfolding of meaning in texts, by expanding the architecture in other dimensions alongside sociological research on knowledge and knower structures (see Maton and Doran, this volume), including the modelling of instantiation and individuation (Martin 2008, 2010).

Because the principle of metafunctional diversity underlies all strata (shown as segmentation by the curved lines in Figure 27.2), instantiation and individuation are often investigated in terms of how meanings across different metafunctions couple and co-articulate. The hierarchy of *instantiation* is a scale of generalisation in language use, and current research in this area seeks to model the intertextual relationships between texts in terms of how texts are sourced from other texts, the instantiation of meaning across modalities and the logogenetic unfolding of texts. The hierarchy of *individuation* involves the distribution of meaning resources in the community, and current research in this area models how linguistic personae affiliate and communities align through texts. This body of research is brought together by the common assumption that features at all strata instantiate and individuate (Martin 2010), as shown in Figure 27.2.

Alongside the hierarchy of stratification introduced earlier in the chapter, Figure 27.2 shows that each stratum in the model can be described along the hierarchy of instantiation from the system of generalised language potential to instances of its use, as well as the hierarchy of individuation from the reservoir of meanings available to the community to the individualised linguistic repertoires. It should be noted with respect to the latter, however,

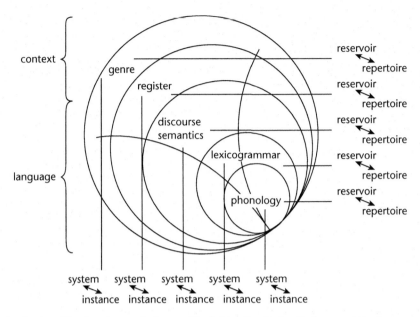

Figure 27.2 Stratification, instantiation and individuation in the Sydney architecture

that despite the persistence of the term 'individuation', there is a current shift in focus from the notion of the 'individual' towards that of shared bonds as the basic unit of description. Owing to space constraints, only a small portion of the research in these two dimensions will be briefly introduced in this section to illustrate the possibilities opened up by the model.

Instantiation

Because stratification, as a theoretical dimension, is concerned with levels of semiotic abstraction in the language system, it leaves the specific selections of features in instances

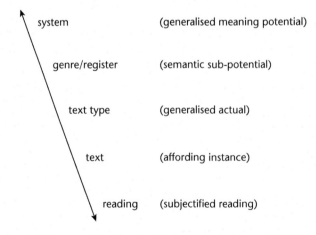

Figure 27.3 Instantiation as a scale of generalisation relating system to instance

Source: Martin (2006)

446

of language use largely underspecified. This is addressed by the dimension of instantiation, introduced by Halliday and Matthiessen (2004) as a cline of generalisation, to account for similarities and differences between registers and text-types. Martin (2006, 2008) expands on the dimension by proposing an additional level of reading to the hierarchy, as shown in Figure 27.3.

Martin also introduces a logogenetic perspective on instantiation by theorising the relation between a source text and its subsequent iteration as a movement further up the cline from the instance towards a more general set of potentiality shared by both texts, before moving down the cline again by making a slightly different set of selections. (The former movement is described as 'distanciation' and the latter, as 'activation'.) The movement up allows the author to trace the association of meanings in the original text by generalising them, so as to draw on a larger set of potential selections available for the production of the subsequent text. The inter-instance relations between source and subsequent texts are theorised in terms of *commitment*, or the extent to which systems are taken up in a text (Martin 2006; Hood 2008).[6] The concept has been variously applied to studies in education (Hood 2008), translation (de Souza 2010) and national identity (Tann 2012b).

Further key concepts associated with instantiation are those of *coupling* – that is, the consistent co-selections of features within the text – and *syndromes* – that is, couplings that are generalised across instances – and hence are higher up the cline of instantiation than the text (Tann 2012b). The concept of coupling has been productively applied in multimodal studies, for example in Painter et al. (2014: 144) to distinguish between the intermodal relations of concurrence (between ideational features across modalities), resonance (between interpersonal features across modalities) and synchronicity (between textual features across modalities). It has also been applied to identity studies to describe semiotic processes of *iconisation* (Martin and Stenglin 2007; Zappavigna et al. 2008; Tann 2012b), in which icons accumulate interpersonal meanings.

Individuation

Because stratification is also concerned with language uses rather than language users, individuation is recently introduced as a dimension to relate the reservoir of meanings available in a community to the repertoires of its members, modelled after the sociological work of Basil Bernstein. The dimension builds on Hasan's extensive work on semantic variation (for example Hasan 1996). While Hasan (1996) and Matthiessen (2007) make a distinction between dialectal (that is, lexicogrammar) and codal (that is, semantic) variations, and locate both on the cline of instantiation alongside registerial variation, Martin (2010) reinterprets both forms of variation in terms of a hierarchy that describes the distribution of semiotic resources among users of language, as shown in Figure 27.4.

The hierarchy of individuation can be read from the complementary perspectives of *allocation* (Martin et al. 2013) and *affiliation* (Knight 2010). Read from top to bottom, the reservoir of meaning resources that are available in a culture are distributed, or allocated, differentially in terms of gender, generation, ethnicity and class, etc. (master identity), familial, collegial, professional and recreational affiliations (sub-culture), to produce individual personae (Martin 2009). Conversely, the negotiation of bonds between speakers by deploying meaning resources allows them to affiliate and form communities of sub-cultures and master identities. Unlike the allocation perspective, which is concerned with the meaning-making resources that are narrowed down for the individual language user of particular coding orientations, the perspective of affiliation treats the bond between language users shared

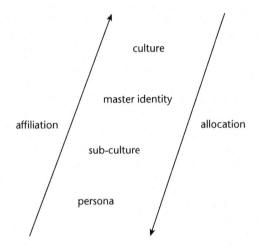

Figure 27.4   Individuation as a scale of identities relating communities to members
Source: Martin et al. (2013)

around particular attitudes as its basic unit and is concerned with how such bonds build up into larger ideological networks (Martin 2010). This model has been applied in forensic contexts, to study the negotiation of identities in youth justice conferencing (for example Zappavigna et al. 2008; Martin 2009; Martin et al. 2013).

Ideology

It has been mentioned already that the Sydney Model has been applied widely to discourse analysis and various areas of social research, focusing particularly on investigating power and ideology. Because the research on community and identity is the current focus in Sydney, a brief examination of an extract from Obama's well-known presidential acceptance speech is presented here to exemplify the kind of analysis enabled by this model.

Contextualising change

When Obama won the US presidential election in 2008 as the nation's first African-American president, his acceptance speech was televised and reported globally to mark a momentous change in US history. The following extract from the speech constitutes a biographical recount[7] of one of his voters, Ann Nixon Cooper, and closes with his famous campaign chant, 'Yes, we can', which establishes his presidency as a necessary conclusion to historical progress and the civil rights movement:

Orientation
This election had many firsts and many stories that will be told for generations. But one that's on my mind tonight is about a woman who cast her ballot in Atlanta. She's a lot like the millions of others who stood in line to make her voice heard in this election except for one thing – Ann Nixon Cooper is 106 years old.

She was born just a generation past slavery; a time when there were no cars on the road or planes in the sky; when someone like her couldn't vote for two reasons – because she was a woman and because of the color of her skin.

And tonight, I think about all that she's seen throughout her century in America – the heartache and the hope; the struggle and the progress; the times we were told that we can't, and the people who pressed on with that American creed: Yes, we can.

Record of Events

At a time when women's voices were silenced and their hopes dismissed, she lived to see them stand up and speak out and reach for the ballot. Yes, we can.

When there was despair in the dust bowl and depression across the land, she saw a nation conquer fear itself with a New Deal, new jobs and a new sense of common purpose. Yes, we can.

When the bombs fell on our harbor and tyranny threatened the world, she was there to witness a generation rise to greatness and a democracy was saved. Yes, we can.

She was there for the buses in Montgomery, the hoses in Birmingham, a bridge in Selma, and a preacher from Atlanta who told a people that 'We Shall Overcome'. Yes, we can.

A man touched down on the Moon, a wall came down in Berlin, a world was connected by our own science and imagination.

Evaluation of Person

And this year, in this election, she touched her finger to a screen, and cast her vote, because after 106 years in America, through the best of times and the darkest of hours, she knows how America can change. Yes, we can.

A text such as this can be analysed in the Sydney Model in terms of a number of system–structure cycles. By framing the progress of history as a biographical recount (as opposed to historical recount or a factorial explanation), the paradigmatic selection at the level of genre translates structurally as the stages Orientation^Record of Events^Evaluation of Person. Each of these stages is then realised as localised choices in register.

The Orientation stage of the biographical recount consists of a setting phase that sets it up as a 'story that will be told for generations' and a comment phase in which Obama reflects 'on all that she's seen'.[8] The field at this point is one about Ann's participation in the election. The setting phase names her, and locates her in time and space as 'a woman who cast her ballot in Atlanta', who was 'born just a generation past slavery', while the comments phase recontextualises her story as part of a greater story of 'the people' and their 'struggle' and 'progress'.

The Orientation is followed by a Record of Events stage that selectively chronicles Ann's 'century in America' as a sequence of significant events, signalled by circumstantial marked Themes that elaborate on America's 'struggles' and 'progress':

At a time when women's voices were silenced and their hopes dismissed . . .
When there was despair in the dust bowl and depression across the land . . .
When the bombs fell on our harbor and tyranny threatened the world . . .

At this point, the field shifts to one of the past and there are two concurrent fields: one of Ann's life; the other of the US civil rights movement, in which the field of American history is projected by the recount of Ann's life in terms of what she witnessed. The mode shifts accordingly from one of language in action (for example 'tonight, I think about . . . ') to one of language as reflection (for example 'At a time when . . . ').

The story finally closes with an Evaluation stage that interprets the 'historical significance of the events' in Ann's life (Coffin 2006: 54) as leading up to Obama's nomination:

> And this year, in this election, she touched her finger to a screen, and cast her vote, because . . . she knows how America can change.

The field has returned to that of the election in the present, while the tenor has developed into one of solidarity with Obama's supporters around Ann's insight on change.

Discourse semantics of progress

From the perspective of the Sydney architecture, these stages and phases constrain the register combinations of the text, each aspect of which relates metafunctionally to specific features in discourse semantics. Hence, in terms of mode, the text is situated somewhere between a prototypical written and spoken text: biographical recounts are typically written (Coffin 2006: 54), although the use of nominalisation in the extract is relatively low as a spoken monologue. Nominalisations such as 'heartache', 'hope', 'struggle' and 'progress' are nonetheless present in textually prominent positions of the text – a feature more typical in a written text – in the comment phase, which functions as the story's macroTheme, to be unpacked in the Record of Events. These grammatical metaphors realise processes as participants, so that the various activities of 'the people' can be construed as a list of phenomena that Ann has 'seen throughout her century'.

In terms of periodicity, the use of ideational metaphors in this way allows the negative appraisal attitudes of 'heartache' and 'struggle', and the positive attitudes of 'hope' and 'progress' to be inscribed in a thematic position, to colour the interpretation of the Record of Events to follow interpersonally in terms of the contrast between these two poles; hence a story about change. Each time period in the Record of Events begins with a marked Theme that picks up on the 'heartache' and 'struggle' as a problem phase, followed by an elaboration of the 'hope' and 'struggle' in a solution phase, and ends with the slogan 'Yes, we can'. In terms of identification, the persistence of Ann's identity chain sets her up as the protagonist of the biography, as shown in Figure 27.5.

As a speech, however, the exophoric reference to the audience at the speech 'we' is presented in the comment phase alongside Ann's identity chain and sustained to the end of the story, thereby recontextualising her biography as a period of American history.

The field of the text involves a chronological organisation of significant events of Ann's life. In contrast to its agnates of personal recounts and autobiographical recounts (cf. Coffin 2006: 53), the text contains specialised terms that refer to historical events, such as 'Dust Bowl', 'Depression' and 'New Deal', as well as references to the historical narrative of the US civil rights movement, such as 'buses in Montgomery', 'hoses in Birmingham', 'bridge in Pettus' and the 'preacher in Atlanta' (Martin Luther King).

At the level of discourse semantics, the field is realised as different activity sequences associated with the two identity chains. Ann Nixon Cooper is associated with relational processes (in bold, below) in the setting phase of the Orientation to establish her identity as simultaneously 'exceptional' and 'like the millions of others':

She's a lot like the millions of others . . .
except for one thing – Ann Nixon Cooper **is** 106 years old.
She **was born** just a generation past slavery . . .
she **was** a woman . . .

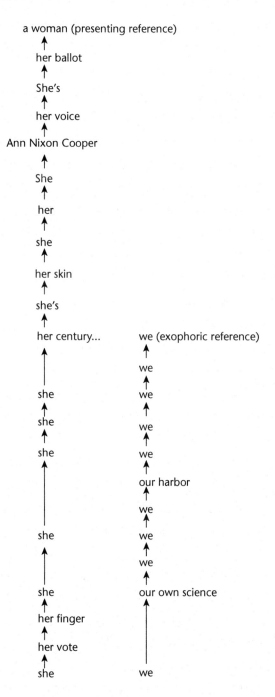

a woman (presenting reference)
her ballot
She's
her voice
Ann Nixon Cooper
She
her
she
her skin
she's
her century...   we (exophoric reference)
                       we
she   we
she   we
she   we
                       our harbor
                       we
she   we
                       we
she   our own science
her finger
her vote
she   we

Figure 27.5 Identification

```
she  +  has seen       +  all
        | (repetition)
she  +  lived to see   +  them stand up and speak out
        | (repetition)
she  +  saw            +  a nation conquer fear itself
        | (meronymy)
she  +  witness        +  a generation rise to greatness
```

Figure 27.6   Ideation

Following this, Ann's role in history is construed as one of an observer, characterised by her activity sequence, which is composed of the mental processes, to 'see' and 'witness' progress in American history, as shown in Figure 27.6.

Alongside Ann's activities, 'progress' in the Orientation is unpacked as the contrast between things that were done to us – 'we were told', 'voices were silenced', 'hopes were dismissed', 'bombs fell on our harbour', 'tyranny threatened the world' – and things that we did – we 'pressed on', 'stand up and speak out and reach for the ballot', 'conquer fear itself', 'rise to greatness' and 'saved democracy'. The meaning of 'progress' is thereby 'committed' as the various activities undertaken by the nation and condensed in the Evaluation stage as 'change'. It was eventually Ann's role as an observer and a knower in light of all this – 'she knows how America can change' – that led her to material action, having 'touched her finger to a screen, and cast her vote'. The text hence invites the American public to partake in this position of knowledge and its values.

Because biographical recounts are designed to align readers with respect to the historical significance of a person in terms of tenor (Coffin 2006: 55), Ann Nixon Cooper is not construed merely as an observer, but as a significant one informed by hindsight. Her processes of perception in the Record of Events culminate as a process of cognition 'knows' in the Evaluation stage, invoking capacity in terms of appraisal (see Martin and White 2005), and flagged by graduation – 'after 106 years in America, through the best of times and the darkest of hours'. Within each phase, the recount is reinterpreted in terms of the identity chain 'we', appraised explicitly in terms of capacity by the recurrent phrase 'Yes, we can'.

Ideology and affiliation

Obama's choices are not arbitrary, from the mental processes of perception that realise Ann's activity sequence of observing and her value as a capable observer, to their realisation of a historical field about emancipation and an affective public monologue, constituting a biographical recount of a voter. The analysis thus far has shown that Obama drew on the meanings that are culturally available. Nonetheless, we may still ask what motivates his choice of these meanings. Martin (1992: 507) proposes another stratum beyond genre that constrains these choices and calls it 'ideology', defined as 'a system of coding orientations constituting a culture'. This initial attempt to account for heterogeneity in speech communities along the lines of generation, gender, ethnicity and class was, however, abandoned subsequently, because it was later felt that the notion of ideology as formulated by Martin does not so much constrain the language system top-down via context, as suggested by stratification, but rather is a variable that influences the different strata in specific ways (for example Banks 2009). The distribution of semiotic resources in communities and the tensions between different discourses are subsequently modelled in the Sydney architecture as distinct dimensions from stratification.

At the stratum of lexicogrammar, processes of perception are coupled with processes of cognition in Obama's text and the participant 'we' is coupled with the modal 'can'; at the level of discourse semantics, Ann's activity sequence of observing history and the identity chain 'we' are coupled with capacity. The co-articulation of these meanings is enabled by Obama's use of biographical recount as a constituent in the macro-genre of his presidential speech. Obama's language of 'progress', which would have once been analysed as 'left protagonist' ideology (for example Martin 1986), is now interpreted in terms of individuation/affiliation, where the couplings at both lexicogrammar and discourse semantics redound to present Obama as a persona who celebrates wisdom, the elderly and the ordinary, and to align his supporters with bonds around discourses on ethnicity, gender and generation. From a semogenetic perspective, his rallying call is condensed in the slogan 'Yes, we can' over the course of the text and eventually reproduced alongside other iconic phrases such as 'We Shall Overcome' over the course of history as part of American identity. In this way, the 'ideological tension' that was once relegated to a single stratum of ideology has been replaced by a more nuanced model of systemic co-selections at all levels of meaning and their persistence as linguistic syndromes both within the community and over the course of time.

Research and social action

Only a partial analysis of this rather short extract may be presented here within the confines of this chapter to exemplify an application of the Sydney Model; it has only begun to scrape the surface of the text and does not do justice to the richness of the multimodal event involving gestures (for example Hood 2011; Martin et al. 2013), music (for example Caldwell 2010) and the use of film techniques (for example Iedema 2001), each of which warrants further examination within the model. Needless to say, there are also variations amongst analysts using the Sydney approach in practice and what can be demonstrated here represents a personal reading of the model. It is nonetheless hoped that this analysis has demonstrated how meaning is made at all levels of language – a core tenet of the Sydney Model – as well as the need for a multidimensional analysis of this kind to account for its complexities. Only then can we begin to ask questions such as: how do meaning-making resources at every level contribute towards community building? What kind of meanings are (differentially) available to its members? What kinds of ideologies are naturalised by its discourse? And what are the powerful forms of language that students need to acquire, to challenge the status quo and construct new realities?

Notes

1 See Moore, this volume, for a message semantics approach.
2 Cf. Bartlett and Bowcher, both in this volume, on the single level of context in Halliday and Hasan's model.
3 See also Berry, this volume.
4 See, e.g., 'Contextualising change'.
5 Cf. Halliday and Matthiessen (1999) on semantic junction.
6 But see Tann (2012a) for a critique.
7 See Martin and Rose (2007) on genre classifications.
8 See Martin and Rose (2007) on genre stages and story phases.

References

Banks, D. 2009. The position of ideology in a systemic functional model. *WORD* 60(1): 39–63.

Bednarek, M., and J.R. Martin (eds). 2010. *New Discourse on Language: Functional Perspectives on Multimodality, Identity, and Affiliation*. London and New York: Continuum.

Caldwell, D. 2010. Making many meanings in popular rap music. In A. Mahboob and N. Knight (eds) *Directions in Appliable Linguistics*. London: Continuum, pp. 234–66.

Coffin, C. 2006. *Historical Discourse*. London and New York: Continuum.

de Souza, L. 2010. Interlingual re-instantiation: A model for a new and more comprehensive systemic functional perspective on translation. Unpublished PhD thesis. Universidade Federal de Santa Catarina and University of Sydney.

Fawcett, R. 1980. *Cognitive Linguistics and Social Interaction: Towards an Integrated Model of a Systemic Functional Grammar and the Other Components of an Interacting Mind*. Heidelberg: Julius Groos.

Gleason, H.A. Jr. 1968. *Contrastive Analysis in Discourse Structure* (Monograph Series on Languages and Linguistics 21). Washington DC: Georgetown University Institute of Languages and Linguistics.

Gregory, M. 1967. Aspects of varieties differentiation. *Journal of Linguistics* 3: 177–274.

Gregory, M., and K. Malcolm. 1981. *Generic Situation and Discourse Phase*. Toronto, ON: Glendon College.

Gutwinski, W. 1976. *Cohesion in Literary Texts: A Study of Some Grammatical and Lexical Features of English Discourse* (Janua Linguarum Series Minor 204). The Hague: Mouton.

Halliday, M.A.K. 1978. *Language as Social Semiotic: The Social Interpretation of Language and Meaning*. Baltimore, MD: University Park Press.

Halliday, M.A.K. 1984. Language as code and language as behaviour: A systemic functional interpretation of the nature and ontogenesis of dialogue. In R. Fawcett, M.A.K. Halliday, S.M. Lamb and A. Makkai (eds) *The Semiotics of Language and Culture, Vol. 1: Language as Social Semiotic*. London: Pinter, pp. 3–35.

Halliday, M.A.K. 1985. Context of situation. In M.A.K. Halliday and R. Hasan (eds) *Language, Context, and Text: Aspects of Language in a Social-Semiotic Perspective*. Geelong: Deakin University Press, pp. 3–14.

Halliday, M.A.K., and R. Hasan. 1976. *Cohesion in English* (English Language Series 9). London: Longman.

Halliday, M.A.K., and R. Hasan. 1980. Text and context: Aspects of language in a social-semiotic perspective. *In Sophia Linguistica* 6: 4–91.

Halliday, M.A.K., and R. Hasan. 1985. *Language, Context, and Text: Aspects of Language in a Socialsemiotic Perspective*. Oxford/Geelong: OUP/Deakin University Press.

Halliday, M.A.K., and C.M.I.M. Matthiessen. 1999. *Construing Experience through Meaning: A Language Based Approach to Cognition*. London: Continuum.

Halliday, M.A.K., and C.M.I.M. Matthiessen. 2004. *An Introduction to Functional Grammar*, 3rd edition. London: Arnold.

Hasan, R. 1977. Text in the systemic-functional model. In W. Dressler (ed.) *Current Trends in Textlinguistics*. Berlin: Walter de Gruyter, pp. 228–46.

Hasan, R. 1983. *Message Semantics Coding Manual*. Mimeo. Department of Linguistics, Macquarie University.

Hasan, R. 1984. Coherence and cohesive harmony. In J. Flood (ed.) *Understanding Reading Comprehension: Cognition, Language and the Structure of Prose*. Newark, DE: International Reading Association, pp. 181–219.

Hasan, R. 1985. Part B. *Language, Context, and Text: Aspects of Language in a Social Semiotic Perspective*. Oxford/Geelong: OUP/Deakin University Press.

Hasan, R. 1996. *Ways of Saying, Ways of Meaning: Selected Papers of Ruqaiya Hasan*. Ed. C. Cloran, D.G. Butt and G. Williams. London: Cassell.

Hasan, R. 1999. Speaking with reference to context. In M. Ghadessy (ed.) *Text and Context in Functional Linguistics: Systemic Perspectives*. Amsterdam and Philadelphia, PA: John Benjamins, pp. 219–28.

Hasan, R. 2009. The place of context in a Systemic Functional Model. In M.A.K. Halliday and J.J. Webster (eds) *Continuum Companion to Systemic Functional Linguistics*. London and New York: Continuum, pp. 166–89.

Hjelmslev, L. 1943. *Omkring sprogteoriens grundlaeggelse*. Copenhagen: Akademisk Forlag.

Hjelmslev, L. 1961. *Prolegomena to a Theory of Language* (trans. F. Whitfield). Madison, WI: University of Wisconsin Press.

Hood, S. 2008. Summary writing in academic contexts: Implicating meaning in processes of change. *Linguistics and Education* 19: 351–65.

Hood, S. 2011. Body language in face-to-face teaching: A focus on textual and interpersonal meaning. In S. Dreyfus, S. Hood and M. Stenglin (eds) *Semiotic Margins: Reclaiming Meaning*. London: Continuum, pp. 31–52.

Iedema, R. 2001. Analysing film and television: A social semiotic account of Hospital – An Unhealthy Business. In T. van Leeuwen and C. Jewitt (eds) *Handbook of Visual Analysis*. London: Sage, pp. 183–204.

Knight, N. 2010. Wrinkling complexity: Concepts of identity and affiliation in humour. In M. Bednarek and J.R. Martin (eds) *New Discourse on Language: Functional Perspectives on Multimodality, Identity, and Affiliation*. London and New York: Continuum, pp. 35–58.

Lemke, J.L. 1984. *Semiotics and Education* (Monograph in Toronto Semiotic Circle Monographs Series). Toronto, ON: Victoria University.

Martin, J.R. 1984. Language, register and genre. In F. Christie (ed.) *Children Writing: Reader*. Geelong: Deakin University Press, pp. 21–30.

Martin, J.R. 1985. Process and text: two aspects of semiosis. In J.D. Benson and W.S. Greaves (eds) *Systemic Perspectives on Discourse, Vol. 1: Systemic Perspectives on Discourse*. Norwood, NJ: Ablex, pp. 248–74.

Martin, J.R. 1986. Grammaticalising ecology: The politics of baby seals and kangaroos. In T. Threadgold, E.A. Grosz, G. Kress and M.A.K. Halliday (eds) *Semiotics, Ideology, Language*. Sydney: Sydney Association for Studies in Society and Culture, pp. 225–68.

Martin, J.R. 1991. Intrinsic functionality: Implications for contextual theory. *Social Semiotics* 1(1): 99–162.

Martin, J.R. 1992. *English Text: System and Structure*. Amsterdam: John Benjamins.

Martin, J.R. 1994. Macro-genres: The ecology of the page. *Network* 21: 29–52.

Martin, J.R. 1996. Types of structure: Deconstructing notions of constituency in clause and text. *Computational and Conversational Discourse* 151: 39–66.

Martin, J.R. 1997. Analysing genre: Functional parameters. In F. Christie and J.R. Martin (eds) *Genre and Institutions: Social Processes in the Workplace and School*. London: Cassell, pp. 3–39.

Martin, J.R. 1999. Modelling context: A crooked path of progress in contextual linguistics. In M. Ghadessy (ed.) *Text and Context in Functional Linguistics*. Amsterdam and Philadelphia, PA: John Benjamins, pp. 25–62.

Martin, J.R. 2000. Grammar meets genre: Reflections on the 'Sydney School'. *Arts: The Journal of the Sydney University Arts Association* 22: 47–95.

Martin, J.R. 2001a. A context for genre: Modelling social processes in functional linguistics. In R. Stainton and J. Devilliers (eds) *Communication in Linguistics: Papers in Honour of Michael Gregory* (Theoria Series 10). Toronto, ON: GREF, pp. 287–328.

Martin, J.R. 2001b. Cohesion and texture. In D. Schiffrin, D. Tannen and H. Hamilton (eds) *Handbook of Discourse Analysis*. Oxford: Blackwell, pp. 35–53.

Martin, J.R. 2006. Genre, ideology and intertextuality: A systemic functional perspective. *Linguistics and the Human Sciences* 2(2): 275–98.

Martin, J.R. 2008. Innocence: Realization, instantiation and individuation in a Botswanan town. In N. Knight and A. Mahboob (eds) *Questioning Linguistics*. Newcastle: Cambridge Scholars, pp. 27–54.

Ken Tann

Martin, J.R. 2009. Realisation, instantiation and individuation: Some thoughts on identity in youth justice conferencing. *DELTA* 25: 549–83.

Martin, J.R. 2010. Semantic variation: Modelling realization, instantiation and individuation in social semiosis. In M. Bednarek and J.R. Martin (eds) *New Discourse on Language: Functional Perspectives on Multimodality, Identity, and Affiliation*. London: Continuum, pp. 1–34.

Martin, J.R., and D. Rose. 2003/2007. *Working with Discourse: Meaning beyond the Clause*. London: Continuum.

Martin, J.R., and D. Rose. 2008. *Genre Relations: Mapping Culture*. London: Equinox.

Martin, J.R., and J. Rothery. 1980. *Writing Project: Report 1980* (Working Papers in Linguistics 1). Sydney: University of Sydney Department of Linguistics.

Martin, J.R., and M. Stenglin. 2007. Materialising reconciliation: Negotiating difference in a post-colonial exhibition. In T.D. Royce and W.L. Bowcher (eds) *New Directions in the Analysis of Multimodal Discourse*. Mahwah, NJ: Lawrence Erlbaum, pp. 215–38.

Martin, J.R., and White. 2005. *The Language of Evaluation: Appraisal in English*. London and New York: Palgrave Macmillan.

Martin, J.R., M. Zappavigna, P. Dwyer and C. Cléirigh. 2013. Users in uses of language: Embodied identity in youth justice conferencing. *Text & Talk* 33(4–5): 467–96.

Matthiessen, C.M.I.M. 1993. Register in the round: Diversity in a unified theory of register analysis. In M. Ghadessy (ed.) *Register Analysis: Theory and Practice*. London: Pinter, pp. 221–92.

Matthiessen, C.M.I.M. 2007. The architecture of language according to systemic functional theory. In R. Hasan, C.M.I.M. Matthiessen and J. Webster (eds) *Continuing Discourse on Language Vol. 2*, pp. 505–61. London and Oakville: Equinox.

Painter, C., J.R. Martin and L. Unsworth. 2014. *Reading Visual Narratives: Image Analysis of Children's Picture Books*. London: Equinox.

Pike, K.L. 1982. *Linguistic Concepts: An Introduction to Tagmemics*. Lincoln, NE: University of Nebraska Press.

Tann, K. 2010. Imagining communities: A multifunctional approach to identity management in text. In M. Bednarek and J.R. Martin (eds) *New Discourse on Language: Functional Perspectives on Multimodality, Identity, and Affiliation*. London and New York: Continuum, pp. 163–94.

Tann, K. 2012a. Committing commitment: Theorizing processes of change. In J.S. Knox (ed.) *To Boldly Proceed. Papers from the 39th International Systemic Functional Congress*. Sydney: The Organizing Committee of the 39th ISFC, pp. 189–94.

Tann, K. 2012b. The language of identity discourse: Introducing a systemic functional framework for iconography. *Linguistics and the Human Sciences* 8(3): 361–91.

van Dijk, T. 2006. Discourse, context and cognition. *Discourse Studies* 8(1): 159–77.

Zappavigna, M., P. Dwyer and J.R. Martin. 2008. Syndromes of meaning: Exploring patterned coupling in a NSW youth justice conference. In A. Mahboob and N. Knight (eds) *Questioning Linguistics*. Newcastle: Cambridge Scholars, pp. 103–17.

456

28

The appraisal framework and discourse analysis

Teresa Oteíza[1]

Introduction

> Harking back to Ochs and Schiefflen's article 'Language has a heart' (1989) perhaps we can envoi by suggesting that alongside having heart languages also ongoingly enact their dialogic soul.
>
> *Martin 2003: 178*

As Martin and White (2005) stated, the purpose of developing an appraisal framework was to expand traditional accounts regarding issues of speaker/writer evaluation, certainty, commitment and knowledge, and also to consider how the textual voice positions itself with respect to other voices and other positions in the discourse. As a result, this theoretical orientation moves us towards an analysis of 'meanings in context and towards rhetorical effects rather than towards grammatical forms' (Martin and White 2005: 94), because the grammar and discourse of language are conceived as a set of resources that 'make' meanings, more than as rules to organise structure (Martin and Rose 2008). Appraisal has to do with the negotiation of meanings among real or potential interlocutors, such that every utterance enters into processes of alignment or misalignment with others, helping us to understand the levels and types of ideological solidarity that authors maintain with their potential readers/listeners. Consequently, one important aspect that has been emphasised by Martin (2000: 143) is not only that appraisal allows the researcher to examine 'how speakers can exploit different ranges of appraisal to construct particular personae for themselves', but also that:

> [T]he expression of attitude is not, as is often claimed, simply a personal matter – the speaker 'commenting' on the world – but a truly interpersonal matter, in that the basic reason for advancing an opinion is to elicit a response of solidarity from the addressee.

Thus appraisal always involves the negotiation of solidarity.

This position about language implies taking a dialogic perspective, which means that every verbal interaction is dialogic, and that the system should be analysed also from a

Teresa Oteíza

dialogic perspective, following Bakhtin's principle that interactions are always socio-culturally situated. This principle echoes the idea that the sign is socially motivated and, for that reason, it is impossible to separate it from the social situation. This takes us to the dialectic relationship between language and context that has been emphasised by Halliday (1978), and by many discourse analysts working with systemic functional lin-guistics (SFL) – that is, the view that language constitutes social context and that it is also shaped by the social context (see Bartlett and Hodge, both this volume).

The appraisal framework therefore aims to provide a comprehensive theoretical and descriptive systematisation of the linguistic resources that can be used to construe the value of social experience, and thereby to achieve a richer understanding of the patterns of inter-personal meaning beyond the manifestation of only emotionality across discourse. This model maintains that intersubjectivity is built by writers and readers who have certain social roles, and who act in determinate social and cultural realms that shape and institutionalise the way in which emotions and opinions are codified through language. In other words, the appraisal framework facilitates the study of the inscribed and evoked codification of intersubjectivity in the discourse, taking into consideration both the epistemological and interpersonal expressions.

According to Thompson and Hunston (2000: 6), evaluation is important and has been a worthy area of study, because it has three key functions in language:

1 to express the speaker's or writer's opinion and, in doing so to reflect the value system of that person and their community;
2 to construct and maintain relations between the speaker or writer and hearer or reader; and
3 to organise the discourse.

These functions can occur simultaneously in the discourse, for example evaluation can both organise the discourse and at the same time indicate its significance.

Because appraisal constitutes a system of interpersonal meanings situated at the level of discourse semantics (see Tann, this volume), it works at a more abstract level than the lexicogrammatical, thus allowing meanings to disperse in the former level and in an ample variety of lexicogrammatical systems. As Martin (2014: 9) states, the discourse seman-tic level 'cannot be seen simply as a list of cohesive ties relating one grammatical unit to another, but as a further level of structure in its own right'. Each level of language is understood as complex patterns of meaning – that is, following the principle of metaredun-dancy (Lemke 1995; Tann, this volume), each level meta-redounds with a lower one, so each stratum (genre, register, discourse semantics, lexicogrammar and phonology) is made from patterns of patterns of the immediately lower level (see Berry, this volume). This notion is of particular importance when dealing with appraisal, since this allows the turn from a gram-matical perspective on evaluation to a complementary perspective founded on the rhetorical effect of evaluative lexis as texts unfold. The appraisal system hence provides a generali-sation of diverse lexicogrammaticalisations that bring feelings together in relation to one another, which in turn allow the description of prosodies of evaluation in relation to genre (Martin 2014). Following this principle, the appraisal framework considers evaluation in a conceptual manner, and takes into account both grammatical and lexical codification and its patterning, or valorative prosody,[2] across the discourse.

Discourse semantic systems are organised by metafunction following the SFL paradigm (see Asp, this volume), which permits us 'to reinterpret from an interpersonal perspective resources that are experientially constituted in lexicogrammar (i.e. mental processes and

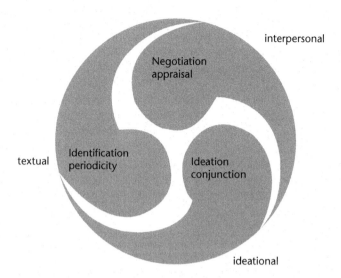

Figure 28.1   The metafunctional organisation of discourse semantic systems
Source: Martin (2014: 10)

states of affection – e.g. *He disliked the approach/He was unhappy about the approach*)'
(Martin 2014: 19), and to explore them, taking into consideration how attitude is realised in
the discourse in a prosodic or cumulative matter. Figure 28.1 illustrates the metafunctional
organisation of discourse semantic systems.

The following sections of this chapter present a brief historical perspective on appraisal,
followed by an overview of the appraisal model and its main research methods. Further, the
chapter offers some of the contributions that have been made since the publication in 2005 of
Martin and White's *The Language of Evaluation: Appraisal in English*, stressing the elaborations and critiques that they have made, and the theoretical and methodological difficulties
that they have encountered when working with the model. These collaborations are organised by field of study, mode and language. Some of the contributions offer a development
of the appraisal framework or present an application of the system, making the connection
to other disciplinary work. Finally, the chapter ends with some proposals for future research
directions related to this interpersonal system and with some suggested software applications that can be useful for conducting appraisal analysis.

Brief historical perspective

The model was initially created in the context of the educational linguistics and literacy
intervention work of the Sydney School, as part of the New South Wales Disadvantaged
Schools Programme led by Jim Martin in the 1980s and 1990s. This work gave rise to
key developments in exploring the language of evaluation in different disciplines taught in
secondary schools and workplace literacy.[3] As Martin (2014) explains, the existing framework for analysing attitude in discourse in different genres was not appropriate for dealing
with the analysis of different types of evaluation that, in turn, allows for an adequate distinction of types of story genre; therefore, it was the work on genre – and initially on narrative
genres[4] and the discourse semantic perspective – that triggered the evolution of a new
approach to interpersonal meaning in SFL.

The main concern of this group of linguists and educators was to better understand the social function of the interpersonal resources and to create a general model that 'could be applied in a systematic way to whole texts from any register, working within the general framework of systemic functional linguistics' (Martin 2003: 171).

This work, which started to build the appraisal model, has been refined up to the present day by many scholars – especially in English as a first or second language, and in different fields of study and languages. According to Martin (2000: 175), this is an unfinished project that needs to be developed with 'new kinds of research orientation – towards lexis (alongside grammar), towards corpus (alongside text), toward prosody (alongside particle and wave), towards solidarity (alongside hegemony), towards multi-modal analysis, including paralanguage, body and image (alongside verbiage)'. Various researchers in the last decade have attempted to follow this endeavour. Some examples of this development are offered later in the chapter, after a general exposition of the *appraisal* system and the presentation of the main subsystems.

Appraisal: a model of evaluation in discourse

The *appraisal* system that operates in the discursive semantic stratum proposed by J.R. Martin and P. White (Martin 2003; White 2003; Martin and White 2005) offers a way of categorising interpersonal meanings that are closely related to the systems of SPEECH FUNCTION and negotiation (Martin 1992; Martin and Rose 2007). Martin (2014: 18) points out that this *appraisal* system would 'complement the interactive turn-taking focus of those two MOOD based systems, highlighting the "-personal" dimension of interpersonal meaning' (Martin 2014: 18). Therefore this model of *appraisal* responds to a development of a social intersubjective perspective on evaluation, and proposes a complementary view of interpersonal meanings beyond grammar and its clause rank interpersonal systems, such as MOOD and MODALITY (see Andersen, this volume).

The *appraisal* framework organises evaluation in three main semantic systems or domains: ENGAGEMENT, ATTITUDE and GRADUATION. This multidimensional framework presents a systematic organisation of 'the semantic resources used to negotiate emotions, judgements and valuation, alongside resources for amplifying and engaging with these evaluations' (Martin 2000: 145). The linguistic analysis is particularly concerned with how evaluation is expressed both implicitly and explicitly, creating valorative prosodies in the discourse that can be codified at a lexicogrammatical level in a wide range of resources. The three semantic systems that organise the *appraisal* framework are presented in the subsequent sections.

System of ATTITUDE

ATTITUDE relates to the ways in which feelings are seen as a system of meanings. According to Martin and White (2005: 42), this system has three semantic areas: emotions (AFFECT), which deal with the expression of positive and negative feelings; ethics (JUDGEMENT), which is concerned with attitudes toward behaviour (to admire or to criticise, to praise or to condemn); and aesthetics (APPRECIATION), which involves evaluations of semiotic and natural phenomena according to the ways in which they are valued or not in a given field. The three systems encode feeling, but AFFECT can be seen as the basic system and the other two as feelings institutionalised as proposals and feelings institutionalised as propositions, respectively. In other words:

JUDGEMENT and APPRECIATION might be interpreted as institutionalizations of AFFECT which have evolved to socialize individuals into various uncommon sense communities of feeling – JUDGEMENT as AFFECT recontextualized to control behaviour (what we should and should not do), APPRECIATION as AFFECT recontextualized to manage taste (what things are worth).

Martin 2003: 173–4

This idea is illustrated in Figure 28.2.

Martin and White (2005) propose that the region of meanings of AFFECT – that is, the semantic resources for construing emotions – can be organised by means of a typology of six variables.

1   Feelings can be positive or negative, following the notion that feelings in general are constructed by the culture as positive or negative experiences:

positive: *the girl was **happy***
negative: *the girl was **sad***

2   Feelings might be realised as 'a surge of emotion involving some kind of embodied paralinguistic or extralinguistic manifestation, or more internally experienced as a kind of emotive state or ongoing mental process' (Martin and White 2005: 47). This distinction between an extralinguistic manifestation and an internal experience is constructed by the grammar as:

behavioural process: *the boy **cried***
mental process: *the boy **disliked** the surprise*
relational process: *the boy **felt sad***

3   Feelings can be constructed as directed at, or reacting to, some specific emotional trigger or as a general ongoing mood. This distinction can be codified by the grammar as the opposition between mental processes and relational states:

reaction to other: *the boy **liked** the teacher* (mental process)
undirected mood: *the boy **was happy*** (relational state)

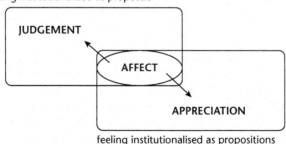

Figure 28.2 JUDGEMENT and APPRECIATION as institutionalised AFFECT

Source: Martin and White (2005: 45)

4   Feelings can be also graded on a scale of intensity – towards a lower- or higher-valued end:

low: *the girl **liked** the surprise*
median: *the girl **loved** the surprise*
high: *the girl **adored** the surprise*

5   Feelings can involve intention, rather than reaction, in relation to a stimulus that is *irrealis* rather than *realis*. This implies making the distinction between feelings that relate to future or unrealised states and feelings that relate to present existing ones. This distinction is realised grammatically with emotive and desiderative mental processes, respectively:

realis: *the girl **liked** the surprise*
irrealis: *the girl **wanted** the surprise*

6   The last variable of this typology of AFFECT groups emotions into the three major subcategories that can be positive or negative – un/happiness, in/security and dis/satisfaction:

in/security: *the boy was **anxious/confident***
dis/satisfaction: *the boy was **fed up/absorbed***
un/happiness: *the boy was **sad/happy***

The expression of AFFECT can be also codified by means of a grammatical metaphor (Halliday and Matthiessen 2004), which includes nominalised realisations of qualities (*joy, sadness, sorrow*) and processes (*grief, sobs*).

The systems of AFFECT, JUDGEMENT and APPRECIATION not only follow the distinction between positive and negative polarity, but also can be classified as direct or implied appraisals. This latter distinction is treated in the *appraisal* model as inscribed and evoked appraisal (*tokens*). An *inscribed* appraisal is explicitly expressed in the text, and is associated with specific lexical items and their graduation, whereas an *evoked* appraisal is manifested in an implicit manner by reference, for example, to a metaphorical language that can provoke a particular valorative meaning. Martin (2000: 155) explains:

[As] far as reading affect is concerned, inscribed affect is more prescriptive about the reading position naturalized – it is harder to resist or ignore; evoked affect on the other hand is more open – accommodating a wider range of reading positions, including readings that may work against the response otherwise naturalized by the text.

The semantic domain of JUDGEMENT, as already mentioned, can be seen as the institutionalisation of feelings in terms of proposals or norms about how people should and should not behave. This subsystem also has a positive and negative dimension, and can be inscribed or evoked in the discourse. Martin and White (2005), following media research made by Iedema et al. (1994), propose a subdivision of JUDGEMENT into two major groups: Social Esteem (values of normality, capacity and tenacity) and Social Sanction (values of veracity and propriety). *Social Esteem* involves admiration and criticism, whereas *Social Sanction* involves praise and condemnation.

The following are some examples of this semantic region of JUDGEMENT, although it is crucial to take into consideration that what counts as appraisal depends on the field of discourse.

Social Esteem:
Normality (how special someone is): *he is **fashionable**/he is **dated***
Capacity (how capable someone is): *she is an **expert**/she is **inexpert***
Tenacity (how resolute someone is): *he is **tireless**/he is **weak***

Social Sanction:
Veracity (how truthful someone is): *he is **honest**/he is **dishonest***
Propriety (how ethical someone is): *she is **humble**/she is **arrogant***

Finally, the subsystem of APPRECIATION, which can be understood as the institutionalisation of feelings in terms of propositions, deals with norms about how products, performances and naturally occurring phenomena are valued (Martin and White 2005). The three variables that authors identified in this semantic domain are related to Halliday's transitivity mental processes of affection, perception and cognition. Therefore APPRECIATION can be divided into our reactions to things (do they catch our attention? do they please us?), their composition (balance and complexity) and their value (was it worthwhile?) (Martin and White 2005: 56). In other words, the appreciation framework 'might be interpreted metafunctionally – with reaction oriented to interpersonal significance, composition to textual organization and valuation to ideational worth' (Martin and White 2005: 57).

Some examples that illustrate these categories are as follows.

Reactions (affection): *The movie was **captivating**/The movie was **boring***
*The movie was **lovely**/The movie was **plain***
Composition (perception): *The argument was **consistent**/The argument was **contradictory***
Valuation (cognition): *The movie was **creative**/The movie was **prosaic***

System of GRADUATION

The subsystem of GRADUATION has to do with the fact that the value of attitudes can be raised or lowered in the discourse. It is possible to intensify or diminish our meanings (Force), or we can 'sharpen' or 'soften' the boundaries of categorical meanings of an experiential phenomenon or attitudinal value (Focus), using words like 'sort of' or 'kind of' and 'real' or 'genuine'. *Focus* deals with non-gradable resources to express graduation and it 'has the effect of adjusting the strength of boundary between categories, constructing core and peripheral types of things (cf. Channel 1994)' (Martin 2003: 175), for example to sharpen the experiential meaning as in *a real policeman* or *exactly four*, or to soften the experiential meaning as in *a policeman kind of, about five* (Martin et al. 2013). This system is expanded later in the chapter by a proposal made by Hood (2010), particularly regarding GRADUATION in relation to experiential meaning, in which items that by themselves are not evaluative, but become evaluative because of the action of graduating words. A proposal can be intensified by, for example, resources of modulation: *it should be taken into account, it needs to be taken into account* and *it absolutely must be taken into account.* GRADUATION and inscribed evaluations should first be specified precisely when doing appraisal analysis, then it is important to explore how these instances irradiate certain evaluation to the rest of the text, infusing negative or positive evaluation in a cumulative manner.

System of ENGAGEMENT

The semantic system of ENGAGEMENT deals with the interpersonal negotiation of the sources of attitudes; it responds to a social dialogic perspective developed by White (2000, 2003). This system allows us to analyse the source or origin of attitudes, identifying discourse as more monoglossic or heteroglossic in orientation (Martin and White 2005, in part inspired by Bakhtin/Voloshinov's work), depending on whether or not and how authors recognise alternative positions in the discourse in relation to their own monoglossic or heteroglossic construals. White (2000, 2003) developed a social dialogic perspective that took resources such as projection, modality, polarity, concession and comment adverbials that 'position one opinion in relation to another – by quoting or reporting, acknowledging a possibility, denying, countering, affirming and so on' (Martin 2003: 174). This system theorises the degrees of heteroglossic space of a proposition that are more or less open in the discourse (opening up alternatives or expanding, or shutting them down or contracting), thus making it possible to determine the speaker's degree of commitment in relation to the appraisal that has been expressed (White 2003; Martin and White 2005).

Finally, when undertaking appraisal analysis, as Martin (2000) emphasises, it is crucial that appraisal analysts declare their reading positions, since evaluations are always influenced by the institutional position from which one is reading.

The general outline of the appraisal system is illustrated in Figure 28.3.

Elaboration of appraisal in different genres and approaches

This section and the next include a presentation of the critical issues that researchers have encountered when working in diverse languages, experiential fields and genres that claim different categories and the adjustment of the semantic systems of the model. The last reports on new directions and elaborations of research conducted from a corpus linguistic perspective, appraisal in academic writing and the growing area of multimodal discourse analysis in conjunction with appraisal, which explores how attitude is constructed from an inter-semiotic view point. More research has been done in other areas that is not possible to present here owing to space constraints.

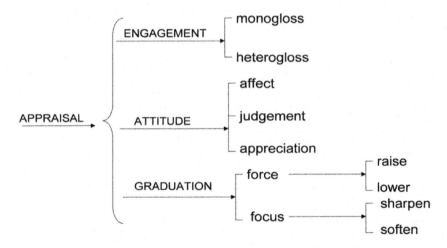

Figure 28.3 Appraisal framework: basic semantic systems

According to Bednarek (2008, 2009) who has completed comprehensive corpus linguistic work on language patterns of ATTITUDE in different registers, including news and academic discourses, corpus linguistic analysis can provide evidence regarding two different aspects of appraisal that need to be considered and which have been overlooked in the framework: the kinds of attitudinal lexis that are used and the kinds of attitudinal targets or types of attitudinal assessment (the entity that is evaluated). Although Martin (2003) has pointed out that an automatised computer-based model has some limitations for analysing evaluative language, especially if we take into consideration the problem of implied evaluation, he recognises – as do many other discourse analysts who work mainly from a qualitative approach – that corpus linguistics analysis of evaluation can contribute to systematising this area of interpersonal meanings and that it has also demonstrated, for instance, how certain grammatical patterns work in discourse.

Work on evaluation from a corpus linguistics perspective (Hunston and Thompson 2000, 2011; Taboada and Grieve 2004; Coffin and O'Halloran 2006; Bednarek 2008, 2009) considers corpora as a research tool. Hunston and Sinclair (2000), for instance, consider that there are particular grammatical patterns that select, and therefore identify, evaluative lexical items, such as evaluative adjectives. Accordingly, Bednarek (2008) emphasises the fact that Martin and White (2005: 260) consider it necessary to complement their qualitative work on evaluation with a more quantitative approach that can 'focus on fewer variables across a corpus of texts'. In her book *Emotion Talk*, Bednarek (2008) takes up the challenge, discussing some aspects of how the appraisal framework maps feelings and deals with them from the perspective of a corpus linguistics and cognitive linguistics.

One of the main contributions that Bednarek offers with her corpus-linguistics exploration of appraisal is the category of COVERT AFFECT, which can be seen as an intermediate category between opinion (APPRECIATION and JUDGEMENT) and emotion (AFFECT). Consequently, Bednarek (2009) postulates that the subcategory of AFFECT should be further divided into OVERT AFFECT and COVERT AFFECT to provide a better account of the emotional responses of Emoters – such as *it makes me feel happy that they've come* or *the people are impatient for a change* – and the resources of indirectly denoting an emotional response or less personalising ones – as in *I find it frustrating* or *this is very distressing for Carol*.

In general terms, after exploring several patterns proposed by Martin and White (2005), Bednarek (2009) concludes that they only partly work to identify specific types of ATTITUDE lexis and that AFFECT PATTERNS seems to be the most promising for conducting an automatic identification of subcategories of ATTITUDE lexis. She offers useful findings in her corpus linguistics work that open new possibilities of study and support some of the findings from qualitative research with small corpuses.

In the area of academic writing in English, especially in research articles, Hood (2010: 2) explores the apparent contradiction of being encouraged as writers on the one hand 'towards objectivity and on the other a requirement to engage critically'. She further develops the graduation categories of Force and Focus to explore the range of discourse strategies by which attitudinal meanings could be graduated by writers to foster a particular reading that tends to subjectify phenomena in a manner that aligns with the writer's view of them. Hood (2010) found that, in academic discourses, attitude tends to be invoked through resources of GRADUATION, enabling writers to subjectify objective meanings. To identify the value invoked, the reader should look beyond the graduated instance to the co-text and the field to determine the *valeur* assigned. Hood states that some resources of Focus enable GRADUATION as degrees of authenticity (*real, truly, pseudo*) and specificity (*general, particularly*), which may have a negative or positive *valeur* depending on the rest of the meaning of the co-text.

In addition, she points out that the categorical boundaries around processes can be softened by encoding lack of completion or actualisation (*tried to show, possible shows*).

Hood (2010) also found that, in academic discourses, attitude is expressed mainly as a nominalised quality, although processes that are infused with attitudinal meaning can also manifest it. Hood's network of GRADUATION as FORCE and FOCUS, as illustrated in Figure 28.4, offers an expansive array of choices that were present in the introductions to the academic articles she analysed. These choices, as Hood (2010) points out, allow authors to flag attitudinal readings rather than express attitude explicitly.

In working with narratives and student's written responses, Macken-Horarik and Isaac (2014) explore the challenge of working in pedagogical contexts with the cumulative and context-sensitive nature of evaluation. They point out that teachers can get frustrated with the 'different interpretations of the many borderline cases' that they encounter when doing appraisal analysis, and therefore Macken-Horarik and Isaac (2014: 67) propose 'a cline of implicitness that relates degrees of reliability to instances of evaluation depending on their textual and/or cultural/institutional environments'. The authors emphasise the high sensitivity to social contexts of evaluative utterances and the fact that, when dealing with narratives, we not only have one source of evaluation, but rather the play of several voices across texts, so that the analysis of the resources of ENGAGEMENT is crucial for understanding the dialogic nature of these texts.

Macken-Horarik and Isaac (2014) raise three important issues, or challenges, regarding the appraisal framework. First is the difficulty of analysing both implicit and explicit evaluation in narrative texts, especially because invoked attitude is crucial in these types of text, as it is also in other literary genres. The second challenge relates to the different orders of evaluation. This implies taking into consideration both local expressions of attitude (unfolding of choices in a text as we read) and also the global patterns of evaluation (weight of evaluative choices from a synoptic perspective), which in turn guide the analyst to better understand how to code the local ones. The third challenge is associated with the culture- and institution-specific nature of evaluation. Because evaluation is a profoundly culturally sensitive business, Macken-Horarik and Isaac (2014: 85) have found it difficult to apply a general system to a register-specific domain, because, as many other researchers have pointed out, 'the system does not give us everything we need'. Macken-Horarik and Isaac

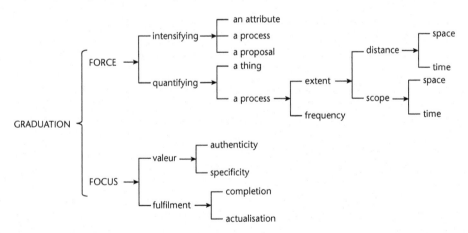

Figure 28.4 SYSTEM of GRADUATION as FORCE and FOCUS

Source: Hood (2010: 105)

propose a methodology for appraisal analysis that stresses, among other steps, the mapping of syndromes of choices in one part of the text against other parts or stages, signalling cases of double- or triple-coding (or coupling between systems), taking into consideration local appraisal choices and also global patterns in which these local choices participate. They suggest working with a cline of implicitness in different environments of appraisal that goes from the most explicit to the most implicit choices of word, wording, phrase, text patterns, culture (with culture being the most implicit in the cline).

Another recent and productive area of working with appraisal resources has been the multimodal approach to discourse analysis and the growing dimension of systemic functional semiotics as a pedagogic tool for multimodal literacy pedagogy. The development of multimodality from an SFL approach can be traced back to the influential book written by Kress and van Leeuwen (2006 [1996]) entitled *Reading Images: A Grammar of Visual Design* (see also Taylor, this volume). Moreover, although the present chapter does not focus on multimodality, it is important to acknowledge the work that has been done by Economou (2014) on adapting some aspects of the subsystem of ATTITUDE to news' analysis and the significant work by Painter et al. (2013) on image analysis of children's picture books – especially in relation to visual focalisation and to intermodal complementarity from a critical multimodal perspective on image–language relations between picture books as animated films (Unsworth 2013, 2014; Thomas 2014). All of this work has been greatly motivated by the necessity of developing multimodal literacy pedagogy from the initial states of primary education in Australia. This work on evaluative meaning and its possibilities of being constructed at least in a bimodal way (verbiage and image) has also permeated critical multimodal discourse analysis on news and popular culture (Economou 2014).

Applications and elaborations of appraisal in languages other than English

Since the publication of Martin and White's (2005) *Appraisal in English*, many scholars have been interested in developing and extending the *appraisal* system to other languages with the purpose of working on discourse analysis and in educational linguistics (Achugar 2008; Vian 2008, 2009; Kaplan 2009; Ngo and Unsworth 2011; Oteíza and Pinuer 2012, 2013; Ngo 2013, to name but a few). In this section, we will present briefly (because of space constraints) only some of these contributions, in Brazilian Portuguese, Spanish and Vietnamese, knowing that more research has been done in this area.

In Brazilian Portuguese, Vian (2008, 2009) has worked from the perspective of the typology of language discussing lexicogrammatical realisations of evaluative instances. Vian takes up the invitation made by Martin and White (2005), who emphasise that the appraisal system may be expanded and taken further, being applied to other contexts.

Vian (2008, 2009) explores the realisation of semantic and lexicogrammatical resources of GRADUATION in a Brazilian Portuguese narrative corpus, and his findings show that the majority of the resources of GRADUATION proposed by Martin and White (2005) in the *appraisal* system can be applied to Portuguese. Vian offers some examples to show other resources that work for Portuguese – and for Spanish, we might add – which are not included in English, such as the nominal group order, the use of several Greek and Latin prefixes, some use of suffixes, use of diminutive suffixes, among others. To illustrate some of these resources, Vian takes, for example, the use of Greek and Latin prefixes that can be employed to intensify the evaluation according to the item that comes after them, as Vian (2008: 815) exemplifies in example (1):

(1) *Já estava **ultra**ligado no reporter . . .*
('He was already **ultra**-attentive to the reporter')

This can also occur with suffixes that can intensify the characteristic of a noun if the augmentative suffix *ão* is added (Vian 2008: 815), as in example (2):

(2) *Eu tinha perdido um temp**ão***
('I had spent **a lot of** time')

Some diminutive suffixes added to certain lexical items can also work to reduce the evaluative force, thus creating meaning of degrading or depreciating in Brazilian Portuguese, as in example (3), or adding an affectionate or tender meaning to a word, as in example (4):

(3) *esses caras fazendo piad**inhas***
('these guys making **silly** jokes')

(4) *começar una vida nova numa cidadez**inha***
('start a new life in a **little** town')

For Vietnamese, Ngo and Unsworth (2011) and Ngo (2013) have demonstrated that the linguistic resources for communicating one's evaluative stances differ significantly from English. Ngo and Unsworth (2011) identify many resources that Vietnamese has for expressing evaluative meanings other than the appraisal resources proposed by Martin and White (2005) for English, such as the inclusion of particles, predicative element-logical passive expressions and classifiers for expressing attitude, and reduplication for GRADUATION. However, as Ngo and Unsworth (2011) highlight, the system of person reference is one of the most commonly used language resources to express stance in Vietnamese.

The system of person reference is inherited from class-structured ideologies of colonial Vietnam and the cultural influence of Chinese civilisation in this country. Therefore, in this lineal organisation of the Vietnamese family, people should behave in accordance to their roles. Ngo and Unsworth (2011) present several resources of this system of person reference, and show how certain words can imply meanings of attitude when used and when not used in certain contexts, and according to the social role and age of the person. For instance, in Vietnamese, the kinship term *bà* ('grandmother') is appropriate when a grandmother is addressing her grandchild – but not using this term can be understood as a negative expression of AFFECT, because it means that the grandmother is denying the blood relationship with her grandchild – or, for example, a young man can use the kinship term *ông* ('grandfather') as a signal of arrogance or superiority over another person. Proper nouns (that is, people's names) are also an important part of the system of person reference in Vietnamese. For example, some middle names are common for males (*Van*) and for females (*Thi*), but for instance, the use of *Thi* by itself 'can be used as a personal pronoun, meaning of "she", but provoking a negative judgement of the woman's capacity as well as propriety' (Ngo and Unsworth 2011: 9). In sum, Ngo and Unsworth (2011) show that the Vietnamese person reference system has the function of evaluating AFFECT and JUDGEMENT, since kinship and status terms can be used to indicate positive or negative affect, and the use of personal pronouns in determinate contexts are signals of evaluation of affection or a judgement of social sanction and social esteem.

For Spanish, several researchers have worked with the appraisal framework to explore different discursive areas, such as: the construction of memories and human rights violations from periods of dictatorships in Latin America in Uruguay and Chile (Achugar 2008; Achugar and Oteíza 2009; Oteíza 2009; Oteíza and Pinuer 2012, 2013, among others); armed conflicts and its representation in the news and political discourses in Venezuela (Bolívar 2007; Kaplan 2009); and the construction of ethnic and language identity (Achugar and Oteíza 2009; Oteíza and Merino 2012).

Oteíza and Pinuer (2013) offer an elaboration of the subsystem of Force in the semantic system of GRADUATION proposed by Hood and Martin (2007) and Hood (2010) to deal adequately with the symbolic representation of time in historical discourses. They also propose the categories of Power, Conflict, Valuation and Propriety as an elaboration of the system network of the semantic domain of APPRECIATION that facilitates taking into account in a more specific manner the appraisal analysis of events, situations and historical processes that characterise discourses in the social sciences (Oteíza and Pinuer 2012). The system of APPRECIATION was initially designed to analyse semiotic products, performances and natural phenomena; however, when dealing with historical processes – especially the categories of Balance and Composition proposed by Martin and White (2005) – it did not adequately apply to the discursive nature of social, historical and cultural phenomena, among others.

The category of *Conflict* deals with the characterisation of societies by means of the different forms of social conflicts that are constructed in historical discourses in a very broad manner, such as tension, opposition and contradiction among values, social relations or many others. The category of historical *Conflict* implies the manifestation of a social, political and/or economic conflict that can be expressed with different grades of radicalism as a cline.

The category of *Power*, which works closely with the semantic category of *Conflict* and also as a cline, is associated with the action and influence of powerful and dominant groups, although power relations are a common component of our societies in general. Social power can be understood as the control that a group or an organisation holds over the actions and decision-making capacity of another group, limiting that group's freedom of action and influencing its knowledge, attitudes or ideologies.

Propriety refers to moral or legal evaluations and follows, in general terms, the orientation of Martin and White (2005) to evaluate human behaviour; however, in this formulation, it is a category that applies to historical processes, events and situations.

Finally, the category of *Valuation* refers to a semantic dimension that is considered in the system of APPRECIATION by Martin and White (2005), although in Oteíza and Pinuer's (2012) design, it has the meaning of the importance and social value that authors attribute to historical events, processes or situations in the discourse.

It is crucial to highlight that these four categories work in a combined form as inscribed or evoked evaluations with which authors build discursive strategies of *historical legitimation* or *historical de-legitimation* in their discourses.

Applications and future directions

The *appraisal* framework is a powerful tool for engaging with discourse analysis because of the possibilities that it offers with regard to the systematisation of interpersonal meanings and the ways in which the negotiation of solidarity between writers and readers legitimate certain positions and social values over others. However, because this model was initially created in the context of educational linguistics and literacy intervention in Australian schools, as previously mentioned, the analytical potential of its application to other fields of study and languages other than English requires careful evaluation. In fact, Martin and White (2005) have emphasised the flexibility of the model and the impossibility of applying it mechanically, especially when working with other languages. Nevertheless, since this model offers an opportunity to examine other fields and languages based on the strong theoretical foundation of SFL, many researchers have seen in this framework a solid and comprehensive analytical tool that has guided their work and suggested new challenges when looking at the manifestation of intersubjectivity in the discourse.

As has been demonstrated in this chapter, exploring appraisal in discourse is a complex endeavour – especially when considering that the patterns of evaluation are built in a prosodic and cumulative manner in texts, and that they can be realised in an inscribed or evoked manner by means of an ample variety of grammatical and lexical realisations. In conducting this analysis, it is worthwhile exploring the computer-based tools for organising data that are currently available for conducting a qualitative and quantitive *appraisal* analysis, such as the UAM Corpus Tool (2.8/3.0) created by Mick O'Donell or the AppAnn system designed by Alhumaidi (2013) to visualise long-range text evaluative patterns. Nonetheless, authors do point out that the use of corpus tools always requires a stage of manual analysis.

Appraisals are made by subjects that are immersed in a social and cultural context who use the potentially evaluative meanings that are available for them and which are realised lexicogrammatically. All of the meanings are realised as dialogic and ideological choices, because 'as language users we make some choices instead of others based on social relations, on the social roles performed in a given context and on the relationship with other interlocutors' (Vian 2008: 821). This 'dialogic soul' enacted by languages, as Martin (2003) highlights, can be seen as an invitation to continue doing research in different knowledge areas, semiotic modes, languages and cultures to contribute to our understanding of our communities and the ways by which we, as social subjects, legitimise and delegitimise specific value systems, and share feelings and opinions with others to build empathy and solidarity.

Notes

1 A note of gratitude for the valuable feedback offered by the editors of this volume.
2 The notion of 'prosody' was taken by Halliday from Firth, who used this term in the level of phonology to signal non-segmental features. This concept was extended in SFL theory to the levels of grammar and discourse semantics. Martin and White (2005) distinguish different patterns of prosody: domination, intensification and saturation.
3 Martin (2000) acknowledges the work that was done in the context of this research project by Caroline Coffin, Susan Feez, Sally Humphrey, Rick Iedema, Henrike Korner, David McInnes, David Rose, Joan Rothery, Maree Stenglin, Robert Veel and Peter White (the Write it Right research team). Martin stresses that, in particular, Joan Rothery and Peter White constructed 'a great deal of the framework' of APPRECIATION and JUDGEMENT, respectively. Later, Martin (2014) acknowledges 'relevant publication' and 'contributions' made by Gillian Fuller on ENGAGEMENT and by Sue Hood on GRADUATION.
4 Based on the work of Labov and Waletzky (1967) on oral narrative analysis and Sinclair and Coulthard (1975) on classroom interaction.

References

Achugar, M. 2008. *What We Remember: The Construction of Military Memory*. Amsterdam and Philadelphia, PA: John Benjamins.

Achugar, M., and T. Oteíza. 2009. 'In whatever language people feel comfortable': Conflicting language ideologies in the U.S. Southwest border. *Text & Talk* 29(4): 371–91.

Alhumaidi, B. 2013. Visualizing patterns of appraisal in text and corpora. *Text & Talk* 33(4–5): 691–723.

Bednarek, M. 2008. *Emotion Talk across Corpora*. Basingstoke and New York: Palgrave MacMillan.

Bednarek, M. 2009. Language patterns and ATTITUDE. *Functions of Language* 16(2): 165–92.

Bolívar, A. (ed.). 2007. *Análisis del discurso. ¿Por qué y para qué?* Caracas: CEC.

Coffin, C., and K. O'Halloran. 2006. The role of appraisal and corpora in detecting covert evaluation. *Functions of Language* 13(1): 77–110.

Economou, D. 2014. Telling a different story: Stance in verbal-visual displys in the news. In E. Djonov and S. Zhao (eds) *Critical Multimodal Studies of Popular Discourse*. New York and London: Routledge, pp. 181–201.

Halliday, M.A.K. 1978. *Language as a Social Semiotic: The Social Interpretation of Language and Meaning*. London: Arnold.

Halliday, M.A.K., and C.M.I.M. Matthiessen. 2004. *An Introduction to Functional Grammar*. 3rd edn. London: Arnold.

Hood, S. 2010. *Appraising Research: Evaluation in Academic Writing*. New York: Palgrave Macmillan.

Hood, S., and J.R. Martin. 2007. Invoking attitude: The play of graduation in appraising discourse. In R. Hasan, C.M.I.M. Matthiessen and J.J. Webster (eds) *Continuing Discourse on Language: A Functional Perspective, Vol. 2*. London: Equinox, pp. 739–64.

Hunston, S., and J. Sinclair. 2000. A local grammar of evaluation. In S. Hunston and G. Thompson (eds) *Evaluation in Text*. Oxford: Oxford University Press, pp. 74–101.

Hunston, S., and G. Thompson (eds). 2000. *Evaluation in Text*. Oxford: Oxford University Press.

Hunston, S., and G. Thompson (eds). 2011. *Corpus Approaches to Evaluation: Phraseology and Evaluative Language*. New York: Routledge.

Iedema, R., S. Feez and P. White. 1994. *Media Literacy*. Sydney: Disadvantaged School Program, NSW Department of School Education.

Kaplan, N. 2009. 'Héroes, villanos y víctimas': La construcción discursiva de personajesen las noticias televisivas sobre eventos conflictivos. In M. Shiro, P. Bentivoglio and F. Erlich (eds) *Haciendo discurso. Homenaje a Adriana Bolívar*. Caracas: Universidad Central de Venezuela, pp. 451–66.

Kress, G., and T. van Leeuwen. 2006 [1996]. *Reading Images: A Grammar of Visual Design*. London: Routledge.

Labov, W., and J. Waletzky. 1967. Narrative analysis: Oral versions of personal expereriences. In J. Helm (ed.) *Essays on the Verbal and Visual Arts: American Ethonological Society, Proceedings of Spring Meeting 1966*. Washington DC: University of Washington Press, pp. 12–14.

Lemke, J. 1995. *Textual Politics: Discourse and Social Dynamics*. London: Taylor & Francis.

Macken-Horarik, M., and A. Isaac. 2014. Appraising appraisal. In G. Thompson and L. Alba-Juez (eds) *Evaluation in Context*. Amsterdam: John Benjamins, pp. 67–92.

Martin, J.R. 1992. *English Text: System and Structure*. Amsterdam: John Benjamins.

Martin, J.R. 2000. Beyond exchange: Appraisal systems in English. In S. Hunston and G. Thompson (eds) *Evaluation in Text*. Oxford: Oxford University Press, pp. 142–75.

Martin, J.R. 2003. Introduction. *Text* 23(2): 171–81.

Martin, J.R. 2014. Evolving systemic functional linguistics: Beyond the clause. *Functional Linguistics* 1(3): 1–24.

Martin, J.R., and D. Rose. 2007. *Working with Discourse: Meaning beyond the Clause*. London: Continuum.

Martin, J.R., and D. Rose. 2008. *Genre Relations: Mapping Culture*. London: Equinox.

Martin, J.R., and P. White. 2005. *The Language of Evaluation: Appraisal in English*. New York: Palgrave Macmillan.

Martin, J.R., M. Zappavigna, P. Dwyer and C. Cleirigh. 2013. Users in uses of language: Embodied identity in youth justice conferencing. *Text & Talk* 33(4–5): 467–96.

Ngo, T. 2013. The deployment of the language of evaluation in English and Vietnamese spoken discourse. Unpublished PhD thesis. University of New England, Armidale, NSW.

Ngo, T., and L. Unsworth. 2011. Vietnamese person reference system as an appraisal resource. In T. Lê and Q. Lê (eds) *Linguistic Diversity and Cultural Identity: A Global Perspective*. New York: Nova Science, pp. 185–206.

Oteíza, T. 2009. Evaluative patterns in the official discourse of human rights in Chile: Giving value to the past and building historical memories in society. *DELTA* 25: 609–40.

Oteíza, T., and M.E. Merino. 2012. Am I a genuine Mapuche? Tensions and contradictions in the construction of ethnic identity in Mapuche adolescents from Temuco and Santiago. *Discourse & Society* 23(3): 297–317.

Oteíza, T., and C. Pinuer. 2012. Prosodia valorativa: construcción de eventos y procesos en el discurso de la historia. *Discurso y Sociedad* 6(2): 418–46.

Oteíza, T., and C. Pinuer. 2013. Valorative prosody and the symbolic construction of time in historical recent national discourses. *Discourse Studies* 15(1): 43–64.

Painter, C., J.R. Martin and L. Unsworth. 2013. *Reading Visual Narratives: Image Analysis of Children's Picture Books*. London: Equinox.

Sinclair, J., and R. Coulthard. 1975. *Towards an Analysis of Discourse*. Oxford: Oxford University Press.

Taboada, M., and J. Grieve. 2004. *Analysing Appraisal Automatically: Exploring Attitude and Affect in Text – Theories and Applications*. Stanford, CA: American Association for Artificial Intelligence.

Thomas, A. 2014. Points of difference: Intermodal complementarity and social critical literacy in children's multimodal texts. In E. Djonov and S. Zhao (eds) *Critical Multimodal Studies of Popular Discourse*. New York and London: Routledge, pp. 217–31.

Thompson, G., and S. Hunston. 2000. Evaluation: An introduction. In S. Hunston and G. Thompson (eds) *Evaluation in Text*. Oxford: Oxford University Press, pp. 1–27.

Unsworth, L. 2013. Re-configuring image–language relations and interpretative possibilities in picture books as animated movies: A site for developing multimodal literacy pedagogy. *Ilha do Desterro: A Journal of English Language, Literatures in English and Cultural Studies* 64: 15–47.

Unsworth, L. 2014. Point of view in picture books and animated film adaptations: Informing critical multimodal comprehension and composition pedagogy. In E. Djonov and S. Zhao (eds) *Critical Multimodal Studies of Popular Discourse*. New York and London: Routledge, pp. 202–16.

Vian, O. 2008. Appraisal system in Brazilian Portuguese: Resources for graduation. *Odense Working Papers in Language and Communication* 29: 825–9.

Vian, O. 2009. O Sistema de Avaliatividade e os recursos para Gradaçao em Língua Portuguesa: Questoes terminológicas e de instanciaçao. *DELTA* 25(1): 99–129.

White, P.R.R. 2000. The appraisal website. Available online at http://www.Grammatics.com/appraisal/.

White, P.R.R. 2003. Beyond modality and hedging: A dialogic view of the language of Intersubjective stance. *Text* 23(2): 259–84.

Systemic functional linguistics and genre studies

Sheena Gardner

Introduction

As children grow, their linguistic resources for meaning-making increase through engagement in an ever-increasing set of culturally appropriate practices – they learn to greet people, to follow instructions, to ask for things they want and to express feelings – and their language develops as a growing resource for meaning-making through interaction in social contexts. In many cultures, they engage with rhymes and songs and stories, and learn to differentiate them. With repeated exposure and social interaction, perhaps through a parent reading a story at bedtime or through regular storytime sessions at nursery, children learn to recognise certain language events as stories; they expect to be introduced to characters and a setting – whether this is three little pigs in a make-believe land, or Katie Morag on a Scottish island, or James in an apartment in Toronto. They expect something terrible to happen – their house to be destroyed by the big bad wolf, granny's tractor to break down or the subway train to stop in James' living room – and, through a series of events, they expect a resolution, so that life resumes, safely and happily. In building up these expectations of how stories develop, children are developing an understanding of the stages through which the 'story' genre unfolds, of the construals of characters and events expected at each stage, and of the language that realises them and the transitions between stages.

There is much disagreement among genre analysts about how best to define, identify and describe genres, but most would broadly agree that 'Genres are abstract, socially recognised ways of using language' (Hyland 2002: 114). They are abstract in the sense that one story does not make a story genre; we have to experience different stories and abstract from them the essence of what makes a (good) story. They are socially recognised and evidence for this often comes from the labels attached to them: *tell me 'a story'*. This is the language of non-linguists making meanings, compared to *give me a full sentence*, which is already the language of those who are looking academically at linguistic features. And they are realised through language. So cultural practices such as having a family meal will also be learned, but where the family sits, what they eat with and how does not necessarily involve language. Of course, there may be language associated with such practices, such as saying grace before a meal, language associated with serving food, appropriate conversation while eating, including ways of commenting on the food and ways of ending the meal. Such an unfolding of talk around a meal may or may not have a label, as 'story' does; then it becomes the work of genre analysts to record and analyse, and explore the possibility of mealtime genre(s), and propose abstract accounts.

Already we see the issues that can arise in the work of genre analysis: which stories should we look at? The most frequent? Popular? Valued? (By whom?) The most 'typical'? Does it have to be 'socially recognised' through an everyday term or can everyday terms sometimes be misleading? (Not every linguistic event labelled 'story' by non-linguists will unfold as outlined above.) Where do genres begin and end? (Does a conversation to choose a story before it is read, or an evaluation after it is finished, belong to the story genre or to a different oral storytelling genre?) And what is the best way in which to relate genre descriptions to the meanings that they construe and the language through which they are realised? And can we identify linguistic features that characterise the genres – that allow us, for example, to tell if a story told in the morning is from the same 'genre' as a different story usually told in the evening? Without linguistic evidence, we cannot identify genres (see Moore, this volume). To put it another way, how much of the language we produce can be described in genre terms? It is perhaps this last question that can best help us to understand different approaches to genre studies within systemic functional linguistics (SFL) and beyond.

This chapter continues with a brief account of the contributions of Halliday's linguistics, Hasan's work on generic structure potential and Martin's addition of a distinct level in the theory for genre analysis, after which it addresses issues associated with the scope of genre analysis and the purposeful nature of genres. The chapter goes on to outline the main contributions of genre analysis to educational linguistics, one of a number of domains in which it has been influential, and then presents research methods used in genre studies. Associated with genre analysis has been an explicit approach to genre pedagogy, which is presented in the chapter on SFL and language teaching (see McCabe, this volume). The present chapter concludes with future directions for genre studies.

Historical perspectives/definitions

SFL is informed both by anthropological insights – that is, that meanings are construed in social and cultural contexts – and by structuralist linguistic insights – that is, that meanings result from differences: 'A language is a resource for making meaning, and meaning resides in systemic patterns of choice' (Halliday and Matthiessen 2014: 23). Where an academic literacies approach to genres would focus on the cultural events and practices (for example Lillis 2008), and an English for specific purposes (ESP) approach to genre would focus on the functional moves and steps in genres as communicative events (for example Swales 1990), SFL focuses on the sociocultural and functional meanings, in cultural and textual contexts, as illustrated in Figure 29.1.

This Janus-like focus is arguably both the strength and weakness of SFL genre theory. In comparison to other approaches, 'Systemic Functional Linguistics (SFL), known in the United States as the "Sydney School", is perhaps the most clearly articulated approach to genre both theoretically and pedagogically, with its basis in Hallidayan functional linguistics' (Hyland 2007: 153).

Two distinguishing features of SFL genre studies are: (a) the detailed, functional linguistic architecture that SFL affords descriptions of the language of genres; and (b) the impact that SFL genre descriptions and pedagogy have had in educational settings from Australia

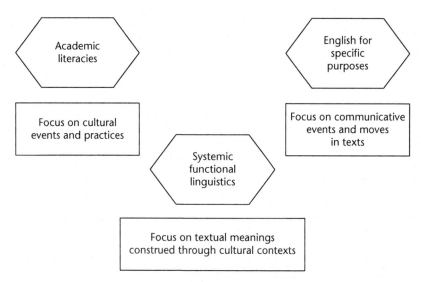

Figure 29.1 Three approaches to genre studies

to Europe, North America and Asia. The focus on functional systems of meanings of texts activated by their contexts of situation and of culture is not straightforward, however, and has resulted in a number of different models of genre and different approaches to genre analysis within SFL, associated with different linguists and different research projects.

Halliday's stratal relations and genre studies

Malinowski's influence shapes the SFL view of linguistics as the study of language 'in its semantic habitat' (Halliday and Matthiessen 2014: 32; Bartlett, this volume); 'The context of culture is what the members of a community can mean in cultural terms' (Halliday and Matthiessen 2014: 33). It is to be approached, practically, from the perspective of context of situation, in which situations, realised through field, tenor and mode, instantiate culture (see Bowcher, this volume):

> Field, tenor and mode variables are the basis for any attempt to develop a taxonomy of situations. At the same time, since text is language functioning in context, the field, tenor and mode variables are also the basis of any attempt to develop a taxonomy of texts operating in situations.
>
> *Halliday and Matthiessen 2014: 35*

Thus while Hallidayan linguistics is essential to descriptions of how genres are realised through contexts of situation in the lexicogrammar, genre is peripheral to Halliday's linguistics. For instance, the term 'genre' does not appear in the index of *The Essential Halliday* (Halliday 2009a). While *genre* is also not included in a list of key terms, it appears briefly under 'Context' (Halliday 2009b: 240). Here, genres and registers are mentioned as functional varieties that are activated contextually, where the context is a stratum 'above' (that is, realised by) the stratum of semantics (Halliday 2009b: 240; see Berry, this volume), as illustrated in Figure 29.2.

Context

→ Semantics

→ Lexicogrammar

Figure 29.2 Realisation relationships between strata

Although Halliday is arguably 'ambivalent about the role of genre in his model, and it is not part of his habitual metalanguage' (Flowerdew 2013: 150), he recognises the detailed work on generic structure potential and semantic patterns in contexts of situation by Hasan and colleagues, as well as the impact of the extensive work on educational genres by Martin and colleagues.

Hasan and generic structure potential

This is not the place to discuss Hasan's very detailed work on context of situation (see Bartlett and Bowcher, both this volume), but it is worth highlighting the code used to present the generic structure potential (GSP), or the formula that describes the 'total range of textual structures available within a genre' (Hasan 1996 [1984]: 53). The chapter on the 'Nursery tale as genre' shows how genre analysis of a corpus of texts progresses from analysis of the generic structure of individual texts to a description of generic structure potential in the corpus.

The basic unit of semantics is the text:

which is organised externally as a unit operating in context: the structure of the context of situation that a text operates in is . . . projected onto the text. . . . For example, in a situation of telling a traditional folk tale, the structure would be (from Hasan, 1984, but slightly simplified):

(Placement ^) Initiating Event^Sequence Event $^{1\text{-}n}$ ^ Final Event (^ Finale) ($^{\circ}$Moral)

. . . Each element, or stage, of the structure of the situation is realized by distinctive semantic patterns. These semantic patterns are realized by distinctive lexicogrammatical patterns.

Halliday and Matthiessen 2014: 43

This GSP of a nursery tale accounts for texts in which Placement, Finale and Moral are optional elements, as indicated by the parentheses (. . .) – and where Initiating Event, Sequence Event and Final Event are obligatory elements. The carat – that is (^) indicates the usual sequence of elements, $^{1\text{-}n}$ suggests that there can be any number of Sequence Events, and the superscript circle – that is, $^{\circ}$ – is used where the order of the elements (here, the Finale and the Moral) can be reversed. This is the basic code, with more details included in the original, such as angled brackets – that is, < . . . > – for discontinuous realisations.

Hasan (1996 [1984]) describes in detail how the Placement element is realised by the semantic features of person particularisation, impersonalisation and temporal distance, where temporal distance is realised by lexicogrammatical locative adjuncts with semantic feature 'far', such as *Once upon a time* or *Once*.

Martin and the genre level

From the 1980s, Martin argued that there should be a level of genre analysis associated with context of culture that is separate from a level of register analysis associated with context of situation and Field, Tenor and Mode, as summarised in Table 29.1.

While SFL maintained a focus on language as a resource for meaning-making – that is, on language as it is used naturally in whole texts – the analysis had tended to focus on the lower levels and to accommodate genre through register variables (see Moore, this volume); 'Halliday . . . treated genre as an aspect of mode; and Hasan . . . derived her obligatory elements of text structure from field and so appeared to handle genre relations there' (Martin and Rose 2008: 16). Two main arguments were central and the acceptance of an autonomous genre analysis was cemented in its uptake in the work on genres in educational linguistics.

Genre analysis as distinct from register analysis

First, treating genres as independent of registers entails that genres can vary independently of registers. The genre level can be described as 'system of staged goal-oriented social processes through which social subjects in a given culture live their lives' (Martin 1997: 13), whereby genres are integral to contexts of culture, in contrast to registers, which are integral to contexts of situation.

The relationship between genres and registers is one of realisation, and thus genre can also be defined as a 'staged goal-oriented process realised through register' (Martin 1992: 505).

There are, in fact, two key respects in which registers can vary independently of genre: the first is where there is register variation across different stages or phases of a genre text; the second is where there is register variation that reflects differences in Field, Tenor and Mode. Thus a children's story genre will be realised through stages the registers of which differ, starting with registers of 'placement' or orientation, continuing with registers of 'complication' and action sequences, each with their own lexicogrammatical realisations.

The realisation of registers through the linguistic systems allows the analyst not only to detail, but also to justify the linguistic choices in meaningful ways. For instance, because the first stage of a children's story gives us the setting and introduces the main characters, we expect descriptive language, usually realised through agentive participants, relational clauses and stative verbs. As events unfold, we expect more material processes to describe the action; in the final stage, we expect evaluative language. These stages can be recognised through the language whether the Field is pigs and houses, or a little boy and a subway train; they can be recognised whether the Tenor is mother to child, or narrator to reader; and they

Table 29.1 The genre level

Level	Focus
Phonology/Graphology	Phonemes/graphemes and syllables/words
Lexicogrammar	Clause
Discourse semantics	exchange or 'paragraph'
Register	stage in a transaction
Genre	whole texts
Ideology	discourses manifested across a range of texts

Source: Martin (1992: 496)

can be recognised whether the Mode is written or spoken, with or without visuals or actions. We will therefore follow Martin in his modelling of genre as a distinct level realised through register (see also Moore, this volume).

Genre as system

The second main argument, a corollary of the first, is that, with genre as a level of analysis, work could begin to identify systems of genres. This work is previewed in detail in Martin (1992) where, for example, he explores Plum's study that contrasts stages in the Narrative, Recount, Anecdote and Exemplum genres (Martin 1992: 565). System networks are proposed, such as +/– expectancy (events in Recounts follow an expected order, unlike in Narratives, where complications arise) and these reappear, refined, in later work on story genres (Martin and Rose 2008: 22).

A different example from university student writing would be +/– recommendations for future action, which differentiates Critique genres from Case Study genres (Nesi and Gardner 2012). Thus the main difference between Critique genres such as book reviews and business evaluations, where students assess the value or significance of an entity from their disciplinary perspective, and Case Study genres, such as patient or company reports, is that the latter include recommendations for future action, whereas the former do not. Evidence for these generic differences can also be seen in the multidimensional register analysis that shows that Critiques and Case Studies are very similar in most dimensions, but differ in that the language of Case Studies – notably, in the recommendation stages – is both more personal and more persuasive (Nesi and Gardner 2012: 47–9; Gardner 2012b).

The development of systems of genres has continued and works well in some areas, but has proved difficult to apply universally.

From a historical perspective, to sum up, genre was not central to Hallidayan linguistics. It was approached via register and generic structure potential by Hasan, whose work informed the framework of optional and obligatory elements that has been widely applied in genre analysis, and who approaches descriptions at the upper levels in terms of contextualisation networks (Hasan 2009: 181). This work, as she admits, has been challenging. In contrast, Martin views culture as systems of genres and, while building these system networks can also be challenging, his separation of levels of genre analysis and register analysis has proved to be the most applicable, or at least the most applied and therefore most influential of genre theories. These applications have been primarily, although by no means exclusively (for example Christie and Martin 1997), in the area of educational linguistics.

Critical issues and topics

Three critical issues in genre studies are now considered.

Less regulated texts

One criticism of genre analysis that may be encountered is that it works well for regulated language contexts, such as educational or legal contexts, or routines such as bedtime stories or buying something in a shop, but it is more difficult to use in contexts in which clear stages in text development are not evident. There is much text analysis that makes no reference to genres and this may be because the genres have not (yet) stabilised (see Bartlett, this volume), or because the effort required to identify and describe genres in some contexts may outweigh the benefits and a focus on register or discourse semantics seems more rewarding. In theory, however, genre analysis should be possible and has proved insightful even in what may initially seem like the most unregulated talk – that is, casual conversation. The key work here is Eggins and Slade (1997), which is also exemplary in its detailed demonstration of a multilevel analysis of spoken texts.

The abstract notion of culture as a system of genres is appealing and sets a research agenda of genre description for decades to come. It is reminiscent of Bloomfield's contention that all language is produced in response to a stimulus and it is only the lack of development in science that prevents us from understanding the detail.

Purpose and stages

Just as the stages of a genre reflect different contexts, so too 'the purpose' and 'goal orientation' of a genre may be conceived in different ways by different users. Telling children's stories may have the purpose of transmitting culture or of putting a child to sleep, and so here again a definition for teachers runs the risk of being fossilised rather than reflecting the context at hand. Purpose has been described as 'what a speaker is trying to accomplish' (Martin 2008 [1984]: 10). It can be glossed in tables such as Table 29.2.

Where the purpose of anecdote relates well to why someone might tell an anecdote, the purpose of narrative relates to the structure – the essential 'complication' stage – and would need to be further unpacked to fit with a more general purpose of stories, such as to 'explore the human condition through storying' (Derewianka 2003: 137). These shifting wordings of genre 'purpose' reflect the responsiveness of genre analysis to different levels, contexts and degrees of delicacy in description; they also raise questions about necessary and sufficient characteristics of genres – for example if a text has the stages of a narrative, is it a narrative, even if its social purpose is very different? A story might be used to teach science, for instance, with its own distinctive purpose and its own unfolding realised in a scientific educational register. Equally, if a text has the purpose of exploring the human condition, but does not follow the narrative stages, is it a narrative? Probably not, because we would not expect the linguistic evidence to support the analysis. This suggests that

Table 29.2 Story genres in the school curriculum

Story genres	Purpose	Stages
recount	recounting events	Orientation Record of events
narrative	resolving a complication	Orientation Complication Evaluation Resolution
exemplum	judging character or behaviour	Orientation Incident Interpretation
anecdote	sharing an emotional reaction	Orientation Remarkable event Reaction

Source: Adapted from Rose and Martin (2012: 56)

despite the issues with stages – or, more specifically, with systems of stages – they are central to genre studies.

Recontextualised genre descriptions

Genre is a highly productive and intuitively useful notion, but it is also slippery. Perhaps because genres are abstractions, operating in the contextual stratum, which can be described as 'recurrent configurations of meanings' (Martin 2009a: 13), there is a pragmatic tendency to modify this account for different audiences:

> In our educational linguistics work with teachers we used a more accessible characterization, namely that of genre as a staged goal-oriented social process:
>
> (i) *staged*: because it usually takes us more than one phase of meaning to work through a genre;
> (ii) *goal-oriented*: because unfolding phases are designed to accomplish something and we feel a sense of frustration or incompleteness if we are stopped;
> (iii) *social*: because we undertake genres interactively with others.

Different accounts of 'genre' for different audiences can naturally lead to variation in use and understanding. It is important to remember that genres are not fixed, but contextually sensitive. This variation is compounded when different analysts focus on different aspects of genre analysis (as we shall see later in the chapter), each of which has its own nuances. As Halliday and Matthiessen (2014: 48) explain, the views from different perspectives may conflict, so most descriptions involve compromise, and these are multiplied for genre when compared with relatively compact units such as phonemes or clauses. Despite these issues, genre studies have flourished in SFL educational research.

Main contributions to educational linguistics and genre

The SFL orientation to appliable linguistics that began with Halliday's work in educational linguistics in the United Kingdom extended to extensive work involving genre analysis and genre pedagogy in schools in Australia and internationally (see McCabe, this volume). These developments are well documented by Derewianka (2003), Martin (2009a), Rose and Martin (2012), Paltridge (2014) and others, but also deserve a recap here.

- *Disadvantaged (primary) schools*: Martin and Rothery's research on written genres in primary schools in the 1980s involved the collection and analysis of all of the texts that pupils wrote in a certain primary school. It showed the predominance of narratives and recounts at the expense of more factual writing. Arguably, this did not prepare children for writing in secondary school. This project led to the specific and explicit teaching of a wider range of genres in schools in Australia and internationally.
- *Writing in the (secondary school) disciplines*: The Write it Right project in the 1990s focused on workplace genres and secondary school genres in English, history, science, mathematics and geography. This included work on subject-based learner pathways and curriculum mapping, and led to dozens of publications, as summarised in Rose and Martin (2012), and studies such as Christie and Derewianka (2008). Table 29.3 illustrates seven of the eleven history genres reported in Unsworth (2000: 248).

Table 29.3 Selected history genres

		Social purpose	Stages
Chronicling history	Autobiographical Recount	To retell the events of your own life	Orientation Record of Events (Reorientation)
	Historical Recount	To retell events in the past	Background Record of Events (Deduction)
Reporting history	Historical Account	To account for why events happened in a particular sequence	Background Account of Events (Deduction)
Explaining history	Factorial Explanation	To explain the reasons or factors that contribute to a particular outcome	Outcome Factors Reinforcement of Factors
Arguing history	Analytical Exposition	To put forward a point of view or argument	(Background) Thesis Arguments Reinforcement of Thesis
	Analytical Discussion	To argue the case for two or more points of view about an issue	(Background) Issue Arguments Position
	Challenge	To argue against a view	(Background) Arguments Anti-Thesis

- *Teaching materials*: These projects led to significant educational activity in the areas of teacher education, curriculum mapping and design, and teaching materials (for example Rose and Martin 2012).
- *Spoken classroom genres*: Christie (1987, for example) extends the focus to spoken classroom genres and macro-genres.
- *Reading genres*: Rose has led developments of an extensive Reading to Learn programme (for example Rose and Acevedo 2006; Rose and Martin 2012). This genre-based literacy programme extends to teacher in-service provision and has inspired experimental research to demonstrate reading gains resulting from interventions.
- *University genres*: Projects that have developed descriptions of genres of university student writing include: Genres of Assessed Student Writing in the British Academic Written English (BAWE) corpus (Gardner and Nesi 2013); the Scaffolding Literacy in Academic and Tertiary Environments (SLATE) project (Mahboob et al. 2010); and Coffin and Donohue's (2014) Language as a Social Semiotic (LASS) approach to learning university student genres.
- *Online materials*: Materials for the teaching of university genres have been developed through the Writing Reports in Science and Engineering (WRiSE) project at Sydney (Drury and Mort 2012), Writing for a Purpose at Coventry (British Council Learn English) and SLATE teacher training materials in Hong Kong.
- *Languages other than English*: Research on genres in languages other than English includes Gruber's projects on student writing in Austria (for example Gruber and Muntigl 2005) and Byrnes' (2012, for example) curriculum development project that puts genres at the heart of teaching of German in American universities.

Research methods

Genre analysis can be approached from many different starting points, each suggesting a different focus of investigation, with related research tools. Some studies have a singular focus, most embrace several dimensions, and few, if any, have seriously undertaken exhaustive analysis of genres from all perspectives.

Analysis can start from the 'top' levels of meanings in context or the 'bottom' levels of wordings, and generally involves 'shunting' between levels and adopting a trinocular perspective from the top, bottom and across the three metafunctions (Halliday and Matthiesson 2014: 48).

Eggins and Martin (1997: 231) suggest that the 'first step [is to] describe the linguistic patterns (words and structures)' to find out about 'the degree of formality' close to spoken or written mode; the next step is to explain the differences. This leads to 'textual prediction and contextual deduction' (Eggins and Martin 1997: 236). This would be in line with a bottom-up corpus-based multidimensional analysis (MDA). Such analysis can identify linguistic patterns as clusters of lexicogrammatical features, but it is hard, if not impossible, to get 'up' to genres without considering purpose and contextual features.

What follows are insights into three accounts into conducting genre analysis that illustrate the crucial shunting between hypothesis forming and linguistic evidence.

First, Martin (2009b: 258–9) describes:

> bobbing up and down between genres and language [and] hopping back and forth between ideational, interpersonal and textual meanings at different levels of abstraction . . . Overall my perspective is top down . . . and across . . . [but] the key is to move around, and not get stuck at . . . the graphological word as in . . . corpus . . . analysis . . . or . . . summary tables of transitivity, mood and theme.

The chapter from which this extract is taken is well worth reading to appreciate the time that genre analysis can take, and why text and discourse analysis is necessary to move beyond initial hypotheses about the purpose and stages of texts.

Eggins' (2004) accounts of genre analyses of service encounters, horoscopes and recipes might be easier examples to start with. Because these are familiar, when we look at the texts, we can use our intuitions to identify and describe stages, each with their own function. Her analysis of the final sentence of a recipe text is telling. She suggests that some readers might want to analyse the sentence *Serve with Greek salad and crusty wholemeal bread* as a final stage, distinct from the 'instructions' that precede it (Eggins 2004: 68). An analysis of the grammatical patterns in the instructions and of this final clause are sufficiently similar to argue that it belongs with the Method (Instructions) stage. Here, as in Martin (2009b), we see how the analysis has to produce a configuration of all three metafunctions – ideational, interpersonal and textual – and not be overly influenced by one.

A third example in which an initial hypothesis is refined during the analysis of field, tenor and mode is in Gardner (2012a), who initially views texts with the same macro-structure (Introduction, Method, Results, Discussion) as belonging to the same genre. Further exploration of texts from across levels and disciplines of study reveals two distinct genres, with different purposes. In one, which tends to be written by students in their first or second year of study, the purpose is to demonstrate familiarity with the methods of the discipline and how they are reported. The Introduction and Discussion sections may be a couple of sentences only, and the decisions about the parameters of the work are often provided by the lecturers. Lab reports are a good example of this. In contrast, there are student projects, often written in the final year, the purpose of which is to demonstrate the ability to conduct a project independently. The Introduction therefore includes the rationale for the study and the Discussion is longer, with the aim of demonstrating the contribution of the findings to the discipline. With examples from psychology, biology and engineering, a pattern emerges of two genres that use very similar section headings, but in which differences in the language used provide evidence of, and explain, their different purposes.

In these three examples, an initial top-down hypothesis was generated, then refined with evidence from the ideational, interpersonal and textual analysis of the lexicogrammar via register associated with each stage of the genre in question.

Table 29.4 indicates the different types of analysis that can inform genre studies.

As Table 29.4 suggests, the SFL architecture is indeed comprehensive. Whether genre analysis starts at the top or the bottom, with one text or thousands of texts, the fundamental

Table 29.4 Analyses that inform genre studies

Aspect	Analysis	Examples
Context of culture: ideology	Critical discourse analysis	Martin (2009b)
Social purpose	Ethnographic methods, such as observation, interviews with experts or insiders, immersion in the community	Gruber and Muntigl (2005); Woodward-Kron (2005); Gardner (2008); Nesi and Gardner (2012)
Macrostructure	Formal structures and functional meanings in headings and titles	Paltridge (2002); Gardner and Holmes (2010)
Genre realisation: discourse semantics	appraisal, ideation, conjunction, identification and periodicity	Martin and Rose (2008)
Context of situation: text typologies, registers	Field, Tenor, Mode; rhetorical functions	Matthiessen et al. (2010)
Discourse semantics: textual metafunction	Method of Development, Marked Themes, Macro Theme and Hyper New	Fries (1995); Davies (1997); Martin and Rose (2008)
Text stages	Rhetorical function and register analysis	Veel and Coffin (1996); Unsworth (2000)
Discourse semantics: lexicogrammar	Lexical density, grammatical metaphor, abstract/institutional participants and causal relations	Veel and Coffin (1996); Christie and Derewianka (2008)
Genre mapping; learner pathways	Mapping genres onto contexts	Veel and Coffin (1996); Unsworth (2000); Coffin (2006); Nesi and Gardner (2012)
Elemental/micro and macro genres	Syntagmatic relations between genres	Christie (2002); Woodward-Kron (2005); Martin and Rose (2008)
Genre families	Groups of genres with similar features	Christie and Derewianka (2008); Martin and Rose (2008); Gardner and Nesi (2013)
Text phases	Lexicogrammatical realisations of Field, Tenor and Mode; Phasal analysis	Martin and Rose (2008); Humphrey et al. (2010)
Lexicogrammar	Corpus linguistic analysis of frequent forms, structures, collocations, key words and MDA	Nesi and Gardner (2012)

aim is to identify patterned evidence, reactances in the grammar for any genres proposed, and to explain how they function as socio-semiotic processes.

Recommendations for practice

The case for genre-based teaching remains strong in general and for literacy teaching in particular (for example Martin 2009a). Although approaches to teaching change and SFL approaches to pedagogy have been accused of being naive in their proclivity to reproduce, rather than challenge, hegemonic discourses (Luke 1996) and for drawing on a linguistic architecture the sophistication of which can be a barrier to teachers (Byrnes 2013), there is still a strong case being made for SFL-style genre-based and genre-informed teaching. Support is found for practitioners in English language teaching (Cirocki 2012), in English for academic purposes (Humphrey et al. 2010; Bruce 2013; Coffin and Donohue 2014; Gardner 2016), in modern foreign languages (Byrnes 2012) and in teacher education generally (Gebhard and Harman 2011). It extends beyond writing to areas such as reading (Rose and Acevedo 2006), assessment (Maxwell-Reid and Coniam 2015), learning in higher education (Coffin and Donohue 2014) and language teaching in general (Paltridge 2001).

In terms of teaching materials, a good place to start is Rothery (1994) or Derewianka (1990, 1996), which are written for teachers and explicitly link the analysis of a number of important educational genres to classroom teaching contexts. More recent genre-based resources, such as those from the WRiSE (Report Genre) Project,[1] the BAWE (Assessed Written Genres) Project[2] and the (genre-based) Writing for a Purpose Project[3] demonstrate more recent applications of genre research in practice.

Ironically perhaps, genre-based pedagogy was first linked with a social justice agenda in Australia – that is, of ensuring that disadvantaged children have access to the same cultural capital as others – yet in the United Kingdom it has been linked with a national literacy strategy (NLS), standardised testing and the enforcement of an hour a day of literacy that starts with shared reading, moves to focused language work and then on to individual text production (Walsh 2006). Thus a pedagogy that was developed to empower disadvantaged children in Australia became something of a straitjacket in England, which was exported to countries including Malaysia and the United States, and has returned to Australia in the NLS guise. Despite concerns and criticisms, it can be argued that the return to an explicit focus on language in schools in England has been beneficial, and that ongoing genre analysis and pedagogy based on real texts in context can be the catalyst for teachers and students to continue to increase their awareness of how meanings are construed through language in context.

Whether or not a genre-based pedagogy is adopted, then, a critical awareness of genres across the curriculum is invaluable for educators at all levels.

Future directions

More of the same

Genre studies have demonstrated their value in helping us to understand how language works in context through genres, and in the application of descriptive accounts of genres and access to instances and examples in educational and institutional settings. Although not addressed in this chapter, they have also been instrumental in developing an understanding of how languages are used to convey ideologies, to develop critical perspectives and to work for social change. One future direction for genre studies is therefore 'more of the same'.

The range of genres not yet analysed in contexts not yet identified is vast; the reasons for pursuing genre studies are also many, as we seek to understand and influence how meanings are construed in cultural contexts as they evolve.

The emphasis has been on educational contexts in English, but the scope for contrastive genre studies across linguistic and cultural contexts, in professional and leisure contexts, is vast and potentially highly enlightening.

New genres to analyse

Most of the genre analysis to date has been conducted on traditional written and spoken texts, but there have been movements towards analysing the genres of digital and social media texts. The way in which teenagers communicate today with the world and with each other presents a challenge for two-dimensional analyses, and one that SFL theory should be able to meet. The work of Baldry (2011, for example) and colleagues has provided a starting point, and there are postgraduate students examining genres such as blogs. Work on multimodal genres and genres that draw on multiple semiotic systems exists, but here again more is possible, and new technologies should provide the flexibility needed to analyse and interpret multiple systems in meaningful ways.

New visualisations of genre analyses

One of the most exciting and challenging areas of development is in the visualisation of SFL analyses. With the increasing power of computers to analyse large corpora and integrate analyses from different perspectives, increasingly complex, multidimensional analyses can be visualised. For example, Alsop has tagged different story genres (anecdotes, recounts, etc.) in a corpus of university engineering lectures from three different cultural contexts (Alsop et al. 2013; Alsop and Nesi 2014) and is able to visualise them all at once, from beginning to end, and to identify patterns of occurrence in the corpus and how they relate to other tagged elements.

Presentations that allow us to zoom in and uncover details of one analysis, then zoom out to see its impact on the whole, or turn around to view a different 'side' or metafunction, are ideal for the shunting and bobbing about across metafunctions and between levels that are deemed essential to uncover the linguistic evidence to support the identification of genres as social-semiotic processes. A three-dimensional interactive representation of analysed genres is therefore an exciting prospect.

Notes

1 http://www.usyd.edu.au/learningcentre/wrise/.
2 http://www.coventry.ac.uk/BAWE.
3 http://learnenglish.britishcouncil.org/en/writing-purpose/writing-purpose.

References

Alsop, S., and H. Nesi. 2014. The Engineering Lecture Corpus: Visualising cross-cultural difference in discourse function. Paper presented at ICAME 35: Corpus Linguistics, Context and Culture. Nottingham, 30 April–4 May.

Alsop, S., E. Moreton and H. Nesi. 2013. The uses of storytelling in university engineering lectures. *ESP across Cultures* 10: 8–19.

Baldry, A. 2011. *Multimodal Web Genres: Exploring Scientific English*. Como, Pavia: Ibis.

Bruce, I. 2013. The centrality of genre in EAP instruction. In J. Wrigglesworth (ed.) *EAP within the Higher Education Garden: Cross-Pollination between Disciplines, Departments and Research*. Reading: Garnett, pp. 25–32.

Byrnes, H. 2012. Conceptualizing FL writing development in collegiate settings: A systemic functional linguistics approach. In R.M. Manchon (ed.) *L2 Writing Development: Multiple Perspectives*. Berlin: Mouton, pp. 191–298.

Byrnes, H. 2013. Positioning writing as meaning-making in writing research: An introduction. *Journal of Second Language Writing* 22(2): 95–106.

Christie, F. 1987. Young children's writing from spoken to written genre. *Language and Education* 1(1): 3–13.

Christie, F. 2002. *Classroom Discourse Analysis: A Functional Perspective*. London: Continuum.

Christie, F., and B. Derewianka. 2008. *School Discourse: Learning to Write across the Years of Schooling*. London: Continuum.

Christie, F., and J.R. Martin (eds). 1997. *Genre and Institutions: Social Processes in the Workplace and School*. London: Continuum.

Cirocki, A. 2012. Genre theory: A horn of plenty for EFL students. *Nordic Journal of English Studies* 11(3): 78–99.

Coffin, C. 2006. Learning the language of school history: The role of linguistics in mapping the writing demands of the secondary school curriculum. *Journal of Curriculum Studies* 38(4): 413–29.

Coffin, C., and J. Donohue. 2014. *A Language as Social Semiotic-Based Approach to Teaching and Learning in Higher Education*. Chichester: Wiley.

Davies, F. 1997. Marked theme as a heuristic for analysing text type, text and genre. In J. Pique and D.J. Viera (eds) *Applied Languages: Theory and Practice in ESP*. Valencia: University of Valencia Press, pp. 45–79.

Derewianka, B. 1990. *Exploring How Texts Work*. Rozelle, NSW: Primary English Teaching Association.

Derewianka, B. 1996. *Exploring the Writing of Genres*. Royston: UKRA.

Derewianka, B. 2003. Trends and issues in genre-based approaches. *RELC Journal* 34(2): 133–54.

Drury, H., and P. Mort. 2012. Developing student writing in science and engineering: The Write reports in science and engineering (WRiSE) project. *Journal of Learning Development in Higher Education*. Available online at http://www.aldinhe.ac.uk/ojs/index.php?journal=jldhe&page=article&op=view&path%5B%5D=183.

Eggins, S. 2004. *An Introduction to Systemic Functional Linguistics*. 2nd edn. London: Pinter.

Eggins, S., and J.R. Martin. 1997. Genres and registers of discourse. In T.A. van Dijk (ed.) *Discourse as Structure and Process*. London: Sage, pp. 230–56.

Eggins, S., and D. Slade. 1997. *Analysing Casual Conversation*. London: Cassell.

Flowerdew, J. 2013. *Discourse in English Language Education*. London and New York: Routledge.

Fries, P. 1995. Themes, methods of development and texts. In R. Hasan and P. Fries (eds) *On Subject and Theme: From the Perspective of Functions in Discourse*. Amsterdam: John Benjamins, pp. 317–59.

Gardner, S. 2008. Integrating ethnographic, multidimensional, corpus linguistic and systemic functional approaches to genre description: An illustration through university history and engineering assignments. In E. Steiner and S. Neumann (eds) *Proceedings of the 19th European Systemic Functional Linguistics Conference and Workshop: Data and Interpretation in Linguistic Analysis*. Available online at http://scidok.sulb.uni-saarland.de/sulb/portal/esflcw/.

Gardner, S. 2012a. Genres and registers of student report writing: An SFL perspective on texts and practices. *Journal of English for Academic Purposes* 11(1): 52–63.

Gardner, S. 2012b. A pedagogic and professional case study: Genre and register continuum in business and in medicine. *Journal of Applied Linguistics and Professional Purposes* 9(1): 13–35.

Gardner, S. 2016. A genre-instantiation approach to teaching English for specific academic purposes: Student writing in business, economics and engineering. *Writing and Pedagogy* 8(1): 117–44.

Gardner, S., and J. Holmes. 2010. From section headings to assignment macrostructure in under-graduate student writing. In E. Swain (ed.) *Thresholds and Potentialities of Systemic Functional Linguistics*. Trieste: Edizioni Universitarie Trieste, pp. 254–76.

Gardner, S., and H. Nesi. 2013. A classification of genre families in university student writing. *Applied Linguistics* 34(1): 25–52.

Gebhard, M., and R. Harman. 2011. Reconsidering genre theory in K-12 schools: A response to school reforms in the United States. *Journal of Second Language Writing* 20(1): 45–55.

Gruber, H., and P. Muntigl. 2005. Generic and rhetorical structures of texts: Two sides of the same coin? *Folia Linguistica* 39(1–2): 75–113.

Halliday, M.A.K. 2009a. *The Essential Halliday*. Ed. J. J. Webster. London: Continuum.

Halliday, M.A.K. 2009b. Keywords. In M.A.K Halliday and J.J. Webster (eds) *Continuum Companion to Systemic Functional Linguistics*. London: Continuum, pp. 229–53.

Halliday, M.A.K., and C.M.I.M. Matthiessen. 2014. *Halliday's Introduction to Functional Grammar*. 4th edn. New York: Routledge.

Hasan, R. 1996 [1984]. Nursery tale as genre. In C. Cloran, D.G. Butt and G. Williams (eds) *Ways of Saying, Ways of Meaning: Selected Papers of Ruqaiya Hasan*. London: Cassell, pp. 51–72.

Hasan, R. 2009. The place of context in a systemic functional model. In M.A.K Halliday and J.J. Webster (eds) *Continuum Companion to Systemic Functional Linguistics*. London: Continuum, pp. 166–90.

Humphrey, S., J.R. Martin, S. Dreyfus and A. Mahboob. 2010. The 3 × 3: Setting up a linguistic toolkit for teaching academic writing. In A. Mahboob and N. Knight (eds) *Appliable Linguistics*. New York: Continuum, pp. 185–99.

Hyland, K. 2002. Genre, context and literacy. *Annual Review of Applied Linguistics* 22: 113–35.

Hyland, K. 2007. Genre pedagogy: Language, literacy and L2 writing instruction. *Journal of Second Language Writing* 16(3): 148–64.

Lillis, T. 2008. Ethnography as method, methodology, and 'deep theorizing': Closing the gap between text and context in academic writing research. *Written Communication* 25(3): 353–88.

Luke, A. 1996. Genres of power? Literacy education and the production of capital. In R. Hasan and G. Williams (eds) *Literacy in Society*. London: Longman, pp. 308–38.

Mahboob, A., S. Dreyfus, S. Humphrey and J.R. Martin. 2010. Appliable linguistics and English language teaching: The Scaffolding Literacy in Adult and Tertiary Environments (SLATE) project. In A. Mahboob and N. Knight (eds) *Directions in Appliable Linguistics*. London: Continuum, pp. 25–43.

Martin, J.R. 1992. *English Text*. Amsterdam: John Benjamins.

Martin, J.R. 1997. Analysing genre: Functional parameters. In F. Christie and J.R. Martin (eds) *Genre and Institutions: Social Processes in the Workplace and School*. London: Cassell, pp. 3–39.

Martin, J.R. 2008 [1984]. Language, register and genre. In C. Coffin, T. Lillis and K. O'Halloran (eds) *Investigating Language in Action: Tools for Analysis – Reader 2*. Milton Keynes: Open University Press, pp. 1–28.

Martin, J.R. 2009a. Genre and language learning: A social semiotic perspective. *Linguistics and Education* 20(1): 10–21.

Martin, J.R. 2009b. Boomer dreaming: The texture of re-colonialisation in a lifestyle magazine. In G. Forey and G. Thompson (eds) *Text Type and Texture*. London: Equinox, pp. 252–84.

Martin, J.R., and D. Rose. 2008. *Genre Relations: Mapping Culture*. London: Equinox.

Matthiessen, C.M.I.M., K. Teruyu and M. Lam. 2010. *Key Terms in Systemic Functional Linguistics*. London: Continuum.

Maxwell-Reid, C., and D. Coniam. 2015. Ideological and linguistic values in EFL examination scripts: The selection and execution of story genres. *Assessing Writing* 23: 19–34.

Nesi, H., and S. Gardner. 2012. *Genres across the Disciplines: Student Writing in Higher Education*. Cambridge: Cambridge University Press.

Sheena Gardner

Paltridge, B. 2001. *Genre and the Language Learning Classroom*. Ann Arbor, MI: University of Michigan Press.

Paltridge, B. 2002. Thesis and dissertation writing: An examination of published advice and actual practice. *English for Specific Purposes* 21: 125–43.

Paltridge, B. 2014. Research timeline: Genre and second-language academic writing. *Language Teaching* 47(3): 303–18.

Rose, D., and C. Acevedo. 2006. Closing the gap and accelerating learning in the middle years of schooling. *Literacy Learning: The Middle Years* 14(2): 32–45.

Rose, D., and J.R. Martin. 2012. *Learning to Write/Reading to Learn: Genre, Knowledge and Pedagogy in the Sydney School*. London: Equinox.

Rothery, J. 1994. *Exploring Literacy in School English* (Write it Right Resources for Literacy and Learning). Sydney: Metropolitan East Disadvantaged Schools Programme.

Swales, J.M. 1990. *Genre Analysis: English in Academic and Research Settings*. Cambridge: Cambridge University Press.

Unsworth, L. (ed.). 2000. *Researching Language in Schools and Communities: Functional Linguistic Perspectives*. London: Cassell.

Veel, R., and C. Coffin. 1996. Learning to think like an historian: The language of secondary school history. In R. Hasan and G. Williams (eds) *Literacy in Society*. London: Longman, pp. 191–231.

Walsh, P. 2006. The impact of genre theory and pedagogy and systemic functional linguistics on National Literacy Strategies in the UK. In R. Whittaker, M. O'Donnell and A. McCabe (eds) *Language and Literacy: Functional Approaches*. London: Continuum, pp. 159–76.

Woodward-Kron, R. 2005. The role of genre and embedded genres in tertiary students' writing. *Prospect* 20(3): 24–41.

Part V

SFL in practice: an appliable theory

30

Systemic functional linguistics and clinical linguistics

Alison Ferguson, Elizabeth Spencer and Elizabeth Armstrong

Introduction

Clinical linguistics has been described as '[t]he application of linguistic theories, methods and descriptive findings to the analysis of medical conditions or settings involving a disorder (or pathology) of language' (Crystal 2008: 80). This chapter first briefly describes the ways in which systemic functional linguistics (SFL) has been applied to various types of communication disorder, before going on to present a comparative critique of the contribution that SFL has made to understanding the nature of these disorders. The chapter then presents a critical comparative appraisal of current and potential application of SFL to intervention for communication disorders, and describes how the study of clinical conditions has challenged and informed the SFL approach.

The application of SFL to speech-language pathology has important consequences for the theoretical understanding of the nature of communication disorder. The predominant paradigms in the field tend to focus on levels of language (phonology, morphology, syntax, semantics, discourse/pragmatics) as providing explanatory ways of locating disorder. Such linguistic approaches also seek to establish the extent to which the language impairment at a particular level validly reflects the individual's function in everyday communication activities.[1] The separation of levels of language has tended to restrict the focus of research and the selection of targets for therapy to either the micro-linguistic (words and wordings) or the macro-linguistic aspects of language (discourse structure). By doing so, the significance of interactions between levels of language in the nature of communication disorder is obscured or seen as an artefactual complication. In contrast, the SFL approach, as discussed by Bateman (this volume), allows for an explicit and detailed description of the multiple strata at each moment. The recognition and identification within SFL of the multiplicity of ways in which the dimensions of language interact provides, as Halliday (2005) suggested, a useful alternative in locating disorder in relation to instantiation. SFL is not a theory of brain function or language learning/remediation, but, as Halliday (2005: 134) suggests:

[B]rain research resonates well with the systemic functional account of language . . . the development of the brain is, in an important sense, the development of language; the basis of neurocognitive activity is a system of connections, not an inventory of symbols . . . ; and 'mind' has a plausible interpretation as the 'personalised brain', the way the individual's brain has developed as a function of that individual's unique pattern of experience (as the idiolect is personalised language, the product of each individual's unique experience of semiosis).

SFL and types of communication disorder

As might be expected, developmental and acquired language pathologies have been the main focus for applications of SFL to the wide diversity of types of communication disorder (see Table 30.1). At the time of preparing this chapter, there have been thirty empirical research reports in the area of adult disorders (reporting on a total of 89 adults with communication disorders and 114 adults without disorder) and seven studies of children with communication disorders (reporting on a total of 115 children with communication disorder and 197 typically developing children) that have utilised an SFL framework. In the area of adult language disorders, there has been a major focus on the acquired language disorder known as 'aphasia', as well as the cognitive-communication disorders seen following traumatic brain injury (TBI) from accidents and dementia, and some preliminary work in relation to right brain damage.

The research in the area of child language has explored developmental language disorders, including those associated with specific language impairment,[2] and as associated with particular medical conditions such as autism[3] and attention deficit hyperactivity disorder (ADHD) (Mathers 2006).

Rarely has the communicative interaction involving severe-profound developmental disorder been investigated from an SFL perspective.[4] Also, disorders of speech, voice and fluency have significant consequences for how the person affected may need to adjust his or her use of linguistic resources – for example to adjust for effort or time pressures – and for how both he or she and his or her communication partners may make use of contextual and co-textual resources to maximise the exchange of meaning. So, for example, the approach of SFL has been used to consider the use of linguistic resources by adults with the acquired neurological impairment of dysarthria (Mantie-Kozlowski 2010), and by adults who stutter before and after successful intervention (Spencer et al. 2009; Lee et al. 2015).

In considering the contribution of SFL to understanding the nature of these communication disorders, it is useful to provide an overview of the main SFL analyses that have been used in the empirical research into communication disorders (see Tables 30.2 and 30.3).

In relation to experiential meaning, the analysis of clause complexes in aphasia can illustrate some of the differences between types of aphasia, for example involving grammatical disorder (such as Broca's non-fluent aphasia) or not involving grammatical disorder (such as fluent anomic or Wernicke's aphasia). More fundamentally, the analysis of clause complexes illuminates the interaction of lexical-semantic retrieval problems that are common across types of aphasia, with difficulties in the formulation of connected language above the rank of clause (Ferguson 2000). The analysis of Transitivity has been applied to the study of aphasia and cognitive-communication difficulties associated with both adults with TBI (Keegan 2012) and dementia (Mortensen 1992), and children with ADHD (Mathers 2005), and has highlighted the pivotal role of the verbal group in an area that has long focused on nouns (Armstrong 2001).

Table 30.1 Empirical studies applying an SFL approach

Areas of practice	Adults	No. of empirical studies	NO. OF PARTICIPANTS		No. of empirical studies	Children	NO. OF PARTICIPANTS	
			With disorder	Without disorder			With disorder	Without disorder
Language	Aphasia (dysphasia) from acquired brain injury (e.g. left cerebral hemisphere stroke)	11	38	26	3	Specific language impairment	82	132
					1	Autism spectrum disorders	41	34
					1	ADHD	11	11
	Cognitive-communication disorder from brain damage				1	Acquired brain injury in childhood (e.g. TBI)	20	20
	TBI	11	26	36				
	RBD	2	7	42				
	DAT	3	5	2				
Multimodal communication	Adults with complex communication needs, e.g. associated with other severe disabilities	0	0	0	1	Complex communication needs, e.g. associated with severe developmental disability	1	0
Speech	Structural	1	1	1	1	Articulatory	1	0
	Neurological (dysarthria, apraxia of speech)					Phonological		
						Neurological		
Fluency	Adults who stutter	2	12	10	0	Children who stutter	0	0
Voice (including intonation)	Functional	0	0	0	0	Functional	0	0
	Organic					Organic		
TOTAL		30	89	117	8		156	197

Key: ADHD = attention deficit hyperactivity disorder; DAT = dementia of the Alzheimer type; RBD = right brain damage; TBI = traumatic brain injury

Table 30.2 Adult communication disorders: examples of SFL analyses

Disorder	Field	Tenor	Mode	Discourse-semantic
Adult language – Aphasia (dysphasia)	Clause complex (Armstrong 1992, 2002; Ferguson 2000) Transitivity (Armstrong 2001, 2005a; Armstrong et al. 2011)	Appraisal (Armstrong and Ulatowska 2007; Armstrong et al. 2011) Tone contour (Ferguson and Peterson 2002)	Cohesion (Armstrong 1987; Ferguson 1992b; Armstrong et al. 2011)	Exchange Structure/Speech functions (Ferguson 1992b; Mortensen 2005)
Adult language – Cognitive-communication disorder from brain damage	Transitivity (Mortensen 1992; Keegan 2012)	Mood/modality (Togher and Hand 1998; Keegan 2012) Appraisal (Sherratt 2007; Keegan 2012)	Cohesion (Müller and Wilson 2008)	Thematic progression (Keegan 2012) Exchange Structure/Speech functions (Togher et al. 1996, 1997a; Togher 2000; Mortensen 2005; Müller and Wilson 2008; Davis et al. 2011; Müller and Mok 2012) Generic structure (Togher et al. 1997b; Togher et al. 2004; Mortensen 2005; Kilov et al. 2008)
Adult speech – Dysarthria	No research reports located	No research reports located	No research reports located	Information Structure, Theme (Mantie-Kozlowski 2010)
Adults who stutter	Transitivity (Spencer et al. 2005, 2009)	Mood/modality (Spencer et al. 2005, 2009) Appraisal (Lee et al. 2015)	Theme (Spencer et al. 2005, 2009)	No research reports able to be located

Note: All involve the analysis of spoken language, except for Mortensen's work, which focuses on written language. Research gaps shaded.

In relation to interpersonal meaning, analyses of Mood and modality and/or the resources for Appraisal have been applied to consider ways in which people with aphasia make use of residual language to express their opinions and feelings (Armstrong and Ulatowska 2007; Armstrong et al. 2011), as well as to consider the potential disruption to interpersonal relationships associated with the reduction in use of these resources in cognitive-communication disorder associated with TBI (Togher and Hand 1998; Keegan 2012) and right brain damage (Sherratt 2007).

It is very apparent that the work of Halliday and Hasan (1976) in the area of cohesion had a substantial impact across much research in the areas of both child and adult language disorders. However, it is also important to note that some of these applied analyses of cohesive devices have been in research that, in other respects, has not been informed more generally by an SFL perspective (Klecan-Aker and Lopez 1985; Adams and Bishop 1989; Jordan et al. 1991). Such studies have tended to use counts of frequency of occurrence of cohesive devices and judgements as to when cohesive ties have been complete or incomplete, in error, or ambiguous. In contrast, studies informed by an SFL perspective have looked to the

Table 30.3 Child communication disorders: examples of SFL analyses

Disorder	Field	Tenor	Mode	Discourse-semantic
Child language – Developmental language impairment (including SLI, ASD, ADHD) and acquired brain injury in childhood (e.g. TBI)	Clause complex (Mathers 2005)	No research reports located	Cohesion (Klecan-Aker and Lopez 1985; Adams and Bishop 1989; Jordan et al. 1991; Fine et al. 1994) Theme (Thomson 2005)	Thematic progression (Thomson 2005)
Child speech	No research reports located	No research reports located	No research reports located	System network, register (Müller et al. 2008)
Child with complex communication needs	No research reports located	No research reports located	No research reports located	Exchange Structure/ Speech functions (Dreyfus 2006, 2008, 2013)

Key: ADHD = attention deficit hyperactivity disorder; ASD = autism spectrum disorders; SLI = specific language impairment; TBI = traumatic brain injury

Note: All involve the analysis of spoken language. Research gaps shaded.

resources for cohesion and how these are used by people with aphasia (Armstrong 1991) and dementia (Müller and Mok 2012). For example, the work of Müller and Mok (2012) highlighted how people with dementia are competent meaning-makers in interaction even in the presence of their characteristic redundancy and tangentiality. Such language output can provide more opportunities for listeners to connect possible intended meaning links. Similarly, Ferguson (1992a) suggested that resources for speaker cohesion are available to help listeners to be able to infer meaning and to guess at the words sought by the person with aphasia. This view of cohesion as a resource for both speaker and listener meanings is a good example of the capacity of SFL to support a strengths-based approach to the assessment and intervention for communication disorders.

Less frequently explored have been the resources for Theme (Thomson 2005; Mantie-Kozlowski 2010; Keegan 2012). Thomson's (2005) findings in children with specific language impairment pointed towards the impact of restricted lexicogrammatical resources on the use of multiple themes and, potentially, the use of the later developing linear (zigzagging) thematic progression in narratives. In speech-language pathology, there is more general familiarity with the constructs around the given–new distinction in models of sentence processing than is realised in the text. By contrast, SFL analysis here presents a textual analysis that highlights the interactivity between and within levels of language.

At the discourse-semantic level, the notion of a move as a semantic unit has provided the study of child and adult communication disorders with a useful alternative to the kind of speech-act analysis that has had a long history in the field. Consideration of the speech functions of semantic moves and their role in relation to the exchange has been given to a range of interactions involving people with different communication disorders. In particular, analysis of exchange structure and generic structure has challenged the prevailing view of cognitive-communication disorder as resting entirely within the individual with dementia

(Müller and Mok 2012) or brain injury (Togher et al. 1996). These studies have demonstrated the improved abilities of the person with a communication disorder when given more socially powerful roles than those usually afforded to them, for example when given the opportunity to be the 'expert' or 'primary knower' of information rather than always being in patient or information-receiving roles.

Even more powerfully, the work of Dreyfus (2011) in relation to partner interactions with a child/adolescent with severe-profound complex communication needs highlights the meaning-making of the listener. With only fragmentary vocalisation and contextually elicited gestural behaviour available from the speaker, the partners were shown to draw creatively on available linguistic and extralinguistic resources to create meaningful and engaging interpersonal interaction through their communication moves. This work extends the boundaries of the SFL approach to further explore the interaction of text and context at a theoretical level. The situation of the non-verbal interactant exemplifies the question raised by Bartlett (this volume) of what aspects of context are to be considered as relevant. Only the utterances of the communication partners are 'entextualised' (as Bartlett describes it), yet Dreyfus (2011) provides a well-supported argument for the exchange of meanings in this situation. Bartlett frames the question as to relevant aspects of context in terms of production, but, as Dreyfus suggests, understanding is informed by systematic use of aspects of context. Her work in describing such system networks links well with the work discussed by Bowcher (this volume) in the quest to develop system networks to describe the internal features of Field, Tenor and Mode. Clinically, the shift in viewpoint highlighting the role of partners in communication has fundamental implications for the focus and nature of speech-language pathology intervention. While communication training for family members and volunteers has an established evidence base in aphasia, work by Togher and colleagues (2004) extended this more widely into community-based training, with the successful trial of an intervention for members of the police force to facilitate their communication skills with individuals with cognitive-communication disorders.

SFL and the discourse of professional practice

In addition to applications of SFL to communication disorders, there have been preliminary applications to research that seek to understand the nature of speech-language pathology practices as a discipline (Ferguson and Elliot 2001; Ferguson et al. 2010), and to adopt a critical discourse analysis perspective towards the discourse of speech-language pathology both amongst professionals (Ferguson and Armstrong 2004; Ferguson 2009; Ferguson 2010) and in the wider community (Ferguson 2013), which is discussed later in this section. Ferguson and Elliot (2001) compared the generic structure and exchange structure in therapy sessions with people with aphasia conducted by a novice student (in her first adult rehabilitation placement), a more experienced student (in her final adult rehabilitation placement) and an experienced, qualified speech-language pathologist. The structure of the session conducted by the novice was linear and in line with standard templates of session plans, following a step-wise progression through greetings, establishing rapport and explaining the planned therapy, through a series of practice tasks, to finish with a statement of required home practice and a farewell. This contrasted sharply with the structure of the session run by the experienced speech-language pathologist, which used a more complex, recursive, embedded structure whereby the sequence of explanation, practice and discussion of home tasks occurred multiple times, interspersed with rapport 'chat', and topped and tailed by greeting and farewell. Analysis of the more experienced student's session showed considerable fragmentation of structure and it appeared that she was attempting to depart from the linear structure, but not yet fully able to control the session as smoothly as the qualified speech-language pathologist. Overall, the three therapists' control of the session was evidenced through their higher proportion of information-giving roles in the exchanges, as well as their frequent use of teaching (delayed primary knower) moves. This pattern was seen regardless of experience.

Ferguson and Armstrong (2004) reflected on the way in which this pattern of control as a desired therapeutic stance is taken for granted – an unquestioned assumption – amongst professionals and is a product of socialisation through the professional education process. Exploring this further, Ferguson (2010) undertook an analysis of the use of Appraisal resources during student learning interactions in discussion with their supervising speech-language pathologist. These learning interactions involved a high proportion of Judgement in contrast with Appreciation. Notably, resources expressing Affect were used only by students and not reflected or initiated by the supervisor. Such a pattern potentially transfers to the clinician–client interaction, in which the clinician predominantly is in the primary knower position, asking questions of the client and evaluating responses primarily through Judgement. This contrasts with a pattern of less formal interaction whereby speakers tend to engage in more joint evaluations in which there is some negotiation surrounding the validity/certainty of a proposition.

The extent to which such acculturation might result in a mismatch between the discourse of clients and their families in comparison with their therapists was investigated by analysing the use of the resources of Transitivity and Mood during in-depth interviews with five people with aphasia, five family members and the eight speech-language pathologists involved in their treatment (Ferguson et al. 2010). When the types of Processes and Circumstances were examined, it was evident that while the speech-language pathologists' talk suggested abstract mental adjustments potentially required as the result of the communication disorder, the individuals with aphasia and their family members were talking about their needs and goals in terms of concrete material and behavioural activities. In other words, the clinicians were focused more on feelings/emotional reactions to the disorder, while the clients and family members were focused on restrictions in their everyday communication activities. While both aspects are noted to be important in the management of aphasia, the study highlighted the way in which the interactants in clinical discourse can often be on different semiotic trajectories.

In looking further into professional discourse, a critical examination of the discourses of communication disability was conducted by Ferguson (2009) through the use of SFL to deconstruct statements of national professional bodies in relation to scope of professional practice in speech-language pathology in Australia, Canada and the United States. The results of analysis of nominal and verbal groups found that, in line with the purpose of the texts, the majority of processes were material. The only Participant Roles filled by clients were as Beneficiary or Goal; never Actors of processes. Taxonomic analysis found that the material processes tended to be abstract, technical or institutional entities. Actions were frequently rendered as nominal, rather than verbal, groups, for example 'screening', 'assessment', 'prevention', 'rehabilitation'. Interestingly, terms such as 'consult', 'negotiate', 'collaborate' occurred only in relation to other professionals rather than in relation to clients. Essentially, the analysis highlighted the professional adoption of scientific discourse (Halliday 2002 [1987]) and it was suggested that this appeared to place the client outside the expressed conception of scope of practice.

Ferguson (2010) later compared a range of selected texts concerned with cognitive-communication disorders following TBI: a personal letter by a person with TBI to a friend explaining the problems; a newspaper article about recovery from TBI; information provided by a support group about TBI designed for family members; information about TBI provided by an advocacy group lobbying for government support; and a scholarly paper about interventions for TBI. It had been expected that there would be differences in medical, as opposed to lay, lexical choices in relation to the text source, but these differences manifested very different perspectives. For example, the person with TBI depersonalised his injuries in describing problems 'in *the* left arm', whereas the newspaper article combined medical terms with emotive choices of Processes – 'caused (his) *frontal lobe* to *slam* into his *skull*' (emphasis added).

The findings from the analyses of practice discourse suggest that there are important differences in the understandings of disorder from 'outside' (as a professional observing the communication) versus 'inside' (as a person with a communication disorder). The possible future directions for such research and application are described in the next section.

Future directions

Possible future directions for such research are fairly apparent from the gaps identified in the foregoing discussion. In relation to the types of communication disorder, it is clear from Table 30.1 that areas yet to receive attention from an SFL perspective include adult complex communication needs (for example those associated with developmental disability) and adults and children with voice disorders (such as those associated with vocal overuse, the presence of vocal nodules, or voice techniques/assistive devices following surgery for laryngeal cancer), and that research into linguistic aspects of stuttering from an SFL perspective could be further explored. In relation to the potential areas for contribution from SFL, it is apparent from Tables 30.2 and 30.3 that there are substantial gaps in our understanding of interpersonal aspects of child language disorders. This is a particularly important area for further attention given that interpersonal aspects of language are a primary site for development in adolescent language and that specific language impairment is known to have long-term chronicity (Brinton et al. 2010).

It is also clear that there has been very little work in the area of communication disorders and SFL in relation to phonology, with the exception of a single case study by Müller and colleagues (2008). Gee (2012) suggested that systemic phonology has strengths at the supra-segmental level, but has been relatively underdeveloped at the segmental level. A number of chapters in this volume offer new possibilities in this regard, both for SFL and for the study of communication disorders, such as Tench's system network for phonology. The work of O'Grady (this volume) might usefully be applied to consider the nature and impact of marked patterns of intonation associated with some voice disorders and following TBI. Similarly, recent developments in relation to rhythmic structure (see O'Grady, this volume) may offer new insights into disorders of fluency. Articulatory and phonological speech sound disorder in children is the core business for speech-language pathologists, and there has been a recent increase in the applications of phonological theory to the field and the inclusion of an SFL perspective is suggested to be a fruitful future direction.

In designing future research applying an SFL approach to the study of communication disorders, it is worth noting the relatively small participant numbers obtained in the research to date (see Table 30.1). Group comparisons involving relatively small numbers are considered in the current medical research paradigm as representing a relatively low-level evidence base. It is suggested that future researchers give careful consideration to ways in which to increase the power of their research design, for example by using cross-institutional collaborations and by making use of rigorous single case designs (such as incorporating concepts of multiple baselines and multiple occasions and contexts of sampling, and larger sample sizes, where possible). These kinds of research designs will be essential to obtain funding and organisational support for the translation and implementation research needed to move the current body of research into clinical practice (some of the future challenges for which are considered in the next section).

However, the most noticeable gap in this critical review of SFL in relation to communication disorders is the limited discussion of how studying the nature of communication disorders may contribute to the approach of SFL. In other approaches to linguistics, the study of communication disorders has been used as a way in which to examine questions such as the psychological reality of theoretical dissociations between levels of language. One such contribution has been Dreyfus's (2006) argument that her findings challenge the boundaries between what can be considered integral to the systemic organisation of language and the so-called extralinguistic. Another contribution has been the work of Armstrong (2005b) and Rigaudeau-McKenna (2005) in relation to the notion of problematic usage of the term, or what might constitute, 'disorder'. Clinical linguistics in general faces a paradoxical dilemma in relation to interpreting language data from language users with a known or presumed pathology. If the theory proposes a notion of grammatical correctness as judged by proficient users (as in the case of generative grammars), or a notion of a normative standard (as in the case of most cognitive-linguistic models), or a notion of cultural appropriateness (as in the case of applied pragmatic models and most other approaches to discourse analysis), then the presence of error or deviation from the norm or appropriate will be interpreted as indicative of pathology. At the same time, language data from individuals with language pathology provides a central empirical plank in the building of theoretical models of language (in particular for models of cognitive-linguistic processing, but also for other models), so that there is an inherent circularity in relation to interpretations of the nature of the pathology observed. Further, language pathology is often seen as providing a test case for testing models of language, which further adds to the dilemma. For probabilistic models such as SFL, the notion of problematic usage has provided a way through this circularity through its focus on understanding *how* the language user is making use of available linguistic and contextual resources to make meaning, which contributes to the central tenets of SFL.

Clinical assessment and intervention

In drawing implications from the research utilising a SFL framework, there are numerous possibilities for both clinical assessment of disorder and subsequent intervention. To date, clinical assessment has been a focus of discussion (Thomson 2003a, 2003b; Armstrong et al. 2012), with only few intervention studies being undertaken using the approach specifically. Research studies have utilised a variety of SFL system networks to explore different aspects of disorders, as we have seen in this chapter. The analyses used have added a different dimension to many already identified features of disorders, such as naming difficulties (seen in the context of the nominal group and implications for cohesion and coherence), 'pragmatic' difficulties (illuminated through exchange structure, speech function, generic structure potential, and Mood/modality analyses), problems with verb retrieval (seen in the context of Transitivity analysis and usage according to genre) and difficulty in maintaining coherent discourse (as reflected in the logical relations between clause complexes). They have also provided new insights at the discourse 'level' in particular, because many prior analyses used in assessment and treatment of communication disorders typically focused on word and sentence phenomena. These analyses can be used clinically to highlight both strengths and weaknesses of an individual's discourse, and the behaviours and contributions of conversation partners.

Of course, the time involved in complex linguistic analysis has often been proposed as a barrier to clinical translation (Togher 2001; Armstrong and Ulatowska 2007). Numerous authors have, however, suggested ways around this barrier. Nickels (2008) discussed the notion of hypothesis testing in clinical assessment in relation to cognitive neuropsychological testing of language skills. She proposed that initial screening of both the spontaneous speech of an individual and his or her performance on a brief battery of language tasks could alert the experienced clinician to particular potential areas of linguistic functioning that warranted further assessment. Those areas deemed to be the most salient were tested in further depth. Olness and colleagues (2012: 57) referred to a similar strategy in discourse analysis regarding what they term 'narrative functionality'. They discussed the importance of ensuring that the *purpose* of assessment is defined by the person with aphasia, while the assessment *process* is based on the clinician's understanding of the nature of the client's disorder and information about the client's contexts of communication. In such assessment frameworks, not all types of analysis or context will form the basis of all assessments; the client's initial presentation will determine the kinds of analyses that might be undertaken. Another way of containing the time involved in discourse analysis is to rate discourse characteristics online from an audio or video tape, rather than from a transcription that would obviously involve more preparatory time. Rating within the context of utterance is a way in which to increase the validity of assessment, although training is needed to establish the reliability of online rating. Linda Armstrong and colleagues (2007) demonstrated successful implementation of this method in a study of aphasic discourse examining both pragmatic and lexical features.

The contributions of SFL to clinical interventions are yet to be fully realised and the potential for SFL may be through the provision of a general framework within which clinicians can navigate to select potentially productive targets for therapy. This notion of a general theory guiding specific therapy targets is well accepted within cognitive-linguistic based therapies (as we will see shortly), but remains relatively untapped in relation to SFL. One of the barriers for implementation is the need for distillation of the approach to enhance its usability. In response, it has been suggested that the complexity of the SFL approach is not a sufficient rationale to explain the difficulties in ready application, because the theory and research informing cognitive-linguistic processing approaches to intervention are no less complex; however, the distillation of this approach has largely avoided reductionism, while providing clarity for the general user.

One of the advantages of SFL for potential treatment frameworks is that it incorporates context as a fundamental theoretical construct. Traditionally, remediation of communication disorders has involved treatment of particular decontextualised linguistic skills, with ultimate outcomes measured in terms of whether these skills, once mastered in a therapy situation, generalise to real-life discourse. In some therapy approaches, generalisation activities are a planned part of therapy process – that is, deliberately changing contexts (for example trips to the shops, telephone calls) and communication partners. However, typically, these activities are chosen without explicit consideration of how the nature of the context of situation affects the lexicogrammatical and discourse-semantic features, and without explicit mapping of Field, Tenor and Mode. Working within an SFL framework, one is working in context from the outset, and therapy targets, tasks and activities may be made more validly and efficiently. The SFL analyses would form part of the assessment and generate information about the linguistic performance of particular communication functions that have a purpose and occur within real communicative contexts with different communication partners. Rather than working on 'verbs', for example, with a client with aphasia, one could work on the material and mental processes required for a recount involving events and actions, and some kind of personal reflection on these (for example Whitworth 2010). The context is embedded in the treatment task. As another example, if a person were having difficulty in giving opinions, communication partners could be trained to elicit evaluative language by engaging in particular genres and being aware of the kinds of language required in this genre. Conversation partner training is of particular relevance in the treatment of communication disorders (Simmons-Mackie et al. 2010), and SFL has much to offer in terms of providing partners with a structure for interactional context and knowledge of the kinds of language they might expect and/or facilitate in interactions with people with communication disorders. The research conducted by Togher and colleagues (2004) demonstrated the usefulness of the approach in working with people with TBI and their conversation partners. They taught principles related to the generic structure potential (GSP) of a service encounter to police officers dealing with individuals with TBI and found significant improvement in telephone service encounters following the training, in terms of the officers' ability to more efficiently establish the nature of the call, respond to queries and successfully finish the call. In turn, the caller with TBI more clearly and effectively articulated the reason for the call (purportedly as a result of the officer's ability to better clarify and control the call through structuring appropriate opportunities for the caller) and was able to terminate the call appropriately.

As an approach, SFL is comfortable with the utility of considering language not only as code, but also as behaviour, and so is a framework with high construct validity when applied to the cognitive-behavioural approaches that predominate in clinical linguistic interventions. This view of language use also resonates strongly with recent neurolinguistic understandings of plasticity in relation to how cognitive processing is shaped by experience in rich everyday contexts.

Conclusion

The contribution of SFL to clinical linguistic understandings of the nature of communication disorders to date relates to the illumination of the systematic bidirectional relationship between specific aspects of context (Field, Tenor, Mode) and the metafunctions of language (Experiential/Logical, Interpersonal, Textual) and how these are realised through available linguistic resources. In a field that predominantly focuses on language as a discrete and modular cognitive 'skill', SFL provides another perspective that enables clinicians to systematically analyse how language works and does not work within interactive contexts. It provides a variety of networks and systems that explore the complex factors that may both facilitate or impede such interactions. SFL highlights that the purpose of such interactions is central to the meanings constructed between the interactants, as is the nature of the relationship between interactants and the potential content that might be conveyed between them. Because variability of performance, and lack of generalisability of treatment tasks and performance to everyday communication situations, are often cited as problems within both clinical and research endeavours (Boyle 2014), SFL can play a role in providing hypotheses to explore such dilemmas and supplies frameworks that directly address them. Translation of SFL principles to clinical practice is an ongoing process. Further work in clarifying both assessment and treatment procedures should yield further insights and uptake by clinicians, and also provide a greater understanding of language impairment in the context of everyday interactions.

Notes

1 For an example, see Ulatowska et al. (2001).
2 For an overview, see Ferguson and Thomson (2009).
3 For a general discussion, see Bartlett et al. (2005).
4 See Dreyfus (2006) for ground-breaking work in this area.

References

Adams, C., and D.V. Bishop. 1989. Conversational characteristics of children with semantic-pragmatic disorder I: Exchange structure, turntaking, repairs and cohesion. *British Journal of Disorders of Communication* 24: 211–39.

Armstrong, E. 1987. Cohesive harmony in aphasic discourse and its significance in listener perception of coherence. In R.H. Brookshire (ed.) *Clinical Aphasiology: Conference Proceedings.* Minneapolis, MN: BRK, pp. 210–15.

Armstrong, E. 1991. The potential of cohesion analysis in the analysis and treatment of aphasic discourse. *Clinical Linguistics & Phonetics* 5(1): 39–51.

Armstrong, E. 1992. Clause complex relations in aphasic discourse: A longitudinal case study. *Journal of Neurolinguistics* 7(4): 261–75.

Armstrong, E. 2001. Connecting lexical patterns of verb usage with discourse meanings in aphasia. *Aphasiology* 15(10): 1029–46.

Armstrong, E. 2002. Variation in the discourse of non-brain-damaged speakers on a clinical task. *Aphasiology* 16(4–6): 647–58.

Armstrong, E. 2005a. Expressing opinions and feelings in aphasia: Linguistic options. *Aphasiology* 19(3–5): 285–96.

Armstrong, E. 2005b. Language disorder: A functional linguistic perspective. *Clinical Linguistics & Phonetics* 19(3): 137–53.

Armstrong, E., and H.K. Ulatowska. 2007. Making stories: Evaluative language and the aphasia experience. *Aphasiology* 21(6–8): 763–74.

Armstrong, E., N. Ciccone, E. Godecke and B. Kok. 2011. Monologues and dialogues in aphasia: Some initial comparisons. *Aphasiology* 25(11): 1347–71.

Armstrong, E., L. Mortensen, N. Ciccone and E. Godecke. 2012. Expressing opinions and feelings in an aphasia group setting. *Seminars in Speech and Language* 33(1): 16–26.

Armstrong, L., M. Brady, C. Mackenzie and J. Norrie. 2007. Transcription-less analysis of aphasic discourse: A clinician's dream or possibility. *Aphasiology* 21(3–4): 355–74.

Bartlett, S., E. Armstrong and J. Roberts. 2005. Linguistic resources of individuals with Asperger Syndrome. *Clinical Linguistics & Phonetics* 19(3): 203–13.

Boyle, M. 2014. Test–retest stability of word retrieval in aphasic discourse. *Journal of Speech, Language & Hearing Research* 57(3): 966–78.

Brinton, B., M. Fujiki and M. Baldridge. 2010. The trajectory of language impairment into adolescence: What four young women can teach us. *Seminars in Speech and Language* 31(2): 122–34.

Crystal, D. 2008. *A Dictionary of Linguistics and Phonetics.* Malden, MA: Blackwell.

Davis, L., E. Spencer and A. Ferguson. 2011. A case study on the communication of older adolescents. *Clinical Linguistics & Phonetics* 25(11–12): 1044–51.

Dreyfus, S. 2006. When there is no speech: A case study of the nonverbal multimodal communication of a child with an intellectual disability. Unpublished PhD thesis. University of Wollongong.

Dreyfus, S. 2008. A systemic functional approach to misunderstandings. Paper presented at the Australian Systemic Functional Linguistics Association Conference, University of Wollongong, July.

Dreyfus, S. 2011. Grappling with a non-speech language: Describing and theorising the nonverbal multimodal communication of a child with an intellectual disability. In S.J. Dreyfus, S. Hood and M. Stenglin (eds) *Semiotic Margins: Meaning in Multimodalities*. London: Continuum, pp. 31–52.

Dreyfus, S. 2013. Life's a bonding experience: A framework for the communication of a non-verbal intellectually disabled teenager. *Journal of Interactional Research in Communication Disorders* 4(2): 249–71.

Ferguson, A. 1992a. Conversational repair of word-finding difficulty. In M.L. Lemme (ed.) *Clinical Aphasiology*. Austin, TX: Pro-Ed, pp. 299–310.

Ferguson, A. 1992b. Interpersonal aspects of aphasic communication. *Journal of Neurolinguistics* 7(4): 277–94.

Ferguson, A. 2000. Understanding paragrammatism: Contributions from conversation analysis and systemic functional linguistics. In M. Couthard (ed.) *Working with Dialogue: Proceedings of the Seventh Biennial Congress of the International Association for Dialogue Analysis, Birmingham, 8–10 April, 1999*. Amsterdam: John Benjamins, pp. 264–74.

Ferguson, A. 2009. The discourse of speech-language pathology. *International Journal of Speech-Language Pathology* 11(2): 104–12.

Ferguson, A. 2010. Appraisal in supervisory conferencing: A linguistic analysis. *International Journal of Language & Communication Disorders* 45(2): 215–29.

Ferguson, A. 2013. A critical discourse perspective on understandings of the nature of aphasia. In M.J. Ball, N. Mueller and R. Nelson (eds) *The Handbook of Qualitative Research in Communication Disorders*. New York: Psychology Press, pp. 173–86.

Ferguson, A., and E. Armstrong. 2004. Reflections on speech-language therapists' talk: Implications for clinical practice and education. *International Journal of Language & Communication Disorders* 39(4): 469–77.

Ferguson, A., and N. Elliot. 2001. Analysing aphasia treatment sessions. *Clinical Linguistics & Phonetics* 15(3): 229–43.

Ferguson, A., and P. Peterson. 2002. Intonation in partner accommodation for aphasia: A descriptive single case study. *Journal of Communication Disorders* 35(1): 11–30.

Ferguson, A., and J. Thomson. 2009. Systemic functional linguistics and communication impairment. In M.J. Ball, M. Perkins, N. Müller and S. Howard (eds) *The Handbook of Clinical Linguistics*. Oxford: Blackwell, pp. 130–45.

Ferguson, A., L. Worrall, B. Davidson, D. Hersh, T. Howe and S. Sherratt. 2010. Talk about goals in aphasia therapy: A systemic functional analysis. *Journal of Interactional Research in Communication Disorders* 1(1): 95–118.

Fine, J., G. Bartolucci, P. Szatmari and G. Ginsberg. 1994. Cohesive discourse in pervasive developmental disorders. *Journal of Autism & Developmental Disorders* 24(3): 315–29.

Gee, J.P. (ed.). 2012. *The Routledge Handbook of Discourse Analysis*. Hoboken, NJ: Taylor & Francis.

Halliday, M.A.K. 2002 [1987]. Spoken and written modes of meaning. In J.J. Webster (ed.) *The Collected Works of M.A.K. Halliday, Vol. 1: On Grammar*. London: Continuum, pp. 323–51.

Halliday, M.A.K. 2005. Guest contribution: A note on systemic functional linguistics and the study of language disorders. *Clinical Linguistics & Phonetics* 19(3): 133–5.

Halliday, M.A.K., and R. Hasan. 1976. *Cohesion in English*. London: Longman.

Jordan, F.M., B.E. Murdoch and D.L. Buttsworth. 1991. Closed-head-injured children's performance on narrative tasks. *Journal of Speech & Hearing Research* 34(3): 572–82.

Keegan, L. 2012. An investigation of the linguistic construction of identity in individuals after traumatic brain injury. Unpublished PhD thesis. Applied Language and Speech Sciences, University of Louisiana at Lafayette.

Kilov, A., L. Togher and S. Grant. 2008. Problem solving with friends: Discourse participation and performance of individuals with and without traumatic brain injury. *Aphasiology* 23(5): 584–605.

Klecan-Aker, J.S., and B. Lopez. 1985. A comparison of T-units and cohesive ties used by first and third grade children. *Language & Speech* 28(3): 307–15.

Lee, A., O. Van Dulm, M.P. Robb and T. Ormond. 2015. Communication restriction in adults who stutter. *Clinical Linguistics & Phonetics* 29(7): 536–56.

Mantie-Kozlowski, A.R. 2010. Dysarthria in conversation: An analysis of information structure and thematic structure. *Journal of Interactional Research in Communication Disorders* 1: 237–52.

Mathers, M. 2005. Some evidence for distinctive language use by children with attention deficit hyperactivity disorder. *Clinical Linguistics & Phonetics* 19(3): 215–25.

Mathers, M. 2006. Aspects of language in children with ADHD: Applying functional analyses to explore language use. *Journal of Attention Disorders* 9: 523–33.

Mortensen, L. 1992. A transitivity analysis of discourse in dementia of the Alzheimer's type. *Journal of Neurolinguistics* 7(1): 309–24.

Mortensen, L. 2005. Written discourse and acquired brain impairment: Evaluation of structural and semantic features of personal letters from a systemic functional linguistic perspective. *Clinical Linguistics & Phonetics* 19(3): 227–47.

Müller, N., and Z. Mok. 2012. Applying systemic functional linguistics to conversations with dementia: The linguistic construction of relationships between participants. *Seminars in Speech & Language* 33(1): 5–15.

Müller, N., and B. Wilson. 2008. Collaborative role construction in a conversation with dementia: An application of systemic functional linguistics. *Clinical Linguistics & Phonetics* 22(10–11): 767–74.

Müller, N., M.J. Ball and B. Rutter. 2008. An idiosyncratic case of /r/-disorder: Application of principles from systemic phonology and systemic functional linguistics. *Asia Pacific Journal of Speech, Language & Hearing* 11: 269–82.

Nickels, L. 2008. The hypothesis testing approach to the assessment of language. In B. Stemmer and H. Whitaker (eds) *Handbook of the Neuroscience of Language*. Oxford: Elsevier, pp. 13–22.

Olness, G., J. Gyger and K. Thomas. 2012. Analysis of narrative functionality: Toward evidence-based approaches in managed care settings. *Seminars in Speech and Language* 33(1): 55–67.

Rigaudeau-McKenna, B. 2005. Towards an analysis of dysfunctional grammar. *Clinical Linguistics & Phonetics* 19(3): 155–74.

Sherratt, S. 2007. Right brain damage and the verbal expression of emotion: A preliminary investigation. *Aphasiology* 21(3–4): 320–39.

Simmons-Mackie, N., A.M. Raymer, E. Armstrong, A. Holland and L.R. Cherney. 2010. Communication partner training in aphasia: A systematic review. *Archives of Physical and Medical Rehabilitation* 91(12): 1814–37.

Spencer, E., A. Packman, M. Onslow and A. Ferguson. 2005. A preliminary investigation of the impact of stuttering on language use. *Clinical Linguistics & Phonetics* 19(3): 191–201.

Spencer, E., A. Packman, M. Onslow and A. Ferguson. 2009. The effect of stuttering on communication: A preliminary investigation. *Clinical Linguistics & Phonetics* 23(7): 473–88.

Thomson, J. 2003a. Clinical discourse analysis: One theory or many? *Advances in Speech Language Pathology* 5(1): 41–9.

Thomson, J. 2003b. Clinical forum reply. *Advances in Speech Language Pathology* 5(1): 69–72.

Thomson, J. 2005. Theme analysis of narratives produced by children with and without specific language impairment. *Clinical Linguistics & Phonetics* 19(3): 175–90.

Togher, L. 2000. Giving information: The importance of context on communicative opportunity for people with traumatic brain injury. *Aphasiology* 14(4): 365–90.

Togher, L. 2001. Discourse sampling in the twenty-first century. *Journal of Communication Disorders* 34(1–2): 131–50.

Togher, L., and L. Hand. 1998. Use of politeness markers with different communication partners: An investigation of five subjects with traumatic brain injury. *Aphasiology* 12(7–8): 755–70.

Togher, L., L. Hand and C. Code. 1996. A new perspective on the relationship between communication impairment and disempowerment following head injury in information exchanges. *Disability & Rehabilitation* 18(11): 559–66.

Togher, L., L. Hand and C. Code. 1997a. Analysing discourse in the traumatic brain injury population: Telephone interactions with different communication partners. *Brain Injury* 11(3): 169–89.

Togher, L., L. Hand and C. Code. 1997b. Measuring service encounters in the traumatic brain injury population. *Aphasiology* 11(4–5): 491–504.

Togher, L., S. McDonald, C. Code and S. Grant. 2004. Training communication partners of people with traumatic brain injury: A randomised controlled trial. *Aphasiology* 18(4): 313–35.

Ulatowska, H.K., G.S. Olness, R.T. Wertz, J.L. Thompson, M.W. Keebler, C.L. Hill and L.L. Auther. 2001. Comparison of language impairment, functional communication, and discourse measures in African-American aphasic and normal adults. *Aphasiology* 15(10–11): 1007–16.

Whitworth, A. 2010. Using narrative as a bridge: Linking language processing models with real-life communication. *Seminars in Speech and Language* 31(1): 64–75.

505

31

Language as verbal art

Donna R. Miller

> [T]he paradox of 'poetic' language [is] that there is *no such thing* . . . but we can all recognize it when we see it.
>
> *Halliday 2002 [1982]: 134, emphasis added*[1]

Introduction

This chapter delineates the framework for the study of 'verbal art', as modelled by Ruqaiya Hasan, pointing towards ways in which it can be compared with 'mainstream' stylistics in terms of strengths and drawbacks. The chapter also provides a circumscribed chronicle of inputs to the model and an illustration of application. Finally, it briefly discusses just how, and how not, corpus linguistics might be usefully merged with what Hasan has dubbed 'social-semiotic stylistics' (SSS).[2]

Core definitions and issues

Vis-à-vis mainstream theoretical-methodological approaches to stylistics, the verbal art framework in systemic functional linguistics (SFL) is significantly distinct. This is unsurprising, given that it sees literature as its sole object of study, rather than extending its brief to other text types, as mainstream stylistics tends more and more to do. This is because its view of what literature *is* is also different and categorically so. For Halliday et al. (1964: 245), '[l]iterature is language for its own sake: the only use of language, perhaps, where the aim is to use language'. Yet although the Hallidayan formula speaks explicitly of 'aim', the observation can be said to be not dissimilar to Jakobson's (1960: 356, emphasis added) definition of his 'poetic function', with its corresponding focus on the factor of the 'message' itself: 'The set (Einstellung) toward the message as such, focus on the message *for its own sake*, is the poetic function of language.' The chapter will return to the vital links between Jakobson and the verbal art framework later. In 1964 – and again in 1971, and 1985 and 1989 – Hasan (1989 [1985]: 91) puts forth an analogous proposition, that 'in verbal art the role of language is central. Here language is not as clothing to the body; it is the body.' Both Halliday and Hasan performed the seminal work that gave us the SFL verbal art paradigm, but it was primarily Hasan's task in the course of the 1970s to better delineate the model.

So there is an essential bone of contention between Hasan's model and those of mainstream sylisticians, one from which most other issues can be seen to stem, and it resides in the verbal art view that literature is 'different' – indeed, 'special': a notion that goes against the grain of what mainstream stylisticians have increasingly tended to posit – that is, that literature needs none other than the sundry tools brought to the analysis of any text type. However, at one level, Hasan (1989 [1985]: 92) very much agrees: she sees the starting point for the analysis of literature as being identical to that for any text. The difference lies in her insistence that the artistic value and status of literature depends exclusively on 'how language functions in the text' (Hasan 1989 [1985]: 91), and that revealing this function requires another, special, level of analysis, more on which below.

The model then is fundamentally incompatible with other approaches, despite certain apparent overlaps in how the discipline is defined. Simpson (2014 [2004]) is particularly exploited in this chapter as the rival yardstick, since his *Resource Book for Students* engages with theoretical aspects that help in setting out the conflicts. The task of extricating the divergences from the convergences, however, is not at all straightforward, because the definitions for key terms range from somewhat to radically divergent and indeed are not always transparent. Disambiguating what is, at times, their polysemous nature is also ticklish at best.

On the surface, Simpson's (2014 [2004]: 3) introductory definition of the discipline throws down no gauntlets to the verbal art camp: 'Stylistics is a method of textual interpretation in which primacy of place is assigned to language.' He even goes on to assert that 'stylistics is interested in language as a function of texts in context' (Simpson 2014 [2004]: 3) and to speak of patterns of language as an index to a text's function – none of which poses a challenge to the verbal art theory. In fact, Simpson's (2014 [2004]: 53) definition of Mukařovskian foregrounding as 'a form of textual patterning which is motivated specifically for literary-aesthetic purposes' is just right. But it is not insignificant that Simpson (2014 [2004]: 106–7) then apparently retracts the definition, presumably since the aesthetic motivation of literature would appear to be at odds with his – albeit admirable and necessary – project of debunking the conventional reverence of the literary critic for literature. Essentially, what foregrounding finally boils down to for Simpson (2014 [2004]: 52) is 'distortion' of some kind: either by deviating from a norm or by bringing it to the fore through reiteration. Much as Halliday (2002 [1971]: 100) had argued against deviation's relevance to stylistics, Hasan (1989 [1985]: 92) unequivocally eschews the notion of foregrounding as deviation, reasoning that deviation is not a characteristic of literature alone.

So the conflict is rooted primarily in that notion of the special nature of literature, which entails there being special requisite characteristics that make a text literature, or verbal art. These will be clarified by degrees directly, but it is worth noting here that Simpson (2014 [2004]: 106–7) candidly, and categorically, disputes this belief:

> To argue for the existence of a distinct literary register is effectively to argue for a kind of cliché, because it would involve reigning stylistic expression into a set of formulaic prescriptions. . . . To claim that literary language is special, that it can somehow be bracketed off from the mundane or commonplace in discourse, is ultimately to wrest it away from the practice of stylistics.

Although negotiation of meaning in this excerpt is clearly being shut down, these monoglossic assertions are plainly debatable. One might answer back that the verbal art theory, while emphatically claiming a special status for the literature text, does not aim at setting confines on stylistic expression nor does it want to isolate it from stylistic study. Ultimately, too, the theory does not argue for a 'literary' register at all; indeed, quite the contrary.

Indeed, Hasan's own work on SFL's modelling of language according to use, or register theory – the SFL view that each instance of language use is rooted in the context of some social situation, which will tend to activate meanings that will tend to be realised in wordings[3] – proved fundamental to (a) her demarcation of verbal art as indisputably a kind of language use in a particular social context, as registers are seen to be, but then also to (b) her conviction that it is *not* a register like any other. Why? Because the context–language connection in verbal art is fraught with complexities to which other registers are simply not heir (Hasan 1975: 54, 2007: 22–3).[4] For this reason, it requires a different theoretical and methodological take.

So, rather than arguing for a distinct literary register, Hasan (1989 [1985]: 94) maintains that literature cannot be defined according to the same criteria as other registers. What is needed, first and foremost, she proposes, is a *shift of focus*: one that will abandon the misguided search for the language *of* literature and focus instead on language *in* literature, on the role it plays, its function *in* the text – that is, on what makes it literature, or 'verbal' art. The essential premise of the verbal art model is that literature is 'created by languaging in a particular way' (Hasan 2007: 16, emphasis original). And that particular way gives us 'language that is artistic and art that is linguistic' (Hasan, in personal correspondence with the author, 15 April 2014). Moreover, in suggesting a way in which to distinguish between what is verbal art and what, most likely, is not, Hasan (1989 [1985]: 101) actually pits 'literary' against 'literature':

> If the patterning [foregrounding] of patterns is consistently utilised for a second-order semiosis . . . then the text in question is a literature text. If, however, such a role is not played by the patternings, then we have a literary text. The recognition of this distinction is important, not least because the techniques for the study and evaluation of the two are not identical.

Again, Jakobson's (1960: 357) thought comes fittingly to mind – this time, on how the poetic function is to be found even outside poetry proper: '[T]he linguistic study of the poetic function must overstep the limits of poetry.' A more, if not fully, detailed description of this special function, in terms of the notion of foregrounding,[5] and also of the model of 'double-articulation' devised for its analysis (Hasan 2007) and the techniques involved, will be provided later in the chapter.

Another word on the nature of the verbal art model at this juncture is, however, in order: SSS is also defined as a 'public discourse' in which an explicit model of language is required as its basis. Such a framework must be 'maximally applicable to the genre [i.e., to literature], irrespective of variations in time, sub-genre, and the critic's response' (Hasan 1989 [1985]: 90). This means simply that any text that qualifies as literature, be it the epic in Old English, *Beowulf*, a Romantic lyric poem, Joyce's *Ulysses*, or a twenty-first-century graphic novel, will be open to the model's techniques of analysis. That may prove consoling for some, but overly tight-reined for others, because 'the model' means '*the* model'. It is uncompromising in that it is not open to methodological input from the proliferation of sub-disciplines, such as feminist stylistics, cognitive stylistics and discourse stylistics, which Simpson (2014 [2004]: 2) sees as enriching the methods of stylistic practice – or even, in theory at least, corpus-linguistics-based, or assisted, stylistics, about which more will be said shortly.

In closing this introductory section, let us candidly acknowledge that the verbal art model is little known, and/or little appreciated, not only outside of SFL circles, but also within them. For many, it is considered (not unlike SFL itself) to be 'daunting' – and needlessly so. Why should this be? Admittedly, SSS relies even for its first-order analysis on the SFL multiple-coding system for the realisation of meanings, and to this 'semiotic system of language' and its hardly popular – in the sense of both widespread and well liked – metalanguage, it then adds a second layer, the 'semiotic system of verbal art', with its own additional metalanguage to learn to wield.

But apart from the metalingual issue, perhaps the verbal art model is simply too holistic, too absolute, for most palates; it also requires painstaking analysis that is extremely systematic and intricate, and so also time-consuming. For its committed practitioners, it may all be well worth it – in fact, mandatory – but there is no denying that it is not 'easy' nor that it will not be content with characterising literature as a question of serendipitously, or even studiously, gleaned isolated patterns of language, but rather insists that such patternings be demonstrated, at a higher order, to be motivated, consistently, and so globally 'significant' – notions that will be further disambiguated next, with a step back in time.

A selective chronicle raising more issues and topics

Space precludes tracing a comprehensive, or even partial, history of the discipline of stylistics and its various 'stages' and offshoots;[6] thus only very limited, if hopefully relevant, comments will be made in this section.

The SSS perspective is not new. As Hasan (2007: 21) points out, 'it actually predates the 1960s' structural stylistics'. She sees the initial approach to the perspective as having been made by the Russian neo-formalists and Prague Circle scholars – especially Mukařovský (1964, 1977, 1978) in his 1928 discussion of 'foregrounding'. For Hasan, 'Garvin's little book' (that is, Garvin 1964) was the first to offer the uninitiated an illuminating glimpse of Prague School aesthetics and she was certainly at least one of the first researchers to use its insights in a full-length study: her unpublished PhD thesis at the University of Edinburgh (Hasan 1964). And while what became contemporary stylistics was emerging and defining itself – and, in the style of any self-respecting discipline, splintering into rival factions– in these early years of the discipline, Hasan – but also Halliday – were actively, if 'differently', contributing to its definition.

If this rough sketch is to make any sense, however, it must be at least somewhat fleshed out. The roots of stylistics go back to the formalist tradition that developed in Russian literary criticism at the turn of the twentieth century – especially within the Moscow Linguistic Circle, whose most renowned member and exponent of the Russian variant of formalism was Roman Jakobson. In 1920, Jakobson emigrated to Czechoslovakia, where a collaboration with Czech literary scholars, foremost among them Mukařovský, began, the Prague Linguistic Circle being established in 1926. That Circle was to give birth to structuralism. Both Jakobson and Mukařovský focused on identifying the formal and functional distinctions between literary and non-literary writing, the former theorising the functions of parallelism and the latter, of foregrounding, and in very similar terms. It is fair to say that these concepts became the cornerstones of contemporary stylistics.

Jakobson's work with the Prague Circle was disrupted by the escalation of hostilities leading up to the Second World War; after some years as an itinerant scholar, he settled in the United States in 1941 – a move that was essential to the spread of his ideas to American, but also European, scholars, as well as to the later development of the new criticism and practical criticism movements in the United States and the United Kingdom, respectively. These were then-novel approaches to literature interpretation focusing on the language of the text. Although there were important differences in their concerns, both were techniques of 'close reading', which enjoyed decades of popularity, albeit that the approach has long been viewed by stylisticians as an outmoded, because inexact and insufficient, analytical paradigm. Halliday's (2002 [1982]: 128) own criticism is of its failure to relate the text to the linguistic system – that is, to meaning potential. This new critical focus on the text itself was also seen as its decontextualised and even dehumanised reification – texts being treated as (even sacramental) objects[7] – in the (negative) opinion of some. It is possible that this is linked to, albeit clearly not solely responsible for, Simpson's apparent fears of the least prescriptivism being allowed to govern the definition and interpretative tools of literature.

Be that as it may, a few words will now be said on the theory and practice of 'linguistic criticism' (Fowler 1986), as opposed to 'literary criticism', since it will help us to link with, and further explain, the reasons why 'specialness' is so vehemently censured by stylisticians today. It will also help us to further associate Jakobson with SSS. To separate the names and work of Mukařovský and Jakobson is difficult and a mistake, as will now be argued in more detail.

Fowler and linguistic criticism

The field of linguistic criticism owes much to the seminal and laudable work – and struggles – of Roger Fowler to wrest literature back from the 'lit crits' as a legitimate object of linguistic study, as the legendary caustic, if also witty, Fowler–Bateson (1967, 1968) debates testify. That said, two particular aspects of Fowler's subsequent ways of thinking should be scrutinised. The first is his take on the definition of what literature is:

> No plausible essentialist or intrinsic definition of literature has been or is likely to be devised. For my purpose, no such theory is necessary. What literature is can be stated empirically, within the realm of socio-linguistic fact. It is: an open set of texts, of great formal diversity, recognized by a culture as possessing certain institutional values and performing certain functions.
>
> *Fowler 1981: 81*

The conflict with Hasan's own exquisitely essentialist definition is obvious, although her SSS perspective does not undervalue the importance of culture and community. Indeed, she says that 'the literature text . . . embodies precisely the kind of "truths" that most communities are deeply concerned with' (Hasan 1989 [1985]: 100). But she does not invest the power for deciding what is or is not literature in the community, whether it be that of the time and place of the text's creation or at a further semiotic social distance (Hasan 2007: 34). This is not to say that the social does not impinge on verbal art: indeed, 'perhaps the most critical part it plays is in the shaping of the ideological orientations of those who write and those who read literature' (Hasan 2007: 25). And a text's endurance as art will hinge on the value that is awarded to it by successive generations of readers: 'The challenge for the creator of verbal art is that the symbolically articulated theme has to be capable of striking a chord in the reader over substantial distances in time and space' (Hasan 2007: 25). Despite these convergences, however, it is the divergences between essentialist SSS and Fowler's viewpoint that remain dominant.

The second aspect of Fowler's thought that might be considered is what, to this author's knowledge, he was the first to call 'the Mukařovský–Jakobson theory', a term coined in the process of his perceptively – and rightly – noting the theoretical intersection of Mukařovský's foregrounding and Jakobson's grammatical parallelism: 'For both of these writers, literary language draws the reader's attention to its own artifices of construction' (Fowler 1986: 73). But Fowler expressly censures their position on the functions and motives of foregrounding, and explicitly sets it up against his own. As suggested in relation to Simpson, the impact of the new criticism and/or contemporary 'lit crit' theories on Fowler's stance should not be discounted. Be that as it may, Fowler was a trailblazer, rightly focused on defending the valuable role of a linguistic analysis of literature against those who derided it. (When one crosses swords with lit crits, a mask is advisable, although visual acuity may then be impaired.)

The relevance of Jakobson's work for SSS, however, is a vital further direction that verbal art studies need to take. To espouse Jakobson's work, even in this postmodern era, is not to advocate an obsessive 'structural' approach to language, because he strongly believed in the inseparability of form and meaning, and was also aware of the vital role of context; rather than a stringent, die-hard structuralist, he was foremost a linguist who was attentive to semantics, semiotics and poetics.[8] Although Jakobson had no functional lexicogrammar with which to substantiate his claims, but simply examples based on traditional grammar and phonology, and although he does not appear explicitly to speak of the role of foregrounding in articulating the aesthetically motivated theme of the work, the analogies between Jakobson's insights and those of Mukařovský – analogies justifiably recognised by Fowler – are simply too many and important to be ignored. In Miller (2012, 2013, 2016), the case is made for recognising – *pace* Hasan's misgivings – that the function of Jakobson's grammatical parallelism must be likened to that of Hasan's patterning of patterns, her foregrounding that 'counts' – that is, the motivated consistency of semantic direction for the symbolic articulation of verbal art, what its art resides in. An illustrative analysis is offered below.

The meeting of like minds

Halliday's own stance on the function of literature with reference to that of Hasan was glossed in the first section of this chapter. Here, something more will be said, not to establish who 'took' what from whom, but rather to show how the ideas of these two scholars on literature and its analysis evolved in largely parallel fashion, as the ideas of like minds in contact will.

Coincidently, perhaps, Halliday spoke of literature being language for its own sake in 1964, the same year in which Hasan wrote her PhD thesis. In 1971, already engaging with Hasan's work, Halliday speaks of Mukařovský's concept of foregrounding in terms of motivated 'prominence' of grammatical features. He proposes twin levels of meaning, both grammatically realised, but one 'underlying' and 'deeper' than the first, 'immediate' level, also glossed as 'subject matter' (Halliday 2002 [1971]: 118–20 *et passim*).[9] The deeper semantic meanings are said, crucially, 'to serve a vision of things . . . The vision provides the motivation for their prominence' (Halliday 2002 [1971]: 104–5).

In Halliday (2002 [1982]: 131, emphasis added), the term 'foregrounding' is replaced by 'de-automatization', with a view to underlining the distinct, if complementary, roles of these two semantic levels from an SFL perspective:

> [W]hat is in question is not simply prominence but rather the partial *freeing of the lower-level systems* from the control of the semantics so that they become domains of choice in their own right. In terms of systemic theory the de-automatization of the

grammar means that grammatical choices are not simply determined from above: there is selection and pre-selection. Hence the wording becomes a *quasi-independent semiotic mode through which the meanings of the work can be projected.*

Without stopping to properly disambiguate the SFL metalanguage here, I would simply draw attention to the two distinct semiotic modes of literature meaning-making being hypothesised and to the fact that these are analogous to the scaffolding of the doubly articulated framework for the analysis of verbal art that Hasan began to model in 1971, which will be properly described directly.

Now, however, it is time for at least a passing reference to what is queried in Miller (2010: 48) as seeming to be a 'politics of exclusion'. Although tribute is ritually paid to Halliday as having been a major influence on the development of British stylistics, it is regularly denied to Hasan. Fowler (1966), of course, was responsible for initially publicising SFL's transitivity system – the main mechanism investigated in the oft-cited Halliday (2002 [1971]) – as a useful stylistic tool. The system has enjoyed wide and repeated application in mainstream stylistics – perhaps because it is seen as being more 'mainstream' itself[10] – but never linked to recognition of the verbal art model. Butler (2003) notes Halliday's influence on a number of monographs on stylistics, including Toolan (1990) and Leech and Short (2007 [1981]). But Hasan's framework is glaringly 'missing' not only from the canonical stylistics scene, but also from the bibliographies of studies by some SFL practitioners. The reasons discussed at the end of the introduction to this chapter are most likely relevant, but perhaps it also has something to do with Halliday simply being harder to ignore and the fact that certain aspects of the SFL model can be integrated into a stylistics textbook without that textbook needing to deal with a holistic 'model' of the kind that Hasan proposes. In other words, perhaps it is because it has been easier to ignore Hasan's authority that it has indeed been largely ignored.

But now to an illustration of that model of double-articulation: of the special functional role that language patterns in literature can be seen to play in construing a specific kind of social meaning exchange, investigated with a mode of analysis that is open to scrutiny – that is, retrievable and replicable.

SSS research methods and practice: a 'taste' of application

The model of double-articulation is reproduced in Figure 31.1.

A full explanation of Figure 31.1 can be found elsewhere,[11] but on the basis of what has been said thus far we can recognise the level of language – the analysis of which, recall, is the same as for any other text type – and the higher level, the first stratum of which, Verbalisation, includes all of the lower and builds upon it, by means of the foregrounding, or 'symbolic articulation', of the 'theme'.

In short, symbolic articulation makes the theme accessible to us – in the same way as, in the semiotic system of language, the lexicogrammar makes the semantics (that is, the stratum 'above' it) accessible to us. If we look at it from 'below', we can see symbolic articulation as the place where the first-order or lower-level meanings are 'added to', or 'expanded upon', or 'heightened', or 'enriched', or 'deepened', and are made 'art'. How it does this is through foregrounding (or the patterning of patterns), the process by which the meanings emerging through analysis of the semiotic system of language are symbolically turned into signs, for the purpose, the aesthetic motive, or 'artistic intention' (Mukařovský 1977) of expressing the theme – a generalisation on the nature of human existence.

Semiotic system of verbal art

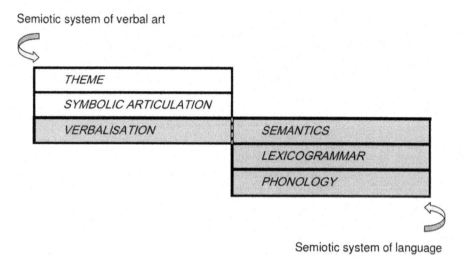

Figure 31.1 Verbal art and language
Source: Adapted from Hasan (1989 [1985]: 99)

A brief example of analysis of the functions of foregrounded patterning in a short poem will allow further aspects of the framework to emerge.[12] The text is William Blake's 'The Garden of Love', which has been adopted in graduate-level stylistics courses to begin to illustrate the framework, since it is perfect for the purpose: a text by an author typically included in English studies curricula in Italian schools, short, straightforward and replete with linguistic mechanisms that 'mean' by construing a tension between features that are backgrounded and foregrounded, and so symbolically articulating its theme, which is then further revealed through probing Blake's own world view, in opposition to that of his contemporary discourse community:

(1)   I went to the garden of love,
(2)   And saw what I never had seen:
(3)   A chapel was built in the midst,
(4)   Where I used to play on the green.

(5)   And the gates of this chapel were shut,
(6)   And *Thou shalt not* writ over the door;
(7)   So I turned to the garden of love,
(8)   That so many sweet flowers bore,

(9)   And I saw it was filled with graves,
(10) And tomb stones where flowers should be –
(11) And priests in black gowns were walking their rounds,
(12) And binding with briars my joys and desires.

With the class, systematic functional analysis of the poem is first performed at the level of the semiotic system of language – that is, of its lexicogrammar as the instantiation of meanings, line by line: a detailed examination of transitivity structure, taxis, the systems of mood, modality and appraisal, Thematic progression, etc., all of which clearly cannot be reproduced here. After ensuing discussion of what the text is purportedly 'about', we move to the higher semiotic order of verbal art, and discuss which of our findings might be reconsidered as evidence of motivated and consistent foregrounding. This means pointing out patternings, to a great degree in terms of Jakobson's grammatical parallelism, and invariably leads us to what emerges as a highly significant semantic location, the final closed couplet, the meanings of which are presaged in the disconcerting lines (5)–(6), with their biblical Decalogue intertext and past participles as Attributes, *shut* and *writ*, and presupposition of Do-ers whose identity is disclosed only at the poem's end.

We start with focusing on patterns of the smallest units on the rank scale, morphemes and phonemes, in terms of meter and rhyme. The text is plainly composed of three four-line stanzas, the first ten lines of which provide imperfect rhythmic parallelism in terms of what is basically trimeter with a mixture of iambs (x/) and anapests (xx/). The last two lines disrupt the pattern with a ponderous tetrameter (iamb+anapest+iamb+anapest) and also by means of caesuras. The rhyme pattern of the first two stanzas is a regular a, b, c, b/ d, e, a, e, with second and fourth lines rhyming, whereas in the third stanza there is no end rhyme at all, but solely *internal* rhyme within the last two lines (*gowns, rounds, briars, desires*). As Taylor Torsello (1992: 50–2) notes, the tension-less sing-song and quasi-infantile predominantly paratactic structure of the text construes a reassuring symmetrical environment that tempts a reader into an acritical appreciation, which the weighty meanings – only fully to the fore and entirely, if metaphorically, made explicit in the final couplet – belie.

In addition to meter and rhyme, foregrounded features in the couplet also include the new, or newly specified, human Agents of negatively appraised action Processes there: the Thematically highlighted *priests*, immediately in conflict with the *I* of the poem, who is now represented as the 'Possessor' of the things being victimised (*my joys and desires*), and so implicitly also as putative Receiver of the generic prohibition *Thou shalt no*t, engraved in cold stone in line 6, as the tables of the Law originally were, of course (Deuteronomy 5.1–22).

In addition, there is a marked focus on tense and time, which is intricately woven into strands of degrees of pastness throughout the text: the couplet gives us the only textual instances of real-time-in-the-past, the progressive form, which confers immediacy, and immovability, to the disturbingly vivid negative actions of *walking rounds* (the way in which military patrols might do) and *binding with briars* (that is, with a negatively figurative thorny, painful and vexatious substance). These distasteful Processes add to the text's numerous lexical strings functioning in negative-vs-positive evaluative tension, but which there is no space to expand upon here.

Thus students see the functions of foregrounded patterning located in a significant textual location and working towards the same kinds of general meanings within the text. Invited to consider their aesthetic motivation – that is, to see these foregrounded meanings as being symbolically articulated by the text for the purpose of expressing a theme – what they formulate is roughly the following generalisation: 'Religion subverts natural freedom/innocence by restricting their expression.'

This theme will undergo only minor modification as a result of the subsequent research into the context of creation of the poem that students themselves perform. Blake emerges as an experimenter with form/technique, his partial rhythms and then-novel rhymes tending to challenge then-current conventions, for example his using the 'lyric' poem as a vehicle of a strangely disturbing message – indeed, for social critique.

And indeed the Blakian cultural paradigm emerges as being in open conflict with the dominant belief and value system of his time: his voice was often candidly raised against social injustice and sexual repression. At the same time, however, he is shown to be very religious, although *un*orthodoxically so. The addition of a single word is, then, sufficient to incorporate these findings in the reconsidered theme: '*Institutionalised* religion subverts natural freedom/innocence by restricting their expression.'

Current contributions and future directions

As Lukin (2015) notes, a summary of some of the Halliday-inspired studies of literary texts can be found in Butler (2003: 445–6, cf. Lukin and Webster 2005; Butt and Lukin 2009). The work of many scholars within the SFL, if not strictly 'verbal art', framework should by rights be mentioned here, foremost among these being Butt, Lukin and Webster in particular on the Australian scene, David Banks in France, and, in Italy, Taylor Torsello and Miller, but also Turci and Luporini. Special mention should also go to Manfredi (2012, 2014) in Italy, and to Lukin and Pagano (2012), the latter in Brazil, for their work on the translation of verbal art.

Looking forward, besides continuing to whittle away at resistance to the verbal art framework, this author's objective of getting Jakobson's grammatical parallelism formally slotted into the SSS approach to the analysis of verbal art – to which much recent work has been devoted (for example Miller 2007, 2010, 2012, 2013, 2016) – will remain a priority. Overcoming Hasan's own misgivings will remain, alas, a mission only partially accomplished.

In addition, Luporini and Miller are continuing to examine the extent to which corpus linguistics can/should be a part of the ongoing development of a rigorous SSS. In brief, the research question addressed is: are corpus-assisted studies of the symbolic articulation of theme within the verbal art framework legitimately and profitably do-able? Quantitative stylistic studies are, of course, not new. In searching for systemic functional linguists on the topic, one finds Bednarek (2008) offering a brief introductory 'Language + Literature + Corpus Linguistics Methods 101' in an SFL perspective, but not a Hasanian one, and Toolan (2009, for example) arguing that using corpus evidence to support qualitative analysis can be useful, as Turci (2007) also demonstrates. Again, however, in neither of these otherwise valuable works is Hasan's model made use of.

A related query is whether foregrounding – at least at a preliminary investigative stage – is quantifiable. We recall Halliday's (2002 [1971]) own explicit caveat that prominence as motivated foregrounding is not tantamount to mere statistical frequency. We ponder the pretty safe bet that systematically tracing the symbolic articulation of theme would appear to require labour-intensive manual analysis – that is, painstaking attention to logogenesis – or to the 'unfolding of the act of meaning itself: the instantial construction of meaning in the form of a text . . . in which the potential for creating meaning is continually modified *in the light of what has gone before*' (Halliday and Matthiessen 1999: 18, emphasis added).

The distinction that Halliday (2006: 298) makes between logogenesis as the instantial construction of meaning in the form of a text and of a corpus is useful here. In the former, a text is being studied as object, whereby it is valued as a discourse in its own right (vs text studied as instrument, whereby its value is as a window on to the system). Clearly, verbal art is the illustration *par excellence* of the former: *a discourse valued in its own right*. Such reflections are not encouraging for corpus approaches. But Halliday has also argued for the validity of 'counting' the linguistic options chosen by an author as a step towards establishing the potentially motivated prominence of patterns in literature. Although foregrounding itself *cannot* be expressed statistically (Halliday 2002 [1971]: 102–3), '[a] rough indication of frequencies is often just what is needed' to evaluate what features deserve further investigation – which is precisely what this chapter suggests as well, keeping in mind, however, that in relying excessively on frequency, one risks missing significant non-frequent foregrounded items, and so vital parts of the full picture.

And so if, on the one hand, it is well known that automatic analyses cannot give us the findings we need at the 'higher' levels of semantics and context (Halliday and Matthiessen 2004: 48–9), no matter what the text type, on the other, perhaps the extent to which patterns (especially those in contrast with an established tendency) are quantifiable would seem to be inscrutable – at least in longer texts – without the (at least initial) assistance of corpus linguistics methods. Hence we continue to study the benefits – and limits – of the venture (for example Miller and Luporini 2015, forthcoming*a*).

These studies investigate in particular the evaluative meanings of certain key words emerging from software-obtained frequencies in J.M. Coetzee's 1986 novel *Foe*. Very succinctly, the results are not discouraging: there is evidence that we have taken some concrete, if hardly giant, steps towards showing that corpus linguistics methods do indeed play a valuable role in SSS analysis, helping with at least the initial identification of patterns that are potentially functional towards articulating the theme, and also that they make SSS research more rigorous, replicable and retrievable (cf. Simpson 2014 [2004]: 4) – that is, guaranteeing statistical significance that cannot be manually achieved in longer texts. At the same time, however, the constant need for co-textualisation by means of growing concordances to logogenetically probe-able lengths continues to prove indispensable. Moreover, as always, the hypothesised theme must still be further substantiated with the aid of research into the context of creation, which, recall, is a vital part of those complexities of the text–context connection that are inherent in literature and which make it a 'register' unlike any other.

As a final point, harnessing Lukin's (2008) arguments for an explicit language-based teaching of literature, and also mindful of the crucial function of enquiry of verbal art asserted by Butt (1996), Miller and Luporini (forthcoming*b*, for example) are also currently focusing on corpus-assisted SSS as an appliable pedagogical stylistics in English as a second language (ESL) teaching/learning.

In closing

While this chapter represents an attempt to adopt an objectively critical stance to the issues presented, a penchant for the verbal art framework may inevitably have seeped through. So here, at the end, that enthusiasm might be further explained with words borrowed from Hasan (2007: 34), which presuppose that the characteristics asserted are positively evaluated:

> The social semiotic model of literature reinstates verbal art as the focal concern of the discipline of literature, treating it as a variety of language use, with its own specific dynamics, its own mode of art construal. Instead of mystifying the nature of verbal art, it offers a framework for its study, which frees the reader from unquestioningly following the opinions of 'authorities'; what is more, it provides a mode of analysis that is open to scrutiny, so that evidence for competing claims can be compared. In this sense the model is enabling. It provides a vocabulary for discussing problems related to the discipline of literature and highlights important questions, many of which have never been asked.

Notes

1 https://benjamins.com/#catalog/books/cilt.15/main. We thank John Benjamins for permission to use the quotation.
2 From 2011 on, Hasan used the term and abbreviation in personal communications with the author. Publicly, she used it only in conference presentations (e.g. Hasan 2013). There are no published instances of its use, although Hasan had planned to write up the 2013 paper and also to discuss it in the final volume of her collected works (forthcoming). Not long before her sad passing, Hasan modified the label social-*semiotic* stylistics to systemic socio-semantic stylistics (personal correspondence with the author, 1 January 2015). The abbreviation, in any case, remains SSS.
3 Cf. Bartlett, this volume, on context, as well as Moore, this volume, on register analysis.
4 Meaning that there are diverse contexts at work: the fictional context created by the text; a context of creation comprising the language, world view and artistic conventions of the time/place of writing, and a context of reception of the reader, all of which dynamically impact on the text and its interpretation and require the analyst's close scrutiny (cf. Hasan 1989 [1985]: 101–3; Hasan 1996: 50–4).
5 Cf. Halliday's (2002 [1982]: 131) preferred term 'de-automatization'.
6 But see, e.g., Miller and Turci (Introduction to 2007) and Busse and McIntyre (2010).
7 These are intricate Marxist-based critical theory issues that are brilliantly elucidated in a diachronic perspective by a semi-anonymous author in herrnaphta (2011).
8 See, e.g., Stankiewicz (1983: 24) and Caton (1987: 223–4).
9 Cf. Hodge, this volume, on Halliday's seminal paper as 'an exemplary piece of discourse analysis'.
10 I am grateful to Gerard O'Grady for pointing out that scholars outside SFL have apparently felt Halliday's transitivity system to be akin to case grammar and so perhaps less of a challenge to non-SFL theory.
11 First and foremost, in Hasan 1989 [1985], with summaries in Miller (2010, 2012, 2013, 2016).
12 This analysis takes many observations from the work of an outstanding scholar who has been, after Hasan and Halliday themselves, a muse over the years: Carol Taylor Torsello (1992). It was proposed in Miller (2010) as well and is reproposed in revised form here with the permission of the publishers.

References

Bednarek, M. 2008. Teaching English literature and linguistics using corpus stylistic methods. Paper presented at the Australian Systemic Functional Linguistics Association 2007. Available online at http://www.asfla.org.au/category/asfla2007.

Busse, B., and D. McIntyre. 2010. Language, literature and stylistics. In D. McIntyre and B. Busse (eds) *Language and Style*. Basingstoke: Palgrave, pp. 3–14.

Butler, C. 2003. *Structure and Function: A Guide to Three Major Structural-Functional Theories, Part 2 – From Clause to Discourse and beyond*. Amsterdam and Philadelphia, PA: John Benjamins.

Butt, D. 1996. Literature, culture and the classroom: The aesthetic function in our information era. In J.E. James (ed.) *The Language–Culture Connection*. Singapore: SEAMO Regional Language Centre, pp. 86–106.

Butt, D., and A. Lukin. 2009. Stylistic analysis and arguments against randomness. In M.A.K. Halliday and J.J. Webster (eds) *Continuum Companion to Systemic Functional Linguistics*. London and New York: Continuum, pp. 190–215.

Caton, S.C. 1987. Contributions of Roman Jakobson. *Annual Review of Anthropology* 16: 223–60.

Coetzee, J.M. 1986. *Foe*. New York: Viking Press.

Fowler, R. (ed.). 1966. *Essays on Style and Language*. London: Routledge & Kegan Paul.

Fowler, R. 1981. *Literature as Social Discourse: The Practice of Linguistic Criticism*. London: Batsford.

Fowler, R. 1986. *Linguistic Criticism*. Oxford: Oxford University Press.

Fowler, R., and F.W. Bateson. 1967. Argument II: Literature and linguistics. *Essays in Criticism* 17: 322–47.

Fowler, R., and F.W. Bateson. 1968. Argument II (continued): Language and literature. *Essays in Criticism* 18: 164–82.

Garvin, P. (ed.). 1964. *A Prague School Reader on Aesthetics, Literary Structure and Style*. Washington, DC: Georgetown University Press.

Halliday, M.A.K. 2002 [1971]. Linguistic function and literary style: An inquiry into the language of William Golding's *The Inheritors*. In J.J. Webster (ed.) *Collected Works of M.A.K. Halliday, Vol. 3: Linguistic Studies of Text and Discourse*. London: Continuum, pp. 88–125.

Halliday, M.A.K. 2002 [1982]. The de-automatization of grammar: From Priestley's *An Inspector Calls*. In J.J. Webster (ed.) *Collected Works of M.A.K. Halliday, Vol. 3: Linguistic Studies of Text and Discourse*. London: Continuum, pp. 126–48.

Halliday, M.A.K. 2006. Afterwords. In G. Thompson and S. Hunston (eds) *System and Corpus: Exploring Connections*. London: Equinox, pp. 293–99.

Halliday, M.A.K., and C.M.I.M. Matthiessen. 1999. *Construing Experience through Meaning: A Language-Based Approach to Cognition*. London: Cassell.

Halliday, M.A.K., and C.M.I.M. Matthiessen. 2004. *An Introduction to Functional Grammar*. 3rd edn. London: Arnold.

Halliday, M.A.K., A. MacIntosh and P. Strevens. 1964. *The Linguistic Sciences and Language Teaching*. London: Longman.

Hasan, R. 1964. A linguistic study of contrasting linguistic features in the style of two contemporary English prose writers. Unpublished PhD thesis. University of Edinburgh.

Hasan, R. 1975. The place of stylistics in the study of verbal art. In H. Ringborn (ed.) *Style and Text: Studies Presented to Nils Erik Enviste*. Stockholm: Skriptor, pp. 49–62.

Hasan, R. 1989 [1985]. *Linguistics, Language and Verbal Art*. Oxford: Oxford University Press.

Hasan, R. 1996. On teaching literature across cultural distances. In J.E. James (ed.) *The Language–Culture Connection* (Anthology Series 37). Singapore: SEAMEO Regional Language Centre, pp. 34–63.

Hasan, R. 2007. Private pleasure, public discourse: Reflections on engaging with literature. In D.R. Miller and M. Turci (eds) *Language and Verbal Art Revisited: Linguistic Approaches to the Study of Literature*. London: Equinox, pp. 41–67.

Hasan, R. 2013. Understanding verbal art: An SFL perspective. Paper delivered to the Third Language Arts and linguistics conference, Hong Kong Polytechnic University, 29–30 September.

Hasan, R. Forthcoming. J.J. Webster (ed.) *Collected Works of Ruqaiya Hasan, Vol. 7: Verbal Art*. London: Equinox.

herrnaphta. 2011. Reification and American literature. *Marxist Marginalia*, 9 January. Available online at http://herrnaphta.wordpress.com/2011/01/09/reification-and-american-literature/.

Jakobson, R. 1960. Closing statement: Linguistics and poetics. In T.A Sebeok (ed.) *Style in Language*. Cambridge, MA: MIT Press, pp. 350–77.

Leech, G., and M. Short. 2007 [1981]. *Style in Fiction: A Linguistic Introduction to English Fictional Prose*. Harlow: Pearson Longman.

Lukin, A. 2008. Reading literary texts: Beyond personal responses. In Z. Fang and M.J. Schleppegrell (eds) *Reading in Secondary Content Areas: A Language-Based Pedagogy*.

Lukin, A. 2015. A linguistics of style: Halliday on literature. In J.J. Webster (ed.) *The Bloomsbury Companion to M.A.K. Halliday*. London and New York: Bloomsbury Academic, pp. 348–65.

Lukin, A., and A. Pagano. 2012. Context and double articulation in the translation of verbal art. In J. Knox (ed.) *To Boldly Proceed: Selected Proceedings from the 39th International Systemic Functional Linguistics Congress*. Sydney: UTS, pp. 123–8.

Lukin, A., and J. Webster. 2005. Systemic functional linguistics and the study of literature. In R. Hasan, C.M.I.M. Matthiessen and J.J. Webster (eds) *Continuing Discourse on Language: A Functional Perspective*. London: Equinox, pp. 413–56.

Manfredi, M. 2012. Description vs prescription in translation teaching: A bridgeable gulf? In F. Dalziel, S. Gesuato and M.T. Musacchio (eds) *A Lifetime of English Studies: Essays in Honour of Carol Taylor Torsello*. Padua: Il Poligrafo, pp. 545–53.

Manfredi, M. 2014. *Translating Text and Context: Translation Studies and Systemic Functional Linguistics, Vol. II – From Theory to Practice*. 2nd edn. Bologna: Asterisco.

Miller, D.R. 2007. Construing the 'primitive' primitively: Grammatical parallelism as patterning and positioning strategy in D.H. Lawrence. In D.R. Miller and M. Turci (eds) *Language and Verbal Art Revisited: Linguistic Approaches to the Study of Literature*. London: Equinox, pp. 41–67.

Miller, D.R. 2010. The Hasanian framework for the study of 'verbal art' revisited . . . and reproposed. *Textus* 23(1): 71–94.

Miller, D.R. 2012. Slotting Jakobson into the social semiotic approach to 'verbal art': A modest proposal. In F. Dalziel, S. Gesuato and M.T. Musacchio (eds) *A Lifetime of English Studies: Essays in Honour of Carol Taylor Torsello*. Padua: Il Poligrafo, pp. 215–26.

Miller, D.R. 2013. Another look at social semiotic stylistics: Coupling Hasan's 'verbal art' framework with 'the Mukařovský-Jakobson theory'. In C.A.M. Gouveia and M.F. Alexandre (eds) *Languages, Metalanguages, Modalities, Cultures: Functional and Socio-Discursive Perspectives*. Lisbon: BonD, pp. 121–40.

Miller, D.R. 2016. Jakobson's place in Hasan's social semiotic stylistics: 'Pervasive parallelism' as symbolic articulation of theme. In W.L. Boucher and J.Y. Liang (eds) *Society in Language, Language in Society: Essays in Honour of Ruqaiya Hasan*. London: Palgrave Macmillan, pp. 59–80.

Miller, D.R., and A. Luporini. 2015. Social semiotic stylistics and the corpus: How do-able is an automated analysis of verbal art? In A. Duguid, A. Marchi, A. Partington and C. Taylor (eds) *Gentle Obsessions: Literature, Linguistics and Learning – In Honour of John Morley*. Rome: Artemide Edizioni, pp. 235–50.

Miller, D.R., and A. Luporini. Forthcoming*a*. Software-assisted systemic socio-semantic stylistics: Appraising tru* in J.M. Coetzee's *Foe*. In R. Wegener, A. Oesterle and S. Neumann (eds) *On Verbal Art: Essays in Honour of Ruqaiya Hasan*. Sheffield: Equinox.

Miller, D.R., and A. Luporini. Forthcoming*b*. Systemic socio-semantic stylistics (SSS) as appliable linguistics: The cases of literary criticism and language teaching/learning. In A. Sellami Baklouti and L. Fontaine (eds) *Perspectives from Systemic Functional Linguistics*. London: Routledge.

Miller, D.R., and M. Turci. 2007. Introduction. In D.R. Miller and M. Turci (eds) *Language and Verbal Art Revisited: Linguistic Approaches to the Study of Literature*. London: Equinox, pp. 1–12.

Mukařovský, J. 1964. Standard language and poetic language. In P. Garvin (ed.) *A Prague School Reader on Aesthetics, Literary Structure and Style*. Washington, DC: Georgetown University Press, pp. 17–30.

Mukařovský, J. 1977. *The Word and Verbal Art: Selected Essays by Jan Mukařovský*. Eds J. Burbank and P. Steiner. London: Yale University Press.

Mukařovský, J. 1978. *Structure, Sign and Function: Selected Essays by Jan Mukařovský*. Eds J. Burbank and P. Steiner. London: Yale University Press.

Simpson P. 2014 [2004]. *Stylistics*. 2nd edn. London: Routledge.

Stankiewicz, E. 1983. Roman Jakobson, teacher and scholar. In *A Tribute to Roman Jakobson 1896–1982*. Berlin and New York: de Gruyter, pp. 17–26.

Taylor Torsello, C. 1992. *Linguistica Sistemica e Educazione Linguistica*. Padua: Unipress.

Toolan, M. 1990. *The Stylistics of Fiction*. London: Routledge.

Toolan, M. 2009. *Narrative Progression in the Short Story: A Corpus Stylistic Approach*. Amsterdam and Philadelphia, PA: John Benjamins.

Turci, M. 2007. The meaning of dark* in Joseph Conrad's *Heart of Darkness*. In D.R. Miller and M. Turci (eds) *Language and Verbal Art Revisited: Linguistic Approaches to the Study of Literature*. London: Equinox, pp. 97–114.

32

Discourse analysis

Bob Hodge

This chapter is written as a guide for readers who want to use systemic functional linguistics (SFL) to analyse discourse, for the wide range of contexts and purposes in which discourse plays a significant role. This gives rise to a double focus: on discourse as an important object of study for many approaches, and on SFL as an especially valuable set of resources for this purpose.

The chapter argues that there is a natural alliance between SFL and one leading brand of discourse analysis, critical discourse analysis (CDA). This alliance could be taken further than it has to date, to benefit both. To illustrate, the chapter will illustrate how well SFL tools and concepts carry out the main tasks of CDA. It also suggests lessons for SFL from CDA that could enhance a common practice.

Discourse and its analysis are potential game-changers for the study of language, and its social uses and functions, and SFL has a major role in this development. Mainstream linguistics in the transformational grammar (TG) tradition was built around a particular account of language as the focus of linguistics, in which language is understood as an autonomous object, interesting primarily for its formal grammar, which is thought to explain the linguistic competence of native speakers. In practice, mainstream (TG) linguistics does not study language much above the level of the sentence nor connect it with social processes.

Linguistics in this tradition is divided between 'theory', primarily grammar, and 'application', following a distinction that goes back to Ferdinand de Saussure, a founder of linguistics. Saussure (1974) opposed *langue* (language) and *parole* (speaking), and proposed language as the primary object of linguistics. Chomsky (1965) made a similar distinction between 'competence' (understanding of language) and 'performance' (realisation of this understanding in actual comprehension or production by individuals).

This fundamental architecture is challenged when the concept of 'discourse' becomes central to the study of language. Discourse includes Saussure's *parole* and Chomsky's 'performance', making them central in theory and analysis. Discourse is always language-in-use, as process and product of social interaction, in conversations or stretches of text, going above sentence level, at which social meanings and forces are often found. When discourse is emphasised in this way, language is not an autonomous object, but situated in, and affecting, institutions of power. For such reasons, discourse analysis has come to be an accessible and attractive field for social science disciplines.

The architecture of SFL makes it better adapted to contribute to this kind of linguistics than any rival linguistic theory, especially mainstream (TG) linguistics. Most characteristic features of SFL are well suited to analysing discourse, as this chapter demonstrates in detail. Discourse analysis will be presented not as a simple 'application' of SFL theory, but as a rich site for elaboration of aspects of SFL theory, a focus for using SFL analysis for many purposes, in many fields to which SFL researchers have already made contributions.

Introductory analysis

Practitioners of SFL and CDA tend to have different balances of description and explanation. For CDA, the primary aim of descriptions of language and context is to explain social contexts and processes (Fairclough 1992). For SFL, description and explanation often concern grammar, rather than social meanings and contexts. Yet these are differences of degree, not kind, aspects of practice, rather than mandated by the respective theories. CDA sometimes lacks a rich descriptive apparatus of language, which SFL can provide. SFL, as a functional theory of language, is stronger if it asks more socially oriented questions about what language in action is doing.

To illustrate this fruitful interplay, we will analyse a short text,[1] using SFL concepts informed by some CDA goals and practices, to show how SFL discourse analysis might look:

> [President Obama]: Good afternoon, everybody. Please have a seat.
>
> It is my great pleasure to welcome Prime Minister Cameron on his first visit to the White House as Prime Minister.
>
> We have just concluded some excellent discussions – including whether the beers from our home towns that we exchanged are best served warm or cold. My understanding is that the Prime Minister enjoyed our 312 beer and we may send him more. I thought the beer we got was excellent – but I did drink it cold. (Laughter)
>
> *White House 2010*

This text illustrates many features characteristic of discourse that are usually not analysed in mainstream TG linguistics. It is six sentences long, not a single sentence, and it illustrates language in action, not points of grammar. Yet the passage is clearly a unit, on a larger scale than the sentence, yet with its own structure. It is embedded in social processes and its analysis can illuminate aspects of society through analysing the language.

The basic SFL metafunctions are a valuable starting point for analysing this as discourse. In this case, the *interpersonal* function is prominent and explains elements that would seem nonsense without that framework. The phrase 'please have a seat' does have some ideational force: attendees are meant to sit down. But interpersonal functions and meanings are the main motive of the phrase. Obama is constructing his audience as a single passive entity, at the beginning of his speech. They accept this construction and obey.

The *textual* function likewise has explanatory value in analysing this text as discourse. Obama is giving an exemplary performance in greeting this visiting head of state, weaving together interpersonal and ideational meanings and functions. Obama introduces what might seem inappropriate ideational material for so serious a genre and occasion: details of what the two men drank, not the major political issues they discussed. Yet the risky tactic paid off, creating a harmonious relationship between the two men and their nations.

SFL's multi-scalar framework is invaluable for analysing this as discourse. A multi-scalar framework is necessary because discourse typically, as here, has different meanings and balances of metafunctions at the various levels that are important for discourse analysis. Just as 'please have a seat' is a whole that has meanings not fully contained in the individual words, so the string of four sentences has meanings and functions that could not be guessed or deduced from the sentences themselves. The whole is a joke; none of the parts in themselves are a joke.

The discursive function of 'political joke' only becomes clear in the context of the speech as a whole, in the occasion in which it occurs. Since all of these are ways in which language has meaning and effects, we can say that a multi-scalar framework, as in SFL, is indispensable for the study of language. CDA practitioners tend to look more freely than SFL practitioners at patterns across large stretches of text, but that is mainly a difference of practice.

CDA tends to be more concerned with interpersonal, social meanings, including big meanings such as power and ideology. SFL can include such meanings, but in practice tends to be less interested in them. Yet the SFL principle that choice is meaning is a useful analytic tool for analysing meanings of all kinds, especially as allied to the signature feature of SFL, system networks. In current SFL practice, system networks are mostly studied as they appear in the grammar, but the principles and conventions are equally useful in discourse analysis to map social and cognitive meanings of options taken by social agents in particular occasions.

In the case of this speech, we can construe, or reconstruct, the options of Obama the speaker, understood not as an individual, but as US President (for example constrained by his office, supported by his team). The other key participants, Prime Minister Cameron and the reporters, likewise all operate within a framework of constraints coming from a common field, tenor and mode. The specific analysis applies only to a select few speakers of English, but the principles throw light on this discursive act as a social phenomenon.

The SFL dictum that choice is meaning is easier to apply in analysis when applied to concrete instances of discourse, as here, because we can ask each time: whose choice? And what meaning does it have? One set of choices of Obama-as-President concern mode, in the triad field–tenor–mode. He is giving a verbal speech, but this mode is complemented by communication in many other modes. He uses paralinguistic resources. Tone of voice and expression are essential to make this recognisably a joke. He and Cameron use dress codes, more formal than two men chatting in a pub, but without indications of rank. This is a multimodal text (Kress and Van Leeuwen 2001).

If meaning is choice, then lack of choice is itself a meaning. There are many meanings here that can be seen as obligatory, for these participants in this kind of occasion: not only the dress codes, but also spatial signifiers, the raised dais, official seals and national flags, separation from the seated reporters, all communicate power and difference. Given that these two men were, at the time, among the most powerful on the planet, the fact that this set of meanings are so constrained is itself socially significant.

A great strength of SFL analysis of choice and meaning is its multidimensionality – its recognition that some choices include many options simultaneously: not either–or but both–and. In network diagrams, this is signalled by curly brackets (or braces – that is, { and }). Inclusive choices are as significant as exclusive ones. By putting together this seamless multimodal package, Obama and his team signify their professionalism. By weaving together a pattern of similar meanings about power and solidarity, formality and informality in a conventional intertextual package, they fulfil the textual function, transmitting a cluster of complementary meanings around that central social message.

SFL also provides a level of delicacy to analysing the discussion about beers. Interpersonal and ideational functions interweave differently at different levels of the text, with different meanings and effects that are of great interest for discourse analysis. At the outset of the passage, Obama chooses interpersonally oriented discourse over the expected ideational discourse (about serious issues of state). This choice, like all choices, has meaning: it implies that, for Obama, social relationships are more important than intellectual content, between him and Cameron, as between the two nations.

The details of the beers can be analysed as an ideational system with interpersonal meanings. The highest category is 'gift': both beers are gifts. The next category is place-of-origin. The choice of home town is a different instantiation of that place for Obama and Cameron, respectively. The social meaning of the place is the same in both cases, although the actual town is different, signifying sameness (both men have the same relationship to a particular town, as well as to a nation) and difference. The gift is a choice of drinks. Beer comes from a set, common to both national systems, which includes spirits and wine. Again, the choice carries an interpersonal meaning of solidarity.

The punchline of the joke introduces a category, temperature, from a separate system, which could be marked by a curly bracket to indicate a simultaneous choice. Obama does not mark this, but the general laughter shows that his choice was meaningful to the audience. In this case, a binary is understood, *warm–cold*. By choosing *cold*, Obama signifies that he rejects *warm*. In rejecting a signifier of English values, he is understood as understanding and rejecting English culture. Analysis of how this works draws on the SFL proposition, enunciated by Halliday (1978), that 'language [is] social semiotic' – that is, an organised resource for making meaning. Obama drew on it to construct his discourse, which SFL enables analysts to construe.

It is crucial for understanding the effect of this passage to know that it is a joke. Cameron laughs and does not take offence. This is because of the system of modality, which nests within the interpersonal system in the grammar. A concern with modality systems is common to SFL (Halliday 1985) in which 'modality' overlaps with 'modulation', and CDA, in which Kress and Hodge (1979) extended the SFL account of modality as a key element for discourse analysis.

In SFL, modality in the grammar expresses the degree of reliability in the utterance, as in verbal auxiliaries such as 'may'. But other parts of discourse also express modality. 'My understanding' and 'I thought' make the modality less certain, indicating a personal judgement that might be mistaken. So although Obama's final clauses are both in the past indicative, which gives them a relatively high modality, the first has the modality marker 'I thought', but the second does not. This signifies that his judgement on the excellence of the beer is just his judgement, whereas his act in drinking it cold is a fact. It implies that the second statement is truer than the first.

Since the degree to which statements are marked as true or certain is crucial to their effect, markers of modality are always relevant for discourse analysis. As this case shows, modality is not completely in grammar and words. How would we (and Cameron, and the audience) know that this statement is not to be taken at face value? Clues may come from genre expectations, which provide background expectations about field (this is a political speech, yet also a personal welcome, so that humour is a possible choice), tenor (relations between Obama and Cameron are constructed by this risky joke as close and intimate) and mode (Obama's voice and other paralinguistic markers signal that this is a friendly exchange, reframing apparent aggression as humour).

This reading of this part of Obama's speech is not intended to be exhaustive, from the point of view of either SFL or CDA. The main point is that discourse analysis asks many important questions about social functions and effects of language in action that SFL is well equipped to answer. Those questions may not always be central questions for SFL and the SFL concepts may not used in their most usual sense, but SFL and CDA discourse analysis complement each other well.

Historical perspectives

Discourse analysis as a broad field has too long and complex a history to give here, in a chapter concerned especially with SFL and its affiliations. However, there are some significant moments and versions of discourse analysis that can help readers to understand the complex relation that developed between CDA and SFL, and options that may usefully exist in the future.

In 1952, American linguist Zellig Harris published three articles on discourse analysis. Harris was regarded as an heir of both the leading linguists of the previous generation, Bloomfield and Sapir, and he was the teacher of Chomsky, soon to be the dominant figure in US and world linguistics. Harris's place in American linguistics should have made his contributions decisive and discourse would have occupied a central place in linguistics.

Harris's (1952) concept of discourse had two distinctive features. Discourse analysis mainly referred to regularities across whole texts, so his enterprise could have equally been called 'text linguistics'. This was an important advance on the sentence-level linguistics before him. Moreover, these were empirically collected actual texts, not the artificial examples commonly used to construct grammars. He also introduced the concept of 'transformations', years before Chomsky did so more famously, although Chomsky's concept was different: an abstract relation between related forms, not an empirical relation between occurring pieces of language.

But Harris's concept of discourse was rejected by the majority of US linguists – and with it was removed from US linguistics a potentially revolutionary new object of analysis, around which the discipline of linguistics could have been redesigned. Yet the concept itself continued an underground existence and it was taken up by major French theorists. Michel Pêcheux (1983) took over much of Harris's concept and methodology, and used it to analyse ideology. Especially after Pêcheux's death, Michel Foucault made the term 'discourse' central to his theory.

Where Harris (and Chomsky) kept their intense interest in issues of ideology separate from their interest in language, Pêcheux and Foucault were not linguists, and they studied conditions and effects of discourse separate from linguistic forms. This had major effects on Anglo-American developments of discourse analysis, leading to a damaging disconnect in the two traditions, discourse theory and discourse analysis. On the one hand, French-influenced discourse theory was concerned with social, not linguistic, facts, and lacked methods to examine realisations of ideology and power in language. On the other hand, Harris's tradition did not connect closely with major social categories and issues.

In this situation, a number of English-based linguists attempted to develop a mediating form of theory to bridge the gap. Critical linguistics (Fowler et al. 1979; Kress and Hodge 1979) drew heavily on SFL to develop a form of analysis of the intersections of discourse and ideology with language. This morphed into CDA, within which Fairclough (1992) built concepts from Foucault into a synthesis of linguistics and social analysis. But although many CDA scholars originated in linguistics departments, they often found their theories marginalised and ignored in the mainstream (TG) linguistics curriculum. More interest in CDA came from outside linguistics, from scholars in sociology, politics, media studies, management and education without backgrounds in SFL or linguistics.

SFL faced a similarly hostile situation between 1960 and 1990, which had consequences for the relation between SFL and different forms of discourse analysis. SFL constantly had to defend itself against accusations from mainstream (TG) linguists that it was not a legitimate form of linguistics. Linguistics itself was collateral damage in a fiercely polemical academic environment riven by factions within mainstream linguistics that has been called 'the Linguistic Wars' (Harris 1995).

In this situation, SFL tended not to declare alliances with other marginalised forms of linguistics such as CDA, and vice versa. However, SFL has become a global force in linguistics, much stronger than seemed possible in the 1980s. The 'Linguistic Wars' are over and SFL is in a strong position to connect with other vital traditions – especially with CDA, as is argued in this chapter.

This context is one reason why what can now be seen as major SFL contributions to discourse analysis were not originally presented in those terms. In this section, we discuss two examples of proto-SFL discourse analysis.

Stylistics as discourse analysis

In 1971, Halliday analysed the language of the novel *The Inheritors* (Golding 1961) in a symposium on stylistics. This context is relevant to an understanding of the history of discourse and its analysis. Stylistics is often seen as a hybrid discipline between literary studies and linguistics, but it took from literary studies something that linguistics itself sorely needed: a concern for linguistic patterns in extended texts, for discourse analysis in fact (see Miller, this volume). A leading figure in stylistics, Leo Spitzer (1948), can be claimed to have pioneered discourse analysis before Harris, under another label.

This deep affinity between stylistics and discourse analysis, as exemplified by Halliday's study, explains why this work can be revisited as exemplary/proto-SFL discourse analysis. Golding's novel presented the clash of Neanderthal and modern humans through the eyes, minds and forms of language of the two species. Halliday identified a recurring grammatical feature in parts of the text representing the Neanderthal world view. Neanderthals had only intransitives; their transitivity system had no option to choose transitives – that is, forms with subjects, verbs and objects representing actions on objects by agents. Modern humans had that fuller system. To put it simplistically, Neanderthals perished because of their defective grammar.

We might draw some lessons here for SFL discourse analysis. First, the fact that the text was fictional does not affect the method: Halliday was analysing English discourse constructed by a novelist, not actual Neanderthal discourse. In analysing this discourse, Halliday looked for patterns over a long text and used fine-tuned grammatical analysis to illuminate these larger patterns. He associated these patterns with specific classes of speaker and context, and explored the cognitive and practical consequences that act as constraints on their behaviour.

This is the other side of the coin of a famous Halliday (1978: 4) assertion: 'Language is as it is because of the functions it has evolved to serve in people's lives.' In Golding's fiction, Neanderthal discourse was as it was because, presumably, Neanderthals had no purpose that was served by transitive forms. But the novel's message is that they needed that purpose, and the language and thinking that enabled it: their linguistic forms not only reflected their habitual behaviours, but also prevented them from developing the new ones they needed. Halliday's SFL discourse analysis not only shows the pattern of choices speakers make, but also reveals what is inhibited or controlled by this discourse. Without using the term, it is *critical functional analysis* – that is, using a functional model to critique forms that were dysfunctional for these speakers.

We can compare the tendencies of Halliday's analysis here with issues around Basil Bernstein's (1970) distinction between elaborated and restricted codes. Bernstein's 'restricted code', the language of working-class speakers of English, had different constraints from Neanderthal language, but the effect is similar. In Bernstein's analysis of 'restricted code' discourse, speakers were socialised into forms of language and thought that did not orientate them to engage in ways of thinking that could grasp the abstract terms of their social position and negotiate its terms.

Bernstein was a sociologist of language and education, not a discourse analyst or SFL practitioner. His theories of the two codes have proved controversial, so it is tentatively suggested here that his theory might have been better supported empirically by reframing it as a hypothesis about forms of discourse and using something closer to Halliday's analysis of *The Inheritors* (see Maton and Doran, this volume).

Bernstein's work was criticised because it seemed to overemphasise the ideational function and the cognitive limitations of 'Restricted Code'. Halliday's analysis also emphasised the ideational function in Neanderthal discourse, but in SFL all three functions are always present. In a careful review of Bernstein's work, Halliday (1978: 105, emphasis original) distanced himself from 'linguistic deficit' theory and saw the value of Bernstein's work in Bernstein's emphasis on 'critical socializing contexts', as these are shaped by 'the variable *function* of language in these contexts'. Hasan (2009) gave an exemplary application of this kind of SFL discourse analysis. She empirically analysed many hours of naturally occurring discourse of families, revisiting Bernstein's hypothesis through a more nuanced pair of oppositions ('higher' versus 'lower' autonomy professionals).

In this form, we can use Halliday's stylistic analysis as a model for SFL analysis of socially effective forms of discourse, treating Bernstein's 'codes' as discourse in this sense. In the interests of a rapprochement between SFL analysis and discourse theory, we can note that Foucault was mainly interested in a critique of the discourse of elite speakers of 'elaborated codes'. We could focus, as Halliday recommends, on contexts of socialisation and later contexts of use, to ask: how do such contexts equip and reward them with forms of language that underpin their formation and role as elites? Bernstein and Foucault could be seen as complementary approaches and perspectives on the highly complex theme of the relations between language and discourse and social class in the social and discursive formation of individuals.

Cohesion

Cohesion is an aspect of language on every scale – but it plays a special role above the level of the sentence, in longer pieces of discourse. It can be regarded as an indispensable aspect of discourse for analysis. Yet until Halliday and Hasan's study of cohesion in English in 1976, there were no models or concepts for analysis of this aspect of discourse. Their study broke new ground for discourse analysis.

Halliday and Hasan (1976) identify many aspects of text that contribute to cohesion, but especially productive is their account of those parts of the text that have the function of reference. These are part of what is often called the 'deictic system'. *Deictic* and the noun *deixis* come from Greek meaning 'to point', and deixis refers to words that point. Halliday and Hasan (1976) make two distinctions: between 'endophoric (in (the text))' and 'exophoric (outside (the text))'. *Endophoric* reference points backwards (anaphoric) or forwards (cataphoric).

Both types increase the cohesion of the text. *Exophoric* references bind the text more closely to the reality to which it refers, but can weaken the cohesion of the text in itself.

This system is multifunctional. The same set of terms is used for all of these functions, producing ample scope for ambiguity of meaning and function. Since this ambiguity is systemic, it is likely that it is functional, as indeed it is. Although these words are small and unobtrusive, they are very frequent. They play a key role in discourse and hence in discourse analysis.

Let us illustrate with an example from the Obama text. Two words, 'the' and 'we', are equally most common (four occurrences). They are both deictics. 'We' shows how slippery their use can be. In its first occurrence, 'we have just concluded', there is endophoric anaphoric reference to Cameron, who was mentioned just previously. However, the other part of this 'we' is Obama, standing exophorically in front of them, as is Cameron. Endophoric and exophoric reference act together to bind the text to itself ('cohesion'), and to its context and referent.

However, the next 'we', 'we may send him more', is no longer endophoric. 'Him' now has that function. This 'we' is more exophoric, referring to the President standing in front of them and to the US people he represents. Obama has interrupted the cohesion of his text. He breaks the solidarity of the 'we' that includes Cameron, to now exclude him, replacing him with Obama's true allies (as he is implying), the American people. Yet his discursive skill is such that the break hardly shows, managed by the textual function.

Gee's (2010) helpful practical guide to discourse analysis emphasises how valuable attending to deixis is for discourse analysts. This is a fruitful point of intersection between SFL and CDA. This instance shows a more general truth: CDA's intense interest in microprocesses of power in language can motivate a functional elaboration of the SFL toolkit for analysing language. Better analysis of discourse contributes to SFL's concern to understand language in all its social uses.

Critical issues and topics

Every dynamic field of research has critical issues, which are usually sites for creative discussions and potential growth. Intersections between CDA and SFL are especially fruitful sites for debate and research into critical issues. This section focuses on some areas in which the two fields converge, with related or complementary takes on similar problems. It also notes some practical lessons for readers of this volume.

Connecting with sociolinguistics

CDA has been criticised for not including more branches of sociolinguistics, limiting its range of tools and concepts for discourse analysis (Blommaert 2005). SFL is open to similar criticisms (see Bartlett, this volume): it is a socially oriented theory of language – a form of sociolinguistics.

Readers: With any concept from sociolinguistics, ask what systems and functions it implies.

Using social theory

CDA explicitly draws on Foucault's work, and implicitly on Marxism, but this is a limited range of theories. SFL remains primarily a linguistic theory, without an explicit social theory, yet it deals with language in social use and needs to develop its own theories of social processes. For instance, Van Dijk (2008), from a CDA perspective, has criticised the SFL understanding of 'context'. Whether one agrees with his specific case, SFL should situate 'context' and other key terms for SFL discourse analysis (such as 'culture', 'ideology') in relation to social theory outside SFL (see Bartlett, this volume). In meeting this challenge, CDA and SFL face similar problems: which social theories, and how incorporate them into a practice centred on the analysis of language and discourse?

Readers: Use SFL discourse analysis to explore any hypothesis, from any social theory.

Critical perspectives

CDA builds criticism into its name. It has been criticised for being too polemical, knowing in advance what its analytic conclusions will be (Widdowson 1998). SFL, in this respect, like most branches of linguistics, tends to present itself as objective and value-free, subscribing to a widespread idea of 'scientific'.

Many SFL scholars engage with political and social issues enacted in and through language, as in the landmark collection of SFL and CDA scholars edited by Young and Harrison (2004). Yet by bringing together distinguished practitioners of SFL (such as Hasan) and CDA (such as Fairclough), this edited collection inadvertently demonstrated the divergent practices of the two fields around engaged criticism. This issue concerns SFL orientation, not theory.

Readers: Ask how critical you want your SFL discourse analysis to be.

The role of verbal language

Both SFL and CDA focus mostly on verbal language; yet SFL includes semiotics in its theory. Halliday's (1978) concept of 'language as social semiotic' was a founding premise for the field of social semiotics; CDA, likewise, has social semiotics in its gene pool. For both fields, the issue is firmly on the agenda. How far should SFL reframe itself as social semiotics? And is CDA tenable in today's multimedia society if it restricts itself to verbal discourse (Taylor, this volume)?

Readers: With every problem, ask whether there is relevant data in other modes.

Disciplinarity

Both CDA and SFL are, in some respects, interdisciplinary, yet they also correspond to communities that close themselves off from all other communities to some degree. In Foucault's (1972) concept of discursive regimes, disciplines function as regimes that control what can be said about what, in what way, by whom, to whom and how. SFL's ideational, textual and interpersonal functions cover similar ground. From both perspectives, we can ask questions about the boundaries currently around both CDA and SFL. For instance, what is the function of the present boundaries between SFL and CDA, or discourse analysis and CDA? Is it driven more by the needs of two communities to remain distinct than from real differences in their programmes?

Similar questions can be asked about the relation of SFL to all other forms of linguistics. Linguistics across all its forms tends to remain distinct from other disciplines, including cognate disciplines such as sociology, psychology and literary studies. A related question concerns terminology: both CDA and SFL are accused of wrapping their meanings in discourse that others find impenetrable, limiting dissemination and uptake.

Readers: Decide as you go how useful disciplinary terms and boundaries are for the problems that you address.

Current research

This section briefly looks at how current work is addressing these questions and issues for the field, especially in discourse-orientated SFL. Note that most of these lines of research are explored in other chapters in this volume.

Key categories in SFL and critical discourse analysis

As discussed earlier, two productive concepts from SFL are Field, Tenor and Mode, and Cohesion. Bowcher (this volume) develops new thinking about Field, Tenor and Mode as categories for analysing discourse, the meanings of which are broadly semiotic. Cohesion (see Clarke, this volume) enables interdisciplinary links with social sciences, as in the work of Butt using discourse analysis to support psychotherapy (Meares et al. 2012).

Strands within SFL

Many approaches within SFL make links with CDA concerns and methods. Genre theory (see Gardner, this volume) synthesised elements from SFL to provide a perspective for analysing sets of text. Martin (2008) and others made genre a central organising principle for analysing and producing discourse in educational contexts. 'Discourse semantics' (see Tann, this volume) is a site at which Martin (2010) explicitly developed SFL for discourse analysis. Part of this emerging field is 'Appraisal theory' (Martin and White 2003), which analyses social meanings and effects in media texts (see Oteíza, this volume).

Beyond verbal language

As indicated earlier, work on multimodality in a social-semiotic framework is developing vigorously, in CDA as in SFL, and in the process is challenging previous compartmentalisation across the field. As stated earlier, Halliday is as much a founding father of social semiotics as of SFL. Kress and Van Leeuwen (2001), leading theorists of multimodality, explicitly ground their work in SFL (see Taylor, this volume).

Research methods and recommendations for practice

This chapter has displayed a practical orientation throughout, to help readers to apply SFL to research and practice where discourse is involved, combining SFL and CDA in a model for practice. Martin and Rose (2007) offer an influential SFL-based practice for discourse analysis. Bartlett (2014) is a helpful SFL guide to critical analysis. These sources can be complemented here by adapting a major article by Halliday (1978), not written as a guide to SFL discourse analysis, which suggests many useful ideas for SFL discourse analysis.

Halliday's article was originally published in a journal of anthropology, not linguistics. This interdisciplinary home gave it a wider scope than is usual in linguistics journals, eliciting qualities especially useful for discourse analysis. Halliday based his observations on three corpora – that is, word lists from three underworld cultures: sixteenth-century

England, and modern Poland and Bengal. He named them 'anti-languages', because they inverted forms and meanings of dominant languages in response to their common contexts, as marginal or incarcerated.

Special forms of language like this can be called a 'discourse' in a similar sense to that in Foucault's (1972) 'discursive regimes'. For Foucault, discursive regimes control who can say what about what topic and what can count as knowledge. Foucault typically had in mind discourses of governance, the language of those who exercise power in society, whereas Halliday here studied the language of outcasts and outlaws, seemingly objects of what Foucault (1979) called 'discipline'. But, in practice, there are many similarities. Halliday's SFL analytic methods are useful tools with which to address Foucauldian questions.

In this spirit, we can adapt Halliday's anti-language article as an eight-step guide for SFL discourse analysis, as follows.

1   *Use actually occurring discourse.* Inconveniently for our purposes, Halliday (1978) did not do this, in this case. As he explained with regret, none of his sources provided examples of discourse in action above word level. However, he asserted the principle and analysed naturally occurring fragments of text from his word lists. Foucault often did not analyse naturally occurring discourse as data. Halliday's successful use of actual, but imperfect, data shows a complementary principle.

2   *Use powerful theories of language and society to interrogate imperfect data.* Halliday used the concept of lexicogrammatical systems as continua to analyse his limited data – mainly words and their translations – and infer processes that respond to the forces and functions of these contexts at other levels. In Obama's case, the analysis earlier in the chapter focused on a naturally occurring piece of discourse, but analysed it similarly to infer general discursive processes and functions.

3   *Relate forms of language ('discourse', genre, register, code) to social conditions and relationships of groups that use it.* Full analyses of Mode in the SFL sense attend to the range of modes and media, in multimodal forms of SFL and CDA. The Obama speech was multimodal. Anti-languages normally incorporate other semiotic modes.

4   *Clarify the main specific functions of the discourse.*   This will be achieved by reference to the social conditions of the group and the relations amongst its members, including key agents (for example in- and out-group prisoners, warders in prisons, nations, leaders, press and audiences in the Obama case).

5   *Analyse specific functions with reference to SFL metafunctions.* In this case, Halliday (1978) noted a dominance of textual and interpersonal functions over ideational – a motivated response to the helplessness of the incarcerated. Foucault lacks a theory of functions. In Obama's speech, we noted his strategic emphasis on interpersonal over ideational functions; in this guide, we have listed specific functions to be analysed before metafunctions. In practice, analysis needs to be dialectic, moving between metafunctions, between more and less delicate analysis. SFL discourse analysis should work out from concrete instances of language in action, with metafunctions providing a framework for examining specific functions.

6   *Look for choices, ask for their meanings and identify the systems that organise them.* This principle applies to choices at every level, down to the lexical. As one instance, Halliday (1978: 164) reported the relation of anti-language *ghōṭ* ('to swallow a stolen thing to avoid detection') to standard Bengali *ḍhōk* ('to swallow'). Members of the Calcutta underworld can say this word, but ordinary citizens cannot. The fact of that choice is its meaning: that, in this respect, underworld members have more choices

than respectable people. All of these principles apply to analysis of Obama's discourse, in which his choices in a shared system of social meanings are primary interpersonal meanings.

7   *Look for transformations and metaphors.* Prisoners use their anti-language to transform their conditions, in language, if not reality. Obama used beers as metaphor for international relations. Halliday (1978) did not use transformations in Chomsky's sense, but he extended the concept of metaphor to cover a wide range of operations (see Taverniers, this volume). In this article, he included phonological, grammatical (including morphological, lexical and syntactic) and semantic metaphors. Halliday reframed metaphor five years before Lakoff and Johnson (1980) published their influential study, a foundational work for discourse analysis in cognitive linguistics.

8   *Arrange forms of language and discourse along a cline.* Clines (that is, continua along which objects are ranged between poles) play a more important role in SFL than in most other forms of linguistics. Here, as elsewhere, they allow for more nuanced and non-binary categories, which correspond more closely to how human language and thought work. Full anti-languages are exceptional, corresponding to conditions under which its speakers are excluded from, and opposed to, the dominant society. But the opposite condition, total unity between all speakers, is equally rare – although this is the condition assumed by Chomsky (1957), who hypothesised ideal speaker-hearers as defining objects of his linguistic theory.

Like Foucault, CDA assumes hostility between dominant and non-dominant speakers, and finds many anti-language features in the discourse of the dominant. Halliday's cline for anti-language can be fine-tuned to include many different forms of discourse, projecting different strategies for SFL discourse analysis. For instance, all forms of academic discourse have some anti-language features, managing in-group solidarity, excluding non-academic others. Mainstream TG fosters an opaque, closed discourse. CDA and cultural theory typically use highly abstract, specialised language. If these positions are all understood as positioned along a cline, it becomes easier to recognise context-dependent differences in the crucial relations between language, form and function. That goal is equally valuable for SFL as for engaged analysis of discourse.

Future directions

This chapter has been forward-looking and speculative, bringing out forms of theory and analysis that currently exist as potential uses of SFL, rather than as dominant practices. In this final section, by way of a conclusion, five predictions can be listed that crystallise tendencies that can be detected now, or which may or should emerge more strongly in the future, as follows.

1   SFL will increasingly engage with discourse (language in action, on every scale, from morpheme to archive, serving every social purpose, in every context) as a primary object for analysis and theory-building.
2   'Discourse' will be increasingly understood in social-semiotic terms as drawing on all resources for making meaning, in all semiotic modes.
3   An emphasis on functions of language in relation to uses and problems of discourse will foster richer developments in SFL, complementing current research strengths in systemic functional grammar.
4   Key SFL concepts will become essential components in a general toolkit for analysing social processes as enacted in discourse (including functional analysis, of metafunctions

and specific functions; system network analyses; rank-and-scale analysis across all levels of discourse; choice as meaning).

5   As SFL becomes an increasingly majority form of linguistics across the globe, it will hopefully increase links and lower terminological barriers across linguistics, with mainstream (TG) linguistics, with CDA and with other disciplines that deal with language-in-use.

Note

1 See White House (2010) for the full speech.

References

Bartlett, T. 2014. *Analysing Power in Language*. London: Routledge.
Bernstein, B. 1970. *Class, Codes and Control*. London: Routledge.
Blommaert, J. 2005. *Discourse: A Critical Introduction*. Cambridge: Cambridge University Press.
Chomsky, N. 1957. *Syntactic Structures*. The Hague: Mouton.
Chomsky, N. 1965. *Aspects of the Theory of Syntax*. Cambridge, MA: MIT Press.
de Saussure, F. 1974. *A Course in General Linguistics*. London: Fontana
Fairclough, N. 1992. (Ed.) *Critical Language Awareness*. London: Longmans
Foucault, M. 1972. The unities of discourse. In *Archaeology of Knowledge*. London: Tavistock, pp. 23–33.
Foucault, M. 1979. *Discipline and Punish*. Harmondsworth: Penguin.
Fowler, R., B. Hodge, G. Kress and T. Trew. 1979. *Language and Control*. London: Routledge.
Gee, J.P. 2010. *How to Do Discourse Analysis*. London: Routledge.
Golding, W. 1961. *The Inheritors*. London: Faber & Faber.
Halliday, M.A.K. 1971. Linguistic function and literary style. In S. Chapman (ed.) *Style: A Symposium*. Oxford: Oxford University Press, pp. 330–68.
Halliday, M.A.K. 1978. *Language as Social Semiotic*. London: Arnold.
Halliday, M.A.K. 1985. *Introduction to Systemic Functional Grammar*. London: Arnold.
Halliday, M.A.K., and R. Hasan. 1976. *Cohesion in English*. London: Longmans.
Harris, R. 1995. *The Linguistics Wars*. Oxford: Oxford University Press.
Harris, Z. 1952. Discourse analysis. *Language* 28: 1–30.
Hasan R. 2009. *Semantic Variations: Meaning in Society and Sociolinguistics*. London: Equinox.
Kress, G., and B. Hodge. 1979. *Language as Ideology*. London: Routledge.
Kress, G., and T. van Leeuwen. 2001. *Multimodal Discourse*. London: Arnold.
Lakoff, G., and M. Johnston. 1980. *Metaphors We Live by*. Chicago, IL: Chicago University Press.
Martin, J.R. 2008. *Genre Relations*. London: Equinox.
Martin, J.R. 2010. *Discourse Semantics*. Shanghai: Shanghai Jiao Tong University Press.
Martin, J.R., and D. Rose (eds). 2007. *Working with Discourse*. London: Continuum.
Martin, J.R., and P. White. 2003. *The Language of Evaluation*. London: Palgrave Macmillan.
Meares, R., N. Bendit, J. Haliburn, A. Korner, D. Meares and D. Butt. 2012. *Borderline Personality Disorder Treated by the Conversational Method*. New York: Norton.
Pêcheux, M. 1983. Ideology: Fortress or paradoxical space? In S. Hanninen and L. Paldan (eds) *Rethinking Ideology: A Marxist Debate*. New York: International General, pp. 31–5.
Spitzer. 1948. *Linguistics and Literary History*. Princeton, NJ: Princeton University Press.
Van Dijk, T. 2008. *Discourse and Context*. Cambridge: Cambridge University Press.
White House. 2010. Remarks by President Obama and Prime Minister Cameron of the United Kingdom in Joint Press Availability. Available online at https://www.whitehouse.gov/the-press-office/remarks-president-obama-and-prime-minister-cameron-united-kingdom-joint-press-avail.
Widdowson, H.G., 1998. *REVIEW ARTICLE* The Theory and Practice of Critical Discourse analysis *Applied Linguistics,* 19(1), pp. 136–151.
Young, L., and C. Harrison (eds). 2004. *SFL and CDA: Studies in Social Change*. London: Bloomsbury.

33

Corpus and systemic functional linguistics

Serge Sharoff

Introduction

Linguistic research requires empirical evidence to give satisfactory answers to questions such as: to what extent a phenomenon X is present in the system of language? Or what is the difference between choices X and Y? Such evidence can be provided by a corpus, 'a collection of pieces of language that are selected and ordered according to explicit linguistic criteria in order to be used as a sample of the language' (Sinclair 1996: 2). A modern computer-based corpus comes with an interface for retrieving appropriate linguistic constructions, such as sequences of word forms, also often lemmas (that is, dictionary headwords) and generic part-of-speech (POS) tags.

With the proliferation of texts in electronic form, linguistic research now has potentially unlimited access to evidence from manually collected corpora, such as the British National Corpus (BNC) (Aston and Burnard 1998), very large generic corpora derived from the Internet (Sharoff 2006b; Baroni et al. 2009) and smaller corpora for specific domains (Baroni and Bernardini 2004) or genres (Nesi and Gardner 2012).

This chapter will explore the field of corpus linguistics, with greater emphasis put on topics specifically related to systemic functional linguistics (SFL). The major topics covered in this chapter are:

1   the historical and genetic links between SFL and corpora;
2   the principles underlying the use of corpora in SFL-based studies;
3   studying language from the lexical end and from the grammatical end using corpora;
4   corpus composition and SFL; and
5   recommendations for corpus use and for enriching SFL theory and descriptions.

Historical perspectives

From the historical perspective, many of the early developments in corpus linguistics have close links with the systemic studies. First, the very notion of collocations was coined by

J.R. Firth (1957 [1951]), with his statement 'you shall know a word by the company it keeps' being arguably one of the best-known quotes in corpus research. Another important milestone was Halliday's PhD thesis completed in Cambridge in 1955 (Halliday 1959), which outlines 'descriptive grammar' of a single text in Chinese – namely, *The Secret History of the Mongols*. That study offered a corpus-based description of word classes, syntactic constructions, collocations and colligations – that is, the relations between words and grammatical patterns of their use. It was also instrumental in developing the first systemic account of grammatical analysis (Halliday 1957). Another historical link comes from the corpus studies performed by Halliday's PhD student, John Sinclair, who started with the English lexical studies project in 1963 and, over the course of the 1970s, moved to development of large corpora for lexicographic investigations. This research provided important contributions to the principles of corpus development and corpus-based lexicography, including the design of the Bank of English and of the *Collins-COBUILD* dictionary (Sinclair 1991). The latter was the first thoroughly corpus-based dictionary, which provided information on meaning distinctions, grammatical patterns of words and their collocations on the basis of their frequencies in a generic corpus. Since then, texts in electronic form have become much more common and this has enormously simplified corpus research. First, large, manually collected corpora were developed in the 1990s, such as the BNC (Aston and Burnard 1998); then, with the proliferation of Internet resources, ever-larger web-based corpora have been created by crawling the web for a number of languages (Sharoff 2006b; Baroni et al. 2009). Some linguistic studies also use interfaces to search engines as a source of corpus evidence. This situation led to numerous corpus studies in SFL research.[1]

The historical perspective also suggests a genetic link between corpus research and SFL – namely, that there are common strands naturally linking SFL research and corpus studies. One of the sources for this link comes from the emphasis made in SFL on social semiotics: language is a social phenomenon that is manifested in production of speech and text (Halliday 1978). This view leads to the system–process–product approach advocated in SFL: each text (this chapter, for example) and each linguistic unit in this text is a product of various processes of text production, an instantiation of a number of choices possible in the system of the English language conditioned by their use in the register of academic chapters. Unlike other kinds of linguistic analysis that emphasise the autonomy of syntax, a socio-semiotic approach to language has to deal with linguistic phenomena instantiated in their context of use, thus naturally promoting corpus-based analysis. As noted by Halliday (1992: 79): 'It seemed clear to me in 1960 that useful theoretical work in grammar was seriously hampered by lack of data.' In this view, the system of language is observable through instantiation, which needs to be quantified through corpus evidence.

Another genetic link between corpus studies and SFL is present in attention to variation. The speakers use language to achieve their communicative goals. The lexicogrammatical properties of their speech vary according to the context of its use, which leads to the concept of register as variation according to use. Another way in which the lexicogrammatical patterns vary comes from variation by the user. For example, it is possible to consider temporal, social or geographical variation (Gregory 1988). Similarly, variation is also at the heart of corpus linguistics: frequencies and patterns can be important by themselves, but the contrast between two kinds of uses is often more informative. For example, the absolute frequency of active vs passive constructions in a large representative corpus provides information about the preferred options in grammar, while variations in their frequency across different registers reveal the possible reasons for choosing between these options.

Critical issues and topics

Frequency and instantiation

When we talk about quantification of evidence, we need to distinguish data coming from different regions on the following cline of instantiation (Matthiessen 2006: 104):

> **Text level** logogenetic patterns with texts as processes, they unfold as meaning is made within individual texts or a group of texts produced in the same context.
>
> **Register level** more generic patterns, which are still specific to an individual register; for example, commands realised as imperatives are possible in instructional texts as well as in scientific articles, but with unequal frequency.
>
> **Language level** such patterns are inherent in the linguistic system, at least at a certain period in time.

In SFL, the natural objects of quantification are the choices in each system and their realisations through lexicogrammatical features. A corpus usually does not contain information beyond the level of linguistic forms; therefore the choices can be easily recognised on more delicate levels of the system. However, less delicate choices can be counted as well if they are recorded through annotation. For example, counting the collocations on a raw corpus is straightforward, while counting the types of process requires explicit annotation of the process types.

A system can have no marked choices – that is, the probabilities of choices are roughly similar – or it can have one unmarked choice, with considerably higher probability. Halliday (1992: 65) gives an example with marked probabilities (example (1)) and suggests that the distribution of the probabilities of marked and unmarked choices as 9:1 is relatively common in the system of language, since this allows a suitable balance of processing efforts in terms of the information-theoretic entropy principles.

(1)   polarity: positive (0.9) / negative (0.1)

Expectations are at the heart of both language production and processing. The frequencies refer to indicative probabilities of the choices to be made within such systems. One can expect a certain ratio of choices of nominalisations in a research article vs a shop encounter dialogue. However, even at the level of an individual text, the expectations expressed in probabilities can vary as the text develops. In a research article, for example, such sections as 'Related work' or 'Research methodology' are likely to vary in their probabilities of choices: considerably more instances of past tense reporting can be expected in the former. In the most extreme case, the 'Bibliography' section will not contain major clauses at all.

Even within a more homogeneous section of a research article, some variations in the probabilities are still possible. Halliday (1992) illustrates logogenetic development of references to the concept of cracking within a scientific article. This starts from *how glass cracks* (*crack* Process; *glass* Actor), goes through *will make slow cracks grow* (*crack* as nominalised caused Actor; property *slow*) and, finally, develops to a fairly complex nominalisation *decrease the crack growth rate* (property nominalised as *rate*). If there is a suitable measure for grammatical complexity, a corpus investigation can test this hypothesis on a large collection of scientific articles.

However, testing such hypotheses is not straightforward. The quantum mechanics metaphor of the wave–particle dualism is quite common in systemic studies: many linguistic phenomena can be described from two viewpoints, which offer complementary perspectives. With respect to corpora, we can notice the duality of description between form and function. Most of the counting by the computer can be done on the basis of forms – that is, the actual word forms as typeset in a text. This can be extended towards linguistic descriptions on a slightly higher level by using information about POS tags and lemmas, so that a search for *left* can produce different results depending on its grammatical environment: *my left hand* vs *he's just left*.

Nevertheless, even this basic generalisation can lead to:

- possible processing errors – an automatic POS tagger might have a systematic bias towards certain interpretations of ambiguous forms as more or less probable, for example *spread* can be more often treated as a noun; and
- uncomfortable design decisions – a POS tagger might define all participial forms as verbal forms, *interested, limited, measured,* so that *interested* will not be present as an adjectival collocate to *parties*.

If we go further away from forms towards their function, we can, with some degree of reliability, detect the more common participant configurations, for example Actor–Process–Goal for material processes. To test the hypothesis concerning development of grammatical complexity within a text, we can use a POS tagger to measure the distribution of lengths of nominal groups. For example, we can detect them by a pattern such as Rule A:

Rule A: (Adj|Noun)* Noun (of (Det|Adj|Noun)* Noun)*

This states that a noun can be preceded by zero or more adjectives or nouns, and it can be followed by a number of other nominal groups after *of*.

In each case, when we generalise forms to their function, we also need to estimate the accuracy of our generalisation procedure manually on a small sample. The standard measures in this case are **precision** – that is, the proportion of *correctly* identified items out of the items a rule *detected* in a text – and **recall** – that is, the proportion of *correctly* identified items out of all items *present* in a text. Precision is inversely proportional to the amount of incorrect items in the output list: cleaner lists correspond to higher precision. Recall, on the other hand, is inversely proportional to the number of items left in a text unidentified: more complete lists correspond to higher recall.

In a corpus of Wikipedia articles on renewable energy (Sharoff 2012), precision of Rule A reaches 95 per cent, with the errors mostly caused by incorrect POS tagging. For example, in a sentence such as example (2), the underlined fragment is identified as a nominal group because *many* has been tagged as an adjective and *spread*, as a noun.

(2) there are *many fragmented spots of high intensity geothermal potential spread across* the continent

However, recall of Rule A is about 60 per cent – significantly lower than its precision – because, in addition to POS tagging problems, a simple pattern like this fails to identify various other postnominal constructions, for example *single-bladed rotor with a teetering hub*, which includes a preposition, *with*, and a form tagged as a gerund, *teetering*. It is possible to expand

Rule A to cover such patterns too, but this should decrease its precision, since its updated version will also apply to such phrases as *to do an experiment with passing high-voltage electricity through rarefied air*.

Investigation from the lexical ends and from the grammatical end

The wave–particle metaphor also applies to the opposition of lexicon vs grammar. One view on the lexicon is to consider it as more delicate grammar (Hasan 1987). In this view, the grammatical systems specify more general configurations, such as the types of clause, their processes and participants, while the lexical choices are specified in more delicate systems following the grammatical choices. This approach has its own advantages, since it starts with small, well-defined oppositions reflecting grammatical choices.

An SFL study from the lexical end starts from lexical patterns and generalises them into more grammatical phenomena, such as transitivity or modality. Research by John Sinclair and his colleagues in the COBUILD project produced considerable evidence about the possibility of describing lexicogrammar from the lexical end. One example concerns detection of a new grammatical class of 'shell nouns' – that is, nouns that need to be expanded in the surrounding text, such as *belief, fact, question, theory of, that* (Hunston and Francis 2000).

Conducting a corpus investigation from the lexical end is considerably easier than one from the grammatical end, since the word forms are immediately accessible to a corpus query. This offers the possibility of creating concordances, frequency lists and collocation lists. Once this information is available, it is possible to classify any regular patterns of use. Even if POS tagging is not entirely reliable and often results in a very coarse model of grammatical functions, basic colligation patterns can be also checked by relatively simple queries. For example, it is easy to use POS patterns to count the types of reporting that follow certain verbs, such as *tell something to someone, tell someone that something, tell someone to do something*, etc. A statistical corpus-based investigation from the grammatical end is also potentially very fruitful, but its progress is hampered by the lack of large annotated corpora in which the grammatical phenomena have been tagged automatically.

Because the two perspectives are complementary, the interpretations often differ when the lexical and grammatical approaches are applied to the same phenomenon. As mentioned, the approach treating lexis as the most delicate grammar provides a useful interface between the two viewpoints. However, many lexical constructions and collocations cross the grammatical ranks, so it is often convenient to describe lexical constructions without a direct reference to their position in the systemic network for grammar. For example, a category such as 'shell nouns' has its meaning only as a part of a wider collocation, such as *arises/comes/follows/stems from the fact that* or *is the question of how/what/who/whether/where*. This combines elements of systemic choices at the levels of clause configuration and clause complex, as well as at the noun level.

Study of collocations is an example of natural lexical patterns that are more difficult to interpret from a purely grammatical viewpoint. The similarity in the meaning of lexically related expressions belonging to different grammatical categories leads to sharing their lexical context. For example, the constructions *lack of* and *to lack* share a lot of their collocates *complete/total/utter lack of ability/confidence/courage/credibility* vs *completely/totally/utterly lacking ability/confidence/courage/credibility*. If language is viewed as setting expectations, then the more obvious expectations are based on lexical collocates: a sentence starting from *Once upon a . . .* needs to be followed by the word *time* irrespectively of grammatical choices. Also, while the grammatical phenomena are relatively parsimonious in terms of choices, by their nature the lexical phenomena require many more choices in the networks (Tucker 1998; Sharoff 2006a).

It is natural that the two views can enrich each other. Hunston (2010: 38) provides an example concerning the contexts of use of the expression *the naked eye*. One can expect that it is usually preceded by *to* or *with* and it occurs in the context of such words as *detect*, *look*, *visible*. What is less predictable is that this particular expression more commonly occurs in the context of negation. As mentioned above, the overall frequency of negation in the system of language is predicted to be around 10 per cent. However, the conditional probability of *invisible* in the four-word context of *to the naked eye* is much higher than expected, as illustrated in the top collocates for the 723 instances of *naked eye* from the British English Web Corpus (ukWaC) listed in Table 33.1. Even though *invisible* is nearly six times less frequent than *visible*, it is about 70 per cent as common as *visible* in this context, with many contexts of *visible* also including *barely*, *not*, *rarely*.

Corpus composition

A corpus provides evidence about the uses of linguistic constructions in a finite sample of documents that it contains. However, it is natural to assume that this evidence can be generalised to a wider body of uses. In addition to statistical requirements for such generalisations, which will be mentioned later, we need to make an important assumption that this wider body of uses is similar with respect to its communicative functions to texts from the corpus that was the source of our evidence. To be able to test this assumption, we have to operationalise the notion of communicative functions by providing an exhaustive list of their types, so that a comparison can be made between collections of different texts.

Approaches to classifying a corpus can start from two different ends: we can follow text-external criteria or we can follow text-internal criteria. The text-external approach is based on parameters related to the context of its production, such as its author, the intended aims of the author or perception by the audience. The text-internal approach is based on parameters related to the lexicogrammatical choices made within texts, such as the use of connectives, conditional expressions or nominal phrases. These two views also need different terminology for describing text classes. Even though researchers often use these terms in various incompatible ways, in this chapter we will refer to 'genres' when considering the text-external view and to 'registers' when considering the text-internal one, unless another terminology is preferred by the author being mentioned (cf. Lee 2001; Biber and Conrad 2009; Santini et al. 2010).

Table 33.1 The most significant collocates of *to the naked eye* and their frequencies in ukWaC

Collocate	In construction	Overall
almost	13	336,594
barely	23	22,116
invisible	212	18,034
just	20	1,747,209
not	72	6,461,794
obvious	13	100,046
undetectable	6	1,157
visible	303	61,649

The wave–particle metaphor is appropriate here again: the two views are directed to the same phenomenon, which naturally combines form and function, but the perspectives are somewhat complementary. If our task is to design a corpus or to compare one corpus with another, we are more likely to use text-external parameters. For example, we can start by postulating the proportion of such genres as Reportage vs Editorials vs Newspaper Reviews (Categories A, B and C, respectively in the Brown corpus). Such categories are reflected in various guidelines for text producers and they are well recognised by the readers, unlike the more linguistically inspired categories such as Narrativity.

However, if our task is to understand the varieties of language use in a corpus, we are more likely to rely on text-internal parameters. For example, we can refer to the choices made in expression of narrative sequences, ways of expressing stance or persuasion and by relating them to the context of their use. Genre analysis of the text-external kind and register analysis of the text-internal kind have attracted considerable attention in SFL research (Bateman 2008; Martin and Rose 2008), as well as in SFL-related corpus studies (Sinclair 2003a).

From the text-external viewpoint, the problem is in designing categories to cover a wide range of parameters describing the variety of texts, which can be considered in a corpus. In his *Introduction to Functional Grammar*, Halliday (1985: xv) defined the aim of his grammatical analysis as being to say 'sensible and useful things about any text, spoken or written, in modern English'. In contrast to this, the existing SFL-based classifications of genres or registers do not cover the entirety of texts in a generic corpus such as the BNC or ukWaC. For example, Martin and Rose (2008) discuss a range of genres centred on different situations of the classroom use. They provide a systemic network that contrasts informing about things (descriptions and reports) vs informing about events (observations, recounts and narratives). Similarly, Bateman (2008) considers a range of visually rich genres, such as newspapers, instruction manuals or field guides, in a multimodal genre space. At the same time, a generic corpus contains many more text types, such as blog entries, annual reports, patents, product reviews, laws, contracts, etc., which also need to be described in some terms. Partly, this is explained by the fact that register analysis is conducted within the stratum of (discourse) semantics, which is not presently covered by an exhaustive list of choices.

Sinclair (1996) responded to the need to describe the composition of large generic corpora by suggesting several text-external dimensions for text classification, including the following six 'intended aims of text production':

- **Information** – reference compendia (Sinclair adds 'an unlikely outcome, because texts are very rarely created merely for this purpose');
- **Discussion** – polemic, position statements, argument;
- **Recommendation** – reports, advice, legal and regulatory documents;
- **Recreation** – fiction and non-fiction (biography, autobiography, etc.);
- **Religion** – holy books, prayer books, orders of service (which label does not refer to religion as a topic); and
- **Instruction** – academic works, textbooks, practical books.[2]

This typology is applicable to a large proportion of texts. However, some classes in this list are too generic: the vast majority of texts are aimed at discussing a state of affairs, so this makes no differentiation between reportage or editorial sections of the newspapers, personal blog entries, political speeches or hotel review forums.

Another important aspect of a text typology – or, indeed, of any annotation scheme – is that it needs to be reliable itself, in the sense that different people performing annotation on the same set of texts are likely to produce the same result, while any disagreement in their annotations is less than what could have occurred by chance (Krippendorff 2004). In the suggested list of the aims of text production, we can expect considerable disagreement between annotators on what counts as, for example, a recommendation (reports), instruction (academic works) or discussion (argument).

One way of achieving reliable assessment of corpus composition is by positioning texts in a genre space (Lemke 1999), so that the genre of a text is assessed through several test questions, such as the Forsyth and Sharoff's (2014) functional text dimensions (FTDs):

> **A1: Argumentative** To what extent does the text argue to persuade the reader to support (or renounce) an opinion or a point of view?
> **A7: Instructive** To what extent does the text aim at teaching the reader how something works?
> **A11: Personal** To what extent does the text report from a first-person point of view?
> **A17: Evaluative** To what extent does the text evaluate something?

A text receives a score (for example from 0 to 1) for each dimension and more than one dimension can be principal – that is, its value close to 1. If 'a register is a syndrome of lexicogrammatical probabilities' (Halliday 1992: 68), a genre can be considered as a syndrome of functional text dimensions.

Annotation studies show that the level of agreement for such dimensions is greater than for atomic genre labels. Also, some of the commonly used genre classes exhibit considerable internal variation: the generic genre class of blog entries, for example, can have fairly different instances along the Argumentative, Instructive, Personal or Evaluative principal dimensions.

Main research methods

The main methods for corpus research involve corpus collection, annotation and querying. Given the abundance of texts in electronic form and availability of large, ready-made corpora nowadays, the collection of ad hoc corpora for a specific task is reasonably straightforward.

Corpus annotation

As for manual annotation, one of the tools commonly used in SFL research is the UAM CorpusTool,[3] which provides ways of designing an annotation schema in the form of systemic networks, for example for annotating clauses for the process types or for polarity. Annotation can be done on several levels, for example for the document, clause and group levels. The tool can search for examples with a particular combination of features and can run statistical analysis comparing data subsets, for example for contrastive analysis of expressions of appraisal across different genres. In addition to purely manual analysis, the UAM CorpusTool can offer some automation in the form of word lists or rules, for example if a clause contains a word-level feature such as passive, the clause will be preselected to be passive-clause at the clause-level annotation stage.

If the annotation procedure uses an untested annotation schema, it is advisable to estimate its inter-annotator reliability by requesting two or more independent annotations for the same collection of texts. Otherwise, any corpus results concerning the difference between the categories of the scheme, for example description vs report in the framework of Martin and Rose (2008), cannot be treated as statistically significant. One of the commonly used reliability measures is Krippendorff's α, which estimates the difference between the actual disagreement and the disagreement by chance.[4] The level of α ≥ .667 indicates an acceptable reliability limit (Krippendorff 2004).

Manual annotation of a large corpus is not feasible. Most often, a basic level of annotation can be achieved by using POS taggers. Some of the commonly used tools for this task are TreeTagger[5] and the Stanford Tagger.[6] TreeTagger is particularly handy, since it comes with a lemmatisation tool and tagging models for a large number of languages. At the same time, the Stanford Tagger can be used together with the Stanford Parser,[7] which can produce basic dependency relations (subject, direct object, prepositional phrases, etc.) for English, as well as for Arabic, Chinese and German. These relations can be used and interpreted by the UAM Corpus Tool in terms of the SFL model to provide a crude first-pass automatic annotation.

Corpus querying

For corpus querying, there is a distinction between stand-alone concordancers, which work directly on user-provided texts, for example AntConc[8] or WordSmith,[9] and client–server interfaces, which usually operate via a web interface with large corpora stored on a server, for example CQPWeb (Evert and Hardie 2011),[10] IntelliText (Wilson et al. 2010)[11] or SketchEngine (Kilgarriff et al. 2004).[12]

In its simple form, making a corpus query is nearly the same as making a search query on the web. However, searching often becomes more challenging because of the need to specify various conditions, such as the possibility to restrict search for lemmas or POS tags, and to indicate possible gaps between words. Many client–server interfaces, including those mentioned above, are based on the Corpus Query Language (CQL), which was developed in the IMS Corpus Workbench.[13] For example, the CQL query to get all examples of the phrasal verb *leave behind* with a possible gap from zero to two words is as follows:

[lemma='leave' & pos='V.*'] []{0,2} [lemma='behind']

With the output of concordancing tools, the next task is to observe the concordance lines such as those in Table 33.2. There are several good introductions to the procedure (Sinclair 2003b; Hunston 2010). The main task is to detect a strong pattern in data, which could be explained by a hypothesis about meanings associated with the query. Usually, hypothesis formulation is accompanied with several more probing queries to test and generalise the pattern observed in the original data sample. This process can be further extended to multilingual contrastive analysis – that is, when we examine the patterns in two languages for potential translation candidates, often close cognates in related languages, and identify the differences between them. For example, even though *absolutely* in English and *assolutamente* in Italian are fairly good translation equivalents, *assolutamente* is often used in negative contexts, which are likely to be translated into English by using *not entirely* (Partington 1998).

When starting any corpus investigation, it is important to remember that corpus linguistics by itself is a tool; it does not provide a theory for investigation. Irrespectively of how 'corpus-driven' (that is, theory-neutral) an investigation is, observing the instances leads to a theory of the underlying system, which in its turn creates the possibility of interpreting the instances.

Another important consideration is corpus and sample size, because, statistically speaking, language consists of a large number of rare events (Baayen 2008). Mega-word corpora

Table 33.2 Concordance lines for *naked eye* in the BNC

oceans seems devoid of plants – at least	**to the naked eye**	; and if weed grows conspicuously on co
reveal patterns not immediately obvious	**to the naked eye**	; an example of this is shown in exerci
pared to buy houses with flaws invisible	**to the naked eye**	, but now we'd fallen for one wi
elaborate colonies, often quite visible	**to the naked eye**	, in which different individuals perfor
e so faint, not a single one is visible	**to the naked eye**	. Another 15 per cent of stars are oran
les being indistinguishable individually	**to the naked eye**	. Clays, the product of chemical weath
or viruses, although still not visible	**to the naked eye**	. Other species of animal are affected
tars the size of Earth and all invisible	**to the naked eye**	. So the Sun is hardly average. And ne
the internal organs looked pretty normal	**to the naked eye**	. There were some granulomatous area on
ible, and the human egg is just visible	**to the naked eye**	. The three key cell structures are the
are small, they are not always visible	**to the naked eye**	. They are revealed in their millions,
limetre in diameter and are just visible	**to the naked eye**	. Unlike the chick they contain no yolk
estern Europe. The mite is just visible	**to the naked eye**	and feeds on honey bees and their grubs
looks as smooth and featureless as glass	**to the naked eye**	but, unlike glass, it is a crystallin

are needed to capture the linguistic properties of even moderately frequent words such as *malicious*, which has 2 instances in the 1 million words of the Brown corpus, 337 in the 100 million words of the BNC and 6,182 instances in the 2 billion words of ukWaC. Data becomes sparser when we consider the frequencies of collocates. A corpus of the size of ukWaC provides some evidence about the patterns of use of *to the naked eye* (see Table 33.1), but even this evidence is not statistically reliable. Statistically significant evidence is not achievable with the 50 instances of this construction in the BNC.

A related issue concerns evidence obtained through corpus use. Corpora do not provide negative evidence – that is, a confirmation that a linguistic phenomenon does not occur. Negative evidence can be inferred only from a non-significant number of examples if positive evidence on a large corpus is overwhelming. Positive evidence suggests that a phenomenon exists, but more attention is needed to the conditions in which it is used, as well as to a comparison against other contexts of use. The number of positive examples is also not a measure in itself; it becomes meaningful only when compared against another value, for example an alternative construction or a different context of use. For example, there are 325 instances of the lemma *acanthus* in ukWaC, but there is no instance of any of the two potentially possible plural forms: *acanthuses* or *acanthi*. However, their absence does not declare their impossibility in the system. Similarly, the presence of 683 instances of the form *advices* in ukWaC indicates that the plural form is possible, in spite of the fact that the dictionaries declare it to be a mass noun. However, this use is much rarer than 452,138 uses of the non-count form and, in the majority of cases, the nominal form *advices* was used in texts from the nineteenth century, language teaching materials as a suggestion to avoid the plural form, or in the specific sense of informing documents, such as *remittance advices*.

For smaller corpora, both positive and negative evidence is less likely to be significant: the difference between three instances of one construction vs six instances of another one is not going to be significant. A conservative estimate for the smallest number of instances for statistically significant results is 30 (Upton and Cook 2001), even if, in many interesting linguistic cases, this is not achievable. However, even greater figures can be misleading for the purposes of generalisation, if the result includes 'confounding' variables, for example most of the instances coming from the same source, either the same text or the same author.

Future directions

As mentioned earlier, corpus linguistics does not provide a linguistic theory in itself; its primary contribution is a set of methods, which can help in developing linguistic theories. Therefore future directions in corpus research have primarily indirect impact on SFL studies by providing tools, rather than research hypotheses.

One of the techniques that has been driving research in automatic natural-language processing (NLP) is statistical machine learning (Manning and Schütze 1999). It has already made considerable impact on the way in which the linguistic resources are produced. An incomplete list of success stories includes POS tagging, syntactic parsing, text classification, information retrieval and machine translation. The machine learning approach starts from some amount of data, which is used to produce automatic annotation of sufficient quality. Sometimes, this data contains a desired annotation level, which serves as an example for annotating more data of the same kind. Technically, this is called 'supervised machine learning'. For example, if some sentences have been annotated with POS categories, the probabilities of the POS sequences detected in them can be used to process any new sentences without annotation to resolve the ambiguities such as *spread* as a noun or as a verb (Manning and Schütze 1999). Similarly, a number of examples of *think* in the sense of 'believe' vs *think* in the sense of 'contemplate' encoded as respectively Mental or Behavioural processes can help in determining correlations with features of the surrounding contexts. In the end, this can annotate verbs in a corpus with their more likely reading, for example Mental or behavioural. Sometimes, we do not have texts at a desired annotation level, while we can still use some more basic linguistic features for inferring statistical regularities at the desired annotation level. Technically, this is called 'unsupervised machine learning'. Biber's (1988) multidimensional analysis is an early example of unsupervised machine learning at the text-classification level, for example making a reliable association of surface-level features such as past-tense verbs or first-person pronouns with narration. Another possible application of unsupervised learning concerns automatic detection of the most common patterns of use for the main processes in the clause, which can lead to a data-driven way of describing the process configurations.

Either approach (or their combination in the form of *semi*-supervised machine learning) has a potential to change the situation with annotated corpora in SFL, improving availability of texts annotated at linguistic levels finer than the POS tags and lemmas as traditional in corpus studies. This should help in providing statistically significant evidence for the distribution of choices and their realisation, such as analysis of process–participant configurations, investigation of appraisal or thematic development. For example, if there is a corpus that has been manually annotated with the types of appraisal group, as well as with their targets and modifiers (Bednarek 2009), and there is a reliable dependency parser, which can link the targets and modifiers automatically in a text (Nivre et al. 2006), then machine learning methods can help in training a classifier that should detect the types of appraisal group in any text. Given that a considerable number of manually annotated resources have been produced within the systemic community since 2000 and given that a large amount of raw text is readily available in electronic form, annotated resources can be utilised to bootstrap systemic research and to provide new kinds of evidence.

Apart from wider availability of texts overall, the web also helps in bringing more *kinds* of texts for linguistic analysis. Among other things, this includes the language of social media, such as Facebook, or traditional news sources enhanced with user-provided comments, as well as user-contributed content on websites such as Tripadvisor or collaborative editing in the form of Wikipedia. Potentially, this provides a far greater amount of data for investigation of linguistic interaction than what was available in the past. However, harnessing this sea of data needs advanced computational methods such as those suggested above.

Another recent development concerns eye-tracking technologies, which are becoming more widely used to link corpus research on the product – that is, the text – to perception research on the process of its interpretation. Eye tracking can detect the amount of time the eye spends on a particular word, as well as possible regressions – that is, cases in which the expected flow of reading is interrupted and the eye returns to a fragment read earlier. The wider availability of eye tracking gives another kind of evidence about what is treated as expected and what is unexpected by the readers, thus reflecting on the marked and unmarked choices.

Notes

1 For an overview, see Thompson and Hunston (2006).
2 A more elaborate exposition of the text-external and text-internal classification criteria is available in Sinclair (1996).
3 http://www.wagsoft.com/CorpusTool/.
4 http://dfreelon.org/utils/recalfront/ is a convenient online interface.
5 http://www.cis.uni-muenchen.de/~schmid/tools/TreeTagger/.
6 http://nlp.stanford.edu/software/tagger.shtml.
7 http://nlp.stanford.edu/software/stanford-dependencies.shtml.
8 http://www.antlab.sci.waseda.ac.jp/software.html.
9 http://www.lexically.net/wordsmith/.
10 https://cqpweb.lancs.ac.uk/.
11 http://corpus.leeds.ac.uk/it/.
12 http://the.sketchengine.co.uk/.
13 http://cwb.sourceforge.net/documentation.php.

References

Aston, G., and L. Burnard. 1998. *The BNC Handbook: Exploring the British National Corpus with SARA*. Edinburgh: Edinburgh University Press.
Baayen, H. 2008. *Analysing Linguistic Data, Vol. 505*. Cambridge: Cambridge University Press.
Baroni, M., and S. Bernardini, 2004. Bootcat: Bootstrapping corpora and terms from the web. In *Proceedings of the Fifth International Conference on Language Resources and Evaluation, Lisbon (LREC 2004)*. Paris: ELRA, pp. 1313–16.

Baroni, M., S. Bernardini, A. Ferraresi and E. Zanchetta. 2009. The WaCky wide web: A collection of very large linguistically processed web-crawled corpora. *Language Resources and Evaluation* 43(3): 209–26.

Bateman, J. 2008. *Multimodality and Genre: A Foundation for the Systematic Analysis of Multimodal Documents*. Basingstoke: Palgrave Macmillan.

Bednarek, M. 2009. Language patterns and ATTITUDE. *Functions of Language* 16(2): 165–92.

Biber, D. 1988. *Variations across Speech and Writing*. Cambridge: Cambridge University Press.

Biber, D., and S. Conrad. 2009. *Register, Genre, and Style*. Cambridge: Cambridge University Press.

Evert, S., and A. Hardie. 2011. Twenty-first century corpus workbench: Updating a query architecture for the new millennium. Paper presented at the Corpus Linguistics Conference, University of Birmingham, 20–22 July.

Firth, J.R. 1957 [1951]. Modes of meaning. In J.R Firth (ed.) *Papers in Linguistics 1934–1951*. Oxford: Oxford University Press, pp. 190–215.

Forsyth, R., and S. Sharoff. 2014. Document dissimilarity within and across languages: A benchmarking study. *Literary and Linguistic Computing* 29: 6–22.

Gregory, M. 1988. Generic situation and register: A functional view of communication. In J.D. Benson, M. Cummings and W.S. Greaves (eds) *Linguistics in a Systemic Perspective*. Amsterdam: John Benjamins, pp. 301–30.

Halliday, M.A.K. 1957. *Some Aspects of Systematic Description and Comparison in Grammatical Analysis* (Studies in Linguistic Analysis). Oxford: Blackwell.

Halliday, M.A.K. 1959. *The Language of the Chinese: Secret History of the Mongols*. Oxford: Blackwell.

Halliday, M.A.K. 1978. *Language as Social Semiotic: The Social Interpretation of Language and Meaning*. Oxford: Blackwell.

Halliday, M.A.K. 1985. *An Introduction to Functional Grammar*. London: Arnold.

Halliday, M.A.K. 1992. Language as system and language as instance: The corpus as a theoretical construct. *Directions in Corpus Linguistics: Proceedings of Nobel Symposium 82* 65: 61–77.

Hasan, R. 1987. The grammarian's dream: Lexis as most delicate grammar. In M.A.K. Halliday and R.P. Fawcett (eds) *New Developments in Systemic Linguistics*. London: Pinter, pp. 184–211.

Hunston, S. 2010. How can a corpus be used to explore patterns. In A. O'Keeffe and M. McCarthy (eds) *The Routledge Handbook of Corpus Linguistics*. London: Routledge, pp. 152–66.

Hunston, S., and G. Francis. 2000. *Pattern Grammar: A Corpus-Driven Approach to the Lexical Grammar of English*. Amsterdam: John Benjamins.

Kilgarriff, A., P. Rychly, P. Smrz and D. Tugwell. 2004. The sketch engine. In *Proceedings of Euralex 2004*, Lorient: Université de Bretagne-Sud, pp. 105–16.

Krippendorff, K. 2004. Reliability in content analysis: Some common misconceptions and recommendations. *Human Communication Research* 30(3): 411–33.

Lee, D. 2001. Genres, registers, text types, domains, and styles: Clarifying the concepts and navigating a path through the BNC jungle. *Language Learning and Technology* 5(3): 37–72.

Lemke, J.L. 1999. Typology, topology, topography: genre semantics. Unpublished manuscript. University of Michigan, Ann Arbor, MI.

Manning, C., and H. Schütze. 1999. *Foundations of Statistical Natural Language Processing*. Cambridge, MA: MIT Press.

Martin, J., and D. Rose. 2008. *Genre Relations: Mapping Culture*. London: Equinox.

Matthiessen, C.M.I.M. 2006. Frequency profiles of some basic grammatical systems: An interim report. In G. Thompson and S. Hunston (eds) *System and Corpus: Exploring Connections*. London: Equinox, pp. 103–42.

Nesi, H., and S. Gardner. 2012. *Genres across the Disciplines: Student Writing in Higher Education*. Cambridge: Cambridge University Press.

Nivre, J., J. Hall and J. Nilsson. 2006. Maltparser: A data-driven parser-generator for dependency parsing. In *Proceedings of the Fifth International Conference on Language Resources and Evaluation, Lisbon (LREC 2004)*. Paris: ELRA, pp. 2216–19.

Serge Sharoff

Serge Sharoff

Partington, A. 1998. *Patterns and Meanings: Using Corpora for English Language Research and Teaching*. Amsterdam: John Benjamins.

Santini, M., A. Mehler and S. Sharoff. 2010. Riding the rough waves of genre on the web. In A. Mehler, S. Sharoff and M. Santini (eds) *Genres on the Web: Computational Models and Empirical Studies*. Berlin and New York: Springer, pp. 3–30.

Sharoff, S. 2006a. How to handle lexical semantics in SFL: A corpus study of purposes for using size adjectives. In G. Thompson and S. Hunston (eds) *System and Corpus: Exploring Connections*. London: Equinox, pp. 184–205.

Sharoff, S. 2006b. Open-source corpora: Using the net to fish for linguistic data. *International Journal of Corpus Linguistics* 11(4): 435–62.

Sharoff, S. 2012. Beyond translation memories: Finding similar documents in comparable corpora. In *Proceedings of the Translating and the Computer Conference*, London.

Sinclair, J. 1991. *Corpus, Concordance and Collocation*. Oxford: Oxford University Press.

Sinclair, J. 1996. *Preliminary Recommendations on Text Typology*. Expert Advisory Group on Language Engineering Standards (EAGLES) Technical Report EAG-TCWG-TTYP/P, June.

Sinclair, J. 2003a. Corpora for lexicography. In P.V. Sterkenberg (ed.) *A Practical Guide to Lexicography*. Amsterdam: John Benjamins, pp. 167–78.

Sinclair, J. 2003b. *Reading Concordances: An Introduction*. Harlow: Longman.

Thompson, G., and S. Hunston (eds). 2006. *System and Corpus: Exploring Connections*. London: Equinox.

Tucker, G. 1998. *The Lexicogrammar of Adjectives: A Systemic Functional Approach to Lexis*. London: Cassell Academic.

Upton, G., and I. Cook. 2001. *Introducing Statistics*. 2nd edn. Oxford: Oxford University Press.

Wilson, J., A. Hartley, S. Sharoff and P. Stephenson. 2010. Advanced corpus solutions for humanities researchers. In *Proceedings of the Workshop on Advanced Corpus Solutions (PACLIC 24)*. Sendai: Tohoku University, pp. 36–43.

34

Translation studies

Kerstin Kunz and Elke Teich

Introduction

Translation studies, or translatology, is the discipline concerned with the theory, modelling and description of translation. Commonly, translation is considered from two (complementary) perspectives (cf. Bell 1991): translation as *product* and translation as *process*. Thus a comprehensive theory of translation will have to account for and explain both of these aspects: the human activity of translation involves interpretation – of a source language (SL) text – and production – of a target language (TL) text. For a linguistic theory to be useful for theorising translation, it needs to be able to describe and model linguistic products – that is, texts in a translation relation – and explain how they are processed (by human or machine). Essentially, then, a linguistic theory suitable for application to translation must be concerned with *language use*. Systemic functional linguistics (SFL) is such a theory. The conception of language use being dependent on context is embodied in SFL in the concept of *register* and SFL provides methods for modelling the context–language relation, as well as for describing single registers in terms of configurations of lexicogrammatical patterns (see Bowcher, this volume; Moore, this volume).

This chapter provides an overview of (a) how translatology has harnessed SFL as a framework for theorising and modelling translation, and (b) the various ways in which SFL has engaged in translation research. In the next section, it provides a brief history of SFL's involvement in translation studies, mainly discussing Catford's seminal work and Halliday's expositions on translation. It goes on to look at SFL's notion of register as a suitable basis for theorising and modelling translation. The chapter then discusses recent research on translation applying SFL for different research objectives such as register variation and regarding grammatical metaphor, cohesion and appraisal. A brief overview of the methods employed in the analysis of translation(s) follows and then we briefly describe the current practices in SFL-based translation research, with a focus on corpus-based studies. Finally, we briefly sketch possible future directions in SFL-based translation research.

Kerstin Kunz and Elke Teich

Historical perspective

The earliest records of SFL-based research on translation date back to the 1950s and early 1960s, with two articles by Halliday (1956, 1966 [1962]) on machine translation. A third early work is Catford's (1965) monograph on a linguistic theory of translation. The 1960s were a very active time in linguistic theory-building and this holds for SFL as well, with a wealth of publications on concepts provided by the theory, as well as applications, one of them being translation. Both Halliday and Catford assume the then-standard SFL model, scale and category grammar, which postulated the levels of context, form (grammar, lexis) and substance (graphology, phonology). While Halliday (1966 [1962]) takes the perspective of machine translation, Catford (1965) aims at formulating a general theory of translation, focusing on the nature and conditions of translation equivalence. The levels discussed as relevant are *form*, relating to linguistic patterning, and *context*, relating to features of the situation in which language operates. At the level of form, the relevant sublevels are *grammar* and *lexis*; within grammar, the relevant category is *rank*. According to Halliday (1966 [1962]: 25), a text and a translation will display *probabilities of equivalence* between the items occurring in them. Using the categories of form and context, as well as rank, Halliday (1966 [1962]) proposes a step-by-step 'algorithm' for translation:

1   selection of a candidate translation equivalent for a given item at a given rank (the item with the highest probability, for example calculated on the basis of frequency);
2   taking into account the conditioning effect of the surrounding text in the source language on the probabilities assumed in the first step and possibly reassessing the probabilities; and
3   considering the structure of the target language and possibly again reassessing probabilities of candidate equivalents.

The second step is described as an operation that starts on the lowest rank (typically the morpheme) and, step by step, moves up the rank scale (word, group/phrase, clause, sentence), thus progressively contextualising an item at higher ranks. This 'model' of translation thus operates within two basic concepts of the SFL model: *stratification* (context, meaning, form) and the *rank scale* (cf. Berry, this volume.

   Catford (1965) provides a formulation of the central goals and components of a theory of translation, and presents some basic reflections on relevant translatological concepts – notably, translational equivalence. According to him, the core task of translation theory is to define the 'nature and conditions of translation equivalence' (Catford 1965: 21). To this end, he defines translational equivalence as (a) a relation that holds between texts (an SL text and a TL text), and (b) a relation that is primarily established at the level of situation (rather than meaning or form). Translational equivalence is thus *not* to be equated with formal correspondence, which is a relation between two languages in the sense that a TL category may be said to occupy the 'same' place in the system of the TL as the given SL category in the TL. Equivalence cannot be formulated in absolute terms, but is contingent on function in context: SL and TL texts are equivalents if they can function in the same situation. The primary unit of translational equivalence is the sentence, since it is directly related to speech function within a situation. Translation equivalence occurs when an SL and a TL text or item are relatable to (at least some of) the same features of situation, in which these features must be *linguistically relevant*. To illustrate this, consider one of Catford's (1965: 37–9) examples. A girl says 'I've arrived': the relevant features in this expression are that there is a *speaker*, an event of *arriving* and a *prior event* that is *linked to* the *current situation*. If translated into Russian as *Ja prishla*, the relevant features are *speaker, speaker-is-female, arrival, arrival-on-foot* and a *prior event* that was *completed*. Even though the Russian translation does not encode the same features, it is an appropriate translation, because there is a large enough overlap in relevant features. To link this back to the conditions of translation equivalence, rather than having the same meaning, SL and TL expressions function in the same situation – that is, are interchangeable in a given situation. The aim of translation is thus to select TL equivalents with the greatest possible overlap in situational range (Catford 1965: 49–50).

Catford thus takes as a basis the fundamental tenet of SFL that language use is ultimately determined by context. Since translation is a particular form of language use, context must play a crucial role in translation as well. To obtain a complete picture of the conditions of translation equivalence, Catford elaborates on two related aspects: *language varieties* and *probability*. Language varieties are reflexes of different contextual settings and, clearly, translation has to accommodate features related to dialect, idiolect or register. Probabilities come into play when we consider that, in translation, there is typically more than one possible TL equivalent, each with a particular probability conditioned by contextual and co-textual factors. The latter could be derived from a large enough corpus of SL texts and their translations (Catford 1965: 31), which is basically the approach taken by statistical machine translation. Human translators are trained in making appeal to contextual and co-textual meaning, and are typically quite good at taking into account the former; (statistical) machine translation can take into account only the latter.

The early works by Halliday and Catford take a linguistic perspective on translation, and they provide only a selective account of translation. As SFL's model of language became more fleshed out over the following decades, it was also harnessed increasingly by translation scholars (as we shall see later in the chapter).

Critical issues and topics

For a linguistic theory to be relevant for translatology, it needs to be a theory of language use. SFL is such a theory and models language use as *choice in context* (cf. Fontaine et al. 2013). Among the various conceptual categories that SFL offers to model language (metafunction, stratification, etc.), the most fruitful one in relation to translation studies has been the notion of *register* (cf. Moore, this volume), which is, of course, inherently connected with choice in context. This is evidenced by a range of works by translation scholars, as well as systemic functional linguists (among others, Hatim and Mason 1990; Bell 1991; House 1997, 2001; Steiner 1998, 2001, 2004; Matthiessen 2001; Teich 2003; Neumann 2013).

The reasons for the notion of register having been so successful in translation studies are, first, that it provides a framework for combining micro-analysis (lexical, grammatical, textual features) with interpretation in sociocultural context. Secondly, using the notion of register has been instrumental in breaking up the boundaries between theoretical, descriptive and applied translation studies. The theoretical strand of translation studies often remains too abstract to be used for the description of translation, let alone for application issues (such as translation pedagogy), and descriptive translation studies is often too anecdotal to provide a basis for theorising. While theoretical and descriptive translation studies are 'indicative', and concerned with describing and identifying the nature of translations, applied translation studies is rather 'imperative' (Halliday 2001: 14), with a focus on translation quality assessment and designing strategies for translator training.[1]

SFL's register model offers a grid into which many concepts and terms used in translation studies can be meaningfully placed (cf. Matthiessen 2001; Teich 2001). One of the earliest works harnessing the notion of register for translation studies is Hatim and Mason's (1990) *Discourse and the Translator*. Their essential contribution is to place translation in the wider context of language variation (including user-related variation – that is, dialect). A similar perspective is taken in House's (1997) work on translation quality assessment. Based on the notion of function in context, she defines two basic translation types, overt and covert translation. *Covert* translation refers to translation functioning as a 'second original', whereas *overt* translation gives recognition to the fact that, for some texts, such as religious, literary, aesthetic texts, functional equivalence cannot be achieved at all. Among the research employing register for translation criticism is Steiner's work over many years (cf. Steiner 1998, 2001, 2004) discussing in great detail the translation relation in selected registers in the language pair English–German.

Research on translation on the basis of SFL's notion of register has provided a lot of insights into *translation as product* (properties of translations, translation relation). However, there is much less work on *translation as process*.[2] Translation must be thought of as a specific kind of linguistic production that is induced by another text (the SL text). The translation process involves 'deconstruing' the SL text, assessing its function in context in the SL and producing a text in the TL that realises a comparable function in context in the TL. This, of course, is quite a complex process, in which interpretation and production are interwoven. Also, it must be assumed that the cognitive processes involved in the comprehension of an SL text, as well as the production of the TL text, are different from comprehension and production in other processing tasks. Since SFL is not a theory of cognitive linguistic processing, other frameworks have to be drawn upon and other methods – notably, experimental ones – have to be employed. Recently, some researchers have addressed this gap by combining product- and process-oriented perspectives (as we shall see later in the chapter).

Current contributions and research

This section shows how selected aspects of SFL are applied to issues in translation studies. We start by discussing the integration of the *register* model and then look at *grammatical metaphor* (Tavernier, this volume), *cohesion* (Clarke, this volume) and *appraisal* (Oteíza, this volume).

As mentioned in the last section, SFL's notion of register (Bartlett, this volume; Bowcher, this volume; Moore, this volume) has been very influential in translation studies. Translation scholars use the register model to describe variation between originals and translations, although for different research objectives. For instance, House (1997, 2001) assesses the quality of translations by comparing the profiles of originals and translations in terms of the parameters of field, tenor and mode. Steiner (2001) enters into discussions on the type and degree of register variation between originals and translations, postulating that translations are a register in their own right. Corpus-based studies, such as Teich (2003), Hansen-Schirra et al. (2012) or Neumann (2013), employ the model as a basis for quantitative studies measuring contrasts in linguistic choice between source and target texts in terms of relative frequency distributions of lexicogrammatical features. This permits identifying preferences for particular co-occurrences of lexicogrammatical features and interpreting them as indicators of register variation. This kind of approach is particularly valuable for translation studies for several reasons. First, the identification of *intra-lingual* variation informs translation studies in terms of systematic knowledge about register variation in translation-relevant registers. For instance, the syntactical structures chosen in instruction manuals, out of all resources available in a given language, differ from those chosen in political speeches.

Second, the identification of *inter-lingual* variation shows that equivalent functions may be instantiated in different languages by groupings of different features (cf. Teich 2003). For instance, lexical repetition and syntactic parallelism may prevail in persuasive registers in language A, whereas imperatives and positive lexis may be preferred in language B. The identification of intra-lingual variation therefore yields knowledge about how languages diverge in terms of patterns that reflect one and the same register, but also knowledge about their commonalities, since there has to be some overlap for texts from two different languages to be assigned to the same (or comparable) registers (cf. Steiner 2001). Knowing about register-dependent variation in the type (for example rank, linguistic level, metafunction) and the degree of equivalence between originals of different languages is essential for elaborating global and local translation strategies that incorporate choice in terms of field, tenor and mode.

Finally, empirical approaches combining the abstract SFL model with quantitative methods provide an insight into the relation of register and *translationese*. The notion of 'translationese' concerns the assumption that translations and originals differ systematically in the use of various linguistic features (Baker 1993; Toury 1995). While some of these features may result from translation errors (and hence be attributable to the translator's lack of competence), the main focus of translation studies has been on so-called *translation universals* or general properties of translations. For instance, it has been observed that translations tend to be more explicit and less ambiguous than their source texts (*explicitation*), for example that they often prefer finite verbal constructions to non-finite ones. Translations tend to be lexically and syntactically simpler than their source texts (*simplification*), for example the number of complex nominal groups is often significantly lower in the translations than in their originals. Moreover translations tend to exaggerate features of the target text language (*normalisation*), for example translations often tend towards a more frequent use of particles than their source texts and the frequencies are even higher than original texts in the same language. At the same time, translations imitate features of the source text language (*shining through*), for example the frequencies found for a linguistic phenomenon often approximate those of their source texts rather than those of original texts in the same language. Evidence of translationese has been demonstrated empirically on the level of lexicogrammar by several corpus-based studies (Baroni and Bernardini 2006; Van Halteren 2008). Some of these works (such as Kurokawa et al. 2009) suggest that the degree of variation depends on the translation direction, for example that distinctive features in translations from German into English differ from those in translations from English into German. Moreover, formal and functional differences between originals and translation may concern only particular registers (cf. Hansen-Schirra et al. 2012; Neumann 2013).

Another notion that has been instrumental in describing and modelling translation is *grammatical metaphor*. Grammatical metaphor concerns the systemic potential of a language to realise a given meaning with a variety of different lexicogrammatical forms (cf. Tavernier, this volume). The notion is used in translation studies to investigate local shifts between originals and translations as conscious or unconscious translation procedures, which eventually are a consequence of the overall translation method (for example overt or covert translation, as we saw earlier). Shifts involve structural translation procedures, such as *transposition* and/ or shifts in semantic perspective (*modulation*) (cf. Vinay and Darbelnet 1958). They may be the result of systemic contrasts between the source and the target text language (cf. Steiner and Teich 2004), diverging conventions across languages according to register (House 1997) or the process of translation itself (Steiner 2004). Steiner (2002) postulates different stages of *(de)metaphorisation* during the process of translation that result in different degrees of metaphoricity between the source text and the translation. In this respect, the study of (de)metaphorisation relates to works on general properties of translation (such as explicitation and simplification). Steiner's observations and hypotheses have been taken up by other scholars and tested with various empirical methodologies (at which we look in the next section). While earlier works have suggested that shifts between translations and originals primarily lead into one direction, for example towards explicitation (Blum-Kulka 2004 [1986]) and/or simplification (Baker 1993), more recent studies show that the language pairs involved, as well as the translation direction, are crucial factors (Teich 2003; Hansen-Schirra et al. 2012).

In the textual domain, Halliday and Hasan's notion of *cohesion* has been used for the study of shifts in translations. For instance, Blum-Kulka (2004 [1986]) postulates that explicitation on the level of cohesion is a general strategy in translation, thus supporting Baker's hypotheses at this linguistic level. Empirical evidence for shifts of cohesive explicitation has been obtained in several corpus-based studies with respect to individual cohesive devices that trigger one of the main types of cohesive relation. For instance, explicitation in cohesion may imply a higher frequency of cohesive devices in the target than the source text, such as conjunctions to mark logico-semantic relations (Olohan 2002). Becher et al. (2009) point to an increased frequency of sentence–initial conjuncts in translations from English into German over time (twenty-five years). This change is related to the dominant status of English, impacting on German originals through language contact via English-to-German translation. Cohesive explicitation may also involve changes from reduced cohesive devices such as pronouns to fully lexical phrases (for example source text: *the President of the United States – he*; target text: *the President of the United States – the President*), as shown in Hansen-Schirra et al. (2012). Again, most studies show evidence that explicitation is a matter of the language pairs involved, as well as the translation direction. Blum-Kulka (2004 [1986]) and also Baker (2011 [1992]) suggest that global changes in thematic structure and coherence are caused in translations through differences in the density of cohesive ties, as well as the number of elements in cohesive chains. These assumptions about shifts in cohesive chains have come to the fore of empirical translation studies only recently (for example Kunz 2010; Kunz and Steiner 2012). By contrast, lexical cohesion has long been recognised as an important notion for the identification of thematic progression in machine translation (cf. O'Donnell, this volume). Machine translation studies show that machine translations contain fewer ties of reiteration than human translations and that machine translations lack semantic variation (for example Wong et al. 2012). Such findings are used to improve metrics designed for the evaluation of machine translation outputs.

In the interpersonal domain, the notion of *appraisal* has been applied in the study of translation (cf, Oteíza, this volume). Appraisal concerns the linguistic reflection of socio-cultural meaning, and refers to the speaker's evaluation and stance in a text by which social interaction with the reader is constantly negotiated in a given communication situation. In translation studies, it is employed to examine patterns of shifts in the speaker's positioning from source to target text and to interpret these shifts in terms of explanatory backgrounds, such as method of translation (overt vs covert) and translation scope. The latter concerns the function of the translation, which is determined by the target text readership and the translation brief provided by the client.[3] Several scholars have shown that appraisal is construed via different language systems through different choices in lexicogrammar. In addition, such studies have revealed that there are cultural differences between languages in terms of the degree to which the meaning of evaluation is instantiated at all.[4] Munday (2012) builds on Martin and White's (2005) model to explore how the different types of appraisal (*attitude*, *graduation* and *engagement*) are inscribed into linguistic instantiations in originals and translations. Munday (2012) applies an innovative combination of quantitative and qualitative methods to show that translators sometimes tend towards neutralisation to the extent that the evaluative force of the source text is lost entirely in the translation. In his analyses, Munday uses appraisal to uncover the translator's own subjectivity and interpersonal 'intervention', and relates it to register and genre, and eventually socioculture.

Main research methods

The specific research methods employed in translatology depend on whether the research carried out is product or process-oriented. Since SFL mainly serves as a basis for product-oriented research, we focus on the research methods employed in this strand of research, which range from the analysis of single text-translation pairs and small samples, to the analysis of corpora. Analysis of single text-translation pairs and small samples of text-translation pairs is essentially qualitative, serving the in-depth discussion of specific translational equivalents, translation strategies and linguistic phenomena relevant in translation (for example grammatical metaphor, Theme–Rheme, etc.). Studies on small samples of text-translation pairs also serve the purpose of refining translation models on the basis of the SFL model.[5] For instance, Steiner (2001) discusses an original advertising text to elaborate on the question of whether translations can be regarded as register variety owing to the differences in field, tenor and mode between source and target texts. Apart from providing insights into translation patterns in particular language pairs and registers, such micro-analytic studies can also serve as a basis for larger-scale, quantitative analyses on the basis of corpora (see Sharoff, this volume).

The design of a corpus to be used in translation research depends on the specific research question. The focus here is on types of corpus that are commonly used in translation studies for indicative, as well as imperative, analyses (cf. Olohan 2004): comparable corpora, translation corpora and parallel corpora (including shadow translations as a particular subtype of parallel corpora).

Comparable corpora are monolingual text collections that consist of a sub-corpus of original texts in a given language and a sub-corpus of translations into the same language as the source language (or several source languages) (cf. Baker 1995: 234). In relation to SFL, this kind of corpus has mainly been used to study features of lexicogrammar and certain aspects of cohesion that are specific to translations as compared to original texts, which are more or less independent of the source texts (as we saw earlier in relation to *translationese*).

Translation corpora are bilingual and consist of two sub-corpora: original texts in a given language and their translations in another language. This corpus type has been widely employed for the study of translation equivalence (recurring translation patterns, translation shifts). Differences between originals and translations have been interpreted as inherently stemming from systemic contrasts of the languages involved and/or register differences. SFL scholars have, for instance, used this corpus design to study contrasts in terms of choices in Theme and process types.[6]

Parallel corpora are understood in translation studies as a combination of translation corpora and comparable corpora: they are bidirectional, containing originals in two languages and their translations into the other language. This design makes it possible to identify (a) contrasts between original texts in two languages, and (b) contrasts between original texts and translations in the same language. In this way, shifts between SL originals and TL translations that result from differences in linguistic systems can be distinguished from translation-induced shifts originating in the process of translation (cf. Teich 2001, 2003; Steiner 2001, 2004; Hasselgård forthcoming). To account for register as a variable in translation, some corpora used in translation studies include samples of different registers (cf. Neumann 2013), for example the Corpus of Translational English (TEC) (cf. Laviosa 1998) is a comparable corpus that follows roughly the design of the British National Corpus (BNC) in terms of registers represented, while the CroCo parallel corpus includes texts from eight different registers in the language pair English–German (Hansen-Schirra et al. 2012).

The notion of *shadow translation* was introduced by Matthiessen (2001: 83) as a kind of 'agnation along the paradigmatic axis', whereby a given instantiation in the source text relates to a set of alternative expressions determined by the systemic potential of the target language; these paradigmatic source text alternatives, in turn, are potential candidates for alternative translation options. Matthiessen's considerations are taken up by Johansson (2007), who uses shadow translations as a particular kind of parallel corpus with multiple translations by professional translators of the same source text. This corpus design serves to study the choice of a particular translation strategy by individual translators and possible preferences in rendering a given meaning across individual translators (Johansson 2007: 20*ff*). Munday (2012) uses this design for exploring differences in translations with respect to the translators' subjectivity in terms of appraisal/evaluation. In recent corpus-based studies, shadow translations are increasingly employed for spotting translation errors in so-called learner translator corpora.[7]

The concept of shadow translations is also applied for studies on the *process of translation*. Empirical data is obtained here from experiments in which different subjects are given the same translation task. For instance, Alves et al. (2011) have shown how SFL notions can be adopted in process-oriented approaches to translation. They take the logo-genetic dimension as a point of departure to examine the translator's choice in the real-time unfolding of discourse. They base their experiments on Bell's (1991) model, which considers translating as a recursive process in which short- and long-term memories interact to decode and encode information at different levels of parsing. This dynamic view on the translation process enhances the notion of *regression paths* – that is, constant online revision and changes in previous translation decisions. The regressions produce so-called macro- and micro-units of translation, in which the meaning of a linguistic unit in the source text undergoes different phases of reformulation during the process of translation. A *micro-unit* in the translation concerns each reformulation separately, whereas a *macro-unit* comprises all reformulations together. Micro- and macro-units are retrievable from keystroke logging, since the data contains recordings of pauses that mark a translation unit, as well as recordings of formulations and reformulations. For instance, the data makes capturing paths of (de)metaphorisation possible. In Alves et al. (2010) and Pagano et al. (2013), further evidence is obtained from eye-tracking data, in which gaze fixation and eye movement are recorded within, and also across, the target and the original text. While keystroke logging identifies problematic parts in the target texts and informs about variation in linguistic choice during the process of translation, eye tracking provides clues about the strategies for solving translation challenges such as grammatical metaphorisation in the target text. To obtain more information about the reasons for translation challenges, Alves et al. (2010) additionally use retrospective protocols in which subjects are interviewed after the translation tasks. Alves (2003) borrows the term 'triangulation' for a combination of these three psycholinguistic methods.

Recommendations for practice

We have seen that SFL provides a suitable model for relating descriptive and theoretical work on translation, and allows combining qualitative and quantitative methods. As with many other areas of language research, in translation studies, we encounter an empirical turn, with corpus-based and experimental methods being increasingly used. One needs to be aware that embarking on empirical research implies a commitment to data. This includes knowledge about how to compile relevant data, how to process this data further, and how to analyse and interpret it. Since experimental studies of translation are still in their infancy, it is too early to speak of an established practice. We therefore focus here on the current practice in corpus-based translation studies (cf. Hansen-Schirra and Teich 2008), which shares many concerns with corpus-based linguistics (cf. Sharoff, this volume) regarding corpus compilation, corpus processing and annotation, corpus query and corpus analysis.

Corpus compilation needs to follow three basic principles: to be suitable for making generalisations about a language (or language variety), a corpus should be *representative* of a given language (or language variety), *balanced* in terms of proportions of text types, genres, registers and media included, and of sufficient *size* (in terms of numbers of words or tokens) so that no linguistic patterns will be missed in analysis. Applied to translation studies, the material should be chosen according to relevance for translation in a particular language pair (for example instruction manuals, speeches or fictional texts, rather than journalistic texts), and it should contain samples of as many different translation-relevant registers or text types as possible. Also, the source language texts included should have been produced by many different authors and the translations should have been produced by different professional translators (or student translators, in the case of learner corpora). One caveat in hand-selecting texts for inclusion in a corpus is that we make a priori assumptions about the text class (register, text type) to which a given text belongs (cf. Hansen-Schirra et al. 2012: 26). This can hardly be avoided, however, and even automatic methods (such as web-as-corpus) cannot avoid biases. In terms of size, translation corpora range from fairly small (around 100,000 tokens) to fairly big (> 1 million). Compared to corpora of general language, corpora in translation studies are relatively small, which is also a result of the restricted availability of text-translations pairs (depending on the language pair) (cf. Neumann and Hansen-Schirra 2005).

In terms of *corpus processing, annotation* and *query*, standard processing steps are sentence segmentation, tokenisation and POS tagging, and, in the case of parallel corpora, text-translation alignment.[8] These steps can be carried out automatically to an acceptable degree of accuracy for many languages. Further automatic processing, such as syntactic parsing, is generally more error-prone, and the results are very variable across languages and text types. If higher-level features (for example functional grammatical categories, appraisal) are of interest, some can be identified by corpus queries, while others need to be annotated manually, or by a combination of queries and semi-automatic annotation (such as by using lexical seeds). For instance, for the annotation of the cohesive *and*, rules can be defined to automatically disambiguate phrase-combining instances from those connecting clauses or sentences. Manual annotation is quite time-consuming, but cannot be avoided in some cases (such as cohesive chains, Theme–Rheme patterns, grammatical metaphor). Here, elaborate guidelines have to be designed to guarantee consistency and inter-annotator agreement needs to be monitored. It is therefore advisable to plan in advance which kinds of manual annotation are really necessary and whether it is perhaps possible to operationalise a given research question at a lower linguistic level (such as by lexical sets, sequences of POS patterns). Tools in use to support manual annotation include the UAM Corpustool (cf. O'Donnell, this volume) or MMAX2 (cf. Müller and Strube 2006).

While most of the foregoing discussion holds for corpora in general, for translation corpora there are two additional considerations: the material included is multilingual (except for comparable corpora) and it may be aligned (in the case of parallel corpora). This means that there is always an additional effort in processing: more than one language needs to be dealt with and text-translation pairs need to be considered. The most reliable type of automatic alignment operates at sentence level. If other units are of interest (which is usually the case, for example when investigating translation shifts), these need to be aligned manually – a process that is again time-consuming – and quality-checking procedures need to be put into place.

The results of *corpus analyses* are typically frequency distributions of selected features that need to be (a) tested in terms of significance and (b) interpreted with regard to a hypothesis. Here, standard statistical tests can be employed to compare such distributions across SL texts and translations (for a parallel corpus), or original texts and comparable texts in the same language (for comparable corpora). If more than one feature needs to be interpreted at a time, machine learning methods such as automatic clustering and classification can be employed (cf. Volansky et al. 2015).

To build a corpus is a fairly costly exercise, especially regarding translation corpora. One should therefore check whether a suitable resource might already be available. For example, for European languages, there is the EURO-PARL parallel corpus containing proceedings of the European Parliament. The most recent version includes originals and translations of 21 European languages, with approximately 60 million words per language (cf. Koehn 2005). For English, there is the comparable corpus TEC, of around 10 million words (Baker 1995). It contains translations into English from a variety of European and non-European source languages, and includes texts from four different genres. One example of a richly annotated parallel and comparable corpus is the German–English GECCo corpus (cf. Lapshinova-Koltunski and Kunz 2014), which includes texts from ten registers, and has been aligned and annotated manually and semi-automatically at word (morphology, parts of speech), syntactic (functional and formal categories at phrase and clause levels) and text (cohesive devices and relations) levels.

Future directions

In future work on translation based on SFL's model of language, the following directions regarding the theory, description and modelling of translation are likely.

For theorising translation, we need to investigate it in the context of other linguistic processes – notably, language contact and language change, since translation is a specific type of language contact and a possible factor in language change (Steiner 2008; Becher et al. 2009; Kranich et al. 2012). For describing translation as product, we need more contrastive linguistic accounts based on SFL, not only at the lexicogrammatical level, but also for semantics and cohesion (for example Johansson 2007; Hasselgård 2012, forthcoming). It would also be desirable to extend the coverage of languages and language pairs, which is fairly limited at the moment, as well as to cover more registers and production types (such as spoken language and interpreting). For modelling translation as process, we need to engage more with theories of cognitive linguistic processing, which analyse language as a kind of human behaviour reflecting mental processes inherent to all human beings. The linguistic features contained in a text are thus regarded as signals provided by text producers to text recipients for how to relate concepts in the mental textual world they create. The signals are governed by the text producer's assumptions about the text recipient's focus of attention, about the status of information of particular concepts (such as given or new, relevant or marginal) or about his or her degree of world or specialised knowledge. For instance, Alves et al. (2010) examine translation behaviour according to professional background and level of expertise (novice translators vs professional translators vs domain experts who are not professional translators) in an experimental setting (cf. Alves et al. 2011; Pagano et al. 2013). So far, this ongoing research has been restricted to the language pairs English–Portuguese and English–German. In an exploratory study, Alves et al. (2010) combine product and process-oriented methods to investigate translation units that are associated with (de)metaphorisation during the process of translation. They use parallel corpora that are annotated on different linguistic levels to identify shifts in metaphoricity. The corpus-linguistic data is then related to psycholinguistic data from a psycholinguistic experiment involving keystroke logging, eye tracking and retrospective protocols. In the long run, work on additional language pairs using approaches combining product- and process-oriented methods is needed to provide a sound empirical basis for generalisations about translation as process and as product.

Notes

1 See, e.g., Kim (2009).
2 See, however, Bell's (1991) attempt at linking SFL to an abstract model of the translation process.
3 See, e.g., Reiss and Vermeer (1984).
4 See, e.g., House (2001).
5 See, e.g., Matthiessen (2001); Munday (2012).
6 See, e.g., Hasselgård (1998, 2004) on an English–Norwegian translation corpus.
7 See, e.g., Kunz et al. (2010) for a corpus setting in which one English original text was translated by student translators into several European languages.
8 Cf. Sharoff and O'Donnell, both this volume, for more details on corpus linguistics in general.

References

Alves, F. 2003. *Triangulating Translation: Perspectives in Process-Oriented Research*. Amsterdam: John Benjamins.

Alves, F., A. Pagano, S. Neumann, E. Steiner and S. Hansen-Schirra. 2010. Units of translation and grammatical shifts: Towards an integration of product- and process-based research in translation. In G. Shreve and E. Angelone (eds) *Translation and Cognition*. Amsterdam: Benjamins, pp. 109–42.

Alves, F., A. Pagano and I.L. Da Silva. 2011. Modelling (un)packing of meaning in translation: Insights from effortful text production. *Copenhagen Studies in Language* 41: 153–64.

Baker, M. 1993. Corpus linguistics and translation studies: Implications and applications. In G. Francis, M. Baker and E. Tognini Bonelli (eds) *Text and Technology: In Honour of John Sinclair*. Amsterdam: John Benjamins, pp. 233–50.

Baker, M. 1995. Corpora in translation studies: An overview and some suggestions for future research. *Target* 7(2): 223–43.

Baker, M. 2011 [1992]. *In Other Words: A Coursebook on Translation*. London and New York: Routledge.

Baroni, M., and S. Bernardini. 2006. A new approach to the study of translationese: Machine-learning the difference between original and translated text. *Literary and Linguistic Computing* 21(3): 259–74.

Becher, V., J. House and S. Kranich. 2009. Convergence and divergence of communicative norms through language contact in translation. In K. Braunmüller and J. House (eds) *Convergence and Divergence in Language Contact Situations*. Amsterdam and Philadelphia, PA: John Benjamins, pp. 125–52.

Bell, R.T. 1991. *Translation and Translating: Theory and Practice*. Oxford: Oxford University Press.

Blum-Kulka, S. 2004 [1986]. Shifts in cohesion and coherence in translation. In L. Venuti (ed.) *The Translation Studies Reader*. London: Routledge, pp. 290–305.

Catford, J.C. 1965. *A Linguistic Theory of Translation*. Oxford: Oxford University Press.

Fontaine, L., T. Bartlett and G. O'Grady (eds). 2013. *Systemic Functional Linguistics: Exploring Choice*. Cambridge: Cambridge University Press.

Halliday, M.A.K. 1956. The linguistic basis of a mechanical thesaurus, and its application to English preposition classification. *Mechanical Translation* 3(8): 1–8.

Halliday, M.A.K. 1966 [1962]. Linguistics and machine translation. In A. McIntosh and M.A.K. Halliday (eds) *Patterns of Language: Papers in General, Descriptive and Applied Linguistics*. London: Longman, pp. 145–58.

Halliday, M.A.K. 2001. Towards a good theory of translation. In E. Steiner and C. Yallop (eds) *Beyond Content: Exploring Translation and Multilingual Text Production*. Berlin and New York: de Gruyter, pp. 13–18.

Hansen-Schirra, S., and E. Teich. 2008. Corpora in human translation. In A. Lüdeling, M. Kytö and T. McEnery (eds) *In Corpus Linguistics: An International Handbook*. Berlin and New York: de Gruyter, pp. 1159–75.

Hansen-Schirra, S., S. Neumann and E. Steiner. 2012. *Cross-Linguistic Corpora for the Study of Translations: Insights from the Language Pair English–German*. Berlin: de Gruyter.

Hasselgård, H. 1998. Thematic structure in translation between English and Norwegian. In S. Johansson and S. Oksefjell (eds) *Corpora and Cross-Linguistic Research*. Amsterdam: Rodopi, pp. 145–67.

Hasselgård, H. 2004. The role of multiple themes in cohesion. In K. Aijmer and A.-B. Stenström (eds) *Discourse Patterns in Spoken and Written Corpora*. Amsterdam and Philadelphia, PA: John Benjamins, pp. 65–88.

Hasselgård, H. 2012. Cross-linguistic differences in grammar. In C.A. Chapelle (ed.) *The Encyclopaedia of Applied Linguistics*. Chichester: Wiley-Blackwell, pp. 1547–54.

Hasselgård, H. Forthcoming. Parallel corpora and contrastive studies. In J. Romero-Trillo and R. Xiao (eds) *Corpus Pragmatics in Translation Studies*.

Hatim, B., and I. Mason. 1990. *Discourse and the Translator*. London: Longman.

House, J. 1997. *Translation Quality Assessment: A Model Revisited*. Tübingen: Narr.

House, J. 2001. How do we know when a translation is good? In E. Steiner and C. Yallop (eds) *Beyond Content: Exploring Translation and Multilingual Text Production*. Berlin and New York: de Gruyter, pp. 127–60.

Johansson, S. 2007. *Seeing through Multilingual Corpora: On the Use of Corpora in Contrastive Studies*. Amsterdam and Philadelphia, PA: John Benjamins.

Kim, M. 2009. Meaning-oriented assessment of translations: SFL and its application for formative assessment. In C. Angelelli and H. Jacobsen (eds) *Testing and Assessment in Translation and Interpreting Studies: A Call for Dialogue between Research and Practice*. Amsterdam and Philadelphia, PA: John Benjamins, pp. 13–26.

Koehn, P. 2005. Europarl: A parallel corpus for statistical machine translation. In *Conference Proceedings: The Tenth Machine Translation Summit (MT Summit X)*. Phuket: AAMT, pp. 79–86.

Kranich, S., J. House and V. Becher. 2012. Changing conventions in English–German translations of popular scientific texts. In K. Braunmüller and C. Gabriel (eds) *Multilingual Individuals and Multilingual Societies* (Hamburg Studies on Multilingualism 13). Amsterdam: John Benjamins, pp. 315–34.

Kunz, K. 2010. *English and German Nominal Coreference: A Study of Political Essays*. Frankfurt a.M.: Peter Lang

Kunz, K., and E. Steiner. 2012. Towards a comparison of cohesive reference in English and German: System and text. In M. Taboada, S. Doval Suárez and E. González Álvarez (eds) *Contrastive Discourse Analysis: Functional and Corpus Perspectives*. London: Equinox, pp. 208–39.

Kunz, K., S. Castagnoli and N. Kubler. 2010. Corpora in translator training: A program for an eLearning course. In D. Gile, G. Hansen and N. Pokorn (eds) *Why Translation Studies Matters*. Amsterdam and Philadelphia, PA: John Benjamins, pp. 195–208.

Kurokawa, D., C. Goutte and P. Isabelle. 2009. Automatic detection of translated text and its impact on machine translation. In Proceedings of *Conference Proceedings: The Twelfth Machine Translation Summit (MT Summit XII)*. Ottawa, ON: AMTA, pp. 81–8.

Lapshinova-Koltunski, E., and K. Kunz. 2014. Annotating cohesion for multilingual analysis. In *Proceedings of the Tenth Joint ACL–ISO Workshop on Interoperable Semantic Annotation*. Reykjavik: ACL/ISO, pp. 57–64.

Laviosa, S. 1998. The English comparable corpus: A resource and a methodology. In L. Bowker, M. Cronin, D. Kenny and J. Pearson (eds) *Unity in Diversity: Current Trends in Translation Studies*. Manchester: St Jerome, pp. 101–12.

Martin, J.R., and P.R.R. White. 2005. *The Language of Evaluation: Appraisal in English*. London and New York: Palgrave Macmillan.

Matthiessen, C.M.I.M. 2001. The environments of translation. In E. Steiner and C. Yallop (eds) *Beyond Content: Exploring Translation and Multilingual Text*. Berlin: de Gruyter, pp. 41–126.

Müller, C., and M. Strube. 2006. Multi-level annotation of linguistic data with MMAX2. In S. Braun, K. Kohn and J. Mukherjee (eds) *Corpus Technology and Language Pedagogy: New Resources, New Tools, New Methods*. Frankfurt a.M.: Peter Lang, pp. 197–214.

Munday, J. 2012. *Introducing Translation Studies: Theories and Applications*. 3rd edn. Abingdon and New York: Routledge.

Neumann, S. 2013. *Contrastive Register Variation: A Quantitative Approach to the Comparison of English and German* (Trends in Linguistics – Studies and Monographs 251). Berlin: de Gruyter.

Neumann, S., and S. Hansen-Schirra. 2005. The CroCo Project: Cross-linguistic corpora for the investigation of explicitation in translations. In *Proceedings from the Corpus Linguistics Conference Series (PCLC)* 1(1).

Olohan, M. 2002. Leave it out! Using a comparable corpus to investigate aspects of explicitation in translation. *Cadernos de Tradução* 9: 153–69.

Olohan, M. 2004. *Introducing Corpora in Translation Studies*. London and New York: Routledge.

Pagano, A., I.L. Da Silva and F. Alves. 2013. Tracing the unfolding of metaphorical processes in translation: Insights from an experimental exploratory study. *Translation and Meaning* 9: 263–75.

Reiss, K., and H.J. Vermeer. 1984. *Grundlegung einer allgemeinen Translationstheorie*. Tübingen: Niemeyer.

Steiner, E. 1998. A register-based translation evaluation: An advertisement as a case in point. *Target*.10(2): 291–318.

Steiner, E. 2001. Intralingual and interlingual versions of a text: How specific is the notion of translation? In E. Steiner and C. Yallop (eds) *Exploring Translation and Multilingual Text Production: Beyond Context*. Berlin and New York: de Gruyter, pp. 161–90.

Steiner, E. 2002. Grammatical metaphor in translation: Some methods for corpus-based investigations. In H. Hasselgard, S. Johansson, B. Behrens and C. Fabricius-Hansen (eds) *Information Structure in a Cross-Linguistic Perspective*. Amsterdam: Rodopi, pp. 213–28.

Steiner, E. 2004. *Translated Texts: Properties, Variants, Evaluations*. Frankfurt a.M.: Peter Lang.

Steiner, E. 2008. Empirical studies of translations as a mode of language contact: 'Explicitness' of lexicogrammatical encoding as a relevant dimension. In P. Siemund and N. Kintana (eds) *Language Contact and Contact Languages*. Amsterdam: John Benjamins, pp. 317–46.

Steiner, E., and E. Teich. 2004. German: A metafunctional profile. In A. Caffarel, C.M.I.M. Matthiessen and J.R. Martin (eds) *Language Typology: A Functional Perspective* (Current Issues in Linguistic Theory). Amsterdam: John Benjamins. pp. 139–84.

Teich, E. 2001. Towards a model for the description of cross-linguistic divergence and commonality in translation. In E. Steiner and C. Yallop (eds) *Exploring Translation and Multilingual Text Production: Beyond Context*. Berlin and New York: de Gruyter, pp. 191–272.

Teich, E. 2003. *Cross-Linguistic Variation in System and Text: A Methodology for the Investigation of Translations and Comparable Texts*. Berlin and New York: de Gruyter.

Toury, G. 1995. *Descriptive Translation Studies and Beyond*. Amsterdam and Philadelphia, PA: John Benjamins.

Van Halteren, H. 2008. Source language markers in EUROPARL translations. In *COLING '08: Proceedings of the 22nd International Conference on Computational Linguistics*, Morristown: Association for Computational Linguistics, pp. 937–44.

Vinay, J.-P., and J. Darbelnet. 1958. *Stylistique comparée du Français et de l'Anglais: Méthode de traduction*. Paris: Didier.

Volansky, V., N. Ordan and S. Wintner. 2015. On the features of translationese. *Digital Scholarship in the Humanities* 30(1): 98–118.

Wong, B.T.M., and C. Kit. 2012. Extending machine translation evaluation metrics with lexical cohesion to document level. In *Proceeding of the 2012 Joint Conference on Empirical Methods in Natural Language Processing and Computational Natural Language Learning*, Stroudsbourg: Association for Computational Linguistics, pp. 1060–8.

35

Interactions between natural-language processing and systemic functional linguistics

Mick O'Donnell

Introduction

Systemic functional linguistics (SFL) views language as human behaviour that takes place in social contexts, as a means to achieve our social goals. SFL is thus an alternative to many other approaches that primarily view language as something that takes place in the minds of individuals.

The socio-functional basis of SFL makes it an ideal model for many applications, such as language education (see McCabe, this volume), critical discourse analysis (see Hodge, this volume), or profiling language use in professional contexts.

The use of computers to process human language is another application area and has become increasingly important in recent years. These applications include, among many others, automatic translation between languages, understanding human utterances and automatic generation of human-readable texts.

This chapter addresses one question: to what degree do the socio-functional characteristics of SFL facilitate such processing of language by machines?

Natural-language processing

Natural-language processing (NLP) can be simply defined as the processing of human language using computers. NLP has its roots in experiments using computers to translate sentences from one language to another, the earliest of which took place in the 1950s, when a single computer could occupy a whole building and had less processing power than a modern digital watch.

From these humble beginnings, the field of NLP has grown into a complex intermixing of subfields and applications. Today, NLP can be divided into two main areas: *text processing*, dealing with written language; and *speech processing*, dealing with the production and understanding of spoken language.

In text processing, three main themes are explored:

- *text analysis* – the conversion of text to a more meaningful form, which includes: *syntactic analysis* (deriving the syntactic structure of text), *semantic analysis* (deriving the propositional meanings of text), *sentiment analysis* (analysing the opinions expressed in a text), *information extraction* (deriving specific facts from a text) and *text classification* (grouping texts together into meaningful categories);
- *text generation* – the generation of natural language from some abstract representation, for example generating descriptions of museum objects from an underlying database listing the class, style, materials, maker, etc., of the object; and
- *machine translation* – taking as input a text in one human language and producing as output a text in another human language.

Speech processing similarly deals with both generation and analysis directions:

- *speech recognition* – the task of converting human voice to a text representation;
- *speech synthesis* – the task of converting text into human-like voice; and
- *dialogue systems* – which combine the above two fields, using speech recognition (and further processing) to understand a human's speech acts and then responding in some intelligent way, usually using synthesised speech.

This chapter will focus on text processing: while some attention had been given to speech processing within SFL, it has been far less central to our concerns.[1]

After examining the three subfields of text processing, the chapter will examine the elements of SFL that make it valuable to NLP and elements of SFL that have led to it being marginalised in recent years. Finally, it will explore how the changing state of NLP offers opportunities for strengthening the role of SFL in the near future.

Text analysis

Syntactic analysis

Over the life of NLP, syntactic analysis has been the area towards which most research has been directed. This is mainly because syntactic analysis has been assumed to be a necessary step in the understanding of text. Syntax is seen as a bridge between text and semantics, and many other text-processing tasks either require, or work better, when, syntactic analysis is done first.

SFL has not been by any means at the centre of this area of research, although there have been efforts in this regard since the beginning of the field in the early 1960s. In the mainstream, most early efforts used phrase structure grammar (PSG). Attempts to parse with Chomsky's transformational grammar failed, owing to the large number of transformation rules needed to handle real text and the exponential process of applying these rules to successive rewrites of the sentence. In this period – that is, around 1962–63 – there was one attempt at parsing with scale and category grammar (Halliday 1961), a precursor to SFL, made by Arthur Frederick Parker-Rhodes and Yorick Wilks (1995), who used it in a small experimental system.

The future of syntactic analysis after this first phase was driven by the need to keep the time spent parsing each sentence to a realistic minimum. One of the most important factors here regards the delicacy of linguistic description. On the one hand, parsers were slowed down because the bare linguistic information used by PSGs (such as 'noun', 'verb', 'nominal phrase', or 'NP', or verbal phrase', or 'VP') did not allow the elimination of alternatives that more detailed syntactic descriptions would catch. For instance, in the phrase *several key members*, the first two words might be recognised as an NP, even though the noun interpretation of *key* does not agree in number with *several*. There was thus a push to increase syntactic delicacy in grammars for parsing, with the first move being the addition of syntactic subcategorisation, for example allowing nouns, verbs and phrases to be subcategorised as singular or plural, and providing rules for each case, such as:

S → NP:sing VP:sing

S → NP:plur VP:plur

At this point of time, there was also a move towards using syntactic functions (Subject, Object, etc.), as well as classes in analysis. One such attempt was by Martin Kay, who was trying to develop a parser for Halliday's grammar of the early 1980s. He gave up on handling system networks, but developed a formalism called 'functional unification grammar', which incorporated elements of systemic grammar (without networks) with ideas of unification from the programming language Prolog (Kay 1979). His proposed grammar used both functional labels and classes for fillers. It allowed for conflation between functions and agreement between elements. This formalism became very central to NLP during the 1980s and 1990s, with various extensions, including many that put system networks back in, although without much credit back to SFL, such as Head-driven phrase structure grammar (HPSG) with typed feature structures.

In regards to the more direct use of systemic functional grammar (SFG) in parsing, there have been only two attempts to use SFG in its full form (parsers for Fawcett's formalism, which is quite different from Halliday's, as will be discussed later).

O'Donnell (1993, 1996a) built a parser for the systemic formalism, as represented by the 'NIGEL grammar', a large systemic grammar of English developed for text generation, principally by Christian Matthiessen (Matthiessen 1983). However, the parser was far too slow with this grammar, so O'Donnell developed a grammar, using the same formalism, but simplifying the description, offering less detail. However, as this grammar grew to cope with real examples, it too began to bog down the parser. The method used in this system consisted of re-expressing the systemic grammar into a form more efficient for parsing.[2] Sugimoto et al. (2005) developed a parser for Japanese using similar principles, with similar problems as their grammar was scaled up.

The main problem relates to the complex nature of an SFG: while most parsers have to deal with only one syntactic function, SFGs allow elements to have multiple functional labels, so that a given syntactic element may need to combine realisation rules associated with different functions (for example Subject conflated with Actor, and perhaps later with Theme). Added to this is the fact that SFGs can assign many features to a unit, not only one or two. The NIGEL grammar may assign as many as eighty features to clause units and forty to nominal groups. A third complicating factor is that the features in a system network may be complexly organised, with disjoint and conjoint entry conditions to system networks. The complexity of processing the system network and conflations of functions makes parsing with SFGs highly computationally intensive.

Other efforts at parsing using SFG have all used some limitation to avoid these problems, such as the following.

- *Using a context-free backbone*: The most common approach has been to use a simpler parser from another formalism to parse each sentence, then apply mapping rules to derive a SFG representation. For instance, Kasper (1988) used a PSG parser to produce a basic syntax tree. Each rule in the grammar specified the corresponding SFG structure to build alongside this PSG structure. This approach has become the standard today and will be looked at more closely later in the chapter. The cost of this approach is that it seems to suggest that SFL is an incomplete language model by itself, requiring another formalism to offer computational analysis applications. However, it is not really an issue of incompleteness, but of overall computational complexity for this application. Additionally, we can argue that SFL analysis adds value that the simpler formalism cannot add and thus that each component of the system takes us to places either by itself cannot.
- *Simplified formalism*: The syntactic formalism of Fawcett's 'Cardiff school' version of SFG is simpler than that of Halliday, in that it allows for only one function label per constituent, with one exception, which is not used in parsing grammars. Conflation is not used and thus parsing is simplified. Additionally, the fillers of these functions are not features from a network, but rather a single class label: *Cl* for clause, *ngp* for nominal-group, etc. As such, parsing is greatly simplified. In a similar vein, O'Donnell (2005) outlines an experimental model using Fawcett's single-function approach, although fillers of these functions are feature selection expressions as in standard SFG.
- *Dependency SFG*: In 2001–03, O'Donnell and his team in a medical informatics company (Language and Computing N.V.) developed a wide-coverage grammar of English using a dependency version of SFL. Dependency grammars do not allow for phrases and clauses, instead describing structure in terms of the functional relations between words, for example in *the cat sat*, *cat* is the Subject of *sat* and *the* is the Deictic element of *cat*. This system provided fairly good results on previously unseen texts (90 per cent of words were correctly connected to their head, with correct syntactic labels) and is currently in commercial use in medical informatics applications.

The rise of statistical parsing

Up to the early 1990s, all work in syntactic analysis was based on the use of hand-developed grammars and lexicons. In the 1990s, the field started moving over to statistical parsing: rather than using a human-written grammar and lexicon, the systems read in a parsed corpus and a grammar is automatically derived from it. For various reasons, these systems outperformed systems with human-coded resources and thus came to dominate the field.

It should be noted that these systems need an annotated corpus (called a 'treebank') to operate and that the first of these annotated corpora were produced by parsing texts with the human-coded grammars/lexicons (with some post-editing of the treebank where needed). In a sense, the knowledge of language that linguists hand-coded into their linguistic resources was then 'exported' in the form of the treebank and the statistical parsers then simply read in this knowledge of language in this alternative form. This process continues today: whenever a member of the team that manages the Stanford Parser finds a sentence that parses wrongly, he or she adds the correct analysis of this sentence to the treebank, manually specified.

Statistically based systems worked best with grammars with few categories. Most commonly, one category is used for each word, for example 'nn' represents a singular common noun, while 'vbn' represents a past-participle verb. SFG, and other grammars with function/feature complexity, offered too much complexity for this approach; hence work with these formalisms became a lot less common.

Statistical systems have, however, become quite robust and they now offer a good basis from which to derive more complex SFG analyses. The term 'backbone' has been used, whereby a simple grammatical parse is used as the skeleton to which more functional information is added.

As mentioned, various computational systemicists are building programs to transform the syntactic analyses produced by these parsers into SFL analyses: Transitivity, Mood and Theme.

The next step for SFL practitioners is to produce our own large treebanks of SFL-labelled analyses and test to what degree the statistical parsers can use them as input to produce SFL analyses directly. To reduce complexity, we can produce separate treebanks for Transitivity, Mood and Theme, and experiment with training parsers over these. Most probably, the Mood analysis (which is most syntactic of the layers) would offer the best possibility for success.

There have been some moves in this regard within the last decade, with, for instance, Elke Teich and colleagues (2008) and Sabine Bartsch and colleagues (2008) pushing strongly for the SFL community to establish shared resource archives. Progress has been slow, however, for two main reasons. First, SFL practitioners have not always been willing to openly share resources that we develop, which slows overall development: there are many SFL-tagged corpora produced by individuals or research projects, but very few are publically available. Second, it has been difficult to establish a representational standard to support ease of resource exchange. In part, this has been because of the problems of finding a single standard that covers all of our needs. Another factor is also the lack of time and funding to hold discussions on standards. An additional issue is that researchers have invested time and effort into establishing their own way of doing things, and are not usually willing to invest the time in converting to a common standard. One partial solution here is for each group to continue working in its propriety formats, but to provide software to convert resources to/from an agreed-upon standard representation for sharing.

Deriving SFG parses from non-SFL parses

As discussed, the focus of SFL work in syntactic analysis of English involves initially parsing a text using a non-SFL parser (such as the Stanford Parser) and automatically converting the parse trees into SFL analyses.

Honnibal and Curran (2007) developed a system that converted the Penn treebank (4.5 million words of English, all syntactically analysed and manually corrected) into an SFL format. Their system produced layers for transitivity, mood, theme and taxis (clause-complexing). While applied only to a treebank, the importance of this system was that the same process could have equally been applied to the output of a structural parser. Details on some layers are sparse: for example, in terms of Transitivity, constituents are labelled simply Participant, Process and Circumstance, a more delicate distinction by process type not being made.

O'Donnell extended the UAM CorpusTool to incorporate the Stanford Parser (Klein and Manning 2003), allowing each English text in the user's corpus to be parsed, producing an NP^VP-style parse for each sentence. These parses can then be converted to separate Mood, Transitivity or Theme analyses.[3] While none of these analyses are perfect (and cannot be, given that the accuracy of the Stanford Parser is less than 100 per cent), results are still useful for applications such as register studies of texts.

Others have also followed this route. For example, Schwarz et al. (2008) report recognising simple Themes (topical Theme, the first element in the clause with experiential meaning) in text parsed by the Stanford Parser, and Costetchi (2013) is producing Mood and Transitivity analyses from this parser.

Mood structures are the easiest to produce from a NP^VP-style syntactic analysis. A small number of pattern-matching rules can identify Subject and Complement, etc., and also features of Tense, Aspect, Voice, Polarity, Modality, etc. One of the grammars provided with the Stanford Parser now identifies syntactic function ('nsubj', 'dobj', etc.), which make the task easier.

Transitivity analysis is more difficult, because an additional resource is required to map verbs onto process type (material, mental, verbal, etc.). The UAM CorpusTool makes use of an internal list of 9,300 verb senses (listing root form of a verb and its process type). Special code needs to be written to resolve ambiguous cases, for example recognising *grasp* as 'mental' where the complement is a clause (or a nominal group with head in a small list of 'idea' nouns), but otherwise as a 'material process'. Costetchi (2013) makes use of Amy Neale's process-type database (see Neale, this volume) for similar ends, mapping onto Fawcett's process-type system.

Performing a full Theme analysis, recognising Textual, Interpersonal and Topical Themes, is also difficult. The UAM CorpusTool examines each constituent of the Mood analysis of a sentence in turn from the left, testing to see if it is Textual or Interpersonal. The first to fail this test is taken as the Topical theme. Themes are basically classified as Textual if the wording of the constituent is on an internal list of common textual themes (144 currently) and Interpersonal themes are recognised in the same way (126 interpersonal markers). This approach actually catches the vast bulk of themes correctly, although the process still has room for improvement.

Ideational analysis

'Semantics' in SFL is taken to cover three types of meaning: ideational, interpersonal and textual. However, in mainstream NLP, semantic analysis is generally restricted to recovering the ideational content of text: the ontological classes of entities and processes, and the semantic relations between them.

Although SFL is a meaning-oriented approach to language, with substantial linguistic work on ideational semantics, there has been very little work on the automatic ideational analysis of text from within SFL – here distinguishing between transitivity analysis, which is a grammatical analysis, from ideational analysis, which is analysis on the semantic stratum.

Part of the reason for computational effort by systemicists in this area has been the lack of SFL-based syntactic parsers; another problem has been a lack of freely available ideational resources. One exception here has been the 'Upper Model', which is a 'system network' of things, processes, qualities and relations, along with realisation rules that set out the types of participant that processes can take on (Actor, Goal, etc.) (Bateman et al. 1989, 1995). This work has been used in various NLP applications, for example as the basis of a large ontology of medicine used in document classification (Ceusters et al. 2004).

However, far more use has been made of semantic resources developed by people outside of SFL. First, Wordnet (Fellbaum 2005) offers a large database of English words assigned to concepts, organised in terms of a thesaurus. This resource, and versions in other languages, has been the most widely used for semantic analysis tasks. Another valuable resource is FrameNet (Baker et al. 1998), a large database providing the semantic dependencies (valencies) for around 10,000 word senses. This resource is based on the work of Charles Fillmore's frame semantics. Various semantic parsers have been produced using this resource, perhaps the best known being that of Gildea and Jurafsky (2002).

SFL does provide some similar resources, such as Amy Neale's process-type database (see Neale, this volume).

Sentiment analysis

In recent years, one of the biggest growth areas for NLP has been in regards to detecting sentiment in text, also called 'opinion mining' and 'affect detection'. Appraisal analysis (Martin and White 2005; Oteíza, this volume) has, to some degree, been picked up by those working in this area, mainly in regards to Attitude. A lot of the efforts in this field have limited themselves to identifying only positive or negative attitude, either in general, or in relation to particular entities (such as to a company, product, politician, etc.). Appraisal analysis allows for detailed identification of types of attitude, ranging over Judgement (evaluation of human behaviour), Appreciation (evaluation of things and processes) and Affect (expression of feelings). It thus allows a wider spectrum of attitude to be distinguished.

Sentiment analysis of whatever kind is difficult, because the value of any one token is very context-dependent: there are big differences between *good* in *He's being good* (positive evaluation of behaviour), *a good wine* (positive evaluation of taste qualities) and *In no way is this good* (negative evaluation of a situation). With delicate programming, we could (to a degree) distinguish between such uses (for example detecting whether the evaluated entity is human or not), but no such program has yet been produced. Most sentiment analysis systems thus do not aim to identify each token correctly, but to detect the overall pattern of sentiment in the text.

Efforts to automatically perform appraisal analysis on real texts include Taboada and Grieve (2004), Whitelaw et al. (2005), Bloom et al. (2007), Sano (2011), Dotti (2012), and Read and Carroll (2012). These systems mostly work with a sentiment lexicon, sometimes specified by hand and sometimes extracted from a manually tagged corpus. Some are limited to adjectives; others deal with verbs, nouns and adverbs as well. The sentiment of a text as a whole is calculated by exploring the percentage of each type of attitude in the text.

Text classification

Text classification involves the use of NLP to automatically assign a class to a text, or part of a text. This is done by comparing the text to the texts in a 'training set' – that is, a corpus of texts in which each text is manually tagged with its class. The usual strategy is to compare the set of words used in the text (the 'bag of words') to the 'bag of words' used in the texts of a given class. The class whose 'bag of words' most closely matches the text is then assigned to the text. Much of the work has aimed at classifying the Field of discourse, for example to separate out emails that address biology rather than physics.

While the 'bag of words' approach is quite powerful, text classification could be improved through the application of register and genre theories from SFL. This could involve using grammatical patterns to help to classify, particularly, issues of process-type patterning (descriptions tend to use relational processes, while recounts tend towards material and verbal processes) and mood (for example imperatives and modalised declaratives are common in instructional texts). Discourse-level patterns may also be of use, for example, applying appraisal theory (Martin and White 2005), Coffin (2002) demonstrates that patterns in Attitude usage can help in classifying history texts in terms of 'recorder', 'interpreter' and 'adjudicator' voices.

One interesting (and successful) application of text classification was within the Scamseek project (Patrick 2006), which scanned the web classifying documents as financial scams or not. The system used SFL as the underlying linguistic framework. The linguists on the team developed a network of sub-registers for scams and labelled each document in the training corpus appropriately. The words and phrases particular to each subclass were associated to the register network, as were some grammatical features. Machine learning was then used to see to what degree each of these wordings or features should count in classification.

Natural language generation and SFL

While the majority of NLP research has focused on text analysis, or translation, some have chosen to focus on the problem of producing natural-language text from an abstract underlying representation.

Text generation from a systemic perspective went through a series of phases. The first involved generating sentences without any user specification, using only a grammar and lexicon either to randomly generate sentences or to generate all possible variants. The first effort in this direction was undertaken by Alec Henrici (1965), a programmer in Halliday's Communication Research Centre at University College London. What was interesting about this work was the use of NLP as a means of verifying the grammar developed by linguists, forcing them to make their specifications exact, consistent and complete.

The second phase consisted of generating a sentence corresponding to a semantic specification of a sentence. The best-known instance of this was the Penman system, developed at the Information Sciences Institute in Los Angeles, within a project headed by Bill Mann (who was also one of the founders of rhetorical structure theory). Christian Matthiessen was the chief developer of the grammar of the system, called 'NIGEL' (Matthiessen and Mann 1985). Using this system, one could specify the ideational content of a sentence in terms of sentence plan language (SPL), and also specify additional information to direct textual and interpersonal decisions in the generation process.[4] The Penman system is now distributed as part of the KPML system (Bateman 1997).

The third phase consisted of efforts to generate whole texts. The text planner generates sequences of sentence plans, which the sentence generator realises as text. Approaches have varied. The simplest systems provide a predefined template for a text, which specifies a sequence of sentence plans with some elements dropped if not relevant (for example DiMarco et al. 1999). Participants and circumstances need to be customised to the particular context of generation.

More advanced text generation systems make use of some theory of discourse structure to control the formation of text, for instance the use of rhetorical structure theory (Mann and Thompson 1988), the earliest work by Hovy (1993) and the ILEX system (O'Donnell et al. 2001).

Up until the late 1990s, SFL influence on the field of text generation was very strong. At this point, however, the growing influence of statistical NLP started to cross over into generation. Langkilde and Knight (1998) explored the use of n-grams to generate optimal natural-sounding sentences and Mellish et al. (1998) explored the use of genetic algorithms to select the best discourse structure for a text. Since then, much of the work in NLG has turned to statistical methods and the influence of the hand-written grammars, which includes all of the SFL work, has been decreasing.

Machine translation and SFL

Machine translation (MT) involves a computer accepting text in one language and outputting a semantically equivalent text in another language. Today, the use of MT is widespread, many browsers and email readers offering on-the-fly translation of textual content and Google Translate allowing free translation of whole documents between some eighty languages. Although current-day automatic translation is not perfect, it is sufficient for gist-translation (that is, enabling a user to understand what the original text says), or to offer a starting point for human translation.

While SFL does not play much of a role in current-day MT, both Halliday and J.R. Firth were involved in one of the earliest MT projects, conducted at the Cambridge Language Research Unit (CLRU) at Cambridge University. Halliday, then a lecturer in Chinese at Cambridge, worked in the Unit, which was funded by the US National Science Foundation to develop an approach to MT that was more semantically oriented than those being developed elsewhere.

Halliday's contribution was in two parts. His first was his proposal to use a multilingual thesaurus for translation (Halliday 2005 [1956]). A thesaurus is organised in terms of concepts (represented by a code number) and each concept is associated with the words that express that concept. The possible translations of a given word can be found by, first, discovering the codes that the word can express, and then discovering, in the thesaurus of the other language, the words that realise those codes. This process can, however, produce many translation possibilities. Halliday's proposal was to use the words around a word in the source language to discern which of the multiple senses were intended (one of the earliest proposals for word–sense disambiguation). For instance, if *plant* were being translated and the preceding term were flowering, then only the senses of *plant* that intersect with those of *flowering* would be used in translation. This idea of using a thesaurus for word–sense disambiguation is still in use today (for example Carpuat and Wu 2007).

Halliday's second contribution was a paper arguing against translation equivalence of syntactic structures across languages, for example that occurrences of a passive in one language should not always be translated as the equivalent of passive in the other language (Halliday 2005 [1956]: 82). When translating a passive clause from English to Spanish, one needs to be aware that the passive is used much less frequently in Spanish than in English; more often, a reflexive form is used (for example, *the glass was broken* would be translated as *el vidrio se rompió*, literally, 'the glass broke itself').

Seeming translation equivalents in fact have distinct contexts of use in each language. Halliday's idea was then to extend the project's language descriptions to identify the contextual conditions under which particular syntactic items are appropriate. He argued that if one could identify all of the determining factors that led the writer of the source text to produce the text that he or she did, then the original text would not be needed in the translation process; one could simply produce a text in the target language appropriate to those determining factors.

In his book surveying MT, Hutchins (1986) devoted more than five pages to the CLRU project and stated that many issues first addressed in that project had become central concerns for artificial intelligence in general. This influence manifested itself most strongly in the group's awareness that, for texts to be properly translated, one needed to take into account the context of situation and also that meaning was a valuable component in language description.

After this strong start, Halliday and his linguistics played little part in MT, with one exception: Erich Steiner and team, as part of the large-scale European translation project,

Eurotra, incorporated a model of Participant Roles into the German component of the system (Steiner et al. 1988).

SFL does not currently play a significant role in MT largely because, as explained in relation to syntactic parsing earlier in the chapter, most approaches today are statistical: the computer is given a parallel corpus (texts and their translations into another language) and uses this to derive valid translations of words or phrases. The programs involved rarely use any lexicogrammatical information, apart (perhaps) from word classes and lemmatisation.

There is some potential use for SFL in more advanced MT, mainly going back to Firth's and Halliday's early ideas on contextually appropriate translation. The approach, outlined earlier, was that a translator should look at the conditions that led the writer of the source texts to choose these features and see what someone writing in the target language would produce under the same conditions. This idea could fruitfully be extended to areas of discourse. A text is not simply a list of sentences; the sentences are formed into a cohesive whole through a number of discourse-level interconnections, such as thematic progression (for example Fries 1981; Forey and Sampson, this volume), cohesive harmony (Hasan 1984) and evaluative style (Martin and White 2005; Oteíza, this volume). When we translate a text sentence by sentence, often these discourse patterns will be disrupted: it may be more natural to take a different element as Theme; elements of cohesive chains may not be realised in the text; or the words used in the translation may have different attitudinal values.

SFL researchers have been addressing these issues in regards to human translation or interpretation, for example Hatim and Mason (1990: 220–2) in relation to thematic progression, Shlesinger (1995) in terms of cohesion and on evaluation, Munday (2012).

The time is now ripe for MT to take these factors into account, to produce translations truer to the source text. However, for SFL to be useful in these regards, we would need various aspects of NLP to be robust. To ensure that thematic progression is maintained in the translation, we would need both automatic recognition of Theme and also reliable reference resolution, and we would need these in both languages. To date, we have reasonably reliable thematic analysis for at least English (as we shall see in the last section), but not for other languages, although it would not be hard to get this working for languages with reasonable syntactic parsers. The state of the art in reference resolution is not so advanced, so this aspect of the task needs to wait for further developments.

Ensuring cohesive harmony is preserved over translation would also depend, to a degree, on reference resolution, to identify co-referential items. A weaker version of cohesive harmony could be identified purely through lexical cohesive chains, without worrying about identifying referents.

Ensuring the preservation of patterns of evaluation in the text is difficult for machines, given that the attitudinal value of a word or phrase is highly dependent on context, as was discussed in relation to sentiment analysis. However, this is one area in which active SFL research is continuing, with results improving each year.

Conclusions: strengths and weaknesses of SFL for NLP

The discussion in the last section should make it clear that while SFL has provided some input to areas of NLP, it has largely been pushed to the side by the advent of machine learning in the 1990s.

It is not a fault of SFL that has led to this marginalisation, but rather the fact that these statistical methods could not cope with formalisms of high complexity. SFL is complex in terms of both the functional layering in the grammar and also the paradigmatic complexity in the organisation of features. Machine learning, particularly in its earliest incarnations, worked best with simple input: one label per element of structure. More recently, the complexity of input to statistical parsers has been increasing, with many systems now accepting as input both a function and a class label per element.

SFL researchers into NLP have been slowly adapting to the necessities of machine learning. As mentioned, we have been using the structural output of non-SFL parsers to produce an initial analysis, and deriving Mood, Transitivity and Theme analyses from this. This has two major consequences for SFL. First, it means that, for computational analysis purposes, we do not need to represent system networks and realisation rules; rather, we need to provide mapping statements between structural representations (for example that a given Mood structure should correspond to a particular Theme or Transitivity structure).

Second, we have been pushed to reduce the complexity of SFL descriptions by separating out the three layers of the grammar, then performing Transitivity, Mood and Theme analyses separately. While Halliday's work has always stressed the separatability of these grammatical layers, all computational implementations of SFG using system networks have needed to interconnect these subnetworks. For instance, the choice of whether to include a Textual or Interpersonal Theme or not are closely tied to the choices related to Circumstance in Transitivity and Adjuncts in Mood. Voice (active vs passive) should only be enterable where Transitivity allows two participants and not with a 'be' or 'have' verb.

Moving forward, the evolving power of statistical parsers means that we do not need to depend on non-SFL analysers for the backbone parsing: with current technology, we can provide a Mood-annotated treebank to train the Stanford Parser, which would allow parsing directly to SFL function structure. Although we would still be limited to one class per element, the features could then be derived from the assigned structure and the lexical items involved. The technology for this is there; we just need to invest the effort in producing the treebank.

While old-style parsers needed humans to specify the grammar (for SFL, a system network and realisation rules), pure statistical parsers take as input simply a range of syntactic analyses. The writing of grammars is a complex task and, as the grammars grow to wide coverage, the complexity – and thus difficulty of writing – becomes unmanageable. With the new systems, we need only to manually tag a corpus of sentences in terms of the Mood function structure and one class label per constituent. We can also use our existing parsers to produce this treebank, manually correcting any errors made. So the job of writing system networks for NLP is probably on the way out; the language description needs only to be encoded into a labelled corpus.

There are further reasons to be optimistic regarding the role of SFL in NLP in the near future. As syntactic analysis is becoming solved, NLP is moving more into the core concerns of SFL: representing of meaning, and the relation between meaning and social context. So the analyses that SFL can produce are of increasing interest to the NLP community. Whether it is deriving the ideational content of a text, detecting attitudes or automating critical discourse analysis, SFL is positioned to play an important role in the future of NLP. All that we need to do is provide the NLP community with the resources that they need: SFL tools for analysis and generation, treebanks for training parsers, sentiment dictionaries to support appraisal analysis, and so on.

In the other direction, SFL is already gaining from progress in NLP. While SFL grammars seem to be too complex to allow parsing in reasonable time with comprehensive grammars, we can make use of the developments in more structural formalisms, which allow reasonably robust parsing. On this basis, a new generation of systemic-oriented computational linguists are starting to automate analysis SFL, currently in terms of Mood, Theme and Transitivity, and will soon move forward into more abstract areas, such as appraisal and thematic progression.

Notes

1 For those interested in pursuing this work, see, e.g., Cleirigh and Vonwiller (1994) on speech recognition and Teich et al. (1997), Bateman et al. (1998) on the speech production side.
2 See O'Donnell (1993) for details.
3 See O'Donnell (2012) on Transitivity and O'Donnell (2014) on Theme.
4 My own thesis work produced a system, called WAG, which followed SPL, but allowed for explicit interpersonal and textual specification (O'Donnell 1996b).

References

Baker, C., C. Fillmore and J. Lowe. 1998. The Berkeley FrameNet Project. *Proceedings of the 36th Annual Meeting of the Association for Computational Linguistics and 17th International Conference on Computational Linguistics* 1(1): 86–90.

Bartsch, S., E. Teich, M. Herke, M. O'Donnell and C. Wu. 2008. SFL corpus and computing colloquium. Paper presented at the International Systemic Functional Congress (ISFC). Macquarie University, Sydney.

Bateman, J.A. 1997. Enabling technology for multilingual natural language generation: The KPML development environment. *Journal of Natural Language Engineering* 3(1): 15–55.

Bateman, J.A., R. Henschel and F. Rinaldi. 1995. *The Generalized Upper Model 2.0* (Technical Report). Darmstadt: GMD/Institut fur Integrierte Publikations-und Informationssysteme.

Bateman, J.A., R. Kasper, J. Moore and R. Whitney. 1989. *A General Organization of Knowledge for Natural Language Processing: The Penman Upper Model* (Technical Report). Marina del Rey, CA: Information Sciences Institute.

Bateman, J.A., E. Teich and A. Stein. 1998. Speech generation in a multimodal interface for information retrieval: The 1 SPEAK! System. In P. Fankhauser and M. Ockenfeld (eds) *Integrated Publication and Information Systems: 10 Years of Research and Development*. St Augustin: GMD/Forschungszentrum Informationstechnik, pp. 149–68.

Carpuat, M. and D. Wu 2007. Improving Statistical Machine Translation using Word Sense Disambiguation. Proceedings of the 2007 Joint Conference on Empirical Methods in Natural Language Processing and Computational Natural Language Learning. Prague, June 2007, pp. 61–72.

Ceusters, W., B. Smith and J.M. Fielding. 2004. LinkSuite: Formally robust ontology-based data and information integration. *DILS* 2994: 124–39.

Cleirigh, C., and J. Vonwiller. 1994. Accent identification with a view to assisting recognition (work in progress). In *Proceedings of the International Conference on Spoken Language Processing*. Wilmington, DE: Institute of Electrical and Electronics Engineers, pp. 375–8.

Coffin, C. 2002. The voices of history: Theorising the interpersonal semantics of historical discourses. *Text*, 22 (4): 503–28.

Costetchi, E. 2013. A method to generate simplified systemic functional parses from dependency parses. In *Proceedings of the Second International Conference on Dependency Linguistics (DepLing 2013)*. Praha: Institute of Formal and Applied Linguistics, pp. 68–77.

DiMarco, C., E.H. Hovy and M.E. Foster. 1999. Layout generation using selection and repair in adapting text for the individual reader. Paper presented at the Association for the Advancement of Artificial Intelligence (AAAI) Fall Symposium on Text Formatting. Stanford, CA, November.

Dotti, F. 2012. Unpublished MSc thesis. Universidad Autónoma de Madrid.

Fellbaum, C. 2005. WordNet and wordnets. In K. Brown (ed.) *Encyclopaedia of Language and Linguistics*. 2nd edn. Oxford: Elsevier, pp. 665–70.

Fries, P. 1981. On the status of Theme in English: Arguments from discourse. *Forum Linguisticum* 6(1): 1–38.

Gildea, D. and D. Jurafsky. 2002. Automatic labeling of semantic roles. *Computational Linguistics* 28:3, 245–88.

Halliday, M.A.K. 1961. Categories of the theory of grammar. *WORD* 17(3): 241–92.

Halliday, M.A.K. 2005 [1956]. The linguistic basis of a mechanical thesaurus, and its application to English preposition classification. In J.J. Webster (ed.) *Collected Works of M.A.K. Halliday, Vol. 6: Computational and Quantitative Studies*. London: Continuum, pp. 6–19.

Hasan, R. 1984. Coherence and cohesive harmony. In J. Flood (ed.) *Understanding Reading Comprehension: Cognition, Language, and the Structure of Prose*. Newark, DE: International Reading Association, pp. 181–219.

Hatim, B., and I. Mason. 1990. *Discourse and the Translator* (Language in Social Life Series). London: Longman.

Henrici, A. 1965. Some notes on the Systemic generation of a paradigm of the English clause. Working Paper for the O.S.T.I. Programme in the Linguistic Properties of Scientific English. Reprinted in M.A.K. Halliday and J.R. Martin (eds.) 1981 *Readings in Systemic Linguistics*, London: Batsford, pp. 74–98.

Honnibal, M., and J.R. Curran. 2007. Creating a systemic functional grammar corpus from the Penn Treebank. In *Proceedings of the ACL 2007 Workshop on Deep Linguistic Processing (DLP)*. Stroudsburg, PA: Association for Computational Linguistics, pp. 89–96.

Hovy, E.H. 1993. Automated discourse generation using discourse relations. *Artificial Intelligence* 63(1–2): 341–85.

Hutchins, W.J. 1986. *Machine Translation: Past, Present, Future*. New York: Wiley & Sons.

Kasper, R. 1988. An experimental parser for systemic grammars. In *Proceedings of the 12th International Conference on Computational Linguistics*. Stroudsburg, PA: Association for Computational Linguistics, pp. 309–12.

Kay, M. 1979. Functional grammar. In *Proceedings of the Fourth Annual Meeting of the Berkeley Linguistics Society*. Berkeley, CA: University of California, pp. 142–158.

Klein, D., and C. Manning. 2003. Fast exact inference with a factored model for natural language parsing. *Advances in Neural Information Processing Systems* 15: 3–10.

Langkilde, I., and K. Knight. 1998. The practical value of N-Grams in generation. In *Proceedings of the Ninth International Workshop on Natural Language Generation*. New Brunswick, NJ: Association for Computational Linguistics, pp. 248–55.

Mann, W.C., and S.A. Thompson. 1988. Rhetorical Structure Theory: Toward a functional theory of text organization. *Text* 8(3): 243–81.

Martin J. R. and P. R. R. White. 2005. *The Language of Evaluation: Appraisal in English*. London and New York: Palgrave.

Matthiessen, C. 1983. Systemic grammar in computation: the Nigel case. *Proceedings of the First Annual Conference of the European Chapter of the Association for Computational Linguistics*, Pisa, pp. 155–64.

Mellish, C., A. Knott, J. Oberlander and M. O'Donnell. 1998. Experiments using stochastic search for text planning. *Proceedings of the Ninth International Workshop on Natural Language Generation*. New Brunswick, NJ: Association for Computational Linguistics, pp. 98–107.

Munday, J. 2012. *Evaluation in Translation: Critical Points of Translator Decision-Making*. London: Routledge.

O'Donnell, M. 1993. Reducing complexity in a systemic parser. In *Proceedings of the Third International Workshop on Parsing Technologies*. Tilburg: Association for Computational Linguistics, pp. 98–107.

O'Donnell, M. 1996a. Input specification in the WAG sentence generation system. Paper presented at the Eighth International Workshop on Natural Language Generation. Herstmonceux, East Sussex, 13–15 June.

O'Donnell, M. 1996b. Sentence analysis and generation: A systemic perspective. Unpublished PhD thesis. Department of Linguistics, University of Sydney.

O'Donnell, M. 2005. The UAM systemic parser. Paper presented at the First Computational Systemic Functional Grammar Conference, University of Sydney, Australia. 16 July.

O'Donnell, M. 2012. Transitivity development in Spanish learners of English. Paper presented at the 39th International Systemic Functional Linguistics Conference, Sydney, July.

O'Donnell, M. 2014. Changes in thematic choice with developing EFL proficiency. Paper presented at the European Systemic Functional Linguistics Conference, Paris, 10–12 July.

O'Donnell, M., C. Mellish, J. Oberlander and A. Knott. 2001. ILEX: An architecture for a dynamic hypertext generation system. *Natural Language Engineering* 7: 225–50.

Patrick, J. 2006. The scamseek project: Text mining for financial scams on the internet. In G.J. Williams and S.J. Simoff (eds.) *Data Mining*. Berlin: Springer-Verlag, pp. 295–302.

Read, J., and J. Carroll. 2012. Weakly supervised appraisal analysis. *Linguistic Issues in Language Technology* 8(2): 1–21.

Sano, M. 2011. Reconstructing English system of ATTITUDE for the application to Japanese: An exploration for the construction of a Japanese dictionary of appraisal. Paper presented at the 38th International Systemic Functional Congress, Lisbon.

Schwarz, L., S. Bartsch, R. Eckart and E. Teich. 2008. Exploring automatic theme identification: A rule-based approach. In *Text Resources and Lexical Knowledge. Selected Papers from the 9th Conference on Natural Language Processing KONVENS 2008*. Berlin: de Gruyter, pp. 15–26.

Shlesinger, M. 1995. Shifts in cohesion in simultaneous interpreting. *The Translator* 1(2): 193–214.

Steiner, E., U. Eckert, B. Weck and J. Winter. 1988. The development of the EUROTRA-D system of semantic relations. In E. Steiner, P. Schmidt and C. Zelinksy-Wibbelt (eds) *From Syntax to Semantics: Insights from Machine Translation*. London: Pinter, pp. 44–104.

Sugimoto, T., N. Ito, S. Iwashita and M. Sugeno. 2005. A computational framework for text processing based on systemic functional linguistics. In *Proceedings of the First Computational Systemic Functional Grammar Conference*. Sydney: Sydney Language Technology Research Group, School of Information Technologies, University of Sydney, pp. 2–11.

Taboada, M., and J. Grieve. 2004. Analyzing appraisal automatically. In *Proceedings of AAAI Spring Symposium on Exploring Attitude and Affect in Text*. Stanford, CA: Association for the Advancement of Artificial Intelligence, pp. 158–61.

Teich, E., E. Hagen, B. Grote and J.A. Bateman. 1997. From communicative context to speech: Integrating dialogue processing, speech production and natural language generation. *Speech Communication* 21(1–2): 73–99.

Teich, E., C.M.I.M. Matthiessen, M. Lam, M. Herke and C. Wu. 2008. IRSFL: An initiative for a repository of SFL resources. Paper presented at the 35th International Systemic Functional Congress (ISFC), Macquarie University, Sydney, July.

Whitelaw, C., N. Garg and S. Argamon. 2005. Using appraisal groups for sentiment analysis. *In Proceedings of the 14th ACM international conference on Information and knowledge management*. ACM, pp. 625–31.

Wilks, Y. 1995. Arthur Frederick Parker-Rhodes: A memoir. Paper given as a Parker-Rhodes Memorial Lecture at the Annual Meeting of the Alternative Natural Philosophy Association, Cambridge, September.

36

Reading images (including moving ones)

Chris Taylor

Introduction

The first important contributions with a systemic functional linguistics (SFL) twist on the concept of 'reading images', a term coined by Kress and van Leeuven (1996), appeared in the 1990s. O'Toole's (1994) *The Language of Displayed Art* can be said in many ways to have set the ball rolling in that it was a genuinely multimodal set, consisting of a book and a CD using a range of semiotic modes to provide an SFL perspective on the interpretation of visual works of art. Kress and van Leeuven's work, both together (Kress and van Leeuven 1996, 2006) and separately (Kress 2003; van Leeuven 2011) expanded the field to examine many types of multimodal text, from school textbooks to bus tickets. The images that were being read were initially largely static pictures, photos, drawings, diagrams, etc. It was the work of Baldry and Thibault, again working together (Baldry and Thibault 2006) and separately (Baldry 2000; Thibault 2000), that was most responsible for breaking into moving pictures and providing an SFL interpretation of video text – first television advertising, but moving into documentary and film – providing Taylor (2004) with the material for an analysis of multimodal texts with a view to their translation.[1] Other writers have produced important work that hinged on multimodal analysis from an SFL point of view (among others, Martinec 2000; Iedema 2001; Lemke 2002; Unsworth 2006) and continue to do so (Martin and Rose 2008; O'Halloran 2008; Martinec and van Leeuwen 2009; Painter et al. 2013), but the abovementioned pathfinders will form the springboard for the approach adopted in this chapter.

Before we begin, it should be mentioned that a number of approaches to multimodality other than SFL have been formulated. The first edition of the *Routledge Handbook of Multimodal Analysis* (Jewitt 2009) suggests that there are three main approaches to multimodal analysis, one being SFL; the others are defined, respectively, as social-semiotic analysis (Machin 2009; Mavers 2009, etc.) and interactional analysis (Norris 2009; Scollon and Scollon 2009, etc.). The former, as well as having a different historical background going back, for example, to Barthes (1977), is less interested in systems and concentrates more on the conscious or unconscious 'sign-maker' in his or her social context, and is interested in how 'meaning potentials are selected and orchestrated to make meaning by people in particular contexts to realize specific social meaning' (Jewitt 2009: 31). The latter, having practically no interest in systems, concentrates on the moment of interaction. Its adherents, according to Norris (2004, quoted in Jewitt 2009: 33), 'set out to understand and describe what is going on in a given interaction (and) analyse what individuals express and react to in specific situations in which the ongoing interaction is always co-constructed'. However, the borderlines between these approaches are not finely drawn, and we see exponents such as Kress, van Leeuwen and Halliday straddling all three, at least to some extent. Certain tenets of SFL would seem to be omnipresent.

Bortoluzzi (2010) discusses what she refers to as 'critical multimodal analysis', based on the tools of critical discourse analysis. In this sense, the question of 'the ideological loading of particular ways of using language and the relations of power which underlie them' (Fairclough and Wodak 1997: 259) is extended to the multimodal sphere. For example, Vasta (2005) analysed advertising campaigns of oil companies, and showed their need to convey discoursally and visually their concern for ethical commitment, seeking consensus and construing a corporate identity.

Most recently, Bateman (2014), also grounded in standard SFL theory, considered multimodality and the inter-semiotic properties of texts and images from a number of other perspectives, including the psycholinguistic approach and the role of rhetoric. Moya (2014) studied the way in which images and words interplay to facilitate young children's comprehension of picture-book stories by analysing the inter-semiosis between verbal and visual elements in nine picture books – although, again, he bases most of his work on SFL.

Scholars in the field of audiovisual translation (AVT) have also attempted to define and analyse multimodal texts, often giving scant recognition to the work alluded to above. Some of these will be discussed within this chapter, but in all cases it is still the interplay of semiotic resources that interests such studies, while wedded to the identifying of the particular 'language' of audiovisuals, the distinguishing of denotative and connotative meanings, the understanding of visual rhetoric, and so on. A particularly insightful semiotic approach to the reading of dynamic images is to be found in Bateman and Schmidt (2012), in which the construal of meaning in films is seen through a choice mechanism at both syntagmatic and paradigmatic levels. The authors show how details of film sequences can lead to the creation of filmic discourse structures and thus to how meaning is made in the cinema.

Static images

Dealing with static images, Kress and van Leeuven, Martin and others looked at representation in school textbooks, among other artefacts, as classic examples of the interplay between visual and verbal texts and the complex sets of relations that bind them together in certain environments. They examined the ideational aspects of classifying and composing in the case of explicit or implicit diagrams, labelled pictures, photographs accompanied by explanations, etc., and how the verbal elements restated, summarised, specified or repeated the information provided in the visual component, or vice versa.[2] Where activities are concerned, and therefore movement of some kind, the use of vectors was discussed, either through explicit means such as arrows or textual configuration, or by less explicit means such as the interpretation of gaze and the use of insets. In terms of textual organisation, Figure 36.1 shows a simplified version of Martin and Rose's (2008: 174) network diagram, based on Kress and van Leeuven's work, illustrating how images are arranged to produce meaning.

Figure 36.1 Network diagram: how images are arranged to produce meaning

Figure 36.1 itself is, of course, a multimodal text, with a simple connection between the verbal and the visual consisting of words, minimal symbolic representation and vectors, which can be expressed solely verbally as follows: relevance tends to emanate from the centre of an image towards the margins, in the sense that the central part is relevant to the whole text, while at the margin the relevance is more specific to certain elements of the text. Given information picks up from preceding images/text or knowledge and tends to appear on the left of an image, followed by New information to the right in the Theme/Rheme pattern. Generalised information, dubbed 'ideal' by Kress and van Leeuven (1996: 193), tends to appear at the top of an image, while more specific or practical information is seen below. Verbal text can be separated from the visual, as in bounded captions or embedded in the main discourse, or it can invade the visual space in the case of internal labels or insets. Finally, where multiple images are involved, some will be more salient and attract initial attention. Appropriate modifications to this model may be necessary when dealing with languages with different writing conventions (Arabic, Japanese, etc.).[3]

A case study

By way of example of the foregoing discussion, Figure 36.2 shows an advertisement for the Mitsubishi Pajero car, as studied by Taylor (2000: 297), who – apart from a detailed analysis of the verbal text as an entity in itself – examined the whole text as a multimodal artefact.

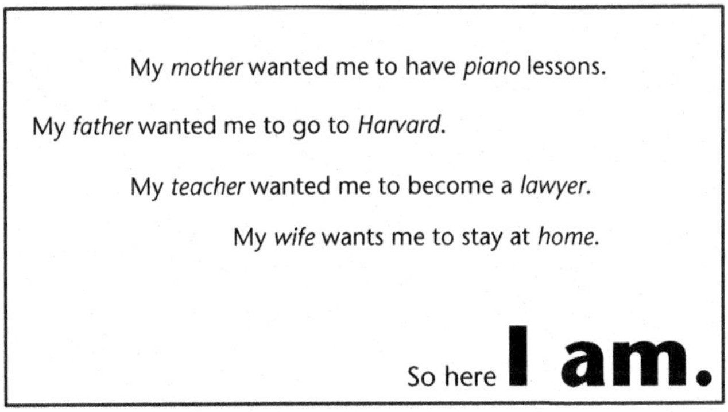

My *mother* wanted me to have *piano* lessons.

My *father* wanted me to go to *Harvard*.

My *teacher* wanted me to become a *lawyer*.

My *wife* wants me to stay at *home*.

So here **I am.**

Figure 36.2   Car advertisement

Taking Kress and van Leeuwen's (1996: 1) concept of 'the grammar of visual design', the text was analysed both in terms of its written text and its non-verbal features – that is, how the two combine to make meaning through information structure (Theme and Rheme, Given and New, cohesive devices, etc.). The written text (see below) on the left of the 'ad' consists of four semantically connected themes – that of pseudo power figures – and four semantically connected rhemes – those of bourgeois values. The clauses are structured according to the Given–New model providing a completely cohesive text.

My mother wanted me to have piano lessons.
My father wanted me to go to Harvard.
My teacher wanted me to become a lawyer.
My wife wants me to stay at home.

This superimposed verbal text first blends in with the rather surreal background. The first four lines provide a sense of perspective, the punchline being foregrounded in a form of semantic hierarchy. This is the eye-catching element that will probably attract the attention of many readers. Among these, the interested reader is given the impression of being in the vehicle with the promise of 'getting away from it all' with the letters composing the slogan *So here I am* written in an exaggerated size. This semiotic construct thus consists of a surreal, and tempting, background, while the product is real and therefore attainable. The two unequal halves of the 'ad' (the picture and the longer written text describing the product) provide the promise and the information, respectively, demonstrating two different kinds of meaning:

(So this 'ad' is) a semiotic unit, structured, not linguistically, but by principles of visual composition . . . verbal text becomes just one of the elements integrated by the codes of information value, salience and framing . . . reading is not necessarily linear, wholly or in part, but may go from centre to margin, or in circular fashion, or vertically . . .

Kress and van Leeuwen 1996: 185

Moving images

The analysis of moving images takes us to the far extremes of multimodality. Films, television programmes, websites, blogs and so on provide examples of texts made up of many semiotic modes, described succinctly by Thibault (2000: 311) as 'texts which combine and integrate the meaning-making resources of more than one semiotic modality – for example, language, gesture, movement, visual images, sound and so on – in order to produce a text-specific meaning'. The creation of the 'multimodal transcription' sprang from Thibault's interest in interpreting such texts – an application refined by Thibault (2000) himself with the analysis of the Westpac advertisement, and by Thibault and Baldry (2006). The original multimodal transcription consisted of a grid of rows and columns showing visual frames captured at predetermined intervals (for example one per second) on the left, followed successively by a description of what is in the frame in terms of salient and secondary items, a description of any movement or kinesic action, a notation of the elements comprising the soundtrack and finally a systemic-functional interpretation. Taylor (2004: 164) then used a modified version of the multimodal transcription as a tool for audiovisual translation. Figure 36.3 shows two rows from a multimodal transcription of an episode of the BBC television series *Blackadder*.

The image in the visual frame (replaced here by a worded version) is described in the next column (VI + kinesic action) in terms of what can be seen and what movement there is, in a variation of the Thibault prototype. The soundtrack then follows, featuring principally the spoken words, with indications as to volume, tempo, intonation, rhythm, etc. The final column contains a translation (into Italian, in this case) for a subtitled version of the programme. The final subtitle is a result of a consideration of all of the semiotic modalities at work in this multimodal text, which can provide clues as to the most appropriate wording, the possibilities for condensation, synchrony with the action, etc.

Clearly, notwithstanding the usefulness of this method in sensitising students to the intricacies of multimodality, 'reading' an entire film in this way would be extremely time-consuming and ultimately counter-productive. For this reason, Gregory's (2002) concept of phasal analysis, further elaborated by Malcolm (2010), allows for a more manageable approach. Their work concerned, principally, written texts but the concept can be easily applied to multimodal material. Consider, for example, a television soap opera such as the well-known *Coronation Street*, which has been shown at least twice weekly on British television for more than fifty

Visual frame (in worded form)	VI+ kinesic action	SOUNDTRACK	SUBTITLE
Blackadder stands in the middle of the room with a bag in his hands. Lord Percy is by the door Baldrick and other servants on the right	Shot 1 CP: stationary/ HP: frontal/ VP: median/ D: MLS; VC: interior of the jail; Percy; Blackadder; Baldrick; Mr. Ploppy/ VS: the bag, exactly in the middle of the scene/ CO: artificial set; VF: distance: median; orientation: Blackadder's and Baldrick's gaze towards Percy **Kinesic Action**: Blackadder orders Percy out by shouting to him/ Tempo: M	{RG} [ ] Blackadder: (**)Go on, (NA)go on// Pause/ Volume: f/ Tempo: F	Sbrigati!
Outside the room Lady Farrow on the left talking to Lord Percy	↓ VF: orientation: Percy with closed eyes, avoiding Lady Farrow's gaze; Lady Farrow staring at him **Kinesic Action**: Percy turns his head and closes the door, keeping his left hand on the handle/ Tempo: M	{RG} [ ] Lord Percy: Em (#) (*)sorry about the delay (NA)madam// Pause/ Volume: n/ Tempo: M {RG} [ ] eh (#) as you know (#) you're about to meet your (NA)husband, whom you'll recognise on account of the fact that (#) he has got a (*)bag over his head// Pause/ Volume: n/ Tempo: M	Ehm,scusate il ritardo.Tra qualche istante potrete vedere vostro marito. Lo riconoscerete dal sacco in testa

Figure 36.3   Two rows from a multimodal transcription of *Blackadder*

years. 'Reading' *Corrie*, as it is affectionately known, requires the reader to follow a number of stories running concurrently, often for months on end. There are people who have watched this programme over a lifetime and have followed hundreds of these subplots. But, in any one episode, the stories intertwine as the camera moves from one scenario to another and then back again, and so on. The different strands can be seen as phases within the single episode and can be recognised as such through the combination of semiotic modalities that distinguish them. Thibault (2000: 320) described these phases as 'continuous and discontinuous stretches of discourse which share ideational, interpersonal and textual consistency and congruity, i.e. consistent selection from the various semiotic systems'.

In other words, as the various stages in the stories appear and reappear, they are identifiable by a series of elements specific to that 'phase' in the overall production, for example (at least some of) the same characters in the same clothes will remain the same, there will be continuity in the settings, the background music may be specific, the dialogue will be congruent with the situation, and so on. This phasal progression may be constituted by a single scene, but almost always it consists of returns to the same scene, or to a connected scene, and can thus be seen as discontinuous in Thibault's terms.

Although Thibault refers to discourse, this term must be seen in its broadest sense, taking account of all the semiotic modalities involved. The sharing of ideational, interpersonal and textual elements involves all modes. Soap operas are a particular genre and can keep discontinuous phases going forever, but also any single film or other screen product can be seen to be divided into, largely discontinuous, phases. Tarantino's *Inglourious Basterds* (2009) is a clear example, as the action constantly switches between well-established phases. Hitler's office, the Basterds' murderous activities, the evil Colonel Landa's devious machinations, the Jewish girl Shoshana's progress through life, the assassination plot, the role of beautiful Bridget von Hammersmark, etc., all intertwine, but maintain specific ideational force (the various stories), interpersonal relations between the protagonists, but also with the audience (hate, disgust, sympathy, humour in varying measure), and textual consistency. The construction of the text is, as explained, in phases that switch, often rapidly, from one to another. These changes between the phases are signalled by what are termed 'transitions' (Thibault 2000), which may take various forms: there may be an immediate scene change, or cinematic techniques may be brought into play such as fade-outs, fade-ins, flashbacks, flash-forwards, or special effects such as dream sequences. All of this assists the 'reader' of the text in unravelling the meaning and in following the plot.

Audio description

Among the various contributions applying SFL to the analysis of film text (Rheindorf 2004; Maiorani 2011), a recent European project – Audio Description: Lifelong Access for the Blind (ADLAB) – has concentrated on a minute examination of the many and varied aspects of *Inglourious Basterds* with a view to producing a set of strategies for the audio description of this film and, by extension, of all films, for the benefit principally of the blind and sight-impaired community in Europe. Audio description in fact consists in the verbal description of film, television programmes, museum exhibits and other cultural manifestations with a visual content that is not accessible to the blind and visually impaired community. It is a technique that clearly requires close attention to the interplay between words and images, because the description has to be inserted in the gaps left by the spoken dialogue. It has been succinctly described by the major American exponent of audio description, Joel Snyder (2008) as 'the visual made verbal'. The fallout from this work has been the identification of a series of 'crisis points' to which audio describers need to pay attention. This analysis also contained an SFL imprint in terms of textual organisation, cohesion, intertextuality and appraisal.

Textual organisation

In terms of textual organisation, the analysis of another film, the late Anthony Minghella's *The English Patient* (1996), indicated how audio description deserves the distinction of being a genre or text type unto itself (see Taylor 2015: 184). The interaction between the visual and the verbal, as observed in the audio description, resulted in some marked theme choices, such as the predominant use of nominal groups, sometimes in isolation for example *The desert. A Red Cross Ambulance*. In terms of theme progression, a more-than-usual use of reiteration is common, with nouns giving way to (exclusively) third-person pronouns. But perhaps the most striking linguistic aspect of audio description is the frequent use of non-finite clauses as theme, usually introduced by participles. In the case of *The English Patient*, we find more than seventy such openers, for example *Passing between them . . .* , *Swathed in blankets . . . . Seated behind the pilot . . .* Compared to similar text types, such as the short story genre, this usage is markedly higher. It would seem that it provides a succinct form of scene-setting when the time factor is crucial:

> It indicates the kind of pre-planning associated with written language. Given that we do and we are while we speak, actors in films can be seen to be doing and being as they speak their roles. But of course the blind cannot see them doing or being, and the non-finite phrases provide that input succinctly.
>
> *Taylor 2015: 184*

Cohesion

In terms of cohesion, a fundamental constituent in discourse analysis that can be considered metaphorically as the glue that holds the text together (see Clarke, this volume). Halliday and Hasan (1976) made a seminal contribution and the cohesive devices that they identified (reference, substitution, ellipsis, lexical cohesion) are as evident in audio description as in other text types, albeit that a more marked use of anaphoric reference, as indicated above, is common. In some texts, cohesive ties are abundant; in others, more sparsely arranged over long stretches of discourse. But this discussion still refers to written (or spoken) discourse, whereas audio description also has to be cohesive with the other semiotic modalities making up an audiovisual text. It has to be cohesive with, and therefore carefully 'read', the images.

The key factor in audio describing has, from the first, been recognised as simply 'what to describe' and how to fit it in if there are time constraints. Clearly, if 'a picture is worth a thousand words', it is not possible to describe everything that can be seen in rapidly changing scenes. The description must connect with the ongoing dialogue and the visibly relevant items on screen, and often swiftly. For this reason, we find many isolated nominal groups such as *A crowded supermarket* or *The New York skyline*.

'Multimodal cohesion' can be seen very clearly in examples of 'anchoring' whereby a visual item unaccompanied by verbal input plays an important part in the storyline. For example, in Eastwood's film *Gran Torino* (2008), a hospital admittance form can be seen lying on a table in the protagonist's house with no indication as to the reason for its presence. Its significance emerges much later in the film, when we learn that the protagonist

Chris Taylor

is going to die. This, as in so many other similar examples used in film and TV series, has a quasi-metaphorical force that is an essential element in the reading of the text. On other occasions, the cohesion is simultaneous, when music or sounds or lighting effects accompany action and dialogue. The chase scene at the beginning of Jim Sheridan's *In the Name of the Father* (1993) is accompanied by the heavy rock of Jimi Hendrix's 'Voodoo Chile', by the bleak pictures of war-torn working-class Belfast, by the imprecations delivered in strong local accents, and by skilful camera work indicating positions of power and rebellion. The Hendrix music and the ice-cream van among the terraced houses also contribute to fixing time and place. A multiple reading is required to gain the full force of the meaning.

Intertextuality

Connected to the concept of cohesion is that of intertextuality. 'Intertextuality' refers to the fact that practically all texts contain elements that can be traced to other texts. Text receivers' understanding of one text will most often depend on their knowledge of others. The connections may be banal, as in the case of everyday expressions, or more pregnant with meaning, when created deliberately by the text producer. In the case of audiovisual texts, the intertextuality is to be found in both verbal and visual form. In all cases, a relation is established between an allusion or reference in the text being received and an element or elements 'alluded to' or 'referred to' in another text. A film viewer will either recognise the marker of the verbal or non-verbal allusion or not, but if so, he or she will relate it to his or her knowledge of other texts and where that element originates.

In terms of purely verbal intertextuality, whenever the expression 'Elementary, dear Smith/Jones/Robinson' is pronounced, it clearly echoes the famous line from Conan Doyle's *Sherlock Holmes* books 'Elementary, dear Watson'. Other references may be more or less well known. Charles Bronson, in *The Stone Killer* (Winner 1973) rebuffs a young girl's amorous offers with 'Another time, another place, another cop', providing an addendum to a much-used phrase. On the other hand, fewer viewers may know that the title of the film *No Country for Old Men* (Coen and Coen 2007) harks back to 'Sailing to Byzantium', a poem by W.B. Yeats. These kinds of verbal ties between texts can be pleasing to an audience when they are recognised and can aid the 'reading' process.

But intertextuality is also present in non-verbal forms. Especially where there is irony or spoof, visible manifestations such as a mysterious-looking castle looming out of the darkness in *Young Frankenstein* (Brooks 1974) apes the scene from so many 'serious' horror films. Even generalised images such as a crowded souk or a row of skyscrapers at the beginning of a film are recognisable to the viewer in establishing immediately that the scene is set in the Middle East or downtown Chicago. These opening sequences often act as macro-themes in the development of a film and appear even before the opening credits.

Appraisal

Appraisal, as analysed and discussed at length in SFL circles (Martin and White 2005; Oteíza, this volume) also impacts on audio description, at times creating controversial stand-offs. It is claimed by many exponents of audio description – particularly the American school (cf. Snyder 2008) – that descriptions must be entirely objective and simply 'say what you see'. Other scholars in the field feel that it is at times helpful, if not necessarily essential, for the describer to use expressions of appraisal, consciously or unconsciously, in his or her portrayals. The argument of the former school is that the blind should have the same experience as the sighted audience and not be 'pandered to' with ulterior explanations or expressions of appraisal. The description should give the blind viewer the information that the normal viewer can obtain visually. Thus if a person on screen is smiling, the latter can assume that that person is happy (obviously the person doesn't say 'I'm smiling'). The audio describer should therefore describe the person's face (*the lips spread and the eyes sparkle*) and leave the blind viewer to realise that the character is smiling. On the other hand, the more flexible approach adopted by many European describers is to save time and possible misunderstanding by simply saying that the person *is smiling*, or even that the person *seems happy*. At this point, the question of appraisal has to be addressed.

Martin and White (2005) originally identified three categories of appraisal – namely, appreciation, affect and judgement. These categories covered the range of ways in which people can express personal (and interpersonal) assessment, from the expression of emotional states, to the forming of ethical judgements, to the evaluating of reality. People express appraisal in various ways, for example through mood structures, by prosodic means and through lexical choice. However, what a person means by what he or she says depends on a number of factors, not all of them linguistic. Word use can be a very slippery domain. As Eggins and Slade (1997: 126) explain:

> The interpretation of the meaning of lexical items is not only dependent on the co-text but also on the socio-cultural background and positioning of the interactants. Appraisal analysis must therefore be sensitive to the potential for different readings or 'hearings' of attitudinal meanings.

But this reasoning can also be applied at an audiovisual level. Eggins and Slade (1997: 126) point towards the difference in meaning of the word *child* in the following two sequences:

Do you have family?
Yes, I have just one child

I can't stand this anymore!
You're such a child!

Similarly (and referring back to the previous example of the smile), depending on the circumstances, this facial gesture can express pleasure, bewilderment, agreement and a host of other attitudes, including evil. The objective description of this gesture would remain the same, but if the co-text and context are not sufficient to disambiguate the meaning, the audio describer has a duty to intervene with an interpretation based on his or her ability to see any possible nuance or clue as to real intent. This is a reading of images that can be practically useful in this context of audio description, but also for translation and for multimodal text analysis in general. These potentially ambiguous scenarios are, of course, generally accompanied by a verbal input. When a person responds to something said and done with the words 'Very interesting', the meaning is often the opposite of the literal interpretation. At times, it is a polite way of saying 'I don't find this interesting at all'; at others, from the mouth of a Bond villain for example, it is a threatening remark. Describing the delivery of this locution as *laconic* or *menacing*, an audio description can avoid time-consuming and potentially confusing physical descriptions. This would be a case of using appraisal to interpret (read) the image and to relay it to a blind audience.

Another case study: The Hours

An example of all these considerations is provided by Stephen Daldry's *The Hours* (2002). The film begins by introducing three spatio-temporal scenarios: Los Angeles in 1949; London in the 1920s; present-day New York. The visual objects enhance these times and places: white-wall tyres on the cars in LA; dowdy dress and middle-class gardens in England; fuzzy hairstyles and leather jackets in New York. Similarly, three different sets of characters are introduced and these 'phases' alternate throughout the film as the action slowly ties them together. The reading of this production is facilitated by the skilful use of the textual resources at the director's disposal in terms of the film techniques that create textuality.

Returning briefly to the purely verbal expression of textual meaning, Eggins (1994: 272) shows how sensitivity to the way in which textual meaning is made is illustrated by the following pair of clauses referring to practices after a blood transfusion:

> But in Switzerland they give you a cognac. Here they give you tea and bikkies.

Eggins (1994: 272) provides five close alternatives to these declarations, pointing out that the experiential meaning carried by the elements of transitivity (actor, process, goal, circumstance) and the interpersonal meaning carried by the declarative mood for giving information, remain the same:

> But they give you a cognac in Switzerland. They give you tea and bikkies here.
> They give you a cognac in Switzerland, though. They give you tea and bikkies here.
> They give you a cognac in Switzerland, though. Here they give you tea and bikkies.
> But in Switzerland they give you a cognac. They give you tea and bikkies here.
> But they give you a cognac in Switzerland. Here they give you tea and bikkies.

But she suggests that none of the other versions 'sound as good' as the first and that the speaker has thus chosen the most effective way in which to express her mild, and slightly concealed, complaint. The textual metafunction is what is at work here. It is the 'enabling function' (Halliday and Matthiessen 2004: 30), 'the level of organization of the clause which enables the clause to be packaged in ways which make it effective given its purpose and its context' (Eggins 1994: 273). The important factor is the ordering of the elements in the clause, which provides the receiver with the signals necessary to construct the cohesive relations between the wording, the context and the purpose of the utterance. The concepts of Theme and Rheme and information structure through Given and New are discussed elsewhere in this volume, and so, as we move to the discussion of textual meaning in moving images, it is necessary only to point towards the questions of theme choice, theme type and theme progression. The presentation of Given and New information, often running parallel with Theme and Rheme structure, is also connected with intonation and realised in the verbal component.

In the case of *The Hours*, the thematic role of semiotic resources other than words is of considerable importance. The introductory phases serve as hyperthemes to establish the three major strands of which the film consists. They do this through images, written words, lighting, perspective, music and innovative cinema techniques. For example, Virginia Woolf, played by Nicole Kidman, bends to wash her face in a bowl. When the figure stands up straight again, it is no longer Virginia, but Clarissa, the character played by Meryl Streep. This is a further example of the effects introduced to underline the basic rationale of the film, as described in the publicity material.

The story of three women in different times, related only by a parallel in their personal lives.

Ideational meaning is expressed principally through the interplay of dialogue and image as the story progresses in its tripartite way, while interpersonal meaning emanates from the viewers' identification of (and with) the depicted scenes. There is both solidarity and disaffection with characters, enhanced by dialogue, supra-segmental elements such as intonation and volume, gesture and facial expression, camerawork and musical effects. Boeriis (2008: 230) makes an interesting contribution to the interpersonal aspects of multimodal analysis by emphasising the multisensory features of film interpretation, including the contribution that can be made from senses other than sight and sound, including the effect of comfortable seating and hot popcorn. The interpersonal component in multimodality is therefore also construed through secondary and tertiary inputs in the 'multisensory understanding of communication' (Boeriis 2008: 233).

But it is the enabling function that ties the text together. In the case of film, this aspect takes on a multimodal dimension as demonstrated by the opening scenes of *The Hours*. The first short scene that we see is the white-wall-tyred car approaching a detached bungalow in a palm tree-lined suburb of Los Angeles on a typically hot summer day. A man gets out of the car, dressed as one would expect a middle-class American man in the late 1940s to be dressed. The caption 'Los Angeles, 1949' is more of a confirmation than an explanation. This is a representation of the first hyperTheme; the scene soon switches to the second hyperTheme, with similar clues emanating from the various semiotic modalities.

Another indication of the skills adopted in constructing textual meaning can be observed in the audio description of *The Hours*. The film features three famous female stars, Nicole Kidman, Meryl Streep and Julianne Moore, and this is also an important part of the whole production. Their names appear in the credits for the benefit of the sighted viewer, but the blind audience has to be informed aurally. During the unfolding of the three hyperthematic strands of the film, the three women are depicted alone, at different times, for a few seconds. At these precise points, the describer says *Nicole Kidman is Virginia Woolf*, and so on for the other two protagonists. This packeting of information is a fine example of 'enabling' and of great assistance in the reading of the film.

Technology

An extremely important aspect of multimodal research and the pursuit of the optimum way in which to 'read images' is that of technological advance in the field. This chapter will look at two important areas: that of computer-assisted analysis (corpora and concordancing); and the relatively new approach through eye-tracking.

Computer-assisted analysis

Baldry, after his early work on multimodal transcriptions, moved into the creation of relational databases enabling the formation of corpus-based alignments of words and other semiotic modes on the model of purely linguistic concordances. His successive versions of the Multimodal Corpus Authoring (MCA) system (Baldry 2002) incorporated a relational database into a corpus system allowing users to search corpora and find alignments of wording with other semiotic resources, such as gesture. His interest has now turned to referencing systems, and the interplay of screenplays, storyboards and film transcriptions as guides to

Storyboard Transcript for In Excelsis Deo. The West Wing Season 1 Episode 10	Teaser; pp. 1–4	Act 1: 2:13–12:59 pp. 4–16						Act 2: 13:00–23:15 pp. 16–30						Act 3: 23:16–27:29 pp. 30–39	Act 4: 27.30–41.38 pp. 39–48. Film ends with credits from 41.38 to 42:13						
Overlay	Episode title at 0:36. Date from 2:13–2:57: *Thursday December 23* at 0:41. Other overlays include names (actors, series creator, episode writers, etc.) from 2:14 to the end of scene 3														Date at 27:30: *Friday December 24*						
Scene	1	2	3	4	5	6	7	8	9	10	11	12	13	14	15	16	17	18	19	20	21
Time-reference	0:0	0:43	2:56	5:12	7:57	8:35	9:27	10:37	13:00	15:24	17:28	19:05	20:05	21:05	23:16	27:30	29:25	32:21	34:31	37:01	37:45
Transcript page-reference	1–4	4	4–6	6–10	10–11	11–12	12–14	14–16	16–20	20–22	22–23	23–25	25–27	27–30	30–33	33–36	36–39	39–42	42–45	45–46	46–48
Location-reference Scenes 15, 16, 17, others = Day; (H = Night; H = White House Hallway)	H	H	North West Lobby +	Korean War Memorial	H + Leo's Office	Press Briefing Room	Toby's Office	H + Josh's Office	North West Lobby	H + Sam's Office	Outer Oval Office	Korean War Memorial	Oval Office	H	Rare Books Store	Underpass Washington Bridge	C.J.'s Office	Outside + Inside Laurie's Home	Leo's Office	Press Briefing Room	Mural Room + Outer Oval Office / Mural Room / Arlington Cemetery + Mural Room

Figure 36.4 Scenes, timings and locations

the understanding of the multimodal nature of screen products. In a volume based on various analyses of an episode of the American television series *The West Wing*, Baldry (forthcoming) introduces a multi-semiotic referencing system in which a grid with rows and columns maps 'acts' on one axis, while scenes, times, locations, characters, thematics and circumstances are mapped on the other. A very simple section is shown in Figure 36.4, indicating scenes, timings and locations (to be followed by character involvement, circumstances, etc.) – a first step on the road to interactive computer-managed referencing systems.

The episode is divided into five distinct 'acts' on the horizontal axis, along with the time duration and page numbers on the storyboard. Vertically, the section first charts the 'text-on-screen' elements, which introduce the actors, etc., and set the scene. There then follow indications as to the scene number, the duration of the scene, its position on the storyboard, where the action takes place, and so on. The cross-referencing that can then be enacted electronically can trace repeated locations, character movements, the matching of diverse semiotic resources such as language and gesture, movement and music, etc.

Eye tracking

When analysing a multimodal text for reasons of translation, for example, or particularly when planning an audio description, it is important to decide which elements are to be prioritised or need prioritising. Intuition may suffice, but a more scientific approach has been provided by eye-tracking studies using, for example, the Tobii computer system. Eye tracking is 'the process of recording the gaze of a person and the movement of the eyes from one point to another' (Saldanha and O'Brien 2013: 136). It has been shown that the number and length of 'fixations' (that is, how long the eye fixes on an object or person) and 'saccades' (that is, the movement between fixations) is indicative of where attention is placed when viewing a picture or film. The order of fixations and 'gaze time' recorded by seeing subjects highlight the elements that attract and retain most attention when viewing either a static or dynamic image. As Wissmath and Weibel (2012: 284) point out, 'eye-tracking is a central tool in visual attention research because eye movements are an overt behavioural manifestation of the allocation of attention in a particular scene and . . . serve as a window into the operation of the attentional system'.

Preliminary studies have indicated that movement attracts the attention more than static features and that 'visual salience' can be triggered by factors such as luminance, contrast, colour or contour density (Henderson and Hollingworth 1998). Lautenbacher (2012: 152) also shows, through eye-tracking experiments, that film audiences look for 'a source of communication on the screen', and fixate on faces, mouths and gaze direction when people are involved. Because the integration of picture, sound and verbal text are inherent to socially oriented meaning-making, film directors already look for visual–verbal cohesion. The audio describer, for example, has to tap into this construct and complete the cohesive whole. Here, the reading of images takes on a whole new importance.

In Figure 36.5, the original frame on the left has been subjected to an eye-tracking experiment (Perego 2012). The frame in the middle shows the main and secondary fixations, and the movements between them (saccades), while the 'heat map' in the right-hand frame captures the concentration of gaze. It can be seen that the face of the person on the left, as a source of communication, is the centre of attention, followed in interest value by the movement of the hands.

The importance of these observations for multimodal text analysts – and particularly for audio describers – should be evident, even though a word of caution is obligatory in statistical terms. This is a relatively recent discipline and the results from a wide range of experiments in varying conditions are needed to come to any definitive conclusions, but the relevance to the concept of 'reading images' has been established. Already, the results of eye-tracking studies have proved useful for subtitlers, who have to juggle written words and images in such a way as to ensure comprehension. Audio describers are following in their wake as they plot how to read the images for the blind in the most helpful and economic way.

Other areas that can benefit from these developments include education and the visual reading by students of educational material, given 'the increasingly integrative use of images in many different types of texts in electronic and paper media' (Unsworth 2006: 55). Particularly in Australia, interest in meaning-making at the intersection of language and image has permeated into the school system. Unsworth (2006) stresses the importance of the need to find a metalanguage with which to facilitate awareness of image–text relations, especially in view of the continual advances in electronic (and iconic) information channels. Eye tracking is also mentioned by Bateman (2014) with reference to photographs included in news items.

Conclusion

This chapter has looked at some of the issues that have been raised and some of the advances that have been made in multimodal text analysis in the search for a meaningful way of 'reading images'. From a consideration of the factors involved in reading static images, the discussion moved rapidly to the taxing question of understanding all that is going on in moving images. Attempts to harness the barrage of semiotic modalities contained within any

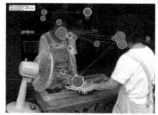

Figure 36.5   Eyetracking

multimodal text have been illustrated – in particular, the multimodal transcription and phasal analysis. SFL approaches, especially with regard to text organisation, cohesion, intertextuality and appraisal, have been discussed as being as relevant to multimodal discourse as to purely verbal discourse. Multimodal text analysis has been considered also in its practical applications, such as those relating to translation and to audio description for the blind – both areas in which the ability to 'read images' is of paramount importance. The significant contribution of technological advances has been illustrated particularly regarding computer applications, concordancing techniques, referencing systems and eye-tracking studies, all of which promise tantalising new discoveries in the years to come in the field of screen media. Indeed, most of the discussion in this chapter has centred on film in its various guises, as the archetypal multimodal text. In fact, the potential for the film medium to enrich SFL theory should not be underestimated: film text provides us with a neatly packaged representation of the metafunctions, processes and, ultimately, genres at work in a more easily observable form than, say, clandestinely watching people's conversations and activities. Questions of textual cohesion and coherence come to embrace the interplay between diverse semiotic modes, and the components of context and register can be observed and, very importantly, re-observed through replaying and freezing. Halliday (2009: vii) reiterates that language is a system of meaning and points to the fact that 'it is likely to appear in very different guises when it is operating in such varied contexts as a classroom, a law court and a surgery'. The 'moving images' of film, whether in the fictitious form of circuit movies or the real-life form of documentaries, cover all of these contexts. It is thus hoped that this medium can continue to act as a vehicle for future discussion of those factors that can inform SFL theory and of how SFL theory can inform multimodal analysis.

Notes

1 See Kunz and Teich, this volume, for other perspectives on translation.
2 Cf. Halliday's (1996) logico-semantic relations of enhancing, expanding, projecting.
3 But see O'Hagan (2010) on the rather haphazard and overladen presentation of material on certain Japanese television shows.

References

Baldry, A. 2000. English in a visual society: Comparative and historical dimensions in multimediality and in multimodality. In A. Baldry (ed.) *Multimodality and Multimediality in the Distance-Learning Age*. Campobasso: Paladino, pp. 41–89.
Baldry, A. 2002. Subtitling dynamic multimodal texts: The development of interactive self-access tools. In G. Iamartino, M.L. Bignami and C. Pagetti (eds) *The Economy Principle in English: Linguistic, Literary and Cultural Perspectives*. Milan: Edizioni Unicopi, pp. 54–62.
Baldry, A. Forthcoming. Multisemiotic transcriptions as film referencing systems. In C. Taylor (ed.) *A Text of Many Colours: Translating* The West Wing. Bologna: Intralinea.
Baldry, A., and P. Thibault. 2006. *Multimodal Transcription and Text Analysis*. London: Equinox.
Barthes, R. 1977. *Image, Music, Text*. London: Fontana.
Bateman, J. 2014. *Text and Image: A Critical Introduction to the Visual/Verbal Divide*. London: Routledge.
Bateman, J., and H. Schmidt. 2012. *Multimodal Film Analysis. How Films Mean*. London: Routledge.
Boeriis, M. 2008. Mastering multimodal complexity. *Odense Working Papers in Language and Communication* 29: 219–36.

Bortoluzzi, M. 2010. Energy and its double: A case-study in critical multimodal discourse analysis. In E. Swain (ed.) *Thresholds and Potentialities of Systemic Functional Linguistics: Multilingual, Multimodal and Other Specialised Discourses*. Trieste: EUT, pp. 158–81.

Eggins, S. 1994. *An Introduction to Systemic Functional Linguistics*. London: Pinter.

Eggins, S., and D. Slade. 1997. *Analysing Casual Conversation*. London: Cassell.

Fairclough, N., and R. Wodak. 1997. Critical discourse analysis. In T.A. Van Dijk (ed.) *Discourse as Social Interaction*. London: Sage, pp. 258–84.

Gregory, M. 2002. Phasal analysis within communication linguistics: Two contrastive discourses. In P. Fries, M. Cummings, D. Lockwood and W. Spruiell (eds) *Relations and Functions within and around Language*. London: Continuum, pp. 316–45.

Halliday, M.A.K. 2009. Preface. In M.A.K. Halliday and J.J. Webster (eds) *Continuum Companion to Systemic Functional Linguistics*. London: Continuum, pp. vii–viii.

Halliday, M.A.K., and R. Hasan. 1976. *Cohesion in English*. London: Longman.

Halliday, M.A.K., and C.M.I.M. Matthiessen. 2004. *An Introduction to Functional Grammar*. 3rd edn. London: Routledge.

Henderson, J.M., and A. Hollingworth. 1998. Eye movements during scene viewing: An overview. In G. Underwood (ed.) *Eye Guidance in Reading and Scene Perception*. Oxford: Elsevier Science, pp. 269–93.

Iedema, R. 2001. Analysing film and television: A social semiotic account of hospital – An unhealthy business. In T. Van Leeuwen (ed.) *Handbook of Visual Analysis*. London: Sage, pp. 183–204.

Jewitt, C. 2009. Different approaches to multimodality. In C. Jewitt (ed.) *The Routledge Handbook of Multimodal Analysis*. Abingdon: Routledge, pp. 28–39.

Kress, G. 2003. *Literacy in the New Media Age*. London: Routledge Falmer.

Kress, G., and T.J. Van Leeuven. 1996. *Reading Images: The Grammar of Visual Design*. London: Routledge.

Kress, G., and T.J. Van Leeuven. 2006. *Multimodal Discourse: The Modes and Media of Contemporary Communication*. London: Routledge.

Lautenbacher, O.P. 2012. From still pictures to moving pictures: Eye-tracking text and image. In E. Perego (ed.) *Eye Tracking in Audiovisual Translation*. Rome: Aracne, pp. 135–56.

Lemke, J. 2002. Discursive technologies and the social organization of meaning. *Folia Linguistica* 35(1–2): 79–96.

Machin, D. 2009. Multimodality and theories of the visual. In C. Jewitt (ed.) *The Routledge Handbook of Multimodal Analysis*. Abingdon: Routledge, pp. 181–90.

Maiorani, A. 2011. Reading movies as interactive messages: A proposal for a new method of analysis. *Semiotica* 187(1–4): 167–88.

Malcolm, K. 2010. *Phasal Analysis: Analysing Discourse through Communication Linguistics*. London: Continuum.

Martin, J.R., and D. Rose. 2008. *Genre Relations: Mapping Culture*. London: Equinox.

Martin, J.R., and P. White. 2005. *The Language of Evaluation: Appraisal in English*. Basingstoke: Palgrave Macmillan.

Martinec, R. 2000. Rhythm in multimodal texts. *Leonardo* 33(4): 289–97.

Martinec, R., and T.J. Van Leeuven. 2009. *The Language of New Media Design: Theory and Practice*. London: Routledge.

Mavers, D. 2009. Image in the multimodal ensemble: Children's drawing. In C. Jewitt (ed.) *The Routledge Handbook of Multimodal Analysis*. Abingdon: Routledge, pp. 263–71.

Moya, A.J. 2014. *A Multimodal Analysis of Picture Books for Children: A Systemic Functional Approach*. Sheffield: Equinox.

Norris, S. 2009. Modal density and modal configurations: Multimodal actions. In C. Jewitt (ed.) *The Routledge Handbook of Multimodal Analysis*. Abingdon: Routledge, pp. 78–90.

O'Hagan, M. 2010. *Japanese TV Entertainment: Framing Humour with Open Caption Telop – Translation, Humour and the Media*. London: Bloomsbury Academic, pp. 70–88.

O'Halloran, K.L. 2008. Systemic functional-multimodal discourse analysis (SF-MDA): Constructing ideational meaning using language and visual imagery. *Visual Communication* 7(4): 443–75.

O'Toole, M. 1994. *The Language of Displayed Art*. Leicester: Leicester University Press.

Painter, C., J.R. Martin and L. Unsworth. 2013. *Reading Visual Narratives: Image Analysis of Children's Picture Books*. Sheffield: Equinox.

Perego, E. 2012. Il tracciamento oculare nella traduzione audiovisiva. In E. Perego and C. Taylor (eds) *Tradurre l'audiovisivo*. Rome: Carocci, pp. 89–120.

Rheindorf, M. 2004. The multiple modes of *Dirty Dancing*: A cultural studies approach to multi-modal discourse analysis. In E. Ventola, C. Charles and M. Kaltenbacher (eds) *Perspectives on Multimodality*. Amsterdam: John Benjamins, pp. 137–52.

Saldanha, G., and S. O'Brien. 2013. *Research Methodologies in Translation Studies*. London: Routledge.

Scollon, R., and S.W. Scollon. 2009. Multimodality and language: A retrospective and prospective view. In C. Jewitt (ed.) *The Routledge Handbook of Multimodal Analysis*. Abingdon: Routledge, pp. 170–80.

Snyder, J. 2008. The visual made verbal. In J. Diaz-Cintas (ed.) *The Didactics of Audiovisual Translation*. Amsterdam: John Benjamins, pp. 191–8.

Taylor, C. 2000. Text analysis and translation: An interactive, self-access computer application incorporating a functional approach. In A. Baldry (ed.) *Multimodality and Multimediality in the Distance-Learning Age*. Campobasso: Paladino, pp. 295–310.

Taylor, C. 2004. Multimodal text analysis and subtitling. In E. Ventola, C. Charles and M. Kaltenbacher (eds) *Perspectives on Multimodality*. Amsterdam: John Benjamins, pp. 153–72.

Taylor, C. 2015. Language as access: Transposition and translation of audiovisual texts as a vehicle of meaning and a gateway to understanding. In S. Starc, C. Jones and A. Maiorani (eds) *Meaning Making in Text*. London: Palgrave Macmillan, pp. 174–94.

Thibault, P. 2000. The multimodal transcription of a television advertisement. In A. Baldry (ed.) *Multimodality and Multimediality in the Distance-Learning Age*. Campobasso: Paladino, pp. 311–85.

Thibault, P., and A. Baldry. 2006. *Multimodal Transcription and Text Analysis*. London: Equinox.

Unsworth, L. 2006. Towards a metalanguage for multiliteracies education: Describing the meaning-making resources of language image interaction. *English Teaching: In Practice and Critique* 5(1): 55–76.

Van Leeuwen, T.J. 2011. Multimodality. In J. Simpson (ed.) *The Routledge Handbook of Applied Linguistics*. London: Routledge, pp. 668–83.

Vasta, N. 2005. Profits and principles: Is there a choice? In G. Cortese and A. Duszak (eds) *Identity, Community, Discourse: English in Intercultural Settings*. Bern: Peter Lang, pp. 429–52.

Wissmath, B., and D. Weibel. 2012. Translating movies and the sensation of 'being there'. In E. Perego (ed.) *Eye Tracking in Audiovisual Translation*. Rome: Aracne, pp. 277–93.

Filmography

Blackadder (1983–89). Written by Richard Curtis.

Gran Torino (2008). Directed by Clint Eastwood.

Inglourious Basterds (2009). Directed by Quentin Tarantino.

In the Name of the Father (1993). Directed by Jim Sheridan.

No Country for Old Men (2007). Directed by Joel and Ethan Coen.

The English Patient (1996). Directed by Anthony Minghella.

The Hours (2002). Directed by Stephen Daldry.

The Stone Killer (1973). Directed by Michael Winner.

The West Wing (1999–2006). Written by Aaron Sorkin.

Young Frankenstein (1974). Directed by Mel Brooks.

Systemic functional linguistics and language teaching

Anne McCabe

Introduction

Systemic functional linguistics (SFL) can trace its conception to questions that Michael Halliday posed from the 1940s as a Chinese teacher 'about the place of the understanding of language in language education, in the broader sense, and also in the more specific narrower sense of language teaching' (Halliday and Hasan 2006: 15). Halliday further writes:

> [A]s a teacher I was a lot more conscious of the need to provide explanations of prob-
> lems faced by the learners, to try to develop some kind of coherent notion of a language,
> how it works, how it was learned, and so forth, in order simply to improve the quality
> of the language teaching.
>
> *Halliday and Hasan 2006: 16*

Throughout this chapter, we will observe Halliday's distinction between language *education*, a broader field encompassing all teaching/learning situations involving language pedagogy, including the mother tongue, and within this, the narrower field of language *teaching*, or the teaching of an additional language once a first language has been learned. Language teaching can further be categorised broadly into second-language and foreign-language situations; in the former, learners live in the society of the second language; in the latter, the additional language is not usually encountered in everyday contexts. For the purposes of this chapter, the term 'L2' will be used to refer to both of these contexts. Steiner (1997: 15) suggests that L2 teaching 'has been one of the shaping influences on SFL, and in terms of SFL's history, some would say THE decisive driving force for the further development of the theory'. However, SFL uptake in language teaching has not been widespread, although it is currently on the rise. This chapter provides an account of SFL in L2 teaching contexts, and an analysis of its drawbacks and potentials for pedagogical purposes.

Anne McCabe

Historical background

Michael Halliday and language teaching

In the 1950s and early 1960s, Halliday maintained his concern with applications of linguistic theory to L2 teaching. In 1960, he wrote the essay 'General linguistics and its application to language teaching', positing the type of description that he found useful for language teaching. Halliday (2007 [1960]: 151) distinguished the linguist's object of study, 'the language', from the object of observation, 'the text', asserting that the linguist 'describes language, and relates it to the situations in which it is operating'. Thus he stressed the need for the description to handle both the system and its relationship to instances of text in contextual use. In setting forth his description for language teaching, as part of the theory of a systemic functional grammar (SFG), Halliday first delineated two main general grammatical categories (see Berry and McDonald, both this volume): the *units* of language, which are interrelated through the hierarchy of the rank system (clause, group, word and morpheme in English); and the *structural elements* of the clause, or the 'abstract functions established to enable us to give a precise account of what can be said or written at the rank of the clause' (Halliday 2007 [1960]: 144). For example, the primary abstract functions of the clause in English, subject, predicator, complement and adjunct, provide the paradigmatic slots of the clause, each of which calls for specific units of language. Or, to illustrate this point from the other way around, the noun belongs to a class of words 'having a certain value, filling a certain place in the structure of the nominal group, which in turn has a certain value in the structure of the clause' (Halliday 2007 [1960]: 151). For Halliday (2006 [1992]: 209, emphasis original), 'a systemic grammar differs from other functional grammars (and from all formal grammars) in that it is paradigmatic: a **system** is a paradigmatic set of alternative features'. This focus on the paradigmatic nature of structure (see Berry, this volume) was not prevalent at the time in L2 teaching. At the same time, Halliday (2006 [1977]: 102) went on to emphasise that '[s]tructural descriptions of sentences do no more than scratch the surface of language', arguing that L2 teaching could benefit from 'the systematic description of the relation between linguistic and situational features' (Halliday 2007 [1960]: 160; Bartlett, this volume).

In 1964, Halliday and colleagues, in *The Linguistic Sciences and Language Teaching*, set out to describe how language – specifically, English – 'works' (Halliday et al. 1964: x) and included the abovementioned concepts. Acknowledging throughout the primary importance of good teaching practice, the authors also argued for descriptions of language that could help to solve problems in L2 teaching. Picking up on Halliday's earlier call for relating linguistic and situational features, the authors brought in the notion of register (see Moore, this volume), or 'variety of a language distinguished according to use' (Halliday et al. 1964: 87). They also argued that learning will take place more readily 'if the language is encountered in active use than if it is seen or heard only as a set of disembodied utterances or exercises' (Halliday et al. 1964: 181).

Halliday's linguistic theory is cited as providing a basis for the communicative approach to L2 teaching – that is, communicative language teaching (CLT) (Brumfit and Johnson 1979; Melrose 1995: 3; Richards and Rodgers 2001: 159–60) – which gathered momentum in the 1970s and became highly influential in the decades thereafter. Halliday's functional, meaning-based approach offered L2 teaching a way in which to move away from a traditional focus on correctness of linguistic form, towards appropriateness of linguistic choices to the context of situation. Brumfit and Johnson (1979) considered Halliday and Dell Hymes to be the two leading theorists whose work inspired CLT. However, Widdowson (200: 202) argues that the 'defining feature' of CLT became 'how language functions externally in context', drawing more heavily on Dell Hymes' (1972) scheme of communicative competence, which includes appropriateness of expression to a given context and situation. Of less interest in CLT was Halliday's notion of the functional motivation of the meaning potential available in the system. One type of syllabus that emerged in early CLT days was the functional-notional syllabus (Wilkins 1976), which grouped functions of language (such as apologising, request- ing, or complaining) and notions (such as general concepts of time, quantity or location) into an ordered plan for classroom presentation, depending on learners' needs. In their applica- tion, Finocchiaro and Brumfit (1983: 33) kept the functions and notions separate from the linguistic structures, arguing that '[a]ny grammatical structure can be used to express any function, and the abstract functional categories of linguists like Halliday have no immediate pedagogical use, as currently formulated'. In sum, CLT was less interested in teaching the language system, or an abstract record of language as the accumulation of instantiations, and more interested in teaching specific instances in use.

At this same time that CLT left aside an SFL focus on the language system, from the mid- 1960s on, Halliday's applied work turned away from L2 teaching and towards his mother tongue English, thus towards the broader field of language education and literacy develop- ment in schools. In the early 1960s, through his encounters with Basil Bernstein, Halliday was drawn to the problem of tendencies relating to social class and educational achievement, which Halliday attributed to differences in children's lived experiences with the functional uses of language in different contexts (Halliday 1978: 25; Bartlett, Painter, and especially Maton and Doran, all this volume). In the 1980s, this focus was taken up in Australia to advance literacy needs in schools and the workplace, especially of learners who came from disadvantaged backgrounds in terms of literacy opportunities. J.R. Martin, Francis Christie and

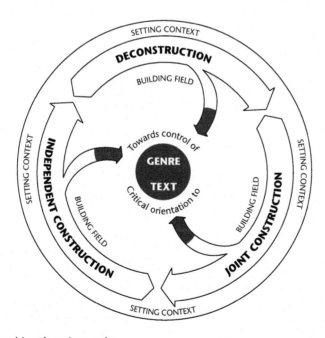

Figure 37.1 Teaching–learning cycle
Source: Rothery and Stenglin (1994: 8)

other researchers drew on notions of genre (Gardner, this volume) and on SFL descriptions of language in creating a genre-based pedagogy (Christie and Unsworth 2005; Martin 2006; Veel 2006). This visible, interventionist pedagogy (Martin 2006) employs a teaching–learning cycle (Figure 37.1) designed to scaffold learners into appropriate and effective understandings and realisations, or production, of genres. For the first phase of the cycle, teachers and students jointly deconstruct a text, while analysing its stages and its linguistic features using SFL concepts and terms. Then, in the first part of the writing phase, teachers and students jointly construct a text in the genre, after which students independently construct their own texts. Throughout the stages of the cycle, explicit attention is given to the field knowledge needed for both understanding and producing the genre, as well as to its social context. Also included is a critical orientation, designed to raise awareness of ideology and power as realised through the language choices made in constructing the genre (Martin 1999: 130).

The next generation of genre pedagogy, 'Reading to Learn' (Acevedo and Rose 2007; Rose and Martin 2012), downplays specialised SFL metalanguage, while focusing student attention on the meanings through 'commonsense terms from everyday folk rhetoric', much like the talk used by caregivers in early child language development (Martin 2006: 111). As the next section shows, both genre-based and Reading to Learn pedagogy, designed for mother-tongue language education in schools, have ultimately provided the means for SFL to grow in pedagogical relevance to L2 teaching.

SFL uptake in language teaching

Genre-based pedagogy, with its intention of helping students to learn more effectively through the school language, has been applied in a number of school contexts to the teaching of English as a second language (ESL) to students whose home language is other than English both in Australia (for example Jones et al. 1989; Gibbons 1993, 2001, 2002; Burns 2001; Marshall 2006; Burns and de Silva Joyce 2007) and beyond. It is, for example, on the rise in the United States for learners of ESL (Gebhard and Harman 2011; Schleppegrell 2013; de Oliveira and Iddings 2014). SFL has also been applied to English as a foreign language (EFL) school contexts, specifically in content-and-language-integrated-learning (CLIL) classrooms, in which English, while not the dominant language of the culture, has become the medium through which subjects such as science and history are taught, providing a context in which learners are both using and learning language. CLIL responds to the perception that, in many foreign-language pedagogical contexts, learners are taught a formal system with little opportunity for using it; at the same time, in CLIL contexts, an explicit focus on language is often missing. Llinares and colleagues (2012), drawing on examples from the bilingual schools project in Spain and in other European contexts, use SFL descriptions of language to illustrate ways in which teachers can provide meaningful explanations of the linguistic system as it is typically realised as text in the disciplines. In Hong Kong, in similar contexts, a number of practitioner-researchers have demonstrated the effectiveness of an SFL approach in the classroom (Firkins et al. 2007; Walker 2010; Maxwell-Reid 2014), with Lock and Tsui (2000) providing useful bridges to SFL descriptions for language teachers.

Similar to these applications of teaching English in school contexts, with respect to L2 teaching of other European languages, the Teacher Learning for European Literacy Education project[1] and the Stockholm Education Administration Reading to Learn literacy project (Acevedo 2010) both use Reading to Learn pedagogy, to 'improve student learning outcomes, particularly for those who are educationally disadvantaged, including second language learners' (http://tel4ele.eu/). For Spanish, SFL genre pedagogy has been used for teaching heritage Spanish speakers in the United States (Achugar and Colombi 2008).

These adaptations of SFL for L2 teaching (McCabe et al. 2015) suggest that it lends itself well mainly to teaching language for specific purposes, given its focus on language use in context for a range of literacy purposes, such as schooling or other specialised applications. Indeed, John Swales' (1990: 2) seminal book *Genre Analysis* cites Halliday et al. (1964) as a cornerstone for research on language for specific purposes, and SFL influence can be seen in English for specific purposes (ESP) – especially English for academic purposes (EAP) – teaching settings around the globe (Coffin and Donohue 2012; Gardner 2012). In more mainstream, general L2 English teaching at the advanced levels, some attention is paid to the textual metafunction (Forey, this volume), using SFL-based concepts such as Theme–Rheme (Alonso Belmonte and McCabe 2004) and the ideational metafunction through, for example, the nominal group (Fontaine, this volume).[2] SFL also shows a very modest influence in L2 teaching of languages other than English (LOTE). For example, Heidi Byrnes (2013) leads a fruitful initiative at Georgetown University in applications of SFL, initially for advanced learners of German and now *ab initio*. In her view, 'learning "the grammar" of a language is not about learning to adhere to rules, but learning to turn experience and human existence into meaning by using the resources that the grammar of a particular language makes available' (Byrnes 2009: 5). This SFL focus has been applied to teaching Chinese as a foreign language at the elementary level (Mohan and Huang 2002), and Japanese as an additional language (Armour and Furuya 2013), which is also taught through a genre-based approach (Ramzan and Thomson 2013).

However, overall, in general L2 teaching, whether taught in schools as a subject in its own right or in language academies/schools, the influence of SFL has been far less, even negligible, despite Halliday's perceived inspiration on CLT. At the same time, one of the criticisms levelled at CLT has been the lack of explicit focus on grammar – or perhaps a lack of connect between communicative activities and focus on grammar (Nitta and Gardner 2005; McCabe and Alonso Belmonte 2006). Polias and Dare (2006: 125) explain that this may be because many teachers have 'limited knowledge of any grammatics let alone functional grammar'. Even when teacher development opportunities in functional grammar are available, Burns and Knox (2005: 256), referring to English L2 teaching, have suggested that SFL 'is still very much in its infancy' and therefore 'considerable tensions exist for language teachers wanting to use SFL when institutional requirements, course material and textbooks, and student expectations are primarily based on dominant traditional grammatical frameworks'. Simply put, '[w]hile traditional grammar is familiar, SFG [systemic functional grammar] requires a different way of thinking about language' (Derewianka and Jones 2010: 10).

A further difference within the field of L2 teaching research is the view of how an additional language is learned, in the sense of how a learner internalises an L2 system – a cognitive viewpoint that has not underpinned SFL theorising in the same way as it has research in second-language acquisition (SLA). Llinares (2013: 31) explains the different perspective of SFL, in which 'there is no sharp distinction between the system and the use of language' – that is, in which the language system is seen as an accumulation of instantiations in use, rather than in the more common view amongst SLA theorists and researchers as an abstract set of rules rooted in the cognitive workings of the mind (Atkinson 2011).

SLA has, over the past decades, been the dominant research paradigm connected to L2 teaching and SFL has not provided a theoretical underpinning for that research. Major SLA handbooks (Doughty and Long 2003; Ritchie and Bhatia 2009) exclude SFL, perhaps because of the mentalist-cognitive bent of much SLA research (Atkinson 2011). At the same time, in recent years, the field of SLA has come to realise more fully the complexity of language *acqui-sition*, or *learning* or *development* – all metaphors that define one's views of language and of the process of developing one's repertoire as a language user. Ortega (2009: 233) explains the different focus of SFL, which 'compels us to redefine additional language learning as semiotic development in an L2, or the development of flexible meaning-making L2 capacities across contexts'. However, she further points out that other linguistic approaches that focus on meaning – namely, cognitive and corpus linguistics – have 'been endorsed more strongly' (Ortega 2009: 234) within SLA studies. Thus 'studies of the actual development of meaning-making capacities in the L2 are still rare' (Ortega 2009: 234).

Halliday (1987: 14) called for descriptions of learner language that would allow researchers to 'be able to represent the system as variable in extent and in elaboration, in order to show how its power increased as the learner makes progress'. Perrett (2000) took up this challenge, describing an approach to analysing learner language of collecting instances of texts over a period of time, choosing the linguistic features to focus on (in her study, speech functions in exchanges) and using system networks to show the choices that learners were able to make at different points in time, thus demonstrating an increasing repertoire of meaning potential. While Perrett built up the systems through the learners' texts, Praxedes Filho (2013) used already-existing clause systems networks (transitivity, mood and theme) to compare texts written by foreign-language learners of English at several different stages of learning with those by first-language writers. This kind of analysis can demonstrate the expanding potential of learners by showing gains in abilities to draw on options within systems and in level of delicacy to more appropriately and effectively approximate language use to context and situation.

These researchers illuminate the difference of an SFL perspective, which centres on the development of meaning potential (Matthiessen 2006), rather than on the cognitive acquisition of an abstract system. An SFL approach emphasises how the learner is socialised into the language through interaction, thus favouring a participation metaphor over an acquisition metaphor (Pavlenko and Lantolf 2000).

Critical issues and topics

Pedagogic grammar

SFL has been downplayed in both the theory and practice of L2 teaching because of a mentalist bent in research related to SLA, on the one hand, and a lack of familiarity with SFL linguistic descriptions, on the other, coinciding with either a traditional focus or a lack of a principled focus on grammar in CLT. At the same time, research has consistently shown that a lack of focus on form in solely meaning-focused learning environments is generally ineffective for second- or foreign-language learning, while a focus on form within meaning-focused tasks and activities is an effective way of helping learners to notice, and thus be able to learn, features of the language system (Doughty and Williams 1998). Language teachers therefore clearly need knowledge about language; a major issue consequently concerns on which descriptions teachers might best draw to explain the system to students, and (for our purposes here) whether SFL descriptions are any more or less helpful in both the articulation and subsequent internalisation of the system by L2 learners.

What, then, are the requirements of an effective pedagogic grammar and how does SFG fit the bill? One important criterion is that a pedagogic grammar should be 'norm-describing' rather than 'norm-enforcing' (Thornbury 2013); descriptions should include explanations of appropriateness to context and not blind adherence to rules. SFL's non-prescriptive descriptions of language as a system of choices fit this criterion. Furthermore, SFL focuses on the meaning potential of language – that is, on what can be said, not on how it should be said. This focus leads to a further advantage of SFL as a pedagogic grammar: descriptions of the meaning potential of a language, in mapping out what can be said, are also, in essence, providing a window onto the societies and culture that the language has grown to serve (Halliday 1970: 173). A pedagogic grammar needs to include semantic values and contexts of use, while at the same time providing properties of paradigmatic and syntagmatic formal patterns (Hasan and Perrett 1994: 205). We have seen, however, that a focus on SFG syntagmatic patterns has been downplayed in applications of SFG to language teaching contexts.

This missing piece of the pedagogy may be related to the complexity of SFL. A pedagogic grammar needs to be based on 'an adequate descriptive grammar of the target language' (Tomlin 1994: 141). Tomlin (1994: 143) further stipulates that a pedagogic grammar 'must provide explicit descriptions of grammatical structure and use in a simple and straightforward manner'; SFG's terms are viewed as 'a veritable maze, very messy and complex' (Bourke 2005: 93). However, the criterion of simplicity is countered by other scholars, because 'the use of simplified rules may be counterproductive' (Westney 1994: 93). In their explanation of a focus-on-form approach, Doughty and Williams (1998: 211–12) argue that:

> [E]very hierarchical level of language – from phonology to morphosyntax to the lexicon to discourse and pragmatics – is composed of both forms (e.g., phonemes, morphemes, lexical items, cohesive devices, and politeness markers) and rules (e.g. devoicing, allomorphy, agreement, collocation, anaphora, and in-group vs. out-group relationships).

In sum, language is a 'complex system' (Doughty and Williams 1998: 212), or, as suggested by the emergentist proposal of language, 'a multi-agent, complex, dynamic adaptive system' (Ellis and Larsen-Freeman 2006: 558). SFL theory does not shy away from the complexity of language, which may make it difficult for teachers and learners who want simplification, especially in the early stages of learning. At the same time, its complexity of description is designed to capture the complexities of language in use, which suggests greater adequacy of description for pedagogic purposes when learners need guidance in lining up the meaning potential of the system with actual instances of language as instantiated in text. Obviously, 'a pedagogic grammar has to be reliable . . . we need to be able to trust its explanations' (Thornbury 2013), as well as its underlying theory of language (Hasan and Perrett 1994: 220). Again, the lack of simplicity and of familiarity may work against trust in SFG as an optimum pedagogic grammar, while its complexity allows for more robust and reliable understandings of language in use.

Furthermore, Macken-Horarik et al. (2011: 11) posit that a pedagogic grammar should offer 'a toolkit for exploring the contribution to meaning of non-linguistic resources'. SFL goes beyond the purely linguistic in allowing for descriptions of multimodal representations or constructions of meaning, and thus for multiliteracies (Unsworth 2001, 2006; Royce 2007: Taylor, this volume), and Polias and Forey (2015) demonstrate the usefulness of applications of SFL in describing a range of meaning-making resources, including images and the body, as they are used for teaching disciplinary subjects through English to L2 speakers. Also, a pedagogic grammar 'should help learners to become independent analysts' (Odlin 1994: 316). These applications take the realm of L2 teaching/learning into fuller considerations of meaning-making and pedagogy to assess the implications of SFL for L2 teaching.

Teaching methodology

As well as a pedagogic grammar, a pedagogy is needed in the language classroom – that is, the term 'language teaching' needs to join ways of focusing on language with methods of teaching it. SFL theorising and research, as we have seen, has often gone hand in hand with theoretical and practical applications in education. The influence of Bernstein in Halliday's work in first-language learning was impetus for the genre-based approach and Bernstein's code theory, in the form of Legitimation Code Theory (see Maton and Doran, this volume), continues to interact with SFL to seek answers to educational challenges, including helping L2 learners to use language more effectively for their purposes (Cheung 2015), providing rich understandings of the construction of knowledge through language in different disciplinary fields. Also, the genre-based approach to language teaching intersects with Vygotskian-based approaches to teaching and learning. Wells (1994) examines the overlaps – amongst others, that of learning through social interaction – and Thorne (2000: 225) highlights Halliday's 'expertly developed' social-semiotic approach to language as formative to his views of SLA. The cycle of teaching–learning involves scaffolding (Bruner 1978), through which a teacher does not simply present knowledge as something to learn in its own right, but rather helps others to perform in a social context, providing opportunities for internalising the knowledge through explicitly labelling what it is learners are doing. Scaffolding moves learners through their 'zone of proximal development', or the distance between the actual and potential levels of development of the individual (Vygotsky 1978: 86). It involves the expert in continually revising where the learner stands with respect to his or her potential to dismantle or strengthen the assistance (Donato 1994: 41). It 'should also result in "handover", with students being able to transfer understandings and skills to new tasks in new learning contexts, thereby becoming increasingly independent learners' (Hammond and Gibbons 2005: 8). Martin (2006: 115) suggests that SFL metalanguage 'is intended to function as permanent ideational scaffolding for text reception and production – a resource to be drawn on when a teacher is not to hand'. This is because of the visible pedagogy, which includes creating a critical awareness of the meaning potential of language choices in context. Phil Chappell (2013: 24), a language teacher-educator, further highlights the usefulness of register variables for teachers:

> SFG provides a rubric for language teachers to plan their teaching around (be they spur of the moment explanations or whole lessons) and for language learners to sort out in their own minds where, when, and how language can be used to successfully communicate across social and cultural settings.

The Reading to Learn pedagogy (Rose and Martin 2012), which, as we have seen, has been adapted to teaching second-language learners in school contexts, posits the strategies, activities and interactions that teachers should implement if they are to engage all students fully to help them to increase their meaning potential in ways that ensure success. Rose and Martin (2012) refer to a 'pedagogic metalanguage' and not a 'pedagogic grammar', because their model includes grammar, discourse, register and genre, and thus is more complete model for a focus-on-form approach. At the same time, Rose (2014) argues that the metalanguage, such as transitivity labels, should not be used simply in place of formal grammar in the classroom as the starting point of teaching, without an accompanying change in the overall pedagogy. The Reading to Learn pedagogy emphasises the use of metalanguage in the classroom only as it serves the understanding of situated meaning-making in text, because 'patterns of language are easier to bring to consciousness if they are encountered in actual texts, in meaningful contexts' (Rose, forthcoming).

Thus, in SFL-based approaches, the text is the starting point, not the linguistic descriptions, which are made explicit only as they help the learners. Jones and Lock (2011) provide examples of how this pedagogy can be applied to different levels in the ESL classroom, using texts as starting points to help learners to notice that grammatical choices are appropriate and meaningful to their contexts. Feez (1999) suggests a text-based syllabus for L2 teaching, which is rooted in genre-based pedagogy. The advantage of this kind of retrospective approach to grammar, whereby 'talking about grammar is postponed until the learners themselves can contribute by bringing to light what they already in some sense "know"' (Thompson 1996: 11), acknowledges that learners of an additional language already have knowledge about the functional nature of language and its meaning-making potential.

Recommendations for practice and future directions

The 'social turn' in SLA research (Block 2003), along with the need for an effective focus on form for teaching language as communication, may bring SFL descriptions into the forefront as an effective pedagogic grammar for L2 teaching. At the same time, teacher training should incorporate direct applications to L2 teaching, not as separate courses on the linguistic descriptions, but as part of an overall SFL pedagogy for L2 teaching, with suggestions for all learner levels. Applications, such as Reading to Learn, which bring together linguistics and pedagogy, can be further adapted to foreign-language contexts, for example with adult learners, who may have literacy skills in their native tongue, but not in the L2.

In addition to 'authentic' texts, such as articles, recipes, letters, and so on, concordances[3] have been suggested as a good tool to use in the foreign- or second-language classroom to provide samples of language in context. At the same time, Widdowson (2009: 207) reminds us that:

> [A]n example is always an example of something, the token of a type . . . You can present any number of real samples of usage by random selection but they are of little help to learners if they cannot realise them as examples.

In other words, 'it is necessary to look at both the system of language and its functions at the same time; otherwise we will lack any theoretical basis for generalizations about how language is used' (Halliday 1970: 142). Thus students need an understanding of the potential of the system and not only of real instances, having available a metalanguage as it serves to tie the two together; therefore teacher-education programmes need to focus on the metalanguage as it best serves the pedagogy. Teachers need descriptions of language to help students in their understandings of choices in text (instance) and in relating those understandings to the system, and back to text/new text, and back to system, *ad infinitum*, as they help learners to expand their register potential in the L2. While the level of the syntagm is sometimes left aside in a focus-on-meaning approach, noticing constituents and their roles in structures can help learners in internalising the forms of the system – that is, 'realisation rules and an account of "surface" syntactic structure are essential accompaniments to the networks of choices of meaning' (Berry 2014: 375). Systemic functional linguists should continue to write pedagogic grammars to bridge teachers' understandings, especially for languages other than English. It is also important for SFL to continue analysing and detailing understandings of how people interact with, and thus learn from, technology, to ensure that the metalanguage and pedagogy are intertwined when drawing on other semiotic resources in the language classroom.

Finally, SFL-based teacher practitioners need to provide evidence from the classroom that the metalanguage + pedagogy is effective for learners, through action research, such as that described by Acevedo (2010), and longitudinal studies, such as those described by Perrett (2000) and Praxedes Filho (2013). Design-based research, through which both the design of an intervention and its implementation are examined to address ways of improving educational practice, has been applied by Schleppegrell (2013) towards identifying specific interactions in the classroom stimulated by SFL-based metalanguage that are beneficial to L2 development. To carry out the SFL programme, based on Halliday's initial interests in both language and pedagogy, it is important for this kind of pedagogy and research to be implemented in a wide range of L2 teaching contexts.

Notes

1 http://tel4ele.eu/.
2 For applications to L2 teaching, see McCabe and Gallagher (2008) and Musgrave and Parkinson (2014).
3 From corpus linguistics: see Sharoff, this volume.

References

Acevedo, C. 2010. *Will the Implementation of Reading to Learn in Stockholm Schools Accelerate Literacy Learning for Disadvantaged Students and Close the Achievement Gap? A Report on School-Based Action Research.* Stockholm: Multilingual Research Institute, Stockholm Education Administration.

Acevedo, C., and D. Rose. 2007. Reading (and writing) to learn in the middle years of schooling. *Pen* 157: 1–8.

Achugar, M., and M.C. Colombi. 2008. Systemic functional linguistic explorations into the longitudinal study of advanced capacities: The case of Spanish heritage language learners. In L. Ortega and H. Byrnes (eds) *The Longitudinal Study of Advanced L2 Capacities.* London: Routledge, pp. 36–57.

Alonso Belmonte, I., and A. McCabe. 2004. The development of written discourse competence in ELT materials: A preliminary analysis. *Revista Canaria de Estudios Ingleses* 49: 29–48.

Armour, W.S., and R. Furuya. 2013. Learning how to mean in Japanese as an additional language. In E. Thomson and W.S. Armour (eds) *Systemic Functional Perspectives of Japanese: Descriptions and Applications.* London: Equinox, pp. 210–53.

Atkinson, D. (ed.). 2011. *Alternative Approaches to Second Language Acquisition.* London: Routledge.

Berry, M. 2014. Towards a study of the differences between formal written English and informal spoken English. In L. Fontaine, T. Bartlett and G. O'Grady (eds) *Systemic Functional Linguistics: Exploring Choice.* Cambridge: Cambridge University Press, pp. 365–83.

Block, D. 2003. *The Social Turn in Second Language Acquisition.* Edinburgh: Edinburgh University Press.

Bourke, J. 2005. The grammar we teach. *Reflections on English Language Teaching* 4: 85–97.

Brumfit C.J., and K. Johnson. 1979. *The Communicative Approach to Language Teaching.* Oxford: Oxford University Press.

Bruner, J. 1978. The role of dialogue in language acquisition. In A. Sinclair, R.J. Jarvelle and W.J.M. Levelt (eds) *The Child's Concept of Language.* New York: Springer-Verlag, pp. 241–56.

Burns, A. 2001. Genre-based approaches to writing and beginning adult ESL learners. In C. Candlin and N. Mercer (eds) *English Language Teaching in Its Social Context.* London: Routledge, pp. 200–7.

Burns, A., and H. de Silva Joyce. 2007. Adult ESL programmes in Australia. *Prospect* 22(3): 5–17.

Burns, A., and J. Knox. 2005. Realisation(s): Systemic-functional linguistics and the language classroom. In N. Bartels (ed.) *Researching Applied Linguistics in Language Teacher Education*. New York: Springer, pp. 235–60.

Byrnes, H. 2009. Systemic-functional reflections on instructed foreign language acquisition as meaning-making: An introduction. *Linguistics and Education* 20: 1–9.

Byrnes, H. 2013. Systemic functional linguistics in the round: Imagining foreign language education for a global world. In F. Yan and J.J. Webster (eds) *Developing Systemic Functional Linguistics: Theory and Application*. London: Equinox, pp. 322–43.

Chappell, P.J. 2013. An introduction to systemic functional grammar. *ETAS Journal* 30(3): 24.

Cheung, E. 2015. Legitimising the knower's multiple voices in applied linguistics postgraduate written discourse. *TESOL International Journal* 10(1): 46–71.

Christie, F., and L. Unsworth. 2005. Developing dimensions of an educational linguistics. In J.J. Webster, C.M.I.M. Matthiessen and R. Hasan (eds) *Continuing Discourse on Language: A Functional Perspective*. London: Equinox, pp. 217–50.

Coffin, C., and J. Donohue. 2012. Academic literacies and systemic functional linguistics: How do they relate? *Journal of English for Academic Purposes* 11(1): 64–75.

de Oliveira, L., and J. Iddings. 2014. *Genre Pedagogy across the Curriculum: Theory and Application in US Classrooms and Contexts*. London: Equinox.

Derewianka, B.M., and P.T. Jones. 2010. From traditional grammar to functional grammar: Bridging the divide. *NALDIC Quarterly* 8(1): 6–17.

Donato, R. 1994. Collective scaffolding in second language learning. In J.P. Lantolf and G. Appel (eds) *Vygotskian Approaches to Second Language Research*. Westport, CT: Ablex, pp. 33–56.

Doughty, C.J., and M.H. Long (eds). 2003. *Handbook of Second Language Acquisition*. Malden, MA: Blackwell.

Doughty, C.J., and J. Williams (eds). 1998. *Focus on Form in Classroom Second Language Acquisition*. Cambridge: Cambridge University Press.

Ellis, N., and D. Larsen-Freeman. 2006. Language emergence: Implications for applied linguistics – Introduction to the special issue. *Applied Linguistics* 27: 558–89.

Feez, S. 1999. Text-based syllabus design. *TESOL in Context* 9(1): 11–14.

Finocchiaro, M., and C. Brumfit. 1983. *Functional-Notional Approach: From Theory to Practice*. Oxford: Oxford University Press.

Firkins, A., G. Forey and S. Sengupta. 2007. Teaching writing to low proficiency EFL students. *ELT Journal* 61(4): 341–52.

Gardner, S. 2012. Genres and registers of student report writing: An SFL perspective on texts and practices. *Journal of English for Academic Purposes* 11: 52–63.

Gebhard, M., and R. Harman. 2011. Reconsidering genre theory in K-12 schools: A response to school reforms in the United States. *Journal of Second Language Writing* 20(1): 45–55.

Gibbons, P. 1993. *Learning to Learn in a Second Language*. Portsmouth, NH: Heinemann.

Gibbons, P. 2001. Learning a new register in a second language. In C. Candlin and N. Mercer (eds) *English Language Teaching in Its Social Context*. London: Routledge, pp. 258–70.

Gibbons, P. 2002. *Scaffolding Language, Scaffolding Learning: Teaching ESL Children in the Mainstream Classroom*. Portsmouth, NH: Heinemann.

Halliday, M.A.K. 1970. Language structure and language function. In J. Lyons (ed.) *New Horizons in Linguistics*. London: Penguin, pp. 140–65.

Halliday, M.A.K. 1978. *Language as Social Semiotic*. London: Arnold.

Halliday, M.A.K. 1987. Some basic concepts of educational linguistics. In V. Bickley (ed.) *Proceedings of the ILE International Seminar on Languages in Education in a Bilingual or Multilingual Setting*. Hong Kong: Institute of Language in Education, pp. 5–17.

Halliday, M.A.K. 2006 [1977]. Ideas about language. In M.A.K. Halliday and J.J. Webster (eds) *The Collected Works of M.A.K. Halliday, Vol. 3: On Language and Linguistics*. London: Bloomsbury, pp. 92–115.

Halliday, M.A.K. 2006 [1992]. Systemic grammar and the concept of a 'science of language'. In M.A.K. Halliday and J.J. Webster (eds) *The Collected Works of M.A.K. Halliday, Vol. 3: On Language and Linguistics*. London: Bloomsbury, pp. 199–212.

Halliday, M.A.K. 2007 [1960]. General linguistics and its application to language teaching. In M.A.K. Halliday and J.J. Webster (eds) *The Collected Works of M.A.K. Halliday, Vol. 9: On Language and Education*. London: Bloomsbury, pp. 135–73.

Halliday, M.A.K., and R. Hasan. 2006. Retrospective on SFL and literacy. In R. Whittaker, M. O'Donnell and A. McCabe (eds) *Language and Literacy: Functional Approaches*. London: Bloomsbury, pp. 15–44.

Halliday, M.A.K., A. McIntosh and P. Strevens. 1964. *The Linguistic Sciences and Language Teaching*. London: Longman.

Hammond, J., and P. Gibbons. 2005. Putting scaffolding to work: The contribution of scaffolding in articulating ESL education. *Prospect* 20(1): 6–30.

Hasan, R., and G. Perrett. 1994. Learning to function with the other tongue: A systemic functional perspective on second language teaching. In T. Odlin (ed.) *Perspectives on Pedagogical Grammar*. Cambridge: Cambridge University Press, pp. 179–226.

Hymes, D.H. 1972. On communicative competence. In J.B. Pride and J. Holmes (eds) *Sociolinguistics: Selected Readings*. Harmondsworth: Penguin, pp. 269–93.

Jones, J., S. Gollin, H. Drury and D. Economou. 1989. Systemic-functional linguistics and its application to the TESOL curriculum. In R. Hasan and J.R. Martin (eds) *Language Development: Learning Language, Learning Culture*. Westport, CT: Praeger, pp. 257–381.

Jones, R., and G. Lock. 2011. *Functional Grammar in the ESL Classroom: Noticing, Exploring and Practising*. Basingstoke: Palgrave Macmillan.

Llinares, A. 2013. Systemic functional approaches to second-language acquisition in school settings. In P. García Mayo, J. Gutiérrez-Mangado and M. Martínez Adrián (eds) *Contemporary Approaches to Second Language Acquisition*. Amsterdam: John Benjamins, pp. 27–47.

Llinares, A., T. Morton and R. Whittaker. 2012. The *Roles of Languages in CLIL*. Cambridge: Cambridge University Press.

Lock, G., and A. Tsui. 2000. Customising linguistics: Developing an electronic grammar database for teachers. *Language Awareness* 9(1): 17–33.

Macken-Horarik, M., K. Love and K. Unsworth. 2011. A grammatics 'good enough' for school English in the twenty-first century: Four challenges in realising the potential. *Australian Journal of Language and Literacy* 34(1): 9–23.

Marshall, S. 2006. Guiding senior secondary students towards writing academically valued responses to poetry. In R. Whittaker, M. O'Donnell and A. McCabe (eds) *Language and Literacy: Functional Approaches*. London: Bloomsbury, pp. 251–65.

Martin, J.R. 1999. Mentoring semogenesis: 'Genre-based' literacy pedagogy. In F. Christie (ed.) *Pedagogy and the Shaping of Consciousness: Linguistic and Social Processes*. London: Cassell, pp. 123–55.

Martin, J.R. 2006. Metadiscourse: Designing interaction in genre-based literacy programmes. In R. Whittaker, M. O'Donnell and A. McCabe (eds) *Language and Literacy: Functional Approaches*. London: Bloomsbury, pp. 95–122.

Matthiessen, C.M.I.M. 2006. Educating for advanced foreign language capacities. In H. Byrnes (ed.) *Advanced Language Learning: The Contribution of Halliday and Vygotsky*. London: Continuum, pp. 31–57.

Maxwell-Reid, C. 2014. Genre in the teaching of English in Hong Kong: A perspective from systemic functional linguistics. In D. Coniam (ed.) *English Language Education and Assessment: Recent Developments in Hong Kong and the Chinese Mainland*. New York: Springer, pp. 87–102.

McCabe, A., and I. Alonso Belmonte. 2006. Focussing on form without formulae? A reflection on grammar teaching. *Estudios de filología moderna* 5(6): 111–20.

McCabe, A., and C. Gallagher. 2008. The role of the nominal group in undergraduate academic writing. In C. Jones and E. Ventola (eds) *New Developments in the Study of Ideational Meaning: From Language to Multimodality*. London: Equinox, pp. 189–208.

McCabe, A., C. Gledhill and X. Liu. 2015. Systemic functional linguistics and English language teaching. *TESOL International Journal* 10(1): 1–10.

Melrose, R. 1995. *The Communicative Syllabus: A Systemic-Functional Approach to Language Teaching*. London: Pinter.

Mohan, B., and J. Huang. 2002. Assessing the integration of language and content in a Mandarin as a foreign language classroom. *Linguistics and Education* 13(3): 407–35.

Musgrave, J., and J. Parkinson. 2014. Getting to grips with noun groups. *ELT Journal* 68(2): 145–54.

Nitta, R., and S. Gardner. 2005. Consciousness-raising and practice in ELT course books. *ELT Journal* 59(1): 3–13.

Odlin, T. (ed.). 1994. *Perspectives on Pedagogical Grammar*. Cambridge: Cambridge University Press.

Ortega, L. 2009. *Understanding Second Language Acquisition*. London: Hodder Education.

Pavlenko, A., and J.P. Lantolf. 2000. Second language learning as participation and the (re)construction of selves. In J.P. Lantolf (ed.) *Sociocultural Theory and Second Language Learning*. Oxford: Oxford University Press, pp. 155–77.

Perrett, G. 2000. Researching second and foreign language development. In L. Unsworth (ed.) *Researching Language in Schools and Communities: Functional Linguistic Perspectives*. London and Washington, DC: Cassell, pp. 87–110.

Polias, J., and B. Dare. 2006. Towards a pedagogical grammar. In R. Whittaker, M. O'Donnell and A. McCabe (eds) *Language and Literacy: Functional Approaches*. London: Bloomsbury, pp. 123–43.

Polias, J., and G. Forey. 2015. Teaching through English: Maximal input in meaning making. In D. Miller and P. Bayley (eds) *Hybridity in Systemic Functional Linguistics*. London: Bloomsbury, pp. 109–32.

Praxedes Filho, P.H.L. 2013. Interlanguage lexicogrammatical fossilization or not? That's an SFL-related question from the viewpoint of choice. In L. Fontaine, T. Bartlett and G. O'Grady (eds) *Systemic Functional Linguistics: Exploring Choice*. Cambridge: Cambridge University Press, pp. 474–92.

Ramzan, Y., and E. Thomson. 2013. Modelling writing: Using the genre approach in the Japanese as a foreign language classroom. In E. Thomson and W.S. Armour (eds) *Systemic Functional Perspectives of Japanese: Descriptions and Applications*. London: Equinox, pp. 243–72.

Richards, J.C., and T.S. Rodgers. 2001. *Approaches and Methods in Language Teaching*. Cambridge: Cambridge University Press.

Ritchie, W.C., and T.K. Bhatia. 2009. *The New Handbook of Second Language Acquisition*. Bingley: Emerald.

Rose, D. 2014. When grammar is not enough: Designing a pedagogic metalanguage. Paper presented at the 41st Congreso Internacional de Lingüística Sistémico-Funcional. Mendoza, Argentina, 14–19 April.

Rose, D. Forthcoming. Building a pedagogic metalanguage. In J.R. Martin (ed.) *Appliable Linguistics and Academic Discourse*. Shanghai: Shanghai Jiao Tong University Press.

Rose, D., and J.R. Martin. 2012. *Learning to Write, Reading to Learn: Genre, Knowledge and Pedagogy in the Sydney School*. London: Equinox.

Rothery, J., and M. Stenglin. 1994. *Spine-Chilling Stories: A Unit of Work for Junior Secondary English*. Sydney: Metropolitan East Disadvantaged Schools Program.

Royce, T. 2007. Multimodal communicative competence in second language contexts. In T.D. Royce and W.L. Bowcher (eds) *New Directions in the Analysis of Multimodal Discourse*. Mahwah, NJ: Lawrence Erlbaum, pp. 361–403.

Schleppegrell, M.J. 2013. The role of metalanguage in supporting academic language development. *Language Learning* 63: 153–70.

Steiner, E. 1997. Systemic functional linguistics and its application to foreign language teaching. *Estudios de Linguistica Aplicada* 26: 15–27.

Swales, J.M. 1990. *Genre Analysis: English in Academic and Research Settings*. Cambridge: Cambridge University Press.

Thompson, G. 1996. Some misconceptions about communicative language teaching. *ELT Journal* 50(1): 9–15.

Thornbury, S. 2013. P is for pedagogic grammar. *An A to Z of ELT*, 24 February. Available online at http://scottthornbury.wordpress.com/2013/02/24/p-is-for-pedagogic-grammar/.

Thorne, S. 2000. Second language acquisition theory and the truth(s) about relativity. In J. Lantolf (ed.) *Sociocultural Theory and Second Language Learning*. Oxford: Oxford University Press, pp. 219–43.

Tomlin, R.S. 1994. Functional grammars, pedagogical grammars, and communicative language teaching. In T. Odlin (ed.) *Perspectives on Pedagogical Grammar*. Cambridge: Cambridge University Press, pp. 140–78.

Unsworth, L. 2001. *Teaching Multiliteracies across the Curriculum: Changing Contexts of Text and Image in Classroom Practice*. Buckingham: Open University Press.

Unsworth, L. 2006. Towards a metalanguage for multiliteracies education: Describing the meaning-making resources of language-image interaction. *English Teaching: Practice and Critique* 5(1): 55–76.

Veel, R. 2006. The Write it Right project: Linguistic modelling of secondary school and the workplace. In R. Whittaker, M. O'Donnell and A. McCabe (eds) *Language and Literacy: Functional Approaches*. London: Bloomsbury, pp. 66–92.

Vygotsky, L. 1978. *Mind in Society: The Development of Higher Psychological Processes*. Cambridge, MA: Harvard University Press.

Walker, E. 2010. A systemic functional contribution to planning academic genre teaching in a bilingual education context. *Language Awareness* 19(2): 73–87.

Wells, G. 1994. The complementary contributions of Halliday and Vygotsky to a language-based theory of learning. *Linguistics and Education* 6(1): 41–90.

Westney, P. 1994. Rules and pedagogic grammar. In T. Odlin (ed.) *Perspectives on Pedagogical Grammar*. Cambridge: Cambridge University Press, pp. 72–96.

Widdowson, H.G. 2009. The linguistic perspective. In K. Knapp and B. Seidlhofer (eds) *Handbook of Foreign Language Communication and Learning* (Handbook of Applied Linguistics 6). Berlin: de Gruyter, pp. 193–218.

Wilkins, D. 1976. *Notional Syllabuses: A Taxonomy and Its Relevance to Foreign Language Curriculum Development*. Oxford: Oxford University Press.

Systemic functional linguistics and code theory

Karl Maton and Y. J. Doran

Introduction

No theory is an island. In the case of systemic functional linguistics (SFL), its most long-standing and intense relationship has been with code theory, a sociological framework originated by Basil Bernstein that has recently been developed into Legitimation Code Theory (LCT) (Maton 2014b). From their beginnings, scholars developing these approaches have engaged in exchanges over a wide range of issues, sparking advances in both frameworks, posing questions to each other and providing fresh insights on persistent concerns. Indeed, in recent years, this dialogue has intensified as SFL and LCT have become increasingly used together in joint analyses of shared data (Martin and Maton 2013; Vidal Lizama 2014; Hood 2016). These genuinely interdisciplinary projects are leading to a growing number of fundamental innovations in both approaches and the emergence of a generation of scholars who are theoretically 'bilingual'. With such intertwined biographies, then, to understand SFL, one must understand its exchanges with code theory.

This chapter explores relations between the two theories, the forms that these exchanges have taken and how they have shaped each other. We consider the past, present and possible future natures of this dialogue. First, we trace the evolving history of exchanges, outline the advances that they encouraged and highlight the foundations each phase laid for future exchanges. Second, we explore current close collaborations between SFL and LCT in which research is productively utilising both approaches in interdisciplinary analyses of shared data. Finally, we consider possible paths for future collaboration, and offer insights into why SFL and code theory are working so effectively together across an ever-widening range of issues, topics and contexts.

A history of dialogue

Exchanges between SFL and code theory can be traced back to the 1960s. During the course of this history, the relationship has evolved as the focus of substantive studies changed and each theory developed. The direction and intensity of influences between the theories have also ebbed and flowed, waxed and waned. Extending Martin (2011), we will highlight five principal phases of exchange that differ in content and form, and thereby serve to illustrate this rich and variegated history. Table 38.1 summarises when these five phases of exchange began and the key concepts at stake in each. Of course, such divisions in a continuously unfolding history are intended to be heuristic, rather than definitive. Identifying distinct 'phases' in an ongoing dialogue between theories that are themselves developing at the same time is not straightforward. Phases overlap one another as conversations continue. Each phase evolves, such that further divisions could be added. What we describe as 'phase I', for example, comprises at least two periods of intense activity between which there was considerable conceptual development ('semantic variation' was coined only in the 1980s). However, our aim is not to make a map as big as the country, but rather to briefly illustrate more than fifty years of dialogue between two complex approaches in a short chapter. Thus, in addition to stating the obvious points that our account is necessarily partial and focused more on how exchanges with code theory have shaped SFL than vice versa, three key attributes are worth briefly highlighting.

1   The progression summarised in Table 38.1 is sedimental: later phases add to, rather than replace, existing phases.
2   The concepts listed are not the only theoretical ideas enacted during these exchanges, but those that we consider most at risk of change in each phase as interdisciplinary dialogue helped to shape each theory's development.
3   This is not a summary of the intellectual history of each theory. Often, concepts central to a phase of dialogue were created separately, earlier and for different purposes. The SFL variable of field, for example, was initially developed in the 1960s (see Bartlett and Bowcher, both this volume) and became a focus of research in educational linguistics during the 1980s (Rose and Martin 2012), but assumed centrality in exchanges with code theory, as a key concept at risk, only during the 2000s (Table 38.1).

Caveats stated, we shall now focus on phases I–III, which established foundations for the current and ongoing intensive collaborations between the two approaches.

Table 38.1 Summary of principal phases of exchange between code theory and SFL

Phase	Period began	CONCEPTS CENTRAL TO PHASE OF EXCHANGE FROM:	
		Code theory	Systemic functional linguistics
I	1960s, 1980s–	coding orientation	linguistic variation, semantic variation
II	1990s–	pedagogic discourse	genre-based literacy
III	Early 2000s–	knowledge structure	field
IV	Mid-2000s–	LCT: Specialisation dimension (specialisation codes, knowledge–knower structures, insights, gazes, etc.)	individuation/affiliation, field, appraisal, etc.
V	2010s–	LCT: Semantics dimension (semantic gravity, semantic density, semantic profiling, etc.), constellations and cosmologies	mode, field, appraisal, grammatical metaphor, technicality, individuation/affiliation, literacy, iconography, etc.

Phase I: exploring variation

A first phase of dialogue had begun in earnest by the 1960s, inspired by discussions among Basil Bernstein, Michael Halliday and Ruqaiya Hasan. This phase centred, on the one hand, on Bernstein's (1971) notion of *coding orientation*, which conceptualised the ways in which actors' dispositions are shaped by their social backgrounds and, on the other hand, what later came to be known as 'semantic variation' – that is, the social distribution of these orientations to meaning (Hasan 2009). This phase was characterised by mutual influence on ways of thinking. For example, Bernstein (1995: 398) later stated that, thanks to discussions with Halliday and Hasan, 'it became possible for me to think about linguistics in sociological terms and sociology in linguistic terms', and that, despite shifting his focus from linguistic to educational practices, SFL 'continued to provide a creative dialogue and tension'.

The phase also involved more directly conceptual relations. In particular, SFL provided a means of grounding Bernstein's early sociolinguistic framework. From the outset, Bernstein had attempted to specify the variation of actors' dispositions linguistically. In 1959, for example, he distinguished 'public language' from 'formal language' through their relative complexity of syntax and frequency of conjunctions, adverbs and adjectives (Bernstein 1971: 31). Such linguistic features were initially characterised in formal and traditional terms, with minimal reference to meaning. However, by the end of the 1960s, Bernstein and his colleagues at the Sociological Research Unit (SRU) in the Institute of Education were engaging with Halliday's meaning-based grammar (Bateman, this volume), developed nearby at University College London. Using these tools, SRU researchers were able to make generalisations across quantitative data. This is illustrated by studies collected in the second volume of *Class, Codes and Control* (Bernstein 1973). For example, Hawkins (1973) focused on the use of reference within the nominal group by 5-year-old children of different social classes. The study utilised Halliday's newly developed (although not yet published) grammar of the *nominal group*, in conjunction with Hasan's distinction between *anaphoric* (looking back), *cataphoric* (looking forward) and *exophoric* (looking out to the situation) reference (Halliday and Hasan 1976). A large set of language data was systematically coded, finding statistically significant differences in language use between working-class and middle-class children. In effect, Hawkins used SFL as a means of translating between code theory and empirical data.

However, SFL did not yet possess sufficient resources for probing the social system to the extent required by code theory. Halliday (1995: 135) later suggested that, at this stage of development, the framework was unable to address the subtle features of grammar critical to the nuanced distinctions needed for sociological concerns with the social distribution of coding orientations. Thus, although already elaborate in comparison with other theories of language, SFL required further development before it could respond to questions posed by code theory. Over the coming decades, SFL would steadily develop its resources in ways that reanimated this exchange.

The SRU, which had brought linguists and sociologists together into close collaboration, was closed by Bernstein during the early 1970s. Nonetheless, Ruqaiya Hasan, who relocated to Sydney in 1976, maintained this focus on semantic variation within a major study of mother–child interactions. Semantic networks were developed that built upon those developed at the SRU (Turner 1973), to be generalisable across language contexts (Hasan 2009). These networks drew upon the rich functional grammar that had been developed by Halliday (Halliday and Matthiessen 2014), allowing Hasan to elaborate the semantic description in ways sufficiently sensitive to explore relations between coding orientation, social class and gender in discourse involving mothers and young children. Using these tools, Hasan (2009) found significant differences between the meanings made by mothers depending on whether the main breadwinner of the household occupied a profession of higher or lower autonomy. Hasan's corpus comprised naturally occurring data rather than responses to interview questions or language-eliciting tasks, as had characterised SRU studies (Bernstein 1973). This represented substantial evidence for the kinds of differences in the meaning-making resources of social classes that Bernstein (1971) had postulated. Such studies have continued, including Cloran's development of rhetorical units to explore aspects of context-dependence and Williams' study of semantic variation in children's joint book reading (Hasan et al. 2007).

Phase I was thus characterised by two principal relations between SFL and code theory. One involved mutual inspiration in viewing their respective objects of study: code theorists began thinking about sociology in linguistic terms and systemic functional linguists began thinking about linguistics in sociological terms (Bernstein 1995). The other involved adaptation of concepts from Bernstein's early sociolinguistic framework to analyse what came to be known as 'semantic variation' and, as a result, the development of more powerful linguistic tools with which to analyse variation in meaning. This phase not only continues to bear fruit, but also laid foundations for decades of exchanges between code theory and SFL that reaches to the current day.

Phase II: theorising pedagogy

During the early 1990s, a second phase of interaction emerged involving the literacy work of the 'Sydney School' (Rose and Martin 2012) and Bernstein's (1977, 1990) theorisation of pedagogic discourse. The exchange centred on the concern of scholars in Australia, including J.R. Martin, Joan Rothery and Frances Christie, with developing a genre-based literacy pedagogy. This pedagogy moves beyond the false dichotomy of didacticism versus progressivism that dominates educational debates in the Anglophone world. The 'teaching/learning cycles' designed to implement this pedagogy enable teachers to integrate guidance, interaction and student creativity through clear stages of interaction (deconstruction, joint construction, individual construction). The aim is for students to gain control of the genres that they must read and write if they are to progress successfully through their formal education and working lives (see Gardener, this volume).

Genre-based pedagogy initially grew out of the language-based theory of learning developed by Halliday (1993) and was strongly influenced by Painter's (1989) research on child language. In terms of dialogue with code theory, Sydney school scholars drew on Bernstein's (1977) concepts of 'classification' (that is, the strength of boundaries between contexts or categories) and 'framing' (the strength of control within contexts or categories) to reflect productively upon shifts made by teachers and students as they moved through the cycles (Martin 2011). These concepts also helped to conceptualise the ways in which genre-based pedagogy drew on the strengths and avoided the limitations of both traditional and progressivist pedagogies (which Bernstein conceptualised as 'visible' and 'invisible' forms of pedagogy) to empower students, many of whom were otherwise denied access to the bases of educational success (Martin 1999).

A second point of dialogue arose from the reception that genre-based pedagogy encountered as it challenged both traditional and progressivist approaches to literacy pedagogy. Proponents became increasingly puzzled by the highly negative responses of a range of commentators. For members of the Sydney school, Bernstein's (1990) account of how pedagogies are sponsored by social groupings whose coding orientations they propagate helped to explain this negative response, while his typology of pedagogies positioned their work as 'subversive' for existing social inequalities. As Martin (2011: 38–9) described:

> We knew as an issue of social justice that we were attempting to redistribute the literacy resources of the culture, so that working class, migrant and indigenous learners excluded by traditional pedagogies and further marginalized by progressive ones could access the powerful forms of discourse they needed to renegotiate their position in society. But until studying Bernstein we did not understand the traditional and progressive debate as a struggle over education between factions of the middle class, and our own 'othered' position in relation to these debates. Bernstein's topology of pedagogies immeasurably clarified our stance and the friction we caused and heartened us greatly in our determination to make our political project succeed.

Phase II thus involved Sydney school scholars 'learning to think sociologically about educational linguistics' (Martin 2011: 40). However, in contrast to phase I, the influence was less mutual. At the time, code theorists knew little of Sydney school work, at least until a 1996 conference at the University of Melbourne organised by Frances Christie (1999) at which Bernstein was a keynote speaker. One reason for this was the geographical distance between the main centres of each theory: principal players were not in close proximity. Moreover, the sociology of education in the United Kingdom was under sustained attack from a series of Conservative governments, leading many sociologists to focus on local survival and discouraging engagement with interventionist research. Nonetheless, the pedagogic work of SFL has continued productively (Rose and Martin 2012; Martin and Doran 2015), providing foundational knowledge and values integral to the training of many linguistic scholars who became central to subsequent exchanges.

Phase III: laying foundations

Energised by two interdisciplinary conferences held at the University of Sydney in 2004 (Christie and Martin 2007) and 2008 (Christie and Maton 2011), a third phase of exchange focused on questions of disciplinarity. This exchange explored the different forms taken by intellectual and educational fields in terms of what Bernstein (2000) conceptualised as 'knowledge structures' and their expression through semiosis – specifically – the register categories of field (accounting for what is happening or being discussed) and mode (what role language and other semiotic systems are playing), as conceptualised by Martin (1992) – and the role of grammatical metaphor and technicality (Martin 2007). This phase gave rise to a renewed dialogue, and raised questions that laid foundations for the intense collaborations that were to follow in phases IV and V.

SFL attempted to come to grips with the semiotic basis for knowledge structures, and thereby to develop the tools to make this visible in linguistic and multimodal texts. However, it became clear that the dichotomous types offered by Bernstein's (2000) model – *vertical discourse* and *horizontal discourse* to conceptualise everyday and academic knowledges; *hierarchical knowledge structures* and *horizontal knowledge structures* to conceptualise different kinds of academic knowledge – needed development. SFL posed questions of code theory as attempts to enact the concepts in research quickly foundered. While good to think with, the concepts proved less useful to analyse with: they were pregnant with questions that required theoretical development to answer (Maton 2014b). Put simply, their defining characteristics were vague or allusive, and the organising principles underlying discourses and knowledge structures were untheorised. The need, then, was for concepts that built on these ideas to excavate the organising principles of different knowledge practices and which could be used in substantive studies. However, the raising of such questions among protagonists once again in close personal contact testify to the significance of this phase. Scholars of each theory were seriously engaging with ideas from the other framework, and engaging in genuine dialogue over how those ideas could help to solve substantive problems of research and practice. This phase thereby prepared the way for a period of dramatic expansion and intensification in exchanges between SFL and what was becoming a revitalised code theory.

Current collaborations

Phases IV and V of exchanges have been characterised by shifts in the focus, form and dynamic of exchanges that mark both new developments and a return to origins. These phases involve Legitimation Code Theory, which extends and integrates Bernstein's framework to provide new tools, foci and avenues of exchange. At the same time, LCT has enabled the enrichment of existing dialogues and involved a return to the kind of intense dialogue that underpinned phase I. This continues a tradition of renovation. Development within each theory has repeatedly refocused exchanges between theories. From the viewpoint of SFL, the emergence of Halliday's functional grammar aided phase I of dialogue with Bernstein's code theory, which in turn sparked its further development and the semantic descriptions of Hasan, Cloran and others. The development of genre by the Sydney school sparked a different form of engagement with code theory in phase II. The search for a semiotic characterisation of disciplinary practices in terms of field, utilising Halliday's development of grammatical metaphor, provoked further interest in code theory by SFL scholars in phase III. Similarly, each phase was shaped by the evolution of code theory, including introducing the concept of 'coding orientations' (phase I), the theorisation of pedagogic discourse (phase II) and the modelling of 'knowledge structures' (phase III).

Phases IV and V have similarly been marked by internal evolution of each theory, although with a difference. The development of code theory into LCT not only introduces new concepts that evoke further phases of exchange, but also does so by extending and integrating concepts central to established phases, shedding fresh light on their concerns. For example, the concepts of 'specialisation codes' from LCT extend and integrate Bernstein's 'classification' and 'framing' (Maton 2014b). They effectively ask whether strengths of classification and framing refer to *epistemic relations* (between knowledge practices and their objects) or to *social relations* (between knowledge practices and their subjects). Similarly, the LCT concept of 'knowledge–knower structures' expands Bernstein's ideas to embrace not only knowledge, but also knowers (Maton 2014b). In so doing, they reveal new modalities of organising principles underlying dispositions and practices, both generating new issues for dialogue and reinvigorating notions of coding orientation, pedagogic discourse and knowledge structures.

A second kind of reinvigorated return is the extent to which SFL and LCT are being used together to analyse the same data. This partly results from a renewed proximity of key protagonists. Martin (2011: 40) emphasises the emigration of the creator of LCT, Karl Maton, to Sydney in the late 2000s as helping to catalyse the kind of adoption and adaptation of concepts within empirical studies that characterised research in phase I. The relationship between SFL and code theory is no longer one of distant influence or exchanging publications, but rather is characterised again by constant creative tension. One result of the growth of studies using both theories is the emergence of a new generation of scholars fluent in both frameworks, precipitating a potential expansion in future dialogue.

Phase IV: specialisation

From the perspective of code theory, phase IV of exchange centres on the LCT dimension of Specialisation, while phase V involves the LCT dimension of Semantics (Table 38.1).[1] In terms of substantive research, the distinction between phases is becoming less clear: many studies use both LCT dimensions alongside SFL. Nonetheless, it aligns with the temporal development of these concepts and roughly aligns with differences in foci for SFL. Phase IV has continued the existing dialogue over education, as illustrated by a growing number of studies that use both theories to explore such issues as academic writing (Hood 2016), popular education (Vidal Lizama 2014), and second-language learning (Meidell Sigsgaard 2013). These studies reveal how legitimate meaning-making has different bases across academic disciplines that require distinct complexes of semiotic strategies. However, education has not been the only focus; another line of enquiry, which we shall discuss here, explores the nature of identity and affiliation in wider society.

Research on coding orientation in phase I had shown that different social groups possess different repertoires of semiotic strategies for communication. Research on identity in phase IV builds on that work by mapping the breadth of resources deployed by people in different situations to understand the distinct personae being performed. This focus on identity and affiliation has utilised more recently developed systems of SFL, such as APPRAISAL (Martin and White 2005) and the hierarchy of individuation/affiliation (Martin 2010, 2012). In similar fashion to research in phase I, many identity studies are utilising LCT concepts as the broader theoretical scaffold with which to interpret and explain findings, and SFL as a means of translating the textual data into forms understandable by those LCT concepts.

Catalysing this research on identity has been a major study by J.R. Martin, Paul Dwyer and Michelle Zappavigna focusing on the restorative justice system of youth justice conferencing in New South Wales, Australia. The research explores how these conferences re-affiliate offending young people into the community by examining their staging, the roles assumed by participants, and the meanings articulated across language and gesture (Martin 2012). Certain participants, such as the young offender or his or her mother, have a range of options in the identities that they can perform. While giving testimony, for example, the young offender can be more or less forthcoming with his or her evidence and more or less remorseful for his or her actions, and these options affect his or her interactions with other participants in the conference. However, as the study reveals, there is no single semiotic feature that characterises each identity; rather, personae are construed through complexes of semiotic phenomena that cut across linguistic and paralinguistic systems. To capture the bases of these multifaceted practices, the investigators adapted 'specialisation codes' from LCT (Maton 2014b). As shown in Figure 38.1, the specialisation plane plots a continuum of strengths of epistemic relations (ER) between practices and their object or focus against a continuum of strengths of social relations (SR) between practices and their subject, actor or author. Each relation may be more strongly (+) or weakly (−) bounded and controlled or, simply put, more or less emphasised as the legitimate basis of practices. Together, these strengths generate four principal specialisation codes and a topological plane with infinite gradations of position.

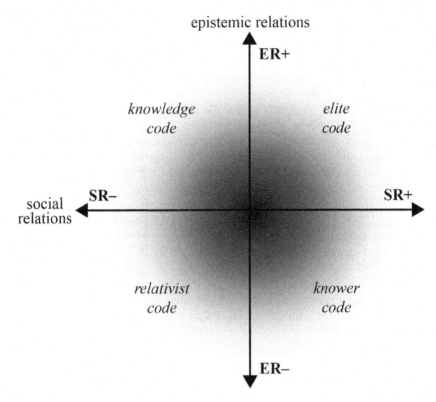

Figure 38.1 The specialisation plane
Source: Maton (2014b: 30)

Linguistic analysis of testimony by young offenders used a wide range of tools across each of the ideational, interpersonal and textual metafunctions. This produced a large set of results that were not self-evidently related. To collect these results into distinct personae, findings were analysed in terms of epistemic relations and social relations. In this particular object of study, epistemic relations (ER+/−) were realised by the ideational meanings of how detailed and forthcoming the young offender was in his or her testimony, and social relations (SR+/−) were realised by the interpersonal meanings of the degree of remorseful attitude expressed by the young offender. By plotting strengths of the ideational (how forthcoming) and the interpersonal (how remorseful) meanings on the specialisation plane, identities were generated to categorise the personae of young offenders. Four principal personae were generated: the *guilty*, who is forthcoming, but not remorseful (ER+, SR−); the *prodigal*, who is unforthcoming (often unable to remember the incident owing to intoxication at the time), but remorseful (ER−, SR+); the *redeemed*, who is both forthcoming and remorseful (ER+, SR+); and the *accused*, who is unforthcoming and only reluctantly remorseful (ER−, SR−). In LCT terms, these are analogous to knowledge codes, knower codes, élite codes and relativist codes, respectively (Figure 38.1). Thus, to develop a generalisable understanding of different performed identities, the study used SFL to translate data into terms that could be engaged by concepts adapted from LCT. This, in turn, made visible the organising principles of personae: strengths of epistemic relations and social relations.

Put another way, SFL revealed the complex array of semiotic resources marshalled by actors to achieve the personae uncovered by adapting LCT.

Such research on identity complements the fast-growing body of educational work using the Specialisation dimension of LCT alongside SFL to build on phases II and III of exchanges. In this research, different relations between the theories often obtain, although studies typically use SFL concepts to explore the complexes of linguistic resources enacted by actors to achieve knowledge practices the organising principles of which are revealed by Specialisation.

Phase V: semantics

The recent advent of phase V (see Table 38.1) has further intensified exchanges between SFL and LCT, again provoking both theories to elaborate their conceptual frameworks. This phase was catalysed by the LCT dimension of Semantics, which is centred on the concepts of 'semantic gravity', or context-dependence of meaning, and 'semantic density', or complexity of meaning (Maton 2014b). These concepts have been used in conjunction with a variety of concepts from across SFL to study a range of issues, including 'critical thinking' (Szenes et al. 2015) and ethnographic writing in the humanities (Hood 2016), and in ongoing PhD studies into museum exhibitions, digital media and mathematics in physics.

Two major studies of cumulative knowledge-building in secondary school classrooms exemplify the intimate and intense nature of dialogue characterising this phase: the Disciplinary, Knowledge and Schooling (DISKS) project, involving J.R. Martin and Karl Maton; and the Pedagogies for Knowledge-building (PEAK) project, led by Karl Maton, J.R. Martin, Len Unsworth and Sarah Howard. These projects have engaged a number of researchers, and have meshed with a series of doctoral studies and other research across linguistics, sociology and education. Both projects explore the basis for knowledge-building through language, educational technology and other multimodal communication through lessons in different subject areas (Martin and Maton 2013). Both projects have brought together LCT and SFL scholars in complementary analyses of shared data. This involves a process of recurrently alternating between parallel analyses, in which each theory separately explores the same phenomenon, and joint analyses, in which results of analyses are related together, raising issues for further parallel analyses.[2]

In contrast to existing phases, here, concepts from one theory are not being adapted by scholars from its companion approach, and neither theory is acting as a means of translation between data and concepts from the other theory. Rather SFL and LCT operate side by side as analytic frameworks providing complementary analyses that are then integrated. Put simply, SFL is enacted to analyse linguistic practices, LCT is enacted to analyse knowledge practices and these are related together to more fully explore the shared problem-situation. Such complementary analyses have not only offered new insights into classroom practice, but also posed questions to each framework, propelling theoretical innovation. As protagonists state:

> [C]ollaborative analysis of shared data raises questions with an immediacy unknown in dialogue at a distance. 'That to be explained' is in plain sight – there is less space for uncertainty or ambiguity, less opportunity to obfuscate or fudge. Under such circumstances, questions can quickly reveal the limits of concepts – they put them to the test.
>
> *Maton et al. 2016: 108*

The resulting theoretical innovation is illustrated by the LCT notion of 'semantic waves' (Maton 2013, 2014a). Semantic waves involve recurrent movements in the strengths of *semantic gravity* (between relatively decontextualized and context-dependent meanings) and *semantic density* (between simpler and more complex meanings) of knowledge practices. A growing number of studies suggest that generating semantic waves is a key to cumulative knowledge-building (Maton 2014a). SFL analysis reveals that such shifts involve a complex coordination of linguistic resources – including, but not limited to, technicality, grammatical metaphor, appraisal and periodicity – and that the selection and relation of these resources vary across subject areas. Thus the phenomenon of semantic waves revealed by LCT cuts across the metafunctions and strata of SFL. That there is no simple equivalence between the concepts of each theory is proving productive. In this case, the need to capture the linguistic resources at play in these complexes of semiotic phenomena so as to understand cumulative knowledge-building have provoked SFL scholars to rethink such fundamental concepts as the register variables field and mode (Martin and Matruglio 2013; Martin 2016).

Martin argues that linguistic theorisation of context-dependence and condensation of meaning is not as well defined or clear as many SFL scholars might assume, and that it varies widely among studies (Martin and Matruglio 2013; Martin 2016). To provide a more comprehensive account, Martin proposes the overarching concepts of 'presence' and 'mass' as linguistic analogues of semantic gravity and semantic density. *Presence* concerns context-dependence and involves *implicitness* (concerning textual resources, such as exophoric reference to the outside situation), *negotiability* (mobilising interpersonal resources, such as the arguability of a proposal or proposition) and *iconicity* (the degree of ideational grammatical metaphor). *Mass* concerns condensation of meaning and accounts for variation in the degree of meaning invoked by an instance of semiosis, embracing *technicality* (distillation of ideational meaning), *iconisation* (condensation of interpersonal meaning) and *aggregation* (consolidation of textual meaning). The concepts of 'presence' and 'mass' thus characterise the full possible array of linguistic resources potentially at stake during changes in the semantic gravity and the semantic density of knowledge practices. Not all resources may be relevant at any one time; which aspects of presence and mass are activated in any given situation is thus a matter for empirical research. While detailed discussion of these concepts is beyond the scope of this chapter, the key point here is that differences between LCT and SFL are productive: concepts from one theory highlight issues previously obscured by the architecture of the other theory.

This is not a one-way street. Joint analyses of classroom practices with SFL underlined the need for more refined means of relating the concepts of semantic gravity and semantic density to empirical data (Maton et al. 2016). To this end, multilevel typologies have been developed that provide fine-grained categories for distinguishing the realisations of different strengths of semantic gravity and semantic density at the level of wording, word grouping, clausing and sequencing in English discourse (Maton and Doran 2016a, 2016b). These 'translation devices' allow LCT to engage with fine-grained analysis of discourse to an extent not previously available in code theory. By exploring these features of knowledge practices within the nature of discourse, they are bringing LCT analyses closer to the kind of detailed exploration of language characteristic of SFL – and the insights offered by each approach are thus able to be more closely related. Similarly, Martin's mass and presence allow SFL to mobilise its vast descriptive array to understand degrees of meaning condensation and context dependence in a more powerful way than ever before. Once more, major advances in each theory have been provoked by engagement with its companion. Moreover, developments driven by close, collaborative analyses of shared data are thereby providing a basis for even closer and more collaborative analyses.

A shared future

What enables this long-standing dialogue to remain fresh and fruitful? Space precludes discussion of the diverse theoretical attributes that have been described as shaping this dialogue (Hasan 2005; Christie and Martin 2007; Martin 2011; Maton 2012). Here, we shall simply highlight how both theories are 'realist', 'relational' and 'risk-taking'. These '3-Rs' describe interrelated features of their ontologies, internal structures and external relations to data; as such, they represent the minimum essential (although not sufficient) characteristics for fecund collaboration.

First, both theories are based on *realist* ontologies that move beyond empirical features to explore underlying organising principles. Neither theory is content with providing empiricist commentary on specific instances. Rather, each seeks to develop means for moving between concrete empirical descriptions and abstract theorisations, to enable findings from different studies to be related and mutually informative.

Second, the approaches both comprise *relational* frameworks that combine typologies and topologies and embrace change. For both theories, semiotic and sociocultural practices exhibit properties, powers and tendencies that are emergent from, and irreducible to, their constituent parts. Rather than understanding meaning-making by aggregating interactions among participants, both approaches highlight the multilayered nature of the social reality realised by any substantive instance. Accordingly, their conceptual architecture reflects this relationality in, for example, emerging hierarchies of stratification, instantiation and individuation of SFL (Bateman and Berry, both this volume), and the stratified notions of 'structures', 'codes' and 'devices' in LCT (Maton 2014b).

Third, both theories put concepts at *risk* through close engagement with real-world problem-situations. Their concepts aim for unambiguous relations to their referents, and are created from and for the exploration of real-world data. As such, every substantive study may prove even well-established and core concepts to be inadequate or in need of fundamental overhaul. Data can 'speak back' to theory, demanding clarification, refinement or revision. Neither theory is a museum piece, to be simply glossed or admired; each is continually modified and developed to account for more phenomena with greater conceptual economy.

Looking to the future, the question remains as to where collaboration may be heading. Conceptual developments inspired by exchanges have taken several forms. All phases have highlighted how each theory may allow its companion to reflect on its own object of study in fresh ways, to think sociologically about linguistics and linguistically about sociology. They have also demonstrated how dialogue catalyses intellectual advance by pointing towards issues requiring further development. More recently, though, innovation is taking a new direction in the form of conceptual development, which can act as a bridge between the approaches. The creation of 'translation devices' for enacting the LCT concepts of semantic gravity and semantic density in analysis of English discourse represents a significant step towards enabling closer joint analyses of data. Conversely, the SFL concepts of mass and presence may offer a means of connecting to those concepts. Martin and Maton (in personal communication) have suggested how the concepts from each theory relate to one another. If we consider each theory as representing a universe of meanings in which individual concepts gain meanings from relations to other concepts and to referents, then 'presence' and 'mass' function as portals between these universes, connecting a wide raft of systems in SFL to 'semantic gravity' and 'semantic density' in LCT. Conversely, the LCT concepts act as portals from the opposite direction by relating their diverse realisations in sociocultural practices across different objects of study to mass and presence in SFL. Each set of portals is sufficiently distanced both from empirical data (thus not too embedded in the phenomena specific to that theory) and from the fundamental principles at the core of each theory (such as strata and metafunction in SFL) to allow movement from one theory toward the other. By moving from the diverse array of linguistic resources to 'mass' or 'presence', and then, through these portal concepts, to 'semantic density' or 'semantic gravity' (and vice versa), one moves from one theoretical universe to another. One is never in both at the same time: the concepts are not a blend of both theories, but rather a means of enabling communication. Such portal concepts represent an exciting possible future for interdisciplinarity: the emergence of genuine means of translation that enable inter-theory movement without theoretical pidginisation or elision. This raises the tantalising question of the possibility of Janus-faced concepts designed specifically to operate in both frameworks. One must always remain mindful that the theories are complementary precisely because of their differences, but these concepts may serve to inspire further developments.

After such positivity, we should highlight that collaboration offers much potential for criticism, confusion and conflict. Such interdisciplinary developments can be terrifying for actors whose status and identity are firmly rooted in the existing state of a theory rather than in the exploration of problem-situations. Such developments can lead to claims that disciplinary purity is being diluted. Dialogue can evoke criticisms that LCT is overly influenced by SFL or SFL research using LCT is overly sociological. Such policing, however, is more concerned with struggles over status than with explanatory power. Nonetheless, criticisms highlight several potential pitfalls to be avoided. These include unclear blendings of the theory, for example where the ideational metafunction of SFL is taken as equating to epistemic relations in LCT, or the interpersonal metafunction is taken as equating to social relations. Although the former concepts may provide insight into one aspect of realisations of the latter concepts within a specific problem-situation, as explored in studies of restorative justice, they are not identical. There is also the potential for the object of study of each theory to be reduced to that of the other – that is, knowledge practices to linguistic practices or vice versa. The gains offered by using the two theories flow not from where one displaces the other, but from where they complement one another. As we have seen, this complementarity provokes creative tension, pushing each theory to develop greater understandings.

The collaboration between SFL and LCT is ongoing, pushing into areas that extend well beyond language in classrooms. Current work is exploring the potential of images in building knowledge, probing the use of mathematics in moving between abstracted theory and tangible instances in the natural sciences, and combining complementary analysis of gestural semiosis in SFL and embodied knowledge in LCT to understand the meaning potential of bodily movement. Each of these areas and many more are being analysed in interdisciplinary studies, with the two theories working in intensive collaboration, offering complementary perspectives. There are still, however, many areas of SFL that have yet to be explored in relation to LCT and there are also as yet relatively underused conceptual dimensions of LCT that will gain much from dialogue with SFL. All of these have the potential to push both theories into new realms. Side by side, the theories continue to march forward into the unknown together.

Notes

1 LCT comprises five 'dimensions', each exploring different organising principles of practice (Maton 2014b).
2 See Maton et al. (2016) on this methodology.

References

Bernstein, B. 1971. *Class, Codes and Control, Vol. I: Theoretical Studies towards a Sociology of Language*. London: Routledge & Kegan Paul.
Bernstein, B. (ed.). 1973. *Class, Codes and Control, Vol. II: Applied Studies towards a Sociology of Language*. London: Routledge & Kegan Paul.
Bernstein, B. 1977. *Class, Codes and Control, Vol. III: Towards a Theory of Educational Transmissions*. 2nd edn. London: Routledge & Kegan Paul.
Bernstein, B. 1990. *Class, Codes and Control, Vol. IV: The Structuring of Pedagogic Discourse*. London: Routledge.
Bernstein, B. 1995. A response. In A. Sadovnik (ed.) *Knowledge and Pedagogy*. Norwood, NJ: Ablex, pp. 385–424.
Bernstein, B. 2000. *Pedagogy, Symbolic Control and Identity: Theory, Research, Critique*. Rev'd edn. Oxford: Rowman & Littleford.
Christie, F. (ed.). 1999. *Pedagogy and the Shaping of Consciousness*. London: Cassell.
Christie, F., and J.R. Martin (eds). 2007. *Language, Knowledge and Pedagogy: Functional Linguistic and Sociological Perspectives*. London: Continuum.
Christie, F., and K. Maton (eds). 2011. *Disciplinarity: Functional Linguistic and Sociological Perspectives*. London: Continuum.
Halliday, M.A.K. 1993. Towards a language-based theory of learning. *Linguistics and Education* 5(2): 93–116.
Halliday, M.A.K. 1995. Language and the theory of codes. In A. Sadovnik (ed.) *Knowledge and Pedagogy*. Norwood, NJ: Ablex, pp. 127–44.
Halliday, M.A.K., and R. Hasan. 1976. *Cohesion in English*. London: Longman.
Halliday, M.A.K. and C.M.I.M. Matthiessen. 2014. *Halliday's Introduction to Functional Grammar*. 4th edn. London: Routledge.
Hasan, R. 2005. *Language, Society and Consciousness*. London: Equinox.
Hasan, R. 2009. *Semantic Variation: Meaning in Society and in Sociolinguistics*. London: Equinox.
Hasan, R., C. Cloran, G. Williams and A. Lukin. 2007. Semantic networks: The description of linguistic meaning in SFL. In R. Hasan, C.M.I.M. Matthiessen and J.J. Webster (eds) *Continuing Discourse on Language, Vol. 2*. London: Equinox, pp. 697–738.
Hawkins, P.R. 1973. Social class, the nominal group and reference. In B. Bernstein (ed.) *Class, Codes and Control, Vol. II*. London: Routledge & Kegan Paul, pp. 81–92.
Hood, S. 2016. Ethnographies on the move, stories on the rise: Methods in the humanities. In K. Maton, S. Hood and S. Shay (eds) *Knowledge-Building*. London: Routledge, pp. 117–37.
Martin, J.R. 1992. *English Text: System and Structure*. Amsterdam: John Benjamins.
Martin, J.R. 1999. Mentoring semogenesis, 'genre-based' literacy pedagogy. In F. Christie (ed.) *Pedagogy and the Shaping of Consciousness*. London: Cassell, pp. 123–55.
Martin, J.R. 2007. Construing knowledge: A functional linguistic perspective. In F. Christie and J. R. Martin (eds) *Language, Knowledge and Pedagogy*. London: Continuum, pp. 34–64.
Martin, J.R. 2010. Semantic variation: Modelling realization, instantiation and individuation in social semiosis. In M. Bednarek and J.R. Martin (eds) *New Discourse on Language*. London: Continuum, pp. 1–34.
Martin, J.R. 2011. Bridging troubled waters: Interdisciplinarity and what makes it stick. In F. Christie and K. Maton (eds) *Disciplinarity*. London: Continuum, pp. 35–61.
Martin, J.R. 2012. *Collected Works of J.R. Martin, Vol. 8: Forensic Linguistics*. Shanghai: Shanghai Jiao Tong University Press.
Martin, J.R. 2016. Revisiting field: Specialized knowledge in ancient history and biology secondary school discourse. *Onomázein*.
Martin, J.R., and Y.J. Doran (eds). 2015. *Language in Education, Vol. 5: Critical Concepts in Systemic Functional Linguistics*. London: Routledge.
Martin, J.R., and K. Maton (eds). 2013. Cumulative knowledge-building in secondary schooling. *Linguistics and Education* 24(1): 1–74.

Martin, J.R., and E. Matruglio. 2013. Revisiting mode: Context in/dependency in ancient history class-room discourse. In H. Guowen, Z. Delu and Y. Xinzhang (eds) *Studies in Functional Linguistics and Discourse Analysis, Vol. 5*. Beijing: Higher Education Press, pp. 72–95.

Martin, J.R., and P.R.R. White. 2005. *Language of Evaluation: Appraisal in English*. Basingstoke: Palgrave Macmillan.

Maton, K. 2012. The next generation: Interdisciplinary research into strange new worlds. Paper presented at 39th International Systemic Functional Congress, Sydney, July.

Maton, K. 2013. Making semantic waves: A key to cumulative knowledge-building. *Linguistics and Education* 24(1): 8–22.

Maton, K. 2014a. Building powerful knowledge: The significance of semantic waves. In B. Barrett and E. Rata (eds) *Knowledge and the Future of the Curriculum*. Basingstoke: Palgrave Macmillan, pp. 181–97.

Maton, K. 2014b. *Knowledge and Knowers: Towards a Realist Sociology of Education*. London: Routledge.

Maton, K. 2016. Legitimation Code Theory: Building knowledge about knowledge-building. In K. Maton, S. Hood and S. Shay (eds) *Knowledge-Building: Educational Studies in Legitimation Code Theory*. London, Routledge, pp. 1–23.

Maton, K., and Y.J. Doran. 2016a. Semantic density: A translation device for revealing complexity of knowledge practices in discourse, part 1 – Wording. *Onomázein*.

Maton, K., and Y.J. Doran. 2016b. Condensation: A translation device for revealing complexity of knowledge practices in discourse, part 2 – clausing and sequencing. *Onomázein*.

Maton, K., J.R. Martin and E. Matruglio. 2016. LCT and systemic functional linguistics: Enacting complementary theories for explanatory power. In K. Maton, S. Hood and S. Shay (eds) *Knowledge-Building: Educational Studies in Legitimation Code Theory*. London, Routledge, pp. 93–113.

Meidell Sigsgaard, A.-V. 2013. Who knows what? The teaching of knowledge and knowers in a fifth grade Danish as a second language classroom. Unpublished PhD thesis. Aarhus University, Denmark.

Painter, C. 1989. Learning language: A functional view of language development. In R. Hasan and J.R. Martin (eds) *Language Development*, Norwood, NJ: Ablex, pp. 19–65.

Rose, D., and J.R. Martin. 2012. *Learning to Write, Reading to Learn: Genre, Knowledge and Pedagogy in the Sydney School*. London: Equinox.

Szenes, E., N. Tilakaratna and K. Maton. 2015. The knowledge practices of critical thinking. In M. Davies and R. Barnett (eds) *The Palgrave Handbook of Critical Thinking in Higher Education*. Basingstoke: Palgrave Macmillan, pp. 573–91.

Turner, G.J. 1973. Social class and children's language of control at age five and age seven. In B. Bernstein (ed.) *Class, Codes and Control, Vol. II*. London: Routledge & Kegan Paul, pp. 135–201.

Vidal Lizama, M. 2014. Theorizing popular education as a knowledge practice: The case of Chile. Unpublished PhD thesis. University of Technology, Sydney.

39

Learning how to mean

Parent–child interaction

Clare Painter

Introduction

With the publication of *Learning How to Mean* in 1975, Halliday presented a case study of early child language development, integrating a developmental perspective into the broader theory of systemic functional linguistics (SFL). He argued there for the functional origins of the mature linguistic system, suggesting that the twin impulses of any infant – to make sense of the world and to share experience with others – explain the gradual creation and use of a language system organised on 'metafunctional' principles (Halliday and Matthiessen 2004: 29). The emphasis in this and much subsequent SFL work on language development has been on the child as a learner; that is, concerned with the child's semantic 'strategies' (Halliday 1993), with the trajectory of the child's changing language system in the first years of life (Painter 2009) and with the crucial role of language in the child's construal of reality (Halliday 1978; Painter 1999a). However, since developmental theory is firmly based on the premise that 'as well as being a cognitive process, the learning of the mother tongue is also an interactive process' (Halliday 1975: 140), it is equally important to attend closely to the role of the adult caregivers in the process, which will be the orientation taken in this chapter.

Within the broader field of child-language studies, a concern with the role of adult caregivers is certainly nothing new. Since the late 1970s, developmental psychologists and linguists have drawn attention to particular features of 'child-directed speech' (CDS) that might render it facilitative for the language-learning child, such as an exaggerated pitch range, syntactic simplicity, semantic redundancy and 'fine-tuning' of the adult 'input' (Gallaway and Richards 1994; Snow 1995). Such work arose in reaction to the influential claims of Chomsky (1975) and his followers that the structural principles of language are innate, and that the speech children hear serves only to provide a 'triggering input' for a hypothetical 'language-acquisition device'. This 'nativist hypothesis' argues that language could not, in any case, be learned from others, since 'the child hears a haphazard selection of sentences and pseudo-sentences and, of course, receives no significant instruction' (Hornstein and Lightfoot 1981: 13). While the notion of an impoverished and haphazard linguistic environment for the young child has been discredited by the work on CDS, the latter has struggled to find acceptable methods for eliciting and recording viable interactive data, for testing observations experimentally, and for demonstrating a cause–effect relation between features of the 'input' and changes in children's speech (Snow 1995).

SFL work on language development is not framed in terms of a response to the nativist hypothesis. And rather than emphasising the nature of adult speech to children, its implicit challenge to nativism consisted in its description of a three-phase process in which an emerging linguistic system is shown to evolve as a functional one serving the child's changing needs. This SFL account relies on naturalistically collected data from four different longitudinal case studies: three of children up to the age of 2-and-a-half (detailed in Halliday 1975; Painter 1984; Torr 1997); and a fourth study continuing the developmental story up to the age of 5, with a specific focus on language as a tool for learning (Painter 1999a). In each case, the data were collected by a parent-researcher using daily pen-and-paper notes and/or regular audio-taped recordings of interactions in a variety of unstructured everyday situations – a methodology aimed at ensuring naturally occurring dialogic, contextualised data.

More recently, the four case studies have been significant in SFL theory as a cornerstone of a 'language-based', as opposed to a psychological, theory of learning (Halliday 1993). In such a theory, learning is seen as a semiotic process and what is learned is correspondingly seen in terms of semiotic construals. The developmental data are important here in providing evidence for how a semiotic system might expand, for example by 'dissociating associated variables, or deconstructing and recombining' (Halliday 1993: 101). They are also important for suggesting strategies used by language-learning children, such as the 'trailer' phenomenon, whereby something new is tried out in a very limited way and then put on the back burner for a while, the child's ongoing use of comparison and contrast, and the child's temporary distinction between 'mathetic' and 'pragmatic' purposes for speech. While the articulation of a language-based theory of learning is a considerable contribution by SFL to the field of education, its continuing focus on the learner runs the danger of de-emphasising the role of the adult in the process despite the theoretical importance of the communicative partner. This, in turn, risks allowing the theory to appear more thoroughly compatible with child-centred, constructivist approaches to education deriving from Piaget's (1977) psychology than is actually the case.

This chapter will therefore use the same case study data to consider more explicitly how SFL views the role of the adult in the child's mastery of language. It will be argued that the adult plays a guiding role here – one that may also be interpreted in terms of the notion of 'scaffolding', deriving from Vygotsky's (1978) psychology – and that what might be termed the 'asymmetrical dyad' is the key to the gradual expansion and reorganisation of the child's linguistic system. As will be shown, this is explained in SFL theory in terms of the relation between system (as a potential for meaning) and the instance (as an occasion of dialogic text), and has implications for language learning later in life.

Interaction before language

Over the past forty years, the picture of the infant drawn from Piaget's work has been radically challenged by new research. Where Piaget (1977) believed that an infant begins in a state of absolute 'egocentrism' and only gradually becomes a social being, a wealth of observational and experimental studies now support the view that 'human selves are born not as individuals but as sociable persons seeking other human selves' (Trevarthen 2009: 511). Fine-grained studies of adult–child interaction in the very earliest weeks and months of life, as reported in Reddy (2008), show that, long before there is any exchange of signs, caregivers and infants interact with each other in what have been termed 'proto-conversations', in which infant gazes, vocalisations, head and body movements are all brought into play in relation to the adult's vocal and facial behaviour, so that '[b]oth actors, adult and infant . . . move together in dialogue, alternating and synchronizing moves to generate cycles of . . . address and reply' (Trevarthen 2009: 512).

Experimental studies (Murray and Trevarthen 1985) show that the infant's behaviour is contingent upon the mother's responses and also that the dyad's communicative history is significant. This is highlighted in Trevarthen's (2005: 70) account of an episode with 6-month-old baby Emma, who has enjoyed a turn-taking game of 'clap-a-handies' with her mother, but who shows 'clear expressions of embarrassment or shame' when the mother is replaced by a stranger who fails to interpret Emma's attempts to show handclapping. The importance of shared communicative experience is clear here and remains a perceptible theme in observations not only of pre-linguistic interaction, but also throughout the language development process.

By the end of the first year of life, the interactions between caregiver and child have progressed to a point at which the child is consistently using specific (but idiosyncratic) vocalisations to bring the outside world into his or her interactions and to make demands on the other or to share interest in something. In terms of the child's language, this is the 'protolanguage' phase, described in detail in the SFL case studies and also discussed elsewhere in the child language literature (for example Blake 2001: ch. 2). In terms of the adult's role with a protolanguage speaker, the two snippets of interaction in examples (1) and (2) indicate typical and repeated patterns. The child's age here and elsewhere is indicated in 'years; months; days' at the beginning of each text. 'H' stands for Hal, the child, and 'M' for the mother.

(1) (1;1;15) (M switches light on)
    H: da!
    M: That's the light, isn't it? The light.

(2) (1;2;0) (M carrying H as they enter room)
    M: Where's the light? Where's the light?
    (H looks at her intently, then up at the light)
    M: It's there, isn't it? Where's the light?
    H: dja (points and looks up at light)
    M: Yes
    H: (points) da
    M: Yes, clever boy.
    H: da; da; da dja; da (points at another light fitting)
    M: Mm, that one's not on.

In example (1), we see Hal taking an interest in something – the ceiling light – and communicating this with his own protolanguage vocalisation *da*. The mother acknowledges his interest and names the item for him. Such exchanges would happen repeatedly when a light came on. By the time of example (2), a fortnight later, Hal has enough familiarity with the word *light* to recognise it and to respond to the mother's invitation to display that knowledge. In this way, through their shared communicative history and the mother's awareness of his interests, Hal is guided into participating in the patterns of dialogue involving statement and acknowledgement, question and answer, well before he himself has the ability to utter a single word of English.

The adult 'tracker' provides scaffolding

It is not necessary to rely on data from SFL case studies to make the point that infants participate in meaningful dialogue well before using the mother tongue. A landmark study of the way in which adults guide children into recognising and responding to 'known answer' questions was published by Ninio and Bruner in 1978. They tracked a single mother ('M') and child ('C') over a period of eighteen months in the context of interacting over picture books, observing the highly predictable and consistent structure of the conversations, as shown in example (3), in which their analysis of the mother's dialogic moves has been reproduced alongside the utterances (Ninio and Bruner 1978: 6–7):

(3)   (1;1;1)

M:	Look!	*(attentional vocative)*
C:	(Touches picture)	
M:	What are those?	*(query)*
C:	(Vocalises and smiles)	
M:	Yes, they are rabbits.	*(feedback and label)*
C:	(Vocalises, smiles and looks up at M)	
M:	(laughs) Yes, rabbit.	*(feedback and label)*
C:	(Vocalises, smiles)	
M:	Yes (Laughs).	*(feedback)*

The similarity to example (2) of Hal and his mother is obvious, and Ninio and Bruner (1978: 8) refer to the repeated and formulaic nature of such conversations as 'scaffolding' dialogues in which 'the set of possible "meanings" is both restricted and shared', facilitating the child's participation. In other words, the predictability of the dialogic structure here, managed by the mother, allows the child to focus attention on particular components of the event – namely, sharing attention to the picture, attending to the common noun name and taking a dialogic turn. As the child develops control of mother-tongue vocabulary, Bruner shows how the adult 'ups the ante', requiring the child to attend to the adult question, to supply an appropriate name in response and to monitor the adult feedback. The mother's ability to pitch her contributions at the appropriate level, of course, depends on the communicative history of the dyad.

In relation to this, Halliday (1980a: 4) makes use of an earlier notion of 'tracking', whereby speakers monitor each other's contributions:

> Now, when we come to study the infant's language development, we find the concept of 'tracking' is fundamental here too. Not only do the caregivers track the *process,* [i.e. uttered speech] they also track the *system.* Child and adult share in the creation of language. The mother knows where the child has got to (subconsciously; she is not aware she has this knowledge).

Although the point being made concerns the crucial role of shared communicative experience and agency is given to the caregiver in Halliday's description, the term 'tracking' itself can perhaps too easily be (mis)read as suggesting that the adult simply follows along passively behind the language-learning child, rather than that tracking enables the adult to guide effectively, as shown in the examples.

The term 'scaffolding', first used in relation to children learning non-linguistic tasks, more obviously assigns a tutorial role to the adult. It is theorised in psychology in terms of Vygotsky's

(1978: 86) ideas about the learner's 'zone of proximal development' (ZPD) – that is, the region between the learner's level of achievement when performing solo in some task and the level that can be achieved under adult guidance or in collaboration with more capable peers. A key point about the metaphor of scaffolding, then, is the attention it draws to the asymmetry of the adult–child dyad: the term is not simply a synonym for interaction or collaboration, but is defined as 'steps taken to reduce the degrees of freedom taken in carrying out some task so that the child can concentrate on the difficult skill she is in the process of acquiring' (Bruner 1978: 19) – an apt description of the adult's role in the snippets of interaction shown here.

One facet of the Vygotskyan argument that learning takes place in the ZPD is that the trajectory of learning is from inter-mental to intra-mental activity, or, in linguistic terms, from dialogue to monologue – something very much in line with the SFL emphasis on the primacy of dialogue (Halliday 1991; Painter 2004). This phenomenon can be readily illustrated from developmental data. In example (4), Hal is a year older than in examples (1) and (2), with hundreds more joint book 'reading' interactions under his belt. In this case, he is sitting on the floor by himself, looking at a picture book and talking:

(4) (2;1;23) (H looks at a picture book by himself)
    H: What's that? (points at picture)
    –   Train.
    –   No. What's that?
    –   Tusk.
    –   That's right. (Loudly) Tusk!

In this monologue, Hal adopts the personae of both child and adult, demonstrating with enjoyment how thoroughly he has 'internalised' their different dialogic roles. Thus not only was the vocabulary item *tusk* learned in the kinds of scaffolded conversations that Ninio and Bruner (1978) describe, but also the dialogic pedagogic genre that continues into formal education as the Initiation, Response, Feedback/Evaluation (IRF or IRE) sequence in classroom discourse (Mehan 1979).

Scaffolding stories

Perhaps the clearest example of the move from dialogue to monologue arises in relation to the scaffolding of stories. One of the most challenging linguistic tasks for a 2-year-old is to manage a monologue that presents non-current experience. When we look at children's earliest 'stories' of their personal experience in the case studies, it becomes evident that caregivers are implicit teachers here too. Example (5), taken from Halliday's (1975: 99) data charting the linguistic ontogeny of his own son, Nigel ('N'), can exemplify:

(5) (Nigel, around 1;9, recalls an outing with Mum)
    N: Bumblebee.
    M: Where was the bumblebee?
    N: Bumblebee on train.
    M: What did Mummy do?
    N: Mummy open window.
    M: Where did the bumblebee go?
    N: Bumblebee flew away.

Again, we can see that the function of the adult's 'questions' is to give the child an opportunity to display what he knows. Because they both shared the experience being related, the parent knows how to pick up the ball when the child throws out a single word and how to frame a question that will elicit a response to take the little story forwards. She then builds on this with further eliciting questions. Such examples show that even when a child has the ability to produce fully formed grammatical sentences, the task of sequencing and structuring a story into a piece of monologic discourse may yet be out of reach. It involves selecting relevant events from memory and sequencing them in such a way that there is some kind of narrative arc: too difficult for Nigel to manage solo at this age, but successfully accomplished in collaboration with his mother.

The importance of shared experience for enabling such scaffolding is shown in example (6), involving Hal at a similar age to Nigel and his mother:

(6) (2;0;0) (H returns from shopping trip with F)
   H: Stick!
   M: (baffled) Stick, eh?
   H: (pause) Horse.
   M: Oh, you've had a ride on a [rocking] horse. (A routine mall event)
   H: Ride on horsey; ride on horsey 'gain!

In this case, Hal's mother cannot help her son to take his initial utterance further because she has not shared his material experience and does not know to what incident *stick* could be referring. Receiving no support, Hal changes the topic and, this time, his mother has some inside information, this being a routine happening. Her 'recasting' of his single word into a more explicit and elaborated grammatical form allows him to continue and make the key point that he had been privileged with an extra ride.

One of the first examples of a scaffolded story in the language development literature is provided in example (7a), Halliday's (1975: 111–12) account of Nigel's story of a visit to the zoo, which was inspirational in an early application of the notion of scaffolding in the context of school education (Applebee and Langer 1983):

(7a) (1;8) (A few hours after a visit to the zoo)
   N: Try eat lid.
   F: What tried to eat the lid?
   N: Try eat lid.
   F: What tried to eat the lid?
   N: Goat . . . man said no . . . goat try eat lid . . . man said no.

Again, although the father had shared the experience, his response implicitly points out the need for an additional grammatical participant in Nigel's original utterance. Having included this key aspect to the story, Nigel adds another event and then, later in the day, reinitiates the story with his mother, who prompts him to take it even further:

(7b) (Later)
   N: Goat try eat lid . . . man said no.
   M: Why did the man no?
   N: Goat shouldn't eat lid (shaking his head *no)* good for it.
   M: The goat shouldn't eat the lid. It's not good for it.

N: Goat try eat lid . . . man said no . . . goat shouldn't eat lid (shaking his head)
      good for it.

All of these examples show how essentially monologic genres, such as personal stories, are initially created in dialogic interaction. The adult is able to play an effective role in each case in which there is shared experience to draw on and, as we have seen, may fail to enable the child to go further where this is lacking.

The system–text relation

So far, the intersubjective nature of early communications has been stressed, together with the significance of a shared communicative history that enables the adult to guide and support the communicative endeavours of the language-learning child. These key features of the enterprise of 'learning how to mean' can be inferred from the textual data, but how this process is explained more generally is in terms of the relation between system and text. In Halliday's (1993: 104–5) words:

> From acts of meaning children construe the system of language, while at the same time, from the system, they engender acts of meaning. When children learn language they are simultaneously processing text into language and activating language into text.

'System', here, refers to the overall 'meaning potential' that is language, with its three levels of discourse-semantics, lexicogrammar and phonology, all of which are realising and construing the context. In the SFL model, this overall system is modelled as comprising, at every level, dozens of individual 'systems', which are sets of opposing options, (such as 'negative' vs 'positive' for the grammatical system of polarity) (see Figure 39.1). 'Text', on the other hand, refers to actual occasions of language occurring in some situational and cultural context. The relation between system and text – between the meaning potential as a whole and the particular choices of meanings, wordings and soundings actualised in an individual text, on a specific occasion – is one of 'instantiation' (Halliday and Matthiessen 2004: 26). In other words, language in its entirety is modelled as a complex set of possibilities for meaning, with any particular instance of speech being the actualisation of specific options on a particular specific occasion.

The significant point in a developmental context is that the spoken instances from which the child is continually making sense of the underlying system are jointly constructed by the child and a conversational partner who has a larger and more complex meaning potential. In other words, in dialogic interaction, where both parties attend to meanings relevant to the child, the child learner produces utterances actualising his or her own linguistic (or protolinguistic) system built to date, but also attempts to construe the utterances of the adult, which emanate from a more developed linguistic system. Most importantly, because features of both the context and all levels of the linguistic system are instantiated in every text, the co-constructed instance can make 'visible' to the child multiple aspects both of the mature linguistic system and of the cultural context.

This last point can be briefly illustrated in relation to a further example of shared picture book reading, this time with an older child, Stephen ('S'):

(8)   (S at 2;7;1 looks at a picture book with M)
      M: (points at igloo) Do you remember what that is?
      S: Mm.

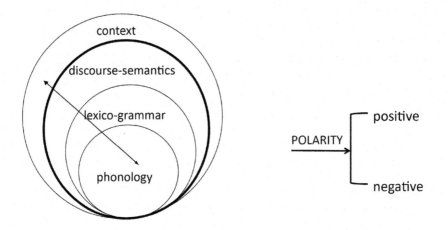

'system' as the overall 'meaning potential'

an individual 'system'

Figure 39.1 'System' in SFL

M: What is it?
S: It's a house.
M: It's a house; special house. And what's it made of?
S: Oh! Snow!
M: Yes, that's right; it's made of ice.
S: Made of ice.
M: And it's called igloo.
S: Igloo.

At the level of **context**, the conversation instantiates yet another occasion of the familiar 'book-reading' pedagogic interaction. At the level of **discourse-semantics**, the co-constructed text instantiates particular conversational moves and speech functions relevant to the genre, while at the level of **lexicogrammar**, the text instantiates relational transitivity (both attributive and identifying processes) and a small range of vocabulary items. And, as with every occasion of speech, a variety of **phonological** choices are actualised. By this time, the nature of the book-reading event and much of the language used will be highly familiar to the child – that is, part of a shared meaning potential, allowing anything that is not familiar (perhaps the word *igloo* or the phrase *made of ice*) to be a greater focus of attention.

It would be quite misleading, of course, to give the impression that the only, or even the main, context of language learning is that of the more consciously tutorial instance, using pictures as prompts. The storytelling examples show how it may well be the child who initiates the dialogue. And where the linguistic focus is on simple naming, it is still just as likely to be the child who initiates an occasion of joint attention, as in example (9):

(9)   (2;8;29) (M and S in the street; S sees a dog)
        S: (points) Look Mummy, baa baa black sheep!

M: Oh, that's not a sheep, that's a dog with a woolly coat.
It's called a poodle. Poodle.
S: Oh, poodle.
(Later)
S: That's not a lamb, no.

The point is not that adults dominate the conversations, but that they collaborate to produce texts that instantiate linguistic choices, some of which are not yet part of the child's own system, but which become available for learning in the course of the interaction.

The direction of adult guidance

Within SFL theory, language development is understood to be a multifaceted process. In Halliday's (1980b: 7) words: 'There are three facets to language development; learning language, learning through language, and learning about language. In a sense, and from a child's point of view, these three are all the same thing.' One way in which the adult's guidance in learning *through* language has been approached in SFL is through 'semantic variation' studies demonstrating how the sociocultural context is unconsciously instantiated in mothers' everyday speech to 3-and-a-half-year-old children (Hasan 2009), work sharing concerns with research outside SFL on 'language socialisation' in different cultures (Schieffelin and Ochs 1986). A second, more developmental, perspective on the adult's role in enabling learning through language is provided by the case study of Stephen, in which a major development is noted in his language between the ages of 2-and-a-half and 3-and-a-half. This comprises a syndrome of features that enable the child's talk to move away from contexts of shared observation and memory (and predictions based on these) to more generalised and hypothetical meanings in textually construed contexts (Painter 1999a, 1999b). What is significant here is that these changes are not simply impelled by the child's own cognitive concerns, but also result from the way in which the adult's conversational contributions implicitly guide him to expand his potential in ways that enable more explicit reflection on the world and on its semiotic construal.

Clearly, in the development of vocabulary, a child is learning about the world through language – learning, for example, what counts as a dog, a ball, a truck or a flower. This is initially done through 'ostensive definition' of the kind already illustrated by the examples in which adult and child point to and name particular entities in the material world or represented in picture books. However, explicit reflection on the meaning system itself requires a number of further developments. Examples (10)–(12) show single instances that are typical of dozens that occurred at around the age of 2-and-a-half. Utterances by the adult with meanings beyond the child's own linguistic system of the time are presented in bold.

(10) (2;5;10) (M arranges flowers in a vase with S's help)
S: Oh, that one hurt me!
M: Oh, be careful! That's a rose and **roses** have thorns, sharp thorns.

(11) (2;7;0) (S holds a strange knitted toy from a friend's toy box)
M: What's that?
S: It's a rabbit
M: Oh yes, **'cause** he's got long ears, hasn't he? And a sort of fluffy tail.

(12) (2;8;18) (S has been singing 'Mary had a little lamb')

    S: Fleece, not feece, no; not teece; not teece. (laughing)

    M: No, not teeth.

    F: (sings) Teeth were as white as snow.

    S: No, not teeth, fleece!

    M: Yes, fleece; **fleece is the wool on the lamb.**
          All the lamb's soft wool is called the fleece.

Construing the adult's language in example (10) requires interpreting reference not only to the materially available flower, but also to an entire class (*roses*), while in example (11), the adult uses 'internal' causality to provide criteria for assigning class membership (*'cause he's got long ears*), a semantic option that will eventually enable the construal of categories with less or non-observable defining criteria. In example (12), a linguistically construed category (*fleece*) is defined in terms of another linguistic construal (*all the lamb's soft wool*) without direct reference to the material setting. These are foundational ways of using language as a tool for learning later in life and the case study of Stephen's language suggests how an adult may unconsciously take opportunities to nudge the child in this direction (see Painter 1999b).

The 'take-up' of adult scaffolding

Most of this chapter has been an attempt to illustrate aspects of the interactions that make visible to children meaning possibilities that lie a little beyond their individual capabilities. In this section, the discussion will turn to how it is that the child can make use of the adult's contributions. Longitudinal data are particularly useful here, since they allow 'first' occasions of the child's use to be noticed, as well as general patterns.

The most obvious way in which a child learner makes use of an adult model is in immediate imitation of it, as with Stephen's use of *poodle* in example (8) or his use of the abstract term *speed* in example (13) below – in both cases, his first recorded use of the item in question.

(13) (4;8;30)

    F: This car can't go as fast as ours.

    S: I thought – I thought all cars could – all cars could go the same –
          all cars could go the same (pause) fast.

    M: The same speed.

    S: Yes, same speed.

This phenomenon is well known and has been referred to as 'Performing without competence' (Clark 1974), when framed in terms of Chomsky's competence-vs-performance dichotomy. As well as enabling the child to produce a meaning that could not be engendered by his or her own system at the time, such imitations presumably allow the child to reflect on the unfamiliar piece of text in an explicit way, perhaps helping him or her to commit it to memory. In SFL terms, '[a] piece of text is construed, and used appropriately, which includes lexicogrammatical and phonological features that have not yet been processed into the system. The system then catches up and goes ahead' (Halliday 1980b: 11).

Rather than being repeated immediately, the novel meaning or structure may initially be stored as a piece of text so that the child produces what Snow (1983) refers to as a 'deferred imitation' – that is, the adult's utterance is replayed on a comparable future occasion. Some

Table 39.1 Adult and child examples of explaining a refusal

Typical texts at age 2	First instances of Hal providing a justification, at 2;3
(14)	(16)
M: Don't you want any tea? Do you want some biscuits and cheese?	M: Want a bit of toast?
	H: No thanks, I not hungry.
H: No.	
M: No? Not hungry. You're not hungry tonight, eh?	
(15) (H pulling M and F by the hands to resume running together)	(17) (M tries to distract H, who is boisterous)
H: Want to run again.	M: Why don't you get the little cars out?
F: No, we can't run any more; Daddy's too tired and Mummy's too tired.	H: Mummy play cars; I can't play cars; I'm too tired.

examples from Hal can illustrate. Table 39.1 aligns typical interactions between parent and Hal at the age of 2, and his very first uses of a particular discourse option three months later.

Examples (16) and (17) are not cases of Hal imitating a lexical item, but of him taking up an additional kind of conversational move: that of justifying a refusal to an offer. It is noticeable that the first times he tries this out, he also uses the same particular explanation that has been used to him, either on his behalf or in response to his own offer. Either the new possibility is available as yet only in the form of remembered text, or managing the new option in the system is facilitated by reusing familiar text. Very often, such deferred imitations are with the original interactants, as here, perhaps with a reversal of dialogue roles, as in example (17). This phenomenon can be regarded as an aspect of the 'interpersonal first' principle posited in SFL work (Painter 2004),[1] which includes the restriction of new developments to interactions in which only the dialogue partners are construed as Subjects and/or to the negotiation of behaviour with the dialogue partner.

There may therefore be three steps in the take-up of the adult contribution. One is the repetition and reuse by the child of text that is engendered by the adult system and could not be engendered by the child's. This may occur immediately within the same conversation, as in example (13), and/or it may occur hours, days or weeks later. Halliday (1975: 112) gives the example of Nigel's co-constructed 'goat' story (example (7b)), noting that, following the conversation, the story is 'repeated as a whole, verbatim, at frequent intervals over the next few months'. Halliday (1993: 104–5) explains that '[t]he effect of [the] ongoing dialectic [of system and text] is a kind of leapfrogging movement: sometimes an instance will appear to be extending the system, sometimes to be lagging behind'. The system would appear to lag behind if the repeated verbatim story were to include features (such as head shaking for a negative in the goat story) that the child's current system has outgrown.

Second, dialogic interaction may lead to eventual instances revealing an expansion of the child's systemic potential, for example to include a new option for a causal explanation. This would be 'extending the system', but often at first with such a new ideational option limited to specific speech functions (for example justifying a refusal, issuing a threat) or with only speech role Subjects/transitivity participants (*I, we, you*).

The most comprehensive take-up, of course, is the third step, in which the child's systemic potential is expanded beyond any such restrictions to include new options that match those of the adult's system. The SFL explanation for how this may occur lies in the nature of language as a system–text continuum:

The system is the underlying potential of a language: its potential as a meaning-making resource. This does not mean that it exists as an independent phenomenon: there are not two separate objects, language as system and language as a set of texts. The relationship between the two is analogous to that between the weather and the climate.

Halliday and Matthiessen 2004: 26–7

Halliday (1992: 26, emphasis added) elaborates as follows:

The system (the climate) . . . is no more, and no less, than the pattern set up by the instances (the weather), **and each instance, no matter how minutely, perturbs these probabilities and so changes the system (or keeps it as it is,** which is just the limiting case of changing it.

In other words, for example, if a young child's observations using specific reference (such as *that dog chased our cat*) are repeatedly responded to by the adult with utterances that elaborate in terms of generic reference (*dogs like to chase cats*), the child's efforts to construe the conversational partner's contribution are likely to 'perturb' the original system and eventually lead the child to try out the new meaning. Probability is a feature of the system and, for both adult and child, the meaning potential changes (or not) in response to the texts being heard and engaged in. Children are able to learn language in untutored conversational interaction because co-constructed instances alert a child to new meaning possibilities that are highly relevant to his or her own concerns at that moment, thus unbalancing the current organisation of the meaning potential.

Applications and future directions

The most salient application of the SFL account of learning how to mean is in the educational field. The case study data demonstrate clearly that building knowledge necessarily involves building the language in which it is construed, which argues strongly for a 'language across the curriculum' approach within the formal education system, in which teaching of subject matter is understood to involve teaching the language in which it is construed. The arguments of the present chapter on parent–child interaction suggest the following four key features of language learning in the home:

1   the **asymmetrical dyad** – children learn their first language in interaction with guidance from a more expert user;
2   **shared experience** – both material and textual shared history provides the basis of successful adult tracking and guidance;
3   **learning about semiosis** – the caregiver guides the talk in directions that enable greater reflection on meaning; and
4   the **jointly constructed instance** – dialogue contingently offers the learner new meanings, available to be used as remembered text or as a basis for extending and reorganising systemic choice.

These features have been the basis for various incarnations of 'genre-based' approaches to teaching writing in schools (see Gardener, this volume). In particular, the idea of a 'joint construction' phase in the writing programme – whereby the teacher scaffolds the children's contributions to a model written text and talks about language as he or she scribes for the class – has been a crucial innovation for both writing and reading pedagogy (Rose and Martin 2012). Since not all joint constructions in the classroom are equally successful, future work will need to focus on deconstructing interactions that encapsulate best practice here (Dreyfus and Martin 2015). Managing pedagogic co-constructions, drawing on examples of the way in which the adult prepares the child for new information with focusing moves (for example *Do you remember?*), unpacks his or her own meanings for the child (*the lamb's wool is called the fleece*) and acknowledges, and/or recasts, and/or elaborates children's responses has already provided some basis for the designing of pedagogic exchanges to facilitate learning to read. These kinds of applications, which also make sense in terms of Vygotskyan theory, are very different from the Piagetian child-centred pedagogy in which only peer interaction is valued, which dominates many segments of the education system in the English-speaking world.

SFL work on learning how to mean has, from the beginning, been significant in providing evidence for the SFL proposal for the functional basis of human language and for suggesting possible routes into a metafunctionally organised linguistic system. There is an acute need for additional longitudinal studies to supplement the currently available data, not only to provide surer ground for generalisations about language learning, but also to provide descriptions of the language-learning experiences of children from a greater range of social and linguistic backgrounds, and of contemporary children, who are growing up in a digital world and a sociocultural milieu with different habits and assumptions about gender, work, leisure and family roles.

Note

1 See also Halliday's (1993: 98) 'magic gateway'.

References

Appleby, A.N., and J.A. Langer. 1983. Instructional scaffolding. *Language Arts* 60: 168–75.
Blake, J. 2001. *Routes to Child Language: Evolutionary and Developmental Precursors*. Cambridge: Cambridge University Press.
Bruner, J. 1978. The role of dialogue in language acquisition. In A. Sinclair, R. Jarvella and W.J.M. Levelt (eds) *The Child's Conception of Language*. New York: Springer, pp. 241–56.
Chomsky, N. 1975. *Reflections on Language*. New York: Pantheon.
Clark, R. 1974. Performing without competence. *Journal of Child Language* 4(1): 1–10.
Dreyfus, S., and J.R. Martin. 2015. Scaffolding semogenesis: Designing teacher/student interactions for face-to-face and on-line learning. In S. Starc, A. Maiorani and C. Jones (eds) *Meaning-Making Processes in Text*. London: Palgrave.
Gallaway, C., and B.J. Richards (eds). 1994. *Input and Interaction in Language Acquisition*. Cambridge: Cambridge University Press.
Halliday, M.A.K. 1975. *Learning How to Mean*. London: Arnold.
Halliday, M.A.K. 1978. Meaning and the construction of reality in early childhood. In H.L. Pick Jr. and E. Salzman (eds) *Modes of Perceiving and Processing of Information*. Hillsdale, NJ: Erlbaum, pp. 67–96.
Halliday, M.A.K 1980a. The contribution of developmental linguistics to the interpretation of language as a system. In E. Hovdhaugen (ed.) *The Nordic Language and Modern Linguistics: Proceedings of the 4th International Conference of Nordic and General Linguistics*. Oslo: Universitetsforlaget, pp. 1–18.

Halliday, M.A.K. 1980b. Three aspects of children's language development: Learning language, learning through language, learning about language. In Y.M. Goodman, M.M. Haussler and D. Strickland (eds) *Oral and Written Language Development: Impact on School.* Newark, DE: International Reading Association, pp. 7–19.

Halliday, M.A.K. 1991. The place of dialogue in children's construction of meaning. In S. Stati, E. Weigand and F. Hundsnurscher (eds) *Dialoganalyse III: Referate der 3 Arbeitstagung.* Tubingen: Niemeyer, pp. 417–30.

Halliday, M.A.K. 1992. How do you mean? In M. Davies and L. Ravelli (eds) *Advances in Systemic Linguistics: Recent Theory and Practice.* London: Pinter, pp. 20–35.

Halliday, M.A.K. 1993. Towards a language-based theory of learning. *Linguistics and Education* 5(2): 93–116.

Halliday, M.A.K., and C.M.I.M. Matthiessen. 2004. *An Introduction to Functional Grammar.* 3rd edn. London: Arnold.

Hasan, R. 2009. *The Collected Works of Ruqaiya Hasan, Vol. 2: Semantic Variation – Meaning in Society and Sociolinguistics.* Ed. J.J. Webster. London: Equinox.

Hornstein, N., and D. Lightfoot. 1981. *Explanation in Linguistics: The Logical Problem of Language Acquisition.* London and New York: Longman.

Mehan, H. 1979. *Learning Lessons: Organisation in the Classroom.* Cambridge, MA: Harvard University Press.

Murray, L., and C. Trevarthen. 1985. Emotional regulation of interactions between two-month-olds and their mothers. In T. Field and N. Fox (eds) *Social Perception in Infants.* Norwood, NJ: Ablex, pp. 177–97.

Ninio, A., and J. Bruner. 1978. The achievements and antecedents of labelling. *Journal of Child Language* 5: 1–15.

Painter, C. 1984. *Into the Mother Tongue.* London: Pinter.

Painter, C. 1999a. *Learning through Language in Early Childhood.* London: Continuum.

Painter, C. 1999b. Preparing for school: Developing a semantic style for educational knowledge. In F. Christie (ed.) *Pedagogy and the Shaping of Consciousness.* London and New York: Cassell, pp. 66–87.

Painter, C. 2004. The 'interpersonal first' principle in child language development. In G. Williams and A. Lukin (eds) *Language Development: Functional Perspectives on Evolution and Ontogenesis.* London and New York: Continuum, pp. 133–53.

Painter, C. 2009. Language development. In M.A.K. Halliday and J.J. Webster (eds) *Continuum Companion to Systemic-Functional Linguistics.* London: Continuum, pp. 87–103.

Piaget, J. 1977. *The Essential Piaget.* Eds H.E. Gruber and J.J. Voneche. New York: Basic Books.

Reddy, V. 2008. *How Infants Know Minds.* Cambridge MA: Harvard University Press.

Rose, D., and J.R. Martin. 2012. *Learning to Write, Reading to Learn: Genre, Knowledge and Pedagogy in the Sydney School.* Sheffield: Equinox.

Schieffelin, B.B., and E. Ochs (eds). 1986. *Language Socialization across Cultures.* New York: Cambridge University Press.

Snow, C.E. 1983. Saying it again: The role of expanded and deferred imitations in language acquisition. In K.E. Nelson (ed.) *Children's Language, Vol. 4.* New York: Erlbaum, pp. 29–58.

Snow, C.E. 1995. Issues in the study of input: Finetuning, universality, individual and developmental differences, and necessary causes. In P. Fletcher and B. MacWhinney (eds) *The Handbook of Child Language.* Oxford: Blackwell, pp. 181–93.

Torr, J. 1997. *From Child Tongue to Mother Tongue: A Case Study of Language Development in the First Two and a Half Years* (Monographs in Systemic Linguistics 9), Nottingham: Department of English Studies, University of Nottingham.

Trevarthen, C. 2005. Stepping away from the mirror: Pride and shame in adventures of companionship. In C.S. Carter, L. Ahnert, K.E. Grossman, S.B. Hardy, M.E. Lamb, S.W. Porges and N. Sachser (eds) *Attachment and Bonding: A New Synthesis.* Cambridge, MA: MIT Press, pp. 55–84.

Trevarthen, C. 2009. The intersubjective psychobiology of human meaning: Learning of culture depends on interest for cooperative practical work and affection for the joyful art of good company. *Psychoanalytic Dialogues: The International Journal of Relational Perspectives* 19(5): 507–18.

Vygotsky, L.S. 1978. *Mind in Society: The Development of Higher Psychological Processes*. Eds M. Cole, V. John-Steiner, S. Scribner and E. Souberman. Cambridge, MA: Harvard University Press.

40

Looking ahead

Systemic functional linguistics in the twenty-first century

Gerard O'Grady and Tom Bartlett

Introduction

Butler and Gonzálvez-García (2014: 25), in their monumental survey of functional linguistic theories, classify systemic functional linguistics (SFL) as somewhat of an outlier. One of the chief reasons for this, they note, is that functional linguistic theories are not usually concerned with analysing texts; SFL, conversely, is a text-oriented model of language (Butler and Gonzálvez-García 2014: 488). As such, SFL does not classify language as an autonomous object. Contra Chomsky (for example Berwick and Chomsky 2016: 81), SFL argues that language did not emerge as a vehicle for structuring thought, but rather as a means of communicating with one's peers.[1] However, the SFL view of communication is richer than that current within the cognitive linguistic framework. Language for SFL is not exclusively representational; equal attention – as this book has made clear – is devoted to non-representational meaning both interpersonal and textual. With the exception of the Cardiff Model, SFL does not focus on language as an embodied intrapersonal theory of language, but rather on language as a shared social-semiotic meaning-making resource.[2]

SFL as a text-orientated, rather than sentence-focused, linguistics is, by nature, appliable. It is a dynamic theory that itself is constantly being expanded through the praxis of language use. With that in mind, the chapters in this volume have shown that while the epistemological underpinnings of SFL theory are solid, the theory itself – as with all good theories – is complete neither in and of itself as a theory nor in its interactions with neighbouring disciplines and real-world issues. The authors in this volume have clarified that there is much to be gained both theoretically and practically from a dialogue between SFL and related or cognate functional theories and related disciplines.

In this volume, we, as editors, tasked our authors with not only critically assessing the current state of affairs, but also offering their expert, but personal, views on the challenges and opportunities that await SFL in the twenty-first century. A number of somewhat permeable themes have emerged from a review of their thoughts, which we have grouped as:

1   interacting/reconnecting with other linguistic theories;
2   revisiting and extending existing theory;

3   extending the description to more languages;
4   conversations with other disciplines; and
5   applications of the theory.

The following paragraphs will offer our reflections on their views.

Interacting/reconnecting with other linguistic theories

A major critique of SFL down the years from friendly and perhaps not-so-friendly linguists has been that its plethora of unfamiliar or idiosyncratic metalanguage has hindered dialogue with other linguistic theories. Yet, as Bateman (this volume) makes plain, there are good theoretical reasons why SFL employs its individual metalanguage. Each theory must make sense in terms of its own aims and philosophical underpinnings. For instance, SFL does not see the need to include an independent level of pragmatics when discussing language in use; SFL adopts what Bateman dubs 'an in-contexts' rather 'an in-texts' approach. As such, it is not focused on what a particular text means in an individual context, but rather upon the text as a realisation of the context. Thus the focus is not on how the speakers performed individual speech acts nor on how they generated and interpreted implicatures, as it would be in a more intersomatically orientated theory of language. Yet this does not mean that SFL is not able to account for pragmatics. An in-contexts description of language entails that all description is contextualised and there is thus no room in an SFL model for an independent pragmatic dimension. The actual language produced in any context and its resultant inter- pretation is an instantiation of the choices that were available in the particular sub-register (Halliday 1978: 40). Context is embedded in the description and not an external factor that is used to make sense of an utterance.

SFL, as a theory, can interact or reconnect with other theories only once its epistemology and ontology – notably, the twin influences of Firth and Malinowski – are understood. It is both a social-semiotic theory of language and one that describes language as a system– structure pair. And as the name of the theory implies, system is the dominant axis. Systemic choices generate structure, although SFL's cline of instantiation entails that every utterance perturbs the probability settings of the system and increases or decreases the likelihood of particular structures being produced in the future.

Yet SFL, as has been alluded to throughout this volume, has been influenced by many of the same theorists whose work has inspired other functional approaches to language – namely, Saussure's (1959: 67) concepts of the duality and arbitrariness of the sign, and Prague school work on Theme, especially Mathiesus (1975: 81–3) and Trávníček (1961). Hjelmslev's (1970: 101–3) content and expression planes have clearly influenced Halliday's concept of interstratal realisation. Matthiessen (2015: 149, emphasis original) states that, if we view grammatical theory from below, 'we can recognize a **family of grammars** with similar properties that includes systemic functional grammar'. This family of unification grammars includes work such as Kay's (1979, for example) functional unification grammar, Bresnan and Kaplan's lexical functional grammar (for example Bresnan 2001), Pollard and Sag's (1994, for example) head-driven phrase structure grammar, Sag's (2012) sign-based construction grammar, categorical grammar (Steedman 2001) and Joshi's tree-adjoining grammar (for example Joshi et al. 1969). Matthiessen (2015) notes, however, that SFL dif- fers from other unification approaches in that it affords primacy to the system. However, as a number of the chapters within this volume indicate, SFL's focus on the system should not obscure potential synergies with other linguistic approaches. For instance, Xin and Cao (2013: 166) have argued for the complementarity of SFL and construction grammars, and specifically recommend that SFL incorporate the notion of construction into its architecture.

Within this volume, a number of authors have made concrete proposals for how SFL can interact with other functional theories and cognate disciplines. Asp, and also Butt and Webster (this volume), have noted some connections with minimalist theory. While minimalist theory aims to explicate what is essential to language to explain why humans are uniquely endowed with a linguistic faculty (Berwick and Chomsky 2016: 94), recent developments in minimalism have seen it implicitly recognise the importance of intrinsic functions and systemic contrasts in language. This, as Asp notes, results in some surprising convergences between minimalism and SFL, although it is worth reiterating that the basic research goals of the two theories remain diametrically opposed. Yet this (albeit partial) convergence means that SFL scholars should be in a position to draw upon relevant evidence gleaned from the minimalist literature when describing the phylogenetic or ontogenetic development of a language. Butt and Webster (this volume) have, for example, not only drawn explicit connections between the Logical Metafunction and Merge, but have also illustrated why, contra minimalism, the richness of language is not distillable only to the Logical Metafunction. Yet, at the same time, while accepting, contra Chomsky, that language evolution is gradual,[3] they have elegantly illustrated how SFL scholars can usefully contribute to the evolutionary debate.

Taverniers (this volume) in her exploration of grammatical metaphor notes that while only Sydney SFL attempts to offer a unified account of different aspects of grammatical metaphor, other linguistic approaches have examined aspects of it under a range of disparate topics, such as factivity, speech acts, shell nouns, adjacency pairs, politeness strategies, etc. It is clear that while SFL scholars of grammatical metaphor have much to gain by familiarising themselves with the relevant non-SFL literature, non-SFL scholars working on aspects of grammatical metaphor would also find their work usefully informed by the unified SFL approach. O'Grady (this volume), in his discussion of intonation, notes the irony that while SFL has by far the richer theoretical description of intonation (and rhythm), tones and breaks indices (ToBI), the current dominant intonational framework, has overwhelmingly produced far more descriptive data. He draws parallels between the two approaches to make ToBI's descriptions more available to those working within SFL. Conversely, it is hoped that SFL-flavoured intonation research will become an increased presence in describing the semio-genetic potential of intonation. After all, SFL alone has integrated intonation into the architecture of language and, unlike other approaches, treats intonation neither as emotional colouring nor in terms of pragmatic force.

In a series of publications, Davidse and her colleagues have applied an approach that draws not only upon core SFL theory (notably, alternations), but also cognitive grammar and constructions and collostructions found in large-scale corpora (for example Davidse 1998, 1999). In this volume, Davidse proposes that the merger of a collostructional approach with a neo-Firthian corpus approach, coupled with SFL work on the semantics of transitivity, is a promising entry point into providing a richer representation of the lexicogrammar. Such an approach has the potential to lead to more granular descriptions of languages both in their own terms and as a basis for cross-comparison work (as we shall see later in this chapter).

Prior to moving on, it is worth emphasising that, in the twenty-first century, SFL must be open to learning from cognate (and, indeed, less related) linguistic theories. Only by so doing will SFL itself be able to productively engage in linguistic debate and help to shape the linguistic agenda. We will return to this point later in the chapter, but first let us describe some areas in which SFL, as an open and dynamic theory, may need to be revised and extended.

Revisiting and extending existing theory

It is a truism that the details of any theory cannot remain fixed: interaction with data necessitates revision of, and perhaps extension or contraction to, existing theory. Within this volume, a number of authors have suggested potential areas in which SFL theory is in need of revision and/or extension. As noted in the last section, Davidse wishes to see SFL descriptions of the experiential metafunction become more granular to reflect theoretical claims about a unified lexicogrammar. This is a challenge that she suggests will require interaction with other approaches.

More controversially, Andersen (this volume) claims that, in the IFG tradition, there is confusion as to whether SPEECH FUNCTION is best treated as a contextual or semantic system. He notes that there is nothing in Halliday's writings that suggests that 'language as doing and language as learning' equates with a distinction between proposal and proposition, and hence to the distinction between speech functions associated with goods-and-services and speech functions associated with information. If goods-and-services are semiotic, then it follows that the distinction between material and semiotic is itself a semiotic construct. In that case, the sole means of differentiating between goods-and-services and information is to classify the latter as linguistic semiosis. Yet this apparent solution itself raises the troubling issue of whether linguistic semiosis can or should be privileged vis-à-vis other semiotic modalities. SFL is an important voice in the study of multimodal communication (see Taylor, this volume), and so its description of semiosis and semio-genesis must rest on firmer theoretical foundations. Andersen suggests that a possible way forward is to detail speech functions by combining descriptions mapped from above with those mapped from below and, in the process, circumvent the issue of distinguishing between information and goods-and-services. In any case, it is clear that further work is required to firm up the theoretical underpinning of SPEECH FUNCTION.

The relevant chapters in this volume have indicated that THEME and its underpinning theory remain a work in progress. Halliday and Matthiessen (2014: 105) state that Theme culminates in the first experiential element, for example participant, process or Circumstance. But at the same time, they gloss Theme as the point of departure for the message (Halliday and Matthiessen 2014: 89). Halliday (1994: 37) offers a slightly different gloss – Theme is that with which the clause is concerned – while others (for example Fontaine 2013: 140) have metaphorically described Theme in terms of a peg upon which the message is hung. The discrepancy between the identifying criterion and the glosses have resulted in some differences of opinion as to whether the Theme can contain more than a single experiential element. Forey and Sampson (this volume), in their overview of Theme in English, suggest that an analyst's decision of what to include as part of the Thematic field depends on his or her focus and aims. While Halliday (2003 [1964]: 38) famously argued in favour of the desirability of competing and coexisting grammatical descriptions designed to suit different aims, his views cannot be equated with theoretical inconsistency within a single grammatical description. Thus, while eminently practical and reasonable in terms of SFL's appliability, Forey and Sampson's suggestion does not resolve the theoretical issues around Theme as a grammatical resource. As such, it must be identified through its reactances in the text rather than the analyst's purposes. The issue of whether Theme is the entry point of a clause or whether it is best conceived as a field that contains a topical element itself motivated by the preceding co-text remains unresolved, as well as the exact form–function pairing in languages other than English (Bartlett 2016). Similarly, the relation between Theme–Rheme and Given–New in English remains somewhat unclear (O'Grady 2016).

While one of the key tenets underlying SFL is that every language must be described in its own terms, this does not mean that the system of Theme should mean something different across languages;[4] it means only that its lexicogrammatical realisation may differ across languages. Arús Hita (this volume) argues that, in Spanish, circumstantial elements do not necessarily exhaust the Thematic potential of the clause. If he were to be proved correct, Theme, at least in Spanish, could potentially contain more than a single experiential element. A more radical solution would, he suggests, be to exclude circumstantial elements that are not Theme-exhausting. Huang (this volume) points out that, in the Cardiff Grammar, because conjunctive elements are not considered to realise a choice, they are not classed as part of the Theme in English. This raises the issue of whether or not Theme–Rheme should be classed as a binary division.[5] We can, in any case, conclude this section by noting that there remain unresolved questions in the study of Theme both in English and in other languages (Bartlett 2016).

Extending the description to more languages

As is well known, almost all early SFL work described English and the realisations of the grammatical categories posited were only intended to apply to English.[6] More recently, SFL scholars have begun to provide descriptions of languages other than English (LOTE), for example Caffarel (2006) on French, Caffarel and colleagues (2004) on a range of eight languages from seven language families, Lavid and colleagues (2010) on Spanish, Li (2007) on Chinese, Teruya (2007) on Japanese and Quiroz (2013) on Chilean Spanish. Recognising the importance of what appears to be a significant typological turn in SFL, we, as editors, commissioned a number of chapters that outlined SFL approaches to the description of LOTE. We did so in the firm belief that SFL theory will be enriched by being tested against non-English data. Caffarel-Cayron (this volume) argues that every language must be described from the standpoint of the language itself. Her description of the French past tense system shows that it has more delicate primary systems and reduced recursivity in the secondary systems compared with that in English. Her description, as well as having obvious resonances for work in translation and especially automated translation (at which we look shortly), helps to deepen our overall understanding of language as a situated social-semiotic meaning-making system of options.

Teruya (this volume) shows the power of an SFL approach in integrating the Japanese honorific system within the lexicogrammar. By so doing, he illustrates the advantages of a unified SFL account over in-texts or formalist accounts that treat honorifics as marked language events. Such accounts, unlike SFL, are forced to rely on external contextual effects such as power and distance; SFL, in contrast, is able to describe the honorific system as a co-system within the Interpersonal metafunction. As Teruya notes, a more delicate analysis of the Japanese Interpersonal systems will help both in establishing the relationship between the various interpersonal systems and, more generally, in advancing the grammarian's dream of uniting lexis and grammar (Halliday 2002 [1961]: 54).

Arús Hita's work on Theme in Spanish raises a number of important theoretical questions for researchers working on SFL descriptions of LOTE. Notably, in this volume he questions the role of Subject. He argues that, unlike in English, Subject is not modally responsible in Spanish, and he questions whether or not Subject should be included within the Interpersonal Metafunction or might be is better treated as part of an independent syntactic structure.[7] Li's description in this volume of the Mandarin nominal group sheds light on the choices available in an analytical language. Baugh and Cable (2012), in perhaps the seminal work in describing the history of English, state that, over the past 1,500 years, English has moved from being a synthetic language towards an analytical one.[8] Consequently SFL analyses of Mandarin such as Li (this volume) have the potential to increase our understanding of the resources that different languages employ when creating scientific texts. Mandarin, like English, employs nominalisations to construe scientific concepts and so a detailed description of the Mandarin nominal group expands our understanding of how processes can be reconstrued as products. Once again, the resonances for translation are obvious.

The preceding paragraphs have, we hope, shown both the urgent necessity for SFL researchers to engage with the description of LOTE and the strength of an SFL approach in so doing. By recognising that every language has its own character (Eco 2008: 109), SFL linguists are in the unique position of being able to provide in-context descriptions for when and where different languages have evolved different choices. Halliday (2010: 18) demonstrates that an SFL approach empowers translators by allowing them to pinpoint the systemic choices that result in moments of translation shift or equivalence across two languages.

The potential for facilitating intercultural communication through the adoption of an SFL framework is obvious, but if the potential is to become an actuality, SFL researchers must first produce detailed and delicate descriptions of LOTE. These descriptions themselves will feed back into the theory and provide for richer theoretical underpinnings for languages (and not only of one language!) as a system of social semiosis. In the current absence of detailed SFL description of LOTE, Teruya and Matthiessen (2015: 443ff) suggest a sensible way of growing SFL-inspired typological work. SFL researchers should use existing typological databases such as the World Atlas of Language Structures (WALS) (Dryer and Haspelmath 2013) to compare and contrast systems across different languages in terms of probabilities, rather than attempting to compare and contrast languages.

Conversations with other disciplines

The typological turn described above opens up a space for SFL to converse with other disciplines. The first is translation theory.[9] Kunz and Teich (this volume) note the increasing influence of appraisal theory (Martin and White 2005) in translation work, and see this as a potential site for developing richer automated translation. To do so, they point out the need for an increase in parallel corpora developed out of contrastive SFL work on lexicogrammar, cohesion and semantics. Intriguingly, they recontextualise translation as a form of language contact, and suggest that there is much to be gained from a dialogue with sociolinguistic accounts of language contact and language change. Because the practice of translation, even machine translation, cannot stop at the skin, Kunz and Teich note the necessity of engaging with psycholinguistic work that studies how hearers interpret the linguistic signals provided by speakers.

Butler (2013: 197) recommends that the Cardiff Grammar – which, uniquely among SFL approaches, views itself as a cognitive-interactive model (Fawcett 1980) – could likewise benefit from interaction with more mainstream psycholinguistic work. The Cardiff

Grammar, like all systemic functional grammars, regards choice as central to meaning, but regards the chooser as the speaker rather than the grammar. Yet, as Butler (2013) notes, while Fawcett (1980) has posited psycholinguistic-sounding components of his model, such as *general planner, discourse planner, micro-planners, reasoned, basic logical form* and *enriched logical forms*, he has not attempted to test the psycholinguistic plausibility of his module. Doing so would extend the Cardiff Grammar, make it more robust and allow it to develop bridges with psycholinguistics with each discipline learning from and informing the other.

To date, SFL work on translation and the development of the Cardiff Grammar have both concentrated on generating computational output, rather than examining how humans engage in semiosis. And while this has led to rich description of languages, as the contributions to this volume have amply demonstrated, it now seems opportune to recast the focus from the system to the speakers. Butler (2013) suggests that embodiment (Hutchins 1995; Gibbs 2005[10]) may represent the common ground between SFL and cognitive science, and enable us to move forward by adopting a combined socio-semiotic and cognitive approach in exploring how ideational meaning is construed, interpersonal meaning enacted and textual meaning composed.

Halliday (1978: 38–9) maintained that linguistics was, if anything, a branch of sociology and famously argued that there was no need to posit a psychological level when describing language.[11] Yet this does not necessarily imply that SFL must stop its investigation of language at the skin. Plausible intrasomatic descriptions of humans operating as semiotic producers/receivers can only add to the rich existing interpersonal accounts of language as a socio-semiotic process. The chapters by Bartlett, Bowcher, Moore and Tann in this volume offer an overview of a state-of-the-art view of SFL work in mapping the relationship between semiosis and context, and different perspectives on the relevance to context of non-linguistic features and the need to take the individual seriously when describing intersomatic semiosis.

The typological turn also necessitates engagement with computational linguistics. O'Donnell (this volume) outlines the historical relationship between SFL and computational linguistics. While SFL was influential in earlier work on natural-language processing (NLP), more recently, as with other linguistic theories, it has been pushed aside in favour of a reliance on statistical algorithms that view language exclusively in syntagmatic terms. And while there can be no doubt that stochastic algorithms have been immensely successful, there are clearly limits to how accurately such grammars can capture meaning. By contrast, SFL, with its richly developed representation of meaning, can produce text analyses, be they ideational, evaluative or cohesive, which shed light on the role language plays in society. O'Donnell suggests that, as computers have become more powerful, previous technical obstacles to SFL-flavoured NLP have dissipated, while at the same time the need for more meaningful automated programs and analyses has increased. SFL, as a theory of praxis, has much to gain in turn from closer interaction with the NLP community, although it is worth reiterating the desirability of a combined future socio-semiotic and cognitive approach. Such an approach could potentially have much to say about who we, as semiotic beings, are and potentially help in the development of human–machine interactions.

The explosion in computational power has also led to the availability of enormous language corpora such as the Bank of English,[12] British National Corpus (BNC)[13] and Corpus of Contemporary American English.[14] Such corpora provide a rich source of data and ensure that theoretical claims about a language are grounded in empirical data. SFL has clearly taken account of the need to ensure that its descriptions are supported by corpus evidence: compare, for example, Halliday's *Introduction to Functional Grammar* in its first

(Halliday 1985) and fourth (Halliday and Matthiessen 2014) editions. Sharoff (this volume) observes that corpus linguistics is not a theory in and of itself, but rather an approach that can help to develop linguistic theory. Yet while this is undoubtedly true, there is a tendency in much corpus linguistic work that has been influenced by Sinclair (1991) to argue that linguistic description should emerge out of the data. This view prioritises the lexis and at least implicitly regards syntactic patterns as the co-occurrence of lexical patterns. Syntax is, in other words, generalised lexis. SFL, conversely, considers lexis to be delicate grammar. The papers collected in Thompson and Hunston (2006)[15] outline a programme for how researchers from both camps could, in theory, meet in the middle. Yet it is worth noting that existing corpus linguistic tools are primarily designed to investigate lexical, and not grammatical, patterns. Thus an SFL-inspired corpus approach that aims to interrogate corpora in terms of register-specific instantiations of underlying systemic choices remains in lieu of software development a potentiality rather than an actuality. The examination of more delicate systems in terms of probabilities across registers[16] nonetheless has the power to reshape not only our view of language potential, but also our understanding of how redundancy fosters or hinders successful communication.

Applications of the theory

Perhaps the most distinctive feature of SFL as a linguistic theory is that it sees itself as an appliable theory (Halliday 1985: 7). As such, theory is not privileged over application. Indeed, as McCabe (this volume) reminds us, SFL grew out of Halliday's difficulties as a foreign-language teacher attempting to explain how language worked. However, despite seeming to be ideally placed as an underpinning for English as a foreign language (EFL) curricula and classroom practice, SFL, as a functional description of system and instance, has not played a significant role in second-language pedagogical theory and practice. As McCabe notes, innovative and successful SFL-inspired educational materials such as the Reading to Learn project[17] could be adapted for use in the EFL classroom. Similarly, in recent years, SFL practitioners have produced SFL-inspired pedagogical grammars and interactive web resources for use in the EFL classroom that describe both the system and the instance.[18] Unlike with currently dominant communicative language teaching (CLT) approaches, learners are not only asked to focus on individual trees, but also given the opportunity to see the tree in its proper place in the forest.

SFL has produced a rich and still-developing theory of context (Bowcher and Bartlett, both this volume) that can be used to describe semio-genetic encounters and, where necessary, develop remedial interventions. Such interventions can occur in a range of institutional sites and be tailored to fit individual purposes, whether that is ensuring the hearing of disadvantaged voices in institutionalised settings or in diagnosing, and hopefully intervening in, language pathologies.

It is to be hoped that SFL interactions with computational linguistics will result in the production of a wide range of automated applications that can facilitate semiosis. Taylor (this volume) shows that SFL theory is an importance influence on multimodal theory and a likely underpinning for (remedial) applications that could be used not only to explicate the meaning of moving and static images, but also to make them more accessible to deaf and blind communities.

This section is short not because we could not speculate on myriad SFL-inspired applications, but rather because we are incapable of imagining the technologies that will emerge over the course of the twenty-first century. Technologies that now seem a normal and indispensible part of daily living have, it must be remembered, emerged only very recently. Facebook and Twitter, for example, date from 2004 and 2006, respectively. SFL scholars, in works such as Maiorani (2009), Ventola and Moya Guijarro (2009), Bednarek and Caple (2012), Zappavigna (2012) and Caple (2013) have been at the forefront of studying the semio-genetic potentiality of such new media. In so doing, they have contributed to the development of SFL theory, while also demonstrating the power of existing SFL theory in describing the construal of meaning in new media interactions.

Conclusion

SFL is a rigorous descriptive theory of semiosis in an age of meaning that has moved on from the notion of the meaning as the transmission of encodable information. Thus SFL practitioners are ideally situated to interpret and guide semio-genetic production in all aspects of human (and machine) interaction. In an age of communication semiotics, it is a – perhaps *the* – necessary science, because without it we are unable to account for how humans make sense of the world, and how they create and interpret meaning. Of all current linguistic or semiotic theories, SFL, imbued with its metafunctional architecture and underpinning notion of choice, is the approach that can provide the fullest account of the construal of meaning. Simultaneously, we can expect SFL theory to continue its development: remaining primarily a theory of text linguistics in a semiotic world in which the concept of text has evolved to encompass representational and interpersonal meaning produced and construed through a range of complimentary modalities.

There is reason to be confidently optimistic that SFL will continue to be an important linguistic theory in the twenty-first century. Matthiessen (2015: 197) reminds us that most, if not all, of the foundational underpinnings of SFL theory have, often without explicit reference to Halliday, gained currency in recent years. Numerous theories now posit a unified lexicogrammar. Probabilistic theories of language have become increasingly fashionable, at least since the publication of Bod and colleagues' 2003 book on stochastic linguistics. With the decline in universal grammar and acquisition-based theories, there is some renewed interest in language development. Prosodic views have largely become dominant in phonology, for example ToBI/metrical phonology (Ladd 2008) and autosegmental phonology[19] (Goldsmith 1990; Scheer 2010). Yet it must be acknowledged that SFL's distinctive view of the primacy of systems over structure has not yet been widely adopted.[20]

In a friendly challenge to SFL, Davies (2014: 9) suggests that the model of SFL can be extended either by deepening the theoretical base through the striving for greater explanatory adequacy or by extending the theory by attempting to describe different phenomena. We humbly suggest that there is space for both approaches[21] and that much may be gained by attempting to reconcile seemingly disparate phenomena within a unified systems-based theoretical framework. Halliday (2013: 16, fn 1) quotes David Butt's report that those working in the physical sciences are desirous of a 'general science of meaning'. It is clear that, because of its orientation towards text and register, its unified lexicogrammar, and its recognition that system and instance co-occur as the outer poles of a cline, SFL theory can be used as a resource to explore all kinds of complex, directed, semiotic activity, including, for instance, gene transfers as conceptualised by endosymbiosis theory (Lane 2015).[22] We see SFL's contribution to a natural science of meaning as a challenge that SFL is both suited to meet and one that will result in a more sharply defined SFL.

Notes

1 For similar and approachable non-SFL views, see Everett (2012: 35), Evans (2015) and Tomasello (2008).

2 For a compatible non-SFL view of cognition, see Hutchins (1995) on distributed cognition.

3 Thibault (2004), despite arguing that semiotic systems including language are advances on prior non-social-semiotic communicative mechanisms, nonetheless sees his SFL position as not dissimilar to that of Hauser et al. (2002). Like Butt (this volume), however, Thibault (2004: 7) would not want to restrict the discussion to recursion or 'language faculty in the narrow sense'.

4 Although, of course, textuality in languages other than English may rely on features that are too remote from what is labelled Theme in English to be classed as Theme. As Bartlett (2016: 147) notes, '[t]he essential point here is not to fit new grammars to old skins'.

5 See Davidse (1987) for similarities and differences between SFL and the functional sentence perspective (FSP) (e.g. Firbas 1992) on Theme.

6 Although, of course, Halliday's initial descriptions and PhD focused on Chinese.

7 See Fawcett, this volume, for a description of the Cardiff Grammar that contains an independent syntax.

8 See also Halliday and Martin (1993) on the use of nominalisations in scientific writing and Cummings (2010) for an SFL description of Old English.

9 See Steiner (2015) for an illuminating overview.

10 Both Gibbs' (2005: 21) and Thibault's (2004: 12) views are underpinned by the Gibsonian perspective that humans' self-perceptions are embodied in our active exploration of the relevant species-specific affordances available at a given eco-social site. For an SFL view, see Thibault (2004).

11 See Hasan (2015: 128–31) and Maton and Doran, this volume.

12 http://www.titania.bham.ac.uk.

13 http://www.natcorp.ox.ac.uk.

14 http://corpus.byu.edu/coca/.

15 The papers emerged out of an International Systemic Functional Congress held at Liverpool University that explicitly attempted to build on perceived existing synergies between SFL and corpus linguistics. It is fair to say, looking back fourteen years later, that the hoped-for connections have not yet fully manifested.

16 See Halliday's (2013: 25) view that systems will likely be equi or skew.

17 https://www.readingtolearn.com.au/#1450398072181-4410d2e7-dbfb.

18 For example, Alan Hess's *Functional Grammar for Teachers* (http://manxman.ch/moodle2/course/view.php?id=4) and the blog *EFL func* (https://eflfunc.wordpress.com).

19 O'Grady (2013: 55) draws attention to the similarities between J.R. Firth's prosodic phonology and autosegmental phonology. Because neither Firth nor Halliday are referenced in the autosegmental literature, we can assume that autosegmental phonology represents a parallel evolution of a prosodic theory.

20 Readers interested in exploring recent theoretical and applied studies of choice as the underpinning concept of SFL are referred to the papers collected in Fontaine et al. (2013) and O'Grady et al. (2013).

21 We must, however, take cognisance of her warning that a theory that wishes to be a theory of everything may well end up being a theory of nothing!

22 Endosymbiosis is a biochemical theory of the emergence of multicellular life. It conceptualises the origin of life itself in terms of a semiotic activity. It is an increasingly accepted theory chiefly associated with biologist Lyn Margulis, who, interestingly, first developed it in the 1960s at the same time that Halliday developed his SFL view that language is a social semiotic.

References

Bartlett, T. 2016. Phasal dynamism and the unfolding of meaning as text. *English Text Construction* 9(1): 143–64.

Baugh, A.C., and T. Cable. 2012. *A History of the English Language*. 6th edn. London: Routledge.

Bednarek, M., and H. Caple. 2012. *News Discourse*. London: Continuum.

Berwick, R.C., and N. Chomsky. 2016. *Why Only Us: Language and Evolution*. Cambridge, MA: MIT Press.

Bod, R., J. Hay and S. Jannedy. 2003. *Probalistic Linguistics*. Cambridge, MA: MIT Press.

Bresnan, J. 2001. *Lexical-Functional Syntax*. Oxford: Blackwell.

Butler, C.S. 2013. Systemic functional linguistics, cognitive linguistics and psycholinguistics: Opportunities for dialogue. *Functions of Language* 20(2): 185–218.

Butler, C.S., and F. Gonzálvez-García. 2014. *Exploring Functional Cognitive Space*. Amsterdam: John Benjamins.

Caffarel, A. 2006. *A Systemic Functional Grammar of French*. London: Continuum.

Caffarel, A., J.R. Martin and C.M.I.M. Matthiessen. 2004. *Language Typology: A Functional Perspective*. Amsterdam: John Benjamins.

Caple, H. 2013. *Photojournalism: A Multisemiotic Approach*. Basingstoke: Palgrave Macmillan.

Cummings, M.C. 2010. *An Introduction to the Grammar of Old English: A Systemic Functional Approach*. London: Equinox.

Davidse, K. 1987. M.A.K. Halliday's functional grammar and the Prague school. In R. Dirven and V. Freid (eds) *Functionalism in Linguistics*. Amsterdam: John Benjamins, pp. 38–77.

Davidse, K. 1998. Agnates, verb classes and the meaning of construals: The case of ditransitivity in English. *Leuvenese Bijdragen* 87(3–4): 281–313.

Davidse, K. 1999. *Categories of Experiential Grammar* (Monographs in Systemic Functional Linguistics 11). Nottingham: Nottingham Trent University, Department of English and Media Studies.

Davies, E. 2014. A retrospective view of systemic functional linguistics, with notes from a parallel perspective. *Functional Linguistics* 1(4): 1–11.

De Saussure, F. 1959. *Course in General Linguistics*. Eds C. Bally and A. Sechehaye. Trans. W. Baskin. New York: McGraw-Hill.

Dryer, M., and M. Haspelmath. 2013. *The World Atlas of Online Structures Online*. Leipzig: Max Planck Institute for Evolutionary Anthropology.

Eco, U. 2008. *Experiences in Translation*. Toronto, ON: University of Toronto Press.

Evans, V. 2015. *The Crucible of Language: How Language and Mind Create Meaning*. Cambridge: Cambridge University Press.

Everett, D. 2012. *Language: The Cultural Tool*. London: Profile Books.

Fawcett, R.P. 1980. *Cognitive Linguistics and Social Interaction: Towards an Integrated Model of a Systemic Functional Grammar and the Other Components of a Communicating Mind*. Heidelberg and Exeter: Julius Groos Verlag and University of Exeter.

Firbas, J. 1992. *Functional Sentence Perspective in Written and Spoken Communication*. Cambridge: Cambridge University Press.

Fontaine, L. 2013. *Analysing English Grammar: A Systemic Functional Introduction*. Cambridge: Cambridge University Press.

Fontaine, L., T. Bartlett and G. O'Grady. 2013. *Systemic Functional Linguistics: Exploring Choice*. Cambridge: Cambridge University Press.

Gibbs, R.W. 2005. *Embodiment and Cognitive Science*. Cambridge: Cambridge University Press.

Goldsmith, J. 1990. *Autosegmental and Metrical Phonology*. Oxford: Blackwell.

Halliday, M.A.K. 1978. *Language as Social Semiotic: The Social Interpretation of Language and Meaning*. London: Edward Arnold.

Halliday, M.A.K. 1985. Systemic background. In J.D. Benson and W.S Greaves (eds) *Systemic Perspectives on Discourse, Vol. 1*. Norwood, NJ: Ablex, pp. 1–15.

Halliday, M.A.K. 1994. *An Introduction to Functional Grammar*. 2nd edn. London: Arnold.

Halliday, M.A.K. 2002 [1961]. Categories of the theory of grammar. In J.J. Webster (ed.) *The Collected Works of M.A.K. Halliday, Vol. 1: On Grammar*. London: Continuum, pp. 37–94.

Halliday, M.A.K. 2003 [1964]. Syntax and the consumer. In J.J. Webster (ed.) *The Collected Works of M.A.K. Halliday, Vol. 3: On Language and Linguistics*. London: Bloomsbury, pp. 36–49.

Halliday, M.A.K. 2010. Pinpointing the choice: Meaning and the search for equivalents in a translated text. In A. Mahbood and N.K. Knight (eds) *Appliable Linguistics*. London: Continuum, pp. 13–24.

Halliday, M.A.K. 2013. Meaning as choice. In L. Fontaine, T. Bartlett and G. O'Grady (eds) *Systemic Functional Linguistics: Exploring Choice*. Cambridge: Cambridge University Press, pp. 15–36.

Halliday, M.A.K., and J.R. Martin. 1993. *Writing Science: Literacy and Discursive Power*. London: Falmer.

Halliday, M.A.K., and C.M.I.M. Matthiessen. 2014. *Halliday's Introduction to Functional Grammar*. 4th edn. London: Routledge.

Hasan, R. 2015. Systemic functional linguistics: Halliday and the evolution of a social semiotic. In J.J. Webster (ed.) *The Bloomsbury Companion to M.A.K Halliday*. London: Bloomsbury, pp. 101–34.

Hauser, M.D., N. Chomsky and W. Tecumseh Fitch. 2002. The faculty of language: What is it, who has it and how did it evolve. *Science* 298: 1569–78.

Hjelmslev, L. 1970. *Language: An Introduction*. Trans. F.J. Whitfield. Madison, WI: University of Wisconsin Press.

Hutchins, E. 1995. *Cognition in the Wild*. Cambridge, MA: MIT Press.

Joshi, A., S. Kosaraju, S. Rao and H. Yamada. 1969. String adjunct grammars. In *Proceedings of the 10th Annual Symposium on Switching and Automata Theory*. Iowa City, IA: IEEE, pp. 245–62.

Kay, M. 1979. Functional grammar. *Proceedings of the Fifth Annual Meeting of the Berkeley Linguistic Society* 5: 142–58.

Ladd, D.R. 2008. *Intonational Phonology*. 2nd edn. Cambridge: Cambridge University Press.

Lane, N. 2015. *The Vital Question: Why is Life the Way It Is?* London: Profile Books.

Lavid, J., J. Arús Hita and J. Zamorano-Mansilla. 2010. *Systemic Functional Grammar of Spanish*. London: Continuum.

Li, E.S.-H. 2007. *A Systemic Functional Grammar of Chinese*. London: Continuum.

Maiorani, A. 2009. *The Matrix Phenomenon: A Linguistic and Multimodal Analysis*. Saarbrucken: VDM.

Martin, J.R., and P.R.R. White. 2005. *The Language of Evaluation: Appraisal in English*. Basingstoke: Palgrave Macmillan.

Mathiesus, V. 1975. *A Functional Analysis of Present Day English on a General Linguistic Basis*. Ed. J. Vachek. The Hague: Mouton.

Matthiessen, C.M.I.M. 2015. Halliday on language. In J.J. Webster (ed.) *The Bloomsbury Companion to M.A.K Halliday*. London: Bloomsbury, pp. 137–202.

O'Grady, G. 2013. *Key Concepts in Phonetics and Phonology*. Basingstoke: Palgrave MacMillan.

O'Grady, G. 2016. Given/New: What do the terms refer to? A first (small) step. *English Text Construction* 9(1): 9–32.

O'Grady, G., T. Bartlett and L. Fontaine. 2013. *Choice in Language: Applications in Text Analysis*. Sheffield: Equinox.

Pollard, C., and I.V. Sag. 1994. *Head-Driven Phrase Structure Grammar*. Chicago, IL: University of Chicago Press.

Quiroz, B. 2013. The interpersonal and experiential grammar of Chilean Spanish: Towards a principled systemic-functional description based on axial argumentation. Unpublished PhD dissertation. University of Sydney.

Sag, I.V. 2012. Sign-based construction grammar: An informal synopsis. In H.C. Boas and I.A. Sag (eds) *Sign-Based Construction Grammar*. Stanford, CA: CSLI, pp. 1–29.

Scheer, T. 2010. Issues in the development of generative phonology. In N.C. Kula, R. Boma and K. Nasukawa (eds) *The Bloomsbury Companion to Phonology*. London: Bloomsbury, pp. 397–446.

Sinclair, J. 1991. *Trust the Text: Language, Corpus and Discourse*. London: Routledge.

Steedman, M. 2001. *The Syntactic Process*. Cambridge, MA: MIT Press.

Steiner, E. 2015. Halliday's contribution to a theory of context. In J.J. Webster (ed.) *The Bloomsbury Companion to M.A.K Halliday*. London: Bloomsbury, pp. 412–26.

Teruya, K. 2007. *A Systemic Functional Grammar of Japanese*. London: Continuum.

Teruya, K., and C.M.I.M. Matthiessen. 2015. Halliday in relation to language comparison and typology. In J.J. Webster (ed.) *The Bloomsbury Companion to M.A.K Halliday*. London: Bloomsbury, pp. 427–52.

Thibault, P.J. 2004. *Brain, Mind and Signifying Body: An Eco-Social Semiotic Theory*. London: Continuum.

Thompson, G., and S. Hunston. 2006. *System and Corpus: Exploring Connections*. London: Equinox.

Tomasello, M. 2008. *Origins of Human Communication*. Cambridge, MA: MIT Press.

Trávníček, F. 1961. O tak zvanem aktualnim cleneni vetnem [On the so called functional sentence perspective]. *Slovo o Slovesnost* 22: 163–71.

Ventola, E., and A.J. Moya Guijarro. 2009. *The World Told and the World Shown: Multi-Semiosis Issues*. Basingstoke: Palgrave MacMillan.

Xin, X., and D. Cao. 2013. Complementarity of systemic functional grammar and constructional grammar. *Canadian Social Science* 9(5): 162–8.

Zappavigna, M. 2012. *Discourse of Twitter and Social Media: How We Use Language to Create Affiliation on the Web*. London: Continuum.

Further reading

Chapter 1 Introduction: reading systemic functional linguistics

No single volume, even one as thick as the current book, can possibly provide a comprehensive survey of the entirety of systemic functional linguistics (SFL). With that in mind, our hope is that this brief chapter, in combination with the other chapters found in this book, will function as a resource enabling deeper exploration into particular areas of SFL theory and practice. The obvious starting point for a scholar interested in learning more about SFL is its seminal text, Halliday's *Introduction to Functional Grammar*. This work, first published in 1985 and then republished in three further editions in 1994, 2004 and 2014, remains the foundational text for SFL. Over the thirty years since its first publication, *IFG* (as it is sometimes known) has been much expanded to the point at which the third and fourth editions have become reference works to be consulted rather than texts to be consumed from cover to cover. As a result, a number of invaluable texts have been written that introduce neophytes to the theory and especially to its grammar. In many cases, they provide a step-by-step guide in how to conduct text analyses.

Bloor, T.M. 2004. *The Functional Analysis of English*. 2nd edn. London: Hodder Arnold.

Eggins, S. 2004. *An Introduction to Systemic Functional Linguistics*. 2nd edn. London: Continuum.

Fontaine, L. 2012. *Analysing English Grammar: A Systemic Functional Introduction*. Cambridge: Cambridge University Press.

Halliday, M.A.K. 1985. *Introduction to Functional Grammar*. London: Arnold.

Halliday, M.A.K. 1994. *Introduction to Functional Grammar*. 2nd edn. London: Arnold.

Halliday, M.A.K. 2004. *Introduction to Functional Grammar*. 3rd edn. London: Arnold.

Halliday, M.A.K., and C.M.I.M. Matthiessen. 2014. *Halliday's Introduction to Functional Grammar*. 4th edn. London: Routledge.

Martin, J.R., C.M.I.M. Matthiessen and C. Painter. 1997. *Working with Functional Grammar*. London: Arnold.

Thompson, G. 2014. *Introducing Functional Grammar*. 4th edn. London: Routledge.

The Martin and Rose titles listed below are readable, comprehensive introductions to the Sydney school and its work in genre analysis. The Fawcett book is an elegant introduction to the Cardiff Grammar and further explicates how the Cardiff Model of SFL differs from Halliday's model. Matthiessen and colleagues is an invaluable resource for understanding SFL's extravagant metalanguage.

Fawcett, R.P. 2008. *Invitation to Systemic Functional Linguistics through the Cardiff Grammar*. London: Equinox.

Martin, J.R. 1992. *English Text: System and Structure*. Amsterdam: John Benjamins.

Martin, J.R., and D. Rose. 2003. *Working with Discourse: Meaning beyond the Clause*. London: Continuum.
Martin, J.R., and D. Rose 2008. *Genre Relations: Mapping Culture*. London: Equinox.
Matthiessen, C.M.I.M., K. Teruya and M. Lam. 2010. *Key Terms in Systemic Functional Linguistics*. London: Continuum.

The books listed above focus, in the main, on the grammar of English; they do not overtly describe the underlying theory. Readers interested in exploring the underpinnings of the theory are advised to consult the most relevant volume of the collected works of Halliday, Hasan and Martin.

Halliday's collected works are available in eleven volumes edited by Jonathan Webster and published by Bloomsbury.

Halliday, M.A.K. 2002. *The Collected Works of M.A.K. Halliday, Vol. 1: On Grammar*. Ed. J.J. Webster. London: Bloomsbury.
Halliday, M.A.K. 2002. *The Collected Works of M.A.K. Halliday, Vol. 2: Linguistic Studies of Text and Discourse*. Ed. J.J. Webster. London: Bloomsbury.
Halliday, M.A.K. 2003 *The Collected Works of M.A.K. Halliday, Vol. 3: On Language and Linguistics*. Ed. J.J. Webster. London: Bloomsbury.
Halliday, M.A.K. 2004. *The Collected Works of M.A.K. Halliday, Vol. 4: Language of Early Childhood*. Ed. J.J. Webster. London: Bloomsbury.
Halliday, M.A.K. 2006. *The Collected Works of M.A.K. Halliday, Vol. 5: Language of Science*. Ed. J.J. Webster. London: Bloomsbury.
Halliday, M.A.K. 2006. *The Collected Works of M.A.K. Halliday, Vol. 6: Computational and Quantitative Studies*. Ed. J.J. Webster. London: Bloomsbury.
Halliday, M.A.K. 2009. *The Collected Works of M.A.K. Halliday, Vol. 7: Studies in English Language*. Ed. J.J. Webster. London: Bloomsbury.
Halliday, M.A.K. 2009. *The Collected Works of M.A.K. Halliday, Vol. 8: Studies in Chinese Language*. Ed. J.J. Webster. London: Bloomsbury.
Halliday, M.A.K. 2009. *The Collected Works of M.A.K. Halliday, Vol. 9: Language and Education*. Ed. J.J. Webster. London: Bloomsbury.
Halliday, M.A.K. 2009. *The Collected Works of M.A.K. Halliday, Vol. 10: Language and Society*. Ed. J.J. Webster. London: Bloomsbury.
Halliday. M.A.K. 2013. *The Collected Works of M.A.K. Halliday, Vol. 11: Halliday in the Twenty-First Century*. Ed. J.J. Webster. London: Bloomsbury.

Hasan's collected works are also edited by Jonathan Webster and are published by Equinox. There will be seven books in total, of which, at the time of writing, four have been published.

Hasan, R. 2005. *The Collected Works of Ruqaiya Hasan, Vol. 1: Language, Society and Consciousness*. Ed. J.J. Webster. London: Equinox.
Hasan, R. 2009. *The Collected Works of Ruqaiya Hasan, Vol. 2: Semantic Variation – Meaning in Society and Sociolinguistics*. Ed. J.J. Webster. London: Equinox.
Hasan, R. 2011. *The Collected Works of Ruqaiya Hasan, Vol. 3: Language and Education: Learning and Teaching in Society*. Ed. J.J. Webster. London: Equinox.
Hasan, R. 2016. *The Collected Works of Ruqaiya Hasan, Vol. 4: Context in the System and Process of Language*. Ed. J.J. Webster. London: Equinox.
Hasan, R. Forthcoming. *The Collected Works of Ruqaiya Hasan, Vol. 5: Describing Language: Form and Function*. Ed. J.J. Webster. London: Equinox.
Hasan, R. Forthcoming. *The Collected Works of Ruqaiya Hasan, Vol. 6: Unity in Discourse: Texture and Structure*. Ed. J.J. Webster. London: Equinox.
Hasan, R. Forthcoming. *The Collected Works of Ruqaiya Hasan, Vol. 7: Verbal Art – A Social Semiotic Perspective*. Ed. J.J. Webster. London: Equinox.

Martin's collected works have been published in China by Shanghai Jiao Tong University Press and are edited by Wang Zhenhua.

Martin, J.R. 2010. *The Collected Works of J.R. Martin, Vol. 1: Systemic Functional Linguistic Theory.* Ed. Z. Wang. Shanghai: Shanghai Jiao Tong University Press.

Martin, J.R. 2010. *The Collected Works of J.R. Martin, Vol. 2: Discourse Semantics.* Ed. Z. Wang. Shanghai: Shanghai Jiao Tong University Press.

Martin, J.R. 2012. *The Collected Works of J.R. Martin, Vol. 3: Genre Studies.* Ed. Z. Wang. Shanghai: Shanghai Jiao Tong University Press.

Martin, J.R. 2012. *The Collected Works of J.R. Martin, Vol. 4: Register Studies.* Ed. Z. Wang. Shanghai: Shanghai Jiao Tong University Press.

Martin, J.R. 2012. *The Collected Works of J.R. Martin, Vol. 5: Text Analysis.* Ed. Z. Wang. Shanghai: Shanghai Jiao Tong University Press.

Martin, J.R. 2012. *The Collected Works of J.R. Martin, Vol. 6: Critical Discourse Analysis/Positive Discourse Analysis.* Ed. Z. Wang. Shanghai: Shanghai Jiao Tong University Press.

Martin, J.R. 2012. *The Collected Works of J.R. Martin, Vol. 7: Language in Education.* Ed. Z. Wang. Shanghai: Shanghai Jiao Tong University Press.

Martin, J.R. 2012. *The Collected Works of J.R. Martin, Vol. 8: Forensic Linguistics.* Ed. Z. Wang. Shanghai: Shanghai Jiao Tong University Press.

Christian Matthiessen's 1995 *Lexicogrammatical Cartography* (Tokyo: International Language Sciences) remains a key source for understanding the power of an SFL approach in mapping out the topography of English grammar. This work is alas currently hard to find.

Two extremely useful books on the architecture of, and the rationale behind, the Cardiff Grammar are the following, both by Fawcett.

Fawcett, R.P. 1980. *Cognitive Linguistics and Social Interaction.* Heidedberg and Exeter: Julius Groos Verlas and Exeter University Press.

Fawcett, R.P. 2000. *A Theory of Syntax for Systemic Functional Linguistics.* Amsterdam: John Benjamins.

Additionally, Fawcett's forthcoming titles *Functional Syntax Handbook: Analysing English at the Level of Form* and *An Integrative Architecture for Systemic Functional Linguistics and Other Theories of Language*, both to be published by Equinox, will be major contributions in illustrating the distinctiveness of the Cardiff approach.

One of our major motivations for compiling this Handbook was our desire to show that SFL is a vibrant and evolving theory. It is no longer – if it ever was – a theory of English grammar nor is it any longer solely grounded in the modality of spoken and written language. As a theory of appliable linguistics/social semiotics, it engages with the world and is itself informed by the world. As such, we asked our authors not only to consider why and how SFL has evolved to its present form, but also to predict the directions in which SFL will evolve over the course of the twenty-first century. Such a brief is, of course, not fully answerable within the confines of a single chapter and so we asked each author to suggest some key readings to which interested readers could refer to broaden their relevant knowledge.

We have on occasion, in the interests of consistency, made some slight alterations to the text supplied by the authors, but have naturally not altered their suggested readings, although space on some occasions as forced us to reduce the number of readings suggested. Where authors were unable to respond to our request for further readings, we have taken the liberty of adding some key readings ourselves.

Chapter 2 The place of systemic functional linguistics as a linguistic theory in the twenty-first century

Butler, C., and F. Gonzálvez-García. 2014, *Exploring Functional-Cognitive Space*. Amsterdam: John Benjamins.
   This work illustrates similarities and differences between SFL and other functional and cognitive approaches to language.

Halliday, M.A.K. 1978. *Language as a Social Semiotic*. London: Arnold.
   In this work, Halliday builds upon the work of Firth and Malinowski to create the framework of a social-semiotic theory of language.

Halliday, M.A.K., and C.M.I.M. Matthiessen. 2014. *Halliday's Introduction to Functional Grammar*. 4th edn. London: Routledge.
   The most up-to-date description of systemic functional grammar.

Chapter 3 What is a system? What is a function? A study in contrasts and convergences

Butler, C., and F. Gonzálvez-García. 2014. *Exploring Functional-Cognitive Space*. Amsterdam: John Benjamins.
   This book usefully compares SFL with other functional/cognitive models of language.

Fawcett, R. Forthcoming. *The Functional Syntax Handbook: Analysing English at the Level of Form*. London: Equinox.
   When published, this will be a clear presentation of Cardiff Grammar, incorporating systems and structural analyses.

Halliday, M.A.K. 2002. *The Collected Works of M.A.K. Halliday, Vol. 1: On Grammar*. Ed. J.J. Webster. London: Bloomsbury.
   This book is a collection of key historical papers in the development of SFL.

Chapter 4 Stratum, delicacy, realisation and rank

Butler, C.S., and M. Taverniers. 2008: Layering in structural-functional grammars. *Linguistics* 46(4): 689–756.
   Provides a detailed discussion of different types of layering, with particular reference to SFL, functional discourse grammar, and role and reference grammar.

Halliday, M.A.K. 1999. The notion of 'context' in language education. In M. Ghadessy (ed.) *Text and Context in Functional Linguistics*. Amsterdam and Philadelphia, PA: John Benjamins, pp. 1–24.

Hasan, R. 2009. The place of context in a systemic functional model. In In M.A.K. Halliday and J.J. Webster (eds) *The Continuum Companion to Systemic Functional Linguistics*. London: Continuum, pp. 166–89.
   These two chapters both discuss the place of context in SFL: Halliday, from the perspective of language education.

Halliday, M.A.K. 2009. Methods – techniques – problems. In M.A.K. Halliday and J.J. Webster (eds) *The Continuum Companion to Systemic Functional Linguistics*. London: Continuum, pp. 59–86.

Matthiessen, C.M.I.M. 2007. The 'architecture' of language according to systemic functional theory: Developments since the 1970s. In R. Hasan, C.M.I.M. Matthiessen and J.J. Webster (eds) *Continuing Discourse on Language: A Functional Perspective, Vol. 2*. London: Equinox, pp. 505–61.

These two chapters cover most of the topics discussed in this chapter: Halliday, at a relatively introductory level; Matthiessen, at a more advanced level.

Martin, J.R. 2013. *Systemic Functional Grammar: A Next Step into the Theory – Axial Relations*. Beijing: Higher Education Press. With an introduction by Halliday, and Chinese contributions by Wang Pin and Zhu Yongsheng.

Provides a step-by-step guide to the drawing of system networks, and discusses the interrelations of system and structure with stratum and rank.

Chapter 5 From meaning to form in the Cardiff Model of language and its use

Fawcett, R.P. 2010 [2000]. *A Theory of Syntax for Systemic Functional Linguistics* (Current Issues in Linguistic Theory 206). Amsterdam: John Benjamins. Paperback edition with new preface and updated bibliography.

This book seeks to answer the question: what theoretical concepts are required for the description of syntax in a modern, large-scale systemic functional grammar? It traces the interplay of both theory and description, and meaning and form, as the theory has evolved over five decades, and it outlines the syntax that is required in a comprehensive description of a language.

Fawcett, R.P. 2013. Choice and choosing in systemic functional grammar: What is it and how is it done? In L. Fontaine, T. Bartlett and G. O'Grady (eds) *Systemic Functional Linguistics: Exploring Choice*. Cambridge: Cambridge University Press, pp. 115–34.

This chapter describes the six answers to this two-part question that have been proposed by SFL scholars, and it explains why the answers proposed here and implemented in the Cardiff Model of language are to be preferred over the others.

Neale, A. 2002a. More delicate TRANSITIVITY: Extending the PROCESS TYPE system networks for English to include full semantic classifications. Unpublished PhD thesis. Centre for Language and Communication Research, Cardiff University.

This thesis provides (a) a history of SFL descriptions of the semantics and syntax of Processes and their associated Participant Roles in English, and (b) an overview of the most fully developed set of system networks available at the time – that is, those of the Cardiff Grammar. This description has been modified in minor ways since this thesis was written, but the major changes introduced in developing the GENESYS generator were all in place by 2002.

Chapter 6 Systemic functional linguistics and the clause: the experiential metafunction

Butler, C. 2004. Representing situations. In *Structure and Function. A Guide to Three Major Structural-Functional Theories, Part 1 – Approaches to the Simplex Clause*. Amsterdam: John Benjamins, pp. 337–448.

In this chapter, Chris Butler offers a thoughtful and instructive survey of the different approaches to the clause's representational semantics in systemic functional grammar, functional discourse grammar, and role and reference grammar.

Halliday, M.A.K. 1967a. Notes on transitivity and theme in English 1. *Journal of Linguistics* 3(1): 37–81.

Halliday, M.A.K. 1967b. Notes on transitivity and theme in English 2. *Journal of Linguistics* 3(2): 199–244.

Halliday, M.A.K. 1968. Notes on transitivity and theme in English 3. *Journal of Linguistics* 4(2): 179–215.

    This trilogy is, and remains, essential reading with regard to the Hallidayan description of process–participant relations in English, which, importantly, shows his agnation heuristics at work to 'crack the code'. These have been republished in *The Collected Works of M.A.K. Halliday, Vol. 7: Studies in English Language* (2009, ed. J.J. Webster, London: Bloomsbury).

McGregor, W.B. 1997. Constituency: The experiential semiotic. In *Semiotic Grammar*. Oxford: Clarendon, pp. 88–136.

    McGregor's chapter about the Experiential Semiotic considers typological evidence for Halliday's generalisation that the ergative and transitive systems of participant roles are relevant in some form to the grammar of all languages.

Chapter 7 The logical metafunction in systemic functional linguistics

Halliday, M.A.K., and C.M.I.M. Matthiessen. 2014. *Halliday's Introduction to Functional Grammar.* 4th edn. London: Arnold.
Halliday, M.A.K., and J.J. Webster. 2015. *Text Linguistics. The How and Why of Meaning.* London: Equinox.
Martin, J.R. 1992. *English Text: Systems and Structure.* Amsterdam: John Benjamins.

    These three volumes provide a detailed outline with worked-through examples of the logical metafunction.

Chapter 8 Interpersonal meaning and the clause

Fawcett, R.P. 2011. A semantic system network for MOOD in English (and some complementary systems). Paper available from fawcett@cardiff.ac.uk.

    An elaborate and rather comprehensive presentation of the system for MOOD in the Cardiff Grammar framework.

Halliday, M.A.K. 1984. Language as code and language as behaviour: A systemic-functional interpretation of the nature and ontogenesis of dialogue. In R.P. Fawcett, M.A.K. Halliday, S.M. Lamb and A. Makkai (eds) *The Semiotics of Culture and Language, vol. 1*. London: Pinter, pp. 3–36.

    Halliday's first (partly theoretical, partly descriptive) account of the current taxonomy of speech functions in the IFG tradition.

Halliday, M.A.K., and C.M.I.M. Matthiessen. 2014. *An Introduction to Functional Grammar.* 4th edn. London: Routledge.

    The most recent description of the clause as exchange in the IFG tradition.

Hasan, R. 1985. *Offers in the Making: A Systemic-Functional Approach.* Sydney: Macquarie University.

    An argument for the offer (as one of the four basic speech functions in the IFG tradition), the book serves partly to demonstrate the appropriateness of the taxonomy for speech functions proposed in Halliday's 1984 article.

Thibault, P.J., and T. van Leeuwen. 1996. Grammar, society, and the speech act: Renewing the connections. *Journal of Pragmatics* 25: 561–85.

    A discussion of the speech functions in SFL in relation to more pragmatic accounts of similar linguistic meanings and an idea for a delicate approach to the description of speech functions, which, in some respects, reflects the approach in Hasan (1985).

Chapter 9 Textual metafunction and theme: what's 'it' about?

Berry, M. 1995. Thematic options and success in writing. In M. Ghadessy (ed.) *Thematic Development in English Texts*. London: Pinter, pp. 55–84.
> Berry illustrates how Theme choices produces effective writing and argues for the importance of raising awareness of Theme among novice writers.

Daneš, F. 1974. Functional sentence perspective and the organisation of the text. In F. Daneš (ed.) *Papers on Functional Sentence Perspective*. The Hague: Mouton, pp. 106–28.
> This seminal work outlines the origin of Thematic Progression. Readers can trace the influence of Daneš' work on SFL views of Theme.

Forey, G., and G. Thompson. 2009. *Text Type and Texture: In Honour of Flo Davies*. London: Equinox.
> This collection is a valuable, up-to-date theoretical account of Theme, including analytical descriptions of Theme in a range of text texts within the wider SFL tradition.

Hasan, R., and P. Fries (eds). 1995. *On Subject and Theme*. Amsterdam: John Benjamins,
> The chapters collected in this volume further explore the influence of Daneš' work on SFL views of Theme.

Chapter 10 Intonation and systemic functional linguistics: the way forward

Beckmann, M., and G.A Elam. 1997. Guidelines for ToBI labelling. Available online at http://www.ling.ohio-state.edu/research/phonetics/E_ToBI/.
> This work is a useful guide for SFL scholars interested in knowing how and why tone and breaks indices (ToBI) coding is as it is.

Bowcher, W.L., and B.A. Smith (eds). 2014. *Systemic Phonology: Recent Studies in English.* Sheffield: Equinox.
Tench, P. (ed.). 1992. *Studies in Systemic Phonology*. London: Pinter.
> These two volumes are the most complete accounts of work in systemic phonology. They include chapters that illustrate the relation between Intonation and other prosodic systems, and Tench provides some systemic-functional intonational descriptions of languages other than English.

Halliday, M.A.K., and W.S. Greaves. 2008. *Intonation in the Grammar of British English*. London: Equinox.
> The most recent account of Halliday's description of Intonation and its place in the grammar.

Tench, P. 1996. *The Intonation Systems of English*. London: Cassell.
> This is probably the best single-volume description of English Intonation.

Chapter 11 Theme in the Cardiff Grammar

Fawcett, R.P., and G.W. Huang. 1995. A functional analysis of the enhanced theme construction in English. *Interface: Journal of Applied Linguistics* 10(1): 113–44.
Huang, G.W. 1996. Experiential enhanced theme in English. In M. Berry, C.S. Butler, R.P. Fawcett and G.W. Huang (eds) *Meaning and Form: Systemic Functional Interpretations – Meaning and Choice in Language: Studies for Michael Halliday*. Norwood, NJ: Ablex, pp. 65–112.
Huang, G.W. 2003. *Enhanced Theme in English: Its Structures and Functions*. Shanxi: Shanxi Education Press.
> Each of these titles describes the Cardiff Grammar's novel approach to the so-called it–cleft construction, and illustrate some differences between the Cardiff and the IFG approaches.

Chapter 12 Transitivity in the Cardiff Grammar

Fawcett, R.P. Forthcoming. *The Functional Semantics Handbook: Analysing English at the Level of Meaning*. London: Equinox.
    The Fawcett handbook will offer the fullest account of the Cardiff Grammar. It will take readers through a Cardiff analysis step by step.

Neale, A. 2002. The Process Type database. Dataset available online at https://www.researchgate.net/publication/273448463_PTDB_-_modified_version_2014.
    This is an invaluable resource for analysing the Process and Participant Roles in English-language texts.

Neale, A. 2011. Alternation and participant role: A contribution from systemic functional grammar. In P. Guerrero Medina (ed.) *Morphosyntactic Relations in English: Functional and Cognitive Perspective*. London: Equinox, pp. 83–112.
    This chapter illustrates the Cardiff Grammar approach to transitivity.

Chapter 13 Theme in Spanish

Lavid, J., J. Arús and J.R. Zamorano. 2010. *Systemic Functional Grammar of Spanish: A Contrastive Study with English*. London: Continuum.
    Chapter 5 of this descriptive grammar of Spanish offers a more detailed account of the Theme-as-starting-element approach in Spanish, as well as a plethora of examples analysed from that perspective.

Moyano, E. 2016. Theme in the Spanish declarative clause: First step for a(nother) systemic description. *English Text Construction* 9(1): 190–219.
    This article is a good example of the most radical challenge to the Theme-as-starting-element approach.

Rose, D. 2001. Some variation in Theme across languages. *Functions of Language* 8(1): 109–45.
    This article provides a comprehensive overview of Theme in different languages, thus creating a useful context for the study of Theme in languages other than English (LOTE).

Chapter 14 Mood in Japanese

Halliday, M.A.K. and C.M.I.M Matthiessen 2014. *Halliday's Introduction to Functional Grammar*. 4th edn. London and New York: Routledge.
    Chapter 4 of this seminal text offers the original and most detailed systemic functional account of the interpersonal grammar of English.

Matthiessen, C.M.I.M 2004. Descriptive motifs and generalisations. In A. Caffarel, J. R. Martin and C.M.I.M Matthiessen (eds) *Language Typology: A Functional Perspective*. Amsterdam: John Benjamins, pp. 537–664.
    This chapter systematically compares and contrasts major interpersonal systems and options in a large sample of languages of the world, including Japanese, which has led to functional generalisations.

Matthiessen, C.M.I.M., K. Teruya and C. Wu. 2008. Multilingual studies as a multi-dimensional space of interconnected language studies. In J.J. Webster (ed.) *Meaning in Context*. London and New York: Continuum, pp. 146–221.
    This chapter investigates the grammaticalisation of the speech functions of moves in dialogic exchanges as a system of MOOD in the context of multilingual studies.

Teruya, K. (2007) *A Systemic Functional Grammar of Japanese*. London: Continuum.

In this chapter on the interpersonal grammar of Japanese, the system of MOOD is described with reference to a number of relevant interpersonal systems.

Teruya, K., E. Akerejola, T.H. Andersen, A. Caffarel, J. Lavid, C.M.I.M. Matthiessen, U.H. Petersen, P. Patpong and F. Smedegaard. 2007. Typology of MOOD: A text-based and system-based functional view. In R. Hasan, C.M.I.M. Matthiessen and J.J. Webster (eds) *Continuing Discourse on Language: A Functional Perspective, Vol. 2*. London: Equinox, pp. 859–920.

In this chapter, a number of languages are systematically compared and unified as a multilingual system network of MOOD.

Chapter 15 The phoneme and word phonology in systemic functional linguistics

Palmer, F.R. (ed.). 1970. *Prosodic Analysis*. Oxford: Oxford University Press.

Palmer offers a clear account of Firthian prosodic analysis and illustrates Firth's influence on Halliday's thinking.

Bowcher, W.L., and B.A. Smith (eds). 2014. *Systemic Phonology: Recent Studies in English*. Sheffield: Equinox.

Halliday, M.A.K. 1994. *An Introduction to Functional Grammar*. 2nd edn. London: Arnold.

Tench, P. (ed.). 1992. *Studies in Systemic Phonology*. London: Pinter.

These three volumes are the best current description of the place of the phoneme in SFL. Of special note are the following chapters.

McGregor, W.B. 1992. Towards a systemic account of Gooniyandi segmental phonology. In P. Tench (ed.) *Studies in Systemic Phonology*. London: Pinter, pp. 19–43.

Young, D. 1992. English consonant clusters: A systemic approach. In P. Tench (ed.) *Studies in Systemic Phonology*. London: Pinter, pp. 44–69.

Tench, P. 2014. Towards a systemic presentation of the word phonology of English. In W.L. Bowcher and B.A. Smith (eds) *Systemic Phonology*. London: Equinox, pp. 267–94.

Chapter 16 Form and function in groups

Butler, C. 2003a. *Structure and Function: A Guide to Three Major Structural-Functional Theories, Part 1 – Approaches to the Simplex Clause*. Amsterdam: John Benjamins.

Butler, C. 2003b. *Structure and Function: A Guide to Three Major Structural-Functional Theories, Part 2 – From Clause to Discourse and beyond*. Amsterdam: John Benjamins.

A comprehensive and detailed comparison at all levels of language of what Butler identifies as 'structural-functional' theories – that is, functional discourse grammar, role and reference grammar, and systemic functional theory – with helpful analyses within each framework using corpus data.

Caffarel, A., J.R. Martin and C.M.I.M. Matthiessen (eds). 2004. *Language Typology: A Functional Perspective*. Amsterdam: John Benjamins.

A collection of 'metafunctional profiles' of the lexicogrammar of a range of languages in an SFL framework, not so consistently organised across the different chapters as to be maximally useful for comparison, but with useful introductory and summary chapters.

Graffi, G. 2001. *200 Years of Syntax: A Critical Survey* (Studies in the History of the Language Sciences 98). Amsterdam: John Benjamins.

A useful account of the rise of syntax as an independent area of study and of the gradual separation between the analysis of sentences and that of word groups.

McGregor, W. 1997. *Semiotic Grammar*. Oxford: Clarendon.

A very thoughtful and carefully argued linguistic framework drawing largely on SFL, as well as other functional approaches, and containing a particularly useful rethinking of the relations between metafunctions and structural types.

Tesnière, L. 1965. *Éléments de syntaxe structurale* [*Elements of Structural Syntax*]. 2nd edn. Paris: C. Klincksieck.

A virtuoso attempt to build a comprehensive grammatical model using a dependency framework, including detailed accounts of the grammar of sentences and groups, and a full treatment of the phenomenon of *translation* – that is, grammatical metaphor.

Chapter 17 The English nominal group: the centrality of the Thing element

Fawcett, R. 2006. Establishing the grammar of 'typicity' in English: An exercise in scientific inquiry. In G. Huang, C. Chang and F. Dai (eds) *Functional Linguistics as Appliable Linguistics*. Guangzhou: Sun Yat-sen University Press, pp. 159–262.

Fawcett, R. 2007. Modelling 'selection' between referents in the English nominal group. In C.S. Butler, R. Hidalgo Downing and J. Lavid (eds) *Functional Perspectives on Grammar and Discourse: In Honour of Angela Downing* (Studies in Language Comparison Series 85). Amsterdam: John Benjamins, pp. 165–204.

The Cardiff Grammar has developed very detailed subsets of types of determiner. These two chapters are key resources in any consideration of determiners in English.

Fontaine, L. 2008. A systemic functional approach to referring expressions: Reconsidering postmodification in the nominal group. Unpublished PhD thesis. Cardiff University.

Fontaine, L. 2012. *Analysing English Grammar: A Systemic Functional Introduction*. Cambridge: Cambridge University Press.

Very few publications have dealt with the nominal group specifically, and even fewer have attempted to account for referring, the system networks and probabilities.

Halliday, M.A.K., and C.M.I.M Matthiessen. 2004. *An Introduction to Functional Grammar*. 3rd edn. London: Arnold.

Much of what has been presented in this chapter has either come from, or been inspired, by Halliday's *IFG*. It is a wealth of information for detail on the Hallidayan account of the nominal group.

Keizer, E. 2007. *The English Noun Phrase: The Nature of Linguistic Categorization*. Cambridge: Cambridge University Press.

This book is listed even though it is not a systemic functional account of the nominal group; rather, it offers an alternative functional approach.

Martin, J.R. 1992. *English Text: System and Structure*. Philadelphia, PA, and Amsterdam: John Benjamins.

Martin's work is an excellent resource that provides an account of the nominal group from a discourse perspective.

Chapter 18 The adjectival group

Downing, A., and Locke, P. 1992. *A University Course in English Grammar*. New York: Prentice Hall.

Downing, A., and Locke, P. 2006. *English Grammar: A University Course*. 2nd edn. London and New York: Routledge.

These titles provide a fuller picture of both the semantics and lexicogrammar of the adjectival group.

Tucker, G.H. 1998. *The Lexicogrammar of Adjectives: A Systemic Functional Approach to Lexis*. London: Cassell Academic.

This book describes the semantics of 'quality' and the syntax of adjectives in a Cardiff Grammar approach, and it is probably the fullest account of this area of English grammar yet published.

Chapter 19 The verbal group

Bache, C. 2008. *English Tense and Aspect in Halliday's Systemic Functional Grammar: A Critical Appraisal and an Alternative*. London: Equinox.

This book critically reviews Halliday's account of English tense in the 'Sydney Model' and explores alternatives, both within and outside SFL – with a special focus on the Cardiff Model and Harder's instructional semantics, respectively. Drawing on this review and exploration, the author proposes his own systemic functional account of English tense, integrating conceptualisations concerning both aspect and type of event ('Aktionsart'). This account challenges the recursive nature of tense systems (in English) and does not assume a rank scale (along the lines of the Cardiff Model).

Halliday, M.A.K. 1976 [1966]. The English verbal group. In G.R. Kress (ed.) *Halliday: System and Function in Language*. London: Oxford University Press, pp. 136–58.

This 1966 working paper, included in Kress's compilation published in 1976, is one of the earliest accounts of the (English) verbal group available from a systemic perspective. The main novelty of this description is its focus on TENSE at group rank, interpreted as a relatively simple system of choices that is recursive in nature. By means of repeated choices, this three-term system is shown to regularly motivate what appears to be a very complex patterning of forms if seen only from the viewpoint of structure (as is the case in traditional approaches to tense).

Halliday, M.A.K., and C.M.I.M. Matthiessen. 2014. *Halliday's Introduction to Functional Grammar*. 4th edn. London: Routledge.

The most up-to-date description of systemic functional grammar in English.

McGregor, W. 1996. Arguments for the category of verb phrase. *Functions of Language* 3(1): 1–30.

This article begins by reviewing key issues in the conceptualisation of the verb phrase in different traditions, raising questions on the need for a 'phrasal unit' of the 'verb class' (as opposed to the 'verb' as the only relevant 'word unit'). The paper then reviews three main arguments against a 'phrasal unit', focusing on the critique directed by Fawcett, within the Cardiff Model, to Halliday's modelling of the (English) verbal group. Drawing on this critique, the author then develops his own proposal of a verbal phrase in a new conceptualisation of this unit within the framework of semiotic grammar.

Chapter 20 The verbal group in French

Caffarel, A. 2006. *A Systemic Functional Grammar of French*. London: Continuum.

Caffarel, A., J.R. Martin and C.M.I.M. Matthiessen. 2004. *Language Typology: A Functional Perspective*. Amsterdam: John Benjamins.

Matthiessen, C.M.I.M. 1996. Tense in English seen through systemic functional theory. In M. Berry, C. Butler, R. Fawcett and G. Huang (eds) *Meaning and Form: Systemic Functional Interpretations*. Norwood, NJ: Ablex, pp. 431–98.

These readings will provide students with additional background on the interpretation of the verbal group and TENSE system in SFL, and the application of the theory to the description of languages other than English and French in particular.

Chapter 21 The nominal group in Chinese

Li, C.N., and S.A. Thompson. 1981. *Mandarin Chinese: A Functional Reference Grammar*. Berkeley, CA: University of California Press.

Li and Thompson adopt a functional approach to analysing the grammar of Chinese. Although published a long time ago, it is still popularly quoted.

Li, E.S.H. 2007. *A Systemic Functional Grammar of Chinese*. London: Continuum.

The first and only book on Chinese grammar from a systemic functional perspective, its main focus is the clausal grammar of Chinese, but it extends into discourse and text analysis in the second part of the book.

Tang, C.C.J. 1990. A note on the DP analysis of the Chinese noun phrase. *Linguistics* 28: 337–54.

A paper that focuses on the Chinese determiner phrase and noun phrase.

Chapter 22 Grammatical metaphor

Halliday, M.A.K. 1999. The grammatical construction of scientific knowledge: The framing of the English clause. In R. Rossini Favretti, G. Sandri and R. Scazzieri (eds) *Incommensurability and Translation: Kuhnian Perspectives on Scientific Communication and Theory Change*. Cheltenham: Edward Elgar, pp. 85–116.

This article is a state-of-the-art example of the study of grammatical metaphor in scientific discourse and includes an overview of subtypes of ideational metaphor.

Halliday, M.A.K., and C.M.I.M. Matthiessen. 1999. Grammatical metaphor. In M.A.K. Halliday, and C.M.I.M. Matthiessen (eds) *Construing Experience through Meaning: A Language-Based Approach to Cognition* (Open Linguistics Series). London: Cassell/Continuum, pp. 227–93.

This chapter gives a comprehensive overview of ideational metaphor.

Simon-Vandenbergen, A.-M., M. Taverniers and L. Ravelli (eds). 2003. *Grammatical Metaphor: Views from Systemic Functional Linguistics* (Current Issues in Linguistic Theory 236.) Amsterdam: John Benjamins.

A collected volume that contains representative chapters on the theorising of ideational and interpersonal metaphor, metaphor in ontogenesis, in scientific discourse, and grammatical metaphor in relation to phonological and semiotic metaphor.

Taverniers, M. Forthcoming. *Grammatical Metaphor as a Construction Type*. London: Equinox.

An in-depth analysis of the emergence of 'grammatical metaphor' in SFL, and a proposal to identify ideational and interpersonal 'grammatical metaphors' as instances of a more general construction type, based on a doubling of (non-metaphorical) semiosis.

Thompson, G. 1996. Grammatical metaphor. In *Introducing Functional Grammar*. London: Arnold, pp. 163–78.

An easily accessible introduction to Halliday's concept of grammatical metaphor, with specific attention paid to the role of grammatical metaphor in the different metafunctions.

Chapter 23 Context in systemic functional linguistics: towards scalar supervenience?

Hasan, R. 2016. *The Collected Works of Ruqaiya Hasan, Vol. 4: Context in the System and Process of Language*. Ed. J.J. Webster. London: Equinox.

The key author on context in SFL is, of course, Ruqaiya Hasan. The fourth volume of her collected works brings together her writings in this area.

Hasan, R. 1995. The conception of context in text. In P. Fries and M. Gregory (eds) *Discourse in Society: Systemic Functional Perspectives* (Meaning and Choice in Language: Studies for Michael Halliday). Westport, CT, and London: Ablex, pp. 183–283.

Hasan, R. 1998. Speaking with reference to context. In M. Ghadessy (ed.) *Text and Context in Functional Linguistics*. Amsterdam: John Benjamins, pp. 219–328.

Hasan, R. 2009. The place of context in a systemic functional model. In M.A.K. Halliday and J.J. Webster (eds) *Continuum Companion to Systemic Functional Linguistics*. London: Continuum, pp. 166–89.

    These three papers are all seminal. Hasan (2009) is the most accessible.

Lukin, A. 2015. Language and society, context and text: The contributions of Ruqaiya Hasan. In W.L. Bowcher and J.Y. Liang (eds) *Essays in Honour of Ruqaiya Hasan: Society in Language, Language in Society*. London and New York: Palgrave, pp. 143–65.

    Annabelle Lukin's chapter in the Festschrift for Hasan offers an excellent overview of Hasan's voluminous work.

Chapter 24 Field, tenor and mode

Bowcher, W.L. 2007. Field and multimodal texts. In R. Hasan, C. Matthiessen, and J. Webster (eds.) *Continuing Discourse on Language: A Functional Perspective Volume 2*. London: Equinox, pp. 619–646.

    In this chapter, Bowcher interrogates the notion of default pairings and the features of ancillary and constitutive as choices in field in relation to multimodal instructional texts.

Bowcher, W.L. 2013. Material action as choice in field. In L. Fontaine, T. Bartlett and G. O'Grady (eds.) *Systemic Functional Linguistics: Exploring Choice*. Cambridge: Cambridge University Press, pp. 318–341.

    This chapter engages with and develops ideas to do with Butt's (2004) and Hasan's (1999) field system networks, specifically the sub-system of Material Action. It also discusses the issue of 'relevancy'.

Bowcher, W.L. 2014. Issues in developing unified systems for contextual field and mode. *Functions of Language* 21(2): 176–209.

    This article discusses some of the issues involved in representing the parameters of context of situation as system networks. It argues that the primary features of the networks should serve as the defining features of the contextual parameters. It brings together previous networks of field and mode and presents two revised system networks – one for field and one for mode.

Butt, D. 2004. *Parameters of Context: On establishing the similarities and differences between social processes*. (unpublished mimeo, Macquarie University).

    In this mimeo, David Butt presents system networks for field, tenor and mode.

Halliday, M.A.K. and Hasan, R. (1985) *Language, Context, and Text: Aspects of Language in a Social-semiotic Perspective*. Geelong: Deakin University Press.

    This foundational volume on Systemic Functional Linguistics includes a description of the concept of context of situation and of the contextual parameters of field, tenor, and mode. It explains the relationship between the contextual parameters, the functions of language, and register, and presents analyses of texts and their contexts of situations.

Hasan, R. 1999. Speaking with reference to context. In M. Ghadessy (ed.) *Text and Context in Functional Linguistics*. Amsterdam: John Benjamins, pp. 219–328.

    The latter half of this chapter presents a detailed discussion of different features within the system of Field, and presents Hasan's argument for the inclusion of "material action", "default" choices and for the place of "ancillary" and "constitutive" verbal action within the field network.

Hasan, R. 2009. The place of context in a systemic functional model. In M.A.K. Halliday and J. Webster (eds) *Continuum Companion to Systemic Functional Linguistics*. London: Continuum, pp.166–189.

> This chapter includes Hasan's argument against the inclusion of "material action" as a subsystem in the field network and presents an up-dated network for field.

Hasan, R. 2014. Towards a paradigmatic description of context: Systems, metafunctions, and semantics. *Functional Linguistics* 1(9): 1–54.

> This article presents a detailed description of the parameters of field, tenor, and mode in terms of system networks, the relations between the parameters and language and register, the analytical and theoretical value of representing field, tenor, and mode as system networks, and the principles underlying this method of their representation.

Matthiessen, C.M.I.M. 2015. Register in the round: Registerial cartography. *Functional Linguistics* 2(9): 1–48. DOI 10.1186/s40554-015-0015-8.

> This article presents a portion of Matthiessen's project which aims to "map" register variation of a language from the perspective of the contextual variables of field, tenor, and mode. In this article, Matthiessen focuses on field, and identifies eight main fields of activity and several secondary fields of activity.

Chapter 25 Cohesion in systemic functional linguistics: a theoretical reflection

Clarke, B.P. 2016. Textual dynamicity as a heuristic for a delicate semantic description of ellipsis patterns. *English Text Construction* 9(1): 99–114.

> This article outline a more detailed discussion than has been possible in this volume of what this chapter claims to be a specific semantic motive (an increase in pace, construed iconically) for a particular patterned use of ellipsis (Subject ellipsis across consecutive clauses) in a specific text-type (one with a fast-paced, second-order field-of-discourse).

Halliday, M.A.K., and R. Hasan. 1976. *Cohesion in English*. London: Longman.

> Halliday and Hasan's *Cohesion in English* remains the standard account on English cohesive devices. It outlines the potential and constraints of each type of cohesion from the perspective of the lexicogrammar.

Martin, J.R. 1992. *English Text: System and Structure*. Amsterdam: John Benjamins.

> Martin's *English Text* is a commendable attempt to show the semantic and contextual relevance of cohesive devices in English. Martin's account here is not without controversy. He sees the majority of cohesive devices in English as the semantics (Martin 1992: 1), rather than as a part of the non-structural lexicogrammatical resources of the language as do Halliday and Hasan (1976).

Yang, X. 2013. Modelling ellipsis in EFL classroom discourse. In Y. Fang and J.J. Webster (eds) *Developing Systemic Functional Linguistics: Theory and Application*. Sheffield: Equinox, pp. 227–40.

> In this chapter, Xueyan (2013: 239) outlines a principled argument that advocates text-type specific inquiries into individual cohesive devices – such work being different in kind from the 'system' accounts of Halliday and Hasan (1976) and Martin (1992).

Chapter 26 Register analysis in systemic functional linguistics

Halliday, M.A.K. 2004. *Collected Works of M.A.K. Halliday, Vol. 5: The Language of Science*. Ed. J.J. Webster. London: Continuum.

> This volume exemplifies Halliday's empirical and theoretical approach to register, focusing on his work on the language of science.

Halliday, M.A.K., and R. Hasan. 1985. *Language, Context, and Text: Aspects of Language in a Social-Semiotic Perspective*. Geelong: Deakin University Press.

   This is an accessible, but theoretically rich, introduction that situates 'register' within SFL theory and remains a classic reference.

Hasan, R. 2014. Towards a paradigmatic description of context: Systems, metafunctions, and semantics. *Functional Linguistics* 1: 9.

   This recent article locates register analysis within the history of SFL's focus on the paradigmatic axis, and links these to Hasan's work on semantic and contextualisation networks.

Matthiessen, C.M.I.M. 1993. Register in the round: Diversity in a unified theory of register analysis. In M. Ghadessy (ed.) *Register Analysis: Theory and Practice*. London: Pinter, pp. 221–92.

   This hugely influential chapter demonstrates the power of register as a theoretical concept, but shows clearly the need for further development and operationalisation of this concept, and is particularly relevant for those interested in computational and/or corpus approaches.

Moore, A. 2015. Can semantic networks capture intra- and inter-registerial variation? Palliative care discourse interrogates Hasan's message semantics. In W.L. Bowcher and J.Y. Liang (eds) *Society in Language, Language in Society: Essays in Honour of Ruqaiya Hasan*. London: Palgrave, pp. 83–114.

   This chapter exemplifies the recent empirical use of semantic networks in the 'register and context' approach to profiling and comparing registers, with extended discussion of end-of-life discussions in palliative care.

Chapter 27 Context and meaning in the Sydney architecture of systemic functional linguistics

Bednarek, M., and J.R. Martin (eds). 2010. *New Discourse on Language: Functional Perspectives on Multimodality, Identity, and Affiliation*. London and New York: Continuum.

Martin, J.R. 2010. *The Collected Works of J.R. Martin, Vol. 2: Discourse Semantics*. Ed. Z. Wang. Shanghai: Shanghai Jiao Tong University Press.

Martin, J.R., and D. Rose. 2007. *Working with Discourse: Meaning beyond the Clause*. London: Continuum.

   These three volumes not only provide detailed illustrations of the Sydney architecture, but also show how and why Sydney school scholars analyse texts.

Chapter 28 The appraisal framework and discourse analysis

Martin, J.R. 2008. Intermodal reconciliation: Mates in arms. In L. Unsworth (Ed.) *New Literacies and the English Curriculum: Multimodal Perspectives*. London: Continuum, pp. 112–48.

Martin, J.R. 2008. Tenderness: Realisation and instantiation in a Botswanan town. *Odense Working Papers in Language and Communication* 29: 30–62.

   In these two contributions, the author explores the complementary roles of three hierarchies that are key from a systemic functional semiotic theory: realisation, instantiation and individuation.

White, P.R.R. 2011. Appraisal. In J. Zienkowski, J.O. Ostman and J. Verschueren (eds) *Discursive Pragmatics*. Amsterdam and Philadelphia, PA: John Benjamins, pp. 14–36.

   This chapter provides an excellent overview of the appraisal framework, written by one of its creators, Peter White, in 2002.

Chapter 29 Systemic functional linguistics and genre studies

Coffin, C. 2006. Learning the language of school history: The role of linguistics in mapping the writing demands of the secondary school curriculum. *Journal of Curriculum Studies* 38(4): 413–29.

Clear and specific exposition of Sydney school genre progression in history, with supporting lexicogrammatical evidence.

Derewianka, B. 2003. Trends and issues in genre-based approaches. *RELC Journal* 34(2): 133–54.
Detailed, insightful overview of issues in teaching through genre-based approaches.

Martin, J.R., and D. Rose. 2008. *Genre Relations: Mapping Culture*. London: Equinox.
One of several volumes by Martin on genre. With plenty of examples from primary and secondary school texts of the main Sydney school genre families and clear explanations, this is a good place to start.

Nesi, H., and S. Gardner. 2012. *Genres across the Disciplines: Student Writing in Higher Education*. Cambridge: Cambridge University Press.
Descriptive account of thirteen genre families found in the British Academic Written English (BAWE) corpus of proficient university student writing.

Paltridge, B. 2014. Research timeline: Genre and second-language academic writing. *Language Teaching* 47(3): 303–18.
Plots the major historical milestones in research on genre theory and pedagogy in relation to second-language writing.

Chapter 30 Systemic functional linguistics and clinical linguistics

The following suggested readings have been selected to illustrate ways in which particular analyses based on different aspects of the SFL approach have been applied to the study of communication disorders.

Armstrong, E. 2001. Connecting lexical patterns of verb usage with discourse meanings in aphasia. *Aphasiology* 15(10): 1029–46.
This paper reports on an analysis of process types produced during recounts of illness and significant life experiences of four people with mild-to-moderate fluent aphasia and four people without brain damage aged between 56 and 80.

Kilov, A., L. Togher and S. Grant. 2008. Problem solving with friends: Discourse participation and performance of individuals with and without traumatic brain injury. *Aphasiology* 23(5): 584–605.
Drawing on SFL understandings of generic structure potential (GSP), this paper reports on the discourse of ten people with mild-to-moderate traumatic brain injury (TBI) talking with ten communication partners without brain damage during a problem-solving task.

Mortensen, L. 1992. A transitivity analysis of discourse in dementia of the Alzheimer's type. *Journal of Neurolinguistics* 7(1): 309–24.
This paper presents a detailed descriptive case study of a 58-year-old woman with moderate dementia. Using an SFL approach, an analysis of transitivity was conducted on her spoken procedural description and recount.

Müller, N., and B. Wilson. 2008. Collaborative role construction in a conversation with dementia: An application of systemic functional linguistics. *Clinical Linguistics & Phonetics* 22(10–11): 767–74.
This paper presents the analysis of speech functions and aspects of cohesion in the natural conversation between an older man with dementia and a man without brain dysfunction.

Spencer, E., A. Packman, M. Onslow and A. Ferguson. 2009. The effect of stuttering on communication: A preliminary investigation. *Clinical Linguistics & Phonetics* 23(7): 473–88.

This paper reports a comparison of a range of analyses based on the SFL approach applied to 5-minute monologues produced by ten people with mild-to-severe stuttering who had not had prior treatment. The analyses looked at grammatical intricacy, and marked and multiple Theme, as well as presence and type of modality.

Chapter 31 Language as verbal art

Banks, D. (ed.). 2011. Comprendre l'incompréhensible: Analyse d'un poème de J.H. Prynne. In D. Banks (ed.) *Aspects linguistiques du texte poétique*, Paris: L'Harmattan, pp. 219–29.

Using SFL tools, Banks illustrates how one of the most 'difficult' poets of the late twentieth century opens up a series of ultimately unverifiable semantic possibilities, leaving the reader in a limbo of meaning indeterminacy.

Taylor Torsello, C. 2007. Projection in literary and non-literary texts. In D.R. Miller and M. Turci (eds) *Language and Verbal Art Revisited: Linguistic Approaches to the Study of Literature*. London: Equinox, pp. 115–48.

Providing corpus evidence from many literary, but also non-literary, texts, Taylor Torsello shows how projection functions as a discriminating factor across genres, across instances of the same variety by different authors and even across different texts by the same author.

Taylor Torsello, C. 2016. Woolf's lecture/novel/essay *A Room of One's Own*. In D.R. Miller and P. Bayley (eds) *Hybridity in Systemic Functional Linguistics: Grammar, Text and Discursive Context*. Sheffield: Equinox, pp. 240–67.

Reading the generic complexity of Woolf's text by way of the metaphor of hybridity, Taylor Torsello incisively probes its selective use of three generic 'templates', and argues the case for Woolf's attempt at creating a 'feminine' style and genre.

Turci, M. 2010. The literary text at the borders of linguistics and culture: A SF analysis of Les Murray's *Migratory*. In E. Swain (ed.) *Thresholds and Potentialities of Systemic Functional Linguistics: Applications to Multilingual, Multimodal and Other Specialised Discourses*. Trieste: Edizioni Università di Trieste, pp. 334–46.

Focusing on the language–culture connection, Turci's analysis follows in the footsteps of Hasan's study of *The Widower*, also by Murray, providing another instance of the value of her analytical model and method.

Chapter 32 Discourse analysis

Gee, J.P. 2010. *How to Do Discourse Analysis*. London: Routledge.

Helpful practical guide to discourse analysis, full of linguistic and grammatical details.

Halliday, M.A.K. 1971. Linguistic function and literary style. In S. Chapman (ed.) *Style: A Symposium*. Oxford: Oxford University Press, pp. 330–68.

Illuminating analysis of discourse by the founder of SFL, from which much can be learnt.

Martin, J.R. 2010. *Discourse Semantics*. Shanghai: Shanghai Jiao Tong University Press.

A systematic application of SFL principles to create a form of discourse analysis.

Chapter 33 Corpus and systemic functional linguistics

The primary goal of this chapter is to introduce some aspects of corpus research within systemic studies. The field of corpus linguistics itself is broader than the scope of the chapter; hence readers are directed to the following important introductory texts.

Flowerdew, L. 2011. *Corpora and Language Education*. Basingstoke: Palgrave Macmillan.
> A book-length introduction that links corpus linguistics to SFL in the context of language education.

McEnery, T., R. Xiao and Y. Tono. 2006. *Corpus-Based Language Studies: An Advanced Resource Book*. London: Taylor & Francis.
> A general introduction into the topic with many useful exercises. A recent massive open online course (MOOC) from the same authors is available online at https://www.futurelearn.com/courses/corpus-linguistics/.

O'Keeffe, A., and M. McCarthy (eds). 2010. *How Can a Corpus Be Used to Explore Patterns?* London: Routledge.
> A handbook in the same series as this volume, introducing number of corpus-related topics.

Thompson, G., and S. Hunston (eds). 2006. *System and Corpus: Exploring Connections*. London: Equinox.
> Various, more specific, topics exploring the link between corpus linguistics and SFL are discussed in this book.

Chapter 34 Translation studies

Teich, E. 2013. Choices in analysing choice: Methods and techniques for register analysis. In L. Fontaine, T. Bartlett and G. O'Grady (eds) *Systemic Functional Linguistics: Exploring Choice*. Cambridge: Cambridge University Press, pp. 417–31.
> Offers further recommendations concerning corpus analysis in the context of register studies.

Bateman, J., R. Kasper, J. Schütz and E. Steiner. 1989. A new view on the process of translation. In *Proceedings of the Fourth European Conference of the Association for Computational Linguistics*. Copenhagen: Association of Computational Linguistics, pp. 282–90.
Steiner, E. 1993. Some remarks on a functional level for machine translation. *Language Sciences* 14(4): 1–15.
Steiner, E., P. Schmidt and C. Zelinsky-Wibbelt (eds). 1988. *From Syntax to Semantics: Insights from Machine Translation*. London: Pinter.
> These three contributions outline some applications of SFL in rule-based machine translation.

Chapter 35 Interactions between natural-language processing and systemic functional linguistics

Matthiessen, C.M.I.M., and J. Bateman. 1991. *Systemic Linguistics and Text Generation: Experiences from Japanese and English*. London: Pinter.
O'Donnell, M., and J. Bateman. 2005. SFL in computational contexts. In J.J. Webster, R. Hasan and C.M.I.M. Matthiessen (eds) *Continuing Discourse on Language: A Functional Perspective*. London: Equinox, pp. 343–82.
Teich, E. 2009. Linguistic computing. In M.A.K. Halliday and J.J. Webster (eds) *Bloomsbury Companion to Systemic Functional Linguistics*. London: Bloomsbury, pp. 113–27.
> These three titles provide the most complete accounts of the evolving relationship between SFL and natural-language processing.

Chapter 36 Reading images (including moving ones)

Jewitt, C. (ed.) *The Routledge Handbook of Multimodal Analysis*. Abingdon: Routledge.
Maszerowska, M., A. Matamala and P. Orero. 2014. *Audio Description: New Perspectives Illustrated*. Amsterdam: John Benjamins.
Mirzoeff, N. (ed.). 2013. *The Visual Culture Reader*. London: Routledge.

These three volumes provide both up-to-date accounts of the state of the art in Multimodality research and illustrate the continuing influence of SFL-inspired research in Multimodality studies.

Chapter 37 Systemic functional linguistics and language teaching

Bloor, T., and M. Bloor. 2013. *The Functional Analysis of English*. London: Routledge.
 An introduction to SFL that is particularly useful for language teachers, with exercises.

Coffin, C., J. Donohue and S. North. 2009. *Exploring English Grammar: From Formal to Functional*. London: Routledge.
 Bridges formal approaches with SFL, text linguistics and discourse analysis; includes exercises and applications to different fields, including second-language teaching/learning.

Derewianka, B. 2011. *A New Grammar Companion for Teachers*. Newtown, NSW: Primary English Teaching Association of Australia.
 A pedagogic grammar that combines more traditional terminology with SFL concepts.

Fontaine, L. 2013. *Analysing English Grammar*. Cambridge: Cambridge University Press.
 A textbook that introduces the structural grammar of English using an SFL approach.

Thompson, G. 2013. *Introducing Functional Grammar*. 3rd edn. London: Routledge.
 An introduction to SFL, with accessible explanations and activities.

Useful websites

Alan Hess, *Stories4Learning*. Available online at http://manxman.ch/moodle2/course/view.php?id=4; see also http://manxman.ch/S4L/intro_en/.
 Explanations of SFL, genre pedagogy and Reading to Learn, including applications and examples, and links to further resources.

Brett Laybutt, *EFL Func*. Available online at https://eflfunc.wordpress.com/.
 Explanations of SFL and experiences of applications to English as a foreign language (EFL) classes.

Leong Ping Alvin, SFL site. Available online at http://www.alvinleong.info/sfg/.
 Accessible systemic functional grammar explanations, with examples and quizzes.

Chapter 38 Systemic functional linguistics and code theory

Christie, F., and K. Maton (eds). 2011. *Disciplinarity: Functional Linguistic and Sociological Perspectives*. London: Continuum.
 Collection of papers using SFL and code theory that were central to phase III of exchanges.

Hasan, R. 2009. *Semantic Variation: Meaning in Society and in Sociolinguistics*. London: Equinox.
 Landmark studies in SFL inspired by Bernstein's code theory.

Maton, K. 2014. *Knowledge and Knowers: Towards a Realist Sociology of Education*. London: Routledge.
 The first monograph setting out two key dimensions of legitimation code theory (LCT), by its founding author.

Maton, K., S. Hood and S. Shay (eds). 2016. *Knowledge-Building: Educational Studies in Legitimation Code Theory*. London: Routledge.
 Primer on using LCT in research (including alongside SFL), with illustrative empirical studies.

Chapter 39 Learning how to mean: parent–child interaction

Halliday, M.A.K. 2003. *The Collected Works of M.A.K. Halliday, Vol. 4: The Language of Early Childhood*. Ed. J.J. Webster. London: Continuum.

Reprints the various papers, constituting 'Learning how to mean', together with all Halliday's subsequent writings on language development.

Painter, C. 2007. Language for learning in early childhood. In F. Christie and J.R. Martin (eds) *Language, Knowledge and Pedagogy: Functional Linguistic and Sociological Perspectives*. London and New York: Continuum, pp. 131–55.

Complements the present chapter by detailing language development from the perspective of the child's own impetus for learning.

Williams, G., and A. Lukin (eds). 2004. *The Development of Language: Functional Perspectives on Evolution and Ontogenesis*. London and New York: Continuum.

A collection of papers on linguistic ontogenesis and phylogenesis, with several chapters addressing language learning in both home and school contexts.

Chapter 40 Looking ahead: systemic functional linguistics in the twenty-first century

Halliday, M.A.K. 2013. *The Collected Works of M.A.K Halliday, Vol. 11: Halliday in the 21st Century*. Ed. J.J. Webster. London: Bloomsbury.

Halliday, M. A. K. 2015. *The Bloomsbury Companion to M.A.K. Halliday*. Ed. J.J. Webster. London Bloomsbury.

These two books, along with the present volume, address the place of SFL in the twenty-first century. The Equinox book series Key Concepts in SFL, edited by Tom Bartlett, Gerard O'Grady and Rebekah Wegener, will provide monographic treatments of key areas of SFL as an expanding twenty-first-century school of linguistics. For full details, see https://www.equinoxpub.com/home/key-concepts-in-systemic-functional-linguistics/.

Index

Hess, A. 665
heterogloss 464
Hidalgo-Downing, R. 75, 197, 212, 282, 656
hierarchically ordered system 30
Higashino, K. 224
Hirschberg, J. 157–8, 161
history genres 480–1
HIV medicine 431–2
Hjelmslev, L. 34, 79, 93, 439
Hodge B. 517
Holland, A. 504
Hollingworth, A. 587
Holmes, J. 483, 487
honorific 214, 217, 220, 227–8, 638;
    honorification 217–27
Hood, S. 447, 453, 466
Hopper, P. 180
Hori, M. 195
Howard, S. 503
Howe, T. 503
Huang, J. 595, 603
Huddleston, R. 52, 55
Hudson, R. 128–9, 211–12, 281–2, 307, 317
Humphrey, S. 483–4, 487
Hunston, S. 458, 465
Hyland, K. 473–4, 487
Hymes, D. 421, 436, 592–3, 602
hyperNew 137
hyperTheme 134–7, 141, 584–5
hypotactic 35, 100, 102, 109, 154, 303–4, 312,
    321, 324, 339, 352, 359
hypotaxis 96, 99, 154, 174, 323

iconography 606
Iddings, J. 523, 594, 601
ideation base 365
ideational 4, 6, 35, 42–7, 60, 69, 100, 110, 125,
    127, 131–6, 138–43, 145, 181, 194–203,
    206–11, 269, 273, 290, 304, 308, 314, 320,
    331, 354–61, 363–9, 380–2, 393–4, 405–7,
    413, 421, 423–4, 443–4, 447, 450, 459, 463,
    482–3, 521–3, 526, 528, 530, 566, 568, 571,
    576, 580, 590, 595, 598, 612, 614, 616, 629,
    640, 658; ideational element 133, 136–43;
    ideational meaning133, 141, 143; ideational
    metafunction 35, 42, 44–7, 131, 140, 595;
    ideational Theme 142, 195–203, 206–11
identity 32, 220, 445–53, 469, 576, 611–13
ideology 448–53
Iedema, R. 453, 459, 575
ILEX 568, 574
images 575–88

imitation 628–9
imperative 117, 215–22, 225–7, 355, 360–1
IMRD (Introduction, Methods, Results,
    Discussion) Genre Structure 482–3
incongruence 60, 70–1, 121, 354–7, 432, 442
independent 15, 32–5, 45–8, 65, 83, 97, 126,
    140, 147, 152–8, 167, 197, 227, 322, 328,
    380, 395, 415, 422, 477, 483, 512, 540, 553,
    594–8, 630, 635, 639, 643, 655
indicative 220–7
individuation 425, 431–3, 442–8, 447–8, 453,
    606, 611, 615; individuative 345–7
inferer 61
inflection 28, 37, 201–2, 215, 248, 252–60,
    310–11, 338; inflectional morphology 28,
    201, 310, 338
influential processes 187–9
information 116, 125, 213, 216, 222, 226;
    Information Unit 147–8; informational
    (strand of meaning) 60, 150–1, 155, 160, 198,
    321
initial position 132–3, 137–8, 141
input 31, 37–8, 59, 61, 70–2, 248, 269, 356, 365,
    427, 506, 508, 562, 565, 570–1, 581, 583,
    585, 603, 619–20, 632
inscribed meaning 458, 462
insert 5, 48–9, 62, 66–7, 152, 223, 34, 580
instance 5–7, 13, 28–33, 36–7, 43–7, 50, 59, 61,
    85–6, 361, 363, 368, 444–7, 465–8, 625–9
instantiation 42, 45, 79, 363, 421, 432, 446–7,
    625, 630
integrated 58, 65, 93, 110, 147, 164, 273, 295,
    309, 338, 367, 375, 387, 390, 393, 395, 420,
    443, 512, 579, 594, 613, 636
intensification 109, 289, 291, 470, 610
Interactional analysis 575
interdependency 314, 395, 443
interpersonal 4, 6, 35–7, 42–8, 52–3, 58, 68,
    89–90, 95, 99–101, 105, 15–19, 125–8,
    131–4, 139, 141–5, 152, 167, 173, 194–6,
    205–6, 210–20, 223–9, 260–3, 269–74,
    276–7, 301, 305–10, 317–26, 335–7, 354–61,
    363–9, 380–2, 405–7, 457–9, 463–5, 482–3,
    521–3, 552–3, 583–5; interpersonal first
    principle 629; interpersonal function 35, 139,
    219–20, 261, 521, 530; interpersonal grammar
    214; interpersonal meaning 131–3, 141, 143,
    215, 217, 220; interpersonal metafunction
    35–7, 42–8, 52, 131, 458; interpersonal
    particles 215, 226; interpersonal resource
    213; interpersonal strategy 226; interpersonal
    structure 195, 220, 206; interpersonal system

offer 116, 120, 218, 225–6
O'Grady, G. 45, 55, 154–5, 159–60, 235
O'Halloran, Kay. 408, 465, 575
O'Halloran, Kieran. 465
Okuda, Y. 214, 222
Olness, G. S. 500, 504–5
Online materials 481, 485
onomatopoeia 249
Onslow, M. 504, 662
ontogenesis 125, 358
open systems 29
optative 221–2, 225–7
optional 30
orbital structure 314, 443–4
organisation of information 155
Organon Model 32–3
orientation of exchange 221, 226
Ormond, T. 504
Ortega, L. 596, 600, 603
orthography 42, 45, 233
Oteíza, T. 467, 469
O'Toole, M. 575
Otsuki, F. 213
Ouhalla, J. 284
overt affect 465, 467

Packman, A. 504, 662
Pagano A. 515
Painter, C. 445, 575, 593
palliative care 430–3
Paltridge, B. 480, 483–4, 488, 662
paradigmatic 27–8, 43, 45, 48, 49, 52, 251, 364, 367, 393–402, 426–9, 432, 592, 597
parallelism 509, 514
parametric phonetics 248
parataxis 303–4
Parker-Rhodes, A. F. 562
Parkinson, J. 600, 603
parsing 542
Parsons, G. 408
participant 80–1, 132, 252, 258–9, 267, 276, 364; participant numbers (for research) 493, 498; Participant Role 82, 87, 178, 180–5, 189, 310–11, 314; participant tracking 200–1
particles 35, 215, 219–20, 223, 307, 314, 468, 551
particularisation 476
particulate structure 443–4, 308, 366
Partington, A. 519, 541
partitive 279
passive 82, 366
patient 496

patterning 507–9, 511–14; patterns 469, 540
Pavlenko, A. 596, 603
Paziraie, M. 408
Pecheux, M 448–53, 524
pedagogic discourse 606–10
pedagogic grammar 596–9,
pedagogical stylistics 516
Penman 58, 71, 568
Penn treebank 565
Perego, E. 587
Perek, F. 91
perfect system 38
periodic structure 308, 443–4; periodicity 139
Perkins, M. 503
Perrett, G. 596–7, 600–3
person 307, 310
personal stories 623–5
Peterson, P. 494, 503
phasal analysis 579, 588
phase 305, 323, 340
phonaesthetics 249
phoneme 233–6, 244–6
phonetics 42, 45–6, 52
phonology 42, 45–6, 51–2, 233–50, 511; phonological hierarchy 235; phonological paragraph 159
phonotactics 236, 247
phrasal verb 307
phrase 251
phylogenesis 358, 368
Piaget, J. 620, 631
Pierrehumbert, J. 157–8
Pike, K. 94, 235, 443
Pinker, S. 85, 90
Pinuer, C. 467, 469
planner 70–2, 365, 568, 640
Plum, G. 400, 403, 422, 437
poetic forms 249
poetic function 506, 508
point of departure 131–7, 143
point of origin 52
polarity 118, 214, 217, 219, 227
Polias, J. 595, 597, 603
politeness 214–16, 220–7, 360, 363
portmanteau morphology 307, 310
Portuguese 306, 467–8
Post-Deictic 276
postmodifier 278–9, 288
postverb 339–40, 344
Poynton, C. 415
practical 391
practical criticism 510